DEMOCRACY AND SECTARIANISM

A political and social history of Liverpool 1868–1939

DEMOCRACY AND SECTARIANISM

A political and social history of Liverpool 1868–1939

P. J. WALLER

Merton College, Oxford

LIVERPOOL UNIVERSITY PRESS

Published by
LIVERPOOL UNIVERSITY PRESS
123 Grove Street, Liverpool L7 7AF

First published 1981

British Library Cataloguing in Publication Data
Waller, Philip J.
Democracy and sectarianism.
1. Liverpool, Merseyside—History
I. Title
942.7′53 DA690.L8

ISBN 0–85323–074–9

This book is published with the
assistance of grants from the
British Academy and the
Twenty-Seven Foundation

Filmset by Willmer Brothers Limited
Birkenhead, Merseyside
Printed by The Camelot Press Limited
Southampton, England

To my parents

Contents

Acknowledgements

For permission to consult particular papers thanks are due to the owners or trustees of the following collections: H. H. Asquith, James Bryce, Sir Henry Campbell-Bannerman, Joseph Chamberlain, Lord Randolph Churchill, the 15th, 16th, and 17th Earls of Derby, T. E. Ellis, Sir A. B. Forwood, A. G. Gardiner, David Lloyd George, Robertson Gladstone, Viscount Gladstone, W. E. Gladstone, Ellis Griffith, R. B. Haldane, Sir W. V. Harcourt, the 2nd Earl of Harrowby, the Holt family, George Howell, Andrew Bonar Law, George Melly, Lawrence Redfern, the 5th Earl of Rosebery, the 3rd Marquis of Salisbury, Sir Archibald Salvidge, J. S. Sandars, Lord Sankey, Sir Leslie Scott, J. E. B. Seely, the 2nd Earl of Selborne, Samuel Smith, and Beatrice Webb; the Home Office, the Roman Catholic Archdiocese of Liverpool, and the Liverpool Steam Ship Owners Association. If a copyright has been infringed, this was unintended and my apologies are clear.

Several theses provided initial guides to my work on certain periods and on particular topics of Liverpool's history, as will be plain from the references. Many librarians and archivists have given valuable assistance, particularly the staffs of Liverpool City Library, the Bodleian Library at Oxford, and the Newspaper Library at Colindale. Individuals have freely given material, advice, or opinions about different questions. Mr. G. D. M. Block, Mr. D. J. Campbell-Smith, Mr. P. A. Clark, Mr. C. S. M. Graham, Mr. R. F. Henderson, Dr. P. J. Joyce, Dr. H. C. G. Matthew, Dr. H. McLeod, and the late Sir Charles Petrie; and Mr. R. Bean, Professor J. Cornford, Mrs J. Howarth, Dr. A. D. Macintyre, Dr. R. I. McKibbin, Dr. K. O. Morgan, Dr. R. E. Quinault, and Dr. J. S. Rowett, bravely read parts or the whole of the book in its different stages. Each has been helpful, as were the anonymous readers engaged by the publishers, in improving the flow of the narrative and in questioning certain judgements. The typing of the work involved many hands, but the final operation was cleanly executed by Terry Sharman. I am grateful to her, as also to Rosalind Campbell of Liverpool University Press who supervised the last lap with commendable despatch. Two institutions merit special mention, Magdalen College and Merton College, Oxford. It seems somewhat absurd to me that I should write of these colleges in an impersonal way; but I must be content to record my gratitude to both Fellowships for providing the freedom and funds to conduct the research for this book. Two individuals from other institutions I must mention more ardently. I thank Patrick Tuck of Liverpool University for his special company in that most special city, and Pat Thompson of Wadham College, Oxford, for his constancy as tutor, critic, and friend. My last regard here is for my wife and children whose efforts to relieve my prison-house labours on this book must be noted but not specified. But they will celebrate the release. P. J. W. 1981

Abbreviations in text and references

D.N.B.	*Dictionary of National Biography.*
E.H.R.	*English Historical Review.*
Ec.H.R.	*Economic History Review.*
I.L.P.	Independent Labour Party.
I.N.L.	Irish National League.
J.M.H.	*Journal of Modern History*
J.S.S.	*Journal of the (Royal) Statistical Society.*
L.C.	*Liverpool Courier* (called the *Daily Courier*, 1863–82, 1922–9).
L.C.H.	*Liverpool Catholic Herald.*
L.D.P.	*Liverpool Daily Post* (called the *Liverpool Daily Post and Mercury*, 1904–16 and the *Liverpool Post and Mercury*, 1916–35).
L.E.A.	Labour Electoral Association.
Liverpool Inquiry	Proceedings and Report of the Liverpool Inquiry, conducted by A. J. Ashton, K. C., under the Police Act of 1909 (published 31 March 1910).
L.L.R.C.	Liverpool Labour Representation Committee.
L.M.	*Liverpool Mercury.*
L.R.	*Liverpool Review* (called the *Liberal Review* before 1883).
L.R.C.	Labour Representation Committee.
L.T.C.	Liverpool Trades Council.
L.T.C. & L.P.	Liverpool Trades Council and Labour Party.
M.G.	*Manchester Guardian.*
N.A.S.F.U.	National Amalgamated Sailors' and Firemen's Union.
N.L.T.	*North Liverpool Times.*
N.P.E.F.	National Protestant Electoral Federation.
N.U.C.C.A.	National Union of Conservative and Constitutional Associations.
N.U.D.A.W.	National Union of Distributive and Allied Workers.

N.U.D.L.	National Union of Dock Labourers.
N.U.W.M.	National Unemployed Workers' Movement.
P.	*Porcupine.*
P.D.	*Parliamentary Debates* (Hansard).
P.P.	*Parliamentary Papers.*
P.S.	*Protestant Standard.*
S.D.F.	Social Democratic Federation.
T.	*The Times.*
T.H.S.L.C.	*(Transactions) Historic Society of Lancashire and Cheshire.*
U.I.L.	United Irish League.
V.S.	*Victorian Studies.*
W.M.C.A.	(Liverpool) Working Men's Conservative Association.

Introduction

Early in the 1930s J. B. Priestley spent a busy day in Liverpool and ended his account of it thus: 'Miserably I decided that somebody else must give a plain fair account of this great city: the task, in the time, was beyond me. So I bought myself a good cigar.'[1] Some ten years (and rather more cigarettes) have been spent on this book. The result is a history of over a century of recent political life in Liverpool. By that concentration on politics Priestley's commission remains unfulfilled here. A title to be considered a history of the city is renounced.

Special problems nevertheless attend the scale and character of this work. The regular paths of historians tend towards other directions—towards biographies, usually reassessments of figures whose careers or legends are reasonably well known; towards sectional studies, of a government ministry perhaps, a party organization, a trade union, or a religious communion; towards specific themes, focusing on the interplay of particular ideas, issues, and movements; and towards single episodes, with the purpose of pleading that an event, once deemed small, should be thought a major watershed, or perhaps the other way round. What these exercises have in common which this book for the most part lacks are generally recognized landmarks and boundaries. Biographies have a preappointed finiteness and unity. There is also a conventional scale to most other historical *genres*, either because their treatment concerns events, people, and organizations of which an amount is already established and understood, or because their significant ramifications extend over a period usually no greater than two or three decades. Much local history does not have those advantages of ready manageability and circumscription. Although its incidents might be of interest to many historians, scholars of allied disciplines, and even the omnibus reader, few of the events or the people described are familiar. Accordingly a major challenge has been, how to convey the range of new information in narrative without sacrificing comment and argument and without damaging structure.

The book does, of course, derive an initial unity from its single location; but this must remain passive, for to anthropomorphize a city is not an acceptable method of historical writing. The structural integrity of this book, therefore, has to be seen more broadly. It lies in the competition of four main parties, Conservative, Liberal, Irish Nationalist, and Labour, for the favours of the Liverpool electorate, and in the reflection of this scene against the national political background from time to time. Without the national quantity local history is parochial history; with it there is a chance that historians

Notes begin on p. 356.

can truly measure political behaviour, for that, after all, takes place on the national and local stage at the same time, sometimes in collusion, sometimes in collision.

Interlocked in this book are sketches of social, economic, and spiritual movements—about problems of disorder, employment, housing, religion—whenever they impinge directly or significantly upon the sense of politicians or upon the outlook and behaviour of the electorate. It is on the latter that much effort has been spent, although perhaps more has been discovered of the former. As every historian knows, the mass of people remain elusive. The problem is not to recover them, for that is impossible, but to reduce the distance of separation and to glimpse some lines of shape and meaning. How best to accomplish this will never be agreed. The method generally adopted here is that prescribed by one who, in part of this period, attempted to understand ordinary people both as a theorist and as a politician, James Connolly: 'A people are not to be judged by the performances of their great men. A truer standard by which the spiritual and mental measurement of a people can be taken . . . is by that picture drawn of itself . . . at the ballot box.'[2]

Notwithstanding this directive, it is worth observing that Liverpool has produced, or provided a forum for, some remarkable personalities. Most were not statesmen—the triumphs of such as W. E. Gladstone and F. E. Smith belonged to Westminster, not Liverpool—and they left few monuments. Some did achieve national reputations. T. P. O'Connor is remembered as an Irish Nationalist, an M.P. for forty-nine years, as a popular biographer, 'the modern Plutarch at £10 a week', and as a newspaperman, the 'High Priest of Personal Journalism'.[3] Then there were the waterfront leaders, James Sexton, an innovator in industrial relations, whose followers reviled his efforts to decasualize labour, and Jim Larkin, a disaster in industrial relations, whose followers extolled him as 'Prometheus Hibernica'.[4] Modern Labour politics in Liverpool have also yielded national names like Bessie Braddock, a proud and pugnacious champion, and physical prodigy. But in a city which almost uninterruptedly for over a hundred years was ruled by the Conservative party it is the Conservative leaders and their auxiliaries who exercise most fascination. Tory Democrats and city bosses like Sir Arthur Forwood, Sir Archibald Salvidge, and Sir Thomas White, and, at another level, Protestant evangelists like George Wise and H. D. Longbottom, all flawed personalities, commanded the course of modern Liverpool.

The importance of that history has still to be argued. Since the nineteenth century Liverpool has been England's second or third largest city. Size establishes no enduring claim to interest: Oscar Wilde was unimpressed by the Atlantic Ocean. There are, however, features in Liverpool's history which demand attention—its ethnic groupings, its ulcerated poverty, its industrial strife, its philanthropy and municipal enterprise, and its caucus systems of political management. Many aspects of urban society in Victorian Britain and after were exhibited in extraordinary dimensions in Liverpool. Sectarian conflict especially injected political life with unusual intensity and moulded the popular Conservatism and immature Labour party which were the hallmarks of Liverpool before the Second World War.

Commercial distribution, rather than manufacture, dominated Liverpool's economy, and had consequences for life in the city. The prevailing characteristics of the labour force were want of formal organization, traditional craft skills, and independence. The concomitants of this casual, impermanent, and relatively unskilled work were irregular wages and irregular ways. According to Sean O'Casey's apophthegm, 'where poverty is, there can never be law or order'; but the jostle for a place to live and work was not all unregulated. Many trades, the dockside trades especially, were riddled with numerous peculiars, which emerged from the singularity of a task and from familiarity with one company or work-place. Thus grain-workers or timber-workers, salt-heavers or coal-heavers, lightermen or bargemen, might have their own society, just as the men who loaded and discharged coasting vessels in the Clarence Dock or who worked for a scheduled transatlantic passenger line like Cunard. Thesc informal labour corporations had purposes in common with many friendly societies and trade unions, aiming to protect their members from three invasions—from employers who tried to exterminate the customs and liberties of a trade, from unconnected workers who tried to penetrate their labour parish, and from cyclical movements of the economy, the fluctuations of which might dictate alterations in the time or price for a piece of work and reduce the number employed. But, though this division cannot always be sustained, these associations were below the level of trade unionism, powerful enough to satisfy immediate and personal needs on 'the ready-money job', but usually impotent to enforce structural changes in the economic condition. The conflict between capital and labour was as guerilla warfare rather than regular manoeuvres, and the conflict within labour itself was as tribal or clan combat. In the nineteenth and early twentieth centuries, Sexton recollected, 'Liverpool had a caste system quite as powerful as India's'.[5]

Associations of immigrant groups, Irish, Welsh, and Scottish especially, gave another semblance of system to the miserable rivalry of individuals, and sectarianism introduced another internecine element or cross-grain into the structure. The Irish were mostly Catholic, but with an aggressive Protestant part, and the Welsh and Scottish were mostly Protestant. It was natural that politicians should seek to utilize these active and persistent divisions for party purposes, but it was often distracting when constitutional issues, or problems of public health, education, and employment, were viewed through ethnic and sectarian spectacles. The way in which Liverpool's political exploiters of religious and national factions were themselves exploited provides a curious continuity amid the many shifts of fortune.

In 1927 the parliamentary debate about the revised Anglican Prayer Book was abruptly ended by a remark of the Labour M.P. for West Ham Silvertown, Jack Jones, that most workers in Britain were more interested in rent books than in prayer books.[6] The course of this transition is a chief theme plotted in this book. This subject, the so-called secularization of politics, has occupied several modern historians but mostly they have concentrated their inquiries within the period from 1890 to 1920. In Liverpool, where the problem of sectarianism was acute enough to evoke comparison with Belfast, the evidence that purports to show the influence of religion in politics much relenting before the First World

War is not very striking. Some 36·8 per cent of the population attended a church in Liverpool in 1851, a sum which shrunk by under 8 per cent in the next sixty years, during which time the total population doubled.[7] The direction of the figures is important to note, for the trend has not been permanently reversed; but equally it should be remembered that the rate of change was not rapid, and that church attendance is an imprecise measure of religious commitment in general and of sectarian feeling in politics in particular. The sectarian rioting in 1909 dwarfed anything seen in the city in the nineteenth century. These eruptions also can be misleadingly titled. Some might argue, as others in the past did, that what was done in the name of religion was atrocious enough to be called pagan and to warrant more rather than less missionary work from the churches. The tensions in Liverpool society, which were manifested in its politics, stemmed not simply from genuine or bastard religiosity, but also from the tendencies towards heterogeneity in that society. National distinctiveness and separate cultural ties were not dissolved and effaced in a melting pot, but sustained by neighbourhood warmth and perpetuated by education over generations. Not that the country Irish or the country Welsh, to take the largest alien groups who settled in Liverpool, remained absolutely as before, impervious to their adopted city. A reconstitution did occur, but this new growth was a hybrid, with singular and common traits, which left the Liverpool Irish and the Liverpool Welsh still shaped as identifiable groups.

The part played by politicians in this also resists simple stylizing. Broadly it might be observed that Conservative leaders were reluctant to shed their sectarian skin because they feared the ensuing ascendancy of socio-economic questions in politics; likewise that Labour leaders were disposed to unsectarian political controversy because they would profit from an unblinkered perception of class interest. In fact sectarianism was not like an article of clothing that politicians might voluntarily wear or cast off. It resembled the mark of Cain, and no politician could much disguise it. Moreover this was not the only obstacle in the way of fashioning class loyalty among working people. As has been noted already about the composition of industry in Liverpool, one workman frequently regarded another as a jealous competitor rather than as a colleague in a common struggle, and the social class ladder did not just contain three rungs, a lower, middle, and upper, but an infinite number of levels, each separated with keenly defended marks of station.

Finally, in this introduction, a place might be found for Lord Chesterfield's encouraging words: 'It is very well known that religion and politics are perfectly understood by everybody, as they require neither study nor experience.' However, in order that this book may be easily intelligible, something should be noted of the constitution by which political life was ruled. To the general reader it cannot be emphasized too strongly that the influence of individual voters traditionally was not equal but varied, according to the possession of wealth and property. Some parts of the electoral system assumed a recognizably modern form earlier than did the franchise: thus the secret ballot was conceded in 1872 and legislation bringing protection against corrupt practices was passed in 1883. But, though the nineteenth-century governing classes feared the power of democracy within their system, a democratic franchise was unrealized before

1928. The cost of contests and of parliamentary life discouraged democratic participation even after M.P.s were first paid in 1911; and the franchise remained limited, by formal property qualifications, by registration requirements, and by sex discrimination. The disqualified and disfranchised constituted a miscellany which included, together with the accredited noble and the certified insane (who are still deprived of the vote), serving soldiers and sailors, paupers, many migrants, living-in servants, single men living with their parents who had not exclusive use of a room, and lodgers in rooms with an unfurnished rental of below £10. Moreover, although there was some participation in local elections after 1869 of women who were rated for poor law purposes, no woman could vote in parliamentary elections before 1918. As for the men, before universal adult male suffrage was conceded in 1918, fewer than six out of ten adult males in towns had the vote and, in a place like Liverpool, with its great numbers of destitute and unsettled, this figure fell considerably below five in ten in certain quarters. The average for the whole city in 1911 was only 49·8 per cent, without making allowance for plural votes.

These last were another now unfamiliar element in the constitution. Before 1918 a man, by owning property in different neighbourhoods, might vote in several constituencies and, in so far as the travelling might be deemed worth while, the staggered dates of a General Election—spread over two weeks—favoured this privileged class.

The measurement of its influence, however, is unavoidably imprecise. The hidden quantity is suggested by the habits of the onetime Liberal minister, Sir Charles Dilke. He made several journeys to vote but, where this was inconvenient, he endeavoured to 'pair' off with Conservatives in those constituencies.[8] The diary of the Liverpool cotton broker, Robert Holt, likewise gives some intelligence about the oddities of the system. Always conscientious, he cast two votes in Liverpool, another in the Stretford division of south-east Lancashire, and another in the Appleby division of Westmorland; but as a Liberal polling in predominantly Conservative seats he rarely had the satisfaction of having backed a winning candidate. Altogether there were perhaps half a million plural voters before 1910, but this is not certain. Their impact is even less susceptible of statistical treatment: how many votes these voters possessed or cast are unknown, and conjecture is not aided by the fact that most sources carelessly fail to distinguish plural voters and plural votes. After 1918 General Elections were held on one day and the plural vote was restricted to one in addition to the elector's residential vote; and in 1948 the plural vote was ended absolutely.

Two other anomalies of the electoral system require statement. One is the local government franchise. Although in regard to women the local government franchise was forward of the parliamentary franchise before 1918, in other respects it was laggard, remaining property-based (the possession or occupation of land or buildings), and insisting on a qualifying period of three months residence, until after the Second World War. Thus while 96 per cent of adult males, and 82 per cent of women aged over thirty, had the vote in parliamentary elections in Liverpool from 1918, and universal adult suffrage nominally prevailed from 1928, only some 61 per cent of the adult population was registered to vote in Liverpool's municipal elections in 1921, and 70 per cent in 1931.[9] The second anomaly concerned few towns apart from Liverpool and obtained for a relatively brief period, 1867–84. This was the Cairns' clause of the Second Reform Act whereby Liverpool, Birmingham, Manchester, Leeds, and Glasgow, each returned three M.P.s but no elector could declare for more than two candidates. This was again intended to impose restrictions on democracy. By refusing to subdivide urban communities, class differences, it was hoped, would be muted, a sense of corporateness would be sustained, and the representation of minorities would be protected. Historians interested in this clause have mostly examined its working in Birmingham, or, rather, its failure to work in Birmingham, following the well-publicized engineering of the Liberal Association there. Under the management of Joseph Chamberlain and Francis Schnadhorst the Birmingham Liberal caucus directed the spread of each Liberal elector's two preferences evenly among the three candidates and enabled them to sweep the city's representation. In Liverpool, except between 1880 and 1882, a Liberal minority member was returned; but again it was apparent that the dominant party—here the Conservatives—began to study the science of electioneering and to essay control throughout the city. The outcome of their deliberations was seen in the redistribution of parliamentary seats in 1885. Thenceforward the charge of Tammany practices came to be levelled as frequently against the Conservatives of Liverpool as against the erstwhile Liberal Radicals of Birmingham. It seemed to those critics paradoxical that the Conservatives could be so successful, without being dishonest, in Liverpool, given the grim circumstances in which much of the population lived and worked. The explanation of this paradox, if such it is, informs this book.

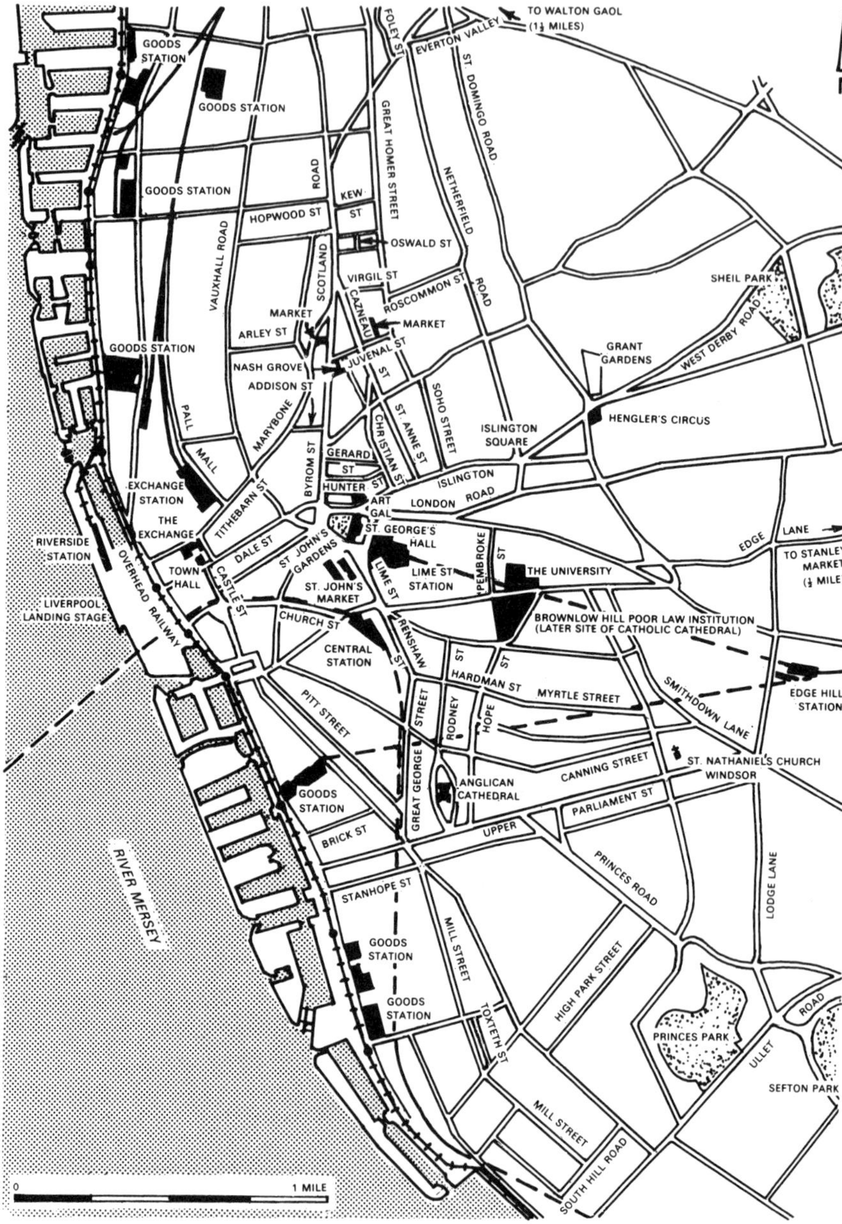

Plan of the inner areas of Liverpool, c.1910, showing the streets and landmarks mentioned in the text

CHAPTER ONE

The character of Liverpool

Every society is judged and survives according to the material and moral minimum which it prescribes to its members. *H. H. Asquith*

It is one of the evils of this day that men are spoken of as classes or masses rather than as individuals. *W. Cooke Taylor*

English society is not stratified in horizontal layers; nor do the working classes form a solid phalanx or mystical brotherhood swayed by one imperious will. The better they are known, the more they are found to comprise an infinite variety of interests, habits, and opinions, among which strong patriotic and Conservative instincts are by no means wanting.[1]
G. C. Brodrick

The growth and work of the port

Irish, American, and colonial trade, and the development of inland waterborne transport, impelled Liverpool's rise. The town contained perhaps 1,000 persons in 1670, and 7,000 by 1710.[2] At intervals in the eighteenth century two different enthusiasts, Defoe and Wesley, admired Liverpool's handsome buildings; but business recognized no responsibility to preserve the past. When Robert Southey visited Liverpool in the early nineteenth century this feature was paramount: 'there is no cathedral, and no castle, gate, town-wall, or monument of antiquity, no marks of decay. Everything is the work of late years, almost of the present generation.' This cycle was continually renewed and by Edwardian times, when much of Georgian and even early Victorian Liverpool had disappeared, writers again lamented the 'commercial vandalism' that destroyed old Liverpool.[3] Not every relic was worth preserving. By 1801 only Castle Street was accounted truly fine; few streets were wide or elegant; most were 'narrow and dirty'. Liverpool had then increased elevenfold, by 1841 another threefold.[4]

Liverpudlians were 'universal merchants', in Irish wool, linen, and beef, American cotton, colonial tobacco and sugar, Midlands metals and pottery, Cheshire salt, and Lancashire coal and textiles.[5] Certain trades reached great

Notes begin on p. 356

proportions. Some reckoned that by 1792 Liverpool engrossed five-eighths of Britain's slave trade, although this trade was not without its fluctuations in volume, profit, and risk; between 1820 and 1850 Liverpool passed four-fifths of England's supplies of raw cotton; and later it commanded the overseas passenger, food, and live cattle trades.[6] But catholicity and diversity remained the trading standard and dictated the physical complement. In 1840 Birkenhead scarcely existed while Liverpool contained sixteen docks. By 1900 forty Mersey docks covered 1,600 acres, with 35½ miles of lineal quay space.[7] The work principally of Jesse Hartley and G. F. Lyster, the docks and warehouses seemed as monumental as the Pyramids.[8] Less fancifully the dock estate represented £42 million capital.[9]

'Busy, noisy, smoky, money-getting Liverpool' was made by merchants.[10] One ecclesiastical visitor in 1795 was amazed by 'this large, irregular, busy, opulent, corrupted town; where so many men and so many women use so many ways and means of gaining and spending so much money . . .'; and a clerk, John Smith, testified that Liverpool was 'frequented solely by *great worms* alias people who think the only end for coming into existence was to scrape together as many bags of the ore as possible'.[11] But Smith knew that Liverpool provided more opportunities than his native Scotland; as did John Holt who, fresh from Lincolnshire, regretted that in Liverpool 'mankind is like a lot of hungry pigs fighting over a trough of milk—everybody seems to be trying to pull the piece of food out of his neighbour's mouth'.[12]

Life in Liverpool moved fitfully with the disposition of trade. A few experienced its generous side. B. R. Haydon was rescued from debt in the 1830s by two notable commissions from Liverpool, to paint *Christ Blessing Little Children*, and *Wellington Musing on the Field at Waterloo*. This led him to laud 'the glorious town of Liverpool', and his impression of Liverpool men, as opposed to the steady and industrious men of Leeds and Manchester, was that they were 'speculators and spirited', albeit 'more idle'. Mostly the text for survival in this world seemed cynicism, about another's position and motives, although the Revd. Francis Kilvert's guide in Liverpool in 1872 was unreasonable when he asserted of his fellow merchants and brokers milling around the Exchange that he did not believe that ten could be found who could pay 15*s*. in the £1.[13]

To some the rhythms of trade were a clatter to the conscience; but others regarded commerce without apology. Southey was impressed by the civic attention and 'princely liberality' of Liverpool merchants; and to B. G. Orchard the merchant was a 'benefactor to humanity'. His boyhood ambition was 'to write an epic in which the progress of commerce would be commemorated'. The poet was soon snuffed out. Instead Orchard compiled a 750-page directory of Merseyside public figures.[14] In this he presented the activities of individual merchants and set some on pedestals, as heroes.

Many more toilers were nameless, and downcast, victims. Society affords little room at the top. Liverpool furnished scant room at the bottom too. Relatively few Liverpudlians found stable employment.[15] Chiefly a commercial and distributive centre, Liverpool did contain an industrial sector;[16] but it too utilized mostly low-paid and unskilled labour. Casual workers were difficult to unionize, while the paucity of skilled trades made them inward-looking and particular about status and privilege.[17] One factory surgeon discerned 'a regular gradation' from 'the best class and strongest looking boys amongst the engineering and ship-building classes', to 'a small and poor type of boy' in riveting works.[18]

Artisans often had a pedigree of craft work and education, nepotism being characteristic of all classes, as Gladstone recognized.[19] However, business rationalization and the Corporation's policy of dock-building squeezed out Liverpool's shipbuilders.[20] Shipbuilding occupied fewer than 5,000 of Liverpool's adult males—about 4 per cent—in 1871. Royden's launched its last vessel in 1899; Birkenhead, Clydeside, Tyneside, and Belfast had come to dominate this work. Some blamed the craftsmen's caste spirit. Sexton, the dockers' leader, likened the Liverpool ship-carpenters to snails who crawled into their shells.[21] The crafts were threatened by the ambience of casual labour. Dock work was 'the last refuge of the unfortunate', the docker 'the Lazarus of the working class'.[22] Social consciousness was sharp. It needed a revolution in attitudes to replace the term 'dock rat' by 'general labourer'.[23]

Conditions of employment varied between and within ports;[24] but in Liverpool the characteristic difference concerned 'shipmen' and porters. Shipmen loaded and unloaded vessels; porters arranged cargoes on the quays. Shipmen were better paid—by 6*d.* a day in 1900—but porters enjoyed more and, perhaps, safer work. Arguably some porters, like weighers and selectors, were more intelligent and reliable; but stevedores who stowed freight performed skilled work. Indeed it is necessary to emphasize that this categorization of work into 'skilled' and 'unskilled' was repudiated by many dockers. Ben Tillett detested the distinction 'not merely because it is untrue, but also because it is patronizing'. Certainly, to the extent that no formal articles of apprenticeship were demanded and the work was mostly irregular, dock labour was not a craft; but Sexton had a point when he argued that, before the days of mechanization, the all-round docker 'required the intelligence of a Cabinet Minister—possibly not a very high standard now—the mechanical knowledge and resource of a skilled engineer, and, in addition, the agility and quick-wittedness of a ring-tailed monkey'.[25]

Dockers were variously recruited, by master stevedores and master porters, by shipowners handling their own stevedorage or porterage or both, and by merchants arranging their own porterage. One reason for this, as the General Manager and Secretary of the Mersey Docks and Harbour Board told Sidney Webb in a moment of rare candour, was 'because it was so much more difficult for the men to strike against a number of different employers'.[26] In the central docks cross-channel shippers employed fairly regular gangs; but for the most part labour was casually engaged daily or half-daily, at 'stands' where foremen behaved like cattle-dealers.[27] Muscle attracted them, although favours could be bought.[28] The foremen's authority was despotic, for gangs had no right to inspect bills for piece-work or tonnage.[29] Not all were vicious—Jim Larkin, for instance was thought honest and sober[30]—but the system facilitated depredations. Theoretically the Dock Board might license any man supported by two householders as a master stevedore or porter.[31]

Contractors were particularly needed by smaller shipping firms, but Sexton deemed them superfluous. Although they hired the men and leased machinery, the shipowner's foreman generally supervised the work. Dockers, therefore, were distanced from their employer, while exposed to his skimping.[32] The *Lancet* reckoned that no one could be a dock-worker for five years and escape disfigurement.[33] Of dockers interviewed by the Royal Commission on Labour, Atkins was without a toe, and grain bags had beaten Sexton's face 'into a mummy'.[34] Certain cargoes—cement, bulk guano, bleaching powder, sulphur, pitch, and hides—always involved hazards; but the vulnerability of dockers was mostly expressed in irregular employment. The supplanting of sailing ships by steam obviated some causes—steamships represented 98 per cent of Liverpool's traffic by 1906, a rise from 16 per cent in fifty years—but the cost of vessels lying idle required that they be turned round quickly. Accordingly steamship owners both demanded sufficient reserves to tackle the maximum work and, from the late 1870s, sought to concentrate the whole operation of discharging, receiving, weighing, and loading, so that a ship was turned round in an average three days instead of four.[35] The same men were, therefore, worked continuously with the result that dockers aged rapidly.[36] Provisioning during long spells was the contractors' responsibility; but Sexton had tasted their hog-wash and suspected that firms vied 'in doing all they could do to crush the labouring men . . .'.[37]

The docks contained seventeen important stands and numerous lesser ones, operating between 6·45 and 7 a.m., and 12·45 and 1 p.m. Men frequented familiar stands; but this impeded that mobility of labour which, paradoxically, employers sought to gain through casualization. Employers could be short-handed, even at slack times.[38]

The 1901 census recorded 19,594 'dock and wharf labourers' in Liverpool, 3,773 in Bootle.[39] What work and wages could they expect? Most observers agreed that the average employment was three days a week. Eleanor Rathbone cited the value of one firms's 'engagement': for its 'regulars' in stevedorage 6*s*. 6*d*., in porterage 5*s*. 7*d*.; for its casuals, in stevedorage 4*s*., in porterage 3*s*. 6*d*. Few worked a statistically average week or received a statistically average wage.[40] Daily fluctuations were excessive.[41] The seasons had not the significance of other outdoor trades, when work was pared. In Liverpool, in 1899, the maximum employment for porterage was on 21 June, for stevedorage on 18 November. Not that winter was without problems, for the unemployed of other industries, particularly of the building trades, competed at the docks. Altogether the casuals' year was a winter lasting twelve months, which spelled poverty even in work. Tillett declared, 'We do not blame our employers for discharging us from three to six months in the year in a manner that cannot be avoided; but . . . while we are at work, they grind us down to a paltry pittance, which allows of no provision for the dark days . . .'[42]

Several trades attracted similar men. Saw-mills, jute-works, and soap-boiling factories provided 'dirty employments'.[43] In 1911 a Committee investigated Kirkdale, Edge Hill, and Toxteth. They were not Liverpool's worst districts. The Committee was interested in wage-earners, not paupers, and it investigated 1,892 males.[44] Most were Liverpool-born, married, and renting accommodation. Some 18 per cent were trade unionists; half were labourers. Most became labourers before they reached adulthood, largely recruited from the class of shop and messenger boys, who received no training for a 'trade'. This underlined an inquiry into the poorer central districts in 1908–9. Of the 2,000 cases then under review, 1,381 began in blind-alley occupations; 837 became labourers before the age of twenty, 1,302 before the average age of thirty-eight. Since over 40 per cent were irregularly employed, thrift was discouraged, and building societies, friendly societies, and co-operative stores in Liverpool maintained precarious existences before the twentieth century.[45]

The most common superior status employment was clerical. An estimated 17,400 clerks were employed on Merseyside in 1870 but 'clerk', like 'docker', was a portmanteau term incorporating many grades.[46] Information about wages is partial but, in the Edwardian period, only about 30 per cent of male clerks crossed the income tax threshold, £160 p.a. About 40 per cent of male clerks, and 95 per cent of female clerks, earned less than £100 p.a. These averages say nothing about the distribution of wages within the range of clerical work, in the law, banking, and commerce, local and national government, on the railways, docks, and wharves. Thus lawyers' offices employed 'the lowest description of talent', with wages at a docker's level; but in banks and insurance companies the clerical labour aristocracy was to be found, some highly skilled clerks who earned respect, status, and promotion to salaries the equal of many independent employers.

Such different clerks were naturally subject to varying pressures, although some general trends can be discerned. The class of 'white-collar' or 'black-coated' worker, the marginal men of the middle class—this includes shop assistants, policemen, post office staff, teachers, and assorted technicians, as well as clerks—was growing both absolutely and relatively from 1860. But, with the provision of widespread elementary education after 1870 and the mechanization of the means of communication in the typewriter and telephone, the supply was often equal to the demand, particularly of those capable of filling the lower grades of clerical work—copying correspondence or marking up ledgers—where the task required little initiative or talent. The increasing employment of two groups, young male apprentices and women, was perceived as a threat to the social status and economic position of clerical occupations; so too was the evolution of capitalist organization as amalgamations brought economies of scale and the regrading (or degrading) of many jobs.

Several writers, not only Marxists, observed a process of 'proletarianization' in the clerical profession. Some 6,700 female clerks (about half were plain typists) worked on Merseyside by 1911, the vast majority being newly employed since 1890. As the dislocations of war accentuated the trend, an absolute decline in the number of male clerks, from 32,000 to 30,000, took place between 1911 and 1921, while the number of female clerks rose to almost 18,000. By 1930 the median wage of adult clerks (60*s.*) on Merseyside was lower than that of skilled manual workers (68*s.* 11*d.*).[47] Although their working conditions, hours, and holidays, were thought generally better and their families smaller, profound fears burdened their lives at work and at home. The organized working class was seen to have obliterated differences of income and to have invaded their suburban retreats.

Those sections of 'white-collar' workers which enjoyed greater security by more specialized skill reacted to this pressure by forming professional associations which, as well as attending to salaries, pensions, and conditions, sought to emphasize their distinctiveness by establishing certificated standards of intellectual ability and efficiency and by eliminating variety of recruitment and practice. This tendency was broadly evidenced by the National Union of Elementary Teachers, which was founded in 1870 and renamed the National Union of Teachers in 1889, and by the National Association of Local Government Officers in 1905, which developed from the Liverpool Municipal Officers Guild of 1896. Public service workers generally were widely organizing between 1890 and 1914—the degree of employment concentration and the impersonal, bureaucratic regulation of their work enhanced a perception of communal interest—but in private employment, apart from some organization of shop workers, an outgrowth of the Early Closing movement, trade unionism was undeveloped.[48]

This was particularly true of ordinary commercial clerks, who were separated by multitudinous grades and locations, and suffocated by conventions of 'respectability'. As a class they were downtrodden, often working in cold, cramped, ill-lit, and insanitary offices; but even when unemployed and in distress few solicited charitable relief.[49] Nor did they organize rallies and 'pass socialistic resolutions against the general order'. They were 'bound by social requirements of which dock labourers know nothing'.[50] The union organization of 'twopenny clerks'—'the unskilled labourers of the middle classes'[51]—was skeletal. The National Union of Clerks was the first organization to appeal to persons in clerical occupations everywhere and to challenge the code of respectability by which clerks identified more with their employers than with other depressed sections of the working class. But a blast of the National Union of Clerks' trumpets did not quickly level the walls of 'respectability', for this sense of identification with employers was not simply pathetic imitation. It reflected conditions of work: respectability and personal connections—they may have been no greater than association in the same religious communion—were essential for getting a start in a business or an advance later. The National Union of Clerks had only 82 members nationally in 1900. There were over 12,000 by 1914, but the Liverpool membership manifested a traditionally retiring disposition so far as politics were concerned, in 1913 defeating a motion to affiliate to the Liverpool Labour Representation Committee by twenty-seven votes to five.

More significant than the National Union of Clerks in Liverpool was the Liverpool Clerks Association, which was established in 1861, had 2,103 members by 1880, and grew fairly regularly to a membership of 5,885 by 1913. This Association provided comprehensive insurance facilities, but it was not a registered trade union and its membership was closed to clerks who were not of proven respectability. Indeed B. V. Kirby, of the N.U.C., claimed in 1936 that the Liverpool Clerks Association 'was not a trade union but a provident society sponsored by big employers in the city'. Likewise N.A.L.G.O. continued to bear marks of its origins, firmly repudiating the label of trade union until 1920, and withholding from the T.U.C. until 1964. Its founder, the Liverpudlian, Herbert

Blain, was Principal Agent of the Conservative party between 1924 and 1927. His first object in the Liverpool Municipal Officers' Guild had been to cultivate a spirit of self-improvement among the membership in order to prove themselves worthy of pensions and other benefits for which they supplicated; and the patronage of the Lord Mayor and Corporation was deliberately sought.[52]

This survey does not comprehend Liverpool's occupational structure, but it adumbrates the difficulties and, to a degree, the uniformity. Life in the city was overlaid with maritime caprices, down to the beachcombing and salvage sales which influenced domestic economies.[53]

Immigrants at odds: the Liverpool Irish, Welsh, and Scots

A port predicates traffic in goods, also in peoples. Liverpool's population was polyglot, 'the Marseilles of England'.[54] Migration shaped its development, inwards as a conduit of aliens, outwards as a sluice for wealth when those with means fled to the suburbs. The Irish dominated the immigrations. The 1881 census distributed Irish-born citizens accordingly: 212,000 in Lancashire, 81,000 in London, 60,000 in Yorkshire, 35,000 in Durham, 24,000 in Cheshire.[55]

The chief conglomeration of Cheshire Irish was in Birkenhead. Together Liverpool and Birkenhead contained some 78,000 Irish-born. Paddy straddled the Mersey as the Colossus at Rhodes. Although the Irish-born, as a percentage of the total population of Liverpool, was ever falling—22 per cent in 1851, 19 per cent in 1861, 16 per cent in 1871, 13 per cent in 1891, 7 per cent in 1901—many in fact claimed that Liverpool was one-quarter or one-third 'Irish' since, as Denvir noted, 'the children and grandchildren of Irish-born parents consider themselves just as much Irish as those born on "the old sod" itself'.[56] Those born in Liverpool's slums were 'sternly Irishized'.[57]

This colony was long-standing. Irish names appear among Liverpool burgesses in 1378, and Catholic historians claim 205 Catholic families (one-sixth of ratepayers) in 1707.[58] The Irish-born multiplied: 5,000 in 1800, 11,000 in 1820, 35,000 in 1840.[59] Ireland's Great Famine drove many more to Liverpool. Thomas Burke warned: 'No man can understand aright the Liverpool of the second half of the nineteenth century, who does not seriously study the dread incidents' of these years.[60]

Some 500,000 Irish entered Liverpool before July 1848. The tide seemed irresistible. When Lord Brougham addressed Parliament in January 1847, 900 arrived in Liverpool daily; when he spoke in April, the number was 3,000. Many re-emigrated but, by spring 1847, 105,000 remained and the Select Vestry of Liverpool complained to Parliament that 'this increase was not one of the people of all classes, but of the poor'.[61] However, many believed with the Earl of Wicklow that Liverpool, having 'benefited more by their Irish commerce than by that of all the rest of the world together', should bear the burden.[62]

The cost must be measured against Liverpool's existing distress. Before the Famine perhaps 30,000 Liverpudlians inhabited cellars and 60,000 inhabited closed courts. Dr. Southwood Smith marvelled that people survived such conditions;[63] but Liverpudlians resisted death for a shorter time than most. Edwin Chadwick reckoned that there 'the mean chances of life appear . . . still lower than in Manchester, Leeds, or amongst the silk weavers in Bethnal Green'.[64] In many cases the court and cellar dwellings, in which disease was so powerfully incubated, had origins stretching back to the 1780s; but civic neglect was one cause for, geologically, Liverpool's facilities for drainage were 'inferior to none'. By the 1840s, however, the Corporation was spending over £100,000 on one magnificent building, St. George's Hall, a sum which would have cleansed half Liverpool's streets in perpetuity, according to Chadwick.[65] The question of public health was therefore one of civic values as much as of medical science or ready cash; but the Famine placed strains on all these.[66] In February 1847 Liverpool's fatalities from what was called 'Irish fever' were 18 per cent above average, in June 2,000 per cent.[67] 'Fever' involved cholera by 1849, recalling previous scourges of cholera in 1832 and influenza in 1837.[68] The Irish districts were ravaged, and thirteen of the twenty-three Catholic priests died.[69]

Health was forfeited, but order was preserved by 20,000 special constables and a military presence.[70] Some feared that rootless Irishmen would turn into revolutionary Chartists. How many of the working men among the special constables were volunteers or were pressed by their employers is debatable, but some made known their attitude. Robertson Gladstone was alarmed when 200 foundry workers, men of some education, refused to become special constables 'on the ground that they neither approve of the Queen, the Aristocracy or the Parliament'; and John Bramley-Moore, the Mayor and chairman of the Corporation's Dock Committee, personally discharged 500 dockers who refused similar duties.[71] If, as Robertson Gladstone supposed, 'a love of our form of Government is fast decaying', a love of Liverpool's swelling Irish population was even more rapidly extinguished as the expense placed on the town grew. Over 173,000 persons—probably 95 per cent Irish—were relieved in Liverpool from 18 to 26 January 1847 alone.[72] Liverpudlians gained a reputation for their predatory and vicious reception of immigrants.[73] John Denvir's mother had 'never heard of sin' until she experienced Liverpool; there was 'no sin in Cor-r-k!'[74] Liverpool's relationship with its unwanted Irish remained flinty, like a 'stony-hearted step-mother'.[75]

Traditionally Liverpool was a catchment-basin for the poor. Irish harvesters were often seen 'with blistered feet, scarcely able to crawl . . . begging for bread and trying to raise the means of getting back home'.[76] Two prominent Liverpudlians once attributed much Irish immigration to love of change and fortune-hunting;[77] but necessity intervened before betterment in inspiring migration in the 1840s. Geography and kinship often distinguished the origins of Liverpool Irishmen, who were largely Ulstermen or Leinstermen, with Connaught harvesters passing through. Generally they mingled as compatriots, but distinctions survived. A builder was reluctant to hire Connaught men because men from the other provinces considered them 'as a lower caste'.[78] Altogether there were few occupational differences among Liverpool's Irishmen before and after the Famine.[79] This was the poor man's imperialism, 'spreading . . . as a kind of substratum, beneath a more civilized community'.[80] One Liverpool priest, Father Murphy, observed two types. Miscreants, fleeing to England, he called 'the scum of the country', and he believed that their degeneration persisted. Another class, 'with a fair character', he believed improved partly owing to more regular employment and 'the good example of their English fellow-labourers'.[81] Other Liverpudlians noted the deterioration of most types;[82] and the 1836 Report had concluded that Irish labourers who settled in Britain maintained their native style of existence, dissipating in drink any increase of income.[83]

Liverpool received other migrant tribes, Scots and Welsh, driven not cataclysmically like the Irish but gradually by employment opportunity.[84] The communities born in Scotland or Wales were roughly equal in size in 1871–81—each about 4 per cent of the total population of Liverpool—but the Liverpool Welsh were cumulatively larger. Liverpool was the 'capital of North Wales'.[85] It had Welsh Mayors in the sixteenth century; and Welshmen settled between Vauxhall Road and the Mersey, an area once nominated 'Welsh town', afterwards 'Little Ireland'.[86] Welsh (and Scots) migrations produced distinct settlements, in Everton, Toxteth, Walton, and West Derby. The 1881 census tabulated 21,563 Welsh-born in Liverpool and 4,871 in Birkenhead, which some converted into 60,000-70,000 Liverpool Welsh.[87] The Lord Mayor in 1900 claimed 100,000 which, if the non-Welsh were deducted from Cardiff, made Liverpool the largest Welsh city.[88]

The Welsh settlement in Liverpool is still apparent. The Liverpool telephone directory in 1975 contained fifty-nine columns of Jones, thirty-six columns of Williams, twenty-eight columns of Davies/Davis, twenty-three columns of Hughes, and sixteen columns of Evans. In the past Welsh cultural influences abounded. Eisteddfodau were held on Merseyside;[89] Liverpool's Mayors after 1884 sat on a bardic chair; the Philharmonic Choral Society was predominantly Welsh; and in 1928 when prisons in North Wales were closed, the concern of M.P.s, that prisoners transferred to Liverpool's Walton Gaol should have Welsh chaplains to minister to them, was disarmed by the reply that complete ministrations already existed and that several prison officers and specially appointed visitors were Welsh-speaking. Reputedly 20,000 Liverpudlians spoke Welsh in their homes in 1900; and a score of Welsh-speaking chapel communities existed.[90]

Welsh quarrymen and miners built many Liverpool docks but house-building and allied trades were the principal Welsh employments. Angleseymen ran Liverpool's biggest building businesses: their speciality was the terraced cottage, supplying the first mass market for cheap housing. Their model, the six- (sometimes four-) roomed cottage, had a scullery, parlour, kitchen, and bedrooms. A bathroom was added after English builders imitated this prototype. The Welsh built quickly but, according to one chronicler, soundly.[91] However, in legend, the term 'jerry-building' originated in Liverpool.[92]

Mutuality, frugality, and diligence, characterized the Welsh community. The North and South Wales Bank was founded in Liverpool in 1836, and its officials provided capital for many builders whose character was known through chapel meetings.[93] Aiding compatriots could entail discrimination against others, and connections were established and maintained between national origins, labour skills, and housing types. In dockland Welshmen confronted Irishmen as immigrant aristocrats. In the 1830s most warehousemen were Welsh, because employers thought Irishmen unreliable. Since warehousemen hired porters,

Welshmen got the best places. Welshmen, Irishmen, and Englishmen (with some Scots) each constituted one-third of porters, but under-warehousemen and regular porters were rarely Irish.[94] Little change occurred in the century. The Warehouse Porters' Union, founded in 1890, was undermined by warehousemen giving preference to men who would lodge with them;[95] and an article in *The Transport Worker* in 1911 specifically denounced 'Welsh warehousemen'. The writer was Irish.[96]

Religious friction

These differences between immigrant groups in Liverpool became dynamic, by party calculations and by the superimposition of Ulster Protestant immigration. Religion, as well as nationality, might distinguish occupational and residential groups. Ulstermen dominated certain shipbuilding trades. The 12 July, which Orangemen celebrated by parades, was nicknamed 'Carpenters Day'.[97] When different groups pursued the same occupation, they might divide, like two societies of coal-heavers, on sectarian lines.[98] 'Religion is love', wrote Beatrice Webb; 'in no case is it logic.'[99] Certainly fanatics will dispute because they are fanatics; nevertheless this mimic holy war merits consideration.

Although Anglicans and Nonconformists were often at odds concerning the established nature of the Church in England, Wales, and Ireland, an Evangelical alliance was discernible as an eclecticism that yoked Anglicans and Protestant Nonconformists against Catholics.[100] Theologically the basis of this Evangelical alliance was an insistence on the sole inspiration of the Bible and belief in man's innate wickedness, together with personal conversion and salvation by faith; and this provoked challenges to church authorities—whether of England or of Rome—wherever efforts were made to dictate a prescribed order of belief and observance upon the individual, which elevated liturgical ceremony and sacramental functions at the expense of preaching, and which included doctrines of Baptismal regeneration and the Eucharistic sacrifice. High Churchmen in the Anglican establishment were naturally suspect when they stoutly proclaimed historical continuities with the Catholic church and placed a 'high' value upon episcopal or priestly authority and sacramental practices. During national crises, which involved pristine Reformation principles and the future of the Protestant settlement generally, this Evangelical alliance was evident even when—as in the eighteenth century—the Anglican and Nonconformist churches institutionally were going their separate ways. These national crises invariably had local repercussions.[101] In 1746 seamen and ship-carpenters led rioters against the Catholic chapel and house of Captain Greene, apparently the only Liverpool Catholic to join the Stuarts.[102] Afterwards relations were friendlier;[103] and the Corporation pensioned a former Jesuit who scripturally defended the slave trade.[104] Deterioration occurred as a reflex of events in Ireland, where land jealousies and competition in the North Armagh linen trade brought a plague of martial bands including, in 1795, the modern Orange Order.

A major influence in Irish politics within three years,[105] in conception the Orange Order was patriotic—*vide* the Dublin lodges' declaration that an Orangeman 'regards every loyal man as his friend, be his religious persuasion what it may'.[106] Orangemen defended 'the old Whig principles' against 'French principles'; but the General Declaration announced an exclusively Protestant association pledged to preserve Reformation principles and the Protestant Succession, and to celebrate annually on 12 July the battle of the Boyne, when William III had defeated James II.[107] Militia regiments and Irish migrations carried Orangeism to England. The first lodges were in Manchester in 1798–9. Liverpool was organized in 1807–8, together with the British Grand Lodge. Many lodges functioned as friendly societies; but the Manchester Orangemen also acted as praetorian guards against radical insurgents and the Liverpool Orangemen engaged in sectarian incitement.[108]

On 12 July 1819 the Liverpool Orangemen paraded with the lamb, ark, and Bibles on poles, and a clergyman officiated while counterfeit Catholic insignia were burned. After clashes with Irish Catholics, the ringleaders were imprisoned.[109] Many M.P.s expressed disgust; one accused the Orange clergyman of 'sedition and blasphemy', and Canning, who had occupied a Liverpool seat since 1812, disclaimed all sympathy with Orange activity.[110] Although Liverpool's freemen voters had an appalling record of corruption and for the most part exhibited no consistent political line—the young Gladstone was 'horribly disgusted' by 'the filthy and foetid character' of the pre-Reform Act Liverpool elections—nevertheless the sectarian factions of 1819 affected political polarization. Liverpool's Whigs championed the imprisoned Catholics; on the other hand, as William Cobbett recognized, the Orangemen were buoyed by 'the unconquerable prejudices' of most Englishmen.[111] The issue of Catholic Emancipation divided Liverpool, with petitions claiming 33,000 supporters and 30,000 opponents.[112] The city's Tory M.P.s exhibited disunity. Gascoyne espoused Protestant Ascendancy whereas Huskisson, backed by Canning's prestige, encouraged emancipation.[113]

The dominant trends were set against toleration. The Whigs' apparent Irish Catholic sympathies inspired in Liverpool a Tory–Protestant connection, which in 1834 welcomed at St. Jude's Church an Ulster parson, Hugh M'Neile. M'Neile has been called 'the real creator' of Liverpool Conservatism. He made it unremittingly sectarian in character by condemning Popery both 'as religious heresy . . . and as political conspiracy'.[114] In 1835 M'Neile formed the Liverpool Protestant Association; but he relied chiefly on demagogy. He was 'a veritable Apollos', who 'made and unmade Mayors as easily as Warwick made kings . . . He ruled by the sheer splendour of his overwhelming eloquence.'[115] He had allies. In 1830 Liverpool contained thirteen Orange lodges, although members cannot be enumerated.[116] There were also issues suited to declamation. In 1827 the Corporation established two elementary schools, with the object of raising Anglican education to the level of dissenters';[117] but, after the Whigs achieved a municipal majority in 1835, Catholic children and scripture were admitted.[118] Protestants reacted strongly, one M'Neilite Tory declaring of the Catholic Bibles that they should be cased in iron chests and cast 'into the lowest sinks of the filth of the Corporation . . .'.[119] Protestantism became the Tories' electoral charm, although other factors—Whig–Liberal dissension, the efforts of the drink trade, and the skill with which registration agents manipulated the franchise—combined to ruin the Whig majority. After the 1841 elections Conservative control of the Council was complete, whereupon most of the 936 Catholic children attending Corporation schools were withdrawn and the three Catholic teachers resigned.

Two Liverpool witnesses of the early 1830s had believed that anti-Catholic prejudice was decreasing;[120] but the continuance of M'Neilite attitudes among Conservatives reinforced the Catholics' desire to build their own schools, and maintained their sense of separateness even after 1870 when the principle of public responsibility for education was conceded. Above all the substantial Irish immigration into Victorian Liverpool aggravated Protestant–Catholic tensions.

Long prevalent were allegations that Irishmen depressed wages. M. J. Whitty, Liverpool's first Head Constable and the founder of the *Liverpool Daily Post*, considered that insufficient English labour existed and that 'the Highland Scotch, and all the Welsh, do and would work for as low or even lower wages than the Irish';[121] but this defence was enfeebled when the Famine multiplied Liverpool's Irish poor. Excess labour swamped the docks, and real wages for many of the Merseyside working class did not improve between 1850 and 1875.[122] The slums bred a 'congenital urge to fight'; and the job competition assumed ceremonial guise. Marchers with green and orange ribbons were 'flaunting their allegiance . . . rather than their belief'.[123]

Some things left Liverpudlians unmoved. Shakespeare was evidently one. When Macready—the foremost actor of his day, after Kean was sunk in drink—played Macbeth in Liverpool, he tried to rescue the performance from a supporting player but, as he confided to his diary, 'the audience were an *old Liverpool audience*, attentive and *very cold*'.[124] Liverpool audiences were warmer upon sectarian matters, and several organizations were splintered by religious factionalism. The Liverpool Historic Society, a debating club established in 1834, specified at the outset, before detailing the forms and procedures of association, '1. Controversial Theology shall not be introduced'. This injunction was unnecessary in those societies which confined their membership to followers of one religious persuasion. An official inquiry revealed the unusual 'prominence of sectarian spirit' among friendly societies in Liverpool. Likewise, although the Liverpool Total Abstinence Society formally abjured 'all sectarian opinions', M'Neile freely denounced teetotallers as revolutionaries and atheists, and separate temperence organizations emerged among Liverpool Catholics and Welsh.[125] M'Neile's Protestant Association also espoused fiscal protection, and this limited the Anti-Corn Law League's appeal in Liverpool. In 1841, following the rumoured murder of Protestant clergy in Ireland, gangs of Orangemen smashed both an Anti-Corn Law meeting and St. Patrick's Church.[126] John Bright reflected that 'Liverpool is too monstrous a thing to affect public opinion except adversely to its own course'.[127]

Political party developments before 1867

Liberalism was a creature of stunted growth in Liverpool.[128] On a number of issues the Liberals seemed careless of local interests. Their prominence in the anti-Slavery movement had been considered treasonable. Similarly, although Nonconformists abhorred Catholic doctrine and education, the Liberals'

Unitarian leaders, by practical help and professions of toleration, were held responsible for the settlement of Popery in Liverpool.[129] Good Samaritans can make inept politicians, and those Liverpool Liberals who supported the North during the American Civil War upset their party by their indifference to local self-interest. Liverpool generally backed the South because of the cotton trade. The *Alabama* and many other privateers were built and manned on Merseyside;[130] and a bazaar in St. George's Hall realized £30,000 to aid Confederate soldiers. It was charity creamed off profits. Vast rewards—and risks—attended blockade-running. Cotton left the South at 3*d*. or 4*d*. and reached Liverpool at 2*s*. 6*d*. per pound.[131]

As fortunes were made and lost some sensed that Liverpool was captured by parvenus, who made its society 'more cosmopolitan and democratic'.[132] This last word indicates a further disadvantage which beset the Liberal leaders. They formed an exclusive set, dominated by the richer merchants, shipowners, and brokers, while the Tories, increasingly from the 1830s, showed an ability to attract tradesmen, particularly small and medium wholesalers, retailers, builders, contractors, and manufacturers, as well as a popular Protestant following. Not that the Tory ascendancy on the Liverpool Council was imperishable, for in the decade from 1858 the Liberals achieved a majority of Councillors in six years and parity in three. Tory control over-all was preserved by the tenacity of their aldermen. Nevertheless the Liberal drive fell short of full blooded commitment. There was a contrast between the Tory bid to wrest control of the Council from the Whigs between 1835 and 1841, and the Liberal bid to wrest the Council from the Tories between 1858 and 1867. In the first period 92 per cent of wards were contested at elections, in the second only 41 per cent. The Liberal merchant élite in general neither worked hard at elections nor saw the need to do so. They would oppose those whom they believed to be unprincipled and depraved, such as councillors who served the drink interest, but they were ready to make exceptions in the case of those who, though Tory, were independent gentlemen like themselves. To raise an electoral army of radical working men against the latter was unthinkable.[133]

The critic and essayist, William Hazlitt, had early exposed the pretensions of the Liverpool Liberal élite. London society, he considered, was meritocratic in character; but in Manchester or Liverpool it was known 'what every man in the room is worth in land or money; what are his connections and prospects in life—and this gives a character of servility or arrogance, of mercenariness or impertinence to the whole of provincial intercourse. You laugh not in proportion to a man's wit but his wealth; you have to consider not what, but whom you contradict.' Hazlitt then pursued a finer distinction, drawing upon his own experience of Liverpool society at intervals from 1790. He was familiar—through his father, a Unitarian minister—with that group of Liberals who imitated the banker, William Roscoe, in zeal for the Italian Renaissance. As an individual Hazlitt accounted Roscoe 'a very excellent man', but as an entity he preferred Manchester to Liverpool society. In the former 'you are oppressed only by the aristocracy of wealth; in the latter by the aristocracy of wealth and letters by turns. You could not help feeling that some of their great men were authors among merchants and merchants among authors. Their bread was buttered on both sides, and they had you at a disadvantage either way.'[134] Here was the chrysalis of Manchester men and Liverpool gentlemen, that contrast of office and factory work.

What Hazlitt judged from a cultural aspect, a modern historian has examined from financial and sectarian sides. Dr. Watkinson has analysed the estates of 159 Liberal Magistrates appointed between 1835 and 1885: they average £160,000. By creed 124 prominent Liberals can be identified as forty-eight Anglicans, thirty-eight Unitarians, nine Independents, five Baptists, five Presbyterians, three Wesleyans, one Quaker, one Positivist, and fourteen Catholics. Another sample of the Standing Committee of Reformers (1831) and of officers of the Reform Club and Liberal Association (1852–85) suggests that Unitarians slightly outnumbered Anglicans. Significant was the Unitarians' strength as in mid-Victorian Birmingham and elsewhere—and the numerical slightness of orthodox Nonconformists in relation to Anglicans.[135]

Family tradition cemented the Unitarians. Mrs Humphry Ward declared that 'Unitarianism in many of its phases looks like the remains of something else'.[136] The Rathbones, previously Quakers, became Unitarian after William Rathbone V (1787–1868) married Elizabeth Greg; but the proprietor of the *Birkenhead News* and *Liberal Review*, Charles Willmer, renounced Anglicanism for Unitarianism after hearing M'Neile's no-popery sermons.[137]

For some Unitarians the creed denoted status.[138] Material and spiritual needs were linked. Charles Beard advised a colleague that success in the ministry in Liverpool derived from familiarity with the cotton market as from sound preaching.[139] Unitarians were charitable; but this the Liberal press over-rated for, subtracting the Rathbone, Holt, and Bowring muscle, a flatulent shape remained. 'Their soft hearts are strongly guarded by their hard heads'—this was true of the Liverpool Unitarians as of many Victorian philanthropists. Moreover it was noted that the Liverpool Unitarians gave offence by forming 'a close clique in the Liberal camp . . . while even as educationalists they have done next to nothing locally compared with the scores of Elementary Schools paid for by their opponents'.[140]

The Unitarians' deep certainty about the superiority of their culture was particularly marked in political controversies over education, for 'no one brought up in the freedom of Unitarian principles can in the least understand the Catholic (Anglican or Roman) point of view that children must have the *right* (as they think) theological opinions drummed into them when unable to really understand for fear that in their more mature age they will not accept these opinions'. The alliance between the Liverpool Liberals' Unitarian leaders and the party's popular Catholic following was therefore never close. The Unitarians' concern for toleration for Catholics was intellectual, a matter of civil rights: the communities were otherwise alien. Richard Holt, for instance, recorded this of the first (perhaps only) Catholic service that he ever attended, by invitation to a full mass to commemorate Archbishop Whiteside in 1921: 'The ceremony lasted two hours and except for a short address eulogizing the deceased was incomprehensible to me:—I had never been to a Roman Catholic ceremonial before but this was worse than I could have expected—tawdry splendour—bowing, scraping, changing clothes, lighting and extinguishing candles—the most miserable performance exactly like the Buddhist priests.'[141]

Protestant Nonconformity in Liverpool was heterogeneous and discordant. Congregationalists and Baptists, Augustine Birrell wrote, were reasonably friendly; but both withheld from the Wesleyans, and between orthodox Dissenters and the Unitarians was 'a great gulf fixed'.[142] Nevertheless, the Nonconformist body as a whole (excepting the Welsh section which, by ethnic ties, was peculiar) was insulated from the general population. Canon Hume illustrated how forty chapels closed in the town centre as a result of the outward migration of prosperous dissenters. By 1862 nine of the deserted chapels were being used by Anglicans, and the Catholic authorities had bought two Nonconformist schools. As the population of Liverpool parish declined, centrally situated Anglican churches closed too—five had done so by 1903, when a Diocesan Commission recommended another six closures.[143] However, the suburban exodus of dissenting communities before 1860 followed from their attachment to the wealthy, since up to that time the population in parts of central Liverpool was still increasing.[144] Not that the Anglican church was exempt from Hume's strictures against class-bound religions. Many churches in central Liverpool had been built to suit wealthy congregations, and, when they moved, their pews remained closed and unoccupied.[145]

These migrations changed the character of districts. Although some professional classes survived in Rodney Street and Abercromby Wards, increasingly the 'pauper' poor occupied the centre. Several parishes were between 75 per cent and 90 per cent Catholic. In one area three-fifths of Protestant families removed house in two years, some several times, and one-quarter moved absolutely. Those that remained were 'an inferior class—poor, ignorant, and godless'.[146]

Social relations chilled as Liverpool divided into broadly single-class zones. Soon after becoming American Consul in Liverpool, Nathaniel Hawthorne developed 'some of the English indifference as to beggars and poor people'.[147] The spread of suburbia did not enhance neighbourliness.[148] Suburbs, by definition, are incomplete communities but the suburbia of Liverpool was rendered almost unnavigable before the 1890s by a poor transport system. When the tram network partly relieved this position it did so in a manner that pointedly emphasized the travellers' circumstances. For fifteen years from 1908 first-class trams operated on certain routes. According to Margaret Cole one in three trams from Sefton Park to the Pier Head had an upholstered lower deck where double fare was charged; but trams were the 'gondolas of the people', and a first-class compartment did not protect its users from lice.[149] The Mersey was another obstacle and, though a railway tunnel was opened in 1886, the Cheshire suburbs maintained an unsociable distance from poor Liverpudlians, who called this 'the land of the one-eyed people'.[150] Because of these topographical disincentives Liverpool's well-to-do had little social life beyond formal occasions at the Town Hall or Wellington Rooms.[151] Before the opening of new political clubs in Dale Street—the Reform in 1879 and the Conservative in 1883—merchants spent secluded evenings at home.

Amid commuting wealth, class relations suffered. The Liverpool party which best adapted when the gulf was widest dominated politics in the period of formative democracy. In 1870 the trade unionist, George Howell, told William Rathbone that the Liberals failed among working men because 'their economics are considered harsh and partial' and their behaviour lacked 'geniality and bonhomie'. To some extent Rathbone himself represented this gap in sympathy. The charity of this merchant and shipowner was legion, but his character was emphatically patrician. Like any Peelite Liberal he was keen to provide 'good government'—especially Rathbone wanted to rationalize the system of local government—but he had set views regarding the role of the state in relief of the poor. He objected vehemently to the democratization of the elections of Poor Law Guardians in the 1894 Local Government Act, because he feared that popular pressure would cause Guardians to abandon 'sound' principles. Self-reliance was the cornerstone of Rathbone's philosophy and, regarding outdoor relief and the test of eligibility, Rathbone remained a man of 1834. Indeed, it was owing to Rathbone's efforts that governments twice republished the classic Poor Law Report in the late-nineteenth century.[152]

Compared with Rathbone's stiff rectitude, fluency characterized the Liverpool Conservative leaders' social behaviour. They were practised in stooping to conquer. They 'mixed with the crowd without assumption of superiority; they have become Freemasons, Oddfellows, Buffaloes, Shepherds, etc.; they have attended Trade Union balls and danced cheerfully with the women . . .'.[153] The Conservatives' ascendancy in Liverpool before 1939 was in part a *tour de force* of five men, Thomas Bold, Edward Whitley, Sir Arthur Forwood, Sir Archibald Salvidge, and Sir Thomas White. These otherwise dissimilar characters had a common touch. Bold, who guided Liverpool Conservatism in the 1850s, lacked oratory, but he could 'adorn the ball room . . . "manage" an old freeman or keep a mob in good humour'.[154] Class distances did not vanish, but some Conservatives, by a conspiracy of social breeziness, made fainter hard lines of exclusion.[155]

While Bold polished his vulgar arts the Liberals were run by such as George Melly, a Unitarian merchant, educated at Rugby, and morally committed to many reforms, like public education, but socially aloof from the working-class electorate. Melly's personal influence disappeared after he won Stoke in 1868, but it was Mellyism in Liverpool that *The Dawn* referred to in 1868 when it complained that the Liberal Association conducted itself snobbishly.[156] Artisan Everton was starved of tickets for the Gladstone meetings, but 'gentlemen' received them unsolicited. Conservatives acted differently, and *Porcupine* asserted that on that side lay 'liberty, equality, and fraternity', on the Liberal side, 'restraint, class distinction, and isolation'.[157]

Several Liberals endeavoured to break this class barrier with a Working Men's Liberal Association in 1873. Its chairman, James Samuelson, patronized Irish and trade union causes, and its object was to return Liberal M.P.s, 'to secure all just political and social privileges for the working classes, and to promote civil and religious equality'.[158] It enrolled 507 members in four branches; but, by the 1874 General Election, its fate was sealed. Liberal leaders who were uninterested, and trade unionists who preferred to separate party and labour matters, crippled it.[159] Conversely the Working Men's Conservative Association expanded in every decade before 1914.

Conservatism, unlike Liberalism, was not foremost a political organization. The Church, throne, peerage, and property great and small provided a natural framework; and social promotions and penalties were for many the bases of party loyalty.[160] Such a system was always open to abuse. John Gorst, for example, alleged that W. H. Smith secured the position of a Conservative leader 'by wholesale bribery and treating of the front bench'. What is certain, however, is that Smith, when his politics were undiagnosed although he had twice considered standing as a Liberal, was rejected by the Reform Club in 1862 but accepted at the Carlton.[161] Whigs withheld from fusion with ordinary Liberals. *Porcupine* cursed this chasm in 1879 when the Liverpool Reform Club's subscription was doubled to ten guineas soon after the Marquis of Hartington opened its new premises.[162] Conservatives by contrast coined social vanity into political force. They recognized that society was plutocratic, they even played with the idea that it was democratic, according to Horatio Bottomley's witticism that 'the most popular form of democracy is that which gives us the right to fraternize upon terms of equality with our social *superiors*'.[163]

It has been argued that intelligent workmen, pursuing not simply material betterment but improved status, were alienated from Tory leaders who 'could not envisage any relationship between party and people other than that of guarded benevolence on the one side and grateful deference on the other . . .'.[164] Several qualifications to this compose fundamental lines in Liverpool's history. First, although the core of Conservatism continued, its presentation altered. That epitome of New Journalism, T. P. O'Connor, who represented the Liverpool Scotland constituency as an Irish Nationalist, once observed: 'The Tory party still remains the party of the monopolists and the selfish, but it has learned that household suffrage means a considerable weapon in the hands of working men, and, accordingly, though it may put its tongue in its cheek, it keeps that tongue very civil whenever it begins to utter opinion.'[165] Furthermore, Liverpool was not a manufacturing town with a spine of skilled workmen who could, *ceteris paribus*, command wages whatever their opinions. Liverpool's social structure was 'honeycombed with purely commercial interests. No one knows where the influence of a single wealthy family may begin or end. The clerk is afraid of losing his situation, the shopkeeper a customer, and so on through the whole gamut from high to low'.[166]

The Liverpool Conservative leader, Arthur Forwood, argued that working men accepted that a leisured and educated class should conduct Government. Even their complaint, that 'our leaders do not come amongst us sufficiently often', indicated 'their good feeling towards those placed in a better position in society'.[167] Not only Conservative working men evinced deferential characteristics.[168] The *Review* knew another 'political coward': 'Let a man only drive a brougham, be reputed to be rich and . . . one of the "good old families", and so the Liverpool Liberal bows down and worships him.'[169]

However, accepting that some working men had social aspirations, there is the question whether this was satisfied in the functional processes of party. One recent historian of the Disraelian era concludes not: the Conservative party extended the franchise to many workmen, but was disinclined to respect their ambitions or to concede a significant part in its organization.[170] Liverpool was an exception to this rule. The Working Men's Conservative Association, founded in 1868, had twelve flourishing branches by 1872 with representation on all committees of the Constitutional Association. Its importance was such that Liverpool politics have to be seen through its lens; but involvement in party organization alone did not slake aspirations.

R. J. White has postulated that 'Anyone with anything to lose, if it is only the opportunity to be idle—these are the Conservatives'.[171] There is the ambition of improving, also the precaution of not losing, status. Lord George Hamilton, a minister in both Disraeli's and Salisbury's Governments, recognized a Conservative as one who was 'more or less contented and happy with his condition'.[172] Change can depress as well as elevate. What, therefore, had Liverpool Conservatives to lose? One late-nineteenth-century political observer stressed that 'Privilege is the mint mark of Toryism, exclusiveness is its life and soul. The doctrine of equal rights must be in everlasting repugnance to it.'[173] This feeling was not confined to those with great possessions. Labourers had their sectional pride, so did the Everton clerk with his poor competence for, as Attlee observed, this man hugged his chains.[174] Not only aristocrats, many lower down feared losing caste. Lord Randolph Churchill recognized the largest of these distinctions when he declared that 'in the minds of the lords of suburban villas, of the owners of vineries and pineries, the mud cabin represents the climax of physical and social degradation'. It symbolized the Irish, those 'white chimpanzees'.[175]

The social alignments in which electors subjectively placed themselves impelled their votes as much as did political events. Liverpool's politics were impregnated with religious-cum-national stereotypes. The W.M.C.A., like many Conservative associations founded in the late 1860s, sought to refute the Reform League's assumption that the entire working class was Radical; it also took as its emblem the maintenance of Protestantism. Tory working men cherished this as self-esteem, believing that England's ascendancy over Ireland was shaped by differences of creed—their Protestantism evoking personal independence, material prosperity, and all civic virtues; the others' Catholicism bringing priest-ridden superstition, lawlessness, and economic fatalism. Marx compared the English proletarians' attitude towards Irishmen with that of 'poor whites' towards 'niggers' in the American South, although with greater deliberation it is clear that the prejudice and hostility were political, cultural, and economic rather than racial.[176] In Liverpool the Conservative party predominated because it 'tended to represent the established and native-born section of the population in a city conscious of wave after wave of immigration'.[177]

Religion was both a shibboleth and fundamentally inspirational. In 1874 the chairman of one ward Conservative Association in Liverpool defined Protestant Ascendancy as 'simply this—it was the ascendancy of truth over error—(cheers)—of light over darkness, of freedom over slavery (much cheering)'.[178] Although certain features, like the system of private pews, indicated the

Church's class scrupulosity, it was an article of faith that the equality of Protestant consciences was complemented by a conservative democracy in the state. Samuel Graves, who represented Liverpool from 1865 to 1873, declared: 'On the King, the aristocracy, and the people rests the constitution, and by the mild influence of a state church these three estates are tied together like the golden thread on which priceless pearls are hung (Hear, hear and great cheering).'[179]

CHAPTER TWO

Incipient Democracy and the Irish Problem, 1868–84

The state of Liverpool would shatter much hope. *Canon Barnett*

You cannot be decently civil to Catholics without offending Protestants, and vice versa.[1] *Lord Derby*

This chapter covers the years between the Second and Third Reform Acts, when the popular voice increased in volume. Problems were publicized rather than corrected. Liverpool Liberals, for instance, responded to the exposure of poverty and crime in their city by a temperance campaign. This was logical in terms of party politics, since the Conservatives were popularly associated with defence of the drink interest; but a temperance campaign was inadequate, if not incongruous, considering the social and economic problems it ostensibly answered.

The Liberals were unable to dictate the movement of Liverpool politics for long. Irish questions began to command most politicians' thoughts. A separate Irish party was formed in Liverpool and the Liberals, after suffering the shock of competition, were forced to come to a *modus vivendi*. The Conservatives, on the other hand, exhibited indignation, but also hesitation. Although they designated their role to be the defence of established national institutions and habits, there was confusion in the definition of these things. A defence of the nation's religion, Protestantism, was only capable of fashioning an alliance of enemies. Anglicans and Nonconformists disputed the type of religious instruction which should be provided in schools, as well as the establishment of the Church of England itself. Moreover many Protestants believed that the most obnoxious of papistical invasions was taking place within the Anglican Church, in the Ritualist movement; and they demanded that the Church be reformed, not merely defended. At the same time all party managers in the 1870s and 1880s considered how much weight to accord the opinions of ordinary voters in their consultations.

Notes begin on p. 365

The General Election of 1868 and the condition of Liverpool

Following the extension of the franchise in 1867 the Reform League assumed that, ' "the operative conservative" being a mere myth', the Liberal cause would be strengthened.[2] In Liverpool, where the electorate almost doubled, to 39,637, radical opinion was less confident. Leading Conservatives had championed household suffrage and, suspecting devilry, the Liverpool branch of the Reform League argued that because of employers' influences 'the Ballot is the great Necessity'. The malady resisted this prescription. The cause was not hard to discover; indeed the same Reformers had noted, 'the Orange element is strong and we believe the majority are Conservative from conviction'.[3]

In the 1868 General Election Conservatives played the Protestant card, defending the Church equally from Disestablishment and Ritualism. The prospect of an Irish Church Bill aroused their strongest opposition, too strong indeed for churchmen like Dr. Thirlwell, the Bishop of St. David's, who saw nothing sacriligeous in reallocating church property, certainly not the 'robbery of God'.[4] There was pungent rhetoric too at the Liverpool Registration Court, where the Conservatives' solicitor, in objecting to voters with Irish names, asserted that Liberals could not distinguish working men and 'the lowest scum of the earth'.[5] One Liverpool Whig, Sir James Picton, however, emphasized that the Conservatives' manipulation of the register and other devices were unnecessary: 'had the voting been by ballot . . . the result would have been the same. There is amongst the lower classes of the English and the Scots an intense dislike of the Irish Catholics, who compete in labour with them, and of whom they certainly see the worst side.'[6]

'The reality of the "Conservative working-man" must now be admitted', said William Rathbone, after Liverpool continued to return two Conservative M.P.s, Samuel Graves and Viscount Sandon.[7] The minority Liberal interest was represented by Rathbone himself: Liverpool had been granted three M.P.s, but each elector was equipped with two votes only. In fact, for an undisguised sense of the dispassionate sameness with which Merseyside entered the era of extended franchise, Birkenhead merits notice. There, even following the secret ballot, the town's principal shipbuilder, John Laird, who 'cared nought for the Trade Unions', increased his majority.[8] The cause of Laird's success had been outstanding in his very first contest of Birkenhead in 1861 when, as one Tory shipwright recalled, men who loathed 'hard old Jock' supported him against 'the son of one of the best of masters', Thomas Brassey. Although they fought bitterly over matters of wages and trade union recognition, men acknowledged Laird's ability to represent and to further the interests of Birkenhead. Industrial disputes, therefore, did not inevitably speed radical politics. Indeed Laird's strong Protestant opinions—he denounced Ritualism as 'sham Romanism'—cut across economic and social class divisions. 'We workmen', the shipwright mused, 'are a mass of anomalies.'[9]

From the 1860s Irish restlessness, and the condition of Liverpool, concerned many politicians. That a 'secret organization' linked Liverpool Irishmen with the Fenians Picton believed 'indisputable'.[10] The police intercepted terrorist traffic;[11] but several Irishmen looked for opportunity to learn the use of arms.[12]

In 1881 a bomb exploded by the Town Hall and the Home Secretary, Harcourt, dispatched troops to Liverpool.[13] The mayor, William Forwood, refused a Gatling gun for his personal use, despite Harcourt's recommendation that they were 'grand things for clearing the streets'. Forwood blamed the sporadic disturbances on Irish Americans: 'the Irish people at large' had no sympathy with them and, when the Prince and the Princess of Wales visited Liverpool, he told Harcourt, they were as heartily received in the Irish quarter as elsewhere.[14]

Nevertheless the Phoenix Park murders, some rumoured, were planned in Liverpool, and Harcourt was urged to apply to Liverpool parts of the Prevention of Crime (Ireland) Bill.[15] The necessity for troops was a fixture of correspondence with the Home Office. William Forwood's brother, Arthur, the mayor in 1878, argued that since Liverpool contained a 'large proportion of the migratory class' a garrison would have a 'salutary effect'.[16] Fenians and migrants, however, were not the only lawless elements. National publicity was achieved in 1874 when, in Tithebarn Street, a citizen was robbed and murdered before an approving audience.[17] The *Daily Telegraph* considered that 'in all the pages of Dr. Livingstone's experience among the negroes of Africa, there is no single instance approaching this Liverpool story, in savagery of mind and body, in bestiality of heart and act'; and *The Times* related terrible statistics of crime, drink, and disease, and concluded that Liverpool's leading citizens neglected their duties.[18]

The Watch Committee permitted the Head Constable, Major J. J. Greig, to expand his force and to increase their patrols. Their number, however, was not the problem.[19] Their organization was over-centralized and their intelligence, measured by literacy, inadequate.[20] This did not inspire confidence. Picton advised respectable persons to carry revolvers; and another Whig, Philip Rathbone, recommended a more extensive use of the 'cat'. If criminals knew 'they would not cause a single unbroken square inch of flesh to be left on their backs, he did not think they would go much further'.[21]

Some reasonable voices countered this clamour. One clergyman offered £1,000 towards improvements in slum areas, and a Kirkdale man wrote that remarks on the brutal temper of the poor ignored the conditions about them—'circumstances calculated to make them savages'.[22] The national urban death-rates in 1861 were headed by those of Liverpool, at 33 per thousand persons. Overcrowding was rife. On average 122 people inhabited every acre of the parish, but about one-third of its total area of 2,200 acres contained non-residential water and business premises. By 1877 living-space was reduced to a half. Thus confined were 200,000 people.[23]

The drink question

A determination for practical social reform was translated into the temperance movement. The outlook of temperance societies was not altogether restrictive. The Church of England Temperance Society (1862), for example, did not require its members to be teetotallers; it emphasized systematic education, with reward schemes, for juveniles; and it encouraged various counter-attractions, such as free libraries, sports clubs, friendly societies, savings banks, and instruction in domestic science and sanitation.[24] There were several notable experiments in Liverpool. The Police Court and Prison Gate Mission—opened in 1879, the first in the country—made contact with thousands each year. On a smaller scale the C.E.T.S.'s Firewood and Mat Factory (opened in 1891) employed under three hundred, and the Women's Shelter (opened in 1887) accommodated under fifty, each year. This provision reflected a not very profound theory of social change, that poor people would cease to frequent public houses or to join street-corner gangs if they were provided with alternative recreation facilities or had contact with well-intentioned middle-class citizens. The pathology of working-class culture was more complex but, in any case, this side of the temperance effort paled in relation to the campaigns to restrict licensing hours by legislation. These campaigns, rather than the patient and private work of social reconstruction, were what elicited the commitment of temperance enthusiasts and, because of this, the reputation of temperance societies tended to be unremittingly austere.

In 1875 2,650 Liverpool ratepayers (including 403 members of the Exchange) petitioned for a town's meeting to consider the relation of drinking to crime; but the mayor refused, believing that they desired to discredit the licensing laws and to dictate to the magistrates. All 68,879 householders were then circularized about a programme which demanded an inspectorate, the rescission of licences following convictions, shorter hours of sale on work-days, and Sunday closing. 51,000 people answered, mostly favourably.[25] A Vigilance Committee notified the Council and Government.

This Committee involved many different sorts. Monsignor Nugent and his sectarian opposite, that stalwart of the Church Association, Canon (later Archdeacon) Taylor, were both exhortatory; and the *Mercury* reckoned that of five or six thousand Liverpool electors whose priority was the Permissive Bill, two thousand were Tories. But the Committee's principals were Thomas Matheson, Alexander Balfour, Stephen Williamson, W. P. Lockhart, and Samuel Smith—Liberals, Scotsmen, and pillars of the Presbyterian Church, Canning Street.[26] Representing the ideal of Christian merchants, they were involved in the Y.M.C.A., Ragged School Union, and most mission work in Liverpool. Balfour was archetypal. He made men 'tremble with his religious earnestness'.[27] His partnership with Williamson revealed their quintessence. Like William and Samuel Rathbone, they reserved a percentage of their profits for religious and benevolent purposes. A self-imposed tax is an opening to cynical suspicions, but Balfour 'would not exchange the proud position of a British merchant . . . for that of the richest landlord proprietor'. Business enabled him to fulfil a Christian's duty—'service'.[28]

There was need to counter services which others rendered. About 12,000 drunks were apprehended in Liverpool in 1874—one-tenth of the country's total—but only three publicans were convicted for offences.[29] Major Greig disliked his constables inspecting pubs because 'temptation is very great on a cold night, and the liquor is held to their lips'.[30] Moreover, bootlegging followed upon the 1872 Act, when opening hours were restricted to between 7 a.m. and 11 p.m.[31] The police claimed to have eliminated this, and illicit stills, by 1875; but both claims were premature.[32]

In 1874 Liverpool boasted 1,929 public-houses, 383 beer-houses (protected by the 1869 Act), and 272 off-licences and refreshment houses. They outnumbered all grocery, provision, furniture, chemist, and stationery shops.[33] Pubs for sale in poor districts were advertised as situated 'in a good drinking neighbourhood'.[34] Herbalists were also numerous for, though such practices were proscribed by legislation in 1875, beer was commonly adulterated. The American novelist, Hermann Melville, had likened 'swipes'—the beer drunk by seamen and the poor in Liverpool—to 'a decoction of spoiled pickles'.[35]

Occasionally this picture of Liverpool was redressed. Though once of the conviction that 'a Liverpool audience is usually dull', Charles Dickens was gratified by the popularity of his public readings and lectures. On his last visit to Liverpool, in 1869, he had noted that 'one of the pleasantest things I have experienced here . . . is the manner in which I am stopped in the streets by working men, who want to shake hands with me, and tell me they know my books. I never go out but this happens'. Dickens, however, did not escape the darker side of Liverpool life. When the Corporation honoured him with a banquet in St. George's Hall, that ended with a cloakroom brawl between drunken dignitaries. The omnipresent brutality horrified those novelists and poets who spent a period of their lives in Liverpool, like Hugh Walpole or Gerard Manley Hopkins, who felt that 'Liverpool is of all places the most museless'. Dinah Mulock gave her account in *A Life for A Life*: 'This Liverpool is an awful town for drinking. Other towns may be as bad; statistics prove it; but I know no place where intoxication is so open and shameless. Not only in by-streets and foul courts, where one expects to see it, but everywhere.'[36] Altogether Liverpool was a writer's by-word for squalor and philistinism and, though adventitious, it seemed appropriate that it was in a Liverpool street that Matthew Arnold collapsed and died in 1888.

Liverpool, 'the most immoral of all immoral places', laid notorious traps for sailors.[37] A Sailors' Home existed from 1852 to protect seamen from extortion, and to provide religious instruction, board, lodgings, and medicine. By 1900 some 7,000 seamen annually boarded there; but pimps, crimps, and prostitutes thronged the doors and forty-six drinking dens stood within 200 yards' radius of the Home throughout the 1870s and the 1880s.[38] Liverpudlians sometimes blamed strangers for the city's drunkenness and crime; but pubs were not only concentrated along the waterfront, and increasingly sailors saved their wages.[39] The *Liverpool Albion* divided the record of arrested drunks into two classes—lodgers in Liverpool under a month, those homeless or inhabiting vessels; and residents over a month. The latter constituted 88 per cent;[40] but another startling feature was the offenders' sex. In 1876 12,156 of 27,529 persons arrested on all crimes were female, a proportion unmatched, *The Times* hazarded, anywhere.[41] Walton Gaol, accommodating 13,000 prisoners annually, was particularly overcrowded with females.

Drunks were reared young in Liverpool. In 1876 352 convicted drunks were aged under twelve; 1,523 from twelve to eighteen; 3,183 from eighteen to twenty-one; and these were the decade's best returns.[42] Samuel Smith concluded that 'this human deposit of vice and poverty is *hereditary*'.[43] He recommended aided emigration.[44] The antithesis of the two nations was glaring in both statistics and solution. According to Smith children were too old at twelve to lose their parents' corrupting influences and needed Christian training before being shipped abroad: 'Decent people cannot be expected to take repulsive children, using bad language and telling lies, to live as inmates of their households. They must be lovable and attractive . . .'[45]

Sociologists might argue that societies get the drunks and criminals they deserve; but Conservatives noticed that the Irish constituted one-quarter of Liverpool but over half of paupers and criminals.[46] One Liverpool Irish woman, a street-trader, sported the national record, being held 356 times for drunkenness, assaults, damage, and begging.[47] Pilferage, unpremeditated violence, and riots, seemed typically Irish crimes.[48] More accustomed to country life, the Irish spiritedly celebrated feast-days, for example, with bonfires on St. John's Eve.[49] When the local chemical manufacturer and Liberal M.P. for Northwich, J. T. Brunner, complained about 'the British Sunday of the slums, with its deadening vacuity, its gluttony, and its debauchery', the *Liverpool Courier* remarked that the horror was 'rather the Irish Sunday than the English one'.[50]

Men invariably recognized 'the Irish quarter' or, as one twentieth-century Liverpudlian put it, 'the unknown regions of the Irish poor', when addressing Liverpool's social problems.[51] This persistence was unusual for, despite disruptions caused by immigration and by no-Popery preachers like Orr, Gavazzi, and Murphy,[52] many Irish people appeared settled in Britain by 1890. The intermixture of Irish in the general population of Birmingham and London was contrasted with the situation in north-country towns, 'where they are more homogeneous, and but rarely marry outside their own creed and nationality'.[53] Numbers partly explained this—the question seemed less that of Liverpool absorbing the Irish, as of Liverpool resisting absorption by the Irish.

Sectarian loyalties

It has been written that 'to be a Catholic was to be a true Irishman; to be an Irishman was to be a true Catholic';[54] but the distinctiveness of Irish nationhood held, though Catholicism might lapse. The prevalence of wakes denoted a folk heritage stronger than avowed religion: the Catholic hierarchy had proscribed wakes regularly from the seventeenth century.[55] Several Liverpool priests during the first episcopal visitation (1855–7) either denied that wakes 'as an abuse' prevailed, or suggested that they had diminished in extent. But many secular observers disagreed;[56] and one priest wrote roundly: 'Subjects to be reprobated, which prevail to an alarming extent in some parts: Wakes, Dancing houses and singing rooms, Ribbonism, the low London trashy corrupting press.'[57] In 1880 Gerard Manley Hopkins cut a miserable figure as a curate at St. Francis Xavier's.[58] What distinguished the Liverpool Irish from Irishmen he had known in Glasgow was their hostility to the city.[59] They seemed unreformed and unreformable; 'the drunkards go on drinking, the filthy, as the scripture says, are filthy still . . .'[60]

Goss, Liverpool's second Catholic bishop, considered that many approached only nominal religion.[61] Inadequate accommodation was partly responsible. In 1851 Liverpool contained nine Catholic places of worship.[62] Most were extempore missions, their condition exemplified by St. Vincent of Paul's with its leaking roof and rotting floor.[63] Ten churches were built between 1850 and 1856, but the battle had been lost in previous decades.[64] The census in 1881 and 1891, when there were twenty-three and twenty-seven Catholic places of worship respectively, recorded 14,483 and 12,348 at Sunday morning services, 9,442 and 12,585 at evening services.[65] Inescapable from these figures was the conclusion that a majority of Catholics was indifferent about expressing their faith by attendance at church.

The interest for historians lies in this: Liverpool exhibited sectarian fervour without widespread religious observance. Other antagonisms were involved. Residual religion, patriotic assertion, and the clannish *camaraderie* of slum neighbourhoods, were knotted together. The *Liverpool Irishman* declared, concerning parades, that 'no self-respecting Irishman, Catholic or Protestant, associates with this ignorant rabble; but, as Orange and Green colours are used, Ireland gets the blame for this rowdyism'.[66] The emblematic and compound nature of the conflict was early apparent. With hostilities aroused by the restored Catholic hierarchy in 1850, priests discouraged St. Patrick's Day parades which 'had greatly degenerated in character and Catholic spirit'.[67]

Protestants also neglected their churches. The census enumerator, Horace Mann, listed some causes: pew-rents and social discriminations; prolix, routine preaching; insufficient clergy and accommodation; and, chiefly, the slum environment.[68] A Liverpool journalist likened the atmosphere inside churches in slum areas to an uncleaned twopenny bath. Before the parsons' religion could begin, the way needed paving by 'the religion of Newlands [the borough engineer] and plenty of sweepers'.[69] Liverpool's fifty-eight Anglican churches recorded 22,610 at morning services on census Sunday in 1881 and about half again at evening services, or 19 per cent of estimated Anglicans.[70] That absenteeism primarily involved working men was illustrated in another survey, instigated by the Anglican Bishop, Ryle.[71] By contrast, the Revd. Richard Hobson's work provided relief from this gloomy picture, as Ryle gladly acknowledged. His parish, St. Nathaniel's, was a witness that the Church of England could attract working people, and as such it merits examination.[72]

Born in Wicklow of Yorkshire stock, Hobson was always 'attached to the Protestantism of Orangeism', although he never joined 'that honourable organization'.[73] Having been a lay preacher with the Irish Church Mission, Hobson in 1864–5 took orders at St. Aidan's College, Birkenhead. The College's Principal, Joseph Baylee, was a noted anti-Romanist; and Hobson the curate demonstrated his puritanism by discountenancing card-playing and dancing in the social round of Claughton parish.[74] Its vicar, R. P. Blakeney, founded the Church Association in 1865 to combat the ritualist English Church Union (1859); and Hobson supported his efforts. In 1868, Hobson took over his first and only parish, St. Nathaniel's, Windsor. This was 'socially and morally the lowest [district] in south-east Liverpool'.[75] Full of brothels and toughs, 'sixteen acres of sin', it contained 4,500 people, growing to 7,000 by 1900, wherein only thirteen families kept a servant and none kept two.[76]

Hobson's first service involved four people in a cellar. The church was consecrated in 1869, but its windows were smashed until they were wired; and the few churchgoers suffered their neighbours' contempt. By 1882, however, Hobson had 800 communicants, 82 Sunday School teachers, 220 church workers, a 600-strong Bible class, and 1,700 Sunday scholars. It was evident from this that churches might attract working people not only as places where religion was celebrated but also by providing community and entertainment, however circumscribed the latter might be by puritan philosophy. Hobson emphasized pastoral visiting, and in 1887 he opened an auxiliary mission where the services were held in Welsh. His conduct of services was always 'simple, hearty', according to Ryle.[77] He spurned ritualism and from the start attracted Orangemen to his church. In 1872 they sought his permission to form a parish lodge. Hobson afterwards recommended that other clergymen rouse 'the latent Protestantism of the masses' by controversial preaching and by association with the Orange Order because, though this particular lodge did not meet his standards, 'it was a factor in the success of the church'.[78]

Sectarian frictions might be awakened with the religiously indifferent.[79] Revivals in the 1870s engendered a Protestant union through common anti-Catholicism. Liverpool had staged revivals before, inspired especially by Robert Aitken, whose devotees established themselves at Hope Street chapel in 1837.[80] His son, W. Hay Aitken, of Christ Church, Everton, shared this enthusiasm: 'We can only reach the masses by sending masses to them'.[81] He welcomed the Americans, Moody and Sankey, in 1875. The preacher of this partnership, which began in 1870, was the unordained Dwight Moody, a nineteen-stone magician of homely religious sentiment; Ira Sankey was the hymnodist. Moody, a Congregationalist, and Sankey, a Methodist, strove to make Christians, not sectarians. Moody's disciple, Reuben Torrey, epitomized this when he called himself an 'Episcopresbygationalaptist'.[82] The Liverpool visit was an interdenominational Protestant effort organized by Hobson and Aitken of the Established Church, Charles Garrett (Wesleyan), Samuel Smith (Presbyterian), and Reginald Radcliffe, whose own missionary work began amid a hail of stones on Scotland Road.[83] In the Victoria Hall, a wooden assembly-room specially built by subscriptions, the Americans magnetized up to ten thousand people nightly for a month. There Smith witnessed 'hundreds of the roughest and coarsest characters in Liverpool melted into tears and earnestly seeking the way of life'.[84]

Some ways were unedifying. Revivals which continued after the Americans' departure brought riots when the congregation invaded neighbouring Irish districts; and processions were suspended as a danger to peace.[85] Not all results were disappointing. Sankey's charm persisted as Moody's evanesced: his hymns attracted some working men away from public houses and into Hobson's Pleasant Sunday Evenings'.[86] Nonetheless, after the Catholic-baiting was exhausted, little remained. At one meeting 2,500 people avowed conversion and, wrote Smith, 'many have stood the test to this day' (1902).[87] But a list of 'converts' was handed to the churches they wished to join. Silas Hocking, a Methodist minister in Toxteth, received twenty names and found that most gave false addresses or recanted. 'Two only were left, young people of my own congregation. My colleagues had a similar experience . . .'[88] Permanent results were not achieved through fly-by-night methods. Moreover religious emotion, unguarded, could be pernicious. The Baptist minister, Hugh Stowell Brown, declared: 'Blind superstition is quite as hostile to Christianity as is infidelity.'[89]

Education and politics

Another concern of the religious at this time, education, speeded party political consciousness. The local shipowner, Charles Booth, estimated that Liverpool contained 25,000 children who neither worked nor attended school; and a Government inquiry, together with the Council's own investigations of 1867, strengthened the case for public provision.[90] Nevertheless, the establishment of a locally elected School Board in Liverpool in 1870 excited controversy, about the type of religious instruction provided and about Clause 25 of the Education Act, which permitted a School Board to pay the fees of poor children attending denominational schools.[91] Two aspects of these debates need general statement. There was no intention that Board Schools should do more than supplement the network of 'voluntary' denominational schools, or that religious instruction should be banished from Board Schools. On the contrary, it was widely held that this last was essential, for 'Education was not merely the imparting of knowledge, but the training of the whole of the child's nature for life, here and hereafter . . .' Undenominational teaching, however, was basically unattractive to every sect. Most men of religion would have endorsed the positive attitude of F. J. Chavasse, the second Bishop of Liverpool, in a letter to the head of the city's Wesleyan Mission in 1902:

> I am glad you are not working on what are called 'undenominational lines'. It is far better in every way that a man should be a good Wesleyan or Presbyterian than that he should be connected with no Christian Church at all. In the one case he receives definite teaching and the benefit of Christian fellowship. In the other case, for the lack of instruction, he is apt to drift into error, or to become a backboneless Christian.

A collision of sectarians and politicians was, therefore, inevitable as the one sought commitment and the other offered compromise, in the form of the Cowper–Temple clause which provided that 'no religious catechism or religious formulary distinctive of any particular denomination shall be taught in schools which receive rate aid'. The statute did not expressly insist that school boards should provide any religious instruction, but those school boards which did without religious teaching were few and mostly in Wales, which reflected the strength not of secularism there, but of the Sunday School system.[92] Accordingly, the kernel of the debate in the country was the undenominational religious teaching prescribed by the majority of school boards.

The Nonconformist–Catholic alliance, which had given the early Victorian Liberal party its base, had always been suspect, being essentially tactical in opposition to the Established Church's privileged position. Now this alliance frayed, as Catholics and many churchmen perceived a common interest seeking public support and protecting their separate denominational schools; but Nonconformists and Evangelical Anglicans equally had a common interest pressing for 'simple Bible teaching' in Board schools. The Liverpool School Board made King James's Bible required reading, to the Catholics' chagrin; and in Exchange ward, with its numerous Irish electorate, J. J. Stitt, a Liberal Nonconformist, was defeated in 1871 following his opposition to the Douai Bible and to payment of denominational fees. The next School Board vacancy found as contenders the Revd. Verner White, an Irish Presbyterian who opposed the Catholics' claims, and Lawrence Baily, a Conservative High Churchman, who supported the Board's course of paying denominational fees for poor children. With Baily commended by the Catholic bishop, the poll had a sectarian character and shook the foundations of both parties.[93]

As the Orange Order and the W.M.C.A. denounced leading Conservatives and Anglicans as Judases and ritualists, it became a set policy of the Conservative party to leave the organization of School Board contests to the religious interests.[94] Politicians might want to quit the sectarians' arena, but sectarians would not quit the political arena and, in a parliamentary by-election in February 1873, Conservatives found it necessary to outbid each other in Protestant credentials. Thus, although the chief political standard of John Torr, the candidate, was the cry to reduce public expenditure, he announced that he had *six* grandfathers buried in a neighbouring churchyard, every one a Protestant.[95] His Liberal opponent, William Caine, was an iron merchant, Baptist, and teetotaller. Several Liverpool Liberals, T. D. Hornby, William Langton, and Robertson Gladstone, had declined to stand; so too had the editor of *The Economist*, Walter Bagehot.[96] Another candidate, Dr. Andrew Commins, representing the Home Rule Association, withdrew; and, in this first election by ballot in Liverpool, Torr won by 1,912 votes. Caine blamed an 'alliance of gin and Protestantism'; but there were more menacing implications. Caine polled 16,790 votes which, reckoning some nine to twelve thousand 'Irish' electors, caused speculation that they could sway Liverpool Liberalism.[97]

One arena of confrontation was the Catholic Club, founded in 1844 by Robert Sheil to counter M'Neile's Protestant Association. When Nonconformists in the city demanded that the Liberal candidates oppose Clause 25, Caine accepted what was essentially an anti-Catholic position; but Rathbone's consent was conditional on the provision of a choice of school. In reaction to the Nonconformists' power in Liberal circles the Catholic Club reluctantly decided to venture independence; but a third candidate threatened Rathbone, who held the minority seat, more than Caine. The Club's Whigs rallied to pass an amendment, withholding from a definite course; but individuals, who favoured the Liberal candidates, canvassed Irish electors. This challenged those inchoate Nationalists who wished to launch Home Rule rather than dispute education matters.[98]

No epithet was more opprobrious to an Irish Nationalist than 'Whig': 'the Tory is regarded as an open enemy; the Whig the treacherous friend . . .'[99] There was imminent the passing of a generation and the curtailment of Whig Catholic influence, in the persons of James Whitty, a Wexford-born merchant with thirty years' service on the Select Vestry, Council, or School Board; C. J. Corbally, Sheil's nephew, a magistrate, councillor, and stalwart of the Catholic Benevolent Society; and John Yates, a convert who became Liverpool's leading Catholic citizen. Clouding their horizon was the Home Rule Confederation, and its Liverpool derivation, founded in 1872 by John Denvir and Alfred Crilly. In 1874, when the H.R.C. counselled abstentions, Rathbone retained the minority seat with 16,705 votes; but Caine's 15,806 was almost 1,000 fewer than his poll in 1873.[100] John Bright sympathized with Caine's desire to quit Liverpool, 'which boro' I think sensible men should avoid'.[101] The election also paralysed the Catholic Club—Whigs were subdued, and Nationalists turned to direct the Irish vote.[102]

The General Election of 1874 and the impact of Irish Nationalism in municipal politics

Conservatives similarly showed disquiet, although the electorate nationally espoused tranquillity as it returned a Conservative Government in the 1874 General Election. Sandon and Torr carried Liverpool, but Protestants were accomplices in William Simpson's campaign as an Independent. An adventurer and onetime bankrupt, who dabbled in business as diverse as tug-boats and catering, Simpson was a temperance worker, a founder of Liverpool's Parliamentary Debating Society, and an early guide of the W.M.C.A. He quarrelled with local Conservative leaders concerning education and temperance; he also voiced labour grievances.[103] His mélange of a programme attracted 2,435 votes. More ominous was the incipient agitation against Ritualism.

By Disraeli's definition Ritualism was 'the practice by a certain portion of the clergy of the Church of England of ceremonies which they themselves confess are symbolical of doctrines which they are pledged by every solemn contract which can bind men to their sovereign and their country to denounce and repudiate'; in an epigram, 'the Mass in masquerade'.[104] The Public Worship Regulation Act of 1874 was designed to punish and to excommunicate Ritualists in the Anglican Church and, during its passage through Parliament, 'party religious feeling' was observed never to have run so high. This excitement was duplicated in Liverpool where the W.M.C.A. denounced the bishops' insouciant attitude to discipline and applauded the local branch of the Church Association whose prosecution, for ritual offences, of the vicar of St. Margaret's, Toxteth, brought his eventual resignation in 1876.[105]

The Conservative–Protestant, and Liberal–Catholic, uneasiness had ramified. In February 1874 two School Board representatives, Samuel Booth (Liberal) and Dr. James Hakes (Church Association), proposed that fees be withheld from children attending denominational schools, since, in Hakes's view, 'Catholics were instructed in such a way as only to fit them for jails or workhouses'.[106] An inter-party combination defeated their proposal; but when one representative of this combination, an Anglican Tory, Dr. William Cross, contested a municipal by-election Orangemen were advised to vote Liberal. Catholics in reply were exhorted to support Cross, who was returned. Out of this confusion, as Liberals and Irishmen collided, it was apparent that the casualty was the interlapping part, Whiggery. At the next Vestry elections John

Prendiville, a Whig Catholic, was abandoned by Liberals who resented his opposition to Stitt in 1871; and Home Rulers proscribed him for his Liberal partisanship in the General Election.[107]

Reminiscing in 1893, the Conservative leader, Arthur Forwood, declared that 'in 1875 the Irish question was little known in Liverpool as affecting Liverpool politics or Liverpool affairs'.[108] In Forwood's mind the turning-point was not associated with any controversy over education, immigration, work competition, or public health: the turning-point came when the subject of an independent Ireland was preached as politics. From 1863 Scotland ward, predominantly Irish, had elected a Welsh Whig, William Williams, who, Forwood said, 'believed in the unity of the Empire for Liverpool purposes'. This phrase captured that underlying co-identity of politicians before 1875, the belief that, though they might differ in many particulars, all worked only in Liverpool's interests in municipal politics. But Williams was not a Home Ruler; as a Dissenter he opposed Clause 25; and as a builder and member of the Land and House Owners' Association he questioned municipal enterprise in working-class housing.

These defaults encouraged Lawrence Connolly, a wealthy fruit broker, to contest Williams's election in 1875. Connolly stood 'as a Catholic, as an advocate of Home Rule for Ireland, and as an advocate of sanitary reform', personifying three disputatious themes. He claimed that Catholics had most to fear from the Liberal party, because Conservatives supported religious education, and 'that was the main point for consideration'.[109] Once victorious, Connolly repudiated this bond and presented the Irish Nationalists' real hopes, that they might proceed to further triumphs against 'the combined influence of Toryism, Protestantism, and Liberal Club-ism'.[110]

Liberals were most threatened. They had alienated Irishmen, and also Welshmen who believed that Williams was brutally abandoned. This latter estrangement was not new. It had been the subject of discussion after Caine's by-election in 1873 when *Porcupine* declared that 'the sooner the Liberals disabused their minds of the idea that Welsh Liverpool is Liberal the better'.[111] Welsh Nonconformists, it was observed, respected an Evangelical Established Church but abominated Puseyism and Catholicism.[112] This hostility Irishmen now endeavoured to mute: they needed to woo, as well as browbeat, Liberals in the interests of Home Rule, and Connolly even suggested that Williams, 'who was a good man, would present himself to another constituency and that the Roman Catholics would support him'.[113]

The Liberals ignored unpleasant omens. Over-all they made two gains in 1875, including St. Anne's ward, where a temperance campaign displaced a Conservative brewer by thirty-nine votes. The Conservatives better appreciated the significance of Connolly's election. Their leader, Edward Whitley, proposed a Whig–Conservative combination to preserve government by 'respectable' people;[114] but Liberal leaders rejected this overture. Some saw the Irish political consciousness, and an apparently effective temperance agitation, as instruments to gain Council control. Several Liberal Ward Associations selected Home Rulers in 1876. One candidate combined a galaxy of titles—Liberal, Catholic, temperance, and Home Rule—but lost by 163 votes in St. Anne's, where the party had won in 1875. Similarly, in Pitt Street, the Conservative Councillor increased his majority against a Home Ruler when only three years before a traditional English Liberal was within two votes of defeating him. The détente between Liberals and Nationalists had disgusted another group, whom the *Courier* called 'Independent Englishmen'.[115] Conservative posters were newly inspiring: 'loyalty to Queen and Constitution . . . and not Home Rule dictation'.

Failing in these compacts, Liberals were not compensated in wards where Whigs and Nationalists competed. In August 1876, in a Vauxhall by-election, Charles McArdle, a cotton broker, temperance advocate, and Home Ruler, was unopposed. This epitomized to Father Nugent' 'the impotency of the Catholic Club'.[116] In the November election the issue was exclusively Home Rule, since both candidates were Irish Catholics. The victor was Dr. Andrew Commins, the popular barrister who was Isaac Butt's predecessor as president of the H.R.C.[117] He lambasted an alliance of 'Tory "sugar", Whig "currant jelly", Orange Lodges and the Catholic Club . . . the very refuse of every party in Liverpool'. Equally strong language prevailed in Scotland ward where the Whig Catholic Councillor, John McArdle, fought the Home Ruler, Dr. A. M. Bligh. Called 'the body-snatcher', Bligh rejoined by accusing McArdle of 'dictation' and 'Tory alliances'. Less than half the electorate voted and Bligh's majority fell 700 below Connolly's in 1875. Victory, therefore, again vindicated the Home Rulers' stand, but it was clear from the election campaign that allegiances were in turmoil. Priests were divided, some accepting new directions, others wishing to reward past services.

The Conservatives reviewed the Liberals' misfortunes. The Liberals according to the *Courier*, had 'played fast and loose with the Irish vote', which had now 'set up for itself, and announced a programme that will be inconvenient for them, if not disastrous . . .'[118] Similarly, Forwood invited the Amalgamated Grand Lodge of Orangemen to study this movement in Liverpool, the 'head centre' of England's Conservatism. He lauded Orangemen as 'the best, the most sober, the most temperate, the most thoughtful, and the most religious of the working men'. Liverpool had need of these stalwarts, to guard against councillors who were elected upon platforms of 'sedition and disloyalty'. Dr. Commins had declared that England's trial in the Eastern Question enabled Home Rulers to state their price.[119] Forwood now assigned patriotism as the Orangemen's preserve. When 'leading members of the Liberal party . . . [were] truckling to and going hand-in-hand about the town with the leading members of the Home-rule party', it was necessary for 'all true men, whether Liberal or Conservative, whether Englishmen, Irishmen, or Scotsmen, to band themselves together . . . as the Orange Association had done'.[120]

Whitley hallowed this marriage. He thanked Orangemen for their support, 'without which no man could lead the Conservative party' in Liverpool. Since Home Rule meant either 'the increase of the Roman Catholic priesthood in Ireland . . . [or] a system without any religion at all', their opposition was total. Orange–Conservative differences of recent years Whitley remembered with 'pain'. He now eulogized Orangemen as model citizens, 'better educated in the main than any other body of working men'.[121] The panoply of respectability covered all who opposed Home Rule politicians, 'the nominees of the riff-raff portion of the most illiterate inhabitants'.[122] The Tory ship-builder, Councillor Thomas Royden, summarized this tactic: 'The real issue at stake was not so much the difference between Conservative and Liberal, as between loyalty to the Throne of the country and sedition.'[123]

Home Rulers continued to capture Council seats where Irish electors predominated. They also contested School Board and Poor Law Guardians' elections. Previously these had been left to professed Catholics without particular politics. Some seats were now challenged, others were not as Whig Catholics shied away. Annually stronger, the Home Rulers also tried to dictate policy to the city's Liberal M.P., Rathbone. In 1877 they demanded that Rathbone by his parliamentary votes should support the release of Irish political prisoners and an inquiry into Anglo-Irish relations since the Union. Rathbone was no Home Ruler; and he objected to pledges, having crossed temperance reformers in this.[124] Doubts about Rathbone's position sharpened with the creation of the Nine Hundred—basically an amalgam of three Liberal associations—in which the Irish were represented. Moreover, the Liberals had a new local leader, the cotton broker, R. D. Holt, whose instincts were towards accommodating the Irish in the interests of party unity. The subsequent municipal elections placed the Liberals within reach of a Council majority;[125] but in January 1880 Torr's death precipitated a parliamentary by-election.

The Liverpool by-election of 1880 and the 'Irish Inquiry'

Several names were connected with the Liberal candidature, including Sir William Harcourt, who had been asked to stand in 1868.[126] Harcourt's moods were electorally promising in Liverpool. His equal dislike of pledges could ease Rathbone's situation; his Erastian Protestantism was second to no Conservative's; and his declarations denoted 'a Whig who talked Radicalism'.[127] Through Harcourt's introduction the naval officer son of the Earl of Dalhousie, Lord Ramsay, was nominated. Ramsay's attractive wife won George Melly's vote.[128] Other conquests were harder because the Conservatives adopted their leader, Edward Whitley, a town Councillor since 1865. Like Melly a product of Rugby, Whitley, however, had a popular touch; indeed many thought him the consummate tea-party politician. His involvement in the common social round of Everton was especially deep, in activities as diverse as Bible classes and hot-pot suppers, Orange lodges and cricket clubs.

Ramsay announced a wide-ranging programme, including land reform and Lawson's local option scheme; but Whitley dulled the temperance issue by advocating Sunday closing and other reforms.[129] The decisive question was Home Rule. Dr. Commins first advised Irishmen to abstain: Whitley personified hostility to the Irish cause, and Ramsay refused to call for an inquiry into a separate Irish Parliament.[130] The new Liberal leader, Holt, was so dismayed by this that he considered withdrawing Ramsay from the contest. He reckoned that 'the priestly section of the Irish Catholics will be with us but unless we can square the Home Rule element we will lose 2,500 votes and the election'.[131]

The position altered on 28 January when Ramsay promised to support an Irish inquiry. The Liverpool Irishmen officially favoured him.[132] But, though

Ramsay was not a Home Ruler because he now accepted the need for an inquiry, the suggestion of a bargain disturbed the Liberal front bench at Westminster and hardened the tendency of ordinary Liverpudlians to support Whitley on personal grounds.[133] Holt wanted Harcourt to speak in Liverpool in order to avert a suggestion that Ramsay and the Liverpool Liberals had been excommunicated by their party leaders; but Harcourt declined, because 'If I held language which pleased the Home Rulers, I should say what I don't think and would do infinite mischief elsewhere'.[134] Moreover, the Whig leader, the Marquis of Hartington, disrupted the principal meeting of Ramsay's campaign by a communication which stressed that he would have refused a comparable pledge.[135] By contrast the Tory speeches were decidedly imperialist, emphasizing 'the integrity of the Empire at home and the safety of the Empire abroad'; and there was also a dash of Protestant bitters, in the interest shown in the Church Association's long prosecution of the Revd. A. H. Mackonochie, which now approached a climax.[136]

Whitley won 26,106 votes against 23,885 in an 80 per cent poll. This was not the first election when an English candidate supported an Irish inquiry;[137] but the issue had never been so controversial. Ripples even reached Eton where young George Wyndham noted 'great rejoicings' at Whitley's victory.[138] A Liberal Unionist party now existed in everything but name. Lord Sefton told R. D. Holt,

> it was '*Home Rule*' that made the *Tories* and *Moderate Conservatives* poll to a man; to say nothing of keeping many moderate Liberals away altogether. If you are to fight again, your candidate must state distinctly that he cannot vote for inquiry into anything that *directly* or *indirectly means* the dismemberment of the United Kingdom or the Restoration of an Irish Parliament. There are plenty of true grievances open to endless inquiry.
>
> If you are really firm I cannot believe the Irish Voters will desert you and you would then have the certain and hearty support of every Liberal in Liverpool and its neighbourhood including moderate men like Lord Derby and
>
> Yours sincerely,
> Sefton[139]

This warning was confirmed in the course of the year. Rathbone's chances of remaining the minority member were slim after Ramsay conceded what he refused; and in March 1880, at the General Election, Ramsay replaced Rathbone, who forlornly fought south-west Lancashire. Sandon, Whitley, and Ramsay were unopposed in Liverpool; but the respite was short, for Ramsay's accession as Lord Dalhousie upon his father's death brought another by-election in August. Some Liberals, unhappy at the recent course of events, made soundings among the Conservative party, trying to exert a proprietary right to the minority seat and to evade the Irish issue by returning Rathbone unopposed; but the Conservatives forced a contest, selecting as their champion Lord Claud Hamilton, a son of the Duke of Abercorn, and an M.P. of fifteen years' experience. Rathbone withdrew, soon to represent Carnarvonshire;[140] but the stopgap Liberal candidate, Samuel Plimsoll, evinced no corresponding keenness to treat with the Irish, and Rathbone's friends accused the local leader, Holt, of having had some 'hidden personal motive' in wanting to get rid of their idol.[141] Hamilton won 21,019 votes against 19,118.

The parties returned to municipal matters. With the Liberals close to a Council majority, several Conservatives again considered the possibility of a municipal truce. Apparently the idea emanated from the Liberal Councillor, J. H. Wilson, and the Conservative, T. B. Royden, who were relatives by marriage; but Forwood—the leader since Whitley entered Parliament—directed the overtures. He regretted that the Irish had divided the city establishment, and he considered it 'detrimental to the interests of the Ratepayers . . . that Gentlemen who have acquired a large experience in municipal affairs should be displaced solely on ground of their political opinions'.[142] Forwood and Holt confabulated about terms, that aldermanships (then held by Conservatives) should be shared and that a redistribution of wards (then biased towards the Liberals) should follow. Beneath his draft of the treaty Forwood wrote: 'Mr Holt personally thinks favourably of above and would advise his friends to accept it provided the next Mayoralty is placed at their disposal.' The horse-trading satisfied points on which the parties had been querulous;[143] but the political climate had changed since 1875 when similar matters were first raised. Whitley, for example, was now 'sure that a return to the old tactics of quietly maintaining our own and not seeking compromises or alliances with others, is the best plan to pursue';[144] moreover, when the Irish suspected new dealings, Holt shunned Forwood and spoke of electing Home Rulers to aldermanic vacancies. This was impossible when the Conservatives' Council majority was reinforced at the November elections. A correspondent to Rathbone summarized the municipal situation: 'Hughes of Everton, as Hughes, beat Vining by 15. Hughes Home Rule candidate, *after Everton knew it*, was beaten by 1,500. Matheson, 100 better than Evans, is beaten by 170 more than Evans, when South Toxteth knew he was the Radical *and* Home Ruler candidate.'[145] Conservatives were minted from moderate Liberals under the impress of Home Rule.

The Liverpool by-election of 1882 and Tory Democracy

The precipice was not yet reached. The Liverpool Liberal party had experienced problems from 1875 which became general only after Gladstone's conversion to Irish Home Rule in 1885. In 1881, following the General Election defeat and Disraeli's death, dissension was more characteristic of Conservatism. Stafford Northcote's leadership of the Conservative party in the House of Commons—like 'some liquid which is so much weaker than water that to add water to it would strengthen it'[146]—provoked both Lord Randolph Churchill's maverick opposition group, the Fourth Party, and disappointment among Conservatives in the provinces.[147] In Forwood's view the Conservative leadership had to attend to the situation in the boroughs, to originate policies, or to sink. Pragmatic first and last, Forwood tackled problems and remedied deficiencies, not as a crusader but as astute politicians disarm opponents. Parliamentary supremacy and municipal supremacy were linked, and Forwood determined to build both.[148]

Born in Liverpool in 1836, Arthur Bower Forwood was a shipowner and a director of an insurance company, moving in the highest provincial society, yet possessing an unvarnished manner which made credible a pretence of belonging to 'the people'.[149] Forwood was immersed in politics from 1868. As Secretary of the Liverpool Conservative Association, his first experiences were of the old hustings when Gladstone, among lesser celebrities, was pelted; but Forwood's interest in administration and party organization suited the modern age which throws mud with discipline. He represented North Toxteth ward from 1871 and, as Mayor in 1878, paid attention to two far-reaching schemes: the foundation of both an episcopal see and a university college.[150] But Forwood's hustling manner and broadening views—particularly with regard to Corporation finance and working-class housing—offended Conservative immovables; and he held the leadership principally in default of an alternative.

In December 1822 Lord Harrowby's death [151] entailed that his son, Viscount Sandon, was translated to the Upper House. The subsequent by-election epitomized the distempers in Liverpool Toryism and regenerative possibilities in Liberalism before Home Rule overlaid them. This was not immediately clear. No Liberal candidate, Holt considered, could equal Ramsay's popularity; and he made these assessments in the event of a contest: 'The Irish would do one of three things—name a candidate, abstain from voting or vote Tory. We don't think many would do the last. (We think this from recent municipal experience). It is quite likely they might name a candidate but we think they might fear exposing their weaknesses. We incline to think their policy would be to abstain from voting. Of course we sh' be beaten . . .'[152]

Holt considered not contesting the by-election, but this would sap the party's enthusiasm. Moreover, *Porcupine* announced that unless a radical candidate was engaged, an independent, James Samuelson, would emerge.[153] Thereupon the selectors advanced the cotton broker, and former president of the Liverpool Chamber of Commerce, Samuel Smith.[154] They excused their hesitation by pretending to have been awaiting a general election to bid for the working-class vote by running Smith with Henry Broadhurst, the Liberal trade unionist who had represented Stoke since 1880; but they dissembled.[155] Councillor Stephen Guion, a shipowner and close friend of Holt, was actually offered the candidature. This confirmed *Porcupine*'s suspicions, for Guion was a moderate 'held in high regard by the Conservative party'.[156] The Liberals, therefore, entered the by-election fractiously. Regarding the 'crotchet-monger' Smith, even the Liberal press concluded that victory was improbable.[157]

Smith, however, pealed the right notes, conservative and progressive, and local Nonconformists admired him as the party at large admired Gladstone.[158] Smith endorsed the Irish Land Act and, while regretting the Liberal Government's intervention in Egypt, he praised the army's 'valour' in an 'unavoidable' imbroglio. His 'chief interest' was 'social legislation for the benefit of the masses'. He recommended shorter drinking hours and local option, since intemperance was 'the chief cause' of poverty; and he demanded better housing, assisted emigration for pauper children, education for street arabs, legislation to free the transfer of property, an extended franchise, and redistribution of seats to the advantage of large towns. The fears stoked by Smith's advocacy of reform were diminished by his emphasizing the question as a defence of class. He associated himself 'with the party of gradual reform, not with that of destruction or revolution. I love our ancient and glorious Constitution, and believe that by adaptation to modern wants it may long remain . . . the bulwark of this empire and the admiration of the world.'[159]

Smith's Protestant reputation vindicated his conservatism. He had written a treatise, *The Credibility of the Christian Religion* (1872), countering Rationalist objections;[160] and he was a noted anti-ritualist and puritan, who campaigned against adornment in churches and nudity in art.[161] Moreover, following Parnell's reaction to the Government's coercion of Ireland, the Liberal party was temporarily relieved of the stigma of abetting Irish sedition. The Liverpool Home Rule Association counselled abstention and moderate Liberals, who had latterly embraced Conservatism, were tempted to support Smith.[162]

On Harrowby's death in 1882 Forwood was visiting America. His party looked headless and the *Liberal Review* had been encouraged.[163] Forwood returned to become the candidate. In Hengler's Circus 6,000 people heard his profession as a 'Democratic Tory'. He criticized Liberal policy towards Ireland, and advocated universal household suffrage, a redistribution of seats, reapportionment of church endowments, temperance reforms, and an extended Employers' Liability Act. Following this Radical trumpet the supporting speaker, Lord Claud Hamilton, confined his comments to Egypt.[164] Forwood's declaration was momentous. Curzon noted that 'Tory Democracy' became common currency after this by-election;[165] but Forwood lost by 17,889 votes to 18,198, giving Liverpool Liberals their first victory in single combat.

The Liberal shipowner, Thomas Brocklebank, exclaimed: 'Victory seemed hopeless and behold! it is here!'[166] From the Admiralty Lord Northbrook was more inquisitive—'What did the Irish do? Are there local reasons? or were the Tories frightened at Mr. Forwood's opinions?'[167] Gladstone partly answered Northbrook when he wrote that 'it is not due to the "Irish vote", for that under present circumstances is of all foundations the most "giddy and unsure" ',[168] a reference which Holt prudently omitted when he publicized Gladstone's congratulations. Smith himself attributed his success chiefly to 'Social Reform';[169] and the Liberal M.P. for Aylesbury, George Russell, deduced that 'modern Liberalism . . . no longer regards the possession of a vote as the be-all and end-all of civic life, but treats it only as a means to an end, and that end the creation of better moral and physical surroundings . . .'[170]

Smith's Liberalism united two traditions, Cobdenite economics and Shaftesbury's philanthropy, as it searched for antidotes to socialism, which thrived in insanitary dwellings, according to Smith, like malaria in swamps.[171] Joseph Chamberlain, watching from Birmingham, agreed that 'probably the most pressing need' was 'the provision of better dwellings' although this would entail 'a bold attack on the so-called rights of property'.[172] Their thesis, of an upsurge of popular feeling intoxicated by the message of 'Social Reform', was too sanguine. Smith was victorious in a poll inferior to the by-elections of February and August 1880. George Melly noted these 'wonderful' figures: 'Smith 1000 worse than Plimsoll, and 6000 worse than Ramsay. *Wins.* and Forwood is 8000 less than Whitley—How they must hate him . . .'[173]

One factor injuring Forwood was speculation about a general election. Since the 1867 Reform Act Liverpool returned three M.P.s, but no elector could cast for more than two candidates. Because only two Conservatives could be returned, who, Whitley, Hamilton, or Forwood, would retire at the next General Election? Forwood publicly accepted the junior position; but Liberal newspapers alleged that Forwood's election now would endanger Whitley later.[174] Consequently Whitley's ward, Kirkdale and Everton, polled 5,000 fewer in 1882 than in 1880. As for personalities, Forwood wrote in the *Contemporary Review* that Smith had provoked no political hostilities, but was celebrated for good works.[175] Privately Forwood impeached Smith's charity: the Y.M.C.A. to which 'Smith had subscribed £7,000 turned out 1000 strong to canvass for him. Within 14 days after the Election he contributed £1000 more—Comment is needless.'[176]

Smith, of course, was a well-known Liberal figure in Liverpool. He had been prominent in the Vigilance Committee and he had defeated David MacIver, the Conservative M.P. for Birkenhead, in Castle Street ward in 1879. Nevertheless Smith's party politics and Forwood's partisanship were different. For fourteen years either secretary or chairman of the Liverpool Conservative party, Forwood's record read as a thick-and-thin man and he excited antagonisms which Smith did not. Cab-drivers were said to have opposed him because his promotion of tramways prejudiced their jobs. Doctors criticized his attempts to compel the notification of disease, shop-assistants his refusal to support their early-closing movement, and working men the wages his firm paid.[177] The drink interest was also doubtful. Licensed victuallers decided only by majority vote to support Forwood as the less hostile candidate.[178]

Forwood, however, was not generally unpopular among working men. That the wages question ruined him was, one workman commented, 'all rot and rubbish'. Forwood's difficulty in this respect, compared with Laird's in Birkenhead, was 'as a wart is to Ossa or Pelion'.[179] The W.M.C.A. applauded his views. By contrast Hamilton was considered 'reckless and flippant', and Whitley, though personally popular, was thought 'a dead failure' politically. Many Conservative workmen wanted Forwood to contest a general election, 'as you would, (even if the party failed to carry two) be worth the other two'.[180] Where Forwood might have suffered respecting working-class votes was through registration anomalies. The suburban removals of respectable artisans could result in temporary disfranchisement, 'leaving the voting power largely in the hands of a lower stratum both in sobriety and intelligence, who are contented to live in some miserable room in a squalid court'. The chairman of the W.M.C.A. was cited by Forwood as one whose mobility resulted in the loss of his electoral right.[181]

The actively treacherous, however, were in another class, for what working men called 'that magnificent speech' in Hengler's Circus, others called 'dangerous' and 'deplorable'—'a direct appeal to the mob as against the upper ten'.[182] The London *Standard* nominated Forwood 'an unpopular candidate with an unpopular programme, and we may add unprincipled programme';[183] and *The Times* agreed that by radical initiatives Forwood neglected to voice Conservative ideas.[184] One correspondent suggested that because Forwood's policies were 'entirely opposed to the traditions of Toryism' his proper place was in the Liberal party.[185] Likewise the *Liberal Review*, generalizing from Forwood's contempt for 'social and political fogeyism', predicted that he would 'abjure Toryism, and become a Democrat pure and simple'.[186] These were pious hopes, reflecting the Liberals' uncertainty in policy. Smith won because of more Tory than Irish abstentions.

Inter-Irish conflict in municipal politics

Isaac Butt had replaced 'Repeal' with the slogan 'Home Rule' for its associations of innocent domesticity.[187] Conservatives nonetheless espied a threat to the Empire and a presentiment of working-class radicalism. This was indicated in Liverpool when Pat Byrne, the 'scavengers' friend', won a Scotland ward by-election in 1883. Once a docker, now a publican worth £40,000, Byrne was a different prospect from Dr. Commins, 'the ready-witted lawyer', or Dr. Bligh, 'the courteous doctor', who lent respectability to the Home Rule cause and thereby failed to satisfy the 'coarse . . . violent, and unscrupulous' aspirations of some Liverpool Irishmen.[188] In November 1883 Joseph Simpson, a Home Ruler and English Catholic, opposed Byrne; and Nationalists retaliated by contesting Vauxhall, which previously John Yates was allowed to retain for fear of inciting clerical opposition to Home Rule. Father Nugent now voiced this;[189] but the new style had support. Bernard Hughes directed Liverpool Irishmen to hearten Parnell by rejecting 'Union Jack Papists' and 'English popinjays'. Byrne himself blamed the quarrel on 'Yates' friends, the English Whigs', and Irishmen like Charles McArdle, 'the mis-representative of Vauxhall Ward', who claimed to want 'a respectable Irish party'. They also endeavoured to obscure Byrne's advocacy of sanitary reform with posters proclaiming 'Vote for Simpson, the Friend of the Poor' or 'Vote for Simpson and Economy, low rates, and the big loaf'. The press had no disguise: electors were warned against men 'who fatten and prosper on agitation' and who aspired to become 'despots and dictators of Irishmen in Liverpool'. The spectacle of a Nationalist fighting Holt in Exchange, 'the centre of commercial intelligence', was horrifying.[190]

The radical Irish vote was dashed. In Vauxhall, where probably 1,200 of 1,500 electors were Irish,[191] Yates, without canvassing won 620 votes against 279; and in Scotland Simpson polled 1,930 against 1,805 although 3,415 electors abstained. The polling hours, 9 a.m. to 4 p.m., effectively disfranchised those unwilling to sacrifice wages; but the grouping of 'moderate' forces was evident. The Liberal chairman of St. Paul's ward gratefully admitted that their councillor had received Conservative votes.

The *Daily Post* now hoped to witness fewer attempts to imbue Irish voters with 'mere race-hatred and implacable resentment', and a greater disposition to credit Liberals with 'just and kindly feeling towards Ireland'.[192] A party metamorphosis had occurred. In 1875 most Home Rulers had been anathema to Liverpool Liberals; by 1883 only the extremists were. This was underlined by Joseph Biggar, the Home Rule M.P. for Cavan, who warned Whiggish councillors in Liverpool that their re-election in 1884 depended upon the Irish National League. He ruled that the Liverpool I.N.L. should appeal 'to the working men, and not to the "swells".'[193]

Internecine war risked all Irish representation. Accordingly principle bent to expediency. Since both Scotland ward branches still tolerated Lawrence Connolly, the I.N.L. Executive supported his readoption; but in Vauxhall ward after the Central, West Derby, and Toxteth, branches of the I.N.L. supported Byrne, and others made representations for McArdle, it declined to interfere.[194] Byrne was eventually nominated at an open meeting. His supporters advocated 'true national principles as opposed to Whiggery and sham Nationality', and his victory spiced speculations about the minority parliamentary seat.

Nationalists estimated that Catholics formed over one-quarter of the Liverpool electorate.[195] *Porcupine*'s conservative estimate—12,000 'Irishmen' among 63,000 voters[196]—hardly checked the assumption that, with unanimity, they might carry a seat. Discord, however, was apparent when Dr. Commins and eight others formed an 'Election Committee', with the object of consulting Parnell and the Irish parliamentary party about a candidature. The Central branch of the Liverpool I.N.L. condemned the caballers as 'unfaithful to Ireland's cause and disobedient to her leaders', and advised local Nationalists to remain unpledged to any candidate until all elements were consulted.[197] This misjudged the leaders' interests. What Parnell and the head of the Irish National League of Great Britain, T. P. O'Connor, required from the Liverpool organization was obedience not democracy.

In 1884–5, therefore, the three parties, Liberal, Conservative, and Irish, awaited a general election facing challenges that decisions, once vested in cliques, should be subjected to popular scrutiny. As Redistribution followed Reform, Liverpool became the largest unit of representation outside London, with nine constituencies. New politics, it seemed, were abroad; but Liverpool, long considered the repository of antediluvian fashions, had already entertained the novelties of politics, Home Rule and Tory Democracy, in by-elections of 1880 and 1882. Significantly both had been scorched in their baptisms.

CHAPTER THREE

Tory Democracy

It is not in the power of any Conservative, however hostile towards me he may feel, to throw the slightest doubt upon the orthodoxy of my political views; and with respect to what may conduce to the ultimate benefit of the Tory party, I conceive that the widest latitude of opinion at the present moment is not only allowable but, indeed, imperative.

Lord Randolph Churchill to Sir S. Northcote, 11 March 1883

I do not believe him to be a Conservative but a mere 'opportunist' looking upon our Party as the one by identifying himself with which he can most easily rise to prominence . . . I have known him since a boy and like his mother I believe him to be entirely without principle.

Lord Claud Hamilton to A. B. Forwood, 30 April 1884; writing about Churchill[1]

A period in which franchise and electoral reform is on a government's agenda—as it was during the second Gladstone ministry between 1880 and 1885—furnishes plentiful evidence of how politicians consider their craft. Ideals and interests are the stuff of politics; so too is the manufacture of favourable electoral conditions. For the Conservatives it seemed that only major surgery could prevent their complete eclipse, following their sound defeat in the 1880 General Election and the death of their leader, Disraeli, Lord Beaconsfield, in 1881. This chapter describes the Conservative party's debates, about policies and personalities, and investigates the part played in their eventual resolution by Arthur Forwood. The rudderless condition of the party at Westminster gave Forwood an opportunity to make known the views of leading Conservatives in the provinces about what direction the party should take. The confidence and authority with which he spoke were somewhat unusual for the times. He was not an M.P. or seasoned academic observer of political affairs. His seniority derived from his status as political manager of the country's most successful Conservative organization. Forwood, by virtue of speaking for Liverpool, and Liverpool, by

Notes begin on p. 373

virtue of Forwood's purposefulness, were commanding the attention of Westminster and seeking a share in political decision-making.

Controversy about Conservative policy and the electoral system

In 1883 Lord Salisbury, an intellectual among 'aboriginal Tories', stated a case of classic ultra-Conservatism.[2] The direction of recent Liberal legislation was sinister. It destroyed 'all confidence in fixed principles'. The result was 'bribery by legislation, the bribery of classes strong in political power at the cost of those who are weak'. The powerful in Salisbury's vocabulary were the enfranchised masses, emancipated by the secret ballot in 1872 and by legislation limiting electoral expenditure and outlawing corrupt practices in 1883. Threatened with a nation split into 'distrustful fragments', he sought to direct politics towards 'objects of national import', not of class and sectional interest.[3]

In 1884–5 these alarms were enlarged. The Conservatives feared another Reform Act detached from a redistribution of seats and one which would flood the counties with urban voters. Some were comforted by the thought that the throne was popular, the aristocracy experienced, and the Church influential; but 'a *proletaire* democracy' might excite ochlocracy in the cities. Political equality and social inequality seemed incompatible. The Commons' ascendancy, it was argued, was 'irresistible'.[4] Only by tactfully waiving their powers of legislative veto, or by encouraging the creation of life peerages, might the Lords survive; otherwise it was 'absurd' to suppose that the hereditary upper house could escape 'its inevitable doom'.[5] Conservatism would be subverted—if Lord Randolph Churchill's estimation was correct—that 'the existence of the party is inseparable from the existence of an hereditary chamber; as inseparable as the latter is from the existence of an hereditary monarchy. These will stand or fall together'.[6]

The structure of representation excited grave concern. By April 1884 the Proportional Representation Society incorporated 170 M.P.s.[7] Ninety were Liberals but most types (except Parnell's Nationalists) were involved including A. J. Balfour, W. H. Smith, Ellis Ashmead-Bartlett, William Houldsworth, and Earl Percy. An anxiety about Ireland and 'inferior' representation united them. This latter had a lusty pedigree. Following the 1867 Reform Act there were complaints about 'the election of a host of local nobodies whose only claims to legislative wisdom have been their success in manufacturing calico, or discounting bills, winning coals, or blowing bottles, or growing turnips'.[8] Fewer M.P.s appreciated 'the best authors on the principles of legislation and government, as well as political history'.[9] They produced more but worse legislation, and their debasement was self-perpetuating. Ignorant M.P.s could not educate ignorant electors.

In 1884–5 several critics, wishing to immunize towns from the contagion of democracy, considered extending Cairns's clause of proportional representation from the 1867 Act.[10] The single-member system threatened, according to the Lincolnshire Tory, Henry Chaplin, to 'vestrify the House of Commons' and, according to the Liberal M.P. for Salford, Arthur Arnold, to produce 'side issues and lessen the parliamentary pride of the community'. It might also hasten that tendency which Bagehot, among many, had warned against: to increase the power of constituency committees over their members, and to substitute constituency government for Parliamentary government.[11]

Especially critical was Leonard Courtney, awesomely remembered by his secretary as the absolute Liberal individualist and acidly likened by the *Daily Mail* to 'an umpire who always gave his own side out'.[12] A junior minister in Gladstone's Government, Courtney believed it obvious 'why the Member for a ward differs from the Member for a town; why a different class of person will be brought forward; why it is impossible to enlist men of the same standing; why it is impossible to confer upon them the same status, the same authority, the same dignity; why they must inevitably be of a lower rank, not merely socially, but morally and intellectually; why it must produce a degradation of representation'.

National power would atrophy with the predominance of sectional interests. Class would no longer permeate class in joint representatives: urban fragmentation would set 'Radicals of the working men's quarter . . . against the professional classes of the more aristocratic quarter'. The Moderate Liberal, G. J. Goschen, also adumbrated this fear that to destroy 'great historical communities' was to incite class politics;[13] and *The Times* endorsed the argument.[14]

That Radicalism would advance was also a conviction of Radicals. Constituency subdivision would cheapen contests and eliminate Whiggery.[15] Some Conservatives predicted absolute devastation: 'If they fear the franchise as the east wind, they have much more reason to fear redistribution, which like the locusts, will devour what the east wind spares.'[16] Lord Claud Hamilton was amazed that Forwood favoured Liverpool's redistribution into nine seats: this spelled 'political suicide'. Hamilton prophesied that Liverpool's representation would alter from two Conservatives and one Liberal, to three Conservatives, three Radicals, two Irish Nationalists, and one Liberal Home Ruler. 'Noisy vestry men' would be ascendant.[17]

Others were less pessimistic. The Moderate Liberal, G. C. Brodrick, wrote that 'Democratic principles must, and will, continue to prevail; but Democratic principles are not quite the same as Radical principles, and a majority of the electors will desire to see them applied in a more or less Conservative spirit'. To change the electorate is not inevitably to change the elected. Boroughs had had household suffrage since 1867 and the Huddersfield Liberal, E. A. Leatham, noticed that with the potential for 'deluging this House with mechanics and working men', voters instead returned well-to-do representatives, because they valued the advocacy and judgement of educated persons. Thus 'we have arrived at the vigour of Democracy, without experiencing . . . the shock of its brute force'.[18] Deference brought the runaway under control.

The working-class Liberal M.P., Henry Broadhurst, understanding this, opposed the single-member principle: 'it will lessen the chance' of working-class M.P.s, he thought. Many labour politicians assumed the opposite, from the advantages of compact constituencies, majorities of wage-earners, longer polling hours, and legislation against corruption. Broadhurst agreed that Radicalism might become 'all-powerful'; but only homogeneous and wealthy mining areas would be able to support working-class M.P.s. Otherwise 'the character of the House would remain much as it is'.[19]

That the tribunes would not themselves be of the people opened other considerations: the manipulation of guileless electorates and the emasculation of Radicalism by 'the aristocratic embrace'. Joseph Chamberlain heralded the advent of popular politicians, released from Whiggish etiquette, particularly in the cultivation of platform performances and programmes.[20] But once Radicals like Chamberlain joined the Government, they became 'a controlling force in a democratic era'.[21] Moreover to those who feared that the masses would introduce leader-fascination into politics was the riposte that Gladstone was already paramount. Perhaps this in an undemocratic Parliament derived from thoughtful appreciation; in a democratic Parliament it would reflect thoughtless hero-worship. Nevertheless, Gladstone's supremacy was 'remarkable for its completeness, its dexterity, and the willing submission with which it was received'.[22] In this case the charisma was not radical. Gladstone was a restraining influence on advanced Liberalism.[23]

Several Conservatives appreciated this. The skilled seducers of the uneducated were not Radicals or politically conscious working men—mahdis in clogs—but the traditional governing class, to whom they habitually deferred in matters of state. If we think about Reform and Redistribution in 1884–5, as many did, that it was another 'leap in the dark', then we should call it a leap in the dark on an unsuspecting passer-by, the working-class voter, by a pack of élitist footpads. The question was not whether the electorate would be beguiled, but who would beguile them. Joseph Chamberlain declared: 'The problem is to give the democracy the whole power, but to induce them to do no more in the way of using it than to decide on the general principles which they wish to see carried out, and the men by whom they are to be carried out.'[24] Likewise Lord Salisbury made popular speeches and promoted 'improvements' in order to underpin property and tradition.[25]

Conservative advantages from single-member constituencies were advertised by Liverpool's Arthur Forwood.[26] He noted that the votes of 'people of position and property' in towns could be overwhelmed if the existing seat distribution continued, or if the *scrutin de liste* was adopted; but in divided boroughs the well-to-do could secure separate suburban representation and also attenuate the working-class vote in mixed business and poor residential constituencies.[27]

> As an electioneer of some experience [Forwood advised Lord Salisbury] against any fancy system of votes—minority or cumulative. We have a crude mass to instruct, and only simple tools should be put into their hands . . . An urban electorate of 300,000 must be dominated by the mass or the poorest on the register. Divided into five—some one or more of the districts will be under the influence of the more intelligent, the various classes living in a great measure apart. A caucus to manipulate a 300,000 constituency and to handle four or five members, is a power that will be felt. Divide this by five each independent they are simply committees of the old sort, of no power beyond their own district and very jealous of interference from extraneous influences. With subdivision the caucus will be broken . . .[28]

In Liverpool Forwood perverted his prescription—there the caucus became a Conservative instrument—but his argument contained general validity. Propertied influences could be asserted through ward committees, and new organizations could be shackled.

When Forwood argued this in 1884 it was partly accepted; when he aired it in 1882 it had been a Tory Democratic opinion. Some suspected that Reform and Redistribution foreshadowed a new Conservatism, appealing to a 'truly national sentiment' against 'the passing delusions of the mob'.[29] Changes in party organization were desirable—this could not remain 'the amateur amusement of the upper class'—but the position of rulers and ruled was quintessentially unchanging in Conservative thought. Curzon wrote that should a Conservative Government be elected 'a Tory Democracy is not merely a phrase but a fact', an argument close to Churchill's view that 'Tory Democracy is a democracy which supports the Tory party'.[30] No possibility other than to define democracy passively—that popular involvement in government should occur only at elections—was open for Conservatives, because an active democracy threatened Conservatism. Accordingly the appearance rather than substance of relations was important; but Curzon scorned 'political acrobatism', the suggestion that a Conservative should become 'a Radical in disguise.'[31]

In this context we need to consider Arthur Forwood and Lord Randolph Churchill—both accused of Radicalism and opportunism—and the evolution of Tory Democracy. This phrase aroused the misgivings of most politicians. Lord Derby, in his Liberal phase, speculated that Tory Democracy was a convenience 'to rally all those people who feel that concessions to Liberalism are inevitable, but who do not like to own themselves beaten'; or else it was a device to impress and to distract the public mind from domestic matters by a 'dashing, adventurous, hazardous, and costly system of foreign policy'. In April 1884 Derby conceded that Churchill was 'improving and very clever; but I cannot imagine that the bulk of the Conservative party will accept him. He seems to me to be keeping open a door between himself and the Radical section, to which, if he has any real opinions, he ought to belong'. But whatever Tory Democracy was, Derby maintained sarcastically, the phrase was 'a capital one, for, being perfectly unintelligible, it does not pledge anybody to anything'. Edward Hamilton, Gladstone's secretary from 1880 to 1885, can be taken to represent his chief's views, and those of the Liberal party, in his captious appraisal of Churchill on 21 May 1884: 'He is evidently playing the game for his own hand entirely—and that game is the association of Tory-ism with democracy, what Dizzie tried once upon a time and failed at.'[32]

Even Tory Democrats disliked the label. In 1882 Forwood declared:

> I did not term myself a Democratic Tory, I was so nominated by my opponents, and I only accepted the term subject to my own definition . . . I did so purposely, for I knew the words Democrat or Democracy, are apt to frighten a good many people . . . Democracy is looked upon as synonymous with revolution, disorder and plunder. To be called a Democrat implies in common parlance Republican, a Socialist or a

> Communist. As a matter of fact however the Democracy simply means the people, and Democratic Toryism may be described as popular Toryism. Democracy does not signify Manhood Suffrage, Household Suffrage, or any special description of Franchise, nor does it mean a Republican form of Government. It simply means that all persons have equal rights before the law, that whatever be the qualification to a vote, it shall be open to attainment by every citizen of every class. A Government conducted by Monarch, Lords and Commons, is as much a democratic form of administration as that of a Republic, provided it is founded on the good will of the people—the Democracy. This happily is the constitution of this country and my Democracy consists in wishing to see these institutions sink deeper and deeper into the hearts of the people—feeling satisfied that the more people are identified with their form of Government the stronger and more permanent it will be.[33]

While Tory Democrats employed clichés that smacked of Radicalism, about 'checking abuses' or even 'measures conceived in the interests of the working class', the kernel of Tory Democracy was the promotion of the traditional creed among a working-class electorate.[34] Tory Democracy changed the pump, not the beer. Forwood affirmed what some—the Undemocratic Tories—doubted: that working men would imbibe their age-old beverage. Forwood wrote: 'If this term means that I have a firm reliance upon and belief in the Conservative instincts of the people, then I am a democratic Tory.'[35] Tory Democrats sought belated popular ratification for traditional institutions and ways of government, while seeking gradually to broaden that governing class by fusing the industrial and commercial aristocracy with the landed aristocracy. This involved different manners, not another creed. Lord Charles Beresford acknowledged Churchill's display: 'We must go with the people and by the people . . . organize and guide the masses and not treat them as scum as the Tories have so often done.'[36]

Were Forwood and Churchill in concert then? Churchill wrote that in the Liverpool by-election of 1882 Forwood discredited the title 'Tory Democracy' because he 'used it without knowing what he was talking about'.[37] This lends itself to various explanations. Churchill did not want Forwood's defeat to extinguish Tory Democracy; and, having then neither met nor corresponded with Forwood, Churchill may have believed rumours that Forwood was a Radical, not Conservative, Democrat. Certainly there were policy differences between Forwood and Churchill at this time. In 1882 Forwood outpaced Churchill in advocating Reform and Redistribution, although the Fourth Party's tactician, the former Conservative agent, John Gorst, was alive to the necessity of identifying with borough opinion on these questions.[38] Churchill only renounced his opposition during the second reading of the Franchise Bill in 1884, not relishing the company of unregenerate rural Tory M.P.s. Afterwards he informed Forwood of his agreement, that 'the only Redistribution which will save the Conservative party from extinction will be equal electoral districts with single members'.[39]

The initial discourtesy shown to Forwood, however, suggests that Churchill believed that he alone understood Tory Democracy's secrets. Churchill's biographers antiphonally echo this. To use Harcourt's jibe, when he heard in 1887 that Churchill planned a Centre party, the biographies suffer from being 'all centre—and no circumference'.[40] None appreciates provincial Conservatism; but, with his booming personality, Churchill was a megaphone at the national level for a provincial colloquium. Tory Democracy was not Churchill's particular invention and, after his political extinction, the movement lost amplification but never stopped talking. Moreover, provincial Tory Democrats distrusted Churchill even as they followed him.

Churchill's missives to *The Times* had borne his thoughts, that maintenance of the monarchy, House of Lords, Union, and Established Church, now concerned practical politicians and if Conservative opinions were to prevail 'they should be represented by, and identified with, a statesman who fears not to meet and who knows how to sway immense masses of the working classes and who either by his genius or his eloquence, or by all the varied influences of an ancient name, can "move the hearts of households" . . .'.[41] Churchill chiefly appealed to grand themes, not justice in details, and summoned deference and paternalism as the reactionary combination. As one critic observed, even as he prepared to expound Tory Democracy Churchill 'showed genuine, hearty, thoroughgoing Toryism of the pre-reform type'.[42] The integral factor was personality. Churchill complained that the present leaders were 'doomed mediocrities'.

Nevertheless personality was not enough. Some formula was required and the new leader's policy was what the old laid down: '*Sanitas, sanitatum, omnia sanitas.*' Churchill credited Disraeli's frippery with:

> a social revolution which, passing by and diverting attention from wild longings for organic change, commences with the little peddling boards of health which occupy and delight the local Government Departments, comprises Lord Salisbury's plans for the amelioration of the dwellings of the poor, carries with it Lord Carnarvon's ideal of compulsory national insurance, includes Sir Wilfrid Lawson's temperance propaganda, preserves and reclaims commons and open spaces favoured by Mr. Bryce, constructs people's parks, collects and opens to the masses museums, libraries, art-galleries, does not disdain the public wash-houses of Mr. Jesse Collings. Public and private thrift must animate the whole, for it is from public thrift that the funds for the largesses can be drawn, and it is by private thrift alone that their results can be utilised and appreciated.[43]

Churchill painted a rainbow by stealing everyone's colours. But who would his party incorporate? Not the Whigs: their 'principles are even more divergent from the modern Conservatives than the principles of the Radical party, and certainly any political victory in which the Whigs bear a part must be to the last degree unwholesome and scrofulous'.[44] So much for Radicals like Labouchere who longed to 'hand this *damnosa hereditas* over to the Conservatives'—until Churchill in 1886 recommended the title 'Unionist', to 'combine all that is best in the politics of Tory, Liberal and Whig'.[45] When W. S. Blunt asked Churchill to define Tory Democracy, he found the oracle in a frivolous mood, willing to hazard that 'it is principally opportunism'.[46]

Lord Randolph Churchill, Arthur Forwood, and the National Union

A party crisis had been imminent in the early 1880s. The Conservatives' borough results in 1880 reflected badly on their electoral management, after the high hopes of 1874. These failures, apparently the result of ignorance as much as policy, sharpened the interest of the spurned agent, Gorst, who now primed Churchill to make a showing in the provinces. In Parliament itself Northcote seemed incapable of striking a firm Conservative line, while the Fourth Party made progressively more inspiriting interventions, in the Bradlaugh, Egyptian, Irish, and Franchise debates. Appropriately in 1883–4 all these issues—the urban Conservatives' discontent at the want of grasp by the party's establishment, franchise reform and Tory Democracy, Churchill's ambitiousness and the party leadership—collected in one arena, the National Union of Conservative and Constitutional Associations.

The leaders seemed unsympathetic to the provincial Conservatives' perfervid moods. Northcote dithered; and Salisbury mused, 'my epitaph must be: "Died of writing inane answers to empty-headed Conservative Associations" '.[47] In April 1884 Salisbury informed Churchill that he and Northcote recognized that the National Union's *raison d'etre* was 'to increase the number of Conservative voters'. Everything else—policy, expenditure, and candidatures—was governed by the leaders and their minions but, to ensure united action the Whips should join, *ex officio*, the National Union's Council.[48] Churchill replied that Salisbury ignored the Birmingham conference in October 1883, which criticized the party organization.

Churchill delineated his understanding of the discontent—that vesting executive power in the leaders, Whips, and other 'irresponsible persons', was 'obsolete' in democratic times; and that 'the centre of organizing energy should be an elected, representative and responsible body', an honest version of the Birmingham Liberal caucus.[49]

Several urban leaders now met Churchill for the first time. Their spokesman, Forwood, told Salisbury that they found Churchill:

> quite a different stamp of a man to what we pictured from his performances in the country. Quick, cool, and thoughtful, with an evident knowledge of what is required to move our large masses—wayward and rather obstinate, but evidently more amenable to reason, than some of us expected. We thought he could be led, once he felt he was not distrusted . . . [and] if Your Lordship could give him a word of assurance or encouragement, the party would secure a loyal, faithful follower.[50]

Two features seem significant. First, provincial leaders had unflattering preconceptions about Churchill, arising from the antipathy between the Fourth Party and their leaders. Second, urban Conservatives desired to forge a connection in high party counsels. Either a responsible role for provincial opinion in the National Union, or someone sympathetic (Churchill or Salisbury or both) in the next Cabinet, would answer their needs.

To Salisbury Forwood sent a copy of his address to the Chairmen of Conservative Associations in nine principal towns. This regretted the party's feud: its acuteness threatened their chances in the next election. Accordingly they would make suggestions about organization 'free from the personal considerations' which had intruded. When Forwood and seven other provincial leaders met Salisbury they affirmed their desire 'not only to improve and strengthen the party organization in the Country, but to see established on a permanent basis unanimity of feeling, unity of action, and loyalty to the recognized party leaders'. No Conservative—including Churchill—wanted the National Union to become a caucus, the provincial leaders asserting as a Conservative axiom the independence of M.P.s. and local associations. They acknowledged that the determination of public policy, general party finance, and candidatures, was the leaders' province—such subjects were 'unfitted for discussion by large, popular bodies'—and they approved a Whips' representative on the National Union's Council. In fact they wanted the leaders to show more interest in party organization, otherwise the National Union was isolated, a mere ornament. Correspondingly the National Union needed to include more provincial parties and to become an effective pipeline of communication. For this it required an annual allocation from the general party funds.[51]

According to its design of relaxing discord, the deputation of provincial leaders also approached Northcote and Churchill. Churchill complimented Forwood on the 'tact and self-sacrifice' which marked the provincial leaders' efforts—a letter which Forwood passed to Salisbury[52]—but their difference proved decisive in arrangements for the Sheffield conference in July 1884. Lord Claud Hamilton meanwhile had been working on Forwood, atrabiliously drawing the picture of a volatile Churchill, prompted by an evil genie, Gorst. He argued that 'so long as Mr. Gorst is Vice Chairman of the Union, Lord Randolph cannot be put back in the Chair'.

Some family hostility perhaps underlined Hamilton's political argument. His sister had married Churchill's brother, the Marquess of Blandford, in 1869; but the marriage was unhappy and a divorce had occurred in 1883 after Blandford, now the Duke of Marlborough, was proved to have committed adultery with the Countess of Aylesford.[53] Hamilton's political position, however, was predictable. He had been Chairman of the National Union (1876–9) when Gorst launched his first serious attempt to make the Council representative of provincial opinion. Although the National Union had been growing throughout the 1870s, its Council had discouraged it from seeking a more prominent role in party management. Hamilton's chairmanship had reflected this chariness of democracy: the Council thought it undesirable in 1877 to imitate those Radicals who had organized popular demonstrations on the Eastern Question, and they refused in 1879 to promote provincial federations of Conservative Associations akin to the Metropolitan Conservative Alliance which Gorst influenced.[54] Hamilton's position remained basically unattractive to Forwood in 1884 but he heeded him when he argued that Churchill's disloyalty to the leaders and their representatives in the organization threatened to pitch the party into 'absolute chaos' at a General Election. Hamilton acknowledged Churchill's usefulness in stumping the country—he too was impressed by Churchill's Birmingham campaign—but he urged the provincial leaders to estimate Churchill's quality by the fact that he had 'only five followers' in the Commons; and he added 'I feel hopeless of any real and permanent good being got out of him till that traitor Gorst is disposed of'.[55]

Hamilton stimulated Forwood's worst fears, of another general election defeat and of the party plagued by personality. Gorst accentuated this by indicating to Forwood that he wanted to press their cause to the finish, warning that 'no executive can be strong unless the persons who compose it are of one mind and of one purpose'.[56] But the provincial leaders were not the samurai of war-lords like Churchill: they wanted a party free from war, which would respect and harmonize every interest, urban and landed. Forwood understood the cost of conflict, and complained about 'the impolicy of making the personnel of the National Union the prominent feature of consideration' because, as he told the Birmingham leader,

> the Conservative party is . . . in a critical position; the Country is thoroughly dissatisfied with the Liberal policy, but those men who form the skirts of both parties, and who by throwing their weight to one side or the other turn the scale of an election, are restrained from joining our forces, because of the uncertainty attending our future leadership and the under-current of personal differences in the rank of our parliamentary representatives.[57]

In July 1884 Churchill sent that list of attainders which Gorst had forecast. Certain men existed 'whose presence on the Council is utterly incompatible with mine. I mean Messrs. Houldsworth, Wortley, Maclean, Chaplin and Lord Percy. Ashmead-Bartlett and others are beneath contempt.' He presented an ultimatum, that if the Conference elected them to the Council, he would leave the National Union.[58] Forwood was shocked:

> If we were to leave off the new Council all the names you proscribe, we should diminish the value of the National Union, just as much as if they were placed on it, and your friends left off. It would be a one-sided unrepresentative affair, one of those bodies which you have so properly decried in the past. I could be no party to support a body so constituted . . . What you really want is a sufficient majority to support your policy, not by the narrow wavering decisions of the past, but by a consistent vote without a previous whip on each occasion. I have had a large experience as Chairman of public committees and so long as I have had the numbers right on my side, I have invited rather than repelled, not only opponents in views, but personal opponents, on my committees. I have found such a plan ensures strength and force to my views from outside . . .

Forwood scrutinized Churchill's roll of execution. For Wortley, Ashmead-Bartlett, and Maclean he made no special plea. Houldsworth was different. Although critical of Churchill, Houldsworth disclaimed any desire to see him leave the National Union or even resign the chairmanship, since Houldsworth too advocated 'a vigorous, able and representative Council'. Moreover as a

Nonconformist and former chairman of the Manchester Conservative Association, Houldsworth represented interests which it would be folly to slight. Forwood recognized that 'Lancashire would resent his removal off the N.U. Let him be ever so much an adversary, against a majority he is powerless.' Regarding others, Forwood knew Chaplin 'as the representative man of the old régime'. He was too considerable to exclude; similarly Percy, Churchill's predecessor as chairman of the National Union. In sum Forwood advised: 'Make a martyr of no one.'[59]

Churchill replied by reiterating ambitions which first attracted Forwood, namely, his desire to produce a Council 'thoroughly representative of provincial opinion . . . What we want to get at are the local leaders, in order to create and preserve constant and harmonious connection between the leaders of the party and the members of the party in Parliament and local opinion.' This happy picture was contradicted when Churchill accused Forwood of intending to pack the Council with 'a strong body of active personal opponents, whose only object on all occasions will be to thwart me and my friends and to place us in a constant minority'.[60]

Although their differences were transparent, Forwood continued to support Churchill's chairmanship. Forwood rationalized this:

> on party grounds. It would be the best reply to the Radical cry of a divided party. His principles, for the National Union, of election not nomination, are those most acceptable to the Country. His plain spoken language has caught the ear of the people. His candidature for Birmingham is more of a national than a local affair, and for a representative body of the party to put him aside would be to prejudice seriously his position in that constituency.

Churchill's image had become part of Tory Democracy; but Forwood had not lost sight of their goal. Unless its Council became representative and was sufficiently financed to undertake important duties of organization, Forwood continued, 'the N.U. will be a danger and not a strength to the cause'. Integral to this was the extinction of the Central Committee: 'Let the Whips and the Leaders be their own Central Committee, consulting whom they like but for a whip to say to an M.P. Oh I will consult Stanhope or I will speak to Chaplin instead of referring to the acknowledged leaders is to open the door to jealousies, and to give an irresponsible body a power detrimental to the public weal.'[61]

Provincial Conservatives did not directly strike at their leaders' policy-making prerogative. They desired to facilitate their access by removing excrescences. Forwood made a final appeal to Churchill: 'Be assured that the men from the country will enter the Council in the distinct determination that it shall rule and not be ruled, that the responsible elective bodies must control and not self appointed committees. I see my way clearly to this result being achieved but we must work diplomatically, so as not to drag across the path a personal red herring.'[62] But the herring was a bloater: Churchill's hugely touchy personality vitiated Forwood's plans. With Churchill's retirement from the National Union, only the question of the Commons' leadership remained, and Forwood supported Hicks Beach's replacement of Churchill in the National Union from the sole motive that 'Beach might *for a time* be a successor to Northcote' in the Commons.[63]

The alliance with Churchill was shaken but not dead. Provincial Conservatives sought that the National Union's Council should become, in Forwood's words, 'a body of a really representative and elective character instead of one which was too much upon a nominated system'.[64] Churchill sympathized with this, but exploited it in his designs on the Cabinet. Winston Churchill wrote that his father was 'not the man to take his decisions from party caucuses'; but 'when he was faction-fighting he fought to win, seizing anything that came along'.[65] Tory Democracy had 'come along'; but party unity and a voice in the Cabinet ultimately counted above organizational reconstruction.

Forwood played almost no part in the affairs of the National Union after July 1884 (although he did not resign from the Council until April 1887). Throughout the crisis in 1883–4 Forwood had cultivated a connection with Lord Salisbury as well as with Churchill. As the flaws in his character were exposed, Churchill's value depreciated; as he emerged as the party's primate, in conjunction with urban Conservative opinion on Redistribution, Salisbury's value appreciated.

Churchill having entered Salisbury's Cabinet, the *Fortnightly Review* complained that 'Democratic Toryism was merged in the common-place opportunism which is called Conservatism'. The take-over bid and asset-stripping are not activities that are new or confined to the business world. Gorst had forecast what was to come in a letter to Drummond Wolff, 4 June 1884: 'I believe Salisbury and the Old Gang are at last opening their eyes to the force of the Tory democracy. The effect will be that they will try to place themselves at its head and oust us from our legitimate position.'[66] Merger, however, had always been one objective of most adversaries and the compromise reached with the party leaders was realistic. The leaders dissolved the Central Committee, they acknowledged that the National Union might contribute something to electoral organization, and they admitted Churchill to the front bench; but both Churchill and the National Union were in a position to be disciplined. Churchill, in the time-honoured device of politics, had seemingly been bought off by having been taken in; and the leaders had granted the National Union the status of a consultative body in the sense in which Ambrose Bierce cynically defined the word 'consult'—'to seek another's approval of a course already decided on'.[67]

CHAPTER FOUR

Tory town—Liverpool in the 1885 General Election

Stringent as the rules of the Birmingham Liberal Association are, they do not seek to exercise anything like so close a control over the deliberation of the Liberal electorate as is actually exercised by the Executive Committee and the Board of Management over the Conservatives of Liverpool.

The Times, 27 October 1885

The leaders of the Radical party in the future may seem wanting in two respects. First, it may be said that the tendency of Radicalism is to pay insufficient regard to the religious sentiments and prejudices of the English people; secondly, that it is the tendency of Radicalism to disregard the patriotic and military instincts of the nation.

Fortnightly Review, July 1883

The Redistribution of Seats Act, 1885, had asserted the principle of the single-member constituency. Exceptions survived, but in a great town this had the consequence of making more striking the political attitudes of the different classes, since social status and residential location were closely bound. Hence the suburban constituency was born, along with the slum constituency, although the latter especially was not homogeneous in Liverpool, through the intermingling of business premises with poor residential property. This chapter maps out the new constituency face of Liverpool in the 1885 General Election. It also examines the manner by which candidates came to be chosen, the criteria of selection, the role of the party leader in the city, and the central and constituency organizations. For Forwood particularly this election was important as a test of his reputation. He had to practise what he preached, to vindicate his commitment to Tory Democracy and to demonstrate that, by a judicious reconstruction of seats, Conservatism might grow into a formidable urban force.

Notes begin on p. 376.

Trade, education, and religion

Pundits were at risk in predictions about the 1885 General Election. Liverpool was awash with a 'flood of oratory', as parliamentary, municipal, and school board, elections coincided; but it was not easy to estimate what issues in the end would register most impact. The leading questions of the later part of Gladstone's ministry, Egypt, Reform, and Redistribution, had receded from prominence during the Conservative Caretaker ministry. Considering the newly fashioned borough seats, an extended rural electorate, and a confusion of policies regarding Ireland—some Liberals advocating repressive legislation and some Conservatives apparently 'cottoning to the Irish demagogues, whom a while ago they would have had no scruple in hanging up in a string'—Councillor Picton felt that 'the novelty of the circumstances utterly defies calculation as to the results'.[1] Mystification existed in government circles too, Thomas Sanderson reported to his former chief, Lord Derby: 'I give occasionally the most contradictory opinions and no one dissents with any strength. I never saw people less decided in their forecasts.'[2]

There were few clues. Northcote, now Lord Iddesleigh, argued that voters, especially new voters, must recognize 'the impossibility of Socialist panaceas for human suffering'. Conservatives had no creative programme. *The Times* approved: it expected the next Parliament to deliver little legislation, but to be preoccupied in containing 'Irish disaffection'.[3] Popular audiences apparently welcomed the Conservatives' insistence on imperial integrity.[4] Businessmen, on the other hand, rejected Liberal ministrations from tangible causes—the trade depression; and Joseph Chamberlain's management of the Board of Trade.[5]

The priority of business federations, like the Liverpool Steam Ship Owners Association—whose fifty members owned one million gross tonnage of shipping—was naturally facility for trade. They disliked philanthropic restrictions which made British shipping uncompetitive; but the Association had regard for safety, by simplifying sound signals for use in fog, building lighthouses, and improving approaches to the Mersey.[6] Trade interests even induced the Association to espouse temperance reform, from a desire to gain sober labour.[7] Regarding shipping reform, the editor of the *Liverpool Daily Post*, Edward Russell, told Joseph Chamberlain that though Liverpool contained 'one or two tough opponents . . . the general tone of opinion is by no means vicious';[8] and William Rathbone reported that Liverpool shipowners would accept a 'workable' bill, being 'much more reasonable than elsewhere'.[9] When the Liverpool Chamber of Commerce discussed the Merchant Shipping Bill, the speeches were moderate, except for 'a ridiculous demonstration of Captain Hatfield, and the animus of Arthur Forwood'.[10] Hatfield was isolated, as one prominent in the coffin-ship racket;[11] but when Forwood questioned Chamberlain's understanding he expressed widespread suspicions. Informed by another Rathbone that '90 per cent of Shipowners would make a good thing at the present time by losing their ships',[12] Chamberlain struck at over-insurance as the key to over-loading, under-manning, poor construction, and unsafe schedules; but Liverpool shipowners resented the inference that they were all 'shipknackers' and 'quasi-criminals'. This, and unenthusiasm in the Cabinet, brought the Bill's withdrawal and a Royal Commission.[13]

When the Liverpool Steam Ship Owners met to elect a spokesman to the Commission, their choice, T. H. Ismay, refused nomination.[14] Other names excited controversy between owners of steam and sailing ships, and passenger liners and freight carriers, although this was not clear-cut since some were involved in many different operations.[15] The difficulty in stating representative opinions and a conviction that 'the Commission must be a fiasco' led Alfred Holt to advise the Association not to offer evidence. The corporate opinion seemed less hostile to particular measures than distrustful of Chamberlain's general attitude.[16] Nevertheless the Association questioned local parliamentary candidates about whether they would reserve 'the Shipowners' responsibility to that which he could personally provide against', and maintain 'the right of freedom of contract between Shipowners and Underwriters and between Shipowners and Merchants', subject to safeguards against fraud, and whether they would reconstitute the Board of Trade to include trading interests.[17]

Most non-Conservative candidates hedged in their replies. Samuel Smith was even considered Chamberlainite in trade policy. James Samuelson was different. He nominated the Board of Trade 'a disgrace to the first trading nation in the world'; but the opinion of one who voiced labour demands hardly attracted the Association. Conservative candidates struck the appropriate notes. The Kirkdale candidate, George Baden-Powell, denigrated 'legislation which saves the lives of sailors by destroying the national industry which enables them to go to sea'; and Lord Claud Hamilton asseverated that the Board impeded the development of the country's resources. He advocated giving to ports like Liverpool 'more central and representative power over all matters connected with their shipping'.[18]

Chamberlain's views on education troubled a wider community. Forwood told Salisbury, 'No party ever had such a friend as Chamberlain. His free education is food for hundreds of votes.'[19] Publicly Forwood displayed piety: 'Free education meant secular education, the bringing up of their children simply as intellectual animals, without the fear of God before their eyes . . .' Piety also contained economy: 1,100,000 children then educated in Board Schools cost £3¼ million p.a.; 2,150,000 children educated in 'voluntary' denominational schools cost the state £1,600,000 p.a. Forwood refused to commit the entire education system to 'that refrigerating machine, the School Board'.[20] The Catholic Bishop of Liverpool, O'Reilly, also fulminated that, following free education, England would be 'robbed of her Christianity'; and Councillor John Yates urged Catholics and Protestants alike to resist 'that socialist, confiscator, leveller, and Oliver Cromwell of the present day, Joseph Chamberlain'.[21]

These elections enabled Catholics to protest against 'the intolerable strain' of having to pay Board School rates while supporting their own Catholic schools.[22] In an unprecedented intervention Cardinal Manning advised Catholics to demand a Royal Commission to review the 1870 Education Act.[23] Liberals at most expressed sympathy. Conservatives gave assurances. This commitment was politic. Denominational education was a Conservative ideal, but 'Rome on the rates' was not. O'Reilly, however, emphasized that while many Catholics in Liverpool would find it 'painful' to sever their long association with the Liberals, 'the calls of conscience are above those of party'.[24]

The connections in Chamberlain's mind between education and disestablishment also fashioned the Conservative cry, 'Church in danger', although it might be interjected, like Carlyle, 'it has seldom been out of "danger" since we can remember'.[25] The Church was a Conservative absolute, 'a matter of life and death to us', according to Salisbury; but the Archbishop of Canterbury, Benson, regretted this party watchword, since 'Liberals will be afraid of meddling with the support of the Church lest it should cause any doubt of their Liberalism'.[26] Disestablishment cries exacerbated tensions in the Liberal party and revitalized the Conservative campaign.[27] They also animated Anglican reformers. This boded ill when later Conservative ministries resisted Patronage and Clergy Discipline Bills.[28]

In Liverpool partisans had already been awakened to protect the Church–State from Nonconformist and Romish perversions. Orangemen had attacked Liberationist meetings in the 1870s, just as the local Church Association prosecuted Ritualists;[29] but when Dean M'Neile died in 1879, *The Times* had declared that the evangelical school, in its exclusive, tasteless, and ignorant form, perished with him.[30] Although *The Times* equally upbraided Ritualists, with their 'childish pratings of Church and priest', its attack had provoked replies from two incarnations of 'the strident bigot of antique Evangelical mould'—Dean Close and the potential Bishop of Liverpool, J. C. Ryle.[31]

The Times erred in pretending that the thunder of extremes had passed. In 1882 the vicar of St. Jude's, Liverpool, the somewhat mentally unbalanced Ernest Fitzroy, was assaulted by anti-ritualist protestors; and in 1885 Dr. Hakes, on behalf of the local Church Association, prosecuted the vicar of St. Margaret's, Bell Cox, for similar violations of evangelical observance.[32] Bell Cox, however, refused to recognize the Chancery Court's authority in ecclesiastical causes; and, despite a sentence of suspension from office for six months, he conducted his services as before. The suit continued before a succession of Courts, effectively until Hakes's death in 1902.[33] Bell Cox was imprisoned for sixteen days in 1887 for contempt, but the Courts' inability otherwise to effect judgement encouraged direct protest. Ryle laid low, after failing to induce Bell Cox to conform by persuasion. He was by now pessimistic about the continuance of an Established Church, and he would not risk episcopal authority on the frailities of the existing legal discipline.[34]

Forwood recognized political significance in these events and cautioned Lord Salisbury for having sent a small donation to Fitzroy's church.[35] Both the Church Association and the Orange Order regarded Ritualism as the General Election's greatest issue.[36] This view Forwood professed to share, in order to contain enthusiasts who wished to place Protestantism before party.[37] However, not every Conservative imitated Forwood's strenuous courtship. Hamilton upset the Orangemen when he attended one of Father Nugent's concerts for the Liverpool poor. Likewise Whitley suffered censure when he opposed a *clôture* on Irish M.P.s.[38]

The Caretaker Ministry and Conservative conflict

A deeper schism between Conservatives had been threatened during Salisbury's minority Government formed in June 1885. Whitley believed it 'a blunder' to take office;[39] and, while he supported Salisbury's course, Forwood advised 'the importance of recognizing what I may term the "party of action" in any ministerial arrangements. The growing feeling in the Country is "progressive Conservatism" and unless its representatives occupy prominent positions . . . it will be a grievous prejudice to the workers in our new and enlarged constituencies.' In personal terms this meant Lord Randolph Churchill. His inclusion in the Cabinet would not involve substantive changes of policy—Churchill only ' "emphasized" the active policy led by you [Salisbury]'—but it would transform the party's image 'if we can only pull the party from under the wheels of mere County and Landed influence, and give to urban constituencies a just share . . .'.[40] Churchill had become Tory Democracy's totem. Salisbury replied carefully: 'I do not know whom you mean by "the party of Action", but, as to Lord R.C. individually, . . . I value his talents very highly.'[41]

Friction resulted, however, as Salisbury's Ministry apparently sacrificed principle for a shadow of power. The Medical Relief Bill, Whitley thought, tended towards 'state socialism';[42] and Forwood depicted the consequence of not disfranchising those treated in Poor Law hospitals:

> Every year we strike off 1,500 names in Liverpool of those who have received this description of assistance. They are the scum of the place, the drunkards, the idle and the dissolute. The respectable decent poor, if they have 1d. in their pocket, can obtain advice and medicine for this fee at our dispensaries, supported by the charitable. If they have no money and can prove respectability our numerous medical charities will care for them on the recommendation of a minister or subscriber. Those who apply to the Parish are the squalid and undeserving, and better almost anything than flood the register with such a class . . .[43]

Embroidered here was an intricate social gradation, demarcating the lower from the lowest, upon which Tory Democracy thrived.

Forwood's 'progressive' and Orange faces were not always compatible. Churchill was invited to speak in Liverpool in July 1885 but, when Whitley and Hamilton would not share his platform, he withdrew. This embarrassed Forwood, who had planned a meeting gathered from all Lancashire.[44] Whitley, usually 'not a very passionate man', found Churchill's character repulsive.[45] The meeting would have served Churchill's self-glorification. Both Whitley and Hamilton described the intended address as 'fulsome', Whitley adding that it 'so ignores Lord Salisbury and the other Members of the Government that it makes it impossible for me to sign it'.[46] Moreover, now recognizing Orange opinion, the M.P.s. denounced Churchill's dealings with the Parnellites.[47]

Forwood spent early August mollifying the individuals and factions involved;[48] but this querulousness about Irish relations was a presentiment of the General Election. Strictly speaking Home Rule was not an issue.[49] Liverpudlians, however, had been concerned ever since 1875–6 when Parnell declared in their city that 'without a full measure of Home Rule . . . no Irishman would ever rest content'.[50] This had worried many protagonists of Reform and Redistribution in 1884–5. Single-member constituencies, it was supposed, would polarize Irish differences;[51] and Hamilton told Forwood 'that Home Rule will be presented to Ireland before many years have passed and woe betide us all then who live over here and are not Papists'.[52]

To the cautious of all colours the Liberal M.P. for London University, Sir John Lubbock, had preached that proportional representation would 'raise and purify' elections, preventing, for instance, Home Rulers from holding the balance in Liverpool:

> We shall give Liverpool, say, eight members because it has 63,000 electors, of whom perhaps 30,000 are Liberals, 30,000 Conservatives, 2,000 Irish Home Rulers, and 1,000 without distinctive political opinions; and I do not understand how any one can really wish that these 3,000 should practically return all the members. We know that generally they join Conservatives, and the result [of single-member seats] would be that 30,000 Liberals would be unrepresented.[53]

Lubbock's arithmetic, however, flattered the Liberals, and his presumptions that Irishmen were dispersed evenly throughout Liverpool, and that many voted Conservative, were unsound.

The Irish vote

Liverpool Irishmen watched as the dice was loaded in constituency boundaries. Their majority in Exchange ward was offset when Lime Street ward was included in the new Exchange division. T. P. O'Connor wanted Lime Street to join Abercromby, thereby integrating 'people of similar pursuits'. He argued that the Irish districts should be segregated to avoid 'confusing' and 'demoralizing' appeals to Irish voters by English politicians. Somewhat disingenuously posing the Tory gospel of community against Irish separatism, Whitley replied that he regarded Liverpudlians 'as a united people'; and Hamilton mimicked him, though he asserted separate representation when it served Protestants in Donegal.[54]

Nevertheless the Liverpool Irish made their electoral preparations. Justin McCarthy, who, living by his pen, knew the value of being agreeable, was invited to contest Exchange.[55] This constituency embraced St. Paul's, Vauxhall, Lime Street, St. Anne's and Exchange wards, which returned eight Conservative councillors, five Liberals, and two Nationalists. Irishmen inhabited every ward but predominated in Vauxhall and Exchange. The residential parts were honeycombed with squalid courts whose origin, Picton considered, was ' "as if a man should cast seed into the ground, and should sleep and rise night and day, and the seed should spring and grow up, he *knoweth not how.*" It might be added— "he careth not how".'[56]

Jerry-builders had evaded the legislation which the Corporation promoted to guide construction. The resultant houses, the Borough Engineer complained, were 'nurseries of disease and death'.[57] Moreover, in places like Addison Street, where the death-rate was 45 per 1,000 persons, the frontage of pubs was one-seventh that of private houses.[58] Chemical works, oil mills, artificial-manure factories, gas-works, and diseased cattle receiving-centres, made living in Vauxhall ward particularly abominable.[59] Business and commerce affected the politics as well as the health of the constituency. Perhaps one-quarter of the electorate in Exchange Division was non-resident.[60] In 1885 two hundred merchants with plural votes had to defend their franchises in the registration court. The Revising Barrister, deeming the objections frivolous, granted 10*s.* costs in each instance. This was beyond the means of the objector, an Irish labourer who fled the court as the orders were made out; and the Barrister reflected sourly how the Nationalists debased political behaviour.[61]

The Irish leader, Parnell, and his chief election organizer in Britain, the newly-wed T. P. O'Connor,[62] made Liverpool their headquarters for the 1885 campaign. One of the first of Parnell's decisions was to withdraw McCarthy's candidature from the Exchange constituency. Parnell was strangely unconfident: local canvassers had been optimistic about winning the seat.[63] A Liberal candidate, Councillor T. E. Stephens, had entered the lists after nomination by the Exchange Division Liberal Association; but on 20 November Parnell presented himself, and Captain O'Shea advanced as another Liberal candidate, with the support of Joseph Chamberlain and the Liberal Whip, Lord Grosvenor. The cuckold's intervention startled many but the *Daily Post* had intimated it. Grosvenor had travelled to Liverpool for a midnight meeting at the North Western Hotel (where Parnell and O'Connor were staying) with the local Liberal leader, Holt. Holt afterwards wrote that he considered it 'an unworthy intrigue and I was very little associated with that disgrace [*sic*] arrangement'.[64] In public, however, Parnell was now busy charging British politicians with gerrymandering the constituencies to deprive Irishmen in Britain of representation. Only O'Connor, who would contest Liverpool Scotland, looked safe; but Parnell threatened that Nationalist M.P.s. might challenge Bootle and three other Liverpool constituencies, Kirkdale, West Toxteth, and Abercromby.[65]

In Exchange Irish canvassers responded to the new circumstances. They directed 'Irishmen' 'to vote for Parnell if he stands, if not vote for Parnell's policy, the balance of power', by supporting the Conservative candidate, L. R. Baily. These manoeuvres produced a confusing impression of Parnell's intentions and Forwood later disclosed that a deputation of three Irish councillors promised him that if Baily withdrew Parnell would visit Forwood's own constituency, Ormskirk, and 'such other constituencies in Lancashire as we might desire', to support Conservative candidates.[66] Forwood peremptorily refused.

Two days before polling Parnell withdrew his own candidature. He promised O'Shea, 'as an Irishman and a Catholic', his support although only Labouchere, Storey, Thompson, and Cowen among Liberals elsewhere in Britain were similarly favoured.[67] Stephens also withdrew, although his name remained on the ballot to seduce thirty-six voters.[68] *Porcupine* had accused Stephens of being 'the cats-paw of men who expect to back him up with Irish Nationalists and Catholic votes while running him under Liberal colours';[69] and O'Connor speculated that his withdrawal was the result of 'a secret deal between Parnell and the Liberal Whip' which, if true, contradicted the Irish party's principles of the time.[70] O'Shea polled 2,909 votes, Baily 2,964.

The debatable feature was the Irish vote. One historian has drawn attention to Irish revolts in several seats, caused by the Liberal candidates' respect for

Catholic education. Parnell's manifesto against the Liberals was obeyed when it coincided with priestly advice.[71] Liverpool, however, was peculiarly placed by Parnell's presence, his machinations and contradictions. His support of O'Shea, countermanding the Nationalists' manifesto, 'astounded' his colleagues;[72] but that manifesto never had much life in Liverpool. Parnell's colleague, Joseph Biggar, had already told Merseyside Irishmen to distinguish personalities, whatever their party: certain Liberals, like Samuel Smith, 'a crawling hypocrite', must be defeated, and apparently friendly Tories, like David MacIver, must be spared.[73]

The Liverpool Liberal leader, Holt, had viewed his party's prospects cheerlessly, believing that Irishmen would vote Conservative;[74] but Lord Derby commented that since 'whoever wins (by the necessary sacrifice) the Irish vote will lose the English vote, . . . the defection of that very slippery lot gives me little concern'.[75] Derby's attitude was apposite—there were few signs in the Liverpool region that Conservative candidates would risk their Unionist support. In the Ormskirk constituency Parnell advised Irishmen to vote Conservative but, since the Conservative candidate, Forwood, had declared Orange sympathies, Parnell was not extensively obeyed.[76] What J. G. Gibson reckoned, that it was improbable that he, an Irish Protestant, would receive any Irish Catholic votes as the Conservative candidate in Walton, might be assumed of most Liverpool seats.[77]

Irish electors were not all drilled Parnellites. T. P. O'Connor's organization of the I.N.L. was such that individual branches would defer to Parnell's chosen executive in the selection of Parliamentary candidates; but this machine was of limited value in educating electors in the complex strategies of 1885. William Redmond believed that no expatriate Irishmen were more true to the cause than Liverpool Irishmen, but local politicians knew how tenuous their organization was, for few had 'joined the National League or any association whatever', and their party press collapsed.[78] The result in Liverpool's Kirkdale constituency said little for the discipline of the Nationalists' organization if their estimate of 2,700 Irish voters was correct. John Redmond was run there—besides Wexford North, which he won—but he received only 765 votes. Probably many Irishmen supported the Liberal candidate, James Samuelson, who had nursed Kirkdale since 1883, and who combined Home Rule sympathies with labour causes.[79]

Tory Democracy in practice

Conservatives won eight of nine Liverpool constituencies. This was Forwood's 'answer to Birmingham'; and the Tory press developed the contrast between Chamberlain's 'reckless and destructive Radicalism' and Forwood's 'progressive, reforming Constitutionalism'.[80] The Liberal *Daily Post*, however, argued that after three years' faltering existence as a Tory Democrat, Forwood had returned to 'the deepest recesses of benighted Toryism'.[81] Similarly the *Review*, while praying for Forwood's emancipation, recognized bonds which kept him Conservative—'his anti-Irish proclivities and his devotion to the Church as a State institution'.[82]

What had become of Tory Democracy? None of Liverpool's Conservative

M.P.s could be considered Churchillites. Indeed in Lord Claud Hamilton, Edward Whitley, J. G. Gibson, and Baron Henry de Worms, Forwood had four men who had strenuously worked to defeat Churchill in the National Union. But men did not have to be Churchillites to be Tory Democrats in Forwood's sense. Moreover, the Liberal press was deceived by the temperateness with which Forwood enunciated Tory Democracy in 1885 as by his excitement in 1882; and, feeling injury, it substituted 'reactionary' for 'radical'. Forwood had not altered what he considered guiding principles—the maintenance of the Constitution and Church–State connection; and 'the promotion of cordial relations between all classes'. Now scorned by Liberals as 'bald and ridiculous platitudes', these were always Forwood's absolutes. Tory Democrats had no academic theory of progress: they treated social problems empirically without asserting principles which conflicted with inherited values. Addressing newly enfranchised electors Forwood called himself 'a practical everyday working man like themselves', 'a thoroughly old-fashioned Tory', and 'a strong upholder of the great institutions of the country'.[83] He emphasized that a conservative democracy was in labour's interest, because the capitalist, meeting 'any trouble, any revolutionary changes . . . could keep his money in his purse, leave the country, and take his money elsewhere'; and that 'withdrew so much labour from the working man'.[84] This smacked of blackmail and intimidation, but also suggested class interdependence, a theme which infused Forwood's defence of the House of Lords as 'the bulwark of the people's liberties against the domination of the majority'.[85] The Radical M.P. for Northampton, Labouchere, might write that 'an hereditary Upper House whose members are drawn almost exclusively from great landowners is the *reductio ad absurdum* of statecraft';[86] but Forwood did not extol uncritical ancestor-worship. He wanted a more representative second chamber.

In important respects, however, the activities of Tory Democrats did not meet their aspirations. Forwood's desire to see the National Union represent Conservative opinion had a corollary for the parliamentary party. Forwood promised to support working men candidates provided certain conditions were honoured: he objected to paying M.P.s, believing that this would encourage 'corruption and jobbery'; he opposed sectionalism, believing that M.P.s should represent all, 'irrespective of trade or class distinction'; and he insisted that the choice was a 'bona fide working man', disparaging 'those in a different sphere of life or calling who offer themselves as candidates especially in the interests of the labouring classes'.[87] This last particular was a stab at Samuelson, the Radical contesting Kirkdale;[88] but the question of working men candidates had currency widely in the Conservative party.[89] In Liverpool the W.M.C.A.'s vitality made the prospects of organizing such a candidature initially better than elsewhere; but ultimately other obstacles proved insuperable.

Four candidates advanced—a schoolmaster, Joseph Williams; a shopkeeper, James Lowry; a warehouseman, Griffith Thomas; and a shipwright, Thomas Graham. Thomas Atkinson, of the W.M.C.A.'s Selection Committee, enumerated their claims and disabilities. Neither Williams nor Lowry was a 'bona fide working man', although Williams was involved in the Parliamentary Debating Society and Lowry in the Trades Council. Thomas was indeed a 'bona fide working man'; but as the W.M.C.A.'s ex-chairman he would alienate non-partisan electors. Atkinson concluded that Graham's candidature would be the most popular: he represented the city's work and he was not considered 'an extreme party man'.[90]

Forwood eschewed interference in these initial deliberations in order to show confidence in the W.M.C.A. He regretted it when the Committee chose Williams.[91] From Graham Forwood learned the inside story. The selection occured at a packed meeting of forty-five men, including many from the Parliamentary Debating Society. Graham formally protested against this 'caucus-ridden vote' and warned that if Forwood allowed it his leadership would be stultified.[92]

The Tory Democracy had demonstrated its irresponsibility; but management was permitted in the rules of the Liverpool Constitutional Association, described by its opponents as 'probably the most complete piece of political machinery in the kingdom'.[93] Each constituency had a council drawn from its ward committees and each ward committee was composed of the chairman, secretary, and ten representatives from each polling district, and three representatives from each branch of the W.M.C.A., Orange Institution, Conservative Temperance Association, or other affiliated societies in the ward, provided that each contained over fifty paying members. This procedure seemed democratic enough; but Clause 15 provided that constituency councils, 'before taking definite steps in matters of primary importance', consulted with the Constitutional's executive. The dependence on the Constitutional was enforced, moreover, by the absence of separate constituency agents. The need to marshal the out-voters in Exchange was a plausible reason for the subordination of the other constituencies; but centralization was positively sought. Since Clause 18 provided that the Constitutional's President was an *ex officio* member of each constituency council and executive (albeit without voting), and Clause 22 empowered him to investigate ward committee proceedings, in practice Forwood dominated the organization.[94] Williams's candidature did not progress beyond the nominating caucus.[95]

Placing candidates in constituencies

In the event most Liverpool constituencies posed candidature problems for the Conservatives, although the sitting M.P.s, Whitley and Hamilton, and the leader, Forwood, were given the pick of the seats. Pundits forecasted that Whitley would choose Kirkdale or Everton, and Hamilton and Forwood West Derby and East Toxteth;[96] but Forwood decided to contest Ormskirk. One councillor told Forwood that his decision fell 'like a thunderbolt upon the party', and the *Review* speculated that Forwood had feared another desertion like 1882;[97] but since he could have chosen a safe seat this argument was grotesque.[98] The *Daily Post* was more perspicacious: Forwood wished to extend his reputation beyond Liverpool; moreover, without personal commitment to a city constituency, he could control Conservative fortunes evenly throughout Liverpool.[99] When considering the several seats Forwood heeded Hamilton's advice, 'to have no local men except first-rate ones'.[100]

One difficulty was Everton, an archetypal artisans' suburb. Everton had been tied to Liverpool by tentacles of terraced cottages following the docks' extension from the 1820s, but the period of most rapid growth was 1851–71, when the population increased by 65,000.[101] The resultant monotonous rows of mostly terraced bye-law housing did not make Everton a slum area: it was 'not exactly squalid—but bourgeois, common, and uninteresting'.[102] The houses seemed brick and mortar replicas of their inhabitants' views—dense, uniform, and unimaginative, although there was injustice in this charge, which was a standard calumny levelled against working-class dormitories by middle-class critics. In fact the dominant political character of Everton was somewhat unusual and required explanation. It was a bastion of 'No Surrender' Conservatism, albeit 'the Goshen of the Cambrian race'.[103] Built principally by Owen Elias, Everton retained its mainly Welsh complexion until an intermixing followed the advent of electric trams.[104] From 1835 to 1866 Everton's municipal representation had been closely contested; but between 1866 and 1868 Conservatives were unopposed and, *Porcupine* declared, these 'fatal uncontested elections beggared Everton Liberalism'.[105] The Liberal press assumed that, with a little exertion, Everton would regain a balanced political composition. The *Daily Post* called Everton Toryism 'a very artificial production', stemming from Whitley's personal popularity and 'the political perversion' of many Welshmen.[106] It considered Welshmen constitutionally Liberal. Their friction with the Liverpool Irish population was discounted.

For Forwood the prospect of a safe seat was clouded by John Houlding's claims. Elias's successor to the cognomen, 'King of Everton', Houlding was once a daily wage-earner; but in 1870 he had founded a brewery. He became chairman of Everton Conservative Association in 1872 and a councillor in 1884. He also served on the Board of Guardians, Burial Board, and Hospital Committee; he was a Freemason, Orangeman, and churchman, and a benefactor also of Nonconformist bodies. Houlding epitomized the parochial patriot. His popularity emanated from 'intimate acquaintance through experience of the condition and requirements of the working classes, absence of any pride of position, and a daily readiness to help in any undertaking, from a school-room concert to a parliamentary deputation'.[107]

Porcupine, usually anti-Tory and especially anti-Drink, supported Houlding in 1884 as one who had 'devoted more time to the ratepayers than almost any other man of his age in public work'.[108] Moreover, Houlding was a 'thoroughgoing democrat', despite unflinching constitutional principles.[109] This distinction perturbed several Conservatives, to whom popularity sounded like criminality. Houlding's colleague as Councillor for Everton and Kirkdale was J. Barkeley Smith, a timber merchant and supine chairman of the Health Committee. The contrast between them is couched in Whitley's mysterious comment, that 'Houlding will hardly do for Everton at least some of our friends fancy not though he would have considerable support from another section'.[110]

Forwood faced a dilemma. As a Tory Democrat, Houlding was a natural ally; but his elevation to parliamentary honours would deepen jealousies; and his trade gave a platform to Liberal opponents. There was also the national movement to consider: a jumped-up brewer, who was 'a little uncertain about his "Hs"', might pass as an agent of Tory Democracy, not as a leader. He personified the prognostication that urban constituencies would return vestry men. In practice, therefore, Tory Democracy was hedged with parentheses. Before constituency associations adopted candidates Forwood and his intimates prepared the nominations. Whitley prescribed Forwood's tactic: 'all these matters . . . [should] be settled as far as possible privately though afterwards the District Committees must be called together before any candidate is finally selected or we may get into a difficulty'.[111]

The first man fancied to balk Houlding's advance was H. S. Giffard, the pugnacious lawyer who had served Disraeli as Solicitor-General. However Giffard became Lord Chancellor in Salisbury's Caretaker Ministry. Without another weighty alternative Whitley offered himself. It seemed a natural step, but Whitley regretted his declining prominence in municipal matters and had wanted to retire from Parliament. However, he won a perfunctory contest, polling 4,535 votes against 2,063 for a member of Liverpool Junior Reform Club.

The problem of Houlding's claims shifted into neighbouring Kirkdale.[112] The docks and railway yards stamped the constituency's character. Densely and toughly peopled, Kirkdale's low life was very low. When a man was kicked to death there in 1885, the *Courier* acknowledged that 'some act of abominable savagery' was a regular occurence.[113] Kirkdale was developed relatively late. When T. Major Lester inhabited St. Mary's vicarage in 1855 the sea view was uninterrupted; and Baines found Kirkdale in 1859 'a healthy and agreeable village' of 9,000 people. By 1900 the district contained 96,000 people, five Anglican, ten Catholic or Nonconformist churches, and eleven schools. Parts of Kirkdale received an overflow of Everton Welsh, vying with an Irish migration from central Liverpool.[114]

The Conservative nomination for Kirkdale evinced Forwood's authority, but also his inability to attract an estimable candidate from outside Liverpool. The constituency Conservative Association wanted a local man, Houlding or Barkeley Smith; but Forwood induced Houlding to withdraw and refused to truckle further to his reactionary wing by underwriting Smith. He contacted several possibilities, including Harland (the Belfast shipbuilder), and a nephew of Lord Iddesleigh. Following their refusals, the Kirkdale Conservative Association again sought Houlding's nomination; but Forwood blocked it by advancing George Baden-Powell.[115]

The manner by which Baden-Powell secured nomination in Kirkdale testifies to the opportunities available to the plausible carpet-bagger in a society where the word of a gentleman often went unquestioned. Baden-Powell's father, though considered by one Archbishop of Canterbury, Tait, to be 'the most talkative of bores', had been Savilian Professor of Geometry at Oxford and a contributor to *Essays and Reviews* (1860), that monument of liberal Churchmen who sought to persuade the Church to accept modern historical criticism of the Bible. The best known now of all Baden-Powells, George's younger brother, Robert—the hero of Mafeking and high priest of the Boy Scouts—had no reputation in 1885; but George Baden-Powell had seen service in the colonies, having recently drawn up a scheme of administration for Bechuanaland in South Africa. This respectable background, together with Forwood's need for a candidate and desire to grow in favour with his party leader, Lord Salisbury, explains why Forwood should have adopted Baden-Powell when he arrived in Liverpool saying that Lord Salisbury had sent him and specially wanted his return to Parliament. This claim was afterwards found to be untrue, but Baden-Powell duped not only Forwood but 3,301 Kirkdale Conservatives, who returned him against 1,981 Liberal-Radicals and 765 Nationalists. Once established in this safe seat, Baden-Powell sought preferment in the colonial service and government. Liverpool benefited not at all. Baden-Powell was uninterested in domestic or constituency affairs; he was a poor attender in the House of Commons, and when he did appear, according to the Whip, it was only to push himself and to demand a good place in debate. Moreover his purse was closed: Baden-Powell never paid his election or registration expenses, even after taking a rich wife.[116]

Just as in Kirkdale, so in the Walton constituency, a district of 'a second-class residential character', Forwood's preferences betrayed an uncritical streak. Initially he favoured Lord Salisbury's twenty-four-year-old son, Viscount Cranborne. The Cecils owned land here,[117] and to advance Cranborne would bring Forwood closer to Salisbury. These considerations dwarfed any knowledge that Cranborne personally had little to recommend him.[118] Cranborne in fact was not available; but, 'before testing the feelings of the leaders in the division', Forwood on his own responsibility continued the search for a candidate.[119] Interestingly, having discounted the possibility of attracting Sir William Hart Dyke, Lord Randolph Churchill also suggested Cranborne's name to Forwood.[120] Eventually Forwood recruited J. G. Gibson, Q.C., Serjeant-at-Law in Salisbury's Caretaker Ministry and, as an orator, a Boanerges.[121] Gibson co-operated in a Liverpool branch of the Imperial Federation League;[122] otherwise he was not a man to identify with Liverpool. His opponent, Augustine Birrell, a barrister and native of Liverpool, designated Gibson 'a frank electioneer. He wanted to get in, in order to get on.'[123] He did both, winning 3,492 votes against 2,500, and in Salisbury's Second Ministry becoming Irish Solicitor-General.

Elsewhere Forwood was less taxed. Hamilton was ensconced in West Derby where he beat the secretary of Exchange Liberal Association, by 4,213 votes to 3,068. Hamilton's programme announced 'uncompromising' defence of the Constitution. Denominational education, imperial sentiment, temperance, and county government reform, provided his gloss. He also stressed the need to make the Employers' Liability Act (1880) compulsory on all employers, although his motives were not selfless as the chairman of the Employers Liability Assurance Company.

In adjacent East Toxteth Councillor Jonathan Hughes had ambitions, but he was inconsiderable compared with Houlding in northern Liverpool. Forwood ignored jealous local men and engaged Baron Henry de Worms, a lawyer and late M.P. for Greenwich. He revelled in the Primrose League; and, as Secretary to the Board of Trade during Lord Salisbury's Caretaker Ministry, he could promise that voice in commercial policy which Liverpool had lacked since Sandon's and Graves's representation. Worms's foreign title—he was the son of an Austrian peer—gave a lever to xenophobes, but he outbid most in denouncing Bradlaugh's atheism and in appealing to British patriotism; and Forwood was delighted.[124]

Worms's first speech in Liverpool delineated the Conservative mission. While opposed to 'measures of revolution' he advocated 'legitimate and fair progress'. He added that 'Tory Democracy might reasonably be supplanted by progressive Constitutionalism', since Democracy was a misused term. Joseph Chamberlain's sense of Democracy, for instance, meant 'being generous with that which does not belong to it'; and against the Gladstonians' slogan of Peace and Retrenchment Worms set their wasteful wars. As for Reform, this was 'as much an act of Conservatives as of the Liberals'; especially it was 'the work of the late Lord Beaconsfield (cheers)'. In the recent National Union controversy Worms had been a partisan of Northcote; but now his 'progressive Constitutionalism' would admit no contradiction between an old and new Conservatism, and 3,598 East Toxteth Conservatives complied.[125] Only 2,608 voters supported the Liberal candidate, a commercial lawyer and Catholic convert, J. C. Bigham.[126]

The parish, Toxteth Park, hardly reflected its name. West Toxteth parliamentary constituency was as depressing as anywhere in Liverpool.[127] Its houses were 'planned slums',[128] brick boxes in courts, with separate cellar dwellings. Drilled in a grid system, many streets remained as pestilential in the 1880s as 1860s and were famed for 'true Protestantism'.[129] Politically, in mid-century, the Toxteths had been dominated by timber merchants.[130] Their grip relaxed as the trade shifted to the northern docks;[131] but Thomas Hughes, a Toxteth councillor from 1878, maintained some of its influence. Tory Democratic preparations had been laid in the High Park Street Club in 1881. Its innovation, an annual subscription not exceeding 5*s*., scandalized some into warning that 'if respectable people do not frequent it, more harm than good will be done';[132] but there was no question of popular manipulation of West Toxteth's Conservative candidature in 1885.

This was foregone to Thomas Bland Royden whose shipyard employed 700 men. Probably Royden was esteemed as the last representative of the once flourishing shipbuilding industry of Liverpool , although the evidence is contradictory. The *Review* and *Daily Post*, before the election, considered Royden 'notoriously unpopular'; but both these Liberal newspapers afterwards attributed victory to his swagger.[133] A Councillor from 1873, and the Mayor in 1878–9, Royden called himself a 'progressive Tory'. He had been a protagonist in the Corporation's Vyrnwy waterworks scheme, whose chaotic administration—criticized by Forwood—illustrated Royden's deficiencies. Royden was smart; he was also superficial.[134] Perhaps Forwood tried to prevent Royden's nomination in 1885, but Royden's local sources of support were firmly based.[135] A Liberal candidate, Thomas Sutherest, also emerged, recommended by Edward Harford and Sir John Lubbock. Sutherest was active in shopworkers', emigration, empire, and temperance, movements; and he advocated protection for railwaymen against overwork.[136] However, no Liberal organization canvassed West Toxteth. Royden won 3,754 votes against 1,771.

In the other constituencies within his *imperium*, Exchange and Abercromby, Forwood again demonstrated a desire to attract gilded names rather than to promote men with a local power-base. Foreshadowed was that party reconstruction which followed the Home Rule schism when Forwood approached the banker, and Moderate Liberal M.P., G. J. Goschen, with a view to his fighting Exchange. Forwood promised him the probable support of both English parties; but Goschen was negotiating an Edinburgh seat. Goschen also feared for his parliamentary position if he represented a 'commercial' rather than 'party' constituency.[137] This was the campaign Forwood planned—running one who was really a business candidate as much as a politician, against the Parnellites. He eventually selected Lawrence Baily, a director of railway, shipping, and insurance, companies, a government nominee on the Mersey Docks and Harbour Board, and a benefactor of churches and charities. Against the serpentine Stephens and O'Shea, even *Porcupine* supported Baily.[138]

Abercromby, another mixed business and residential area, the Liberals had earmarked for Samuel Smith. In April 1885 the *Review* considered Smith so popular that he might be unopposed; but this was too sanguine. Smith had estranged both commercial and Parnellite opinion, and the *Courier* alleged that he 'represents the free educational mania which threatens denominational schools'.[139] Moreover the balance of party power in the constituency was tilted against Smith: the six wards returned eleven Conservatives and seven Liberals. In 1882 Lord Claud Hamilton had lectured Forwood about the inopportuneness of announcing 'a new departure' against an opponent like Smith.[140] This was not repeated in 1885. The candidate, William Lawrence, was a Wiltshire squire with Jamaican interests. His father had been vicar of St. Luke's and his grandfather chairman of the Liverpool and Manchester Railway.[141] Lawrence himself had modest abilities—the *Review* considered him imbecile [142]—but he enticed the business-minded with his distaste for expensive social legislation, and won 3,789 votes against 2,982.[143]

Only Scotland division resisted Conservatism. There the Nationalist, T. P. O'Connor, received 2,724 votes against 1,474. Forwood had refused to court humiliation in a constituency 'as Irish as if . . . in County Tipperary'.[144] Accordingly no official Conservative candidate was presented, although an Independent put in an appearance—M. N. Woodard, a son of the Manchester canon who founded the Woodard schools, where the sons of the middle classes were reared in the High Church ethos. O'Connor's reputation, from his past five years in Parliament, representing his home town of Galway, was that of a radical obstructionist. This was the Home Rulers' outer skin. In truth O'Connor was a steadfast parliamentarian, although it was an improbable speculation in 1885 that ultimately he would sit as Father of the House of Commons. Now, in the selection for Liverpool Scotland, O'Connor was Parnell's nominee: the local ambitions, of Pat Byrne and Bernard Hughes, were overruled.[145] By preferring Liverpool O'Connor surrendered his Galway seat, whither the carnival of Captain O'Shea's candidature removed.[146] It was sensible that O'Connor, the I.N.L.'s head, should take the Nationalists' sole English seat. Financially too, the Scotland constituency was attractive, being among the cheapest returns.[147]

The measure of the Liberals' failure

Excluding Scotland division, Conservative candidates won 59 per cent of the poll throughout Liverpool. Forwood had paced Tory Democracy to match the constituencies' rhythms, allowing it a canter in the Toxteths, restraining it by the bit in Kirkdale and Everton, and curbing it altogether in Exchange and Abercromby. The Liberal stable was nobbled by Parnellites where it was not already out of condition. Liberal constituency associations had been formed; but many were lifeless and, Holt wryly declared, 'If anything unpleasant in connection with our political party has to be done, it is generally put upon my shoulders'.[148]

The Liberals' inadequacy was not immediately obvious. The *Liverpool Courier* was Conservative but otherwise Liberals owned three of Merseyside's four daily newspapers, the *Liverpool Daily Post*, *Liverpool Mercury*, and *Birkenhead News*. The *Daily Post*—known as 'the local Hansard'[149]—and its subsidiaries, the *Echo* (an evening paper) and *Weekly Post*, sold 3,250,000 copies per month in 1885. Liberals also owned the weeklies—*Porcupine* (Russell, the *Daily Post*'s editor and proprietor, was among its original partners); and *Liverpool Review* (part of Willmer's *Birkenhead News* group).[150] The printed word could not replace party organization, although some newspapermen had a hand in deprecating the old cabalistic arrangements. Thus the *Mercury*'s editor, John Lovell, led an open meeting of Abercromby Liberals in denouncing procedures which stifled party life in the city.[151] The General Election overshadowed the municipal elections and twelve of sixteen retiring Councillors were unopposed in November 1885; but in Rodney Street ward the Liberals' disputatiousness was exhibited when Philip Rathbone was challenged by Liberal malcontents from Abercromby.

Rathbone, retired from the insurance business, was a *poseur* who managed the Fine Arts Committee. Even his friends thought him as 'eccentric as a March hare and a very unreliable quantity'.[152] To Radicals he epitomized Whiggery at its worst. *Porcupine* noted Rathbone's 'wavering towards Conservatism'; accordingly, although it questioned his extreme temperance views, *Porcupine* supported Rathbone's Radical opponent, Nathaniel Smyth.[153] A tradesman and one-time Chartist, Smyth intended to destroy 'the old order of things at the Reform Club'; but the *Review* defended Rathbone's tradition of public service, observing that 'Liberal principles do not exist in order that the caucus may reign . . .'.[154] Rathbone survived, but the Liberals' internal strife was expensive—St. Peter's ward went Conservative for the first time since 1856 after Liberal business voters with dual qualifications deserted St. Peter's and exercised their option to cast in Rodney Street.[155]

As a result of such pressure Radical Liberals had won constituency independence in 1885. The old Management Committee was dissolved and with it went a means of controlling constituency disputes or of inspiriting constituency activity. Except in Exchange and Abercromby autonomy, without subsidies or direction from the centre, meant premature burial or persistent fractiousness. Holt did not aspire to Forwood's authority and he was inconspicuous apart from formally presiding at important meetings and providing financial support for the constituency association in West Derby, where he lived.

The difficulties that resulted were typified in Kirkdale. Five polling districts had elected delegates to an inaugural General Council of Kirkdale Liberal Association in June 1885. Its Executive subsequently sought a parliamentary candidate, entertaining three names. One was James Samuelson, already campaigning as an Independent: other agencies, attracting errant and distempered Liberals, had emerged while the central Liberal Management Committee was supine. Approached by a working men's deputation in June 1883, Samuelson had stood in lieu of a satisfactory trade union candidate. His campaign stimulated the Liverpool Industrial Union which, with a general committee of 350, filled the vacuum created by the Trades Council's studious neutrality in party politics and by the W.M.C.A.'s refusal to sink party differences in a working men's candidature.[156]

Samuelson challenged these working men's organizations when he asked, 'Who set class against class? Who set sect against sect? Who had for twenty—aye, fifty—years fanned the fanatic flame of religion? . . . Who had induced the Orange carpenters at the North-end to look upon their fellows at the South-end as their natural enemies? The Roydens, the Forwoods, and the Tory employers of labour had done so . . .' Samuelson exhorted Liverpool working men to exercise their political power for higher wages, and not to believe that 'their happiness and prosperity depended on their fighting the Irish'.[157]

Samuelson's efforts long encountered hostility from traditional Liberal organizations, which strenuously sought not to acknowledge his existence;[158] but in August 1885 Kirkdale's Liberal Association had required the Industrial Union to submit his name for official selection.[159] His rivals were not openly known, although probably one was Robert Hudson, the Association's chairman. Samuelson's campaign, however, was not easily diverted and, since the Management Committee was now defunct, an arbitrator, John Morley, had been engaged.[160] He mediated by post, and favoured Samuelson as a potential winner. The key to his decision was W. S. Caine, who valued Samuelson's temperance opinions; but Morley was not alone in his calculation, for the *Daily Post* belatedly observed that Samuelson's campaign had brought many working men to a state of embryonic Liberal faith.[161]

Samuelson was officially adopted in Kirkdale, but Morley had crippled constituency Liberalism by flouting the principle for which the Kirkdale Association fought. It had not questioned Samuelson's strength but asserted that a constituency must freely exercise selection.[162] As it was, the official support now given to Samuelson dispelled the nimbus of a non-party working men's candidature. Forwood observed that Samuelson's disguise 'as a labour representative, independent of party politics . . . attracted to him the support of some weak-kneed Conservatives'. When, however, he avowed 'his extreme party views' Tory working men rallied to Baden-Powell.[163]

The mismanagement in Kirkdale epitomized the Liberals' inadequacy generally throughout Liverpool . The history of Salisbury's Caretaker Ministry was 'practically that of a prolonged election campaign';[164] but the Liverpool Liberals were unprepared and desperate to find candidates.[165] Their organization, moreover, failed in the task of education. Lectures and literature were limited by lack of funds, even where party workers were available; and problems in registration were long-standing.[166]

The age of the electoral register—the qualifying date for its annual revision was 15 July—obviously had an impact on the turn-out of voters. The 1885 General Election was conducted upon a register only four months old: no general election before the First World War was based upon a fresher register.

Nevertheless some 10,000 Liverpudlians annually risked disfranchisement through removals of two kinds, of artisans or tradesmen towards and within the suburbs, and of the poor within the centre. Even a steady, sober man in regular and reasonably paid employment, like a railway porter and cargo checker, David Brindley, made frequent short-distance removals within a small area. Brindley moved a dozen times between 1882, when he arrived in Liverpool from the Cheshire countryside, and 1890–1, when his diary ends. His homes, all in Everton–Kirkdale, were within 1½ miles of his work and seem to have been dictated by changing family circumstances and by a desire to live close to particular friends. The students of his diary reach this conclusion:

> The four-stage pattern of residential mobility seen in these moves must have been typical of many migrants to nineteenth-century cities: first, bachelor lodgings, initially with relatives; then, secondly, with a landlord; thirdly, following marriage (and briefly in Brindley's case) in rented apartments; fourthly (and finally), in a series of rented houses, all in the same locality and of a similar style and cost.[167]

Evidence of an impressionistic kind exists of other mobile groups who were in less favourable circumstances than Brindley. The Liverpool Domestic Mission had reported in 1859 that under one-quarter of its neighbours inhabited the same house or street over two years.[168] Mobility among the Irish and labouring poor generally did not reflect an upward social movement of low-income groups so much as their demoralization. John Hobson noted that 'the city poor are a wandering tribe', and Beatrice Webb that they resembled 'the circle of suicides in Dante's Inferno; they go round and round within a certain area'.[169] Conditions of irregular employment, but also undischarged debts and responsibilities, caused removals. Some slum denizens preferred to lose their vote rather than to answer 'the summons of the School Board inspector or the threats of local shopkeepers'.[170] Probably many 'flitters' were Irishmen—Charles Booth described them as 'alike shiftless, shifty, and shifting'[171]—but the Liberal organization was hard pressed to trace these prospective Gladstonians.

In 1885, therefore, the Liverpool parties had entered the General Election troubled by divisions, but the Conservatives, by completeness at city and constituency levels of organization, were composed as the Liberals floundered. *Porcupine* offered a prognostication. Whiggery and old Toryism were moribund. The future lay between a Tory and Radical Democracy; but a 'Tory Democracy which will recognize that England is for the English—aye, and Ireland for the Irish—which will not be afraid of much that is revolutionary, but yet will uphold the Queen and Constitution, may find itself face to face with a democracy which will not pledge itself to uphold anyone or anything if once their usefulness be disproved'.[172] The error of one assumption, that Tory Democracy might admit Irish Home Rule, invalidated the other, that Toryism could not divert Democracy.

CHAPTER FIVE

Home Rule and party reconstruction, 1886–7

If he is not mad, he is a *Traitor*.

Sir D. Probyn writing about Gladstone, 4 February 1886

So long as the Irish question is not settled, the Tories must have the pull in the country, and the Radicals must remain discredited and disunited.

H. Labouchere to J. Chamberlain, 1 January 1886[1]

. . . the Liberal Unionist movement had its origin in currents of thought that were prevalent before ever the subject of the Union was raised as a party question, and their object was the putting of some limitation upon the imperious and meddlesome policy of Mr. Chamberlain in forcing upon the Liberal party unripe principles and indigestible measures.

A. H. Bencke, letter in the Liverpool Daily Post, *5 November 1897*

The Gladstonian and Unionist appeals

In February 1885 Gladstone dismissed 'Tory Democracy' as 'demagogism . . . living upon the fomentation of angry passions, and still in secret as obstinately attached as ever to the evil principle of class interests'. Despite the noisy slogans Gladstone had believed then that 'there is no crisis at all in view'.[2] By November 1886 Gladstone was writing differently: politics were in a critical phase.[3] In the interim Unionism—the opposition to Irish Home Rule—had animated Tory Democracy. The spectacle to Whigs and moderate Gladstonians was disagreeable. Emphatic Conservatism excited Radicalism.

Whiggery, Conservatives naturally understood but electorally needed to deny. Balfour once depicted 'the lukewarm and slippery Whig, whom it is so difficult to differ from and so impossible to act with'.[4] The Whigs' attachment to the Liberal party, it seemed, expressed the duty of sleeping dogs: even a move to slumber in the Conservative party was too demanding. This was not a complete picture of the Lancashire magnifico, the 15th Earl of Derby. He was continually plagued by doubts; nevertheless he was as good a Liberal as most, if that meant that he wanted the party to stay together under Gladstone's leadership. Derby

Notes begin on p. 383

had been in favour of the Liberal Government taking the initiative in the Bradlaugh controversy by passing an Affirmation Bill; he had acknowledged the realities of the situation in Egypt; and he had accepted an extension of the franchise in 1884, while respecting his fellow peers' disapproval. But the Home Rule crisis admitted no possibility of accommodation for Derby. He had suspected that Gladstone would declare for Home Rule ever since a conversation with him in October 1885. The result for the Conservatives would be 'such a cry as they never had before'. The result for the Liberals would be that 'we should be where Fox and North were in 1784'. If Gladstone pressed Home Rule the party would split; if Gladstone was forced to retract, he would resign the leadership and the party would still split. 'It is altogether a muddle!', Derby told Harcourt.

Nevertheless Derby was clear that he could not countenance a parliament in Dublin, with control of the police. This would be a betrayal of men of property whom the Government had a duty to protect. Derby foresaw anarchy in large parts of Ireland and soon 'a general refusal to pay rents'.[5] In February 1886 Derby informed the Liverpool leader, Holt, of his conclusions: 'the split in our party will be wide and deep'. He added, 'I shall take as little part as possible till I see some prospects of our coming together again'. Since Holt was Derby's 'authority on all political subjects connected with Liverpool', Derby was now more than ever isolated at Knowsley for Holt, while unhappy about infinite Irish crises, supported Gladstone.[6]

Derby had never taken an active part in Liverpool Liberal politics—beyond attending the annual banquet at the Reform Club and lending his horse and carriage to convey visiting celebrities during their speaking engagements—and it is certain that the redistribution of constituencies in 1885 would have reduced his participation and influence, come Home Rule or not. When Kirkdale's Liberal Association sought Derby's financial aid in March 1886 it was nine months old; but Derby was unaware of its existence, although a property-owner in Kirkdale. He asked another grandee, Lord Sefton, about its credentials; and Sefton approached Sir Thomas Brocklebank; but they knew nothing. Sefton elevated their ignorance into bliss: 'in the present uncertain and very dark state of the political situation, I think we may very well withhold our *Names* and our *Money*: we shall e'er long have to oppose Parnell and the Irish Division in this County, which will make a split in many clubs and associations'.[7]

One who rejected measured sloth was Albert Bencke. A barrister, Bencke had been the Liberals' treasurer in south-west Lancashire, England's largest constituency until redistribution vivisected his province. Like all Whigs he revered the politics of social influence and despised the caucus; nevertheless Bencke wanted to expand Whiggery's base.[8] Before the 1885 Election Bencke had noticed that 'disaffection was widespread among moderate Liberals'; many had drifted into Conservatism 'through fear of the Radicals rather than on account of confidence in the Tories'.[9] Bencke sought to reorganize Whiggery, as a sanctuary from both Lord Randolph Churchill and Joseph Chamberlain, 'the Ignatius Loyola' and 'Ultramontane Spirit' in English politics'.[10]

This ambition remained phantasmagoric until Gladstone overturned the political world by embracing Home Rule. While his nominal generals, Derby and Sefton, retreated, Bencke marshalled his reserves. This complicated the movement towards a Unionist structure in Liverpool, for, Forwood told Salisbury, although 'considerable disaffection' existed among Liberals, 'party loyalty and Gladstone Worship . . . [were] very weighty factors'. He suggested that these might be overcome if 'a scheme of large municipal or local self government' was formulated with the Whigs' agreement. The Constitutional Association and W.M.C.A. broadcast Unionist resolutions; but Forwood eschewed 'a special party demonstration, as such at this juncture would do more harm than good, by pushing the Whigs who are now on the fence, once again into their brethren's arms . . .'.[11]

It was difficult to harness the aristocrats' sense of self-preservation. Derby doubted whether a Unionist demonstration would be supported: 'fear of the Irish voter is strong among those whose opinions I can learn'.[12] Nevertheless in May 1886 a Liverpool Liberal Unionist Committee was formed. Bencke was secretary and treasurer. William Oulton became its chairman after Sir Thomas Brocklebank and T. D. Hornby waived the privilege. Oulton was a railway contractor, a former chairman of the Reform Club, and a Wesleyan member of the School Board. Once 'the hope of the Democracy', then the stern critic of Irish Land Bills, Oulton was now deemed reactionary.[13] Actually he was a natural committee man, an operator not a philosopher of parties. His committee numbered immediately a hundred members, including renegade Holts and Rathbones, W. P. Lockhart, Thomas Matheson, the Earle family, A. H. Brown, John Patterson, and Edward Browne;[14] and Derby's name was soon appended.

Only a few months before the rift Robert Holt had organized a dinner at the Reform Club to celebrate two honours bestowed through Gladstone's Government, the Order of the Garter for Lord Sefton and a baronetcy for Thomas Brocklebank. Now he was surprised that 'so many of our most valued and respected supporters', including Sefton and Brocklebank, had forsaken 'all previous association and family history' and become 'paper Unionists'. He believed that 'they were showing an unworthy fear and distrust of the Irish'; but for those with little faith in the Irish capacity for self-government, the British Parliament's supremacy and the Queen's veto were protected under the Gladstonian scheme. Moreover, 'from all previous history one feels so satisfied that if the Tory party comes into Power they will eat all their previous professions and to dish the Radicals propose the very measures the Whigs profess to consider so destructive'. Accordingly Holt aimed 'to smooth down differences and forget hasty and angry words', and he hoped that the 'strange alliance' made by the Liberal Unionists would be temporary. The seceders, for their part, claimed to be true to the quintessential principles of Liberalism, by placing 'patriotism and duty before all other considerations'.[15]

Bencke valued this manifesto as proof that Liverpool contained 'a Liberalism beyond and superior to that of the Caucus, the Radical clubs and the wire-pullers, which is determined to make a firm stand to defend its opinions'.[16] He was mistaken. Peddling Moderate Liberalism under Unionist guise, Bencke dismayed those Whigs who wanted to underplay, not exacerbate, disagreements with former colleagues. The contrast between a Moderate Liberal and the Whig which Alfred Milner once drew for G. J. Goschen was applicable in some measure to Bencke's situation: '. . . a real Moderate Liberal is a man whose moderation is based on principle, as strong, maybe stronger, and better digested than that of the more advanced men. But the moderation of the Whig is the result not of Moderate principles but of the accident of birth and of having no principles at all'.[17]

Bencke, to Sefton's displeasure, had '*a bee in his bonnet.*' Sefton preferred collaboration with Brocklebank, whose seventy-two years and taste for the quiet life symbolized Sefton's requirements of associates.[18] Thus Bencke, who once informed Derby that he considered him 'the natural leader' of Moderate Liberalism in Lancashire, was not considered its natural organizer. Sefton told Derby of his hope that the Liberal Unionist Committee would 'find some way of *shunting* our friend Bencke'.[19] Through T. D. Hornby's influence the Committee appointed a party agent—James McComb, once secretary of both Liverpool and South-West Lancashire Liberal Associations—and subsequently Brocklebank and H. H. Hornby replaced Bencke as, respectively, secretary and treasurer.

For Bencke Unionism proved treacherous, for the Liberal party openly devastating. The *Review* lamented that 'Liberalism in Liverpool was so chaotic, so broken-down, and so helpless'.[20] Leadership was absent. Holt limply waited on events. His character was inscribed in a letter to Gladstone: 'I wish we could do more to help you in your efforts to place the relations of the English and Irish on healthier footing—but you must not expect much from Liverpool. The Tories are too strong for us, but we go "pegging away"—perhaps some day things may change even here.'[21]

The feet were no more inspiring than the head. The *Review* declared, 'The average Liberal will not do a "hands turn" for his party'. As another General Election approached, gains and losses were tabulated with more equanimity. The money-bags had departed, to the regret of 'those who live for dinner parties and "at homes" but they never had . . . much influence with the masses'. Free from enervation Gladstonians might assume robustness, while 'the worst the Liberal Unionists will do will be to abstain from voting, and in a few cases to vote Tory'.[22]

The Whigs' unwillingness to become an extinct species or to accept mutuations made living with Conservatives difficult. Forwood applied his arts to smooth the passage of Liberal seceders, by giving them 'some feeling of security against our taking an undue party advantage of their actions'.[23] Since both Whig and Radical Unionists wished to preserve their mortgage on Liberalism, Forwood recommended some progressive gestures—'such as appeal to the working classes'.[24]

The potency of Gladstone's name remained an obstacle. Liverpool's attitude to its famous son was equivocal. The compiler of *Liverpool's Legion of Honour* wrote sourly that Gladstone 'will not let Liverpool claim him, but keeps apart, rarely coming hither, and declaring that he is a pure Scot'.[25] Gladstone's last political visit was in 1868; but in 1872 he had delivered the prize-day address at Liverpool College. A paean to Liverpool's aggrandizement was tempered by an admonition about the need to support the sciences and humanities. Gladstone hoped that Liverpool, like Florence, would become renowned for its cultivated commercial families. He rejoiced that one of his brothers, Robertson, his nephews, and one of his sons, by engaging in commercial pursuits furthered this end.[26]

For those Liverpudlians who accepted this consanguinity Gladstone in June 1886 planted a tree at his brother's house.[27] The axeman in him emerged in his speech at Hengler's Circus. There the twin elements of Gladstone's power, noted by Walter Bagehot, the didactic impulse and the contentious impulse, were demonstrated. Gladstone emphasized that he differed from the Whigs not upon one policy but by entire outlook. He did not assert that 'the mass of the people who do not and cannot give their leisure to politics are necessarily and on all subjects better judges [but] . . . where the leading and determining considerations that ought to lead to a conclusion are truth, justice, and humanity—upon these, gentlemen, all the world over, I will back the masses against the classes (Loud cheers)'.[28] Gladstone did not favour the democratic politician, but he respected the democratic General Will.

The Conservatives fashioned their counter-campaign. During Salisbury's Caretaker Ministry in 1885 Hamilton had threatened that if Conservatives trifled with Home Rule, he would join any party of resistance.[29] His warning became superfluous. The Conservative party filed into the last ditch of the Union. Lord Randolph Churchill epitomized this proclivity—in July 1885 he had been so suspect of courting the Irish that Hamilton sabotaged his Liverpool meeting; in February 1886 his Unionist demonstration preluded a violent summer in Belfast.[30]

The same deliberate preaching to the converted occupied Conservatives in Liverpool . The Revd. T. K. Morrow asked members of the North Toxteth branch of the W.M.C.A. whether Gladstone should be allowed to surrender the empire's 'fairest province', Ulster, to a 'disloyal, yea, a hellish crew, appointed and promoted by the Romish priesthood?' Morrow drove the subject home when he speculated that Liverpudlians might benefit by seeing 'the riff-raff of the Irishmen that now infested their lanes take flight at once, under the idea that they would get a share in the scramble for the land and possessions of the landlords and farmers'.[31] This exacerbated basest jealousies and interlocked the interests of poor Protestant and threatened magnate.

Propagandists recognized that Ireland, the scene of crime, needed stage villains. Parnell and Gladstone received star billing while John Morley, the Liberal Chief Secretary and belletrist, was described as having found in the French Revolution 'valuable examples for public policy'. Here was another Robespierre, regicide, and 'believer in revolution', seeking a compact with 'the moonlight marauder and the fanatic priest'.[32] A new short-hand emerged: Unionists became 'Loyalists', Gladstonians 'Disloyalists'.[33] Forwood, considering the position of English Catholics, sensed the dangers of such simplification and he informed Lord Salisbury:

> There is not that attraction to us that the free education question created, and some sympathy exists with what is in a measure regarded as the cause of their co-religionists in Ireland. In my opinion Ulster and loyal questions should not be treated simply as a protestant matter, but the

many Union Catholics should have a word of sympathy. No doubt it is a very delicate subject to handle, but upon what may be said many wavering votes depend.[34]

The General Election campaign

The 1886 General Election in Liverpool turned on the thesis in Worms's address, that 'an imperious Minister, by invoking, in the name of democratic instincts, a spirit of class hatred and racial animosity, had endeavoured without any mandate from the constituencies, to carry a measure which, in the specious garb of justice to Ireland, meant in reality the disintegration of the Empire'.[35]

The Baron's pugnacity was unslaked: East Toxteth Liberals remained passive after trouble was expected from Liberal Unionists.[36] Similar considerations persuaded Liberals to abandon West Toxteth and Everton. Elsewhere contests were mostly perfunctuory, although the general decline in turn-out was caused by the staleness of the register, now 11½ months old, as well as by Liberal disenchantment.

In Walton the *Review* contrasted the party organizations—the absence of Liberal, and abundance of Tory, literature and canvassers.[37] There Gibson's poll decreased by 620 votes: the Liberals slumped by 819. In West Derby Hamilton increased his majority by 115 but again the turn-out fell. In Kirkdale Baden-Powell defeated Ralph Neville, a local barrister. The lingering wounds of Samuelson's candidature in 1885 undermined Neville's hopes in 1886: Kirkdale's Liberal Association was 'dispirited and factional'.[38] In these three constituencies the turn-out was down, on average, 15·2 per cent, to 62·7 per cent, but the Conservative share of the poll rose to 61·1 per cent.

Mechanical for opposite reasons was the contest in Scotland constituency. The Irish sharpened their work in tracing registered voters, and Scotland was the sole Liverpool constituency in 1886 to record an increase in turn-out from 59·3 to 61·4 per cent.[39] O'Connor added 230 to his majority, against a Liberal Unionist, Arthur Earle, whose brother, killed on the march to Khartoum, was Liverpool 's principal martyr to Imperialism.[40]

There was the prospect initially of more serious competition in Abercromby, which Gladstone was invited to contest. Ultimately the sitting Conservative M.P., Lawrence, faced Sir Thomas Brassey, who left his seat at Hastings.[41] In a slightly reduced turn-out of 70·3 per cent, Brassey pulled Lawrence's majority 68 below that of 1885; but Lawrence still took a comfortable 55·7 per cent of the poll.

In Exchange constituency the Liberal Association was thought demoralized by Parnell's late conspiracies and by recent Whig defections. The *Review* anticipated victory only in the unlikely event of Robert Holt standing;[42] but, adding together O'Shea's and Stephens' polls of 1885, the seat was poised on a margin of only nineteen votes, and Conservatives and Whigs were not yet working partners. Several names were connected with the Gladstonian ticket, including Hugh Childers and W. S. Blunt, before it went to David Duncan, a shipowner with South American interests.[43] Unseated after a petition at Barrow in 1885, Duncan was none the less attractive to business voters. Edward Russell considered Duncan to be upstanding, 'a four square man, who went through the world fearing God, and trying to do his duty'.[44] He won 2,920 votes against 2,750. He added to O'Shea's poll 11 votes; but Baily's support had declined by 214. Although most businessmen were Unionist, several waverers could be decisive, if the resident Irish remained virtually constant.[45]

Seven victories in nine constituencies was no bad record and Forwood, unopposed in Ormskirk, became Financial Secretary to the Admiralty as Lord Salisbury formed a new Government. The first steamship-owner in that position, Forwood wanted to bring business experience to navy administration, although in the management of government contracts it was the shipbuilders' business methods, particularly their cartel, that gave Forwood his ministerial headache. In the Government Forwood was a new shoot; however, 'the roots of old weeds permeate the ground in many directions', he observed of the Front Bench. He welcomed the Conservatives' communion with Liberal Unionists, 'as an advantageous check as well as spur to our fossils and do nothings'; but personally he was not taken with the prospect of office. He believed that 'the aggressive M.P. is stronger than the ragged minister' and 'the leading politician outside the House has more influence than his M.P. inside'.[46]

Locally Forwood's ascendancy seemed complete. The *Daily Post* had observed that Liverpool Conservatism owed to Forwood everything it did not owe to 'old-fashioned darkness and bigotry'.[47] The *Church Review* developed this mixed compliment: it applauded his 'capacities for organization' and how 'as a progressive Conservative he has retained the support of the Orangemen, without yielding to their prejudices'. Thus, although Forwood was not an Orangeman, one Liverpool lodge bore his name.[48]

Orangemen naturally confirmed Unionism; but Protestant dissent was to grow as Ritualism was unchecked by Salisbury's Government. Demonstrations already affected St. John's Toxteth, whose vicar, R. F. Herring, belonged to the English Church Union. Although his services were mostly plain and read rather than intoned, he faced eastwards during the confession of the Apostles' Creed. Considering this act an 'abomination' protestors either faced west or made a noisy exodus from the church. Early in 1887 a crisis was reached when churchwardens jostled with the vicar and extinguished the altar candles, to prevent their church becoming 'a house of Baal'. Their subsequent trial under the Brawling Act embarrassed the magistrate, who dismissed the case on a technicality.[49]

Orangemen in this 'religious' capacity Conservatives still neglected. Orangemen in their 'political' character Conservative leaders usually patronized but in 1886 they had been missing from the 12 July celebrations which followed the General Election. This risked one foundation of their strength, for that 'roughness in the grain of Orange Toryism' needed controlling by close association: Catholic homes and chapels in Toxteth had recently suffered attack.[50] Perhaps the Conservative leaders reckoned that the Liberal Unionists' support made the Orangemen superfluous, but many Liberal Unionists were incompletely committed. They might still support a Gladstonian Liberal in a municipal election, although some of their former colleagues did not care for their ways. Edward Russell told Gladstone that what was wanting was 'not means or grounds of reunion but a disposition among the [Liberal] Unionists to reunite, or to do anything but vomit forth threatenings against the Irish people'.[51] The political world in Liverpool was thus in flux in December 1886 when David Duncan died.[52]

The Goschen by-election and Unionist rancour

The vacancy which Duncan's death created in Exchange coincided with Lord Randolph Churchill's resignation from the Cabinet, after his failure to curb increased expenditure on the armed services. As the scourge of Gladstone, the defender of established institutions, and the representative Tory Democrat, Churchill was a valuable property; but his disputatiousness was unnerving for the party. Churchill seemed incapable of performing in a team. His impact on party, observed Sir William Harcourt, was further proof of the infinite divisibility of matter. Now Lord Randolph Churchill's nuisance was more evident than his worth. In this drama all his impolitic aspects coalesced—from the moment when he composed his resignation in Windsor Castle, to the Queen's consternation ('Written on my own paper?!');[53] to that in which Lord Salisbury jumped at his resignation 'like a dog at a bone'.[54] The new Chancellor of the Exchequer, the Liberal Unionist, G. J. Goschen, was Churchill's antipole. When Churchill had been made Leader of the Commons, Goschen was staggered, 'for it is a premium on the arts by which he has risen into notoriety . . . [As] he imitated Dizzy at a distance, so men of even lower moral may imitate Churchill.'[55] This was directed not at Tory Democracy but at a personal style.

Goschen, however, was without a parliamentary seat. His name had long been connected with Liverpool's Exchange constituency. In 1885 he had checked developments; but at the 1886 General Election his nomination had been blocked by Conservatives.[56] During the first months of Unionist co-operation Goschen was uneasy. Irish questions only concerned him as part of the larger issue of government in a democratic era but, when exchanging opinions with Lord Salisbury, he struck the Balfours as 'more Tory than Uncle Robert!'[57] Goschen liked safety and did not relish the prospect of contesting Exchange.[58]

Forwood, however, nourished support and the Exchange Conservative Association, 'sinking any minor difference of political opinion' in order to preserve the Union, sought Goschen's candidature. The Liberal Unionists issued a similar invitation; indeed, according to Holt, showed themselves 'more furiously devoted to Goschen, Salisbury etc. than the Tories themselves'.[59] Conversely the Gladstonians considered several claimants, including three ex-ministers, Lord Edmond Fitzmaurice, Sir Arthur Hayter, and George Russell. There seemed reason for optimism in the Unionist camp: a business requisition favoured Goschen, and there were 260 fewer registered voters since the General Election, mostly the result of Irish removals. Irishmen, moreover, questioned the Gladstonians' right to the candidature, believing that a Nationalist would have more success.[60]

The Liberal selection narrowed to two—Fitzmaurice and the local barrister, Ralph Neville. Fitzmaurice refused on personal grounds to fight Goschen. This left Neville but, as the recently defeated candidate in Kirkdale, he was considered by the I.N.L. to be 'hopelessly weak'. The Exchange Liberal Association also was disappointed that 'no local man of position on 'Change or a statesman' had been found. The Liberal leader, Holt, however, had more confidence in Neville;[61] and he was still officially without an opponent. A deputation, including Forwood, had travelled to London only to experience Goschen's temporizing. Goschen disliked mixing with the party at large; but finally he accepted the invitation to fight Exchange on condition that 'a prolonged personal canvass will not be expected of him'.[62] These agonies support Childers' observation that Goschen took longer to reach decisions than anyone he knew.[63] His grudging manner gave his candidature a bad start. Liverpool Conservatives were unaccustomed to genuflexion, in religion or politics.

The platform work in Goschen's campaign was assigned to *prima donnas* among the local M.P.s, like Worms, who advised electors 'to sink consideration of party names' and to defeat 'those who truckled to treason and made alliance with the avowed enemies of the Queen and the would-be destroyers of the Empire'.[64] Worms's trenchancy underlined Goschen's deficiencies. His published address described a lifelong Liberal who resisted Home Rule less, it seemed, from manly Unionist spirit than from sickly Whiggery. Moreover, it was plumaged with egoism, an essay in how not to change sides.[65]

The Liberals concentrated on the Unionists' vulnerable areas—the *argumentum ad hominem*, and the constituency's interests. Edward Russell hoped that Gladstone might induce Harcourt or Morley to visit Liverpool, 'take the buttons off their foils, and do their worst with Goschen'.[66] Harcourt and Morley kept away, but Russell's designs were appeased by W. Summer's acrostic:

G was the gumption for which he was famed,
O the obstruction that many folks blamed,
S was the skill that secured Tory cheers,
C his concealment of Liberal ideas.
H was the heat against any reformer,
E was his excellence as a performer,
N was the end of a curious story when he went to the poll half Whig and half Tory.[67]

Neville described Goschen's code as 'Faith, hope, charity, and property, but the greatest of these is property'. Goschen's replacement of Churchill was emphasized, that Salisbury's Government was not only tottering, but exchanging the modishness of Tory Democracy for Whiggish obsolescence. The chairman of Exchange Liberal Association declared, 'they did not want a cool and calculating financier . . . [but] a man who could be touched with wide and generous sympathies, who could feel and legislate in the interests of the poor of this country, far more so than legislating in the interests of Egyptian bondholders'.[68]

Neville also tested Goschen's commercial support by alleging that a 'carpet-bagger' might betray their interests. The suggestion was powerful because the Post Office had temporarily deprived the Cunard and White Star lines of mail contracts, placing them with the North German Lloyd. Although the Post Office was only reacting to the cartel operated in this traffic since 1877 by the Liverpool lines, it discontinued services which, in Cunard's case, stretched back forty-six years. The Chamber of Commerce fought the decision, and Forwood recognized 'a considerable feeling of resentment'.[69] Since every American mail meant £1,000 in local wages, xenophobia was a promising line of attack. The *Daily Post* asked, 'Who handed over British mail bags to the fellow-countrymen of Mr. Goschen?'[70] This was a wilful misrepresentation because the real beneficiary was the port of Southampton, and the North German Lloyd invariably used British-built ships and British crews; but Lord George Hamilton considered this propaganda decisive.[71]

Goschen's campaign lacked equivalent edge. He spent little time in Liverpool and by polling day the I.N.L.'s canvassers had removed Irish reservations about Neville.[72] 5,670 of 8,171 electors polled in 1886; now, in a reduced electorate, 6,427 polled. The Liberal majority dwindled from 170 to 7; but Liberals everywhere and, according to Harcourt, Treasury officials, exulted at the news of Goschen's defeat.[73] Some Unionists alleged that impersonations had tipped the scales, and they considered petitioning; but Goschen quickly found a metropolitan seat. This left only the resentments. *The Times* thundered about Goschen's 'rejection by the Irish rabble'; and it lamented that extension of the franchise which had empowered them.[74] For Forwood defeat was particularly sour, having enticed a leading minister to trust to the soundness of Liverpool Conservatism. Forwood remembered Goschen's failure as 'a black page in the history of Liverpool and it looked worse as the days progressed'.[75] The more he brooded the more he considered the problem of the Unionist alliance—the Whigs had money, but Tory Democracy needed workers.

CHAPTER SIX

Municipal problems, 1886–90

> Ours is pre-eminently a partisan age; no plan for the improvement of Society can be proposed that is not viewed by all parties in its relation to politics, with little or no respect to its intrinsic merits.[1] *W. Cooke Taylor*

Vehement Unionist and Protestant declarations in the early 1880s had been responsible for consolidating the Conservatives' ruling position in the municipal administration, after it faltered in the 1870s. However, once the immediate danger of Irish Home Rule had passed, the Conservative party's record in government was subject to scrutiny, from its own adherents as well as from its nominal party opponents. The Liverpool Conservative party was no monolith, for it harboured within it different social groups whose economic interests and sectarian opinions were not always coincident.

The first section of this chapter considers the impediments which Forwood encountered in directing the Liverpool Conservative party to respond in an enterprising way to problems of city government. To some extent social reform was non-party in character. It was not a politically controversial goal to want a healthful society and to minimize the depredations of preventible diseases. The result, by prolonging the working life and well-being of the population, would be to add to the stock of national wealth. However, advances in public health, in order that society as a whole, and dependent sections in particular, might not suffer, were ineluctably controversial because of the resultant trespass upon established rights and previously untrammelled freedoms in the ownership of property and management of business. Forwood readily recognized this difficulty but did not shirk the challenge. He declared: 'Liverpool is a very remarkable illustration—if any justification is needed—of the necessity of public control, to ensure health and to save the toiling thousands from the evil consequences which the avarice and greed of individuals might inflict.'[2]

Unfortunately for Forwood those who resisted this course were not manifest

Notes begin on p. 386

public enemies or unconnected individuals. They were persons whose activities government had traditionally tolerated and protected, and they included individuals within his own party who had a title to be thought true Conservatives, for 'the Tories have always been opposed to the three principles of compulsion, centralization, and confiscation'.[3] Arguably these were policy guide-lines rather than sacrosanct principles, but they could not be infringed with impunity by a party leader. The concern of this part of the chapter is to show Forwood first stepping boldly, then being forced to tread warily, in those realms where public, private, and party interests chafed against each other.

The same theme infuses the last section of the chapter, which reviews the Conservatives' relations with their Orange allies. 1886 had been a year in which a siege mentality predominated among the Unionists but, when Home Rule was checked, the allies had leisure to scan the spectrum of their interests. Disharmonies were exposed, particularly by the Orangemen's stand in School Board elections in which the Conservative party, by reason of its chequered and variegated sectarian complexion, could not give absolute commitment to the Protestant cause. Forwood might well have agreed with the Radical, Henry Labouchere, that 'they are utter humbugs, these worthy Orangemen';[4] but a cavalier character was inadmissible in a party leader. Again Forwood was driven into an accommodation.

Party politics and public health

In 1886 sixteen Liberal and five Nationalist councillors faced a Conservative group of twenty-seven councillors and sixteen aldermen. No enthusiasm connected the Liberals' municipal and parliamentary performances in Liverpool and the *Review* demanded 'a robust municipal policy', which all who sought to act as Liberal representatives should endorse.[5]

Many Conservative councillors were also inert. Then there was Forwood, 'the mainspring of all municipal work', admitted one Radical. Forwood directed the Finance and Insanitary Property Committees, and led the Council. He was an excellent advertisement for his party but a poor reflection on his colleagues. One workman, Thomas Graham, complained to Forwood: 'none of the first class men assist you in personally working the wards; unpleasant work most certainly, but it is *essential* to *success* . . . Good heavens in your person you are expected to be a combination of Atlas and Achilles.'[6]

The issue whether, having been elected by parties, councillors should practise partisanship in Corporation matters, was central when Forwood joined Lord Salisbury's Government. He continued to lead the Finance Committee but conceded leadership of the Council to Barkeley Smith and the Insanitary Property Committee to Thomas Hughes. Smith's regular attendance was his only sign of activity; but Hughes was accounted 'a Radical by nature and a Conservative by accident'.[7] Concerning the Union and State-Church Hughes was decidedly Conservative; but he was a municipal reformer, seeking powers of compulsory purchase and to tax unoccupied land. A revised rating system and redistribution, even abolition, of wards, Hughes believed would ensure superior councillors. Forwood's reforming instincts differed in manner not extent.

Forwood wanted progress attributed to Conservative rule. Hughes resisted the argument that party rule and civic improvement were inseparable.

Disagreement was marked when Smith found little glory in being leader if no-one followed. He threatened to retire from the Council unless he was better supported. Hughes spurned him: he 'had not been returned by Tory votes alone' but by men who valued his independent judgement. The issue was referred to the caucus of Tory councillors; but, Hughes asserted, there was no 'connection between Conservative principles and the general policy of sewage and roadmaking pursued by the Health Committee'. Smith's self-regard had provoked Hughes, but Forwood's direction was also questioned. Both he and Whitley attended this meeting; but councillors would not commit themselves beyond an 'understanding' that collective party behaviour was expedient.[8] The insanitary state of Liverpool nevertheless demanded some intervention by the Conservatives, the majority party since 1841. Reference to these problems will suggest why Forwood ultimately agreed to limit his party's municipal responsibility.

From 1842 the Council had assumed rudimentary powers over public health and house-building.[9] Parliament was increasingly responsive to such requests by local authorities, although at the same time it was sensitive to the hostility of many ratepayers. Public inquiry was one precursor of public action. In 1871, for example, the Council commissioned Drs. Parkes and Burdon-Sanderson, who recommended the proliferation of water-closets and noted the vast numbers—perhaps one-fifth of Liverpool—inhabiting 'court' slums.[10] Having half a million citizens in 1880, Liverpool was dignified as a city with an episcopal see; but misery, not magnificence, characterized the lives of some 70,000 people occupying 14,472 houses in 2,531 courts which were condemned as unfit for habitation.[11] Bye-laws in 1869 had permitted inspections to combat overcrowding in sub-let and lodging houses; but their owners were not compelled to register. The system depended upon 'chance information' and the medical officer's diligence. By 1884 some 15,000 were registered, but the effectiveness of inspection was doubted.[12]

As a pioneer in many aspects of public health administration, superficially the Corporation's record was satisfactory. Following local legislation of 1846 Liverpool had appointed England's first Medical Officer of Health, Dr. Duncan. He was succeeded before 1924 by Drs. Trench, Taylor, and Hope; but their appointment was not uninfluenced by political favouritism, and their work was not immune from political pressures.[13] Dr. Taylor, for instance, was formerly a Conservative Councillor. He resigned in 1893, six months after the Liberals achieved power;[14] and his successor, Dr. Hope, was related to the then Liberal leader, Edward Evans.

Forwood refused to speculate whether the M.O.H.'s election by the Council curtailed his independence;[15] but, originally, not only 'improvers' but 'dirty' parties might advance appointments, preferring to control a M.O.H. than to be controlled from Westminster. Many councils—including Liverpool's until the Home Secretary argued otherwise—insisted that a M.O.H. retain his private practice. This ensured cheapness and curtailed his meddling.[16] Dr. Trench, for example, had been an 'ardent sanitary reformer', but he could not overcome the councillors' dislike of widespread clearances and minicipal housing or, it was alleged, their property interests.[17] Trench thus exhibited caution.

Expense was a scriptural text for inactivity; and no M.O.H.'s machinery was adequate. In 1895 the city boundaries were extended to incorporate Walton (population 56,067), West Derby (38,528), Toxteth (28,435), and Wavertree (15,098). Previously these Sanitary Districts had separate M.O.H.s who maintained their private practices, and only Walton's Sanitary Inspector was certificated. Without clerical and professional staff these district duets had undertaken no large-scale programme.[18]

The notification of infectious diseases was both tardy and irregular.[19] Disease was locked in certain quarters and regenerative. In 1882, Dr. Taylor reported, Liverpool contained 2,684 'infected and dirty houses'—984 more than in 1875. Whole districts were 'plagued as the cholera-smitten cities of India'.[20] The health authorities' impotence resembled that of the police, who occasionally encountered blockaded streets, wherein disorder reigned. People denied that illness existed, to checkmate bureaucratic prying. Minimal furniture stood behind windows screened with paper or rags. In courts containing four to sixteen houses one Corporation tap and trough-closet served every inhabitant. Scavengers cleaned these every morning; by noon they were disgusting.[21] Toilets were mostly used for excrements; otherwise people urinated in the yard or, as Pat O'Mara's father favoured when drunk (which was often) from the window.[22] The stench by night, one Irishman reported, would 'raise the roof off his skull'.[23] Some causes of ill-health were obvious—deficient amenities combined with environmental hazard.

Councillors and health officers in Liverpool, however, would not establish their own hospitals for infectious diseases, on financial grounds and because their management might engender political, social, and religious contentions. The Local Government Board's disapproval, and recurring epidemics—of typhus (1865), cholera (1866), relapsing fever (1870), and smallpox (1870–1, 1876–7),—did not shake this conviction that Boards of Guardians could manage without municipal interference.[24] Consequently, during the smallpox outbreak of 1883–6, victims were treated in workhouse or voluntary hospitals, which were badly equipped; and infection spread from where it was ostensibly cured. Even after the Corporation assumed some responsibility—in 1893 the Port Sanitary and Hospitals Committee was established—the Local Government Board maintained that existing isolation arrangements were inadequate in Liverpool. Controversy broke out afresh in the 1902–3 smallpox epidemic.[25]

To mitigate the problems of Victorian towns required an enlarged staff of trained public servants and a revised concept of local government. Many radical publicists, like George Sims, attacked the belief that 'all Englishmen have to do to help the denizens of the slums and alleys is to put their hands in and pull out a sovereign or a shilling. It is legislation that is wanted, not almsgiving. It is not a temporary relief, but a permanent one, that can alone affect, in any appreciable manner, the condition of the one-roomed portion of the population of great cities.' London alone contained 'a Norwich full of prostitutes; a Huntingdon full of known criminals; two Nottinghams full of folk without homes'.[26] Many towns wanted 'a Lisbon earthquake, or a Stuart fire, to give the opportunity of reconstruction'.[27] In Liverpool the work done only highlighted what remained to be done. The Health Committee's vigorous insufficiency resembled a child's attempt to empty the Mersey with a bucket.[28]

One deterrent was the notion of individual responsibility. This invited debate: '*Is it the pig who makes the stye or the stye that makes the pig?*'[29] Poverty had an interactive and accumulative character. Drink drove men to slums; slums drove men to drink. Low wages restricted the choice of housing; misapplication enhanced their misery. Being 'never a shilling ahead of the world',[30] slum dwellers purchased minute quantities—'their groceries by the ounce, their meat or fish by the half-penn'orth, their coal by the hundredweight or even by the pound',[31] which turned out more expensive. Higher wages might not encourage people to different ways or better lodgings, while migrancy discouraged pride in a home.[32] Vandalism was rife: taps became scrap-metal, ashpits became fuel. Lord Shaftesbury said, 'You go up the rickety staircase, and you see the filth, but it is not their filth; it is the filth of the family that has just preceded them'.[33]

Slums denied hygiene: damp walls cannot be scoured, rotting floorboards cannot be polished. Many houses were inadequate *before* they were occupied.[34] The nineteenth-century poor understood the parable in which everything passed by on the other side. Improvements in sanitary, lighting, and cooking facilities first went to upper economic groups, but even in the better property the spread of household utilities was slow, in part because of the availability of cheap domestic servants. Labour-saving devices were less popular when it was only the servants' labour that was saved. The problem for many working-class people was different. Their homes were not only without servants and household utilities, they were poorly provided with 'even the barest necessities, not only of cleanliness, but of decency'. The landlord, some argued, was the 'prime cause' of this misery; but it was questionable how many prospered by slum property (except through the rising value of land or by compensation for demolitions) since bad housing was bad business.[35] Rents went unpaid. Lawlessness was certainly one cause of default, but equally many people were simply too poor to afford an economic rent. The agent for one Liverpool street, containing fifty houses, declared: 'My book shows a weekly rental of £8; I never get more than £2; and I think myself lucky if I can extract a shilling from tenants of a three-shilling house.' The Radical journalist, Hugh Farrie, said of the slum landlords: 'They get little, and they do nothing.'[36]

Some suggested that municipalities should compile and make accessible a register of owners, as a step towards a reform of the land laws. 'The evil of land monopoly', as James Sexton called it, continually exercised radicals of all description. A Labour M.P. after 1918, Sexton asserted that 'the leasehold system has created the slums, because property-owners, having to pay big prices for the land, and having a lease on it for only a limited period exact during that period the highest possible rents and at the same time allow the property to deteriorate'.[37] In Liverpool the Corporation itself owned one-third of the parish, where residential property was 'unsatisfactory in the highest degree'; and much was subdivided, among persons who lived on the difference between the interest on the mortgage and the rent they extracted from tenants.[38] This complicated a thesis of rich landlord or lease-holder exploiting poor tenant. Sometimes the poor fleeced the poor.

Reformers were further demoralized by the agencies of redress. City Corporations seemed only more corrupt or inefficient Little Pedlingtons. Literature cast local officials alike as part idiot and part crook. It was always fashionable to deride municipalities: in the *Ragged Trousered Philanthropists* the Council of 'Mugsborough', known as 'The Forty Thieves', contained two parties, 'Brigands' and 'Bandits'. Few men in public life considered local government a major question, beyond paying lip-service to the view that it was potentially a great educator of a sober democracy. William Rathbone was an exception. He entered Parliament in 1868 intending to devote himself to this. He was prepared not to be discouraged by the argument that 'Local Government was not regarded as "Politics" ', but he had not bargained for the poverty of information about local government even on such essential matters as the total rates of Liverpool. A report of a Commons Select Committee, headed by Goschen, in 1870 was influential in demanding improvements in the quality of this information, but mostly it only served to highlight the deficiencies. A consolidated rate and uniformity in the system of assessments and accounts were needed: the 'clumsy inequity', the 'inconveniences and wasteful management' of local taxation were 'a national scandal'.

Rathbone personally spent £4,000 on research and legal aid in drafting legislation. He believed that the continuing division of work, between Councils, School Boards, Boards of Guardians, and other agencies, deterred the best men from entering local government. He aimed to concentrate all local government into a single representative body which would delegate particular functions to committees but meet once or twice a year to debate questions of principle and to allocate the budget. Rathbone had allies in a small group of interested county M.P.s from both parties—two Liberals, Lord Edmond Fitzmaurice and Albert Grey, and three Conservatives, Clare Read, Albert Peel, and J. R. Yorke. Different ministries occasionally paid attention to their ideas; but only Rathbone of this group survived to hold his seat during the turmoil of Redistribution and Home Rule in 1885–6, and, thus isolated, Rathbone himself retired in 1895, wearied by 'ploughing the sands'.[39]

Political factors were decisive for, while few excused the confusion in local government, few welcomed an extension of national government. John Stuart Mill observed that centralization was 'the subject not only of rational disapprobation, but of unreasoning prejudice . . . resisting even the most beneficial exertion of legislative authority to correct the abuses of what pretends to be local self-government, but is, too often, selfish management of local interests, by a jobbing and *borné* local oligarchy'.[40]

Political considerations predetermined both men and measures. Liverpool's Town Clerk, H. E. Clare, liked to think that the Council Committees selected their chairmen from personal confidence;[41] but many Councillors contemplated re-election, and the Corporation officials, respecting a party majority in the Council, might not report uncomfortable facts or proceed as needed. The constraint was clear: 'There is the question of the rates going up'.[42]

Some believed that municipalities should have been made to furnish specific information showing what was done and undone, so that Governments had the data upon which to arraign them.[43] But no consensus about their duties existed. Many poor people distrusted municipal action, from what cause is uncertain, but the involvement of the police in some sanitary administration cannot have helped the popularity of public health. At all levels of the argument, however, principles were mixed with prejudices. Thus many—the influential Liverpool Land and House Owners Association among them—felt it wrong for Corporations to build and let houses at lower rentals than cost; and, without a determination to act in a public capacity, private builders remained mostly undisturbed. The St. Martin's Cottages (1869) in Liverpool , some of the country's first Council houses, were intended as models for private builders; and the Victoria Dwellings (1885) advanced only after 'attempts to carry out a scheme by private enterprise completely failed'.[44]

The Liverpool Corporation had pioneered compulsory purchases in legislation in 1864. Before 1875 it bought 635 court-houses, but £72,000 went in compensation, £10,000 in legal charges, and £24,000 in damages to adjoining properties. The compensation, Forwood agreed, was 'much greater' than owners 'morally' deserved. Some wanted prices calculated by actual receipts of rent; but the 1864 Act allowed owners to demand separate arbitrations of value, and the Council found it cheaper to pay most claims than to seek compulsory purchase orders from a tribunal.[45] Small ambitions and timid practice proved expensive. The 1864 Act was 'a complete failure',[46] and new powers were sought in 1882, which halved the legal costs per house bought by the Corporation. Nevertheless fundamental questions of compensation, betterment, and development rights remained as obstacles to local authority clearance of slums and provision of housing. The general Housing of the Working Classes Act of 1890, for instance, based compensation on the fair market value and directed the arbitrator to reduce compensation where the rental was inflated by overcrowding and where the property constituted a nuisance or was unfit for habitation; but, before the 1919 Housing Act, some compensation for the buildings, as well as the site, had to be paid, and no government subsidy was available for new housing.

Forwood became interested in these questions as an adventure in Tory Democracy. He emphasized rehousing the dispossessed. Demolitions had been undertaken since 1864, but the Council could build only by taxing the ratepayers or by borrowing from the Public Works Loan Commissioners, at what were considered unfavourable terms.[47] However, as chairman of the newly created Insanitary Property and Artisans Dwellings Committee in 1883, Forwood produced a programme which for the first time envisaged council-housing as an essential part of Liverpool's housing stock. Over 14,000 insanitary houses existed according to the criteria of 1864, that is, of a court or back-to-back type. Forwood calculated that for the Council to demolish these houses and to rehouse two-thirds of their inhabitants would cost up to £1½ million, but the burden to the rates from the Corporation's building might be limited to an annual charge of about one penny in the pound if one-third of the properties were remodelled.[48]

Demolition and house-building had to harmonize, otherwise overcrowding was exacerbated; but many people wanted rehousing near the docks, their livelihood. By law, however, the smallest cottage required forty-six superficial yards of land: only 8,000 cottages could be built on land then occupied by over 14,000. Forwood concluded that cottages must yield to flats.[49] Private builders, however, specialized in terraced cottages with weekly rents, for four rooms of 4–5*s*., and for six rooms of 7–9*s*. Accordingly families accepted lodgers and, with insufficient amenities, slum characteristics rapidly proliferated in new houses. This argued to Forwood that the Corporation should set the example by itself building flats in central Liverpool. Moreover he weighed this choice: how best to accommodate workmen 'at a *Rental* of *ONE Shilling per Week per Room*. This shilling rental is the all-important factor, for no man with a family ought to occupy less than three rooms, and 3*s*. is as much as the average Liverpool workman can afford to pay.' In linking the housing question and that of income Forwood exhibited his realism, but it was a connection that gave little cause for optimism. The real issue was poverty not slums: slum housing simply reflected the distribution of economic power in society. In addition Forwood recognized 'a moot politico-economic problem, whether if we improve house accommodation out of the public purse, thus making rents abnormally low, we shall induce increased numbers to come to the town, and so increase the present over-supply of labour'; but he was prepared to accept the risk.[50]

Previous experiments were unsatisfactory. The St. Martin's Cottages were 'much shut in and gloomy'. The Council Committee which scrutinized different designs had aimed 'to get as many houses on the land as possible'.[51] Their poor construction was reflected in the annual repairs bill; and the lowest rent for three rooms, 3*s*. 6*d*., fell short of Forwood's ideal. However, a resident caretaker collected rents and enforced sanitary arrangements. That the Corporation could supervise property efficiently encouraged Forwood further.[52]

Forwood's showpiece was the Victoria Dwellings, 272 tenements and 12 shops at Nash Grove, opened by Sir Richard Cross in October 1885. The Corporation's stock of tenements was now doubled, at a cost of £68,000, or twice that expended on the St. Martin's, Arley Street, and Gildart's Gardens dwellings.[53] Many visitors were impressed—including a deputation from Glasgow, that other pioneer of council housing—but the argument about rents had been lost. The minimum for three rooms exceeded 4*s*. Later the 16th Earl of Derby protested that the Corporation should never have built apartments which attracted 'a superior class of workmen, who did not want to be nursed by anyone, and who were quite capable of taking their own part'.[54] This fact was important and diminished the Corporation's satisfaction when the death-rate of Nash Grove fell from 44 to about 20 per 1,000 in the next decade, for those who moved into Nash Grove in 1885 were not those who had been displaced in the clearances there of 1875–6. Some argued that the dispossessed had drifted into the workhouse or aggravated overcrowding in Scotland ward. Forwood replied that 'the population there is so enormous that it would have no appreciable affect';[55] nevertheless teachers, clergymen, and shopkeepers complained of disturbance to the community.[56]

Official pride was humbled. Appearing before a Royal Commission, the Liverpool City Engineer was overborne by George Godwin who asked, regarding the 14,000 court-houses 'incapable of sustaining healthful life' and the considerable population not rehoused years after clearances, 'why is it that the corporation always seems about to do something and are never doing it?'[57] The best affirmative Forwood could give was that 'like all pioneers, we had a great deal to learn, and we could only learn by experience'.[58] In fact the experience was so chastening that, while demolitions proceeded, the Corporation built only another hundred apartments, in Juvenal Street, in the next decade.

Forwood turned his resourcefulness in another direction. He sought both to augment the Corporation's coffers and to strike at slumdom. He differed from most advocates of leasehold reform—from Lord Randolph Churchill to Henry Broadhurst—by asserting the Corporation's rights over its large tenants instead of empowering leaseholders to convert tenure into freehold. Originally leases covered three lives and twenty-one years, subject to renewals fines and a small annual rent; but a seventy-five years standard was introduced in 1824. Forwood challenged this in the 1880s: the Corporation drew only ¼ per cent revenue from an estate which had rocketed in value with the expansion of the business quarter to an estimated £12½ million, for its fines favoured those who renewed under twenty-five years in order to ensure a regular current income.[59] The Leaseholder's Association retorted that what Forwood claimed was benefit of unearned income because the Corporation's possessions had increased in value from the lessees' expenditure, not from its own development. That Forwood claimed tolls for the community, not an individual landlord, hardly deflected their fervour.

Several councillors—being also leaseholders—maintained that £10½ million of the estate's value belonged to the leaseholders; therefore the Corporation was entitled to income only from the remainder.[60] Moreover, the Leaseholders' Association threatened impeachment if the Corporation adopted Forwood's intentions since by prescriptive usage they claimed the right to renewals on the 1824 scale. An alternative was to dispose of Corporation property by a system of perpetual ground-rent payable annually. This idea apparently originated from an auctioneer and estate agent, Owen Williams, who represented the Land and House Owners' Association; but it was a scheme that contained problems. Valuations varied; and if conversion was optional, lessees might delay and depress the Corporation's revenue below its annual average of £40,000.[61] In 1887–8 the Council received two reports. A Finance Sub-Committee proposed to continue the existing renewals, while offering terms for leaseholders to purchase reversions. The Leaseholds Committee considered this too favourable: it recommended heavier fines and their investment in annuities.

As the Council rejected the Leaseholds Committee's report Forwood returned from Westminster to contest the alternative. Liverpool's future was at stake, since the estate enabled them to undertake public works. He reminded councillors that they represented 500,000 inhabitants, not 5,000 lessees. Their transactions were unequal: 'The lessees knew that the Corporation were [*sic*] cornered for money; they knew that the Council were [*sic*] relying upon getting a certain income from fines year by year in order to avoid the levying of a borough rate . . .' Moreover the reversions were unsaleable to anyone but the leaseholders.[62]

This speech consummated a succession of retreats since Forwood had broached a programme of municipal initiative. He had laboured mostly alone, discouraged by important sections of his party, and without proper legislative aids. Reform, particularly in the direction of welfare provision, could not be considered apart from its uncongenial corrolary, increased public expenditure. Forwood, it seemed, had been slow to appreciate Castlereagh's dictum, that people had an 'ignorant impatience of taxation'. Having learned, however, Forwood smartly changed course. He advised Conservatives that 'they should not too far identify themselves with the policy that might be adopted in municipal matters by the City Council'. It was more prudent to have the party judged by its certain position on 'questions of the union and foreign policy' than by its doubtful attitude regarding 'leaseholds, waterworks, or any other municipal question'.[63]

Forwood acknowledged that his party was unsuited to win elections by its social conscience. Grand national themes, not painstaking municipal work, were his party's *forte*. From 1888 he tailored his speeches accordingly.

Unionist doubts

Although deadened by disengagement from reformist illusions, Tory Democracy thrived in public relations. Paternal personalities enveloped the party with decent popularity. Arthur Forwood—or his wife—was credited with having originated the custom of afternoon receptions and teas at the Town Hall during his mayoralty in 1878–9; but David Radcliffe's mayoralty between 1884 and 1886 established a new standard of hospitality. Called the 'People's Mayor', he was the first in 130 years to be re-elected to an immediate second term. By entertaining at the Town Hall some 5,000 working men Radcliffe had 'gratified a section of the community not previously recipients of such attention'.[64] This Hal had not forgotten Falstaff, and at Christmas 'deserving poor' received through the different clergy a thousand 'hot-pots', each enough for eight or ten people. William Simpson had begun this tradition modestly in 1876 with a hundred hot-pots, but Radcliffe established its large scale. The dockers' leader, Sexton, later complained that 'it breathes contemptuous and vulgar patronage'; [65] but it appears to have been genuinely popular. The climax of Radcliffe's mayoralty was a knighthood when the Queen opened the International Exhibition in 1886.[66]

The politics of Tory Democracy remained problematical. The 1887 municipal elections were inconclusive with only two contests, in Great George Street, which Liberals captured by eleven votes, and St. Anne's, a Conservative gain by seventy-seven votes. There the accusation that the Tory party represented Great Grog lost its potency, for the victor defended brewing as a legitimate trade.[67] Indications elsewhere were discouraging. In West Derby the W.M.C.A. complained of Councillor Lunt's snobbishness;[68] and in Abercromby Forwood's dilemmas were clearly posed—whether municipal contests should be party contests, and whether their manifesto should be imperial or local in content. Superimposed was Orange discontent in which Thomas McCracken played an increasing part.

A wealthy wine merchant born in Belfast, McCracken was a founder of the Junior Conservative Club in 1880, a former chairman of Low Hill W.M.C.A. branch, and the secretary of the Hot-Pot fund. The *Review* called him 'a real people's man';[69] but he came forward to contest Abercromby in 1887 as a large ratepayer who detested extravagence. He declared that his imperial opinions were Conservative, but 'politics would never count with him in municipal affairs'.[70] This split the ward's Conservative representatives: Councillor Morris deprecated McCracken's ambitions, but Alderman Grindley, a clubable independent, welcomed them. Forwood used his influence—the W.M.C.A. branch supported the sitting Councillor, G. H. Ball, in preference to McCracken; the Constitutional Association censured Grindley; and McCracken withdrew his candidature when threatened with expulsion from the party.[71] H. C. Gillmore, a Liberal, assumed his mantle as an Independent Ratepayers' candidate; but he too withdrew after a technical objection.[72] This avoided issues and left resentments. Forwood had little cause for jubilation in Jubilee Year.

The Liberals were also unsettled. Few Gladstonians wanted to embrace the radicals or to break irrevocably with Whig Unionists. Perhaps the Liverpool Liberal leader, Holt, should not have been surprised when the Marquis of Hartington declined to dine with the Liverpool Reform Club;[73] but, so far, Holt had no cause to feel that politics would sully the intercourse of polite society. From the record of his diary Holt never sat down with any Irish politician, local or national, at his or their homes, but he continued to exchange dinner parties with Lord and Lady Derby, the Brocklebanks, the Earles, and other leaders of Liverpool and West Lancashire society. Brocklebank indeed warmed to Holt's conciliatory tone and regretted that some Liberal Unionists were 'wanting in tact to omit civilities to well-known Liberals, though they may not be in accord with my own views while these members seek to honour men of the extremist Nationalist Party. I may plainly say I object to Dillon, Healy etc. while I respect Lords Rosebery and Granville. If the Irish Question could be out of the way it would be a very fortunate circumstance.'[74]

The Gladstonians' moderation was demonstrable in June 1888 when Radicals at the Liverpool Reform Club proposed to invite the Nationalist M.P., John Dillon, to an official dinner. The Liberal Unionists, although separately they numbered only sixty, carried an amendment that the invitation be private. They benefited from an aspiration shared by several Gladstonians that the Club might remain comprehensive; but the *Review* reviled 'the noble army of lunchers whose political principles are not strong enough to govern and control their social instincts'.[75]

Gladstonian lunchers were a formidable force. In 1888 the Club served 55,000 meals.[76] Several Radicals resigned, enraged by the lunchers' political pusillanimity; but the retreat became a rally when Parnell's defence against Pigott and *The Times* raised a new leader, Edward Evans. Evans lived in Cheshire, but he championed a Municipal Reform Association in Liverpool and exercised power in Abercromby, where his firm of wholesale druggists was situated. Evans was not altogether radical but he had qualities which Holt lacked—energy, and a trust in organization. His election as chairman of the Reform Club in 1889 symbolized a more determined Gladstonianism and, significantly, Parnell was the guest of honour at an official reception that December, despite critical murmurs.[77]

Some Liberals were stirring even before Evans's advent, for St. Anne's ward was won in November 1888 in a 75 per cent poll. The municipal economy was a leading issue and the *Review* noted portentously that St. Anne's was 'a microcosm' of the city's conflicting populations. That many combined to reject 'the old and debased order' was considered 'most hopeful'.[78] Sectarian difficulties, however, had been mostly avoided by the unusual character of the Liberal Home-Rule candidate: McMillin was an Ulster Presbyterian. Moreover, his victory injured the moderate school. As chairman of Rodney Street Ward Liberal Association, McMillin employed its organization in his contest of St. Anne's. This stranded the Rodney Street Councillor, Philip Rathbone, and the *Daily Post* mourned the defeat of one who placed 'public interest before popular applause'.[79]

Protestant pressure

The *Daily Post*'s lament had more relevance to the Conservatives' troubled relations with Protestant partisans. Most Orangemen belonged to the 'artisan class', and disturbances regularly attended their sectarian celebrations.[80] In Liverpool, between 1886 and 1889, thirty instances of riot occurred; and, after an Orange attack on one Nationalist meeting in which Councillor Byrne was injured, the Council debated the question of law and order.[81] Many Conservatives were frankly unmoved; but frequent tumult could not be ignored. The Improvement Act (1842) had empowered the Mayor to warn marchers about street obstructions, and in 1852 the magistrates had exhorted the police to prevent sectarian parades. This was *ultra vires* but, by agreement, 'aimless' processions had ceased, and formal marches on key days, for instance, 17 March or 12 July, were allowed from club headquarters to points of departure from Liverpool provided that bands were silent and insignia concealed. These restrictions were mostly observed until Home Rule revived hostilities. In 1886 the Liverpool Corporation sought special powers. These were not unique—a Party Processions Act had applied in Ireland (1833–43, 1850–72)—but Liverpool's application was modest, seeking to prohibit party bands from certain streets at certain times. However, the Government would not countenance local interferences with liberty and Liverpool's powers remained the same—the ultimate sanction of the Riot Act.[82]

The Conservative party seemed caught. Either it abetted riot or it suppressed its supporters. One answer was to argue that the Orangemen's position was 'defensive': they 'banded themselves together for mutual safety', to avoid being 'exterminated'.[83] The Conservatives pandered to Orange convictions, from sympathy and expediency. Sabbatarianism, for instance, was integral to the Orangemen's code and furnished opportunities of inter-class co-operation. Opening the Walker Gallery on Sundays was not a party question, but the Council divided largely by parties as Nationalists introduced this motion annually from 1888.[84] Anti-Sabbatarian Conservatives mostly avoided the debates.[85]

Orangemen also influenced School Board elections. The Liverpool Board, reflecting sectarian interests in the city, contained six Catholics, five Anglicans and four Nonconformists. In 1888 only the Catholic congregations were united and their candidates led the poll with 25,000–28,000 votes each. By contrast, the Anglican list contained both Evangelicals and the Ritualist Bell Cox; but an Orangeman, Harry Thomas, surpassed every official Church candidate with 22,426 votes. Special positions invalidated a precise equation of School Board parties with political parties, and from the start of the School Board in the 1870s, when the damaging potential of ritual differences became clear, the Liverpool Conservative party had not officially involved itself in these elections. Curiously, although the Liberal leader, Robert Holt, for the most part regretted the politicization of municipal affairs, in the case of School Board elections he thought it best to admit their political character: 'It is the old cry of civil and religious Liberty which was and still is the main plank in all Liberal creeds, and as you can't get the Tories to accept this view of the question why not identify the position now as in our Fathers' times with our political creed.'[86] The political significance of Thomas's victory arrested the attention of the Conservatives. Their party was in religion hermaphrodite and unappealing to masculine Orangemen, whose experience was of Conservatives snubbing them once they attained power. Conservatives, the *Protestant Standard* reflected, 'would support the devil himself if it answered their purpose'.[87]

Discord was also evident within the Conservative party organization. The W.M.C.A. was founded, among other objects, 'to unite in maintaining Protestantism'; but, from allegiance to the Union, the W.M.C.A. had been patronized by Catholics like P. E. J. Hemelryk. A wealthy cotton merchant, settling in Liverpool in 1862, Hemelryk's credit had soon blossomed. He was a shareholder in the exclusive Wellington Club and introduced polo locally; he served as Dutch Vice-Consul and, on behalf of the Chamber of Commerce, promoted a continental telegraph. Like his business partner, Hornby, he was first a Liberal; but in 1886 he had turned Unionist. He became a member of the Constitutional Association's Political Committee and vice-chairman of Wavertree Conservative Association (in Bootle Division).[88] There he had sponsored a branch of the W.M.C.A. and was elected its president. Workmen gave their labour freely to build the club, which seemed a model affair, 'dry' and practically self-supporting. In 1888 the Prime Minister, Lord Salisbury, visited Wavertree to advertise Tory Democracy. His speech observed 'how enormously the temperature of political feeling . . . [was] intensified by constant converse with those who hold the same convictions'.[89]

If a club's pride and purpose was to convert supporters into fanatics, then Wavertree W.M.C.A. was virtuous and effective. Many of its 150–200 members were Protestant fundamentalists and supporters of the Bootle M.P., Colonel Sandys. When Sandys began to deliver anti-Catholic diatribes at the club Hemelryk resigned from reasons of conscience. Sandys's part in this drama was significant. He was the *ne plus ultra* of reaction, combining the worst of Colonel Sibthorp and C. N. Newdegate.[90] His world was uncomplicated. Trade unions, he declared, were 'the curse of the country'; and he bemoaned the abolition of flogging as part of the discipline of the army, in 1881. The Grand Master of the

English Loyal Orange Lodge, Sandys also denounced the Open Church Association as 'savouring of Romanism'.[91] His will entreated his heirs 'to avoid betting, gambling, horse-racing, and card-playing', and declared void the succession of his estate to a Catholic or descendent marrying a Catholic, so that his family might escape 'the evil results which inevitably . . . follow upon the spirit of Romanism'.[92]

Sandys's representation of Bootle was appropriate. Bootle, incorporated as a borough in 1868, invariably excited the derision of Liverpudlians.[93] When B. S. Johnson, a Bootle mayor, contested Kirkdale in 1895, Salvidge recited a pantomine song, 'the wild man of Bootle has come to town'.[94] Bootle was a nadir vital to Liverpool's *amour propre.* If Liverpool's officials were imperfect, at least they were above the Bootle Town Clerk who embezzled £24,000.[95] If Liverpool was rough, at least its violence paled by 'Brutal Bootle'—'where the bugs wear clogs'.[96] For Liverpudlians, wogs began at Bootle: Bootle people, like the 'heathen Chinese', had ways which were 'more peculiar than pleasant'.[97] Again, though its slums were shocking, Liverpool contained some handsome districts. Bootle displayed only 'dirty streets, deserted mansions, public-houses, brick-fields, and waste-land'.[98] Bootle was the squalid face of Liverpool; but it had not always been so. Gladstone remembered wild roses once growing there; Sir William Forwood recalled 'few more charming spots'; and bathing vans still dotted Bootle sands in 1851.[99] In 1861 Bootle contained 6,500 people, in 1871 16,000, in 1881 27,000. New docks brought another 16,000 residents by 1885.[100] Politics in Liverpool and Bootle were transilient: Bootle's Irish centre was outnumbered by the Conservative majority among Wavertree and West Derby freeholders.

In challenging the Liverpool Constitutional Association in 1888 the Orangemen used Sandys's intransigent Protestantism as a gauntlet. In December James Lynch, the Provincial Grand Secretary, notified James Thompson, the Conservative agent, that Orange representatives were quitting the Constitutional. They accused Conservative leaders of truckling to Catholics and Ritualists, failing to support Thomas for the School Board, and ignoring Sandys's celebration of the tercentenary of the defeat of the Spanish Armada. Lynch summarized the severance: 'Orangemen are Protestants first; after that they are politicians.'[101] This bared a weakness in Conservative armour. Although it was improbable that Orangemen would vote Liberal, they might venture independence.

Forwood recited the Association's rules. The Constitutional was not founded to promote sectarianism; it was not responsible for expressions by individuals; Bootle was outside its jurisdiction; and its policy was not to interfere in School Board elections. Forwood regretted the Orangemen's departure when they needed steadfastness to maintain the Union and to 'protect that loyal minority in Ireland, which is so largely composed of Protestants'.[102] He invited the mediation of Lord Arthur Hill, a Conservative Whip and Orangeman. He subsequently accepted the Orangemen's demand for fifteen representatives on the Constitutional's General Council and proportionate representation on the Executive. He criticized, however, a Committee of the Orange Order, established by Henry Skewes, the Deputy Grand Chaplain, which intended to vet future candidates. The Constitutional's decisions could not be referred to a subsidiary organization.

In 1889 the Orangemen affirmed their independence and nominated Thomas in Scotland ward.[103] Tactically, Forwood noted, this was 'an unfortunate fight' which discredited Orange Conservatism by demonstrating its weakness in that district.[104] Although Thomas advocated increases in scavengers' wages and a redistribution of wards, his campaign was principally sectarian, exhorting 'Protestant electors . . . to fight the Fenian Lynskey'.[105] Afterwards, at a by-election in South Toxteth, Thomas sought official Conservative nomination. Instead a fruit broker, James de Bels Adam, was selected. Thomas's nominators on the ward Conservative Association committee agreed to support Adam; but Thomas blamed Forwood for his failure and came out independently. Another candidate, a Gladstonian, John Thomas, existed; and to prevent confusion Irish voters were asked to consider Harry Thomas as 'Old Harry'.[106] Old Harry had willing workers in Orange leaders like Latta, Lynch, and McCracken, and in prominent evangelical churchmen like Dr. Hakes and Canon Lester. To the Deputy Grand Master of the Orange Order this contest prefigured a national Protestant campaign.[107]

The *Review* analysed the schism. Harry Thomas was 'the instrument of democracy' fighting 'not against Conservative principles but against the "swells" of the party, who think that because they have money they have a right to place and power'. Thomas, at the age of thirty, had already risen in trade to master plumber and in the Orange Order to Grand Master of Liverpool Province and Grand Treasurer of England; but the *Review* distinguished this 'advocate of reform' from the 'truculent bigot of the past'. It discerned 'a closer identity of interest' between the Conservative and Liberal masses than between each and their parties' 'currant jelly element'.[108]

The Gladstonians incorporated some democratic patter in their campaign, regarding the corporate estate and the Tory aldermanic ring. They accused the Docks Board of diverting trade to the northern docks and of feasting in ways 'that should bring the blush of shame to their cheeks'.[109] Immorality further exercised Liberal consciences—Samuel Smith intervened to asseverate that Liverpool winked at vice while other cities expelled it.[110]

Both Liberals and Orangemen underestimated their opponents. Criticism of the Docks Board's menus did not shake Adam's promise to berth more vessels in the south end. Adam was a popular employer. The Fruit Porters' Union, whose foundation he aided, praised him for 'paying the highest rate of wages of the port, besides giving assistance in cases of sickness and death'.[111] Moreover Adam, a Presbyterian, ridiculed Ritualist churches as theatres.[112] The Tory organization steeled itself to resist Orange dictation.[113]

Adam won 1,734 votes, John Thomas 1,699, Harry Thomas 398. Some Orangemen made allegations of conspiracy;[114] but more obvious had been their exaggerated hopes. The Deputy Grand Master had scaled the heights of delusion by believing that Orangemen composed 'one-third of the electorate of the kingdom'.[115] Liverpool in fact contained about 17,000 members of the Orange Order, but how many were enfranchised was debatable. South Toxteth, where they were relatively strong, had about five hundred. Forwood scornfully declared that 'the Orange party had no power and were scattered up and down the city like the four winds of heaven'.[116]

Every Toxteth Orangeman, however, had not supported Harry Thomas. The *Protestant Standard* distinguished two classes, 'Christian Protestant Orangemen' and 'nominal Protestant, political Orangemen'.[117] The former embraced independent representation on class and sectarian grounds; the latter waived everything to preserve the Union. McCracken now dropped his intention of contesting West Derby ward;[118] and Orange militants turned to registration work and propaganda.[119] In December 1889 Lynch launched another penny weekly, *The Loyal Orangeman*. This designated Home Rule 'a diabolical plot of the Papacy' and threatened civil war;[120] but it also denounced, often without syntax, Ritualism, Socinianism, Atheism, Socialism, and Republicanism. The Pope—'this hoary-headed monster in human shape'[121]—retained his primacy in the Orangemen's black museum, but Ritualists ran him close. A class element was pronounced:

> The Ritualists are mainly supported by the upper and wealthy classes, who concentrate all their worship of God on the greatest display of images, fanfare of trumpets, the screeching and twisting of intoned white-sheeted service; not so with the middle and working classes, who remain true to the ancient protestant worship of Almighty God, pure and undefiled, such as was proclaimed to the world by Wycliffe and Luther, the blowing of trumpets, and lamp-post candles, the adoration of images and white night-gowns, would not help in assisting Ritualists to Heaven; but it is a certain and near cut to the other place . . .

This 'bitter lesson' was pointed to all '*loyal* Orangemen': 'Conservatism is Popery of the deepest stain, when it is "ritualistic" in the Church.'[122] The Orangemen's Conservatism was conditional on the Conservatives' Orangeism.[123] Equally menacing was the Protestant Alliance, founded in November 1889. Colonel Sandys, the chairman, considered its influence: it embraced both Anglicans and Nonconformists and, 'though not primarily political [it] would hardly fail to exercise political effect, where *any* Government made concessions to Rome'. The present Government's course, apparently leading to Irish University endowment and sending an envoy to the Vatican, dismayed Sandys: ' "*Quem Deus vult perdere, prius dementat*" is the only way I can account for it . . . these things will wreck this administration.'[124] Unfortunately for Liverpool Conservative, as staunch members reconsidered their allegiances, they lacked the consolation that their traditional party opponents were in disarray.

CHAPTER SEVEN

Labour Emergence and Conservative Retreat, 1889–91

> No member shall use unbecoming words or references to any other member's religious opinions, or nationality, or antecedents, it being a fundamental principle of the Union that all men are brothers.
>
> *Rule 19 of the National Union of Dock Labourers*

> The city of Liverpool has some of the worst vices of the worst American cities. It has municipal patronage used for political purposes, and it has its 'boss' in the shape of the right hon. Gentleman the Secretary to the Admiralty.[1]
>
> *T. P. O'Connor, talking about A. B. Forwood*

This chapter has two concerns—to introduce labour as an organized force in both industrial and political spheres, and to depict the dissolution of the Conservatives' Council majority in Liverpool, after an uninterrupted rule of half a century. With regard to the first the study is as much of what maimed organized labour in Liverpool, as of what spurred it forward. The late 1880s and early 1890s are memorable as a period of trade union formation, particularly in the transport and distributive sectors of industry; but the sizeable labour surplus and casual terms of employment made union control in these trades speculative and doubtful. Independent labour power in politics was likewise conditional. The established parties confirmed their position in an age of extended franchise not only because of their financial superiority and range of experience but, quite simply, because many working people shared their values. Although henceforth a labour presence became increasingly distinct, it was only another factor, not the governing factor, in Liverpool politics.

The late 1880s and early 1890s also witnessed a recrudescence of the Liberals' 'moral' campaigns—for temperance and civic purity—when the Conservative party was disheartened by conflict over social reform and church policy. That the condition of Liverpool was in need of improvement had the status of a truism; but the Liberals' appraisal of problems of vice, drink, and crime, was

Notes begin on p. 391

questionable. Certainly they were right to focus attention on positions of public trust held by men with vested interests to serve. W. S. Caine, for instance, had been struck by the lax superintendence of licensing regulations during the mayoralty of A. B. Walker in 1873–4 and 1876–7, and he was 'strongly inclined to think that a policeman whose wages are at the rate of 24 shillings a week may be very largely influenced by the fact that the chief magistrate of Liverpool, at present, is the owner of 78 public-houses'.[2] The question, however, went deeper than that of individual morality or of impartial execution of law. Public action, in housing and employment, was required on a scale either unperceived or intolerable to ordinary Liberals. In any case, for all the fuss it raised, the Liberal 'purity' campaign met with qualified electoral success. More important in accounting for the Liberals' increasing municipal strength was the bias of the electoral system. The Conservatives were under-represented because ward boundaries had not been revised to accord with the movement of population to the suburbs. Since this system favoured the Catholic working class of central Liverpool, the result was once more to fuel sectarian political animosities.

Municipal politics and the Trades Council

Liverpool Liberalism seldom enjoyed cause for rejoicing. Its pessimists never languished from unemployment. Nevertheless 1889 gave signs of recovery when Evans established a Federal Council, with five representatives from every constituency.[3] The Mugwumpism of Melly and Holt had ended. Under new management a programme was billed 'for the people, for the poor'. Democratization of the elective system was cardinal, with declarations to abolish plural voting, reform registration, and pay M.P.s. Land reform was promised, concerning primogeniture, tithes, death duties, leaseholds, and mining royalties. The manifesto also pontificated about Privilege. Specifically it advertised Welsh disestablishment and, vaguely, 'measures as may from time to time be necessary to redress existing inequalities in the distribution to the parties concerned of the results of co-operation between capital and labour'.[4] Another section embraced municipal affairs, regarding auditing and the corporate estate. Liberals apparently had no views on ward redistribution, housing, municipal trading, or labour representation.

In twelve contests in the November 1889 municipal elections the Liberals gained three seats, St. Paul's, St. Peter's, and Rodney Street. Among the uncontested wards was Castle Street, where the Conservatives supported the Liberal Unionist, H. H. Hornby. The Gladstonian revival had not abated the errancy of Liberal Unionists; moreover, the Gladstonians' gains occurred in central wards of declining population. None had an electorate over 2,500 or afforded a majority over 100; and the candidates had a familiar look. Philip Rathbone, defeated in Rodney Street in 1888, won St. Paul's in 1889.[5]

Both Conservative and Liberal parties advanced candidates with little title beyond an ability to pay expenses, but in the Conservative party they were often ornaments, for their organization involved practical men, with or without money. By contrast Liberal magnates hampered their party's working. The Liberals did benefit from some Irish electioneering;[6] but an assertion that the

Nationalists' organization in Liverpool 'by 1885 had assumed the character which it was to retain up to 1914' neglects the factious fluctuations.[7] Under George Lynskey, a Galway-born solicitor, active initially in branches of the Young Ireland Society and Land League, the Liverpool I.N.L. had sixteen branches by 1890, involving 10,000 members, mostly voters;[8] but better organization brought friction in wards where Liberal majorities required Irish *claqueurs*.

In St. Anne's in September 1889 delegates from four clubs—the ward Liberal Association, Gladstone Club, Shamrock League, and I.N.L. (Michael Davitt branch)—met to nominate a candidate. Disagreement ensued and the Nationalists scorned the selection of a slum-landlord, H. C. Gillmore. They advanced Jacob Grant as an Independent against 'official Liberalism'. Several differences distinguished their campaigns. Gillmore paraded his Catholicism, at which Grant, a Jew, observed that the electors required someone in the Council not in a pulpit; and, while Gillmore was exercised about rising rates, Grant emphasized labour grievances. Both Liberal candidates lost to the third runner, A. J. J. Bamford, a wealthy provision merchant and self-styled Democratic Tory. His 640 votes surpassed Grant's by 27, Gillmore's by nearly 400.[9] The I.N.L. (Central branch) blamed the defeat on indiscipline 'caused by the want of a central authority'; but not only the selection method, the type of candidate was also the subject of dispute. All three St. Anne's contestants paid their expenses. Liverpool needed, so the *Review* deduced, 'half-a-dozen robust and square-headed labour candidates'.[10]

It was not clear how labour representation could develop. The failure of Samuelson's and Williams's parliamentary candidatures in 1885 had highlighted the traditional parties' difficulties in reaching an accommodation over this; and, at the municipal level, the narrowness of the social groups from which town councils were drawn reflected the obstructions placed upon most working men by the conditions of their employment. More than this independent working-class representation was beleaguered by occupational, political, and religious divisions. Labour confronted the established parties as Manchu China confronted industrial Europe, a 'huge mummy empire by the hands of custom wrapped in swathing bands'.[11] Thus a branch of the Social Democratic Federation had begun in Liverpool in 1882, with Sam Reeves, a coremaker, and John O'Brien, a coachbuilder, as its luminaries. They advanced three impecunious candidates in the municipal lists, but defective nomination papers eliminated them.[12] Thereafter this S.D.F. branch was comatose.[13]

The winters of the mid-1880s provoked riotous demonstrations by the unemployed in London. They also turned Liverpool dockers from hungry men into angry men.[14] Distress was severest in the south-end, as new northern docks provided some work. A Dock Labourers' Relief Society operated a form of labour bureau;[15] and the Toxteth Aid Society supplied the desperate with food.[16] However the Charity Organization Society had discovered no 'exceptional' distress;[17] and the *Daily Post* echoed it by censuring outdoor relief—'when the funds of the committees are exhausted we shall hear less of distress in Toxteth Park'.[18] The Town Council was equally stolid. It could only support utilities which had statutory authority. It could not invent undertakings to absorb seasonal unemployment. As for the Poor Law Guardians, who had no organic relationship to other local government bodies, their relief work for married men consisted of breaking eight hundredweights of stones for 1*s*. 6*d*. at such hours as prevented them looking for work elsewhere.[19] Others were offered the workhouse.

In these circumstances some turned to schemes of political self-help, even the 'Utopian and impracticable';[20] and on Sunday 19 September 1886 an audience assembled off Toxteth Street to hear J. Hunter Watts (London S.D.F.), Reeves, and O'Brien. Their handbill contained, to *The Times*, 'a series of suggestive questions': for example, 'You who suffer, are you prepared to die by inches without a murmur?'[21] An unusual retort was made by Orangemen, returning from a Church parade. They invaded the meeting. What provoked them is unclear: they might have been incited by the offence to their Sabbatarianism, also because Labour leaders were invariably Home Rulers. The Orangemen, however, were themselves attacked by Catholic bands. Amid uproar the Socialist speakers charged the authorities to introduce a statutory eight-hour day, provide remunerative relief works for the unemployed, supply free meals to under-nourished children in Board Schools, and build healthy working-class dwellings;[22] but the Orangemen drowned these resolutions by singing the National Anthem. Similar incidents were to recur.[23] The Orangemen practised Lord Salisbury's preaching that 'all the politics of the moment are summarized in the word "Ireland"'.[24]

Less demonstrative work was tackled by the Liverpool Trades Council, founded, under different name, in 1848.[25] Under its revised rules in 1888 members agreed 'to unite for the protection of labour, and to cultivate a good understanding between the Employers and the Employed'. This supposed no irrevocable differences, although many historians have observed the fundamental opposition to orthodox economics among mid-nineteenth-century trade unionists, in regard to the operations of a free market for labour and wages. At the same time many values—Conservative and Liberal—were shared, and Rule 12 of the L.T.C. proscribed 'party or political matters unless bearing upon labour questions'.[26] The L.T.C. was not widely representative of Liverpool labour. Its affiliated societies in 1887 consisted of engineers, printers, tailors, saddlers, bookbinders, railwaymen, gilders, cabinet-makers, sawyers, brush-makers, boot-makers, mast and block makers, and upholsterers. These represented 3,000 workers; and the L.T.C., levying 2*d*. per member annually, some of which went unpaid, was destitute.

Politics remained enveloped in traditional denominations. Politically active workmen bypassed the L.T.C. Liverpool's first working-class councillor, J. G. Taggart, was an Irish Nationalist and, with his colleague, Thomas Kelly,[27] he remained the only one until 1905. Winning Vauxhall ward in January 1888, Taggart claimed to have 'imbibed treason with his mother's milk'. He was born in Tyrone in 1861 before his family 'tramped' to England. As a boy Taggart worked in the north-east coalfields; but in 1879 he became a labourer in Tate's Liverpool refinery and in 1889 an estate agent's collector at 30*s*. a week. He retained contact with the ambience of manual labour as District Secretary of the

Gasworkers and General Labourers Union. Attending Council meetings cost him wages, but he regularly appeared to oppose a housing programme of demolitions without ready accommodation for the dispossessed. Ireland remained the alpha and omega of Taggart's creed—'all social and labour questions are part and parcel of Home Rule'[28]—but not only the city establishment closed against the combination of Home Rule and labour assertion which Taggart embodied.[29] The L.T.C. also mistrusted his advocacy, for Taggart, as a Nationalist, was a 'politician'.[30]

The L.T.C.'s first positive step towards representation was in the 1888 School Board elections. This arose from an interest in evening classes for workmen's children and in working-men's scholarships to the University College; but 1888–9 was also the L.T.C.'s boom year when the affiliated societies increased to twenty-one and the membership to 10,000.[31] Numbers, of course, were no criteria of strength. The Sailors and Firemen claimed 800 members but since under 200 paid subscriptions and the branch's expenditure exceeded its income, the secretary supplicated the L.T.C. to record a notional account for 300 members and to postpone demands for fees.[32]

Nevertheless certain newcomers to the L.T.C. were significant, like William Matkin, the Carpenters' and Joiners' delegate and local secretary of the Labour Electoral Association. This body had founded a Liverpool branch in 1887, whereupon it soon made political overtures to the L.T.C., although it encountered opposition led by the upholsterers' veteran delegate, George Maxwell.[33] By August 1888 co-operation was related to the School Board elections. The L.T.C. nominated its secretary, Henry Pearson (Typographers'), and the L.E.A. William Newcomb, a workingman jeweller;[34] but members of the L.T.C. were circumspect. George Parkin, the president, declared that they should advocate 'economy and efficiency, and not let their hard-earned money be wasted'; but he emphasized that 'the School Board was not a party or a political body . . . They would not be going out of their sphere in taking this step.'[35] However, neither candidate made an impression by advocating non-sectarian education. Newcomb polled 4,331; Pearson 2,779. Since each elector could cast fifteen votes (reflecting the size of the School Board), their failure was abject.[36]

The L.T.C.'s reluctance to assert new principles was evident in this episode. Contention was renewed as particular occasions arose.[37] In 1888 the L.T.C. supported agitations against sweating and the Sugar Bounties;[38] but a municipal by-election in Lime Street in August 1889 was contested for labour by the L.E.A. alone. The candidate, a piano manufacturer, John Bond, was a sixty-two-year-old former Chartist, and one-time secretary of the Liverpool Reform League. Although he criticized the Liberals' failure to achieve a radical working-class base, privately he still had hopes that the Liberals would honour his service by a magistracy. When this ambition was thwarted his interpretation—that the Liberals spurned him because he was 'too ardent a supporter of Home Rule and the Cause of Labour'—ignored his ambiguous posture.[39]. Now, in 1889, he polled 299 votes against 472 for the Conservatives. The press gave little publicity to the contest, and what vote can be accredited to Labour causes—Bond had been active in the tramwaymen's disputes that summer—is uncertain because he still worked in the ward Liberal party and his programme of 'pure' government struck common chords.[40]

'New Unionism' and strike action

Neither Bond's example, nor evangelism—Henry George lectured in Liverpool[41]—were as powerful in producing the political involvement of labour bodies as the strikes of seamen in June–July 1889, and of dockers in February–March 1890. Matkin drew a moral: 'seamen should return men of their own order' to Parliament so as to improve their conditions of work.[42] He also congratulated the union on joining the L.T.C. because only by combination with other trades would labour's cause be advanced. This argument was endorsed when the L.T.C. denounced the Poor Law Guardians for allowing shipping companies to recruit blacklegs from the workhouse, and when it urged the T.U.C. to demand 'immediate legislation' to prevent foreign pauper and contract labour from flooding many trades.[43] Moreover the L.T.C. established a five-man Committee to attend emergencies; and, although representatives were changed half-annually, it was indicative that political activists were first elected.[44]

Groups of unskilled workers took heart. In September 1889 a tramwaymen's deputation appeared before the L.T.C. to delineate grievances about hours, stoppages from wages, and victimization of trade unionists. However, there were limits to the L.T.C.'s authority and sympathetic exertions. With less than one-third of tramwaymen unionized, the L.T.C. could not realistically support a proposal to boycott the Company's vehicles; and the conventional alternative of representations was rendered ineffectual by the Company's refusal to negotiate.[45]

This year of widening responsibility culminated in the L.T.C. sponsoring Matkin in West Derby ward. Lincolnshire in origin, Matkin had experience of the London Working Men's Association and allied Education and Peace Movements.[46] He now muted his politics—the L.T.C. would not sanction them— and he fought simply for labour representation, a fair-wages clause, and economical management in Corporation business. The last contest in West Derby (in 1884) had brought out 3,589 Conservatives against 3,015 Liberals; but in a 43 per cent poll Matkin now recorded only 1,602 votes against 2,953 Conservatives. Liberals evidently did not equate their cause with Labour even though, on the other side, Conservatives and Orangemen were at loggerheads. In a December by-election in the same ward the Conservatives had difficulty in finding a candidate, until Forwood pressed George Rodway, the Constitutional Association's solicitor. This time the Liberal ward organization pledged its support of Matkin, while complaining that he was twice thrust on them without consultation; but both votes fell, Rodway's to 2,384, Matkin's to 1,566. The Nationalist Councillors, Taggart and Connolly, had addressed Matkin's meetings, and Forwood emphasized that Conservatives had two classes of Home Rulers to fight, Gladstonians and Labour candidates.[47]

The dockers' strike completed this phase of definition, locating Labour on one side of politics rather than remaining supra-political. Sectional antagonisms were apparent when 2,163 members of the Carters' Union, largely Protestant, considered whether to join the strike and 1,700 declined.[48] In 1936 Sexton recorded that this strike was engineered by employers endeavouring to crush the nascent union.[49] In 1892, however, Sexton said that the strike began from 'disaffection among the men at the conditions only'.[50] Possibly London's example stimulated both sides; but trade revival in the late 1880s, creeping unionism in Liverpool's south-end and Birkenhead, and the desire to level up and standardize conditions following the introduction of mechanization and steamships, all hastened confrontation.[51]

Unionization among dockers was undeveloped, owing to the fragmentary nature of dock work and recruitment to it. Sexton once wrote of 'the caste system throughout the dockers' fraternity which led to the creation of almost innumerable small clubs and societies all hostile to each other'. The funds of many of these associations were managed so badly—being divided either annually or every few years—that only with difficulty could they meet the limited purpose of sick and burial clubs.[52] None could confidently claim port-wide membership or permanence. A Liverpool and Birkenhead Stevedores, Quay Porters, and Dock Labourers Union and Benefit Society had played a part in resisting a general reduction of wages in 1879–80 by strike action, but it was plentiful only in title by the mid-1880s. Another relic, the Clarence Dock Club, amalgamated with what became the Mersey docks' premier union—the National Union of Dock Labourers, founded in Glasgow in 1889.

The N.U.D.L. was not registered as a union until March 1890. Its structure was skeletal, but Irish strivings gave it sustenance. Both the General Secretary, Edward McHugh, and the president, Richard McGhee, were executive members of Glasgow's branch of the Irish Land League. Neither man actually founded the N.U.D.L. and its business was initially unco-ordinated.[53] McHugh heard of the Liverpool strike after it began, although posters had appeared in his name, suggesting that the union could afford 13*s*. strike pay to members. These were forgeries; but various demands were abroad—specifically, wage increases for grain-workers; and, generally, that union rules should regulate the labour market.

The strike endured for a month.[54] Its importance drew visits from the prominent Socialists, Tom Mann and Cunninghame Graham, although this association perhaps discredited the strikers.[55] McHugh also affected militancy, from necessity of keeping the union afloat. The mayor's offer of arbitration was rejected.[56] As 13,000 blacklegs were imported, McHugh feared that the Liverpool docks might become 'a slaughterhouse'; but Donald Kennedy, of the Employers Labour Association, and other magistrates imposed heavy sentences on intimidators; licensing hours in Bootle were restricted, and soldiers garrisoned the docks.[57]

The recent tramwaymen's agitation had shown how the press might summon public support, but McHugh seemed unconcerned: 'Whether newspapers are with us or not, we have reached that stage now that we know our own business, and are determined to do it.'[58] In fact exhaustion, not business, moved the strikers who settled through the medium of McGhee's friend, Michael Davitt. A Catholic educated by Wesleyans, Davitt was without sectarian quibbles;[59] but his Fenian past marked him. The broad movement of Liverpool Labour receded. The Irish Nationalist particular again overlaid it.

Sexton declared that Davitt's settlement favoured the men with '40 per cent' better conditions.[60] According to the Board of Trade, the strike failed.[61] The test was how many men remained trade unionists and how long agreements were respected. War was waged over the 'button' worn by subscribed unionists. The Employers Labour Association was strong enough to ban union men: it represented thirty substantial shipowners and twenty master stevedores and porters, and employed three-fifths of Liverpool's seamen and dockers. The N.U.D.L.'s Merseyside membership as a result slumped from 15,000 to under 6,000. The core worked in the south-end where companies were either relatively small or such as Alfred Holt's and R. P. Houston's, who honoured agreements reached before the strike. By 1891 most of the old conditions were resumed. The work was still dangerous, the hours were irregular, and the union was balked.

Some men retaliated with 'ca' canny' methods, systematic go-slow and shoddy working. This was potentially demoralizing; but, when Sexton became General Secretary in 1893, the N.U.D.L., if small, seemed 'very virile spiritually'. The strength was in the parts, not in the whole. Sexton later reflected, 'It was bad for me, when I took office, that McGhee and McHugh had granted a very large measure of Home Rule to dockland, with the consequence that every branch and every twig looked after its own affairs . . .'[62] Much depended on an avoidance of controversy although, paradoxically, strike action had been important in winning men's allegiances.[63] In the 1890s, without a major dispute, the Union consolidated itself. In 1902 five Merseyside branches involved 9,500 men, but some 3,000 were behind with subscriptions;[64] and the 1905 strike raised the same claim as 1890, that of port-wide union recognition.

These factors raise questions about motivation. The efflorescence of 'New Unionism' among general workers excited the politically committed.[65] The N.U.D.L. proclaimed that 'for the first time in the history of the labour world, distinctions of nationality and religious creed and political party and colour of skin were set aside, and the common brotherhood of the workers asserted and vindicated . . . the *utter helplessness and uselessness of capital without labour*'.[66]

In fact strikes were initiated usually by the rank and file, not by the precariously placed officials of insecure unions. McHugh, like Havelock Wilson in the seamen's dispute, found that to lead a strike which had begun spontaneously was less dangerous than to oppose one.[67] Evangelism followed this realization. McGhee claimed that in Glasgow unionized dockers worked fifty-four hours a week at 7*d.* normal time and 10*d.* overtime; whereas non-unionized Liverpool dockers worked irregularly, were underpaid and underfed. McGhee did not advise another strike now in Liverpool, but if one arose 'as a last resource', he promised '£200 a week from Glasgow' and 'the whole financial support of the union throughout the country (Applause)'.[68]

This was bravado, for that underemployment persisted, which negated unity and strength. One victim of trade union intimidation, unemployed for five weeks, declared that with a wife and five children he could not buy bread, let alone a 'button'.[69] McGhee and McHugh soon resigned, criticized for their ignorance of the dockers' circumstances. Attacks on officials, as on non-union men, denoted frustrated, unconfident organizations. At this time John Burns addressed the London Dock, Wharf, Riverside and General Labourers' Union, concerning the 'crisis' in their movement: 'members were getting tired of the chronic agitation . . ., the constant petty strikes, the repeated large meetings, and the ever-recurring demonstrations'. They required 'time for building-up and solidifying. They had more pluck, energy and enthusiasm than the old unions, but now they needed more money and more caution.'[70] Industrial peace might be more profitable than industrial war.

Conciliation Boards had existed in previous decades in sections of several trades. In iron-making the high cost of strikes, through heavy capital investment in plant, and the need to accommodate to fluctuating prices, were compelling factors; in the hosiery, lace, and the boot and shoe trades the desire to regulate competitive piece-work and to protect employment in a period of stagnation, influenced the Conciliation movement. In Liverpool the Cotton, Corn, and General Warehouse Porters, Seamen and Firemen, Amalgamated Railway Servants, Carters, Mersey Flatmen and Watermen, all invited Lord Brassey's assistance in establishing Conciliation Boards. A committee resulted, of workmen and employers; but by 1891 only Carters' and Warehouse Porters' included arbitration clauses in their rules. Shipowners and dockers refused to send representatives. The shipowners' preference, a 'free' labour market, and the dockers' ambition, a closed shop, were antithetical. Moreover neither the men's union nor employers' associations could compel their members to observe uniform conditions and wages, and the strike settlement in 1890 was as fragile as the arbitration in 1880, when an attempt to establish a permanent Board of Conciliation had been aborted by mutual mistrust and recrimination.[71] Nevertheless some sought a dialogue. Sexton believed that both sides were 'wasting valuable time in fighting one another when they ought to go to the root of the evil'. He proposed the docks' municipalization, dispensing with contractors; eight-hour shifts leading to the abolition of systematic overtime; and a government department of arbitration.[72] It was a common hope that strikes and lock-outs, like duels, would become superannuated; but politicians preferred voluntary tribunals to Government interference.[73]

Co-ordination was first required between workmen. Sexton later alleged that the L.T.C., 'representing the would-be aristocratic artisans, whilst not actively opposing the dockers' strike, looked askance at it as at something which really ought not to be encouraged'.[74] During the strike Sexton had no official capacity; and his memory was partial. In 1889 the L.T.C. had recognized the N.U.D.L. and invited its membership. However, the dockers had not affiliated, and this made the L.T.C.'s position difficult when strike occurred. Sympathy was expressed and military intervention condemned; but the L.T.C. was estranged by the same posters which distressed McHugh.[75] These disdained the L.T.C.'s right to interfere. However, McHugh, McKeown (of the Birkenhead branch of the N.U.D.L.), and Cunninghame Graham attended the L.T.C. and repudiated the posters. Relations thereafter were less taut—the L.T.C. selected five delegates to assist the dockers' negotiations and in July 1890 the N.U.D.L. affiliated. By 1891 the L.T.C.'s 121 delegates, representing 47 trades and 46,168 members, made it the largest Trades Council outside London. While regretting that friction which had been 'magnified by irresponsible charlatans under the supple "aristocracy of labour" cry', the L.T.C. proclaimed that 'the old and new are being drawn together by an irresistible affinity'.[76]

Despite all this controversy, however, the impact of the Liverpool strikes on the established political parties was slight. Most M.P.s held aloof. Generally this was inconsequential, but some dockers had resented it in O'Connor and Neville. There were reported moves to displace them.[77] As for the Conservatives, Royden did not endear himself and some considered that the seamen's leader, Havelock Wilson, might contest his seat.[78] By contrast, Forwood sympathized with the docker's predicament, but he suspected that the strike had retrograde results in a 'thirty or forty per cent' additional surplus of dock labour.[79] Subsequently Forwood warned that 'dangerous doctrines were being preached by the new school of trade unionists—the Burns, Mann and Tillett type of demagogue', who intended to restrict employment to union men. Non-unionists, he added, would be cast into the workhouse.[80] Forwood's changing mood can be explained by the self-publicity of New Unionists, also by the exigencies of party warfare as Liverpool Conservatives defended their Council majority.

Local scandals: vice, crime, drink, and vested interests

In 1890 Richard Armstrong published *The Deadly Shame of Liverpool.* For six years the minister of Hope Street Unitarians, Armstrong had been politically active since his first incumbency, at Banbridge, Co. Down, where his concern to ensure justice for Catholics gained him the title 'Papish Armstrong' and aroused Orangemen to smash his windows. His admirers thought of him as 'an heroic man, and one of the very few . . . [who] would under circumstances have gone to the stake in support of their principles'.[81] Armstrong was certainly outspoken: *The Deadly Shame of Liverpool* alleged that most citizens 'cared little for the poverty and the squalor, *the knitting together of the wholesale liquor trade, of drunkenness, and of prostitution on an enormous scale, in one vast, compact interest, and the power which that interest has obtained within the governing bodies of Liverpool*'. He pointed an especially accusing finger towards Alderman John Hughes, who dominated the Watch Committee and Licensing Bench. Hughes had extensive financial investments in the drink trade and acted as legal adviser to the principal brewers, Sir A. B. Walker and Robert Cain. The police, Armstrong concluded, were supine, and public men irresponsible.[82]

Armstrong's indictment detonated the parties.[83] Conservatives mobilized against his 'lying pamphlet', to Forwood's dismay since to defend the indefensible was no political position. One choleric Conservative, A. M. Jackson, of St. Paul's ward, criticized the publicity, not the accuracy, of the allegations, asserting that Radicals gloried 'in calling Liverpool an immoral town (cries of "disgraceful")'. He castigated the *Daily Post*'s habit of reporting the particulars of a 'filthy' court case, adding, 'Strong men like themselves might read them without any harm. But he asked how often had they, before they left their homes in the morning, seen fit to hide their daily papers from their children?'[84] A Tory speaking his mind never spoke much for the Tory mind—except that some force remained in the ploy of blackening opponents as civic traitors.

Prostitution was a problem aggravated in a port where single men came to seek work, not early marriages, and found many domestic servants. Then there were the slums—poverty and overcrowding, apart from the clients' preference, caused juvenile prostitution.[85] The workhouse and Lock Hospital annually admitted 1,000 persons with venereal diseases; but those who were treated or recorded by these institutions represented relatively few of the afflicted.[86] In 1889 443 brothels were 'known to the police', a reduction, the Liverpool Head Constable claimed, from 830 in 1871.[87] The law, however, conferred on the police no power to visit. An Englishmen's brothel was his castle, observed the police surgeon, Dr. Lowndes. Of twenty-three persons proceeded against for keeping a brothel in 1884–5, eighteen were discharged.[88] James Larkin, born in Liverpool in 1876, declared that 'some of the most respectable citizens' controlled the brothel industry.[89] The Corporation was the reversioner of several Lime Street brothels, which were rented higher than artisans' dwellings;[90] and the Watch Committee tolerated this until, in 1888, 'ere the doom of Sodom falls upon us', the magistrates appointed a committee of inquiry.[91]

Official statistics were unsound. One Head Constable of Liverpool once said about 'crimes known to the police': 'the figure is one on which to place very little reliance because it is what I call a discretionary statistic; the man who has to prepare that figure can put down pretty much what he likes'. Glasgow recorded 2,631 cases of solicitation; but its Chief Constable denied that Glasgow contained over 1,500 prostitutes, for only fourteen brothels were 'known to the police'.[92] Although reformers would not admit it, the intelligence of Liverpool's police compared favourably. They proceeded against brothels under specific circumstances, where very young girls lived, where robbery or disorder occurred, where a brothel opened in a respectable street, or where neighbours would substantiate a complaint.[93] The known brothels were localized;[94] but, since 2,275 prostitutes were charged with disorderly conduct in 1885, estimates of Liverpool's population of prostitutes began at over 4,000.[95]

Some origins had been indicated in a report of 1853, concerning 1,123 Liverpool prostitutes: 44·2 per cent were born in Ireland, 26·3 per cent in Liverpool, 18·5 per cent elsewhere in England, 4·3 per cent in Scotland, 4·7 per cent in Wales, 1·3 per cent in the Isle of Man, 0·7 per cent abroad.[96] Priests in 1836 had contradicted the assistant overseer's observation of the preponderance of Irish prostitutes in Liverpool; but Dr. Duncan noted then, and Dr. Lowndes fifty years later, that besides being most numerous 'Irish' whores were generally 'the lowest and most degraded class'.[97] Many operated from 'free and easies'—pubs with singing and dancing licences.[98] The Watch Committee possessed the key to action in this question, but one magistrate believed that 'if the masses were polled they would be unanimously in favour of putting down these abodes of vice, because it was, unfortunately, from the ranks of the masses that these unfortunate girls were chiefly recruited. Those who were responsible for leading astray these girls were, as a rule, taken from the ranks of the classes.'[99] Thus politicians belatedly tackled the problem of vice, the dimensions of which had been familiar to many casual observers for decades.[100]

Violent crime also disturbed Liverpool's authorities. Certain districts had suffered from gang warfare in the 1860s; and, in the protection racket of street bookmakers, the Scotland Road gang known as the 'High Rippers' deposed the 'Bootle Bummers' in 1885. In one week the North Dispensary treated 176 cases of wounds or violent fractures. None involved prosecution, and journalists juggled with arithmetic: 9,000 cases of unpunished violence annually in Liverpool's north-end alone. There was sensationalism—the Head Constable accused newspapers of exaggerating the *organization* of violent crime—but many citizens had 'no faith in the protection of the police'.[101]

How were thugs identified? In the 1860s they were recognizable for their flat faces, thick necks, and white trousers up-turned over greasy boots.[102] In 1885 the 'corner-man' sported his 'blue jacket, greasy pants, and a tight cap, with a large muffler'.[103] By these descriptions most workmen were suspect. Evidence that criminality in Liverpool was growing, constant, or diminishing, is unsatisfactory. Violence frequently attained spasmodic peaks. Between May and July 1892 an exceptional number of street fights was recorded; but this year registered an overall decrease in violent crime.[104] Fights in slum courts, involving men, women, and children, were commonplace.[105] Reporting them was a matter of political capital as Liberals framed their indictment of Tory rule.

Their reportage also reflected controversy in the legal world as a result of the policy of leniency and light sentences idealistically pursued by C. H. Hopwood, the Recorder of Liverpool from 1886. Hopwood was the antipole of Mr. Justice Day, a judge whose severity was notorious; but it was Day's capital punishment of the High Rippers' ringleader that destroyed the gang by 1887.[106] For historical usage, however, a stereotype of Liverpool crime would contain the frustration of underemployment and the elemental anger of slum life, with sectarian prejudice superimposed. One example was the homicide of a coal-heaver, Luke Crean, whom a woman dispatched with an axe. Crean and some mates, finding no work on one Monday morning in 1901, went to drink in a pub off Roscommon Street. Later their argument, involving six men and two women, who shouted 'I am a true blue and no surrender' or 'St. Patrick for ever', developed into the fatal fight. A similar case had appeared before the summer assizes in 1878. Again a street fight, involving drunken men and women, led to a docker being beaten to death, this time with a poker. His assassin shouted, 'You bloody papes here's the heart's blood of an Orangeman'.[107]

The failure to control drink, more than whoredom and violence, constituted the principal accusation against the municipal administration. The Duke of Albany, visiting Liverpool , nominated drink 'the only terrible enemy whom England has to fear';[108] and Samuel Smith proclaimed that Liverpool worshipped Beer as Ephesus worshipped Diana.[109] According to the coroner, the only clock many Liverpudlians knew after twenty years of national education was 'the closing hour of the public houses'.[110] Temperance was among the most influential Victorian movements. Its adherents included camp-followers but often zealots. George Isaacs recalled that 'whilst broadminded in matters of religion and politics', his father was 'intolerant almost to bigotry on the drink question';[111] and one Liverpudlian, Alexander Guthrie, who advocated temperance in everything, won the nickname 'Alexander the Less'.[112]

Radicalism was one conclusion of involvement in temperance politics. Benjamin Townson, a pillar of the Town Mission and Y.M.C.A. who died in

1888, had been the first doctor in Liverpool to defy the medical opinion of his day and to treat acute disease without alcohol. Several of his patients, connected with the drink trade, withdrew from his practice when he advocated temperance from public platforms; but Townson was uninfluenced, for he 'had no class feeling. The poor clerk or shopman who was trying humbly to serve his God had as much interest in his eyes, and was esteemed as worthy of his friendship as the rich City merchant who could drive his carriage and pair. . . .'[113] To many the brewers' vested interests symbolized the irresponsibility of unchecked capitalism; indeed by 1905 seventeen of the fifty companies with the largest capital in Britain were concerned with brewing. The pastor of Pembroke Street Baptists, Charles Aked, declared that 'the war is not with individuals, but with a system'. He added that without 'a consecrated endeavour to kill the public house', Labour was condemned to sterility. Liverpool working men were 'soaked in bad Protestantism and worse beer'.[114]

Temperance had had a hold in Liverpool from the beginnings. A Society met there in 1830; and John Finch, an Owenite iron merchant, contributed to Preston Temperance Society, the foundation group of English teetotallers.[115] The Liverpool Society had American origins, but American influences were otherwise detrimental in the profusion of 'long bars' catering for 'perpendicular drinking'.[116] T. H. S. Escott reviewed the results by 1885: 'twenty years ago the habit of drinking during business hours was comparatively unknown at Liverpool; now it is so common as scarcely to attract attention'.[117] 1876, however, was the record year of arrests—20,551—for drunkenness in Liverpool, and this was coincidental with the maximum average per capita beer consumption nationally.[118] Among males the classes were discernible. In 1888 the list was, as usual, headed by labourers (5,630), followed by 'the unfortunate' (1,913), sailors (805), carters (468), and those with no trade (3,955), among whom were several 'gentlemen'.[119] Most were not habitual drunkards: 11,157 were first offenders, 413 second offenders.[120]

No statistics conveyed the extent of dissipation, but many assertions existed; for example, George Sims reckoned that 'more than one-fourth of the daily earnings of the denizens of the slums goes over the bars'.[121] A recent estimate suggests that expenditure on drink as a percentage of total consumer expenditure on goods and services, at current prices, fell from a peak of over 15 per cent in the mid-1870s, to about 12 or 13 per cent in the 1880s and 1890s, and to about 8 or 9 per cent by 1910. Since the proportion would decrease as income increased, these figures underplay the part occupied by drink in working-class budgets; none the less the significant trend was a decline in the amount spent on drink from the late nineteenth century as a range of cheap consumer goods became available, to say nothing of the impact of temperance opinion, education, and alternative leisure opportunities.[122]

The subject might also be approached in reverse, by asking not how much did working people actually spend on drink but how little need working men drink before pitching their families into destitution, and by considering variable criteria of choice and circumstance. *Porcupine* in 1885 offered a silver watch to the workman who described the lowest weekly wage sufficient to maintain a wife and five children. The winner, a Kirkdale docker, supplied a budget for 21*s*. Bread, potatoes, and meat scraps formed its staple; but 3*d.* was allocated for tobacco, 1½*d.* for ale. Other budgets between 24*s.* and 35*s.* were more prodigal on food and predicated a wider society, with school, church, and club subscriptions, and money spent on clothes and newspapers. One included 10½*d* for tobacco and 2*s.* for beer in a budget of 34*s.* because 'life is not worth living for unless you have some pleasure'.[123]

A considerable item was always rent, accounting for about 15 to 20 per cent of income. The winning budget devoted 3*s.* 6*d.* to this; that of 34*s.* spent 5*s.* 6*d.*; but both seem unrealistic sums if seven persons were to be housed without overcrowding. A railway porter, David Brindley, spent 5*s.* to 5*s.* 6*d.* per week at this time on rented accommodation in terraced bye-law housing in Everton and Kirkdale; but there were no children in Brindley's marriage, and he rarely took a glass of beer. The dilemma was accurately posed by one entrant to *Porcupine*'s competition, who sought

> a house with three bedrooms, a parlour, and kitchen. Some people would, perhaps, laugh at a working man having a parlour, but let this be comfortably furnished, and there would be considerably less working men wandering about the streets and frequenting the public houses; but those things were not to be had in Liverpool except you pay 7*s*-6*d* or 8*s.* per week—unless you walk a considerable distance out of town when you will get one for 6*s.*

The connection between accommodation and alcohol was primary. The less a man spent on his home, the more he spent outside his home. Happiness—solvency—lay in a huddle about the hearth. The poor, being public drinkers, dominated the lists of drunkards. Robert Blatchford, the editor of the *Clarion*, enumerated other reasons: '1. The labourer is often in a low state of health. 2. The labourer does not drink with any caution or method. 3. The labourer does not get pure liquor.'[124]

Results, not causes, most concerned the authorities. Liverpool's Medical Officer of Health noted that 'the misery and degradation and destruction of human life consequent upon excessive and uncontrolled indulgence in alcohol are the saddest features which sanitation has here to contend against, and the most hopeless. . . .'[125] Of children born of drunken mothers, 55·2 per cent died under two years old, as against 23·9 per cent born of sober mothers in similar circumstances. Another horrifying record (1883–90) was of 1,132 children suffocated in sleep by drunken parents; but this primarily indicated overcrowding.[126]

The tentacles of drink embraced most aspects of living. Pawnbrokers and moneylenders were a common sight in poor districts. In the early 1920s, when social workers began making investigations of their practices, prior to seeking legislative control, the size of the problem was uncovered for the first time. About 1,380 persons were registered as moneylenders in Liverpool. Some 85 per cent of these were women, who often ran a greengrocery or clothes shop together with their moneylending business; and there was almost no protection against their charging exorbitant interest on tiny advances, and bullying their debtors into buying articles which they did not want or could not afford.[127] Absenteeism from work was also considerable but only scattered references summon its magnitude.[128] The same was true of disorderliness. Scotland Road, with proportionately more pubs than most Liverpool streets, was notorious for its brawls;[129] and at Anfield, where John Sheepshanks ministered before becoming Bishop of Norwich, men drank heavily on pay days but 'no notice was taken until they began to fight in the streets with fenders snatched from their firesides. At that stage the Vicar was sent for to restore order.'[130]

Under-employment, slum housing, disease, and disorder conjoined in the syndrome of drink. Not all Liberals, however, were sympathetic to the vociferous teetotal fringe or to the alternative culture of the temperance world. The former local leader, Robert Holt, once had the misfortune to stay in a temperance hotel which he found a 'rather seedy place'. The clientele were 'ugly and unattractive', and Holt was 'curious to know why teetotallers are so plain looking and such ravenous and coarse feeders'. Holt defied the temperance faction in 1889 by seconding a Conservative motion to honour Sir A. B. Walker with the Freedom of the City: he considered brewing a legitimate trade and felt that Liverpool should acknowledge Walker's munificient gift of the Art Gallery. Likewise, when mayor in 1893, Holt made a determined attempt at public impartiality when, within a fortnight, he attended the Licensed Victuallers Ball and gave the Church of England Temperance Society 'tea (reluctantly) in the Town Hall'.[131]

Nevertheless Holt, and most Liberals, equated the Conservative party and the drink interest. They believed that the public house network contained the key to Tory successes in Liverpool. Ignoring the profounder forces at work, the Liberals proposed changes in the complexion of the magistrates' bench and in their administrative procedures. Although under one-third of Conservative magistrates were councillors and, strictly speaking, licensing was divorced from Council politics, the Liberals complained that the Liverpool and Bootle benches were packed, like the County Bench whose emphatic Unionist complexion was designed by the Lord Lieutenant, Sefton.[132] But when John Hughes had become a Liverpool alderman he had had some Liberal support. When he graduated to the Watch Committee, Liberals divided 8 to 3 in his favour. They now complained that Hughes should not have joined the Licensing Committee. This seven-man body was supposedly elected by all eighty-six magistrates, but only nine Liberals and nine Conservatives bothered to attend. Voting by ballot, they gave Hughes sixteen votes. If distinctions are to be made, they seem less between parties than between the negligent and the actively interested.

On most questions neither party could claim a superior record. Before 1878 public house inspections were undertaken by ordinary constables who made 80,000 visits annually; but, following the Vigilance Committee's campaign, a special force was appointed. It made 250,000 inspections annually, without deriving a corresponding decrease in drunkenness or increased prosecution of publicans. Its superficial surveillance and its independence of normal police accountability, while being exposed to 'the enormous monetary interests' in the trade, convinced the Head Constable that the special force should be disbanded in 1889.[133]

Some Liberals, like Robertson Gladstone, long shared this belief privately;[134] but he and other Liberal magistrates had to their credit the 'free trade' experiment between 1862 and 1866, when they granted licences to most applicants, believing that laws of supply and demand would adjust the number of pubs and relieve the bench from dispensing valuable patronage. Few schemes achieve perfection, but this was a perfect failure, as large brewers expanded their empires of 'tied' houses.[135] The 'free trade' in licences was discontinued; but the Bench's philosophy remained *laissez-faire*. Few checked that conditions of licences were recorded or obeyed: for example, that licensees did not open back doors, or add bars and vaults, or that a beer off-licence did not cover a jug trade. When evidence was brought against a tied pub, the magistrates made the Company change its manager. They did not revoke the house, as when owners and licensee were the same.[136] This insouciance bred Citizens' Associations;[137] but the size of establishments and different standards of policing invalidated correlations between numbers of pubs and convictions for drunkenness. Liverpool had more convictions for drunkenness and less pubs per 1,000 persons than many large towns.[138] The discrepancy made sense only in the context of Liverpool's slum and labour problems.

The purity campaign and party politics

The Liberals pressed the moral issue in municipal elections. Their candidate in February 1890 at a Lime Street by-election, T. D. Laurence, owned a temperance hotel and the *Daily Post* attributed his success—the first Liberal victory in Lime Street for over twenty years—to criticism of the Watch Committee regarding 'public order and morality'. Publicans agreed;[139] but politics should not be ignored. The Conservative Councillor's views on imperial matters were part of the contest; and Laurence was upheld by exceptional Irish effort in a 71 per cent poll.[140]

Naturally, temperance advocates boasted of converts among Irishmen too. In May Pat Byrne's death brought a by-election in which two Nationalists competed.[141] Thomas Kelly, a commission agent, with temperance opinions, carried the official nomination against P. J. Deery, a publican with a brother in the priesthood. The dispute, however, concerned the right of Lynskey's clique to represent the I.N.L.'s authority in municipal matters. Deery's occupation was not determinant.

The temperance campaign persisted into the main municipal elections in November 1890.[142] Before the October Assizes appeared a man who had been served drink while intoxicated, and who had afterwards beaten his wife unconscious. This case, the judge declared, illuminated 'a great many crimes' in Liverpool, and he regretted that he was not trying the publican as well as the wife-beater. He also berated the owner, who 'did not manage the house himself—he was too respectable to do so—but put others in to do his dirty work'.[143] This almost supplied the Liberal party's manifesto. Temperance was its Trojan horse to capture the Town Hall.

The 1890 municipal elections were city-wide. Only St. Peter's returned its member (a Liberal) unopposed. One change, in St. Anne's, was foregone as

Liberals and Nationalists resolved divisions which cost them victory in 1889. The defeated Conservative was a brewer; but this hardly diminished the purely political causes of Grant's victory.[144] The only other gain, in Abercromby, reflected the conservatism of the Liberal candidate, a coal merchant, John Lea. The significant issue here was sabbatarianism; and on this the ward Conservative party was divided.[145]

Where Temperance succeeded in 1890 Liberalism failed to prosper. In a 57 per cent poll North Toxteth returned an Independent, Willink; but he was a renegade Conservative who declared that 'both sides had been willing to sink their differences for one great cause'.[146] The result was actually worrying for Gladstonian Liberals because in 1889 a Nationalist had lost heavily there.

The Toxteths were the focus of temperance propaganda. From 1880 Lord Sefton's agents had operated prohibition in the Windsor Street–Admiral Street area.[147] According to William Crosfield and Samuel Smith, the health of the district was thereby transformed.[148] However, most of the houses were above-average rental and equipped with cellars, and several large and profitable pubs stood on the perimeter of the dry zone. F. E. Smith later observed: 'the thirsty inhabitants of Toxteth are indulged at the expense of their neighbours, while they continue to adorn the perorations of teetotal speeches'.[149] One brewer offered five licences elsewhere in exchange for one there;[150] and, when the Bench licensed some premises on South Hill Road in 1890, 800 householders and every Liberal licensing magistrate protested. The licence belonged to Robert Cain whose legal adviser was Alderman John Hughes.[151] Later, when he applied to enlarge his property, this was granted by Alderman Thomas Hughes (also of Toxteth) using his casting vote.[152]

The defence of these interests in South Toxteth fell to Joseph Ball. He was first elected in 1878 as a fervid Orangeman and municipal reformer. By 1890 both traits had lapsed. The Irish Nationalist leader, Lynskey, called Ball 'an indefinite article, even the Tories being unable to say who or what he was'.[153] In fact self-interest guided his politics. A magistrate, he was absent when the South Hill Road licence came before the bench;[154] but he now proclaimed that 'the voice of the people must be heard' and that 'no one having even an indirect interest in the drink traffic shall be eligible for the licensing bench or Watch Committee'.[155] Doubts about the *Liverpool Citizen*'s verdict that Ball was 'one of the most serviceable tools of the ruling clique' were erased when Ball refurbished the 'No Surrender' platform.[156] His supporters also made play of allegations that his Liberal opponent, Joseph Brunner, employed alien labour.[157] Ball polled 1,939, Brunner 1,845. The Nationalists' canvass was perhaps crucial: Orange Toxteth rejected Home Rule, come temperance or not.

Other Conservative candidates elsewhere proved their soundness in defence; and in West Derby ward Labour representation was again essayed by Matkin. In 1890 the L.T.C. had clarified its ventures by revising Rule 12. Religious topics remained inadmissible but a two-thirds majority of delegates might now permit political discussions where they directly affected working-class interests.[158] Matkin himself was honoured by being president of the T.U.C. which met in Liverpool in 1890. However, the *Daily Post* styled him a 'Liberal candidate'. Matkin denied this—he was 'a Labour and ratepayers' candidate pure and simple'—but a Liberal candidate withdrew from West Derby and Matkin inherited his cause.[159] His performance improved—he polled 2,525 votes against 2,978—but he attributed his defeat both to working men attending football matches and to misrepresentations by temperance propagandists.[160]

A Liberal administration was pending. The Council in November 1890 contained twenty-five Liberals or Nationalists, one Independent, twenty-one Conservatives, and one Liberal Unionist. Sixteen aldermen maintained the Conservatives' over-all control. This might not have been admirable but it was legal. Although in the County Councils aldermen were elected by councillors alone, in borough councils, until the Municipal Corporations Amendment Act, 1910, aldermen were elected by councillors and non-retiring aldermen. The Conservative majority in the Liverpool Council was preserved by this device until 1892, when eight aldermen retired. On the other hand, their Liberal opponents were unusually placed as a 'progressive' party since their majority among the Councillors derived from unreformed ward boundaries rather than the electors' confidence.[161]

The Conservatives also endeavoured to stave off Liberal Council control by adopting some Liberal men and measures, and by exposing them in an unfavourable light. Holt was invited to chair the Watch Committee.[162] When he refused, the Liberal Unionist, H. H. Hornby, stepped forward, and the Conservatives pilloried Holt for shirking municipal work.[163] The municipal administration also attended to the problem of vice when in December 1890 the Bishop, supported by every Anglican clergyman in Liverpool, memorialized the Watch Committee to expel debauchery.[164] Accordingly, the Head Constable was directed to prosecute all brothels known to the police.[165] This was a surrender to the Vigilance Committee, and the subsequent campaign endorsed the view that 'there was nothing so bloodthirsty as philanthropy on the war path'.[166]

The *Daily Post* reckoned that the police eliminated immediately 300 of 342 known brothels. By November 1891 only twelve brothels were reported.[167] The Liberals' puritans concluded that the campaign was absolutely successful; but there had been 810 prosecutions between December 1890 and September 1891. Some Conservatives claimed that the number of brothels had actually increased to 468. Prosecution occurred without considering the circumstances of prostitution. The result was pharisaism. As one prostitute asked, after eviction from brothels, where would they go?[168] Some reopened business elsewhere. Property owners criticized the Watch Committee for having scattered, not suppressed, prostitution.[169]

The prostitutes' parasites were also alarmed. Islington tradesmen and shopkeepers complained of decreasing profits after local brothels were closed.[170] Many prostitutes, now homeless, wandered the streets. Solicitations increased;[171] and the police were undiscriminating in their suspicions of female pedestrians until a jeweller's servant, accused of prostitution, won £35 damages.[172] Others were too discriminating. It illustrated Liverpool's sectarian hypersensitivity when even the reclamation of harlots floundered on denominational differences: some refuges would not receive Catholics with Protestants, since 'the mixture renders due discipline difficult to maintain'.[173] Few sections of Liverpool's establishment could review 1891 with pride. The Head Constable's predictions about the dispersal of vice were fulfilled. Moral reform was impeded.[174]

The electorate was unimpressed. Following a by-election in North Toxteth ward, when Willink rejoined the victorious Conservatives, the *Review* acknowledged that 'despite the side issues of teetotalism, purity, and the rest', politics still governed municipal contests.[175] Aked's charge, that 'Liverpool had been ruled by publicans, prostitutes and Tories',[176] was read for what it was, a partisan utterance.

Party disharmonies

The Conservatives

The Conservatives had other difficulties to attend, besides the purity campaign. Their claim to have improved the sanitary condition of the city was upset when the 1891 census announced Liverpool's depopulation from 552,425 to 517,980.[177] This depressed the death-rates—to 27·8 rather than the estimated 23·6 per 1,000—since the Health Committee had been guilty of a 20 per cent error by following the Registrar-General's reckoning, that the population was still growing, to about 620,000.[178] The region in fact showed a decennial increase of 5·83 per cent but Liverpool had declined by over 6 per cent.[179]

The Conservatives' administrative record thus hung in the balance; and the Council group was demoralized. With Forwood at Westminster the leadership was in commission; but the commissioners did not command. *The Courier* blamed the city's vivisection into wards and constituencies: there was 'no centre of cohesion, nothing but parochial policy in its narrowest and most cramping aspect'.[180] Isaac Morris, an ex-Councillor, developed this theme: 'We have a splendid organization, plenty of willing workers, a good cause, but no recognized leaders.'[181] He indicted the Liberal Unionists for being lackadaisical, but others blamed irresponsible Conservative licensing magistrates (like Morris himself): the party would revive if its leaders exhibited 'moral worth'.[182] The discussion crystallized into criticism of Forwood, the absentee general.[183]

Forwood had not been absolutely withdrawn. November 1890 brought the coincidence of Balfour's Liverpool meeting and O'Shea's divorce. The occasion of Balfour's visit, Oulton told Derby, promised to be 'the most successful political gathering ever held in Liverpool.'[184] Balfour, the Chief Secretary for Ireland, spoke about his Ministry's achievements and intentions;[185] but Forwood, following him, struck the keynotes for Liverpool. Forwood's speech betrayed no understanding of Irish nationalism but it marked the progress of Conservative politics since Irish questions first mattered in Liverpool. The civic patriot remained, but he was adorned with imperial and class embroidery. Forwood appreciated that the Irishmen of Liverpool's professional classes endorsed Balfour's policies to become almost honorary Englishmen, 'citizens of one empire'. He reprobrated 'ignorant' Irishmen, who benefited from the enterprise of the city without feeling loyalty towards it. This group threatened to destroy

English society along with the Union: they were 'a race alien to themselves and hostile to their country'.[186]

The exposure of Parnell in the O'Shea divorce suit added fuel to the Conservative case. Parnell's Lucifer-fall inspired Forwood to take the worst as typical:

> It was only when Mr. Parnell's profligacy in his private life was legally exposed, and then only, after some hesitation, Mr. Gladstone thought his value as a political tool was gone that he must be deposed from office. There is an old saying that when thieves fall out honest men get their due; so it is that day by day, first one and then the other of the Irish parties give us information as to their past transactions that amply justify everything that has been asserted by the most rabid Unionists.[187]

The Irish and the end of Parnell

Parnell's humiliation stunned Liverpool Irishmen. They emerged with a definition of nationalism untarnished by personal considerations. This advertised that Unionism, even sweetened by kindnesses, would not convert Irish souls. When divorce proceedings had been initiated, the Liverpool I.N.L. affirmed Parnell's leadership.[188] The divorce verdict made loyalty more an act of faith;[189] but the *Daily Post* was initially satisfied that Parnell's amour did not affect his leadership.[190] Having a 'horror of "Faction"', this was also T. P. O'Connor's reaction, although the first declarations of those on the fund-raising tour in America merit little significance.[191]

Anti-Parnellite letters soon made their appearance in the press. This roused the president of the Joseph Biggar branch of the I.N.L. in Liverpool, Patrick Kearney, to announce that, 'compared with other nations, the Irish nation happens to have a balance of morality to its credit sufficient to cover the lapses of Mr. Parnell a thousand times over: and, indeed, history will hardly notice these lapses. But it will truly say of our leader that he was the man of his age to achieve the greatest good for his people with the least means at his disposal; that he found Irishmen serfs and left them freemen.'[192] But to invoke history's judgement implied an obituary.

Councillor Kelly might declare that Parnell's withdrawal would be disastrous, and the St. Paul's I.N.L. branch might scorn 'the Pigottest Press'; but others summoned a more faithful talisman—the Manchester Martyrs—and the Central branch, by sixty-one votes to three, from 'high moral principle, and in the best interests of our country', rejected Parnell.[193] The Liverpool I.N.L. splintered.[194] Parnell's manifesto appeared and O'Connor loyally responded; but after Gladstone's rejoinder the *Daily Post* turned, convinced that Parnell's 'political treachery is as great as that . . . proved against him in the Divorce Court'.[195] Personal issues bowed before the consideration of whether an election could be won under Parnell's leadership. Many concluded not.[196] Parnell's 'Caesarism' was broken, the Liberal Unionist, Bencke, gloated;[197] and, following the North Kilkenny by-election, that 'Culloden of the last of the pretenders', the Parnell branch of Liverpool I.N.L. took William O'Brien's name.[198]

Protestant responses

Not every Conservative reacted to these events in the manner of Forwood. Some unusual positions were adopted by those who attended to the recent Orange revolt, the most astonishing thing, to the *Liverpool Citizen*, since Balaam's ass broke into human speech.[199] The local Tory agent, James Thompson, asked, 'Why was Mr. Parnell rejected, and why were all the priests of Ireland against him? He had done his duty, but it was simply because he was a Protestant that he was kicked now he was down.'[200] Thenceforward a myth prospered, of Parnell 'the sturdy Protestant'. In time even the *Protestant Standard* defended Parnell from 'infamous' allegations that he sympathized with crime: 'He loved his country, and he hated the priests, of whom he said they would be hunted out of Ireland like rats when Home Rule was obtained.'[201]

Conservative–Orange relations were not, therefore, fundamentally improved by Parnell's eclipse. McCracken still advised Orangemen not to ally themselves too closely to any party; and another recorded the Orangemen's 'uncompromising antagonism' to 'Ritualists and Atheists' as to 'Parnellites and McCarthyites'. The Liberal press observed that the Unionists' interest in Orangeism was declining;[202] but 1891 stands out as the year when Archibald Salvidge and George Wise, two Protestant Conservatives who later dominated Liverpool, first became generally known. A director of Bent's Brewery, Salvidge, then aged twenty-eight, was the W.M.C.A.'s vice-chairman; and, though he was not an Orangeman, he declared on the Glorious Twelfth in 1891 that his principles were the same, because the W.M.C.A.'s premier rule required a member 'to be a sound Protestant'.[203] By contrast George Wise, then aged thirty-five, had no official position. Bermondsey born, the nephew of John Pounds (the accredited originator of Ragged Schools),[204] Wise was reared on Spurgeon's preaching and Ryle's tracts. Having shaken off a brief spell of scepticism he took a Christian Evidence course and in 1888 moved to Liverpool, where evangelicals like R. H. Lundie, Samuel Smith, and Archdeacons Taylor and Madden, patronized his meetings.[205] As 'the celebrated Anti-Infidel lecturer',[206] Wise delivered some five hundred addresses in Liverpool and Ryle presented to him a set of his works. In 1891 the local merchant and lay-reader, J. A. Bramley-Moore, announced that Wise would stay in Liverpool to work 'against unbelief, whether it be infidelity, rationalism, or popery'.[207] That last word presaged a new departure.

The National Protestant League also promised militancy. The Revd. C. H. Wainwright (of Blackpool) had organized this body in 1890 as an electoral agency of the Church Association.[208] By July 1891 fourteen Lancashire branches existed, forty-four altogether. The first Liverpool branch was formed at the Revd. Richard Hobson's church, St. Nathaniel's, and Wise delivered the inaugural lecture.[209] He invited Methodists, Presbyterians, and Baptists, being 'Protestants to the backbone', to join Evangelical Anglicans in resisting Popery and Ritualism. Bramley-Moore called this Wise's 'first Protestant lecture, as such, in this town'.[210] The *Review* registered a note of caution when it warned Wise against tarnishing his Christian Evidence programme by 'tirades about doctrine and church polity';[211] but Wise's erudition distinguished him from the common orator and the *Protestant Standard* anticipated Wise's 'very brilliant future'.[212]

The municipal administration

As yet the Conservatives' Popish connections were irritating rather than indictable. McCracken and Forwood argued about state-endowed Catholic colleges; but in the 1891 municipal elections, in Abercromby, McCracken engaged the pump and poured drenching abuse upon the Liberal party.[213] It was greatly needed: Abercromby's Councillor, Dr. Marsh, had no 'more qualification for council work than his own carriage horse'.[214] The Water Committee's chairman from November 1890, Marsh's amiability excused his incompetence until February 1891 when John Hughes, seeking sanctuary from the Watch Committee, supplanted him. This go-round of discredited personalities, from one municipal chair to another, epitomized the Conservatives' tergiversations in defence of their majority.

Every Conservative seat was contested in 1891, but Forwood now argued that 'party did not enter into municipal matters one iota'. He adumbrated this case by stating that

> party government in the Council was impossible because the Council was an administrative, and not a legislative body. It had simply to carry out acts of Parliament passed in another place. To make party government in the Council they must have all the work done by one party only, whilst the second party was doing nothing; and he would like to know the voter in Liverpool who would be content to see his municipal representative simply going into the Council-chamber once a month to listen to what his opponents had done (Laughter).[215]

Two different interpretations of local government are suggested by this, although probably only one was meant by Forwood. This was that councillors forgot their party politics and judged issues on their merits; and, in recent controversies—concerning the leaseholds system, an independent audit, and the management of the Vrynwy waterworks—the considerable cross-voting supplied evidence for this view. Another construction, however, was that whether councillors behaved as party politicians or not mattered little because Liverpool was managed by 'a close ring of officials'. This view, of government by experts, naturally appealed to Harcourt Clare, who served Liverpool Corporation as Deputy Town Clerk from 1883, and as Town Clerk from June 1895. It also satisfied the officer mentality of the Fabians, Sidney and Beatrice Webb, to whom Clare boasted upon leaving Liverpool to serve the Lancashire County Council in 1899.

No senior civil servant exists as a mere functionary but Clare's evaluation of his position was that of the 'General Manager' of the Corporation, the arbiter of policies. No committee passed outside his scrutiny. As Deputy Town Clerk he ordered the Corporation's parliamentary business and looked after the management of the debt; and as Town Clerk he claimed to be the architect of the city's expansion of its boundaries in 1895. The actual legal business of Town Clerk Clare delegated. Nothing was more calculated to elicit the Webbs' admiration than the conception of this 'masterful and resourceful' bureaucrat, driven by a 'desire for efficiency'. Clare's contempt for democracy was unabashed. Democracy was ignorant, inefficient, and indecisive; moreover, democracy was potentially corrupt, for Clare feared, as municipal trading was expanded, Corporation employees could wield a dangerous influence electorally. In fact, since Clare was a partisan Conservative, it seems probable that what control he exercised over the Corporation's non-political business was allowed because his conceptions disagreed little from Forwood's. His successor was not to claim so much for the office.[216]

The town hall bureaucracy, however, was not at issue in 1891. The electoral argument concerned the role of political parties in local government. Here Forwood's case was as disingenuous as the Liberal manifesto which blamed the Conservatives for everything, for although councillors enjoyed a lax whip, elections were fought on party grounds. The Town Clerk asserted that the alderman's impartial civic sense outweighed this;[217] but their record invalidated his idealization. All Liverpool aldermen at this time were Conservatives, and in many controversial matters—the selection of committee members; the wages and conditions of Corporation workmen; sabbatarianism—they 'voted in a solid phalanx in support of privilege and against progress and reform'.[218]

Against this the Liverpool Conservatives could argue that their monopoly was not unique. In Leeds, Leicester, and Nottingham, all aldermen were Liberals. Moreover, the Liberals' majority among Liverpool councillors was hardly democratic, since it depended on inequitable ward distribution. An electorate of 741 in Pitt Street and of 24,270 in Everton returned three councillors each. Forwood denounced this in characteristic terms—the Liberals gave 'Home Rulers in some of the wards thirty votes in comparison with the honest man, and the man who owned his house in Everton one vote'.[219]

The 1891 municipal elections and Labour's stultification

In 1891 the Liberals made two gains, predictably in inner wards. A manifesto received the assent of Radicals but others quarrelled with its proposals. The imbalance was plain in the party's victories—J. A. Doughan, in Exchange, criticized the Corporation for building insufficient council houses; George Grierson, in St. Peter's, disputed the principle of municipal housing, moved perhaps by his own property interests.[220]

Labour added to the discolouration of issues. The seamen's leader, Havelock Wilson, exhorted Liverpudlians to reject Toryism;[221] and the L.T.C. joined the Nationalist councillors, Taggart and Kelly, and the Liberal, Grant, in a campaign for a Fair Wages clause in Corporation contracts. The L.T.C. also demanded an eight-hour day (Labour's standard remedy for unemployment at this time),[222] and a tighter policy of immigration. The L.T.C. was quite broadly xenophobic, although the settled population of foreigners in Liverpool was not large. Nevertheless the immigrants' habit of clustering in certain areas and trades made them noticeable and, for the most part, resented. An exception was the group of Germans employed on the heavy manual labour side of the sugar refining industry: their work was so exacting as to be unattractive to most native labourers. The group that particularly provoked hostile reaction was the Jews. Not all of the 4,000 Jews in Liverpool were foreign but it was the entry of East European Jews into tailoring, cabinet-making, and other 'sweated' trades that caused the L.T.C.'s anti-alien campaign at this time. Several delegates were also disappointed that their agitation did not specifically include the Chinese—'bob-tailed people'—whose launderies were said to be 'springing up like mushrooms' throughout Merseyside.[223]

These emotions attracted the L.T.C. to a conservative, if not Tory, view;[224] but its part in politics as a representative body had still to be defined. In 1891 the L.T.C. considered contesting every ward until ambition bowed to finance. The election committee recommended three contests—Everton and West Derby, which were fought in 1890, and Vauxhall, whose Councillor, Dr. Commins, had criticized labour's cause in the dockers' strike. The L.T.C., however, left Commins alone after the I.N.L. threatened to retaliate in West Derby. An Independent, Hugh McAleavey, eventually contested Vauxhall without the L.T.C.'s support. He incorporated labour grievances in his Parnellite candidature, but was crushed after allegations of Orange plots.[225]

The L.T.C. still hesitated on the threshold of politics. Kaney (Pattern-makers) and Reeves advocated independent representation; but William Winterburn (Tailors) believed that 'if they did not consult the political organizations . . . they would get fewer of the friends of labour in the Council'.[226] The L.T.C. compromised by appointing delegates to question all municipal candidates about union requirements in corporation contracts;[227] but the traditional parties were unaccommodating. In West Derby Councillor Cookson dismissed Matkin as 'the catspaw of the Radical party' and proclaimed that while he extended the hand of fellowship to labour, he refused 'to supply every demand of the working classes'.[228] Cookson was worried more by the 'purity' campaign than by Labour. He purchased temperance support by dissociating his ward party from Houlding, the Conservative brewer who defended Everton against the local leader of the Sailors' and Firemen's Union, Nicholson.[229] Both Conservative candidates had Protestant workmen's support. Indeed the W.M.C.A.'s president, Charles Wycherley, felt no embarrassment about Matkin's criticism that the W.M.C.A. was 'a semi-religious body . . . for none but sound Protestants were admitted'; and the Orange Order backed Houlding.[230]

Confusion rent the Labour side. Houlding called the L.T.C. 'a Radical camp in disguise'; but one workman claimed that 'three-fifths of that body (at least) are Tories pure and simple';[231] and another demanded all-party opposition, asserting that 'while Tories sweat the land, Radicals sweat the labour'.[232] The L.T.C.'s president hoped that party politics could be ignored while they advocated 'reforms which will remove abuses from which working men and ratepayers (Tory and Liberal) suffer alike;[233] but the contests never developed in this fashion.

In Everton a Liberal councillor, Benjamin Johnson, campaigned for Nicholson by asking electors to choose between 'the party of extravagence and monopoly, and the party of reform, progress and purity'; and the L.T.C. itself advocated economy in Liberal parlance.[234] When Houlding appealed to a democracy of drinkers—'he had been abused by the teetotal party, but claimed to be a temperate man, and liked a glass of good beer (a voice: "So do I") and did not think England was anything the worse for brewing good beer'—there seemed something in Edward Whitley's claim that his was 'the cause of the working man, against cant, humbug, and hypocrisy'.[235] Nicholson's meetings, addressed by temperance zealots, were interrupted by Tory working men singing the National Anthem.[236] Nicholson was unimpressive even as a trade unionist. Houlding, the president of the Carters' Union, contrasted its smooth, cheap operation with the faction-ridden, and financially mismanaged N.A.S.F.U.[237] Half the electors polled, and Nicholson received 5,588 votes against 7,120.

The various sources of Nicholson's support provoked debate in the L.T.C. Nicholson ingeniously argued that he kept within instructions because Nationalists, teetotallers, and Liberals had allied with him, rather than he with them; but he now threatened to quit the L.T.C. for it had 'landed him in a contest and then deserted him'.[238] The L.T.C.'s instinct, however, was for harmony. Nicholson was appeased and the question of how far politics were admissible in labour affairs remained unsolved.

CHAPTER EIGHT

Protestant–Conservative conflict and the General Election, 1892

> We ask the question, what [Liverpool M.P.] . . . has done anything to advance Protestant truth, or to check Ritualism and Popery . . .; and we warn Protestant working men against the attempt that will be made to swindle them by fair words and smooth speeches, which are as worthless and as hollow as bubbles of soap. Protestant Standard, *5 December 1891*

> The fact was that the Irish question was not genuine; it was simply kept afloat by paid agitators . . . The men to whom Mr. Gladstone proposed to hand over Ireland had been tried—many of them—by a committee of England's wisest judges, and the verdict was that they were associated with criminals of the worst class, and that if they did not commit the crimes themselves they lent their moral countenance and weight to them.
> *R. P. Houston, M.P., reported in* Protestant Standard, *4 June 1892*

The centre of political interest in 1892 was the July General Election. For the Liverpool Conservative party the critical question was its ability to harness Protestant electoral power. Forwood found in the new chairman of the W.M.C.A., Salvidge, a man capable of using the Protestants' popular strength in reinforcement of the party rather than—what some Orangemen wanted—as an independent arm to twist in directions which would be painful for the body of the party. Whatever Forwood's ideal wishes in this—church affairs never elicited his enthusiasm—by 1892 he had little choice. His interest in social reform brought him trouble from men of substance within his own party, and the Liberal Unionists' following was neither so sizeable nor so steadfast as the Conservative party needed if it was to be compensated for a stand against intolerant sectarianism.

The Conservative–Protestant detente in 1892 was to a degree counterfeit. The Liberals' dogged loyalty to Home Rule for Ireland ensured that outstanding Conservative–Protestant differences over Church polity were shelved in order to defend the Union; but the Protestants' patience was not inexhaustible, for they

Notes begin on p. 401

would seek to redeem the credit they had for so long extended to the Conservative party. Forwood's response was twofold. He acknowledged Protestant concerns; he also tightened his grip upon the party organization. A contrast with the Liberals is marked, as we observe their efforts to check an unruly regiment, Labour. Lip-service was paid to Labour sentiment but, in the Liverpool Kirkdale constituency, it was evident that no Liberal organization had the power to corral Labour activity.

Controversy on the School Board and in the party organization

Partisans and patricians were increasingly estranged. After Henry Tate and William Rathbone had been admitted as Freemen of Liverpool in June 1891 a requisition signed by four Liberal councillors and a Nationalist proposed that the Liberal leader, Gladstone, be similarly honoured. The equation of Gladstone and Liberalism was popularly absolute, but iconolatry bred iconoclasm. Although Edward Whitley and Sir William Forwood expressed their confidence in Gladstone's ability to behave himself if he came to Liverpool to receive the Freedom, their Conservative Council colleagues would not permit the motion to proceed at a time when a General Election was pending.[1]

School Board matters also divided Conservatives. Dr. Hakes, who represented the Church Association on the Board, disputed the appointment of a Catholic clerk; but Harry Thomas, the Orangeman, commended it, having made an arrangement to support Catholic nominations to administrative positions as they supported his.[2] Hakes now denounced Thomas's complicity and, although the Orange executive officially readopted Thomas as their candidate, William Gilbert, a tea dealer, entered the School Board elections in November as an independent Orangeman.[3] Neither Gilbert with 1,177 votes, nor Thomas with 15,894, was returned. The beneficiary was Archdeacon Taylor's churchwarden, William Roberts, who appeared on the official Anglican list and, as an Orangeman, attracted dissentients in his 27,938 poll. Altogether 520,000 votes were recorded in these School Board elections, as against 357,000 in 1888. Since each elector might cast fifteen votes, the exact increase of public interest was indeterminable; but the Church's candidates polled 98,851 more votes, the Undenominationalists' 52,987 more, the Catholics' 10,948 more.[4] Evangelicals controlled the Church's list: Roberts took the official ticket from the ritualist Bell Cox, who suffered defeat as an Independent.[5]

These elections turned upon the issue of Industrial Schools in which Catholics accounted for 886 of 1,222 pupils. Canon Honeyburne, of the Church Association, complained that ratepayers' money furnished the Catholic children with images of the Virgin Mary. These children were of 'the lowest and most degraded class from which cornermen and criminals were made. Their parents cared nothing for them so long as they were not only educated, but fed and partly clothed by the public.'[6] But, although Honeyburne exhorted electors to 'curtail the power of Rome', electoral enemies sometimes united on the Board. The Anglican and Catholic majority sought, William Oulton complained, 'to make the efficiency of the lowest voluntary school the level of School Board education'.[7] Industrial Schools lay outside the Cowper–Temple clause of the 1870 Education Act, by which 'non-denominational teaching' was required; but where no denominational education was allowed the Board moved slowly—for example, in evening continuation and higher-grade schools. One educationalist declared regarding secondary education: 'Liverpool has allowed itself to remain, as compared with its rivals, in the state in which its port would have been had little been done to deepen the channels of the Mersey.'[8] Voluntary effort by denominationalists remained the norm. Only 43 of Liverpool's 156 elementary schools were Board Schools.[9]

Some candidates, like Oulton, campaigned simply as Educationalists. Oulton was no secularist. Education, he believed, was inseparable from religious principles. Nevertheless he wanted 'an education contest', not 'a strife of sects'.[10] In 1891 he topped the poll with 41,351 votes and seemed set to succeed Samuel Rathbone as an impartial Chairman. Instead the denominationalists combined to elect Canon Lester, whose 'antagonism to the School Board system' was unconcealed.[11] He remained chairman until the Board's abolition.[12]

Another interest in the 1891 School Board elections had been the performance of two L.T.C. candidates, Potter and Rouse, and two Socialists, Newcomb and Reeves. They campaigned to improve technical education, provide free meals, reduce officials' salaries, abolish 'unnecessary prosecutions', and enforce union conditions on builders; but everything paled in the light of Newcomb's declaration that 'the time given to Bible lessons might be better employed'.[13] They received 8,000 votes combined.

Inspired by their School Board successes, militant Protestants mounted a serious intrusion into politics in 1892. They accused the Conservatives of dishonesty towards their sectarian support, and sensed an opportunity when Whitley died on 14 January—the same day as Cardinal Manning.[14] Whitley vacated both a parliamentary and Council seat. The circumstances resembled those of 1885 when divisional organizations had essayed independence; and the Liberal press again presented Houlding's claims.[15] This was rather obvious politics—if Houlding stood, Liberalism might profit by a defection of Tory teetotallers;[16] and when Houlding declined to emerge, ostensibly because of advancing years, Forwood was suspected of having placed pressure on him, and of having 'driven another nail into the coffin of what is called Democratic Conservatism'.[17] However, Houlding's eminence rested on a deficiency of rivals.[18] Among those refusing to be considered as candidates were Lord Claud Hamilton, Lord Skelmersdale, Councillor Barkeley Smith, and William Taylor (one of the Archdeacon's sons). Everton's Executive Committee eventually balloted only two names—David MacIver, and John Willox who was adopted.[19] The editor of the *Courier* and a director in Cope's tobacco factory,[20] Willox had never previously spoken from a political platform; but an unpolemical disposition suited Forwood's requirement. When he broke silence, he bowed to Everton as Liverpool's 'premier' seat, to Forwood as his mentor, to the Union as the *leitmotiv* of party gospel, and to Protestantism as his electoral salvation.[21] The *Protestant Standard* endorsed his nomination as, by dormancy, did the Liberals.[22]

The succession to Whitley's municipal seat was effected without similar consent, for a substantial Conservative wing—not merely Orangemen—revolted against the 'official clique'.[23] Forwood's nominee, a shipowner, Ralph

Leyland, was not well chosen. He had represented Exchange ward (1888–91) first as a Liberal, then as a Liberal Unionist, finally as a Conservative;[24] and part of Everton Conservative Association reacted by advancing McCracken as an Independent. Although 'a staunch Conservative in Imperial affairs', McCracken announced that municipally he was 'not the nominee of a party, but the representative of the ratepayers of all classes'.[25] McCracken's supporters caricatured the struggle as between Tory democrats and aristocrats, but in fact voiced Liberal criticisms of the Conservative Corporation.[26]

In this contest the Liberal party was officially inert, but Councillors Grant and McMillin openly backed McCracken.[27] This was foolish because if McCracken secured Liberal votes the Orangemen would be encouraged 'to further promulgate their doctrines of bigotry [and] racial hatred' in elections.[28] It also enabled Conservative officials to parade the scarecrow of 'Party Loyalty'. The party agent, James Thompson, declared that McCracken was neither Conservative nor Orange but the 'tool' of 'two of the most contemptible members of the Radical party'. This won several converts, among them Harry Thomas, who initially led McCracken's deputation. Leyland exhibited his siren beauty: 'He was a Conservative, a supporter of the Established Church (cheers), a temperance man (cheers), and a strong Unionist (renewed cheers).'[29] He polled 4,712, McCracken 3,288.[30] Many Liberals abstained—Houlding alone recently polled 7,120 in the same ward—and Leyland was pessimistic about retaining Everton if McCracken and a Liberal candidate stood in November.[31] The *Daily Post* concluded that Forwood needed to 'conciliate the Orangemen instead of calling them traitors and braving their hostility'.[32]

Retreat was not Forwood's favourite course. He asserted the Constitutional Association's right to reject any candidate, even one unanimously adopted by a constituency;[33] and he instructed the Abercromby and Rodney Street branch of the W.M.C.A. to expel McCracken.[34] Supporters of McCracken in other Conservative bodies were also disciplined, but this only uncovered the extent of that support, amid Orange Lodges and Conservative working men.[35] The Abercromby Conservative Club for its part offered to censure McCracken; but when Forwood insisted on expulsion the chairman, Morris Jones, and a prominent member, Colonel Morrison, resigned.[36]

Humbling subordinate Conservative associations Forwood found easier than bridling the Orange Order. Four of its fifteen representatives on the Constitutional's Board of Management were clearly implicated in McCracken's candidature. The Constitutional delivered an animadversion about them, which the Provincial Grand Lodge scorned by electing McCracken to a vacancy in its representation on the Constitutional's Executive.[37] In April 1892 the Management Board confirmed some alterations to its rules. The presidency of the Association and chairmanship of the Management Board were separated. Although the Board might elect the president chairman, this reflected doubts about an over-centralized leadership.

The *Daily Post* speculated that Forwood would be relieved of the chairmanship and left the presidency, *honoris causa*.[38] It was observed that Liverpool Conservatives were 'as minutely sub-divided as the Irish members of Parliament'.[39] They contained at least three camps—the benighted Tories, who disliked the Government's consideration of 'free' education, working-class housing, and old age pensions; the 'official' section, incorporating Forwood and 'comparatively few personal friends and supporters'; and a large amorphous group, including political 'moderates' and the drink interest, who questioned Forwood's reliability. However, a world separated discontent and regicide. With no obvious rival, with a general election imminent and the municipal majority perilous, this was not an appropriate time to change leaders. Moreover the Constitutional would not sacrifice its leader to satisfy a body it despised, the Orangemen.[40]

The Liberal press had misread the crisis. Especially it jumped to the conclusion that Forwood was finished. In fact he remained president and chairman of the Constitutional. Rather more significant than the theoretical division of these offices was the alteration of other rules. One empowered the Constitutional to sever any affiliated body if, according to two-thirds of a quorum of fifty members, it contravened the party's interests; and another allowed two-thirds of a quorum of thirty members to expel any delegate. In May seven Orangemen were expelled, and the Provincial Grand Lodge withdrew its remaining delegates. The Liberal press now remembered that it loathed 'these obscure hysterical pietists' more than it loathed Forwood: 'they are persons of the most ignorant class; they have neither brains, nor money, organization nor influence . . . Orangemen cannot help voting Tory; and the more they are kicked by intelligent Tories, the more staunch their fidelity comes'.[41]

As a General Election approached Forwood spared the rod, professing 'his good opinion' of the Orange Association.[42] In July 1892 the Orangemen decided that whatever their differences with the Constitutional, they must defend the Union.[43] But Protestantism and Unionism were now separate accounts: the preservation of the Union did not answer the question of Ritualism. The Protestant agitation had entered another phase following the Church Association's prosecution of Edward King, the Bishop of Lincoln, for ritualist practices. The judgement in this case in 1890 by the Archbishop of Canterbury, E. W. Benson, permitted lighted candles on the altar, the singing of the Agnus Dei, and the use of the mixed chalice, although this could not be mixed ceremonially. The Archbishop insisted that manual acts of consecration should be visible to a congregation and he forbade the sign of the Cross in the Absolution and final Blessing; but High Churchmen interpreted the verdict over-all as a substantial gain. Conversely the Church Association complained that the Archbishop's Judgement had reversed previous rulings by secular courts and by the Judicial Committee of the Privy Council and 'dangerously trenched upon the Prerogative of Parliament', The Church Association no longer sought to curb Ritualism through the ordinary courts; it sought parliamentary action, through electoral pressure. Thus the Liverpool Protestant Alliance, advocating 'Protestantism before party politics', questioned parliamentary candidates about a variety of Protestant safeguards, in the King's Declaration and Catholic Emancipation Act, about diplomatic relations with Rome and public expenditure on Catholic education as well as about Ritualism.[44]

Prayer mats warmed Tory feet; they might smart like hot coals. So Forwood discovered in West Toxteth when Royden, in poor health, retired. Among several claimants the favourite was T. H. Ismay, Liverpool's premier shipowner—of the White Star Line—and a Liberal Unionist.[45] Ismay had a reputation for charity—on his fiftieth birthday, in 1887, he had donated £20,000 to found a Seamen's Pension Fund[46]—but his political life was stymied by indecision. The *Review* backed Thomas Hughes for his brusque integrity, but in November Hughes withdrew.[47] Soon Lord Charles Beresford was mentioned:[48] the press thought in Forwood's terms, of a title in order to preempt a strong local bidder.

This was Robert Houston, born in Bootle of Renfrewshire stock in 1853. He had little formal education but, having served an apprenticeship as an engineer and shipbuilder, he had established a firm of South American merchants whose vessels provided employment at the south-end.[49] The 1890 dockers' strike had made Houston's popularity: he would not join the Employers' Labour Association, and he paid union wages and gave financial aid to strikers' families. This was a mark not of his humanity but of his business acumen, for he was a shipowner who profited by exploiting the weaknesses of Conference rings in the South American and other trades.[50] Now, in politics, Houston was the Orangemen's nominee[51] in a game in which Protestantism was the knave, and democracy the ace, of trumps. The deck was stacked: Salvidge held both cards.

Until Salvidge's advent, his son wrote, 'the Liverpool democracy had votes, but no leader and no cause'.[52] Houston's candidature quickened Salvidge's establishment and Thomas Hughes's decline as a power in Tory Toxteth. Already they had clashed in 1889, when the chairmanship of a polling district had been vacant. Salvidge, then known as 'a licensed victualler of the superior type' and the leader of the South Toxteth branch of the W.M.C.A., had defeated Hughes's nominee.[53] Subsequently Hughes worked to limit democratic activity in West Toxteth. In 1891 the constituency council was reduced from fifty-six to five members, over whom Hughes presided. Salvidge marshalled the reaction, advancing Houston's candidature through the South Toxteth W.M.C.A. without consulting the smaller North Toxteth branch, reputedly under Hughes's control.[54] Houston was forced on the constituency council in March 1892; and, at the Constitutional Association, Forwood attempted to delay the ratification of his candidature.[55] This proved unacceptable: Salvidge carried Houston's nomination by thirty-six votes to sixteen.[56] Forwood was defeated on his doorstep and rumours of his resignation circulated.[57] Forwood, however, accommodated to defeat by absorbing the victor. In April 1892 Salvidge succeeded the ailing Wycherley as the W.M.C.A.'s chairman.

This new partnership, of Forwood and Salvidge, gave effect to Forwood's essayed change of emphasis, the diminution of Social Reform and exaggeration of Unionism. Salvidge's contribution was to re-unite Unionism with Protestantism. It was symbolized by developments in Everton ward. In the February by-election Salvidge had supported McCracken against Leyland; in the main municipal elections in November Leyland retired and was replaced by Austin Taylor. There was no question of Taylor's credentials, as Conservative—he was a respected shipowner—and as Protestant—he and his family were pillars of the Church Association.

The General Election campaign

One clarion for the 1892 General Election was sounded by the new candidate, Houston: the granting of Home Rule 'would mean civil war in Ireland. (Applause and a voice: "We would help them".)' The Liverpool Orangemen, 'that very important and powerful body' in Houston's opinion, would not 'stand quietly by and see their kinsmen and the loyalists of Ulster massacred and slaughtered'.[58] Church disestablishment in Wales was another election issue since Houston's Liberal opponent, Ellis Griffith, courted both national minorities. He spoke in Welsh, to rally West Toxteth's (claimed) 1,000 Welsh voters;[59] but both Toxteth constituencies rallied to the Tory watchwords, 'Liberty, Union, Now and for Ever, One and Inseparable'.[60] In fact the cue of the Liverpool contests had been taken from the Bootle M.P. Colonel Sandys, when he announced that 'Ruling Ireland was like controlling a savage dog'.[61]

Remembering the Indian Mutiny when he had slept with a revolver to discourage murderous sepoys, Sandys gave his Liverpool audience a recipe for disciplining an inferior animal. Some reported Sandys as having said that the 'Irish were like savage dogs, and ought to be muzzled';[62] but the significant feature was that Sandys was among the most popular of the regional M.P.s.[63] His Protestant backbone was rigid. He had refused all dealings with a Catholic Home Secretary (albeit a member of the Conservative Government), and now he warned against Jesuit influences in the press and 'Romanizing' in Anglican institutions.[64] Sandys believed in 'a great Romish conspiracy to trample down the liberties' of Britain.[65] He was not alone. Forwood dismissed the Liberals' Newcastle programme and affirmed that 'the real issue was Home Rule'.[66] Sandys drew Protestant law-and-order arguments; Forwood added an economic warning, that Home Rule, 'would banish capital from Ireland . . . [and] large bodies of men now finding employment in Ireland [would] compete in the English labour market'.[67]

Blood and thunder speeches about Ireland diverted attention from two other questions—education and temperance. The Archbishop of Canterbury supported Free Education 'warmly';[68] but many clerics echoed the Bishop of Liverpool, Ryle, who declared at the Diocesan annual meeting, 'I always dislike it, and dislike it still'.[69] Forwood had opposed Free Education as a feature of the Radical Programme in 1885, but now he commended it to Conservatives because he feared that a Liberal Government would kill voluntary schools by making education free in Board schools only.[70] This gamesmanship did not satisfy every Conservative. In Liverpool the critics included the Abercromby and West Derby M.P.s, W. F. Lawrence and W. H. Cross, as well as Sir William Forwood, who smarted at this 'death-blow dealt at the Conservatism of the country'. He feared its encouragement of 'democratic and socialistic principles', and he would rather the Conservatives languish in Opposition than surrender 'one tittle of the religious education of the people'.[71] The *Review* replied that 'parroting catechisms and learning by rote Church dogmas have as little to do with the formation of the Christian character as the three R's have to do with the equipment of a Shakespeare';[72] but merry cynicism was a minority taste. The

Courier thought Sir William represented most Conservatives, although it was demonstrable that better school attendance would result from lowered fees.[73]

Temperance provided another challenge. Although Harcourt privately criticized the amount of support which temperance workers gave the Liberal party, he elevated the drink question to national saliency, asserting that 'Temperance is the backbone of [the] Liberal Party *vice* Nonconformity retired'.[74] In his Tory Democracy speeches Forwood had advocated Sunday closing legislation which made allowance for travellers: 'It is a working men's question, and I believe that class in Liverpool desire such a measure.'[75] Now, in 1891, Forwood proposed to blacklist licensees who traded via irregular entrances. Following a conclave of brewers' representatives and Conservative magistrates, the bench compromised by legalizing such sales until 6 p.m. Many pubs continued illicit sales, but 123 back or side entrances were closed entirely.[76] Forwood had given publicans the opportunity to co-operate with 'those who, whilst wishing to promote temperance and good order, are averse to interfere with the legitimate rights of a respectable trade'.

Accordingly Forwood, 'a practical, not a theoretical, temperance reformer', scorned Radical advocates as faddists and pharisees.[77] The Direct Veto League was out-manoeuvred. Forwood championed the working man's ability 'to have a glass of beer on Sundays if he wanted it, as well as himself, who could afford to have a glass of beer in his cellar'.[78] Tory Democracy now had meaning as a commonalty of pleasure uniting rich and poor. It defended physical enjoyment against the 'moral' improvement of a conventionally minded bourgeoisie. Forwood told Lord Salisbury: 'The [Liberal] Unionists worked better with us than ever before, and their help gave us one possibly two seats . . . Vetoists and other faddists pushed their isms very hard but without appreciable effect, and our politically well educated people cannot now be caught by promises or deceived by the lies so freely distributed.'[79]

The Unionist alliance had been less harmonious than Forwood suggested. The Liberal Unionists of Liverpool resented 'never being consulted about anything by the Conservative leaders'. Viscount Wolmer, the Liberal Unionist Whip, had been inclined to dismiss the distemper as 'a want of tact on somebody's part', and he warmed at the prospect of a Liberal Unionist contesting Exchange;[80] but, as their municipal majority declined, the Liverpool Conservatives had not been able to afford to squander largesse. H. H. Hornby remained the sole Liberal Unionist Councillor. There were other reasons for parsimony. To recover the Exchange constituency Conservative registration agents had made 800 objections and 500 claims compared with the Gladstonians' 300 objections; but Forwood criticized the Liberal Unionists' contribution. He exhorted merchants 'to throw off their apathy, to come to the meetings, and to take some interest in the work of the party. He oftentimes got disgusted when he saw men who preferred their own enjoyment, and going home to their ease and comfort, to doing anything for the party and the good of the country.'[81] Many Liberal Unionists, however, were apprehensive about Free Education and the Government's 'apparent want of grip in dealing with [Irish] obstruction'.[82]

Liberal Unionists still frequented the Liverpool Reform Club. At one banquet Lord Derby made the startling announcement that 'the ideas of 1886 are out of date'. He applauded the Gladstonians for desiring prosperity to Ireland, howsoever they differed as to means; and he advised Liberal Unionists 'to act with the Conservative Government as long as they thought right, but let them keep their own separate organizations'.[83] In fact the Liverpool Conservative and Liberal Unionist Associations appointed a joint electoral committee in preparation for the General Election;[84] but, although Forwood adopted more gracious manners,[85] the allies were not confidants.

The Liberal Unionists occupied the fool's paradise. Bencke, vigilant but morbid, recognized this, although his power to effect a remedy was gone. His arch-enemy in the Liberal Unionist Association had been T. D. Hornby, the chairman of the Docks Board who died in 1892. When Sir Thomas Brocklebank relinquished the Secretaryship in 1888, Bencke coveted it; but Hornby passed over Bencke's claims and transferred the post to the Political Committee's responsibility.[86] Without a portfolio Bencke became a confessor to those Liberal Unionists who were 'disheartened by the inaction of our Association'.[87] Only its finances were encouraging, after the treasurer, H. H. Hornby, requested an assistant. Richard Steel filled this position, more accurately both positions: he did all the work.[88] Bencke considered that Steel's importance, like his own, went unrewarded by leaders who snubbed him socially; but Steel's exchequer did not make an army: 'We are a body of Colonels wanting privates and not only is there no recruiting but many a captain and lieutenant deserts to the enemy if for no other reasons than because our own party "shows no fight" and men become sick to death of doing nothing.'[89] The officers' inertia was epitomized by the Brocklebanks: Sir Thomas, the vice-President, was aged seventy-eight; Mr. Thomas was absorbed in business; and Harold was a sportsman. Death had removed John Patterson, Richard Lowndes, and Enoch Harvey; and A. H. Brown M.P. had left Liverpool. Neither Derby nor Sefton wanted Bencke's services—his immodesty was intolerable—but activity had been replaced by sterility.[90]

To contest Exchange constituency the Liberal Unionist Association selected T. H. Ismay, but when a deputation met him he surprised it by declining to stand.[91] No-one had troubled to divine Ismay's purpose before the party was committed and Conservatives smarted at their allies' ineptitude. Later Forwood brutally summarized Ismay's claim to honours in a letter to Lord Salisbury: 'Nobody would grudge him a Peerage, but nobody would care whether he had one or not.'[92]

It was difficult to find another candidate. Oulton and Sir William Forwood were mentioned, but it was June 1892 before the Unionists adopted J. C. Bigham. Although by now the northern circuit's leading advocate, Bigham was an uninspiring choice politically, being remembered as East Toxteth's Liberal candidate in 1885. In fact neither party nor domestic politics excited Bigham, who sought entry to Parliament for legal preferment.[93] He promised to attend to the interests of West African traders; but their want of confidence was shown in approaches to Alfred Jones, of Elder Dempster's, to encourage him as an Independent.[94] Irish demonstrators also gave Bigham a rough time;[95] and, if municipal results were pertinent, his candidature was hopeless—four wards returned Liberals or Nationalists; and Lime Street was poised. Bigham's hopes rested on the sitting M.P.'s past unpopularity, for Neville, like most Parliamentary lawyers, would not impeach the Attorney-General for his behaviour in the episode of the Pigott forgeries.[96] The *Review* had then found 'the pusillanimous and soulless condition of Liverpool Liberalism' personified by Neville.[97] By 1891, however, Neville had adopted more advanced positions, lending his advocacy to the L.T.C.'s agitation against sweating.[98] Without the drama of Goschen's by-election Neville dropped 496 votes but his majority rose to 66. The Orangemen blamed Bigham's poor performance upon jealous Conservative officials: the chairman of constituencies where plural voters resided had not encouraged their polling in Exchange.[99]

Five divisions were contested with some seriousness and three (the Toxteths and West Derby) as diversions. A Catholic tenant farmer, James Middlehurst, also contested Ormskirk to 'waste Mr. Forwood's time': wirepullers at Liverpool Reform Club stood his expenses.[100] The hopeful predicted Liberal victories in Exchange, Walton, Abercromby, and Kirkdale; but the extra voters would be difficult to find, for the electoral register, as in 1886, was 11½ months old. The Liberal machine gave no cause for optimism. Robert Holt, touring the Committee rooms during the elections, 'had little hesitation as to how the contests were going. Our people seemed very limp. The only Committee Rooms where earnest work was going on were the Irish districts.'[101]

The outer divisions were unattainable. In West Derby, in August 1888, W. H. Cross had succeeded Lord Claud Hamilton without contest.[102] Orange malcontents worried the Conservative Association there;[103] but no Liberal champion had been able to take advantage of it, since the fractiousness at the Liberals' Edge Hill and Low Hill clubs was reportedly even more bitter.[104] Holt supported them financially, but declined their nomination in 1892. Accordingly Councillor Frederick Smith, a solicitor who made a fortune dabbling in shares (including those of Bent's Brewery), laboured for 2,925 votes and defeat by 1,182.[105]

Everton and Walton seemed also invulnerable, although in the former Orange dissidents were held responsible for a slump of 581 votes in the Conservative poll. P. W. Atkin, a lawyer, Birkenhead born, improved the last Liberal total by 102 votes, with a programme which included a galaxy of promises for Labour;[106] but 1,789 votes separated the parties. Initially, in Walton, the Liberals' hopes were small: the by-election there in January 1888, after J. G. Gibson had accepted an Irish judgeship, had been dispiriting. Forwood nominated another lawyer, Miles Mattinson, who had been a Churchillite in the National Union controversy;[107] conversely the L.E.A. considered their secretary, T. R. Threlfall, their president, John Wilson, and the North Wales Quarrymen's leader, W. J. Parry.[108] Parry visited Liverpool, courting the Liberal executive and Walton Welshmen; but the L.E.A. and Liberal Association never reached agreement and Mattinson was unopposed.[109]

Both Forwood and Mattinson had boasted of this demonstration of the working men's confidence in Unionism and Tory Democracy;[110] but there were 1,579 new electors by 1892 and Mattinson had been replaced. His successor, James Henry Stock, was a barrister who acted the squire after an Oxford education and the inheritance of his father's fortune, made in the cotton market.

He also had Irish Conservative connections through his wife, a Kavanagh, whose father had been Lord-Lieutenant and M.P. for Co. Carlow. Stock cultivated popular feelings against alien immigration; otherwise he defended the Church and Union, Peace, Progress, and Prosperity.[111] The first Liberal candidate was more impressive. Thomas Heller was secretary of the National Union of Teachers, but failing health necessitated his withdrawal.[112] He was replaced in March 1892 by Dr. B. W. Richardson, F.R.S., a temperance controversialist and sanitary reformer, the author of proverbs like 'National health is national wealth'.[113] Although a sprightly sixty-four, Richardson was old to begin a political career, and Stock improved the Conservative majority.[114]

The challenge in Abercromby was less foregone. W. B. Bowring, a merchant-shipowner, Unitarian, and president of the United Kingdom Alliance, was a power in Liverpool Liberalism, although his humourlessness and caution were unlovable, even to his family.[115] Facing a majority of 739, his prospects from municipal results were promising—the six wards returned fourteen Liberals, three Conservatives, and one Liberal Unionist. Bowring endorsed the Newcastle programme and added, with rare passion, that his election would avenge the city's snub to Gladstone over the Freedom. Lawrence's supporters nevertheless polled more rigidly than in 1886. The majority against Bowring—'unexpectedly heavy', according to Robert Holt—made the point starkly, of the Unionists' recuperation by fighting Home Rule howsoever other trends exposed their debilities.[116]

This verdict was confirmed in Kirkdale, as local trade unions manifested a political awareness.[117] Edward McHugh, T. R. Threlfall, and William Matkin had been considered for contests in Kirkdale and West Derby.[118] In September 1891 the L.T.C. nominated Threlfall alone, although Reeves claimed that the Liberal Federal Council had adopted Threlfall six months before, 'to prevent a more thorough labour candidate being brought out' and his posters advertized a Liberal and Labour candidate.[119]

The L.E.A.'s secretary, Threlfall had previously fought Sheffield (Hallam), and in 1892 Walton, Deptford, Woolwich, and a Birmingham constituency considered his qualities; but he chose Kirkdale after an invitation from 1,200 electors.[120] The L.E.A. aimed to return *bona fide* workmen M.P.s, who would form a Labour pressure group within the Liberal party. This was not incongruous, because many workmen shared Liberal attitudes of self-improvement, temperance, and moral reform. In fact the eccentric seemed those like Keir Hardie who stood as independent Labour candidates while holding many Liberal aspirations. Threlfall questioned the efficacy of independent representation after the traditional parties had begun to take up working-class questions. A class integrity existed in the trade unions: Threlfall resisted its dilution in alliance with middle-class Socialist theorists.[121] But, until manhood suffrage and payment of M.P.s obtained, an independent Labour party was folly because its candidates would impede 'the only party which is likely to pass such laws', i.e. the Liberal party.[122]

Porcupine summarized Threlfall's candidature differently, as a test of the electors' deference. 'Men in silk hats', it alleged, won more working men's votes than men 'in corduroy breeches'.[123] The contest never achieved this neatness.

Any opponent of Conservatism in Kirkdale had an uphill struggle. The Liberal organization was defeatist.[124] Threlfall embarked upon a painstaking canvass, emphasizing that Home Rule was 'pre-eminently a Labour Question. A contented Ireland would be peopled by three times its present population. This would create for this country a vastly improved market, would prevent the constant migration of workers into our large towns, and would make both countries stronger and more prosperous.'[125] Kirkdale had been schooled in another interpretation. Gladstone's Home Rule fixation involved the postponement of labour questions, Baden-Powell declared, whereas the Unionists' 'Rule of Law and Order' made Ireland 'more prosperous than she has been for many a long year, and thus of increasing commercial value to Great Britain'.[126] There were other aspects. Matkin, speaking for Threlfall, discountenanced attempts 'to stir up religious bigotry';[127] but this closed the stable-door after the horse had bolted. McCracken and other Orangemen, despite differences with the Constitutional, disputed Threlfall's pretension as a working men's candidate;[128] and while he stumbled over the L.T.C.'s set questions,[129] Baden-Powell in his address tempted the labour-minded elector by professing to favour 'such domestic reforms of the Poor Law, including the substitution of Age Pensions for the Workhouse—the important matter of the Registration of Electors—and of sound Temperance Legislation'.[130] He added to his 1885 poll 449 votes and Threlfall improved Samuelson's and Redmond's polls by 27; but the total electorate had increased meanwhile by some 1,200. It was argued from this that many Liberals had either abstained or opposed Threlfall. One Kirkdale workman called these Liberals 'a lasting disgrace'; and Matkin said as much to the L.E.A.[131] Notwithstanding his title of 'Gladstonian and Labour', Threlfall ended more Labour than Liberal.

A concern for labour matters also occupied factions in Scotland Division. The Unionists opened rooms in Virgil Street, providing concerts, lectures, and literature 'of the true patriotic stamp'.[132] More unusual, Luke Bagnall, an Orange member of the W.M.C.A., was said to have confabulated with Parnellite working men in the constituency.[133] The Nationalists' fissure had had an effect of bringing into notice local labour issues, in contrast to the Westminster-centred strategy of the I.N.L.;[134] but T. P. O'Connor replied to this mood by renewing his radical youth, advocating manhood suffrage and payment of M.P.s.[135] His opponent, Vesey Fitzgerald, advertized Tory radicalism but principally relied on the register which was 1,000 down since 1886.[136] O'Connor, however, won a majority of 1,190.

Taking stock of Forwood and the Orange revolt

Amid national defeat the Liverpool Conservatives had held seven seats. In some their superiority increased. Partly the success was organizational: their agency, the largest in the country, had conducted a house-to-house survey since 1886.[137] Then there was Forwood's captaincy. He now had national distinction. He had served six years as the Admiralty's spokesman in the Commons and, more unusual, he was the first serving town councillor to become a Privy Councillor. His party's plaudits, none the less, were reserved. Forwood, the city boss, was a 'hustler of the first order'. He had 'a rare driving power as an administrator and reformer, but not the knack of making himself popular'. As a minister, he confronted the Navy Controller, Admiral Graham, who was 'an excellent official, but he early felt the burden of his office, and he did not like Forwood'.[138] Few others liked him. The Chancellor of the Exchequer, Goschen, had not wanted to take on Forwood as Financial Secretary to the Treasury; and Balfour, perhaps symbolically, misspelt his name, 'Forward'.[139] Forwood was a misfit at Westminster, steeped in municipal business so long that he once addressed the Speaker as 'Mr Mayor'.[140] He personified Liverpool politics which, as Home Rule was pressed into another Bill by the incoming Liberal Government, developed more crudely in its translation of national affairs.

The General Election in Liverpool ended as it began, on notes of Orange dissension. The Liverpool lodges celebrated the Glorious Twelfth in 1892 at Lathom Park, but few of the Orangemen visited Ormskirk (which polled after Liverpool) to rally Forwood's supporters.[141] The Orangemen were not so shy when they returned to Liverpool, and many citizens were appalled by the injuries to persons and damage to property that were itemized in accounts of the rioting.[142] Not every Conservative journal joined in this condemnation. *The Tory*, for one, apparently still viewed the Orange card as a trump: it made light of the disturbances and exhorted Orangemen to make the Twelfth more 'glorious' by holding their main celebration in the city rather than outside.[143]

Subsequently changes occurred in Orange officialdom. Harry Thomas, considered a 'politician' after his desertion of McCracken in the Everton ward by-election, joined the Orange Grand Council on the strength of votes of representatives from other provinces. Only one Liverpool delegate supported him;[144] but McCracken in pique resigned all his positions in the Order, including the Deputy Grand Mastership of Liverpool Province. He would not associate with a body which included Thomas.[145] The political revolt connected with McCracken was now checked; but it hardly affected Protestant aggression on the streets. More significant than McCracken's eclipse was the *Review*'s announcement in September that sectarian fights, resulting in injuries to a hundred people, had been ignored by daily newspapers.[146] The July eruption was not exceptional: sectarian violence was so familiar that pens tired of describing it.

CHAPTER NINE

The Liberal Corporation, 1892–5

> There are . . . a few exceptionally able men amongst the . . . [Liberal] party. But it must be confessed they have not proved themselves a match for their Conservative rivals. They have taken a second place, not from a lack of capacity but because they have not worked as hard. They have not had the knowledge the Conservatives have possessed; and in municipal matters knowledge is power.
>
> Socialists must work hard to make municipal dealings with the unemployed avenues to the higher life, not grudging utilization of pauper labour.[1]

The years 1892–5 saw a Liberal municipal administration in Liverpool. This drove the Conservative leadership back upon its denominational support, and at the same time proved a test of Liberal progress in municipal policy and in their relations with Labour. On either count the Liberals failed. Protestant Tory Democracy was a more resilient force; and the first rays of a Labour alternative began to show.

Liberals, Labour, and Irish Nationalists

In September 1892 *The Tory* doubted whether England contained 'a filthier city or a filthier and squalid people . . . than Liverpool';[2] but Forwood, before he left on a journey, part business, part holiday, to America, took care of his political scavenging.[3] The Liberals, he declared, were winning municipal elections by trickery.[4] In the five largest wards 55,000 electors returned fifteen councillors; in the remaining eleven wards 17,000 electors returned thirty-three councillors.[5] In 1891 the Liberals and Nationalists killed a petition to redistribute the wards, asserting that this must await reform of the aldermanic system; but Forwood projected the Conservatives as guardians of democracy, the Liberals as defenders of privilege. Inequalities were widening annually—from 1870 the eleven small wards had decreased in population almost 20 per cent; the other five increased

Notes begin on p. 406

almost 100 per cent. Suburban expansion was widespread: this was 'a great national and imperial question, and not a mere local question'.[6]

Retrospectively, however, the most important local development in 1892 was the foundation of an Independent Labour Party and Fabian Society. The London Fabians had sought to educate Lancashire workmen in alternatives to orthodox Liberalism and revolutionary Socialism; but the Liverpool branch of the Fabian Society organized its own lectures and tracts, and the national secretary, Pease, considered its members 'I.L.P. in personnel and policy, and Fabian only in name'.[7] John Edwards presided over both Fabian and I.L.P. clubs in Liverpool; Reeves was the Fabians' vice-president and the I.L.P's chairman; and Sexton, on the Fabians' executive, was among the first hundred in the country to join the I.L.P.[8] One recent historian of the Fabians states that the Liverpool body numbered seventy or eighty before 1904.[9] In fact 110 members existed in 1893, with thirty satellites in Birkenhead.[10] Though tiny, they constituted a nucleus of activists whose goal was neither permeation nor industrial strife, but independent political representation for labour. They were temperamentally not ideologues. As Keir Hardie observed of the I.L.P. and New Unionism, these things would have emerged had Marx and the rest never lived: 'Increase of political power made this inevitable.'[12]

In July 1892 the Liverpool Fabians considered contesting four wards previously ignored by Labour—St. Anne's, St. Paul's, Great George Street, and Pitt Street—until the local branch of the L.E.A. criticized independence carried to 'a suicidal pitch of unreasonableness', and practically directed workmen to vote Liberal.[13] The Fabians halved their provocation: the Sailor's and Fireman's official, Connorty, abandoned his canvass of St. Anne's after he judged the Liberal–Nationalist candidate impregnable; and Matkin abandoned Pitt Street when Catholics anathematized his views on education. For St. Paul's ward South Toxteth was substituted. Several L.T.C. delegates participated in these debates but, although the L.T.C. ratified the candidatures of its president, Kaney (Fabian), and vice-president, Rouse (I.L.P.), there were doubts about challenging, for the first time in Liverpool, both major parties.[14]

In Great George Street (985 electorate) Rouse, a joiner, confronted a Liberal majority and confusion of credentials, since the Conservative candidate, James Lowry, was an ex-president of the L.T.C. Lowry's Tory Democratic programme proposed more public baths, cheaper water, higher wages for corporation workers, and a union-rates clause in municipal contracts. He also approved Joseph Chamberlain's 'Labour Programme', particularly his advocacy of pensions and immigration controls.[15] The L.T.C. expressed similar concerns: the meeting which endorsed Rouse's candidature denounced competition from pauper aliens.[16] Lowry also advocated temperance and an equal party division of aldermanships. Rouse had little to interest labour votes which Lowry did not promote, except independent representation. Even this was obscured—Nationalists believed that a Labour candidate who fought a Home-Ruler must be crypto-Conservative.[17] The Liberal polled 481, Lowry 248, Rouse 20.

The South Toxteth contest reproduced these features. *Porcupine* alleged that the L.T.C. was privy to a Conservative conspiracy and that Kaney belonged to the W.M.C.A.[18] This was denied, but the *Review*, two days before polling, insisted upon Kaney's falsity.[19] His advocacy of better health administration, evening Council debates, and municipalized gas, found 154 supporters.[20] The Conservative Councillor polled 1,923, a Liberal 1,624. Irish equivocation, and ultimate hostility, caused Labour's rout. Kaney advocated Home Rule and amnesties for political prisoners but, at the local I.N.L. branch, a resolution to support Kaney was rejected for another which, while sympathizing with Labour's cause, declared that their country had first call.[21]

The Liverpool Irish followed Lynskey's advice, to 'remember they were Irishmen first and Liverpudlians after'—a statement which, several Conservatives claimed, illustrated the Nationalists' improper attitude to municipal affairs.[22] Labour's image invited burlesque. Lynskey said about George Crane's Conservative address in Scotland which exhorted men of all beliefs to promote civic improvements: 'it might be inferred that he was a Labour candidate, and not a politician at all (derisive laughter)'.[23] Nationalists had reacted to recent sectarian strife by distrusting gestures of communion.[24]

The first Liberal administration for fifty years

Twelve of the sixteen wards experienced contests in the main municipal elections of November 1892. Castle Street (Liberal Unionist), Pitt Street, Rodney Street (Liberal), and Vauxhall (Nationalist) councillors were unopposed. Fog discouraged high polls, but Abercromby and Lime Street went Liberal. In several wards the Conservatives presented a palpably ragged electoral army. In St. Anne's there were Orange abstentions;[25] and Rodney Street Conservatives endorsed the Liberal councillor, Archibald Williamson, who wanted civic service, not party time-service, to qualify aldermen. These anti-Forwood Conservatives believed that 'there has been too much politics introduced in the municipal chamber to the prejudice of the public interest';[26] and the *Daily Post* designated the elections 'a great victory for morals, as well as a great Liberal victory'.[27]

The party victory was more apparent. The Liberal/Nationalist group now had an over-all Council majority, which it immediately exploited by dispossessing the Conservatives' eight retiring aldermen. Six Liberals and two Nationalists were elevated instead. It was just as well that their majority was thus reinforced, for the aldermanic creations necessitated by-elections, in which Liberal reverses occurred in St. Paul's and Rodney Street, where Conservatives recovered their partisanship. In the other four by-elections Nationalists or Liberals held but they were embarrassed by *Porcupine*'s allegation of a 'breach of faith to the Labour Party'. Before the main municipal elections several Liberals professed to welcome Labour representation, but the results had apparently justified those who believed that Labour was too paltry to humour. Pitt Street's Liberal Association now rejected Matkin's candidature and St. Peter's rejected Newcomb's, although the Liberal Federal Council and party leader pressed for a gesture.[28] Fighting independently, the Labourites polled under ninety votes.

The new Corporation assumed shape as Liberals appropriated the mayoralty and chairmanships of key committees. Five Nationalists became deputy-chairmen (the first time Nationalists held office on any Committee); but several chairmanships remained unchanged—Hornby retained the Watch Committee's hot seat; Sir William Forwood led the Library, Museum, and Arts Committee;[29] and Barkeley Smith still governed the Health Committee, despite Taggart's protests that Smith had led 'the worst department of a rotten and fraudulent Corporation'.[30] Smith's reappointment signified an indifference to improvements when these confronted the Liberal priority of cheap government.

The Conservative reaction

Arthur Forwood would not lend his reputation to a Liberal administration. In January 1893 he resigned from the Finance Committee, preferring 'the outs watch the ins' rather than a 'happy family principle' of government.[31] Financial questions provoked acrimonious debate. Bowring, the Finance Committee's new chairman, expected £29,000 deficit in the city fund but £45,000 surpluses from renewals and exchequer contributions. He imitated Forwood's previous practice by transferring £12,000 to the city fund, treating the leaseholds fines as current income, despite the fact that in the elections Liberals had stigmatized this as 'mismanagement'. They had also promised greater efficiency by separating estate from finance management; but this was not implemented and Forwood sneered that 'Liberalism represented the spirit of envy, the ideals of hypocrisy, and the passion for lies'.[32]

Several Liberals had also whispered about jobbery. W. H. Watts in particular had accused the Insanitary Property Committee (under Forwood) of excessive compensation of slum-landlords, among them the Conservative alderman, Hugh Nicholson. Unfortunately Watts was 'a little bit confused in his figures' and inaccurate about circumstances.[33] In a libel action Forwood won £300 damages, which he donated to the Constitutional Association.[34] The Conservatives' competence was vindicated by rebutting charges of corruption. Watts' general complaint, that 'the state of confusion is enough to deter the strongest and most heroic man from undertaking the task of governing the city',[35] was emasculated.

The Liberals' attitude on ward redistribution was also impaired when they created aldermen entirely from their supporters. Even Liberal newspapers condemned this as 'immoral and unworthy';[36] but when redistribution proposals were again raised in January 1893 only one Liberal, Bowring, was present in the Council chamber. He snapped infelicitously that the Liberal party would not 'sign a petition which they did not believe would be of advantage to the city or to themselves'.[37] Moreover, when Forwood lodged a petition from ratepayers in the under-represented districts and Parliament refused to enact by private member's measure what belonged to a public bill, the suggestion that the Liberal Government was an accomplice in the Liverpool manoeuvres was damaging.[38]

Forwood was unrelenting. He exonerated his administration; he impaled Liberals on the ward question; and what was lacking in argument the second Home Rule Bill compensated in emotion. A parliamentary by-election in West Derby early in 1893, following W. H. Cross's death, illustrated this.

Several Liverpudlians were potential candidates, including the former mayor, Adam; but the last general election had unseated C. T. Ritchie (President of the Local Government Board), Walter Long (Ritchie's Parliamentary Secretary), and Viscount Cranborne, whom the Central Office reportedly favoured.[39] In fact, soon after the 1892 election, the Conservative whip had tried to persuade Baden-Powell to vacate his Kirkdale seat in Ritchie's favour, but Baden-Powell had wanted a firm promise of a government position.[40] Ritchie was no more successful now in West Derby, when a poll of the Divisional Council gave Long thirteen votes, Ritchie eleven, Adam ten, Cranborne one.[41]

Long himself was surprised by his adoption, but his biographer implies that Long was Forwood's preference by citing 'a characteristic telegram', reading 'Excellent Selection; able, diligent, influential'.[42] The telegram might have been characteristic, for it was disingenuous. Forwood had been abroad. He was not hostile to Long but wanted Cranborne.[43] West Derby, Forwood told Cranborne's father, Lord Salisbury, was a

> working class division where men of status are few and far between. It was to assist districts so placed, in their selection of candidates, that our central association was formed. Under its rule the Chairman and Honorary Secretary are ex officio members of the Divisional executives, and as such have much influence. I was absent and thus practically the Divisional Council were left to their own devices. One of the members is a Wiltshire man and he ran Long rather vigorously. I believe someone mentioned your son's name but quite casually and without authority, when another man said he was an advanced Ritualist. There was no-one who could reply that he sat in the same Church as Cross or in any way a word.[44]

Long was a leader of Tory squires. In part he never matured: to bat in a Harrovian cricket victory over Eton was absolute happiness. He was no luminary; but he had some political shrewdness. This made him 'a clever man for stupid people', a 'master mediocrity'. He recognized that few in West Derby wanted him because he was Walter Long. Others ran the place: they wanted any well-to-do and sympathetic member.[45] The Orangemen were more explicit, arguing that they must 'stand steadfast to the cause of Imperial unity and Protestant principles' and resist 'the tendency of Gladstonian legislation . . . to hand over the government of Ireland to the Romish priests'.[46] Cookson, the constituency chairman, was an Orangeman; and Long was accommodating. He designated Home Rule the 'one question paramount'; he lauded religious education, and he reprehended disestablishment. Otherwise he was a 'progressive Conservative' who would apply necessary remedies, without raising unrealizable hopes.[47]

The Liberals were divided. The Federal Council's reluctance to promote a contest provoked secessionist language from the West Derby constituency council.[48] Temperance questions provided their opportunity. The chairman of Bath Brewery, Long was an author of compensation clauses in the Local Government Bill.[49] He opposed Sunday closing and local option, and the Church of England Temperance Society and Conservative Temperance Association criticized his candidature, although he belonged to the former organization.[50] The Liberals, therefore, nominated Daniel Shilton Collin, a tea-broker and agent for Pegrams.[51] His parents and wife were prominent in the temperance world. Since teetotallism was integral to Collin's upbringing, business, and marriage, his opinions about alcohol were naturally vehement. The pulpit of Pembroke Street Baptists was annexed for the cause, indeed so abused by Collin that Forwood accused him of blasphemy.[52] Collin seemed a crank. In the 1888 School Board elections he had polled one vote above the Socialist, Newcomb; and in the 1892 General Election he had contested Birmingham East against a Liberal brewer. Now, two days before polling, the National Conservative Temperance Union supported Long, reckoning that local option was inoperable.

Temperance was only a stalking-horse in a party war. Collin's programme, which Forwood called 'Pegram's Progress', included Home Rule, disestablishment, law reforms, industrial protection, shorter working hours, and payment of M.P.s and returning officers' expenses. Long discountenanced hours legislation and salaried representatives but, regarding unemployment, he proposed the 'emigration of English workmen and the prohibition of alien immigration'. Fabians were advised to support Collin, who concluded that his 'objection to Mr. Long was not that he was a brewer, but . . . that he was a reactionary politician, and a representative of the very worst type of Toryism'.[53] Long won 3,632 votes against 2,275, increasing the last majority in a lower poll. The posters summarized the campaign, especially the W.M.C.A.'s proclamation which condemned 'those who were by false cries trying to induce the people to play into the hands of the Separatists'.[54]

Emphatically Liverpool echoed Salisbury's admission that he had 'not the slightest wish to satisfy the national aspirations of Ireland'.[55] During the Home Rule debates in 1893 Forwood warned Parliament not to treat talk of civil war as 'theatrical'. Shipbuilding and insurance companies had curtailed their Irish business, and banks had advised customers to withhold credit from Ireland until the Bill's fate was known. Should it pass, England would overflow with the unemployed of Ireland's bankrupt industries.[56] These considerations roused the Galway M.P., Nolan, to observe that Forwood had struck a new line by discussing Home Rule in terms of 'trade jealousies'; but that he expected this from Liverpool, whose Conservatives 'were some of the narrowest people in their views that could be found in the United Kingdom'.[57] Forwood, however, was not markedly original: that industry would collapse was a common Conservative threat regarding socialist strikes as well as Home Rule. Trade itself was officially less vocal. When Liverpool's Chamber of Commerce was asked by Dublin's to agree that the Union was essential to Ireland's prosperity, it eschewed party comment.[58]

Forwood's speeches confirmed the faithful in their faith; and in April 1893 Lord Randolph Churchill made his overdue visit to Liverpool.[59] His sepulchral voice hardly reached his audience;[60] but he thrice croaked that Ulster would fight and be right.[61] There were other exhibitions. In Hope Hall the Protestant lecturer, George Wise, welcomed Miss N. F. Cusack, a former nun who lectured about 'the iniquity, treachery, and cruelty of that abominable system'.[62] Edith O'Gorman (Mrs Auffray) preceded her in 1889, and Miss Beatty and Madge Moult succeeded her in 1903 and 1909. 'Escaped Nuns', even doubtfully sane, stirred ordinary Protestants, even the unchivalrous.[63] The rule of obedience symbolized Rome's slavery (it facilitated 'the commission by a Sister of the foulest crimes'); the vow of poverty supplied Rome's avarice ('It is a grand scheme for relieving English ladies of their money'); and stories of sexual transgressions made 'a Briton's blood boil with righteous indignation'.[64]

Blood boiled, sometimes flowed, freely enough in Liverpool . The *Protestant Standard* was incessantly sensational. A disturbance during an Irish Guardians' election evoked this headline: 'Home Rule in Practice: A Mob Headed by a Priest.'[65] Forwood was equally defamatory. Opening the Liverpool Junior Conservative Club in 1893, he claimed that since the Gladstonians were supported only by 'the lowest strata of society . . . such as the Irish corner rough, too idle to work, too much of an inebriate to find employment, and too impecunious to find a permanent home', they 'favoured control of Ireland being placed in the hands of the most rowdy element of Irish society'.[66] Leading Conservatives now enthusiastically patronized Orange demonstrations;[67] and a municipal revival was engineered. Liberal 'purity' was bogus. Prostitutes had been scattered, not suppressed, and Councillor Clarke 'protested against the quiet, orderly, residential streets of West Derby, which had hitherto been pure, being made the tipping ground for the moral rubbish of the city'.[68]

The city centre, stained with vice, was equated with the Irish issue; and in the redistribution controversy suburbans vented their spleen. Forwood objected to Liverpool being controlled by

> men who regarded the English as foreigners in Ireland, and whose countrymen in Liverpool were certainly foreign in many of their ways to the ideas and principles of his hearers. (Applause). The influx of the Irish into Liverpool brought poverty, disease, dirt and misery, drunkenness and crime, in addition to a disturbance in the labour market and the cost to the ratepayers of an enormous sum of money ('Hear, hear', and a voice—'What about the Polish Jews?')

To the W.M.C.A. Forwood emphasized one question—'Was Liverpool to be governed by the Irish Nationalists? (Cries of "No" and "Send them home").' But he elaborated, wishing Liverpool 'to be governed by Liverpool men whether they were born in Scotland, in Ireland, in Wales, or in Liverpool , so long as they remained and conducted themselves as part of the great community, and desired to get into the Council in order to have Liverpool governed for Liverpool purposes only'. Welshmen and Scotsmen, he noted, 'became good citizens', leaving their national fads outside the Council chamber; but 'it was different with the body of Irishmen—(a voice: "Papists")'. Forwood observed of his oratory that it was his habit 'to call a spade a spade'. Thus he pelted the Irish pariahs. His conditions were ignored: the Tory Democracy took its hero's licence as the pith of truth.

The Liberals, when they were not presented as the Irishmen's dupes, exhibited only their misconceptions and broken pledges. Expenditure was reduced by curbing slum clearances. The Liberals, Forwood declared, failed to recognize 'that Liverpool must be a progressive city, and that they must always have a debt of magnitude, and that sinking funds could be used for new works'. Labour was snubbed, Forwood noting that 'there was none so Radical on the platform as the

Gladstonian orator . . . [but] none so conservative as to who he mixed with in the drawing room of his home'.[69]

Forwood's asperity had consequences within his party. Thomas Hughes's principle of independent judgement in municipal matters—he retained the Licensing Committee's chairmanship against Forwood's wishes—was washed away in party tides. From the Liberal side Robert Holt had watched with alarm and distaste Forwood's assumption of 'the pure party politician's position'. Forwood had returned from his long absence as a minister

> in a very furious and irritable state—he misses no opportunity of saying the bitterest things—there seems no desire on his part to do anything to promote a good feeling and assist wise local legislation, but his every effort is to dish the policy introduced into the Finance Com: affairs, a policy which has the support and approval of Mr. Thomas Hughes and Mr. Radcliffe. Mr. A. B. Forwood has rallied to his standard the outside and extreme members of the Tory party and since his return a very different tone has been imparted into our Council proceedings.

Forwood 'seems to have lost much courtesy of manner and all tact and conception of the attributes of a considerate gentleman', Holt wrote again in April 1893; and his diary thereafter regularly noted the stormy Council meetings—there was 'always a row when he [Forwood] puts in an appearance'—and Forwood's parade of himself and the Tory party at the expense of 'what is best for the City as a whole'. Holt found some consolation in thinking that 'our leaders and candidates are less vulgar and less purposely inaccurate' in their electioneering, and that Forwood 'has lost much of his influence among the better class Tories'. He was not supported by every Conservative in Council meetings and Holt was cheered to learn, when dining with the new Lord Derby, a Conservative, that 'A. B. Forwood [was] not a favourite'.

Another witness, however, was also monitoring Forwood's progress, and he, the W.M.C.A.'s leader, Salvidge, was more interested in Forwood's standing with the working classes than with the proprietors of Knowsley. Salvidge observed cynically that Forwood had never been so popular with the Conservative ranks, while those such as Hughes had 'too much faith in Radical promises'.[70] The Liverpool W.M.C.A. was the country's strongest Conservative working men's organization. Some five or six thousand members[71] each paid 1*s.* annually to one of eighteen branches, and each branch paid 3*d.* per member to the Central Committee. The W.M.C.A. was mostly self-supporting—Salvidge even discouraged wealthy men from sending large donations—but only one branch sold intoxicants. This demonstrated the W.M.C.A.'s vitality since, according to Charles Booth, workmen's clubs could not survive without bars.[72] Prestige and ambition fired Salvidge's W.M.C.A. when working men had the opportunity to become district officers; and continual activity sustained them, with 'lectures, dances, concerts, picnics, anything and everything, to keep our men, *our workers*, together and at fighting pitch'.[73]

Staunch Conservatives had prophesied ruin when workmen were admitted to the organization; but Forwood believed that if the leaders were as active as the followers, the balance of authority would remain. As in the National Union's struggles, so locally Forwood was orthodox in believing that decisions should be made at the top; unorthodox in his advocacy of powerful organizations to transmit decisions. The ring of condescension, that tocsin of old Conservatism, did not disappear from Forwood's political thought: he would speak to and for the democracy, but resisted democratic dictation. When, in 1887, the Constitutional Association had testimonialized Forwood as 'almost the first of public men [who] called their attention to that remarkable phenomenon of the present day, the Tory Democracy', Forwood replied: 'He, like them all, believed in the people—(cheers)—but the people must be educated—(hear, hear)—and it was a duty incumbent upon each one to do what he could to bring the truth before the masses . . .'[74] He reiterated this position in 1893: 'They were governed by the democracy and, above all things, it was most desirable that democracy should be truly, honestly, and fairly instructed.'[75] Conservative leadership required not only attendance at the immersion of the Great Unwashed; it also involved mixed bathing.

Labour's reaction

The Liberals were doubly unfortunate in the timing of their municipal administration. The Conservatives fashioned vicious electoral charges; and severe unemployment placed most corporate authorities under stress. In November 1892 the Liberal–Nationalist Councillor, Clancy, a plasterer, approached the L.T.C. on behalf of the unemployed, imploring it to organize demonstrations and to demand relief works.[76] Two Fabian delegates persuaded the L.T.C. to adopt Clancy's suggestion, but another meeting afterwards rescinded it. The majority of delegates viewed the unemployed with suspicion and even hostility, from a belief that the unemployed 'take the place of trades unionists if they get the chance'. The flatboatmen's delegate actually doubted whether there were any involuntary unemployed.[77] Faced with such attitudes the dockers' leader, Sexton, wrote that 'in the interest of the thinking trade unionists the sooner they [the L.T.C.] disband the better'.[78]

This was a controversial season for Sexton. Early in 1893 his appointment as Liverpool Correspondent of the Government's *Labour Gazette* was questioned by Forwood on account of his 'extreme views as to the ownership of property by private individuals, the limitation of individual incomes, and the collective ownership of all means of production'. Although the President of the Board of Trade replied that the Gazette published only 'facts of interest to workmen, and not the opinions held either by Local Correspondents or by any classes of the community', Sexton was asked to resign.[79] Meanwhile his dispute with the L.T.C. ramified when, together with Reeves, he proposed that Liverpool 'follow the example of Carlisle, Medway, and London Trades Councils and federate with the I.L.P.'.[80] Several delegates to the L.T.C. protested that they could not cast a political vote; and the Liver Assurance Collectors' delegate complained that the I.L.P. intended to advance a social revolution, but many were satisfied with their present condition.[81]

Although the L.T.C. participated in a local Labour Representation Committee, formed in December 1893, its annual report reiterated that it was a trade union organization rather than a political body. Running candidates solely on trade union lines was antithetical to the intentions of Socialists and the L.T.C. withdrew from joint action in 1896.[82] This was the lingering death of Sexton's motion but prophets of gloom had gathered from the first. One working man wrote that the I.L.P.'s programme would never find acceptance in Liverpool, 'where political rancour and religious prejudice runs so high, especially, among working men themselves'.[83] In Bradford the I.L.P. was nicknamed 'The Impudent Little Party'.[84] In Liverpool it might have been 'The Impossible Little Party'.

The unemployed wanted work not politics. Perhaps a million or more were unemployed in England in 1893.[85] Several unions of skilled workers recorded over 10 per cent unemployed.[86] The proportion of Liverpudlians below 'the poverty line' (the magic £1 per week), the *Daily Post* reckoned was 40 per cent. 59,000 men were directly engaged in port-work, which could engender a chain reaction of unemployment, pitiless in conditions of normal under-employment. Building workers, laid off in winter, traditionally competed in the docks; but this alternative was closing, as some shipping companies recruited a more regular force and as the N.U.D.L. began securing preferential treatment. In 1893 a master stevedore observed that there were about double the men needed for work. Most earned 10*s.* per week and less.[87]

Workers were idle; charity was busy. In February–March 1893 the Central Relief and Charity Organization Society granted help in kind up to 3*s.* in 11,109 cases, or twice the number recorded during the whole preceding year. Although it had enlarged its operations by establishing workshops and by experiments in labour redeployment, it was obsessed with distinctions of 'deserving' and 'undeserving' poor. Being determined to arrest fictitious mendicancy and promiscuous almsgiving, it often withheld relief for inadequate reasons, and there were certain categories of people, like deserted wives, whom in no circumstances it would help.[88] Eleanor Rathbone's verdict was that the Central Relief Society made no 'permanent material visible improvement in Liverpool'. Little could be achieved by purely voluntary organizations; but the Central Relief Society was ill equipped with its 'patronizing coal-and-blanket, Sunday-School-treat-type' of philosophy, and with its staff of 'lower middle-class people, very willing and interested, but not highly educated, and quite untrained'.[89]

Equally sharp and dogmatic, Beatrice Webb believed that 'social questions are the vital questions of the day: they take the place of religion'.[90] In Liverpool nothing overtook fratricidal religion. Sexton criticized dockers who allowed 'political and religious bigotry and ignorance' to divide them;[91] but his own upbringing illustrated the tendency. Sexton's Fenian father raised his six children on 'hatred—bitter and boundless hatred' of everything British.[92] After various dead-end jobs on both sides of the Atlantic, Sexton had discovered a vicarious purpose working for the I.N.L., until Parnell's exposure. One of Sexton's brothers became a schoolmaster (eventually a headmaster) in Liverpool; but Sexton himself was taught by political and working experiences, and in 1891–2 he claimed to be exclusively a trade unionist. Having discovered that 'the political sentiment and bigotry of the working community have been traded upon and pandered [to] by a gang of political hucksters . . . I am no longer a party man'.[93] Sexton's political agnosticism ended as he accepted socialism, but it was in this mental flux that he joined the unemployed's struggles.

Having failed to move the L.T.C. the unemployed found support among Fabians; and, apparently on the initiative of a fruit porter, Joe Hart, an Unemployed Association was formed. Sexton became its chairman, Hart its secretary, and James Samuelson a trustee. At a Temperance Hotel, Hunter Street, the Association opened a labour bureau. Two thousand men, mostly labourers, occasionally a clerk, registered.[94] The police harassed the bureau, and its funds were uncertain after subscriptions from Samuel Smith, Neville, O'Connor, Willox, several councillors, and sympathizers were exhausted.[95] Another privately run bureau on Great George Street was equally destitute; and together they advocated municipal agencies to command the confidence of employers and men.

The existing public provision was negative, even malevolent, in attitude. The Poor Law Guardians restricted direct relief to widows aged over sixty. Other applicants were offered 'the House' but, as Sexton recognized, working men 'had a perfect horror of the poorhouse, and would rather die in a ditch than ask the assistance of the Poor Law because the conditions it imposed were degrading in the extreme'.[96] Nevertheless 37,000 Liverpudlians annually became paupers; and almost one-third of the manual labour class died in the workhouse. [97] In the 1860s a merchant had nominated the Liverpool workhouse 'the biggest house in Town'; in 1873 Picton acclaimed it the biggest workhouse in England; and in 1886 *Porcupine* thought it the biggest in the world.[98]

As a structure the workhouse was impressive; so too were some developments on the medical side, and the Corporation was content to leave hospital treatment mostly under the Guardians' control. Thus in the 1860s the Liverpool Guardians were renowned for their advances in nursing; and in 1897 they asked permission of the Local Government Board to provide an up-to-date operating theatre. This, as the tuberculosis specialist at the hospital later recalled, was a fateful decision because the Local Government Board acknowledged that the Guardians' hospital provision was not restricted to the destitute but was supplying services which a local—or national—health authority should have undertaken. It remained a fact, however, that by law any person who entered a Poor Law institution was officially a pauper. Although by 1920 some fifty Poor Law infirmaries in Britain were quite dissociated from the workhouse administration, the taint of charity had not been removed, and this arrangement—quite apart from the generally poor equipment in these hospitals—was deemed 'out of tune with democracy'.[99]

On the workhouse side the Liverpool Guardians had been noted in mid-century for their achievements in economy; in the 1880s for dabbling in resettlement schemes and introducing marginal improvements in food; and in 1905 for dropping 'Workhouse' from the official address, in an attempt to mitigate the stigma. This administrative record was also tarnished. In 1885 the governor, a bankrupt, was charged with defalcations of £419; and overcrowding in the workhouses was never stemmed. In 1902 the Toxteth workhouse used padded rooms as dormitories.[100] There was also partiality in religion. Protestants worshipped in a specially built church, but Catholics, although twice as numerous, used the dining-hall.[101] One inmate, Pat O'Mara, recalled the pervading despair, like 'a lost city'.[102] The Clerk to the Select Vestry, Henry Hagger, summarized the Guardians' policy in 1894: to protect the ratepayers 'we give a man relief in a form he is unwilling to take'. Asked by the Lord Mayor if he had any suggestions for easing unemployment, Hagger replied: 'Unfortunately, my lord, I have none.'[103]

In March 1893 the Corporation opened relief works at Pall Mall, partly influenced by the Local Government Board's circular indicating distress among those who ordinarily did not seek relief.[104] The Hunter Street Bureau acted as contractor and in a month supplied 189 men who worked from three to six days at 4*s*. per day. Under 250 men were found other work by the two bureaux; but they affronted militant sections of the N.U.D.L. and N.A.S.F.U., who suspected that they provided the Shipping Federation with blacklegs for use during the strike at Hull.[105] Sympathetic strikes were threatened in Liverpool; but only minor stoppages occurred, and these from different causes—the N.U.D.L.'s desire to control labour in the Wapping Basin and King's Dock.[106] The scabbing question was shortly answered, although not before Sexton implied that the L.T.C. had complicity in it.[107] The Shipping Federation had its own register.[108] By 26 April 850 scabs had gone to Hull; and more applied when wages of 30*s*. were rumoured.[109] Some suspected crimping;[110] but potential employment was compulsion enough.

The Unemployed Association was discouraged. The Shipping Federation in a week found twice the number of jobs two workmen's bureaux found in a month.[111] The Corporation's Water Committee, in the Pall Mall works, did more than most by advancing its schedule; but among the workmen some Irish harvesters were discovered. Corporation foremen could not differentiate them from Liverpudlians.[112] The L.T.C. was deeply suspicious and, by fifteen votes to six, refused to advocate a municipal exchange, even with Sexton's proviso that it must exemplify union principles. The majority echoed Reeves, who would not trust a Corporation Committee to run 'a home for lame dogs'.[113] Later, however, the L.T.C. agreed to request a labour exchange as defined by the 1890 T.U.C.

An overture was made to the Corporation's Finance Committee, demanding that a Labour Committee be formed to help 'the respectable unemployed as far as possible'. This would contain seven councillors, seven employers, and seven workmen.[114] Many councillors, perhaps, shared the opinion of the Nationalist Alderman, Dr. Commins, that the public provision of employment smacked of 'state socialism'; however, no member of the Finance Committee voted against the suggested Labour Committee. Few saw utility in it but it committed them to little. When the L.T.C. met the Finance Committee again, only two Liberal councillors bothered to attend. Reeves ridiculed their assertion that the Corporation had no outstanding work: many streets 'had not been paved since Adam was a boy'. The Council, it seemed, showed determination only as a buffer and Reeves cursed the fact that it could rely on 'an ignorant electorate, which voted according to party passion'.[115]

A municipal exchange was urgently required as the workmen's bureaux had since found work for only 120 from 6,474 applicants. Ninety town councils now operated exchanges and the L.T.C. estimated that its administration would cost £300 per annum. The Town Clerk doubted whether this could legally be found from existing funds;[116] but the called-for Labour Committee convened on 8 December with Kaney, Parkin, Reeves, Rouse, and Sexton among the labour representatives. The Council representation, entirely Liberal, agreed to establish a municipal exchange.[117] No real change of heart was exhibited; but demonstrations had taken a militant turn under John O'Brien of the S.D.F., H. Squires, a painter who had succeeded Hart as secretary of the Unemployed Association, and Bob Manson, a theatrical Irishman.[118]

The Corporation registry opened on 4 January 1894. By 26 January it had found work for thirty men, mostly skilled, from 2,000 applicants.[119] Reacting to this unimpressive record, fewer registered although the number seeking relief had grown.[120] City councillors met the unemployed with the cynicism of Disraeli who believed that 'receiving a deputation is like sham marching: an immense dust and no progress'.[121] Squires and O'Brien accused the Corporation of recruiting non-Liverpudlian policemen and placing clothing contracts with 'Russian Jews and other sweaters';[122] but S. Wade, a commission agent, proposed a public inquiry of recognized persons in order to investigate the whole question.[123] Demonstrations were suspended as Wade's idea was adopted, a compromise in lieu of deadlock.

The Commission met in July 1894. It consisted of the Lord Mayor (Bowring), a cotton broker, A. A. Paton, George Cox of the Central Relief Society, two university men, Professor Gonner and Professor Jenks, three councillors, John Houlding, Thomas Hughes and H. H. Hornby, two clerics, Canon Lester and Richard Armstrong, Charles Rouse of the L.T.C., and three women social workers, Misses Ronald, Melly, and Gordon. They reported in October, having called fifty witnesses. Concerning the number of unemployed, the Commission believed accuracy impossible, owing to 'the fluctuating nature' of port-work.[124] Individuals coloured the jigsaw. Barnabas Bain, of the Town Mission, had never encountered more 'respectable unemployed';[125] and William Grisewood, of the Central Relief Society, described 'a permanent surplus of considerable dimensions'.[126] Working men witnesses supplied particular information. Councillor Taggart declared that 32·9 per cent of 2,711 regional members of the Gasworkers and General Labourers Union were unemployed;[127] and, although in some respects N.U.D.L. members had advantages over outsiders, Sexton reported that 50 per cent of unemployed dockers were trade unionists.[128]

Several factors required differentiation, particularly the exceptionally unemployed from the permanently underemployed. The latter were mostly aged over forty-five.[129] Thomas Parr, of the Warehouse Porters' Union, declared that his trade employed 9,000 in winter and 6,000 in summer. When he gave evidence (30 July) 2,000 had been idle for three months and 2,000 had little work. Likewise the Docks Board's warehouse manager, W. S. Brice, reported that the slackest months were August, February, and March, and that the maximum he employed in 1893 was 2,782, the minimum 337.[130]

The Commission approached the problem schematically, defining 'unemployed' as those 'substantially without remunerative work for several months'. It observed 'two distinct classes': (*a*) 'steady and capable men and women who could and would really do work if they could find it'; (*b*) those who 'are incapable of doing, or refuse to do, steady work up to the average standard in quality and quantity'.[131] Most witnesses accepted these categories, but differed about their composition. Mission workers emphasized the spuriously unemployed. The Revd. J. Gamble declared that half of those whom he dealt with deliberately avoided work;[132] and Bain believed that those individuals who took part in agitation and demonstrations were 'unreal' unemployed—'men who lived upon their mothers, their wives, their children, and women of ill-fame, men who allowed their aged mothers to work for them and who would not turn out of bed if they could help it before ten o'clock any day'.[133] Others refuted this calumny. The cargo superintendent of the American (formerly the Inman) Line, which had recently transferred many steamers to Southampton, reckoned that those unemployed through 'personal disabilities physical or moral' were insubstantial.[134]

In balancing opinions the Commissioners had clear partialities. Neither Gamble's nor Bain's thesis was cross-examined; indeed Armstrong encouraged them with the reflection that 'a great deal of the poverty was caused by men spending their time and money in the public houses'.[135] The Commissioners joined in Class (*b*) those unemployed through intemperance and 'restlessness' and those unemployed through ill-health or age. Moreover, among 'the most powerful contributory factors' was 'injudicious and indiscriminate charity'.

Trade unions were also accused of inviting unemployment by 'unjust attempts to secure the monopoly of particular markets'.[136] The dockers' strike, Bain believed, brought 'a great deal of local suffering' and diminished the work available to the unskilled and middle-aged.[137] Brice agreed that many were permanently displaced by immigrant blacklegs, including 'men who had been from three to twenty-seven years in the Dock Board's employment who, sympathizing with or terrorized by the dock labourers, had stopped work, and had never got back again'.[138] The Commission suggested arbitration boards to obviate strikes and lock-outs. Immigration, however, was a causal factor upon which all agreed. Bain blamed the Jews; O'Brien denounced publicans who scoured Ireland and Scotland for workers at smaller wages and at their board; and Parr criticized the preference Welsh warehousemen showed to compatriots. The Tramways Company, likewise, was rebuked for recruiting non-local labour.[139] Other factors were the substitution of women and boys for men in certain trades, and the decline of Liverpool ship-building, although this was too late to halt.[140]

Concerning remedies, the Commission wanted 'a strong and permanent representative Labour Committee' to press its prescriptions 'as opportunity occurs'. It recommended fewer hiring 'stands' for dock labour but ignored Sexton's wish that employers utilize the N.U.D.L.'s telephone.[141] It hoped that employers, by establishing labour-clearing centres, would guarantee employment to more men. Weekly, as well as daily, rates would need negotiation; but registration might deter immigrant labour.

Liberal fancy shaped other recommendations, concerning temperance restaurants, labour colonies, the emigration of unemployables, and discriminate almsgiving. For 'the idle, dissolute, and criminal section', the stricter enforcement of poor laws and statutes against vagabondage was recommended; and the opinion of missionary witnesses that more work could be provided if older men accepted less pay appealed as an alternative to pensions. All 'political' recommendations made by witnesses—concerning Irish Home Rule, and various types of nationalization—were ignored.

Wade, the author of the Commission, criticized its narrow references and endorsement of 'lower wages'.[142] From the start working men suspected its imposture—several trades refused to supply evidence[143]—and at the end no other conclusion was possible. Most recommendations the Commission was powerless to enact; but bad faith was demonstrated where it had some influence, regarding the municipal exchange. This remained a register of unemployed. No attempt was made to ascertain men's capabilities or to contact employers.[144]

Thus the Corporation proceeded as before, with studied aversion. The Liberals attracted the obloquy pent up against traditional Conservative practices. Liberal rule was epitomized by the three Liberal mayors between 1892 and 1895. In February 1893 Holt had listened with sympathy for an hour and a quarter to his first deputation of unemployed. He could not decide how exceptional was the distress but he was sorry not to be able to put food in their stomachs or work in their hands. He grew impatient as the deputations were repeated. He was determined that the unemployed should have no control over the direction and nature of relief; he was disturbed by 'wild socialistic talk'; his casting vote defeated the scavengers' demand; and, in a report of one local Labour Conference submitted for the Corporation's approval, he lamented 'the absence of good criticism . . . as really I felt it was impossible as sensible and practical business men to endorse all that was recommended'.[145] Holt's successors hardened the mould. Bowring gave a wooden reception to more deputations; and Watts opposed a relief fund with the brutal observation, 'let them go to hell'. In his view the unemployed were the naturally idle and improvident.[146]

As in the large questions of public policy, so in the smaller matter of civic honours the Liberals' attitude to Labour was niggardly. About two dozen magistrates were appointed to the Liverpool bench in 1892–3 by the Liberal Government, after consultation with Robert Holt, Edward Evans, and T. P. O'Connor. The Catholic-cum-Nationalist interest was recognized and appeased without much ado: it could easily furnish some half-a-dozen names which would stand the test of respectability. The Labour interest was more intractable. After much misgiving William Matkin in 1892, and George Parkin in 1893, were elevated to a Bench which then consisted of 113 magistrates. Trade unionists were disappointed. This working-class representation was a token, whereas employer domination remained a fact: the I.L.P. and N.A.S.F.U. claimed that sixty-one Liverpool J.P.s were shipowners, an important matter considering the numerous cases involving interpretation of the Merchant Shipping Acts which came before the Bench. The Liberals, however, pretended that neither trade interests nor party *per se* were factors in appointments. So far as the Labour element was concerned, Evans was anxious to establish the principle of working-class magistrates, but his support of Matkin and Parkin was negative, in that others recommended by trade unions, in his opinion, would '*never* do'. Thus he discountenanced the N.U.D.L.'s nomination of James Sexton and Thomas Kilkelly: he considered them 'really rather obnoxious agitators and living on it'. Holt was even less enthusiastic. He regarded the question of working-class magistrates not as a principle but as an insurance that 'the Labour party act loyally towards the Liberal party'. When it came to the point of forwarding names Holt was stuck. His quandary evinced an essential Liberal philosophy: 'Good working men are difficult to find—for if "good" they speedily cease to be ordinary working men and become masters.'[147]

Criticisms crystallized

The reaction of Labour and Conservative opponents to the Liberal administration was uncannily close. Reeves recognized that while the Tories moved slowly in housing matters, the Liberals scarcely moved at all. This was 'typical of the class to which they mostly belonged. The typhoid fever dens of Liverpool were ordered to remain in order that the rates might be saved, and that the councillors who own many of these places should not be inconvenienced'. Forwood supported this view: 'a narrower spirit dominated the Council. Small property owners controlled its policy', and they condemned the poor 'to live in slums . . . in order that a little cheap popularity might be secured by apparently reduced rates'.[148]

The need to redistribute the wards also continued to excite argument. In April 1894 the Liberals placed a scheme before the Local Government Board. Rateable value, not population, determined their proposals. Wards within the old parish would be distributed on the basis of electorates of two thousands each, suburban wards on the basis of electorates of three or four thousands, because the parish contributed 60 per cent of the rates. Forwood disputed this assertion that 'a man's value in the constituency was to be regarded by the amount of rates he paid, and not by his existence as a citizen'.[149] The Everton Liberal Club supported him on this issue. More melodramatically, Hornby resigned his municipal offices, having been displaced from the Committee which deliberated the scheme of ward redistribution. Hornby suspected gerrymandering and named several Liberal councillors.[150] Possibly Hornby was precipitate, but the W.M.C.A. supported his allegation of 'political wirepulling' and denounced the slight to one of Liverpool's good old names'.[151] Just as Disraeli, with sincere dishonesty, once entered his profession as 'patriotism',[152] so the Liverpool Conservatives idealized themselves as champions of their city's patrimony. Liberals were parricidal. The *Courier* asserted about Hornby: 'He had no party interest to serve, and he spoke in the interest of the community and justice . . . Mr. Hornby is banished from municipal life because he would not pay tribute to "Irish ideas"'.[153]

The false syllogism of Liberal—Home-Ruler—civic traitor Forwood presented with cartoon extravagance. He exhorted '*the adherents of both political parties*' to repudiate government by the 'nominees of the most ignorant and irresponsible inhabitants of the city . . . . This danger was all the greater because it was hid behind a veil of respectability which the names of Holt, Bowring, Rathbone, and Picton, leading Gladstonians, conveyed to the minds of the unthinking multitude.' Mordantly Forwood cited *The American Commonwealth*, a treatise by James Bryce, then a Liberal Minister, to draw the moral that Irish electors espoused venal politicians. When Irishmen controlled New York, they lined their pockets. Liverpool could suffer likewise from 'an absence of proper interest in public affairs by the better educated and more intelligent of the respectable working and middle class population'. Already there had been signs of jobbery: Lynskey had sought the salaried coronership in 1891 and Irish public health officials allegedly prevented slum clearances because removals meant the dispersal of Nationalist voters. Forwood encouraged 'the real residents of Liverpool , who believed in Liverpool first and Liverpool last, to say with determined voice that they would have none of the domination of this class of man'.[154]

The enemy was branded. He was not yet hanged because an electoral truce was observed in 1894 while new wards were negotiated.[155] Labour or, as Robert Holt saw it, 'some foolish independent (self-advertising) working men', dissented from the party truce. The L.T.C. accepted the L.L.R.C.'s resolution to 'protest against the unholy alliance between the Liberals and Tories' by contesting every ward.[156] These troublous years had marked the L.T.C. Its offices were now contested, although their political nature was not paramount: Seniority, personal character, and the delegates' society, mattered greatly. These subtleties were etched in the L.T.C.'s elections of October 1893. J. H. Naylor (Coachbuilders') who advocated non-political representation, defeated Sexton for the presidency, by thirty-three votes to twenty-eight; but Sexton became vice-president by thirty votes to twenty-one for John Shannon (Carpenters' and Joiners'), an avowed non-political. Socialists held the presidency for the next year—Sexton from March to October 1894, Reeves thenceforward to March 1895. But Shannon had become secretary, a position he occupied for another decade; and Rule 12 still limited discussions of 'party or political matters'. It was applied, ironically, by Sexton in July 1894, when he quashed a resolution applauding a parliamentary speech by Keir Hardie.[157]

Sexton, however, shaped the decision to break the municipal truce in 1894. He recalled the Liberals' accusations linking Labour and 'Tory Gold' in 1892; and he observed how 'the party of political purity should so far forget their purity as to shake hands with the Tory Party—their rampant enemy—so as to demonstrate their love for the Labour party by crushing it out of existence'.[158] Delegates were stirred, not to advocate Socialism, but to expose the Liberals' blandishments. The L.T.C. listed the Corporation's 'many acts of betrayal': the condition of its employees, the contracts given to non-Liverpool firms, and the refusal to find remunerative work for the unemployed. The Council had also encouraged M.P.s to oppose the Hours of Labour Bill; and, while exempting individuals like Grant, the L.T.C. accused councillors of 'attempting to "nobble" the local members of Parliament, in their own interests as employers'.[159] The Council was dominated by 'rich merchants and rack-renting slum property owners': the sixty-four members included eighteen merchants, shipowners, and brokers; twenty-six tradesmen and manufacturers; seven lawyers; three doctors; two architects and surveyors; two commission agents; two wine merchants; one brewer; one retired tradesman; one master carter; and one trade union secretary. Fifty-five councillors lived outside Liverpool, 'away from the slums from which they drew their incomes'.[160]

Money for a city-wide campaign was not forthcoming; nor were candidates. Sexton and Matkin, for example, declined to contest St. Anne's.[161] Only three official candidates emerged; and none made an impression. Naylor's contest of Everton was typical of the mortification, for the Carters' Union and several Liberals openly supported the Tory, Houlding.[162] Moreover, O'Brien expressed the unemployed's impatience with the L.T.C. by standing simultaneously in five wards. A labourer, Michael Egan, also contested Exchange; but these candidatures were annulled because of forged nominations. In November O'Brien stood not for election but on trial. He received six months hard labour for corrupt practices.[163]

This was Labour's crowning humiliation after two years of trade depression and unsympathetic Liberal rule. What the S.D.F.'s founder, H. M. Hyndman, said about strikes might have applied generally to Labour's agitation: 'it was like using Brown Bess against Maxim Guns'.[164] Hyndman advised that Labour redouble its determination to control local administrations; but Labour in Liverpool divided over practical matters, large and small, as the controversies over the unemployed, and demarcation disputes between skilled and unskilled unions, illustrated.[165] The N.U.D.L. left the L.T.C. in 1894; it did not reaffiliate until 1906. By 1896 the L.T.C.'s representative membership, 35,000 was 11,000 less than in 1890–1. Mostly this drop mirrored the hard times and was to some extent unreal, since Birkenhead branches began a separate Trades Council in 1892; but the L.T.C.'s failure to recruit also reflected its disputed role.

CHAPTER TEN

Conservative supremacy in Greater Liverpool and Forwood's last years, 1895–8

> Like every successful public man, the Right Honourable Sir A. B. Forwood has his enemies, of course; but he is also rich in the possession of hosts of friends; and were there only more such considerate and large-hearted men as Sir Arthur in the world we should hear far less of the cry of socialism, and everyone would be far happier and better.
>
> He is certainly short of the instincts of a Gentleman and carries his political bias too far so as to be unjust to others.
>
> No man in the kingdom, below the Cabinet Minister rank, has had more to do with the development of Tory Democracy.
>
> He has been a most expert Tory wire-puller, as all the world knows.[1]

In 1895 Liberal governments crashed both nationally and locally. In Liverpool in the general election, as sectarian and ethnic associations hardened, and in the municipal elections, as ward boundaries were redistributed at last, the Conservative party scored imperious victories. But it is a classic feature of empire that extinction shadows extension. About the Conservative supremacy in Greater Liverpool there were marks of temporariness and incompatibility. There was potential conflict, for example, in the fact that while the Conservative party machinery became ever more centralized the restructuring of the wards had given an accent to variety and differentiation. Men with a cause felt even less compunction in parading before a ward of 3,500 electors than one of 35,000. Accordingly, both Protestant and Labour factions were encouraged by the redistribution and subdivision of wards to claim recognition as entities independent of the Conservative and Liberal establishments. In government too Forwood's writ was not absolute. During his absence as a junior minister before 1892, and during the Liberal municipal administration subsequently, men of ambition entered the Liverpool Conservative party with their own views about

Notes begin on p. 411

policy; and in 1898 a vote on the future of the tramways was understood as a repudiation of Forwood's Council leadership.

The General Election of 1895

In 1895 Liberals were as lively as wrung chickens who mimic immortality before they collapse. The party's head was twisted three ways, by Rosebery stumping against the Lords, by Harcourt foaming about temperance reform, and by Morley pandering to Home Rule. The electoral register was fully twelve months old as Parliament dissolved on 6 July. Liverpool polled on 18 July, the last day the Liberal mayor could choose. It reflected his party's unreadiness. Moreover, when the local Liberal leader, Evans, declared that candidates with great commercial connections would contest the divisions, this reflected the Liberals' indifference to labour questions.[2]

Both tendencies were highlighted in Abercromby. When the shipowner, Councillor Williamson, declined nomination, the Liberal constituency association resolved 'that in view of the important commercial interests of Liverpool, [which] Mr. Lawrence alone of the sitting members has taken any pains to advance', it would not contest the seat.[3] Thus, in the constituency with the smallest Conservative majority in Liverpool, Liberalism capitulated.

Undoubtedly Lawrence had solicited this support. In 1893 his entry in *Dod's Parliamentary Companion* was altered to read 'Independent Conservative', not 'moderate Conservative'; and this nomenclature remained until 1901, when it reverted to unadorned 'Conservative'. Lawrence's reward in 1895 was Robert Gladstone's signature, among those of other Liberal businessmen, on his nomination papers;[4] and, without further need to appease deferential opponents, Lawrence revelled in one-dimensional Conservatism. He observed that more illiterate voters were registered in Nationalist and Liberal seats than in Unionist seats. 'It proved', said Lawrence, 'that the less you know the less Unionist you are.'[5]

Commercial intelligence had not always benefited Conservatism—in Exchange ward in 1892 Liberal Unionists had assisted Holt against a Conservative opponent[6]—but the Unionist alliance had been hallowed in support of Hornby's allegations of malpractices by the Liberal Corporation in 1894. The party organizations did not merge finally until the Liberal Unionists' agent, McComb, retired in 1907; but now they issued a joint manifesto and centred their electoral operations in the Conservative offices.[7]

Forwood's onslaught against the Liberal–Irish Corporation had reaffirmed his leadership; nevertheless the 1895 General Election campaign opened with a blow. Forwood was excluded from Lord Salisbury's Third Ministry, formed in June. Knowledge that places were scarce in Hotel Cecil did not soften the hurt, and Forwood's letter to Salisbury contained a rebuke—'the position would have been more palatable had it been accompanied by a friendly word'—and a notification that after the General Election he would retire from active politics. Forwood had barely entered his tent before the post brought Salisbury's 'friendly word'—baronetcy. With becoming modesty, Forwood interpreted his elevation as 'a compliment to Liverpool *not to me*';[8] but some deduced that Forwood had cashiered the Tory Democrat.[9] His speeches were weighted in defence of the Union, Church, and Lords.

Forwood, however, also talked of legislation which would enable working men to own their homes and to have security in old age; moreover, he was among several Unionists whose schemes anticipated the Workmen's Compensation Act (1897). The law on accident liability was 'incomplete and uncertain in its action, defective in its machinery, and doubtful in its interpretation';[10] but in 1894 Forwood devised a Bill which contained 'an entirely new departure'.[11] Although a workman might seek damages under common law, Forwood wished to avoid litigation by ensuring compensation in all accidents, which employers could gauge in the cost of business. The 1897 Act was narrower—it excluded agricultural labourers, seamen, domestic servants, carters, building workers, and waterfront workers. Forwood would have included 'all working people'. This comprehensiveness was typical of his decided manner, especially his view, expressed in 1886, that 'permissive legislation was a mistake as a rule'; he thought that if the Legislature considered it necessary to lay down certain principles which should regulate the relations between man and man, between landlord and tenant, or between employer and employed, it should not make these measures permissive but should make them compulsory'.[12]

Neither Forwood's Bill nor the 1897 Act was perfect. Employers were not compelled to insure to protect their workmen's compensation; and trade unionists feared that employers might relieve their burden by reducing wages.[13] Trade unions, however, might benefit by fewer demands on their sick and burial funds; and the Webbs noted the boldness of Conservative thinking, which seemed 'to give the go-by to all the old controversies.'[14] In Liverpool Forwood's scheme was advertised to the W.M.C.A. with different trimmings. Salvidge denounced 'paid agitators' before sermonizing on the text of class interdependence; and Austin, the vice-president, observed that such measures would curb 'that terrible evil of Socialism, which was the curse of the present day'.[15]

Forwood remained a 'progressive' Conservative, although the Liverpool elections did not turn on these matters. Sectarianism loomed large. One Labour delegate previewed its dimensions from the School Board elections: '"Socialist"—the only one in 1894 gains 2,906 votes—Top score for the "Church" 67,000! Tilting at windmills?'[16] In 1892 the Board had censured school managers who circularized parents about free education.[17] Edward Russell speculated that 'the wish to make Free Education unacceptable arises from fanatical sectarianism', and that consequently the Board was unpopular.[18] The Board, however, in conjunction with the Poor Law Guardians, was still assisting necessitous parents with their children's fees at voluntary schools; and the electorate endorsed this. Likewise the Board's successor after 1902, the Liverpool Education Committee, charged fees in 65 of 161 schools, for reasons of economy and 'to bolster up the denominational schools which otherwise it would be difficult to make pay'. About a dozen of the sixty public elementary schools which were still charging fees in Liverpool in 1915 were opened after the 1891 Free Education Act.[19]

Theoretically the defence of religious education attracted Catholic voters to

Conservatism. Cardinal Vaughan made this a test question; and the Catholic Bishop of Liverpool , Dr Whiteside, proclaimed 'the right of denominational schools to an equal share with Board Schools of public moneys'.[20] Forwood recognized the Catholic interest;[21] but this was rare. Although they defended denominational education, few Conservatives outside Exchange Division explicitly courted Catholic support. The risk of alienating Protestants was obvious; and those pietistic Irish Catholics who stomached Tory Orangeism were probably few.[22]

To many Liberals the House of Lords was as Birrell described it, a Tory pocket borough; but, by rejecting Home Rule, Welsh Disestablishment, and temperance legislation, the House of Lords became heroic to Conservative working men. Salvidge organized a demonstration to acclaim as 'the tried and trusted working men's friend' Lord Dudley, the great mine-owner whose contracting-out amendment emasculated Asquith's Employer's Liability Bill.[23] The peers were credited with protecting Tory Democracy from the Commons' rampant factionalism.[24] This implication, that the Liberal victory of 1892 was fraudulent, achieved credibility by reference to the over-representation of Ireland; and this constituted the Conservatives' answer to Radical proposals to abolish plural voting.[25] A Wadham undergraduate, F. E. Smith, told the W.M.C.A. that Liberalism meant 'One Englishman one vote, one Welshman one vote and a tenth, and one Irishman three votes'.[26] Forwood depicted some possible consequences of ending plural votes. Seven Liverpool constituencies would be little affected; but Abercromby would have an Irish majority and the electorate of Exchange would be half of West Derby, Everton or Kirkdale, giving 'each Irish Nationalist elector . . . an equal power . . . to two of the English Unionist working men electors'.[27]

In the same vein the Bootle M.P., Colonel Sandys, lectured Lord Salisbury that 'the first duty of the Government is to *reduce the representation of Ireland to that of London* . . . Our policy has too long been dominated by illiterate voters in Ireland driven to the poll by terrorism and Romish priests . . .' Salisbury's Government must 'crush Home Rule for ever . . . *no matter who objects*'. Sandys's 'savage dogs' speech of 1892 was no aberration. He wanted to make an anti-Irish policy cardinal, because a programme of social reform was 'too tame for a fighting majority'.[28] Sputtering, Sandys appraised Salisbury's appointment of the Catholic Duke of Norfolk as Postmaster-General: 'people object to have the Post Office and the Telegraph in the hands of the Jesuit secret police, who thereby know all the secret policy of the Government, the movements of Troops and Fleets and police, as well as the private affairs of individual members of the community . . . .' Sandys's spirit was Elizabethan: *semper eadem*. But he could not be disregarded. Sandys represented many when he demanded 'more firmness in dealing with Ireland . . . no matter how they cry out, it is the only way to rule them, they are the very last race on earth to give way to, hoping to conciliate thereby'.[29]

More broadminded candidates submitted before this prejudice. Personally, Willox 'did not allow differences of creed, country, or politics to interpose if he could do any good in the social life of Everton'.[30] This virtue evaporated amid the boiling Protestantism of his supporters. At Willox's re-adoption meeting one

Evertonian reminded him of the controversy concerning Cromwell's statue at Westminster. Accordingly Willox donned the trappings of bloody Protestantism, furious that Irish Nationalists should consider 'the man of iron, of faith, of patriotism, and of Protestantism' unworthy of honour. Willox demanded 'more of Cromwell's courage and more of his religion'.[31]

Ultimately, in the Unionist party, a Sandys lurked inside most Willoxs.[32] Among Orangemen doubts remained. They had formed a committee to take, if necessary, an independent part;[33] but, come the General Election, their concern was not whether to sell themselves to the Conservative party, but that harlotry should not seem cheap. A speech of Councillor Roberts, the Deputy Grand Master, pointed the way; and on the Glorious Twelfth lodges urged their members to withstand 'the popish Separatists and their contemptible tools the Gladstonians'.[34]

Conservative candidates paid them well. At a time when privately Baden-Powell was displaying most ignoble characteristics in seeking a government post, in the Admiralty or Colonial Office, he declared in Liverpool that he 'placed religion in the forefront of all political work'.[35] The Liberals, he alleged, sought 'the pulling down of churches, the secularization of schools and property, the confiscation and robbery of churches and money devoted to the service of their God'.[36] The religious trump protected his hand in other suits. Having opposed the inclusion in Factory Acts of ships at dock, he faced the N.U.D.L.'s disapproval.[37] His Liberal opponent, Benjamin Johnson, was a respected employer, with experience as Threlfall's campaign chairman in 1892;[38] but a class difference marked them and Baden-Powell rightly suspected that working men would not follow Johnson as Threlfall.[39] Kirkdale's I.L.P. abstained.[40] Baden-Powell polled 68 more votes, Johnson 305 fewer: the majority rose to 1,350.

West Toxteth showed similar proclivities. Although chiefly a south-end employer, the Conservative M.P., Houston, also held berths in the north docks, where the N.U.D.L. accused him of combining with other shipowners to refuse employment to union members. Conservative canvassers therefore placarded the constituency with notices which stated that Houston employed union men, or which recited previously friendly letters from Sexton to Houston's Company.[41] Houston viewed West Toxteth like a fief. Had he been unopposed, he exclaimed, he would have donated his election expenses to local charities: thus, '£500 has been lost to the poor of Toxteth through the Radical party (Hoots and Hisses)'.[42] Houston also flourished 'the bloody and dusty old rag of religious animosity', as his opponent, William Mulholland, said.[43] A lawyer, practising in Liverpool for twenty years, Mulholland was a brother-in-law of the Lord Chief Justice, Lord Russell of Killowen. To Houston, however, he was 'the Roman Catholic and Home Rule Mr. Mulholland'; and he urged the 'Protestant boys of Toxteth' to give Mulholland 'what Paddy gave the drum—"a rale good batin"'.[44]

Houston enlarged his majority from 1,125 to 2,057. Since 1892 he had attracted only six more votes; the Liberals slumped by 826. Mulholland had carried a double indemnity as an Irish Catholic: Houston's last Liberal opponent, Griffith, was a Welsh Nonconformist. When he addressed Toxteth about labour questions, Mulholland learned from an Orange docker that 'The Lord himself need not come here asking for anything unless he is of the right colour'.[45]

The cockpit of the General Election in Liverpool in 1895 was as usual Exchange. Illness prostrated the twice victorious Liberal, Neville; but his replacement, Bowring, had established credit with local Irish Catholics when, as Lord Mayor, he had entertained Cardinal Vaughan.[46] This advertised to others that Bowring had lost caste.[47] The Unionists' constituency chairman declared that Bowring was favoured 'by the disloyal and by the ignorant'. 'Educated and religious Irishmen' supported the Unionist candidate, Bigham.[48] Both Bigham, who was a Catholic convert, and Tory Catholics like Hemelryk, explored the putative rift between Catholics and Liberals; and, when T. P. O'Connor addressed Bowring's meetings, hecklers asked him if he preferred Liberalism to Catholicism.[49]

Bowring lost by 254 votes. His poll was ninety-one below Neville's in 1892, and the Reform Club gave 'Three groans for the Tory priests'.[50] Some Conservatives believed this interpretation; but against it Councillor Doughan claimed that 'the Irish Catholic vote went solid for Bowring'.[51] Other factors were important—138 more votes were polled in a smaller electorate. The latter was explained by slum clearances and by unemployment—several Irishmen were disfranchised after receiving parish relief.[52] The former testified to the degree of commercial collaboration in Bigham's candidature, possibly in response to the Government's part in the Indian cotton duties controversy, which made Lancashire a centre of Conservative reaction generally in 1895; and the Liverpool Junior Reform Club retaliated by expelling those Liberal Unionists still frequenting its premises.[53]

Elsewhere Liberalism was routed. In Walton Stock was unopposed, although he was a slack parliamentarian, criticized by his own party;[54] and candidature problems crippled the Liberal associations in Everton, West Derby, and East Toxteth. In Everton Willox was unopposed, and in West Derby the former local leader, Robert Holt, refused the Liberal nomination.[55] Holt was sixty-three years old and refusal was invariably his way now. This negativism had recently assumed a perverse grandeur when Holt, with his family's approval, cancelled the honour of a baronetcy from Rosebery's outgoing government.[56] Holt was unlucky enough to have Beatrice Webb, his sister-in-law, record the torpor of his old age: 'his small-mindedness and secretiveness has degenerated into a restless kind of vanity, and undignified love of social esteem. It is pathetic to see his little mind always reverting to the glory of having refused a Baronetcy. Oddly enough, it was his position of Mayor which fostered his instinct of self-importance—one would have thought his social position was too big for that.'

In fact there was injustice in this judgement. Holt was to prove steadfast to his brand of Liberalism in opposition to the Boer war; and, as for standing for Parliament, he was always modest about his intellectual quality. He had gone straight into the family business as a youth, and now he did not want to step outside local politics—'the bare idea of success terrifies me. What sh^{d} I do if I had to go to London and dance attendance at the House of Commons. No, it would not suit me.' Only 'those of first-rate abilities and opportunities ought to go to London', was Holt's view.[57]

In lieu of Holt the West Derby Liberals advanced Oscar Browning, the Cambridge historian who had once taught at Liverpool College. Although prim, Browning was not without valour. Agnosticism was spreading among the Fellowship at King's and Browning reacted by hanging a crucifix in his anteroom, 'to fwighten the agnoggers', he said.[58] The West Derby electorate was not so susceptible to charms and Walter Long, now President of the Board of Agriculture, delivered the largest Tory majority in any Liverpool constituency since 1885.

In East Toxteth, too, the sitting Conservative M.P., Worms, was not troubled by a stop-gap Liberal candidate, a barrister, C. Y. C. Dawbarn. Degenerate Liberals cried 'Vote for an Englishman' in order to counter Worms's advocacy of immigration controls; but Dawbarn's standard noises, about temperance, disestablishment, and the House of Lords, Worms silenced by remarking that 'Ireland had been too long the spoiled child of England, and the electors must no longer allow themselves to be carried away by any clap-trap'.[59] Even T. P. O'Connor's majority in Scotland division tumbled against W. G. E. Macartney, 'a Tory of Tories, an Orangeman of Orangemen, and a bigot of bigots'.[60]

Temperance had fared no better than Home Rule and Lords reform as Liberal causes. Defending his seat at Derby Harcourt was dashed by the question, 'who took the duty off the Irishman's whiskey and put it on the Englishman's beer?'; and in Liverpool publicans backed the Conservative party to protect their livelihood.[61] Canvassers announced that Local Veto would mean £33 million extra annual taxation and two million unemployed; and 41,000 Liverpudlians petitioned against the Bill. These defeats, and the Peel Report on the licensing laws in 1899, persuaded leading Liberals henceforth to moderate their commitment to the temperance movement.[62]

Labour had been equally confounded in the General Election. The L.T.C. and Unemployed Association had demanded legislation to enable Guardians to create employment during exceptional distress, and to protect from disfranchisement electors who received poor relief.[63] Seven I.L.P. branches now existed, in Breckfield, Edge Hill, Kensington, Old Swan, Kirkdale, West Toxteth, and Wavertree; but their non-political work most impressed Sexton, who designated the Liverpool I.L.P. an 'amateur dramatic society'.[64] Sexton's 415 votes in Ashton was no testimony to professionalism; likewise the Liverpool S.D.F., with a hundred members, was unfitted for elections.[65] Even the irrepressible was dampened. O'Brien, of the S.D.F. and, more recently, of Walton gaol, failed to beg sufficient funds to contest Exchange.[66] Labour enthusiasts were humiliated to discover 'more men lounging at the public-house corners than inside at our meetings'.[67]

Conservatives, however, stirred men by a simple recipe. It took no flights of philosophy to recognize that some required little provocation to resist whomever and whatever was associated with Irish nationalism and Roman Catholicism, and to promote whomever and whatever perpetuated their degradation. In 1895 Liverpool and its environs breathed Conservatism, a feat which Forwood boasted nationally.[68]

Ward redistribution brings new conditions of municipal politics

The Conservative control of Liverpool culminated in the municipal elections of November 1895. Following redistribution there were twenty-two wards in place of the previous sixteen. Pitt Street, St. Paul's, Rodney Street, and Lime Street vanished by absorption into St. Peter's, Vauxhall, Great George Street, Abercromby, and St. Anne's. This diminution of Liberal/Nationalist strongholds was offset by dividing Scotland ward into North and South; but representation increased outside the old parish. Everton and Kirkdale made six wards—Sandhills (3,197 electorate), Kirkdale (6,023), Everton (4,716), Netherfield (4,276), St. Domingo (4,519), and Breckfield (3,964). West Derby was trisected into Edge Hill (4,572), Kensington (4,027), and Low Hill (4,030); and North and South Toxteth became Dingle (5,213), Granby (3,866), Princes Park (3,841), and Brunswick (3,093). Greater Liverpool was represented in six additional wards, South Walton (3,625), North Walton (3,103), Fairfield (3,199), West Derby (2,963), Wavertree (2,372), and Sefton Park (3,718). Electorates were more equal than before, but five of seven wards within the old parish had under 2,300 voters, from the Liberals' consideration of rateable value, not population, as a criterion of redistribution. However, the revised roll of 97,873 voters made Liverpool the country's largest municipal constituency.[69]

Control of this Council was crucial. Forwood issued a pamphlet, *Three Years of Radical and Nationalist Misrule*; and Evans revamped his thesis about fifty years of Conservative 'mismanagement'.[70] The critical question concerned party in municipal affairs. Forwood betrayed some ambivalence. He wrote, concerning temperance, that 'no party can claim any monopoly of the causes for improvement' and, concerning prostitution, that 'to introduce party in connection with such a subject is a disgrace to our common humanity'. But, to 'secure the best men of the city for public work', party considerations mattered for, 'whether they fought as Unionists or not, Home Rulers would fight as Home Rulers, and between the Radicals and the Nationalists there was no promise of continuity of action for the public good'.[71]

An accusation of ethnic politics did not embarrass Lynskey who maintained that he promoted Liverpool's prosperity consistently with Irish Nationalism; moreover, while Council parties existed, '200,000 Irishmen had a right to fair representation'.[72] Others reversed Forwood's charge of Tammany practices. A Liberal Councillor, John Henderson, asked if Liverpudlians wished to establish 'the dictatorship of Mr. A. T. Salvidge and Sir A. B. Forwood . . . [and] to make the City Council the seat of power for the intolerant section of the Tory party?'[73]

The W.M.C.A., however, did not scrutinize every Conservative candidate and not every Councillor followed Forwood. R. Ripley reminded St. Anne's electors that he had voted against his party on occasions, 'thus showing his impartiality'.[74] There was also Thomas Hughes. As chairman of the Parliamentary Committee, Hughes had lent minority Conservative support to the Liberal scheme of ward redistribution. J. S. Harmood-Banner, a new Conservative Councillor, compared Hughes's position to 'a man who has had to assist in cutting a suit of clothes which did not fit'; and C. W. Jones, a Liberal shipowner contesting Wavertree ward, asserted that Hughes 'hoped that his party would not have a majority' because, with Forwood returned to power, 'Hughes' influence would be gone'.[75] However, though Hughes was indeed 'very irate' when Forwood attacked the Liberal redistribution scheme, the two men were no longer rivals in any significant sense. The cleaner image with which Hughes's chairmanship invested the Licensing Committee benefited Conservatism where it was vulnerable; and Hughes's opportunities to disrupt party organization, where Salvidge had checked him since 1892, were remote. Accordingly, we find Forwood in 1895 reminding Lord Salisbury that Worms had recommended a knighthood for Hughes; and in 1896 he shunted Hughes aside from active leadership in the Council by arranging his second term as mayor.[76]

Forwood could afford generosity. The 1895 municipal elections, he apprised Lord Salisbury, were 'on strict party lines', and his party increased from twenty-nine members (including eight aldermen and one Liberal Unionist) in 1892 to sixty-four (including four aldermen and two Liberal Unionists) in 1895. The Liberal–Nationalist representation declined from thirty-three (including seven aldermen) to thirty-two (including nine aldermen). Liverpool's Conservatism was at last presented realistically and it was expected that, in regular circumstances, this majority would be sufficiently sizeable to deprive elections of keenness for a decade.[77] Publicly Forwood lamented the eclipse of a genuine Liberal party. Before it adopted Irish policies, it was led by 'broadminded men and worthy citizens'. Otherwise Forwood polished the image of democratic Conservatism. Working men, he emphasized, gave them victory.[78]

This was reflected in the dismissal of third-party hopes. Out of over 150 candidates some twenty-five were not from established parties. They represented many causes, but about half had Labour colours. A 'new and more advanced class of men' apparently had joined the L.T.C.;[79] but a fair-wages clause remained its public ambition. *Bona fide* clauses had been adopted by the Poor Law Guardians and School Board, but not by the Corporation. However, the L.T.C.'s decision to confine candidatures to those who ran 'on purely trade union lines' was not strictly upheld. Reeves was criticized for this,[80] but his 726 votes in Edge Hill exceeded the sum of the L.T.C.'s four other candidates. More wards required more funds; but many of the L.T.C.'s affiliated unions were in permanent arrears and opposed a capitation fee of more than 2*d.* A dismal postscript to Labour's adventures followed at Christmas when Matkin, Liverpool's first working-class magistrate, was charged with drunkenly assaulting a constable.[81]

Their own disparate sections, rather than their nominal opponents, troubled the Conservatives. Council parties were not whipped with parliamentary discipline and only thirty-five Conservative Councillors had sat before. Moreover subdivision engendered wards where Orangeism was the password. St. Domingo and Netherfield returned six Conservative councillors who were Orangemen; in addition an Independent Orangeman in Netherfield attracted 781 votes. The party's brewing connections and Forwood's promotion of the W.M.C.A. also presaged difficulties; but now, in Dingle ward, Forwood intervened strongly and directed the expulsion of several critics from party membership.[82]

Altogether the tendency inherent in the creation of Greater Liverpool was to reinforce the caucus management of the Conservative party. The Constitutional Association's annual levy on M.P.s, aldermen, and councillors, produced sums which were insufficient to support independent agencies in constituencies and wards, but sufficient to maintain a central agency. This agency now became stronger as successes in new wards brought more subscriptions. Before 1895 the Constitutional was often in some financial difficulty; henceforward it remained solvent. Moreover, while the agency's role was ostensibly to execute arrangements and decisions made by polling district, ward, or constituency, committees, inevitably the party leader used its universal involvement as a lever of dictation.

Personality and policy disputes in the Conservative administration

Lord Derby was invited to become the first Lord Mayor of Greater Liverpool. The origin of this is difficult to pinpoint. Members of the Liberal merchant plutocracy had espoused the idea before their party majority was reversed in the municipal elections. Robert Holt had been dismayed both by the increasing partisanship of politics and by the antics of their party's most recent choice of Lord Mayor, Watts. A draper, Watts was wealthy but socially 'second class'. His first public engagement had brought him out in 'magnificent scarlet robes trimmed with sable fur and cocked or rather three-cornered hat. Awful swell. I believe the verdict is one of approval but really I cannot fancy such outlandish dress for civilized human beings.' In proposing Derby as Watt's successor at a Liberal caucus Holt therefore 'used the argument of his high position and that possibly such an appointment would raise the tone of municipal councils', although this view was not then endorsed. On the Conservative side Forwood was moved by a sense that Derby was a catch politically. The other aspect hardly mattered. Forwood had not much interest in Lord Derby's polite society. Derby fulfilled Forwood's purpose of decoration without independent inspiration. Like his son, the 'King of Lancashire', the 16th Earl suited a town hall better than Westminster but, when it came to the vote, the Irish Nationalist councillors formally opposed his adoption. Thus Lord Derby became the *English* mayor of Liverpool by eighty-two votes to eleven.[83]

The labyrinth of party favour was less tractable than the ceremonial. The W.M.C.A. petitioned Forwood to advance Salvidge to a vacant aldermanship but Forwood failed, despite a laboured intimation to Conservative councillors that Salvidge was 'a thorough representative of the working classes'. Some refused Salvidge because of this; others were unsympathetic because Salvidge was not a councillor. They would pitchfork Derby into the mayoralty; but Salvidge encountered rivals for the aldermanship—Herbert Campbell, a Toxteth councillor, and Hornby, who had rejoined the Council in 1895. Of the Conservative councillors thirty-five favoured Hornby; Salvidge found seventeen supporters, Campbell eight.[84] Whatever Salvidge's estimation of Council membership relative to control of party organization, they now seemed indivisible.[85] He removed his disadvantage at a by-election in Low Hill. A magistracy followed and, appropriately, the aldermanship was achieved when Salvidge replaced Forwood in 1898.[86]

The creation of Greater Liverpool had been undertaken from administrative necessity but, to secure the assent of the Local Boards it swallowed, the Corporation conceded differential rating for the next fifteen years. The new areas were consumers as well as producers of revenue. Residents and representatives alike complained of the 'lack of public enterprise' in outer wards.[87] This was common to many cities. There was no 'intelligent anticipation' of urban growth; and newly incorporated areas, previously without stringent sanitary administrations, reproduced on city outskirts 'the slum characteristics which are the despair of the civic reformer in its heart'.[88]

The Liberal interregnum had provided few foundations for a new Liverpool. The Liberals' object, to reduce the rates, involved starving municipal departments and ignoring thorny problems in the sinking fund. To relieve a debt of £50,000 the Conservatives levied a rate; and in 1898 they reversed the policy in the Corporation Stock, pursued since 1880, by returning to a system of redeemable bonds.[89] Forwood advocated a broad strategy, despising the view that low rates should be the *summum bonum* of administration. He wanted to extend recreation space, to review the road system, to replace insanitary property, and to forge an alliance between the Corporation and Docks and Harbour Board in order to cheapen charges and to expand trade.

The boundary extension widened the Council's responsibility but also permitted adventures in house-building. The supply by private enterprise had slackened from over 1,000 houses built annually before 1885 to 265 in 1895.[90] In 1896 over five times this amount was completed, and three years of expansion followed. This supply was outside the Council's control; but until now the Council's houses had been mostly occupied by relatively well-to-do artisans.[91] From 1898, therefore, the Insanitary Property Committee reached agreement with landlords and builders by reaffirming Forwood's original proposition of 1883, that the Corporation would restrict its dwellings to displaced families. Implicit was that the municipality gave up competition in the housing market.[92]

Thenceforward to 1915 the Corporation utilized the Housing of the Working Classes Act of 1890 to build 2,400 tenements compared with 523 previously; and by 1913 only 2,771 'insanitary' dwellings remained, although the criteria were unchanged from 1864.[93] The ambition was to diminish discrepancies between Liverpool's worst district, Exchange, and its healthiest, Sefton Park, with death-rates of 36·9 and 9·9 per 1,000 respectively at the end of the century. Nevertheless in 1911 Liverpool still enjoyed 'the unenviable reputation of possessing the worst slums of any English city'.[94]

The Council's conception remained limited. It would not go beyond rehousing those dispossessed by its demolitions, although in its operations Liverpool was in advance of other municipalities. Between 1865 and 1914 private enterprise demolished 11,000 houses, mostly to make way for business premises, while the Corporation demolished another 10,700.[95] The houses built by private enterprise were invariably let at rentals too high for former court residents. The Corporation could not legislate for this, or for human choice in regard to its own dwellings. After 1897, in seven schemes which displaced 7,259 people, 72·91 per cent entered municipal dwellings. The remainder excited the deputy surveyor's indignation: 'They have idle, indolent ways . . . There are certain people whom no corporation or body of persons can help.'[96]

Certainly a prejudice existed against the barrack life in flats;[97] but one builder noted the wages question—'People do not live in slums for choice, they do not starve for choice, are not dirty for choice. When a man loses employment he may be respectable; then he gets half-starved—[and his] wife gets disheartened. If you consider what poor working men have to go through do you wonder they become careless? There is no margin for them to save.'[98] The Housing Committee's chairman accepted that 'the first duty of a municipality was to the poorest poor'; but even the minimum weekly rent for a one-room Corporation tenement, 1*s*. 9*d*., was beyond the means of some.[99] In these circumstances council housing, until 1919 without government subsidy,, was unlikely to expand in principle and scale. Before 1914 Liverpool's capital expenditure was £1,163,000. Rents barely covered maintenance costs, and an annual deficit of £30,000 accrued.[100]

Improvement derived as much from developments in suburban-city transport as from the provision of Council housing. When the well-to-do went further afield, central properties fell to smaller wage-earners. A Tramway Company started in 1865; but the Corporation controlled its streets and in 1880 purchased the lines. Thereafter the Corporation leased them to the Company, nominated a director (Forwood), and negotiated fares.[101] Under the Liberal administration the lines had fallen into disrepair and the Company gave notice holding the Council responsible for damage to vehicles and loss of traffic. Forwood now had the choice of renewing lines for horse traction or changing to motor power. Economy and increase of traffic demanded electrical power; but this placed the Corporation and Company at odds over expenditure. Forwood concluded that the Corporation should acquire the Company.[102] To buy and reconstruct the network, he estimated, would cost £1 million with an underground system, £1,300,000 with an overhead system. Either was feasible: the Electric Supply Company was municipalized in 1896.[103] In 1897 the Tramway Company was purchased. Thereafter councillors debated the sort of electrical traction.

These technical disputes concealed a challenge to Forwood's dictation of policy. In the last ten years, during Forwood's absence as a Minister and the Liberal interregnum, new men had entered the Conservative party. Charles Petrie and William Rutherford were types Forwood was warned against on the Generating Station (Tramways) Committee—'too many of the clever and ambitious men in the Council have been placed upon it'.[104] In May 1898 Rutherford's views about the best tramcar created a sensation in the Council when Forwood's recommendations, as chairman of the Tramways Committee, were rejected. Forty councillors were absent from the debate. Regarding this as an expression of no confidence or, as Robert Holt thought, merely out of temper, Forwood resigned from the Council.[105]

This did not end Forwood's leadership of Liverpool Conservatism. Councillor Hampson argued that, without a municipal portfolio, Forwood would 'be better able to guide and criticize'; and the party agent, James Thompson, was forthright:

> your action in the interests of the party is well timed as, for a leader to suffer the humiliation you have had from time to time, is impossible and encourages the relaxation of party discipline resulting in chaos. I know what some of them say; one has gone so far as to assert that he will be the Leader in the Council before two years are over—If *such a thing were possible* our position in Liverpool is doomed.[106]

Forwood was not seriously entreated to withdraw his resignation: the party leadership and Council leadership was an undesirable combination. Salvidge alone suspected that Forwood might abdicate both positions. His perplexity radiated disingenuousness: 'I fail to see upon whom your mantle will fall so as to maintain the credit, you have established, to the City and the Party.'[107] In fact Salvidge's speculation was not premature. Forwood died in October 1898.

It is tempting to think that this crisis was manufactured. The evidence, however, will not run to this conclusion. Of course Forwood's dominance excited peevishness, and the leadership's most controversial characteristic, the elevation of the W.M.C.A., had not been unimpeded. Forwood had failed to make Salvidge an alderman; and Salvidge complained that W.M.C.A. officials were excluded from Town Hall social functions and from the platform at important political meetings.[108] But, though Rutherford had replaced Forwood as chairman of the Tramways Committee, in August 1899 he too resigned.[109] The type of tram was still disputed. Rutherford also clashed with the city engineers, by preferring contract to Corporation labour for the work of laying lines.[110] This talent for publicity was the mark of a soloist, and Rutherford raised suspicions about his loyalty to the party when he embarrassed his successor, Petrie, with his championship of tramway workers' grievances.[111] Rutherford's record suggests inexperience, rather Forwood's chance assassin than part of a coherent conspiracy.

The municipal tramway turned out better than many suspected, into 'the most successful system . . . in England', according to Rutherford.[112] Gladstonian Liberals, like Robert Holt, and old-school Conservatives, like the Overhead Railway Company's chairman, Sir William Forwood, vaunted the virtues of private capital against Municipal Trading and predicted disaster from cheap fares;[113] but the rates profited by nearly £½ million by 1914.[114]

The change from horse to electric traction was a transport revolution.[115] Politics rarely undergo obvious metamorphosis; but Sir Arthur Forwood's demise augured novelties.

CHAPTER ELEVEN

Poverty and Protestantism: Salvidge in control, 1898–1900

God seemed very far away in Liverpool. *Hugh Walpole*

The question was formerly asked if there was such a thing as a Conservative working man, but if honourable Members will go to Liverpool, they will see 8,000 of them all subscribing members of the Working Men's Conservative Association. Are they seeking to obtain old age pensions or employers' liability legislation, or anything to better their own position in life? No; they are deeply concerned on one subject, and one subject alone, and that is the danger to Protestantism and the danger to the national Church. They are staunch Conservatives, but they place their religion above politics.
Charles M'Arthur, M.P.

Forwood's death closed an era in the history of modern Liverpool. His twenty-seven years of Council service and eighteen years of Conservative leadership were a tribute to the unsparing strength rather than the prepossessing nature of his personality. The best judgement of his career was recorded in the diary of one who disliked Forwood personally and who abominated his political partisanship. 'What he decided to do he worked at till he did it', wrote Robert Holt. After the death of this gaunt man the Liverpool Conservative party entered a period of irresolute and unauthoritative leadership. Amid shifting and uncertain forces Protestantism stood out as one apparently sure source of loyalty from the Conservative democracy. Accordingly Salvidge, in association with the Protestants' spokesman, George Wise, propelled the W.M.C.A. into a position of command over the Conservative organization. But politicians had to beware of simulating indignation for Protestant audiences. Babble breaks down when faced with fundamentals. The Protestant concern about Catholic power had an imperial ring to it, but also a domestic note, which Archdeacon W. F. Taylor sounded with brutal directness: 'We do not want the priests in our homes with our wives and children.'

As well as the sectarian animation of Liverpool politics, this chapter also highlights the continuing poverty of much Liverpool life. Public concern and

Notes begin on p. 416

policy was channelled in two directions. Relief might be given to the individuals and families that poverty scarred; but a priority was to ensure that society as a whole was protected from the depredations of the malformed and misused. Lord Macaulay's warning was still heeded: 'The Huns and Vandals who will destroy our civilization are being bred, not in the wilds of Asia, but in the slums of our great cities.' In fact this fear was proved baseless at the turn of the twentieth century by Charles Booth, who concluded from his statistical inquiry into the London poor that, though the slums indeed contained barbarians, 'the hordes . . . do not exist . . . they are a handful, a small and decreasing percentage: a disgrace but not a danger'. Misery he observed aplenty—reckoning some 30 per cent of the population living in poverty—but he protested against the common confusion of the residuum, that group of 'occasional labourers, street-sellers, loafers, criminals, and semi-criminals,' with other classes of the poor and very poor, the casual labourers, underemployed, unemployed, old and helpless. In this respect the children of the poor were important, and in this chapter attention is paid to the design of voluntary societies and statutory bodies, that the next generation should be an improvement on the last.[1]

Private charity and public policy in civic welfare

The poverty of Liverpool life was measured politically by indices of drunkenness. In 1889 16,042 drunks were convicted, in 1895 5,305. The Head Constable credited improvement to a zealous Bench, rigorous inspections, trade depression, slum clearances, the extension of sport, education, benefit societies and transport, and the diminishing practice of 'subbing' wages.[2] Other explanations exist, such as the emergence of an alternative pattern of expenditure on cheap imported foodstuffs and mass-produced articles.[3] There was also a suspicion that the Liverpool public was supplied with comforting information. The 7,800 persons treated in dispensaries for wounds or injuries sustained through drink outnumbered the drunks arrested by the police in 1895. The Unitarian minister, Richard Armstrong, bluntly called the police statistics 'farcical'. In fact it was a useful rule-of-thumb concerning police statistics to reckon that the reliability of the record varied according to the seriousness of the crime. A policeman would have no hesitation in apprehending a thief or vandal as a public menace, but he might regard a drunk only as a minor nuisance, to be ignored or ushered on his way. Different people employ different standards of drunkenness. The Liverpool police generally were instructed to arrest when the suspect was deemed 'incapable' but this guidance was not sure. It was notorious that many 'drunks' escaped proceedings.[4] In the absence of trustworthy statistics, therefore, witnesses of Liverpool life relied on impressions—the 'evidence' before their eyes. According to this criterion Liverpool had not been transmogrified. Indeed it remained, one Poor Law Guardian observed, 'a reproach to all'.[5]

This wretchedness was variously viewed. The Unemployed Association was concerned that in Liverpool 'thousands of men were walking the streets in a starving condition'.[6] The sight of children, as traders-cum-beggars, disturbed more.[7] Bessie Braddock found the poverty 'difficult to describe . . . without making it seem incredible': 'a kid with shoes was an event . . . and thousands were stunted from lack of food like ragged shrubs in the Arctic'.[8]

Few tokens of a society's values are better than its regard for children. Conventional standards of authority allowed parents or guardians to maltreat children with relative impunity. Animals had protectors long before a Liverpool town's meeting, in 1883, founded the Society for the Prevention of Cruelty to Children.[9] Its first report, of six month's work, classified 378 cases brought before it into 'immorality' (12), 'violence' (50), 'cruel neglect' (106), beggary and exposure (210). Putative causes were distinguished: sixty-five cases where parents were dead; twenty-four where children were deserted; seventeen where step-parents were 'unkind'; seven where children were illegitimate; eight where parents were imprisoned; fifteen where mothers were prostitutes; and 202 where 'drink' seemed significant. Others were assigned reasons of temper: only twenty-two were acknowledged to derive from 'poverty'.[10] This emphasis on character, not circumstances, was archetypally Victorian.

The Liverpool S.P.C.C.'s prosecutions were few—three from 378 cases in 1883–4; 113 from 3,774 cases in 1909[11]—since it cherished the family principle. The early cases were mostly settled either by placing children under the School Board's supervision (141 cases) or by leaving parents under visitation from the Society (120). Others were committed to Industrial Schools, Emigration Homes, private homes, hospitals, with relations, or in domestic service. Samuel Smith, a founder of the S.P.C.C., cultivated the emigration schemes. About 3,000 destitute children had been helped to emigrate from Liverpool before 1895.[12] For many the sea itself, not what lay beyond, was spellbinding.[13] The respectable agency of escape, the Seamen's Orphanage (1869), trained merchant navy officers. Leading shipowners supported its school ships, the *Indefatigable* and *Conway*.[14] In contrast the Olive Mount School maintained the *Akbar* (for Protestants) and the *Clarence* (for Catholics). Reformatories rather than training ships, they broke boys into ordinary seamen. The *Clarence* was investigated in 1894–5 for neglect of health, the *Akbar* in 1910–11 for alleged brutality.[15]

Children and play, usually affinities, demanded organization by Victorians. After 1877 many cities had 'Fresh-Air' or 'Country Holiday' Funds.[16] Some brought entertainments to the slums. Liverpool's Cinderella Club was among several inspired by Blatchford's *Clarion*,[17] and, from 1897, the Food and Betterment Association held summer concerts in slum streets. Financing these organizations was difficult. When Canon Lester begged money on the Exchange on behalf of Liverpool 's Ragged Schools and the Kirkdale Child Charity, 'the flags [pavements] were cleared as though there was a downfall of rain'.[18] The Food and Betterment Association owed its director, H. Lee Jones, £950 by 1899. In 1898 it had distributed 275,000 meals, and 43,400 persons attended its sixty-three street concerts.[19] These finished neutrally with 'Auld Lang Syne', not the National Anthem; and *Porcupine* condemned this truckling to Irish and Socialist opponents of the monarchy.[20] Some charity workers in Irish districts intended to save souls before stomachs.[21] The right religion might banish poverty, so Silas Hocking, who had been a Methodist minister in Toxteth, stressed in a novel, *Her Benny*. An account is worth giving: *Her Benny* was a best-seller for many years after its publication in 1879.[22]

The protagonists are nine-year-old Nelly Bates, who sells matches, and her brother, ten-year-old Benny, who carries bags at the Mersey ferry. They abscond from their drunken father and stepmother. Living on the streets Benny is tempted to steal but restrained, once by Nelly and once by a dim remembrance of their mother's faith. Their neighbourhood contains Scotland Road, which policemen never patrol alone and where rent-collectors are intimidated; and Hocking explains many miseries, like overcrowding, by personal viciousness.[23] The waifs are befriended by grandmotherly Betty Barker, who introduces them to her much-worn Bible. Dwelling in narrow poverty the children are as ignorant of their city as of the gospel—Benny believes that the Infirmary 'wur the 'ouse the Queen lived in'. He becomes acquainted with its realities when Nelly is run over. A nurse tells Benny, 'if your sister leaves you she'll be better off, and will not have to tramp the streets in the cold and wet'. Nelly has a pauper's burial.

Hereafter Benny is adopted by Mr. Lawrence, a merchant with a young daughter, Eva; and Benny, earning several shillings in Mr. Lawrence's office, ruminates about 'poor Liverpool boys who by perseverence and honest toil, had become wealthy men, and were now occupying high and honourable positions'. This is Hocking's sermon, the open society. It favoured the elevation of working people—one at a time. Benny learns to write; he attends Sunday School; and he alters his elocution so as not to be 'a disgrace to the gentlemen who employed him and the butt of the clerks'. However, a different test intervenes--£5 is missing in the office and Benny is suspect. He cannot keep his job, although insufficient evidence exists for prosecution. Rejecting suicide in the Mersey (where his father drowns while intoxicated), Benny quits Liverpool. He seeks work in surrounding villages but, when people learn that Benny is from Liverpool, they slam their doors—'they wanted no thieves nor pick-pockets in their employ'. For six years Benny works on a farm; and at night-school he is educated and Christianized. Nearby are merchant properties, including that of Eva Lawrence's relations, the Munroes. Conveniently Benny rescues Eva and Mr. Munroe from their runaway carriage. Munroe offers Benny employment in Manchester, telling him, 'I commenced as a clerk at the desk, and what I have accomplished there is no reason why you may not'.

Eva recognizes Benny. The tale is out—the £5 was mislaid, not stolen—and Benny is welcomed for, as Eva's cousin says, 'he has the bearing of a gentleman . . . I expected we were going to be highly amused at his behaviour and his dialect . . . but really he speaks quite correctly'. Benny returns to Liverpool with the Lawrences. Everything falls into place, and that place gets higher as Benny marries the boss's daughter and becomes a partner in the firm. In his leisure Benny teaches at Sunday School, introducing 'ragged and neglected children' to 'a bright future that might be theirs if they would be industrious, truthful, and honest'.

Hocking was not artless. Contrasted with Benny is Perks, who graduates from beggary to crime and dies in prison. Perks is incredulous that Benny could have 'kep' honest . . . an' kep' in Liverpool'. Hocking emphasized that moral cowardice distinguished Perks but, as Perks on his deathbed recognizes a 'loving Saviour, who was ready to forgive the vilest', he speculates whether 'society had made him what he was, and was to some degree responsible for his wickedness'.

Benny's morality was exceptional.[24] The Head Constable of Liverpool noted the existence of young criminal brotherhoods—'six boys together committed thirteen cases of house-breaking in Wavertree; a band of nine systematically stole sugar from the docks; and fifteen formed a gang for stealing goods outside of shops'.[25] Aimless, underemployed lads, leaving school at fourteen, discarded 'all parental authority. They get congregating about street corners at night time . . . they chew tobacco and smoke and their highest ambition is to get drunk . . .' The Head Constable was clear about Liverpool's position in the criminal league: 'no city can compare with it in juvenile crime' or, it might have been added, in most other categories of offences. At the turn of this century the gaols of Liverpool contained one-ninth of the total prison population of England, one-seventh of those aged between sixteen and twenty-nine, one-third of reformatory inmates, and nearly one-third of all reconvicted ex-reformatory inmates. In 1898 some 900 Liverpool children aged under sixteen were arrested on indictable offences, and another 400 on non-indictable offences. There were various attempts to curb the size of this group. Some success was claimed for corporal punishment. In five years 489 boys were whipped; 135 were reconvicted; of these forty-four were whipped again, and only ten of these were subsequently reconvicted. The School Board was also enlisted to pacify and to socialize young criminals: the case was strong for a more subtle and varied system of sentences, probation, and reform. As for the potential criminals it seemed indisputable that more preventive work was required—'crime decreases in proportion to the care taken of the young, and this care, if an apparent expense at the moment, saves in the long run'.[26]

Nevertheless until such groups as the Police-Aided Clothing Association began in 1895, shoeing and clothing 15,000 children by 1903, the picture in *Her Benny* was genuine—of travellers encountering ragged children at all hours.[27] Gradually they were 'forced out of sight', into 'less conspicuous neighbourhoods'; but Rupert Brooke, for one, had no trouble finding an urchin in 1913, whom he paid, to wave him off from the quay; and barefoot and ragged children were still common in Liverpool in the 1920s and 1930s.[28] Their evidence had long been offensive to some citizens: 'rags and half-nakedness should be treated as indecency, and such misery taken off the streets; the circumstances of each investigated, and, if in absolute poverty assisted; and decency of attire insisted upon at the expense of the individual when possible, but at the expense of the city if necessary'.[29] This depicted it like a job for the scavenging department, sweeping up individuals as litter.

Complaints, however, stimulated the Watch Committee.[30] Its warnings about serving drink to children under thirteen years became a bye-law in 1899 in order to destroy the carrying trade.[31] From 1898 the Corporation also licensed street-trading by children, the Home Office tolerating this innovation because 'no town . . . contains so difficult a population as that of Liverpool'.[32] The licences, mostly issued free, distinguished children exempt and not exempt from school; and regulations governed behaviour and hours. The Corporation originally demanded that children from bad backgrounds reside in approved lodgings; but Catholic Councillors wanted children to lodge with persons of the same creed. Being unwilling to undertake such detailed supervision and inquiry, the Corporation attenuated this clause. Without compulsion children avoided authorized lodgings; but although Boer War news tempted children out late selling papers, trading during school hours and at night diminished. By mid-1900 the licences totalled 1,146 (979 boys; 167 girls) of whom 257 attended Board, 228 Anglican, and 661 Catholic, schools. Some 161 children were summonsed for unlicensed trading, and 345 were reported for breaches of regulations. Fifty licenses were revoked; but mostly the regulations had desired effects. Ten towns sought similar powers, and in the Liverpool Corporation Act of 1930 the regulation was extended to include such as van boys and errand boys under eighteen years of age.[33]

Another consequence of destitution was considered by the Government's Physical Deterioration Committee, that many offering military service were not fit to be shot. This was not new—sixty years before it was noted that Spitalfields weavers were 'descending to the size of Lilliputians. You could not raise a grenadier company amongst them all.'[34] The phenomenon was now concentrated, not diffused; but two tendencies seemed marked. Children of 'the respectable artisan class', or country-bred children, were healthy and well-developed; but the entirely city-bred children of labouring stock had 'deteriorated very much'.[35]

On the debit side was evidence of rickets, ringworm, ophthalmitis, tuberculosis, deformity, rotten teeth, rapid ageing, and sterility; and Liverpool's lunacy rate, 5·9 per 1,000 persons, was thought 'phenomenally' high. On the credit side schools and charities disseminated principles of hygiene and nutrition. Absolute deterioration was arrested. The Committee was investigating a wasted previous generation. Dr. Young described casuals at the docks, 'undersized men' now in their maturity, whom he used to inspect as factory boys. Then they appeared 'with bare feet, ignorant, illiterate, dirty, and mentally deficient. I do not say that they are idiots or lunatics, but without the brightness and quickness of intellect you find in young people now.'[36] A gradually rising standard of living and improved diet had curtailed the virulence of major infectious diseases in the late nineteenth century;[37] moreover the provision of Education Acts, Factory Acts, slum clearances, public parks and baths, and school medical inspections, in fact the whole expanding network of public health administration before 1914 was clearly registering an effect, although the facilities for treatment remained much fewer than those of diagnosis.

Not every advance was consolidated, and not every advance was an improvement. Winston Churchill declared during the Second World War, 'There is no finer investment for any community than putting milk into babies'. However, the right kind of milk was essential. At the turn of the century the Liverpool Corporation hoped to combat infant mortality by supplying sterilized milk to poor people at a nominal price; but sterilization destroyed the nutritive value, along with the bacteria.[38] Impure milk was a besetting problem. With the Mersey Railway Tunnel opened in 1886 Liverpool's milk might come from as far away as North Wales. In 1898 the Corporation appointed the country's first City Bacteriologist; and, by an Act of 1900, it was empowered to inspect and to license dairies and cowsheds outside its boundaries. The administration comprised one veterinary surgeon, five inspectors conversant with animal diseases, three who investigated the condition of cowsheds, and three who collected samples.[39] The twelve ostensibly controlled 802 shops, distributing 30,000 gallons per day, and 12,000 cows in 442 cowsheds, within and without Liverpool . Tubercular milk remained a problem well beyond the First World War.[40]

To blame the Corporation's health department was unrealistic. Dr. Nathan Raw, the tuberculosis specialist at the Poor Law Infirmary in Mill Road, called for Government action to control the pasteurization of all cow's milk, and in addition to provide a national system of hospitals, to inaugurate comprehensive housing and child care schemes, and to finance medical and scientific research. A city health department like Liverpool 's needed this support because its authority invariably confronted a vested interest.[41] Thus each M.O.H. had regretted that the meat eaten in Liverpool was slaughtered in the Abercromby district, in premises rented from the Corporation; and the Health Committee between 1850 and 1880 reduced the licences by almost a half. The death-rate of people living within 500 yards of the abattoirs averaged 36 per 1,000; and pressure accumulated against renewing the surviving leases in 1889.[42] However, death-rates alone proved nothing. Slaughterers complained that 'the abattoirs have now to bear the sins of the wretched hovels that the Corporation have at length been shamed into demolishing'. They also argued that their removal would increase costs and reduce the working classes' ability to buy meat.[43]

When the Council refused to confirm the Finance Committee's support of the M.O.H., it was evident that two interests collided. Some 330 doctors in and about Liverpool petitioned against the leases; but 2,650 property-owners counter-petitioned to save a trade whose employees brought custom to local shops.[44] The Council renewed the leases, until 1926 when the site was so 'monstrous . . . medieval, rat-ridden, and thoroughly insanitary' that it kept business away.[45] This episode illustrated the health authorities' dependent position. Trade interests directed them from preventive into consequential activities, a group of rat-catchers not town-planners.[46]

The anti-Ritualist movement

Amid this continuing poverty, Liverpool's political and religious authorities were also diverted. 'True Protestantism' implied mysterious distinctions. Sir David Gamble recognized that his son's views 'would be called rather low Church in the Diocese of Lincoln or Southwell, but . . . rather high in the Diocese of Liverpool'.[47] 'Ritualist' was a portmanteau term of abuse equating those clergymen who used liturgical ceremony sparingly with crypto-Catholics.[48] The offence of these High Churchmen in the view of Evangelicals was their revival or introduction of Roman Catholic ceremonial and sacramental practices in the Church of England and their elevation of the clerical and episcopal offices at the expense of 'saving religion'. According to the Church Association's investigation of ritualist societies the Liverpool Diocese contained thirty-four clerical members of the English Church Union, nine members of the Confraternity of the Blessed Sacrament, and four members of the Holy Cross. Sixty-three clergymen used the eastward position, thirty-five used the mixed chalice, three used incense, twelve used vestments, and twenty-four used altar lights, in their churches.[49] This tally was comparatively the fewest of any diocese—the Church Association listed altogether 9,600 'Ritualist' clergy—but Liverpool was not peaceful.

Ryle's episcopacy evinced the difficulties. Ryle's reputation was founded by a penny tract *What Do We Owe To The Reformation?* (1877), a question he answered thus: England gained 'a true idea of Christian worship', delivered from 'the degrading tyranny and swindling impostures of the Romish priesthood'. Downrightness made Ryle, apart from Spurgeon, the most popular Victorian tract writer and the doyen of evangelicals.[50] When appointed bishop he declined to make 'a guy of himself' and discarded the cope and mitre;[51] but gestures could not solve Ryle's problems. In 1880 his diocese had contained a mere 179 beneficed clergy and 125 curates amid 1,100,000 people. Only twenty-five churches had endowments; the rest subsisted on fees, pew-rents, and offertories.

Ryle connected Ritualism with working-class indifference, and commended 'aggressive evangelization' in church and mission room. The parochial system was fossilized and, 'as to excessive decoration, I believe the intelligent working man regards it as childish . . .'.[52] Before ordination in 1841 Ryle had considered entering Conservative politics and, as bishop, he reflected how an infidel people 'have nothing to lose by a general scramble', fomented by 'talking meddlers who delight in setting labour against capital'.[53] The integrity of the rule of law in both civil and religious establishments was a prime consideration. One famous Protestant writer, Walter Walsh, significantly defined Ritualists as '*Ecclesiastical Anarchists*'.[54] A divided Church, which tolerated disobedience, would begin a general slide; and Ryle wanted Parliament to abolish the episcopal veto, which virtually closed the door to a layman initiating proceedings against a clergyman for offences of doctrine or ritual, and to establish lay tribunals which would define formulary and rubric.[55]

Ryle's preaching belied his infirmity:

> Once let Popery put her foot again on the neck of England, and there will be an end of all our national greatness. God will forsake us, and we shall sink to the level of Portugal and Spain. With Bible-reading discouraged—with private judgement forbidden—with priest-craft re-established—with auricular confession set up in every passage,—with monasteries and nunneries dotted over the land,—with women everywhere kneeling like serfs and slaves at the feet of clergymen—with men casting off all faith, and becoming sceptics,—with schools and colleges made seminaries of Jesuitism,—with free thought denounced and anathematized:—with all these things the distinctive manliness and independence of the British character will gradually dwindle . . .[56]

Such pronouncements made understandable Dean Church's opinion that 'The Bishop of Liverpool surely is an obnoxious to all High Churchmen as the Bishop of Lincoln can be to any Low';[57] but Ryle's failure to check 'Ritualism and priest-craft' in his diocese only excited militant Protestants against the episcopacy, since even 'the best among them do nothing'.[58] Forwood had told Lord Salisbury that Ryle 'as a man is esteemed and respected but as a Bishop he is failure wearing but one pair of official spectacles'.[59]

This was not strictly true. On accepting his bishopric Ryle had given up nominal partisanship and resigned from the Church Association, with which he had recently shown some tendency to disagree, over 'What Diversities Of Opinion, Practice, And Ritual Are Justly Tolerable Within The Pale Of The Established Church Of England'.[60] Nevertheless his visceral strength of expression encouraged activists like George Wise, whose commitment was confirmed in 1897 in debates with Father Donnelly and the Revd. John Wakeford. In 1898 Wiseites demonstrated at St. Catherine's, Abercromby, St. Margaret's (Wakeford's church), and St. Thomas', Toxteth, where allegedly ritualism had driven workmen from the congregation.[61] Wise was also prominent in the Protestant Reformation Society, but his activities occasioned the resignation of the president, Maurice Darby. A hot gospeller turned lukewarm, Darby condemned Wise's 'campaign of flagrant abuse and inflated bigotry', as likely to provoke 'bloodshed, and civil war'; but Wise claimed, although he fought Ritualism, his agitation against Rome 'had not taken definite shape'.[62]

Anti-ritualist feeling was formalized in July 1898 with the foundation in Liverpool of a Churchmen's Council and Laymen's League. The first was mainly a churchwarden's and clerical body; the Laymen's League was more political. Its ancestry lay in memorials to the Government on ecclesiastical questions during previous decades.[63] While it might be thought that theological matters are peculiarly the province of clergymen, the Laymen's League argued that such an assumption of authority was inconsistent with true Protestant principles, and it promoted a Church Discipline Bill to extirpate the Mass, Confessional, and other offences, by abolishing the episcopal veto and substituting for imprisonment inhibition or deprivation. A bishop could exercise disciplinary powers before proceedings began and he would be represented at the lay tribunals. The plaintiffs might be any two Anglicans in the diocese.

The League's chairman, Austin Taylor, was the second son of a respected Archdeacon of Liverpool.[64] After a Cambridge education he had entered the shipowning business of his uncle, Hugh Evans, who was president of the Church Association's Liverpool branch in the 1880s. This pedigree explains Taylor's 'lurking sympathy with fanatics because they were the only people, as a rule, who got anything done'.[65] His determination made him 'the Hampden of the Protestant and Constitutional cause', although his partisanship had been too strong for some when he had referred to Gladstone's 'indecently prolonged existence'.[66]

Equally startling was Taylor's and Wise's intervention, in August 1898, in a Southport by-election called by Curzon's appointment as Viceroy of India.[67] Southport was marginal when Curzon first stood in 1886, but he built a majority of 763 by 1895.[68] Now Sir Herbert Naylor-Leyland defeated Lord Skelmersdale by 272 votes. Naylor-Leyland cannot be thought personally popular. His defection from the Conservative party and receipt of a baronetcy from the Liberal government had been considered scandalous in 1895; but Curzon's force was missed, and holiday absenteeism, controversy over leaseholds, and wavering Liberal Unionists, conspired towards the Conservatives' failure.[69] Naylor-Leyland, however, had satisfied the anti-Ritualists' demands, while

Skelmersdale resisted the Church Discipline Bill. This difference, *inter alia*, was important. The disaffection 'not only of Churchmen but of Protestants generally' exceeded the Government's estimation.[70]

The pelting style was maintained with a lecture in Liverpool by the secretary of the newly formed Imperial Protestant Federation, Walter Walsh. His classic work, the *Secret History of the Oxford Movement*, (1896), which had achieved 22,000 sales and a fourth edition in 1898, furnished the argument that Protestantism and national prosperity were inextricable. Ritualism was foreign and demoralizing: 'Ritualists supply Popery in the Church of England as some Irishmen supply whisky—without a *licence*.' Walsh indicated a spiral of infamy: 'The Tractarians prepared the ground, the Puseyites planted, the Ritualists watered, and the Pope has reaped the harvest.'[71] The success of this teaching was manifested when Protestant hecklers sought to deny the Revd. Wakeford freedom to reply to Walsh's charges.[72]

Wise meanwhile acknowledged that the assault on Catholicism had begun, by founding the British Protestant Union to fight 'a trinity of evils—Romanism, Ritualism and infidelity'.[73] Wise's patron, J. A. Bramley-Moore, had just died and Wise parted from two bodies with which he had worked since coming to Liverpool.[74] He left the Christian Evidence Society and was dismissed from the Y.M.C.A. Wise criticized the Y.M.C.A. for allowing its Foley Street building—practically the public hall of Kirkdale—to be used for a Catholic bazaar. The Y.M.C.A. made counter-allegations: moneys which Wise collected as a teacher inflated his Protestant campaign. Moreover the Y.M.C.A. discountenanced 'controversial lectures because the inevitable result of such in a district like this is too alarming to be entertained'.[75]

Protestants also disputed election tactics. Salvidge had defended McCracken's stand in Everton in 1892; but now he criticized militants who desired to oust from the Council Conservatives like Alderman Bartlett who openly despised their claims. The antagonists arrayed their arguments, the uncompromising Orangemen supported by Wise's Protestant Union, Salvidge by the Laymen's League and Forwood's prestige.[76] As for the W.M.C.A. members voted to sever all ties with Alderman Bartlett; but larger questions of public policy were harder to settle. Several delegates proclaimed that 'religion could not be separated from politics' and that 'politics dissociated from religion would be a miserable thing not worth fighting about'; but Salvidge carefully reviewed the position.[77] Local government was irrelevant to the Protestant cause: only Parliament could curb Ritualism and if Protestants were to persuade 'all moderate and right-thinking men efforts must be made to avoid any appearance of bigotry or persecution'.[78]

The subsequent municipal elections were generally quiet. Liberals made one gain in 1897, two in 1898; but the average poll fell from 55 per cent to 44 per cent since, with their majority, many Unionists lacked urgency.[79] Sectarians were not so sluggish. One Evertonian avowed that 'the election of a Catholic would introduce a plague spot into the ward' and that 'Catholicism produced stunted intellects'; and in Dingle ward Salvidge rallied 'every religious man, whether Liberal or Conservative'.[80]

By January 1899 Salvidge's designs were clearer as the W.M.C.A. questioned the Prime Minister and local M.P.s concerning the Church Discipline Bill. Lord

Salisbury was studiously non-commital;[81] but the Abercromby, West Toxteth, Exchange, and Kirkdale M.P.s, Lawrence, Houston, M'Arthur, and MacIver,[82] embraced the Bill. Less than enthusiastic was A. F. Warr, who had represented East Toxteth from November 1895, after Worms became Lord Pirbright. The son of a canon, and former vicar of Childwall, Warr was keener to give Liverpool an independent University than independent Protestantism.[83] He promised to support the Bill's second reading, but intended to propose amendments in committee. Salvidge accepted Warr's position; but many W.M.C.A. delegates showed impatience with Warr's suggestion that the Church was designed to include different opinions.[84]

The Walton and Everton M.P.s, Stock and Willox, were also unhappy. Stock procrastinated about replying, and Willox disputed the efficacy of fresh legislation; but they eventually capitulated before the W.M.C.A.'s assertions 'that the chief cause of recent ritualistic excesses has been the episcopal veto, and that there can be no security for the laity unless they have proper access to the Courts . . .'.[85] Only the West Derby M.P., Long, remained impervious. Action was, for the moment, deferred but anti-Ritualism had introduced into Liverpool politics a disquieting stratagem. M.P.s had mostly subordinated judgement to a partial body, the W.M.C.A. Accredited political agencies were aping 'popular' Protestant organizations in direct action.

This was emphasized when Wise accused the Bishop of evading his responsibility to 'correct and punish the disobedient'.[86] Recently Ryle had exhorted two curates at St. Agnes's to resign for preaching the necessity of confessionals; but the Revd. John Wakeford gained national publicity for the case by offering to employ the offenders at St. Margaret's.[87] In this case the two arms of a bishop's authority—the paternal and the judicial—seemed nullified; and this exhibition of Ryle's helplessness nourished sympathy for the militants. The *Review* urged the Protestant Party to 'brawl on, and make those deaf and dotard bishops hear'.[88] Led by an Orange band, on Palm Sunday 1899, demonstrators protested at seven churches against what Wise called the 'illegal procession', Via Crucis. At St. Margaret's they abused Wakeford as 'Pope John of Anfield' before encountering police batons. Nevertheless the militants claimed success since intimidated congregations concealed their palms.[89]

In May 1899 the Exchange M.P., Charles M'Arthur, moved the Church Discipline Bill's second reading in the House of Commons. His speech, prizing the Reformation, was an illustration of man's enslavement in mythology; but he achieved a fair statement of a prejudice. A malapropism ('five bishops even allowed themselves to be incensed in churches') lowered the tone preparatory to his tirade against confessional practices which 'weakened the moral fibre and invaded the sanctity of family life'.[90] M'Arthur was heard sympathetically until the Attorney-General demonstrated the Bill's capacity for oppression. An amendment in his name passed without division: it criticized the creation of fresh offences but promised legislation if the bishops' failure to secure clerical obedience continued. This had been manufactured with a view to appeasing both Lancashire Conservatives and Liberal anti-Ritualists like Harcourt. The Church Discipline Bill itself fell by 310 votes to 156.[91]

Repercussions ensued in another Southport by-election, as Naylor-Leyland died. The Conservatives pitted Charles Balfour against Sir George Pilkington, the former M.P. (1885–6) and mayor. Circulars proclaimed that Balfour opposed ritualism; but the Layman's League scrupulously defined its Protestantism. Pilkington supported the Liverpool Bill absolutely; Balfour, a Scots Presbyterian, endorsed its intention but disliked its encouragement to informers. Moreover, although opposed to formal relations with the Vatican, Balfour felt that 'exceptional circumstances' might necessitate sending an Ambassador; and he welcomed a state-aided Catholic University in Ireland.[92]

To the surprise of many Conservatives the Church Association and Laymen's League resolved to elect Pilkington, whose programme included Disestablishment; but this, it was claimed, would expel from Parliament bishops who undermined their Church.[93] Pilkington's Home Rule principles were less digestible and Ryle's opinion was publicized, that he would not support a Home-Ruler. Bewildered by such conflicting advice several members resigned from the Laymen's League's Southport branch.[94]

The Unionists had not all the disadvantages of the 1898 by-election; moreover, Catholics might react in Balfour's favour. The *Catholic Times* applauded his uprightness, although it was suspected that four-fifths would still follow Pilkington.[95] *Ceteris paribus*, Protestants held the scales. The Laymen's League was particularly influential among the 1,385 electors of Waterloo (virtually Liverpool suburbia), and there *The Times* observed disenchantment with Conservatism.[96] Pilkington polled 5,635 against 5,052.

The struggle for power in the Liverpool Conservative Party

Within Liverpool the Church Discipline Bill's rejection had more momentous consequences than those observable in Southport. The West Derby M.P., Walter Long, expressed dislike of Ritualist services; but he retained a belief in episcopal discipline and, as a Cabinet Minister, he could not support legislation tending to Disestablishment. Salvidge concluded, 'Poor Long will have to quit West Derby'.[97] The constituency party twice demanded that Long support the Church Discipline Bill or forfeit its confidence.[98] When he followed the Attorney-General's line, the business of his removal began. In August 1899 the polling district committees denounced him; in September the constituency executive arraigned him. Conciliatory speeches from West Derby's Conservative councillors, Cookson, Petrie, and Clarke, were discountenanced; and Long compounded error by lecturing John Ashworth, of the Kensington W.M.C.A., upon definitions of 'ritualist' and the merits of Lord Hugh Cecil. He was condemned by twenty-seven votes to fifteen.[99]

Later, when Long visited the central Conservative Club in Dale Street where several councillors applauded his stand, *The Times* speculated that he might not surrender his seat.[100] The drift of events was more truly captured in G. K. Chesterton's cheerful satire:

> Walter, beware! scorn not the gathering throng . . .
> It suffers, but it cannot suffer Long.

The prospect of Long's deprivation disturbed every Liverpool M.P. 'No

Englishman', Houston reflected, 'likes to be coerced.'[101] Salvidge's commitment, proclaiming that he would prefer the Church disestablished than disloyal, astonished his party; but the *Review* reckoned that, as 'the mouthpiece of the working men', Salvidge would vanquish opposition.[102] This was tested in moves by Councillor W. T. Burgess, who was chairman of the Constitutional's Political Committee. Burgess had circularized members resident in Southport to support Balfour. Later Taylor's action—not Salvidge's since, officially, only the Laymen's League acted in Southport—was discussed by the Management Committee. Burgess's efforts to expel Taylor were balked;[103] but to advance their programme Taylor and Salvidge could not act without the Liverpool Conservative party. They wanted opportunity to capture it at the top as well as in the ranks for, Taylor told Salvidge, 'the classes are a complete clog on Protestant assertion and must be shaken off at all costs'.[104]

The denouement came not by Taylor's design but through Salvidge's impetuosity. Moving a fair-wages clause in Corporation contracts, supported by Liberals, Nationalists, and 'Tory Democrats', Salvidge confronted the new Council leader, Hughes, and heatedly asserted, 'I have never known Sir Thomas Hughes to advocate anything in the interests of the working man'. Hughes, though a year previously he promoted Salvidge's aldermanship, retorted that Salvidge was 'an individual of no standing and no position'.[105] Salvidge soon apologized to Hughes; but his opponents briefly stirred. Warr exploited this difference in order to resign as a vice-president of the W.M.C.A.;[106] and H. Burley, of the W.M.C.A. branch in Granby ward (in Warr's constituency), declared that Salvidge was 'too often getting at the upper ten'. Working men wanted a voice in matters but did not want 'to run the whole show'. Burley suspected that Salvidge wished 'to get into the shoes of the late Sir Arthur Forwood'; but his criticisms hit the wrong notes. Deference was not the mood of those who bathed in Salvidge's ambitions for himself, the W.M.C.A and Protestantism. Ashworth, Long's hunter, felt that the W.M.C.A. had few friends in the City Council or party leadership, and he wanted a showdown with 'these vindictive autocrats'.[107]

The schism extended when the East Toxteth Constituency Council, managed by Councillor Burgess, approved Warr's resignation from the W.M.C.A. by forty-five votes to seventeen. The minority mostly consisted of W.M.C.A. representatives.[108] The W.M.C.A. now equated 'ritualists' and 'aristocrats'.[109] Ironically Liverpool's Levellers were no proto-Socialists but antediluvian Protestants, annoyed that in the Animal Farm of Conservative politics the cart-horse was not getting his due. The Constitutional Association, comprehending men of all religious beliefs, would not censure their Government's omission;[110] but the W.M.C.A. argued that as a constitutional party the maintenance of the Protestant Church must be their priority.[111] That Conservatism represented something else—devotion to a social, above a religious, state—was difficult to press on unphilosophical workmen. Sir William Forwood gave it magisterial expression when he contrasted Salvidge's assertiveness with the subordination of previous W.M.C.A. chairmen. The crisis, he gestured, must be settled 'with a wise but with a firm and a strong hand'.[112]

Hands were abdicating, not wielding, leadership. The Constitutional's stop-gap president after Arthur Forwood's death, Sir Edward Lawrence, now resigned.[113] He recommended that Lord Stanley (the potential 17th Earl of Derby) succeed him. Taylor and Salvidge, however, argued that, as a Whip, Lord Stanley had been a teller against the Church Discipline Bill; moreover, he could not give time to local matters. Thomas Hughes essayed appeasement. Although his own Conservatism was 'founded in his churchmanship', he asked anti-Ritualists to be patient with the Government.[114] Patient patricians and impatient plebians tested their strengths. On the Constitutional's Management Committee fewer than ten of the seventy-seven members were workmen and their amendments, respectively to negate or to postpone Lawrence's recommendation, mustered only thirteen and eighteen votes, against forty-one and thirty-six.[115]

The W.M.C.A. reviewed its position. Salvidge scorned Sir William Forwood's 'impudent interference' and claimed that the Constitutional, disliking the W.M.C.A.'s alliance with the Laymen's League, had exploited his row with Hughes. Regarding Lord Stanley, he asked, 'Did it mean a Government Whip to whip Protestants into line in Liverpool?'[116] The party seemed racked, and the prospect of his organization in ruins brought the party agent, James Thompson, to swear, 'We will kill this infernal Protestantism'.[117]

Salvidge was also shaken, by allegations of Roman influences in his own household. Salvidge's wife was a Catholic, although they were married by that unimpeachable Protestant, the Revd. Richard Hobson, and their children were brought up as Protestants. Salvidge now pledged that 'no Roman Catholic priest had ever crossed the threshold of his door'. This jarred with his claim that the W.M.C.A. campaigned not against people who differed in religion, but 'to prevent a clergymen who ate the bread of the Church of England from practising and preaching an alien doctrine'. Salvidge, however, held on, while Hughes resigned the Council leadership.[118] Charles Petrie replaced him. At forty-six, he was fifteen years younger than Hughes. He was also better mannered but, so Robert Holt felt, 'not strong enough for a turbulent party as the Tories have become'.[119]

In December 1899 the Management Board considered its executive's recommendation of Lord Stanley. A trump was needed and the Kirkdale M.P., MacIver, produced it in a voice from the grave. Arthur Forwood had written to him in July 1898 in terms which deprecated both church brawlers and 'self-styled priests'; but Forwood had advocated 'exhausting every other means . . . to check abuses before appealing to Parliament, composed as it is of men of all sects and creeds many of whom are bitterly hostile to our Church'.[120] The Constitutional now, as Salvidge earlier, sought legitimacy by the mantle of their lost—and ambiguous—leader. Lord Stanley became president of the Constitutional Association by 114 votes to 40. The Board had 300 members: those absent from this midday meeting were mostly workmen. The Tory Democracy, some claimed, had been disfranchised;[121] but a search for unity followed.

One course was obvious. Britain was at war; indeed December 1899 was the blackest month for British forces in South Africa. The Everton M.P., Willox, unfurled the flag: 'John Bull had one characteristic—that if he blundered at the beginning, he came out right in the end.'[122] When Lord Stanley visited the Constitutional, he attempted a vindication: his Protestantism was such that if 'a Bill had been brought forward for creating a Roman Catholic University for Ireland he would not have held office for twenty-four hours'. Then followed the patriot: 'There was one religion they all held at the present moment—the religion of their Queen and people . . .'[123]

Salvidge and Taylor now echoed Lord Stanley's sentiments, while reserving their judgement on Church questions; and the W.M.C.A. compensated for what it lost in its assault on the Constitutional by ambushing individuals with whom it had outstanding accounts. Taylor replaced Warr as the W.M.C.A.'s vice-president and threatened to fight him at a General Election. Accordingly Warr bowed to Salvidge's terms, of a public confession of his misguided ways.[124]

In the case of the West Derby M.P., Long, the valedictions were too advanced. James McKinney, the Orange vicar of St. Silas's, declared from the pulpit that 'no vote should be given to a milk and water candidate'.[125] The municipal electorate responded warmly to this advice as Protestant Conservatives won resoundingly in West Derby. One, Samuel Higginbottom, was among the few Conservative Councillors who voted against Lord Stanley's presidency of the Constitutional Association.[126] The West Derby constituency organization, meanwhile, had been purged of Long's sympathizers.[127] Long eventually resigned, to avoid the deeper humiliation of not being readopted; and Higginbottom succeeded him as the parliamentary candidate.

The General Election of 1900

Liberal–Nationalist schism and the Boer War

The W.M.C.A.'s control of Liverpool 's representation was contested by other Conservatives, but hardly by Liberals. The 1900 General Election witnessed a Liberal presence in only two Liverpool constituencies, Exchange and Kirkdale. No fighters were forthcoming elsewhere, despite the leaders' mendicant appeals.[128] Edward Evans accepted that 'they were only a little clique working among themselves'; and Alderman Paull noticed that men preferred 'golf, billiards, or some equally useless pursuit' to Liberal politics.[129] New talent was not attracted to defeat..

Hitherto, by virtue of the Irish Nationalists' persistence, the Liberals' registration work had improved in central Liverpool ;[130] but the 1890s was a decade of mounting distemper among Nationalists. The *Catholic Herald* asked: 'Beyond making City Councillors for the Liberal party and jerrymandering seats in safe Irish wards for the favoured few, what has the Irish Nationalist League of Liverpool done . . .?'[131]

Lynskey in particular attracted personal attacks. When he attended the Lord Mayor's garden party on the occasion of the Queen's Jubilee he was taunted with the sobriquet, 'Jubilee Jeremy'; but there was more to the disputes than this. The organization that Lynskey had built up was suspect. Several I.N.L. branches, like the Michael Davitt, were worked *sub rosa* as Liberal organizations.[132] By contrast the Ninety-Eight, West Toxteth, and North Liverpool , branches now asserted independence. Their efforts were unavailing in two municipal by-elections early in 1899 when 'Liberal-Irish spies, agents, [and] hacks' succeeded in returning 'Catholic Liberal' and 'Liberal and Nationalist' candidates without opposition; but Councillor Burke had given the cue, that the Irish Nationalists in Liverpool had been 'too slavish' to the Liberals and should face both English parties.[133]

The break occurred as Burke became party secretary and Council whip. In June 1899 Liverpool 's Nationalists withdrew from formal co-operation with the Liberals.[134] This was a relief rather than an embarrassment to many Liberals. The Irish M.P.s' speeches during the Boer War were distasteful, and the Liverpool Reform Club cheered the Marquis of Northampton when he suggested at a meeting there that Home Rule be suspended from the Liberal programme. Sir Edward Russell told the Liberal leader in the House of Commons, Campbell-Bannerman, that even Edward Evans, 'whose business and practice it has been for years to cultivate and coincide with the Irish', echoed Northampton's opinion. Russell himself was critical of this reaction but he did not boldly controvert it in the *Daily Post*, reckoning that the remedy was in Irish hands, and that 'nearly all English and Scottish Liberals want what Lord Northampton said to be generally said. Partly this is to get rid of a chain which they find galling; partly they think, which I doubt, that, separated from the Irish they would get some Liberal Unionists back and get new support from the sort of electors who waver from election to election.'[135]

Russell here did not mention a third consideration, that those who cared little for Home Rule and who gave some thought to Liberal reunion personified their hopes in Lord Rosebery. Many viewed this tortured talent as still a real contender for that Liberal leadership which he had resigned in October 1896. Edward Evans, and Russell himself, paid private, sometimes public, obeisance; the *Liverpool Mercury* was classified as Roseberyite before it was taken over by the Home Rule *Daily Post* in 1904; and among the Liberal Unionists, the egregious Albert Bencke sought to realize his life's ambitions under Rosebery's mantle. Being, like Rosebery, out of love with the existing party system, it was Bencke who in early 1900 best summarized the hopes that Rosebery inspired:

> I am a Liberal Unionist and have never left any of my Liberal clubs and moreover am extremely dissatisfied with the leadership of Balfour and Chamberlain . . . The fact is that I am like yourself a Moderate Liberal and I trust a patriot and am by no means disinclined to return to the Liberal fold provided that there was a Liberal fold whereunto to return. Such a fold has to be created! What the country wants is a great Whig leader who thinks more of her than of his party. The nation is intensely dissatisfied with the Tory democratic alliance and still more disgusted with the Radicals. The Nation wants a Palmerston with more principle than Palmerston and a more profound intellect.[136]

A Roseberyite Liverpool Liberal party would not mend the rift with the Nationalists but make it irreparable. For a time, however, municipal politics seemed to be moving in that direction, for the Irish–Boer association crippled even patriotic Liberal/Nationalists like Joseph Clancy. When Clancy, the president of the Michael Davitt branch, fought St. Anne's ward Salvidge attributed his unexpected defeat to the Conservatives' Liberal support.[137] Councillor Grant's resignation followed. He explained that since a Liberal in St. Anne's depended upon Nationalist votes he as an Englishman could not represent it. The Conservative press crowed that he had done 'what many Liberals are thinking secretly in their hearts'; and the Liberal *Review* assented.[138]

Patriotism encouraged the scoundrels to desert Home Rule; but they were not unprovoked. Irishmen, declared Taggart, 'rejoice at England's misfortune because she is responsible for all of ours'.[139] *Porcupine* nominated the pro-Boers 'a heterogeneous collection of Anarchists, Socialists, Revolutionists, Screeching Sisters, and cranks of every description'.[140] Heterogeneous they were: those who advocated a Day of National Humiliation and Prayer included Samuel Smith and the Catholic Bishop. The Labour movement contributed to a branch of the South African Conciliation Committee Edwards (its president), Reeves, Morrissey, Manson, and Jeannie Mole;[141] and the *Labour Chronicle* blamed this 'villainous' war on conscienceless capitalists.[142] However, Sexton's articles in the Tory *Courier* probably represented a wider body of opinion. He was neither jingo nor pro-Boer. He questioned the causes of war and the banner of 'Boer slave-owners', but he felt the thrill of British military recovery, and speculated that enlistment might ease unemployment and advance labour's value.[143]

Among Nonconformists the pro-Boers were predictable—the Unitarian minister, Richard Armstrong, and the Baptist minister, Charles Aked, who believed that 'khaki-worship is an imbecility'.[144] Others, like John Thomas, the pastor of Myrtle Street Baptists and a supporter of Wise, were markedly loyal.[145] In fact several prominent Nonconformists joined Evangelical Anglicans in the Liverpool Patriotic Society, devised by the Revd. James McKinney to counter Aked's and Armstrong's 'treachery'. The minister of Sefton Park Presbyterians, John Watson, addressed recruiting rallies and even justified the war providentially.[146] Watson's congregation contained influential men of both parties—Sir Edward Russell, Charles Petrie, W. W. Rutherford, John Lea, and John Japp—and in April 1900 Watson became Moderator of the Presbyterian Synod.

The Liverpool Reform Club housed few pro-Boers, but they included members of the Holt, Bowring, Brunner, Meade-King, Rathbone, Muspratt, Crosfield, and Hargrove, families. This Gladstonian plutocracy dwarfed Edward Evans, a Liberal Imperialist, and immobilized the party at the General Election. As the relief, first of Ladysmith, then of Mafeking, was announced, Liverpool was buried under flags; sirens and foghorns blew continually; business ceased; there were fireworks, banquets, tireless processions, and collections to honour Baden-Powell. Apart from the drunkenness it was all 'very un-English.'[147] Evans did his best in the conditions. He exhorted voters to remember Liberal self-government when discussing a Boer settlement; he also advertised constitutional reforms, housing problems, temperance, religious equality, and popular control of education. This manifesto, however, made less newspaper copy than John Morley's anti-war speech at Oxford. The *Courier* stated, 'the man or the party not Imperial is impossible'.[148]

Beaconsfieldism had returned to roost with Joseph Chamberlain and 'a bragging pirate democracy'.[149] In pointing to 'The Queen or Kruger' Chamberlain realized his deepest traits: 'no one is his equal in getting the length of the foot of the British vulgarian . . .'.[150] Indecent haste characterized the Government's timing of the General Election—the register was over fourteen months old—but the Unionists nestled in patriotic folds. The statement made by the M.P. for Liverpool Exchange, M'Arthur, that 'the majority of the Liberal party have offered bitter opposition to the War', was typical.[151]

The Liberal Party and the anti-Ritualist question

To deflect the allegation that their party was peopled by the unpatriotic some Liberals pondered anti-Ritualism as a party cry. Education matters partly provoked these thoughts. Catholic authorities were believed to have been 'squared' by Lord Salisbury's Government with the prospect of a Catholic University in Ireland endowed from public funds and, according to Robert Holt's information, several priests in Liverpool were influencing their flocks to vote Conservative in 1900. Party opportunism was another factor in the Liberal's thinking. The *Review* noted that 'the aristocrats and democrats of the Liverpool Tory party' were divided by Church questions, and it suggested that 'Liberals have everything to gain . . . by supporting the Salvidge-Taylor wing'. But the *Review* also considered the anti-Ritualist movement 'really a Liberal one'. None personified this conviction more than the former Liverpool M.P., Samuel Smith, who still kept a home in Liverpool and sat in Parliament as the member for Flintshire. Surveying the Anglican constitution Smith was satisfied that the Thirty-Nine Articles were wholly Protestant, but he identified about one-tenth of the Prayer Book as Romish. This 'unnatural compromise' could not continue. In Smith's view 'the great bulk of the laity are Protestant and would reform the Prayer Book if they got the chance and start a pure Protestant Church to which Nonconformists would have little objection. Our objection is not to moderate Episcopacy but to *Sacerdotalism* and the latter is twin sister to Romanism and melts into it by imperceptible stages.'

Smith's programme turned upon the need to take education out of the hands of Romanizing clergy and to establish a representative lay body to control the Church's property and endowments and to reform the Prayer Book. Ultimately Parliament would be dispossessed of its powers over the Church because it was no longer competent to decide doctrine or ritual. Seventeenth-century parallels poured from Smith's pen—the nation's religion was threatened by dangers greater than any since the days of Archbishop Laud; there was a call for another 'Pride's Purge'; the task was the most gigantic since the Revolution of 1688—but the political present and future were not absent from his calculations. The Conservative leaders, he wrote, 'are bound to the Bishops and the head of the Government and his family are steeped in sacerdotalism'. Since Lord Salisbury's Government would not act, the Liberal party must. 'There is far more ripeness for a Protestant reformation in England now', Smith had written in September 1898,

> than there was for Irish Home Rule in 1885, when Mr. Gladstone by his transcendant genius forced it on the Liberal Party. Home Rule in its

> Gladstonian form is practically dead. Mr. Gladstone's generous desire to repair the wrongs of Ireland has borne fruit in a hundred ways, and most of the clamant wrongs of Ireland are now redressed. Possibly at some future time it may be safe and expedient to grant Ireland a Parliament but Great Britain will not have this policy now, and it greatly needs and wants thorough going changes in a Protestant direction . . . There is no party issue of much moment before the nation just now. It would purify and re-invigorate political life to have a clear issue put before us, something that will give play to the deepest convictions of men on the greatest of subjects. The controversy that will follow would educate the people as nothing else would. It would draw them away from the frivolities and trivialities of modern society and restore to public life the earnestness and dignity it had in the times of Cobden, Bright, and Gladstone. Moral issues appeal far more deeply to the British nation than international or commercial questions do. We run the risk of an access of jingo-ism if we have not some great moral issue put before us. That issue is now simmering in a multitude of minds; it only needs the enchanter's wand to give it concrete form.[152]

Smith was appealing to the then Liberal leader, and the party's best-known voice in anti-Ritualist matters, Sir William Harcourt, to launch a Protestant campaign in the country. So too was the editor of the *Liverpool Daily Post*, Russell, although only a few months before he had taken Rosebery's side against Harcourt in their squabble, and still hoped that Rosebery might leave retirement and give the Liberal Party a confident lead in foreign affairs. Now, in October 1898, Russell advised Harcourt to collect his letters to *The Times* on church affairs, and to 'publish them cheap'. In Russell's view 'the old evangelical system of religion and "redemption", though discredited and disused in the Church, is *still* the popularly accepted view of "saving religion", and lies latent and capable of being effectually appealed to'. Russell cited the opinion of a High Church vicar in Liverpool , who had made no impact on three-quarters of the 'good, hard-headed fellows' belonging to his working-class parish: they 'don't care twopence about religion at all; but they to a man hate "Popery" intensely'. Russell reckoned that this experience was common and 'if by any accident an election turned on it many of them might vote according to their hatred of Popery, to whatever party they might belong'. From observation Russell believed that 'the working classes hate most the Mass; the middle classes hate most the Confessional'.

Both Russell and Smith considered the organization, as well as the programme, of a Protestant campaign. Russell's contribution was to write a letter of introduction to Harcourt for the Laymen's League's leader, Austin Taylor, which Taylor used to arrange a secret meeting at Harcourt's Hampshire home in December 1898.[153] Smith, similarly, sought 'to smooth as much as one can the party of Protestant Nonconformists and unite them in one phalanx with Protestant Churchmen—this is a combination no government could resist but it is not easy to bring about'. One problem at the parliamentary level was how 'to unite the Protestant feeling on both sides of the House leaving out

Disestablishment on one side and Erastianism on the other'; but more discouraging altogether was the inappropriateness of the Liberal party as a vehicle, and Harcourt as the manager, of a Protestant campaign. It was difficult to erase memories of the Puseyite Gladstone, to whom evangelicals attributed 'the growth of the Romanizing influence';[154] and Harcourt's prestige was dimmed from December 1898 when he resigned the Liberal leadership. By 1900 Harcourt considered new legislation on Church discipline futile if the old was unenforced.[155] Moreover there was the Boer War. Patriotism as well as Protestantism mattered from late 1899 and Harcourt was stamped as an opponent of British policy in South Africa.

The Protestant–Conservative campaign

The Liberal anti-Ritualist campaign, then, never flowered in the 1900 General Election; but the efforts that Smith, in particular, made in Liverpool during 1898 and 1899 possibly benefited the Salvidge–Taylor Conservative wing by alerting Nonconformists to

> strengthen the Protestant cause in the National Church. I am willing to work with those inside the Church to purify it and I am constantly telling my Nonconformist friends to help the Protestant laity of the Church of England and so well is this understood in Liverpool —the most Tory place—that I am now constantly asked to attend Protestant *Church* meetings. I am quite in sympathy with these dear friends—we don't differ materially in anything. I am not one of those rabid dissenters who hates the Church and want to pull it down.[156]

Not everyone had discarded the hope that the Church might cleanse itself, and considerable interest was aroused in 1900 by the appointment of a new Bishop of Liverpool , Francis J. Chavasse, once principal of Wycliffe Hall.[157] Compared with Ryle, his lusty predecessor, Chavasse was tiny, hunched, and valetudinarian; but Wise, who had feared the translation of the Bishop of Stepney, was optimistic that Chavasse would extirpate 'the blasphemous sacrifice of the Mass, and the abominable confessional'.[158] Militancy was suspended while Chavasse settled in, and his first address sounded the theme Evangelicals desired: 'A lawless church will soon lead to a lawless state; and the swift Nemesis of lawlessness is ruin.'[159]

Salvidge and Taylor were not becalmed. In August 1900 they requested a Protestant 'war chest' of £20,000. They received £10,000 quickly. Membership of the Laymen's League had multiplied in Liverpool ; but Taylor officially limited its goal to another Church Discipline Bill and checked the tendency to join 'other Protestant agencies against Roman Catholicism'.[160] Nevertheless an Imperial Protestant Federation, formed in 1898, embraced twenty-one organizations including the Church Association and Orange Order. It aimed to return 150 M.P.s pledged upon Reformation principles.[161] There were some setbacks in publicity, as when the Earl of Portsmouth criticized the Conservatives' uninterest in reform and blunders in the war, and regretted that Liberal Unionism had become 'a mere device for obtaining Liberal votes for Conservative uses'.[162] Portsmouth had been the Laymen's League's President from mid-1899, when Taylor ostentatiously produced him at a garden party for the W.M.C.A. His defection was embarrassing for, although the League was ostensibly non-party, its Liverpool campaign was integrated with Conservative demonstrations.

The Walton M.P., Stock, also caused irritation by dissenting from some of the Laymen's League's proposals. He perhaps reckoned, since W.M.C.A. delegates constituted a minority of Walton Conservative Council, that his candidature would go forward. But the timid and amorphous opinion which sympathized with him would not engineer division at an Election; and Stock was forced to accept the Laymen's League programme, 'a death-bed repentance' Taylor coldly observed.[163] Like Warr, Lawrence, Higginbottom, Willox, and Houston, Stock was bound to the Laymen's League and returned unopposed. Their consciences were stained with class interests. Houston preferred business to religion; but now he trumpeted his evangelicalism.[164] Equally Higginbottom, who had made a fortune as a colliery owner and the co-founder of Douglas Steamers, calculated his Protestant dividends. A Wesleyan Methodist, he cultivated unimpeachable views on Anglican discipline. This, and 'week end trips to the Isle of Man to all his supporters', isolated critics of his attitude on labour questions.[165]

The topical politics of 1900 were unrelentingly Conservative. Richard Cherry Q.C., the Liberal candidate contesting Kirkdale, asked if voters desired to 'postpone all social legislation . . . by the waving of the Union Jack as a party emblem'.[166] His Unionist opponent, MacIver, mentioned no domestic item except Protestantism; but this, and monotonous patriotism, brought him 4,333 votes against 1,738. The Liberals' enervation was especially evident in Exchange, traditionally a marginal seat. In November 1897 Charles M'Arthur, a former president of the Chamber of Commerce, had maintained the Liberal Unionist representation by fifty-four votes.[167] Thereafter he entrenched himself among Protestants and businessmen: he was the author of *The Evidences of Natural Religion* as well as of works on marine insurance.[168] These qualifications, in the freakish conditions of 1900, put M'Arthur ahead by 1,297 in a 64·4 per cent poll. His 2,811 votes probably registered the Unionists' optimum. The electorate in this central constituency was dwindling—7,060 in 1897, 6,718 in 1900—and M'Arthur improved his total only by a hundred votes. His new majority depended upon 1,100 Liberal abstentions.

In 1900 Liverpool's marginal constituency was Scotland, where T. P. O'Connor confronted the Conservative, W. W. Rutherford, and dissentient Nationalists led by Austin and Frank Harford. The Harford brothers, in business together as drapers, denounced their accredited leaders' Liberalism. They had displaced Lynskey from the Council and now commanded South Scotland's representation. Municipal grievances were beginning to be differentiated from nationalist ideals. For two decades now Irish Councillors had participated in Corporation work, taking particular interest in housing questions; and there was not that subjugation to parliamentary leadership as existed in the heyday of Parnell. Moreover, from 1898, local-born councillors outnumbered the Irish-born among Liverpool's Nationalist group.[169]

In the General Election, although five branches of the United Irish League passed resolutions deploring factionalism, Austin Harford advanced as an Independent.[170] O'Connor's wealth and Babylonian living excited puritan strictures; and it was also said that O'Connor ignored 'the north-end slum dwellers', while Harford had been working among them.[171] The jealousy of fellow journalists did not improve O'Connor's public standing; and this quarrel encouraged the Conservative seducer. Rutherford paraded his Irish ancestry; he supported the Nationalists' housing policy; and he wondered how Liberals could sympathize with the Boers since 'under Kruger there was not liberty for Roman Catholics'. Alone among Unionist candidates Rutherford courted the L.T.C.[172] He was a paragon of Tory Democracy, promising pensions sufficient to keep the aged from the Workhouse.[173] Principally, however, Rutherford was Patriot writ large, travelling in a carriage drawn by khaki-coated ponies.[174] His chance went when Harford withdrew; but, by polling 2,044 against 1,484, O'Connor received his smallest mandate.

Tory Democrats sought to punish the Irish Nationalists by other means. Councillor Taggart was expelled from the Corporation's Estates Committee and Lancashire Asylums Board, although he remained on the Health Committee. Salvidge, whose younger brother died in the war, demanded that the Council exclude Taggart 'from the society of loyal men'. The W.M.C.A. and Orangemen agreed—'a pro-Boer, a rebel, and a traitor' should not sit with 'respectable persons who honour their Queen'—but this demonstration did not win every Conservative's approval.[175] Motivated more by a distaste for the persecutors than by a love of the persecuted, Hughes, Bartlett, and the Constitutional caucus sought Taggart's reinstatement. The contest for ascendancy in Liverpool Conservatism was thus reopened.

CHAPTER TWELVE

The Protestant crisis: Salvidge out of control, 1900–3

Clergymen are not perhaps the most reasonable of mankind, but they are not more unreasonable than political enthusiasts. *A. V. Dicey*

The line between religious monomania and insanity is not easy to draw, nor is it easy to say whether intense ignorance or invincible prejudice be the moving force. *Samuel Smith M.P.*

Luther; your responsibility is great indeed, for the closer I look the more clearly do I see that you overthrow the Pope—and set the public on the throne.[1] *S. Kierkegaard*

George Wise and John Kensit

In November 1900 Forwood's policy, to abstain from School Board elections, was reversed as Salvidge strove to capture every outpost of Conservative power. His unlikely knight was the Protestant lecturer, George Wise. Nominated by the British Protestant Union, Wise was without official Church backing; but, with Salvidge's and Taylor's *imprimatur*, he polled 107,063, over double any other candidate's votes. All were astounded. In the Liberals' opinion, according to Richard Holt, Wise 'had no qualifications for the work and a large part of his supporters were merely the public house Tories who have a domestic feud with the more respectable section of their party, and use professions of extreme protestantism as a cloak'. On the Conservative side Thomas Hughes regarded it in the same light. He resigned from the Council, declaring that the Liverpool Conservative party had descended so low that he could not rub shoulders with it.[2]

Trivial talk often takes a serious turn. The argument whether the twentieth century began in 1900 or 1901—both the Pope and the Kaiser favoured 1900—was settled for Britons by Queen Victoria. Her death in January 1901 inaugurated another age. Sir Edward Russell's instinct was that 'she would have lived capable to ninety but for a degrading South African War'. These were private thoughts. In public to wallow in or to resist Royalist sentiment made or

Notes begin on p. 423

unmade reputations. Most clergymen revered the Queen's piety; but the Baptist, Charles Aked, from his pulpit in Liverpool outspokenly deplored King Edward's licentiousness.[3] Equally Samuel Smith offended Protestant loyalists by thinking the Coronation Declaration anachronistic.[4] From an open-air meeting Wise telegraphed his thanks that Edward would 'repeat the Protestant declarations against the Romish doctrine of the mass and the worship of saints and the Virgin Mary'.[5] The Protestant Reformation Society heard Archdeacon Taylor and Alderman Roberts resolve likewise. The populace outdoors, and the respectable inside, shared opinions.

By Easter 1901 the credit which the militant Protestants had extended to the new bishop, Chavasse, had expired. Though he advocated more adequate representation for the laity in church government and enunciated the principle that 'the clergy exist for the church, and not the church for the clergy', the Wiseites reprobated his tolerance of 'Popish altars' and encouragement of a Liverpool cathedral.[6] The previous bishop, Ryle, had believed that the diocese had more pressing deficiencies;[7] and Wiseites asked, 'did ever the drones of a cathedral hive assist in . . . slum work?' Ritual—'Pharisaical display, prayer and praise by etiquette'—would banish religion. Working men opposed the building of a cathedral, 'the Bishop's church—the church of the rich'.[8] Class differences paralleled ritual differences; and Wise kept the limelight.

In May 1901 he stumped Islington Square, nearby a Jesuit seminary and many Catholic homes. The subject of Jesuit intrigue attracted audiences whatever the weather.[9] Wise's demonstrations now included mock Catholic rites, which so provoked Catholic spectators that the deputy Head Constable, Dunning, summonsed Wise not to lecture near Islington Square. Instead he harangued crowds on St. George's Plateau, until removed for his own protection. In court he was bound to keep the peace for twelve months. He might lecture in public halls but not outdoors.[10] The trial had political importance: the Nationalist, Alderman Lynskey, was prosecuting counsel, and the Conservative, Councillor Rutherford, defended Wise.

Wise had been transformed from an inconvenience into the key to a sectarian imbroglio. There was nothing outwardly fascinating about this grey-haired, lisping bachelor. Wise was robust but short and bespectacled. He usually wore a frock-coat, white tie, and slouching hat which on Sundays became the orthodox 'stovepipe'. A crude earnestness compensated for an insignificant presence. Moreover, Wise understood both religious salvation and what it was to be the centre of interest.[11] He was a terrible trifle.

Wise's publicity restored the Orangemen's energy. A mob stormed St. Francis Xavier's, marchers clashed on London Road, and two priests suffered assault. Wise demanded a rejuvenated working-class Orange Order, free from aristocratic shackles. Tory Democracy became, by Wise's transmutation, 'a Protestant democracy': the Orange Order would advance both progressive politics and Protestant rights.[12] But what of their existing party allies? Councillor Rutherford, who on the Glorious Twelfth lambasted Jesuitism as 'the curse of civilization and humanity', later in July entertained W.M.C.A. officials at his home. Both he and Austin Taylor showed that among the faithful the pretence of toleration was dropped: Taylor now argued that they must not make any attempt to conciliate 'Roman Catholic and Ritualist sentiment'.[13] Ambitious Liverpool Conservatives were plainly preferring to court the W.M.C.A. rather than the Constitutional. This had dangers for, while professing Protestant fundamentals, they were still labelled as members of a party whose Government ministers were 'traitors to the Protestant cause'.[14]

Formal party opposition to Conservatism in Liverpool remained feeble. The Liberals were combative chiefly as self-flagellants. The Irish were defensive. In 1901 O'Connor campaigned for the first time in municipal elections, to answer critics of his absenteeism and to evoke national consciousness in second and third generation Liverpool Irish. Salvidge had discontinued Forwood's policy of discouraging Conservative candidates from contesting Irish wards. Thus Taggart's municipal service was almost buried in Imperialist propaganda; but elsewhere Irish Councillors easily held against unfamiliar Conservative opponents, to gladden anti-Salvidge hearts at the Constitutional.[15]

From the twenty-two contests in the 1901 municipal elections party strength was unchanged: seventy-nine Unionists faced forty-one Liberals and Nationalists. The Conservatives' gain in St. Anne's countered their defeat in Netherfield, where George Sturla, an Independent anti-Home Rule Liberal, advocated welfare policies. Although he eventually joined the Conservatives in 1905, Sturla epitomized the character of the contests in 1901—a 'struggle against bigotry and religious intolerance'.[16]

The medieval aura was maintained by a minor outbreak of bubonic plague.[17] How far the sectarian infection had penetrated Conservatism was suggested by the election of a temporary Council leader to replace Petrie, the new Lord Mayor. The West Derby M.P., Councillor Higginbottom, proposed Austin Taylor; but Petrie proposed Robert Hampson, who won forty votes against twenty.[18] Hampson was a solicitor (his firm represented several brewers), and the party whip. A traditionalist—Conservative first and Orangeman second—Hampson in addition defeated Rutherford in the contest for the chairmanship of Everton Conservative Council, after Houlding died in March 1902.[19]

Personalities also impeded Salvidge. It was now apparent that the West Toxteth M.P., Houston, would not appear on platforms with him. The details of their hostility are obscure, but both could be bullheaded. We can believe Houston's wife, a former harpy, Poppy Radnall, when she called Houston 'a hard nut'.[20] Perhaps Houston's alleged profiteering in the Boer War divided the men.[21] However, though this rift continued until Houston's death in the 1920s, its political consequences were marginal because, as Salvidge acknowledged, Houston still 'played the game whatever his private feelings may have been'.[22] Some reverberations were detectable at the W.M.C.A.'s general meeting in January 1902, when a few members contested Salvidge's re-election to the chair; but the meeting's main business was to hear M.P.s register their Protestant declarations.[23] Salvidge, abetted by the Association's secretary, a pugnacious and intolerant Scotsman, Sam Barton, was forging the W.M.C.A. into a unitary instrument. This, at any rate, was the complaint of one branch secretary, who was forced to resign following a ruling that Catholics could not belong to the W.M.C.A.[24]

The W.M.C.A.'s relations with the Constitutional Association were less clear-cut. Salvidge told the Sandhills branch of the W.M.C.A. that 'peace had been restored not by compromise, but because all sections of the Conservative party recognized that the general body of the electorate were with them . . . .'[25] He cited the Constitutional's Annual Report for 1900, that when the Boer War ended the Liverpool Conservative party would expect the Government to eradicate Ritualism, as the Attorney-General had promised in his amendment to the Church Discipline Bill of 1899. But a compromise had been made which involved slowing the Protestant agitation to a pace which the Liverpool Constitutional Association could manage. This was apparent at the Constitutional's general meeting in 1902. Major operations against the Boers had ceased; accordingly Orangemen wanted the Constitutional to restate its commitment. They were checked by the Everton M.P., Willox, feeling that it was 'most inconsiderate' to press the Government 'in season and out of season'. This argument of expediency, which Salvidge and Taylor had denounced in 1899, did not now receive their rebuff. Instead Taylor echoed Willox, while Salvidge brooded about the corn duties and necessity for controls against foreign competition.[26]

This token salute to Protestantism by its principal Conservative allies signified their awareness of a fundamental incompatibility. Salvidge had used Protestant sentiment to establish himself, seeing also, perhaps, that by it the Conservative party might eschew progressive social policies. To Protestants, however, the Conservative party was merely a vehicle for legislation proscribing Ritualism. Politics were secondary in their considerations and important only in determining whether coercion or cajolement would best serve their end. The *Protestant Standard* advised Protestants not to waste time appealing to Conservatives;[27] and the Church Association advertised for a Protestant electoral roll, beginning 'Now that the War is over, the Protestant Question must come first . . .'.[28]

Nevertheless the *Protestant Standard* did not welcome every means of independence; and this probably influenced Salvidge to proceed more regularly. The initiative was slipping from responsible hands. John Kensit had arrived in Liverpool . His character can be gauged from the accusation levelled at Wise, that he aimed to out-rival Kensit.[29]

Born at Bishopsgate in 1853, Kensit had a High Church upbringing before he adopted Methodism and completed a sectarian salmon cycle by re-entering the Anglican Church. Business boomed for this one-time draper's assistant, now a publisher of evangelical tracts, when he exhibited in his shop window in Paternoster Row, Romish hair-shirts, scourges, and penitential lashes.[30] He had been a stalwart of the Hoxton and Bethnal Green branch of the Church Association from its inception in the mid 1870s; and in 1889 he founded the Protestant Truth Society. Unlike its Catholic counterpart, no clergy supervised its work and no accounts appeared until 1895 when, exposed by *Truth*, Kensit audited a report himself.[31] Its funds supported his contests in London School Board elections; and he launched the Wycliffe Preachers to peregrinate the country denouncing ritualist clergymen. Kensit achieved notoriety by staging the first of these protests, in January 1897, at the Bishop of London's confirmation;[32] and he repeated this drama several times.[33]

Kensit's Liverpool Crusade dismayed the *Protestant Standard.* Although it relished scandal about Catholics,[34] it preferred electoral pressure and legal prosecutions to Kensit inciting a mob. When a Wycliffe Preacher proclaimed 'To Hell with the Pope', the *Protestant Standard* wished that he had prayed instead for the Pope's conversion.[35] It shared Archdeacon Taylor's ambivalance. He disliked indecorous demonstration but applauded Kensit's profession 'to preach the pure gospel'.[36] The Bishop of Liverpool , however, seemed unambiguous: 'I often am ashamed of the unwise and unchristian conduct of some who call themselves Protestants.'[37]

Wise, not to be outdone by Kensit, briefly collaborated with Arthur Trew, who was free after a year's imprisonment for inciting riot in Belfast. In September 1902 they led Orange marchers into battle with Irish Catholics at Seaforth. John Kensit also had an ally, his son and namesake until, refusing to abstain from street meetings for a year, his son received three months' imprisonment.[38] As Kensit junior entered Walton Gaol, 20,000 people attended a Wiseite protest; and Kensit senior petitioned the Government that his son was degraded by having to parade with Catholic prisoners.[39] Particular incidents—the smashing of a window because it displayed Wise's portrait—betokened high feeling.[40] Wise was also aggrieved when the mission hall, where he was conducting a harvest service, was stormed.[41] But he would not moderate his course at the behest of 'a wild and bigoted Roman Catholic mob'.[42] Most Protestant lecturers claimed to abominate Catholicism and pity Catholics. In Birkenhead, however, Kensit attributed most pauperism, crime, and debauchery to 'besotted Romanists'. Afterwards, at the Ferry, he was felled by an iron file.[43] He died several days later, on 8 October, but the degree to which the pneumonia and meningitis that brought about his death were caused by the wound was disputed.[44]

The next day his son was released, following solicitations made by the Exchange M.P., M'Arthur, before the Home Secretary. Salvidge, the stipendiary magistrate, and others, had supplied testimonials. Kensit's release was unconditional, a triumph, he proclaimed, for free speech.[45] Officiating at a service commemorating his father were Archdeacon Taylor, Canon Woodward, and Canon Hobson. The Bishop of Liverpool had another engagement, although he had called at the Infirmary when Kensit was first admitted.[46]

The police charged John McKeever,[47] aged nineteen, with Kensit's murder. F. E. Smith was the Crown Prosecutor, in popular opinion representing Protestantism as in 1901 when he had argued Wise's Appeal against the deputy Head Constable. Conflicting medical evidence and confused eye-witnesses allowed McKeever's acquittal, and he was carried shoulder-high in triumph through the streets. This ugly parade made McKeever more than ever a marked man. In 1903 he was arrested for disorderly behaviour at a Wiseite meeting and fined for threatening a laundress who called him 'Kensit's murderer'. The magistrate advised him to emigrate.[48] Protestants might have relished his execution, but alternatives existed. In Exeter Hall, London, the surviving Kensit inaugurated 'the battle of the Second Reformation', for 'the system which impelled the throwing of a cruel weapon at his father's head was the same as that which put to death the noblest of their forefathers'.[49] Liverpudlians received similar embellishments: Kensit, said his son, was slain by a 'cruel priestly hand'. His dying words were recalled: 'No Compromise.'[50]

Fact withered as fable flourished. Twenty years later Kensit still related how his father 'was murdered by the dastardly hand of Rome'.[51] At his funeral panegyrists found Kensit worthy of comparison with Knox, Huss, and Bunyan;[52] but few martyrs have been more dispensable. The Protestant show rolled on callously. Even as Kensit's audience melted into tears in Exeter Hall, Liverpudlians were spellbound by Master Jack Cooke, 'the boy preacher' (he was in fact aged seventeen) advertised as 'an enigma to some, and a wonder to all'.[53]

Sectarian controversy and two parliamentary by-elections

Meanwhile Liberals licked their wounds. Campbell-Bannerman's animadversion in June 1901 about the British army's 'methods of barbarism' in the Boer War created international sensation. In Liverpool Austen Chamberlain referred to Campbell-Bannerman staining his country's flag;[54] but this Unionist reaction was predictable. The interest lay in the Liberal party's response for, though Campbell-Bannerman had sought merely to question the specific tactic of block camps, his Liberal Imperialist wing considered the speech symptomatic of basic differences about their party's character and ambitions. In August Evans offered to resign the Liverpool leadership but, from these depths, he was increasingly hopeful that Rosebery's Chesterfield speech in December would settle the party's course.[55] In a powerful address which belied the hesitations of a wretched insomniac, Rosebery declared that 'the nation that cannot produce an alternative Government to this one is more fit to control allotments than an Empire'. He was not concerned to make a stand on the issues of the war. He called instead for Liberals to wipe clean their party programme in pursuit of one of national efficiency and he repeated this position in a speech in Liverpool in February 1902.[56]

Privately, to Lord Sefton, Rosebery communicated his

> anxiety to see formed a stable Liberal and imperialist party. The country is Liberal and imperialist in its tendencies. But many have been alienated by Little Englandism and fears about property. As to Little Englandism that seems to have shrivelled to its proper proportions, and property is much stronger than the forces which attack it. What I really dread is a reaction against this Government of so violent a kind that sound Liberals could not be associated with it. The only remedy for this lies in the Liberal League, which offers the alternatives of measured and practical progress.[57]

To some Liverpool Liberals, like Allan Bright, the Liberal League—the cave for Liberal Imperialists which Rosebery founded on 24 February 1902—denoted only 'the rowdyism of the pothouse and minstrelsy of the music hall';[58] but one creative argument for the party concerned the future settlement with the Boers. To influence this pro-Boers and Liberal Imperialists needed communion; and, after his re-election as leader of the Liberal party in Liverpool, Evans pretended that consensus existed between Rosebery and Campbell-Bannerman. One dissentient from his position, an Irish Nationalist, inserted reality between this miraculous fraternity. Rosebery and Campbell-Bannerman remained poles apart on Home Rule for, while Campbell-Bannerman might be persuaded to embrace a 'step-by-step' approach to an Irish solution, the proposal of a 'clean slate' was abhorrent.[59] This difference was mirrored locally in Liverpool. Throughout 1901–2 Edward Evans hoped that the Liberal party would draw together around Lord Rosebery, Robert Holt that it would draw together against Lord Rosebery. The resolutions of the Reform Club were carefully drafted at this time and a balance of offices brought some forbearance—the Liverpool Federal Council's secretary was a Liberal Leaguer; the treasurer had been anti-war—but the division was impossible to mask.[60]

Nationally the Gladstonian section of the Liberal party rallied as the 1902 Education Bill goaded Nonconformity. A few Liberal Leaguers publicly applauded the Bill's embodiment of 'efficiency' but mostly they tamely surrendered to the old cry. 'It is not an Education Bill', said James Bryce; 'It is a Voluntary Schools Relief Bill.'[61] Its main provision was the substitution for a locally elected School Board of an Education Committee of the town or county council. The majority of members of this Committee would be taken from the Council and the rest, the male or female nominees of non-party bodies, would be co-opted. All elementary and secondary education was to be consolidated under this single authority, but the dual system was perpetuated by a distinction between 'provided' and 'non-provided' schools. The former were the old Board Schools, whose maintenance and curriculum were determined by the local authority, and in which religious instruction was predominantly 'simple Bible teaching' of the undenominational type; the latter were the old 'voluntary' schools which, if their buildings and secular curriculum were approved, would now universally receive rate-aid while retaining their definite denominational character in respect of religious instruction. Without this transfusion of money the denominational schools would perish even more swiftly in the next decade than in the last. Church dignitaries offered opposition to the introduction of local authority scrutiny over the religious instruction given in their schools—indeed, the Archbishop of Canterbury, Frederick Temple, pushed himself to the point of collapse during the debate in the House of Lords—but the Act did no more than provide that one-third of the managers of non-provided schools should be appointed by the local authority, and the Church on the whole won the bargain over the division of building and maintenance costs between the public purse and the denomination itself.[61]

Among Nonconformists, especially in Wales and in rural areas with a single Church school, the Act provoked rebellion against the apparent confirmation by local authority adoption of an unpopular education régime; but in Liverpool rate-aid for voluntary schools had been anticipated, and the Anglican and Catholic–Nationalist public mostly welcomed relief. The proportion of Liverpool children attending the Corporations' elementary schools as opposed to 'non-provided' schools rose by 10 per cent before 1914; but this was still under 50 per cent of the total roll. Many Protestant Nonconformists grumbled, but in its deference to denominational education the Liverpool Education Committee represented majority opinion in the city. In any event the Liverpool branch of the Passive Resistance League was crippled by the unpopularity of its organizer, Aked.[62] His New Year's sermon, entitled 'Our Cowardly War', resulted in his windows being smashed.[63] This incident illustrated, as Kingsley Martin recorded of his father's experiences, that 'it was not politics in the pulpit that men objected to, but the kind of politics'.[64]

A parliamentary vacancy opened in East Toxteth constituency in October 1902. Warr gave personal reasons for his resignation; but Protestant intrusions had dismayed him. The Conservatives nominated Austin Taylor, the Liberals Councillor Herbert Rathbone. Both demanded army reforms, Rathbone particularly criticizing the class character of officers. Both were free traders, although Taylor accepted modifications to maintain the mercantile marine's supremacy.[65] Concerning Ireland, Taylor opposed Home Rule while Rathbone trimmed. Concerning education, Taylor sought to protect consciences in single-school rural areas, having in mind the case where the church school was dominated by ritualist clergy.[66] Rathbone complained that the Education Bill imposed 'taxation without adequate representation' and failed to ensure that religious instruction accorded with parents' wishes. Both ran fads—Taylor advocated closer colonial ties; Rathbone advocated temperance, and Welsh disestablishment.

All this suggested an orthodox contest. The interest lay backstairs. The constituency Conservative Council had considered five names—Austin Taylor, his brother William Taylor K.C., Sir Alfred Jones, Alderman Burgess, and W. W. Rutherford. After Salvidge induced William Taylor and Burgess to withdraw, a ballot gave Austin Taylor thirty-three votes, Rutherford twenty-two, Jones twenty. This majority for two Protestant Conservatives, on a council which recently supported Warr's defiance of Salvidge, suggested that the W.M.C.A. had packed it through a manipulation of Polling District Committees.[67]

This engineering provoked reactions. At the municipal elections in November 1902 two of only three Conservative defeats in the city occurred in Toxteth; and O. C. Williams and Philip Lloyd, prominent Toxteth Tories, resigned their party offices and resolved to vote Liberal.[68] The Constitutional Association ratified Taylor's nomination with few dissentients,[69] but the complaint was undisguised. Williams criticized 'leaders who have bowed to the power behind the throne'; and Lloyd reprobated their 'cringe to the Lord High Dictator'. They hoped to avenge Balfour in Southport and Long and Warr in Liverpool, and to 'raise Tory politics to a higher and nobler platform'.[70] They attracted other disgruntled Conservatives. Fred Saunby, onetime Councillor of St. Anne's, thought it 'impossible to conceive a more intolerant dictator' than Salvidge; and Councillor McGuffie, of Warbreck ward, appealed to Conservatives to elect Rathbone and to quash 'any "bossing" nonsense in Liverpool'.[71]

A shipowner whom Taylor had displaced as chairman of the Housing Committee, McGuffie never shirked controversy. He was suspected of pro-Boer tendencies; and he sought to make welfare matters the party's priority. This meant, negatively, a purge of publicans and their lawyers from Corporation Committees. It also entailed municipal enterprise. McGuffie inspired the incorporation of Garston into Liverpool , believing that this district had 'immense industrial possibilities'.[72] Passionately he exhorted workmen to '"squelch the clique now", for industrial developments and increasing the wage-earning opportunities of the people are foreign subjects to the clique'.[73] In January 1903 McGuffie joined East Toxteth Conservative Club, the cave of dissent; but his principles were exceptional.

Most Tory renegades considered religion not wage-packets. One declared, 'People can record their convictions in the ballot-box but rabid Protestantism should not be brought into the political arena. I know dozens of Roman Catholics and many Jews in the division who are good Conservatives, and why should they be insulted in the party clubs by such men as follow Alderman Salvidge?' Bigotry was ungentlemanly. Tactical, not ethical, differences were exhibited. One rebel, who admired Salvidge's command 'as a party manager', criticized his 'turning what should be a broad national platform into a narrow sectional platform. That was what brought the Liberal party to disaster'.[74] Salvidge, however, denied that the W.M.C.A. dealt in 'slavish politicians'. As for principles, 'the old Conservative cry was "Church and State"'.[75]

Although prominent in this colloquy, sectarianism was not broadcast on the hustings. Kensit's death made politicians wary; but a rumour that his son might stand conveyed Protestant impatience.[76] As he hedged over the Education Bill Taylor aroused the Protestants' distrust of 'a clever political party man';[77] and, encouraged, Liberals questioned the Laymen's League's influence in Liverpool.[78] Rathbone even suggested that the League was partly responsible for Kensit's death;[79] but their rebels' sense of party loyalty, not their sectarian qualms, was the target of Conservative apostrophes.

Championing an official programme Salvidge was unimpeachable. The former West Toxteth M.P., Royden, defended him at the Constitutional; Warr denied that Salvidge forced his resignation; and Long was somehow induced to write on Taylor's behalf.[80] Joseph Chamberlain telegraphed a beat of imperialist drums; the Prime Minister, Balfour, urged East Toxteth to forget minor issues; and the Liverpool Conservative agent, Thompson, concocted a circular alleging that Rathbone favoured entire church disestablishment.[81] These vessels paled alongside the diversionary craft which the new president of the Constitutional Association, Lord Stanley, launched. He eulogized Salvidge's services but also dangled the prospect of an inquiry into grievances, *after* Taylor's return.[82] Lloyd for one responded by discontinuing opposition. Taylor polled 3,610 votes, Rathbone 3,233.

Although the electorate was 850 larger since the last contest (1895), Taylor attracted slightly fewer votes and Rathbone 1,500 more. Taylor thanked 'the working classes', not 'villadom', but was satisfied to have won 'the last constituency which I should have chosen from a tactical point of view to test the Protestant issue . . .'.[83] The margin was less important than the fact of victory. 'We can afford to give the Liberals a seat for this time only', one rebel had advised, 'but we cannot afford to sit any longer under the rule of a few autocratic dictators.'[84]

This interpretation was confirmed. In December 1902 the West Derby M.P., Higginbottom, suddenly died. Long's expulsion from this seat already signified the W.M.C.A.'s omnipotence there. The Conservative Council leader, Petrie, presented faint competition, but the constituency committee picked Rutherford as Higginbottom's successor.[85] A popular Lord Mayor, Rutherford had opened the Town Hall between 17 and 20 November, and entertained 7,650 people.[86] He retired in January 1903 to stand for Parliament and the 'Father' of the Council, Sir William Forwood, became his mayoral warming-pan. Liberals crabbedly noted that Rutherford 'might just as well wear his chain of office at the husting'.[87] This set the tone of the contest, and polling day saw Rutherford driving through the streets in 'an open landau with four horses [and] postillions, two men behind and two outriders blowing trumpets'. Salvidge cheered these antics, proclaiming that Rutherford 'was the first Lord Mayor to break down class prejudice, and to recognize that the Town Hall belongs to the people'.[88] Certainly Rutherford was the first *Lord* Mayor to imitate Sir David Radcliffe; but the presence of working people in the Town Hall on four days hardly spelled democratic possession.

Rutherford was intent on promotion. He exhibited sternness regarding Home Rule, Imperialism, and Protestantism, and welcomed every other wind to blow votes his way. The Government dodged pensions and the taxation of urban ground values; but Rutherford championed both in his programme.[89] He sympathized with trade union grievances, desiring to extend the Workmen's Compensation Act, to limit the employment of foreigners and Lascars on British ships, and to allow absent seamen to exercise the franchise. The W.M.C.A. busily promulgated anti-alien legislation.[90]

Among the Liberals the Holt family stirred. The ageing Robert Holt was President of the West Derby Liberal Association and, after failing to attract Lord Sefton's brother, Richard Molyneux, and the cotton broker, A. A. Paton, Holt's eldest son, Richard, the constituency chairman and Federal Council's treasurer, became the candidate.[91] A typical scion of a merchant dynasty, he had added refinement to the stock by an education at Winchester and Oxford; but it was his American wife, rather than Richard himself, who impressed his aunt, Beatrice Webb. Though admittedly 'a shrewd, pleasant, and public-spirited man', Beatrice Webb had castigated Richard Holt for his 'parrot-like prejudices against all new ideas', when she visited Liverpool in 1899. 'In political intelligence', she concluded, 'he is still a child.'[92] No one, however, could accuse Beatrice Webb of being unprejudiced, and it says much for Richard Holt's mettle that he could survive such an aunt. The Holt family, in fact, treated Beatrice Webb with affectionate, if mystified, tolerance. Robert Holt had even contrived to have a cheerful time at Beatrice's wedding in 1892—'though there were many criticisms in confidence'—acknowledging that 'Beatrice looked remarkably well being for once tidily dressed'. The Other One, the cerebral Sidney, was liked by the younger Holts and Richard, after a talk with Webb in 1900, had been 'much interested and largely converted to a scheme for improving the labouring classes by a minimum wage'. This Fabian enthusiasm did not last. The political child developed views of his own and by the time of the 1903 by-election Richard Holt was ready to put his aunt and uncle in their place: 'The Webbs of course are very Imperialistic, with a great idea of spending money so as to please the working classes. Not to my idea a very high minded type of political opinion though accompanied by most devoted work in the public interest.'[93]

Holt's campaign in West Derby opened badly. On imperial matters his manner, so as not to upset the tender unity of the Liberal party, was hesitant and, concerning Ireland, opaque—'legislation must be passed to enable Ireland to deal with purely Irish affairs. By this he did not mean an independent Parliament or any nonsense of that sort.' This scarcely encouraged the constituency's 800 Irish Catholic voters, whose support for Liberalism was already frayed by their general acceptance of the Conservatives' Education Act; and Rutherford perfidiously suggested that the Liberals preferred to air their fanaticism rather than to see children educated. Needing a cry, Holt dusted the slogan 'Peace, Retrenchment, and Reform'.[94]

Rutherford's enterprise was most keen in Ritualist questions. A Presbyterian, he applauded the Church Discipline Bill; but Holt, a Unitarian, had scruples. Privately he was in no doubt that the best expression of religion in politics was 'simple Christianity' and he blamed sacerdotalism for causing 'apathy and littleness' in politics. Publicly, however, he would do no more than voice disapproval of Church lawlessness: he would not interfere in another communion's affairs.[95] Rutherford, a Freemason and Orangeman, received support from both organizations;[96] and Holt's delicacy was scorned by Wise and E. G. Stafford, a former Liberal, now regional chairman of Kensit's Crusaders.[97] According to the Protestant Alliance, 600 West Derby voters placed Protestantism first.[98]

Windows in the Liberal headquarters were broken;[99] but politically the major diversion was provided by Labour. For the first time a Liverpool constituency seemed attractive—candidates in the last municipal elections had won 1,800 Labour votes in West Derby.[100] N. Donovan, who had contested Low Hill ward, declared that with dearer bread, unemployment, and a judge-made law, they must smash Conservatism. He despised the Tory choice in West Derby—Rutherford was a 'bungholer'—compared with whom any Liberal was respectable. While rebuking Donovan's language, the L.L.R.C. agreed to explore the situation.[101] Frank Rose, of the Engineers', and Sexton were potential candidates; but a Radical attack on the 'subserviency of the Liberal party to a few rich men' complicated matters.

It was rumoured that the local Baptist minister, the Revd. Charles Aked, would stand as an Independent.[102] Although W. B. Lewis, who nominated Aked for the official Liberal candidature, afterwards led Holt's campaign, Aked's standing was not ephemeral.[103] In twelve years his Sunday congregations had grown from under a hundred to over three thousand, consisting principally of lower-middle and middle-class Liberals who found at Pembroke Street Chapel 'opportunities for service which the atrophied, exclusive nature of local politics denied them'.[104] Aked denounced the 'competitive system' in economics and morals; he sought 'a Socialism which is bounded by the Ten Commandments and the Sermon on the Mount'. Although he spoke of municipalizing or nationalizing 'our industries and our wealth-producing and distributing agencies', his views emanated not from doctrine but, the Revd. John Watson once wrote, from the marrow of his bones.[105] His disciples—like the trainee teacher, Ethel Annakin, who married Philip Snowden[106]—embraced social missionary work (or social climbing) before Socialism.

Aked capped his quilted creed with egotism. He alone, he asserted, could win West Derby.[107] In fact he wrecked Labour's chances when time was short owing to the Tories rushing the writ. The I.L.P.'s chairman, Bruce Glasier, thought that Aked's independent candidature might elicit Labour's 'hearty support' and even funds;[108] but Sexton dismissed the idea. He wanted a trade-union Labour party, represented by trade unionists.[109] Amid dissension the L.L.R.C. would not venture out.

This side-show had interesting repercussions. Rutherford believed that Labour's intervention would injure him more than Holt;[110] but, with the note of class representation removed, different claims were made. Protestantism induced the Carters' Union to recommend Rutherford; but Holt's company had a reputation of co-operation with the N.U.D.L. Rutherford monopolized anti-alien prejudice; but Holt advocated the right to combine for collective bargaining and to strike.[111] This provoked another sensation, when Richard Bell, the general secretary of the Amalgamated Society of Railway Servants, and chairman of the L.R.C., recommended Holt.[112] With 3,000 railwaymen in West Derby, the Liberals were delighted; but local Labour leaders contended that Bell acted without the L.R.C.'s authority.[113] The discord was finally personified by Aked, who approved Holt's programme but preferred Rutherford's decisiveness.[114]

Rutherford polled 5,455, Holt 3,251. The *Daily Post* had questioned Rutherford's popularity and both Richard Holt and his father, who had predicted a Tory majority no larger than between five hundred and a thousand, felt that the constituency had been 'debauched' by Higginbottom's treating in the past and by Rutherford's now. The Tory organization, constantly at work in the constituency, was superior. The Liverpool working man, Robert Holt concluded, 'clearly wants more education. The canvassers said it was surprising to find street after street occupied by voters who seemed to know little or nothing of [the] Education Bill and seemed to care precious little about the question now so fully before the Country.' Other Liberal witnesses were more generous: the *Review* saluted 'A Triumph of the Democracy'.[115] The singular Demos was Salvidge, and the *Daily Post* made obeisances in a squib:

> Thy party leaders, though they writhe and squirm,
> Know well thou hast them in thy grip so firm:
> The Protestant-cum-Pagan rabble rout
> Will swallow all thou say'st without a doubt;
> The Beer-and-Bible cult hath thee enshrined
> Among the choicest products of its kind.
> All 'ale![116]

The anti-hero drew his own conclusions. The strength of Liverpool Conservatism lay in 'men of democratic tendency, personally identified with the masses'.[117] The dissidents had been confounded. McGuffie, who had supported Holt, now began to speak of the potential economic benefits of Home Rule.[118] The W.M.C.A. returned his subscriptions.[119] McGuffie was henceforth politically dead. Predators assembled. In December 1901 Thomas Bell, a Liberal Unionist, had applauded McGuffie's efforts to rid the Unionist party of Salvidge's 'Tammany organization'. In June 1903 Bell, now chairman of Warbreck Conservative Association, moved that McGuffie had forfeited the ward party's confidence and should relinquish his councillorship.[120] Salvidge's reflections on the utility of human nature in politics are not known.

The West Derby result apparently exposed the Liberals' policies as well as inadequate organization. 'Peace, Retrenchment, and Reform', to which the Holt family especially were wedded, the *Review* characterized as 'Surrender and Scuttle, Parsimoniousness and Promises without performances'. Cobdenism and Gladstonianism were obsolete. The party needed 'to pull their policy right up to date'.[121] But Liberals could be excused confusion. For what programme except Salvidge's suited a democracy which was illiberal, inegalitarian, and fratricidal?

An independent Protestant party emerges

In 1903 Protestants made an issue of 'free speech', when the Liverpool police endeavoured to restrain Wise. Sectarianism was unsavoury, but 'free speech' was respectable. M'Arthur, Archdeacon Taylor, and the Church Association, avidly denounced 'designing bigots' who strangled Protestant liberties. They demanded special sites for public meetings.[122] In March the Council began inquiries. Twenty-six sites had been approved in London and nine in Manchester; but the Watch Committee's chairman, Alderman Maxwell, warned that Liverpool contained 'certain factions, religious and political, which for their own sakes ought to be kept as far apart as possible'.[123] Wise's designs were apparent in the application of the George Wise Crusade (as his open-air movement was now styled) to use St. Domingo Pit. Everton, Wise claimed, was over 90 per cent Protestant;[124] but nearby the Pit were the Catholic bishop's residence, St. Edward's seminary, two convents, and three Catholic churches with congregations totalling 12,500.[125] Catholic residents petitioned against Wise's application; and the new Head Constable, Leonard Dunning, accepted its inadmissibility.[126]

Dunning advanced matters by summonsing Wise. According to the police, Wise's lewd assertions—for example, that priests lived 'with harlots' and 'rob the poor' to feed their bastards—incited disorder.[127] Wise had three days to consider whether to cease open-air speaking for a year or be gaoled for two months. The Wiseites' bellicosity was broad enough to include avowed friends. When the Orangemen's chaplain, Theodore Howard, advised Wise and his followers to abstain from demonstrations while the Council debated their applications, some fifty Wiseites brawled in his church.[128]

Wise himself was shrewder. His vilifications at open-air meetings, which the police recorded, were missing in public halls, where the press was present. He indulged in excesses, paradoxically, with wariness. He would not upset, until he out-manoeuvred, respectable support. The 'free speech' agitation flattered him and he chose imprisonment.[129] In gaol he was privileged to wear ordinary clothes, order meals, and keep books. One acolyte considered that Wise might write another 'Pilgrim's Progress';[130] but Wise did not display to the world the humanity, literary skill, and imagination that would be required to produce a rival to Bunyan's humble masterpiece.

The British Protestant Union, which held ninety-three meetings in Liverpool in 1902, and the George Wise Crusade, merged as the George Wise Defence Committee. Their petition for Wise's release attracted 63,000 signatories, including Councillors, M.P.s, and clergymen. M'Arthur observed 'great indignation'; Rutherford visited Wise in prison and the Lady Mayoress brought flowers.[131] In a more sinister move the Defence Committee hired a London lecturer, Albert Stones, at £2. 10*s*. per week plus 15*s*. for lodgings.[132] Violence returned to the streets and inside churches.[133] When protestors invaded St. Thomas's, demanding 'another Oliver Cromwell' to end 'idolatry', the churchwardens prosecuted them, hoping to discourage the 'constant state of siege' they had suffered from 1898.[134] One wonders how English civilization impressed W. F. Cody ('Buffalo Bill'), whose Wild West Show visited Liverpool at this time.[135]

According to the chaplain of Ireland's Orangemen, 'Liverpool had reached a crisis in religious matters'. He advised Protestants to pack the churches and 'leave no room for the idolater'; and his narrow suspicion inspected Edward's visit to the Pope—'they should watch the King from this time, and the moment he gave evidence of a complicity with Rome he forfeited his right to the occupancy of the British throne (Prolonged Applause)'.[136] Socialists were tame beside these regicides. Their language was hyperbolical: small men became heroes, prepared to 'set Liverpool on fire' at Wise's side.[137]

In May 1903 the National Protestant Electoral Federation was formed in Liverpool , under the chairmanship of Thomas Massey, an Orangeman. It aimed to harmonize the proliferating organizations, and to put into action the slogan of 'Protestantism before party'. Its immediate inspiration was the Council's change of heart in the allocation of sites. A committee had recommended several, although it obliged Dunning by discountenancing St. Domingo Pit;[138] but the Council refused to proceed, despite Salvidge's efforts. The Nationalist Councillor, Lynskey, exclaimed against Wise's obscenities, 'How could I, as a Catholic, having two brothers as priests and two sisters as nuns, hear such language, without throwing at the speaker the first brick at hand?'[139] Lynskey's colleague, Byrne, echoed him: special sites would promote 'sectarian licence in which every idea of true liberty would be killed'.[140]

A by-election defeat in Anfield ward for Charles Rutherford, the M.P.'s brother, registered the Protestant reaction at the Council's failure to accede to their demands. Several members of the W.M.C.A. repudiated their leaders, particularly Austin Taylor who, having read Wise's speeches, had found them offensive to 'all who value the cause of true religion'.[141] Moreover, in this election the N.P.E.F. linked arms with the Liberals in denouncing the Education Act.[142] The W.M.C.A.'s secretary deduced that the Conservative party in Liverpool could not win without Protestant working men.[143]

In June Wise was released. Sixty thousand people followed him from the gaol to St. Domingo Pit which, by occupation, became the Protestants' forum.[144] In July mobs disputed the Glorious Twelfth in Liverpool , while Wise visited Belfast, requesting Protestant solidarity.[145] Gangs seemed permanently afoot, and the *Protestant Standard* cried enough: religion was being 'trailed in the gutter by a rowdy, godless element to whom Roman Catholicism and Protestantism are merely names . . .'.[146] The visiting American Evangelists, Torrey and Alexander, gave no respite. Their revivals reputedly made 4,000 converts locally;[147] but Liverpudlians did not lack animation. The Americans' mission synchronized with fighting in Islington Square when Wise burlesqued Catholic rites and exhorted 40,000 Protestants to lay claim to speak at Old Swan, a Catholic quarter. As Dunning again summonsed Wise, Wiseites importuned the Lord Mayor to prevent his 'malicious prosecution'. However, having denounced Dunning as a cat's-paw, Wise eventually pledged to withhold from where the police thought disorder might result.[148]

Protestants exacted reparations from the Conservative party in the municipal elections in November 1903. They contested four seats and won three. Their failure, Dr. J. P. Waddy, lost by one vote in Breckfield. In Garston Fred Maddocks, a Kensitite, polled 631 against 510 Liberals and 458 Conservatives. In St. Domingo William Gilbert, an Orangeman, beat the Lord Mayor designate, Hampson, by 1,627 votes to 1,102. In Kirkdale Wise defeated Councillor Russell-Taylor by 2,424 votes to 1,526. Wise exulted that he would 'knock out' the Kirkdale M.P., MacIver, and reduce the Head Constable's salary: Protestantism had made him 'master of the situation'.[149]

The Conservatives blamed bad weather; but 58 per cent of St. Domingo had polled, and 66 per cent of Kirkdale, without Liberal candidates. Russell-Taylor's expenses were the highest in Liverpool. Hampson too outspent his opponent. Wise rightly boasted that the people were with the N.P.E.F. Wise knew his Protestant constituents. He regularly visited their homes, even braving Catholic mobs;[150] and his meetings attracted thousands, exceptional for a municipal contest.[151]

The Protestants' political inspiration had not grown uniformly. Enthusiasm was continuous but its acuteness was often adventitious. During the East Toxteth and West Derby parliamentary by-elections Wise had lost attention; and when he had interrupted the Prime Minister, at a meeting in February 1903, he had been hooted.[152] Wise's resurgent popularity stemmed from the controversy over sites for public speaking, Dunning's 'persecution', and the indiscretions of Ritualists themselves. In March the Rev. John Wakeford had lambasted the Church Discipline Bill as the progeny of a city managed by an Orange-Conservative Tammany organization. His peroration was an insult: to oppose this Bill he appealed 'from Liverpool drunk to England sober'.[153] Wise had returned to favour as Conservatives defended their character.[154] Possibly Orangemen were a body 'which cannot be discredited, because they have no credit to lose',[155] but Wakeford erred in believing that 'not one respectable Christian of any denomination has joined the agitators'.[156] Protestant meetings involved 'the solid, respectable middle class';[157] and their mainstay was the W.M.C.A., composed of respectable artisans. Disorderly elements were included, but clergymen and M.P.s too. It signified that 'in the middle and working classes there is a deep, earnest desire' to extinguish Ritualism.[158]

Protestantism alone had not given the Wiseites victory. Russell-Taylor had petitioned for Wise's release from gaol and supported the Protestants' demand for sites. Certain reports might have been damaging: a speaker accused Russell-Taylor of attending a Ritualist church; but this he denied.[159] What none could deny was the extraordinary compound in the N.P.E.F.'s general programme. This opposed the Education Act, 'the dumping of Jesuits and foreign monks and nuns on our country', and an endowed Catholic University for Ireland; and it advocated another Church Discipline Bill, the inspection of convents, temperance reform, and 'everything that has for its objects the honour of God, and the good of man'.[160] Wise's particular municipal programme included council housing and cheaper transport, and he had condemned councillors' extravagance.[161] Likewise Maddocks denounced Liberalism and Toryism as 'kipper and red herring politics', and he advocated an eight-hour day for Corporation employees, contracts for local firms, and Council housing at 1*s.* per room.[162] Waddy had recommended licensing reform; and Gilbert criticized Hampson's expensive failure to incorporate Bootle with Liverpool.[163]

Most importantly Protestant candidates had profited from Nonconformist discontent with the Conservatives' Education Act.[164] This legislation, moreover, had threatened to divide Catholics and Liberals. T. P. O'Connor specially toured Merseyside to warn Catholics against 'throwing in their lot with the Tory party and the Anglican Church';[165] but that some disregarded him was suggested by one Liberal, a Baptist, who complained of being 'driven into the Wiseite party by the action of the Roman Catholics who deserted the Liberal candidates in Old Swan, Great George, Abercromby, Everton, and Netherfield . . .'.[166] Finally, amid trade depression, there were the resignations from the Cabinet of Joseph Chamberlain and the Free Fooders that autumn. Invited to Liverpool by Salvidge, Chamberlain dilated upon nationalism, shipping interests, and democratic consciousness: Free Trade was 'a manufacturers' and a middle-class movement'. Fiscal matters were beyond municipal affairs; but candidates for the Council could hardly ignore issues which divided local M.P.s, with MacIver embracing Protection and Taylor Free Trade. Salvidge's commitment to Chamberlain's 'wild and ill-digested proposals' was staggering. When the Unionists' elder statesman, Viscount Goschen, followed Chamberlain to Liverpool to defend Free Trade at the Chamber of Commerce, he found that his invitation to an official dinner at the Conservative Club was cancelled. There had also been a Lord Mayor's reception for Chamberlain; there was none for Goschen, and the city establishment smarted at Salvidge's impudence.[167]

Where no Protestant candidate stood the N.P.E.F. had recommended twelve candidates from established parties. Only four were Conservative.[168] Two fought without hope of winning Liberal–Nationalist strongholds. Thus Dr. Hill (Abercromby), and A. S. Collard (Dingle), were the only Conservative councillors in 1903 with official Protestant backing. Without Protestant candidates, however, Protestant votes were undisciplined. In Princes Park ward the N.P.E.F. had favoured the Liberal, Max Muspratt; but the incumbent Conservative councillor, H. C. Dowdall, nonetheless emphasized the Protestant cause, approved their sites, criticized the police and Education Act, and demanded that the Corporation should not employ Catholics. Dowdall polled 1,206, Muspratt 1,090. Paradoxically Dowdall was probably rescued by his

Protestantism, without Wise's approval; and a similar situation materialized in Edge Hill.[169]

Only three of the N.P.E.F.'s Liberal recommendations achieved election. Two represented West Derby ward, but Protestantism was not the determining factor there. In Fairfield the N.P.E.F. supported Frank Joseph, apparently from radical motives for Joseph, a stalwart of the Food and Betterment Association, detested sectarianism. His concern was for 80,000 Liverpudlians below the poverty line.[170] He converted the last Conservative majority of 421 into a Liberal majority of 773; but the disaffection was not exclusively Protestant. Repercussions from the East Toxteth parliamentary by-election were evident in the opposition to Salvidge from non-sectarian Conservatives.

Thus the N.P.E.F.'s individual impression was obscured. The Conservatives' choler was not. Their Council leader, Petrie, denounced the Protestants' 'ingratitude' and defiantly advanced the unseated Hampson to the mayoralty.[171] A place, representing Aigburth, was soon found for Hampson; but other by-elections, following the November aldermanic elections, were troublesome. The N.P.E.F. nominated David Williams in Walton and Robert Griffiths in Princes Park.[172]

The first successes had been intoxicating. The Revd. James McKinney had predicted that 'Balfour's Government would be shaken'.[173] Some Protestants, especially Wise and Maddocks, were more intoxicated than others. They decided policy and selected candidates *ultra vires*. McKinney, Waddy, and others, left the N.P.E.F. when Wise pointedly made Salvidge the subject of the succeeding by-elections. McKinney defended Salvidge's 'staunch Protestantism' and that of the Conservative candidate in Princes Park, J. Lockhart Bailey, a churchwarden at St. Paul's.[174] Wiseites nevertheless disrupted Bailey's meetings. In a 72 per cent turn-out Muspratt polled 1,101, Bailey 857, Griffiths 728. Muspratt had gained only eleven votes since 2 November. Walton registered a more definite result, with 1,548 Conservative votes against 754 Protestants.

Wise reacted furiously to these setbacks. McKinney, he declared, had capitulated to 'Beer, barrel, and bung'; moreover, he would 'stagger humanity' by revelations about McKinney's treachery. The Protestants' readiness to devour each other was staggering enough. McKinney had led Wise's Bible Classes during his imprisonment and in the main municipal election in Kirkdale he had vigorously supported him, declaring that 'he could not understand a Protestant giving a vote for Toryism', and that the N.P.E.F. 'would clear out the City Council . . . [and] turn Liverpool upside down'.[175] When Liverpool was overturned a mob was evident underneath. McKinney became acquainted with it when militants led by Councillor Maddocks brawled in his church, St. Silas's. In Birkenhead the Bishop of Chester recited Wesley's imprecation, 'God deliver us from reforming mobs';[176] but fractiousness continued. An Orange Lodge affiiliated to St. Silas's sided with McKinney; and E. G. Stafford quit the N.P.E.F. to conduct his Wycliffe Crusade independently in Garston.[177]

The N.P.E.F. now officially discountenanced rowdyism, while reaffirming Wise's *démarche*.[178] This was not maladroit because it stimulated Conservatives who had tolerated Salvidge only because they assumed that he was *persona grata* with the Protestant masses. Even friends began to doubt. One told Lord Stanley, 'I have no ill will towards Salvidge, if anything it is the contrary, neither am I indifferent to the Church question, but the better class of Unionists will hold back so long as he rules or seems to rule'.[179] Political beer scandals in November–December further embarrassed Salvidge;[180] and a letter to the *Daily Post*, signed 'Conservative Expediency', observed that although Salvidge's party services were great, his 'withdrawal for a time might be the greatest'.[181] Salvidge's enemies rejoiced. McGuffie recognized that Salvidge was reaping fruits of his sowing; and he exhorted the Wiseites to 'burst up the Alderman Salvidge Unionist caucus, and let Liverpool prosper'.[182] Moreover the *Protestant Standard*, long depressed by mob violence, regained its Wiseite tongue to pronounce the most damnable of verdicts: 'if William of Orange was alive today Alderman Salvidge would not be found walking the chalk line along with him'.[183]

Salvidge performed different prodigies of rectitude, moving the argument to that beloved Tory issue, anarchy versus 'law-abiding citizenship'. He admitted that Conservatives 'had not done all they could for Protestantism' but, regarding Wise's party, he never dreamt that 'those who claimed free speech would deny it to others'.[184] Salvidge was so contrite that he undertook a purge of Wise's partisans from W.M.C.A. branches in Edge Hill, Walton, Scotland, and St. Domingo.[185] According to Salvidge, under a hundred members were disaffected.[186] Expulsions excited resignations in sympathy;[187] and Orange representatives reportedly considered resigning from the Constitutional Association in protest against the Education Act, a new Coronation Oath, and the Duke of Norfolk.[188]

The W.M.C.A. nevertheless affirmed Salvidge's leadership;[189] and rescue work continued at a Kensington by-election in December 1903. The Conservative champion was Sir Thomas Royden, the former M.P., once 'Protestant Tommy of Toxteth'. His reappearance in municipal affairs signified the critical situation. The error of electing an absentee president of the Constitutional was admitted; and Royden was to succeed Lord Stanley in May 1904. A tough campaigner, Royden browbeat an N.P.E.F. deputation which sought to discover his Protestant opinions; and men who had hitherto been dissidents now announced that the N.P.E.F.'s activities were discrediting Protestantism.[190] The N.P.E.F. backed Royden's Liberal opponent, J. L. Langford, a Wesleyan lately defeated in West Derby; and desperadoes, led by Maddocks, broke up a meeting addressed by the constituency's M.P., Rutherford.[191] Royden polled 1,383, Langford 1,063, in a 53 per cent turn-out; but the militant Protestant contribution cannot be estimated, since Catholics evidently disapproved of Langford. The previous Liberal candidate in Kensington (in 1900) had polled 886 against a Liberal Unionist's 1,067.

Royden's election closed four years of schism in Liverpool Conservatism. In reviewing Protestant–Conservative relations Wise provided an outline and punch-line:

> When he was allied with the official Conservative party, when he and many of his workers were members of the Working Men's Conservative

> Association, nothing that he did was described as unlawful or wrong. Not a word did Alderman Salvidge say in public against him until he began to fight the Conservative party on the one hand and the Liberal party on the other, and did his best to form a fourth party in the City Council . . . They had not changed their methods, they had not changed their character, they had not changed their delivery of speech—and yet he was that day described as a rowdy, a law-breaker and a disturber of the peace.

Invited to define Salvidge's Protestantism, Wise replied, 'Convenience'.[192]

CHAPTER THIRTEEN

Dissolving Protestantism and Burgeoning Labour, 1904–6

A new party has now arisen in Parliament whose great object is to promote expenditure. I refer, of course, to the Labour party. Their general policy includes many projects which whether good or bad would entail profuse demands on the public exchequer. *W. Jeans*

The election of a Socialist to any public body is only valuable in so far as it is the return of a disturber of the political peace.[1] *J. Connolly*

In the Edwardian period Labour established a foothold in Liverpool politics. Partly this was a consequence of trade union activity, partly because an outside stimulus existed in the Labour Representation Committee, forerunner of the national Labour party. There were also encouraging signs locally, in the developing disenchantment of Liverpool Irishmen with the Liberal party and in the attention paid to Labour issues by the Nationalists' Council group. Increasing numbers of Liverpool Irishmen were second or third generation: their knowledge of poverty in Liverpool was actual, while their vision of Irish Nationalism was dreamy. Likewise the Conservatives' pretensions to represent the interests and ambitions of Protestant working men had been exposed in recent years. This state of flux and Labour's first successes in municipal elections in 1905 are detailed in this chapter, which concludes with an examination of the 1906 General Election. Nationally the Liberal party's most resounding triumph, in Liverpool the Liberals' advances were marked for their superficiality. The Liverpool Conservative party substantially held firm because, though the Ritualist controversy of the last seven years had been painful and distracting, Salvidge and Wise realized that in the interests of the Conservative party and popular Protestantism it was better to mend rather than to end their association. Protestant Tory Democracy was renewed.

Inter-sectarian conflict

By December 1903 Wise had several guises—educationalist, evangelist, councillor, convict. Now came Pastor Wise. His adherents bought a Welsh

Notes begin on p. 429.

Methodist chapel in Netherfield Road North, renaming it the Protestant Reformers' Memorial Church.[2] Wise had the city's largest congregation. His gift was for attracting rough-grained people into church activities. His Bible Class, a thousand strong, contained many reclaimed drunkards.[3] It marched five times each year and was like the Vatican Guard, an army which rarely fought, until in 1909 two members broke ranks to assault a woman who waved a green flag.[4] Becalmed degenerates were as sirens to Victorian moralizers, and it is no surprise to find the *Daily Post*'s editor, Sir Edward Russell, paying homage to Wise's work.

In other respects too Wise was attractive to Liberal Nonconformists. Indeed it has been suggested that Wise's agitation was really Nonconformist. One Liverpool Conservative in the 1930s insisted that only about two hundred of the eight thousand members of the W.M.C.A. at the turn of the century were Anglican communicants; that the 'Protestant Reformers' were 'as remote from Canterbury as from Rome . . . [and] as "unconstitutional" as the Romanists whom they denounce'.[5] Exactness in nomenclature, however, is less important than Wise's evident intention of polarizing evangelical Protestant forces. In this ambition he had earnest encouragement from many Liberal Nonconformists, although even a partial success in this would bring confusion to existing political party lines. Nevertheless men like Russell lent respectability to Wise's cause. Russell valued 'the spiritual continuity' that England had enjoyed from the state–church connection; but he was 'a frank Erastian' Protestant who in the end advocated Disestablishment as the only way to expel sacerdotalism from influence in the Church of England.[6] Russell epitomized the perplexity of many Liberal Nonconformists in Liverpool when he eulogized Wise on two accounts, as 'a good pastor' who fought drinking and gambling—'the worst enemies of all classes'—and as a crusader who upheld 'their Reformation birthright' against that 'large portion of the Church of England [which] was corrupted . . . by the terrible fancy for degenerating into medieval religion'.[7]

From Wise himself the disagreeable was never distant. Thus his conversion to the Protestant cause of one Catholic, S. Monks, only abetted a divine appointment to offend. Kept from penury by the Crusade's moneys, Monks lectured against the Catholic system in a manner the police thought obscene.[8] The character of Wise's crusaders was also reflected in their revision of Sankey's hymn, 'Dare to be a Daniel!', 'Dare to be a Wiseite!', they sang, 'Dare to stand alone, Dare to be a Protestant, And to Hell with the Pope of Rome!'

Wise's control was incomplete. A single Protestant empire was impossible after his collisions with Salvidge and the Orange chaplains, Howard and McKinney; moreover, Stones, the lecturer whom the Crusade had drawn from London, did not react kindly to the subordination and wage-cut he had suffered on Wise's release from gaol. He demanded an 'interest' in Wise's Church; yet he failed to account for his own collections. In Toxteth in 1904 Stones declared his independence from Wise's Crusade while promising still to co-operate in the N.P.E.F.'s political work.[9] This controversy raised embarrassing questions about the movements' finances;[10] but the Protestant Reformers' Memorial Church was self-supporting, apart from some small donations, and Wise's stipend was derived by the Nonconformist envelope system. He denied that money taken at open-air meetings swelled his pocket.[11]

As a result of the altercation with Stones, Wise lost any title to direct south-end Protestantism. Some might argue that anarchy, rather than Stones, reigned in Wise's stead—riots disturbed Toxteth in the spring of 1904; in addition were individual assaults, executed under the pretext of religious differences[12]—but Stones reported 'far larger crowds and double collections since the split'.[13] He relished advertisement. His photograph sold for 3*d.*; and animus against the police attracted the rougher disciples.[14] Stones flourished because he defied Wise. Militants in the city's south-end seized the opportunity to deny that 'Protestantism in Liverpool was a one-man movement';[15] but, just as Wise took lessons from both Kensit and the Welsh revivalist, Evan Roberts, so Stones aped Wise.[16] There was also muscularity in his Christianity. He '*feared nothing*',[17] and once thrashed an Irish labourer who assaulted him.[18]

Wise was much that Stones was not; especially, he sat on the Council, although this was double-edged since Protestantism was irrelevant to most Corporation work. The Revd. Wakeford believed that because of this Wise's faction must die;[19] but the *Review* predicted, from Wise's record on the School Board, that he would make a 'progressive' councillor and champion Liverpool's interests 'regardless of party or creed'.[20] Wise in fact was an active critic of extravagance, and he shamed many councillors by his contact with constituents. At his ward gatherings he might lament the paucity of Cromwells in the Council; he also genuinely endeavoured to inform people about public affairs.[21] His busyness ensured that his term on the Council enhanced rather than damaged his popular reputation. However, the regular minister of a Dissenting congregation, as Wise had become in December 1903, was ineligible as a Councillor and Wise could not seek re-election in 1906.[22]

Meanwhile Catholic counter-aggression to the Protestant Crusade grew. A Nationalist-inspired 'Sunday Music in the Parks League' opposed Sabbatarian restrictions; and several Protestant homes in West Toxteth were wrecked in rioting. Sectarian strife cost, in police overtime, £650 in 1903, £770 in 1904.[23] The Head Constable noted that disturbances used to be 'caused by crowds passing to and from places of meeting, crowds with some semblance of organization, and a nucleus of perhaps well-meaning persons, followed by mobs over whom the leaders exercised no control'. During 1904, however, disturbances occurred 'without special occasion or warning. Almost nightly through the summer the sound of a drum from one side or the other would bring out two angry crowds . . .'[24]

This elemental character of the sectarian conflict complicated the policeman's lot, since it was difficult to predict where violence would occur. Precautions were taken on 639 occasions in 1904; in 80 force was necessary. Eighteen incidents were designated 'riots'; several, mainly in the south-end, were serious. The police attempted to restrain factious marchers, but Stones bluntly declared that 'he had yet to learn that processions were illegal or that the police could map out a course for them'.[25] None the less, at least one section of public opinion, the shopocracy, supported the police. In May 200 south-end ratepayers petitioned against sectarian processions, claiming danger to the public and 'a struggling trading community'; and in September the Watch Committee demanded notification as to times, routes, display of emblems, and playing of music.[26]

Wise, who soon afterwards was charged with obstruction, wanted a judicial inquiry.[27] The Head Constable and Town Clerk travelled to London but the Home Office would not recommend legislation when bye-laws already covered nuisances of noise and insulting language.[28]

Protestants continued to buffet the authorities, although the Bishop of Liverpool warned that their activities made 'the great name of Protestant stink'.[29] In November 1904 the Conservatives lost another municipal seat to the Protestants, and four to the Liberals. Protestant candidates again stressed welfare questions.[30] Only H. Porter in St. Domingo succeeded, by 1,518 votes against 1,323 (a 63 per cent poll); but Protestants scored 976 in Netherfield, 1,119 in Breckfield, 685 in Kensington and 900 in Princes Park. Subsequently, in Toxteth, Stones was involved in several violent incidents; and riots disturbed Garston throughout 1905.[31]

Salvidge takes to Tariff Reform

The situation with regard to the Protestants, Salvidge admitted, was 'uncontrollable'.[32] This seemed true at a parliamentary as well as municipal level. MacIver's confidence that he could continue to enjoy undivided Protestant support in Kirkdale had collapsed;[33] and Taylor, a devoted free trader, had begun an 'opportune dive' into waters far removed from the majority of his party.[34] In April 1904 Taylor moved to discuss the appointment of a Royal Commission to inquire into Ecclesiastical Discipline.[35] This, he maintained, was a diversion: legislation on ritual disobediences, not further evidence, was required. The terms of reference of the Commission were also unsatisfactory. It was directed to investigate 'breaches or neglect of the Law relating to the conduct of Divine Service in the Church of England and to [investigate] the ornaments and fittings of Churches'. But as Samuel Smith declared on another occasion, 'it is not a mere question of millinery, it is a question of fundamental doctrine'; and Balfour had rejected the Church Discipline Bill in 1899 on this ground, that it did not cover doctrine.[36] The Government must now reckon with the Protestant Party's complaints, warned the Exchange M.P., M'Arthur; but Taylor's tactics, in insisting on carrying the debate about the Commission to a division, mystified and estranged his Liverpool colleagues. MacIver thought that it would only encourage enemies of the Church and Government; and Rutherford taunted Taylor with 'playing for his own hand', having strayed from Conservatives in fiscal matters.[37] Moreover, Taylor's absolute repudiation of the Commission forestalled their plans to increase its Evangelical membership. The outcome, defeat by 179 votes to 90, seriously weakened the Protestants' parliamentary position. Rutherford, however, soon retracted his personal aspersions against Taylor when he found that Taylor remained a hero of Conservative Protestantism locally.[38]

These quarrels resuscitated complaints about the usurpers of Liverpool Toryism. Critics at the Constitutional Association inwardly echoed McGuffie's diagnosis that leaders 'of the right sort' were wanted.[39] Salvidge reconsidered his strategy. Protestantism had slipped among Conservatives like a fire-ship amid moored galleons, and Salvidge looked to navigate his fleet away. There was tacking to be done. Speaking in Liverpool in 1902 Lord Rosebery had enunciated quasi-Unionist views, and many Liberals sought 'step-by-step' approaches to Home Rule. Salvidge had no intention of letting 'that question sleep awhile'.[40] In May 1904 he declared that 'never was the danger of the Irish Nationalists becoming supreme greater'; and he advocated Redistribution to trim Irish representation.[41] Reviving the issue of Home Rule might redirect Protestant passions to Unionist politics.

There were other attractions that Salvidge could cultivate. An Aliens Bill was recently scuttled. Salvidge observed: 'The foreign sweater could grind his slaves unchecked, the British worker could be turned out of his home into the streets to make room for the alien immigrant, and this by the direct act of the Radical party in Parliament.' In addition to 'free trade in pauper and criminal aliens', Salvidge also opposed 'Free Trade in merchandise'.[42]

Never a visionary, Salvidge placed deals before ideals. His 'conversion' to Tariff Reform is not romantic. The engagement, not the end, was cardinal. The Protestant trick had a twofold genius. It crystallized religious and nationalist strife and confined class warfare within the purviews of Conservatism. Sponsorship of this agitation was halted in 1903–4; but the theme of Protection promised continuing prestidigitation, with Conservatives championing working-class interests against the 'lower-middle-class fraud, called Liberalism or "Free Trade"'.[43]

Recklessness distinguished Salvidge's intiatives. He built palaces of opportunity without checking the ground for subsidence. In 1898 he had committed the Liverpool Conservative party to anti-Ritualism without waiting for consent. In 1905, at an Everton parliamentary by-election following Willox's retirement, Salvidge bellowed Chamberlainite Protection instead of whispering Balfour's compromise version.[44] Salvidge's candidate, the Council's Finance chairman, J. S. Harmood-Banner, echoed Chamberlainite sentiment favouring pensions.[45] The Liberals were optimistic: their candidate, a barrister, W. H. Aggs, was an ex-Conservative free trader. Moreover Everton was untried since 1892.

In January 1905 Protestants had returned their sixth councillor against Conservative opposition; but Harmood-Banner was a self-styled 'Reformation candidate', who denounced ritualism, an endowed Catholic University for Ireland, and a revised King's Declaration. He satisfied the Laymen's League, Church Association, and Orange Order; but Aggs also supported Church Discipline. The N.P.E.F., therefore, adopted a neutral position; but Wise, Maddocks, and the Birkenhead Kensitites' leader, T. Major Thompson (an ex-Liberal), joined Aggs's platform to castigate a 'contemptible, ignoble, and vicious' Government, run by Romans and brewers.[46] Salvidge endeavoured to stem a desertion by affirming that 'Protestantism was the first plank' of the W.M.C.A.[47]

The tariff argument otherwise occupied politicians' thoughts. Whether electors matched their interest is debatable: a Free Trade Union propagandist protested that nowhere could rival Everton's 'dense political ignorance'.[48]

Everton based its decision on a confidence in Salvidge, not in horoscope economists. In a 63·4 per cent turn-out Harmood-Banner received 3,854 votes, Aggs 2,543. Aggs polled 378 more than Atkin, Harmood-Banner a hundred less than Willox, in 1892. This was hardly singular, but *Porcupine* deduced that the Protestant ranks had ditched Wise. Several Orange lodges sought to discipline Wise, Maddocks, and Thompson, for their subversive politics.[49] In April, however, at the Poor Law Guardians' elections in Kirkdale, Protestants led by Wise swept the lists. *Porcupine* now declared that Wise would determine the parliamentary representation at the next General Election.[50]

This pendulum swing in Wise's reputation reflected commotion in the Protestant campaign. With Wise in Kirkdale, Stones in Toxteth, and Kensitites in Garston, Birkenhead, and Bootle, the agitation drifted in parochial detachments. The N.P.E.F. could not bind competitive and jealous Protestant leaders. Salvidge, possessing the machinery of the W.M.C.A., remained a Protestant power, and his manifesto of May 1905 was seductive. It claimed for *local* Conservatives an 'unquestionable' record, despite opposition from 'a body arrogating to itself the distinctive name of the Protestant Party'. Even as he chided independent Protestants, Salvidge censured his Government's failure to recognize the nation's Protestantism. Balfour's ostrich attitude had provoked a twin Conservative revolt, on Protestantism and tariffs.[51]

The national assembly of Orangemen resolved that only candidates pledged against Home Rule and Disestablishment should receive Protestant support in the forthcoming General Election; but the Liverpool delegation deemed the declaration against Disestablishment 'unwise', for it removed one resort against Ritualism; and Wise deprecated entangling alliances in a lecture on 'How the Tory party tried to strangle the Orange Order'.[52] Conservative dissemblers had been exposed before and the new M.P., Harmood-Banner, was now tested by allegations that he attended a ritualist church, was anti-Sabbatarian and had secretly endowed the Woodard Schools.[53] There seemed little firmness or consistency of purpose in the Protestants' politics. In March 1905 the Liverpool branch of the Church Association resolved to adopt Henry Miller (the national secretary) in Everton at the General Election;[54] but by October Harmood-Banner was presiding over the inaugural meeting of the Association's winter campaign. Wise interrupted this meeting in order to interrogate the M.P. upon Protestant attitudes. Several Orange lodges criticized Wise's methods, and the *Protestant Standard* declared that Wiseite rowdies were 'no more Christians than the dogs that run the streets'.[55] The previous issue, however, had published one of Wise's lectures expounding 'the Principles of Theology'.[56] The *Protestant Standard*'s ambivalence was common. Opening a bazaar at Wise's Church, Samuel Smith 'could not say he would stand by him in all his performances, being naturally a man of peace'; but Smith admired Wise's 'strong convictions'. Moreover, Wise was 'solving the problem of how to get people to church'.[57]

Politically Wise was out on a limb, but it was in Salvidge's interest to renew dialogue with as many Protestant fragments as possible. In October 1905 he contracted that he would not oppose a Protestant candidate in St. Domingo ward, if the Protestants allowed Kirkdale's Conservative councillor a straight fight against Labour. St. Domingo Conservatives were advised accordingly, but the ward secretary rebuffed Salvidge by stating that they regarded the Protestant as 'our only political opponent'.[58] They defeated him by 1,406 votes to 1,059. Protestantism was also humbled in Breckfield ward, where a Protestant candidate, a builder, James Taylor, opposed the Conservative councillor, Louis Cohen. Anti-semitism marked the Protestants' campaign although Taylor maintained that Cohen was opposed not because he was a Jew but because he represented 'a party which has betrayed the Protestant cause, which is tied up with the liquor interest, which has little or no consideration for the working man, and which has recklessly wasted the ratepayer's money'.[59] Certainly Cohen had alienated dockers during the summer strike; but he was a teetotaller and, in many respects, a progressive employer.[60]

The only other Protestant candidate in the 1905 municipal elections was William Singleton, a master carter and a trustee of Wise's church. Against Nationalist opposition in Sandhills ward Singleton combined the strengths of Protestantism and Unionism; but the Protestants had no unqualified triumph. The N.P.E.F. worked towards the Liberal gain of Edge Hill, but financial questions dominated the elections. Salvidge was quiet amid this controversy.[61] The Liberal leader, Evans, stated that the Corporation was bankrupt, owing £450,000 on current account; Harmood-Banner replied for the Conservatives by conjuring a £270,000 surplus and contributing a sting, that Evans's office-boy could have corrected his figures.[62]

Both parties drew selectively from reports of the elective auditors, one of whom publicly supported Evans.[63] The elections were running the Liberals' way anyhow. The Corporation had missed an opportunity to buy Rivington watershed for £60,000 in 1900. When it later went to arbitration against the new owner, W. H. Lever, it purchased part of the estate for £138,000, spending another £20,000 in fees.[64] The Liberals' promise to apply 'ordinary business methods' in municipal management was attractive by contrast.[65] Increased rates had propelled significant shifts in allegiances.[66] In 1895 West Derby, Toxteth, Kirkdale, and Everton, voted solidly Conservative; in 1905 the Liberals won Low Hill, Edge Hill, Wavertree West, Kensington, Garston, and Warbreck, and retained recent gains in Princes Park, Sefton Park East, and West Derby. Statistics of health, crime, and housing, could be found to undermine the Conservatives' propaganda that Liverpool was 'a better and happier place in which to live'. Ratepayers accepted the Liberal protest that they had not value for money.[67]

Under these currents the Protestant cause sank; but Wise promised a 'reorganization of forces which ultimately would . . . win victories all along the line'. As democrats they could not support the Conservatives' extravagance; but as Unionists, they could not support Liberal–Nationalists. Accordingly, if their independent position was to develop, 'every Protestant should be a labour man . . .'.[68] This speech denoted two aspects of Wise. He was only part politician, and electoral setbacks had not diminished his bumptiousness. Thus he disregarded the Head Constable's warning concerning processions: 'he cared not one jot about it'. Also Wise was an opportunist, quick to appreciate the emergence of a fifth Council party—Labour.

A Labour presence in municipal politics

Sexton, wearing on his mutilated face the hardships of dock life, had been the N.U.D.L.'s General Secretary since 1893. His chief difficulty was 'with the chaotic want of discipline, the ignorance and petty jealousies within our own ranks, rather than with the employers'.[69] In June 1905 a dispute arose over seven foremen at Harrison's—shipowners with berths in the south-end—who were behind with their trade-union contributions. When several unionists struck, Harrison's took the Employers' Labour Association's line that they must return as 'free labourers'.[70] Their allies, the Shipping Federation, supplied nine hundred blacklegs; and a phalanx was formed against the strikers.[71]

The Lord Mayor, a Liberal, John Lea, intervened after two weeks but did no more than state the employers' case.[72] James Larkin, one of Harrison's foremen, scorned Lea's intercession. A charter member of the I.L.P., Larkin preferred to 'chew the grass in Sefton Park' than surrender.[73] Lea claimed that many dockers disliked the strike. Some evidence supported him;[74] but the L.T.C. rallied to the 611 strikers, many of whom were the cream of dock-workers. This was an asset as Harrison's boats incurred delays.[75]

Harrison's replied by riding roughshod through various sanitary, safety, and truck, acts in arranging blackleg labour. Parliamentary protests by Labour's D. J. Shackleton and by the Labour–Nationalist, J. P. Nannetti, were anaesthetized by the President of the Local Government Board, Gerald Balfour, and by his secretary, Bonar Law. The Government passed the buck to the Corporation and Medical Officer of Health, to the Watch Committee and Head Constable, to the Dock Board and Harrison's, who did what they liked.[76] Their sheds were used as unauthorized lodging-houses. In the City Council Taggart moved that the Health Committee prosecute them. Wise seconded him. When the division bell was rung and the Conservatives, Burgess, Ball, and Cohen left their teas, their right to vote was disputed since they were absent when the motion was put. On being ruled in order, the trio opposed the motion, which failed by two votes. From the gallery dockers swore retribution against a Council 'bought by the shipowners'.[77]

Not everyone was hostile. A Relief Fund, started by Councillors Harford and Byrne (Nationalists), Roberts and Boote (Liberals), had Conservative support too.[78] £600 in trading coupons relieved 308 wives and 957 children. The N.U.D.L. expended £2,000, including £500 from the National Federation of Trades.[79] This threatened to complete Harrison's object by bankrupting the union. On 11 September the men returned without union badges.[80]

There were few tangible gains to show from striking. Larkin, bitter at the start and more bitter at the end, had formed another union branch, claiming 1,200 members. He left Harrison's: the N.U.D.L.'s executive gave him an official appointment, although Sexton objected.[81] Everyday conditions were unaffected. In February 1905 an accident had incapacitated a docker, Murphy, employed by Lamport and Holt. In April he was awarded 14*s*. 6*d*. per week, half his average wage. In May his employers argued that Murphy might undertake light work. Although the docks provided little light work, the judge considered Murphy's capacity theoretically improved. He reduced the award to 12*s* 6*d*.

Murphy appealed, but his suit was dismissed with costs.[82] As Will Crooks observed of another case, 'the man with a wooden leg hasn't a wooden stomach'. In Harrison's racking six hundred families for ten weeks, and in Lamport and Holt spending months of litigation to cut a cripple's pension, Liverpool's labour relations were inscribed.

The dockers' strike had bred some strong reactions. Several candidates' addresses in the subsequent municipal elections advocated municipalization. Ben Tillett once deprecated the Mersey Docks and Harbour Board 'because the same class of man is removed from a private capacity to do more mischief in a public one'.[83] Before 1857 a Corporation committee had administered the docks and diverted some revenues for municipal purposes, to the neglect, many substantial trading interests argued, of the port's facilities. But, with the establishment of a public trust, the port was governed by a Board of twenty-eight members. Four were chosen by the Board of Trade and twenty-four by parties who paid dues. Apart from vacancies caused by death or resignation, Governments reappointed the sitting representatives as their term of office expired, and this practice was uncontroversial until the inter-war period when pressure accumulated from Labour M.P.s anxious to appoint a Labour representative.[84] As for the non-government representatives, Sir William Forwood thought that Liverpudlians were proud of the Board, and that the rivalry for berths and facilities was intrinsically healthy. Certainly small investors, of under £50, were attracted by the Board—T. P. O'Connor claimed that it was 'a favourite investment of what you might call the lower middle class'.[85] But membership of the Board, 'the blue ribbon of the commercial world',[86] was sometimes achieved by faggot-votes (there were some 3,000 electors by 1914); and critics complained that the city was unrepresented in the body which controlled its economic life. The Board could claim to have pursued adventurous policies of dock-building, but its apparent feebleness over the Manchester Ship Canal and the concern expressed by Irish M.P.s about facilities for their cattle trade brought unwelcome publicity in the 1890s.[87] In 1893 the American (formerly Inman) Line transferred its main operations to Southampton; and the White Star Line was to follow in 1907. Geography was against Liverpool as British companies saw in Southampton a more convenient base from which to compete in the continental passenger traffic to America. There was some incompatibility in being both a major passenger port and a distributive centre. The expensive works required for the largest liners might necessitate higher dock dues all round, which would alienate other business. Liverpool's tea and wool trades had already been lost; the timber trade was in trouble, and the grain trade was attracted to Barrow and Hull.[88]

Porcupine was unsympathetic to the Docks Board's difficulties, and nominated it '*the* enemy of Liverpool'. It exhorted citizens to depose that 'wretched oligarchy';[89] but this was not practical politics in 1905. More relevant electorally were labour questions within the City Council's competence. Salvidge did not naturally consider industrial causes, but he would assess their political recoil. This calculation sickened Richard Holt by its cynicism: 'The Salvidge party are playing a very astute Tammany game—Liberal measures in everything that does not affect the pockets of the public house. Councillor Burke gave an instance or two of cases where this section of the Tory party offered to carry motions set down by Liberals if they were allowed to move them and get the kudos. Otherwise they would throw them out.'[90]

In 1901, however, the L.T.C. had praised Salvidge's efforts to protect dockers by Factory Acts;[91] and now, in 1905, Salvidge promoted a minimum daily wage (4*s*.) and paid holidays for Corporation workmen who, with the expansion of local government services, were becoming an important sub-section of the electorate. It was reckoned by 1917 that one man in thirteen on the Liverpool electoral register was a municipal employee of one kind or another. Of forty-seven members who opposed the minimum wage in 1905, forty-four were Conservatives; of sixty-two supporters sixteen were Conservatives. Of thirty-four who criticized paid holidays, thirty-three were Conservatives; of fifty-five advocates nine were Conservatives. This conflict with his own party explains Salvidge's discomfort, as a Tory Democrat, during the elections.[92]

Three Labour candidates emerged—Sexton in St. Anne's, John Wolfe Tone Morrissey in Kensington, and J. S. Ratcliffe in Kirkdale. Conditions were favourable: labour questions were topical and neither Protestants nor Catholics were content with the established parties. The Protestant councillor, Maddocks, even believed that he could join Labour without forsaking Protestant ambitions.[93] In Ulster the Sloan–Crawford manifestos had mooted a Protestant Labour movement;[94] and in Liverpool's Breckfield ward Protestants and Catholics showed signs of co-operation, although whether from common labour sympathies or from anti-semitism was unclear. Nevertheless two Orangemen, James Taylor and James Quick, organized the Liverpool Right to Work Committee in protest against the inadequacies of the 1905 Unemployed Workmen's Act.[95]

On the other side the Liberals' equivocations about Home Rule and intention 'to rob us of our Catholic schools' alienated many Catholic workers;[96] and the Nationalist party's sub-divisions increasingly reflected local labour aspirations. In 1905 the United Irish League promoted James Bolger, a shipping contractor, in North Scotland;[97] but the ward branch disputed its right to dictate selection and advanced Michael Phelan, a publican. The U.I.L. cried 'treason' and 'corruption', but Phelan pressed local issues and won 809 votes against 713. T. P. O'Connor had supported Bolger. It signified his high opinion of party loyalty and his relative ignorance of Liverpool Irish interests. But to conclude that he was 'politically defunct' was optimistic.[98]

Sexton's vicissitudes made this appear less of a family quarrel. He first considered contesting Dingle ward in south Liverpool as a protest against the Corporation's supineness during the dock strike.[99] His moving to St. Anne's arose from opportunities presented by the retiring Councillor, Clancy. Known for his 'hanging between the Nationalist heaven and the Liberal earth', Clancy really sought a radical firmament.[100] St. Anne's was traditionally inconstant. Before the Ballot and Corrupt Practices Acts it had exhibited exceptional venality;[101] afterwards its shifts denoted the subterranean activities of managers of Irish clubs. Sexton's candidature in 1905 provoked several resignations from the U.I.L. branch;[102] but against a Conservative the experimental Nationalist–Labour alliance performed as soundly as a Liberal–Nationalist team. The xenophobic ring of some of Sexton's pronouncements—against Jewish and Chinese immigrants—was a reflection that liberal values counted cheap besides jobs and housing;[103] and this rugged electioneering gave the impetus to Sexton's victory by 884 votes to 709.

Catholic connections also consecrated Labour's candidature in Kensington ward. Morrissey had a brother in the priesthood. The Conservatives considered Morrissey's forenames. They desired 'a loyal representative'; anyone called Wolfe Tone should canvass the Scotland wards.[104] The Conservative candidate, Dr. Hill, had been defeated by a Protestant in a St. Domingo ward by-election that January. He now decided to eschew sectarianism and to stand on his record in municipal health. Morrissey was qualified to refute him. As a city auditor since 1901 (the first Socialist to be elected to public office in Liverpool), Morrissey had exposed civic mismanagement and his critique was distributed among voters.[105] Morrissey's preeminence in this controversy undermined the third candidate in the Kensington contest, a Liberal, Benjamin Wilson. Wilson claimed to be the only *bona fide* Labour candidate—Morrissey was an insurance agent, Wilson a master tailor—but he languished with 659 votes. Morrissey polled 1,137, Hill 1,076. That Morrissey's and Sexton's successes were Labour-cum-Nationalist was implied by Ratcliffe's failure in Kirkdale. His campaign for independent labour representation ignored other faiths, whereas his Conservative opponent, the chairman of the Hospitals Committee, Dr. Utting, was a Wiseite sympathizer.[106]

Although dominant—with sixty-nine Council members against forty-seven Liberals, thirteen Nationalists, five Protestants, and two Labour—the Unionists had lost ten seats in two years. When the party defended its municipal record without effective sectarian incitement it palpably failed. Conservative discredited Conservative. The East Toxteth rebels of 1902 now campaigned as a Citizens' Association, promoting 'better government . . . irrespective of party or creed';[107] and Salvidge was scalded by their publicity. Williams proclaimed that he 'left the Conservative party because it failed to realize its responsibility to the people'; and Burley emphasized, 'By one man the best Conservatives were being driven out of public life'.[108]

Labour's victories in Liverpool had coincided with the party's first major breakthrough into local government. Altogether sixty-six councillors were returned; but, scattered amid several boroughs, they seemed doomed to humdrum activities. A *Clarion* columnist suggested a Municipal Intelligence Bureau to co-ordinate their work and to cultivate independence of Town Hall bureaucracies. The Fabians' Local Government Information Bureau, which had aimed to provide this service in the past, needed rejuvenation; but an alternative was that provincial L.R.C.s trade information.[109]

Unemployment was a more immediate concern. Morrissey estimated 20,000, *Porcupine* 30,000, unemployed in Liverpool that winter.[110] The Conservatives' answer was Protection. The Council leader, Petrie, proposed to give preference in Corporation work to residents of over two years' standing. Taggart translated this, 'No Irish need apply'; and Sexton joined the Nationalists in deriding 'parochial narrowness'. After frigid reconsideration, the Conservatives insisted upon a qualification of one year's residence.[111]

The range of public provision for relief of unemployment had scarcely broadened since the last severe test in the 1890s. The municipal labour bureau was dormant. The Council did, however, establish an Unemployed Committee, as permitted by the 1905 Unemployed Workmen's Act. This specified forty members—eighteen councillors, fourteen Guardians, and eight persons experienced in relief. The Committee provisionally included three Nationalist and two Protestant councillors, but only two Labourites—Rouse and Gerrard, the L.L.R.C.'s chairman and secretary.[112] They would sit, as members experienced in relieving distress, with two representatives of the Central Relief and Charity Organization Society and one each from the Salvation Army, Police-Aided Clothing Association, friendly societies, and Women's Council. Since many sufferers were dockers a significant omission was Sexton's name. His offence was outspokenness during the recent dock strike; and although after his election to the Council Sexton was eventually included, Labour remained under-represented.[113]

This grievance faded as the Committee's limitations became known. The Council's order to prefer workers of twelve months' residence was binding; and the temporary work was designed, according to the President of the Local Government Board, for the 'élite of the unemployed,' that is, those unemployed who, in the Committee's opinion, should not come under the Poor Law.[114] The Committee could promote emigration and farm colonies; but expensive experiments were unlikely since their costs were mostly defrayed by the rates.[115] An economic justification of public works was lacking. Some trade unionists had an instinctive appreciation of possible counter-cyclical, multiplier effects of public works, but the financial aspects seemed intractable and their case was primarily based on the abstract moral principle of the right to work.[116] In the immediate future, then, public works were to have less appeal for politicians as a palliative for unemployment than national insurance, financed partly by workers' and employers' contributions. Liverpool's Labour Councillors were soon disenchanted with the Unemployed Committee. Morrissey deplored the Council's deceptions and lack of inquiry. Sexton blamed the Government (which had refused exchequer-aid) rather than the Council. In his capacity as a trade unionist he pressed on with plans of clearing houses for dock labour.[117]

Agitation about unemployment nonetheless developed. The leader of the S.D.F., H. M. Hyndman, visited Liverpool and called General Booth, of the Salvation Army, 'a canting old kangeroo'; but the unemployed were not measurably relieved.[118] They spawned their own leaders in the Liverpool Right to Work Committee. Among them was Robert J. ('Valdo') Gibbon, a former circus-performer with a reputation from the London unemployed riots of 1886.[119] One of Gibbon's children, before the age of two, was said to be capable of opening steel handcuffs without a key. Socialism was Gibbon's Houdini trick to release the unemployed. Demanding a living wage, Gibbon led a march on London. With the geography of a snake the marchers proceeded across the Midlands, at each stage expecting to recruit more support. They were disillusioned. The contingent remained small; subscriptions were dissipated on drink; and their reception by London labour organizations never materialized.

Back in Liverpool, Gibbon denounced the Right to Work National Council—

'these nonsensical, humbugging lot cannot do anything for the workers either in this city or in any other'.[120] Meanwhile the L.L.R.C. participated in the Liverpool Unemployed Committee to prevent it becoming free labour agency. The Committee would not insist on union rates and, although some historians view the Unemployed Workmen's Act as the first legislative recognition of government responsibility for the unemployed, divorced from the question of poor relief, the L.L.R.C. concluded that the Act was 'a back-handed slap at organized labour'.[121] We might leave the unemployed preserved in two moods. Despite Gibbon's *débâcle*, men were said to be wanting a Deliverer, 'a second Will Crooks'[122]—or perhaps George Wise. Unemployment also inspired business opportunity. This was ablaze in one advertisement: 'Much has already been written in the local Press this season as to the want and poverty existent in the poorer quarter of Liverpool. Worse, however, than a famine in the land is a famine in the body . . .'[123] Bile Beans might cure constipation; but where were Morison's Pills, as Carlyle named simpletons' panaceas, for unemployment?

The 1906 General Election

Labour's bid

Attention shifted to the pending General Election. Labour's preparations were made by the Liverpool Labour Representation Committee (L.L.R.C.), which began as the Trades Council's Ways and Means Committee in June 1903. T. A. Wood, a stonemason, was the first chairman; Sexton was among the trustees. They sounded sixty-five societies and unions (150 branches) about contributing an annual minimum of 3*d* per member for political purposes. Twenty-seven societies, totalling 10,000 members, answered affirmatively; another dozen were sympathetic. Five societies refused outright to make a contribution; the rest as yet expressed no opinion.

Labour's political organization was as effective as the trade unions' interest allowed it. In Liverpool the unions were only half engaged. Nevertheless, the Kirkdale contest advanced the L.L.R.C.'s maturation. Boiler-makers constituted the strongest local union and in 1903, over two years before the General Election was due, the L.L.R.C. had adopted James Conley.[124] Labour's satisfaction had then been sullied by Wise's election as a Councillor for Kirkdale. This seemed a bad omen; and several Liverpudlians had advised the Boiler-makers' General Secretary, D. C. Cummings, to withdraw Conley. Cummings recognized that a poor performance by Conley might strengthen some of his executive who 'belonged to the old political parties';[125] but, though Wiseites disturbed Conley's first public meeting, his campaign mounted.[126] The L.L.R.C. appointed polling district secretaries in 1904 and Gerrard, as Conley's agent, registered 300 voters. By 1905, having distributed handbills and held meetings in profusion, the L.L.R.C. confidently rejected compacts with Liberals or Nationalists.[127] Opposing an unabashed Protectionist in the Conservative M.P., MacIver, Conley did not dilute his programme for Liberal support. He extolled manhood suffrage, nationalized industries, pensions, and a state solution to unemployment; and he exhorted electors to 'sink all differences of party interest, all religious bigotry (loud applause), and strive to break down the barriers of capitalism and landlordism (applause)'.[128]

Sectarianism was not dismissed as Conley wished. MacIver called himself a Reformation candidate. He abused the Royal Commission which investigated Ecclesiastical Discipline, a Liberal Cabinet which included Catholics, and 'ignorant Home Rulers, who voted as their priests directed'.[129] Conley lacked 592 votes in a 65·2 per cent poll on a miserably wet day, and the L.L.R.C. showed a £221 deficit which the Boiler-makers' were reluctant to shoulder.[130]

Early in 1905 there was no prospect of another Labour contest;[131] but in December West Toxteth's Liberal candidate fell into business difficulties and withdrew. In his place the I.L.P. nominated Sexton, who gladly abandoned his canvass of Hull. The Liberal constituency council agreed not to advance another candidate, although one dissentient, belonging to the N.U.D.L., considered that Sexton could not combine a political career consistently with his obligations as General Secretary.[132] The Liberal leader, Evans, however, applauded Sexton as a free-trader and Tory critic; and the *Weekly Post* declared that, despite his preference for the title 'Labour', Sexton 'must be called a Liberal'.[133]

West Toxteth contained some 2,800 unionized workers and Sexton assailed Houston's parliamentary record in labour matters.[134] As an employer Houston had discountenanced the N.U.D.L. since 1904 but, regarding the larger question of trade union privileges, it is uncertain how far public opinion was concerned to establish the right to strike and to picket without penalty. Restrictive legal decisions in the 1890s and after had a popular foundation.

Chinese 'slavery' in South Africa was another emotional issue for Labour and Sexton's election agent, Larkin, dramatized this in a mock funeral.[135] Houston had more practical aids, in an extensive canvassing machinery; moreover, being part buffoon and part megalomaniac,[136] Houston was an experienced politician. His address muddled his position on tariffs and emphasized that alien immigration would 'reduce wages, drive British-born men and women out of employment, and greatly increase Pauperism'.[137] Houston advocated a rigid Aliens Act, together with 'Protestantism, progress, unity, and Imperialism'. As a Catholic, Sexton suffered every defamation, Houston working on the principle that 'the man who never made an enemy, never made anything'.[138] Here Houston made victory, by 781 votes in a 71·5 per cent poll. Sexton commented, 'The dockers weren't all true to my labour standard'. Moreover, 'the Dingle boys beat the Protestant drum till the sheepskin nearly burst'.[139]

Liberal stimulants

Different considerations influenced contests between the established parties. The Drink Question was again thought important. The 1904 Licensing Act the Liberal temperance wing bitterly opposed as a setback for the cause of popular control. This legislation had coincided with the ascendancy in the Liverpool Conservative party of Salvidge, the manager of Bent's Brewery. This connection was marked even by Liberals who had never been devoted to the temperance cause, like the former leader, Robert Holt. He was dismayed by the strength of the Tory organization and by the 'large staff of canvassers they can command through their Public House interest'; and in 1906 he pleaded that all elections should be held on the same day, and that that day should be made a holiday when every pub was closed.[140]

The drink issue, however, really became central to the General Election in Liverpool when eight Unionist members of the Licensing Committee in December 1905 sued the editor of the *Daily Post*, Sir Edward Russell, alleging criminal libel. This was an unusual, and very serious, move by the plaintiffs, who used their positions as public persons to bring a criminal action, for which the penalty might be imprisonment, rather than a civil action for damages as private citizens. W. F. Taylor and F. E. Smith, both prominent Conservatives locally, represented the licensing magistrates; Rufus Isaacs and E. G. Hemmerde, both well-known Liberals, defended Russell. He had asserted that the magistrates obstructed temperance reform at the behest of a trade-influenced Conservative party. The suit's significance was clear. Isaacs, in his summing up, declared, 'it is a political case and nothing else'; but the plaintiffs' clumsiness in court somewhat diminishes his later boast that this case constituted 'the greatest triumph of his forensic career'.[141]

It was disclosed how a Unionist majority had been engineered on the Liverpool Licensing Committee, established by the 1904 Act. Regarding these partisans Sir Thomas Hughes, the independent chairman, almost despaired. He declared about one licence, 'If you pass that you will pass anything'.[142] The Unionists had rejected a Liberal proposal, imposing the maximum levy on public houses, and Hughes's compromise of three-fifths. They operated half the maximum, deriving £18,500. The smaller the compensation fund, the fewer licences the committee extinguished. In 1905 it condemned twenty-nine from a black list of eighty-two. Some magistrates were deeply involved, like the deputy chairman, Isaac Morris, who handpicked Conservatives for the Committee. Morris Jones was one such tool. He never attended the inspection of premises but always voted. He voted on evidence presented and, in divisions, supported the majority—his party colleagues.[143] Sir William Forwood, the chairman of Lancashire Licensing Committee, acknowledged that Hughes's achievements depended on the *Daily Post*'s support.[144] Salvidge was silent, but the trial thwarted his efforts to dissociate his trade from politics. The verdict, Russell's acquittal by a jury reputedly containing eight Conservatives and four Liberals, was popular. Pulpits rang with purity's victory. More obviously Liberalism triumphed.

No party in office for ten years can pretend to popularity. In fiscal matters Conservatives were especially disadvantaged. They spoke through Balfour and Chamberlain, as brotherly as Cain and Abel. Already Balfour seemed a liability. Lloyd George observed 'not a man but a mannerism'.[145] Balfour sought obscurity; Chamberlain courted publicity. In the Liverpool Conservative camp MacIver aggravated differences by asserting that the shipping community was mostly Protectionist.[146] Rebutting him were J. M. Laird for shipbuilding, Arthur Haywood for the cotton trade, Edward Paul for the corn trade, and two Cunard directors.[147] One, Sir William Forwood, had led the local Unionist Free Food League since its establishment in December 1903.[148]

Officially the Liverpool Unionists were Chamberlainites, but M'Arthur seemed a free food troglodyte and Lawrence was opaque. Their best chance was to couch economics in images of patriotism, 'so "piping-hot"—hot with anger against the foreigners; hot with enthusiasm for our colonies—that the delirium grows'.[149] The novelist, Robert Tressell, observed that what workmen called 'the "Friscal Policy", the "Fistacal Policy", or the "Fissical Question" was a great Anti-Foreign Crusade'.[150] Tariff Reform would provide and protect employment.

Many shipowners felt both alarm and envy when they considered foreign competition: alarm at the 'subsidies of immense value', by which foreign governments stimulated their shipping, and envy at the way in which foreign shippers were relatively unsupervised in their management of men and machinery. This engendered a retaliatory spirit in Liverpool and the Steam Ship Owners' Association lobbied Balfour for assistance in the export market.[151] Nevertheless, business conservatism mostly affirmed free trade as if it determined Liverpool's commercial eminence; and Councillor Byrne carolled this canticle on behalf of ordinary working people—'Protection for Liverpool means industrial suicide'.[152]

Both commercial constituencies, Exchange and Abercromby, went Liberal. Exchange's electorate (5,891) was 1,169 down since 1897, the last serious contest. The *Courier* believed that businessmen still overwhelmingly supported M'Arthur; but Salvidge recognized commercial discontent.[153] Having become what *Punch* called Balfour—'A Free-Tariff-Trade-Reformer'[154]—M'Arthur endeared himself to neither Chamberlainites nor traditionalists. His vagueness was scorned as 'Protection and water'.[155]

M'Arthur's only consolation was that his Liberal opponents could not expect complete Nationalist support.[156] The conviction of the candidate, Richard Cherry, that Home Rule remained integral to Liberalism,[157] was countered by the speech at Liverpool Reform Club in November 1905 by the future Cabinet Minister, R. B. Haldane. Liberals, he said, required 'a majority independent of the Irish members. Their ideals were not the same in education, in temperance, and in other things'. Home Rule was 'an impossibility' until a state of industry was established in Ireland and until sectarian aspirations in education were suppressed. Englishmen had 'a want of confidence in the way in which the people of Ireland might use the power placed in their hands'. Ireland, therefore, must be maintained imperially.[158]

This unsparing speech shook Cherry's Nationalist support. Moreover, as T. P. O'Connor told his party leader, Redmond, Liberal–Nationalists faced 'vehement hostility' from the Catholic Church.[159] Cherry was not a Catholic and, while Lynskey supported him, the Nationalists' education champion, Councillor Burke, opposed him. On the other hand, the Liberals' want of commitment to Home Rule enfeebled the Unionist alliance. Redmond might assert that this was 'the supreme political question';[160] but Home Rule was less of a sensation in 1906.[161] This liberated the Unionist Free Traders, who deserted M'Arthur as Cherry triumphed by 121 votes.

In Abercromby the Unionists were insecure before fiscal matters hastened their overthrow. Polling between 3,500 and 3,800 votes Lawrence had won no majority greater than 831 since 1885; but the electorate had fallen from 9,137 to 7,418. Following these suburban migrations the municipal representation was transmogrified. In 1895 Abercromby returned nine Conservative and three Liberal councillors; by 1905 these positions were reversed. Abercromby Unionists exhibited no enthusiasm. The constituency chairman, Isaac Morris, suffered from his exposure in the Russell trial and the organization had stagnated.[162] Lawrence had owed his past successes to an ability to satisfy businessmen. He now declined to categorize himself fiscally, and businessmen were niggardly about trust in 1906.[163] Lawrence's disguise contrasted with his opponent's frankness. Major-General J. B. Seely, the former Hughligan, had quit the Conservative party on account of differences over tariffs and Chinese labour.[164]

Lawrence tried to compensate elsewhere. He believed that to make the Unemployed Workmen's Act efficient 'would throw a burden on the rates'. This appealed to the parsimonious community; so too did his hesitation concerning state pensions.[165] Lawrence, however, had little opportunity to stimulate anti-Irish feeling: Seely showed no Gladstonian bias.[166] Moreover, minorities like the Jewish colony were repelled by Lawrence championing an Aliens Bill.[167] Seely scored 2,933, Lawrence 2,734, in a 76·4 per cent poll.

The Tory hold

In constituencies without considerable commercial interests voters responded to fiscal arguments when they were arranged with familiar trappings. In Walton the issue was fought between two barristers—a Tory, F. E. Smith, apparently 'the most brilliant and broad-minded' of Liverpool's candidates;[168] and a Liberal, E. G. Jellicoe. Smith, born on Orangeman's day 1872, published a nine-point address containing four sectarian references, about Ireland, education, disestablishment and disendowment, and ritualism. The *Protestant Standard*, however, reckoned that Smith's priority was 'to look after No. 1'. It clearly scented that novelettish quality about Smith which Cynthia Asquith later described so well—that of 'a magnificent bounder . . . the Zeppelin-like cigar always in his mouth and the reliefs of good living on his face'.[169] Liverpudlians suspected Smith as once they suspected Canning: 'We never loved brilliancy from our hearts in Liverpool. We have tolerated it at times for the sake of other qualities by which it has been accompanied; but we were always anxious to get rid of it.'[170] Smith's very candidature betokened cynical manoeuvre, 'the greed of ambition with a capacity for intrigue'.[171] He had been destined for defeat in Scotland

Division until Stock was induced to tire of Church Discipline and to make way in Walton.

Fortunately Smith confronted an opponent who also projected the thunder and lightning of personality. Jellicoe's 'screaming tirades' had alienated members of Fairfield ward Liberal Association by June 1905; but he did not proceed circumspectly. Balfour he called 'the long-wriggling worm', Chamberlain a 'Judas' and 'panjandrum of trust-mongers and combines'; and a vote for Smith was, in Jellicoe's opinion, a vote for 'Rand slave-owners'.[172] Inevitably Jellicoe questioned Smith's involvement in the Russell suit. That Smith instigated the plaintiffs from political motives was also alleged by the Liberal leader, Evans; but Jellicoe, in downright fashion, proclaimed that Smith was the brewers' runner.[173]

Thus, whereas most Conservatives regarded the fiscal question as reason for caution, Smith keenly turned to it. A debate, 'Should working men support the Conservative party?', found Smith championing the W.M.C.A. against W. H. Lever, the soap-king and president of Liverpool Junior Reform Club. This phenomenon had long exasperated Liberals. The Conservative working man, the *Review* once declared, was 'an unnatural abortion, having Prejudice and the Parson as his parents. Whenever the Conservative working man opposes a question that question is morally certain to be right.'[174] Likewise the *Daily Post* pronounced that the Conservative working man 'resents any well-directed attempt at improving the social condition of the masses'.[175]

The Smith–Lever debate was less vehement. With Labour at their shoulders, neither man disturbed the legend that the working-class lot had vastly improved.[176] Against Jellicoe, however, Smith repudiated Cobdenism, 'the creed which detested trade unions, which loathed the colonies, which made false prophecies, which had swollen the list of our poor relief, and had filled our streets with displaced British labour'.[177] Jellicoe remained traditional in his concept of State activity: 'they could not benefit their unemployed by Government grants, municipal help, or by robbing the rich'.[178] Tariff reform, Smith maintained, would 'not add one farthing to the cost of living of the working classes, while it will go far to alleviate the miseries of unemployment'. His Government would also restrict alien immigration.[179] Walton had been uncontested since 1892, when the Unionist majority was 1,214. Subsequently this working-class dormitory had sprouted nearly 5,900 more voters. Municipally it returned ten Conservatives and eight Liberals; now Smith polled 5,862, Jellicoe 5,153, in a 74 per cent turn-out.

West Derby experienced practically a repetition of the 1903 by-election. *Porcupine* reckoned Rutherford 'the boldest and most courageously democratic' of Liverpool's M.P.s[180] The less impressionable eye of the Liberal leader, Edward Evans, discerned a 'mountebank', who personified the worst faults of a bad Government. But in his 'bumptious and vulgar' way Rutherford understood electioneering. Every constituent received his Christmas card, and the W.M.C.A. worked as always. By contrast on the Liberal side Richard Holt found the same want of organization that had prevailed in 1903. He recorded in his diary in March 1905: 'Started electioneering in the quiet way—organizing committees and getting names and men. Virtually I have to manage my own election, which should really not be the candidate's work.'[181] Rutherford also contrived with some success to sympathize with labour questions. The L.T.C. complimented his 'go-ahead characteristic':[182] he was an honorary member of the Amalgamated Society of Railway Servants and advocated a Railway Hours Bill. Rats could be scented beneath Rutherford's platform. He denounced the use of Chinese labour in the Transvaal, yet supported his party on this question because he would not entrust the Empire to Campbell-Bannerman.[183] He was also averse to Labour M.P.s: they 'had never done a stroke of work in their lives'. Most Labour candidates were 'not *bona fide* working men, nor *bona fide* trade unionists, but merely irresponsible agitators'.[184]

One 'agitator', Morrissey, now represented Kensington ward. Rutherford was unlikely to attract Morrissey's supporters, or the constituency's many postal workers, whom the Postmaster-General, Lord Stanley, had called 'bloodsuckers'. Rutherford, however, advocated their cause: he valued agreement, not coherence. Trade union legislation, nationalized transport, national insurance, pensions, female suffrage, better education, land reform, compulsory purchasing powers for municipalities, and an expanded navy—Rutherford's programme exuded Tory Democracy. He also declared that 'existing taxes have reached their limits'. He wanted income tax replaced by a tariff on foreign manufactures, although Rutherford avoided the term 'Protection', since he would not tax raw materials and food.

In an exchange about future betterment, Rutherford's opponent, Richard Holt, airily repeated Campbell-Bannerman's declaration that the 'work before a Liberal Government was not Free Trade, because that would be settled by the general election, but the great social reforms which the nation so urgently required'.[185] Rutherford turned to emotional side issues. Concerning immigration, he had long advocated controls. Now he remarked that if the Government expelled Chinamen from the Transvaal, it should prohibit their employment on Holt's boats.[186] Moreover, Rutherford refused 'to go across the street to solicit a Catholic vote'.[187] Holt picked up 349 votes since 1903, and Rutherford dropped eight; but in the city's highest poll, 77·4 per cent, Rutherford won a majority of 1,847. This was the man whose election as the Constitutional's vice-chairman in June 1905 signified to *Porcupine* 'new and progressive life for that ponderous body'.[188]

Like Rutherford, Harmood-Banner followed the formula of his recent by-election. His staple pronouncements were the Union, Protestantism, and Protection, in that order. He also championed Chinese labour as 'an absolute necessity' because it brought 'large orders for work to this country by the production of gold'.[189] His opponent, Aggs, attacked the myopia of Liverpool workmen whose

> political faith . . . commenced with hot-pots, continued with hot-pots, and ended with hot-pots. The steam of the hot-pots obscured their view of the Tory mountain; if at any time the steam rolled away, and the people down below began to bestir themselves, the Tories from their mountain

> lowered down a tempting bait, labelling it sometimes Home Ruler, sometimes Pro-Boer, or Alien Immigrant, and the people grew so excited . . . that they forgot all about their real rights and wrongs and neglected to drag down the Tories from their mountain of vested interests and monopolies. It was not hot-pots they wanted, but houses—houses to live in and wages to live on, and the means to produce happiness in their lives.[190]

Aggs won most of the 4 per cent increase in turn-out since 1905, but trailed by 1,065 votes.

Except for a mechanical challenge in Scotland division, Liverpool experienced no other contest. Austin Taylor, 'that delightful creature', as Lord Stanley called him, was unopposed as an Independent. He had criticized Chinese 'slavery', and deserted his Government as a Free Trader unable to follow either Chamberlain or Balfour. East Toxteth's Conservative Council had censured him and in October 1903 Taylor behaved properly and resigned. This was kept secret, though Stanley thought then that there was no prospect of getting Taylor to continue, and that the shipowner, Sir Alfred Jones, would surely replace him.[191] In fact Taylor was still in his place in 1906, and in the General Election he cunningly combined causes: 'No party which becomes either Protectionist or Priest-ridden will command my support.'[192]

The Conservatives' decision not to re-adopt or to oppose Taylor was effectively taken by Salvidge. 'Should the Tariff Reform League try to displace the acknowledged leader of Protestantism in Parliament', Salvidge argued, 'it might well end in strengthening Taylor's position and rousing hostility to Tariff Reform in quarters where no such hostility exists.'[193] Following his re-election, Taylor presided at a Church Association lecture entitled, 'Protestantism Before Party';[194] and in February 1906 he joined the Liberal benches. Not having re-adopted him the Liverpool Conservatives could not technically demand his resignation. Wise asked him to retire and fight a by-election to validate his independent Protestantism but, although the month of March passed grimly—F. E. Smith's maiden speech pilloried Taylor, and he suffered the deaths of his wife and father—he was not yet dislodged.[195]

Conclusions

The lesson here, that in a confrontation Protection bowed before Protestantism, renders suspect Salvidge's statement to Chamberlain that 'the democratic constituencies went solidly for those candidates who supported your programme in its entirety'.[196] Workmen remained firm and businessmen wobbled. Rutherford also believed this;[197] and Lord Stanley's observation in 1903, that 'Liverpool has gone Joe mad—they won't look at anybody unless he swallows Joe's whole hog', was affirmed by a Tariff Reform League report in 1908, that 'the masses in Liverpool were moving decidedly, but they still had great difficulties with merchants and other leading men'.[198] However, for workmen to elect Unionists who happened to be Protectionists did not prove that Protection was the pre-eminent attraction.

The *Daily Post* complained that the prototype of many Liverpudlians could be found in Belfast: 'the hopeless electors', whose first interest was sectarianism, had carried Liverpool Conservatives to victory.[199] This sentiment, however, was not exclusive to the Tories. T. P. O'Connor used it profitably to bind the Nationalists' factionalism. His opponent, A. A. Tobin, a Liverpool-born lawyer, advocated Protection; but O'Connor decided the terms of the contest—'As Colonel Saunderson and the Orangemen ruled the Tory party in Ireland, so George Wise and the no Popery gang ruled the Tories in Liverpool . . . If Mr. Tobin was a member of the City Council, and if he was to be friendly to the Catholic schools he said he wanted to protect, would he not have to run away at the first tap of the no Popery division by George Wise (applause)?'[200] O'Connor set his supporters dancing on Bloody Balfour's political grave—'the man who did John Mandeville to death, who applauded the Mitchelstown slaughter, who defended Plunket when he told his police not to hesitate to shoot; that man who made his first political fame by the coercion of Ireland, lies in the dust . . .'.[201] O'Connor's majority nearly trebled in a 68 per cent poll.

Wise's passivity had not muffled sectarianism in particular constituencies, and nationally anti-Ritualist propaganda reached a climax. Following another Church Discipline Bill's rejection in 1903, Protestants had claimed a part in several Unionist by-election defeats, especially at Brighton;[202] and in May 1905 Taylor, M'Arthur, MacIver, Rutherford, and others, had appealed for £30,000 towards a national campaign.[203] What significance to place on their arrangements is difficult to estimate. The Laymen's League had formally affiliated to the Church Association in 1902, and a Northern Council of the Church Association was created in 1906 out of the Laymen's League and Manchester Protestant League; but the purpose of uniting Protestant electoral work was hardly achieved. Much waste remained. By 1905–6 the Laymen's League had five branches in the Liverpool area, the Church Association had five, the National Protestant League four;[204] and there were also bands of Wiseites and Wycliffe Crusaders. However, the Church Association claimed to have a roll in every English constituency, committees in 310 constituencies, and 366 local and seven regional agents. They interrogated candidates about Ritualism and Home Rule, not about Disestablishment. Altogether 322 M.P.s gave pledges: another sixty-one were 'sympathetic'. Some thirty-one of Lancashire's seventy-eight M.P.s had supported Church Discipline in 1903. In 1906 sixty-one Lancashire M.P.s pledged support for this legislation. None who opposed the 1903 Bill was returned.[205]

Protestantism and Unionism were generally united in Liverpool; but independent strivings occurred in Birkenhead where Kensitite Orangemen deprecated their Unionist chiefs.[206] Later in 1906 the Ecclesiastical Discipline Commission reported. It condemned various practices, especially 'elaborate spectacular ceremonial', but it concluded that the Anglican law of public worship was 'too narrow' for modern tastes (which Wiseites disputed); and that the disciplinary machinery was ineffectual (which Wiseites maintained as a commonplace). The Church Association criticized a recommendation that the Convocations devise another ornaments rubric, since half the members were Ritualists; and the Laymen's League discountenanced a suggestion of an ecclesiastical court of appeal to replace the Privy Council's jurisdiction.[207] Wise also scorned these recommendations but considered that the Commission's evidence of ritualism in 559 cases 'justifies everything that the extreme Protestant has said . . .'. The Commission itemized only one Liverpool church (St. Thomas', Toxteth) using incense although, according to Wise, eight or nine existed before his agitation.[208] One result of the Commission was that the Convocations explored Prayer Book revision (the first since 1661); and this was to provide plentiful fare for Wise's eventual successor, H. D. Longbottom. A more immediate result was that politicians tacitly ceased to attempt to force conformity in public worship.[209] The anti-Ritualist movement was obsolete.

Political conclusions were also drawn from the General Election. The W.M.C.A., that 'party parliament of the proletariat',[210] had rescued Liverpool Unionism again. On the other side the local Liberal party claimed to value speeches by its leaders—Campbell-Bannerman visited Liverpool in this election, just as Asquith was to do before the first 1910 election—but what the Liberals needed was to capture electors individually in the wards. The *Daily Post*, however, refused to commend the Conservatives' methods—'Intelligent Liberal working men' should not require 'free hot-pot suppers, picnics, and periodical symposia', but should 'regard principle a good enough thing to work and fight for'.[211] The Liberal conception of political society was of a debating club in which unclouded reason triumphed. The Conservatives recognized the electorate's animal rather than intellectual qualities. Cattle required herding and wanted food, not for thought, but instead of thought.

To others this argument was redundant, because Liberalism seemed moribund. With shrewdness amid pungent misrepresentation George Bernard Shaw wrote that in 1906 Liberals stood for conservatism:

> for the good old nineteenth century; for Free Trade; for a careful disclaimer of Home Rule; for the Gladstonian ideal of a reduced or even extinguished Income Tax; for honest John Morley's promise to do nothing in the direction of the millennium that could possibly put a penny on the rates. No Socialists these, but plain, steady, contented men, who have battled their way for twenty years through a seething surf of new ideas, and come out exactly as and where they were in 1880.[212]

The policy-book of young Conservatives, *The New Order*, curiously echoed Shaw from evidence of municipal politics where, without a rigid party system, 'men adapt themselves more quickly to the actualities than in Parliament'. Thus Conservatives and Liberals were making 'common cause against the intruding Labour Councillor'.[213] Certainly some Conservatives were identifying as their enemy not Liberalism but Socialism, which 'narcotic-like, has drugged the spirit of patriotism'.[214] Tariff reformers particularly exhibited scant loyalty to the existing party system. They would 'steer a middle course, by propounding a policy which will preserve the institution of property, together with reasonable individual liberty, and at the same time secure to the wage-earners, by means of discriminating Government interference in industrial organization, a more just proportion of the wealth they produce than they have enjoyed under the Liberal regime of Free Trade'.[215] Emotion directed more responses. This was that spectre of Socialism as 'an uprising of the uneducated, suddenly breaking into houses, their clumsy feet on the mantelpiece, their clumsy hands seizing and destroying all beautiful and pleasant things'.[216]

Conservatives might lock up their daughters; but the working classes would determine their state. According to Councillor Morrissey, some had already decided: he claimed that four-fifths of Labour recruits in Liverpool were Conservative working men.[217] Similarly Sexton prophesied that if Salvidge continued to democratize Liverpool Conservatism he would destroy it. Sexton assumed that the W.M.C.A. would insist on electing working-class Councillors and M.P.s but, although many conventional Conservatives disliked Salvidge's pushiness, it was recognized that sharing party power with the W.M.C.A. was 'the very thing to preserve its ascendancy'.[218] Moreover, democratization was not infinite. The W.M.C.A. did not highly regard working-class representation. Forwood had discovered this; and Salvidge experienced little pressure.

Before 1914 no working-class Conservative became a Councillor, although the status of members generally declined.[219] The Liberal leader, Evans, had believed that working men in West Derby would rally to a party which had John Burns in its Cabinet—an 'ideal member' of their class, 'one who knew all their wants'. 'This fact alone', he concluded, 'ought to win West Derby for Mr. Holt'.[220] Richard Holt failed in West Derby, and the Conservative working man continued to confound appraisal.

CHAPTER FOURTEEN

Socialism and sectarianism, 1906–10

> The question is wh[ich] party makes most blunders. A. J. B[alfour] is I soberly believe the most unskilful leader (out of Parlt.) since Wellington. Asquith seems to be the next worse. Which will make the biggest mess?[1]
>
> *Lord Hugh Cecil*

> The Socialist programme is one of undiluted atheism, theft, and immorality, and the once great Liberal Party has become only the kept party of the Socialists, and has ceased to have any identity of its own.
>
> *Duke of Rutland*

> The main question for Liverpool has from time immemorial been only the struggle between a live Italian priest and a dead Dutchman.[2] *Frank Rose*

This chapter carries further the slide towards extinction of the Liberal party in Liverpool. Even where no Labour candidate stood it was in opposition to Labour-Socialism that a Conservative candidate principally addressed himself. As a creed apart from Free Trade or Irish Nationalism, Liberalism was without vigorous life in Liverpool. The Conservative party recovered ground, having harnessed its Protestant auxiliaries once more; but a nasty outbreak of sectarian violence, which enforced the segregation of poor Protestant and poor Catholic colonies in the city, clouded the party's successes in the 1910 general elections.

Tarnishing Labour's image

In March 1906 Wise's congregation was stoned, and a Protestant mob in retaliation attacked two strangers in the area who wore shamrock—but who turned out to be Irish Church Missionaries. Archdeacon Madden felt that these incidents showed the true face of Wiseitism—'nothing else than brickbats and rowdyism'. 'Bastard Protestantism', he wrote, 'disgraces our city . . .'[3]

In 1906, however, Wise ceased his outdoor campaigning. Until 1908 he did

Notes begin on p. 437.

not again speak at St. Domingo Pit on Catholic matters.[4] He was preoccupied with lecturing against modern biblical criticism.[5] Atheism and Socialism were his targets. This, and the want of policy displayed by the Protestants' Council group, confirmed the evidence of the General Election, that Protestantism was conforming with Conservatism.[6]

After the municipal elections in November 1906 only two Protestant councillors remained. The *Protestant Standard* still campaigned to subject convents, like lunatic asylums, to inspection;[7] but, with the advent of a Liberal Government, the sectarians' interest in education had channelled conflicts towards the established parties. Labour also suffered by this.[8] In Kensington ward in 1906 Labour polled 350 fewer votes than in Morrissey's pioneering victory of 1905. The over-all turn-out fell by 300, but the Conservative's support increased by 700. The absence of a Liberal candidate made the difference. Either the straight fight with Labour drove many otherwise inert Conservatives to poll or, as was suspected, most Liberals positively preferred a Conservative to a Labour candidate. Labour's propagandists were spasmodically active—Keir Hardie and Robert Blatchford spoke in Liverpool—but no issue naturally served their aspirations. Unemployment tested Labour as well as civic organizations. It was a slender hope that *Clarion* vans distributed politics with soup.[9]

The Conservatives gained five municipal seats in 1906. There were chiefly two causes. One was the publicity given to the Liberals' Education Bill, introduced into the House of Commons in April 1906 by the President of the Board of Education, Augustine Birrell. In July the Bill was passed to the House of Lords, who 'mangled, tortured, [and] twisted' it before the Government withdrew it in December. The original bill had declared that after 1 January 1908 no public elementary schools would be recognized except those provided by the local education authority. The existing non-provided denominational schools would have to be transferred to the local authority, which would appoint all teachers. As regards religious instruction, qualified staff might give only undenominational, simple Bible teaching—'Birreligion' the wits now called it, being neither religion nor irreligion. 'Special facilities' were granted for denominational teaching in the transferred schools, but this would be outside school hours and at the denominations' expense. This gave to Nonconformists in single-school rural areas the protection for which they had been calling for many years, especially since the 1902 Education Act. Others saw it as a Bill which virtually emasculated the Church and established Nonconformity. However, in urban areas with over 5,000 people 'extended facilities' were granted whereby denominational teaching in transferred schools was permitted if the parents of four-fifths of the children demanded it, and if the denomination paid for that part of the teacher's time. This was devised primarily as a concession to the Liberals' Roman Catholic following, although naturally it included the many Anglican schools too. In fact neither section was placated. The churches would lose control of their buildings and teachers to local authorities which were permitted, not compelled, to grant the 'extended facilities'. The case could be envisaged where a Nonconformist-dominated local education authority might refuse these privileges. The supporters of the churches reacted in a predictable manner. Some Anglican bishops, including the primate, Randall Davidson, sought amendments but were conciliatory to a point; others, including the High Church bishop of Birmingham, Charles Gore, and the evangelical bishop of Manchester, E. A. Knox, demanded absolute rejection. The latter, nicknamed Hard Knox, expressed the unyielding militancy of the North of England by organizing thirty-two special trains to carry 10,000 demonstrators to London. Eventually the Anglican and Conservative majority in the House of Lords pulled together to mutilate the Bill and thus fire the first shot in the brewing constitutional conflict between the two Houses of Parliament. The Catholics, for their part, were not gifted with such destructive powers, but they did all that was possible by way of protest. The Irish Nationalist M.P.s voted against the Bill in the House of Commons and, so the Holts alleged, many Catholics in Liverpool cast against the Liberals in the November municipal elections.[10]

The second cause of the Tory success in these elections was more unusual, stemming from the exposed weakness of a Liberal campaign on the slums question. In 1905 new methods of council-house construction, using concrete blocks, had induced the Tory *Courier* to ask, 'Is the Housing Problem Solved?' Although 9,000 court-houses awaited demolition, the city had registered its lowest annual death-rate, 19·2 per 1,000 persons.[11] Optimism was soon checked. In September 1906 the death-rate returned to 28·6 and the Medical Officer of Health, Dr. Hope, declared that 'no city in Christendom' exhibited comparable squalor.[12] The *Courier* and *Daily Post* responded with surveys of slumdom, like those of 1883.[13] They found few changes—the same stench, the same dungeon-like dwellings, and the same trough-closet serving forty people, in the same areas—around Great Homer Street, Soho, and Hornby Street, although here and there were council houses. The *Daily Post* chiefly blamed drink. The director of the Food and Betterment Association, H. Lee Jones, criticized the 'cowardice' of this judgement. 'Industrial reform, and not temperance reform', he declared, 'is the premier need'; but the *Daily Post* had wide support.[14] When Edward Evans announced that Liberals must make 'these social matters' their municipal cry, many crusaders assumed that temperance would suffice.[15]

Conservatives reacted differently. The opinions of the *Courier* columnist, a teetotaller, were changed by his investigations. Now he blamed principally irregular employment, low wages, and ignorance about domestic economy, child-care, and hygiene.[16] George Wise still denounced drink;[17] but others, like Rutherford, advocated labour decasualization. Regarding intemperance, Rutherford's remedy was not to close the pubs but to improve them as social centres. The Liberals would kill, not multiply, the pleasures of the poor; and Rutherford joined causes in his peroration, that to blame Conservative Councillors or poor people for the evident misery was to libel both.[18]

Not all Conservatives absolved the poor so readily as themselves. The Housing Committee's deputy-chairman, a builder, John Morris, criticized drinking, pawnbroking, and gambling; but he also vaunted the Conservatives' record and promised that by 1910 'very few' court-houses would remain.[19] Compared with the Liberal administration of 1892–5, Petrie added, the Conservative party 'proved itself vastly superior [in] demolishing "fever dens"'.[20] Alderman Roberts went further: since insanitary property was the

M.O.H.'s responsibility, 'if anybody was to blame for the slums it was Dr. Hope'. He sensed intrigue: Hope and Evans were 'near relations'.[21] Thus, as the campaign advanced, Liberals shrank from their original battle-cry.[22]

Temperance solutions were morally satisfying and administratively cheap. Many electors studied the rates. Robert Killip, a butcher who in 1899 described himself as 'a Protestant, Conservative, and Christian Socialist', in 1906 led the Toxteth Ratepayers Association, demanding non-party municipal government for 'better administration and greater economy . . . and a happier and purer citizenship'. These ideals were incompatible. Evans observed, 'they should be prepared to spend a vast sum of money'. Their return would be measured not in cash but in community health.[23]

This 'democratic neoliberalism of the twentieth century', as Asquith called it, 'had little in common with Gladstonian liberalism'.[24] Nevertheless the old Liberal concern for retrenchment clouded the new Liberal vision; and the Liverpool Liberals' electoral defeat did not encourage a re-examination of their argument. In 1907 the *Daily Post* commissioned George Sims to analyse slumdom. He reinforced the lesson that 'drink is the enemy'.[25] The poor themselves nominated different enemies, in hostile demonstrations against the city's Chinese colony. Past electioneering—that 'foreigners' (whether Irish, Jews, or Chinese) brought disease, housing shortages, unemployment, and national decline—had stimulated violence. The M.O.H. and Liberals were isolated, as Conservatives and some labour groups acted confraternally. Problems of class, commerce, and culture were rewritten in a racial shorthand to ease political expression.[26]

The L.L.R.C., on the other hand, was more introspective as it reviewed its organization. Its relationship with the Bootle L.R.C. was defined as 'exclusively fraternal and not financial';[27] but personalities bound them. The Carpenters' and Joiners' delegate, Arthur Short, was a Bootle councillor, president of the Bootle L.R.C., and secretary (1906–12) of the L.L.R.C.[28] For much of 1907 the L.L.R.C. argued about how to spread its resources in registration work. Labour organizations were always poor. The L.T.C.'s secretary was reporting that forty-one societies (almost half the affiliations) were in arrears with subscriptions.

In September MacIver's death created a vacancy in Kirkdale. The L.L.R.C. accepted the Boiler-makers' nomination of their secretary, John Hill. Encouraged by Labour–Socialist victories in recent by-elections at Jarrow and Colne Valley,[29] some hundred open-air meetings were held in Liverpool by polling day (27 September).[30] Nearly twenty Labour M.P.s appeared, including Ramsay MacDonald and Arthur Henderson. They designated this the biggest fight in Labour's history.[31] Hill's Socialism was 'naked', exclaimed a horrified *Courier*; but Hill also espoused temperance and free trade. Salvidge hurriedly summoned his stump orators—Rutherford, who quit a tour of Russia, and F. E. Smith, who abandoned Winston Churchill on holiday in Italy. The Unionist candidate was Charles M'Arthur, the staunch Protestant and aspen Tariff Reformer, converted after his defeat in Exchange in 1906. One hundred and forty vehicles were at his disposal; the W.M.C.A. mobilized 500 canvassers; and the Tariff Reform League and Church Association were active. But against unprecedented opposition other tactics were required. Salvidge had wired headquarters—'It is not sufficient to call the Socialists names. Send us arguments.'[32] The result was the better argument of worse names, 'a campaign of calumny'.[33]

This was not intrinsically new. MacIver's last public pronouncement was that Socialist pickpockets would drive capital abroad.[34] The novelty of Salvidge's campaign was the thoroughness of vilification. Some aspects mirrored yahoo sensibilities: a refuse-cart toured the streets labelled 'Hill's motor-car full inside'.[35] Others reflected conscientious homework, especially the ubiquitous leaflet *What Socialism Really Means*. This announced that 'Socialism would destroy family life'. Moreover, 'no man could rise', since everyone would be 'STATE-planned, STATE-run, STATE-crushed'. Socialism, it was implied, caused present hardships: 'the workhouse is the nearest thing we have to Socialism'.

Many electors' primary education in Socialism was by Conservative pedagogues. One leaflet, which was distributed in abundance during the by-election, cited atheistical works, like *God and My Neighbour*, by the editor of the *Clarion*, Robert Blatchford.[36] Blatchford's opinions were raw meat for parsons' sermons,[37] and the *Protestant Standard* chorused that Socialism would generate 'absolute infidelity', 'the grossest immoralities', and 'rivers of human blood'. The Devil, it said, was Socialism's 'master leader'; and, despite Hill championing Bible teaching and criticizing secular education, it felt that no 'Christian Conservative or Liberal' could support him.[38] Temporarily the argument had shifted from Protestantism against Catholicism to religion against atheism, 'a Holy War . . . with an over-proportion of drummers'.[39]

Catholic and Liberal voters were an important quantity. Hill had opposed a Liberal at Govan in 1906; but now Kirkdale's Liberal executive unofficially supported him.[40] The Catholic vote was ambiguous. Hill was a Home Ruler and the U.I.L. applauded this; but some Labour propagandists were less than delicate in their consideration of Irish sensibilities. Frank Rose wrote roundly in the *Clarion* that all Liverpool's M.P.s were Tories, 'including he who sits for the Scotland part of it'—T. P. O'Connor. This by-election, moreover, coincided with the Catholic Truth Society's conference, which heard Socialists defined as 'militant materialists' who aimed 'to destroy the idea of God'.[41] Some recommended Catholics to espouse social reform, but the Catholic Bishop of Liverpool recognized virtue's ignorance. Priests informed him that young parishioners, 'striving to know their rights as working men, often imbibed poison from the publications of Socialists and ended by losing their faith'. The Bishop, however, trusted the national characteristics, 'for we were conservative and slow to take up new ideas'. Regarding current politics he knew that most Catholic working men were Liberals but the Government's attitude to denominational education was alienating them. The north of England would mount a successful 'Pilgrimage of Grace' using the voting weapon.[42]

M'Arthur polled 4,000, Hill 3,300. The congratulations that poured on Salvidge were uniform, that a working-class constituency had repelled Socialism.[43] Rutherford paused to bestir the 'smug respectable middle classes'; but this was only his way of appreciating the W.M.C.A.[44] Ramsay MacDonald concluded that Labour would never progress in Liverpool until Orangeism was broken;[45] but, while Orangeism led, all slings of religion had hurled stones. 'The main question', the *Church Times* noted, 'was the religious and moral character of the Socialist movement. Blatchfordism lost the election.'[46] Blatchford was perturbed;[47] but Sexton acquitted him—'rotten organization did the trick'—while chiding his old-fashioned ways. Sexton was now 'a responsible local legislator' and union leader, with a 'technical knowledge and experience' which a crude publicist like Blatchford lacked.[48] Appropriately Sexton's pen-name was 'Citizen', Blatchford's 'Nunquam'. Men who sought places in the community were superseding Labour's mavericks.

The enthusiasms of this by-election dominated the municipal elections in November 1907. In Kirkdale ward Labour polled 847 against 1,584 for Councillor Paris, who did battle in the armour of 'Conservative and Protestant'. No independent Protestant councillor survived. The twenty-six contests in 1907 constituted the widest conflict since 1895 and the Conservatives gained another six Liberal seats. Denominationalism was a recurring factor—on the one side Catholics were seen to have deserted Liberal candidates, on the other side the Anglican Bishop and the Church Schools Association had not been so active in a campaign since the days of School Board elections.[49]

Expelled by these factions, the L.L.R.C. in 1908 examined the prospects of a local newspaper. Propaganda, however, is ineffective without broad initial agreement between the propagandists and the propagandized. Religious questions gnawed at loyalties. Thus the Carpenters' and Joiners' central branch agreed to support Labour representation, but denied use of their funds 'for propagating Secularism'.[50] The L.L.R.C. now confined its call for secular education to Corporation schools; and it was sensitive to misrepresentation. It alerted the press that John Walker, contesting Netherfield, was a self-styled 'Protestant and Labour' candidate and that it 'emphatically' opposed religion in politics.[51]

These protestations did not guarantee immunity. Councillor Russell-Taylor predicted a fusion of 'Constitutionalists' against 'Socialists', believing that 'a moderate Liberal would vote for a moderate Conservative (A voice: "No soft soap"). Every Socialist was bound to be irreligious (several voices: "It's a lie").'[52] The election results affirmed Russell-Taylor. In Kensington ward in 1905 Morrissey had polled 1,137 Labour voters against 1,076 Conservatives and 659 Liberals. In 1908, facing only Conservative opposition, he polled 1,203 against 1,641. Morrissey boasted that he had converted progressive Liberals and driven the retrograde into Conservatism. More prosaically his agent demanded more candidates to prevent the concentration of conservative forces.[53]

Unemployment also took its toll. The L.T.C. nominated 1908 'starvation year'.[54] The insouciance of public authorities was reviled but Labour M.P.s were not absolved. One visiting M.P., Pete Curran, was booed by local Social Democrats; and the L.L.R.C. unfavourably compared the Parliamentary Labour Party's efforts with those of Victor Grayson, the Socialist firefly whose disquieting manner had been formed by his upbringing in Liverpool.[55]

But unemployment was a peripheral issue when Conservatives fought Liberals in thirteen of Liverpool's fourteen municipal contests in 1908. In a 57 per cent poll Conservatives triumphed for the third consecutive year, gaining six Liberal seats and Morrissey's. Why Sexton was unopposed was unclear, but it was expedient to indict the Liberal party for advancing 'pernicious doctrines'.[56] This association did not affect Max Muspratt who, with Evans ill, led the Liberals' campaign. As a large employer in Vauxhall and a champion of Catholic schooling, Muspratt was said to be 'hero-worshipped' by the Irish. Other Liberal candidates were not so fortunately placed: several were vulnerable when the Conservatives, to avoid controversy concerning municipal trading, echoed the Catholic School Managers' grievances about the Government's most recent Education Bill. Birrell, the centre of the storm over the 1906 Education Bill, had become Chief Secretary for Ireland: this Bill's nominal author was Reginald McKenna, although during 1908, when Asquith took over Campbell-Bannerman's Government, he too was replaced at the Board of Education by Walter Runciman. The treatment of Church schools was again the vital matter. McKenna's Bill recognized only one category of public elementary school, under local authority control, wherein the prescribed religious instruction was of the undenominational kind. Church schools in a single-school parish would have no choice other than to be transferred to the local authority: elsewhere they might contract out of the council system and receive a government grant, not rate-aid. Church schools which were compelled or did agree to be transferred might provide denominational instruction at their own expense to children whose parents called for it. The Bill's opponents included the National Union of Teachers, who disliked the contracting-out principle; mostly they were Anglican and Catholic churchmen, who demanded statutory facilities for denominational instruction in transferred schools, and more generous financial provisions regarding the present settlement and future building of contracting-out schools. As in 1906, so in 1908 most Anglican bishops—noting the accelerating slide, nationally, of children from church to council schools—were dedicated to finding a compromise over particulars; but, when the Representative Church Council met in December and recorded its decided objections in principle, the Government withdrew its Bill.[57]

The Liberal Councillors and candidates defeated in Liverpool since 1906—mostly young men—were a reserve which no party could afford to lose, and Muspratt reflected that if the Conservatives continued to return 'mediocrities and nonentities upon all kinds of false issues they would have a City Council of which they would be less and less proud'. One of the Liberal Councillors defeated in 1908, a dentist, Arthur Black, gave this valediction:

> It seemed to him when he considered what was his master passion . . ., namely, the redemption of the children of the city, almost a comedy that a man should come and attack him on that very issue, and so distribute his literature that there went an impression through the ward [Abercromby] that he was either an atheist or something of the sort, and would blot out religion from the schools.[58]

'Socialist'—in Tory jargon, infidel and thief—was affixed to every reformer who threatened vested interests. Harmood-Banner called the 1908 Licensing Bill 'gross and abominable robbery', and he refused to contribute to a motor-car for the Bishop of Liverpool, one of the Bill's defenders.[59] M'Arthur was more judicious. The Kirkdale by-election taught him that they must fight Socialism with social reform. Accordingly, though he found the Old Age Pensions Bill 'hastily drawn and so full of ambiguities', he welcomed its 'small beginning'.[60] George Wise also attended to the Socialist menace. In 1908, in the Sun Hall, Kensington,[61] Wise debated 'That the problem of modern poverty can be solved by Socialism only', and 'That Socialism, being practical atheism, is not worthy of public acceptance'. Since Wise equated Socialism with confiscation, he declared 'Christian Socialism' impossible. Reform by co-operative means, or 'Social Christianity', he welcomed. He still claimed to be 'a labour man' and in common with many in the L.T.C. and L.L.R.C. held that the Labour party should disentangle itself from political Socialists—'the absurd blending of Labour with Socialism will defeat the admirable and laudable object of the labour party, and will tend to drive the more moderate into the ranks of the historic political parties. Labour should stand alone and independent. Labour should not be the tool in the hands of revolutionary socialism . . .'[62]

A city torn by sectarian civil war

Sectarian strife also drew out Wise. In February 1908 M'Arthur's Ecclesiastical Disorders Bill was rejected by Parliament;[63] and in September Wise petitioned the Government to prevent a Eucharistic Procession in Westminster.[64] The pending revision of the King's Declaration also alarmed Protestants.[65] Wise addressed 20,000 people about this in January 1909;[66] and in June the West Toxteth M.P., Houston, regaled his constituents with stories of counter-Reformation atrocities. Jesuits, he asserted, worked to reclaim England for Rome by subverting the Church and throne. They were now abetted by 'Socialism, with its infidelity, lawlessness, and lack of nationality'. The bulwark against this fate—for 'Popery and poverty were synonymous'— was 'the British constitution of Protestantism and patriotism'.[67] Such speeches aggravated long harboured hostilities. When a Home Office Commission investigated the sectarian rioting which was unleashed in Liverpool in 1909 one attorney pleaded that they consider only that year's events. The Commissioner agreed. Though the precipitating incidents of the riots would inevitably seem trivial in content, the Commission could not amplify their context unless it was willing to embark on a study of 'the cause of human nature'.[68] Official authorities—government and police— and professional men—lawyers and academics—each have their own interpretation of riots and their significance, whether clinically exact and finite, or broad with implications for the fabric of society. But, though apparently uneloquent eruptions, violent disturbances do betoken a kind of political language. As Martin Luther King has asserted, 'Riots are the voice of the unheard.'

On 9 May 1909 the Holy Cross Catholic church commemorated its diamond jubilee. The church received permission from the Corporation's Health Committee to erect an altar in Marybone; and the Head Constable, Dunning, accepted the processionists' promise not to carry the Host or other emblems and to parade only in Catholic streets. Nevertheless the parish was festooned with Catholic bunting; the Stations of the Cross were carried; and the procession abutted several Protestant chapels. Wise's Bible Class marched on the same day:

Protestants refused to defer to the Catholic presence on the streets. At wayside altars (all, except at Marybone, were illegal) disturbances occurred. The processionists numbered 4,540, but altogether 150,000 people, including the Italian colony,[69] participated. Subsequently, Protestants charged that Dunning had either deceived them or been deceived.

In the following fortnight Wise was assaulted; and Orange and Catholic marches occurred in defiance of Dunning's request for restraint. These incidents were dwarfed by the preparations to defend or impede a march of St. Joseph's Catholic church on 20 June. The Orangemen's determination to resist 'illegal processions' was shaped at a conference of lodges by Richard Briggs, a foreman printer and official of Wise's church and Crusade Committee. Briggs's connection is pertinent because Wise's own suggestion at this meeting, that Protestants abstain from action, was rejected. Wise could have been preparing an alibi: his moderation was neither in character nor sustained on 20 June.[70]

The Head Constable, Dunning, went on holiday. His deputy banned emblems from the St. Joseph's parade; and the route was restricted. Orangemen, however, assembled in the Juvenal Street area. One later expressed disappointment at the turn-out;[71] but this was relative to the army of seven hundred policemen, including thirty mounted. Following an unscheduled march of three hundred Catholics, singing partisan songs, a scuffle developed outside a pub, and fighting spread. Without a magistrate to read the Riot Act Chief Superintendent Smith addressed his force: 'Go for the buggers and give them hell.'[72] Twelve policemen were injured, some badly. One combatant was John Walker, soon to be elected a Protestant Councillor. He was knocked senseless while his son was apprehended for brandishing a paperhanger's knife. Walker junior was among fifty-five arrests (thirty-four Catholics and twenty-one Protestants).

This was a prelude for civil war. The week brought 130 convictions for offences against property, and 81 for violent assaults. Houses were marked to denote the creeds of their inhabitants, and beatings and looting ensued as partisans aimed to enforce in the Netherfield and Scotland areas a monopoly of faith.

Most clergymen had experienced difficulties before but, said Father Fitzgerald, this was 'simply terrorism'.[73] Many parishioners asked Fitzgerald not to call, because his presence in their homes would attract hostility. Priests at St. Antony's—the church was on Scotland Road, but the parish extended into Netherfield Road—knew 157 Catholic families (833 individuals) who fled from 'Protestant' streets.[74]

There were Protestant victims too. The parish of St. Martin's-in-the-Fields, which included Scotland and Vauxhall Roads, was four-fifths Catholic. Here relations were customarily tense—the vicar had ceased open-air missionary work in 1907 to avoid being stoned—but now the church school was stormed and 110 Protestant families left the neighbourhood. The vicar claimed that most were neither Orangemen nor Wiseites, but the Catholics 'did not stop to discriminate'.[75]

The casual brutality of many incidents was illustrated when, before onlookers, a carter was beaten to death in Hopwood Street. Likewise two employees of William Singleton, a trustee of Wise's Church were beaten, with a policeman nearby.[76] Even a cordon was penetrable, as one Orangeman discovered after having been intimidated to quit his job at the Palatine Oil Cake Mills. Despite the protection of six policemen, a woman hit him with some tongs.[77] The Silcock Oil Cake Mills became equally intolerable for fifty Protestants among the five hundred employees. Menaces were blood-curdling: a carter removed from Oswald Street after 'several women threatened to tear the so-and-so bowels out of my missis'.[78] During the Inquiry in 1910 witnesses were cowed; a Catholic school was attacked; and Lynskey, the Catholics' counsel, received threats to his family. Even the court-room was not immune: the second day's hearing was interrupted by no-popery cries.

Recurrent characteristics indicated certain patterns. The Head Constable, Dunning, believed in a cycle, almost routine, of riot.[79] He asked Wise's Bible Class to refrain from parading on 27 June. Wise, agreeing only to alter his route, was instantly jailed. Hours later Wise promised to abandon his procession. Two Conservative councillors provided half Wise's sureties.[80] Rioting occurred anyway. The stoning of the convent at Everton Valley was by so-called 'scratch bands'—individual Orangemen leading others who were not of the Order. The police regularly complained that while Orange officials might respond to their appeals or directions, they could not control their hangers-on.[81]

Otherwise the violence seemed explicable only by Santayana's maxim that fanaticism consists in redoubling the effort as the aim is forgotten. The most inoffensive circumstance gave provocation, for example, a Protestant presence in Catholic areas, or vice versa. The sectarian inheritance was represented by one witness, Catherine Achilles, whom the Commissioner asked if she was Irish. She replied, 'No sir, I am a Protestant'. He had to rephrase his question to learn that she was English.[82] Many a mind was suffused with Wise's teaching, as was apparent in the cross-examination, concerning Jesuitism, of Ralph Rattray, a chain-worker and youthful Wiseite:[83]

> 6269. What did you hear [at St. Domingo Pit] about the Jesuits?
> —A. I have heard on two or three occasions that they were not a set of people who attended to the welfare of the British Protestant nation . . .
> 6271. Tell me something else you heard.
> —A. I remember one phrase they used. It is taken from Ignatius Loyola.
> 6272. What was it?
> —A. As regards if the Jesuits know a thing to be black and they swear it is white they will do so to suit their own particular purpose . . .
> 6274. Anything else?
> —A. I cannot remember for the minute.
> 6275. Just try and think—anything about being pernicious?
> —A. I don't remember. I don't understand what pernicious means.
> 6276. Have you heard anything about [the Jesuits] having to be driven out of England?
> —A. Yes, sir . . .
> [Then, asked what else he could remember]
> The WITNESS: I think they were untruthful . . .
> 6287. MR. LYNSKEY: What was said about Cardinal Manning?
> —A. Cardinal Manning said they were here in the country, and he said they were glad to be here as they had a great fight here, and it was their

desire to bend, and to break, and to subjugate this imperial race—when once conquer in England, Romanism would be supreme in the whole world.

Wise spoke through Rattray as if on the stand himself. Wise, 'this strange enigma',[84] was the key to the imbroglio. Two Wises were observed—the pastor, engaged in good works; and the hot-gospeller, pugnacious and processioning, sneering and jeering at another's faith.[85] Wise did not cause Liverpool's sectarianism; he activated it. Policemen and clergymen agreed that relative peace existed until Wise began open-air speaking. Although from June 1909 Father Fitzgerald could not enter Netherfield Road at all, before that he was invariably insulted.[86] When Fitzgerald had arrived in Liverpool in 1892 the street-door of his church was always open; following Wise's agitation from 1898 Fitzgerald closed it and conducted his services from the bottom of the church, 'to keep people from shouting through the door, throwing stones, bottles, and sticks'. Without Wise's activities at the Pit, Fitzgerald believed peace was possible, 'even in Everton'.[87] Although the 1909 disturbances mostly occurred in northern Liverpool, open-air lectures and riots were similarly correlated in south Liverpool. Father McKinley, ministering in Toxteth since 1897, had suffered 'worse than a stray cat or dog'. The presbytery was regularly attacked and McKinley considered arming himself with a revolver.[88]

The open hostility of sects was partly Wise's responsibility, and continuing strife depended on his moods. The Anglican bishop, Chavasse, and fifteen vicars of disturbed parishes, condemned the habit of martial processions and expressed confidence in the authorities;[89] but Wise accused the police of partiality: 'To be a Protestant to-day was to be treated with contempt; but to be a Roman Catholic . . . was to be treated with respect.'[90] Provocatively Wise announced that 'if the present Jack the Ripper is a Roman Catholic which I believe he is, and if he was to go to Father Fitzgerald and say he had murdered two or three women, and the police were to call on Father Fitzgerald and ask him if he had seen Jack the Ripper, Fitzgerald would say, No'.[91]

In August 1909 Wise received four months' imprisonment upon refusing to abandon the Bible Class parades for twelve months. 100,000 people accompanied him to the prison gates.[92] The intention in imprisoning Wise, declared the *Protestant Standard*, 'is to gag Protestantism and remove all objects out of the way . . . of the Church of Rome'.[93] M'Arthur and Rutherford demanded an inquiry. No professional compunction as a solicitor prevented Rutherford from prejudging Dunning. He announced that the police were 'badly commanded' and behaved with 'unnecessary brutality'. He added that Wise, 'a personal friend', was 'a respectable citizen', and 'few men have done more by personal character and by their influence to elevate and improve the masses'.[94] Wise was released on bail, pending an appeal.[95]

Meanwhile gangs consolidated denominational uniformity, street by street, workplace by workplace. A Protestant Defence Committee, founded by the Orange Order on 24 June, tabulated 550 Protestant families forcibly evicted by October.[96] S. G. Thomas, its secretary, ardently criticized the police.[97] In August the Catholic bishop, Dr. Whiteside, sanctioned a Catholic Emergency

Association.[98] Both sides professed peace, but their manifestos were tendentious.[99] Wise actually demanded 'preferential treatment for all Protestants'.[100]

In October Wise lost his appeal against the Head Constable's prosecution, despite F. E. Smith's pleas; and he returned to jail. Dunning's pertinacity increased his own unpopularity and Wise's following.[101] After Wise's preliminary incarceration in August, 20,000 regularly attended the Pit and the Bible Class gained 400 members. Of thirty-eight cases of violence upon property in October twenty-five occurred soon after Wise's re-imprisonment; and at the Pit nightly gatherings took place. Speakers scorned the Catholics' 'wafer God' and 'penny-in-the-slot blessing machines'; and Richard Pollock, a hardened bigot from Belfast, proclaimed that all convicts, paupers, and whores were Catholics.[102] This competition in excesses was halted by Wise's release on 27 November, pending a Home Office Inquiry; but the armistice was spurious.[103] A Sun Hall meeting, celebrating Wise's freedom, attracted multifarious Protestants, including Kensit; and the *Protestant Standard* marvelled at the 'cohesion between Protestant Churchmen and Protestant Nonconformity . . . against their common foe—the papacy'.[104]

The General Election of January 1910

Amid this turmoil elections were fought. In Netherfield in November 1909 John Walker defeated Alderman Rutherford—the West Derby M.P.—who had advised Wise to avoid jail by giving sureties. Walker disparaged Rutherford's timidity but his victory seemed ludicrous when the Crusade afterwards praised Rutherford's assistance of Wise. Possibly the ambiguous ascriptions of Walker's Protestant Labour Club accounted for his success; but official Labour candidates lost in Kirkdale and Low Hill wards.

Rutherford's defeat indicated that tension remained between Protestantism and Unionism. The *Protestant Standard* now argued that if the priests' 'dictatorial power' was broken 'Irishmen are fully capable to manage their own affairs'. For Conservatives the importance of imperial defence, the need to preserve a social and economic system, and a sense of innate superiority, justified Ireland's subjugation. The *Protestant Standard*, however, maintained that successive English Governments, by respecting Catholic education, were 'the chief cause of rivetting the chains of Popery on the Irish nation'.[105] 'Simple Bible education' would obviate popery; and after the House of Lords rejected Birrell's Bill, 'the best Education Bill that was ever formulated', the *Protestant Standard* advocated Radical constitutional reform.[106] Moreover, although a pro-Unionist manifesto was launched, the Liverpool Orange executive did not unanimously support it.[107]

How many of Liverpool's 15,000–20,000 Orangemen were anti-Conservative in the January 1910 General Election is debatable. Kirkdale's Labour candidate, A. G. Cameron, spoke in the Protestant Reformers' Memorial School;[108] but the Laymen's League and Protestant Alliance evaded Unionist–Protestant differences by requiring candidates to preserve the King's Declaration, to initiate inspections of conventual establishments, and to oppose

Ritualism in churches and schools, parades of Catholic images, and the settlement of Catholic orders expelled from abroad.[109] The bishop, Chavasse, also required electors to reject candidates who opposed Anglican education or promoted disestablishment;[110] and Salvidge organized a rally which was 'as much a Protestant demonstration as a Unionist demonstration'.[111] Labour propagandists were attacked in Netherfield Road; but the scheduled rally was trouble-free despite the philippics. Harmood-Banner proclaimed Liverpool's resistance of Home Rule, even by civil war.[112]

The press noted that Liverpool's elections involved considerations which mattered little elsewhere.[113] Winston Churchill asked Liverpudlians to 'be true to Free Trade, resist bread and meat taxes, and scorn the insolent pretensions of the Lords'; but F. E. Smith simply countered, 'Liverpool stands by Belfast'.[114] Religion, complained the *Daily Post*, was 'used without scruple as a political weapon'.[115] Salvidge was otherwise unconfident of success. Tariff Reform, professedly 'a great ideal', yielded to 'the necessity of preserving the Union'.[116] Since 1906 both sides had propagandized strongly, with Churchill, Wyndham, and Lloyd George, visiting Liverpool.[117] The Chamber of Commerce even passed a resolution against Protection. Salvidge minimized its significance;[118] but the business community's spokesmen insisted that 'Protection in any form is inimical to shipping'.[119] Accordingly Salvidge disguised the strictly fiscal properties. His propaganda dispatched Protection in the manner most appealing to the mass—TAX THE FOREIGNER; MAINTAIN OUR OWN INDUSTRIES. Tariff Reform skulked behind the Empire and Home Defence.[120]

Conservatives blamed their urban defeats on the Budget's land-tax proposals.[121] The Budget's liquor tax also galvanized excitement, and the Bartenders' Union intervened in the Liverpool elections by advocating the Shop Hours Bill and abolition of the living-in system. The union joined the L.T.C., which condemned brewers and publicans who intimidated their employees at elections.[122] According to the *Daily Post* most Liverpool pubs were Tory committee-rooms; and 1,000 barmen were sent by brewers from North-West Manchester to repay Salvidge's services against Churchill in the 1908 by-election. These mercenaries mainly canvassed Abercromby and Exchange but also West Toxteth and Kirkdale.[123]

The L.L.R.C. faced other difficulties. The intelligence that moderate Liberals voted Conservative against Labour made the Liberal party want to fight Kirkdale until the L.L.R.C. threatened to contest Exchange and Abercromby.[124] Cameron, of the Carpenters and Joiners, was selected to fight Kirkdale in June 1909, by thirty-six votes against eleven for Sexton; and, although a Liberal canvassed until 5 January 1910, Cameron's rhetoric dominated attention. This climaxed when he credited M'Arthur with 'the blackest and most inhuman record' of any Kirkdale M.P.[125] Cameron's Protestantism was a hindrance to those Unionists who customarily denounced Labour as a vehicle for Catholicism or Atheism; but the best he could do was to narrow the margin of defeat to 223 votes. Allegiences had been hardened by rioting. West Toxteth, which Sexton again contested, was also unyielding. Illness kept Houston from the rites, but Orangeism sustained him.[126]

Elsewhere, in Everton, the opponents of 1905 and 1906 repeated their motions before Harmood-Banner lengthened his majority to 1,706. A tradition was maintained with Harmood-Banner's title of Tory Democrat. The *Daily Post* explained this as one who 'advocates Radical measures and votes against them'.[127] Nevertheless, while denouncing Socialism, Salvidge advocated the rating of land values, and free school meals for poor children.[128]

Social reform was the Liberals' platform in Walton; but its effect was lost in division. Two Liberal candidates stood, Frank Joseph with official backing, E. G. Jellicoe with independent hopes and a hint of Unionist intrigue.[129] Jellicoe maintained that, having spent some £2,000 in the 1906 General Election, he had a claim to the local Liberal Association's consideration; but Lloyd George stigmatized his 'wrecking and selfish candidature', and he suffered several indignities for 481 votes.[130] Joseph polled 5,513, Smith 6,627.

The West Derby contest also had a malodorous air: Rutherford's honesty was not beyond question.[131] His 'political incongruities' amazed many Liberals and not a few Conservatives.[132] Rutherford's title was 'Democratic Tory': 'Tory because he believed in the maintenance of the constitution and in the British Empire, and democrat because he believed in government of the people by the people.'[133] He repeated his idiosyncratic programme of 1906, with reservations about nationalizing railways; he dilated upon naval rivalry and Tariff Reform; and, chastened after his municipal defeat, he deplored sectarianism. Electors were notified that the landlords' increment tax, imposed by the Budget, would burden tenants.[134] Rutherford won 5,190 votes against 3,682.

The unpredictable constituencies were East Toxteth, Abercromby, and Exchange. East Toxteth experienced its first contest since 1902. Austin Taylor retired, and John Lea and Edward Marshall Hall K.C. contested the succession. Pundits prophesied a Liberal victory, partly from the Free Trade influence exerted by Taylor, partly from Lea's personality; but both the public and private faces of this colliery director and temperance worker reflected his 'intellectual and spiritual limitations'.[135] His faithful recitation, that the Lords' rejection of the Budget was 'the supreme issue', was disregarded by Marshall Hall who expatiated on Ulster and foreign war. He won by 285 votes. The victorious party and candidate were more than usually pleased. For the Conservative party victory testified that, despite Taylor's errancy, it could still pull the Protestant vote; and for Marshall Hall, membership of Parliament boosted a flagging legal practice.[136]

The Unionists also regained Abercromby, by 526 votes. Colonel R. G. W. Chaloner[137] had nursed the seat since 1907, his brother, Walter Long, having educated him in Liverpool's pecularities. It was 'a very funny place', also 'a most enthusiastic place', where candidates had better rely on their managers.[138] Chaloner was a power in the Church Association;[139] and his opponent, Seely, without like accoutrements, was defeated. In fact, sharing Herbert Gladstone's opinion that 'Liverpool was well-nigh a hopeless place for any Liberal', Seely had only defended his seat because to have quit would have damaged every Liberal contest in Liverpool.[140]

In the Exchange constituency, however, Max Muspratt showed what could be achieved in Liberal colours by campaigning single-mindedly for Catholic education.[141] He won by 161 votes but in the process found that several business associates deserted him. Although a free-trader, the Docks Board's chairman, Robert Gladstone, supported the Conservative candidate, Leslie Scott, K.C.[142] Merchants in Exchange disparaged Liberal Socialism, and did not like to be regarded as an appendage to Scotland Division, where O'Connor won emphatically.

Protestant Conservatism rampant

The General Election results in Liverpool mostly satisfied Salvidge; but his health collapsed. Others also found Liverpool unmanageable. To the Head Constable, Dunning, Liverpool was 'a hell upon earth'. He complained on behalf of his constables that citizens 'could not get for 25*s*. a week a man with the manners of a Lord Chesterfield and the wisdom of a King Solomon'.[143] In their rates bills Liverpudlians were being made to understand the price of unruliness. In 1909 police overtime cost £18,877. Additional expenses, including riot damage, totalled £12,000. The Home Office Inquiry cost £3,277.[144]

The future was more important. The Home Office's Commissioner hoped that sectarian processions might only be allowed on petition to the Lord Mayor and that a Committee, representative of the parties and factions involved, might forward conciliation. Wise, however, would not abandon open-air meetings, though he promised to submit to the police a list of speakers at the Pit.[145] Territorial rights had been mapped, and neither denomination brooked trespass. Rank sometimes impressed Tory Democrats, but where the Catholic bishop was concerned, Protestants were sans-culottes. In June 1910 Dr. Whiteside was stoned by a Protestant mob after laying the foundation of St. Alphonso's church.[146]

In July Kirkdale suffered another by-election. Religion was politics. The late M.P., M'Arthur, Wise proclaimed, 'died a martyr to duty'.[147] The new Unionist candidate wore his countenance. Colonel Kyffin-Taylor, Austin Taylor's brother, was a potentate of the Church Association and Protestant Reformation Society.[148] Posters called him 'the Unionist and Protestant candidate', and Wise endorsed his nomination.[149] The campaign, coinciding with the Glorious Twelfth of July, was preceded by rioting in Islington.[150]

No upper class inhabited Kirkdale. The élite consisted of small shopkeepers, ship-repairers, boiler-makers, and engineers. The rest were 'casual labourers of a lamentably ignorant type'.[151] To the Protestant section Kyffin-Taylor addressed himself, pealing his hatred of Catholicism and the 'national importance' of maintaining the King's Declaration. F. E. Smith criticized trade unions' compulsory political levy; but other speakers dramatized rather than widened the issue, 'between the Constitution and Revolution'. Kyffin-Taylor purported to stand 'For God, for King and for Liberty', while his Labour opponent, Cameron, was accused of designing 'the abolition of religion . . . the abolition of the Monarchy . . . and tyranny and slavery for the working classes'. 'We stand on this platform', said Salvidge, 'to prevent the people of Ireland from ruling

Kirkdale'; and the National Protestant League flayed 'Asquith's taskmasters, otherwise the Irish and Jesuit treason-felony mongers', who conspired 'to place a Roman Catholic upon the throne'.[152]

Kirkdale's understanding of this was epitomized by one, Frank McAleer, who, charged with smashing a window, declared, 'I did it for my religion'.[153] Disturbances were numerous, although when the McAleers operated in handfuls it was hardly newsworthy. A typical case during the by-election involved four men and a woman who wrecked another's house because it contained a picture of the Pope. The judge commented: 'How people can imagine that any cause or religion is promoted by abusing one another and by riot I cannot conceive.'[154] The inconceivable to Mr. Justice Pickford was routine to Liverpool Unionists, whose most enthusiastic meetings featured sectarian leaders.

Kyffin-Taylor's personification of Protestant Conservatism was, Salvidge observed, 'a bitter disappointment to his opponents'.[155] But sectarian strife damaged property as well as reputation. Ratepayers were represented at the Home Office Inquiry; and shopkeepers composed jeremiads about respectable families migrating. The fanatics who remained were less sedulous in paying debts.[156] Accordingly Cameron seized the chance to project Labour as a party of responsibility. Labour did not begin its campaign until the day after the Glorious Twelfth, and it mostly avoided street meetings. Exceptions proved the soundness of the rule. On 16 July Protestant intruders disturbed one open-air Labour gathering, and Wise deliberately addressed a meeting near Labour's headquarters. It ended with stone-throwing.[157]

The Labour party shied away from the streets, but its campaign was not otherwise reticent. Cameron's speech had muscular emphasis. 'The Tories',he noted, 'were appealing to the lowest and the bitterest and the most brutal feelings.' Labour represented 'practical Christianity'; but Salvidge, who had 'turned a somersault from a brewery into the pulpit', and the Anti-Socialist Union, 'talked about Socialism meaning atheism and free love'. They were 'paid liars who would sell their mother for a pot of beer'.[158] By threatening to 'break Mr. George Wise's power' Cameron abandoned prudence.[159]

There were, of course, other issues. A Free Trader, Cameron maintained that Protection would intensify unemployment. His answer was social reform, from 'the Labour and Socialist party'. This was a rare admission of Socialism, marking a change from the 1907 by-election.[160] It reflected the desire to attract Liberals. The Liberal party, however, refrained from formal support, and a condescending speech from Allan Bright only aroused Labour's hackles. The Gladstone League and Free Trade Union gave indirect support: they valued a cause, not the candidate.[161] Celebrities neglected Cameron's platform: only Ramsay MacDonald flitted across. Moreover, although Cameron favoured Home Rule, his party kept it quiet, so there was no supporting Nationalist campaign.

The parties ended on notes of self-vindication. Wise denied that he was a Conservative hireling: 'He was very democratic and a believer in the Budget . . . [and would] support any Protestant candidate, irrespective of political party.' He 'always worked in the interests of the people', he said, and 'was in debt through helping the poor'.[162] Cameron surpassed him by climbing on the cross:

'I am only a plain carpenter. Remember the Carpenter of old, how He was persecuted as I am persecuted, and by the same class of men who belong to the Tory party today.'[163] 3,427 voters joined Cameron at his Calvary; 4,268 hammered in the nails. 370 fewer electors polled since January: terrorism had increased removals.[164] Kyffin-Taylor, however, polled within sixty-five of the best Unionist score.

Salvidge thanked his party workers; but the press coverage evoked mixed feelings. The *Courier* had sneered and scared, as when it described Cameron riding 'in a "swanking" car preaching motor cars for the million at each point'.[165] Thus plaudits for the *Courier*—but a slap for *The Times*: Salvidge disliked its reporters' bias.[166] He returned to the architects of victory. Among them Wise and the Protestant working men were pre-eminent. Kyffin-Taylor was grateful too: 'I say may God bless him, and may he go on with his Bible Class purifying everybody around him.' Wise rejoiced: 'this is Liverpool's reply to the Commissioner's report.' Labour's evaluation was similar. One party official warned that until they destroyed Wise's 'pernicious power' their movement was annulled.[167]

Wise was the cynosure of both sides. Few paused to consider another party. Liberalism was again ignored in a critical engagement. Only Marshall Little, at the Junior Conservative Club, noticed 'the defunct Liberal Party'.

The by-election had two postscripts. Kyffin-Taylor recognized his mandate, 'that in a Protestant country we should have a Protestant King'.[168] His maiden parliamentary speech was upon the King's Declaration Bill; but the new King, George V, was inclined towards Tim Healy's opinion, that some Conservatives wished the old Declaration retained, 'not because it is pleasing to the Protestant so much as because it is offensive to the Catholic'.[169] The Prime Minister, Asquith, maintained that by altering only the tone the Bill did not materially alter the succession, although the Church Association complained that Asquith eviscerated the Declaration, and the *Protestant Standard* that the Liberal Government had 'sold England to the papacy'.[170] The Bill became law on 3 August. Nationally, then, the Kirkdale by-election was a wonder of immeasurable insignificance.

Locally it afforded insights into sectarianism. Peace would not be achieved simply by enforcing the law or smoothing errors of theology. A realignment in political bases was required, to strip the rival mobs of party favour.[171] Significantly when the authorities had acted strongly—as in quelling the initial riot of 20 June 1909—Unionist politicians demanded an inquiry. When that Home Office Commission vindicated the police, Unionist politicians derogated it by applauding the marked culprit, George Wise.

The face of contrition was assumed. Catholics abstained from processions for a year after the Home Office Inquiry; and Orangemen promised to reduce their thirty *official* processions to four and to consult the police concerning routes. However, when one lodge repudiated promises which 'played into the hands of the police', the Provincial Grand Lodge sanctioned bands to parade monthly without regalia for any Protestant organization. Consequently S. G. Thomas, a leader in conciliation, resigned his membership of the Order.

The Watch Committee displayed its concern by drafting a Bill to regulate processions; and Lord Derby, opening a bazaar at Wise's Church, advised Protestants to be sure that 'the lessons learned in the Church were not forgotten in the streets'.[172] This was ambiguous: the manner of preaching sometimes provoked or authorized sectarian violence. Geographically separatism in Liverpool was a hard fact which sentiment would not unfreeze. Between the Catholic and Protestant zones Great Homer Street was the frontier, a local 'No man's Land'.[173] One humorist revised the Protestants' song, 'Dare To Be A Daniel', to 'Dare To Go Down Scotty Road'.[174] The humour was that there was only this line. The root problem was identified at the Inquiry. Asked who thronged St. Domingo Pit, Thomas answered, generally artisans, but Wise also had 'many sympathizers amongst the higher class'.[175] This association was as romantic as that of Dr Crippen and Ethel Le Neve.

The municipal scene and the General Election of December 1910

In November 1910 twenty of thirty-five municipal wards were contested. Although the Liberals made three gains the Unionists formed a majority of eleven among councillors alone. The L.L.R.C. adjusted to adverse legal decisions, especially the House of Lords' judgement in the Osborne case in December 1909 which, by rejecting the unions' privilege of compulsory political levy, sapped the Labour party's income.[176] Nevertheless the L.L.R.C. again contested Kirkdale and Low Hill; and it met eighteen times in 1910 compared with fourteen in 1909.

Wealthy friends helped to maintain Labour's electoral activity. At the I.L.P.'s invitation the L.L.R.C. promoted Edward Whitley, the former Conservative M.P.'s son, in Edge Hill and A. K. Bulley, a cotton-broker, in Kensington.[177] Bulley made no impression against S. M. Hutchinson, the Lord Mayor-elect;[178] but Whitley polled 1,001 votes, against 952 Unionist, 69 S.D.F., and 8 Independent Socialist opponents. Whitley's election, Sexton wrote, signified 'a great change in public thought';[179] but sidestepping the class problem was not its solution, since this depended on Labour's ability to enlist radical 'gentlemen'.

The L.L.R.C.'s advance was as precarious as Whitley's health. In February 1911 he retired. Although in Labour qualifications W. R. Blair was a worthy successor—Liverpool's leading Co-operative Society worker—he lacked Whitley's name and polled 843 votes against 1,017. Whitley's choice of issue had been judicious—the Corporation estate was a favourite Liberal complaint. Blair encountered competition for this Liberal support and sectarian appeals which Whitley had avoided. The Unionist, Bennet Brough, called himself a 'Protestant out and out'; and Councillor Russell-Taylor importuned 'all moderate Liberals who were heartily sick of Socialist doctrines'. These he defined as Atheism, 'the annihilation of liberty', and 'the levelling down of the entire race of humanity'.[180]

Dividing these contests was the December 1910 General Election. The electoral register was 16½ months old, but the Liverpool Unionists' organization was steeled in readiness.[181] Conversely the Liberals' hope, that education was spreading enlightenment in Liverpool, was unsupported by party equipment.[182] Everton had not even a Liberal candidate—Harmood-Banner was among sixteen unopposed English borough M.P.s. His colleagues decided the issues to secure their election, Unionism and Protestantism; and though the *Guardian* complained that Liverpool echoed Belfast not Lancashire, this playing down of Tariff Reform, particularly of food taxes, presaged Lancashire's revolt in the Conservative party in 1913.[183]

T. P. O'Connor observed 'the different horses the Tories rode'. At Southport they professed to further Catholic liberties; but in Liverpool, except Scotland division 'where it would not have been quite safe', they emphasized 'hatred of the religion of the Roman Catholics'.[184] The inconsistency of Lord Derby's homily in October and Conservative speeches in December was downright; but every Unionist majority in Liverpool increased. Exchange division was recovered after Balfour's declaration, that he would not introduce Tariff Reform without a referendum, elicited the enthusiasm of Unionist Free Traders.[185] Mostly the Unionists encountered dispirited opposition. The L.L.R.C.'s quandaries were typical. The Carpenters' and Joiners' withdrew Cameron from Kirkdale. The Ayrshire Miners' secretary, T. McKerrell, was adopted on 25 November; but the L.L.R.C. risked its reputation with an unknown candidate presented at short notice.[186] In West Toxteth no Labourite emerged, after a feeling, shared by elements in the L.L.R.C. and by the national secretary, that Sexton was unsuitable.[187] A Liberal gathered the baton without much running: T. F. Molony, K. C., was a Dublin Catholic to whom Muspratt had been preferred as the Liberal candidate in Exchange in January.

Salvidge's afterthoughts

Walter Long and Salvidge corresponded about their successes. They applauded Balfour's referendum pledge concerning tariff reform, although Chamberlainites thought it a bitter pill.[188] For both men opposition to Home Rule was unflagging in electoral efficacy.[189] This discussion was not casual. For Long directly and Salvidge indirectly it concerned the party leadership. Salvidge's son accounted 1911 'the critical year' in his career.[190] His organization set an example to the rest of the Conservative party by its democratic basis. *The Times* deduced that 'the more local organizations can be weaned from the habit of depending for support on headquarters, the more efficient they become'.[191] But issues, records, and expectations mattered along with organization. Salvidge understood that Liverpool, a demi-monde, was an inappropriate calculus for national success. To Long he generalized from Liverpool experiences; but he retreated when faced with the prospect of supervising national machinery—'things do not run on the same lines in all parts of the country. A thing I have to remember is that though Liverpool politics are more complicated they are always more alive because of religious feeling and the Nationalist and Orange factions.'[192]

In February 1911 Balfour appointed Salvidge to a committee to investigate party organization. Concurrently Salvidge examined for Lord Derby the Manchester Unionist Association.[193] It was hazardous to launch into national politics. It was prudent, because historical connections remained, to establish Liverpool as the bridge between Ulster and Lancashire.

CHAPTER FIFTEEN

Strife, 1911–14

August, 1911, was ideal strike weather. It was far too hot to work
H. Gosling

We hold that the sympathetic strike is the affirmation of the Christian principle that we are all members one of another. *J. Connolly*

The sympathetic strike is an abomination and utterly destructive of friendly relations between master and man in any trade. *R. D. Holt*

A dead quarrel for which neither the country nor the [Unionist] party cares a damn, outside of Ulster and Liverpool.[1] *F. E. Smith*

This chapter focuses on the series of labour disputes which paralysed Liverpool in the summer of 1911. The inspiration of the strikers is considered and, though syndicalist ideologues were loth to admit it, industrial violence and sectarian violence were connected. Subsequently, a reconstruction of the casual labour market was embarked upon but labour leaders risked their authority in this; and, though many Liverpool Liberals increasingly chose to embrace the Conservatives in industrial matters, the Labour party could not enlarge its representation without tackling the unpalatable realities of sectarianism. However, as civil war in Ulster was only narrowly averted, Conservatives themselves apprehended the consequences of excessive or unrestricted sectarian identification by 1914.

Sectarian strife

The Bootle by-election in March 1911 marked the turn of the tide for Bonar Law. 1910–11 was a memorable time for him in which he experienced the misery and elation of political life. In November 1911 he would replace Balfour as leader of the Unionist party, but now he was without a parliamentary seat, having failed in the last General Election to win North-West Manchester for

Notes on p. 443.

Tariff Reform. Lord Derby, after some ponderous conspiracy, finally came to Bonar Law's rescue, and Colonel Sandys was persuaded to speed his retirement from Bootle.[2]

Of some 25,000 potential electors, about 2,600 were plural voters. Only 8,713 electors inhabited Bootle itself. Wavertree and West Derby freeholders predominated. Thus although Bootle was unconnected with Liverpool's organization—Salvidge once wrote that some 'stupid jealousy' always existed—the W.M.C.A. canvassed for Bonar Law.[3] Moreover, the Tariff Reform League employed a cinematograph, held seventy-one open-air meetings, and distributed 4,000 posters and 200,000 leaflets.[4] Had not Bonar Law been, according to his opponent, the Liverpool chemical manufacturer, Max Muspratt, 'the archangel of Tariff Reform', the Liberals might not have contested Bootle;[5] but the electors hearkened to other rivalries. Sandys had flourished by Protestantism. Now Bonar Law delighted the Orangemen by designating the Parliament Bill the 'Home Rule in Disguise Bill', and for the first time in his career he responded to the Church Association's questions. Accordingly the Nationalists encouraged Muspratt to style himself the 'Irish candidate'.[6] North Liverpool witnessed renewed rioting as Bonar Law polled 9,976 votes against 7,782.[7]

The continuing violence stimulated the Head Constable to make another appeal about processions.[8] He was supported in a letter, which the Revd. Stanley Rogers originated, from Anglican and Nonconformist clergymen.[9] Significantly Rogers omitted from the letter, which a month previously attracted no signatories, a demand that Wise cease open-air speaking.[10] Wise was too powerful to accuse directly. The *Protestant Standard* declared that his church needed five times more space; and many clerics candidly admired him.[11]

The spring of 1911 brought a series of assaults upon Protestant workmen in Vauxhall, and the Protestant Defence League blamed equally the police and mongrel Catholics.[12] In reprisal Netherfield Protestants conducted another purge of Catholics from their neighbourhood, and the second anniversary of the 1909 riot was celebrated by fighting.[13] Certain combatants were known, like a milkman, James Glendenning, who by now had accumulated a lengthy police record, involving house-wrecking and assaults on Mormons as well as on Catholics.[14] He was imprisoned; but judicial rigour no more curbed the violence than did neighbourliness. Mrs. Sawey, for fifteen years a boot-repairer in Netherfield Road, removed after Protestants attacked her. She was reputedly the last Catholic resident in Netherfield Road.[15] Afterwards attacks were directed against persons who, though of the right religion, wore the wrong colour in the wrong place.[16]

The Catholic bishop in May 1910, and Alderman Taggart in July 1911, petitioned against Wise's speaking at the Pit.[17] Their protests were unavailing. Kyffin-Taylor asserted that only Catholicism feared argument; and Wise, confident in this defence, refused to abandon free speech 'at the dictation of the Roman Catholic hooligans of the Council, the ruffianism of the Catholic Defence Association, or the tyrannical demands of the Church discredited by her unequalled persecution of the Jews, the infamies of the Inquisition, her bloody deeds of St. Bartholomew's Massacre, and her martyrdom of John Huss and

Savonarola, Latimer and Ridley'.[18] As this tirade was published rioting was renewed in Edge Hill.[19] It prefaced Merseyside's greatest industrial confrontation, the transport strikes of summer 1911. This needs emphasis because Syndicalists claimed that sectarianism disappeared in cathartic strikes.[20]

The Transport Workers' strikes

Probably a spell of low unemployment, following a decade of declining real wages, unleashed labour activities which observers invested with shibboleths, in *Punch*'s witticism a turn from 'Sidneywebbicalism' to Syndicalism.[21] There were numerous stresses, between labour and capital, unions and politicians, union leaders and members, unionized and non-unionized labour.[22] Contemporary with pointers towards Ulster rebellion and international war, the transport strikes of 1911 alarmed some more than even the General Strike of 1926;[23] but temperamental, not ideological, ascriptions best summarize the unrest. Impatience was the prevailing mood and incontinent protest the form. The President of the National Sailors' and Firemen's Union, J. Havelock Wilson, told the T.U.C.: 'He was a Syndicalist and a Parliamentarian. He made no attack on the Parliamentary Party, but they could not depend alone on political action.' This was common to men like T. E. Naylor (London Compositors') who denied Syndicalism and Noah Ablett (South Wales Miners') who propagated it.[24]

The nominal authors of the Liverpool strikes in 1911 were Havelock Wilson and Tom Mann, an ill-assorted pair with lengthy, but blemished, records of labour activism. Wilson had been an intermittent M.P. for Middlesbrough for twelve years: he was now stricken with arthritis and persecution mania. Mann had had many careers in many organizations in many countries. His personal habits, as much as ideological differences, had dictated his movements. Thus he resigned the I.L.P.'s secretaryship in 1897 to the relief of those who felt that licentiousness was not the best advertisement for Labour politics. But, if Mann's personality made him a less than prudent politician, he could be a magnetic figure on a platform addressing rough and discontented men, 'with his black hair, his flashing eyes, and his tumultuous speech peppered with expletives'. His latest reputation was as an exponent of Industrial Unionism, playing a part, with Ben Tillett and others, in forming the National Transport Workers' Federation in 1910, although the unified command which the title suggested was absent from this cumbersome association of some thirty bodies. The Federation was reluctant to abet Wilson's preparations for a strike in 1911 and he went ahead, it was said, in the mood of a gambler making his last throw.[25]

Wilson's intentions were widely known: Reuters predicted a seamen's strike about Coronation time. Many shipowners believed that any strike would be minor; but Liverpool was potentially the employers' Achilles Heel in a national fight. The original fifty companies in the Employers Labour Association had dwindled to thirteen by 1909. Many employers had different interests by virtue of the scale and type of their business—consider, for example, the different concerns of transatlantic passenger lines, owners of cargo steamers transporting perishables, and coastal traders—and in several cases since 1890 they had negotiated separate bargains according to need with their seafaring and dockside work forces.[26] They had no interest in forging a united opposition by challenging the men as a class.

Already the decline in union membership among seamen, which had deepened in the decade from 1896, had ended. The N.S.F.U. had grown from 7,000 to 12,000 since 1906, of whom 4,000 were from Liverpool.[27] They had allies in the Ships' Stewards, Cooks, Butchers, and Bakers Union, founded in 1909. Half its 4,000 members were from Liverpool, including James Stephenson, the president, and Joe Cotter, the militant secretary whom Cunard's had sacked for agitating against foreign labour on British ships.[28] Increased wages, improved conditions, and general union recognition were the objectives; and on 14 June the strike broke among five hundred firemen at Liverpool's North Docks. Mann, in Liverpool from 13 June, directed activities which soon became 'out of the ordinary'.[29] Dealing individually, major companies like Cunard's, Elder Dempster's, Booth's, and Holt's, conceded a general increase of 10*s*. per month.

Porcupine noticed 'a stupid strike' but King George's Coronation monopolized the attention of the press as 165,000 persons, one-fifth of Liverpool, enjoyed civic hospitality.[30] Those feted included four hundred seamen. Individuals were generous: the West Toxteth M.P. and shipowner, Houston, amplified his normal treating of constituents. Sectarianism intervened, however, as Catholics declined Houston's invitations.[31]

The Coronation, not the strikes, also engaged the I.L.P.'s newspaper, *Labour Leader*. Fenner Brockway, who wrote on labour matters, explained this initial reticence: the *Labour Leader*, like the Shipping Federation, had been gulled into not taking the men seriously, since most port-workers were non-unionized.[32] This was changed, as first seamen, dockers, and carters, then railwaymen and engineers, at Liverpool and most ports except London, exhibited solidarity to press their demands. On 28 June a dock strike began when dockers refused to work a White Star boat except by union rules. On 3 July work was resumed as shipowners' and union representatives reached preliminary agreement and set out to reach a permanent settlement of casual labour problems in a Joint Committee.[33]

Porcupine was wrong to denounce 'the tyranny of the Trade Union leaders'.[34] Violent strikes, Ramsay MacDonald observed, had erupted 'against both the authority of the State and of the Trade Unions'.[35] In 1911 the sheep led the goats. A leader like Sexton who, Mann wrote, 'would have preferred to wait a season', was tested when 8,000 dockers suddenly joined his Union and launched demands.[36] Sexton's feelings were evident in his play, *The Riot Act*, which was first produced in 1914. It had some literary merit, although modelled too closely on Shaw and Galsworthy, especially on the latter's *Strife* (1909), which also found an audience at the newly opened Liverpool Repertory Theatre. Both *Strife* and *The Riot Act* portrayed fanaticism in the conflict of capital and labour; but Sexton's allusions were indiscreet and the Lithographic Printers' demanded that the L.L.R.C. censure him.[37]

Three figures dominate *The Riot Act*—Cunliffe, the Quayside Workers' dedicated general secretary; Maddocks, a 'fanatic' with one watchword, 'solidarity'; and Waring, a tribune begot by chaos. Cunliffe was Sexton, Maddocks Mann, and Waring anyone of the 'irresponsibles' who harried

Sexton, with traces of Larkin. Their identity is less important than the problems they personify. Foremost was the viability of general strike. Cunliffe complains that Maddocks' 'solidarity' 'lacks one essential item—discipline'.[38] Strikes are declared and Cunliffe reluctantly takes up the men's case, from the opinion that they were better with him than without; but Syndicalist slogans permeate and, without funds, the strikers even secede from Maddocks's attempted direction. The men are the masters; no one man is master. Cunliffe deduces 'that the mob, which calls itself Democracy, is a bigger tyrant and a greater despot than the Capitalist system it so vigorously denounces, with the additional disadvantage that it is an unmitigated ass'.[39]

Men are gullible. They strike 'because someone . . . came over the hatch . . . told them to put their coats on and come up to Hell out of that and they, of course, come'.[40] Waring, their mouthpiece, is imbued with a brute's falsity, a natural leader of the 'ne'er-do-wells, and those who had adopted unemployment as a profession'.[41] He is a bad worker. The gang Waring belongs to 'was always a man short'.[42] The Strike Committee is no better for its faith in the 'general body'. Its bovine devotions are pernicious, since medical supplies to the city's hospitals are cut. By opening negotiations Cunliffe saves the strikers from themselves; but he loses his life, symbolically crushed between the mob and troops.

By the close *The Riot Act* illustrated not Liverpool in 1911, but Sexton's ego. One character exclaims that 'all the money in the Union, or in the whole Trade Union movement, is not enough to recompense for his services. He's simply wasting his opportunities . . . when he could secure an appointment where his ability would be adequately recognized; where he would be free from the turmoil, intrigue, and petty jealousy he is subject to, and where his salary would be quadrupled.'[43] In the thankless task of union leadership the leader who craved an acclamation composed his own.

Both Sexton and Mann in their recollections exaggerated the intimacy of the strikers. When George Milligan, Sexton's second-in-command of the N.U.D.L. and a stern Catholic critic of Socialism, allied on the Strike Committee with W. H. Jones, the leader of the mostly Protestant Carters Union, a convergence of sectional interests, rather than syndicalist ideals, bound them. Carters occupied the strategic position between dockers and railwaymen, and could best immobilize Liverpool.[44] By 1911 many firms refused to honour agreed rates or to recognize the Carters Union. Motor lorries threatened the trade with extinction, and carters demanded assurances that drivers would be recruited from their union. These needs made carters appreciate solidarity: 'Should the Carters ask the Dockers not to load or unload the motors, the day of the motor, for the time being at any rate, is over in Liverpool.'[45]

Likewise many dockers grasped federation because their days were numbered. Officially they demanded a minimum 8*d.* per hour, 1*s.* overtime, and some application, catered to seasonal demands, of a six-hour day; but many were upset by the prospect of progressive decasualization, in Sexton's clearing-house scheme. The 'one-ship-one-stand' system was profligate. Most employers now accepted that they might gain by a regular work-force; indeed large companies, like Cunard, White Star, and others, had been employing some permanent men by weekly wages for two decades. Some dockers, however, at both ends of the employment pendulum were suspicious. 'Aristocrats' cherished their freedom of working long spells and relaxing; the under-employed feared displacement.[46] This caused conflict within the N.U.D.L. after common demands were won.

The railwaymen's action had no equivalent local causes.[47] As the railways had ceased to expand from the 1880s the railwaymen's wages and opportunities of promotion relatively contracted, and lower-grade employees, paid between 17*s*. and 22*s*., found over 1*s*. deducted for company 'benefits'.[48] Railway profits, £47 million in 1910, were the largest ever, but costing problems were acute. Whereas shipping companies could and did raise their passenger and freight rates to recover the costs of their wage settlements with seamen and dockers, railway companies had encountered parliamentary regulation of their rates in two decades when their working expenses, on wood, coal, and steel, had progressively risen. Accordingly, most railway companies were unwilling to countenance unionization and wage demands by their men.

On 5 August 1911 1,200 Lancashire and Yorkshire Railway goods porters struck at Liverpool. The Company's carters and London and North Western railwaymen joined them. Union leaders who mentioned conciliation were barracked. Subsequently clerks endeavouring to shift perishable goods, and policemen escorting convoys of milk, were attacked.[49] Blacklegs settled in Edge Hill; but Mann and the N.U.R.'s General Secretary, J. H. Thomas, discussed with the authorities means of preserving order. Thomas, like Sexton, was a union leader uncomfortably placed between workers who suspected compromise and companies who would have none.[50]

The authorities in Liverpool, however, could not wait on events in the docks and on the railways, and the Home Office was asked to prepare the military.[51] In a sentence deleted from the published correspondence between Liverpool and London the Head Constable, Dunning, wrote: 'But the failure of the Shipping Federation to stand out against the men's demands by importing labour proves pretty well that there is no free labour available, and it seems to me that the only alternative to conceding the men's demands is closing down, a thing which is hardly to be contemplated.'[52] Officially the Government intervened to safeguard food supplies;[53] but Keir Hardie recognized the hiatus: 'It meant that if these railway directors refused to do what the Government itself does, namely, to receive the officials of the trade unions, the military forces were to be placed behind them to enable them to persist in their refusal. Then we are told that is not taking sides.'[54]

The occupation of Liverpool began on 10 August with four hundred soldiers, and extra policemen drawn from Leeds, Birmingham, and Ireland; but hot weather encouraged people to stay outdoors, and disturbances continued.[55] On 11 August, as more squadrons arrived, the railway companies administered a counterpunch by reopening Brunswick and Edge Hill stations. Foodstuffs were carted, with a police, military, and magistrates' escort; but the companies rejected the Corporation's suggestion of a reconstituted Conciliation Board since workers on sympathetic strike were out of court. As dockers boycotted railway-borne goods (three-quarters of all traffic), the N.U.D.L. was told to influence men to return according to recent agreements, or face a lock-out.[56] The closure of the docks followed. Sexton was powerless against the union malcontents, 'men of vicious instinct who strove to exploit the ignorance of newcomers';[57] moreover, 'Bloody Sunday' had inflamed tempers.

90,000 people had been attracted by the Strike Committee's demonstration on St. George's Plateau.[58] Two accounts circulated of how trouble began. Either policemen cudgelled spectators from window-sills; or strikers upset a cart, believing its driver was blacklegging.[59] Two hundred people, including twenty policemen and 'many innocent persons', were injured in the ensuing riot. The Birmingham special constables were unrestrained; but Mann wrongly asserted that no newspaper justified their violence.[60] *The Times* declared that although 'many respectable people' were batoned, this was 'an object-lesson of the folly of mixing with criminals and rioters'.[61] It defended what Labour leaders decried as 'medieval'[62] means of policemanship because labour disputes were interwoven with traditional struggles, between religious sects and between slum denizens and the authorities.

After people had fled from St. George's Plateau—leaving a hundred arrested—riot continued north of Lime Street where, behind barricades, residents withstood the police for thirty-six hours.[63] One policeman died from injuries received here;[64] and *Porcupine* lambasted 'squeamish' critics of 'Bloody Sunday'. Only the authorities' severity prevented a 'reign of terror'.[65] The Strike Committee had called out all transport workers—75,000 men—following the docks' closure. More troops arrived, and magistrates licensed special constables and warned 'respectable people' away from disturbed areas. Soldiers were engaged during the night around Great Homer Street. They fired twelve shots on magistrates' orders; but no civilian casualties were reported.[66]

Dunning belittled this incident;[67] and the Home Secretary, Winston Churchill, informed Parliament—'the important point is that the riot is not one which originated with the strikers, but that disorder and riots sometimes occur in those parts of Liverpool where sectarian difficulties exist'.[68] To Dunning this experience was normal; the strike was unusual. The Labour M.P., George Barnes, expanded the lesson: while Conservatism and sectarianism governed Liverpool the trade unions' influence towards peaceful negotiations was feeble.[69]

On 15 August two men were shot dead and three wounded when 3,000 people attacked prison-vans containing arrested rioters.[70] The escort of thirty-four soldiers and sundry policemen was overawed. Stones were the rioters' prevailing weapons but soldiers alleged that some fired guns.[71] It was in the military's interest to exaggerate the opposition; but, as mobs elsewhere wrecked tram-cars or erected barricades, Lord Derby forwarded to the Home Secretary the Lord Mayor's cry that Westminster should realize that 'a revolution was in progress'.[72]

Over 2,300 soldiers now patrolled Liverpool, and another company was summoned.[73] Ferries, trams, and suburban trains operated with interruptions, but the Strike Committee controlled most transport movements. Even the postmaster sought permission to ship overseas mail.[74] The Committee's writ was absolute, except for the food convoy which left Edge Hill daily. It was an insufficient breach. Shortages affected the Isle of Man,[75] and the Millers' Association declared that without coal, wheat, and flour supplies Liverpool would shortly be without bread. This, and the threatened national railway strike, inspired *The Times* headline, 'LABOUR AGITATION GONE MAD'.[76]

The Scotland Road district remained in ferment. Walton Gaol was full. Shops and public houses were shuttered, but determined looters checked only when troops assumed the firing position.[77] The giant of violence, pent in the slums, had broken loose as Liverpool lay helpless. *Porcupine* recognized 'the crimson flag of anarchy';[78] and the *Daily Mail* echoed it when its reporter was assaulted. One army officer described their tormentors: 'They are not strikers; they have no calling or trade; they are simply hooligans who will pillage, murder, burn, or riot without hardly any provocation.'[79] The *Review of Reviews* summarized everyone's distress when it entitled Liverpool, 'A Nightmare of Civilization'.[80] However, there was method in the madness when shops belonging to persons of one religion were looted while another's in the same area survived.[81]

The Strike Committee called out tramway and brewery workers, both inadequately unionized; and there were fears of an epidemic as Corporation scavengers and seventy electricity workers also struck. The former Unionist candidate in Scotland Division, T. Ockleston, organized four hundred public-school men as volunteer stokers at the power station.[82] Even with army protection these high-spirited Hercules could not satisfactorily replace the downtrodden workmen, and businesses requiring electricity were affected.[83]

Gas still illuminated most areas and the Gasworkers and General Labourers Union, recognizing that its members constituted only a tiny minority of the 1,700 workers at the Liverpool United Gaslight Company, counselled restraint, so no sympathetic strike occurred in this quarter. Fears remained, nonetheless, for those businesses and wealthy residential districts exposed to 'darkness and pillage' during electrical failures.[84] Some 4,000 special constables were enrolled, many pressed by corporations, like the 592 tramwaymen, 492 Dock Board employees, and 179 Cunard workers.[85] A battleship and cruiser arrived. The Lord Mayor wanted sailors to work the power station and ferries but the Government refused.[86] Their instructions were to protect ferries and dock property.

Suffocation by armour took effect. Isolated attacks on shops and pubs occurred on 18 August but no general riot. Journalists safely toured Scotland Road in daylight; and shipowners urged dockers to return to work. They were promised union rates throughout the port and advised that the Joint Committee was the place to air outstanding questions. Mann replied in conciliatory tones, although *Porcupine* considered him 'as cruel as the worst friends who disgraced France'.[87] The Home Office also acted, nominating a three-man investigation. This really resulted from the Home Office Commissioner's recommendations during the 1910 Inquiry into the Wiseite riots. Sectarian disturbances remained its brief, but it now included class strife. The trio, T. P. O'Connor, Kyffin-Taylor, and D. J. Shackleton (the Home Office's Labour adviser), were not ideal nominations. The Stipendiary Magistrate and Justice's Clerk complained that the local M.P.s might excite rather than allay sectarianism. However, their role was limited, because the national railway strike ended on 19 August. The Government promised a royal commission to investigate the operation of the 1907 agreement and the companies pledged themselves to abide by its recommendations.[88]

Improvement followed. Trams ran in daytime, with only the Great Howard

Street route suspended; several liners sailed; and local railwaymen voted overwhelmingly to return to work. However, the Strike Committee demanded universal reinstatement and, when the Tramways Committee refused to reinstate strikers unless they disavowed their union, solidarity was renewed. The streets were again unsettled;[89] and magistrates demanded additional powers, convinced that 'the present systems of picketing and intimidation are almost the sole factors in preventing a universal settlement . . .'[90]

The problem was not simply the Tramways Committee pursuing reprisals, convinced, as the chairman, Petrie, put it, that 'we had beaten them [the strikers] hollow'. The vacancies created by the minority of tramwaymen who struck had been filled already; moreover, 'loyal' tramwaymen, having suffered intimidation, declared that they would not work with reinstated former strikers.[91] The chasm between Conservative working men and the Labour movement was plain; but it only confirmed the failure to unionize tramwaymen following municipalization in 1897. Then the L.T.C.'s president had exasperatedly called tramworkers the 'scrap-heap of society.'[92]

The deadlock maintained antagonisms. The Corporation conceded reinstatement to electricity workers and repairmen at the tramworks but, as businessmen petitioned the Tramways Committee to maintain the ban against uniformed tramwaymen, Mann sounded the Transport Workers' Federation about extending the fight.[93] The Board of Trade sent its conciliator, George Askwith, to Liverpool;[94] yet within twenty-four hours the strike ended.

Salvidge had deprecated anything which focused hostility on the Conservative party.[95] What Mann's menaces found immovable, an electioneer's calculations shifted. The Tramways Committee resolved to reinstate strikers, whenever men were required, and subject to the general manager's satisfaction.[96] Mann accepted compromise realistically;[97] but Liverpool's scourge was already supplanted in attention by its saviour. The Liberal, Alderman Bowring, and the Kirkdale M.P., Kyffin-Taylor, publicly congratulated Salvidge upon his stand against the Tramways Committee; and Wise described Salvidge's encounter as 'a fight between the democratic and aristocratic parties'.[98]

The compromise reached regarding the tramwaymen should not obscure the fact that, for the most part, public authorities and private employers did not relax their position of ultimate advantage following the strikes. Salvidge's device was accepted; but most businessmen believed that 'there can be no lasting peace until the methods of the Liverpool Strike Committee and the National Transport Workers Federation have been definitely discredited . . .' Richard Holt had been appalled by the 'recklessness' of the Strike Committee in risking starvation for 'comparatively trifling grievances'. He recorded in his diary: 'As far as I can observe nothing has been obtained by the strike—all the concessions having been made before. Indeed thanks to the very firm attitude of the shipowners, led by Alfred Allen Booth with Lawrence [Holt] as his right hand man I consider the position of the employers was stronger after the strike than before.'[99] Shipowners were exacting in negotiations with the N.U.D.L., which undertook not to support men who broke agreements. Pinched faces at the docks demonstrated a submission of sorts. Troops challenged rioters for the last time on 24 August.

They had withdrawn, except for one batallion and squadron, by 28 August. Special constables served until October, when the Watch Committee founded a permanent reserve of a thousand men.[100]

Political responses to industrial and sectarian violence

Accountancy occupied public men following the strikes. The Council's bill, including claims for damages and injuries in the strike, was £21,000; and 'Bloody Sunday' was re-enacted in debate. According to Sexton, soldiers had behaved like 'indecent brutes' and, according to Harford, policemen like 'bashi-bazouks'. The U.I.L. had petitioned the Government to amnesty persons convicted during the strikes.[101] When Walker, the Independent Protestant councillor, echoed this, the disturbances' dual nature was recaptured. But three hundred policemen had been injured also: the Council accepted its liabilities and voted £2,000 in gratuities to policemen and 'loyal' tramwaymen.[102]

The Council also received its annual Health Report. A comparison of July–September in 1911 with that period during the previous five years showed 843 more deaths. Dr. Hope blamed the interrupted food supply, piled-up garbage, and damage to grids and gutters. The report was a tract against general strikes which, another M.O.H. deduced, must be dealt with by the criminal law. 'Strikers', he added, 'in their ignorance, were led to a wholesale massacre of their own children.'[103] Mann, the modern Herod, defended himself before Liverpool railwaymen; and Sexton and Ramsay MacDonald deprecated Hope's bias.[104]

Dr. Hope was also challenged professionally. One leading medical authority enjoined fellow doctors to sympathize with men who demanded a living wage.[105] The intention of preventing general strike was more common. Shipowners lobbied the Government to repeal sections of the Trades Disputes Act concerning picketing; and arrangements were made to promote this in private members' legislation. Wiser voices concluded that Merseyside needed new industries, but punitive legislation enchanted many politicians. F. E. Smith's declaration in 1911, that pickets who stood for 'the right to prevent work' should be checked, reflected a widespread belligerence in labour matters.[106] Personal ambition, the poor electoral prospects of the existing Tory party nationally, and the hope of enlisting conservative elements in the Liberal party in support of a federal solution to the Irish problem, such factors had stimulated Smith's interest in Coalition proposals during the constitutional crisis between 1909 and 1911; so too had his desire to maintain the Osborne Judgement (1909) which restrained trade unions from supporting a political party financially without the positive assent of its members. To resist the Labour party's pressure to reverse the Osborne Judgement, in Smith's opinion, 'would go far to justify the coalition if it stood alone . . . I have some knowledge of the [Conservative] party and will pledge my judgement that the whole party will support with enthusiasm the attempt "to save Asquith from Keir Hardie".'[107]

In fact there was much that was fictional about labour strength. Picketing, the Webbs perceived, 'is a mark not of Trade Unionism, but of its imperfection', that is, the inability of unions of semi-skilled and unskilled men otherwise to protect their members' jobs from being taken by blackleg labour.[108] The *Transport Worker* tabulated the spread of union membership among Liverpool transport workers, from 24,500 to 91,000 between May and October 1911.[109] There was an angler's tendency to exaggerate his catch. Unions were not strengthened by thousands joining under the impression that plentiful funds existed for strike pay. While for the most part the unions had won port-wide recognition, the strikes impoverished the unions and landed them with members whose understanding of union aims was loose.

The sense of national fraternity among dockers, let alone all transport workers, was weak. The wage claim pressed by Ernest Bevin before Lord Shaw's Court of Inquiry in 1919 was the first call for a national rate in the docks; but prior to this, according to Sexton's reckoning, 'these were at least twenty-two organizations professing to care for the casual dock worker'. In 1894 Sexton had experienced the failure to eliminate the competitive jurisdictions of different dockers' unions by amalgamation of the two largest, the N.U.D.L. and the Dock, Wharf, Riverside and General Labourers' Union. It failed 'because of the ignorance and prejudice of the rank and file, often fostered and exploited for the benefit of local officials who feared the consequences to themselves'. To a marked degree these difficulties, especially the resistance to centralized command and finance, remained to plague the Transport and General Workers' Union following the war. Formal federations, like the T.G.W.U., or informal compacts, like the so-called Triple Alliance of 1914, which saw some concert between the National Union of Railwaymen and the Miners' and Transport Workers' Federations, grew up because industrial action by one section of these workers invariably had consequences for the rest. This created the simulacrum of a general strike. In fact preparation for a general strike formed no part of these unions' purpose, although there was some awareness that benefits might result from the *threat* of a united action.[110]

Now, after the 1911 strikes, the Liverpool branch of the N.U.D.L. faced gradual decasualization with a large dissident element among its 30,000 members. The strike had been no vote for the authority of union leaders.[111] Indeed their task was made more difficult in several respects. Direct action provoked attempts to manacle unions by legislation, while encouraging men to value quick results. Moreover, sectarianism had not been expunged. Labour's 'solidarity' was impermanent.

Kyffin-Taylor, the Housing Committee's chairman, argued that rehousing would insure quietude.[112] It seemed an appropriate psychological moment to promote improvements; but there was a circular aspect. Politicians pronounced their duty to bring sectarian peace, the churches their mission to bring civic peace. Churchmen had exercised little influence during the strike. Half the Anglican clergy were on holiday during August but the Bishop declared that many urban dwellers resisted alike 'the laws of God and man', being ever ready to 'riot . . . plunder and maim and destroy'. The well-to-do were also transgressors—their 'selfishness, unsympathetic attitude, [and] absorption in getting money or in seeking pleasure are some of the chief causes of the present labour troubles'.[113]

This was a homily for all seasons. Meanwhile O'Connor and Kyffin-Taylor organized a conference of political and sectarian representatives. Salvidge participated after Lord Derby, the chairman, pressed him; but his pessimism was compounded as Wise defined the condition of his association.[114] He would not surrender his rights as 'an Englishman and a Protestant';[115] or, it seemed, his thirst for publicity. The wide sweep of the Conference's brief was reflected in its other members—the Anglican and Catholic prelates; Colonel J. P. Reynolds (Conservative councillor and chairman of the Catholic Emergency Association); Taggart, Harford, and Lynskey (Nationalists); Walker and Holden (Orangemen); Stanley Rogers (Congregationalist); and Sir Benjamin Johnson (the new local Liberal leader).[116]

Wise soon exhibited his 'old vicious, mountebank tricks' which mocked the Conference's ambitions.[117] To the Protestant Truth Society he declared that 'all the strife in Liverpool for the past two years had been caused by members of the Catholic Defence Association'. Moreover, Kensit had returned, advocating Carson's case for Ulster and 'Cromwellian methods' against Ritualist bishops.[118] The Conference resolved to promote a Bill to regulate demonstrations. Wise understood that political collusion could perforate legislation, but one recommendation won his approval, that to prohibit any meeting should require the Watch Committee's consent. Wise called this 'a splendid safeguard' against the tyranny of one official—a transparent reference to the Head Constable.[119] Soon Dunning resigned. He had had enough of Liverpool and feared a nervous collapse.[120]

As the Conference met, the political parties would normally have been preparing for the municipal elections; but the Liberal, Alderman Bowring, proposed a truce.[121] Those councillors who were retiring or wanting re-election were fairly equal—thirteen Liberals, thirteen Conservatives, three Nationalists and one Labour—but more than a token towards sectarian peace and the saving of £8,000 motivated the leaders of the established parties. They presumed that a truce would 'dispose of Socialist threats'; but Labour was revivified by opposing a Liberal–Conservative coalition.[122]

Penury prevented a city-wide challenge but the L.L.R.C. co-operated with the L.T.C., Transport Workers' Federation, I.L.P., and S.D.F., to advance fourteen candidates. They demanded reinstatement for all tramwaymen, the adoption of the Provision of Meals Act, and medical treatment of schoolchildren. Concerning the city's finance, they advocated economical management to raise the salaries of lower officials, and an inquiry into Corporation leaseholds. The promotion of new industries and female suffrage completed their cardinal points; but their concern for all oppressed workers included the police. As propaganda this was sensible but it reflected grievances which before 1911 brought Labour some constables' votes.[123]

The manifesto eschewed wildness; but inevitably the contest was bitter. *Porcupine* viewed Labour's challenge as 'proof of their unfitness' for government. In case memories failed, it applied the branding-iron: 'all the Labour candidates were associated with the disastrous strike'.[124] The Conservatives Council leader, Petrie, held the Strike Committee responsible for 'sickness and disease and death'. He alleged that the Labour party paid Mann £4 a week—'no doubt Mr. Mann found his job much easier than working with a pick and shovel'. The

Labour supporters who broke up Petrie's meeting only illustrated to Conservatives 'what might happen . . . if the Socialists gained control'.[125]

Agitators who had led men with genuine grievances into 'a suicidal course' also concerned Salvidge; but during the elections he presented Conservatives as fair-minded men who would 'stimulate industries rather than drive capital away'. Equally the West Derby M.P., Rutherford, allowed Labour some honest intention but prophesied that in a Socialist polity all would become 'servants of a bureaucracy . . ., the slaves of ignorant, and therefore of brutal, masters, scoffers at morality, and scoffers at God Almighty'. The thesis was robot politics: Labour councillors would 'take their orders from men like Mr. Tom Mann'. The Liberal–Conservative platform contained 'no party politicians'.[126]

This 'unpolitical' assault on Socialism had many abettors. During the strike the *Protestant Standard* had revealed basic antipathies to trade unionism—'a system of secular popery'.[127] Wise, accepting 'radicalism' while abjuring Socialism, was more circumspect. His Bible Class had condemned the soldiery and supported the railwaymen; and Wise advocated a tramwaymen's union.[128] The strikes placed Protestant workmen in novel circumstances; but Wise had admonished one Orangeman who proclaimed that henceforth they should place labour questions first.[129] Wise argued that Mann's writings signified 'the worst possible gospel', and in the municipal elections he embraced Salvidgeite Conservatives.[130]

Metternich once tried to educate the Duke of Wellington to regard as blessings the radical disturbances which followed the Napoleonic Wars: 'the effects of such violence crises', he wrote, 'always turn in favour of the good party'.[131] In Liverpool in 1911, however, industrial rioters did not instantly enthrone political reactionaries. The Liberal–Conservative propaganda (primarily Conservative, since eleven of the fourteen Labour-contested seats were Conservative) overstepped credulity. Not everyone detected bloody revolution in Labour candidates like George Nelson, a co-opted member of the Education Committee; in W. R. Blair, of the Co-operative Society; or in T. J. Hickling, of the Postmen, who declared that 'he was not a Socialist, nor was he a supporter of secular education'.[132] No Labour candidate was unknown in his ward. Most had done public work. Seven were elected in polls averaging 57 per cent. The peaks were scaled by W. A. Robinson in a 73 per cent poll in Garston, and by Sexton in a 66 per cent poll in St. Anne's. Only in St. Domingo was victory fortunate. There an independent Conservative split the anti-Labour vote.

Sexton trusted that 'the common platform of labour' would annul sectarianism. But seven Labour councillors faced eighty-one Unionists, thirty-four Liberals, fourteen Nationalists, and one Protestant: they could make a noise, not the millennium. They joined unimportant committees and failed to introduce evening debates.[133] One trend was encouraging. The Liberals had lost two municipal seats and more intangibly as Conservative accomplices. The Whip's office now leaked a report that the 'gasconading' Colonel Seely and other well-known Liberals would contest Liverpool at the next General Election, assuming that six Unionist seats were vulnerable.[134] Their plans included a sustained effort in registration. Seely's forced resignation, after the Curragh incident, and the First World War, intervened before this strategy could be tested; but the Liberals' local failings argue against any sensational recovery by outside salvage operations. Indeed Liberals broadly were far from robust in constitution or confident in direction. Lloyd George had an unflagging appetite for office and power, and he was brewing his Land Campaign in the years before the war, with a significance for the towns in its references to housing, a minimum wage, and land usage in the public interest; but the implications of these questions could not be confined within vague arguments about the places of country and city within the economic system. Industrial issues, particularly the roles of capital and labour, were central and could not be ducked now that trade union membership and influence had greatly grown; and political issues, particularly the flight from constitutionalism to conflict in Ireland, and the franchise, were outstanding. Two of the earliest engineers and spokesmen of Liberal 'progressivism', J. A. Hobson and C. P. Scott, in 1914 recognized a need for drastic party reconstruction: they were 'beginning to feel . . . that the existing Liberal party is played out and that if it is to count for anything in the future it must be reconstructed largely on a labour basis.'[135] But labour unrest everywhere, from the mines to the docks, gave no promise that the trade union movement would ever again comfortably settle under Liberal leadership as it had in Gladstonian days.

Industrial unrest renewed and Larkinism

Industrial relations remained disturbed. Many felt like Austen Chamberlain, that 'we shall never have settled peace until one struggle at least has been fought out to a finish'.[136] Liverpool's unrest resumed a violent character in the strike, from May to August 1912, at Wilson's bobbin factory in Garston.[137] The infant Warehouse Workers Union demanded recognition and increased wages; and Tom Mann was back in Liverpool, following his imprisonment for publishing the 'Open Letter to British Soldiers'.[138]

Garston had a past of sectarianism, but the strike at Wilson's renewed the best of 1911 in signs of Protestant and Catholic co-operation.[139] Although Mann made a religion of working-class organization,[140] not all were incorporated. Strikers and police again clashed, significantly on the anniversary of 'Bloody Sunday'. The City Council refused to institute an inquiry. Accordingly the L.T.C. made an electoral issue of police 'barbarism'. This was unwise: the rioting alienated many ratepayers and shopkeepers.[141] In an 83 per cent poll Joseph Cleary (the Warehouse Workers' leader) attracted 757 supporters, but 1,127 flocked to the Conservatives.

Strife in the docks overshadowed this dispute. Under Sexton's system of clearing-houses registered dockers could collect their weekly wages in sum; but it predicated decasualization and coincided with the beginnings of National Insurance.[142] Both events betokened one movement which many men wished to resist, the growing influence of bureaucracy in their lives. That other bodies—the police, schools, tax inspectors—might seek to use the clearing-house registers was obvious and, though Sexton shared this objection, his authority to implement the scheme was questioned.[143]

Some claimed that two-thirds of the N.U.D.L. opposed the clearing-house scheme.[144] At its inauguration on Monday 15 July 1912 only 1,000 men applied for work. This surprised even pessimists since 11,000 had registered. As the Union officially condemned the strike, most men resumed work; but on the following Monday dockers in north Liverpool struck, after delays on pay-day. Some 2,000 Birkenhead dockers had remained out since the previous Monday; but Liverpool's south-end, where the Union was traditionally strong, and Bootle, persevered.

The local Labour paper, *Forward,* upbraided 'miserable, puny, wasteful, sectional strikes', for they discredited trade unionism and alienated even friendly employers.[145] A lock-out had ensued in Birkenhead. As blacklegs were imported, the divorce between Sexton and the ranks widened.[146] In July he prosecuted two dockers who nominated him 'an unprincipled lying thing, a creature of the employers, an enemy of the working class'.[147] One of Sexton's libellers was a delegate of his own union, who had only joined the N.U.D.L. during the 1911 strike.

Sexton had repudiated Larkin's calumnies in 1909 and, significantly, this libel first appeared in Larkin's paper, the *Irish Worker.*[148] Considering his struggles on behalf of these downtrodden and fickle workers, and the vituperation he received, the whining tone of sections of Sexton's autobiography is understandable. Partly the attacks reflected Sexton's weakness for high company, particularly Lord Derby, whose humour he tickled with recollections of his father's poaching at Knowsley. In 1912 Sexton, and every Labour councillor except Robinson, offended the L.L.R.C. by endorsing the Freedom of Liverpool for Derby; but Sexton alone flaunted the L.T.C.'s injunction to boycott the ceremony.[149] *Forward*'s headline announced 'Sexton Dines with Derby. Latest Phase of Flunkeyism'; and correspondents likened Sexton to Pecksniff and Judas.[150] Differences concerning industrial procedure exacerbated this hostility. In October when Ben Tillett censured Liverpool's failure to support the London dockers' strike, the cry went up—'The men were with you', 'Sexton was to blame'.[151]

Sexton maintained his position. Statistically the case for some decasualization was sound. Greater security for more men, not decasualization for all, was Sexton's objective. Indeed he always maintained that absolute decasualization was impossible. 'Time and tide', he observed in 1920, 'wait for no man', and dock work 'takes its own period from the fluctuations of export and import.'[152] The clearing-house scheme attacked the casual system obliquely, by regulating entry to the trade rather than evicting those already in.[153] All with experience of dock work were allowed to register. A year's trial showed that 7,387 worked in under thirteen weeks, including 2,138 who never worked; 4,836 worked in fourteen to twenty-six weeks; 5,228 in twenty-seven to thirty-nine weeks; and 14,020 in over forty weeks, including 8,805 who worked in forty-eight weeks or more.[154] The new scheme, however, was incomplete since the Docks Board refused to participate and ten master-stevedores among the sixty-five contracting employers insisted on paying wages separately and 'subbing' Saturday workers.[155] Moreover, many men would not move freely about, because mobility seemed like blacklegging; but some control was exercised by tallies differentiating 'Company' from 'Clearing-House' men (the former were regulars) and it was hoped that lads beginning employment would find a full week's work.[156]

Unofficial action impeded progress. Blacklegs were disbanded in mid-August as the Birkenhead dockers adopted Sexton's scheme; but this crisis was superseded by Saturday stoppages, which began in the south-end and by April 1913 regularly affected the whole port.[157] After 7,000 men were idle on 3 May, employers threatened to terminate agreements since negotiations were useless with a union which had 'no power to control the men'.[158] Liverpool worked normally on 10 May. At Birkenhead was deadlock; but the N.U.D.L. recovered face at its annual conference when an overwhelming majority instructed Birkenhead to conform.[159]

Relations remained thus uneasy before the First World War. Tremors from the great Dublin strike in 1913 rocked the English labour movement, especially in Liverpool whose son, Jim Larkin, was the soul of Dublin's struggle. Some Liverpool railwaymen 'blacked' Dublin goods, but capitulated after a lock-out. Their union denied them support. Larkin styled the railwaymen's leader, J. H. Thomas, 'the double-dyed traitor'.[160] On the other hand 300 blacklegs were recruited in Liverpool by 12 November 1913, and more followed them to Dublin, all, Larkin said, 'camp followers who robbed the dead and dying'.[161]

Larkin was 'trumpet-tongued' and unorthodox.[162] Labour party and trade union officials he flayed as 'quidnuncs', 'fools', 'mummies', 'hypocrites', men who had forgotten what it was to work at the bench, in the docks or on the footplate. Larkin was a leader who abhorred leadership. He aimed to get the ranks to appreciate their power, to 'tell their leaders to get in front or get out'. He reviled constitutional encumbrances: 'Man does not live by contracts drawn up by employers' hirelings. Man lives by bread. To get bread one must work and if one works one is entitled to say under what conditions one will work.'[163] Larkin's challenge echoed 1911 but that sympathy was exhausted.

The T.U.C. met in September 1913, following fighting in Dublin and Larkin's arrest. Sexton demanded the restoration of civil rights and 'a very rigid inquiry' into police behaviour.[164] He wished to satisfy the N.U.D.L.'s emotional support of Larkin, without a practical alliance. He defended liberal principles not Larkinism. When Larkin evangelized England, this difference hardened. Funds were freely subscribed and the L.T.C. condemned the Dublin employers; but delegates disagreed about inviting Larkin to speak. One advised that this would 'cause friction'; another suggested James Connolly's name instead; but a motion to invite the Dublin strike leaders found only three supporters.[165]

Larkin nevertheless came. In November he visited his mother-in-law in Bootle and addressed the Clarion Club.[166] He returned in December, alleging that Havelock Wilson was conniving with the Shipping Federation, and that Liverpool resented him because he was clean.[167] Cotter, the L.T.C.'s vice-president, counter-attacked on behalf of the seamen's unions but was censured by the L.T.C. which sought a middle ground. It would not accept Larkin's accusations, but it was embarrassed by the irrefutable fact that Larkin was 'doing his best for the workers of Dublin'.[168] However, at a specially convened T.U.C., the 'petty personalities' exploded and English labour leaders confirmed their repudiation of the methods of 1911.[169]

The future of the Liverpool Labour Party

Prosaic problems bemused Liverpool's Labour movement. In 1910–11 Labour's poll in the municipal elections rose from 4,129 to 12,231; in 1912 it dropped to 9,353, in 1913 to 7,400.[170] Labour lost every contest in 1912–13. In the negative electors considered the question, 'Are trade union leaders, basket-makers, railwaymen, Socialist spouters, and shop-assistants capable of administering the health and happiness' of 750,000 Liverpudlians? For city managers they chose Conservatives—not Liberals, for there was indignation that no Liberal faced Labour opposition, with the 'honourable exception' of H. R. Rathbone.[171] As an electioneer in these years Salvidge made reference to 'paid agitators' in the Labour party; but his fellow leader, Petrie, surpassed him in slander. He advised women in Breckfield ward, if 'the Socialist candidate' was elected, to imagine their 'husbands coming home on Saturday with their free love and no wages'.[172] The Fabian minister of the Baptist chapel in the Kensington district, Herbert Dunnico, retorted, 'What about the bloated Tory capitalists who employed girls at starvation wages, and thereby drove many on to the streets? When these men made their foul and loathsome charges he felt like saying to them, "Take your hypocrisy to hell, where it came from".'[173] They took it to the polls.

After the 1912 municipal elections the L.L.R.C. and L.T.C. summoned 'all the progressive bodies' to a joint committee. This upset those who favoured a trade union party.[174] The L.T.C., L.L.R.C., and I.L.P., agreed to meet quarterly from April 1913; but it was difficult to tailor Labour politics to municipal requirements. A competition of ideologies was counter-productive; but new issues rarely appeared. This was Salvidge's purpose. He resisted pay rises for the Corporation's chief officials, 'to prevent the so-called Labour men being provided with a popular electioneering cry'.[175] Labourites agitated to amend the Fair-Wages Clause: and the Joint Committee of Labour bodies demanded that the Corporation allow the British Socialist Party (the recharged S.D.F.) the right of public meeting.[176] Neither issue broadened their appeal and Salvidge sneered that the Labour Party could not be considered labour's representative.

These electoral disappointments surprised many Labourites. The Revd. Dunnico had prophesied in 1912 that the Conservatives were doomed 'because they could no longer beat the big sectarian drum'.[177] That October Liverpool's private act of Parliament, regulating processions, became law; but sectarians had not been disfranchised. Another Home Rule Bill and Welsh Disestablishment were before Parliament in April 1912 and, though F. E. Smith asserted that many Tories would accept Disestablishment and only discountenanced Disendowment, Salvidge was not particular when he arranged with Wise that Conservative councillors would pursue Protestant policies.[178] Rallies cemented the agreement.

Labour had no equivalent device, being torn by loose Catholic associations and by accusations of atheism. A manifesto of the Catholic Bishop of Salford, signed by George Milligan (Liverpool N.U.D.L.) among others, execrated Socialism and raised the possibility of forming Catholic trade unions. Concurrently Orangemen in Garston denounced their Labour councillor,

Robinson, who was a Catholic. The L.L.R.C. heard about these movements from James Murphy, the defeated candidate in St. Domingo in 1912. Having presented Labour's case at Wise's Debating Society, Murphy urged the L.L.R.C. 'to adopt Orange candidates, saying that politics was a dirty game and we must play it like the Liberal and Tory parties—that the Nationalist Party in the Council were [sic] no good to us and we must play up to the Orange Leaders and so place them in a dilemma'.[179] The L.L.R.C. revolted from the choice: an alliance with either sect would negate Labour's doctrinal pretensions. Murphy's suggestion was also compromised by his controversial conduct, as a Larkinite and outspoken critic of the parliamentary Labour party.[180]

In one sense, however, Murphy triumphed. The reflex of collaborating with Orangemen was collision with Nationalists. Industrial strife generated disputes about the Irish party's role. Larkin had repeatedly declared that 'Home Rule does not put a loaf of bread into anybody's pocket'; and Liverpool men asked, 'How is Home Rule going to benefit the Irish slum residents in the vast Scotland Road area, the Liverpool-born Irish docker, with all the uncertainties and perils of his employment; the underpaid ships' firemen, the bottom dog of the mercantile marine; or the anaemic girl slaves in the factories . . .?' Home Rule would not alter these industrial conditions. Liverpool Irishmen required 'something more than mere political reform'.[181]

In November 1913 at a Great George Street ward by-election the L.L.R.C. decided to brave Nationalist opposition for the first time. Joseph Cleary was nominated and the Nationalists resolved in retaliation to oppose every future Labour candidature; but an expectation of co-operation was held out if Cleary now withdrew. One Catholic Labourite, Milligan, wanted the L.L.R.C. to surrender. Instead it advanced—to humiliation. Cleary polled only 72 votes against 468 Conservatives and 478 Nationalists; and the L.L.R.C. instituted an inquiry into his failure.[182]

By 1914 Labour's catalogue of activity seemed conspicuous for calamity upon calamity. These continued—in February the Labour paper, *Forward*, was crippled by a fine of £2,000 for libelling Fairrie's Sugar Works; and the records of several of the Labour councillors elected in 1911 were considered poor.[183] The movement was more redoubtable than this suggests, for still Labour took the argument to its rivals who were compelled to accommodate to a body which might be knocked down, but never knocked out, by defeat. The Irish party, for example, increasingly took care to divine its supporters' industrial interests, a tendency which was to ease their transition to the Labour party when the Irish party was sapped by concessions over the nationalist issue in the 1920s.

This can be illustrated by two incidents in 1914. One concerned the Liverpool United Gaslight Company's Bill. The company refused to recognize the Gas-workers' and General Labourers' Union, and sought parliamentary approval for a scheme of co-partnership, which promised bonuses for the workers and cheaper gas for the consumers. The union had begun to recruit members in the company's six gas stations from 1910 but progress had been made only in one by 1914. Probably a majority of gas workers lived in Scotland division—where there were three gas stations—and the local Nationalist leaders, Harford and Burke, canvassed them before T. P. O'Connor defended the Company's Bill in parliament against Labour's criticism that the company denied its workers the right to organize and paid them lower than average wages for the industry. On the other hand, concerning a Mersey Docks and Harbour Board Bill, O'Connor took a different line. Though he was a member of the Board, he allied with the Labour party in regretting that the Board refused to enter into collective bargaining or to join the Joint Conciliation Board of masters and men which had been in existence since 1911. What inspired his change of course was clear: some 85 per cent of Dock Board employees were trade unionists by 1914, whereas only a minority of gasworkers were.[184]

By riding the trade union wave the Labour party was inching up the beach, pushing its opponents' defences further and further back. With the reversal of the Osborne Judgement in 1913 the L.L.R.C.'s affiliated societies grew from twenty-three to fifty; and now it resolved to construct ward associations, and to campaign among union branches. A five-man standing committee co-ordinated meetings, literature, and a house-to-house canvass. In June the L.L.R.C. heard reports from everywhere except Wavertree West, Low Hill, and Old Swan. Mostly the reports confirmed the serious situation, that there remained a dearth of workers; but new members were emerging, and Breckfield was ready to call its first ward Labour party meeting.[185]

Soon the First World War intervened and this slow and patient party recruitment was put in jeopardy. The L.L.R.C. was approached about an all-party electoral truce. A narrow majority of delegates accepted its necessity; but the L.L.R.C. resolved to 'continue their work in the wards in order that we should not be caught napping' when war ended.[186] In evident strength Liverpool's Labour party had reached the youthful stage. This was the state, too, of the electoral system: until 1918 all adult males were not enfranchised. However, one precondition of Labour's development was established in Liverpool. Labour had mostly disentangled its organization from Liberalism by 1914.

The Unionist Party's disquiet

The Conservative party still dominated Liverpool, although this Goliath was vulnerable to problems of national leadership, tariffs, and Ulster. To Salvidge the machine's integrity, not policies, came first. Theodore Roosevelt once expressed this attitude thus: 'There are no politics in politics.'[187] Some issues none the less required resolution. The anti-Ritualist offensive had passed—the Laymen's League's protest was unavailing as Parliament gave birth to more bishops[188]—but the Ulster question was burning. Although in 1910 prepared to face difficulties in Liverpool by committing Ulster to a federal Ireland if he could achieve his price of a coalition government at Westminster, F. E. Smith in 1911 reaffirmed Liverpool's dedication to Carson's cause.[189] Marshall Hall, the East Toxteth M.P., also galloped. He proclaimed that with the likelihood of 'Civil War in Ireland' their party leader, Balfour, was 'too much of a gentlemen' for their needs.[190] In the following month, November 1911, the Conservative party ditched Balfour and ranged itself behind Bonar Law, a Presbyterian with Ulster connections and a forthright 'new style' of address.

Locally, in Liverpool, Salvidge was concerned that an irresponsible movement should have responsible leadership.[191] In September 1912 he transferred an anti-Home Rule rally from St. George's Plateau to Sheil Park, at Lord Derby's request, in order to minimize possibilities of disorder;[192] and in 1913 he discountenanced a demonstration to be addressed in Liverpool by Lord Willoughby de Broke. He told Lord Derby that if the demonstrators wanted 'volunteers to go to Ulster in case of a row this ought to be done in a quiet and solid manner and not by stirring up the mob whose only view of helping Ulster would be to leave riots and disturbances in Liverpool'.[193]

Salvidge distinguished between demonstrations which incited lawlessness in Ulster, and demonstrations which incited lawlessness in Liverpool; but he was increasingly pessimistic that Liverpool 'might easily turn out to be a second Ulster' unless some Irish settlement was forthcoming. In March 1914 certain reports indicated that 3,000 Liverpool Nationalists had received military training, a counter to Liverpool's Ulster Volunteers, said to number only half as many; but earlier, when Carson had visited Liverpool, F. E. Smith had promised him 10,000 Liverpudlians in three ships, and rumours of even greater numbers of potential combatants reached the King.[194] Whether we can credit Salvidge, as Tim Healy credited Carson, that his 'influence has acted as a safety-valve for the Orangemen',[195] is doubtful. As the movement became more extreme, those who sought control assumed the same tone. There was little moderation in Salvidge's speeches by June 1914. 'We have every reason to go any length in supporting Ulster', he said; 'The Unionists would consent to no compromise.' Especially they would not treat with 'a despotic Government', run by Nationalist and Socialist 'place-hunters' and 'self-seekers'.[196] Salvidge was an electioneer, not a peace-maker.

This calculation was evident in Salvidge's part in the resolution of the Conservative party's position on tariffs. The new leader, Bonar Law, was a committed Tariff Reformer as well as a determined Unionist and in 1912 the Tariff Reform League had played on this loyalty, seeking to attain a primacy in the party programme, by arguing that Lancashire was '*the* part of England in which the question of Home Rule is of least value to the Conservative Party'.[197] Lancashire might well have been responding to other electoral inducements, and Liverpool was not Lancashire; but Salvidge spoke for Liverpool and Lancashire when he declared that they could not 'endanger the Ulster cause for the sake of insisting on the full gospel of Tariff Reform . . . In the existing prosperity of this country it would be madness to expect to defeat the Government on a free trade and free food issue.'[198] Salvidge met Bonar Law, who accepted his position. Food taxes would be dropped at the next election; and, if the party won, the Dominions would be consulted about what duties would ensure effective preference. But these would not be imposed without another election.

Bonar Law's continued leadership required his submission. The conviction that Tariff Reform was an impediment, Austin Chamberlain recorded, 'had spread to all but a few stalwarts'.[199] After this little remained of the Conservative programme except opposition to Home Rule, Disestablishment, and Liberal–Socialist finance. An exclusively reactionary stance was fraught with danger; but the Unionist Social Reform Committee, which reported in 1914, came up with few ideas. It broadly welcomed an extension of the Conciliation and Wages Board machinery, trumpeted a historical Tory Democracy, and berated Cobdenite Liberalism for its selfishness and indifference to the needs of both the State and labour. Two Liverpool M.P.s were involved in this Committee's report, Leslie Scott, and F. E. Smith, who sang the common cause of 'the saner Trade Unionism and the wiser Conservatism'.[200] The party, however, was rescued from the danger of its doubt and drift by a greater danger, war, in Europe, not Ulster.

CHAPTER SIXTEEN

'Our miscellaneous and slightly conservatively-minded democracy', 1914–28

If the P.M.'s new Party is to have any kind of success it will have to build itself up on National Health as an alternative to the more thorough policy of Socialism. We must at least get a minimum of health even for Capitalism.
Beatrice Webb

As I watched L.G.'s Cabinet—watching each of its members under a microscope—I felt I was in a thieves' kitchen. Nobody seemed to have any principles. There was the most awful cynicism. Perhaps it was all due to reaction after the War. *Stanley Baldwin*

Reorganization is bureaucracy's defence against reform.[1] *R. Strausz-Hupé*

This chapter takes the story from the First World War. The change in party fortunes was drastic. The Labour party, long unable to tap the full reservoir of working-class votes while the franchise was undemocratic, settled the ground vacated by the Liberal party and, less decisively, by the Irish Nationalists in the 1920s. On the Conservative side Salvidge was increasingly shorn of his sectarian armoury. Wise died in 1917, although he had a pretended successor in Pastor Longbottom; the W.M.C.A.'s membership slumped; and the remaining Irish Nationalist questions ceased to dominate, though they might still distort, other electoral issues. This chapter ends with Salvidge's death, as the dictator suffered the ignominy of a rebellion by his M.P.s.

Liverpool in the First World War

The war claimed 13,500 Liverpudlians.[2] Local particulars remained but more experiences were shared. The slums, once 'almost self-contained communities',[3] were being opened. Government was inquisitive. In September 1915 the Munitions Tribunal fined 236 Birkenhead shipyard workers who, through absenteeism, disputes, and general dilatoriness, had lost thousands of hours'

Notes on p. 450.

work in twenty weeks. The men prophesied that 'there'll be a revolution in this country', for workers were not 'slaves';[4] but those who banished leisure were rewarded. For his assistance in restricting licensing hours Salvidge was knighted. During and soon after the war these controls were extended nationally, the alcoholic content of beer was reduced, and punitive taxation was imposed on spirits. The Drink Question was thus politically answered: 'nowadays our national drink is bad tea', moaned J. B. Priestley by 1933. Government purchase, which was accepted in principle by Lloyd George and Bonar Law in 1915, had been rendered unnecessary, likewise National Prohibition as practised in America throughout the 1920s. In 1922 Lloyd George reckoned that under 20 per cent of people wanted some action in this once famous Liberal cause. The Labour party especially was cool about it—with some notable exceptions, like Arthur Henderson who in 1927 considered resigning from the National Executive when it dropped from the party programme any reference to the topic.[5] Emphatically labour questions, and the economy, had long since dominated the thoughts of practical politicians.

Liverpool's war effort centred on the docks, which became congested as southern ports closed. Merseyside's share of the nation's imports rose from 25 per cent in 1911–14 to 33 per cent in 1915–20; but shortages occurred of berths, transport, and labour. According to the N.U.D.L. some 7,000 experienced dockers joined the forces before there were reserved occupations, and three-fifths of their replacements soon quit. Some inducement to dock work existed in the wage increases of 1*s*. per normal workday; but that the Liverpool docks remained congested argued that factors other than the increase in business were involved. The chief transport problem was the want of co-ordination and system; likewise the chief labour problem was how to undo the habits bred by casualization. Wage increases inspired some men to work shorter hours for the same basic wage, rather than harder or longer, although this question is fogged with prejudice and rumour. Some believed that the licensing restrictions brought about an increase in drinking at home. The West Toxteth M.P., Houston, asserted that increased wages encouraged intemperance, and he objected to drunks being merely fined—'I would suggest . . . that during the War drunkenness should be made a crime against the State, to be punished accordingly. I heard the other day of a working man lighting his pipe with a £1 note. What punishment would a fine be upon him? Evidently he attached very little value to money.'[6]

Patriotism had to be lined, as well as the pocket. In 1915 a Dockers' Battalion was established for union men above enlistment age but wanting to expedite Government work. Some 1,200 dockers by 1918 were earning their normal wages plus Army pay, which guaranteed 42*s*. The Government and various shipping companies defrayed the additional expenses. The conception and management of the Battalion belonged to R. F. Williams, a South Wales mining company secretary who had moved to Liverpool in 1909 as the first Divisional Officer of Labour Exchanges. Lord Derby nominally commanded, but Sexton was the Battalion's inspiration. In 1913 the N.U.D.L. had resolved to resist international war by international strike. Its changed mind Sexton ascribed to the Germans' atrocities and 'diabolical plot for world domination. This was not a capitalist war, not a war of aggression, but a war of defence'.[7] The N.U.D.L.

matched Sexton's ardour in recruiting, even at the risk of alienating the L.L.R.C.;[8] and observers of the Dockers' Battalion marvelled at this transformation of the roughest members of the working class.[9] Predictably, however, its preferential position excited jealousies. Ordinary dockers did not care to work with the Battalion, and labour generally demanded compensation for soaring food prices and irksome government controls. Wage increases were won either progressively or by *force majeure*.[10]

Agreements about the dilution of skilled labour were reached in Mersey shipbuilding, plumbing, and boiler-making trades in 1916; but engineers took national strike action in 1917.[11] The national emergency was also exploited in an unofficial strike by crews of four transatlantic liners in Liverpool in September 1917. This, and government pressure, resulted in the Shipping Federation, N.S.F.U., and Ships' Cooks and Stewards Union, meeting together to found the National Maritime Board and to establish the first nationally standardized wage rates for this work. The Employers Association of Liverpool stood apart from this Board until 1 January 1920; and internecine quarrels among the seamen's unions, exacerbated by Havelock Wilson's unyieldingly individual style of leadership, continued for another decade. Nevertheless a new structure of labour relations in the shipping industry had been born. Likewise the adoption of 'ca' canny' methods by railwaymen on Merseyside in November 1917 forced the pace of negotiations after the National Union of Railwaymen and Railway Executive failed to resolve a demand of 10*s*. and an offer of 5*s*. and bonuses. J. H. Thomas called the Liverpool action 'anarchy'; but 6*s*. was won, plus bonuses.[12]

The war at home extended beyond industrial management. After the sinking of the *Lusitania* in 1915, claiming 1,198 lives, *The Times* signalled for reprisals against an enemy of 'demented Barbarians'.[13] A polite start had been made in Liverpool when enemy aliens were expelled from the Cotton Association and Exchange News-room.[14] The sinking of the *Lusitania*, with its predominantly Liverpudlian crew, awoke sharper tempers. German submarines came within five miles of Liverpool during the war, and Houston sought to encourage the arming of merchant ships by offering £2,000 for each submarine they sank, up to a total of fifty'. The 'hideous modern Hun' was like the pirate of old, according to Houston. He deserved summary execution: 'legal subtleties and diplomatic niceties' could not deter such crimes.[15] The sinking of the *Lusitania* also moved Lord Derby to be explicit: 'This country calls no longer for men to fight an honourable foe. It calls for men to hunt down a race of cold-blooded murderers.'[16]

Wrecking two hundred German shops on Merseyside occupied three days. Enemy aliens were interned for their safety; but the City Council resolved not to recognize their claims for damage and the Cotton Association resolved that no member should trade directly or indirectly with Britain's enemies for ten years after an armistice.[17] Liverpool's Conservative M.P.s were most aggressive on such issues, seeking to root out alien directors or shareholders from British companies, and to restrict business with Germany after the war. The intention was to 'make it difficult from them to recuperate, destroy their credit, take over their world trade'. These notions arose naturally from the circumstances of the blockade and patriotic zeal; they also attuned to the ambitions of erstwhile Tariff

Reformers. Significantly it was a Free Trade Liberal, Richard Holt, who predicted that a Germany economically impoverished by punitive tariffs or indemnities would become more militaristic; but the war witnessed a flight from liberal values on all sides. When Holt expressed his preference for 'perfect freedom of contract' instead of wage boards and like controls, the Labour benches erupted with cries of 'Worst paid labour' and 'Grind them down'. His defence of a voluntary system of military service was equally rudely received by the 'Tory-jingo knock out blow lot'. Chaloner, the Abercromby M.P., asserted that conscientious objectors 'should be deprived of all rights of citizenship'.[18] Pacifists were despised. Thus employees at Bibby's Oil Mills struck rather than work with conscientious objectors, and even George Wise needed to refute rumours that he had German ancestors.[19]

By 1916 seven hundred from Wise's Bible Class had enlisted, but the Protestants' political work continued. The Church Association denounced the Government's relations with the Vatican, and Wise accused Southern Irishmen of cowardice and treachery.[20] Only illness pared his energy. From 1914 two curates aided his mission, first H. D. Longbottom, and second T. B. Wilmot, a Kensitite. Wise died on 29 November 1917. For a year the Protestant Reformers tolerated Wilmot before the church enticed Longbottom from a ministry at Leytonstone. In August 1919, at St. Domingo Pit, he affirmed that Protestantism 'thrives in the strong winds of opposition'.[21]

Wise was dead; other faces disappeared too. In 1918 Sir Thomas Hughes vacated the chairmanship of the Licensing Bench after twenty-six years; and Stanley Rogers left Westminster Road Congregational Church after forty-one years. In the constituencies D. F. Pennefather succeeded Kyffin-Taylor in 1915;[22] and J. S. Rankin replaced Marshall Hall in 1916.[23] The Conservative agent since 1886, Thompson, also retired. His assistant, Edward Murch, replaced him. Salvidge always recognized Thompson's 'genius for electioneering', but he had found him personally unctuous.[24] Salvidge worked better with Murch, who was his man completely and made others bristle. Inhabiting a different dark room, T. P. O'Connor became President of the Trade Board of Film Censors in the year of the Easter Rebellion.[25]

O'Connor had held high hopes at the beginning of the war, that 'this War is a War for the liberation of the masses of the German people as well as the liberation of Europe generally'. Ireland was the first, and greatest, of his disappointments in this respect. Kitchener's refusal to countenance brigades specifically made up from the Irish Volunteers dampened recruitment from Ireland; and, with the conscription issue pending, rebellion erupted in 1916. O'Connor asserted that 'the Sinn Fein rebellion was largely an anti-Conscription rebellion'; but an exact determination of cause was soon academic: 'When that rebellion started, 90 per cent of the people of Ireland condemned and repudiated it; but when repression was in progress the sympathies of the 90 per cent were on the other side.' The note of resignation in O'Connor's voice thereafter was understandable. As he pointed out in 1920, he had been making the same speeches to Parliament for forty years, against coercion and for a free and constitutionally united Ireland. He was now a witness, not to the triumph of his ideals, but to 'the bloody harvest'.[26]

In Liverpool there was already a post-Victorian generation, looking with new eyes. Between the young and old lay a passage of death. Amid the crape, juveniles excited unfavourable comment. The Head Constable admonished the looseness of young girls. American soldiers conquered them by cash; but some married, 'economic romances' O'Mara called them.[27] Boys were busy too. In 1915 Liverpool's Juvenile Court registered a 32 per cent increase in cases. The magistrates and Education Committee blamed a decay in parental control. Their recommendations reflected the new and old criminology, the remedial and deterrent schools. They encouraged scout movements and other counter-attractions; but they sought to birch all young male offenders and to increase the prescribed strokes.[28] Although by 1925 the total offences, 9,596, were the lowest (except for 1915) since 1905, 56 per cent involved young persons. A new society has new crimes: the injured in Liverpool's road accidents surpassed the number convicted of drunkenness by 1929.[29] Modern facilities multiplied: the number of telephones in Liverpool increased from 19,042 in 1912 to 41,098 in 1931. In suburbia Charles Pooter of Holloway was maturing into George F. Babbit of Zenith.

The decline of the Liberal plutocracy

Changes of outlook between generations and their impression on politics resist incisive descriptions, but some traces can be drawn. In this case the war was only one of many influences. A generation is commonly defined as about thirty years, and this is the world that requires reflection if we pause and take stock of the changes in post-war Liverpool. One frequent lament is that the new generation is spiritually inferior to the old but we might examine this adage through the record of one leading Liverpool family and the light which it sheds on the society about it.

Beatrice Webb, visiting her sister-in-law's, the Holts, in 1899, had considered the family 'commonplace in outlook and mediocre in ability'. Most of the new generation—Robert Holt had five sons and three daughters—seemed without a sense of personal fulfilment through public service. Inherited wealth had incubated private vanity and a passion for frivolous pleasure. In fact there is little evidence for this sharp condemnation. It is true that Ted Holt, who was twenty-one in 1899, emigrated to become a rancher in New Zealand, but this was hardly a soft option, and every generation has its wanderers or adventurers. Another brother, Phil, who was twenty-three in 1899 and not known for his steady application, nevertheless volunteered to fight in South Africa and then returned to qualify as a barrister. He eventually threw up a legal career to enter the family firm of cotton brokers, with his elder brother, Bob. This conformed remarkably to the pattern of the previous generation where, out of several sons, most would turn to business, with or without inspiration. Usually only one carried the family standard deep into public or political life. In the case of Robert Holt's sons this was Richard, who was thirty-one years of age at the time of the Webbs' visit. He shortly proved himself as ready to take on public responsibilities as many of his father's generation. In fact, by entering Parliament in 1907, he demonstrated that he was less shy of the wider political world; in addition he served as president of the Free Trade Union and as chairman of the Mersey Docks and Harbour Board. A similar account can be made for that other representative family of Unitarian plutocrats, the Rathbones. Eleanor Rathbone held notions of public work quite as strong as her father, William; likewise Herbert Rathbone followed on from his father, Philip.

There was also continuity between the generations through the religious community to which these families belonged. With a sense of almost inevitable succession Richard Holt in 1903, 1915, and 1918, became president of the Liverpool Domestic Mission, chairman of the Ullet Road Chapel Council, and president of the British and Foreign Unitarian Association. Changes none the less had taken place within the Liverpool Unitarian community and were registered in Robert and Richard Holt's lives. Quite how close the Unitarian community had been bound up with the Holts can be illustrated in the translation of the chapel from Renshaw Street to new premises on Ullet Road in 1899, where Robert Holt had built his own house in 1878. Betty, Robert Holt's second daughter, even married the minister in 1913. But both Robert and Richard Holt were conscious that others did not seem 'to hold to the faith of their ancestors or to value the position . . . as members of one of the old Unitarian families of this town'. The meeting that determined the new chapel's character in 1899 was 'unsatisfactory and disappointing' and made Robert Holt 'apprehensive of the Future of the Congregation'. White surplices were adopted for the choir, but a liturgy prepared by the minister, Dr. Klein, was barely considered before rejection—clearly an interest or competence in these matters was generally moribund. Most disheartening of all, the congregation decided to name their new building, Ullet Road Chapel, rather than Sefton Park Unitarian Church; and Robert Holt felt keenly the pusillanimity of this decision.

He was not relieved by what he discovered elsewhere. In 1900, when revisiting Rochdale, where the Holt family originated, Robert Holt was told that though a loyal congregation of ordinary working folk remained 'the old well-to-do families who used to attend have died and the younger branches are mostly indifferent. It seems the same story at all our Churches.' The Ullet Road Chapel soon bore out this foreboding. In 1903 the disappointed Dr. Klein gave up trying to influence the congregation and resigned. Richard Holt, with the vigour of a young man, thought that Klein had not tried hard enough, while his father, in his last years, prayed that Klein's successor would 'bring the congregation together with a little more fellowship and common interests than have late characterized our church work'. In fact the involvement of the great families with chapel life continued to drain away, in a steady, unspectacular fashion. After one service, just before Christmas 1924, Richard Holt could record as an event that he had sat between Sir John Brunner and Hugh Rathbone—'such of the old fashioned Unitarian gentry as still survive'.

Two great changes did separate Robert and Richard Holt, however strongly they shared other traits. These were their education and financial positions. It was usual for those of Robert Holt's generation to go straight into business, into the family concern directly or into an allied venture. Thus Sir William Forwood's father had disabused him of ambitions of Cambridge, arguing that 'a university training would spoil me for a business career'. Part of Robert Holt's timidity in public life outside Liverpool stemmed from this deprivation, a feeling of being only 'half-educated'. The attitudes of the merchant shipowning and broking classes in Liverpool changed almost completely in this respect, and the passage of their offspring through the great public schools and universities became familiar. It was a sign of the times in 1904 when Robert Holt's second son, Bob, organized the first reunion dinner of Wykehamists in Liverpool, and about forty attended. An artless snobbery perhaps rubbed off on their fathers. Robert Holt proudly noted the 'earnest cultured gentlemanly manner' of his eldest son in public debates. He also discussed the proposed Ullet Road chapel in this fashion in 1893:

> Our new church should be different to other places of worship in the neighbourhood and we suggest for serious consideration a reproduction of one of the College chapels. Red-brick outside and inside the large stately hall appearance: with handsome fittings and good seating. Also an excellent vestibule—for monuments etc.—but not to repeat the church form of architecture as at Hope St. which is not suited to our service.

Taxes began to bite this class for the first time in the twentieth century, especially in the post-war period. This might seem a promiscuous mis-statement considering the sumptuous style which Robert Holt's family inherited and maintained, with their large well-staffed houses in Liverpool, their holiday homes in the Lake District and Wales, their generous charitable gifts, and their business interrupted with regular bouts of expensive sport—golf, polo, and shooting. In 1919 Richard Holt remained quite capable of calling in Agnew's and buying a Gainsborough landscape that took his fancy for £350; and in 1925, without thought of cost, he donated £1,000 towards a war memorial in the cloister of his old school, Winchester. He had noted of the Ocean Steam Ship Company's general meeting in 1916 that 'the shareholders were so pleased'; and with reason—steamer earnings amounted to £1¼ million and a bonus of 10 per cent was announced, on top of a dividend of 25 per cent. But these days of swollen profits did not last: the company's debts multiplied in the 1920s as the trading position worsened. In 1923 Richard Holt sold his London home, 63 Lowndes Square. He was no longer in Parliament, but this had not provoked the sale: 'with present taxation I cannot afford it'. This was a phrase never found in Robert Holt's diary, but it began to recur in Richard's, particularly with regard to luxuries, of which politics was becoming a notable one. The possibility of general elections, as in 1924, began to be feared because of the financial strain, and by-election contests, as in North Cumberland in 1926, were deplored: 'A beastly nuisance—three weeks hard work—£800 expense at least and . . . a jolly holiday interrupted too.'

In Robert Holt's working life standard rate in income tax was below 1*s*. in the pound before 1900, and for half the time it was 6*d*. or under. Between the wars it never fell below 4*s*. and for nine years it was 5*s*. or more. Below £2,000 earned income the standard rate prevailed; thereafter supertax or surtax was imposed, taking toll at various stages from 9*d*. to 9*s* 6*d*. on the excess in some five income brackets up to £30,000. In 1913–14 the exchequer netted £43·9 million (26·8 per cent of total receipts) from income tax, and £3·3 million (2 per cent) from supertax or surtax; in 1927–8 these categories produced £259·4 million (37·9 per cent) and £68·5 million (10 per cent), and in 1937–8 £297·9 million (35·6 per cent) and £57·1 million (6·7 per cent).

With a subject as exceptionally rich as Richard Holt there was so much fat left on that the ribs would take time to show. It was not the same with the moderately wealthy who in pre-war days were able to cut considerable figures in Liverpool society and politics. The cachet of assured position in Liverpool society had been membership of the Wellington Rooms, which were designed by Edmund Aiken with Adam-style decorations and opened at the end of the Napoleonic wars. There each year some five or six exclusive balls had been held, Liverpool having a social circle, punctuated with a debutante season and other fancies, quite like London. In the nineteenth century the only remarkable changes in this annual round were fashions in consumption and appearance. Crinoline dresses and poke bonnets went out, champagne suppers came in; but by the 1920s there were more important trends to notice than that men's beards had been shaved and women's hair bobbed or shingled. A style of life was at stake. In November 1922 the Wellington Club's trustees decided to sell the premises to a syndicate which proposed to inaugurate general entertainments. Richard Holt regretted that 'Liverpool society is so depleted and spiritless that they could not keep the club going as heretofore in spite of the heavy increases in expenses through rates and general charges'; but many members failed to share his concern. They 'desired nothing except to get their money out'. However, in the contract of sale the club had reserved the right to use the rooms six times a year at £25 per night, and Richard Holt mounted a further rescue operation. He organized a new Wellington Club with a scratch committee and succeeded in attracting 250 members with the promise of three balls each year. The first, in January 1923, was a social and financial success: but the popular use to which the new owners put the Wellington Rooms began to be felt. By March 1927 Richard Holt thought it time to call the experiment to an end: 'the place is filthy and scarcely fit for gentlefolk. It must be given up and I dare say I shall never go there again. It is painful to think of this collapse of Liverpool Society and to reflect on what the place was thirty years ago.'

Through Richard Holt's eyes it is possible to witness the erasure of a traditional way of life, particularly as he made such great efforts to withstand the process. This is also true of politics. In Richard Holt's career the extinction of the historic Liberal party is embossed, like a memento of Pompeii trapped in Vesuvius's lava. In August 1897 when Richard and Elizabeth Holt had returned from their honeymoon to his father's house at Sefton Park, some fifty West Derby Liberals called with a surprise gift of a silver salver, to which the newly-weds replied with refreshments of sandwiches, cake, and champagne. Likewise, following his first parliamentary contest in 1903, Richard Holt had given a reception for some 700 Liberal party workers and the then leader of the Liverpool Liberal party, Edward Evans, had presented a diamond and pearl necklace with pendant, on their behalf, to Elizabeth Holt. This relationship is not easy to describe—to call it deferential gives it an ugly ring of condescension on the one hand and of servility on the other, without paying regard to simple expressions of courtesy and respect—but it mostly disappeared after the war.

The erosion occurred from both sides. The politicians altered. In 1929 Richard Holt attended the meeting of general election candidates in London and was 'horrified by the type of man chosen as Liberal candidate—mostly professionals—no one of any standing so far as I can judge'. Liberal politics had been too long in the grip of 'clever men of bad character'. Richard Holt now found it difficult to get his opinions published in the press; likewise, Parliament seemed to have become closed, the forum only of those who were prepared to act as satellites of some 'big politician'. The cause of this, in Holt's opinion, lay with the Lloyd George Coalition—'a gang of men united by no common principle of public policy'—wherein the 'villainy', the 'roguery and the dirty ways of the Welshmen' had free play. 'He has been a bad influence in public life', Richard Holt recorded of Lloyd George in 1923; 'vain—spiteful—treacherous—untruthful and dishonest—the man is evil. How can he live as we know he does live on any income he has honestly come by?' But Lloyd George not only lived well, he also bought power or, at least, in 1926–7 he bought the Liberal party when its financial position and electoral prospects were so desperate that it would take money on Lloyd George's terms. Not only Lloyd George's strength, Asquith's weakness was also corrupting. Liberalism has not much backbone or integrity when it was personified by such as Asquith and his wife. The former, once noble, now worthless, ended his days 'living on the charitable subscriptions of persons many of whom were political opponents'; the latter was simply 'awful—covered with paint—a dreadful women whom one is ashamed to see in the house'.

The politicians showed themselves unworthy of the people's confidence. The people had also let down the politicians. 'To me', wrote Richard Holt in 1919, 'it seems that after the war the one thing needful is steady attention to the "daily round—the common task"; and yet apparently it is the one thing no one can do.' The attitude that resulted in strikes for shorter hours and more money Holt found 'amazing'; but he knew who was to blame. The Labour party, he wrote, 'is fundamentally a class movement representing the wish of the manual workers when organized in Trade Unions to get the leading places in Government filled by "our lot". These people look on big places as perquisites in which all classes of the community should get their share:—they do not conceive of the office as a trust to be held by the most competent man.'

Amid this dereliction of politicians and people it was up to Richard Holt himself to do what he could to preserve Liberal values. So far as economic and financial management was concerned he set about this task with a will. In 1914 he had organized a parliamentary corps of 'businessmen and some survivors of the Cobden-Bright school of thought against the ill-considered and socialistic tendencies of the Government finance'. Holt noted that 'a great many of the Cabinet secretly agreed with us—*inter alia* [*sic*]—McKenna and John Burns'; and they succeeded in knocking a penny off the income tax. But Holt recognized the magnitude of their over-all struggle: 'We have certainly travelled a long way from the old Liberal principle of "retrenchment" and I deeply regret it. The more I see of socialistic developments the less I like them—the stronger I feel in favour of leaving individuals the maximum of personal freedom including the right to make a thorough mess of their own affairs.'

The First World War instead made a mess of Liberal finance. Selective tariffs were imposed; and the Government continuously overspent, while at the same time regulating prices in 'foolish attempts . . . to please the wage-earning classes'. The burst of the post-war boom in 1921 gave Richard Holt some hope: 'the financial situation is getting too serious and difficult for quackery, and economic reality is beginning to assert itself. Trade is very bad, prices falling and unemployment is widespread for which I see no remedy but lower wages, better work, and lower prices. The great dole system is on its last legs as money cannot be found any longer for this expenditure—the taxpayer is at the end of his tether.' It was time to eradicate that 'semi-socialistic element attached to the Liberal party who believe that the State ought to support the unfortunate and incompetent . . .'. In fact while Richard Holt demanded a return to 'simple principles', of free trade, a balanced budget, 'a period of sobriety and low taxation', the Liberal party nationally sought deliverance through 'stunt producers' like Lloyd George—first his 'preposterous land policy' of 1925, then his 'reckless promise' in 1929 to cure unemployment within twelve months, involving 'all sorts of public works financed by a loan which will only add to the difficulties of all legitimate trade by enhancing prices and wages'.

The fortunes of the Liberal party nationally by this time had moved beyond Holt's always marginal influence, but between 1920 and 1928 he was president of the Liverpool Liberal Federal Council, in effect the local Liberal leader as his father had been forty years before. He sought to revitalize the party by an insistence that Liberals adhere to their principles and turn aside from the degrading quarrels of their leaders; but in fact he hastened the local party's decline by having too little faith in Liberal principles apart from those of finance. Under Richard Holt the Liverpool Liberal party lost all claim to be a party of franchise and constitutional reforms. Votes for women failed to interest him; indeed, where 'flappers' ' votes were concerned, positively upset him, though he admitted that their cause was 'unanswerable as a matter of abstract justice'. More generally Holt doubted the wisdom of the principle of self-determination having observed the 'social convulsion' that followed the Bolshevik Revolution in Russia and the power of the Labour party in Britain, and the 'uprising of the inferior civilization against the superior' that followed the nationalist successes in Ireland and China. Holt, therefore, not only stood by while the Liverpool Liberal party's old connection with Nationalist and Labour groups was snapped, he welcomed the severance. He laid down his electoral strategy in 1921 with pitiful pride and myopia: 'The Liberal party must concentrate their efforts on the outer districts and rally the better class of citizen against the Irish-Labour efforts to exploit the ratepayer and the Tory dictatorship of Salvidge.' The Liverpool Liberal party had become a conservative, class-bound, suburban rump, excluded from all vital areas of power and interest in the city.

In using the Holt family as a mirror of change over generations in Liverpool various features have emerged, but two are outstanding.[30] One is a personal account. In Richard Holt there was too much consciousness about tradition for comfort, adaptation, and survival. The public service of the old Liberal Unitarian families was not so much exhausted as superannuated. The political world had left them behind. This announces the second conclusion, a commentary on post-war party struggles. The historic Liberal party was no longer a contender for power in Liverpool.

Salvidge meets new conditions

The political moods of the post-war world had been glimpsed in the by-election in Liverpool's Abercromby constituency in June 1917, following Chaloner's elevation as Lord Gisborough. Salvidge engineered the nomination of Lord Edward Stanley, Derby's twenty-two-year-old son.[31] He remained in military service; but the National Federation of Discharged and Disabled Sailors and Soldiers promoted an opponent, F. B. Hughes, who campaigned against the Act for the re-examination of discharged men.[32] The N.F.D.D.S.S. also advocated comprehensive pensions, training, and employment for ex-servicemen; and Hughes criticized 'unwarranted' rises in prices. Optimistically he courted businessmen, 'because the war is costing 8 millions a day and ought to be run on better business lines'. The N.S.F.U. and two buccaneerish Liberal M.P.s, Hogge and Pringle, supported him; but the Coalition Liberals, and Labour 'patriots' like Sexton, supported Stanley, 'the Government candidate', as Lloyd George styled him. Irish Nationalists officially remained unattached.

The W.M.C.A. was active in repudiating Hughes's claim to be 'a soldier of democracy against a soldier of autocracy',[33] but oratory moved few votes. Hughes, christened 'Two-minutes Hughes' on account of his concise exposition, was a chatterbox compared with his twice-wounded opponent, who never appeared during the course of the election. Stanley's published address discounted premature peace but promised employment for the vigorous and care for the wounded. A feminine trio, of Stanley pedigree, decorated his platform, but MacPherson, the Under-Secretary for War, did some ardent speaking and the knightly boss, Salvidge, was busy. He needed to cook the accounts when they exceeded the allowed election expenditure; but his office prepared a handbill alleging that eleven of Hughes's nominators were aliens, upon which his 'ex-soldier support melted away'. Salvidge was satisfied when Stanley won 2,224 votes against 794; but he estimated post-bellum prospects cheerlessly. A 'nasty strident, undisciplined note among the opposition' made Salvidge contemplate events in Russia.[34]

Salvidge was also alarmed by Electoral Reform. Leslie Scott argued that proportional representation would reduce the power of the caucus, and guarantee fairness and stability in the vital period of post-war reconstruction.[35] Though Scott claimed that he had always favoured proportional representation, Salvidge found his opinions 'disgraceful' in their ingratitude to the organization that returned him to Parliament. Salvidge resisted any attempt by the Coalition to 'throttle' Unionist caucuses as if they were 'unclean things'. They were the 'vitalizing power' which protected 'the people with any capital or interest at stake' and prevented 'demagogues' from manipulating elections.[36]

Salvidge, and various trade associations, defended the business vote before the Boundary Commission in 1917.[37] Salvidge also refused to experiment with proportional representation. In the City Council he defended the 'poor man's' ability to enter Parliament, since single-member constituencies were cheaper than electoral provinces;[38] but he argued more dexterously before the Assistant Boundary Commissioners, picturing what would happen if Nationalists had to campaign in 'the Protestant districts of Everton and Kirkdale', and vice versa. The Nationalists agreed and, except F. E. Smith and Scott, Liverpool's M.P.s followed Salvidge's direction.[39]

Parliamentary elections, 1918–19

The General Election, in December 1918, nevertheless exhibited new features in Liverpool. The recent enfranchisement of adult males, after six months residence, and of many women aged over thirty, increased Liverpool's electorate to 344,816, or four times that of 1910; and redistribution, based on the antiquated 1911 census, increased the constituencies from nine to eleven.[40] Abercromby was absorbed into Exchange but new divisions, Edge Hill, Wavertree, and Fairfield, were created. Changes also occurred in the local Conservative party. Petrie was ill and incapable of exerting even a marginal check on Salvidge, who became leader of the Council and, in 1919, chairman of the Constitutional Association.[41] F. E. Smith told Lloyd George that the W.M.C.A. and Salvidge were '*Pivotal.* The Tory Party cannot refuse what they endorse.'[42] Although fascinated by Lloyd George,[43] Salvidge deferred to none in Liverpool. He was willing to allow Coalition Liberals one or two seats, so long as he dictated the allocation. Wavertree and Walton, with sizable Liberal electorates, Salvidge was prepared to concede; but he would not tolerate a demand for Wavertree, Fairfield and Exchange. Accordingly Major Cohen defeated a couponed-Liberal in Fairfield;[44] and all constituencies (except Scotland) returned Unionists.

Liverpool retained much singularity. Pennefather in Kirkdale, Harmood-Banner in Everton, Rutherford in Edge Hill, Houston in West Toxteth, Smith in West Derby, even Dr. Nathan Raw[45] in Wavertree, all were to some extent political Protestants. In Walton, Warden Chilcott, Smith's yachting friend, succeeded him where Bonar Law was not attracted;[46] and in Exchange sectarianism glowed as Scott defeated Harford, whose nominators included four priests. One trade unionist remarked that Evertonians 'were still blaming the Pope for causing the war'; but the Diocesan Council, with the Free Church Council, appealed for sectarian peace. What fraction of the Unionists' majorities derived from sectarianism is indeterminable. Pennefather, fiercely defending Ulster Protestantism, polled 10,380 votes against 5,012. Nevertheless his Labour opponent suspected that 'the religious bogey is nearly dead' and, when the Church Association questioned candidates about ritualism, Prayer Book revision, and Vatican diplomacy, it found that 'many expressed ignorance on the subjects at issue'.[47]

Ignorance does not disable political expression. It can strengthen its assertion. A consummation of xenophobic prejudice was achieved during the general election in the campaign to extend the Aliens Restriction Order of 1914. Disembowelling dachshunds was not enough when alien waiters, domestic servants, teachers, shopkeepers, and their families remained to be deported or debarred. F. E. Smith warmed to his theme when addressing a Liverpool audience once more:

> I tell you that when the history of the last twenty years comes to be written it will be found that of every twenty Germans who settled in this country eighteen were spies. Clear them out. That is the policy of the Coalition Government. (Cheers). At this moment there are waiting in Holland about 20,000 aliens—Poles, Russians, and persons of mixed blood and German fusion, with their tickets ready to come back to this country . . . Here is a great question of national policy. Do we want them? ('No'.) What is the good after winning this great war if we cannot keep England for the English? (Cheers.) What do we want with the waiters who were spying and with the professors who were teaching and spying all the time?[48]

For many businessmen the dismantling of war-time controls was the priority. Liverpool numbered among its Conservative M.P.s some rugged exponents of *laissez-faire* capitalism. The shipping millionaire, Robert Houston, declared: 'It must be remembered that it was not State control, it was individual effort and individual enterprise that has made this nation what it is.' In pursuit of national retrenchment he recommended not a capital levy but 'the abolition of all Employment Exchanges and their costly staffs'. Houston's solution to his own, rather than the nation's, financial problems was only discovered after his death. He had established domiciliary rights in Jersey in order to avoid death duties. Among his colleagues, in the patriotic flush of 1914, Rutherford had been predictably forward in inveighing against profiteering in Government contracts; but after September 1915, when the excess profits duty was introduced, he surrendered the limelight to Pennefather, Scott, and, especially, Harmood-Banner, who thundered: 'A more infamous, a more unenlightened, extravagant, ruinous, demoralizing measure has never been brought before the country.' In truth, there was much to criticize about the duty but, in the six years of its incidence, it produced 25 per cent of the exchequer's total revenue. As for Harmood-Banner personally, though he was able to buy Richard Holt's London house in 1923, his mining interests—inherited from his father-in-law—were increasingly unremunerative. He remained chairman of the Finance Committee of Liverpool Corporation, and he recommended to the nation's financial managers, as well as the repeal of the 'immoral' excess profits duty, a controlled inflation to reduce the National Debt, printing more money and lowering interest rates and income tax.[49]

Money matters, then, in one form or another, dominated the 1918 General Election. Coalition candidates threatened to make a war profiteer of the whole nation by demanding drastic reparations from Germany. The Labour party embarked on the equally hazardous course of distinguishing the illegitimate from the legitimate profits made at home. This was less generally popular and, though it was eventually crystallized in the issue of the Capital Levy in the 1922 and 1923 General Elections, leading men of the Labour party—Ramsay MacDonald and Philip Snowden—feared its electoral consequences. There was discord concerning election issues but, so far as Labour was concerned, singlemindedness about election strategy. Nationally there were no compacts with another party. Labour's independence from the Liberal party was a matter of fact, not a matter of debate, although Richard Holt's speculation remained to be proved, that 'many Liberals are drifting to the Labour party, bitten with the idea of State interference, and as a consequence of the destruction of political interest due to the so called party truce and the infernal coalition'.[50]

The Liverpool Labour Party[51] contested seven divisions in 1918 and the N.F.D.D.S.S. fought Everton. Under 60 per cent of the nation's electorate voted (including an average of only one serviceman in four); and the Liverpool Labour party polled 36,087 votes (41,866 counting Everton) without success. In 1917 Alderman W. A. Robinson had become leader of the Liverpool Labour party, although the secretary, Fred Hoey, was considered the stronger presence.[52] Hoey had censured Sexton's collaboration with other parties in recruitment;[53] and, although Sexton was supported by the Dockers, Seamen and Ships' Stewards Unions, which seceded from the L.T.C. until September 1918, his voice in Liverpool was muted upon his election for St. Helens.[54] During the war the L.L.R.C. and L.T.C. had co-operated and grown in public confidence from their work concerning rising prices and military service;[55] and the two bodies merged in 1921. Marriage did not bring harmony but it facilitated an eventual dissemination of constituency associations.[56] In this the party locally reflected the party at large. By adopting a new constitution in 1918 Labour aspired to become a national party with a mass individual membership and a network of branches, but the trade unions' power at the centre was recognized, with their block votes and money wielding the influence at conference, on the party executive, and over the selection of candidates.

Early in 1919 West Derby fell vacant when F. E. Smith became Lord Birkenhead upon his elevation to the woolsack. Many applicants, including Christabel Pankhurst, wanted a safe seat; but Sir Reginald ('Blinker') Hall, the ex-director of Naval Intelligence, succeeded. He had spent thirty-six of his then forty-eight years in the navy, crowning his war-work by the decipher of the Zimmerman telegram, which had given Americans the final spur to war in 1917. But in domestic party politics Hall was an unenlightened beginner. A non-Tory was 'either a German, a Sinn Feiner or a Bolshevist'.[57] His combination of diehard denseness and religious fervour established his fitness to represent Liverpool. He galvanized nationalism and scorned the League of Nations. Otherwise his speeches contained stock phrases about reconstruction. Hall's adversary, the L.T.C.'s president, Councillor George Nelson, spoke out against conscription, food taxes, and Tariff Reform; but many Liberals embraced Hall. Of the 31,310 electors in this mixed suburb, two-fifths were women and 7,000 were absent. Nelson cut the majority from 6,004 to 1,392, but the poll decreased from 55·1 to 34·3 per cent. Few seemed enthusiastic about their right to vote or, as Carlyle once phrased it, their 'twenty-thousandth part of a master of tongue-fence in National Palaver'.[58]

Industrial unrest and the police strike

Notwithstanding the West Derby by-election, 1919 was not a passionless year in

Liverpool. Tobacco and food rationing (except of sugar) ended, but mounting discontent among miners and strikes in most ports led some to think that revolution approached. The Cabinet was informed that seven hundred rifles were concealed in Liverpool and, as it debated the organization of a citizens' army to guard against industrial sabotage and class war, ministers presumed that neither the Labour party nor the trade unions could be relied upon to take part against insurgent members of their class.[59] This misrepresented many on the Labour side—Sexton, for example, in his maiden parliamentary speech, remonstrated against Communist trade unionists, those 'honest fanatics' whose cure was 'worse than the disease'[60]—but even policemen grew fanatical as their standard of living declined.[61] A Liverpool branch of the National Union of Police and Prison Officers had started in 1918 during the Metropolitan police strike; but in 1919 the Government drastically limited their right to combine. The L.T.C. considered sympathetic action, despite opposition from those with memories of police 'brutality' in 1911; and the N.U.P.P.O. called its strike on 31 July.[62] Conservative newspapers cried 'mutiny';[63] but the strikers, many of them ex-servicemen, bravely sacrificed jobs and pension rights in the cause.[64]

Tanks, warships, and 2,500 troops arrived in Liverpool and 730 special constables were enrolled. The London Road–Scotland Road area became a war zone. The Riot Act was read; one man was shot dead; and pubs and shops were plundered, to the tune of £150,000. One thief observed 'respectable-looking men and women' among the looters. Apparently not everyone shared Cynthia Asquith's inhibitions: she considered herself unimaginative in not knowing how to take advantage of the absence of police during the London strike in the previous year.[65] Three hundred and seventy alleged looters were tried in Liverpool, fifty in Birkenhead. Rain, and military strength, brought quiet. The strike's zenith was reached on 4 August—1,056 strikers from a force of 19,000 Metropolitan policemen, 57 from 1,170 in the City of London, 118 from 1,365 in Birmingham, 932 from 1,860 in Liverpool, 106 from 225 in Birkenhead, and 63 from 77 in Bootle.[66] Apart from one policeman in Wallasey and seventy-four prison officers in London and Birmingham, none struck elsewhere.

In proportion to its force Merseyside was the key. Outside authorities placed the worst construction upon this fact. The Commissioner of the Metropolitan Police, General Sir Nevil Macready, wrote:

> I fancy the high proportion of men of the Liverpool Police who went on strike was due to the presence of many Irishmen in the force, a class of men who are always apt to be carried away by any wave of enthusiasm. During the time I was Commissioner I refused to enrol Irishmen in the force on the grounds that in their own country the Royal Irish Constabulary offered openings to any who wished to become the upholders of law and order.[67]

To add to their burdens Liverpudlians became pedestrian as tramwaymen also struck. This was a sectional as much as sympathetic action;[68] but militant dockers and railwaymen raised protests against the Government's attack on trade unionism. A Strike Committee directed affairs and a radical display seemed possible—2,000 painters struck on 13 August; a bakers' strike withdrew bread supplies; and various Liverpool unions mooted a three-day strike from 20 August.

The authorities none the less were adamant against reinstatement and the police strikers were isolated by the Desborough Report recommending improvements in pay and conditions. Sexton—a member of the Desborough Commission, as well as of the Liverpool Watch Committee—announced that the N.U.D.L. would resist a token strike; and warehousemen and the District Federation of Shipbuilding and Engineering Trades (representing 40,000 men) were of like mind.[69] Salvidge, behind Liverpool's resistance, was flattered by Lloyd George's disingenuous observation that this was 'perhaps the turning-point in the Labour movement', redirecting it 'from Bolshevist and Direct Actionist courses to legitimate Trade Unionism'.[70] In November the N.U.P.P.O. reported 3,000 members idle. Alternative employment was scarce and the L.T.C. and L.P. unavailingly lobbied Parliament and the Home Office about reinstatement through the 1920s.[71]

Municipal politics and surviving sectarianism

Three police strikers were Labour candidates in the 1919 municipal elections. Two, Charles Burden and Jack Hayes (the N.U.P.P.O.'s general secretary), were elected. Ten gains were made altogether, which gave Labour twenty councillors and two aldermen. Salvidge had shivered at the ease of Labour's earlier by-election victories, on an anti-profiteering platform; but a sober appraisal revealed Labour's insecurity. Two wards were won on minority votes in three-cornered fights; some Labourites ostentatiously declared themselves Communists, proclaiming the need for strike action; and only one ward featured Labour and Nationalist competitors.[72] Irish votes were unpredictable without Nationalist candidates—Harford recommended Labour because it championed national self-determination, but Taggart resisted Labour's education programme. Sixteen Nationalists formed the weakest party. The anti-socialist Coalition predominated, in the shape of twenty-five Liberal and eighty Conservative members; and in 1920 they won resoundingly as Salvidge took the offensive, for 'Constitutionalism v. Revolution and Anarchy and Labour Extremists'. The Coalition convinced the electorate, especially women, that Labour's success would 'add still further to the burdens we are already carrying'.[73] None the less Salvidge, who became a K.B.E. in 1920, was not absolutely comforted. The Conservatives' association with the mercurial Lloyd George disturbed many Orangemen, and the Protestant Councillor, Walker, was re-elected.

For the Protestants, as for any other section of society, the problem was to regroup after the dislocation of the war. Longbottom's followers in the Protestant Reformers' Memorial Church held an undying interest in Catholic and Irish questions. By 1921 the Church's activities evoked shades of the pre-war Wiseite dynamism. The allied adult recreational and educational facilities, and boys' and girls' guilds, penetrated deeply into the lives of ordinary working people in Kirkdale. The Church's secretary, Richard Briggs, informed Salvidge:

> There are fourteen organizations connected with the Church, and on Sunday afternoon every place is fully occupied, and a gathering of about 700 men meet in the Church. The Sunday School, comprising 800 scholars, is crowded out, also a Primary class in a small room and two women's classes. During the week Christian Endeavour Societies meet, also Debating and Literary Societies. We have also an Economic Study Class to counteract the extreme element of the Labour Party. This class holds open-air meetings almost every night throughout the city and district. We are not in a position to pay an assistant, all the work being carried on by a band of loyal workers, bearing all their own out-of-pocket expenses.[74]

By contrast the established engine of Protestant power within the Conservative party, the W.M.C.A., was run down. The Edge Hill M.P., Rutherford, might affirm that the W.M.C.A. still represented Protestantism, but the warpaint dressed a decaying frame. By 1916 the W.M.C.A. had only three or four thousand subscribing members; and after the war the twenty-five branches were considered 'skeletons'. 'Tory jingoism died on the battlefield', it was observed, and the young were joining trade unions. There were other alarming portents. Under one-fifth of Liverpudlians were churchgoers. No more than in the Victorian period could church attendances be interpreted as an exact index of inner spirituality or of sectarian impulses in politics, but the trend towards a more secular society had deepened and the pace of change had accelerated. In six decades from 1851 church attendances in Liverpool, in proportion to population, declined less than 8 per cent from 36·8 per cent, when the total population doubled from about 375,000 to about 750,000. Now, in under two decades from 1912, church attendances declined a further 10 per cent when the total population rose by another 100,000. For the Protestant denominations the decline bore a similar character—the faithful residuum tended to be the young and old, single rather than married, women rather than men, and anything but working class. The Catholic Church, on the other hand, could squeeze some satisfaction from the figures. The authors of the *Social Survey of Merseyside* in 1934 were in no doubt that the Catholic Church had succeeded best in maintaining congregations composed of persons of all types. In fact they argued that those classes who were the least frequent attenders at most other churches were the best supporters of the Catholic Church—families of manual working-class type.[75]

The shrewder politicians responded to these trends. Petrie had wanted to establish internment camps for Sinn Feiners found in Britain, and terrorist activities in Liverpool in 1920 had buoyed diehard Conservativism; but the days were gone when the party could rest its case on such incidents. Salvidge was looking to the secular side of politics. He had tried to make the W.M.C.A. a forum for Coalition patriotism by admitting non-members to its annual meeting in 1917.[76] The Liberal–Nationalist alliance was practically sundered and, with Southern Ireland's self-government negotiated in 1921, one more hurdle was jumped. Catholic Conservatives in Liverpool welcomed a settlement. The Protestants were more implacable but it fell to Salvidge, at the National Union conference, to adjust the political framework. While recognizing that Liverpool supported Ulster 'whatever the merits of the case', he would not exploit this to disrupt the Coalition. Salvidge even forgot his plainness in an emotional speech, contrasting the Die-hards in the 'security of a Conference' with soldiers who might 'die hard in grim reality' in Ireland. The speech seemed crucial. The conference remained loyal to the leadership of Austen Chamberlain and the Coalition. In fact Salvidge left little to the chance of his oratory. There is evidence that he had packed the hall with Liverpool delegates who, fresh from municipal election successes, valued the partnership with Liberal Coalitionists and were keen to shape conference opinion in the same way.[77]

Three weeks later the Irish Free State was created; but signatures cannot recast parties. Among the unreconciled Sir James Craig, the first Prime Minister of Northern Ireland, memorialized Liverpool's Ulster Association 'to fight for Liberty and the honour of the British flag'; and Sir Henry Wilson, the former Chief of the Imperial General Staff, speaking in Liverpool shortly before his assassination, drew two choices, Britain either watched Ireland explode or governed it imperially.[78] Pennefather too warned Parliament that Protestant feelings in Kirkdale 'may rise to a point of danger' from concern about Ulster's boundaries;[79] and in the 1922 municipal elections Protestant candidates reappeared in the lists. Walker retained Netherfield, but a Protestant victory in St. Domingo in 1921 was not repeated. The surprise lay elsewhere. Assuming that the Nationalist party was defunct, the Labour party prepared to inherit its following. Instead the elections reduced Labour's Council group to five members. Where seats fell, Conservative majorities surpassed the Labour and Nationalist polls. Nevertheless Labour's misunderstanding was real. An Irish settlement did not terminate the interest of 200,000 Liverpudlians in Catholic concerns. Under the archepiscopate of Keating, who succeeded Whiteside in 1921, the Catholic Church progressively adopted the Nationalist party to combat 'divorce, interference in Catholic schools, and the Revolution'.[80]

Reconstruction: housing and employment

Other questions of pre-war Liverpool—housing and employment—returned to plague politicians. The Corporation had saluted war by suspending schemes of improvement. The tradition of Christmas hot-pots ended in 1915, ostensibly because of 'the absence of distress'; and only 616 houses were demolished and 994 houses were built between 1915 and 1920 (half the annual average, 1900–14) when the population grew by 40,000.[81] In the immediate post-war period, however, the Lloyd George Coalition was prodigal by Gladstonian standards in its spending on social services. The deputy secretary, Tom Jones, captured the atmosphere in the Cabinet in a letter early in 1919:

> Several [ministers] were drawing rather long faces and piling up the financial bogey and the P.M. forced the Ministers to tell him how much they could spend in the next twelve months. The bill came to

> £71,000,000. He then asked: 'Supposing the War had lasted another year, could we not have raised somehow or other another £2,000,000,000?' It was blank nonsense to talk of a bagatelle like £71,000,000—a cheap insurance against Bolshevism.[82]

In 1919 the Liverpool Corporation planned under Addison's Act (the first to grant an Exchequer subsidy to council housing) to build 14,000 houses within three years. As an expedient 500 huts, formerly the American base, were converted into dwellings for 2,000 people. Grand schemes soon surrendered before rising costs and a shortage of skilled bricklayers and plasterers. In 1920 the Corporation lowered its ambitions, seeking to build 2,000 houses within two years; but the M.O.H. reported in 1924–5 that the city had 10,000 houses fewer in proportion to population than in 1914.[83] Altogether the Corporation built 5,808 houses under Addison's Act, 829 under Chamberlain's 1923 Act, and 13,448 under Wheatley's 1924 Act. Three-quarters of all houses built in Liverpool in the 1920s were Council houses. By 1931 they housed one-eighth of Liverpool. By 1939 the proportion was one-sixth, after another seven estates, comprising almost 10,000 houses, had been completed. Altogether the Corporation owned about 39,000 dwellings.[84]

These figures concealed much social change, policy vacillation, continuing shortages and distress. No council houses before 1914 were suburban; 96 per cent were in the 1920s. This migration was indicated by the closing of fourteen Anglican churches in the central wards. However, an inquiry among 1,206 families in six depressed areas disclosed that while 84 per cent wished to quit insanitary homes only 38 per cent wished to change neighbourhoods.[85] Most council-house rents were above what poorer wage-earners customarily paid; and with dearer food in suburban shops, and tram fares, many tenants were pinched. Eleanor Rathbone declared that some families returned to a single-room slum.[86]

From 1918 until 1922 one precondition for council tenants was to be an ex-serviceman, with at least two children. This arithmetical factor remained practically constant between the wars. The Housing Committee was still basing its assumptions on an average family of 4·25 persons in 1938. Generally, from a variety of causes—more widespread contraception, the great reduction in infant and child mortality, a change of attitude—the average family had declined since Victorian times. Nevertheless exceptions existed and Liverpool was the chief exception. Its birth-rate in 1931 was the highest among the large towns and cities. In that year it was observed that Liverpool Corporation had done a great deal to house small families, especially clerks', and little for large families, especially labourers'.[87] In 1927, as the subsidy fell by 30*s*. per house, the Council decided to develop two central sites with flats. This defied the preference for cottages;[88] and the plantation of new areas was shortly resumed. Four thousand acres in Speke and Croxteth were bought from Lord Derby before 1932, when the Corporation had a waiting-list of 20,000 applicants; and 30,000 people were housed at Huyton, just outside the city boundaries, without a single community centre.[89]

The Huyton estate, and many others with their lamentable want of facilities, were testimony to the fact that, though the scope of its activities had broadened, Local Government as a conception was not yet transformed. One critic, G. D. H. Cole, wrote of Local Government in the inter-war years that it was still

> in general assumed that its functions should be essentially residuary and that it should deal only, or at any rate mainly, with indispensable tasks that could be performed with even tolerable adequacy neither by self-help on a voluntary basis, nor by philanthropy, nor by profit-seeking enterprise. This was surely a skinflint way of regarding it, and one which could not possibly lead to the building of decent communities . . . Instead of treating it [Local Government] as the scavenger of the abuses with which no other agency can or will deal, we ought to regard it as the master-architect of the fabric of community living, in city, town and village, and in the regions within which city, town and village are comprised.

This conception of local government activity was obscured by the central government's concern for economy in such measures as the Housing (Financial Provisions) Act 1933, which ended grants for new housing on two grounds, that the housing shortage was so far conquered, and that interest rates and construction costs were sufficiently lowered to cater for future needs. Neither argument was convincing to members of the Liverpool Housing Committee.[90]

Every inquiry only served to highlight problems. The average of 28 per cent of working-class homes containing a bath concealed discrepancies between Inner Liverpool (4 per cent in Exchange, rising to 15 per cent in Edge Hill) and Outer Liverpool (60 per cent). The statistics of agglomeration hid similar divisions. In the 1921 and 1931 censuses the average density of Liverpool, 37·8 and 34·5 persons per acre respectively, exceeded that of most towns, and in certain areas strikingly so. Netherfield contained 227 persons per acre in 1931 and Everton, Low Hill, and St. Domingo over 150.[91] Thus the £17 million which Liverpool Corporation spent on housing in the 1920s did not buy absolute relief. One issue impressed politicians: council houses accommodated only a minority of families from inadequate dwellings. The promised 'houses fit for heroes' too often remained the same 'flea-ridden, bug-ridden, rat-ridden, lousy hell-holes'.[92]

Many aspects of Liverpool's housing thus aroused controversy. A scandal in the Housing Committee's management of contracts was uncovered in 1921 by the Ministry of Health's Inspectorate; and it was confirmed in the courts that the Corporation overpaid the contractors for its Garston housing scheme by £300,000.[93] Mostly, however, the Corporation faced difficulties not of its own making and not within its capacity to change: the price of land, the inability of private enterprise to build houses at economical rents, and government policy regarding powers of compulsory purchase, rent restriction, and subsidies for clearance and reconstruction. Moreover, with all its faults, the programme of house-building relieved unemployment. Merseyside's 23 per cent increase of insured building workers (1924–31) placed this among few industries which expanded faster on Merseyside than elsewhere. In October 1920, 14,888 unemployed were registered in Liverpool; in February 1921, the post-war boom having truly broken, there were twice as many, 29,239. In August 1922

Liverpool still had 30,800 unemployed (13 per cent of insured workers); Birkenhead had 10,000 (26 per cent) and Bootle 10,300 (19 per cent). The stress was in shipbuilding (11,151 unemployed) and distribution (19,968).[94] The causes lay beyond Merseyside, but relief questions excited controversy within, as well as between, the parties.

Among the Conservatives the proposal in 1922–3 to build a major road to Manchester—the East Lancashire Road—found Salvidge in a quandary. It would provide some employment and benefit traders in cheaper carriage; but if more freight shifted to the roads, the railway rates would have to be reduced. The Corporation, therefore, would suffer a loss of revenue, while supporting a new capital expenditure.[95] Labour, on the other hand, was embarrassed by the Communist-led Unemployed Workers' Movement, demanding work or substantial maintenance. The Movement won some concessions from the Council; but on 12 September 1921 demonstrators occupied the Walker Art Gallery. The police forcibly evicted them. Fifty of the 156 arrested had sustained injuries, and the leaders, who included the Revd. Vint Laughland, Robert Tissyman, John Braddock, and his future mother-in-law, Mary Bamber, went forward for trial. The police tactics, rather than the allegations of Communist influences, shocked the Recorder, E. G. Hemmerde, who therefore sentenced the leaders of the demonstration to a token of one day's imprisonment.[97]

Conspiracy was not confined to Communists. Several shipping companies, including Cunard, Brocklebank, and the Anchor Line, gave financial support and encouragement in the early 1920s to counter-revolutionary bodies like the British Empire Union, which used a variety of illegal methods—provocation, forgery, and theft—to combat socialist and communist influences in the labour movement. The B.E.U.'s object appealed to many besides frightened businessmen and right-wing extremists. The N.U.D.L.'s Liverpool secretary, the unswerving Catholic George Milligan, was a member of the B.E.U., as was W. B. Smithwick, one of the leaders of the police strike. In the same way several Labour politicians publicly denounced the Art Gallery demonstration, and the L.T.C. and L.P. refused to allow the Unemployed Movement to affiliate. Electorally the Labour party understood that a Communist taint was damaging; in fact the Communist threat was ephemeral. As the Deputy Secretary to the Cabinet, Tom Jones, had argued to Lloyd George in 1919, 'Bolshevik propaganda in this country is only dangerous in so far as it can lodge itself in the soil of genuine grievances'. The C.P. soon sought economies as its membership declined, and the introduction of 'democratic centralism' portended rigidity. The Braddocks, foundation members, responded by quitting the C.P. in 1924.[98]

Party politics in flux, 1922–6

Restlessness characterized party politics at national and local levels. A. J. P. Taylor has written that the 1922 Election was a plebiscite against Lloyd George as the 1918 Election was a plebiscite in his favour.[99] Salvidge had wanted an election early in the year, and publicly regretted anything which might upset the Coalition;[100] but in October the Conservative party ditched Lloyd George.

Salvidge, with Scott, Harmood-Banner, and Chilcott, was disappointed.[101] By Austen Chamberlain's instrumentality Salvidge, in the Dissolution Honours, became a Privy Councillor—unusual for one not an M.P.—but by pinning his reputation to the continuance of the Coalition he had exposed his position. He now covered himself in the elections by pressing Ulster's boundary claims against the Irish Republic. He exhorted Liverpool's Orangemen to quash 'anarchy and revolution', and to return 'ten loyal constitutional Protestant members' to Parliament.[102] However, Salvidge was safe if Lord Derby was correct, that opinion was not against the Coalition, but against a Liberal leading it.[103]

In fact the target of Tory wrath in Lancashire was not Salvidge but Lord Birkenhead, when he accused Lord Derby of wanting to succeed Lloyd George.[104] This embarrassed Sir Harold Smith, K.C., who replaced Raw as the Conservative candidate in Wavertree. As an aspiring M.P., Smith understood his duty: he aligned with Derby and repudiated his brother.[105] The Tory predominance in Liverpool remained. Chilcott and Pennefather were unopposed; and in East Toxteth Rankin defeated Eleanor Rathbone.[106] Less certain was Leslie Scott in Exchange. Since March 1922 he had served Lloyd George as Solicitor-General (without a seat in the Cabinet). Wanting the Coalition to continue in order to deal with the question of the French in the Ruhr and 'to stem the principles of communism and nationalization' at home, Scott had been bound in honour to decline Bonar Law's offer of the Attorney-Generalship when the new Conservative ministry was formed in October. He now faced Joe Devlin, whom he called 'an interloping Nationalist'. Devlin, however, was officially Independent. The 'duodecimo Demosthenes', Devlin had been gerrymandered from Belfast following Ulster's reduced representation at Westminster; but Scott preferred to draw attention to the fact that Devlin and his colleagues boycotted the Ulster Parliament. 'Nationalists will not help Ireland,' said Scott; 'they express no desire to help England, and they cannot help Liverpool.' Nevertheless only exceptional organization and expense saved Scott's seat. The local Conservative agent, Murch, made a special appeal to women voters in the out-districts, the wives of businessmen in Exchange; and the efforts of Sir James Reynolds, the constituency chairman and one of the city's leading Catholics, brought disharmony among former Nationalist voters.[107]

Elsewhere Labour contested seven Liverpool seats, bypassing O'Connor on the national agent's advice.[108] The party's performance in Parliament between 1918 and 1922 had seemed even poorer than that between 1906 and 1914. Its members never impressed as an alternative Government, being inadequate or inattentive in debate, and lacklustre and leaderless with MacDonald unable to find a seat on account of his anti-war record. But this was deceptive because Labour was incomparably stronger as an electoral force in the country, with a class and national appeal which the wrangling remnants of Liberalism could not rival. The party nationally would have preferred to have polled on a Saturday, not a Wednesday; nevertheless, the polls generally were 20 per cent above 1918. Only Joe Gibbins in West Toxteth, J. H. Hayes in Edge Hill, and Joe Toole in Everton, pulled the Conservative majorities below 5,000; and Everton evidenced revived sectarianism.[109] But, with an unstable national situation, few Liverpool seats were reliable.

In March 1923 a by-election in Edge Hill, upon Rutherford's retirement, finally rewarded Labour's efforts in Liverpool. The Conservative Constituency Association bridled as the Government, through Derby's and Salvidge's agency, foisted a candidate on them—J. W. Hills, a Treasury Minister who had lost Durham in the General Election. Moreover, Protestants were vexed over Ulster and a rumour that the King would pay a state visit to the Pope; and, with high unemployment—33,921 unemployed were registered in Liverpool that January—and the Ministry of Health's wrestling with local authorities over rents and the housing subsidy, the climate was altogether unfavourable to the Conservatives.[110] Hills had a reputation as a progressive Conservative; but Hayes increased Labour's score by 780, sufficient for a majority of 1,050 in a 58·1 per cent poll. This was a 12·4 per cent decline in turn-out. Salvidge had failed to rally the hosts of the W.M.C.A. He had evoked that spirit of 1907 when Labour had been repulsed in Kirkdale; but it was Labour now that attracted the volunteer canvassers, including members of the Civil Service Clerical Association who claimed Hills's scalp in their struggle against the Treasury over the issue of starting pay for temporary clerks.[111] Sexton was incredulous that Labour had won a Liverpool seat—but Hills was the third minister defeated within days.[112]

The L.T.C. and L.P. returned its first M.P. amid municipal humiliation. In November 1923 it slumped to its post-war nadir of four Council members. Seven unemployed fought official candidates.[113] The L.T.C. organized demonstrations but barely co-operated with the Unemployed Movement until, in 1925, a Joint Committee was formed. The local N.U.W.M. branch afterwards affiliated to the L.T.C. but its delegates could not vote. Laying the Communist bogey was desirable but a witch-hunt was for special palates, like Herbert Morrison's in London.[114] Although the L.T.C. and L.P. opposed the affiliation of the Communist party, the decision of the 1924 Labour Party Conference to ban individual Communists was not immediately respected. Communists still elicited sympathy, like Harry Pollitt, whom 'fascists' prevented from speaking in Liverpool. Only in June 1926, when the executive expelled its Communists, did the L.T.C. obey party directives.[115]

Progress, with limping gait, also occurred in Labour–Nationalist relations. In 1923 the two parties confabulated but Labour could not contemplate an alliance which entailed surrendering several central wards to the Nationalists and alienating the Protestant working class elsewhere. In any case, Labour believed in the Nationalists' obsolescence. The U.I.L. held its last annual convention in 1918. Factionalism or individualism, not organization and coherence, now marked the Nationalists. Individuals gave contradictory signs. Some, like David Logan, joined Labour; some conspired with Conservatives in education policy; others called themselves Irish Democrats, an independent rump managed by Harford; and at Westminster O'Connor attempted to project something of everything. With regard to Ireland O'Connor had little new to contribute, except to announce his conversion to proportional representation, whose advocates he had previously ranked with the 'one-ideal fanatics'—'Vaccinationists, anti-vivisectionists, Pussyfoots, and other faddists'. In some ways O'Connor respected the past, as 'an old Free Trader in the cause of freedom and of the masses of the people'. Protection he described as 'a collar of steel which wealth will put around the neck of Labour, and it will squeeze and squeeze until it makes Labour paralysed'. The radical in O'Connor was not petrified. He gave independent support to the first Labour government—for which a privy councillorship was the reward—and, before the General Strike, he criticized the Baldwin government for its failure to reach accommodation with reasonable trade unionists and to reconstruct the coal industry on lines recommended by several Royal Commissions since the war. From 1923, however, Catholic education replaced Ireland as O'Connor's main theme at Westminster. The existing division of provided and non-provided schools he denounced as 'a social as well as a religious inequality; a discrimination against the people who are poor and are asked to pay more than the rich'. It was reckoned that in three-quarters of a century the Liverpool Irish had spent £800,000 on this work. O'Connor himself had played a part in raising £40,000 in the last decade or so, mainly from his own constituents.[116]

With matters thus undecided, the parties had considered the General Election in December 1923. The Conservative leader, Baldwin, went to the country with a programme of tariff reform. He had a dual purpose, to fight unemployment and to emphasize the end of the Coalition. Already, however, Lord Derby had predicted that in a Tariff Reform election 'Labour or a Free Trade party would sweep Lancashire'.[117] In Bootle and Birkenhead (East) Liberal candidates had been successful in 1922, after Labour candidates had been withdrawn.[118] Lord Derby now rephrased the issue and invited Lancashire to choose between 'Constitutionalism and Socialism'.[119] Salvidge concurred in this: Baldwin's programme caused 'dissatisfaction and misgiving'. Conservatives would not fight for tariffs as they would fight against 'Socialism and a capital levy'.[120] Indeed Salvidge swore that those responsible for a tariff reform election 'might just as well have rolled tons of dynamite into Liverpool to uproot the Conservative party'.[121]

Hall, the principal Conservative agent since March 1923, was blasted out of West Derby. His defeat, according to Tom Jones, was received with 'Much jubilation . . . in the more wholesome political circles'.[122] This was a reference perhaps to the part played by Hall in circulating extracts, about homosexual practices from Sir Roger Casement's diary in order to frustrate his chances of a reprieve from execution in 1916. With Labour's covert support the leader of the Liberal rump on Liverpool City Council, Sydney Jones, had beaten Hall by 1,990 votes.[123] Wavertree also went Liberal, in a three-cornered fight; but it was the Edge Hill contest that epitomized the post-war ethos. There the N.U.P.P.O.'s former secretary, Hayes, who still pressed for the reinstatement or compensation of police strikers, repulsed Oliver Stanley, Derby's youngest son. Uneasy about tariffs, Stanley had considered withdrawing; but Derby thought that he might win with a Conservative social policy.[124] Derby ruined this plan by himself becoming an issue. Hayes attacked Derby's ground-rents for 'strangling economic life' in the city. Derby rejoindered that a capital levy would kill business. He added that 'taxation was too high', and he might have to quit Knowsley Hall. Harry Walker, contesting Everton, irreverently offered to fill Knowsley with needy Liverpudlians.[125]

The turn-out in Liverpool in 1923 averaged 63·8 per cent in six contests, compared with 69·7 per cent in eight contests in 1922. In Everton Labour lost by 1,510, in West Toxteth by 139. These were straight fights. The Liberals presented no candidates apart from their two victors. In Exchange an Independent, Councillor Grogan, promoted free trade, labour policies, and denominational education, and ran only 229 votes behind Scott. Four sitting members were unopposed, including T. P. O'Connor, who employed himself at Harrow supporting Oswald Mosley.[126] Walton, Fairfield, and East Toxteth were also uncontested; but *The Times*'s prediction that Liverpool would return ten Unionists was awry.[127]

Lord Derby's worries represented Conservative depression. Before the poll he had feared a landslide like 1906; afterwards he feared the Conservatives' extinction if a Labour ministry received Liberal support.[128] In fact 1924 passed blithely. Labour was not Bolshevist; a 'progressive' alliance of Labour and Liberal was eschewed by Labour; and Lord Derby's horse won the Derby, the first time since 1787 that the family triumphed in their eponymous race. That political cornerman, Salvidge, also began rearranging the Conservative party's features. Never again, he announced, would the party be 'hustled by the central office'. He lambasted Baldwin's 'terrific political gamble', his 'shockingly faulty' channels of consultation, and his ignorant advisers. Salvidge rejected suggestions that he take over the national party organization. His object was to influence policy, not to be 'a mere manager of machinery'.[129]

Salvidge remained a Protectionist, but this commitment he was prepared to waive rather than injure the fight against Socialism. With a mandate from Liverpool Constitutional Association Salvidge spoke emphatically: provincial party organizations had 'an undoubted right to have a say on policy'.[130] The Manchester meetings, of Lancashire and Cheshire Unionist Associations, were forums for dissent;[131] and Baldwin apparently capitulated. A general tariff would not be submitted again unless the country clearly demanded it. The party chairman, F. S. Jackson, also resolved that the provinces would be better represented on the party executive, and that a six-man committee, equally appointed by the National Union and party leader, would advise on policy; but this never materialized and Baldwin, though perhaps more sensitive, remained untrammelled in control of policy.[132]

Salvidge indicted Baldwin for being 'autocratic'. Locally this case was made against Salvidge. Scott had denounced caucus politics in 1917; now he and Ernest Stacey, a stockbroker who acted as Stanley's agent in Edge Hill, founded the 1924 Club to counteract the W.M.C.A. This they disliked for its Orangeism, also because it empowered working men against the party paymasters, businessmen, and 'gentlemen'.[133] Equally they censured Salvidge for the fact of defeat—Liverpool had a poor Conservative record in 1923. West Toxteth, vacant in May 1924 as Houston retired, exemplified the decline. The majority had dwindled—6,233 in 1918, 4,721 in 1922, 139 in 1923—but Houston had held the representation 'as a sort of freehold', practically independent of the Constitutional, and Salvidge and the central agent, Murch, seized the chance to reverse the tide. A special appeal for funds was launched; and Salvidge advanced as the candidate his henchman in the W.M.C.A., Tom White. An Orangeman and councillor for St. Domingo, White was, in Salvidge's view, the only man capable of winning the seat, with the possible exception of Sir Thomas Royden.[134]

Born in Liverpool in 1887, White had been a merchant seaman before becoming a publican (although he neither drank nor smoked) and afterwards a paper merchant. His first rates bill had stirred an interest in politics. He became a Poor Law Guardian, promoting the Liverpool Boards' amalgamation. Now he contested West Toxteth as a 'democratic Tory' and a suspended tariff reformer.[135] The Conservative case, however, assumed rodomontade proportions on 7 May when Winston Churchill returned to that platform after twenty years. Speaking in Liverpool, he invoked all classes to resist 'the fallacies of Russian and German Socialism'.[136] A telegram from Baldwin simplified the Tories' rhetoric, stating that Labour's 'aim is Socialism'.[137] Its disadvantage was in making Labour's intentions clearer than it did itself.

All classes did not join the crusade. Some demeaned the supernal debate by considering practical issues. After both candidates were questioned about the Safeguarding of Industries Act, McKenna duties, and Proportional Representation, Liberals were advised to vote Labour. Salvidge retorted that 'if the official Liberals of Liverpool are going to be the allies of the Socialist Party, then . . . this election will have done a good thing. It will have drawn the badger and shown us where we are.'[138]

Where the Tories were in West Toxteth was by the exit. White was ill, whereas Labour's candidate, Gibbins, was contesting his native constituency for the third time. Housing headed his appeal. West Toxteth had seen few new homes. Houses condemned ten, twenty, and thirty years before were still standing. Otherwise Gibbins showed pride in Snowden's tax-cutting Budget as an example of 'what will be done when the Labour Party has full control'; and Salvidge again bitterly regretted Baldwin's decision to call the last General Election, for it had enabled Labour 'to distribute the surplus which we had accumulated'.[139] White polled nearly 600 more votes than Houston in 1923 but Gibbins won by 2,471. Five Liverpool seats now returned non-Conservatives.

Labour's Irish relations remained fickle. One Liverpool Irish leader, P. J. Kelly, sought a three-year union of 'progressive forces' (Liberals, Labour, and Irish) to terminate Conservative power. Otherwise Kelly threatened Labour's Council seats.[140] Sniffing the electoral winds, Labour rejected compromise: the former Nationalist, David Logan, had recently won a North Scotland ward by-election for the Labour party. Moreover, a full-time secretary, W. H. Barton, had been appointed to knit Labour's ward activities; and in the November municipal elections Labour made the first gains since 1919.[141] Two seats were wrested from Conservatives. Elsewhere, in South Scotland, Kelly was beaten. Sandhills also fell. Both Labour victors were ex-Nationalists. This portended another problem, the incompatibility of Labour's secular and Catholic personalities.

National and municipal politics converged in 1924 with a General Election on 29 October. Ramsay MacDonald was at his most slippery as his Government came to grief in its handling of the Campbell Case. Leslie Scott saw a great issue embodied here, that the Government interfered with the course of justice for political reasons; but the chance of an easy cry, of Communist machinations, impressed more Conservatives. T. P. O'Connor, on the other hand, thought that to dissolve Parliament on such an issue—'this miserable tempest in the tiniest little teapot ever introduced into political life'—could only damage public respect for all parties.[142] O'Connor, however, was returned unopposed; so too, in spite of his narrow majority, was Scott. He had accepted Catholic policy. Scott's walk-over released some 5,000 business voters in suburban divisions. This advantaged the Conservatives; but they were without a party newspaper as the *Courier* took an increasingly independent line, finally breaking with Salvidge when he opposed Sunday music in the parks in deference to the Protestant clergy.[143]

Salvidge, moreover, would not co-operate with independent Liberals after White's defeat. This upset ex-Coalitionists like Muspratt. Spurned also by Asquithians, they eventually became Conservatives. As in most boroughs, so in Liverpool, the Liberals were no longer a municipal force; and in 1924 their parliamentary representation ended too. Salvidge had counteracted Rathbone's and Jones's special attraction, of being local businessmen, in his choice of candidates, and they not only lost Wavertree and West Derby but were driven into third place. In 1927 Liverpool's Reform and Junior Reform Clubs merged, after forty-seven years' separate existence; and in 1931 the Club closed altogether.[144]

A concern for food prices, not the jumble of parties, was said to have been uppermost in electors' minds in Liverpool in 1924; and the incoming Conservative Government responded with a Royal Commission. But 1924 was not without significance in the party history of Liverpool. Labour had assumed the opposition to Conservatism. In 1923 it contested four seats; in 1924 nine. The turn-out was generally 10 per cent above 1923, and two seats, Everton and West Toxteth, recorded swings against the tide to Labour. Labour retained Edge Hill and West Toxteth, but the newcomers among the M.P.s were Conservative. On Pennefather's recommendation Everton selected Colonel H. C. Woodcock, a Bristol merchant and Evangelical; Wavertree chose J. A. Tinne, a local merchant and churchman; West Derby returned Sandeman Allen, the Chamber of Commerce's chairman; and East Toxteth promoted A. E. Jacob, whose biscuit factory employed 2,000 people at Fazakerley. Jacob's odyssey reflected party trends. A Liberal councillor from 1906 until 1912, he re-entered the Council in 1918 as a Conservative. Excepting O'Connor, who scorned mortality, only Scott among the Liverpool M.P.s had been returned before the war. If any political break can be measured by personalities, 1924 marked a divide from the past.

Nationally moods were also set. Baldwin conceived his task to instruct new M.P.s in 'the limitations of parliamentary government'. This was not Salvidge's view. He believed that the Government had a duty 'not to reduce the income tax, but to carry out their social programme of housing and widows' pensions and other measures for the relief of the under-dog'.[145] Viewed from Liverpool, Baldwin the Prime Minister was even less malleable in policy than Baldwin the party leader. This reflected another tendency. The provinces, as decision-makers, were moribund. Liverpool's ability to attract the new industries it needed was virtually nonexistent before the Rating and Valuation Apportionment Act of 1928 (implemented by the Local Government Act of

1929) because Liverpool, like any depressed area, suffered the consequences of its own poverty in high rates.

What boldness remained in the 1928–9 derating legislation was due to the Chancellor of the Exchequer, Churchill. His original plans, growing from a seed planted by Harold Macmillan, conceived of economic revival by relieving farms, factories, and railways of rates, amounting to one-quarter of all rates. The money to be disbursed by the Exchequer in compensation of local authorities was to come from various economies, particularly in the naval estimates, and from new taxes, on petrol and on business profits. However, other Conservative ministers feared what might become of a profits tax in the hands of a future Labour government; and the Minister of Health, Neville Chamberlain, jealous and obstructive, insisted on a partial rather than full remission of rates in order to preserve industry's financial interest in economical local administration. The resultant legislation did not constitute a sensitive instrument. The principle of selectivity was little observed. The de-rating, to one-fourth their net annual value, applied to all manufacturing businesses, and freight-transport, irrespective of scale, market, and location. Local authorities were compensated for the loss of revenue by a new block grant from the central government based upon the formula of 'weighted population', that is, weighted by an index of relative needs and ability, including the proportion of children and unemployed, and density of settlement, as well as rateable value. Many critics, however, regretted the lost opportunity to recast the whole system of local government finance by replacing rates, which were regressive in tendency, with a more equitable form of taxation, like income tax, which was progressive in character. G. D. H. Cole, indeed, nominated the De-rating Act as 'perhaps the worst of all inter-war measures. De-rating, in spite of the compensating grants paid out of the Exchequer, has acted to the detriment of small householders and of shopkeepers, and has reduced the rating system to the last absurdity of unfair incidence.' However, while the rates remained, changes in valuation and assessment were necessary, for example, to relieve owner-occupiers of houses built since 1914; and, regarding industry, there was force in Cole's argument that open subsidies were preferable to tax remissions.[146]

Although impotent to determine the framework of local government finance, Salvidge was not absolutely deprived of initiative in local government in the 1920s. He conducted Liverpool's negotiations with central government departments concerning a Mersey Tunnel, which was now linked with the East Lancashire Road scheme.[147] On behalf of the Docks Board Richard Holt composed a jeremiad about financial irresponsibility—the proposed Wallasey branch struck him as a particularly 'absurd waste of money'—but in recognition of the scheme's importance Salvidge received the Freedom of Liverpool in 1925, when Princess Mary visited the city and ceremonially sunk the tunnel's first shaft.[148] The tunnel was opened by the King in 1934 and, though it cost one-third over the original estimate, a fillip was given to the idea of a Merseyside federation of local authorities, co-operating in matters other than transport.[149] Some unemployment was also relieved, but not Catholic and Protestant competition.[150]

In 1925 the Catholic Archbishop, Keating, criticized discrimination in civic offices. Just as in Belfast, so in Liverpool, no Catholic had ever been Mayor. The likelihood, to T. P. O'Connor, seemed as good as the chance of a Christian becoming Caliph of Bagdad. Keating also wanted aid for education. The Board of Education described eleven Liverpool schools (two Council, four Catholic, and five Anglican) as 'unsuitable for continued recognition and incapable of improvement'; and thirty-one schools (only four of which were Council schools) required radical repair and fewer pupils.[151]

Improving 'non-provided' denominational schools was not ostensibly a party action; and it was not a Catholic but a Church of England school, St. Clement's, in which a floor collapsed in 1934 injuring 120 children and some adults during a school entertainment. Moreover, the consequences nationally of a thinly financed education system were clear. As one academic had observed in 1917, 'We have fought this war with the very minimum of brain power and we really cannot afford to manufacture unskilled workers at the rate we are doing'. The President of the Board of Education, H. A. L. Fisher, had introduced legislation in 1918 which aimed to broaden and extend the existing system of public education. Schooling for all under fourteen was made compulsory; the Board of Education increased its financial responsibility to some 50 per cent of local authority expenditure; and a network of 'continuation' schools was conceived, in which part-time education was available up to sixteen. In addition some free places at secondary schools and 200 state scholarships to universities were established; and teachers had their salaries regularized by the Burnham scale. Two obstructions, however, prevented swift and secure advances. One was Fisher's carelessness as an accountant, and the Geddes economy axe found education an easy prey. The continuation schools were cut down and the result of making schooling compulsory up to fourteen was an increase of class size when money was scarce for building new schools. Inequality in education opportunities, therefore, remained a national reproach that was all the sharper for being most marked in the poor districts. On Merseyside in the late 1920s some 25 per cent of children in Wallasey went on to receive secondary education, but only 11 per cent in Liverpool and Birkenhead. Another obstruction was the religious problem. Education would not expand as a priority of government spending while the sectarian aspect was unresolved. The Fisher Act of 1918 ignored this difficulty. Grounds for optimism existed but were slight. The churches were alarmed by declining membership and, through adversity, an impetus was given to the idea of Protestant reunion. Conversations about this foundered in 1925 on the vital matter of Orders; nevertheless, hopes of a *rapprochement* remained current. Regarding education, meetings between Churchmen and Protestant Nonconformists took place in 1919–20. The Archbishop of Canterbury, Davidson, wanted to end the dual system of 'provided' and 'non-provided' schools, feeling that the longer a settlement was delayed the poorer would be the terms that the churches would eventually receive. He repeated the three articles of his position—that religious instruction must be an essential part of education, that it must be taught by properly qualified and committed teachers, and that it must have definite doctrinal content. The Nonconformists, however, still would not tolerate denominational teaching in Council schools; and the Catholics for the most part remained isolated, retaining a profound hostility to all association with local authorities.[152]

On the other hand, the Catholics, even more than the Anglicans were in need of a political solution to relieve their financial plight. In Liverpool the vehicle that Keating adopted to promote his views made the question especially contentious: the Irish party was turned into the Catholic Representation Association. Keating cast his purple over the party to obliterate its 'Red' tinge. Some members like Kelly now deserted to Labour; but old Nationalist wards returned C.R.A. councillors, some overwhelmingly. In North Scotland ward Monsignor George beat the ex-Nationalist, now Labour, Councillor, by 3,465 votes to 617. Keating demanded that Labour and the Irish factions place Catholicism first and, although the C.R.A.'s representation diminished in 1926, a priest defeated Labour's leader, Robinson.[153]

Politically active Catholicism goaded Protestant militancy, but this was predictable too from the Prayer Book controversy.[154] Longbottom held open-air demonstrations about this and, following one incident in High Park Street, he was legally bound over not to kindle religious strife.[155] Longbottom's ardour was not singular: the Home Secretary, Joynson-Hicks, and the Solicitor-General, Inskip, stirred what remained of Evangelicalism within and without Parliament. Joynson-Hicks spoke in Liverpool, moving versatilely in theme from the Reformation to Bolshevism.[156] In the 1926 municipal elections Protestant candidates gingered Conservative sectarians. Walker had Conservative support in Netherfield; but in Fazakerley ward, which Longbottom contested, Salvidge directed the Conservative candidate to fight Socialism, not split the vote on Protestant and Catholic lines. Religious questions, he said, did not concern the Council. Longbottom fought hopelessly, but he had established a claim to Conservative support; and later that November he won Breckfield.[157]

Demoralization: the General Strike, unemployment, sectarianism

On the industrial front the years up to 1926 are chiefly memorable for the huge number of working days lost in national stoppages, largely owing to the failure of collective bargaining readily to accommodate to swift fluctuations in prices and wages. The General Strike in this respect exaggerated and exhausted a trend. The Liverpool part in the General Strike has been described elsewhere,[158] but its salient characteristics should be mentioned—labour's preparedness in establishing a Council of Action in 1925; the response of most workers, except tramwaymen and electricity workers, to strike in 1926;[159] the dockers' vulnerability to blackleg labour; and the seamen's difficulties, faced by Havelock Wilson's resort to the courts to enforce his refusal to bring the N.S.F.U. out on official strike. In 1911 and 1919 the Government soon despatched armour to Liverpool; in 1926 two battalions and two battleships arrived before the strike. Some volunteers, and some special constables 'foolish enough to wear plus fours', were menaced by strikers; but there was little 'beautifying' of Liverpudlians with batons.[160] Violence in previous disputes had indicated high feeling; peaceableness now did not register indifference. A large minority of the L.T.C.

condemned the T.U.C.'s General Council for abandoning the miners; and several hundred workers in the Liverpool flour-milling industry were not reinstated after the strike.[161]

During the strike political and industrial activity was co-ordinated. Individual Councillors, as trade unionists, were busy; and three regional M.P.s, Hayes, Gibbins, and Sexton, joined the Council of Action, whose secretary was the Liverpool Labour party's secretary. Mostly, however, the strike seemed a disaster for the Labour movement, which emerged plainly defeated and divided.[162] After the Trades Disputes Act (1927)—that 'foolish aggravation of feeling just when industrial relations seemed to be settling down'—post-office engineers, railwaymen, and woodworkers disaffiliated from the L.T.C. Other unions needed encouragement to contract in the political levy. Some, like the Liverpool Cotton Workers', had not even awaited the Act to discountenance the Strike by their disaffiliation;[163] but in other respects the General Strike left little permanent mark on the industrial scene. Revolution was not abandoned by the majority because it had never been embraced by the majority; and unions had been losing membership since 1920, although what significance should be ascribed to this is debatable. The membership that was shed may have been that of the fickle and uncommitted; but the decline also reflected changes in the country's occupational and regional structure. Some traditional industries of the North, where trade unionism was established, notably coal, textiles and shipbuilding, suffered relative or even absolute decline, while the expanding industries—not all of these were 'new' industries—in the Midlands and South-East, notably motor vehicles and components, electrical goods, chemicals, artificial fibres, building, and a host of consumer, service, and distributive trades, were industries without union traditions or difficult to organize. The vital aspect of industrial relations, union recognition by employers, was not dramatically disturbed by the General Strike and, although the experience was undoubtedly chastening, it was likely that the ensuing years would have been relatively peaceful and free of national stoppages in any case as price fluctuations became less violent and structural changes in the distribution of employment deepened.

In the subsequent municipal elections in Liverpool Labour's Council group increased to nineteen representatives. Two C.R.A. and three Conservative seats were gained, as well as Longbottom's. Out of a total Council of 151 this was hardly a vote of confidence and, rather than approval of Labour's action in the General Strike, the elections probably registered the discontent among Conservative voters with rising rates, from expensive housing projects and poor relief. Nevertheless, the amplified Labour voice brought tumult to Council meetings.[164]

Unemployment remained a contentious issue. 1927 was nationally the decade's best year; but Merseyside could show 52,000 insured unemployed. Two local sources of employment had ceased. In December 1925 H.M.S. *Rodney* was launched. Salvidge and Derby has used their influence in winning the contract for Cammell Laird's; but it was the second of two battleships authorized under the Treaty of Washington. No others were allowed until 1931. In February 1927 the Gladstone Dock system was completed. Richard Holt was one of only two surviving members of the Docks Board's Works Committee which had initiated the project in 1905. In vain he had protested against the 'want of financial courage' which delayed its completion. This 'doubled the cost besides depriving us of the earnings we should have got in war time'. It now resembled 'the tomb of Mausolus reconstructed'.[165]

Trade and employment prospects were gloomy, and budgetary management was haywire. When Government is sterile, local authorities merely tinker. Improvised measures were discouraging. Farmers stated that the men sent from Liverpool's Labour Exchanges contributed less than a boy on his holidays; and at the Chamber of Commerce speakers blamed the 'dole' for the unemployed's reluctance to emigrate. In fact, of the £17 million permitted maximum expenditure under the 1922 Empire Settlement Act less than £4 million was actually spent by 1928. Merseyside's contribution was paltry. Of the 210 unemployed men who applied for training for settlement in Australia or Canada in 1926–7, twenty-one eventually withdrew, and seventy-three were unacceptable to the Dominion authorities.[166]

Many of the features which strike historians as typical of the 1930s' depression were apparent throughout the 1920s. The number of unemployed was already straining the agencies of relief. The West Derby Board of Guardians was overdrawn in its account of current expenses by £650,000 by 1925. It had been paying an annual average of £15,000 in interest charges since 1922 when, as was widespread, the old controls of the Poor Law, in giving assistance only to the sick, aged, and unemployable, had broken down, and the able-bodied unemployed were relieved too. The rates were thus burdened because the Government's Unemployment Insurance Fund was inadequate to the need. Unemployment insurance had been devised as a grant to help a man over temporary unemployment, and as a supplement to his savings. It was inappropriate where depression set in and never lifted. The debates, which were to grow in stridency in the 1930s, were now joined: whether, when unemployment occurred from national or international causes, the relief of unemployment was properly a local charge; whether rough lines of equity could be observed in assisting the unemployed while recognizing different titles to benefit, spurring labour mobility, and preserving initiative through personal contributions; and what level of welfare and social services expenditure could the budget tolerate.

In the Liverpool corner of this national picture the colours were dark with despair and rancour. Already there had been inquiries into juvenile unemployment, compelled by the knowledge of some six or seven thousand youths, hanging about the docks, walking the streets, or getting into trouble. Already merchant seamen protested against the employment of aliens, which was such that by 1931 the Labour M.P., David Logan, could exclaim that half of the meagre shipping that entered Liverpool was manned by 'coolie labour, black labour, and chinks'. Even for those in work there were unfamiliar pressures. Dockers had become income-tax payers, a sign of war-time wage-increases and inflation. Dockers were also brought within the folds of national insurance legislation. The benefits of this were not transparent. Sexton complained that bureaucracy had gone too far when dockers had to carry their trade union, health insurance, and unemployment insurance, cards. 'If you go on piling up all these additional burdens', he told parliament in 1920, 'you will soon have the dockers and other workers going to their employment equipped with an attaché case in order to carry the documents they are expected to have upon them.'[168]

For those without work problems were naturally greater. In 1914 about 29,000 dockers found some work in Liverpool. In 1930 the number of registered dockers was 21,000; in 1938 no more than 12,000, pruned by trade depression, by steady mechanization, and by gradually reducing the number of tallies, so that registered dockers might obtain more employment and higher wages. Dockers who found no work, being on call twice a day, had to sign the unemployment register twice a day and, although the National Joint Council for Dock Labour had this under inquiry from 1931, the inconvenience remained throughout the inter-war period.[168]

Inconveniences might be bearable, but sneers were insufferable. The Edge Hill M.P., Hayes, criticized the press for referring to the unemployment benefit as the 'dole', because this was not a charity but receivable by right by all insured persons; but the press was echoing, not manufacturing, an attitude, quite apart from the fact that long-unemployed persons soon began to outstrip their entitled benefits. The systematic examination of the status of the unemployed by Labour Exchange staffs or by statutory relief bodies was another source of humiliation, but it seemed beyond human ingenuity to devise a way of determining whether an applicant was genuinely seeking work, whether he was qualified for various benefits, or whether he would have to turn to the poor law, without questioning the applicant himself. In Socialist folklore Labour Exchange staffs, Poor Law Guardians in the 1920s, and Public Assistance Committees in the 1930s, conducted their interrogations and exercised the means test with fiendish relish; but this is not the whole account. Two Liverpool Labour councillors and M.P.s., Joe Gibbins and David Logan, who were Guardians in the 1920s and chairmen of Public Assistance Committees in the 1930s, never ceased to complain of the 'damnable and iniquitous system' which they were bound to apply. Moreover, the Liverpool Public Assistance Committee was one of only two—the other being Chester—that exercised the power of co-optation, and in one individual, Dorothy Keeling of the Personal Service Society, it found a representative who throughout the decade protested against hard and unsympathetic dealings and against the Ministry of Health's policy. But even the charitably disposed and the independent-minded were made servants of the system. In 1939 Conservative councillors questioned Miss Keeling's credentials and voted to discontinue the Corporation's annual £200 grant to her society. However, the want of freedom within which all administrators of the poor laws operated had already been emphasized in 1933 when a tradition of twenty years' standing—the dispensing of a little extra food and fuel by the Liverpool Guardians for a fortnight at Christmas and the New Year—was stopped after an objection raised under the 1930 Public Assistance Order, which tightly restricted special allowances and punished deviations by a surcharge on individual members of Public Assistance Committees.[169]

Government was the main target for complaints. Economy was the goal of governments in the 1920s, just as it was to be in the 1930s, and the consequence was the same—a shift of the burden from national exchequer to local rates. The

1926 Conservative budget, which ate into the health and unemployment insurance funds, was typical of many. Sexton likened its method to 'pinching the pennies out of a dead man's eyes at a wake'. That Lazarus should be resurrected, not robbed, was a common cry, and Gibbins added his measure, that the government did little to relieve unemployment but much to prevent the unemployed from drawing relief by 'harsh and cruel regulations'. The government, however, did recognize the need in 1930 to change the name 'poor law' to 'public assistance.' At the same time it commissioned another Labour Exchange to be built at Everton. The 72,518 registered unemployed in Liverpool and Bootle were severely testing the staffs at the four existing exchanges, and on one famous occasion in 1929 the Garston Exchange had to close when insufficient money had been drawn from the bank to meet the claims. There were also public works, and in the five years up to 1931 the Unemployment Grants Committee approved thirty-seven schemes submitted by Liverpool Corporation, of an estimated cost of £788,000, and three schemes by the Docks Board, of an estimated cost of over £2 million. However, the number of Liverpudlians directly employed at any one time on state-aided schemes was under 2,000 in the 1920s and under 4,000 in 1930 and 1931.[170]

In 1927 the Liverpool Guardians reduced their scales of relief, to save £40,000 for the rates.[171] Although Longbottom, Labour, and C.R.A. members deprecated economies which 'starved women and children', they were hardly more inventive of solutions or prodigal of relief. Posturing produced no results. When Labour councillors in a gesture of self-denial and sympathy with the unemployed moved that the annual civic luncheon be abandoned, Salvidge replied that no Corporation feasted less at the ratepayers' expense. He added, 'these Labour men, when they attend the T.U.C., stay at the most palatial hotels and drink more champagne in a day than I would drink in five years'. Similarly, at Christmas 1927, when the N.U.W.M. demanded more generous allowances, the Guardians' Finance Committee, including Longbottom, refused even to consider proposals from 'a deputation of wild men'.[172]

Longbottom's political position depended on surviving sectarianism, not on his adoption of radical views. 'If the Catholics were in power', he warned, 'there would be no Protestant schools'; but in 1927 the Protestant party was halved when one councillor was defeated. Protest by demonstration returned, but this exposed the Protestants' inadequacy.[173] When Parliament rejected the revised Prayer Book in 1927 and 1928 success was galling, for another of the Protestant party's *raisons d'etre* had expired. Every Liverpool M.P., except O'Connor and Jacob, who were absent from the debates in Parliament, voted against the new Prayer Book. Party ties were suspended: Hayes personally was uninterested but he faithfully reported the wholehearted opposition from Protestants of all classes in Liverpool, and he joined Pennefather in acting as a teller for the Noes in both divisions. Protestantism, then, was not so much in danger from the Malines conversations or from the Prayer Book revision, as Longbottom maintained, as from its own indistinctness and derangement.[174] In 1928 independent Protestantism was effaced from the Council when Walker lost Netherfield.

This depletion of Protestant strength, gradual since Wise's death, was hastened by the C.R.A.'s disbandment. Archbishop Keating had died, and his successor, Richard Downey, forbade the title 'Catholic' to a political party and banned priests from electoral activity.[175] The C.R.A. now took the title 'Centre' party, but of its nineteen Council members five retired rather than face Labour opposition. Altogether Labour gained eleven seats (five Centre, four Conservative, one Protestant, and one Liberal) which gave it thirty-six representatives.

The Conservative revolt against Salvidge

Momentous changes occurred in the Liverpool Conservative party in the late 1920s. In 1927 the Exchange M.P., Sir Leslie Scott, led every Liverpool Conservative M.P., except the Walton M.P., Chilcott, to repudiate Salvidge's tutelage.[176] They demanded full-time constituency agents to relieve—and undermine—the central agent, Murch, and altogether criticized Liverpool's singular political organization. The Chamber of Commerce and trade associations welcomed their case, according to Sir William Forwood; but Salvidge found 'disgraceful' and 'baseless' the suggestion that he bossed a caucus. Instead he accused the M.P.s of attempting 'to abrogate the powers of a democratic organization'. The Prime Minister appealed for peace; and the issue mostly dropped from public attention.[177]

So basic a challenge to the premises on which Salvidge's leadership rested could not be conveniently buried. Thirty years before, the M.P.s argued, when the Irish question dominated politics and Orangeism swept everything before it, it was comparatively simple, if registration was maintained, for the Constitutional's officers to manage elections in most Liverpool constituencies and wards. Two factors had transformed the situation. The rise of Labour altered the political debate, and the growing number of electors widened the political ambit. In 1928, when women would be accorded the same franchise as men, the average size of Liverpool's constituencies would be nearly 45,000 or six times those of 1914. It seemed imperative to have more decentralized authority, more independent vitality in the constituencies, and more money for propaganda. The Constitutional's everyday working had long depended on its elected municipal and parliamentary representatives—each M.P. was expected to give £200 per annum to the Constitutional, as well as to pay his election expenses—but 'in these democratic days', the M.P.s said, 'it is inconsistent and short-sighted to act so as to confine the selection of M.P.s to those with long purses'.[178] This was skilful pleading. The M.P.s posed as democrats against an autocratic Salvidge. In fact they were annoyed that their purses did not buy them power.

Salvidge did not make it difficult for those who contended that he was a crusty boss. 'M.P.s come and M.P.s go', he mused, 'but the organization goes on for ever.' Nevertheless, Salvidge had wisdom, believing that the danger to the party was its acceptance of pedigree or money, without other distinctions, as qualifications to rule. Salvidge would not give positions to men 'merely because they had been to public schools. They must share the dust as well as the palm. I had never had any use for the old Tory prayer, "God bless the Squire and his relations and keep us in our proper stations".'[179]

The seven M.P.s., it seemed to Salvidge, were reformers only in wanting to model Liverpool after other Conservative organizations where their class dominated the counsels. This observation had general validity, although it did not do justice to individuals. The Exchange M.P., Scott, was a most clamorous reformer. He was a Conservative who did not rest on the *status quo*. Social and industrial peace were his goals and what characterized his efforts was the principle of incorporation. He advocated women's suffrage and proportional representation to leaven the electoral system, and a simple and cheap system of land transfer to extend the property-owing class, especially to include more of the trade unions and Labour party. This would 'disincline them to revolution' and 'cut the ground from under the feet of the bolshevists'. Scott claimed to believe in 'the complete *bona fides*' of the Labour party, and his equitableness was sufficiently convincing for the Labour party to consider proposing him as Speaker of the House of Commons in 1928.

'Progress is of the essence of the Coalition policy', Scott had declared in 1919. A member of Lloyd George's wartime Reconstruction Committee, Scott shared Lloyd George's instinct for a conjunction of Conservative and Liberal opinion. This remained sharply apparent even after the 1924 General Election when the free trade Liberal party perished at the polls. 'Let the body die, and let its great soul come and find a haven of rest inside the Unionist party!', was Scott's plea. 'We are all social reformers today', he argued; 'before the War, the Unionist Social Reform Committee was a mere fraction of the party. Today it is the whole party.'

There was more to Scott's thought than the vapour about Tory Democracy and Beaconsfieldism which Baldwin made fashionable. Like a jazz band Scott provided free expression in a host of projects. Regarding housing he recommended a betterment tax, and wanted the clarification of compulsory purchase powers and greater powers of town planning. The 1925 Housing Act introduced the betterment principle and the 1932 Town and Country Planning Act and the 1933 Local Government Act were to proceed further along these lines; but on the whole they had limited utility, and the argument was not crystallized before the Uthwatt Committee in 1941–2 recommended the nationalization of development rights, thus setting the framework of financial provisions in post-war planning. The 1926 Factories Bill, on the other hand, Scott regarded as the epitome of Conservatism: it aimed 'to bring the worst employer up towards the level of the best'. Scott was sure that Conservatism rested on private enterprise and profit but he made this 'short statement of Conservative policy—the maximum freedom for the individual *plus* control by the State so that he shall not harm others'. Like most parliamentary lawyers Scott sought to outlaw the General Strike and his contributions to the question of industrial relations reflected his inexperience in this area—for instance, he espoused the idea of a compulsory cooling-off period, before a strike was joined, especially in the essential services sector, during which inquiry could be made and public opinion marshalled. Scott made greater contributions in less dramatic questions, which nonetheless impinged on the lives of many people. In the Money-lenders' Bill, 1926, he strove to protect the poor from being trapped by exorbitant interest rates in small transactions.

Scott was not markedly original—his ideas about strikes, for instance, had Canadian analogues and had been advocated previously by the former Edge Hill M.P., Rutherford, among others. Moreover, Scott's reforming impetus was vitiated by conceit and by a knack of rubbing too many Conservatives the wrong way. Scott's challenge to Salvidge's authority in the Liverpool organization dated effectively from his exclusion from high government office in 1924. Scott had an extraordinary appetite for politics. He had been in torment in 1913–14 when it had seemed that a heart complaint might necessitate his retirement after only three years in the House of Commons. 'My whole soul was in political life', he had then written to Bonar Law; and he was deeply wounded when Baldwin passed him over for the Attorney-Generalship in 1924. At the very least he had expected the Solicitor-Generalship—his claims, he thought, were 'immeasurably greater than Inskip's'—and he groaned that the Conservative premier was blind to his past sacrifices and services. During the Coalition he neglected a lucrative legal practice and estimated that he lost £100,000 directly or indirectly by devotion to government work. It also rankled that others took the credit—as he thought Lord Birkenhead did, over his reconstruction of the whole system of land conveyancing—and that his colleagues did not appreciate the significance of his contributions to the shipping industry, to agriculture, or in the 1923 Mines Working Facilities Act, that 'great bulwark against nationalization, as it removes many of the worst grievances which afford the nationalizers a pretext for attacking the present system.' But though Baldwin may have given Scott cause to believe that he would eventually shunt Inskip aside, the decade after 1922 proved a politically dark and unrewarding period for Scott, illuminated only by his elevation to the Privy Council and by a highly paid brief to advise India's Chamber of Princes in 1927–8. He replaced Lord Donoughmore as chairman of the committee on ministers' powers in 1931; and his fortunes revived further after 1935 as a judge of the Court of Appeal. He had been a contemporary at Rugby, and remained a friend, of the paramount Conservative of the time, Neville Chamberlain; and as chairman of the Committee on Land Utilization in Rural Areas in 1941–2 he returned to work of a comparable nature to that of the First War. But he had then long since severed his Liverpool connection.[180]

There was a better marriage of personality and political purpose in the West Derby M.P., John Sandeman Allen, who was knighted in 1928. He had special trading interests in East Africa; and he served on the City Council, paying particular attention to technical and commercial education. His ability was most well known as chairman of Liverpool Chamber of Commerce from 1923 to 1926, and as a principal in both British and International Chambers of Commerce. Up to 1930 Allen opposed a general tariff on food taxes, but not from a doctrinaire position. He emphasized, 'We want everything dealt with on a purely business basis'. Accordingly he supported the safeguarding policy in the 1920s and defensive subsidies, to prevent certain trades from extinction, in the 1930s; but these actions, he argued, could only provide temporary relief. His goal was bilateral or multilateral agreements between nations.

Allen did not neglect Liverpool's immediate needs while he sought to improve Britain's long-term trading position. He welcomed the derating movement in the late 1920s and, amid the 1930s depression, pressed Liverpool's claim as a distressed area, although he agreed with the National Government's pursuit of economies and was never enthusiastic about recommending the nationalization of unemployment relief or the equalization of rates. Allen in the end achieved little, but he eschewed the contemptible and considered remedies in a responsible manner. Thus, while he encouraged moves to develop the empire—his son had settled in Canada—he condemned as cruel and economically misguided sending the unemployed blindly from Britain simply because they were temporarily unwanted at home. In this he was right: an examination of the 1929 Colonial Development Act reveals a panic measure, in which a relationship between colonial development and improving exports and employment in Britain was assumed rather than proven.[181]

Only another of the seven Liverpool Conservative M.P.s who opposed Salvidge in 1927–8 might sensibly be construed as a reformer and he, the Fairfield M.P., Cohen, was a special case. An invalid, having lost both legs at Ypres in the later stages of the war, Cohen devoted himself to the British Legion, of which he was treasurer and parliamentary spokesman. On the wide range of matters concerning ex-servicemen, particularly the disabled, Cohen was a determined lobbyist. His professed hope was to keep these questions out of party politics, although this was not advanced by his aspersions against the Labour party, that it showed no solicitude about the welfare of ex-servicemen and contained members with dishonourable war records.[182]

Apart from Scott, Allen, and Cohen, the Liverpool Conservative M.P.s had no title as reforming or democratic Tories. This remark also includes Salvidge's only supporter in 1927–8, the Walton M.P., Chilcott, who had waxed rich in a way that the Prime Minister, for one, considered reprehensible. Chilcott was 'of the [Sir Robert] Horne type , picking up £1,000 here and £1,000 there' from director's fees in several City companies.[183] The Walton seat had come Chilcott's way originally out of his friendship with Lord Birkenhead, with whom he shared many interests, especially a relish for expensive living. Chilcott owned a grotesquely grand yacht, a Hampshire estate with private golf course, and a Corsican castle where he hunted wild boar with hounds and a mounted entourage wearing pink and carrying pikes. The Chilcott-Birkenhead connection was cemented in the early 1920s by a common appetite for the *louche* world of Maundy Gregory, the honours broker and owner of the Ambassador Club; but in 1926 Chilcott had exploited his friendship and alleged influence with Birkenhead, then Secretary of State for India, to deceive a group of Indian princes into parting with £100,000 to establish a political fund under Chilcott's direction. Chilcott's enterprise was not publicly exposed but Birkenhead henceforth considered him as a 'sewer rat'. Regarding Liverpool, Chilcott's interest in his constituency was nil, apart from the promotion of personal wealth which the contacts and title of M.P. facilitated. He seems to have taken Salvidge's side because Salvidge had proved capable of delivering the votes, and because he disliked Scott personally. Chilcott had spoken (or tabled a question) only once in the parliamentary sessions of 1921, 1924 and 1925 and never spoken in those of 1922, 1923, 1926, 1927 and 1928.

Jacob, the East Toxteth M.P., was almost as speechless. His zeal was limited to pressing for decimalization and selective tariffs. The Wavertree M.P., Tinne, was also narrow in his concerns. A representative of the 'well-abused plantocracy', he was born in British Guiana, with which his family had been connected for five generations. He was unshakeable in his belief that the prosperity of the colony depended upon the planters; but, though he served as parliamentary private secretary to the President of the Board of Trade in 1927–8, he was not forward in speaking on the theme of Liverpool, its interests and people.

By contrast with this trio, the Everton M.P., Woodcock, was an active parliamentarian, but his special interest was in the armed services and he voiced no popular views. He wanted to penalize voters who abstained in elections; he thought private enterprise superior to municipal enterprise in all departments; and he demanded the abolition, or stricter supervision, of grants to the Workers' Education Association after its official journal, *Highway*, in 1928 contained articles on the coal industry by R. H. Tawney and the Labour M.P. for Mansfield, F. B. Varley, which, in Woodcock's view, were 'nothing but propaganda for Communist purposes'.[184]

The last of Salvidge's antagonists, the Kirkdale M.P., Pennefather, was busy as Westminster on matters of trade and finance; and he could always be stirred to defend Ulster or to cast suspicion on the Vatican. But he was fierce opponent of the capital levy in the early 1920s; and, in regard to Liverpool's problem of high rates, he was no friend of government intervention, preferring instead the assisted emigration of the unemployed. His only remarkable position was his concern to halt the diminishing influence of the business vote by enfranchising each limited company, of which there were 95,000 compared with 86,000 private companies, in 1925. In this Pennefather spoke for many Liverpool businessmen. The chairman of Exchange Conservative Association, the cotton broker, Sir James Reynolds, was even more downright when he represented Exchange in parliament between 1929 and 1932. To abolish the business vote, he predicted, would push Britain 'one more step to eventual economic disaster'. He added, 'I feel that democracy has gone a great deal too far for this country. I would prefer another maxim: "The man who pays the piper calls the tune".'[185]

Thus the conflict between Salvidge and the seven M.P.s in 1927–8 was mostly about power. Compared with other Conservative organizations subscribers exercised little influence in Liverpool. At the bottom the polling district committees were open to election by all known Conservatives; at the top Salvidge would have no M.P.s on the Constitutional's Board of Management which, Sir John Sandeman Allen claimed, was packed with Salvidge's personal supporters and the nominees of allied clubs and societies.[186] The representation which was assigned to the W.M.C.A. and Orange Order was at the centre of the controversy. This, the M.P.s maintained, did not reflect their diminished importance. It was also impolitic, the M.P.s sharing the opinion of Sir James Reynolds—who was that oddity in Liverpool, a prominent Conservative and a prominent Catholic—that there existed 'vast numbers of Catholic working men' who, without party calls, were drifting towards Labour on account of the W.M.C.A.'s sectarianism. If this was removed Reynolds predicted that the Conservatives would benefit from the Catholic working man's natural affinity over religious education, and his distaste for Socialism. Allen went further: he claimed that 'a great majority of the Orangemen vote today for the Labour–Socialists', while the W.M.C.A.'s spirit was 'repugnant to the business world'.[187]

Although Salvidge earlier had admitted to Lord Derby that the W.M.C.A. was crumbling, he now made few concessions. The Constitutional Association, he said, had no religious test but equally it had no authority to change the W.M.C.A.'s rules; the idea that 'the old time Catholic Home Ruler is now straining at the leash to enter the Conservative Party' was 'balderdash', although there was nothing to prevent the formation of a Catholic W.M.C.A.; and, close to a General Election, in which the Prayer Book would be an issue, it was folly to offend Protestant feeling.[188]

The reluctance of many businessmen to engage in Liverpool Conservative politics was another matter. Salvidge had observed in 1926 that the wards were so big that election expenses were an impossible strain for many candidates in a period of commercial depression. Two years earlier Salvidge had considered the parliamentary difficulties. Since 1918 he had raised £16,000, but two big contributors, Colonel Ritchie, who was Lord Mayor during the police strike, and Sir William Cain, the brewer, had recently died. The number of other contributors was few; moreover, they would not generally subscribe to the Constitutional, but only to personal appeals for special purposes—General Election or By-Election funds, for example. Salvidge thought it possible to extend the circle of contributors, 'but it only means that we should have people giving us £5 notes, and really one does not want such people to be able to talk about what they have done'.[189]

Salvidge's Special Election Funds were not at issue. The controversy concerned the amount of money raised for the everyday running of the organization in the city. In the 1920s the Constitutional's annual expenditure was £3,000, of which perhaps 70 per cent went on the wages of the secretary and party agent, Murch, his assistant, W. N. Malcolm, and their small clerical staff. The loss of seats had been felt since the Constitutional depended on its elected representatives' subscriptions and, Salvidge contended, the central agency would be starved of another £1,600 if they were to establish constituency agents.

The problem, in Salvidge's opinion, was not fundamentally organizational. It was Government policy that lost elections: Edge Hill in 1923 and West Toxteth in 1924 had been decided by attitudes on rents and housing. Nevertheless, organization could blunt or sharpen the effect which policies created, and Salvidge maintained that a central agency was necessary to co-ordinate the city's effort. Constituency agents would not halt the Conservatives' decline in Liverpool any more than they had averted the Liberals' eclipse; instead they would bring waste, jealousy, and friction. The M.P.s, however, stuck to their argument. The amount of money which the Constitutional raised, and the solitariness of the central agency, were 'ridiculous' for a city like Liverpool. Birmingham's Conservatives, they instanced, raised £10,000 per annum—£7,000 by their Central Association, £3,000 by their Constituency Assoociations.[190]

Salvidge was being indicted for his Caesarism and alienation from most businessmen. Even an admirer of Salvidge's 'wonderful powers', Alderman Richard Rutherford, acknowledged that Salvidge latterly 'was going off the rails' for, in contrast to the Labour party, 'the avenues to enter the organization were kept closed'.[191] The crux was Salvidge's attitude to the 1924 Club which, according to Allen, was composed of 'excellent material'—'the business leaders of the future'. This would be a source of strength if Salvidge would welcome it into the official organization.[192] Salvidge, however, found it easier to dislike the actuality of the 1924 Club than to appreciate its potentiality, for its moving spirit was Scott, whom Salvidge thought egotistical, officious, and disloyal. Scott's political judgement was poor, according to Salvidge; he meddled in matters which did not concern him; he told tales to the Prime Minister, the party chairman, and the press; and he had a bad habit of inviting Ministers and other distinguished visitors to address his Club and to ignore the official organization.[193] While Scott was organizing the M.P.s' case Salvidge would think often of the 1924 Club and in personal terms.

This was a danger which Lord Derby, who was originally brought into the controversy as a mediator, was anxious to avoid, for he was convinced of the necessity for constituency agents, to strengthen the parliamentary against the municipal side of the organization. Moreover, while Derby wanted to involve more businessmen in the Liverpool Conservative party he too suspected Scott of 'self-aggrandisement' and 'absolute disloyalty'. Scott was insufferably 'pompous', 'the stupidest man and the most tactless I have ever had to deal with.'[194]

Accordingly when the M.P.s and Salvidge met at the Conservative Club on 28 May 1927, with Derby in the chair, it was Allen, not Scott, who was charged with putting the M.P.s' case. Salvidge had insisted on the presence too of representatives from the organization (mostly allies), Murch, Malcolm, Rutherford, White, and the eleven constituency chairmen. J. C. C. Davidson, the party's national chairman, also attended, but as an observer, for Salvidge would not tolerate an official investigation.[195]

Although Derby and the M.P.s ideally wanted separate constituency agents, practical considerations predicated a co-ordinated system, in which a central agent retained some importance. Derby, however, suggested that co-ordination might be achieved through a President's Advisory Council, consisting of the Constitutional's chairman (Salvidge), two members of the Board of Management, two councillors, and two M.P.s. Salvidge was careful not to reject this. Instead he observed that 'it would be an unofficial committee, not provided for in the rules', and he proposed a larger body, with two representatives of the Women's Federation and two of the W.M.C.A.[196]

This May meeting gave Derby and Allen a chance to assess the situation. Scott had contended to Derby that 'the Constitutional Association has become a mere paper organization' and that 'the whole work of the Association is in fact done by Salvidge and Murch, who are practically autocratic'.[197] Derby and Allen now more or less confirmed this. The organization had evolved differently from what the rules prescribed: for instance, the Constitutional's Executive Committee, which should have met monthly and governed the party funds, had been virtually dispensed with on account of its unweildy size; and divisional councils, instead of being the governing body in each constituency, had been overshadowed by the Constitutional. Derby and Allen assessed the prospects for reform. Among the constituency chairmen only Dr. Richardson, of West Derby (Allen's constituency), welcomed constituency agents. Derby and Allen explained the other chairmen's hostility by their being a 'very poor class' of person, ignorant of the experience of other cities, too satisfied with past results, and too concerned with showing loyalty to Salvidge. Allen asserted that these chairmen did not represent many 'thinking workers' in their constituencies, and Derby confidently reckoned on the support of 'the whole of the best people of Liverpool' if things ever came to a smash with Salvidge.[198]

This did not do justice to the chairmen's case, which emerged more clearly at a further conference in November. Mere pique certainly moved some to share White's opinion that the M.P.s wanted agents in order to relieve themselves of work; and Alderman J. G. Paris—the one-time Protestant Conservative councillor, now chairman of the constituency council in Kirkdale—accused the M.P.s of wanting to provide jobs for the smart set of London Central Office. Profoundly Salvidge and the constituency chairmen objected to agents being appointed by M.P.s: a party organization must control its paid officials. Although in other respects hostile to Salvidge, the party's national chairman, Davidson, endorsed this principle as essential for continuity and progress. Accordingly, Derby and the M.P.s acknowledged that a constituency agent should be chosen jointly by the Constitutional's chairman, the appropriate M.P. and constituency chairman, and that the nomination should be ratified by the constituency council and Constitutional's Executive.[199]

That Salvidge should accept any kind of constituency agent in principle might be thought a triumph for Derby and the M.P.s. Salvidge had been put in a difficulty, with a general election pending and the majority of his M.P.s disaffected. Derby had impressed this on Salvidge. Unless an M.P. was permitted some personal representative in his constituency, 'no young candidate of good standing would come to Liverpool . . .'. Derby added, with some duplicity:

> You cannot look at our Members of Parliament for Liverpool and be particularly proud of them. With the exception of Sandeman Allen who is an able business man and Tinne who is a very nice fellow, the rest really do not count and yet I am certain that unless we do something in the Agent line before the next Election you may not get even these to stand and your next lot would be worse than the first.[200]

It had been a consequence of Salvidge's management that the quality of Liverpool's M.P.s was low. Even when some were honoured it reflected little credit. W. W. Rutherford, for example, had been knighted in 1918 for his services at the bridge table, where he kept Bonar Law amused; and Houston's baronetcy in 1921 had staggered Derby, who thought that Houston's 'only real public service was to have his yacht anchored off Gairloch so that some of the P.M.'s guests could occasionally dine and sleep on board'.[201]

Salvidge could not suddenly cast around for another seven M.P.s in 1927. Initially he tried bullying. In March he had directed a meeting of the

Constitutional Association to censure the M.P.s' 'irregular and unconstitutional' demands and to affirm the existing system.[202] When the M.P.s held firm Salvidge tried appeasement. Derby and Allen mistook this for a substantial concession. When Salvidge dined, in secret, with Derby and Allen at Knowsley prior to the conference on 28 May, Derby felt that Salvidge was 'in great funk' lest their conclave should become known. Both Derby and Allen now reflected that perhaps it was not Salvidge, but others, who violently opposed their schemes. Salvidge's difficulties, Allen wrote, were with 'his Frankenstein'; and Derby speculated that Salvidge was 'a cat's-paw', either 'afraid of his own people' or flattered by them, for 'he is one of the vainest men I have ever come across', he added nastily.[203] The sequel revealed how little Salvidge had conceded or would concede.

Salvidge would have nothing to do with raising funds for constituency agents. It was agreed that Derby would launch an appeal; but Salvidge, and one M.P., would join Derby as trustees to administer the fund, provided the Constitutional's Executive agreed.[204] The fund, however, never reached an amount such that its administration might be a subject of dispute. A critical delay occurred when Derby's only daughter was killed in a hunting accident. Derby stayed abroad for several months, suffering his bereavement in Cannes; but Derby in any case was not naturally diligent. He aimed at an initial fund of £5,000 and personally promised £1,000 to which Reynolds promised another £500; but between November 1927 and September 1928 activity was virtually suspended. Derby admitted to Robert Topping, the party's Principal Agent, that he had 'to a certain extent let the Liverpool M.P.s down'. When Derby at last moved again, with Allen's prompting, Salvidge's obstructiveness reduced them to despair.[205]

In the first place Salvidge introduced Henry Mond with a view to replacing the dying Jacob in East Toxteth at the General Election. Salvidge had chosen shrewdly. Mond, an ex-Liberal M.P., was a director of I.C.I., which employed 11,200 persons locally; and he was strongly opposed to both constituency agents and the 1924 Club.[206] In Mond Salvidge had another Chilcott, to sow discord among the M.P.s. Salvidge also launched his Special Election Fund. This clearly took priority over the agents' question, and few men would contribute twice. But Salvidge's further demand, that a quarter of the amount which Derby raised should directly benefit the Constitutional, was the death-blow. In October 1928 Derby and Allen shelved the question.[207]

The position was transformed by Salvidge's death on 11 December 1928. The editor of the *Observer*, J. L. Garvin, who was a Birkenhead man in origin, wrote that Salvidge was 'one of the biggest men in England', although 'never widely enough appreciated'.[208] In fact what reputation he had shattered with his death. He left almost no money. The published residue was fictitious, for several creditors waived their claims from sympathy for Salvidge's family, or perhaps from an unwillingness to publicize the fact that the Liverpool Conservative party had been managed for several decades by a virtual bankrupt.[209] Salvidge's financial position had long been embarrassing. Slow horses and a second establishment were expensive tastes; but now Lord Derby, with Alderman Rutherford as his agent, organized a Testimonial Fund to support and provide medical aid for Lady Salvidge and her haemophiliac son, Stanley, who subsequently wrote his father's biography. Derby aimed at a minimum of £10,000. He himself generously contributed £1,000 but was under no illusions that the rest would be easily achieved. The commercial depression was against it, as was the subject himself, for Salvidge 'was never on good terms with what I call the richer people in Liverpool'.[210] Bitter memories were cherished of this 'rabble-rouser' with his 'hectoring, not to say bullying, manner', who managed an organization which was 'diametrically opposed to the old families and everything for which they stood'. [211] Salvidge represented vulgar power. His conjunction with Wise had never been forgotten. Wise, that 'combination of Uriah Heap and Titus Oates',[212] and Salvidge, 'the nearest to a Tammany boss that we have in this country',[213] seemed Conservative at the expense of Conservatism.

About £8,700 was contributed or promised before Derby closed the Testimonial Fund in October 1929. The bankruptcy of Salvidge's political work had always taken precedence in Derby's thoughts. He had written to Allen in January:

> . . . Salvidge's death has left everything in absolute chaos and the whole organization has got to be remodelled. It ought to have been done as we wished it to be done last year but as you know as well as I do, it was no good attempting it with Salvidge resisting it. I see now why Salvidge did resist it. If we had gone into the matter we should have found how entirely a one man show it was and how he had regularly and consistently broken every rule and regulation of the Constitutional Association. However, we have got to do the best we can and I hope we may pull through.[214]

It was time for traditional Conservatives to turn their hands to organization. The machine might survive M.P.s; but would it survive Salvidge?

CHAPTER SEVENTEEN

Removing 'sectarian cobwebs', 1929–39

Everyone can look back and say 'I have been an idiot'. Only a few people can look forward and say 'you are going to be an idiot'.

J. Ramsay MacDonald

Deficient in brains and starved in money, it is a miracle that the Labour Party steadily grows in voting power. The impression left on the observer's mind is of a slow underground social upheaval, moving independently of leaders or organization—propelling a lower strata of society into a more dominant position. This soulless momentum gives a certain colour to the materialist conception of history. But will this mass momentum continue if leadership fails?[1]

Beatrice Webb

This chapter demonstrates that, though a trend towards Labour and away from the Conservatives was established by 1929, the old character of Liverpool politics was not easily eradicated. Salvidge's successor, Sir Thomas White, struggled to rescue the Conservative machine; and Labour faced the fact that, in superseding former Irish parties, it must still attend to Catholic claims and interests. Economic slump in the long run, perhaps, advanced fellow feeling among Liverpool's working classes, but in the 1930s sectarian jealousies, which survived in certain quarters, might still be stirred.

White plays Salvidge's hand

Salvidge's presence in elections, the party agent, Murch, once wrote, was 'a magnet and cue' to the Conservative masses, which 'no other form of persuasion could equal'.[2] Despots, conventionally, cannot be replaced; but such was the disenchantment with Salvidge that few desired a mere replacement. Just as a family solicitor takes charge following a bereavement, Lord Derby assumed the presidency of the Constitutional Association. His difficulty was that an ersatz Salvidge so obviously existed. This was Tom

Notes on p. 460.

White, who had been knighted in 1928 as chairman of the Central Rating Authority for England and Wales.

White had been Salvidge's intimate, his deputy in the machine, and the W.M.C.A.'s vice-chairman, 'popular with a considerable section of the rank and file, especially the less educated'.[3] White so resembled Salvidge that he even filled Salvidge's position at Bent's Brewery. Salvidge's critics were also White's critics. White's political methods, Sir John Sandeman Allen asserted, were unacceptable. He was intolerant and 'would not command confidence with most who could help financially'. Derby would not recognize any good qualities in White. He felt that he was 'loathed by all the better class people in Liverpool'.[4]

Mostly, however, even his enemies admitted that White had a real grasp of municipal work and, though he showed some reluctance—he thought of moving to London as a rating expert[5]—his election as leader of the Council and chairman of the W.M.C.A. was almost a matter of course. His rival among the senior councillors was Alderman Sir Max Muspratt. Muspratt was a government nominee on the Docks Board and had the necessary connections in the business world; but he was unpopular with the rank and file and effectively disqualified, as an ex-Coalition Liberal, by not joining the Conservative Club until Salvidge's death.[6]

The logic of the situation was for Derby to depart from the Salvidge system by separating municipal and imperial politics, for a concentration of power was detrimental where the leader was labelled as chairman of the W.M.C.A. As Sir James Reynolds wrote, 'We want someone who is not prejudiced on the Orange side'.[7] Derby placed in commission the chairmanship of the Constitutional and established a President's Council, hoping to kill the practice of one-man management before undertaking a comprehensive revision of the constitution.[8]

Derby's original conception of the President's Council was a small body of only some half-a-dozen respected senior men or officers; but this was hard to reconcile with his professed concern to rouse the initiative of constituency chairmen, women, young people, and businessmen. Derby, therefore, conceded that these elements had claims to representation, despite personal misgivings regarding Major Harrison of the W.M.C.A. and Ernest Stacey of the 1924 Club.[9] Derby also doubted whether to include Reynolds, on two grounds: first, because gout made him irascible and slightly crazy; second, because he was a Catholic. Derby did not want to garland his reform movement too soon with provocative associations.[10] However, the very foundation of a President's Council was provocative. White informed Derby of the 'simmering dissatisfaction': the President's Council had not derived from the will of established party bodies but from the whim of a few individuals.[11]

Derby's difficulties deepened. An Advisory Council could not be self-acting; but Derby could not pay it undivided attention. Indeed it was undesirable that Derby, the Lord Lieutenant of Lancashire from 1928, was involved in active party politics. He sought, unavailingly, to induce a distinguished shipowner, Sir Percy Bates or Sir Thomas Royden, to become titular president of the Constitutional.[12] With a General Election pending, both the Advisory Council and the Constitutional's Board of Management needed an acting chairman, and someone had to give Murch his daily instructions. Everything pointed to White for these positions, which he assumed in January 1929. Allen immediately foresaw a 'reversion to the old and hopeless idea of one-man prominence'.[13] Derby mollified him by considering a three-man sub-committee; in fact Derby had sold the pass. Though he entreated White to overhaul the organization and to pay regard to youth, he promised not to interfere in White's executive work. His advice would always be available, but he placed himself in White's hands over whether to continue as president.[14]

In the arrangements for the 1929 General Election White and Murch were in the saddle. Partly this development was unavoidable for the M.P.s had always accepted that a General Election Fund should be discreetly raised and controlled. Accordingly Richard Rutherford, the Hon. Treasurer of the Constitutional, never saw these accounts, which were outside the ordinary audit.[15] But Allen would not have applauded Derby's choice of phrase when Derby discussed the management of the 1929 General Election Fund with Murch:

> I know of course what Sir Archibald's methods were and I wish we could find somebody who would take the same responsibility that he did. What do you think about giving it to White to deal with? I am sure that it must be in one man's hands and that must be the hands of a man who does not talk and I fear that Alderman Rutherford certainly does not fulfil that qualification. If therefore we could arrange that all money should be paid into a Central Fund from which from time to time cheques could be drawn and paid to you or Sir Thomas, and left entirely to your discretion as to how the money was spent, I am sure it would be a good thing. No account would have to be asked of you and we should have to accept, and I would readily do it, your receipt for the money as being a guarantee that the money was well and properly spent.[16]

Small wonder that Murch was soon calling White the 'Acting Leader of the Party.'[17]

The new leadership's first test had come quickly as Jacob's health further deteriorated. He vacated East Toxteth in February 1929. Only one ward had a preponderantly working-class population, returning one Liberal and two Labour councillors. Three other wards were absolutely Conservative. The candidate, Henry Mond, was preselected by Salvidge. White and Murch ran his campaign from the Constitutional. They had little to do except point Conservative supporters to the poll and quash Mond's suggestion that he approach the other parties about giving him an unopposed return until the General Election, when the electorate would expand with another eleven or twelve thousand women.[18]

Industrial peace and industrial rationalization inspired Henry Mond and his father, Sir Alfred Mond, now Lord Melchett. In pursuit of the first goal Melchett had envisaged a national campaign, in conjunction with moderate trade union leaders and with Lord Derby as President; but the movement had been halted by the bitter feelings which the Trades Disputes Act aroused. The second goal was just as controversial. Melchett was accused of having a 'bias towards ruthless American methods'; and in the Liverpool shipping industry rationalization spelled unemployment to men who had already witnessed a transfer of Atlantic liners to Southampton and of head offices to London. Melchett in fact was a radical exponent of trust capitalism, who had introduced profit-sharing schemes into his business with a view to ensuring high productivity and banishing Socialism, which he abominated for its destructive and impractical nature. Accordingly, though he was Lloyd George's Minister of Health (1921–2), Melchett had broken with Lloyd George in 1925 when he considered that his land proposals tended in a socialist direction; and he had joined the Conservative party in 1926, asserting that the Liberal party's position in politics had become 'futile and sterile'. Men must resist Liberalism's 'demonstrated futility' and Socialism's 'demonstrated dangers', his son now observed filially.[19] In an economic emergency, to avoid a general reduction of wages Henry Mond favoured a tariff on foreign manufactured goods and 'a policy of Imperial insulation'; but mostly he appealed to governments to observe different priorities. Two forces were responsible for Britain's economic decline, the 'orthodox Free Trade View' and the 'orthodox Treasury View'. Industrial interests should be put before financial interests, and Mond advocated an extension of credit to rationalized industries by squeezing the unrationalized. The whole taxation system, in his opinion, was wrong: if taxation was used to redistribute wealth industrial progress would be halted by the injury to capital and effort. 'What you want to arrive at', Mond thought, 'is not national redistribution, but national prosperity, with high wages, and in order to get high wages you have got to have good prices and low taxes'.[20]

Undaunted, the Liberal candidate in the East Toxteth by-election, Abed Roberts, echoed Lloyd George's boast that he could reduce unemployment to normal proportions within twelve months; and Labour's candidate, a lay preacher, Alderman Cleary, hardly seemed the dangerous man of Mond's imagination. He deprecated 'scare statements' regarding Labour's financial intentions, and advocated raising the school-leaving age, adequate pensions, an international forty-eight hours week, the scientific utilization of land, a unified coal industry, public works, and trade expansion.[21] Altogether the by-election had an ailing look, personified by Lord Birkenhead's last appearance at the hustings. In a 61 per cent poll the Conservatives dropped 6,447 votes, Labour 57. The Liberals numbered 2,000 more. Mond won, but for the first time Conservatives constituted a minority in East Toxteth. In the Government's record on unemployment a sufficient explanation existed.[22]

The General Election in May 1929 brought a resurgent interest. Approximately democracy had arrived, in which women preponderated. Less than ten years previously one Liverpool M.P. had warned against lowering the age qualification of women electors from thirty to twenty-one by reminding Parliament of 'what happened to Samson once when he gave away the source of his strength'; but this step was now mostly uncontroversial.[23] Delilah could not be blamed for Britain's industrial decline.

White and Murch directed the Conservative performance in Liverpool, although without being able to choose much of the script or cast. None of the six new candidates was bred by them, and several brought controversy in their train. For example, Geoffrey Watson, a retired businessman whom Allen had recommended to West Toxteth, demanded decasualization in the docks and restrictions against unskilled immigrants from Ireland. In Walton the argument concerned the character of the candidate rather than his policies. Chilcott, the retiring M.P., and Alderman R. C. Herman, the constituency chairman, had conspired to fix the candidature without consulting anyone else. They sought a man who had money and who liked to spend it; and, after several mishits, they presented Reginald Purbrick, who had made a fortune from Australian dairy products. Purbrick was an advocate of co-operation in industry, but co-operation on his terms. He had no time for those who espoused theories of new social, political, and industrial systems; and he applauded the 1927 Trades Disputes Act for preventing trade unions from establishing 'soviet government'. Purbrick had no political experience and no connection with Liverpool except by his purse strings. Derby told Murch: 'I hate to think of a Liverpool seat being bought and that is what it comes to.'[24]

For most of the new Conservative candidates the problem was sectarianism. White and Murch attempted a diversion. The Council had braved the Bolsheviks in 1928 by excluding Russian petrol from Corporation contracts; now it was reported that Liverpool Conservatives felt that 'the dominating issue is no longer unemployment, but Socialism and its threat to the nation's security.' However, one concern was Catholic education after the Archbishop, Downey, questioned fifty-nine parliamentary candidates in the Liverpool region about whether they would welcome equal treatment for denominational and provided schools. Three replied with qualified affirmatives, thirty-eight with assentation.[25]

In the Exchange division Scott retired in favour of his constituency chairman, Sir James Reynolds who, Scott predicted, would 'carry the Catholic vote and the business vote'.[26] In 1929 Reynolds was Privy Chamberlain to the Pope. His main political interest, like Downey's was to prevent the Catholic vote moving towards Labour. To this end he contributed to the expenses of Centre candidates in municipal elections, and suggested that the Conservatives nominate Harford for the mayoralty.[27] Reynolds' opponent, Labour's leader, Robinson, was also a Catholic; but he rejected Downey's inquiry. After a violent contest, which Reynolds won by 209 votes, Labour considered petitioning, alleging a priest's intimidation of electors.[28]

Allen was certain that Reynolds won where Scott would have lost; but Reynolds' ostentatious Catholicism upset White who wanted to maintain an equilibrium between sectarian factions in the Exchange constituency association. He was also nervous about Longbottom's capacity to direct the militant Protestant votes elsewhere.[29] Everton particularly occupied White's thoughts. By 1929 all except one of Everton's wards had turned Labour, and the parliamentary seat seemed lost if the sitting M.P., Woodcock, contested it.

Derby disliked Woodcock. He thought him 'half-witted' and 'one of the most unpopular men in the House'; but these were no disqualifications to represent Everton. Woodcock was reasonably diligent at Westminster. His real problem was that he could not get on with his constituency chairman, Councillor A. M. Urding, or with Murch, and he would not pour money into the debt-ridden constituency clubs.[30] Woodcock had been casting about for another seat, without success, but Derby and White insisted that he retire in March 1929.

White picked Margaret Beavan to replace Woodcock. She had a high reputation as the director of the Liverpool Child Welfare Association which, White reckoned, might reflect credit upon the Conservative party, although Labourites remembered her visit to Italy, as Liverpool's first female mayor, when she carelessly adopted the fascist salute.[31] Miss Beavan would have preferred to contest West Toxteth which, she claimed, Salvidge had promised her. Everton did not attract her. It had not a 'clean' reputation politically; her health was poor; and she would need Derby's financial support in any event. Derby gave this, though he disliked her standing for parliament, fearing that she might jeopardize her life's work by identification with one party.

This proved to be the case. Miss Beavan was downcast by an acrimonious campaign in Everton and died eighteen months later. She especially blamed Longbottom—'a nasty creature'. White, having talked with Longbottom, persuaded her to withdraw her commitment to Downey on the education question. What form this bargain took is obscure, but Miss Beavan felt 'betrayed by Longbottom. Had he not broken faith and openly abused the Catholics and caused press sensation—the Archbishop—who seemed to have amazing confidence in me— would have stood by me—even in spite of my concession.'[32] Derwent Hall Caine, a son of Sir T. H. Hall Caine, the Manx novelist who had once lived in Liverpool, defeated Miss Beavan by 1,667 votes.[33]

The education issue was unrewarding for the Conservatives in the constituencies where sectarianism mattered. Watson, striving for the Orange vote in West Toxteth, was the only Conservative to join Miss Beavan in rejecting Downey's position. By contrast only one Labour candidate—Elijah Sandham, the I.L.P. candidate who won Kirkdale[34]—affirmed Catholic policy. With Labour holding Edge Hill and West Toxteth, and gaining Everton and Kirkdale, Liverpool barely remained Conservative in 1929. Four of the six Conservative seats had unhealthy majorities.

The religious question was not everything. Although four out of the five Liberal candidates in Liverpool complied with Downey's position, their preoccupation was in weaning suburbia from Conservatism. 37,816 Liberals declared themselves but every candidate found third place. Labour inspired what enthusiasm there was in 1929. Margaret Beavan likened their devotion to that of Crusaders: 'They are willing to make any sacrifice—week in, week out—for Socialism. Possibly they have only this *one* cause which demands sacrifice—most of us have many—but we have to face the fact that the Political outlook has so entirely changed that other methods are necessary . . .'[35]

It was debatable whether the Labour party contained a preponderance of truculent Socialists whom the existing political system could not accommodate. Jack Hayes, the one-time mutinous policeman, now returned to constabulary duties as Vice-Chamberlain of H.M. Household in the incoming Labour Government. Lord Derby, however, was not in a position to fashion and implement any new methods which Miss Beavan might have had in mind to revitalize the Conservative party. White and Murch had relieved Derby of much labour and responsibility in the General Election. He had also relieved himself of several of the principles for which he had been fighting. He had no illusions about White and Murch. Both had made plain their dislike of the proposed reforms of the organization. Previously, Derby had considered White to be 'villainous' and he had wanted to discharge Murch because 'personally I dislike him very much indeed and distrust him'. Now, Derby appreciated their appetite for work. Allen and others still warned him that White and Murch were 'wedded to the old idea'; but Derby replied that White was 'a real good fellow', 'loyal' and 'helpful', and though Murch's manners remained 'shockingly bad', he too was 'running quite straight and very loyal'. 'It is hard', Derby informed Tinne about Murch, 'for a man to suddenly change and I do not think that we can expect in his case that the change from rudeness to suavity will be a very quick one'.[36]

In December 1929 Derby weakly told Allen that Murch had become 'almost painfully civil' to him; but by then Derby was bound, out of consideration for the reformers, to essay Murch's removal. He acknowledged that numerous people 'won't give one single penny or help in any way so long as Murch is there'. Accordingly Derby asked White to consider pensioning Murch: 'You and I appreciate Murch's value,' he wrote; 'I never used to like him and there is nothing much in the man himself to like except his intense loyalty to his Chiefs. Personally I think he is the best agent with the worst manner I have ever known.'[37] But White would not ditch Murch, and Derby retreated.

The consequence of Derby having given White and Murch freedom to act was seen in the constituencies. Perhaps it was true that 'archaic as the Rules may be, they could not restrain active Divisional life if there was a will for it;[38] but, at a time when the future of constituency agents was in the balance, the central office held the master hand. In April 1929 Alderman Haigh resigned the chairmanship of Wavertree constituency association. After more than a decade of service he left a dormant organization. He himself described 'the great amount of apathy, want of workers, and of co-ordination in the Division'.[39] Muspratt was coaxed into replacing Haigh for the period of the General Election: the reformers wanted to give J. F. Brackell, Tinne's recent appointment as secretary of the division, a sympathetic chairman. After barely two months of work Brackell told Derby that Wavertree's organization had been deliberately run down to facilitate control by the Constitutional's office. Only three of the twenty-four polling district committees were functioning; the ward organization was ruined; and the few voluntary workers, being unable to stand Murch's dictation, retired from political life.[40]

Exchange was the only other constituency to have ventured independence. Scott had wanted to appoint an agent in 1927 but Derby and the national chairman, Davidson, restrained him since the negotiations with Salvidge were then at a tender stage.[41] Members of the 1924 Club, none the less, infiltrated into the constituency organization. The chairmen of St. Peter's, Great George, Vauxhall, and Exchange wards were either members or sympathizers; and the secretary of the 1924 Club, Stacey, became deputy chairman of Exchange division and acting election agent. Stacey was a capable organizer, an author of a new constitution for Birkenhead Conservative Association; but his tactlessness outrivalled Scott's. He made no secret of his ambition to expel the 'old gang' and become chairman of the Constitutional.[42] Derby was annoyed by Stacey's pushiness but he begged White to 'make more use of the young men than

Salvidge did. He resented the 1924 Club and I agree with him. It exists as a Club solely for the purpose of glorifying Leslie Scott and Stacey, but there are a lot of very capable young men in it who individually would be of the greatest use to us and Stacey himself would be of use if he would not give himself such airs'.[43]

In playing up to both sides in the Liverpool struggle Derby remained constant only to the reputation of 'Genial Judas', which he had won as Director General of Recruiting some fifteen years before. In January 1929 he threatend Scott that he would resign if Stacey was put on the Advisory Council against his wishes; but in April Derby joined the 1924 Club and in June hoped to place Stacey on the Advisory Council himself.[44] By then Scott had retired with heart trouble and recommended that Reynolds succeed him as Conservative candidate in Exchange. Derby had his doubts, about both Reynolds's health and his evident Catholicism. The Protestant element in Exchange was not large but it was strong in the constituency organization and its leader, Roberts, had defeated Stacey in a contest for the constituency vice-chairmanship. Muspratt also suspected others of disliking Reynolds's succession. White and Murch, he alleged, were quite prepared for Reynolds to lose Exchange, and for Tinne to lose Wavertree, 'as an example of what happens to the independent minded Conservative member'. Derby, however, would not face White with this accusation.[45]

The situation in Exchange reached a crisis early in 1930 as the constituency chairman, Sir Arnold Rushton, was dying. Members of the 1924 Club implored Derby to secure Stacey's replacement of Rushton, and to continue as president of the Constitutional, otherwise 'a vast body of honest opinion' would be left at the mercy of White and Murch. White, however, told Derby not to interfere. The 1924 Club was checked. Stacey became the constituency vice-chairman, but only by allowing Roberts the chairmanship unopposed; and the 1924 Club's candidate for the deputy vice-chairmanship was defeated, at an exceptionally large constituency meeting, by ninety-six votes to forty-eight. Reynolds, who only a few months before prided himself on being independent of the Constitutional, was now warned by White not to overvalue the 1924 Club or to exacerbate sectarian difficulties by demonstrations of his Catholicism.[46]

Defeat for Stacey was also defeat for Derby, since Derby meanwhile had employed Stacey in drafting a constitution to embody the ideas that had developed from his exchanges with Allen. After the 1929 General Election Derby had reopened the question of a reorganization with a bluff assurance which had never characterized his dealings with Salvidge, and which soon disappeared from his dealings with White. 'I am convinced of one thing', Derby had proclaimed, 'that the Working Men's Conservative Association as at present constituted is no use. Half the men are socialists and we are relying on a broken reed when we think they could be of use to us.' While some central representation might be arranged, Derby's recommendation was entire constituency independence—each with its own secretary or agent, and its own working men's, women's, and young Conservative associations.[47] White, predictably, was unimpressed. Derby had been exceptionally maladroit. Allen counselled Derby to proceed cautiously, aware that White's and Murch's management of the General Election gave them an advantage: their industriousness and knowledge secured for them the confidence of most constituencies, despite the generally poor results.[48]

The conspiratorial nature of the opposition to Salvidge was now resumed against White as Derby and the M.P.s met for discussions at Westminster. Allen was the guiding intelligence, but Stacey's help was formally sought by Derby in September 1929, and Topping, the principal agent, was also consulted. Their ambitions were clarified: to eliminate the direct representation of the Orange Order, diminish the W.M.C.A.'s influence, and enlist the support of Catholic working men; to rouse and give influence to the majority of Conservatives outside the clubs and societies by restricting membership of the Constitutional to subscribers; to permit the constituencies to have their own funds and salaried officials; and to liberate parliamentary from municipal politics in Liverpool by disconnecting ward and constituency associations and by making councillors and aldermen ineligible as officers of polling district, ward, or constituency, associations. Some of these ambitions, however, would have to be modified or dropped if they were to effect a smooth transition from the existing organization.

Much depended on Derby, but Derby now wanted only to effect the smooth transition of himself out of Liverpool politics. The occasions when he considered resigning the presidency were many, and by October 1929 he had his valediction in draft, advising the Constitutional to cultivate constituency responsibility, to face the religious problem—and to elect White as the next president.[49] Derby did not then resign, but he considered it again, in letters to Topping and Tinne, in November and December. By then his spirit was so abject that his reason for wanting to resign was that he felt the force of White's objections to the reform proposals.[50]

Derby instead ended the year trying to satisfy Allen by composing a circular to all constituency chairmen. Derby had promised the Constitutional's Board of Management that he would seek a generally agreed scheme of reform; until then he urged the constituency chairmen to work the existing constitution, insist on constituency authority, and inspirit their polling district, ward, and constituency meetings. White, however, would not tolerate bombast. Since 1885, he corrected Derby, polling district, ward, and constituency, officials had always discussed their arrangements with the Constitutional's central agency, which had then executed them.[51]

The New Year, 1930, brought worse when Stacey, White, and Murch quarrelled about whether White, as chairman of the Constitutional's Board of Management, was entitled to be called 'the party leader'. Derby's response again was to threaten resignation; but White would not let Derby go, since this would leave an impression that Derby had made another attempt at reorganization and that he had blocked him.[52] Derby was floundering now, but his chances of being able to quit rose sharply when Stacey met White and, in the course of discussing his new constitution, casually remarked that he had visited Topping in London. White was furious and wanted the new constitution immediately placed before the Board of Management and voted on. He himself boldly defended the existing constitution as giving adequate provision for constituency life.

Derby welcomed this clash of White and Stacey. It gave him a plausible case for resignation, and he could pass the blame for his failure to press reform. 'Sir

Thomas White', Derby told Allen, 'like Salvidge, so hates the 1924 Club and Stacey in particular, that he has done everything he can to prevent our arriving at any solution of our troubles.'[53] Derby, however, still wished to save face by avoiding a direct vote between White and himself—though he boasted to Stacey that he could win such a vote—and he persuaded Reynolds to propose, and Muspratt to second, a resolution that White and Allen be commissioned to prepare a scheme of reorganization. In the event of difference they should refer to the party's national chairman and, after consulting the constituency chairmen, submit their scheme to the Board of Management.[54]

When White was entrusted with the preparation of reform, albeit watched by Allen, reform was virtually dead. Stacey's reaction, having been blocked in Exchange and now at the Constitutional, was to cling more keenly to his only remaining source of power, the 1924 Club. He became its president in October 1930 but his every move reflected its failure. The age restriction was relaxed, to include older men; formal recognition from the Conservative Central Office in London was sought, to ease the raising of funds; and effort was directed towards the outlying districts, Liverpool itself having been mostly surrendered to White and Murch. Overtures were made to Sir Oswald Mosley and Lord Lloyd, Stacey seeking to command almost any Liverpool organization, whether for the Fascists or for Conservative critics of Baldwin's India policy; but the commission never came. By January 1934 members of the 1924 Club preferred party loyalty to Stacey's restlessness, and the Club was wound up.[55]

Though some skirmishes remained, White had won Salvidge's war.

Religion and the Liverpool Labour party

Liverpool's Conservatives had no monopoly of internecine war. The Labour party also slipped into factionalism, and religion was again a source of the conflict. Criticism that O'Connor remained unchallenged in the General Election was annulled by his death in November 1929. David Logan became the new 'Member for the Scotland Yard Division'.[56] He was a Liverpudlian of Scottish–Irish origins who had lived all his life in the Kew Street area of Scotland Road. By trade he was a pawnbroker, although previously he had worked on the river and in the theatre. As the chairman and an alderman of the Labour party in the constituency Logan was well placed to succeed O'Connor; in his erstwhile Nationalist credentials and in his robustness—he was to hold the seat for thirty-five years—his succession was natural too. Most fitting of all was Logan's deep Catholic faith. He had founded a chapter of the Knights of St. Columba with the aim, his critics said, of catholicizing the Liverpool Labour party or, at least, of ensuring that the Labour party might not subvert Catholic principles.

Logan had no patience with sectarianism rooted in national mistrust. He often pleaded in the 1930s for the reconciliation of England and Ireland, and he tried to extend the 1936 Public Order Bill, which banned the exhibition of fascist uniforms, to prohibit the parade of bellicose Orangemen and Catholics. But upon fundamental principles of his faith Logan was ultramontane. His maiden parliamentary speech rebutted a Labour party proposal to repeal the laws against blasphemy. He spoke of the 'great religious fervour' of his constituents and added: 'To me God means everything and all things, and I feel that in this House and in the Government of this nation it is essential that we should understand what true religion means.' Soon after, in 1931, Logan divided from his party again, over the Education Bill, and he was in the dismal minority which voted against certain local authorities being permitted to continue the Sunday opening of cinemas, theatres, and concert-halls. In 1932 he opposed any facilities for divorce, even where one partner had been incurably insane for over five years; and in 1935 and 1936 he objected to government money being spent to spread information about birth control. This 'scurrilous literature', he declared, 'is only fit for the gutter. It is not fit for decent homes to have any knowledge of.' Logan himself had ten children.[57]

An impression that Logan was exclusively a Catholic champion in Parliament would be false—he was the most active Liverpool M.P. on questions of unemployment relief and housing—but the accession of quondam Nationalists and eternal Catholics made Liverpool's Labour party a bipartite creature, whose Catholic and secular halves often clashed.

Municipally, in 1929, Labour achieved its inter-war peak. Fifty-seven Labour Council members faced seventy-nine Conservatives, fourteen Liberals, seven Centre representatives, and one Independent. The Conservatives' over-all majority was one, but in practice they depended on the co-operation of the Liberals. They shared with Labour neither the chairmanships nor deputy-chairmanships of thirty Committees and thirty-eight Sub-Committees. Callowness thus characterized the Labour group. Moreover, Catholics composed over one-third of Labour councillors between the wars. Safe in former Nationalist wards, they were even a majority in Labour's years of setback, 1924, 1930–1, 1936–8.[58] Arguably the Catholicism of many electors and elected came before their Socialism. Labour inherited rather than won Nationalist seats: the outstanding feature of the 1920s had been the failure of the Labour party to sweep aside the Church-protected remnants of the old Nationalist party. Elimination having failed, accommodation was tried; but the potential for disharmony was plain, as Catholics, while strong in Labour's Council group, composed under one-eighth of the L.T.C.'s executive.[59]

In 1929–30 the nine-acre site of Brownlow Hill Workhouse went on sale as the Corporation undertook the administration of poor relief. Labour councillors divided, by twenty-three votes to eighteen, in recommending that the Housing Committee develop the site. The opposition was Catholic, inspired by Archbishop Downey's enthusiasm for building 'a cathedral in our lifetime'.[60] The Poor Law Guardians, however, had rejected the Catholics' offer of £100,000: their reserve figure was £125,000, although the Ministry of Health approved a price not under £100,000.[61] When the Corporation would not sanction a factory on the site or develop it itself, the Catholic bid stood alone. Though Longbottom declared his preference for 'a poison germ factory' instead of a Catholic Cathedral, the Finance Committee commended the Catholic offer.[62] The Council endorsed it by eighty-eight votes to twenty-seven. Sir Edwin Lutyens's models for the cathedral—designed to be second only to St. Peter's at Rome in size—were soon displayed;[63] but sectarian differences had been re-animated.

Thirty-two Labour members, including the party leader, Robinson, finally voted to accept the Catholic offer; nineteen opposed it. Two Catholic Labourites had approved of Robinson's line without voting; nineteen Catholic Labourites voted with him, none against.[64] That same month the Labour Government's Education Bill was advertised. Church schools did not have the facilities to meet the objective of raising the school-leaving age to fifteen, without special financial aid; and the conclusion was clear, that the Bill would lead to many Catholic children being taught in non-Catholic surroundings. Downey exhorted his flock to rebel.[65] Rupture was inevitable as the L.T.C. insisted that Labour councillors accept a secular educational position.[66]

Three councillors in Great George Street, and one in Vauxhall, seceded. They styled themselves 'Democratic Labour', endeavouring to attract ex-Nationalist colleagues. A different seceder was Olive Hughes, who found that St. Anne's ward committee would not readopt her after she supported the Cathedral site. She stood independently, confirmed by various Catholic bodies, against the official candidate, Bessie Braddock. Mrs. Braddock pluckily pressed a campaign for more homes, not priests.[67] She won, but elsewhere Labour lost five seats to Conservatives, four (uncontested) to Democratic Labour, and one to a Protestant. The party seemed shattered on the left also, for in an Edge Hill ward by-election an I.L.P. candidate defeated the official Labour candidate. The victor, Tissyman, was the retiring councillor; he had resigned the L.T.C.'s vice-presidency, remonstrating against irresolute leadership. A Conservative won Edge Hill in November through divided Labour votes; and the L.T.C. expelled the I.L.P. branch.

A finale occurred when the Labour group deposed its leader. It was unhandsomely done—Robinson was absent, fighting (and losing) a parliamentary by-election in Shipley—but he had crossed the L.T.C. once too often. Robinson thereafter sulked until he won a parliamentary pension in 1935, representing St. Helens, a substitute Sexton. The leadership of the Liverpool Labour party passed to Luke Hogan, who was less punctilious but naturally Catholic (Robinson was a convert). He was also more matey, full of eloquence and beer, the chairman of the Liverpool Council of Action during the General Strike.[68] Both Robinson and Hogan were officials of the N.U.D.A.W. and, with the Braddocks also members, it was among the most influential, if inconsistent, of trade unions in Liverpool politics.[69]

The legacy of the Cathedral site controversy and of the collision between the L.T.C. and Labour Council group was an apparently endless feud in which Labourites 'hated each other far far more than they hated the Tories'.[70] Several constituency parties, Scotland, Edge Hill, and West Toxteth, which sided with Robinson, engaged in a protracted dispute concerning affiliation fees.[71] These were side-shows in a generally destructive performance. Regarding the participants Reginald Bevins is a solitary, though partial, guide. The Braddocks were reticent in print, but Bessie in speech in 1936 nominated Bevins (then a Labour councillor) 'anti-working class'. Bevins likened the monthly Labour meetings to 'an exercise in apartheid', where members segregated themselves according to religion and prejudice. The left-wingers, he claimed, were 'open or secret members of the Communist Party', but the Irish Catholics 'always won because they were the big battalions'. Those in the middle were impotent.[72]

Neither crypto-Communists nor Catholics could dominate singly both the L.T.C. and Council group. They could impede; but Hogan's leadership rested on union 'moderates' as well as Catholics. In measuring the Church's power in Liverpool politics at this time it is useful to consider the past. J. H. Whyte's assessment of the electoral activity of the Catholic clergy in nineteenth-century Ireland seems generally applicable: the clergy could tap a large stock of affection which might result in a candidate whom they supported polling better than he would otherwise have done; but mostly they 'could lead their people only in the direction that they wanted to go'.[73]

The suspicion of Catholic power aroused Protestant warhorses. Six candidates enlivened the 1930 municipal elections; and in December Longbottom started a newspaper, the *Protestant Times*. He won a three-cornered contest in St. Domingo; others (including Mrs. Longbottom) registered a collective failure of 9,000 votes but their intervention, White believed, prevented the Conservatives from gaining several seats.[74] In centenary celebrations of the Liverpool–Manchester Railway citizens recalled that Liverpool staged the country's first substantial steam-driven railway service. Coincidentally violence in Netherfield ward evidenced that Liverpool was the last English city to allay sectarianism. There could be no community spirit, according to the Anglican bishop, Dr. David, when Catholics would not join Protestants even to sing hymns at the Cenotaph.[75] The Bishop also deprecated speakers of the Catholic Evidence Guild and priests who, by 'relentless pressure' upon non-Catholic partners, brought 'bitter unhappiness' into mixed marriages.[76]

Downey replied that he had closed the Guild's pitches not because its speakers mocked Anglican formularies, but because Protestant hooligans made trouble at their meetings. Moreover, he snubbed David's invitation to an ecumenical service—'an Archbishop of the Catholic Church can hardly be expected to accept the spiritual leadership of an Anglican Bishop'.[77] Some Liverpudlians responded to this exchange. Protestant mobs buffeted Downey and stormed a presbytery.[78] In 1931 David proclaimed that the Catholics' activities again threatened 'our liberties and our peace', but he exhorted Orangemen to expose these invasions by publicity, not by 'angry language and vengeful deeds'.[79] He claimed that the situation in mixed marriages had improved following his recent publicity. This was optimistic. Downey believed that David had exploited malicious hearsay in order to 'stir up the Orange drum'.[80]

After Downey's invective against the Labour Government's Education Bill,[81] sectarianism again moved politicians. In January 1931 an amendment, deferring the Bill until it aided denominational schools, passed against the Government. The sensitivities of Liverpool's Labour M.P.s were demonstrable—Sandham supported his Government, but Logan, Caine, and Gibbins, defended Catholic claims by voting with the Conservatives. Logan's outspokenness in particular angered several of his Labour colleagues who, equally forthright, told him to 'Go to Hell'; but the issue still plagued the party at a by-election in February 1931, following Mond's succession as Lord Melchett.[82] Labour advanced Charles Burden, the candidate in 1924. He advocated aid to denominational schools, whereas Cleary, who had twice contested East Toxteth in 1929, opposed it. This manoeuvre reflected Labour's internal disquiet but was politically pointless because East Toxteth was hardly a Catholic stronghold and economic issues were alienating Labour's support.[83]

Burden's brief was for a Socialism which, *The Times* commented, was 'barely distinguishable from advanced Liberalism'; but he asserted that 'capitalism is bringing the nation to ruin'.[84] On Melchett's recommendation the Conservatives nominated Patrick Buchan-Hepburn, Winston Churchill's former secretary.[85] Although Buchan-Hepburn studiously followed Baldwin's line on India, he imitated Churchill by denouncing Labour's alleged preference for Russian over Empire trade, and by calling the Trades Disputes Act (Amendment) Bill 'the Bill to promote further and better strikes'.[86] The Prime Minister, MacDonald, theatrically scorned this attempt 'to rouse the 1926 spirit of class enmity'; in fact Churchill was less reactionary in this question than was supposed. Ever since 1925, when he first developed a position, he envisaged the reversal of the trade union political levy as part of a package which would also include a treasury grant towards cheapening the cost of parliamentary elections.[87] Now, however, both parties engaged in humbug since, to common knowledge, the Trades Disputes Act (Amendment) Bill would be emasculated in Committee stage. More importantly, this by-election demonstrated the extent of the electorate's disillusionment before the Labour Government collapsed. The Conservatives held their 1929 (General Election) sum of 17,000; Labour plunged from 9,904 to 5,550. Moreover 9,287 Liberal votes disappeared despite Churchill's belief that their 'self-respect' would not permit abstention.

This feature was repeated in a June by-election in Wavertree, when Tinne retired. His successor was Ronald Nall-Cain, a barrister son of the chairman of Walker-Cain, the brewers. He had been a potential candidate in East Toxteth in February. He defended denominational education; but Labour's candidate, Sam Treleavan, represented Nonconformist traditions and as a consequence received little help from his party.[88] Without a candidate the Liberal party officially abstained. Treleavan satisfied key points of the Liberals' questionnaire, but leading Liberals like Sir Benjamin Johnson, who had voted for Tinne in 1929, again supported the Conservatives. Many had been upset by the Government's land tax. Baldwin called this 'a tax of the most vicious kind', which penalized those who 'committed the crime of buying property'.[89]

The Tory alternative, as enunciated by Nall-Cain, was to develop the Empire, institute tariffs, and 'tax the foreigner'.[90] Nall-Cain was a product of Eton and Magdalen, and not yet thirty. His pulse beat steadily to the rhythms of class, not to the quixoticism of youth. His answer to the national crisis was 'rigid economy' and reductions in income tax. He was impressed now by Mussolini's repeal of death and estate duties, to stimulate agriculture; later in the 1930s he was impressed by the Nazi extirpation of Communism.[91] He received 18,687 votes, an increase of 1,800 over the 1929 sum. Treleavan's poll fell from 13,585 to 10,042; and 9,000 Liberal votes evaporated. White speculated that perhaps 1,500 Liberals and even some Labourites voted Conservative; but militant Protestants in Garston were thought to have gone the other way.[92]

The years of depression

The East Toxteth and Wavertree by-elections were a presentiment of the 1931 General Election. MacDonald, scorned as the Prime Minister of a National Government by his erstwhile Labour colleagues, had braved unpopularity before. His opposition to the 1914–18 war had cost him the leadership of the Labour party, membership of his golf club, and eventually his seat in Parliament; moreover the press, led by *John Bull*, had conducted a vituperative personal campaign, not sparing the details of his bastardy. That stand upon his principles had been forgiven by 1922; this time the obloquy prevailed beyond his extinction. One Liverpool Labour M.P., Hall Caine, followed MacDonald in support of the National Government, but no Everton party respected his loyalty. Cries of 'Twister' and 'Traitor' engulfed Caine and the Dominions Secretary, J. H. Thomas, who visited Liverpool to speak for his side. Thomas was roused, not to tackle unemployment but to discipline the unemployed. He retorted to the hecklers, 'No greater need for a National Government can be given than that this hooliganism must and will be dealt with. . . . This is always the attitude of people who know they are whacked. It is the surest sign of success'.[93]

Thomas had beseeched Lord Derby to effect the withdrawal of Conservative opposition to Hall Caine. Nothing should weaken their 'firm front against the wreckers', as Thomas now styled his former party. This, however, was impossible. If the Conservatives withdrew, Longbottom would stop Hall Caine with a Protestant candidate. Moreover, many Conservatives, including Derby himself, had not forgiven Hall Caine's offensiveness to the late Margaret Beavan during their contest in 1929. Hall Caine eventually achieved third place behind the Labour candidate, Treleavan, and the Conservative victor, Councillor Frank Hornby, whose Meccano symbolized the miniature economic enterprise of the day.[94] Altogether there was little National Government sentiment among Liverpool Conservatives. Allen was alone in publicly criticizing Hornby's candidature; and White's speculation that MacDonald himself might be invited to speak in Liverpool drew this reply from Derby: 'I doubt whether he could come but I am told that the man is such a mass of nerves now that he really might not be of much use to you.'[95]

In August 1931 the Liverpool Chamber of Commerce had advised MacDonald to institute economies; in September the Council's Finance Committee ceremonially slaughtered the education estimates.[96] The Public Assistance Committee followed by rejecting the unemployed's demands for increased relief. With specious equity the Council reduced the Lord Mayor's allowance by 10 per cent to £2,700; and Reynolds joined those plutocratic penitents who waived their Parliamentary salary.[97] Labour lost every Liverpool seat, except the imperishably Catholic Scotland division, where Logan was confident of beating all-comers, 'from the Prime Minister downwards'.[98]

This, in a curious way, was a tribute to MacDonald's past achievement. For all his personal flaws—his solitariness, shyness, suspicion and prickliness—between 1900 and 1914 and again between 1922 and 1931 MacDonald had been the principal architect of Labour's parliamentary policy and personified the party's credit in the country. Himself a classless figure, with a rich and romantic vein of oratory, he had been able, without apparent contradiction, to present a class-conscious Labour party to a class-divided electorate as a party that would heal, repair, and remove class wounds by evolutionary progressive Socialism. Now all this was undone. In 1931, at the age of 65, MacDonald changed from a venerated Gladstone of Labour into an impious Lloyd George at the head of a Tory-dominated Coalition, and this metamorphosis dealt destruction to his former party.

In East Toxteth and Wavertree the Conservative majorities outstripped the Conservative polls in recent by-elections. Including Hornby, five new M.P.s emerged. C. E. R. Brocklebank, the shipowner, won Fairfield; Clyde Wilson, a local-born barrister, now chairman of the L.C.C.'s Entertainments' Committee and the foremost anti-Sabbatarian lobbyist, won West Toxteth; and Sir John Hugo Rutherford, the chairman of the Corporation's Housing Committee and a candidate in 1929, gained his father's former seat, Edge Hill. Robert Rankin, a shipowner, won Kirkdale: he too had been defeated in 1929, and he was the brother of the former M.P. for East Toxteth.

Kirkdale had enjoyed Longbottom's candidature, representing 'Protestant Democracy'. His politics were difficult to define. Derby was sure that Longbottom was 'an out and out Socialist'; White was equally sure that Longbottom was 'a Liberal and Free Trader'. Excitement blessed his cause in 1931. Kensit returned (he was invited, originally, to contest Everton); mobs stoned Downey; and Longbottom could make a plausible case, with Reynolds in Exchange and the Corporation favouring the Catholic cathedral, that the Conservative party had become lukewarm on Protestant matters.[99] Longbottom also personalized economic issues, blaming unemployment, slums, and high rates on Irish immigration. He proposed five year's residence before eligibility for relief.[100]

By ordinary standards of political contests Longbottom was a wild card, but his Labour opponent, the sitting M.P., Sandham, matched his abnormality. Sandham's contempt for Parliament's efforts in the economic crisis was supreme. His maiden speech in 1929 expressed the opinion that 'we could do more of a practical nature in a city council in a day than we can do here in a week'; but Sandham's speciality was interrupting, not making, speeches. His sole contribution to the Coal Mines Bill debate in 1930 was the question. 'Why need we have all this piffle?' He was unconcerned with Free Trade or Protection and, though he had some thoughts on over-production and under-consumption, the fundamental need, in his view, was to abolish the capitalist system. With his own party Sandham was ever at war, especially with the 'office-conscious snobs'. In 1930 he had been pilloried for a breach of parliamentary privilege after a speech to the I.L.P. in which he made several charges: that M.P.s used House of Commons' stationery in writing promotions for their personal profit; that drunkenness was rife among Labour M.P.s; that Labour M.P.s took bribes to pass doubtful legislation; and that the taking of bribes was in keeping with the traditions of the House.[101] The accumulated hostility of his own party made Sandham virtually a non-starter in the 1931 election and though he polled 9,531 to Longbottom's 7,834, the Conservative, Rankin, was returned with 14,303 votes. Rankin's tally meant that he was that rare Conservative who polled less in 1931 than in 1929, but Longbottom had clearly attracted many Protestant Labourites.

For a decade now politics were decided. Labour's emergence was halted. In the 1931 municipal elections every Conservative candidate won, except in Brunswick, and White counted a Conservative Council majority of twenty-seven over all other parties.[102] The congratulations were muted. Merseyside in 1931–2 boasted 110,000 insured unemployed, 30,000 uninsured unemployed, and 90,000 underemployed. One-third of insured males were unemployed; but, counting women and youths, the over-all average was 28 per cent.[103] Ports inescapably suffered by global depression, but Britain's northern ports suffered more, and Liverpool most.[104] At the same time as the nation's traffic slumped over-all between 1919 and 1939, Liverpool lost an annual average of 1 per cent of its trade to other British ports. Before Britain left the gold standard shipowners reported freights one-fifth below, and costs three-fifths above, pre-war levels. They risked a loss on every working ship. Raw cotton alone accounted for half Liverpool's fall in imports since 1924.[105]

What unemployment was attributable to the Depression, what was normal for any port-city, and what stemmed from Merseyside's abnormality, was debatable; but structural alterations would not work miracles overnight. Thirty-seven per cent of Liverpool workers were engaged in production, compared with the 63 per cent national average.[106] In the 1920s this was applauded: a Corporation booklet argued that Liverpool had escaped disfigurement by an absence of manufacturing industries.[107] But new industries were not answers if they required highly skilled labour, since they might add to the population without relieving the unemployed.[108] The expansion of the armed services and civil defence construction work in the late 1930s were more traditional ways of reducing unemployment; but about 50 per cent of the 3,692 Liverpudlians seeking to join the army in 1936, and about 30 per cent of the 6,000 Liverpudlians seeking to join the Army, Navy, or Air Force in 1937, failed to meet the medical or physical standards.[109] In 1932 Professor Caradog Jones had concluded that it was 'beyond reasonable hope' to absorb the existing unemployed within ten years. This prediction was confirmed: in 1935 Merseyside had 97,000 insured unemployed, in 1939 80,000.[110] The unemployment rate remained above 18 per cent, double the national average.[111]

The Ministry of Labour, Liverpool Juvenile Employment Committee, and Council of Social Service, recommended raising the school-leaving age, transfer schemes, and training-centres.[112] Their attention was focused on the young: 46 per cent of applicants for public assistance in Liverpool were under thirty-five years old. The national average for this group was 32 per cent. In 1934 Liverpool contained 13,000 unemployed aged between fourteen and twenty-one. Many were 'long-unemployed' and had been cynically used. Hundreds of van and errand boys started work, for cheap rates, at the age of fourteen, and then were sacked when they reached the insurable age of sixteen.[113] However, Junior Instruction Centres, operating since 1923, had enrolled 1,090 boys and 990 girls; and between 1933 and 1935 the Liverpool Y.M.C.A. and Education Authority made efforts to train and place 600 boys in agriculture. In 1936 three new centres, costing £37,000, involved 1,500 boys and 900 girls; and in 1939 a training-centre opened for 150 unskilled men, aged between nineteen and thirty-five.[114]

Economies, not reconstruction, engaged the authorities' strongest inclinations. In 1932 the Corporation made cuts of £5 million, mostly in health and education administration.[115] That September demonstrations took place against the Birkenhead Public Assistance Committee. Shops and houses were damaged, and the police allegedly pursued reprisals against the demonstrators in their homes; but riot was rewarded. Increases were conceded for several categories of unemployed.[116]

The trouble spread to Liverpool and a demonstration in Islington Square, where a meeting of the unemployed had been in conflict with the police in 1931, also ended in riot.[117] Among those charged with incitement was John Braddock, a councillor of three years' standing. Maxwell Fyfe, a rising star in the local Conservative party, led the prosecution; and E. G. Hemmerde, the former Liberal and Labour M.P. and stipendiary magistrate who had frustrated the police harassment of unemployed demonstrators in 1921, defended Braddock. Thirteen policemen positively identified him. Some had known him for twelve years but two factors unsettled these lynx-eyed lawmen. One was that the demonstration was Communist-organized and Braddock had quit the C.P. in 1924. The second was that Braddock did not attend the demonstration. Three councillors, including Longbottom, and other witnesses pleaded that they had met Braddock elsewhere. Nevertheless, Braddock was sentenced to six month's imprisonment. In November he was re-elected councillor; in December he left jail after a successful appeal. The police admitted to having mistaken him; but the Watch Committee refused an inquiry.[118]

The Braddocks had now arrived politically. Born in the Potteries, John had been thinking of emigrating to Canada when he settled in Liverpool in 1915. He initially found work as a wagon-repairer but, after persistent unemployment, he became an agent for the Co-operative Insurance Society in 1926. He was a big man, and Bessie Bamber, whom he married in 1922, was a rosy-cheeked, heavy-jawed creature, of legendary girth. The onetime Communist M.P., Walton Newbold, used to address her as 'the Six B's—Big Bonny Beautiful Bugger Bessie Bamber'.[119] The Braddocks understood declamation: Bessie once brandished a megaphone in the Council to get a proper hearing. But lest they appear only melodramatists through popular memories, one might cite John's summons of the Town Clerk in 1933 to supply accounts of payments made to councillors.[120] The Braddocks pertinaciously championed common people in a Council overloaded with the wealthy.[121]

An early associate of the Braddocks was Sydney Silverman, a solicitor and a pacifist who had gone to jail for his beliefs. Although not a councillor until 1932, he contested Exchange in January 1933 following Reynolds's death. Silverman, however, was a Jew, and White regarded it as 'a blunder of the first magnitude' for Labour to ignore the susceptibilities of the large Catholic vote. He did not make the same mistake. He selected Colonel J. J. Shute, Reynolds's partner in business and philanthropy, though it needed Derby's persuasion before Shute consented to stand. Unlike Reynolds, Shute was not prepared to be directed by

Stacey and the 1924 Club; but like Reynolds he was an eminent Catholic, friendly with the Centre party, which roosted in Exchange ward, and with the Democratic Labour party, which occupied Great George Street and Vauxhall. Altogether some ten Catholic councillors, several priests and laymen, publicly reproved Silverman for opposing state-aid for Church schools. His Socialism was brazen. The National Government he called 'a Tory dictatorship of the most reactionary kind'. He opposed retrenchment and tariffs; moreover, he wanted the means test abolished and unemployment relief made wholly a national charge.[122]

By contrast Shute was cautious. He deployed a steady, undemonstrative business mind in the many and varied spheres in which he was active—witness his chairmanship of the Liverpool Repertory Theatre for twenty years—and tariffs he now described as an inevitable, not ideal, step.[123] MacDonald and Baldwin demanded a 'national effort' against 'reckless partisan fights'; but the Government poll fell from 24,038, to 15,198 and Labour rose from 10,894 to 12,412. White was glad to have won: he had predicted disaster if a Samuelite Liberal stood, and throughout the contest he detected no enthusiasm for the Government among businessmen. White, however, exploited this in his desire to regain the grasp on the Conservative machine that Salvidge once had. There were still traces of constituency independence in Exchange, and White blamed this for the relative absence of propaganda and cars to draw the out-voters. Not enough use had been made of the Constitutional's central office, and White emphasized the lesson for Derby: 'I am more than ever convinced that to separate the various divisions in Liverpool would be a tactical mistake for the Party as the position of divisions like Edge Hill, Everton, West Toxteth, and Kirkdale would be quite hopeless and defenceless were they without the resources which can be posted for the common benefit of the city as a whole.' In White's opinion Shute's victory was not political but personal. Silverman went even further: sectarianism, he said, had triumphed over politics.[125]

Silverman's verdict had justification. The National Economy Act and Finance (No. 2) Act (1931) saved £9½ million partly by transferring burdens onto ratepayers. Liverpool spent £260,000 more in unemployment relief in 1932 than 1931. The Town Clerk and City Treasurer suggested that, without further grants, an equalization fund might operate nationally; and a colloquy of Labour parties on Merseyside recommended uniform, levelled-up, scales of relief and pressed the Government to make unemployment a national charge and to reinstitute grants-in-aid for public works.[126] Immediately after Silverman's defeat the Liverpool Conservative party adopted these cries and joined the protest of other northern boroughs with rates of over 14*s.* in the pound, in a deputation to the Minister of Health, Sir Edward Hilton Young.[127]

In April 1933 Young promised £1½ million to aid distressed areas, pending a long-term scheme. Half was derived by reducing the block grant to wealthier areas, equivalent to a halfpenny rate;[128] but the whole was insufficient.[129] The division between prosperous and poor Britain was bared. Young represented Sevenoaks; Sir William Ray, who led the Economy Committee, represented

Richmond. Ray's Committee opposed the additional grant, arguing that if local authorities in the distressed areas cast off their sluggishness economies of £40,000,000 per annum were possible 'without diminishing the efficiency of the social services'.[130]

The 1930s are not remembered for the hunger marches of Home Counties' Conservatives. Young's pretended long-term scheme, the Unemployment Insurance Bill, announced in December 1933, made unemployment a national charge but the claim that distressed areas were specially relieved was spurious, since the grant-in-aid was shared by poor and wealthy towns. White criticized the 'sharpness in this injustice', and the 'callous indifference' of the Chancellor of the Exchequer, Neville Chamberlain. Moderating his tone somewhat, White denied that Liverpool was 'rebellious' or that the Government's action affected his Conservatism; but, regarding housing, shipping, and unemployment, White was thoroughly disgruntled.[131]

The burden having shifted from the insurance fund to the rates, the cost of unemployment in Liverpool in 1935–6 was three-and-a-half times that in 1931, and over twelve times that in 1922.[132] The Government was compelled to reconsider the position, and the Unemployment Assistance Acts of 1934 and 1935 were designed so that the Government eventually would shoulder almost 95 per cent of the financial burden of able-bodied unemployed. But it would not assume total responsibility, from a belief that good local administration would be maintained by sharing the cost; and even a 5 per cent charge to the rates was a disincentive to the new industries which distressed areas needed to attract. Moreover, considerable hardship attended the reassessment of benefits as transitional payment cases and those absolutely on poor relief were transferred from the Public Assistance Committees to the Unemployment Assistance Board—the first date of transfer was dragged out from October 1934 to 31 March 1936; the second was not appointed until 1 April 1937—and these delays meant that the Liverpool rate-payers still had to find £400,000 for relief in 1937.[133] However, not everyone viewed the issue from White's side. As the rates rose to 18*s*. 2*d*. in 1936, businessmen in Liverpool denounced the Corporation's 'extravagence' not the Government's inequity.[134]

Although in common fate Liverpudlians divided still in sectarian matters.[135] In 1932 anti-Ritualist Protestants brawled in St. Paul's church, Stoneycroft, and interrupted the English Church Union's assembly; and sabbatarians again rallied to defeat Sunday games and music in the parks and Sunday trading on council estates. Around the Glorious Twelfth of July a priest was assaulted and Catholic institutions were damaged, although the Anglican cathedral also suffered. The bishop, David, exhibited surprise but the Catholic archbishop, Downey, believed violence inevitable when men preached 'the gospel of religious hatred'.[136] Wiseite traditions remained, as demonstrators protested against commemorative crucifixes being placed in St. George's church, Everton;[137] but the Protestants were not without their own martyrolatry. October 1932 was the thirtieth anniversary of John Kensit's death. The Corporation sanctioned a Protestant Truth Society rally in Sheil Park; J. A. Kensit lectured in the Philharmonic Hall; and the iron file which struck his father was displayed to the curious.[138]

Catholics also stirred as Downey crusaded against 'the godless, soulless philosophy of Karl Marx'.[139] All creeds had this enemy; but the Merseyside Church Crusade in 1933 was an Anglican affair, celebrating ten years of David's episcopacy. The crusaders nudged the people, in incongruous settings like a boxing bout and football match, in order to 'combat the materialist philosophy of the day'.[140]

Denominationalism resisted combat. When the chancel of the Anglican cathedral was consecrated in 1924 and arrangements were made for joint services with Nonconformists, as 'Protestant Christians, children of the Reformation', Canon Raven declared that the cathedral should not be 'a glorified Parish Church' but above sectional and divisive influences.[141] Unity between Nonconformists and Churchmen against 'that grim spectre', secular education, had been the theme of Chavasse's valediction in 1923;[142] and in 1933 Dr. L. P. Jacks, the former Liverpool minister, now of Manchester College, Oxford, became the first Unitarian to preach in the cathedral, at non-liturgical services. Afterwards the Dean invited Lawrence Redfern, minister of the Ullet Road Unitarian church, to preach at the Assize Service. This the bishop disapproved, distinguishing between the 'special' services at which Jacks preached and the 'regular' service which Redfern addressed. He was not alone in his concern: the chapter was inundated with protests when the service ended. Canon Lancelot, of Birkdale, fulminated that the cathedral was not a 'civic temple' where anyone might get a hearing: the invitation was 'utterly subversive' of Anglicanism.[143] *The Times* opened its columns to the adversaries. Among them Lord Hugh Cecil raged toweringly. He nominated the episode 'a scandal in the face of Christendom' and petitioned the Archbishop of York, William Temple.[144] In 1934 the bishops of the Northern Province, sitting in the Upper House of York Convocation, upheld Cecil's charge: they repudiated the invitation, not reckoning Unitarians as 'members of a Christian Communion' on the ground that they denied 'the doctrine of the full deity of Jesus Christ'.[145] Dean Inge, in retirement, commiserated with Redfern: 'It is a pity that the Bishops are so timid. They all hold season tickets on the line of least resistance.'[146]

Elections did not primarily revolve upon sectarian matters, but Protestant candidates contested St. Domingo, Dingle, Netherfield, and Kirkdale wards. Their campaign had economic pretensions in demanding immigration restrictions. In 1932 Mrs. Longbottom joined her husband in the Council; in 1934 their party became a trio. All represented St. Domingo. Elsewhere Protestant votes were variable—five candidates in 1933 polled 8,000; eight candidates in 1934 polled 6,500. This was a small toll upon the Conservatives; and Downey's Pastoral in 1934 gave further incentive to the Liverpool Conservative party to resign their Orange pedigree, with its declaration that 'the Catholic church will always be anti-Communist but will be tolerant of any political group not anti-church'.[147]

Labour gained six Council seats in 1933, fifteen in 1934; but no party had sure credentials. A distribution of spoils did not quiet dissent. In 1934 Labour provided its first mayor of Liverpool, F. T. Richardson, of the Postmen:[148] and Freedoms of the City honoured one member from each party—White, in recognition of the completed Mersey Tunnel; Bowring, in recognition of his civic generosity;[149] and Sexton, in recognition that if Buggins waited, his turn would come. The Whip was withdrawn from Silverman and Bessie Braddock when they criticized these honours; and the Labour leader, Hogan, complained that members' personal and sectarian jealousies and inattention to Council business ruined Labour's prospects.[150]

Randolph Churchill champions anti-caucus Conservatives

Hogan's consolation, as he reviewed the ragged condition of the Liverpool Labour party, was that the Conservatives were also locked in self-conflict and mutual recrimination. The West Derby M.P., Allen, who had taken the lead in the revolt against Salvidge's and White's authority between 1927 and 1930, had soldiered on with hopes of effecting a reorganization. 'It is a case of walking very warily', he told Derby in 1931, 'and I almost feel I have not a sufficiently "long spoon".' White had trusted to his own obstinacy and the weight of tradition to tire and defeat the reformers; but Allen showed pluck and pertinacity. In April 1933 they had finally bared their disagreement before the Constitutional Association's Executive. A large majority rejected Allen's proposal to base the organization on a subscribing membership, however token; and the Orangemen retained their representation. Allen was recompensed by a new rule enabling constituencies to raise their own funds and appoint salaried secretaries; but such officers would organize the constituencies in conjunction with the Constitutional's staff. This new rule was practically otiose. Only Exchange by 1935 had taken advantage of it. Elsewhere neither the money nor the will existed to found an agent system.[151] Allen, moreover, was nudging seventy years of age, and on the point of death.

White and Murch had preserved the central machine; but they were shaken in 1935 as Nall-Cain succeeded his father as Lord Brocket and had to vacate the representation of Wavertree, where once Tinne tried to stir constituency independence. The 61,053 voters were double those of 1918; and two candidates quickly emerged. The Labour candidate, Cleary, had been adopted in 1932; and a solicitor, Artro Morris, championed Liberal critics of Labour's 'ignorance of finance, its cowardly attitude on free trade, and its worship of the god of State'.[152] They disputed fiscal matters before a Conservative appeared. This was James Platt, a cotton merchant but a stranger to politics. The debate shifted to the Government's record. Economic historians find no necessary illogicality in demonstrating that the 1920s and 1930s were a time of quite fast economic growth and generally improved living standards, as well as a time of high unemployment and particular distress; but, to popular audiences, the Government's claim to have brought prosperity, when some 22 per cent of Liverpudlians, and two million nationally, remained unemployed, seemed grotesque. Labour's leader, George Lansbury, summarized his party's case, that 'the Government's mad schemes for paying people not to produce are the economics of Bedlam'.[153]

A rogue infant, Randolph Churchill, now interrupted the regular party contest, shaking his father's rattle against the government's India policy and throwing tantrums of his own against the Liverpool caucus.[154] He also demanded the rejection of 'men who have been against the British Empire' in the first World War and General Strike, especially 'the same Socialist Prime Minister who was responsible for bringing Great Britain to the verge of bankruptcy'. That Randolph Churchill considered Ramsay MacDonald an active Socialist in 1935 indicated his singularity. He claimed only Conservative support, being, as his father had observed some six years earlier, 'a bitter Tory'. He wanted to boost Lancashire cotton and Mersey shipping; and he demanded a stronger Air Force, speedier rehousing, credit-financed public works, and 'a live Conservative Party, appealing to youth and served by youth, free from the taint of Socialism, and independent of caucus influence'.[155]

A kind of Tory Democrat, Randolph Churchill evoked the shade of his grandfather and namesake. There was the same passionate insistence on quintessential Conservative values, including the Englishman's inalienable right to be rude to people of every social class. A special part of Randolph's malignity was reserved for White personally. These were his 'shock tactics', and mostly unfair. White, for instance, had done much to present to the Government Liverpool's case as a distressed area; but one of Randolph's complaints, that Liverpool's politicians relied upon religious sectarianism, hit a sensitive nerve, for this was a fact of life that many wished away.[156] Randolph's personal flouts White dealt with easily: he sued him and the *Sunday Dispatch* for libel.[157] But a Government with a majority of four hundred threatening 'disciplinary action' against this debutant only validated Winston Churchill's caricature of Platt as one of those 'rich, tame, futile men' whom party managers advanced into Parliament. Randolph himself spoke of the 'vile party caucus'. His connection with the local anti-White movement was not new. In December 1932, when Reynolds's death created the by-election in Exchange, Reynolds's son had nominated Randolph as an alternative to Shute.[158]

The Liverpool Conservative caucus exhausted its repertoire. The 3,000 strong Liverpool Junior Conservatives formally renounced their deliverer; canvassers came from Cheshire; Lord Stanley, Sir Anthony Eden, Sir Thomas Inskip, R. A. Butler, and Ernest Brown, addressed meetings; and Platt castigated 'cranky intellectuals' who imbued working people with 'Socialist schemes divorced from reality'.[159] However, Sir Joseph Nall (M.P. Hulme), who originally promised to support Platt, appeared for Randolph because of 'the shameful betrayal' in India and the Cabinet's 'complacent attitude' towards economic problems; and, backed by Rothermere's press, Churchill's case mounted. No gravestone was left unturned. Lady Long celebrated Randolph on behalf of her dead husband, Walter Long, who had been ousted from his seat in West Derby by Protestant critics thirty-five years earlier. She now appealed to electors to recognize 'the real Conservative cause'; and even Stanley Salvidge, to White's dismay and disgust, favoured Randolph.[160]

A bewildering poll gave Cleary 15,611 votes, Platt 13,771, Churchill 10,575, Morris 4,208. The turn-out fell from 75 to 72·3 per cent; but Labour polled 6,000 more than in 1931. Cleary attributed his success to the Government's failure to subsidize council housing, and especially to the muddle and delays in transferring the burden of unemployment relief from the rates to the national exchequer. Together with the boos which prevented Malcolm MacDonald from speaking for Platt, Cleary's poll suggested that few National Labourites remained.[161] Liberals too were incoherent. Richard Holt, now Sir Richard, only confused Liberal voters by denouncing the government's 'policy of extravagence, protection, and thinly-disguised Socialism'; and Morris forfeited his deposit.[162] The surprise was the rebel Conservative vote. It is difficult to assess the number upset about India. So far as party activists were concerned the Constitutional's Board of Management had approved the Government's India policy and Baldwin's Conservative leadership in June 1933 by 130 votes to 3; and the Constitutional's Central Council had reaffirmed this in November 1934 by 62 votes to 18. Purbrick was the only Liverpool M.P. to dissent, but he had always opposed Baldwin and, despite the money that he lavished on Walton, a poll of the constituency association found him in a minority of eighteen, against forty-seven supporters of Baldwin, in a motion of censure on the Conservative leader. Some now blamed Garston's dissident Orangemen for Platt's defeat, but Randolph Churchill's supporters were probably chiefly young people who, without established political convictions, embraced his audacity and name. *The Times* sourly regarded this 'girlish enthusiasm', but admitted that people demanded 'definite and coherent' policies.[163]

From Liverpool's Wavertree Randolph Churchill bore his torch to South London on behalf of another Independent, Richard Findlay, an ex-R.A.F. officer, who contested the Norwood by-election. The official Conservative candidate there was Duncan Sandys, who shortly became Randolph's brother-in-law. Findlay had espoused Fascism because he was 'sickened' by Conservative leaders who 'perverted the power of the party to adopt Socialist measures'; he had left the Fascist party because of its anti-Semitism and because 'its policies were far more left wing' than he appreciated. He now hailed Randolph Churchill's fight to purge the Conservative party's 'caucus management' and to revive 'those Imperial doctrines which Mr. Disraeli proclaimed'.[164] This fascinated 2,698 voters and lost his deposit.

Chastened by Norwood's raspberry, Randolph Churchill returned to Liverpool. He marshalled a hundred workers 'on democratic lines' but was unhorsed, by jaundice which necessitated his cancelling engagements, and by the Constitutional Association which rejected his application for membership.[165] In June 1935 Baldwin replaced Ramsay MacDonald as Prime Minister, one study in still-life instead of another; but it obviated one of Randolph's grievances. The next month brought two more parliamentary by-elections in Liverpool.

In West Derby, vacant by the death of Sir John Sandeman Allen, Maxwell Fyfe, the Constitutional's vice-chairman, was unopposed.[166] The Labour offensive was concentrated on West Toxteth, after White rejected the Conservative Central Office's recommendation of a National Labour candidate. Instead he advanced J. W. J. Cremlyn, a sixty-year-old lawyer, Bootle Welsh in origin. Randolph Churchill gladly seized the opportunity of making more mischief for White, and of working his way back into official Conservative favour. Informing the press that Liverpool's Conservative organization lacked 'drive', Randolph grandly lent Cremlyn sixty canvassers to withstand 'the sinister and insidious forces of Socialism which would plunge the nation into bankruptcy and involve us in a bloody war'. This did not relieve what White knew as 'the most depressed area of our depressed city'.[167] Annually since 1931 the Labour candidate, Gibbins, had dealt with 15,000 grievances from his former constituents; and a 53·9 per cent poll made him M.P. in fact, by 14,908 votes against 9,565.

This dismal Conservative performance gave Randolph his chance at the General Election. White recognized that the Government's industrial policy had lost West Toxteth and made Everton, Kirkdale, and Edge Hill vulnerable. He had written to MacDonald and others in May 1934, to the Conservative Central Office in January 1935, and again to Baldwin in May, emphasizing that 'there is a sullenness pervading the ranks of our supporters which alarms me'. White tried to overcome this by insisting that his candidates in Liverpool make known their determination to press the Government to relieve the rates of the entire unemployment charge. He also helped to negotiate a reduced rent for Cammell Laird's, so that it could compete for orders with lower tenders. To his satisfaction the Liverpool Labour party opposed the latter.[168]

Lord Derby, however, was more impressed by Randolph Churchill's stand against White's organization. This epitomized the energetic independence which constituencies ideally ought to show. Derby and Winston Churchill had been estranged in 1934, when Churchill brought before the Committee of Privileges charges of improper conduct against Derby and the Secretary of State for India, Hoare, alleging that Derby had nobbled Lancashire cotton manufacturers to alter a submission to the Joint Select Committee on Indian Constitutional Reform which had expressed alarm for the future of their trade in the light of the Government's India White Paper. Now, however, with Winston Churchill's prompting, Derby worked to reconcile White and Randolph. In this Derby was extraordinarily insensitive to White's feelings. Randolph did not help by proposing to contest a Tory-held municipal seat, at which even Derby showed some exasperation—'Really Randolph Churchill is too stupid for words'. Derby persevered, and White and Randolph met at Knowsley in October. Randolph now withdrew his threat to contest Wavertree against Major P. S. Shaw, a cousin of the last Conservative M.P. Instead he was officially adopted in West Toxteth, Derby subscribing £200 towards his expenses.[169]

Randolph's campaign attracted all the publicity. He promised to turn Parliament upside down in Liverpool's cause; but the overturning did not occur at Westminster. Several stewards, windows, cars, and a hat belonging to Mrs. Sandys, were casualties in the violence which attended Randolph's appearances.[170] His supporters canvassed with Union Jacks but the young Churchill failed by 16,539 votes to 18,543. He was not to entertain Liverpudlians again, leaving immediately to buzz about Malcolm MacDonald in the Ross and Cromarty constituency.

The Government seemed barren. While few lamented Ramsay MacDonald, 'that queer, vain, simulacrum of a statesman', who was now politically buried at Seaham, few cheered Baldwin, that 'pale reflection of everyone's perplexities', who led the new Ministry. Baldwin invariably flavoured his speeches to his audiences' taste, but was it promising when he announced in Liverpool that '*laissez-faire*' was as dead as the slave trade?[171] Men looked about them for signs of the handiwork of government dynamism. Some were appalled by what they saw: 'Sir, I am fifty-two and only associate Baldwin with a memory of poverty, want, and hunger. In 1935 I saw children begging for left-over sandwiches outside a Liverpool sugar refinery, and women scratching for cinders in the ash tips of my works. This memory I connect with Mr. Baldwin and I cannot erase it.'[172]

Nevertheless, some nimbus of National Government remained and by 1934–5 the cuts imposed in 1931, especially in unemployment benefit, had been removed. The Liverpool poll fell by 4·7 per cent, but Wavertree, Fairfield, Walton, West Derby, and East Toxteth, recorded Conservative majorities of over 7,000. In Exchange Shute increased his majority to 4,412: his erstwhile opponent, Silverman, carried Nelson and Colne and Simon Mahon was Labour's stop-gap candidate. Bessie Braddock afterwards replaced him. Her husband had refused an invitation to contest Everton, which he represented municipally. By not risking his job, he sacrificed an M.P.'s salary for life, since Councillor B. V. Kirby, the L.T.C.'s president, won the seat by 177 votes. His programme highlighted the need to restore the housing subsidy, to abolish the means test, and to relieve distressed areas of all unemployment charges: but this was Labour's sole gain.[173] Hayes failed by 301 votes to recover Edge Hill. There the doughtiness of Conservatism was symbolized when rowdies at one meeting broke a gas chandelier. As men fled and women fainted the National Anthem was sung.[174]

The last sectarian rally

National issues, locally interpreted, had predominated in the 1935 General Election in Liverpool; but sectarianism was also represented. In the municipal elections, which prefaced the General Election, Hogan ascribed Labour's three losses to a Protestant–Conservative compact. The W.M.C.A.'s religious test had long been under criticism from sections of the Conservatives, but White observed: 'Whether we like it or no, . . . there are many thousands of electors in Liverpool who will, if the need arises, put Protestantism before their politics, and it would be simply madness on my part if I told the people of Kirkdale, Everton, or West Toxteth, that the Conservative Party has ceased to care for religion or for Protestant interests.' In 1934 and 1935 the Conservatives' Council control had depended on minority support, from stray Liberals, Centre Catholics, or Protestants. When Longbottom threatened to advance twelve candidates in the 1935 municipal elections, White persuaded the Conservative councillors to elect Longbottom to an aldermanship and to accept that another Protestant, Dunbar, should succeed to Longbottom's Council seat in St. Domingo ward, making the Protestants a faction of four. In return the other Protestant municipal candidates withdrew. Likewise Protestant candidates refrained from Walton and Everton in the General Election; but Longbottom would not abandon Kirkdale.[175] His address, otherwise a *réchauffé* of 1931, sought a mandate against the possibility that the Corporation might rehouse dispossessed Catholic families from other districts in St. Domingo. Longbottom polled 1,157 less than in 1931. Rankin, the Conservative M.P., having affirmed Catholic education policies, polled 3,763 fewer votes than in 1931; but Labour rose by 452.

Longbottom's campaign had been constricted, compared with 1931, by a smaller budget, which was further depleted when Bessie Braddock sued him for slander. Longbottom did not delight ladies of the Left but, though it cost him money, he might have been thankful that Mrs. Braddock took to the courts rather than imitated Councillor Mrs. Hamilton, who slapped his face.[176]

It was debatable whether the Protestant pact was necessary for the Conservatives to retain control of the Corporation. White and Murch exerted themselves in propaganda, distributing 50,000 pamphlets; and White acknowledged that Hogan made several 'tactical blunders', especially an incautious boast that Labour would run the Red Flag above the town hall and pack the magistrates' bench. Longbottom's support, moreover, did not bring peace to the Conservatives. The Exchange M.P., Shute, threatened to resign from the party. This taxed White's political resource, but he quieted Shute in a masterly epistle. White personally deplored Longbottom's attacks on Catholics, but he recognized that with a Council following of three Longbottom had a claim to an aldermanship as good as the Centre party. White reminded Shute that the Conservatives on five occasions had voted members of the Centre party to aldermanships. The Labour party, on the other hand, evinced no respect for minorities, and three years hence the Conservatives would have to re-elect three Centre aldermen, otherwise they would not survive. Furthermore, White had diverted £350 from his meagre General Election Fund in 1935 to run a Catholic Conservative candidate in Scotland division; and municipally he had contributed towards the expenses of Catholic candidates in St. Anne's and Great George wards. In sum White claimed to have protected Catholic as well as Protestant interests.[177]

White's pretension to defend both sects against a mercilessly secular Labour party was, however, unrealistic. In the first place many Labourites were affectionately disposed towards Catholic interests, just as many Conservatives were traditionally champions of Protestantism; secondly, Protestants and Catholics infrequently recognized their common Christianity. What White himself once remarked of Exchange division was applicable generally to Conservatives in Liverpool: 'Our trouble is to do justice to both sects without incurring the suspicion of either.'[178]

Now, in 1936, sectarians scrutinized the new Education Bill which permitted grants of 50 to 75 per cent to build or recondition non-provided secondary schools, so that the church schools might meet the demands of the Hadow Report (1926), whose recommendation about raising the school-leaving age to fifteen was scheduled to take effect in September 1939. The churches complained of the insufficiency of the grants and feared an extension of local authority control of appointments. Downey, in particular, mourned the churches' 'unequal struggle'. The Liverpool Labour M.P.s, Logan, Gibbins, and Kirby, cast against the Bill. This placed the sole Catholic among Liverpool's Conservative M.P.s in a dilemma, but Shute was not easily driven to divide from his Government and he predicted that it would not be long before non-provided schools were given the same financial aid as council schools for the limited purpose of providing more secondary school places.[179]

Liverpool's anti-Ritualist protestors also left hibernation. In March 1936

'Cromwell's Ironsides' scorned the bishop's authority and disrupted services in Sutton parish.[180] Sectarians were determinedly separatist. Downey instructed the forty Catholic voluntary workers in the Liverpool Personal Service Society to resign, following its decision to inform non-Catholics about birth control. Likewise Hogan criticized the Council's decision in 1935 to give a grant, for the first time, to a birth-control clinic, which had been providing advice for the past ten years.[181]

Protestants set the pace of succeeding municipal elections by connecting unemployment burdens and Irish immigration. They won Netherfield from Labour, which lost three seats altogether. The anti-Labour vote, 89,086, was the highest since 1931; the pro-Labour votes, 57,089, decreased by 10,000 since 1935.[182] International tensions rippled the surface of local politics, reinforcing inchoate waves. During the Spanish Civil War the Great George Street Labour party was Catholic and Nationalist inclined; neighbouring Exchange Labour party was Republican. Liverpool was among several fascist recruiting centres. R. Reynell-Bellamy, the northern agent, was Liverpool-born. Fascists occasionally contested a ward and, in 1936, a parliamentary candidate was adopted in Wavertree.[183] But the fascist cause was not popular. Their parades were attacked in Liverpool and Bootle in 1936;[184] and Mosley was felled by stones in October 1937.[185]

The Conservatives made gains in the 1936 municipal elections despite a valedictory blast from Randolph Churchill's banditti. A pamphlet indicted Liverpool Conservatism for stimulating 'Religious prejudice, Class jealousy, and Caucus formation'. The party machine, framed by Forwood and Salvidge, had passed to mere technicians like White and Murch—'With "high politics" they have no contact; national issues they disregard; and local needs are just so much bagatelle.'[186] The pamphlet failed to find a Liverpool printer, but a Manchester firm was rewarded by selling 4,000 copies in a fortnight. Its authoress, Barbara Whittingham-Jones, wished to combat Socialism but first advocated that Liverpool Conservatism be reformed. Murch in fact retired in 1936, after twenty-three years as secretary and agent, and forty-five years' service altogether to the Constitutional; but his departure heralded no new dawn. Lord Derby grumbled about the persistence of the 'old gang'; but White insisted that Murch's deputy and echo for eighteen years, Malcolm, succeeded. Among Malcolm's many attributes which White indicated to Derby, one was that he knew Liverpool's sectarian problems intimately.[187] This was appropriate for, rather than implement the Education Act, White rekindled anti-Catholic flames.

In 1937 the Catholics asked the Liverpool Education Committee for a 75 per cent grant-in-aid in order to provide more senior school places. This meant £540,000, and half would directly burden the rates. The L.E.C. recommended 66 per cent; but when the issue was debated in the City Council Labour members demanded the maximum and Conservatives nil. In seeking to avert another charge on an already overburdened local exchequer, White had renewed old tribal rhythms of 'Rome On The Rates'. The Conservatives subsequently gained eleven seats (eight Labour and three Liberal) in the municipal elections; but the Corporation would have to place unaccommodated Catholic children in its schools. Liverpool was the only large authority refusing a grant and the Board of Education reported that its schools would lack 22,000 places if the school-leaving age became fifteen in 1939. Thirty-four public elementary schools in Liverpool featured on the Board of Education's black-list of schools with defective premises at the end of 1935, and the Board now charged the L.E.C. to delineate its total programme, of elementary and secondary education. In a reply drafted by White the Town Clerk detailed thirty-six elementary schools, with 32,000 places, provided since 1918, despite economic difficulties. He demanded the Board's assistance, not criticism.[188]

In January 1938 White died. Longbottom conducted his burial at sea. White's successor was Alderman A. E. Shennan. He had joined the Council in 1920—only one year after White—and served on the Housing Committee, as chairman of Fairfield division, and as the party's chief whip. Allen, considering possible successors to Salvidge in 1928, had noted Shennan's speaking abilities and popularity with the rank and file, and concluded: 'May develop leadership if character strong enough.' In 1938 Maxwell Fyfe, now Allen's successor as M.P. for West Derby, considered Shennan the only leader in view. Again Liverpool's municipal and parliamentary leaderships were joined as Shennan became leader of the Council and chairman of the Constitutional; but Derby's optimism, that a devolution of power might be achieved, still burned as he made a final stab at White's memory in a letter to Earl Winterton, the Chancellor of the Duchy of Lancaster, in June 1938—'Shennan is a very good fellow. He has got many difficulties in front of him as White was such a dictator that he kept everything in his own hands. Shennan is, I am glad to say, bringing in a lot of people to help him . . .'[189]

In the immediate crisis Shennan flew Orange colours; and the party's education policy continued. In April 1938, by seventy-five votes to fifty-four, the Council rejected aid to voluntary schools and instructed the L.E.C. to provide alternative accommodation. An unusual situation had materialized: Conservatives acted as secularists, Labour as clericalists. The no-grants majority consisted of sixty-eight Conservatives, four Protestants, and three Labour. The Labour trio was non-Catholic and two represented Garston where Orangeism thundered; but Labour's virtual solidarity was surprising. Demanding the grant were thirty-seven Labour, six Liberal, six Centre, and five Conservative councillors, but only twenty-seven of them were Catholics. Seven Labour councillors who had opposed the planting of the Catholic cathedral on the workhouse site in 1930 now supported the 'Catholic' side. Only Cleary, Labour's deputy leader, opposed both.[190]

In September 1938 the Board of Education redoubled its pressure by withholding a specific grant to Liverpool of £15,000 per month (equal to a sevenpenny annual rate). This was justified not by the 1936 Act but by section 17 of the 1921 Act, regarding the L.E.C.'s failure to provide sufficient elementary school accommodation, especially in dockside areas. The Board's maxima were forty pupils in classes wholly or mainly of children over eleven years of age, and fifty in classes of children wholly or mainly under eleven years. Of 3,243 classes in Liverpool's public elementary schools in 1938, nine contained over sixty pupils and 284 between fifty and sixty; and of 1,389 classes containing between forty and fifty pupils 288 had a majority over eleven years. At Westminster the Labour M.P. for Shoreditch, E. Thurtle, congratulated the L.E.C. for resisting the 'extortionate demands of the churches', but Logan—who was a member of the L.E.C.—feared the recrudescence of sectarian strife. He, therefore, retracted his opposition to the 1936 Act and supported the Board's action. His view now was that the 1936 Act was not permissive but mandatory: the L.E.C. had no choice but to reach agreement with the church schools in order to achieve Parliament's object of raising the school-leaving age. In this controversy, however, the Liverpool Labour Party discovered an apostate. Reginald Bevins, who had failed in seeking adoption as parliamentary candidate in Exchange in 1936, quit the party, asserting that it should not support the Board's dictation.[191]

This remained the election issue when Shennan pledged that his party would never employ the rates to build sectarian schools.[192] The Conservatives won another six seats (five Labour, one Liberal) in the 1938 municipal elections. These defeats returned Labour to its citadels, holding ex-Nationalist wards and losing wards similar in socio-economic class but not in religion. The party's commitment to the Catholic position, and the loss of seats that ensued, enraged Protestant Labourites to complain to the party's National Executive Committee. Two courses were open to the National Agent, Shepherd, who had long been disquieted by the performance of Hogan's clique in Liverpool. Either he could wait for Hogan to pull the noose round his neck and let the party die of inanition, or the most reprehensible constituency parties—Exchange, Scotland, and West Toxteth—might be closed down and allowed to lie fallow for a while before reconstruction on a new basis. But, though it was suggested that Herbert Morrison might conduct an official inquiry, the feeling was that Hogan's cronies were too strongly entrenched to uproot, and the matter was shelved.[193]

Release came when Shennan received legal advice that the Board of Education could legitimately withhold moneys.[194] He was also threatened by a ratepayers' rebellion. In 1938 27,000 petitioned Parliament, and Ratepayers' Associations considered nominating candidates, having deduced from the parties' sectarianism their 'inability to administrate economically'. In May 1939 the Council agreed, with one Protestant dissentient, to build fifteen schools, costing £900,000 and that they should be leased to the church authorities (chiefly the Catholics) at £10,000 per annum. The Corporation would appoint teachers, but the churches could veto those whose duties included religious instruction. This peculiar arrangement, the Senior Public Elementary Schools (Liverpool) Act, by which schools 'provided' by the L.E.C. were to be deemed 'not provided', became law in July 1939.[195]

A disconsolate decade was etched in the last year of peace. The Anglican bishop criticized the acceptance of 80,000 unemployed in Liverpool as 'normal'.[196] The unemployed themselves emphasized this when the N.U.W.M. held a 'lie-down' demonstration in Lime Street.[197] Their protest was for modern times, halting traffic for fifteen minutes. In August 1939 Huyton tenants 'struck' against rent increases, and women 'picketed' with perambulators.[198] It heralded the new poverty, possessing but not plentifully. Some did not change: a report on employment repeated allegations about Irishmen accepting lower wages and Irish gangers giving preference to labourers who were indebted to them.[199] The Irish remained out of step, as the I.R.A. protested with lonely and inefficient violence.[200] In July a woman deposited 'Paddy Regan's dinner' at a workmen's hut, but this 'dinner' ticked and was thrown into the dock.[201] It was a prolegomenon to the real food parcels and bombs in the war.

CHAPTER EIGHTEEN

The Second World War and after

The old opinions in religion, morals, and politics are so much discredited in the more intellectual minds as to have lost the greater part of their efficacy for good, while they have still life enough in them to be a powerful obstacle to the growing up of any better opinions on those subjects. When the philosophic minds of the world can no longer believe its religion, or can only believe it with modifications amounting to an essential change of its character, a transitional period commences, of weak convictions, paralyzed intellects, and growing laxity of principle, which cannot terminate until a renovation has been effected in the basis of their belief, leading to the evolution of some faith, whether religious or merely human, which they can really believe; and when things are in this state, all thinking or writing which does not tend to promote such a renovation is of very little value beyond the moment. *Autobiography of John Stuart Mill*

Settling accounts

Liverpool suffered ninety air attacks between August 1940 and August 1942, including a 'blitz' in May 1941.[1] Outwardly there was political peace. Sydney Jones, one of eight Liberal Council members, remained Lord Mayor from 1938 to 1942 when Austin Harford, the octogenarian Independent, succeeded him. Harford was Liverpool's first Catholic mayor. Lord Derby congratulated Shennan on having broken with tradition. White had resisted Derby's and Reynolds's pressure for this same concession in 1929.[2] Then it might have had some significance. Now it was merely a tribute overdue, to none more than Harford who died in office.

Some had suspected a ruse to remove Harford from the Licensing Bench, where he upset the brewers; but sharp practice was not a Conservative monopoly. John Braddock replaced Cleary as Labour's deputy leader in 1943, an exchange which Hogan directed.[3] Four councillors, however, changed to Labour colours—G. H. Dunbar, who quarrelled with Longbottom over the education grant; a Centre councillor, noticing the tide; and two Conservatives,

Notes begin on p. 467.

one of whom, Dr. Richard Clitherow, won the Edge Hill parliamentary constituency in 1945.

Faith in an approaching millennium is commonly frustrated, but there were indications that Labour's moment was coming. The question of welfare services occupied the minds of the L.T.C. Pragmatism did not absolutely overtake quixoticism and pro-Communist feeling grew after the Nazis invaded Russia; but Liverpudlians entered the twentieth century by ceasing to observe the Sabbath. Under the pretext of amusing war-workers Liverpool's cinemas were liberated on Sundays from May 1941, and the parks from July 1943. Longbottom glowered, the Anglican bishop doubted, but the Catholic archbishop approved. Some oddity remained. Thus, notwithstanding the Sunday Trading Act (1937) which permitted the Sunday sale of newspapers, tobacco, and confectionery, shopkeepers on the Liverpool Corporation estates were prohibited from Sunday opening by a clause in their tenancy agreement.[4]

Sabbatarianism was fading, sectarianism dimly glowed. In 1940 councillors wrangled over the rent of a school leased to Catholic authorities; and Downey steeled his flock to maintain their schools. By contrast, nationally, the Protestant denominations reached a concordat. A significant illustration of this was the joint deputation of Anglican and Free Churchmen to the new President of the Board of Education, R. A. Butler, in 1941, in order to secure better religious instruction in *all* schools. According to the then Archbishop of Canterbury, Cosmo Lang, the assault on Christian civilization by Nazi Germany wonderfully concentrated their minds on this issue. Lang's successor from 1942, William Temple, determined to maintain the dual system of council and church schools; but by now 399 of the Board of Education's black-list of 700 schools were Anglican establishments and some new settlement was vital if the long-deferred desires of raising the school-leaving age and of freeing and re-stratifying the educational ladder were to be implemented after the war. Regarding the church schools, the Government's White Paper in 1943 offered 50 per cent of the cost of reconditioning and maintenance and, though the Nonconformists' grievance about single-school country areas still simmered, the subsequent Education Act of 1944 embodied many of their desires and laid to rest a great part of the century's old controversy. Religious teaching was made a statutory obligation for all schools, which would open with a daily act of corporate worship and include periods of religious instruction at other times, although the usual Conscience clause accompanied this provision. Religious knowledge was recognized as a qualification for Teachers' Certificates, and would be tested by H. M. Inspectors. Much of the friction in the dual system now disappeared, and was symbolized by the substitution of new terms, 'controlled' and 'aided' schools, for the sharply separate old terms, 'provided' and 'non-provided'. Butler's sincerity was unquestioned when he appealed in Parliament to denominationalists 'to dismiss from their minds the wholly unwarrantable view that the Government desire either to tear away church schools from unwilling managers or to force them inhumanely out of business'. Liverpool was not forgotten. The general 1936 Act, and the particular Liverpool Act of 1939, remained available, enabling managers of church schools to receive grants of up to 75 per cent of the cost of works or equivalent assistance, without prejudice to the 50 per cent Exchequer grants offered in the 1944 Act. The Liverpool Labour party was relatively cool in temper, and would not venture again near the electoral abyss of 1937–8, although its education policies remained somewhat singular compared with the national party. Many would argue that the 1944 Act accentuated class divisions and perpetuated social inequalities by leaving untouched the fee-paying private schools and by promoting within the state system selection tests for secondary education. Nevertheless, the opportunities for individual upward social mobility which were furnished by the '11-plus' examination had cumulative effects that were far from limited. In Liverpool the sense of separateness, which prevailed in the Catholic community, still persisted with the maintenance of Catholic schools; but its parochial strength increasingly slackened with the imposition of the grammar, technical, and secondary modern, school divisions. By the early 1960s it was observed that 'the gradual disappearance of the social homogeneity of Roman Catholicism in Liverpool has been sharply accelerated in recent years. The sons and daughters of working-class families now attend universities in increasing numbers. A single family may experience in a few years changes which were previously accomplished over several generations.'[5]

The war ended in May and a General Election followed in July 1945. The register was incomplete and Liverpool's turn-out, 68 per cent, and swing to Labour, 6·5 per cent, were below the national average.[6] Nevertheless party dominance was reversed: Labour won eight of eleven seats. Logan, in Scotland division, was actually unopposed, as were candidates in only two other British constituencies.[7] Conduct at political meetings apparently improved.[8] Not that expressions were temperate. With Longbottom fighting Kirkdale and Bessie Braddock Exchange, opponents were chastised with a customary ferocity, but aspects of both contests indicated that sectarianism was subsiding. The war's toll had reduced Longbottom's canvassers. He advertised social betterment as well as Vatican diplomacy, Irish treachery, Catholic education, and Prayer Book revision, but polled 2,601 votes, 13·2 per cent compared with almost 25 per cent in 1931 and 1935.

In Exchange the Conservatives' record of the late 1930s impaired the rapport which the sitting M.P., Shute, once had with Catholic voters. Mrs. Braddock won by 639 votes, although she had informed Catholics and businessmen that their interests must bow to those of working people generally.[9] Some 2,292 business premises voters survived among 26,732 electors. Assuming that three-quarters of the business vote was cast and that two-thirds voted Conservative, it has been calculated that on four occasions from 1922 Conservatives thereby won Exchange.[10] This franchise ended in 1948, but Mrs. Braddock was extraordinary. She courted opposition, within and without the Labour party, but no contest from 1945 to her death recorded a pro-Conservative swing.[11] To run the gauntlet of Mrs. Braddock promised promotion in the Conservative party. In 1946 Reginald Bevins accused her of complicity with Communists. Following their inconclusive law-suit, Bevins was adopted at a by-election in Edge Hill and, in 1950, he won the new constituency, Toxteth.

Bessie Braddock's bounce brought her attention which rightly should have focused on her husband, John, who took control of the Liverpool Labour party after 1948. The local government franchise had been more or less aligned with the parliamentary franchise in 1945 and another facility was granted in 1949 when residence on a 'qualifying date' (10 October) became acceptable for registration purposes as an alternative to residence during a 'qualifying period' of three months; but the Liverpool Labour party under John Braddock embarked on few new initiatives to attract the widened democracy. Perhaps decades of opposition had deadened Braddock, but few leaders will spurn a formed following. Hence the irreligious Braddock devoted himself to the old Irish Catholic districts in central Liverpool. This refrigerated his rebelliousness and committed him against electoral change. Early in the 1950s, for example, he opposed a redistribution of wards, which would curtail the influence of the depopulated city centre.

The Labour party machine in the 1950s, such as it was, bore an uncanny resemblance to the Conservative machine in the 1920s. The suburban movement in both periods undermined established sources of support. Both parties employed only one full-time agent. Power was centralized and personalized. Instead of Boss Salvidge stood Boss Braddock. In 1970 the L.T.C. and L.P.'s agent and secretary, Simon Frazer, recalled that 'the organization was poor and intentionally kept poor to keep out the "wrong" sort of candidate'. Unlike Salvidge who had White, John Braddock died in 1963 without political issue. The leadership fell to Bill Sefton. A member of the Council from 1953, Sefton had been proscribed by Braddock for his Bevanite views in foreign affairs; but it was the marked difference between the men in Liverpool affairs which ultimately mattered. As an opposition leader, Braddock had wielded power only within his party; but between 1955 and 1961 Labour controlled the Liverpool Council for the first time. Braddock became chairman of the Corporation's most important committee—Finance and General Purposes—but he seemed interested in power mainly for the control over his party which patronage brought him. An insularity and intolerance, an obsession with loyalty and discipline, appeared his outstanding characteristics. As leader of the Council from 1963 to 1967, Sefton was more outward-looking. Especially he embraced plans of modernization, in education, housing, and transport.[12]

With the redistribution of parliamentary seats in 1950, the Liberals' ineffectualness, and the absence of novel or peculiar issues, Liverpool's politics increasingly registered national moods. The constituencies were reduced from eleven to nine, of which the Conservatives won five in the 1950 General Election, despite weak organization.[13] No change occurred in 1951, when most majorities increased—Labour in Labour-held seats, Conservative in Conservative-held seats.[14] The trend was for each party to have two safe seats (Labour, Exchange and Scotland; Conservative, Garston and Wavertree) while five were more marginal.[15] In 1955 Norman Pannell won Kirkdale for Conservatism, but no other seat changed, although J. V. Woollam (who had fought Scotland in 1950) replaced Maxwell Fyfe in a 1954 by-election.[16]

The scene was static in the 1959 General Election: R. M. Bingham replaced Sir H. V. A. M. Raikes but Garston was unquestionably Conservative.[17] In 1964, by an average 8 per cent swing, Labour gained four seats—James Dunn won Kirkdale, Richard Crawshaw Toxteth, Eric Ogden West Derby, Eric Heffer Walton; and, at a by-election in Scotland, Walter Alldritt replaced the nonagenarian Logan. Differential economic prosperity perhaps explained Labour's successes: Liverpool might never have had it so good as in the 1950s, but other areas were undoubtedly having it better. Labour's victories in Liverpool were consolidated in 1966; moreover, in 1970, when few seats in Britain swung to Labour, five were Liverpudlian.

Unionist malfeasance in Ulster might have had some influence on the Liverpool elections;[18] but the parallel between Liverpool and Belfast had really ceased with the growth of a strong Labour party and the acceptance of Catholic participation in government. Liverpool's intractable problems were no longer sectarian. This was clear from the Scotland by-election in March 1971. Slum clearances had halved the electorate from 56,000 in 1955 to 25,000. As Britain's eleventh smallest constituency Scotland was ripe for redistribution, a factor which perhaps shaped Alldritt's decision to retire. The succession was contested between Councillor Frank Marsden, formerly the Labour constituency agent; Barry Porter (Conservative), a Birkenhead solicitor; and a 'Labour and Anti-Abortion' candidate, Peter Mahon, who had represented Preston South for Labour until 1970. A member of the family which dominated Labour politics in Bootle, Mahon was upset not to have won the official nomination of the Scotland constituency.[19] He tried to take advantage of the fact that Marsden was the first non-Catholic to bear Scotland's non-Conservative candidature; but inflation, unemployment, housing, and strikes were the sovereign issues, and Mahon was routed.[20] In the slums removed for the highway to a second Mersey tunnel, sectarian identities were buried. At the 1971 Conservative Party Conference Porter declared that this by-election 'convinced him that electors could forget their differences as Protestants and Catholics and vote instead for people and parties'.[21]

The previous twenty years had dislocated an earlier century's history. Some pages fluttered unbound. Longbottom had become Lord Mayor in 1950, and the Catholic archbishop, Heenan, was stoned in Robsart Street in 1958.[22] There were six Protestant councillors between 1946 and 1951, but only one by 1958–9. Longbottom was rejected in 1956. He rejoined the Council in 1960 after the Education Act aided new Catholic schools and Heenan advanced the cathedral.[23] Thereafter Protestant representation fluctuated between two and six but Longbottom—for a decade Grand Master of England—was expelled from the Orange Order in 1961.[24]

Orange lodges in Liverpool were neglecting political work. Longbottom burned with undiminished fire. He had had difficulties in securing new premises after his church was blitzed in 1941 but, before his death in 1962, he was campaigning against Britain's entry in the European Economic Community, fearing the surrender of religious and political sovereignty. He remained an inflexible Fundamentalist. His son-in-law, the succeeding leader of Liverpool's Protestant Party, Ronald Henderson, emphasized that 'his greatest love was preaching the evangel'.[25] The Protestant Party continued to breathe old life into new issues. It joined the British Constitution Defence Committee, allied with the Revd. Ian Paisley, to resist Ulster being submerged in Eire and Britain in

Europe. Its slogan was dank: 'Socialism leads to Communism, Ecumenism to Popery. We reject both.'

The life sustained by the W.M.C.A. was equally feeble. White was the last leader associated with it. Although Derby and Maxwell Fyfe, successive presidents, maintained a superficial sparkle, Shennan declined to be chairman of the W.M.C.A. in 1938. From a membership of some eight thousand at the turn of the century, it had shrunk to a body of fewer than seven hundred by 1936. One secretary gave his opinion in 1969 that the W.M.C.A. was 'declining very fast due to working men showing more interest in Socialism';[26] but, more basically, the W.M.C.A.'s appropriateness had gone. Political and demographic redistributions had purged the slum wards' fetid antagonisms.[27] Without popular coherence the ward was an ineffective political vehicle, although a resurgent Liberal party challenged this.[28] The Conservative leader after 1966, Alderman McDonald Steward, espoused business efficiency and comprehensive planning, not nationality or religion, to enchant a majority;[29] and, faced with Liberal successes and Labour Council control, in 1972 the Conservatives issued notice to the Protestant Party to join them or be beaten.[30]

The new society

The political game requires a selective memory. In the *Liverpool Constitutional Association Centenary Souvenir* (1948) the W.M.C.A. was described only as a body which 'laid stress on certain principles which they considered fundamental'. Protestantism was not mentioned explicitly there, or in a note by the Liverpool Conservative Agent in 1971. He wrote that the W.M.C.A.'s rules 'were not in line with present day thinking'.[31]

These furtive comments do not explain why the tradition of aggressive Protestantism was discarded; but it seems reasonable to surmise that some felt it distasteful, others merely useless. Increasingly people were discovering alternatives to, or surrogates for, religion. There was a variety of modern fetishes, devotions, rituals, and loyalties, which were cultivated and shared by politicians, doctors, scientists, industrialists, advertisers, artists, writers, and entertainers; and the old ethical order and conformity was loosened. Aldous Huxley, who had advanced this theme in several essays written between the wars, observed that none of the substitutes offered the universal embrace of religion, but each in turn took over some part of previously religious territory.[32]

Among the most glamorous and powerful of these idolatries was the prestige of science and technology and, in the make-believe world of perpetual modernization which post-war politicians inhabited, the past excited less reverence. Streamlining had become the substitute superstition. Liverpool's economic structure was radically altered. Change had been initiated before the war. Food processing and artificial fibre manufactures were established at Fazakerley; the Speke industrial estate was begun; and several large employers were welcomed, like I.C.I., Dunlop, and the football pools promoters, Littlewood's and Vernon's, although these last provided jobs mainly for women. In 1947 the persons employed in transport and associated work on Merseyside still constituted more than twice the national proportion. The diversity of work now evident on Merseyside came after 1949 when the region was declared a Development Area, a status which was renewed in 1963 and 1966. The conditions of this aid were changed in 1971 but under considerable protest for, throughout much of the post-war period, Merseyside's unemployment rate remained $2\frac{1}{2}$ times the national average.

As communications were improved, with the electrification of the railway to London in 1966, with motorways stretching from the city's edges, with another Mersey tunnel completed, and with an underground railway due to open in the late 1970s (a project, incidentally, which had been frustrated by want of government support in 1935), Liverpool assumed the trappings of a modern regional capital. The property boom of the late 1960s and early 1970s engendered a great expansion of office, hotel, and shop space; some traditional trades, like flour-milling and sugar-refining, expanded in scale; and, most of all, the whole area burgeoned with new employment, in the engineering and petro-chemical industries, telecommunications, electronics, plastics, and motor vehicles. After the opening of the Tranmere Oil Terminal in 1960 the Mersey became the third largest of Britain's oil ports; but the expansion was insubstantial in several respects. Both Cammell Laird's and the Docks and Harbour Board faced insolvency and required rescue by 1970; the new Anglesey moorings for tankers threatened the Mersey's new oil interests; rationalization in the sugar and steel industries augured a slackening traffic of both through the port; the inner motorway, planned in 1962 to encircle the city centre and to link the docks directly with the M62, was abandoned in 1975; and branches of Plessey telecommunications in Kirkby and Speke were doomed to closure through lack of Post Office orders in 1977. The depression deepened in 1978: Birds Eye's meat pie factory at Kirkby, British Leyland's TR7 car plant at Speke, and the Lucas Group's Victor Works at Wavertree, all were added to industry's condemned list. Over 5,000 jobs were involved at these works but, whether a factory was crippled by strikes, like Leyland's, or free of strikes for twenty-two years, like Lucas's, the tendency towards rationalization in giant combines seemed always to single out the Liverpool limb for amputation. Unemployment on Merseyside already stood at 11·3 per cent, nearly twice the national average, before the announcement of these threatened closures. By January 1980 the unemployment rate had reached 12·7 per cent. Some 40 per cent of these had been unemployed for over a year, and school-leavers' prospects were equally miserable. The future for Liverpool now seemed not that of an expanding provincial capital but, according to one local M.P., a decline to the status of a 'shanty town', unless the Government was induced to reverse the trend by an industrial strategy that advanced beyond short-term expedients.[33]

The nature of work was not changed after 1945 without disquiet. The chief reputation of the labour forces remained their unreliability and low productivity. In the docks decasualization occurred as part of the Devlin plan in 1967, but piece-working brought numerous minor stoppages, and the completion of the Seaforth Docks in 1972, with its huge investment in container and bulk cargo traffic, was heralded with a prolonged dispute over the grain terminal, and a failure to draw off the trade of the southern ports. In 1975 the specialized machine-tool manufacturer, Cross International, completed its first five years on Merseyside with handsome profits and no strikes; but this was rare enough to be singled out by the press as an event. Other industrial newcomers to Merseyside have not always been fortunate.

The difficulty of adapting ex-dockers and the like to assembly-line work is obvious; but, it may be argued quite apart from the industrial structure, work will remain unsatisfactory while homes are disturbed. An eyrie in one of the 'Mersey Mountains', as the towers of flats are called, is not most people's concept of an ideal home. Many of the recent party disputes have focused on the future of the old residential areas, whether they should be obliterated or reconstituted, with houses or flats. The City's first Planning Officer, soon after appointment in 1964, declared that 'some 60 per cent of the city's 205,000 dwellings date from before 1920 and in 1961 approximately 79,000 of these were unfit'. But already the plight of the new was being compared with the plight of the old. Few would recommend life on the new estates at Kirkby, Netherley, and other places, where, so the joke cruelly ran, even the dustbinmen needed to travel about in pairs. People don't go there, it was said, they're sent. 'Modernization' had apparently brought only new piggeries for old.

As a result, tenants' and residents' associations were formed against the despotism of the planners, demanding priority for repairs and amenities. This way too the Liberals rode to power, mobilizing small men in a phalanx against bigness. 'Pavement politics', 'drains and dustbins', was their party opponents' contemptuous estimation; but they were made to recognize that, in the words of the Conservative leader, 'minorities of different people on different issues collectively add up to a majority'. This was belated confirmation of a fundamental need in local government, which G. D. H. Cole identified some twenty years before:

> If we stand in need of larger units for co-ordinated planning, for the administration of certain services which imperatively require regional management, and for the regional supervision of some other services which can be effectively managed over relatively small areas, I am sure we stand fully much in need of more small-scale Local Government, over areas narrow enough for contact between the electors and the *elected bodies*, as well as the individual elected persons, to be close and responsible.[34]

A hundred years previously a country parson, the Revd. Francis Kilvert, spent three days in Liverpool. He recorded in his diary, 21 June 1872: 'Liverpool left upon my mind an impression of ragged Irish barefoot women and children. Enormous wealth and squalid poverty, wildernesses of offices and palatial counting houses and warehouses, bustling pushing vulgar men, pretty women and lovely children.' The particular incidents and the idiosyncracies of the observer alter, but some startling contrasts remain. The deterioration of inner Liverpool has become very pronounced. Some 15 per cent of the land is derelict. No mythical liver bird symbolizes modern Liverpool, but a different creature, the bulldozer with caterpillar tracks. A study of the mid-1970s recorded that the city's worst area contained 18 per cent unemployment, compared with the 8 per cent city average; 13 per cent immigrants (4 per cent average); and 10 per cent large families (6 per cent average). Both crime and overcrowding were three times the city average, and the want of standard housing amenities twice the average. Public expenditure averaged over all districts of the city was, however, 50 per cent higher than in the worst district, and the Council was spending £1·3 million per year to repair the depredations of vandalism.[35]

Previously, when the city centre teemed with population, the tensions that sprang from their deprivation found a religious and nationalist form, and a resolution was achieved not by addressing their social and economic needs or by conciliating the communities but by channelling their conflict towards the political parties. Now the communities are dispersed or dowered with different interests, for sectarian identifications have relaxed. By 1975 only about 2½ per cent of Liverpudlians attended Anglican services, and eighteen churches had closed in central Liverpool in the previous ten years. The new bishop, David Sheppard, emphasized, as his predecessors had done, that a missionary situation existed; and parsons were directed to proselytize men at their place of work and to establish Christian settlements in areas like pagan Toxteth, 'the most uninsurable place in Great Britain'.[36]

Sectarianism and nationalism, as elements of Anglo-Irish competition in Liverpool, have dwindled but racialism, as an element in the struggle between poor white and coloured communities in the wastelands of central and south Liverpool, has shown signs of re-emerging as too many people chase too few jobs. During the Second World War West Indian immigrants had swollen the number of adult male blacks in Liverpool from about 500 to 3,500, although in part Liverpool's coloured community remains Afro-English and old-established. Clashes between blacks and whites occurred in May–June 1919 and again in July–August 1948, although to call certain incidents race riots is to imply that particular acts of aggression represent the broad attitudes of the communities. Black seamen, munitions workers, engineers, electricians, and others, recruited during full employment in the war-time emergencies, suffered from the competition of ex-servicemen when the demand for labour was slackening. The prolonged high levels of unemployment in the 1970s threatened to replicate certain of these conditions as youths organized their workless leisure in gangs which took a visible identity from colour. Some parallels exist between the sense of injury and frustration felt by Irish communities in Liverpool from the 1840s and the grievances about status and security felt by coloured communities from the 1940s. There was the same tendency to be supplied with shabby and expensive housing; in work to be left the dirty jobs, to be accused of accepting lower wages and inferior conditions, to be overlooked in promotion, and to be more vulnerable to redundancy and unemployment; in social relations the same tendency to isolation, clustering in certain districts; and in habits and behaviour to be thought outlandish, passionate, and disorderly. In numbers the new immigrants are less considerable than the old Irish, but colour and race lend a novel and aggressive distinction to them, which is hardly softened by the Liverpool wit that calls a negro a 'smoked Irishman'.[37]

But the solutions to the problem of city government which the local political parties offer more and more depend on national government policies, on national economic factors, and on professional administrators. This was emphasized by a well-publicized interim report of the Inner Areas Studies team in 1977. This included Liverpool 8 in its purview, along with Small Heath in Birmingham and Stockwell in London's Lambeth borough. It made recommendations which would further trench upon local initiative in the planned regeneration of decayed and abandoned urban areas. Whitehall departments, of Industry, Employment, Education, Environment, and Housing, would control the levers of policies designed to restore manufacture, raise incomes, expand the rate-base, and repopulate the inner areas of cities. The *ad hoc* and speculative character of past housing schemes was disavowed; but the integrated policy which was now advocated by some students of urban problems was politically contentious, on account of the reallocation of resources which it demanded. That some of the existing subsidies of the rents of council-house tenants and of the mortgage payments of owner-occupiers might be transferred was one possibility; another, as the Housing Centre Trust proposed, was the national aggregation of the mortgage part in council housing, so that the prosperous municipalities would shoulder some of the burden of the poor municipalities.[38] But, whatever course is favoured, it seems unlikely that the municipal corporation will emerge as the paramount authority in either its conception or its execution.

Not that the city council will be removed from all responsibility, for it fulfils a vital purpose for the national political parties. If things ever go well it is permitted some minor share of the credit, so that it may continue to perform its essential role of taking a major share of the blame when things go badly. Annual local elections act as breakwaters for the tide of public feeling to batter against and to spend some of its force. The Labour party's Harrogate conference on local government in 1977 exemplified this. With high rates of inflation and unemployment and the Government's cuts in public expenditure, local authorities were placed in a trap, needing to raise the rates in order to maintain declining services. Delegates were appalled by an announcement that the rates in Liverpool might rise in April by 40 per cent and council-house rents by an average of £1 per week; but the party's general secretary, Ron Hayward, was quick to caution those Labour infantrymen in the forthcoming local elections who might be tempted to desert or to blame their generals in Whitehall. 'You do not win local elections by attacking your own government', he declared. 'The electorate are not fooled. They believe in collective responsibility for our policies, even if we do not always believe in it ourselves.'[39]

The tradition of a participating, amateur democracy has, therefore, been maintained, although the conviction that local government is too serious a business to be left to the elected councillors has gained. Much local government work is administrative, not legislative, and in the exercise of these delegated powers a multiplicity of officials beckon and deprecate, check and co-ordinate, manage and direct. The interlocking of local and central government in public health and social services provision developed in the nineteenth century with the inculcation of national minimum standards by official regulation, removal, and restraint; but it hardened after the First World War with government subsidies for housing, unemployment benefits, regional policies for industry, and national policies for transport and fuel. At the same time the once geographically discrete city, in which most people's work and pleasure were contained within walking distance of home, was pulled apart, gradually from the 1860s with surburban tramways and railways, and rapidly from the First World War with mass-produced motor vehicles. Inner urban decay and suburban sprawl melted Liverpool with Merseyside. In April 1974 the new metropolitan County Council of Merseyside was born, governing over $1\frac{1}{2}$ million people in an area of 250 square miles. Where once it was hard to define Merseyside, now it was hard to distinguish Liverpool.

Notes

INTRODUCTION

1 J. B. Priestley, *English Journey*, 1934, p. 250.

2 Quoted in C. Desmond Greaves, *The Life and Times of James Connolly*, 1961, paperback 1972, p. 287.

3 *L.R.* 24 June 1899; Viscount Gladstone, *After Thirty Years*, 1928, p. 186 n.1.

4 J. Sexton, *Sir James Sexton, Agitator*, 1936, *passim*; E. Larkin, *James Larkin*, 1965, *passim*; S. O'Casey, *Drums Under the Windows*, 1945.

5 R. Samuel, 'The Class Struggle and Work-Place Collective', unpublished paper; H. Gosling, *Up and Down Stream*, 1927, pp. 144–5; Sexton, *op. cit.* pp. 109–13.

6 *P.D.*, 5th ser., vol. 211, col. 2652.

7 See Table 2.4 of H. McLeod, 'White Collar Values and the Role of Religion', in G. Crossick (ed), *The Lower Middle Class in Britain 1870–1914*, 1977.

8 R. Jenkins, *Sir Charles Dilke*, 1968, pp. 192–3, states that Dilke had nine votes (in 1885); N. Blewett, 'The Franchise in the United Kingdom, 1885–1918', *Past and Present*, no. 32, 1965, p. 44, that Dilke had six.

9 R. I. McKibbin, H. C. G. Matthew, and J. A. Kay, 'The Franchise Factor in the Rise of the Labour Party', *E.H.R.* xci, 1976, pp. 723–52; local election figures from I. Budge, and C. O'Leary, *Belfast: Approach to Crisis*, 1973, p. 175.

CHAPTER 1

1 H. H. Asquith in 1901, quoted in Lord Snell, *Men, Movements, and Myself*, 1936, p. 86; W. Cooke Taylor, *Notes of a Tour in the Manufacturing Districts of Lancashire*, 1841–2, 3rd edition 1968, p. 308; G. C. Brodrick, 'The Progress of Democracy in England', *Nineteenth Century*, Nov. 1883, reprinted in *Literary Fragments*, 1891, p. 181.

2 H. J. Dyos and D. H. Aldcroft, *British Transport*, Leicester, 1969, p. 45; D. Defoe, *A Tour through England and Wales*, Everyman edition, vol. ii, p. 256; H. Peet, *Liverpool in the Reign of Queen Anne*, Liverpool, 1908, p. 16; W. Smith (ed.), *A Scientific Survey of Merseyside*, Liverpool, 1953, p. 120; C. W. Chalklin, *The Provincial Towns of Georgian England*, 1974, p. 20.

3 Defoe, *op. cit.* pp. 68–9, 255–9; *The Journal of the Rev. John Wesley*, Everyman edition, vol. ii, p. 292; W. G. Herdman, *Pictorial Relics of Ancient Liverpool*, Liverpool, 1878, vol. i, p. iii; R. Southey, *Letters from England*, 1951 edition, p. 222; Peet, *op. cit.*, p. 12.

4 W. MacRitchie, *Diary of a Tour through Great Britain in 1795*, 1897, pp. 42–3; W.

Smith *op. cit.*, pp. 120, 122. The tonnage of vessels using the port of Liverpool doubled every fifteen years between 1749 and 1857. See Gomer Williams, *History of the Liverpool Privateers with an Account of the Liverpool Slave Trade*, 1897, pp. 621–2.

5 Defoe *op. cit.*, p. 256. On Liverpool's rising prominence, P. G. E. Clemens, 'The Rise of Liverpool 1665–1750', *Ec.H.R.*, 2nd ser. xxix, no. 2, May 1976, pp. 211–25; A. Holt (ed.), *Merseyside*, Liverpool, 1923, pp. 28–47; S. Derrick, *Letters*, 1767, vol. i, pp. 15–30; *Svedenstierna's Tour of Great Britain 1802–3*, Newton Abbot, 1973, pp. 169–73; A. Bryant, *The Age of Elegance 1812–1822*, 1950, p. 138; L. M. Cullen, *Anglo-Irish Trade 1660–1880*, Manchester, 1968, pp. 43–4, 56, 71–2, 89, 134–7.

6 *Liverpool and Slavery by a Genuine 'Dicky Sam'*, Liverpool, 1884; Newcastle, 1969, chaps. xiii–xv; F. E. Hyde, B. B. Parkinson, and S. Marriner, 'The Nature and Profitability of the Liverpool Slave Trade', *Ec.H.R.*, 2nd. ser. v, no. 3, 1953, pp. 368–77; F. E. Sanderson, 'Liverpool and the Slave Trade: A Guide to Sources', *T.H.S.L.C.*, vol. 124, 1972, pp. 154–76; J. R. Harris (ed.), *Liverpool and Merseyside*, 1969, p. 183; R. Perren, 'The North American Beef and Cattle Trade with Great Britain, 1870–1914', *Ec.H.R.*, 2nd ser., xxiv, no. 3, 1971, pp. 430–44; W. H. Davies, *The Autobiography of a Super Tramp*, 1908; new edition, 1964, chaps. x–xii.

7 Gomer Williams, *op. cit.*, p. 62; *L.D.P.* 27 Dec. 1905; W. Farrer and J. Brownbill (eds.), *The Victoria History of the County of Lancaster*, 1911, vol. iv, pp. 41–3.

8 R. Muir, *A History of Liverpool*, Liverpool, 1907, p. 301; J. McCarthy, *A History of our Own Times*, 1879–80, vol I, p. 89; E. de Selincourt, *The Letters of William and Dorothy Wordsworth*, 2nd edition, Oxford, 1970, vol. iii, part ii, p. 573; L. Mumford, *The City in History*, Pelican edition, 1966, p. 479; Dyos and Aldcroft, *op. cit.*, pp. 251–5; *The Journals & Miscellaneous Notebooks of Ralph Waldo Emerson*, Harvard, 1973, vol. x, p. 178; J. Q. Hughes, *Seaport*, 1964, pp. 1–39; F. E. Hyde, *Liverpool and the Mersey*, Newton Abbot, 1971, chaps. 5, 7. On the engineer of Liverpool's first dock—the enclosed Wet Dock, opened in 1715—see H. Peet, *Thomas Steers*, 1932.

9 B. G. Orchard, *Liverpool's Legion of Honour*, Birkenhead, 1893, p. 221; *P.* 13 Jan. 1906.

10 Dr. Currie to James Mason, 21 May 1804, in W. W. Currie (ed.), *Memoir of the Life, Writings & Correspondence of James Currie M.D., F.R.S., of Liverpool*, 1831, vol. i, p. 360.

11 MacRitchie, *op. cit.*, p. 45; John Smith to Jane Smith, 18 April 1810, MS. letter in possession of the Forman family. John Smith became a New York banker; he was the uncle of Samuel Smith. On the want of culture among Liverpool's tradesmen, see *Miss Weeton's Journal of a Governess*, Newton Abbot, 1969, vol. i, pp. 169–70.

12 C. R. Holt (ed.), *The Diary of John Holt*, Liverpool, 1948, p. x. On Holt see John Holt and Co. (Liverpool) Ltd., *Merchant Adventurer*, n.d. 1950; J. Holt, *The Early Years of an African Trader*, 1962; B. Porter, *Critics of Empire*, 1968. On Scots migrations see A. Redford, *Labour Migration in England, 1800–50*, Manchester, 1926, pp. 117–18.

13 T. Taylor (ed.), *The Autobiography and Memoirs of Benjamin Robert Haydon*, 1926 edition, vol. ii, pp. 627, 644; W. Plomer (ed.), *Kilvert's Diary*, 1969 edition, vol. ii, pp. 211–12.

14 Southey, *op. cit.*, p. 223; Orchard, *op. cit.*, p. ix.

15 Muir, *op. cit.*, p. 306; Cooke Taylor, *op. cit.*, p. 13; T. Baines, *Liverpool in 1859*, 1859, pp. 5–6; Herdman, *op. cit.*, vol. i, p. xiii.

16 Among the largest industries were Cope's tobacco factory, employing 1,400 mostly women, *L.R.* 17 and 20 March 1886; Mathew's paint factory, *L.R.* 13 Feb. 1886; Price's candle factory, *L.R.* 13 July 1886; Noblett's sweet factory, *L.R.* 20 Nov. 1886; soap factories, *L.R.* 23 Oct. 1886, Farrer and Brownbill, *op. cit.*, vol. ii, pp. 399–403; sugar refineries, T. Jones, *Henry Tate 1819–1899*, revised edition, 1960; saw-milling, and foundry work. Flour-milling and the chemical industry grew in the nineteenth century,

but two craft industries for which Liverpool was once celebrated—pottery and watchmaking—were mostly extinct. See G. Chandler, *Liverpool*, 1957, pp. 331–46; H. B. Lancaster, *Liverpool and her Potters*, Liverpool, 1936; Harris, *op. cit.*, pp. 1–15; S. Lewis, *A Topographical Dictionary of England*, 1831, vol. iii, pp. 98–110.

17 *P.P.* 1894, xxxv, p. 30.

18 *P.P.* 1904, xxxii, Qs. 2057–8, Dr. T. F. Young. The same was true of women's work, the best class finding employment in tobacco manufacture, confectionery, and dry-cleaning, the poorest—mostly Irish—in rope-making, sack-mending, and jute factories. See A. Harrison, *Women's Industries in Liverpool*, 1904, pp. 13–14.

19 *P.P.* 1904, xxxii, Qs. 2062, 2065; Gladstone cited in O. Anderson, *A Liberal State at War*, 1967, p. 120.

20 Harris, *op. cit.*, pp. 167–75; J. Masefield, *The Wanderer of Liverpool*, 1930; E. C. Woods and P. C. Brown, *The Rise and Progress of Wallasey*, 1960 edition, pp. 196–9.

21 *L.D.P.* 7 Oct. 1899; *T.U.C. Annual Report*, 1890, pp. 41, 58; J. H. Clapham, *An Economic History of Modern Britain*, 1926, vol. i, pp. 212–13.

22 Sexton, *Agitator*, p. 225; B. Tillett, *Memories and Reflections*, 1931, p. 102; J. Sexton, *The Riot Act*, 1914, p. 84.

23 Tillett, *op. cit.*, p. 88.

24 On London see H. Llewellyn Smith and Vaughan Nash, *The Story of the Dockers' Strike*, 1890, p. 19 ff.; J. Lovell, *Stevedores and Dockers*, 1969; G. Stedman Jones, *Outcast London*, Oxford, 1971.

25 E. Rathbone, 'Report on the Results of a Special Inquiry into the Conditions of Labour at the Liverpool Docks', *Transactions of the Liverpool Economic & Statistical Society*, 1903–4, p. 20; Tillett, *op. cit.*, p. 20; Sexton, *Agitator*, p. 67; *P.D.*, 5th ser., vol. 113, col. 1015.

26 Interview with M.H. Burton 1899, Webb Local Government Collection, vol. 148.

27 *L.R.* 7 Aug. 1889; W. Greenwood, *How the Other Man Lives*, 1939, p. 59; Tillett, *op. cit.*, p. 76; *Liverpool Domestic Mission Society, 23rd Annual Report*, 1860, pp. 61–62.

28 Sexton, *Agitator*, p. 72; Sexton's serialized autobiography, *Manchester Empire News*, 27 Dec. 1925; the Earl of Woolton, *Memoirs*, 1959, p. 20; C. R. Fay, *Life and Labour in the Nineteenth Century*, 1920; reprinted Cambridge, 1947, pp. 222–3.

29 *P.P.* 1892, xxxvi, Q. 13579, Sexton, xxxv, Q. 234, Brien.

30 Larkin, *op. cit.*, p. 8.

31 Sexton, *Agitator*, p. 68.

32 *P.P.* 1892, xxxvi, Qs. 13579, 13612, Sexton.

33 *P.P.* 1892, xxxv, Qs. 3675, 396, McCarthy.

34 Ibid., Q. 897, Atkins; *P.P.* 1892, xxxvi, Q. 13580, Sexton; Sexton, *Agitator*, chap. x. *The Labour Annual*, 1896, p. 217, contains photographs of Sexton before and after his accident.

35 *Liverpool Steam Ship Owners Association Annual Report*, 1879–80, p. 2; Minutes, 16 Feb. 1880.

36 Rathbone, *op. cit.*, p. 23.

37 *P.P.* 1892, xxxvi, Q. 13579, Sexton.

38 *L.D.P.* 14 Dec. 1905.

39 Rathbone, *op. cit.*, p. 32.

40 Ibid., pp. 37, 44, 49; *P.P.* 1884–5, xxx, Q.13328, Forwood; Sexton's letter in *L.D.P.* 16 Dec. 1905.

41 Rathbone, *op. cit.*, p. 34.

42 B. Tillett, *The Dock Labourers' Bitter Cry*, 1889, p. 5; B. Tillett, *A Brief History of the Dockers' Union*, 1910, p. 11.

43 *P.P.* 1904, xxxii, Q. 2070, Young.

44 *L.C.* 1 May 1911.

45 E. F. Rathbone, *William Rathbone*, 1905, p. 384; *P.P.* 1874, xxiii, pt. ii; W. H. Brown, *A Century of Liverpool Co-operation*, Liverpool, n.d. 1929.

46 B. G. Orchard, *The Clerks of Liverpool*, Liverpool, 1871, p. 10. Specifically commercial clerks numbered 10,961 in Liverpool and Birkenhead in 1881—*P.P.* 1883, lxxx, p. 34. On the difficulties of analysis, from the censuses' failure to distinguish personal occupation and industrial role, see W. A. Armstrong, 'The Use of Information about Occupation', in E. A. Wrigley (ed.), *Nineteenth-Century Society*, Cambridge, 1972. On the class generally see G. Crossick (ed.), *The Lower Middle Class in Britain 1870–1914*, 1977.

47 Orchard, *Clerks*, pp. 25, 51; G. L. Anderson, 'The Recruitment, Apprenticeship and Mobility of the Mid-Victorian Clerk: A Study of the North and South Wales Bank, 1850–75', *The Welsh History Review*, vol. 7, 1975, pp. 341–56; F. D. Klingender, *The Condition of Clerical Labour in Britain*, 1935, pp. 11–26; S. F. Bullock, *Robert Thorne*, 1907.

48 E. H. Phelps Brown, *The Growth of British Industrial Relations*, 1959, Papermac edition, 1965, pp. 47–48, 60–61, 172–3, 218; H. A. Clegg, A. Fox, and A. F. Thompson, *A History of British Trade Unions since 1889: Volume 1. 1889–1910*, Oxford, 1964, pp. 215–29, 469; H. Finer, *English Local Government*, 3rd edition, 1946, chap. x; G. L. P. Anderson, 'A Study of Clerical Labour in Liverpool and Manchester 1850–1914', unpublished D.Phil. thesis, Lancaster, 1974, *passim.*

49 Orchard, *Clerks*, p. 37; J. W. Diggle, *The Lancashire Life of Bishop Fraser*, People's Edition, 1891, p. 356; *P.D.*, 5th ser., vol. 309, 2542–6, B. V. Kirby.

50 *T.* 4 Feb. 1886. Liverpool's clerks, for example, complained of the gregariousness of Bank Holidays—*P.D.*, 3rd ser., cccxxv, 1150–3, Lawrence.

51 Hugh Farrie quoted in M.B. Simey, *Charitable Effort in Liverpool in the Nineteenth Century*, Liverpool, 1951, p. 101.

52 Orchard, *Clerks*, pp. 48–49; Clegg, Fox, and Thompson, *op. cit.*, p. 223; *P.P.* 1872, xxvi, Q. 23890–924, Harding; *P.D.*, 5th ser., vol. 309, 2542–6; Anderson, 'Study of Clerical Labour', pp. 196–7, 205–6, 292–303; A. Spoor, *White-Collar Union*, 1967, pp. 13–15, 47–49.

53 M. Cole, *Growing up into Revolution*, 1949, p. 23; Sir W. B. Forwood, *Recollections of a Busy Life*, Liverpool, 1910, p. 8

54 T. H. S. Escott, *England: Its People, Polity and Pursuits*, 1885, p. 85.

55 *P.P.* 1883, lxxx, p. 53; J. Denvir, *The Irish in Britain*, 1892, pp. 383–4, 434.

56 J. Denvir, *The Life Story of an Old Rebel*, Dublin, 1910, p. 2; *P.P.* 1857–8, ix, Q. 5901, Hume; J. A. Picton, *Memorials of Liverpool*, 1903 edition, vol. ii, pp. 504–5; T. Burke, *Catholic History of Liverpool*, Liverpool, 1910, pp. 234–5; *L.C.H.* 6 Feb. 1903; W. S. Jevons, *Methods of Social Reform*, 1883, p. 213.

57 P. O'Mara, *The Autobiography of a Liverpool Irish Slummy*, 1934, p. 75; J. Brothers, *Church and School*, Liverpool, 1964, pp. 41–42.

58 Muir, *op. cit.*, p. 304; R. J. Stonor, *Liverpool's Hidden Story*, Birchley Hall Press, 1957, Appendix III.

59 *P.P.* 1836, xxxiv, Appendix G, p. vii.

60 Burke, *op. cit.*, p. 81.

61 *P.D.*, 3rd ser., lxxxix, 770–1, xci, 810, xcii, 58.

62 *P.D.*, 3rd ser., xcii, 60.

63 *P.P.* 1844, xvii, Q. 985. For estimates of slum and cellar dwellers see M. W. Flinn (ed.), *Report on the Sanitary Condition of the Labouring Population of Great Britain by Edwin Chadwick 1842*, Edinburgh, 1965, p. 6 n.6; W. H. Henderson and W. H. Chaloner (eds), *Engels: The Condition of the Working Class in England*, Oxford, 1958, p. 43 n.2; J. P. Mayer (ed.), *Alexis De Tocqueville, Journeys to England and Ireland*, 1958, p. 110; Chandler, *op. cit.*, pp. 409–10; Simey, *op. cit.*, p. 11; J. H. Treble, 'Liverpool Working-Class Housing,

1801–1851', in S. D. Chapman (ed.), *The History of Working-Class Housing*, Newton Abbot, 1971. I.C. Taylor, 'The Insanitary Housing Question and Tenement Dwellings in Nineteenth-Century Liverpool' in A. Sutcliffe (ed.), *Multi-Storey Living*, 1974, pp. 43–44 n.7 corrects some past mistakes.

64 Flinn, *op. cit.*, pp. 223–4; E. C. Midwinter, *Social Administration in Lancashire 1830–1860*, Manchester, 1969, pp. 74–75.

65 *P.P.* 1844, xvii, p. 186, Holme; *The Stranger in Liverpool*, ninth edition, 1829, pp. 64–73; I.C. Taylor, 'The Court and Cellar Dwellings: The Eighteenth Century Origin of the Liverpool Slum', *T.H.S.L.C.*, vol. 122, 1970, pp. 67–90; W. Carter, *Some Results of Recent Sanitary Legislation*, Liverpool, 1886, pp. 11–12; B. D. White, *A History of the Corporation of Liverpool 1835–1914*, Liverpool, 1951, pp. 25–26.

66 On public improvements undertaken in late eighteenth-century Liverpool, M. C. Buer, *Health, Wealth and Population in the Early Days of the Industrial Revolution*, 1926, pp. 84–86; White, *op. cit.*, chap. iv.

67 Burke., *op. cit.*, p. 84; Simey *op. cit.*, pp. 41–43; O. MacDonagh, *A Pattern of Government Growth 1800–60*, 1961, p. 33.

68 C. Creighton, *A History of Epidemics in Britain*, 1894; new edition, 1965, vol. ii, pp. 140–1, 206–7, 388, 826, 847; Midwinter, *op. cit.*, 70–71; S. G. Checkland, *The Gladstones*, Cambridge, 1971, p. 237.

69 *L.R.* 22 Aug. 1885.

70 Muir, *op. cit.*, p. 305. On the quality of Liverpool policemen, E. C. Midwinter, *Law and Order in Early Victorian Lancashire*, Borthwick Papers no. 34, 1968, pp. 21–29.

71 R. Gladstone to W. E. Gladstone, 22 March 1848; Burke, *op. cit.*, p. 92; Orchard, *Legion*, pp. 197–8; F. C. Mather, *Public Order in the Age of the Chartists*, Manchester, 1959, pp. 82, 84, 115–16, 194; J. Bright, *Selected Speeches*, Everyman, 1907, p. 71. Cf. J. H. Treble, 'O'Connor, O'Connell, and the Attitudes of Irish Immigrants towards Chartism in the North of England 1838–48', in J. Butt and I. F. Clarke (eds.), *The Victorians and Social Protest*, Newton Abbot, 1973, pp. 33–70.

72 *P.D.*, 3rd ser., lxxxix, 598–9.

73 MacDonagh, *op. cit.*, p. 39. On the defrauding of immigrants, see *The Catholic Institute Magazine*, Nov. 1857, pp. 53–64; Revd. A. Hume, *Suggestions for the Advancement of Literature and Learning in Liverpool*, Liverpool, 1851, pp. 19–20; A. Behrend, *Portrait of a Family Firm*, Liverpool, 1970, pp. 137–8; T. Coleman, *Passage to America*, 1972, Penguin, 1974, *passim*.

74 Denvir, *Life Story*, p. 26.

75 Denvir, *Irish in Britain*, p. 9; J. E. Handley, *The Irish in Modern Scotland*, Cork, 1947, chap. 2.

76 Burke, *op. cit.*, p. 63; Handley, *op. cit.*, chap. 6; J. E. Handley, *The Irish in Scotland 1798–1845*, Cork, 2nd edition, 1945, pp. 36–56; Redford, *op. cit.*, chap. viii; MacDonagh, *op. cit.*, p. 22.

77 *P.P.* 1836, xxxiv, Appendix G, pp. 21, 29, Whitty and Holme. Whitty, Liverpool's first Head Constable, held similar views on crime, that it was due not to poverty but to the attraction of criminal life—see J. J. Tobias, *Crime and Industrial Society in the Nineteenth Century*, Pelican edition, 1972, pp. 179–80.

78 *P.P.* 1836, *op. cit.*, Holme.

79 Compare Holme's occupational survey, ibid., pp. 29–30, and the survey in *P.P.* 1893–4, cvi, p. 62.

80 *P.P.* 1836, *op. cit.*, p. iv.

81 Ibid., Appendix G, p. 24; cf. Derrick, *op. cit.*, i, p. 24.

82 *P.P.* 1836, *op. cit.*, pp. 18, Duncan, 20, Whitty, 22, Glover, 23, Fisher, 27, Falvey; *P.P.* 1877, xi, Q. 8313, Father Nugent.

83 Ibid., p. xiii; cf. A. W. Coats, 'The Classical Economists and the Labourer', in E. L. Jones and G. E. Mingay (eds.), *Land, Labour, and Population in the Industrial Revolution*, 1967, pp. 111–12.

84 J. R. Jones, *The Welsh Builder on Merseyside*, Liverpool, 1946, *passim.*

85 Ibid., p. 31; W. Smith (ed.), *op. cit.*, pp. 1–11.

86 G. R. Jones, 'Liverpool and the Influence of North Wales', *Liverpool Daily Post*, Centenary Edition, 1955, p. 110.

87 *P.P.* 1883, lxxx, p. 363; *L.R.* 28 Jan. 1893. R. W. Jones, of the Liverpool Welsh National Society, wrote of 70,000 or 80,000 Welsh in Liverpool in a letter to Samuel Smith, 23 Aug. 1892, now in the James Bryce Papers, UB34.

88 *M.G.* 19 Sept. 1900.

89 National Eisteddfodau were held in Liverpool in 1840, 1851, 1864, 1884, and 1900, and in Birkenhead in 1878 and 1917. For an account of the 1840 Eisteddfod, see H. M. Walmsley, *The Life of Sir Joshua Walmsley*, 1879, pp. 120–1.

90 *L.R.* 5 May 1900; *T.* 18 Sept. 1884; *The Liverpool Review*, vol. v, no. 1, Jan. 1930, pp. 480–1; R. Jones, *The Poetical Works of the Rev. Goronwy Owen, with his Life and Correspondence*, 1876, vol ii, p. 94; *P.D.*, 5th ser., vol. 214, 1207–8; E. G. Ravenstein, 'On the Celtic Languages in the British Isles; A Statistical Survey', *J.S.S.*, vol. xlii, 1879, p. 621 n.

91 J. R. Jones, *op. cit.*

92 Ibid., p. 163; *Notes and Queries*, 7th ser., vol. ix, p. 507; vol. x, p. 116; vol. xxii, p. 376. The *Oxford English Dictionary* records that 'jerry-built' first appeared in 1869, origin unknown.

93 J. R. Jones, *op. cit.*, pp. 12–13; Anderson, in *Welsh History Review*, *op. cit.*, pp. 342–5.

94 *P.P.* 1836, *op. cit.*, pp. 28, Holme, 31, Dover.

95 *Labour Chronicle*, 1 Jan. 1895; *P.P.* 1892, xxxvi, Qs. 12009, 12079–80 (Parr).

96 E. Flynn in *The Transport Worker*, Aug. 1911.

97 Denvir, *Life Story*, *op. cit.*, p. 23. It is impossible to enumerate the Irish Protestants in Liverpool. Canon Hume reckoned them equal to the number of English Catholics—about 2,000 in 1851. *P.P.* 1857–8, ix, Q. 5901.

98 Sexton, *Agitator*, p. 109; *L. C.* 26 Oct. 1894; E. Taplin, *Liverpool Dockers and Seamen 1870–1890*, Hull, 1974, pp. 10–11, plays down the sectarian differences among dockers.

99 B. Webb, *My Apprenticeship*, 1926, p. 90.

100 G. B. Shaw, *John Bull's Other Island*, 1907, Preface; F. L. Cross and E. A. Livingstone (eds.), *The Oxford Dictionary of the Christian Church*, Oxford, 1974. The agreements and disagreements of the Evangelical alliance in the 1840s are explored in G. I. T. Machin, 'The Maynooth Grant, the Dissenters and Disestablishment, 1845–1847', *E.H.R.* lxxxii, Jan. 1967, pp. 61–85.

101 R. Clifton, 'The Popular Fear of Catholics during the English Revolution', *Past and Present*, no. 52, Aug. 1971; R. Sayers, *The History of Everton*, Liverpool, 1830, p. 416; R. C. Jarvis, 'The Town of Liverpool in the "45" ', *T.H.S.L.C.*, vol. 108, 1956, pp. 63–82; *The Stranger in Liverpool*, 9th edition, 1829, p. 83 and Appendix.

102 Stonor, *op. cit.*, pp. 30–31.

103 Wesley, *Journal*, ii, p. 292; iii, p. 192; *The Stranger in Liverpool*, *op. cit.*, p. 82. However see Parkinson, *op. cit.*, chap. 11.

104 Currie, *op. cit.*, p. 135; *Liverpool and Slavery*, *op. cit.*, chaps. x–xi; R. B. Walker, 'Religious Changes in Liverpool in the Nineteenth Century', *The Journal of Ecclesiastical History*, vol. xix, no. 2, Oct. 1968, p. 199.

105 H. Senior, *Orangemen in Ireland and Britain 1795–1836*, 1966, pp. 22, 274; Budge and O'Leary, *op. cit.*, chap. 1.

106 *The Orange Institution*, 1813, p. 13.

107 Ibid., pp. 15, 22; Senior, *op. cit.*, Appendix A; M. W. Dewar, J. Brown and S. E. Long, *Orangeism*, 1967, p. 113.

108 Senior, *op. cit.*, chap. vii.

109 Ibid., p. 171; Picton, *op. cit.*, i, p. 355.

110 *P.D.* 1819-20, xli, col. 896, Bennet, 948, Canning.

111 E. M. Menzies, 'The Freeman Voter in Liverpool, 1802-1835', *T.H.S.L.C.*, vol. 124, 1972, pp. 85-107; W. E. Gladstone to Robertson Gladstone, 17 Dec. 1830, 2 June 1831; Cobbett quoted in Senior, *op. cit.*, p. 216.

112 Picton, *op. cit.*, i, p. 414; G. I. T. Machin, 'The Catholic Emancipation Crisis of 1825', *E.H.R.* lxxviii, July 1963, p. 471.

113 'An Old Stager' (J. Aspinall), *Liverpool a Few Years Since*, 1852, chap. xxii et seq.; Checkland, *op. cit.*, chap. 9 ff.; C. R. Fay, *Huskisson and his Age*, 1951, chap. xii; P. J. V. Rolo, *George Canning*, 1965, pp. 94-98, 161-3, 187; L. Melville (ed.), *The Huskisson Papers*, 1931, pp. 124-6, 188-94; B. Whittingham-Jones, 'Liverpool's Political Clubs 1812-1830', *T.H.S.L.C.*, vol. iii, 1959, pp. 117-38.

114 B. Whittingham-Jones, *The Pedigree of Liverpool Politics*, Liverpool, 1936, pp. 34-35; R. L. Hill, *Toryism and the People 1832-1846*, 1929, pp. 58-61; and G. A. Cahill's articles on the Tory-Protestant connection in *The Catholic Historical Review*, vol. xliii, Oct. 1957, pp. 273-308, and *The Review of Politics*, vol. xix, Jan. 1957, pp. 62-76.

115 C. Bullock, *Hugh M'Neile and Reformation Truth*, 1882, p. 15; Sir Edward Russell, *That Reminds Me*, 1899, p. 133; G. H. Francis, *Orators of the Age*, 1847, p. 413; J. Evans, *Lancashire Authors and Orators*, 1850, p. 182; G. R. Balleine, *A History of the Evangelical Party in the Church of England*, 1908; new edition, 1933, p. 202; *P.P.* 1857-8, ix, Q. 5816, Archdeacon Jones. Manning considered M'Neile more eloquent than Canning—E. S. Purcell, *Life of Cardinal Manning*, 1896, i, p. 64.

116 *P.P.* 1835, xv, Appendix 20. p. 145; also cited in Senior, *op. cit.*, Appendix C.

117 J. Murphy, *The Religious Problem in English Education*, Liverpool, 1959; and Murphy's articles in *T.H.S.L.C.* vol. 116, pp. 167-95, vol. 118 pp. 105-38.

118 Walmsley, *op. cit.*, chaps. viii, ix, xiii. On the franchise, see J. L. Hammond, 'The Social Background 1835-1935', in H. J. Laski, W. I. Jennings, and W. A. Robson (eds.), *A Century of Municipal Progress 1835-1935*, 1935, p. 41.

119 Quoted Murphy, *op. cit.*, p. 248. As one example of Protestant literature, see *Auxiliary Explanatory Notes for the use of the Children of all Sects who are to be Instructed at the two Corporation Schools, Liverpool, from the 'Irish Bible Selections, with Notes' !!*, Liverpool, 1836.

120 *P.P.* 1836, *op. cit.*, Appendix G. p. 24, Father Wilcock, p. 27, Mark Falvey.

121 Ibid. pp. 20-21, Whitty, p. 37, Hodgson, p. 38, Dover, p. 40, Muspratt; T. Carlyle, 'Chartism' (1839), in *Critical and Miscellaneous Essays*, 1869, v. pp. 351-2.

122 Sexton, *Agitator*, p. 68; A. T. McCabe, 'The Standard of Living on Merseyside, 1850-1875', in S. P. Bell (ed.), *Victorian Lancashire*, 1974, chap. 6; A. L. Bowley and G. H. Wood in *J.S.S.*, vol. 68, 1905, pp. 126-9, 132-3, 608-11.

123 O'Mara, *op. cit.*, p. 80; Woolton, *op. cit.*, p. 31.

124 W. Toynbee (ed.), *The Diaries of William Charles Macready, 1833-51*, 1912, ii, p. 451.

125 *P.P.* 1874, xxiii, pt. ii. pp. 223, 229-30, 286; P. T. Winskill and J. Thomas, *History of the Temperance Movement in Liverpool and District*, Liverpool, 1887, chap. xii; B. Harrison, *Drink and The Victorians*, 1971, pp. 167-8, 173.

126 Burke, *op. cit.*, p. 67. On the divisions in the Tory ranks, between Protestants and Protectionists, owing to Lord John Manners's candidature in the 1847 General Election, see C. Whibley, *Lord John Manners and his Friends*, 1925, vol. i, pp. 238-42; W. E. Gladstone to R. Gladstone, 5 Feb. 1846; R. Gladstone to W. E. Gladstone 4, 6 Feb. 1846. Dr. H. C. G. Matthew kindly supplied me with the Gladstone correspondence relating to Liverpool in the 1840s.

127 Quoted G. M. Trevelyan, *The Life of John Bright*, 7th edition, 1914, p. 201. Richard Cobden equally despaired of Liverpool—see A. Briggs (ed.), *Chartist Studies*, Papermac, 1965, p. 354 n.l. For the Liverpool merchants' doubts about Peel's free trade policy see H. Reeve (ed.), *The Greville Memoirs*, 1888, vol. vi, p. 100; and *Report of 2nd Annual Meeting of the Liverpool Constitutional Association*, 1850.

128 C. D. Watkinson, 'The Liberal Party on Merseyside in the Nineteenth Century', unpublished Ph.D. thesis, Liverpool University, 1967, p. xxiii; Farrer and Brownbill, *op. cit.*, iv, pp. 27–28, 33–36; Sir L. Namier and J. Brooke, *The History of Parliament: The House of Commons 1754–1790*, 1964, pp. 317–8; R. Sedgwick, *The History of Parliament: The House of Commons 1715–1754*, 1970, pp. 270–2.

129 E. F. Rathbone, *op. cit.*, p. 9; 'An Old Stager', *op. cit.*, pp. 60, 155–9; *Liverpool and Slavery*, *op. cit.*, chap. x; Anne Holt, *Walking Together*, 1938, chap. viii; W. Smith, *op. cit.*, pp. 148–64; J. R. Harris, *op. cit.*, passim; Currie, *op. cit.*, i, pp. 110, 500; I Sellers, 'Liverpool Nonconformity 1786–1914', unpublished Ph.D. thesis, University of Keele, 1969, pp. 271–87; Seller's article on the Roscoe circle in *T.H.S.L.C.*, vol. 120, pp. 45–62; S. G. Checkland, 'Economic Attitudes in Liverpool, 1793–1807', *Ec.H.R.*, 2nd. ser., v, no. 1, 1952, pp. 58–75; Burke, *op. cit.*, pp. 68–69.

130 At least thirty-six blockade-runners were built on Merseyside—see M. Ellison, *Support for Secession: Lancashire and the American Civil War*, Chicago, 1972; McCarthy, *op. cit.*, iii, chap. xliv; and R. C. Jarvis, 'The *Alabama* and the Law', *T.H.S.L.C.*, vol. iii, 1959, pp. 181–98.

131 S. Smith, *My Life-work*, 1902, pp. 26, 33–35; W. O. Henderson, *The Lancashire Cotton Famine 1861–65*, Manchester, 2nd edition, 1969, Appendix A, pp. 75–76; T. Ellison, *Gleanings and Reminiscences*, Liverpool, 1905, pp. 322–9.

132 *P.* 28 Dec. 1867; Forwood, *op. cit.*, pp. 53–55, 60; H. McLachlan, *Records of a Family 1800–1933*, Manchester, 1935, p. 41; Henderson, *op. cit.*, pp. 14–16, 25; *Kilvert's Diary*, *op. cit.*, 20 June 1872; S. Marriner, *Rathbones of Liverpool 1845–73*, Liverpool, 1961, pp. 120, 148.

133 D. Fraser, *Urban Politics in Victorian England*, Leicester, 1976, chap. 6.

134 W. Hazlitt, *Table Talk: or Original Essays*, 1931 edition, essay xx, pp. 203–4; G. Chandler, *William Roscoe of Liverpool*, 1953, xxxv. E. L. Griggs (ed.), *Collected Letters of Samuel Taylor Coleridge*, vol. i, Oxford, 1956, pp. 339–40, vol. iv, 1959, pp. 669–70, 735–6, for an agreeable view of the Roscoe circle and a disagreeable view of Hazlitt.

135 Watkinson, *op. cit.*, pp. xxvii–xl, Appendices A and D; Sellers, *op. cit.*, chap. 9.

136 *Spectator*, 11 Aug. 1894. See also W. Copeland Bowie, *Unitarian Churches in Great Britain and Ireland*, Essex Hall pamphlet, n.d. 1906, p. 5; B. Hereford, *A Brief Account of Unitarianism*, British and Foreign Unitarian Association pamphlet, 1903, p. 2; J. P. Trevelyan, *The Life of Mrs Humphry Ward*, 1923, pp. 153–5.

137 E. F. Rathbone, *op. cit.*; W. Willmer, *Family Business*, Birkenhead, 1961.

138 K. Martin, *Father Figures*, 1966, Penguin edition, 1969, p. 15.

139 McLachlan, *op. cit.*, p. 55; Anne Holt, *op. cit.*, p. 223; *D.N.B.* Supplement, vol. 1, pp. 154–6.

140 Orchard, *Liverpool's Legion of Honour*, *op. cit.*, pp. 48–49.

141 Richard Holt's diary, 1 Nov. 1906, 6 Feb. 1921.

142 A. Birrell, *Some Recollections of Early Liverpool*, Liverpool, 1924, p. 8; A. Birrell, *Things Past Redress*, 1937, p. 13.

143 A. Hume, *The Church of England: the Home Missionary to the Poor*, 1862, pp. 13, 16–17; *L.C.* 27 Jan. 1903; H. Peet, *Brief Historical Notes on the Churches of St. George and St. John, Liverpool*, Liverpool, 1900.

144 R. Lawton, 'The Population of Liverpool in the mid Nineteenth Century', *T.H.S.L.C.*, vol. 107, 1956; W. R. Ward (ed.), *The Early Correspondence of Jabez Bunting*

1820–1829, Camden Fourth Series, vol. 11, 1972, pp. 118–28, 203; K. S. Inglis, *Churches and the Working Classes in Victorian Britain*, 1963, pp. 62–64.

145 *P.P.* 1857–8, lx, evidence of Archdeacon Jones, and the Revds. A. J. Tomlin and A. Hume, *passim*.

146 A. Hume, *Ecclesiastical History of Liverpool*, Liverpool, 1881 p. 40; *P.P.* 1857–8, *op. cit.*, Qs. 5151–5288 Revd. Tomlin, 5821 ff. Archdeacon Jones, 5841 ff. Canon Hume; *P.P.* 1887, xxx, Qs. 50238–364, L. Conway.

147 *Passages from the English Note-books of Nathaniel Hawthorne*, 1870, vol. i, pp. 59, 69–70. Hawthorne was Consul in Liverpool from 1853 to 1857, and unhappy both in his duties and in his surroundings—see *Our Old Home*, 1863, vol. i, pp. 1–59, vol. ii, pp. 185–239.

148 Bullock, *op. cit.*, p. 206.

149 Orchard, *Legion*, p. 60; Cole, *op. cit.*, p. 23; R. Hoggart, *The Uses of Literacy*, 1966 edition, p. 145; R. E. Blackburn, *Liverpool Tramways*, 1968; D. C. Keeling, *The Crowded Stairs*, 1961, p. 13.

150 O'Mara, *op. cit.*, p. 4; 'An Old Stager', *op. cit.*, p. 32. Birkenhead contained about 100 inhabitants in 1800; 8,000 in 1841; 60,000 by the mid 1860s. It became an incorporated borough in 1877. Although the Cheshire suburbs were not extensively developed until after the laying of new railway lines in 1896, Wallasey doubled in size every twenty years of the nineteenth century, having over 50,000 inhabitants by 1900. See Baines, *op. cit.*, pp. 136–7; C. R. Fay, *Round about Industrial Britain 1830–1860*, Toronto, 1952, pp. 86–98; J. M. Lee, *Social Leaders and Public Persons*, Oxford, 1963, p. 25; Woods and Brown, *op. cit.*, p. 7; H. S. J. Raikes, *The Life and Letters of Henry Cecil Raikes*, 1898, pp. 165–6, 251–2.

151 Orchard, *Legion*, p. 51; Forwood, *op. cit.*, pp. 60–63; Sir J. W. Nott-Bower, *Fifty-Two Years a Policeman*, 1926, pp. 101–2; Picton, *op. cit.*, ii, p. 237; 'An Old Stager', *op. cit.*, chap. xi; G. T. Shaw, *History of The Athenaeum, Liverpool 1798–1898*, Liverpool, 1898.

152 E. F. Rathbone, *op. cit.*, pp. 270–1; interview with William Rathbone, 1899, Webb Local Government Collection, vol. 148.

153 Orchard, *Legion*, p. 50.

154 *Pen and Ink Sketches of Liverpool Town Councillors*, Liverpool, 1866, pp. 132–3. The vast majority of 'freemen' voters, generally over 70 per cent, cast for the Tories, although their proportion in the electorate declined from 25 per cent in 1835, 20 per cent in 1841, 14 per cent in 1853, to under 10 per cent in 1858. See C. A. Collins, 'Politics and Elections in Nineteenth-Century Liverpool', unpublished M.A. Thesis, Liverpool University, June 1974, pp. 45–46, 104.

155 See Forwood's speech at a people's concert, *L.C.* 21 Nov. 1885. For this reason, that it was based on social influence, was precariously opportunist, and had no true respect for democracy, moderate Liberals, or Whigs, feared Tory Democracy more than Liberal Democracy—see G. C. Brodrick, *Literary Fragments*, 1891, pp. 505–7.

156 *The Dawn*, 13 Oct. 1868.

157 *P.* 21 Nov. 1868. P. Searby, 'Gladstone in West Derby Hundred: The Liberal Campaign in South-West Lancashire in 1868', *T.H.S.L.C.*, vol. iii, 1959, p. 157 ff. exaggerates the personal grudge of *Porcupine*'s editor, Hugh Shimmin. On Shimmin see Simey, *op. cit.*, pp. 53–58.

158 *L.C.* 5 Feb. 1873.

159 *L.C.* 27 Jan. 1874; letter from J. Bond in *L.M.* 5 Dec. 1892.

160 G. C. Brodrick, *Political Studies*, 1879, pp. 258–9; 'A Liberal', 'The Social Discipline of the Liberal Party', *Fortnightly Review*, June 1883, p. 768; T. H. S. Escott in J. Chamberlain *et al.*, *The Radical Programme*, 1885; new edition, 1971, ed. D. A. Hamer, pp. 41–42.

161 J. E. Gorst to Lord R. Churchill, 22 Sept. 1883, Churchill MSS. 1/1/170; Viscount Chilston, *W. H. Smith*, 1965, pp. 58–59.

162 *P.* 8 and 15 Feb. 1879, cited in Watkinson, *op. cit.*, pp. 449–50.

163 Quoted in J. Symons, *Horatio Bottomley*, 1955, p. 20.

164 Paul Smith, *Disraelian Conservatism and Social Reform*, 1967, p. 265.

165 T. P. O'Connor, *Sketches in the House*, 1893, p. 162. On O'Connor's journalism, S. Morison, *The English Newspaper*, Cambridge, 1932, chap. xv.

166 *L.R.* 18 May 1899.

167 A. B. Forwood, 'Democratic Toryism', *Contemporary Review*, Feb. 1883, p. 299.

168 Cf. E. A. Nordlinger, *The Working-Class Tories*, 1967, p. 84; R. McKenzie and A. Silver, *Angels in Marble*, 1968, pp. 227–8.

169 *L.R.* 18 May 1899.

170 Paul Smith, *op. cit.*, p. 323.

171 Quoted in McKenzie and Silver, *op. cit.*, p. 29 n. 26.

172 Lord George Hamilton, *Addresses*, 1880.

173 H. Dunckley, 'The Conservative Dilemma', *Contemporary Review*, Jan. 1883, p. 150.

174 C. R. Attlee, *The Labour Party in Perspective*, 1937, pp. 283–4; P. Addison, *The Road to 1945*, 1975, p. 261.

175 *P.D.*, 3rd ser., cclxxxviii, 857. See the speeches of the Liverpool M.P.s, Whitley and Hamilton, ibid. 861–73, 1368–9. 'White chimpanzees' is Charles Kingsley's description in 1860—see F. Kingsley, *Charles Kingsley*, 1876, vol. ii, p. 107.

176 Marx to S. Meyer and A. Vogt, 9 April 1870, in *Karl Marx and Frederick Engels on Britain*, Moscow, 1962, pp. 551–2.

177 D. C. Jones, *op. cit.*, i, p. 45.

178 *L.C.* 2 Feb. 1874.

179 *L.C.* 21 Oct. 1868.

CHAPTER 2

1 S. A. Barnett to Mrs. Courtney, 29 January 1884, quoted in H. Barnett, *Canon Barnett*, 1919, vol. i, p. 170; Derby to Disraeli, 15 Sept. 1874, quoted E. E. Buckle, *The Life of Benjamin Disraeli, Earl of Beaconsfield*, 1920, vol. v, pp. 346–7.

2 *The Political Crisis* (Pamphlet among the Reform League Branch Reports 1868; Howell Collection).

3 See letter from John Bond (secretary of Liverpool Reform League) in *L.M.* 5 Dec. 1892. The Reform League Branch Report on Liverpool includes a list of trade unionists and their putative politics. Lancashire Conservatives did not fear the ballot—see Buckle, *op. cit.*, p. 123.

4 Buckle, *op. cit.*, pp. 18, 59–65; *P.D.*, 3rd. ser., cclxi, 1531–3 (W. Rathbone); *L.M.* 14 Oct. 1868; *L.C.* 18 Nov. 1868; *L.D.P.* 14 June 1869 (supplement); Harrowby MSS., 2nd. ser., vol. 1. fols. 253–4, 276–81, 289–91; *The Church Association Monthly Intelligencer*, Sept. 1867, p. 86, Nov. 1867, pp. 118–20; W. Jeans, *Parliamentary Reminiscences*, 1912, pp. 27–31.

5 Quoted Watkinson, *op. cit.*, p. 340. The Revising Barrister had to consider three-eighths of the register in Liverpool—9,000 objections, 6,000 claims—and the whole operation took three weeks. See *P.D.*, 3rd. ser. cxciv. 975–7, ccxiv. 665–6 (W. Rathbone).

6 J. A. Picton, *Sir James A. Picton*, 1891, p. 315; Harrowby MSS., 2nd. ser., vol. 1. fols. 46, 48, 53; *P.P.* 1868–9, viii, Qs. 3299–3515 (A. B. Forwood).

7 *P.D.*, 3rd. ser. ccxviii, 298. W. W. Bean, *The Parliamentary Representation of The Six Northern Counties of England*, Hull, 1890, p. 328 for the distribution of the votes by wards.

8 *L.C.* 30 Oct. 1874; H. J. Hanham, *Elections and Party Management: Politics in the Time of Disraeli and Gladstone*, 1959, p. 73.

9 *The Church Association Monthly Intelligencer*, March 1874, p. 104; T. Graham to A. B.

Forwood, n.d. (Dec. 1882), Forwood MSS. 19 M62/31. See also V. S. Pritchett, *A Cab at the Door*, 1968, p. 44, on the admiration of hard masters; and J. E. Mortimer, *History of the Boiler-makers Society*, 1973, vol. i, pp. 64–66 on Laird's struggles with shipyard unions in the 1860s.

10 Picton, *op. cit.*, p. 303; Sexton, *Agitator*, pp. 30–34, 57–59.

11 *P.D.*, 3rd. ser. cclxiii, 1750–4; *T.* 30 and 31 March 1883; and, for Glasgow explosions, J. E. Handley, *The Irish in Modern Scotland*, Cork, 1947, p. 274.

12 Denvir, *Life Story*, p. 166; Greaves, *op. cit.*, p. 20.

13 Liverpool Summer Assize Depositions, 1881, Public Record Office: Assizes 52/4, nos. 25, 26; W. B. Forwood to Lord Sandon, 10 June 1881, Harrowby MSS, 2nd ser. vol. l. no. 124.

14 Forwood, *Recollections*, p. 89; W. B. Forwood to Sir W. V. Harcourt, 10 Sept. 1881, Harcourt MSS. 210, fols. 73–74. William Forwood was knighted in 1883—see *The Diary of Sir Edward Walter Hamilton*, Oxford, 1972, vol. ii, p. 443, where the editor, D. W. R. Bahlman, mistakes William for his brother, Arthur, and compounds error by calling Arthur 'Albert'.

15 A. G. Gardiner, *The Life of Sir William Harcourt*, 1923, vol. i, pp. 438, 448.

16 HO 45/9339/21762, Public Record Office.

17 *T.* 7 Jan. 1875.

18 *Daily Telegraph*, 17 Dec. 1874, quoted in J. Ruskin, *Fors Clavigera*, Letter 49, Jan. 1875; *T.* 26 Dec. 1874.

19 *T.* 25, 26 Dec. 1874; *P.P.* 1877, xi, Qs. 62–63, 146 (Greig); V. A. C. Gatrell and T. B. Hadden, 'Criminal Statistics and their Interpretation', in E. A. Wrigley (ed.), *Nineteenth-Century Society*, Cambridge, 1972.

20 Nott-Bower, *op. cit.*, pp. 39, 89; E. C. Midwinter, *Old Liverpool*, Newton Abbot, 1971, chap. 3. In the absence of formal training, however, the Liverpool force was unusually deliberate in inculcating a sense of duty in its police recruits—see T. A. Critchley, *A History of Police in England and Wales, 900–1966*, 1967, pp. 148–50.

21 *T.* 7 Jan. 1875.

22 *T.* 5, 11, 16 Jan. 1875.

23 W. L. Sargent, 'Certain Results and Defects of the Reports of the Registrar-General', *Journal of the Statistical Society of London*, June 1864, pp. 200, 218–19; *T.* 11 Jan. 1875 and 4 Dec. 1877.

24 The Church of England Temperance Society reached its peak membership in Liverpool diocese, over 54,000, in 1887. It had dwindled to half this by 1897. Always the majority of members were juveniles. See *C.E.T.S. Annual Reports, passim.*

25 *T.* 2 Feb., 14 May 1875. There were demonstrations against as well as for restrictions—see *P.P.* 1877, xi, Qs. 241–2 (Grieg), 503–5 (Lawrence); and Harrison, *op. cit.*, pp. 267, 273, 276.

26 *L.M.* 25 Jan. 1873, quoted in C. A. Collins, *op. cit.*, p. 196; *Jubilee Memorial of Canning Street Presbyterian Church, Liverpool 1846–1896*, Liverpool, 1896; S. Smith, *My Life Work*, 1902; *W. P. Lockhart: Merchant and Preacher*, by his wife, Liverpool, 1895; P. T. Winskill, *Temperance Standard Bearers of the Nineteenth Century*, 1897, vol. i, p. 78, vol. ii, pp. 182, 232, 447–8; A. Balfour, *Licence Reform*, 1876; I. Sellers, 'Nonconformist Attitudes in Later Nineteenth-Century Liverpool', *T.H.S.L.C.*, vol. 114, 1962, pp. 222–4.

27 R. H. Lundie, *Alexander Balfour: A Memoir*, 2nd edition, 1889, p. 27.

28 Ibid., pp. 37, 42, 51. The Rathbones began with a 10 per cent toll of their profits for charitable and public purposes, and later raised it—see S. Marriner, *Rathbones of Liverpool 1845–73*, Liverpool, 1961, pp. 4, 120;.

29 *T.* 25 Feb. 1875; B. D. White, *op. cit.*, p. 105.

30 *T.* 2 Sept. 1875. Liverpool policemen traditionally accepted tips, free drinks, and Christmas boxes—*P.P.* 1920, xxii, Qs. 1983–6, Dunning, 3563–5, Miles.

31 The 1872 Act gave magistrates the discretion to fix opening-time between 6 and 7 a.m., and closing-time between 10 and 12 p.m. This was withdrawn by the 1874 Conservative Government and in Liverpool opening-time was put back to 6 a.m., to catch men on their way to work—see J. Samuelson, *Drink and Compensation*, 1903, p. 29.

32 *T.* 13 Sept. 1875; L. Masterman (ed.), *Mary Gladstone (Mrs. Drew) her Diaries and Letters*, 1930, p. 403.

33 *P.P.* 1875, xxxvi, Police Reports; *T.* 26 June 1876, 29 Nov. 1877; Harrison, *op. cit.*, p. 58. A simple correlation between the numbers of pubs and convictions of drunkenness is untenable—see *P.P.* 1877, xi, Appendix C (2), p. 339.

34 *T.* 25 Dec. 1877.

35 H. Melville, *Redburn: His First Voyage*, 1848, vol. i, p. 268.

36 W. Dexter (ed.), *The Letters of Charles Dickens*, vol. iii, 1938, pp. 283–5, 501–9, 716–9; K. J. Feilding, *The Speeches of Charles Dickens*, Oxford, 1960, pp. 384–93; C. Dickens, *The Uncommercial Traveller and Reprinted Pieces*, Oxford, 1958, chap. v; H. Walpole, *The Crystal Box*, Glasgow, privately printed, 1924, chap. iii; C. C. Abbott (ed.), *The Correspondence of Gerard Manley Hopkins and Richard Watson Dixon*, Oxford, 1935, p. 42; D. Mulock, *A Life for a Life*, 1860 edition, p. 181. Two of Hopkins's finest poems, 'Felix Randal' and 'Spring and Fall', emerged from his misery in Liverpool. It should also be noted that Arnold attempted to instil 'a spirit of lucidity'—a feeling for intellectual truth—in Liverpool's money-making classes. See his *Liverpool Address*, 1882, in M. Arnold, *Philistinism in England and America*, Ann Arbor, 1974, pp. 74–88.

37 *Our Mercantile Marine*, by an ex-officer, Congleton, n.d. 1870, p. 38; P. E. Razzell and R. W. Wainwright (eds.), *The Victorian Working Class*, 1973, pp. 272–4.

38 E. W. Hope (ed.), *City of Liverpool: Handbook*, Liverpool, 1903, pp. 82–83; W. Plomer (ed.), *Kilvert's Diary*, 1969, vol. ii, 21 June 1872, pp. 214–15; *P.P.* 1877, xi, Q. 8216, Father Nugent; *P.D.*, 3rd ser., ccliii, 381–4, W. S. Caine; *The Liverpool Sailors' Home Annual Report*, 1888, pp. 7, 12; J. Havelock Wilson, *My Stormy Voyage Through Life*, 1925, p. 62.

39 *T.* 2 Sept. 1875. The Sailors' Home opened a temperance room in 1883. Dockers were sometimes paid off in pubs—see C. R. Fay, *Life and Labour in the Nineteenth Century*, 1920, Cambridge, 1947, pp. 222–3.

40 *T.* 25 Dec. 1874.

41 *T.* 26 Nov. 1877.

42 Ibid. and *T.* 3 Dec. 1877.

43 S. Smith, 'Social Reform', *The Nineteenth Century*, vol. xiii, May 1883, p. 900.

44 Smith, *Life Work*, pp. 40, 90–91, 158–63; G. Stedman Jones, *op. cit.*, chap. 16.

45 Smith, 'Social Reform', *op. cit.*, p. 909, cf. K. Heasman, *Evangelicals in Action*, 1962, pp. 102–5. Canadians shared Smith's distinction between the destitute child and the workhouse child. Smith's work, in Mrs. Birt's Emigration Home, in Liverpool stimulated the Catholic and Anglican churches to establish their own societies. See *P.P.* 1896, xliii, Qs. 16207–375, Smith.

46 Denvir, *Irish in Britain*, p. 435; *P.P.* 1877, xi, Qs. 8195, Father Nugent. Cf. L. P. Curtis, *Anglo-Saxons and Celts*, New York, 1968, p. 59. n. 39.

47 *P.P.* 1897, xxxv, Q. 12263, T. E. Sampson.

48 *P.P.* 1836, xxxiv, Appendix G. p. 20, M. J. Whitty.

49 *T.* 9 July 1877.

50 *L.C.* 29 June 1891; Walmsley, *op. cit.*, p. 53.

51 *T.* 25 Jan. 1884; *P.P.* 1836, *op. cit.*, p. 27, W. Dillon; Maxwell Fry, *Autobiographical Sketches*, 1975, p. 50.

52 Denvir, *op. cit.*, p. 261; Handley, *op. cit.*, chap. iv; E. R. Norman, *Anti-Catholicism in Victorian England*, 1968, p. 18; Hanham, *op. cit.*, pp. 303–8; *P.* 13 July 1867.

53 Denvir, *op. cit.*, p. 415; *T.* 5 Aug. 1936. C.f. J. Foster, *Class Struggle and the Industrial Revolution*, 1974, pp. 211, 243–6; P. J. Joyce, 'Popular Toryism in Lancashire 1860–90', unpublished Oxford D.Phil. thesis, 1975, chap. 3; J. M. Werly, 'The Irish in Manchester, 1832–1849', *Irish Historical Studies*, xviii, no. 71, March 1973, pp. 345–58. Catholics were willing, however, to be married by Puseyites—see *P.P.* 1857–8, *op. cit.*, Q. 5288, Revd. A. J. Tomlin.

54 W. Herberg, *Protestant-Catholic-Jew*, Anchor edition 1960, p. 146; cf. McCarthy, *op. cit.*, iv, p. 230.

55 S. O'Suilleabhain, *Irish Wake Amusements*, Cork; translated 1967.

56 *N.L.T.* 3 Jan. 1885; *The Liverpool Wasp*, 30 April 1880; *P.P.* 1836, *op. cit.*, p. 10, G. Forwood; *P.P.* 1868–9, xxxii, Q. 7836, Dr. Trench; Farrar and Brownbill, *op. cit.* iv, p. 52.

57 Archives of the Archdiocese of Liverpool: First Visitation Series Oct. 1855—Oct. 1857, Lancashire County Record Office; *The Institute*, April 1858, pp. 1–6, June 1858, pp. 123–31. For a rosy view, see J. Pope Hennessy, 'What do the Irish Read?', *The Nineteenth Century*, June 1884.

58 C. Devlin (ed.), *The Sermons and Devotional Writings of Gerard Manley Hopkins*, Oxford, 1959, p. 10.

59 C. C. Abbott (ed.), *Further Letters of Gerard Manley Hopkins*, Oxford; 2nd edition, 1956, pp. 248–9.

60 Quoted Devlin, *op. cit.*, p. 10.

61 Burke, *op. cit.*, pp. 203–4; Inglis, *op. cit.*, pp. 122–30. For wild optimism, see *The Catholic Institute Magazine*, Nov. 1855, pp. 33–35.

62 *P.P.* 1852–3, lxxxix, p. 92.

63 Archdiocesan Archives, First Visitation, *op. cit.* The church was solidly built by E. W. Pugin in 1856–7. See also Woods and Brown, *op. cit.*, pp. 90–91.

64 Burke, *op. cit.*, p. 71; Inglis, *op. cit.*, p. 125; S. Gilley, 'The Roman Catholic Mission to the Irish in London', *Recusant History*, vol. 10, no. 3, Oct. 1969, pp. 124–5.

65 *L.D.P.* 17 Oct. 1881, 24 Nov. 1891. C.f. *P.P.* 1852–3, *op. cit.* For criticism of the figures, see R. B. Walker, *op. cit.*, p. 211; G. A. Beck (ed.), *The English Catholics 1850–1950*, p. 80; O. Chadwick, *The Victorian Church*, part ii, 1970, pp. 226–9.

66 *The Liverpool Irishman: or Annals of the Irish Colony in Liverpool*, Liverpool, 1906, p. 6.

67 Burke, *op. cit.*, p. 111. Cardinal Wiseman was stoned in Liverpool—see McCarthy, *op. cit.*, ii, p. 87.

68 *P.P.* 1852–3, *op. cit.*, pp. clviii-clxi; Inglis, *op. cit.*, pp. 48–57. In sixteen districts of Liverpool, containing 148,695 people, there was church accommodation for 18,110 (a ratio 1:8), of which 7,366 sittings were free (a ratio 1:20). St. Anne's ward and the Toxteths were the most under-provided—see *P.P.* 1857–8, ix, Qs. 5162–3, 5179–82, 5195, 5856, 5860, 5788.

69 H. Shimmin, *Liverpool Sketches*, 1863, pp. 120–1.

70 *L.D.P.* 17 and 19 Oct. 1881. Gladstone was 'much excited' by the figures—see *Hamilton's Diary*, *op. cit.* i, p. 181.

71 J. C. Ryle, *Can They be Brought In?*, 1883, p. 5. For a description of St. Simon's parish, 'the head-quarters of Prostitution', see J. R. Conor, *The Struggles of an Infant Parish*, 1854.

72 R. Hobson, *What Hath God Wrought*, 1903, pp. 147–8.

73 Ibid., pp. 3, 32.

74 This was not unusual—see Inglis, *op. cit.*, pp. 74–78; L. Masterman, *C. F. G. Masterman*, 1939, p. 11. On Baylee see *P.P.* 1857–8, ix, Qs. 5019–150.

75 Hobson, *op. cit.*, p. 50.

76 *L.C.* 16 March 1901.

77 Ryle, *op. cit.*, p. 44; Chadwick, *op. cit.*, p. 240; Orchard, *op. cit.*, p. 384.

78 Hobson, *op. cit.*, pp. 79, 123, 151; *P.P.* 1857–8, ix, Qs. 5019–150, J. Baylee; *The Church Association Monthly Intelligencer*, Nov. 1871, pp. 307–11, Dec. 1875, p. 423. Hobson had been made a canon of Liverpool by the time of his death in 1914.

79 *P.P.* 1857–8, ix, Q. 5913, C. Groves; *The Evangelistic Record*, 1 Oct. 1867.

80 Picton, *Memorials*, ii, p. 232; B. Gregory, *Autobiographical Recollections*, 1903, pp. 108–12; Winskill, *Temperance Standard Bearers*, i, pp. 40–41.

81 J. H. Morgan, *The Christian Workers' Association*, 1885, p. 11; J. E. Orr, *The Second Evangelical Awakening in Britain*, 1949, pp. 156–8, 240–1. On missions and open-air work in 'rough and riotous neighbourhoods' in Liverpool, see *The Evangelistic Record*, 1 Sept. 1867, et seqq.

82 Quoted in J. W. White, 'The Influence of North American Evangelism in Great Britain between 1830 and 1914 on the Origin and Development of the Ecumenical Movement', unpublished Ph.D. thesis, Oxford, 1963, chap. 4, p. 6. Sellers, *Liverpool Nonconformity*, pp. 37–38 considers Torrey more narrowly sectarian than Moody.

83 H. Johnson, *Stories of Great Revivals*, 1906, pp. 202–4; Winskill, *op. cit.*, ii, p. 350; Heasman, *op. cit.*, pp. 44, 253.

84 Smith, *Life Work*, p. 93; G. A. Smith, *The Life of Henry Drummond*, 1902 edition, pp. 82–85. Other commentators suggest that working people were little represented in the audiences and that the revivals' most important contribution was their encouragement to middle-class mission and temperance work—see Sellers, *op. cit.*, pp. 27, 29; Heasman, *op. cit.*, pp. 140–3; B. Harrison, *op. cit.*, pp. 171, 304.

85 *T.* 30 March 1875.

86 Hobson, *op. cit.*, p. 228. On the P.S.A. movement, see Inglis, *op. cit.*, pp. 79–85.

87 Smith, *Life Work*, p. 93.

88 S. K. Hocking, *My Book of Memory*, 1923, pp. 51–52; S. Pearson, *Service in Three Cities*, 1891, p. 25; P. T. Marsh, *The Victorian Church in Decline*, 1969, p. 248. Moody and Sankey returned to Liverpool in 1883; Gipsy Smith held missions in 1889, 1892, and 1894—see *Jubilee Memorial of Canning Street Presbyterian Church, Liverpool 1846–1896*, *op. cit.*, p. 21. One of Moody's and Sankey's 'converts' was the atheist Charles Bradlaugh's brother, Robert, who had never renounced the Anglican faith—see H. B. Bonner, *Charles Bradlaugh*, 1908 edition, i, p. 350.

89 Russell, *That Reminds Me*, p. 159.

90 *P.P.* 1870, liv, pp. 398–446; T. S. and M. B. Simey, *Charles Booth, Social Scientist*, Oxford, 1960, pp. 46–47; *The Catholic Institute Magazine*, March 1857, pp. 253–8; G. Melly, *Recollections of Sixty Years, 1833–1893*, Coventry 1893, p. 137; G. Melly, *The Children of Liverpool and the Rival Schemes of National Education*, Liverpool, 1869; B. D. White, *op. cit.*, pp. 141–3.

91 Clause 25 was repealed in 1876 and the obligation of assisting poor parents was transferred to the Poor Law authorities. Liverpool's School Board, however, continued to operate this facility, spending altogether £1,000 p.a. on school fees, about £800 going to voluntary schools. See *P.P.* 1887, xxix, Qs. 32, 384–8, E. Hance; B. D. White, *op. cit.*, pp. 147–8.

92 *The Guardian*, 6 Aug., 15 Oct. 1902; E. Halevy, *History of the English People in the Nineteenth Century*, 1961 edition, vol. v, p. 164 n.l, vol. vi, p. 67 n.l.

93 Picton, *Memorials*, i, p. 538; Whittingham-Jones, *op. cit.*, pp. 43–45. On White see Orr, *op. cit.*, p. 156; Sellers, *op. cit.*, pp. 65–66; *Canning Street Presbyterian Jubilee Memorial*, *op. cit.*, pp. 119–20.

94 C. A. Collins, *op. cit.*, p. 193.

95 Feuchtwanger, *op. cit.*, p. 71 n. 63; J. Newton, *W. S. Caine M.P.*, 1907, p. 56.

96 A. Buchan, *The Spare Chancellor*, 1959, p. 149; Anne Holt, diary, 31 Jan. 1873.

97 Newton, *op. cit.*, p. 59; J. D. Crawford, *Reflections and Recollections*, 1936, pp. 20–21; *L.D.P.* 28 Jan. 1874.

98 Burke, *op. cit.*, pp. 212–13.

99 R. B. O'Brien, *The Life of Charles Stewart Parnell 1846–1891*, 1898, i, p. 90.

100 For the distribution of votes by ward, *L.C.* 3, 6, 7 Feb. 1874.

101 J. Bright to W. S. Caine, 15 Dec. 1877, quoted Newton, *op. cit.*, pp. 64–65.

102 Burke, *op. cit.*, p. 230.

103 *L.C.* 29 Jan. 1874, 2 and 4 Feb. 1874. On Simpson's temperance work, B. D. White, *op. cit.*, pp. 109–110; Winskill, *op. cit.*, ii, p. 430; Winskill and Thomas, *op. cit.*, p. 84; Smith, *Life Work*, p. 106. On Simpson's patronage of working-class causes, R. Bean, 'Aspects of "New" Unionism in Liverpool 1889–1891', H. R. Hikins (ed.), *Building the Union*, Liverpool, 1973, pp. 101–3; E. L. Taplin, *Liverpool Dockers and Seamen, 1870–1890*, University of Hull, Occasional Papers in Economic and Social History no. 6, 1974, *passim*; and Taplin's sketch in J. M. Bellamy and J. Saville (eds.), *Dictionary of Labour Biography*, ii, 1974.

104 Quoted in W. Jeans, *Parliamentary Reminiscences*, 1912, pp. 78–79. Privately Disraeli referred to Ritualist practices as 'high jinks' (Buckle, *op. cit.* v, p. 315). Gladstone never forgave Disraeli or the Archbishop, Tait, for their part in framing the 'inquitous' Public Worship Regulation Bill—see *Hamilton's Diary*, *op. cit.*, i, pp. xlvii, 86; G. W. E. Russell, *Malcolm MacColl*, 1914, chap. v; Feuchtwanger, *op. cit.*, pp. 99–100.

105 S. Childers, *The Life and Correspondence of the Right Hon. Hugh. C. E. Childers 1827–1896*, 1901, i, p. 230; *The Church Association Monthly Intelligencer*, May 1872, pp. 78–79, 90, March 1874, p. 103, May 1874, pp. 166–71, Nov. 1874, pp. 389–93, Dec. 1874, pp. 399, 439–42, May 1875, pp. 166–7, March 1876, p. 73. One of the architects of the Public Worship Regulation Bill, the Lord Chancellor, Cairns, was married to Hugh M'Neile's niece.

106 Quoted in Burke, *op. cit.*, p. 214.

107 The poll remained open for the extraordinary length of twenty-six days, during which the Guardians experimented with different polling hours, 10 a.m. to 4 p.m., 2 p.m. to 8 p.m., 3 or 4 p.m. to 9 p.m. See *P.D.*, 3rd ser., ccxlvi. 1668–71, Rathbone.

108 *L.C.* 9 Nov. 1893.

109 *L.C.* 27 Oct. 1875.

110 *L.C.* 2 Nov. 1875. See also B. O'Connell, 'The Irish Nationalist Party in Liverpool, 1873–1922', M.A. Thesis, Liverpool, 1971, pp. 33–36.

111 Quoted in Watkinson, *op. cit.*, pp. 382, 384. See also *L.C.* 13 Nov. 1868; *L.D.P.* 13 Oct. 1868; *L.C.* 2 Feb. 1874.

112 *P.P.* 1857–8, ix, Q. 5136, Revd. J. Baylee; T. S. Raffles, *Memoirs of the Life and Ministry of the Rev. Thomas Raffles*, 1864, pp. 85–86. Cf. E. Morgan, *Memoir of the Reverend John Elias*, Liverpool, 1844, pp. 117, 142, 184, 198–201; J. Chamberlain to H. Labouchere, 3 Jan. 1886, quoted in A. L. Thorold, *The Life of Henry Labouchere*, 1913, p. 278; P. Searby in *T.H.S.L.C.*, 1959, *op. cit.*, pp. 152–3. As one illustration there is St. Saviour's school, Everton, where the instruction was of a 'distinctly denominational character', although probably half of the 340–80 children at the school were dissenters. Their parents, mostly respectable working class—joiners, masons, pilots, bricklayers, shopkeepers, and the like—objected not to the religious instruction but to the few children of 'the wastrel class', who attended the school, associating with their own children. See *P.P.* 1887, xxix, Qs. 22040–581, E. Horsfield.

113 *L.C.* 2 Nov. 1875. Williams won St. Paul's ward in 1877. He retired in 1880 aged sixty-seven.

114 *L.C.* 9 Nov. 1893.

115 *L.C.* 2 Nov. 1876.

116 Quoted in Burke, *op. cit.*, p. 216.

117 Orchard, *Legion*, pp. 246–7; Denvir, *Life Story*, p. 172; J. W. Lowther, *A Speaker's Commentaries*, 1925, i, p. 140.

118 *L.C.* 2 Nov. 1876.

119 *L.C.* 27 Oct. 1876.

120 *L.C.* 3 Nov. 1876.

121 *L.C.* 7 Nov. 1876.

122 Letter in *L.C.* 1 Nov. 1876.

123 *L.C.* 26 Oct. 1876.

124 E. F. Rathbone, *op. cit.*, pp. 254–61, 292–5; Watkinson, *op. cit.*, pp. 364–5; Cooke and Vincent, *op. cit.*, p. 432. Rathbone's views on temperance legislation are best captured in *P.D.* ccxxix, 17 May 1876. He walked out of the Wales Local Option debate in 1891—see K. O. Morgan, *Wales in British Politics, 1868–1922*, University of Wales Press, 2nd edition, 1970, pp. 97, 117.

125 Anne Holt, diary, 20 April 1877, 1 Nov. 1878. The Council, some three weeks before the 1879 municipal elections agreed to promote a parliamentary bill to obtain new water supplies from Vyrnwy, about 70 miles from Liverpool in Montgomeryshire. More water was welcome but there were always ratepayers who criticized expensive municipal works; and the Tories lost eight council seats.

126 Watkinson, *op. cit.*, pp. 333–6; Gardiner, *op. cit.* i, pp. 181–4; F. Archer to Sir W. V. Harcourt, 6, 10, 20 June 1868; S. G. Rathbone to Harcourt, 23 March, 1, 7, June 1868; Harcourt to Archer, 13 June 1868, Harcourt MSS. 202, fols. 52–54, 62–64, 67–69, 74–83.

127 Gardiner, *op. cit.* i, pp. 273–8, 229, 357.

128 Melly, *Recollections*, pp. 78–79.

129 Whitley opposed local option; moreover, his record as a licensing magistrate dissatisfied the zealots. Whitley's mother was a Cheshire Greenall, *P.D.*, 3rd ser., ccliii. 381–4, Caine; *Dod's Parliamentary Companion.*

130 *T.* 26 Jan. 1880.

131 R. D. Holt to Sir W. V. Harcourt, 25 Jan. 1880, Harcourt MSS. 209, fols. 12–14.

132 *T.* 29 Jan. 1880; Holt to Harcourt; 29 Jan. 1880, Harcourt MSS. 209, fols. 16–17.

133 Lord Ramsay to R. D. Holt, 9 Feb. 1880, Holt MSS; Gardiner, *op. cit.*, i, p. 360; *T.* 31 Jan 1880.

134 Holt to Harcourt, 2 Feb. 1880, Harcourt MSS. 209, fols. 18–19; Harcourt to Holt, 2 Feb. 1880, Holt MSS.

135 Watkinson, *op. cit.*, p. 465; Lloyd, *op. cit.*, pp. 17, 40; *The Annual Register 1880*, pp. 5–6; letter from Hartington, 3 Feb. 1886, quoted in Russell, *MacColl*, p. 373.

136 *T.* 5 Feb. 1880. The Church Association's prosecution, for ritual practices, of Mackonochie, vicar of St. Alban's Holborn, began in 1867. In 1879 the Court of Appeal decreed that he be suspended from office for three years; and in 1880 the Bishop of London ordered the sequestration of his living. For Liverpool's interest—*The Church Association Monthly Intelligencer*, Feb. 1880, pp. 58–59, June 1880, p. 173.

137 See list of English 'Home Rulers' in O'Brien, *op. cit.* i, p. 124 n.l.

138 J. W. Mackail and G. Wyndham, *Life and Letters of George Wyndham*, 1924, vol. i p. 130.

139 Lord Sefton to R. D. Holt, 8 Feb. 1880, Holt MSS.

140 Rathbone's difficulties hardly bear out Professor Vincent's description of an 'astute machine politician' or 'city boss'—see J. Vincent, *The Formation of the British Liberal Party 1857–1868*, 1966, Pelican, 1972, pp. 72, 123.

141 Anne Holt, diary, 22, 29 July, 7 Aug. 1880. Both Holt and Samuel Smith refused the candidature—see Holt's draft letter to the Liberal Management Committee, 28 July 1880, Holt MSS; Smith, *Life Work*, p. 130. Dalhousie contributed £1,000 towards Plimsoll's fight—Dalhousie to Holt, 1 Aug. 1880, Holt MSS.

142 A. B. Forwood to Holt, 18 Aug. 1880, Holt MSS.

143 Idem 24 Aug. 1880.

144 E. Whitley to Viscount Sandon, 4. Nov. 1881, Harrowby MSS., 2nd. ser., vol. 1, fols. 246–8.

145 Quoted E. F. Rathbone, *op. cit.*, p. 304. Liberals ascribed their municipal defeats to Forwood's 'fraudulent device' in encouraging voters with duplicate qualifications to vote in two wards; but Liberals had employed the same tactic in 1879–80—*P.D.*, 3rd. ser., cclix, 1230–2, 4th. ser., iv, 607–8, 619–20, 630–1. Tory councillors in St. Paul's and Lime Street wards were also indicted for bribery—see Anne Holt, diary, 25 Oct. 1880, 2 March 1881.

146 Mr. Gladstone's opinion, 3 Feb. 1881—quoted in Masterman, *Mary Gladstone*, 1930, pp. 217–18.

147 A. B. Forwood to Lord Salisbury, 16 April 1882, Salisbury MSS; A. J. Balfour, *Chapters of Autobiography*, 1930, p. 140; T. H. S. Escott, *Randolph Spencer-Churchill*, 1895, p. 89.

148 A. B. Forwood, 'Democratic Toryism', *Contemporary Review*, Feb. 1883, p. 297.

149 *P.* 28 Nov. 1885. On Forwood's paternal grandfather, George, see J. Hughes, *Liverpool Banks and Bankers 1760–1837*, Liverpool, 1906, p. 195.

150 On the University, Orchard, *Legion*, p. 105; Farrer and Brownbill, *op. cit.* iv, pp. 53–54; C. H. Reilly, *Scaffolding in The Sky*, 1938. On the episcopal see, Forwood MSS., Bundle 30; on the choice of Ryle as first bishop, Sandon to Forwood, 15 April 1880, Harrowby MSS., vol. 1095, fols, 204–6; Ryle's own version in *L.C.* 27 March 1900.

151 On Harrowby, who represented Liverpool between 1831 and 1847, see L. Strachey and R. Fulford (eds.), *The Greville Memoirs 1814–1860*, v, 205; A. B. Cooke and J. R. Vincent (eds), *Lord Carlingford's Journal*, Oxford, 1971, p. 75.

152 R. D. Holt to Sir William Harcourt, 16 Jan. 1882, copy Holt MSS.

153 *P.* 25 Nov. 1882.

154 Sellers, *op. cit.*, p. 84.

155 *P.* 20 Nov. 1884.

156 *N.L.T.* 26 Dec. 1885; Sir W. B. Forwood, *Reminiscences of a Liverpool Shipowner 1850–1920*, Liverpool, 1920, p. 42; L. H. Powell, *History of the Liverpool Steam Ship Owners' Association 1858–1958*, 1958, p. 10.

157 *L.R.* 25 Nov. 1882, 2 Dec. 1882.

158 Orchard, *Legion*, p. 642.

159 Address in *L.R.* 2 Dec. 1882, and Smith, *Life Work*, Appendix vi.

160 Smith's pamphlets on Catholic and other religious questions had over one million circulation—Smith, *op. cit.*, p. 360.

161 *P.* 11 Sept. 1900 nicknamed him 'Mr. Psalmuel Smith'.

162 *T.* 6 Dec. 1882; *The Annual Register 1882*, p. 181; B. O'Connell, *op. cit.*, p. 55.

163 *L.R.* 2 Dec. 1882.

164 *T.* 5 Dec. 1882.

165 *Fortnightly Review*, May 1885.

166 Brocklebank to Holt, 10 Dec. 1882, Holt MSS.

167 Lord Northbrook to Holt, 10 Dec. 1882, ibid.

168 Gladstone to Holt, 12 Dec. 1882, ibid. See also, *Hamilton's Diary*, i, p. 373.

169 Smith, *Life Work*, p. 139; S. Smith, 'Social Reform', *The Nineteenth Century*, May 1883, p. 896.

170 G. W. E. Russell, 'A Protest against Whiggery', *The Nineteenth Century*, June 1883, p. 926.

171 Smith, *Life Work*, p. 137.

172 J. Chamberlain to E. R. Russell, 22 Jan. 1883, Chamberlain MSS. 5/62/4. Parts

of this letter are quoted, but not in the context of Smith's victory, in J. L. Garvin, *The Life of Joseph Chamberlain*, i, 1935, pp. 384–5, and P. Fraser, *Joseph Chamberlain: Radicalism and Empire*, 1868–1914, 1966, p. 48. John Morley, in the *Pall Mall Gazette*, drew the same conclusion—see D. A. Hamer, *John Morley*, Oxford, 1968, p. 158.

173 Melly to Holt, 7 Dec. 1882, Holt MSS.

174 *L.R.* 25 Nov., 2 Dec. 1882.

175 A. B. Forwood, 'Democratic Toryism', *op. cit.*

176 A. B. Forwood to Lord Salisbury, 20 Aug. 1883, Salisbury MSS: Smith, *Life Work*, pp. 89–90.

177 *L.R.* 16 Dec. 1882; Forwood's speech at the W.M.C.A., 29 Jan. 1883, Forwood MSS., Bundle 39; Anne Holt, diary, 12 Dec. 1882.

178 *T.* 6 Dec. 1882.

179 T. Graham to A. B. Forwood, n.d. (Dec. 1882), Forwood MSS. 19 M62/31.

180 Ibid.

181 A. B. Forwood, *op. cit.*, p. 300.

182 Lord Claud Hamilton to A. B. Forwood, 14 Dec. 1882, Forwood MSS. 19 M62/26; Hamilton to Lord Harrowby, 14 Dec. 1882, Harrowby MSS., 2nd. ser., vol. 1, fols. 265–8.

183 Quoted in A. B. Forwood, *op. cit.*

184 *T.* 9 Dec. 1882.

185 'A Poor Radical' to A. B. Forwood, 11 Dec. 1882, Forwood MSS. 19 M62/24.

186 *L.R.* 30 Dec. 1882, 10 Nov. 1883.

187 O'Brien, *op. cit.* i, p. 67.

188 *L.R.* 11 July 1885.

189 Burke, *op. cit.*, p. 218.

190 *L.D.P.* 1 Nov. 1883.

191 *The Nationalist*, 8 Nov. 1884.

192 *L.D.P.* 2 Nov. 1883.

193 *Irish Programme*, 24 May 1884.

194 Ibid. 1 Nov. 1884.

195 Ibid. 10 May 1884.

196 *P.* 17 May 1884. McCalmont gives an electorate of 61,326 in 1884—see J. Vincent and M. Stenton (eds.), *McCalmont's Parliamentary Poll Book 1832–1918*, Brighton, 1971, p. 180.

197 *Irish Programme*, 17 May 1884.

CHAPTER 3

1 Quotations from the Forwood Papers.

2 McCarthy, *op. cit.* iv, p. 20. Salisbury's article, 'Disintegration', *The Quarterly Review*, Oct. 1883; reprinted in P. Smith (ed.), *Lord Salisbury on Politics*, Cambridge, 1972. See T. H. S. Escott's attack, *Fortnightly Review*, Aug. 1884, p. 162.

3 *Quarterly*, *op. cit.*, pp. 562, 566, 569. Cf. Lord Dunraven, 'The Future "Constitutional" Party', *Nineteenth Century*, April 1883, pp. 679–99; G. C. Brodrick, 'Democracy and Socialism', *Nineteenth Century*, April 1884, reprinted in G. C. Brodrick, *Literary Fragments*, pp. 185–211.

4 (Percy Greg), 'Redistribution and Representative Democracy', *Quarterly*, July 1884, pp. 230, 235–8, 240. Cf. A. Jones, *The Politics of Reform 1884*, Cambridge, 1972, pp. 58–59.

5 T. H. S. Escott in J. Chamberlain *et al.*, *The Radical Programme*, 1885, new edition,

Brighton, 1971, pp. 19, 45–49; H. Broadhurst in *Fortnightly*, Feb. 1885, p. 155; W. Bagehot, Introduction to the 1872 edition of *The English Constitution.*

6 *Fortnightly*, May 1883, p. 619. Cf. Smith, *Life Work*, pp. 153.

7 *Nineteenth Century*, April 1884, pp. 713–15 gives the names. Whitley, the Liverpool M.P., was sympathetic—*P.D.*, 3rd. ser., cclxxxvii, 801–4, 28 May 1884. On the P.R.S. see A. Jones, *op. cit.*, pp. 95–103.

8 Quoted in Earl Grey, 'The House of Commons', *Nineteenth Century*, March 1884.

9 Ibid., pp. 517, 519.

10 On the Cairns's clause, see p. xix. Disraeli disliked the device (see Buckle, *op. cit.* iv, p. 115); so did J. S. Mill, an advocate of radical proportional representation—see J. S. Mill, *Autobiography*, 1873, New York edition, 1964, p. 210. Together with the 'cumulative' voting procedure in School Board elections, Cairns's Amendment was blamed for the rise of party machines—see A. L. Lowell, *The Government of England*, 1920 edition, i, p. 483.

11 *P.D.*, 3rd. ser. ccxciv, 710; A. Arnold, 'Parliamentary Reform', *Fortnightly*, Feb. 1884, p. 175; A. Arnold, 'Is This the Bill?', ibid., Nov. 1884. p. 593; W. Bagehot, 'Lord Althorp and the Reform Act of 1832', 1877, in N. St. John-Stevas (ed.), *Bagehot's Historical Essays*, 1971, p. 177.

12 Quoted in G. P. Gooch, *Life of Lord Courtney*, 1920, pp. 352, 441. Cf. M. I. Cole (ed.), *Beatrice Webb's Diaries 1912–1924*, 1952, p. 121.

13 *P.D.*, *op. cit.* 671, 674, 718, 721, 1826. Cf. T. J. Spinner, *George Joachim Goschen*, Cambridge, 1973, pp. 94–98.

14 *T.* 2 Dec. 1884. Courtney had written leaders for *The Times*, 1864–80.

15 T. H. S. Escott, 'The Revolution of 1884', *Fortnightly*, Jan. 1885, p. 3. In fact, following Redistribution, the city as a powerful political community was broken, and with it went the hopes of a classless 'constructive' Radicalism. For criticisms of Radical presumptions, see D. A. Hamer (ed.), *The Radical Programme*, 1885, new edition, 1971, pp. xxxv–xxxvii.

16 Letter (W. A. Hunter), *T.* 17 Sept. 1884.

17 Lord C. Hamilton to A. B. Forwood, 2 Dec. 1884, Forwood MSS. 19 M62/26.

18 G. C. Brodrick, 'An Address', 19 Nov. 1885, in *Literary Fragments*, 1891, p. 511; *P.D.*, *op. cit.* 1825–6. Leatham, a brother-in-law of John Bright, was an outspoken opponent of women's suffrage.

19 *Fortnightly*, Feb. 1885, p. 150.

20 *Hamilton's Diary*, ii, pp. 666–7; J. Chamberlain (ed. C. H. D. Howard), *A Political Memoir 1880–92*, 1953, pp. 115–19.

21 T. H. S. Escott in *Fortnightly*, Dec. 1884, p. 725.

22 G. W. E. Russell in *Fortnightly*, Jan. 1883, p. 18. Cf. Smith, *Life Work*, p. 534; T. P. O'Connor, *Memoirs of an Old Parliamentarian*, 1929, i, p. 53; *Hamilton's Diary*, i, p. 188; D. A. Hamer, *Liberal Politics in the Age of Gladstone and Rosebery*, Oxford, 1972, chap. iii. Russell had written equally of Disraeli's magnificence in the 1870s—see Buckle, *op. cit.* v, p. 511.

23 Viscount Gladstone, *op. cit.*, pp. 364–5.

24 Quoted in Balfour, *op. cit.*, pp. 220–1.

25 See P. Smith, *Salisbury*, pp. 21–109; *Hamilton's Diary*, ii, p. 697.

26 A. B. Forwood, 'Redistribution: Electoral Districts', *Contemporary Review*, Oct. 1884, pp. 582–3.

27 Forwood's letters, *T.* 27 Aug., 1 Nov. 1884.

28 A. B. Forwood to Lord Salisbury, 20 Oct. 1884, Salisbury MSS.

29 'A Candid Conservative' in *Fortnightly*, Jan. 1885, p. 52.

30 G. C. T. Bartley, G. N. Curzon, in ibid., May 1885, pp. 614, 625, 627–8; W. S. Churchill, *Lord Randolph Churchill*, 1907 edition, p. 240.

31 *Fortnightly*, p. 629.

32 Sir T. H. Sanderson and E. S. Roscoe (eds), *Speeches and Addresses of Edward Henry XVth Earl of Derby*, 1894, ii, p. 126; Derby to Sir W. V. Harcourt, 17 April 1884, Harcourt MSS. 213, fols. 31–32; *Hamilton's Diary*, ii.

33 Speech to the W.M.C.A. 29 Jan. 1883, copy in Forwood MSS., Bundle 39.

34 Cf. Disraeli's Guildhall speech 1874, and Gorst's reflections in 1907, quoted in Buckle, *op. cit.* v, pp. 351–2, 369.

35 *Contemporary Review*, Feb. 1883, p. 298.

36 Quoted in R. R. James, *Lord Randolph Churchill*, 1959, p. 113.

37 Lord R. Churchill, 'Elijah's Mantle', *Fortnightly*, May 1883, p. 621.

38 W. S. Churchill, *op. cit.*, Appendix iii, p. 846; J. E. Gorst to Lord R. Churchill, 29 Jan, 5 Feb. 1883, Churchill MSS. 1/1/105,107.

39 Lord R. Churchill to A. B. Forwood, 17 Oct. 1884, Forwood MSS.

40 Quoted in Gardiner, *op. cit.* ii, p. 586.

41 *T.* 9 April 1883; also quoted in W. S. Churchill, *op. cit.*, p. 199. Cf. Churchill's election address, *T.* 28 June 1886.

42 W. Jeans, *Parliamentary Reminiscences*, 1912, p. 123.

43 'Elijah's Mantle', *op. cit.*, p. 621.

44 Ibid., p. 617. Cf. Feuchtwanger, *op. cit.*, p. 36; Gorst, *op. cit.*, p. 133.

45 Labouchere in *Fortnightly*, March 1883 p. 375; Churchill quoted in Chilston, *W. H. Smith*, pp. 206–7.

46 Quoted in W. S. Adams, *Edwardian Portraits*, 1957, p. 79. Cf. Escott, *Randolph Spencer-Churchill*, p. 367. In considering this story, as also Blunt's account of Churchill's Irish sympathies, 'it should be remembered that Randolph was a bold talker who probably did not take Blunt very seriously as a politician'—R. B. McDowell, *British Conservatism 1832–1914*, 1959, p. 124.

47 Quoted in Lady G. Cecil, *Life of Robert Marquis of Salisbury*, iii, 1931, p. 108.

48 Copy of correspondence between Salisbury and Churchill, April 1884, Forwood MSS. 19 M62/23. On the National Union controversy see J. Cornford, 'The Transformation of Conservatism in the late Nineteenth Century', *Victorian Studies*, 1963–4, pp. 35–66.

49 Churchill to Salisbury, 3 April 1884, copy, ibid. Cf. Forwood's opinion of the Birmingham caucus: 'No true Conservative desired such a political engine (hear, hear), but to win they must have an efficient organization which, while permitting complete freedom of action to supporters, should nevertheless afford them every encouragement to record their votes.' Speech to Liverpool Constitutional Association, *T.* 20 May 1884.

50 A. B. Forwood to Lord Salisbury, May 1884, Salisbury MSS. The letter has no precise date, but the context would indicate very early May.

51 Idem 4 and 6 May 1884; 'Memo of the Proceedings of a Conference held in London on 8th May 1884', Forwood MSS. 19 M62/23.

52 Lord R. Churchill to A. B. Forwood, 11 May 1884; Forwood to Salisbury, 13 May 1884, Salisbury MSS. Northcote also wrote in approval of the memo—see letter to Forwood, 14 May 1884, Forwood MSS.

53 H. A. Doubleday and Lord Howard De Walden, *The Complete Peerage*, viii, 1932, p. 503. Dr. R. E. Quinault drew my attention to this point.

54 *Minutes. N.U. Conference 1876, 1877; N.U. Report 1877* p. 2; *N.U. Report 1879*, p. 1.

55 Lord C. Hamilton to A. B. Forwood, 16 May 1884, Forwood MSS. That Forwood pursued this with Gorst is indicated by Gorst's letter to Sir Henry Drummond Wolff, 4 June 1884, quoted in H. E. Gorst, *op. cit.*, pp. 294–5.

56 J. E. Gorst to A. B. Forwood, 4 June 1884, Forwood MSS.

57 A. B. Forwood to J. S. Hopkins, 24 June 1884, copy, ibid.

58 Lord R. Churchill to A. B. Forwood, 5 July 1884, ibid.

59 A. B. Forwood to Lord R. Churchill, 6 July 1884, copy, ibid. See also W. H. Houldsworth to Lord R. Churchill, 17 July 1884, Churchill MSS, RCHL 1/4/448.

60 Lord R. Churchill to A. B. Forwood, 10 July 1884, Forwood MSS.

61 A. B. Forwood to W. H. Houldsworth, n.d., copy, ibid.

62 A. B. Forwood to Lord R. Churchill, 11 July 1884, Churchill MSS. RCHL 1/4/445.

63 Idem 28 July 1884, RCHL 1/4/457.

64 Forwood to Churchill, n.d., copy Forwood MSS.

65 W. S. Churchill, *My Early Life*, Fontana, 5th. edition, 1965, p. 55.

66 *Fortnightly*, Dec. 1885, p. 718; H. E. Gorst, *The Fourth Party*, 1906, pp. 223–5.

67 A. Bierce (ed. E. J. Hopkins), *The Enlarged Devil's Dictionary*, 1967, p. 46.

CHAPTER 4

1 Diary, Oct. 1885, quoted in Picton, *Sir James A. Picton*, pp. 376–7.

2 T. H. Sanderson to Lord Derby, 1 Nov. 1885, Derby MSS. A. B. Cooke and J. Vincent, *The Governing Passion*, 1974, p. 3, note that no senior politician forecasted a Tory victory and that Harcourt and Childers came close to guessing the exact party strengths.

3 *T.* 23 Sept. 1885.

4 *L.R.* 18 July 1885; *Quarterly*, Oct. 1885, p. 568; George Baden-Powell's letter, *T.* 22 Oct. 1885, cited in B. H. Brown, *The Tariff Movement in Great Britain 1881–1895*, 1966 edition, p. 64n.

5 See speeches of Whitley, Hamilton, and MacIver—*P.D.*, 3rd. ser., ccxciii, 668–76, cclxxxv, 1050–1, cclxxxviii, 753–7, ccxc, 358–61, ccxciii, 673, 1456–7, 1590–5, ccxciv, 121–7.

6 *Liverpool Steam Ship Owners' Association Annual Report*, 1898–9; Powell, *op. cit.*, pp. 18–20. The Association was founded in 1858. It had twenty members in the 1860s, sixty-two by 1914. At the turn of the century its members owned 21 per cent of the total British steamship tonnage, 26 per cent of that with a speed of twelve knots and more, 29 per cent of that over 3,000 tons, and 50 per cent of that over 5,000 tons.

7 *Annual Report*, *op. cit.*, 1889–90, p. 10; Association Minute Book pp. 603, 685. However, a move in 1892 to persuade the Docks Board to remove all public houses from its estate failed. The Board would go no further than encourage coffee-houses (of which there were then four) as counter-attractions to the many licensed premises. See *L.D.P.* 29 July 1892.

8 E. R. Russell to J. Chamberlain, 5 March 1884, Chamberlain MSS. JC2/14/58.

9 W. Rathbone to J. Chamberlain, 11 March 1884, ibid. JC2/14/65. Rathbone had spoken for the Liverpool Steam Ship Owners' Association against the practicability of many of Plimsoll's suggestions of legislation in 1875–6—*P.D.*, 3rd. ser., ccxxiii 557–70, ccxxi, 161–2, 428–35.

10 *L.D.P.* 24 March 1884, press cuttings, Chamberlain MSS. JC2/14/122. Forwood was to be a member of the Select Committee which studied the Employers' Liability Act (1880) Amendment Bill—see *P.P.* 1886, viii.

11 Men disputed how many ships Hatfield had lost—see Chamberlain MSS. JC2/14/123; *P.D.*, 3rd. ser. cclxxxviii, 694–6, 1507–9, ccxc, 348–61.

12 Quoted in J. Chamberlain to W. E. Gladstone, 8 March 1884, in J. Chamberlain (ed. C. H. D. Howard), *A Political Memoir 1880–92*, 1953, pp. 102–4.

13 Garvin, *op. cit.* i, pp. 428–30.

14 Liverpool Steam Ship Owners' Association meeting, 12 Nov. 1884.

15 Letters in *L.C.* 12, 18, 24 Nov. 1884; *L.M.* 17 Nov. 1884; *L.D.P.* 19 Nov. 1884.

16 Liverpool Steam Ship Owners' Association meeting, 5 July 1885. Cf. G. Alderman, *The Railway Interest*, Leicester, 1973, chaps. 6, 7.

17 Ibid. 20 Oct. 4, 6,, 21 Nov. 1885. C.f. the opinions of J. H. Beazley, former chairman of Liverpool Steam Ship Owners' Association, *P.P.* 1886, viii, Qs. 6092–6, 249; *P.P.* 1887, xliii, Qs. 18320–744; the views of J. Williamson, Liverpool merchant and shipowner, *P.P.* 1886, xxiii, Qs. 11175–294; and *Report of the Liverpool Steam Ship Owners' Association upon the Proposals of the Board of Trade with Reference to Merchant Shipping Law and Proposed New Maritime Courts*, Liverpool, 1883.

18 Liverpool Steam Ship Owners' Association meeting, 21 Nov. 1885.

19 A. B. Forwood to Lord Salisbury, 20 Oct. 1885, Salisbury MSS. Cf. Cooke and Vincent, *op. cit.*, pp. 12–14.

20 *Ormskirk Advertiser*, 16 Oct. 1885; *Manchester Examiner*, 20 Aug. 1885. See also Forwood's speech at Litherland, *L.C.* 20 Sept. 1894.

21 *Ormskirk Advertiser*, 12 Nov. 1885; *L.C.* 13 Nov. 1885. Cf. Canon M'Neile of Liverpool, who was inclined to 'attribute the considerable development of socialism to the teaching in board schools'. *P.P.* 1887, xxix, Q. 34401.

22 Burke, *op. cit.*, p. 242.

23 C. H. D. Howard, 'Manning and Education', in J. Fitzsimons (ed.), *Manning: Anglican and Catholic*, 1951, p. 106.

24 Quoted in Burke, *op. cit.*, pp. 242–3; *L.D.P.* 23 Nov. 1885.

25 T. Carlyle, 'Signs of the Times' (1829) in *Critical and Miscellaneous Essays*, 1869, ii, p. 315.

26 Salisbury in *T.* 12 Nov. 1885; A. C. Benson, *The Life of Edward White Benson, Archbishop of Canterbury*, 2nd. edition, 1900, ii, p. 64.

27 Lord Selborne, *Memorials Part II, Personal and Political 1865–1895*, ii, pp. 181–7; 'Church and State', *Quarterly Review*, Jan. 1886; Russell, *MacColl*, p. 177; Masterman, *Mary Gladstone*, p. 484.

28 Benson, *op. cit.*, ii, pp. 72 ff., 102.

29 Watkinson, *op. cit.*, p. 421. On the Liberation Society see Buckle, *op. cit.*, v.p. 25; Marsh, *op. cit.*, p. 244; Diggle, *op. cit.*, pp. 21–3; Vincent, *Formation of the Liberal Party*, p. 105; D. M. Thompson, 'The Liberation Society, 1844–1868' in P. Hollis (ed.), *Pressure from Without*, 1974, pp. 210–38.

30 *T.* 31 Jan. 1879, C.f. R. G. Wilberforce, *Life of the Right Reverend Samuel Wilberforce, D.D.*, 1882, iii, p. 190; Bowen, *op. cit.*, chap. iv.

31 *T.* 6 Feb. 1879.

32 *T.* 19, 21 Sept. 1882; *The Church Association Monthly Intelligencer*, March 1881, pp. 79–83, Dec. 1882, pp. 334–5. On St. Margaret's see *L.R.* 7 Aug. 1886; *Liverpool Citizen*, 4 June 1890; Prestige, *op. cit.*,pp. 28 ff., 59.

33 *L.R.* 17, 24 Jan., 7 Nov. 1885, 24 March 1888, 18 Oct. 1890; *T.* 26, 27 Jan., 12 July 1886, 17 March 1887; *P.* 5, 29 Nov., 6 Dec. 1902.

34 *The Church Association Monthly Intelligencer*, Oct. 1880, pp. 272–3; *The Church Review and Church News*, 27 March, 2 April 1885; and M. C. Church, *The Life and Letters of Dean Church*, 1895, pp. 322–4 for Ryle's unpopularity with High Churchmen. The Bell Cox case, like the Ridsdale, Tooth, and Green cases, wrecked the Public Worship Regulation Act—see Bowen, *op. cit.*, chap. 3; Selborne, *op. cit.*, i, chap. xviii, ii, pp. 75–79; Chadwick, *op. cit.*, chap. vi.

35 A. B. Forwood to Lord Salisbury, 28 Dec. 1884, Salisbury MSS.

36 *L.C.* 9 May 1885; letter in *L.C.* 14 May 1885.

37 *N.L.T.* 16 July 1884; *L.R.* 18 July 1885; *P.D.*, 3rd. ser., cclxxxvi, 1796–7; *The Church Association Monthly Intelligencer*, April 1883, pp. 79, 92–94, Nov. 1883, pp. 302–3, Jan. 1884, pp. 2–6.

38 *P.* 13 Dec. 1884, 7 March 1885.

39 E. Whitley to A. B. Forwood, 23 July 1885, Forwood MSS. On the Conservatives' decision to take office, Cooke and Vincent, *op. cit.*, pp. 261–9.

40 A. B. Forwood to Lord Salisbury, 9 June 1885, Salisbury MSS.

41 Salisbury to Forwood, 10 June 1885, Forwood MSS.

42 Whitley to Forwood, *op. cit.*

43 Forwood to Salisbury, 16 May 1885, Salisbury MSS. Forwood's tone altered by 24 July 1885: he wrote to Harrowby, mocking Whitley's fears and recognizing that 'It was a wise move to take the Relief cry out of the Radical hands'. Harrowby MSS., 2nd. ser., vol. 1, fols. 257–8. William Rathbone in 1879, and Dr. Commins in 1884, had introduced similar Bills, drawing upon their Liverpool experiences—*P.D.*, 3rd. ser., ccxliii, 623–6, cclxxxix, 859–62, Cf. B. Abel-Smith, *The Hospitals, 1800–1948*, 1964, pp. 129–31.

44 Forwood to Churchill, 12 June 1885, Churchill MSS, RCHL 1/5/627; Churchill to Forwood, draft, RCHL 1/6/757; Churchill to Forwood, 29 and 30 July 1885, Forwood MSS.; Forwood to Salisbury, 29 July 1885, Salisbury MSS.

45 Whitley to Forwood, 31 July 1885, Forwood MSS.

46 Whitley to Forwood, 23 July 1885; Hamilton to Forwood, 23 July 1885, Forwood MSS. Whitley at the last moment agreed to attend the meeting—see Forwood to Churchill, Churchill MSS. RCHL. 1/6/754—but Hamilton was unrelenting.

47 Ulster Unionists distrusted Churchill. They regarded him as 'ministerial' not Orange—see R. Lucas, *Colonel Saunderson M.P.*, 1906, pp. 113, 240. On the Conservatives' explorations of local government for Ireland see Viscount Gladstone, *op. cit.*, pt. iii, chap. 5; W. S. Blunt, *My Diaries*, New York, 1921, ii, p. 124; A. Jones, *op. cit.*, chap. 4. The *Standard*, 31 July 1885, together with letters in 1 Aug. 1885, delivered an extraordinary personal attack on Churchill, who believed it officially inspired and linked to Hamilton's and Whitley's boycott in Liverpool—see Churchill to Forwood, 12 May, 31 July 1885, Forwood MSS.; Forwood to Churchill 1 Aug. 1885, Churchill MSS. RCHL 1/6/763; Cooke and Vincent *Lord Carlingford's Journal*, pp. 131–2; Cooke and Vincent, *Governing Passion*, pp. 279–80.

48 *L.R.* 1 and 8 Aug. 1885; Forwood to Salisbury, 3 and 6 Aug. 1885, Salisbury MSS.; resolution of Liverpool Constitutional Association, 30 July 1885, Churchill MSS. RCHL 1/6/759.

49 Balfour, *op. cit.*, p. 191; Cooke and Vincent, *Governing Passion*, chap. 2.

50 Quoted R. B. O'Brien, *op. cit.* i, p. 102.

51 L. Courtney, 'The Seats Bill', *Fortnightly Review*, Jan. 1885, p. 33; Gooch, *op. cit.*, pp. 242, 245.

52 Hamilton to Forwood, 12 Dec. 1884, Forwood MSS. 19M 62/26. Hamilton was writing from Barons Court in Ireland.

53 *Nineteenth Century*, April 1884, pp. 707–9.

54 *P.D.*, 3rd. ser., ccxcvi, 1361, 1364–6, ccxvii, 1073–5.

55 Charles Russell was also offered the candidature—R. B. O'Brien, *The Life of Lord Russell of Killowen*, Nelson edition, 1909, p. 196. In his several books of recollections McCarthy fails to mention his candidature in 1885, although he informed Mrs. Praed that he had spoken in Liverpool in August 1885 'without having received a single brickbat'—J. McCarthy and Mrs. Campbell Praed, *Our Book of Memories*, 1912, p. 19.

56 Picton, *Memorials*, ii, pp. 122–3. The quotation is from Mark 4: 26–27.

57 Quoted H. Shimmin, *The Sanitary Aspect of Philanthropy*, Liverpool, 1866, p. 11. See also J. N. Tarn, *Five Per Cent Philanthropy*, Cambridge, 1973, pp. 7–8.

58 *P.D.*, 3rd ser., ccliii, 381–4; also in.Newton, *op. cit.*, p. 82.

59 Picton, *op. cit.*, ii, p. 77; Shimmin, *op. cit.*, p. 22.

60 References to this vary—one historian, using the 1888 returns, records 18 per cent

of Exchange and Abercromby as non-resident, adding that Exchange came to have proportionately more than Abercromby—P. F. Clarke, *Lancashire and the New Liberalism*, Cambridge, 1971, p. 114. In 1894, however, Walter Long declared that of 7,134 electors in Exchange 1,451 lived in adjoining county constituencies and 1,155 in other Liverpool constituencies; and Abercromby contained 3,378 non-residents in an electorate of 8,678. Again in 1906 W. W. Rutherford was evidently referring to Abercromby and Exchange when he mentioned two Liverpool constituencies with 25 per cent and 30 per cent plural voters. *P.D.*, 4th. ser., xxiv. 121–2, clxiii, 438.

61 *T.* 22 Sept. 1885.

62 O'Connor had just married Elizabeth Paschal, the daughter of a Texas judge. See E. O'Connor, *I Myself*, 1910.

63 Burke, *op. cit.*, p. 244.

64 *L.D.P.* 16 Nov. 1885; R. D. Holt, diary, 10 July 1895. Mrs. O'Shea had been the intermediary between Grosvenor and Parnell. See K. O'Shea (Mrs. C. S. Parnell), *Charles Stewart Parnell*, 1921 edition, p. 189; L. W. Brady, 'T. P. O'Connor and Liverpool Politics 1880–1929', unpublished Ph.D. thesis, University of Liverpool, 1968, p. 157.

65 *M.G.* 23 Nov. 1885. O'Connor claimed that Parnell consulted no-one in this decision—*Memoirs*, ii, p. 7. O'Connor's reminiscences, however, notably ignore Parnell's own candidature.

66 Open letter by A. B. Forwood, 9 Aug. 1893, to local press. See also A. B. Forwood to Lord Harrowby, 20 Nov. 1885, Harrowby MSS., vol. 1, 2nd. ser., fols. 259–61.

67 *M.G.* 24 Nov. 1885. O'Connor, *op. cit.*, remembered this as 'humiliating'.

68 Stephens soon left Liverpool altogether. See *L.R.* 9 Oct. 1886; Watkinson, *op. cit.*, pp. 565–6.

69 *P.* 14 Nov. 1885. Cf. *P.* 31 Jan. 1885 for Stephens's previous popularity.

70 *Irish News*, 21 May 1923; O'Connor, *op. cit.* ii, pp. 9–10. The Manifesto O'Connor remembered as 'an open and passionate plea to the Irish electors of Great Britain to vote for the Tory candidates'. This accords with what Labouchere told Chamberlain, 12 Nov. 1885, that 'T. P. O'Connor is strong for supporting the Tories', quoted in Thorold, *op. cit.*, p. 242; but it differs from what O'Connor wrote to Labouchere on 16 Nov. 1885. Then he noted the Nationalists' quandary, having to weigh Gladstone's sympathy and Hartington's hostility; therefore 'we may go entirely one way or make exceptions in favour of some of the candidates' (letter among Viscount Gladstone papers, B. L. Add. MSS. 46015, fol. 54). Cf. O'Connor's account of Parnell and O'Shea in 1925, quoted in R. Deacon, *The Private Life of Mr. Gladstone*, 1965, pp. 145–6. Parnell, from a letter which he wrote to O'Connor on 16 Nov. 1885, was also still in doubt whether to plump for the Tories—Cooke and Vincent, *op. cit.*, p. 67.

71 C. H. D. Howard, 'The Parnell Manifesto of 21 November, 1885 and the Schools Question,' *E.H.R.*, Jan. 1947.

72 O'Connor, *op. cit.*, ii, p. 10.

73 *The Irish Programme*, 24 May 1884. Smith was not a Home Ruler, although he eventually followed Gladstone rather than his friend, W. S Caine—Smith, *Life Work*, pp. 196, 229–31, 282. MacIver, Birkenhead's M.P. from 1874, was a Fair Trader like the Parnellites. Moreover, he had supported Captain Nolan's motion in May 1884 for a reduction of the tea duty and increase of the wine duty; and in October 1884 he was one of few Conservatives to support Churchill and the Irish party in demanding inquiry into the Maamtrasna murder case. However, MacIver did not stand in 1885 and later, as M.P. for Liverpool Kirkdale, he made a name as an anti-Catholic. Parnell, none the less, spoke in 1885 in Birkenhead on behalf of the Conservative, General Sir E. Hamley, who was elected. See *The Life of James W. Alsop*, by his wife, Liverpool, 1926, p. 48.

74 Holt expected Liverpool to return 8 Tories and 1 Nationalist—'in fact 9 Parnellites!", R. D. Holt to Lord Derby, 19 Nov. 1885, Derby MSS.; and Holt's diary, 12 Nov. 1885.

75 Derby to Holt, 22 Nov. 1885, Holt MSS.

76 *L.C.* 1 Dec. 1885. Cf. S. Koss, *Sir John Brunner, Radical Plutocrat 1842–1919*, Cambridge, 1970, p. 63.

77 J. G. Gibson to A. B. Forwood, 30 June 1885, Forwood MSS. Against this there is E. R. Russell's view that the Liberals lost three Liverpool seats (unspecified) because of the Irish voting Conservative; and James Sexton claimed in 1919 that he voted Conservative in Liverpool in 1885—the first time he exercised the franchise—because of T. P. O'Connor's instructions. *P.D.*, 5th ser., vol. 115, 1703–12; *T.* 3 Dec. 1885. See also M. Kinnear, *The British Voter*, New York, 1968, pp. 13–14.

78 B. O'Connell, *op. cit.*, pp. 63–65; *The Irish Programme*, 22 March 1884, 26 July 1884; J. A. Jackson, *The Irish in Britain*, 1963, p. 123.

79 C. A. Collins, *op. cit.*, p. 281.

80 *L.C.* 26 Nov. 1885; *Liverpool Express*, 11 Sept. 1885.

81 *L.D.P.* 11 Sept. 1885.

82 *L.R.* 13 June 1885.

83 *Ormskirk Advertiser*, 16 Oct. 1885.

84 *L.C.* 30 Nov. 1885.

85 *Ormskirk Advertiser*, 16 Oct. 1885, 29 Oct. 1886.

86 *Fortnightly Review*, Sept. 1884, p. 325.

87 A. B. Forwood to R. Foote (chairman of the W.M.C.A.), 17 April 1885, quoted in *N.L.T.* 25 April 1885. Foote was a mineral-water manufacturer whose public life was directed more to the Board of Guardians than to Council or Parliamentary politics.

88 *L.R.* 9 May 1885; Samuelson's reaction in *L.C.* 2 June 1885.

89 Viscount Chilston, *Chief Whip: The Political Life and Times of Aretas Akers-Douglas 1st Viscount Chilston*, 1961, pp. 175–8; W. S. Churchill, *op. cit.*, pp. 250–1. Lord Randolph Churchill, however, was thoroughly antagonistic by 1892—see *L.D.P.* 17 Oct. 1892.

90 T. Atkinson to A. B. Forwood, 6 May 1885, Forwood MSS.

91 A. B. Forwood to R. Foote, 12 May 1885, copy, ibid.

92 T. Graham to A. B. Forwood, two letters, one dated 'Wednesday morning', the other 12 May 1885, ibid.

93 *L.D.P.* 12 Feb. 1892; *T.* 27 Oct. 1885.

94 *L.C.* 30 June 1885.

95 See Williams's correspondence with the W.M.C.A.'s secretary, *L.C.* 23 June 1885.

96 Lord C. Hamilton to A. B. Forwood, 3 and 13 March 1885, Forwood MSS.

97 T. Hughes to A. B. Forwood, 9 June 1885, ibid.

98 *L.R.* 13 June 1885.

99 *L.D.P.* 9 June 1885. The Conservative Central Office, later, also took the view that 'no Chairman of a party ought to think of contesting a seat in his own area'. Quoted in N. Blewett, *The Peers, the Parties and the People*, 1972, p. 276.

100 Lord G. Hamilton to A. B. Forwood, 3 March 1885, Forwood MSS.; *L.C.* 30 June 1885.

101 On Everton's growth, see R. Lawton's articles, *T.H.S.L.C.*, vol. 107, p. 97, and with C. G. Pooley, *T.H.S.L.C.*, vol. 125, p. 165; Sayers, *op. cit.*, p. 85; Farrer and Brownbill, *op. cit.* iii, pp. 20–22; Herdman, *op. cit.*, ii, pp. 41–45; Koss, *op. cit.*, pp. 9–10.

102 Picton, *Memorials*, ii, p. 323.

103 Ibid., p. 353.

104 J. R. Jones, *op. cit.*, p. 31; Dixon Scott, *Liverpool*, 1907, p. 96.

105 *P.* 22 Nov. 1884. Between 1835 and 1867 41 per cent of municipal elections were

uncontested in Everton. The Conservatives won altogether 60 per cent of Everton seats in that period. See D. Fraser, *op. cit.*, pp. 219–22.

106 *L.D.P.* 14 Sept. 1885. Cf. E. Evans Jr. to T. E. Ellis, Jan. 1890, Ellis MSS 862.

107 *L.R.* 26 May 1888.

108 *P.* 8 and 15 Nov. 1884.

109 *L.R.* 2 June 1888.

110 E. Whitley to A. B. Forwood, 23 Feb. 1885, Forwood MSS.

111 Ibid.

112 *T.* 26 Oct. 1885. Owing to the maldistribution of wards Everton and Kirkdale parliamentary constituencies made up one municipal ward.

113 *L.C.* 29 June 1885. Cf. the art of 'purring' (kicking as a sport) in R. Challinor, *The Lancashire and Cheshire Miners*, Newcastle, 1973, pp. 246–9.

114 A. H. Grey-Edwards, *A Great Heart or The Life of Canon Major Lester*, 1906, pp. 23, 194; Picton, *op. cit.* i, pp. 407–8; Baines, *op. cit.*, p. 113. Cf. Farrer and Brownbill, *op. cit.* iii, pp. 35–40; *Miss Weeton's Journal of a Governess*, vol. i, section iii.

115 *L.R.* 11 July 1885, 8, 15, and 22 Aug. 1885, 12 Sept. 1885, 10 Oct. 1885.

116 A. Akers-Douglas to J. S. Sandars, 27 Aug. 1895, Sandars MSS. c. 727, fols. 16–17. On Baden-Powell's father, see E. G. W. Bill, *University Reform in Nineteenth-Century Oxford*, Oxford, 1973, pp. 90–92; Bowen, *op. cit.*, pp. 165–6.

117 The Prime Minister's mother was a Liverpool Gascoyne—see Cecil, *op. cit.* i, pp. 6–7; Farrer and Brownbill, iii, pp. 22–28.

118 Cranborne's political debut in Liverpool was in 1880, to open a Junior Conservative Club. Forwood thought him bright and intelligent. See A. B. Forwood to Lord Sandon, 1 April 1881, Harrowby MSS., vol. l, 2nd ser. fol. 83. The opinion of other witnesses was sharply adverse—see T. P. O'Connor quoted in H. Fyfe, *T. P. O'Connor*, 1934, p. 167; H. W. Lucy, *A Diary of the Salisbury Parliament 1886–1892*, 1892, p. 395.

119 A. B. Forwood to Lord Salisbury, 21 Feb. 1885, Salisbury MSS.

120 Lord R. Churchill to A. B. Forwood, 14 and 27 April 1885, Forwood MSS.

121 Lord G. Hamilton, *Parliamentary Reminiscences and Reflections 1886–1906*, 1922, p. 63. Gibson's brother, Edward, Lord Ashbourne, was also endowed with a loud voice. See A. B. Cooke and A. P. W. Malcomson, *The Ashbourne Papers, 1869–1913*, Belfast, 1974, p. 31.

122 *T.* 16 July 1885.

123 A. Birrell, *Things Past Redress*, 1937, p. 105. A letter from Birrell to his election agent, 12 Dec. 1885, is in the Bodleian, Oxford, MSS. Eng. lett. e. 118, fol. 57.

124 A. B. Forwood to Lord Salisbury, 20 Oct. 1885, Salisbury MSS.; Robert Holt, diary, Sept. 1885.

125 *T.* and *L.D.P.* 18 Sept. 1885. Cf. Salisbury's article, 'Disintegration', *Quarterly Review*, 1883.

126 Viscount Mersey, *A Picture of Life*, 1941, chap. i; J. D. Crawford, *Reflections and Recollections*, 1936, pp. 39, 62–66.

127 *L.R.* 4 Sept. 1886. Cf. Farrer and Brownbill, *op. cit.* iii, pp. 40–45; A. Holt (ed.), *Merseyside*, p. 42.

128 F. Vigier, *Change and Apathy: Liverpool and Manchester During The Industrial Revolution*, Massachusetts, 1970, p. 174.

129 Shimmin, *Liverpool Sketches*, p. 103 ff.; *P.P.* 1884–5, xxx, Qs. 13454–6, 13502, H. Farrie.

130 *Pen and Ink Sketches of Liverpool Town Councillors*, Liverpool, 1866.

131 F. A. Latham, *Timber Town*, Liverpool, 1967, *passim.*

132 *The Toxteth Observer*, 29 Jan. 1881.

133 *L.R.* 14 and 28 Nov. 1885; *L.D.P.* 14 Sept. 1885, 9 March 1892.

134 *L.R.* 24 March, 8 Dec. 1883, 5 Sept. 1885. The Vyrnwy reservoir was first

discussed in 1876, authorized in 1880, and opened in 1892. See W. B. Forwood, *Recollections*, pp. 102–5; Hope, *City of Liverpool* pp. 194–6.

135 *L.C.* 17 June 1885; *P.* 14 Nov. 1885; *L.R.* 12 Sept. 1885.

136 Harford was general secretary of the Amalgamated Society of Railway Servants. See Sutherest's letter, *T.* 23 Sept. 1885. Lubbock was prominent in the shop hours movement and, according to him, of 2,000 shops circularized in Liverpool, 1,770 favoured and 200 opposed the Early Closing Bill (1888). See *P.D.*, 3rd ser., cccxxv 1101, 1150–3; and W. B. Whitaker, *Victorian and Edwardian Shop Workers*, 1973, chap. 6.

137 G. J. Goschen to A. B. Forwood, 22 March 1885, Forwood MSS. Goschen had made a speech in Liverpool, 11 Feb. 1885. To bring Goschen and the Hartington Whigs into the Conservative fold was also Northcote's ambition—see A. Jones, *op. cit.*, chap 2; T. J. Spinner, *op. cit.*, Chap. 6.

138 *P.* 14 Nov. 1885.

139 *L.R.* 11 April 1885, 28 Nov. 1885; *L.D.P.* 13 Nov. 1885; Smith, *Life-Work*, pp. 153–4. Smith had joined the Conservatives in resisting the Nationalists' ambitions regarding the boundaries of Exchange and Abercromby—*P.D.*, 3rd ser., ccxcvii, 1078–9.

140 Lord G. Hamilton to A. B. Forwood, 14 Dec. 1882, Forwood MSS.

141 R. E. Carlson, *The Liverpool and Manchester Railway Project 1821–1831*, 1969, pp. 69–70.

142 *L.R.* 7 Nov. 1885.

143 Smith returned to Parliament in March 1886, representing Flintshire.

144 Birrell, *op. cit.*, pp. 101–2. On Scotland division, its rapid growth 1830–50, see J. H. Treble, 'Liverpool Working-Class Housing, 1801–51' in S. D. Chapman (ed.), *The History of Working-Class Housing*, Newton Abbot, 1971, pp. 170–1.

145 Charles Russell, Tim Healy, and Thomas Sexton were also mentioned. See *L.C.* 30 June 1885; *The Nationalist*, 20 Dec. 1884; *L.R.* 18 July 1885; *L.D.P.* 14 Sept. 1885.

146 C. C. O'Brien, *Parnell and his Party 1880–90*, Oxford, 1957, pp. 166–84.

147 O'Connor spent £147. Only the two Northampton seats, where Labouchere and Bradlaugh spent under £270, were cheaper. Everton was the country's fifth cheapest seat, Whitley spending £188—see *The Tory*, 13 Aug. 1892.

148 R. D. Holt to Lord Derby, 19 Nov. 1885, Derby MSS.; A. B. Forwood to Lord Harrowby, 20 Nov. 1885, Harrowby MSS., vol. l, 2nd. ser., fols. 259–61.

149 *L.D.P.* 24 Oct. 1872.

150 T. Graham to A. B. Forwood, 13 May 1884, Forwood MSS. On Russell see Orchard, *Legion*, pp. 605–11; on Willmer, see W. Willmer, *Family Business*, Birkenhead, 1961.

151 *P.* 3 Oct. 1885; *T.* 27 Oct 1885; *L.R.* 6 Nov. 1886. Russell's *Liverpool Daily Post*, it is worth noting, also favoured Chamberlain's Unauthorized Programme. See C. A. Cooper, *An Editor's Retrospect*, 1896, p. 393, for Gladstone's disappointment.

152 J. Evans, *The Conways: A History of Three Generations*, 1966, p. 85; J. Willett, *Art in a City*, 1967, pp. 41–48; Robert Holt to Richard Holt, 20 Sept. 1893, 920 DUR 14/1/167.

153 *P.* 10 and 17 Oct. 1885. Winskill and Thomas, *op. cit.*, p. 83.

154 *L.R.* 12 Sept. 1885.

155 *P.* and *L.R.* 7 Nov. 1885.

156 *N.L.T.* 27 Feb. 1884; 19 March 1884; *T.* 11 Feb. 1884. E. L. Taplin's sketch of Samuelson in Bellamy and Saville, *Dictionary of Labour Biography*, ii, p. 329, suggests that Samuelson was officially adopted by the L.T.C. Certainly Alexander Clarke, the L.T.C.'s secretary, spoke well of Samuelson's campaign (see *Report, 18th Annual T.U.C.*, 1885, p. 33); but, according to its rules, the L.T.C. could not display party political favour. The L.T.C.'s Minute Book I shows only cordiality towards Samuelson. See also Watkinson, *op. cit.*, pp. 375, 392–3, for the L.T.C.'s position in the 1870s.

157 *N.L.T.* 27 Feb. 1884.

158 *P.* 26 April 1884, 5 July 1884.

159 Taplin, *op. cit.*, says that Samuelson 'sought adoption' by Kirkdale Liberal Association. In fact the initiative was from the Association. See James Ure to R. Hudson, 12 Aug. 1885, letter published in *N.L.T.* 5 Sept. 1885, Ure, the Industrial Union's president, was a member of the A.S.E.

160 John Bright was approached before Morley but he refused to interfere—see *N.L.T.* 19 Sept. 1885. Morley had spoken in Liverpool in 1883 and was well received—see Smith, *op. cit.*, p. 144; F. W. Hirst, *Early Life and Letters of John Morley*, 1927, vol. ii, pp. 169–71.

161 *L.D.P.* 2 Sept. 1885.

162 *Kirkdale Liberal Association, First Annual Report*, 16 Feb. 1886.

163 *N.L.T.* 17 Oct. 1885; *L.C.* 21 Nov. 1885. In fact Samuelson had never concealed his radical views—see *T.* 25 June 1883.

164 Cecil, *op. cit.* iii, p. 262.

165 Birrell, *op. cit.*, p. 101.

166 *Kirkdale Liberal Association, First Annual Report, op. cit.*; A. Baker to Lord Derby, 15 March 1886, Derby MSS.; Watkinson, *op. cit.*, pp. 403–4; James McComb, Liverpool Liberal Agent, cited in H. J. Hanham (ed.), *The Nineteenth-Century Constitution 1815–1914*, Cambridge, 1969, p. 284.

167 *L.R.* 21 Sept. 1889; N. Blewett, 'The Franchise in the United Kingdom 1885–1918', *Past and Present*, no. 32, Dec. 1965, pp. 27–56; R. Lawton and C. G. Pooley, 'David Brindley's Liverpool: An Aspect of Urban Society in the 1880s', *T.H.S.L.C.*, vol. 125, 1974, pp. 149–68.

168 Simey, *op. cit.* p. 10; S. K. Hocking, *Cricket: A Tale of Humble Life*, 1886, p. 212. The Liverpool Domestic Mission was founded in 1836, under Unitarian influence.

169 J. A. Hobson, *Problems of Poverty*, 1895, p. 13; diary entry, May 1887, in B. Webb, *My Apprenticeship*, 1926; pp. 256–7. Cf. Stedman Jones, *op. cit.*, pp. 81–88; M. Anderson, *Family Structure in Nineteenth Century Lancashire*, Cambridge, 1971, pp. 41–42.

170 *T.* 3 Nov. 1897.

171 A. Fried and R. M. Elman (eds.), *Charles Booth's London*, 1969, pp. 5, 40, 60.

172 *P.* 21 Nov. 1885.

CHAPTER 5

1 Quoted in A. Ponsonby, *Henry Ponsonby*, 1942, p. 355; Thorold, *op. cit.*, p. 278.

2 Quoted in J. Morley, *The Life of William Ewart Gladstone*, 1911 edition, vol. ii, pp. 412–13. Gladstone attributed the degradation of Conservatism to Disraeli's leadership—see letter to G. C. Brodrick, 23 July 1874, quoted in Brodrick, *Memories*, pp. 242–3.

3 See Gladstone to Harcourt, 16 Nov. 1886, in Gardiner, *op. cit.*, ii, p. 12.

4 Balfour to Salisbury, 24 March 1886, in Balfour, *op. cit.*, p. 221, Cf. T. E. Kebbel, *A History of Toryism*, 1886, new edition, 1972, pp. 319–20; and Northcote quoted in Feuchtwanger, *op. cit.*, pp. 185–6.

5 Derby to Sir W. V. Harcourt, 7 Feb, 30 Dec. 1883, 11 Sept., 17 Nov. 1884, 4 Jan. 1885, 8, 10, Jan. 1886, Harcourt MSS. 212, fols. 14, 74–75; 213, fols. 72–75, 138–9; 214, fols. 2–3; 215, fols. 13–16a.

6 Derby to R. D. Holt, 5 Feb., 17 March 1886, Holt MSS.; Holt to Derby, 6 Feb. 1886, Derby MSS. On Derby's loneliness and equivocations in 1885–6, Cooke and Vincent, *op. cit.*, pp. 126–31.

7 Derby to Holt, 17 March 1886, Holt MSS.; Sefton to Derby, 30 March and 1 April 1886, Derby MSS.

8 Orchard, *Legion*, pp. 167–8.

9 A. H. Bencke to Lord Derby, 12 Sept. 1885, Derby MSS.

10 Idem 25 Sept. and 5 Nov. 1885, Derby MSS.; and Bencke's letter in *L.D.P.* 5 Nov. 1897.

11 A. B. Forwood to Lord Salisbury, 22 April 1886, Salisbury MSS.

12 Derby to Forwood, 7 May 1886, Forwood MSS.

13 *L.R.* 24 April 1886.

14 See Alsop, *op. cit.*, pp. 49–55.

15 Robert Holt, diary, 2, 8 July 1886; *L.R.* 19 May 1886. Among the 'other considerations' which moved some Liberal Unionists were the tax ideals of the Liverpool Financial Reform Association, which was now broken, although it struggled on until 1914—see W. N. Calkins, 'A Victorian Free Trade Lobby', *Ec.H.R.*, 2nd. ser., xiii, p. 103.

16 Bencke to Derby, 6 and 10 May 1886, Derby MSS.

17 Milner to Goschen, 21 Aug. 1884, quoted Spinner, *op. cit.*, p. 100.

18 Sefton to Derby, 24 May 1886, Derby MSS.

19 Bencke to Derby, 5 Nov. 1885; Sefton to Derby, 4 June 1886, enclosing letter from T. D. Hornby, Derby MSS.

20 *L.R.* 29 May 1886.

21 R. D. Holt to W. E. Gladstone, 28 Jan. 1887, B. M. Add. MSS. 44500, fol. 71. Cf. William Rathbone's description of Holt in Rathbone to James Bryce, 30 Sept. 1892, Bryce MSS. UB 34.

22 *L.R.* 27 March 1886, 29 May 1886, 12 June 1886. The local Liberal leader's brother, Alfred Holt, was one who voted Tory—see Robert Holt, diary, 8 July 1886.

23 A. B. Forwood to Lord Salisbury, 14 May 1886, Salisbury MSS.

24 A. B. Forwood to A. Akers-Douglas, 15 July 1886, quoted in Chilston, *Chief Whip*, p. 82. Writing to Lord Randolph Churchill, 31 July 1886, Forwood specified Local Government, Railway Rates, Employers' Liability, Coal Mines, Merchant Shipping, Small Debtors, Land-Law and Allotments, legislation, Churchill MSS, RCHL 1/13/1606.

25 Orchard, *Legion*, p. 50. Cf. Morley, *op. cit.* i, pp. 17–18.

26 W. E. Gladstone, *Address delivered at Liverpool College, December 31st 1872*, 1873, pp. 17, 30–31. On this speech see A. Ramm (ed.), *The Political Correspondence of Mr. Gladstone and Lord Granville 1868–1876*, Camden 3rd ser., vol. lxxxii, pp. 367–8. Gladstone did not greatly exert himself in practice to make Liverpool a cultural capital, being severe with Canon Gore in the 1890s when Gore suggested that Gladstone found a new library there rather than at Hawarden—see Prestige, *op. cit.*, p. 173. Ironically what prevented Liverpool from becoming the City Beautiful was the expansion of the business quarter which swept away most traces of antiquity—see H. Peet, *Liverpool in the Reign of Queen Anne*, Liverpool, 1908, p. 12.

27 *T.* 28 June 1886.

28 W. Bagehot, 'Mr. Gladstone' (1860), in N. St. John-Stevas (ed.), *Bagehot's Historical Essays*, 1971, pp. 243–4; *T.* 29 June 1886. For different receptions of the speech see T. P. O'Connor, *op. cit.* ii, pp. 42–43; Robert Holt's diary, 28 June 1886; *Mary Gladstone's Diaries, op. cit.*, p. 390; Alsop. *op. cit.*, pp. 52–53; Brodrick, *Literary Fragments*, pp. 256–62.

29 *P.* 9 Jan 1886. In 1899, when out of Parliament, Hamilton again reconsidered his Conservative allegiances, this time outraged by what he felt to be the Conservatives' flabbiness in defence of property and capital—see Alderman, *op. cit.*, p. 172.

30 See Budge and O'Leary, *op. cit.*, chap. 3; Lucas, *op. cit.*, p. 99. Churchill was distressed by that summer's terrorism in Belfast, and the Ulster Unionist leader, Colonel

Saunderson, endeavoured to exonerate the Orange Order by blaming the rioting upon adolescent hooligans—see letter, 10 Aug. 1886, Churchill MSS. RCHL 1/14/1653.

31 *L.R.* 3 April 1886. Cf. A. V. Dicey, *England's Case Against Home Rule*, 1886: new edition, Brighton, 1973, p. 147. Morrow was vicar of St. Phillip's, Hardman Street, and a member of the Church Association.

32 *Quarterly Review*, Jan. 1886, p. 264, April 1886, pp. 559–60, 575.

33 For Gladstone's anger at this, see Gardiner, *op. cit.* i, p. 559.

34 A. B. Forwood to Lord Salisbury, 16 June 1886, Salisbury MSS.

35 *T.* 12 June 1886.

36 *L.R.* 5 June 1886.

37 *L.R.* 10 July 1886.

38 R. D. Holt to Lord Derby, 18 March 1886, Derby MSS.

39 *L.R.* 29 May 1886; B. O'Connell, *op. cit.*, p. 157.

40 *T.* 10 and 12 June 1886; *L.R.* 26 June 1886. Major-General William Earle died on the march to Khartoum. A statue was erected from public subscriptions and unveiled by Lord Wolseley, see *L.M.* 17 Dec. 1887. The sculptor, Charles Bell Birch, was also responsible for the statue of Disraeli in front of St. George's Hall.

41 *T.* 10 June 1886; *L.R.* 26 June 1886, 10 July 1886.

42 *L.R.* 19 June 1886.

43 *T.* 10 and 12 June 1886; *The Liberal Year Book 1887*, p. 130.

44 *L.D.P.* 1 Jan. 1887. See also R. H. Lundie, *Alexander Balfour*, 2nd. edition, 1889, p. 24.

45 Correspondence in *T.* 6 July 1886. Kinnear, *British Voter*, p. 20 has different figures and a different conclusion.

46 S. Pollard, 'Laissez-Faire and Shipbuilding', *Ec.H.R.*, 2nd ser. v, no. 1, 1952, pp. 98–114; A. B. Forwood to G. Melly, 12 July 1886, Melly MSS. 31: 5908.

47 *L.D.P.* 9 June 1885.

48 *The Church Review and Church News*, 4 Dec. 1885; *The Loyal Orangeman*, 11 Jan. 1890.

49 *L.R.* 15 and 22 May 1886, 30 Oct. 1886, 6 Nov. 1886; *T.* 28 Feb. 1887, 1 March 1887.

50 *L.R.* 10 and 17 July 1886, 7 and 28 Aug. 1886.

51 E. R. Russell to W. E. Gladstone, 6 Nov. 1886, Gladstone MSS. B. L. Add. MSS. 44499, fol. 137.

52 R. D. Holt to Gladstone, 24 Dec. 1886, concerning temporary harmony to celebrate Gladstone's birthday at Liverpool Reform Club, B.L. Add. MSS. 44499, fol. 260. On the gradual estrangement of friends at Liverpool Reform Club, Alsop, *op. cit.*, *passim.*

53 T. Sanderson to Lord Derby, 5 Jan. 1887, Derby MSS.; M. V. Brett (ed.), *Journals and Letters of Reginald, Viscount Esher*, vol. i, 1934, p. 132.

54 Churchill's phrase quoted in M. Bonham Carter, *The Autobiography of Margot Asquith*, 1962, p. 48.

55 G. J. Goschen to A. L. Bruce, 22 Aug. 1886, quoted to A. D. Elliot, *The Life of George Joachim Goschen, First Viscount Goschen 1831–1907*, ii, p. 97, Cf. Mr. Gladstone's reaction—'an insult to Parlt.', in Masterman, *Mary Gladstone's Diaries*, p. 392.

56 *T.* 1 Jan. 1887.

57 Quoted in B. E. C. Dugdale, *Arthur James Balfour, 1st Earl of Balfour*, 1936, i, pp. 118–19. Goschen's arguments against a Unionist coalition were tactical rather than fundamental, fearing in reaction a democratic union—Goschen to A. Austin, 28 Dec. 1886, in *The Autobiography of Alfred Austin 1835–1910*, 1911, vol. ii, pp. 250–2. See also Cooks and Vincent, *op. cit.*, pp. 84 ff.

58 A. Akers-Douglas to Lord Salisbury, 1 Jan. 1887, quoted in Chilston, *Chief Whip*, p. 106.

59 *T.* 7 Jan. 1887; Robert Holt, diary, 19 Jan. 1887.

60 *L.D.P.* 7 Jan. 1887, *T.* 8 Jan. 1887.

61 *T.* 8, 11 Jan. 1887; Robert Holt, diary, 7, 10 Jan. 1887.

62 *T.* 12 Jan. 1887.

63 Told in Russell, *That Reminds Me*, p. 28. Childers can be considered an authority in such matters because he, according to Harcourt, also could never make up his mind. See Cooke and Vincent, *op. cit.*, p. 348.

64 *T.* 13 Jan. 1887.

65 Address in *T.* 13 Jan. 1887; *Annual Register 1887*, pp. 4–5.

66 E. R. Russell to W. E. Gladstone, Gladstone MSS., B.L. Add. MSS. 44500, fol. 35.

67 *L.C.* 27 Jan. 1887. W. Summers represented Huddersfield, 1886–93.

68 *T.* 15 Jan. 1887.

69 A. B. Forwood to Lord Salisbury, 20 Nov. 1886, Salisbury MSS; Forwood to Lord R. Churchill, 26 Nov. 1886, Churchill MSS. RCHL 1/17/2068; *The Chamber of Commerce of Liverpool, 37th Annual Report*, 1887, pp. 24–32; H. Robinson, *Carrying British Mails Overseas*, 1964, pp. 247–50.

70 *L.D.P.* 26 Jan. 1887.

71 Hamilton, *op. cit.*, p. 56. The Postmaster-General disputed this—see Raikes, *op. cit.*, chap. xxii.

72 O'Connor, *op. cit.* ii, pp. 117–18; Robert Holt, diary, 26 Jan. 1887.

73 *L.D.P.* 28 Jan. 1887; Gardiner, *op. cit.* ii, p. 30.

74 *T.* 27 Jan. 1887.

75 *L.C.* 2 May 1888.

CHAPTER 6

1 W. Cooke Taylor, *op. cit.*, p. 299.

2 Quoted in Simey, *op. cit.*, p. 108.

3 Kebbel, *op. cit.*, p. 405.

4 Quoted in Thorold, *op. cit.*, p. 314.

5 *L.R.* 17 and 24 July 1886, 18 Sept. 1886.

6 *P.P.* 1884–5, xxx, Q. 13493, H. Farrie; T. Graham to A. B. Forwood, 13 May [1884], Forwood MSS.

7 *L.R.* 21 Jan. 1888.

8 *L.D.P.* 11 and 13 Oct. 1887. On the strength of Tory fossils *vis-à-vis* Tory radicals, Robert Holt's diary, 9 Nov. 1887.

9 For accounts of public health in Liverpool before 1870 see. B. D. White, *op. cit.*, chaps. iv, v, and viii; Midwinter, *Old Liverpool,* chaps. 5, 6; J. H. Treble in Chapman, *op. cit.*, chap. v; J. L. and B. Hammond, *The Bleak Age*, Pelican edition, 1947, chaps. v, xii.

10 Shimmin, *The Sanitary Aspect of Philanthropy*, p. 16; White, *op. cit.*, pp. 37, 49, 52–53; *Liverpool Town Planning and Housing Exhibition 1914*, Liverpool, 1914, p. 117; Hope, *City of Liverpool* p. 166; *P.P.* 1868–9, xxxii, Q. 7712, Dr. W. S. Trench, 2,229, J. Rayner.

11 *P.P.* 1884–5, *op. cit.*, Q. 13592, C. Dunscombe.

12 Ibid., Q. 13366; *P.P.* 1868–9, *op. cit.*, Q. 7795 ff., Dr. Trench; *Report, 18th Annual T.U.C.*, 1885, p. 41.

13 Orchard, *Legion*, p. 666. The Coronership was another example of party patronage in Liverpool—see F. W. Lowndes, *Reasons why the office of Coroner should be held by a member of the Medical Profession*, 3rd edition, 1900; W. Lewin, *Clarke Aspinall*, 1893, pp. 182–5, for the strong Protestant and Unionist opinions of Liverpool's long serving

Coroner; Robert Holt's diary, 21 Dec. 1891, for the election of Aspinall's successor, Sampson.

14 *L.C.* 5 May 1893.

15 *P.P.* 1884–5. *op. cit.*, Q. 13710.

16 B. D. White, *op. cit.*, p. 65; R. Lambert, *Sir John Simon 1816–1904 and English Social Administration*, 1963, pp. 100–1; A. S. Wohl, 'Unfit for Human Habitation', in H. J. Dyos and M. Wolff (eds.), *The Victorian City: Images and Realities*, 1973, vol. ii, pp. 603–24.

17 *P.P.* 1884–5, Q. 13480, 13520, 13544, T. E. Stephens. Forwood denied the allegations, ibid. Qs. 13740–1, 13657–8. Cf. Sexton *Agitator*, pp. 89–90.

18 E. W. Hope, *Report on the Extension of the Boundaries and Health Administration in Liverpool*, 1895. Cf. *P.P.* 1868–9, *op. cit.*, Qs. 7770–2 Dr. Trench; W. Carter, *Report of the Health of West Derby*, 1875, 1877, 1878; Finer, *English Local Government*, p. 259.

19 *P.P.* 1884–5, *op. cit.*, Qs. 13347–50 Forwood; B. D. White, *op. cit.*, pp. 121, 127; E. P. Hennock, *Fit and Proper Persons*, 1973, pp. 234–5; J. L. Brand, *Doctors and the State*, Baltimore, 1965, pp. 60–62. Dr. Carter, West Derby's M.O.H., opposed compulsory notification, see *Report, 1881*, pp. 7–8; but when Bolton and other corporations pioneered this in local acts from 1877 it was generally adopted after the Infectious Diseases (Notification) Act of 1889.

20 *L.D.P.* 5 Nov. 1883.

21 *P.P.* 1884–5, *op. cit.*, Q. 13343 (Farrie). Liverpool first gained continuous supplies of water when the link with the Rivington watershed was opened in 1857, and extended in 1865 and 1875. After new supplies were drawn from Vyrnwy, in 1894 the Corporation stipulated that all new houses should have at least one tap. Liverpool drew under 3 million gallons of water per day in 1846, nearly 19 million in 1891, nearly 27 million in 1902. See G. A. Pumphrey, *The Story of Liverpool's Public Services*, Liverpool, 1940, p. 131.

22 O'Mara lived in several courts, in Stanhope and Brick Streets—see O'Mara, *op. cit.*, *passim.*

23 Quoted in Midwinter, *Social Administration*, p. 72; and in J. A. Jackson, *op. cit.*, p. 49.

24 B. D. White, op. cit., pp. 119–23; E. W. Hope, *Health at the Gateway*, Cambridge, 1931, pp. 10–11. Of 2,600 deaths from cholera in Lancashire in 1866, 2,122 were in Liverpool, Midwinter, *op. cit.*, p. 116. Nevertheless Liverpool Workhouse was praised for its hospital service—*P.P.* 1867–8, lx, pp. 437–41.

25 *P.P.* 1884–5, *op. cit.*, Qs. 13347–50, Forwood; *P.D.*, 4th ser., vol. 146, cols. 1379–80, vol. 147, col. 222, vol. 151, col. 83.

26 George Sims quoted in P. Keating (ed.), *Into Unknown England*, 1976, p. 85; A. White, *The Problems of a Great City*, 1886, p. 13.

27 W. L. Sargent, 'Certain Results and Defects of the Reports of the Registrar-General', *Journal of the Statistical Society of London*, June 1864, p. 200.

28 *L.D.P.* 5 and 6 Nov. 1883.

29 Pamphlet quoted in *P.P.* 1884–5, *op. cit.*, Report p. 14.

30 Ibid., Q. 5767; Shimmin, *Liverpool Sketches*, p. 116.

31 J. A. Hobson, *op. cit.*, p. 11. Cf. Fried and Elman, *op. cit.*, pp. 46, 49; E. J. Hobsbawm, *Industry and Empire*, 1968, p. 135. Poor people also bought minute quantities because food would not keep—see J. L. and B. Hammond, *op. cit.*, p. 72.

32 *P.P.* 1884–5, *op. cit.*, Q. 13649, C. Dunscombe, 4358, H. Wright.

33 Ibid., Q. 39.

34 Mumford, *op. cit.*, p. 530; Tarn, *op. cit.*, p. 114; *P.P.* 1887, xxix, Q. 29249, Miss F. Calder.

35 H. Lazarus, *Landlordism*, 1892, pp. 5–7, 41, 52, 57. H. J. Dyos and D. A. Reeder, 'Slums and Suburbs', in Dyos and Wolff, *op. cit.* i, pp. 380–1, cite George Bernard Shaw's,

Widowers' Houses, 1892, as an illustration of the profitability of slum tenements. Lickcheese, Sartorius's rent-collector, boasts, 'It's been calculated on the cubic foot of space, sir, that you can get higher rents letting by the room than you can for a mansion in Park Lane'. G. B. Shaw, *Plays Unpleasant*, Penguin edition, 1965, p. 60. This seems a dramatic simplicity. Sartorius complains about the wanton destruction of his property and the impossibility of expending money on repairs if he is to profit from a weekly rental of 4*s*. 6*d*. (ibid., p. 71). Significantly he moves into the compensation racket as the profitable side of slum ownership. On compensation scandals see Stedman Jones, *op. cit.*, pp. 200–2; *The Radical Programme*, *op. cit.*, pp. xxiii, 81–89.

36 *P.P.* 1884–5, Qs. 13483–4. One attraction of cellars was the relative ease with which their inhabitants could escape paying rent—M. J. Whitty, in *Report of a Committee of the Manchester Statistical Society on the Condition of the Working Classes*, 1838, p. 10.

37 *P.P.* 1904, xxxii, Q. 9148, M. Garnett; *P.D..*, 5th ser., vol. 114, 1914–17, J. Sexton.

38 *P.P.* 1884–5, *op. cit.*, Qs. 13441–2, 13672, 13719, 13725, 13729, 13731, Forwood, Cf. J. H. Treble, *op. cit.*, on the numerous small builders and landlords before 1851, in Chapman, *op. cit.*, pp. 191–2; and *P.P.* 1868–9, *op. cit.*, Q. 7715, Dr. Trench.

39 R. Tressell, *The Ragged Trousered Philanthropists*, Panther edition, 1967; R. H. Inglis Palgrave and John Scott, articles 'On Local Taxation', *J.S.S.*, vol xxxiv, 1871, pp. 111–235, 281–333; interview with W. Rathbone, 1899, Webb Local Government Collection, vol. 148; V. D. Lipman, *Local Government Areas 1834–1945,* Oxford, 1949, chap. iv.

40 J. S. Mill, *Autobiography*, New York, 1964, p. 144.

41 *P.P.* 1894, xvii, Q. 10136. For the contrary view see T. M. Shallcross, *Municipal Shortcomings: The Example of Liverpool.* 2nd. edition, 1904.

42 *P.P.* 1904, *op. cit.*, Q. 8825, Dr. Ashby.

43 Ibid. Q. 10258, C. S. Loch.

44 The City Engineer, quoted in B. D. White, *op. cit.*, p. 133; Tarn, *op. cit.*, pp. 62, 89–91. The Liverpool Land and House Owners Association was tied in with the Liberty and Property Defence League—see N. Solon, 'Laissez-Faire as Dogma', in K. D. Brown (ed.), *Essays in Anti-Labour History*, 1974, chap. 9.

45 *P.P.* 1884–5, *op. cit.*, Qs. 13380, 13484, 13660–2, Forwood. William Rathbone estimated that to avoid legal expenses Liverpool Corporation paid owners of insanitary property 50 per cent more than they deserved—*P.D..*, 3rd. ser., ccxxiii, 759.

46 *P.P.* 1884–5, *op. cit.*, Qs. 13402–8, Sir Charles Dilke's phrase.

47 Ibid. Qs. 13426 ff., 13733, Forwood; *P.P.* 1868–9, *op. cit.*, Q. 7757, Trench; Tarn, *op. cit.*, p. 62. In 1903, because of the difficulties local authorities were faced with financially, the maximum period for repayment of loans to the Public Works Commissioners was extended to eighty years.

48 A. B. Forwood, *The Dwellings of the Industrial Classes in the Diocese of Liverpool and how to Improve Them*, Liverpool, 1883, pp. 29–30; *The Pall Mall Gazette*, 7 Nov. 1883.

49 Forwood, *op. cit.*, p. 20. See also I. C. Taylor, 'The Insanitary Housing Question and Tenement Dwellings in Nineteenth-century Liverpool', in A. Sutcliffe (ed.), *Multi-Storey Living*, 1974, chap. 3.

50 *P.P.* 1884–5, *op. cit.*, Qs. 13419–20, 13684, Forwood; Forwood, *op. cit.*, p. 25; W. Carter, *Some Results of Recent Sanitary Legislation, with Suggestions as to its Safe Extension*, Liverpool, 1886, p. 28.

51 Forwood, *op. cit.*, p. 22. F. Turton, the Deputy City Surveyor, admitted in 1903 that these cottages could not have been built under later bye-laws—see Hope, *City of Liverpool*, pp. 167–8, 170–1.

52 *P.P.* 1884–5, *op. cit.*, Q. 13425. See also A. Errazurez, 'Some Types of Housing in Liverpool 1785–1890', and J. N. Tarn, 'Housing in Liverpool and Glasgow: the Growth

of Civic Responsibility', in *Town Planning Review*, vol. xix, no. 2, Spring 1946, pp. 57–68, vol. 39, no. 4, Jan. 1969, pp. 319–34.

53 Hope, *City of Liverpool*, pp. 171–3; *L.D.P.* 21 Oct. 1885; J. F. J. Sykes, article on working-class housing, in *J.S.S.*, vol. 64, June 1901, pp. 189–264. Forwood tried to get Lord Salisbury to perform the opening ceremony—Forwood to Salisbury, 29 July 1885, Salisbury MSS.; Salisbury to Forwood, 31 July 1885, Forwood MSS.

54 C. M. Allan, 'The Genesis of British Urban Redevelopment with Special Reference to Glasgow', *Ec.H.R.*, 2nd. ser., xviii, no. 3, 1965, pp. 607–9; *L.M.* 18 Sept. 1895. The previous Lord Derby, the 15th Earl, held similar opinions, believing that state or municipal housing would initiate 'universal and undisguised pauperism'. See speeches in Liverpool 1871–2, in Sanderson and Roscoe, *op. cit.*, ii, pp. 129–35, 171.

55 *P.P.* 1884–5, *op. cit.*, Q. 13709.

56 *Liverpool Town Planning & Housing Exhibition 1914*, p. 117; Denvir, *Irish in Britain*, p. 435.

57 *P.P.* 1884–5, *op. cit.*, Qs. 13632–9. On Godwin, the editor of *The Builder* between 1844 and 1883, see G. Godwin, *Town Swamps and Social Bridges*, 1859; Leicester, 1972, Introduction by A. King, pp. 7–22; Tarn, *op. cit.*, *passim.*

58 *P.P.* 1884–5, *op. cit.*, Qs. 13653–8.

59 *T.* 5 Jan. 1888; *The Stranger in Liverpool*, 9th edition, 1829, p. 63; Aspinall, *op. cit.*, p. 102; Chalkin, *op. cit.*, pp. 98–112; *P.P.* 1886, xii, Qs. 8847–9, E. Ryde; D. A. Reeder, 'The Politics of Urban Leaseholds in Late Victorian England', *International Review of Social History*, vi, 1961, pp. 413–30.

60 *L.C.* 7 June 1888. About one-third of councillors leased Corporation property—see *P.D.*, 3rd ser. cclxix, 206–8 (E. Whitley).

61 *T.* 24 Jan. 1888; Orchard, *Legion*, pp. 712–13; letter from W. B. Forwood, *T.* 26 Jan. 1888, Sir William Forwood was chairman of the Leaseholds' Committee—see Forwood, *Recollections*, pp. 109–11.

62 *L.C.* 7 June 1888. Several freeholds were sold (raising £180,000) and pockets of this type of tenure appeared all over the estate, to the disadvantage of the Corporation's later area redevelopment; but the 1824 system otherwise continued with the consequence to the Corporation of shrinking revenue, until 1 January 1920, when it was replaced by leases of ninety-nine years and by the application of proper valuation principles in each case—see H. H. Hough, 'The Liverpool Corporate Estate', *Town Planning Review*, vol. xxi, no. 3, Oct. 1950, pp. 237–52.

63 *L.C.* 1 May 1888.

64 Orchard, *op. cit.*, p. 564; Anne Holt, diary, 19 Jan. 1881.

65 *L.C.* 23 Dec. 1899.

66 On Radcliffe, *P.* 7 Nov. 1885; *L.D.P.* 11 April 1907. On the hot-pot tradition, *L.R.* 5 Jan. 1899; Orchard, *op. cit.* On the International Exhibition, and the undignified squabbles excited by Radcliffe's knighthood, *T.* 11 and 12 May 1886, 28 Oct. 1886, 10 Nov. 1886, 4 Dec. 1886; Nott-Bower, *op. cit.*, p. 63; *The Letters of Queen Victoria*, 3rd ser., 1930, vol. i, pp. 125–8; *The Parrot*, 11 Nov. 1887; Robert Holt, diary, 6–12 April 1886.

67 *L.D.P.* 28 Oct. 1887.

68 Letter from 'Tory Democrat', *L.D.P.* 20 Oct. 1887.

69 *L.R.* 1 and 29 March 1890.

70 *L.D.P.* 15 Oct. 1887.

71 *L.D.P.* 18, 19, 20, 21 Oct. 1887.

72 *L.D.P.* 22, 26, 27, 28 Oct. 1887.

73 Hartington to Holt, 7 May 1888, Holt MSS.

74 Brocklebank to Holt, 7 June 1888, ibid.

75 *L.R.* 9 June 1888.

76 *L.R.* 2 Feb. 1889. There were 606 club members on 1 January 1889, but only about half were regular attenders.

77 Orchard, *Legion*, pp. 297–9; Robert Holt, diary, 19 Dec. 1889. Evans had been secretary of the National Parnell Expenses Fund.

78 *L.R.* 3 Nov. 1888.

79 *L.D.P.* 2 Nov. 1888; Robert Holt, diary, 1 Nov. 1888.

80 *L.C.* 13 July 1888.

81 *L.R.* 4 Feb. 1888.

82 *L.D.P.* 26 July 1892.

83 *L.C.* 13 July 1888.

84 Letter in *L.C.* 7 Aug. 1888; *L.C.* 8 March 1888. On the want of public walks and gardens open on Sundays in Liverpool, J. L. and B. Hammond, *op. cit.*, p. 128. On the aspect of inter-class co-operation, B. Harrison 'Religion and Recreation in Nineteenth-Century England', *Past and Present*, no. 38, 1967, pp. 98–125.

85 *L.R.* 14 Dec. 1889.

86 Robert Holt's diary, 31 Oct. 1897.

87 *L.R.* 3, 10, 17 Nov. 1888; *T.* 15 Nov. 1888; *P.S.* 14, 21 Sept. 1889.

88 Orchard, *Legion*; Hemelryk's letter in *L.D.P.* 6 Nov. 1897.

89 *L.C.* 15 Jan. 1888.

90 *Liverpool Citizen*, 16 July 1890. On Sibthorp and Newdegate, pillars of perfect prejudice, *D.N.B.* xiv, pp. 329–30, xviii, p. 188.

91 *L.R.* 11 May 1889; *L.D.P.* 22 Jan. 1906; *P.D.*, 4th ser., lxxxi, 591–2. The Open Church Association aimed to rid the Church of England of the pew system.

92 *T.* 17 Nov. 1911. These are Clauses 22 and 23 of the will, Somerset House reference 1722, 14 Nov. 1911.

93 Scott, *op. cit.*, pp. 106–7.

94 *L.R.* 12 July 1895.

95 *L.R.* 21 Jan. 1885; *T.* 1883, *passim.*

96 *The ABZ of Scouse*, Liverpool, 1966; reprinted, 1970, p. 13. On Bootle toughs see *L.R.* 31 Jan. 1885, 27 July, 3, 10 Aug. 1889; *L.C.* 1 Nov. 1898; *L.D.P.* 22 Dec. 1892; P. M. Young, *A History of British Football*, 1968, p. 138; Midwinter, *Old Liverpool*, p. 134; *N.L.T. passim.*

97 *L.R.* 4 Sept. 1886.

98 *L.R.* 21 Feb. 1885.

99 Morley, *op. cit.*, i, pp. 21–22; Forwood, *Recollections*, p. 5; *L.C.* 8 July 1903; Farrer and Brownbill, *op. cit.* iii, pp. 31–35; A. Austin, *Autobiography*, i, pp. 27–28.

100 Letters by G. H. Croxden Powell, in *T.* 2 Jan. 1885, *N.L.T.* 24 Jan. 1885.

101 J. Lynch to J. Thompson, 10 Dec. 1888, in *L.C.* 23 Nov. 1889.

102 *L.C.* 23 Nov. 1889.

103 *L.C.* 16 July 1889.

104 *L.C.* 23 Nov. 1889.

105 *L.D.P.* 19, 28 Oct. 1889.

106 *L.D.P.* 25 Nov. 1889.

107 Letter by W. J. Austin, in *L.D.P.* 22 Nov. 1889.

108 *L.R.* 23 Nov. 1889, 19 July, 9 Aug. 1890.

109 *L.D.P.* 20 Nov. 1889.

110 *L.D.P.* 21 Nov. 1889.

111 Letter by W. Draze, in *L.C.* 31 Oct. 1891. See also Adam's obituary, *L.C.* 31 May 1897.

112 *L.D.P.* 19 Nov. 1889; *L.C.* 23 Nov. 1889.

113 *L.D.P.* 20 Nov. 1889.

114 *L.D.P.* 25, 26 Nov. 1889; letter by H. Skewes, in *L.D.P.* 27 Nov. 1889.
115 *L.D.P.* 22 Nov. 1889.
116 *L.D.P.* 27 Nov. 1889; *L.R.* 30 Nov. 1889.
117 *P.S.* 6 July 1889.
118 *L.C.* 23 Nov. 1889; *L.D.P.* 5, 6 Dec. 1889.
119 Resolution of the Star of the North Lodge, in St. Anne's ward—*L.D.P.* 30 Nov. 1889.
120 *The Loyal Orangeman*, 21 Dec. 1889.
121 Ibid. 4 Jan. 1890.
122 Ibid. 28 Dec. 1889.
123 Ibid. 25 Jan. 1890.
124 T. M. Sandys to Lord Salisbury, 14 and 29 Nov. 1889, Salisbury MSS.

CHAPTER 7

1 Rule 19, National Union of Dock Labourers, Trades Union Congress Library; T. P. O'Connor talking about A. B. Forwood, *P.D.* 4th ser., vol. iv, col. 633.
2 *P.P.* 1877, xi, Qs. 773–4.
3 *L.R.* 18 May 1889. The Federal Council was homeless until it moved into Cook Street late in 1890.
4 *L.R.* 31 Aug., 5 Oct. 1889.
5 *L.R.* 26 Oct., 9 Nov. 1889.
6 *L.R.* 30 Aug., 6 Sept. 1890.
7 Brady, *op. cit.*, p. 152.
8 *L.R.* 28 June, 30 Aug. 1890.
9 *L.R.* 31 Aug., 7, 14, 21 Sept., 19, 26 Oct. 1889; *L.D.P.* 29 Oct., 2, 4, 5 Nov. 1889.
10 *L.R.* 31 Aug. 1889.
11 Sir John Bowring, quoted in J. McCarthy, *A History of our Own Times*, 1879–80, iii, p. 11.
12 C. A. Collins, *op. cit.*, p. 266. *Forward*, 27 Aug. 1912 contains some recollections of these contests.
13 W. Hamling, *A Short History of the Liverpool Trades' Council 1848–1948*, Liverpool, 1948, p. 31. The Liverpool S.D.F. was re-founded in 1892, principally by Joseph Goodman, one-time secretary of the L.T.C. Reeves was not connected with the new body—Bellamy and Saville, *Dictionary of Labour Biography*, i, pp. 282–5.
14 *P.* 20 March 1886; Sexton, *Agitator*, pp. 80–1.
15 *L.R.* 11 Sept. 1886; Simey, *op. cit.*, pp. 111–12.
16 *L.M.* 15 July 1886.
17 *Liverpool Central Relief and Charity Organization Society, 23rd Annual Report*, 1885–6, pp. 7–8. The distress was reflected in applications: 11,549 in 1882–3; 13,576 in 1883–4; 28,128 in 1884–5; 30,042 in 1885–6; 22,904 in 1886–7; 18,253 in 1887–8; 12,954 in 1888–9. The C.O.S.'s failure to perceive 'exceptional' distress was due to its recognition of a normally overstocked labour market and by comparison with 1878–9 when 35,073 applicants had been forthcoming. Nevertheless, the C.O.S. opened soup kitchens in the winter months between 1884 and 1887; it organized penny dinners in schools in the poorest districts; and it admitted over 1,000 men to its workshops, compared with under 500 in 'normal' years. For evidence of distress among Liverpool engineers, boiler-makers, ironfounders, bricklayers, carpenters and joiners, plumbers, and typographers, see *P.P.* 1886, xxii, pp. 10, 19, 24, 44, 58, 66, 84–85.

18 *L.D.P.* 3 Sept. 1886.
19 *T.* 3 Sept. 1886; *L.M.* 3 Sept. 1886.
20 *L.R.* 18 Sept. 1886.
21 *T.* 20 Sept. 1886.
22 *T.* 20, 21 Sept. 1886.
23 Hamling, *op. cit.*, p. 31.
24 Speech, 5 March 1887, quoted in Churchill, *Lord Randolph Churchill*, p. 697.

25 Hamling, *op. cit.*, pp. 15–18. On the role of Trades Councils, E. H. Phelps Brown, *The Growth of British Industrial Relations*, Papermac, 1965, pp. 240–4.

26 L.T.C. Minute Book II; S. G. Checkland, *The Rise of Industrial Society in England 1815–1885*, 1971 edition, pp. 415–16; R. Harrison, 'The British Working Class and the General Election of 1868', part ii, *International Review of Social History*, vi, 1961 pp. 103–9; R. V. Clements, 'British Trade Unions and Popular Political Economy, 1850–1875', *Ec.H.R.*, 2nd ser., xiv, 1961, pp. 93–104.

27 Orchard, *Legion*, p. 430, sourly described Kelly's mission as 'the advocacy of wages above the market value'. In fact temperance was his principal passion and his politics were Liberal—see T. Kelly to J. Bryce, 22 Jan. 1894, Bryce MS. UB 34.

28 *L.R.* 9 Feb. 1889, 13 Dec. 1890, 13 Jan. 1894; *P.* 19 May 1906. Brady, *op. cit.*, p. 283 wrongly states that Taggart was first elected in 1895 and B. D. White, *op. cit.*, p. 188 that Taggart was a docker and first elected in 1892.

29 Orchard, *Legion*, p. 659. Taggart ultimately accorded to the archetype of Nationalist councillor, becoming a self-made businessman. By 1910 he owned an estate agency. See B. O'Connell, *op. cit.*, pp. 114–17.

30 *L.C.* 25 Oct. 1889.

31 *L.M.* 7 April 1889. Technical education in Liverpool, despite considerable efforts, remained inadequate from the want of sound elementary education on which to build. See G. W. Roderick and M. D. Stephens, *Scientific and Technical Education in Nineteenth-Century England*, Newton Abbot, 1972, chaps. 3 and 5.

32 W. Nicholson to H. Pearson, 29 Dec. 1888, Picton Library, Liverpool, 331 TRA 5/4/2. In fact the union sent only one delegate to the L.T.C. in 1888, which, according to Rule 3, denoted less than one hundred paid members.

33 L.T.C. Minute Book II, 30 Nov., 1 Dec. 1887.

34 On Newcomb (b. 1849), his promotion of industrial organization among tramwaymen, scavengers, postmen, gas workers, and railwaymen in Liverpool, see essays by E. L. Taplin and R. Bean in H. R. Hikins (ed.), *Building the Union*, Liverpool, 1973, pp. 58, 108 although there is some contradiction concerning Newcomb's connection with the Knights of Labour.

35 L.T.C. Minute Book II, 24 July, 17 Aug., 5 Oct. 1888. Parkin represented the A.S.E.

36 Pearson's contest brought censure from his union, which did not re-elect him as a delegate in January 1889. Consequently the L.T.C. had to find another secretary—Joseph Goodman (Lithographical Society)—but he too was withdrawn by his union within two years when his views, as a Marxist Social Democrat, were considered unrepresentative.

37 L.T.C. Minute Book II, 5 Oct. 1888, 3 May 1889.

38 On the Sugar Bounties, which led to the closure of several refineries in Liverpool by 1900, see *L.D.P.* 12 April 1889; *P.D.*, 4th ser., lxxxvii, 946–7 (C. M'Arthur); B. H. Brown, *op. cit.*, chap. 2. As for sweated workshops, the *Lancet*, May 1888, listed 230 in Liverpool. Their prevalence dated from the mid 1870s and was blamed on machinery and pauper (Jewish) immigration. *P.P.* 1889, xiii, Appendix A; *P.P.* 1889, xiv, pt. 1. evidence by H. S. Richmond, J. B. Goodman, J. Allen, S. Bloch, and A. Davies.

39 See Bond's letters to J. Bryce, 4 Jan. 1893, 3 March 1894, seeking a magistracy, Bryce MS. UB 34; Watkinson, *op. cit.*, pp. 330–1, 528.

40 *L.R.* 10, 17 Aug. 1889; E. L. Taplin, 'The Liverpool Tramwaymen's Agitation of 1889', in Hikins, *op. cit.*, pp. 55–71.

41 L.T.C. Minute Book III, 25 June 1889; Smith, *Life Work*, pp. 148–51, Appendix iv.

42 Newspaper cutting in L.T.C. Minute Book II, May 1889.

43 Ibid. III, 30 Aug. 1889; Havelock Wilson, *op. cit.*, pp. 78–79, 127–8, 143–5.

44 L.T.C. Minute Book III, 25 Sept. 1889.

45 Taplin, *op. cit.*, pp. 62–63.

46 *L.R.* 21 Dec. 1889; Orchard, *Legion*, p. 497.

47 *L.D.P.* 6, 9, 16, 18 Dec. 1889; L.T.C. Minute Book III, 6, 10, Dec. 1889; *L.C.* 25 Oct. 1889.

48 *L.R.* 22 March 1890. The Union Secretary defended the decision in *L.R.* 29 March 1890. Some 500 carters engaged in unofficial action on behalf of the dockers—see R. Bean, 'The Liverpool Dock Strike of 1890', *International Review of Social History*, xviii, 1973, pt. 1, p. 65. The Mersey Quay and Railway Carters' Union (founded in 1889–90) had 4,433 registered members in December 1890, but only 2,780 in October 1891—*P.P.* 1890–1, lxxix, p. 670; *P.P.* 1892, lxxiii, p. 577.

49 Sexton, *Agitator*, p. 94.

50 *P.P.* 1892, xxxvi, pt. ii, Q. 13589.

51 Llewellyn Smith and Nash, *op. cit.*, p. 104; R. Bean's articles in Hikins, *op. cit.*, pp. 99–118, and *International Review of Social History*, *op. cit.*, pp. 51–68; Taplin, *Liverpool Dockers and Seamen 1870–1890*; E. Rathbone in *Transactions of the Liverpool Economic and Statistical Society 1903–4*, pp. 25.

52 Sexton, *Agitator*, p. 109; P. H. J. H. Gosden, *Self Help*, 1973, pp. 23–26, 180–9.

53 McHugh's testimony in *McHugh* versus *Kierman* libel action, heard in Liverpool—*L.D.P.* 19 Dec. 1890, E. M. Shepherd, first president of the Barrow branch of the N.U.D.L., mentions some faint contact with Liverpool in 1890—*P.P.* 1892, *op. cit.*, Q. 13551.

54 Sexton, *Agitator*, p. 95, wrote of 'seven long and sickening weeks'. Mr. R. Bean drew my attention to this discrepancy.

55 *Liverpool Citizen*, 2 April 1890; C. Watts and L. Davies, *Cunningham Graham*, Cambridge, 1979, pp. 90–1; J. Saville, 'Trade Unions and Free Labour: The Background to the Taff Vale Decision', in M. W. Flinn and T. C. Smout, *Essays in Social History*, Oxford, 1974, pp. 254–8.

56 Mott-Bower, *op. cit.*, p. 157.

57 *Liverpool Citizen*, 19 March 1890. On Kennedy, 'an omnipresent detector of idleness' among his employees, see Orchard, *op. cit.*, p. 431; on the Employers Labour Association, founded in February 1890, see R. Bean 'Employers Associations in the Port of Liverpool, 1890–1914', *International Review of Social History*, xxi, 1976, pt. 3.

58 *Liverpool Citizen*, *op. cit.*; Hikins, *op. cit.*, pp. 68–70, for the role of the *Mercury* and *Review* during the tramwaymen's dispute.

59 T. W. Moody, 'Michael Davitt and the British Labour Movement 1882–1906', *T.R.H.S.*, 5th ser., vol. 3, 1953; F. Sheehy-Skeffington, *Michael Davitt*, 1908, reprinted 1967, pp. 147–8.

60 *P.P.* 1892, *op. cit.*, Qs. 13600–1. The details of the settlement are obscure but a later version of them is reprinted in Taplin, *Liverpool Dockers*, Appendix D.

61 E. Rathbone, *op. cit.*, p. 25; C. Bradlaugh, 'Force or Conciliation in Labour Disputes', in J. Samuelson (ed.), *Subjects of the Day*, Aug. 1890, p. 129; J. Burnett (Labour Correspondent of the Board of Trade) in *J.S.S.*, vol. 55, 1892, p. 128.

62 Sexton, *Agitator*, pp. 103, 107, 113. Nationally the N.U.D.L.'s membership

slumped from nearly 25,000 in December 1890 to 13,000 in December 1891—*P.P.* 1890–1, lxxix, p. 680; *P.P.* 1892, lxxiii, p. 592.

63 The Bootle assembly of the Knights of Labour ceased to rival the N.U.D.L. in this district following the strike—H. Pelling, 'The Knights of Labour in Britain, 1880–1901', *Ec.H.R.*, 2nd. ser., vol. 9, 1956–7, p. 322.

64 This is conjecture. The subscription was 3*d.* per week but members might be twelve weeks in arrears without forfeiting full membership—Rathbone, *op. cit.* According to the T.U.C.'s record, the N.U.D.L. declined from 14,000 to 12,000 members, 1891–1902, and was then static until 1911. The Dock, Wharf, and Riverside General Labourers' Union declined from 40,000 to 14,000, 1891–1900.

65 Tillett, *Memories* pp. 116–17; preface to 1892 edition of *Engels: 'The Condition of the Working Class in England'*, ed. W. O. Henderson and W. H. Chaloner, Oxford, 1958, p. 371; and, for an opponent of trade unionism, Brodrick, pp. 193–4. In one sense New Unionism merely reflected the self-conscious novelty of the 1890s, when not to be new was to be nothing—see Holbrook Jackson, *The Eighteen Nineties*, 1913, Penguin edition, 1939, p. 24.

66 *N.U.D.L. Annual Report, Year Ending 30 June 1891*, pp. 12–13, T.U.C. Library. Cf. Llewellyn Smith and Nash, *op. cit.*, p. 164.

67 S. Maddock, 'The Liverpool Trades Council and Politics 1878–1918', University of Liverpool, M.A. thesis, 1959, p. 69; Havelock Wilson, *op. cit.*, chap. xviii.

68 *L.D.P.* 28 Nov. 1890.

69 *L.D.P.* 20 Nov. 1891.

70 *Dock, Wharf, Riverside and General Labourers' Union, 1st Annual Report, 30 Sept. 1890*, pp. 4–5, 8. Cf. Llewellyn Smith and Nash *op. cit.*, p. 167; H. A. Clegg, A. Fox, and A. F. Thompson, *A History of British Trade Unions since 1889*, Oxford, 1964, i, p. 93; Stedman Jones *op. cit.*, pp. 315–21, 346–8.

71 Liverpool Steam Ship Owners' Association Minutes and Letter-Book, May–June 1880; *P.P.* 1892, *op. cit.*, Q. 12056, T. Parr; J. Samuelson, *Boards of Conciliation in Labour Disputes*, 1891, p. 23; Bradlaugh in *Subjects of the Day*, *op. cit.*, pp. 121–2. An arbitration system operated from 1874 in Liverpool's building trade, and was also the goal of the Coremakers' Society—see Clapham, *op. cit.*, iii, 1932, p. 175; *Dictionary of Labour Biography*, i, pp. 282–5. On the iron, hosiery, lace, and boot and shoe trades, see Clegg, Fox, and Thompson, *op. cit.*, pp. 21–26.

72 *P.P.* 1892, *op. cit.*, Qs. 13586, 13605–6, 13617–22. Cf. J. Sexton, *A Criticism of the Workmen's Compensation Act*, Liverpool, 1900, p. 14; *P.P.* 1892, xxxv, Q. 647, T. McCarthy; B. Tillett, *The Dock Labourers' Bitter Cry*, 1889, p. 6.

73 L. L. Price, 'The Position and Prospects of Industrial Conciliation', *J.S.S.*, vol. 53, Sept. 1890, pp. 420–59; *P.P.* 1892, xxxv (Report), p. 100; Sir Michael Hicks-Beach in *L.C.* 19 Feb. 1891.

74 Sexton, *Agitator*, p. 95.

75 L.T.C. Minute Book III, 7 March 1890.

76 *L.T.C. Annual Report March 1890–March 1891*, preamble. Havelock Wilson cited the L.T.C.'s activities in contradiction of John Burns's charge that Trades Councils were supine. The L.T.C., said Wilson, was 'organizing women, scavengers, and any who desired to be organized. (Applause)'. *Report, 23rd Annual T.U.C., 1890*, p. 32.

77 *Liverpool Citizen*, 23, 30 April 1890; *L.R.* 12 April 1890. O'Connor subscribed merely one guinea towards the relief of strikers' families. Later, however, he won the dockers' thanks for his efforts in Parliament to ensure their inclusion in Workmen's Compensation Acts—Sexton, *Agitator* pp. 84–85, 126, 297.

78 *Liverpool Citizen*, 30 April 1890.

79 *L.C.* 10 March 1890.

80 *L.M.* 22 Sept. 1890.

81 Richard Holt's diary, 10 Jan. 1905; Orchard, *op. cit.*, p. 136; G. G. Armstrong, *Richard Acland Armstrong: A memoir*, 1906; Sellers, *op. cit.*, pp. 258–62; Snell, *op. cit.*, p. 34. Armstrong believed in the indissolubility of 'religious and political Liberalism'—quoted in Koss, p. 17 n.l.

82 R. A. Armstrong, *The Deadly Shame of Liverpool*, Liverpool, 1890, pp. 3–5, 16–17. His italics. See also *P.D.*, 4th ser. iv, 641–2, S. Smith and A. B. Forwood; *L.R.* 12 Sept. 1891.

83 *L.D.P.* 16 Oct. 1890; Armstrong's reply to Tory critics in *L.D.P.* 31 Oct. 1890. Samuel Smith sent £20 towards the cost of distributing 15,000 copies of Armstrong's pamphlet during the elections—G. G. Armstrong, *op. cit.*, p. 104.

84 *L.D.P.* 31 Oct. 1890. On the campaign against the publication of 'indecent' evidence—Smith, *Life-Work*, pp. 236–7, 252–4, Appendix ix; *Church of England Purity Society, 4th Annual Report, April 1887*, pp. 13–14.

85 *P.P.* 1871, xix, Q. 12878, Mrs. J. Butler; W. Acton, *Prostitution*, 2nd. edition, 1870, p. 295; *Liverpool Domestic Mission Society, 23rd Annual Report*, 1860, p. 19 ff.; Havelock Ellis, *Impressions and Comments*, 1914, p. 44. 36 per cent of occupied unmarried females aged over ten in Liverpool were domestic servants in 1900—A. Harrison, *op. cit.*, p. 17.

86 F. W. Lowndes, *Prostitution and Venereal Diseases in Liverpool*, 1886, pp. 41–49; *P.P.* 1882, ix, Dr. Lowndes. The treatment of syphilis was by mercurous products which were potentially dangerous. Medical advances came after 1905 with the Wassermann reaction and the discovery of salvarsan. Not until 1916, under the Local Government Board's regulations, were Corporation Hospitals Committees obliged to provide for the treatment of venereal diseases. The Government granted 75 per cent of expenditure.

87 Nott-Bower, *op. cit.*, pp. 141–2; *L.D.P.* 23 Dec. 1890.

88 Lowndes, *op. cit.*, p. 10. The Vigilance Committee initiated proceedings against individual prostitutes, not against brothels, under the Vagrancy Act. The number of cases rose from 67 in 1869, to 301 in 1870, 3,388 in 1871; they continued between 2,000 and 4,000 annually throughout the 1870s. Another 1,300 to 2,500 cases were brought against prostitutes annually in the 1870s under laws relating to disorderly conduct. Laws concerning the abatement of nuisances afforded opportunities to proceed against brothels, and from 1885 brothel-keeping was a statutory offence. The difficulty, however, was in proving guilty knowledge or wilful connivance by the owner of the premises used as a brothel. See *P.P.* 1882, *op. cit.*, Qs. 12162–9 and Appendix 29, Dr. Lowndes; *P.D.*, 4th ser., xxxi, 1034–5; C. Rover, *Love, Morals and the Feminists*, 1970, p. 69; J. L. and B. Hammond, *James Stansfeld*, 1932, p. 169.

89 Quoted in Larkin, *op. cit.*, p. 5.

90 *L.M.* 26 May 1888, 14 June 1888.

91 Thomas Matheson in *L.M.* 16 May 1888. The Vigilance Committee of the 1870s now worked in the Association for the Repression of Immorality—see its memorial to the Corporation, *L.C.* 5 June 1888.

92 Sir Leonard Dunning, speaking as H.M. Inspector of Constabulary, *P.P.* 1920, xxii, Q. 1465; Nott-Bower, *op. cit.*; letter from W. Boyd, Chief Constable of Glasgow, *L.D.P.* 16 Oct. 1890. Boyd made a similar statement in 1900, which was uncritically accepted by the National Vigilance Committee—see Smith, *Life Work*, pp. 602–3. The Glasgow authorities had earlier boasted that their local Police Act (1870) brought an enormous reduction in prostitution without recourse to the Contagious Diseases Act—see *P.P.* 1881, viii, Qs. 7386–7, 7655, evidence of Glasgow's Chief Constable, McCall; *P.P.* 1882, ix, Qs. 2836 ff., Dr. Patterson, of Glasgow Lock Hospital. Liverpool's Dr. Lowndes was sceptical—*P.P.* 1882, *op. cit.*, Qs. 12104–563. Certainly, before 1870, Glasgow was notorious for street solicitation—Josephine Butler herself was importuned there, see *P.P.* xix, Q. 12968.

93 *L.M.* 28 Nov. 1889.

94 *L.R.* 21 July, 11, 18 Aug. 1888; *P.P.* 1857–8, ix, Q. 5187 for the Rector of Liverpool describing St. Peter's parish—twenty-one of its thirty-one brothels were in one street. Josephine Butler argued that the Contagious Diseases Acts scattered prostitutes amid respectable working-class districts, *P.P.* 1871, *op. cit.*, Qs. 13010–13.

95 Lowndes, *op. cit.*, p. 7. In year ending 29 Sept. 1885, 128 known prostitutes were proceeded against on indictment, and 5,240 summarily, in Liverpool. These were not necessarily individuals. Except for London no other town had anything like these figures *P.P.* 1886, lxxii, pp. 94–95. Lowndes's estimate in 1886 was 1,000 higher than his estimate in 1882, see *P.P.* 1882, *op. cit.*, Qs. 12173, 12179; but neither is reliable owing to the amount of casual prostitution. Josephine Butler reckoned that one-sixth of Liverpool's prostitutes practised for about two years and then either married or set up in trade, commonly with a sewing machine, *P.P.* 1871, *op. cit.*, Qs. 12949–56.

96 Quoted in Lowndes, *op. cit.*, p. 3. Cf. *The Stranger in Liverpool*, p. 69.

97 *P.P.* 1836, xxxiv, Appendix G, pp. 10 G. Forwood, 18 Dr. Duncan, 23 Revd. P. Wilcock; Lowndes, *op. cit.*, p. 4.

98 *L.D.P.* 27 March 1889; B. Harrison, *op. cit.*, p. 324. William Tirebuck (1854–1900), the Liverpool novelist, depicted a 'free and easy' in *Dorrie*, 1891, chap. xxx. This novel, about a Liverpool prostitute, could find neither reviewer nor retailer in Liverpool when first published—see Hall Caine's preface, W. E. Tirebuck, *Twixt God and Mammon*, 1903.

99 Thomas Cropper in *L.M.* 28 Nov. 1889. Seduction by wealthy men was probably an inconsiderable cause of most working-class prostitution, although Mrs. Butler accounted it responsible for the fall of several daughters of tradesmen, and even of clergymen, *P.P.* 1871, *op. cit.*, Qs. 12879, 12931.

100 On the persistence of gross prostitution in Liverpool throughout the nineteenth century, see Midwinter, *Old Liverpool*, p. 55; *The Journals and Miscellaneous Notebooks of Ralph Waldo Emerson*, vol. x, 1847–8, Harvard, 1973, pp. 333, 550–1; J. Ruskin, *Fors Clavigera*, letter 48 (Dec. 1874).

101 *N.L.T.* 29 Aug. 1885; *L.R.* 7, 28 Aug., 4 Sept., 9, 16 Oct. 1886; Shimmin, *Liverpool Sketches*, pp. 119–20; *P.D.*, 3rd ser., cccxxvii, 974, W. F. Lawrence. Novelists carried this exaggeration of organized crime to the extreme—see A. Morrison, *A Child of the Jago*, 1896, chaps. 5, 24; Sir A. Conan Doyle, *The Memoirs of Sherlock Holmes*, Penguin edition, 1967, p. 239.

102 Shimmin, *op. cit.*, p. 122.

103 *L.D.P.* 22 Dec. 1885.

104 *L.D.P.* 12, 26 July 1892, Cf. B. D. White, *op. cit.*, p. 110.

105 *L.D.P.* 4 July 1895.

106 *L.R.* 13 Nov. 1886; J. D. Crawford, *Reflections and Recollections*, 1936, pp. 59–60.

107 *L.C.* 18 July 1901; deposition by Mary Mannan, illiterate, Public Record Office, Assizes 52/2.

108 *T.* 28 Jan. 1884; Diggle, *op. cit.*, pp. 193–4.

109 Smith, *Life Work*, p. 108.

110 *L.D.P.* 18 Nov. 1891. The coroner, Clarke Aspinall, was a vice-president of the Church of England Temperance Society. He died in December 1891. See *Church of England Temperance Society Annual Report, 1891*, p. 28.

111 Quoted in G. G. Eastwood, *George Isaacs: Printer, Trade Union Leader, Cabinet Minister*, 1952, p. 25.

112 *P.* 16 Dec. 1905.

113 *Benjamin Townson*, by his daughter, n.d. 1895, pp. 79, 88, 96.

114 P. L. Payne, 'The Emergence of the Large-scale Company in Great Britain, 1870–1914', *Ec.H.R.*, 2nd ser., xx, 1967, pp. 519–42; C. F. Aked, *Changing Creeds and Social Struggles*, 1893, pp. 189, 196, 230; *Liverpool Opinion*, 19 May 1906. Cf. John Finch quoted in Winskill and Thomas, *op. cit.*, p. 24.

115 N. Longmate, *The Waterdrinkers*, 1968, chaps. 4, 5; Winskill and Thomas, *op. cit.*, chaps. 2, 3; R. B. Rose, 'John Finch, 1784–1857: A Liverpool Disciple of Robert Owen', and J. Murphy, 'Robert Owen in Liverpool', *T.H.S.L.C.*, vol. 109, 1957, pp. 159–85, vol. 112, 1960, pp. 79–103.

116 *P.P.* 1897, xxxv, Qs. 11311–3, A. T. Davies.

117 Escott, *England*, p. 88.

118 *T.* 17 Nov. 1877; D. Butler and J. Freeman, *British Political Facts 1900–1960*, 1963, p. 236. A higher consumption may have existed in the 1820s or 1830s, from the amount of illicit distilling, brewing, and traffic, which official statistics cannot measure.

119 *L.D.P.* 14 Nov. 1888; J. Samuelson (ed.), *The Civilization of our Day*, 1896, p. 228 n. The police were also considered irresponsible drinkers—*L.D.P.* 25 Oct., 6 Dec. 1888; *P.P.* 1920, xxii, Q. 10399, Dunning.

120 *L.D.P.* 14 Nov. 1888.

121 G. R. Sims, *How the Poor Live, and Horrible London*, 1889, p. 135; J. Rowntree and A. Sherwell, *The Temperance Problem and Social Reform*, 1899, pp. 3–26.

122 A. E. Dingle, 'Drink and Working-Class Living Standards in Britain, 1870–1914', *Ec.H.R.*, 2nd ser., xxv, no. 4, 1972, pp. 608–22.

123 *P.* 23 Jan., 6 Feb. 1886. Cf. Rowntree and Sherwell, *op. cit.*, pp. 419–20; Diggle, *op. cit.*, p. 118.

124 Lawton and Pooley, *op. cit.*, pp. 149–68; 'Nunquam' (Robert Blatchford), *Merrie England*, 1894, p. 73. Cf. *Liverpool Town Planning and Housing Exhibition 1914*, p. 131; S. Reynolds, *A Poor Man's House*, 1909, pp. 268–9; J. Burnett, *Plenty and Want*, 1966, on adulteration; A. White, *The Problems of a Great City*, 1886, pp. 155–6.

125 Quoted in *L.R.* 5 June 1900.

126 *Liverpool Citizen*, 18 June 1890; Shimmin, *op. cit.*, chap. 1; *L.R.* 31 Jan. 1885; *P.P.* 1897, *op. cit.*, Q. 12202, T. E. Sampson; *Toxteth Observer*, 24 Dec. 1881; H. R. Jones, 'The Perils and Protection of Infant Life', *J.S.S.*, vol. 57, 1894, pp. 38–42.

127 *P.D.*, 5th ser., vol. 194, cols. 1605–13; Keeling, *op. cit.*, pp. 58–61.

128 *Toxteth Observer*, 24 Sept. 1881; J. J. Baker, *The Economy of Temperance*, 1909, pp. 20–21; H. R. Jones, *op. cit.*, pp. 78–79.

129 *L.R.* 29 May 1886.

130 D. E. Muir, *Lift the Curtain*, 1955, p. 18.

131 Robert Holt's diary, 28 Nov. 1887, 9 Nov. 1889, 27 Jan., 12 Feb. 1893.

132 *P.P.* 1897, *op. cit.*, Q. 11191, A. T. Davies; *P.D.*, 4th ser., iv, 641–2, S. Smith; R. D. Holt to J. Bryce, 12 Sept. 1892; W. Poulson to Bryce, 23 Sept. 1892; J. Bright to Bryce, 12 Nov. 1892; Bryce's Cabinet Memoranda, 12 Feb. and 7 March 1893, Bryce MSS.

133 Report, 14 Nov. 1889, quoted in Nott-Bower, *op. cit.*, p. 135.

134 R. Gladstone to J. G. Livingston, 4 Aug. 1875, quoted by Forwood, in *L.M.* 28 Oct. 1895.

135 On the controversy over the 'free trade' experiment, see Winskill and Thomas, *op. cit.*, pp. 64–69; *P.P.* 1877, xi, Qs. 263 ff., S. Rathbone, 402 ff., E. Lawrence. Reformers were divided—William Rathbone defended it, *P.D.*, 3rd ser., ccxxix, 17 May 1876; but Wilfrid Lawson, speaking at Birmingham, 17 Feb. 1864, called it 'a total failure', Bodleian, ref. no. 1687 and 61 (30); and Samuel Smith, in 1892, called it 'a deplorable blunder', *P.D.*, 4th ser., iv. 642. On Sir A. B. Walker's multimillion-pound fortune, see Orchard, *op. cit.*, pp. 688–91.

136 *P.P.* 1897, *op. cit.*, Qs. 11318–20, 11365–71, 11517, A. T. Davies, 12088–119,

12147–52, Miss H. M. Johnson; A. T. Davies, *A Survey of Liverpool's 144 Lapsed Licences, and What it Teaches*, 1897, p. 2; *P.D.*, 3rd ser., cccliii, 1369, W. B. Rowlands.

137 Davies, *op. cit.*, p. 4; A. T. Davies, *The Relation of Municipal Action to Morals*, 1899, p. 9.

138 *L.R.* 22 Aug. 1891.

139 *The Liverpool Brewers' and Victuallers' Journal*, 1 March 1890.

140 *L.R.* 1, 8 March 1890.

141 *L.R.* 7, 28 Sept. 1889, 17, 24, 31 May 1890; B. O'Connell, *op. cit.*, p. 139.

142 Goschen's Budget in April 1890 revealed that 1889–90 was the most drunken year since 1874–5. £2½ million out of the £3¼ million surplus derived from drink. See H. W. Lucy, *op. cit.*, 1892, p. 262 ff; Lady Raleigh (ed.), *The Letters of Sir Walter Raleigh 1879–1922*, 1926, i, pp. 144–5, for an account of John Morley's Liverpool speech on Ireland and temperance reform.

143 Quoted in *L.D.P.* 29 Oct. 1890.

144 *L.R.* 23 Aug., 13 Sept. 1890.

145 *L.R.* 27 Sept., 4 Oct. 1890.

146 *L.D.P.* 3 Nov. 1890.

147 *P.P.* 1897, *op. cit.*, Qs. 11581–9, A. T. Davies.

148 Ibid., Q. 11776, W. Crosfield; Smith, *op. cit.*, p. 129. On Crosfield, Liverpool businessman, Liberal M.P. Lincoln 1892–5, see Orchard, *Legion*, p. 258.

149 F. E. Smith, *Speeches Delivered in the House of Commons and Elsewhere 1906–1909*, Liverpool, 1910, p. 62. Cf. Rowntree and Sherwell, *op. cit.*, chap. 3 and pp. 213–14.

150 *P.P.* 1897, *op. cit.*, Q. 11767, W. Crosfield; Cf. *P.D.*, 4th ser., lxxxv, 273–4, S. Smith.

151 Orchard, *Legion*, p. 223.

152 *L.D.P.* 21 Oct. 1891.

153 *L.D.P.* 29 Oct. 1890.

154 *L.R.* 11 Oct. 1890.

155 *Liverpool Citizen*, 15 Oct. 1890.

156 Ibid. 8, 29 Oct. 1890.

157 *L.R.* 22 Nov. 1890. Cf. Koss, *Brunner*, pp. 66, 174.

158 Cf. *L.T.C.* Minute Book, ii, Jan. 1888, iii, March 1890.

159 *L.D.P.* 25, 27 Oct. 1890. Cf. Maddock, *op. cit.*, p. 113.

160 *L.D.P.* 3 Nov. 1890. Matkin made a similar complaint in 1893 when Everton F.C. declined to play in a benefit match for the unemployed. He moved 'that we recommend working men to support their various Trades Unions instead of running after Football clubs'. Carried unanimously. L.T.C. Minute Book, 29 Nov. 1893.

161 *L.R.* 18 Oct., 8 Nov. 1890.

162 *L.C.* 22 Oct. 1890; *L.R.* 12 Sept. 1891; Robert Holt's diary, 13, 23 Nov. 1890.

163 *L.C.* 10 Nov. 1890.

164 *L.M.* 9 Dec. 1890.

165 Nott-Bower, *op. cit.*, p. 144.

166 Lyulph Stanley's reaction to Samuel Smith's proposal to flog persons guilty of sexual offences against children—*P.D.*, 3rd ser., ccc, 744.

167 *L.D.P.* 30 Oct. 1891.

168 Letter in *L.D.P.* 17 Dec. 1890.

169 *L.D.P.* 23 Dec. 1890.

170 *L.C.* 20 Jan. 1891. There had always been tradesmen to exploit the unfortunate. The male bastards of Liverpool prostitutes had been sold to master-sweeps as climbing boys—see Clapham, *op. cit.*, iii, 1932, p. 415.

171 *L.C.* 20 June 1891; *L.D.P.* 23 Dec. 1890.

172 *L.M.* 5 March 1891; *L.C.* 3 July 1891.

173 Quoted in *L.R.* 28 Feb. 1891.

174 Nott-Bower, *op. cit.*, p. 145. A. B. Forwood, in an open letter sent to the press, 26 Oct. 1895, accounted the number of prosecutions of brothels as follows: 722 cases in 1891, 850 in 1892, 949 in 1893, 742 in 1894.

175 *L.R.* 21 March 1891.

176 *L.D.P.* 22 Oct. 1891.

177 *P.P.* 1883, lxxviii, pp. 193–4; *P.P.* 1893–4, civ, p. 171; *T.* 22 June 1891.

178 *T.* 13 June 1891; N. A. Humphreys, 'Results of the Recent Census and Estimates of Population in the Largest English Towns', *J.S.S.*, vol. 54, June 1891, pp. 311–40.

179 *P.P.* 1893–4, cvi, pt. iv, p. 14; D. C. Jones, *op. cit.*, i, pp. 59–65. Liverpool was the only large town to decline absolutely, 1881–91, though several suffered a decline in the rate of increase. The size of the Registrar-General's errors in his estimates—in the 1890s he was to err by 50,000 in the other direction, in Liverpool's case—led the Royal Statistical Society and the Society for Medical Officers of Health to make a deputation to the President of the Local Government Board in 1904, asking for a quinquennial census—see *J.S.S.*, vol. 67, June 1904, pp. 272–81.

180 *L.C.* 30 April, 2 May 1891.

181 Letter in *L.C.* 3 May 1891.

182 Letter from 'True Loyalty', *L.C.* 5 May 1891.

183 Letter in *L.C.* 4 May 1891.

184 W. Oulton to Lord Derby, 18 Nov. 1890, Derby MSS.

185 *L.C.* 19 Nov. 1890.

186 *L.D.P.* 18 Nov. 1890.

187 *L.C.* 30 April 1891.

188 Brady, *op. cit.*, p. 255.

189 *L.D.P.* 19 Nov. 1890.

190 *L.D.P.* 18 Nov. 1890.

191 W. O'Malley, *Glancing Back*, 1933, p. 124; F. S. L. Lyons, *The Fall of Parnell 1890–91*, 1960, p. 75; *L.D.P.* 20 Nov. 1890.

192 *L.D.P.* 21, 22 Nov. 1890.

193 *L.D.P.* 24 Nov. 1890.

194 *L.D.P.* 25, 26 Nov. 1890.

195 Lyons, *op. cit.*, pp. 320–6; *L.D.P.* 1 Dec. 1890.

196 Lyons, *op. cit.*, p. 179.

197 Letter in *L.D.P.* 6 Dec. 1890. The branch activity of the Liverpool I.N.L. was irreparably disjointed from this date. By 1896 only 2,500 members were noted. B. O'Connell, *op. cit.*, pp. 152–60.

198 *L.D.P* 15 Dec. 1890. At North Kilkenny Sir John Pope-Hennessy (Anti-Parnellite) beat Vincent Scully (Parnellite) by 2,527 to 1,365. See J. H. Whyte, 'The Influence of the Catholic Clergy on Elections in Nineteenth-Century Ireland', *E.H.R.* ccxcv, April 1960, p. 256.

199 *Liverpool Citizen*, 26 Nov. 1890.

200 *L.D.P.* 14 July 1891.

201 *P.S.* 7 May 1910, 4 March 1911. Parnell denied having used the expression 'Papist rats'—R. O'Brien, *op. cit.*, i, p. 192.

202 *L.D.P.* 14 July 1891; *L.R.* 18 July 1891.

203 *L.D.P.* 14 July 1891.

204 R. Griffiths, *Life Story of Pastor George Wise*, Toxteth, 1909.

205 *Proceedings and Report of the Commissioner, Police (Liverpool Inquiry) Act 1909* p. 733.

206 *P.S.* 7 June 1890.
207 *P.S.* 18 April 1891.
208 *P.S.* 22 Feb. 1890.
209 *P.S.* 18 July 1891.
210 *P.S.* 24 Oct. 1891.
211 *L.R.* 24 Oct. 1891.
212 *P.S.* 5 March, 7 May 1892. Wise's lectures on 'Theosophy', delivered to the Y.M.C.A., are reported in *P.S.* 12 March 1892 et seqq.
213 *L.R.* 19, 26, Sept. 1891.
214 *L.D.P.* 21 Oct. 1891; *L.R.* 24 Oct. 1891.
215 *L.C.* 26 Aug. 1891.
216 Interview with H. E. Clare, 1899, Webb Local Government Collection, vol. 148; Beatrice Webb's Diary, vol. 20, 10 Oct. 1899, Webb MSS.; B. D. White, *op. cit.*, p. 182; Orchard, *Legion*, p. 234; Robert Holt's diary, 5, 23 July, 2 Aug., 6 Sept. 1899. On the importance of town clerks in the progress of certain corporations, A. L. Lowell, *op. cit.* ii, p. 179.
217 *P.P.* 1894, xvii, Qs. 10064, 10075, H. E. Clare.
218 *L.D.P.* 25 Oct. 1892.
219 *L.C.* 26 Aug. 1891; *P.D.*, 4th ser., iv, 616–28, A. B. Forwood.
220 *L.C.* 28 Oct. 1891; *L.R.* 28 Nov. 1891.
221 *L.D.P.* 3 Nov. 1891.
222 *L.D.P.* 28, 30 Oct. 1891. The L.T.C. instructed Sam Reeves to vote 'the whole hog or none' in the 'Eight-Hour Day' debate of the T.U.C. in September 1891. Reeves observed, only half humorously, that the L.T.C. was 'a most Conservative and most respectable body', but that he had converted it on this question. *Report, 24th Annual T.U.C., 1891* p. 52.
223 *P.P.* 1889, v, Qs. 289–321, evidence of H. J. Hagger, Clerk to the Liverpool Vestry; *P.P.* 1889, xiii, Appendix A; *P.P.* 1889, xiv, pt. i, evidence of H. S. Richmond, J. B. Goodman, J. Allen, S. Bloch, A. Davies; L.T.C. Minute Book iv, 19 June 1891. The first Chinese laundry on Merseyside was Yee Chin's laundry at Newington in 1886, see *L.C.* 11 Dec. 1906. Sixty-three existed in Liverpool and Birkenhead by December 1906—*P.D.*, 4th ser., vol. 167, col. 132.
224 The L.T.C. questioned the Prime Minister and all Liverpool M.P.s on their attitude to immigration. The replies were reported at the L.T.C.'s 3 July meeting. Royden and Baden-Powell failed to reply on this occasion; but Royden's only recorded communication with the L.T.C., in March 1890, was on this subject. Whitley's, Royden's and O'Connor's hostility to the employment of foreign labour is preserved in their letters, Picton Library, Liverpool 331 TRA 5/4/4–6.
225 *L.D.P.* 26 Oct., 2 Nov. 1891; B. O'Connell, *op. cit.*, pp. 68–70, 187.
226 L.T.C. Minute Book IV, 4 Sept. 1891.
227 Ibid. 2 Oct. 1891.
228 *L.D.P.* 15 Oct. 1891.
229 *L.D.P.* 28 Oct. 1891.
230 *L.D.P.* 17 Oct., 2 Nov. 1891.
231 Letter from J. W. McGovern, *L.D.P.* 20 Oct. 1891.
232 Letter signed 'Consistent Platform', *L.D.P.* 15 Oct. 1891.
233 Letter from Charles Doeg, *L.D.P.* 16 Oct. 1891.
234 *L.D.P.* 13, 23 Oct. 1891.
235 *L.D.P.* 27 Oct. 1891.
236 *L.D.P.* 31 Oct. 1891.
237 *L.D.P.* 27 Oct. 1891. On the N.A.S.F.U., B. Mogridge, 'Militancy and Inter-

Union Rivalries in British Shipping, 1911–1929', *International Review of Social History*, vi, 1961, pp. 376–9; Havelock Wilson, *op. cit.*, passim.

238 L.T.C. Minute Book IV, 4 Dec. 1891.

CHAPTER 8

1 *T.* 22 Dec. 1891; letter from Sir. W. B. Forwood, *T.* 24 Dec. 1891. There was a precedent for the assurances which many Liverpool Conservatives demanded. The Gladstonian majority in Glasgow had extracted pledges from the Unionists when Lord Salisbury received the Freedom of the City, that the occasion would not be marked by a party demonstration. Letter, *T.* 28 Dec. 1891. Gladstone was to receive the Freedom of Liverpool in 1892. See Robert Holt's diary, 3 June, 13, 21 Dec. 1891, 14 Sept., 12 Oct., 3 Dec. 1892.

2 *L.R.* 17 Jan. 1891; *L.D.P.* 13 Nov. 1891.

3 Letters from 'Ex-Orangeman' and 'Mountjoy', *L.D.P.* 6, 13 Nov. 1891; *L.D.P.* 24, 27 Oct. 1891; *P.S.* 14 Nov. 1891.

4 *L.D.P.* 19 Nov. 1891.

5 Letter from Canon E. M'Neile, *L.D.P.* 12 Nov. 1891.

6 *L.D.P.* 13 Nov. 1891. Industrial schools were established by Sandon's Education Act, 1876, 'to deal effectively with the children of drunken and dissolute persons, for whom the ordinary fines under the Education Acts and the imprisonment following non-payment appeared to have no terror'. *Liverpool School Board Annual Report, 1888*, p. 5. By 1890 there were five such schools in Liverpool, four of them Board-managed.

7 *L.D.P.* 14 Nov. 1891. Cf. *P.P.* 1887, xxix, Qs. 32262–70, E. Hance, 34098–103, E. M'Neile.

8 M. E. Sadler, *Report on Secondary Education in Liverpool*, 1904, p. 11. Sadler had been commissioned by J. W. Alsop, the Liberal Unionist deputy-chairman of Liverpool Education Committee. Alsop afterwards did much to rectify the neglect of secondary education in Liverpool. See Alsop, *op. cit., passim.*

9 Hope, *City of Liverpool,* p. 243. Less than 37 per cent of Liverpool children were taught in Board Schools, compared with 67 per cent in 19 other large towns—*Liverpool School Board Report for the three years ending 25 November 1900*, p. 84.

10 *L.D.P.* 12, 13 Nov. 1891.

11 Oulton quoted in *L.D.P.* 14 Nov. 1891; *L.R.* 5 Dec. 1891. On Samuel Rathbone, the guiding spirit of the Board for its first two decades, see interview with Hance (clerk to the School Board) in the Webbs' Local Government Collection, vol. 148.

12 On Lester see obituary in *L.D.P.* 4 Nov. 1903; A. H. Grey-Edwards, *A Great Heart*, 1906. Oulton, in fact, became chairman of Liverpool Education Committee, 1903–13.

13 *L.D.P.* 13 Nov. 1891; *L.R.* 21 Nov. 1891. The number of prosecutions by Liverpool School Board visitors in 1886 was 3,700, and they applied for 1,761 attendance orders. See *P.P.* 1887, *op. cit.*, Q. 32132, E. Hance. The enforcement of attendance was increasingly successful in Liverpool—in 1871 only 52·7 per cent of registered pupils attended; in 1892 85·2 per cent; in 1924 91·3 per cent—Pumphrey, *op. cit.*, p. 160.

14 *P.S.* 5 Dec. 1891.

15 *L.R.* 23 Jan. 1892.

16 *L.D.P.* 22 Jan. 1892; *T.* 23 Jan. 1892.

17 *L.R.* 3 Jan. 1892; *L.D.P.* 27 Jan. 1892.

18 Letter from 'Newcomer' (a working-class Tory), *L.D.P.* 3 May 1891.

19 *T.* 27 Jan. 1892; *L.D.P.* 1, 3 Feb. 1892.

20 Willox had married Thomas Cope's widow in 1888.

21 *L.D.P.* 5 Feb. 1892.

22 *P.S.* 13 Feb. 1892. Three city councillors, R. D. Holt, Eli Brooks, and J. R. Grant, and the Welsh lawyer, Ellis Griffith, had been mentioned as possible Liberal candidates. *L.R.* 23 Jan. 1892; *T.* 5 Feb. 1892; *L.D.P.* 15 Jan. 1892. Griffith's name was raised first in 1890. His election expenses would have been paid locally, but his friends mostly regarded Everton as hopeless. Eventually he contested West Toxteth in 1892—see Ellis Griffith MSS. 352, 357, 380–1; Thomas Ellis MSS. 729, 862, 1928.

23 *L.R.* 20 Feb. 1892.

24 *L.D.P.* 6, 8 Feb. 1892.

25 *L.R.* 13 Feb. 1892.

26 *L.D.P.* 10 Feb. 1892.

27 *L.D.P.* 15 Feb. 1892.

28 *L.D.P.* 12, 13 Feb. 1892.

29 *L.D.P.* 13 Feb. 1892.

30 Two other candidates received votes: Patrick Kelly (Independent Nationalist) 205, and William Saxton (Conservative Temperance) 31.

31 *L.D.P.* 7 April 1892.

32 *L.D.P.* 17 Feb. 1892.

33 *L.D.P.* 6 Feb. 1892.

34 *L.D.P.* 20 Feb. 1892.

35 *L.R.* 27 Feb., 12 March 1892; *L.D.P.* 8 March, 14 June 1892.

36 *L.D.P.* 26 Feb., 7, 8, 10 March 1892; *L.R.* 19 March 1892.

37 *L.D.P.* 5, 8, 17 March 1892.

38 *L.D.P.* 23 April 1892.

39 *P.* 21 May 1892.

40 *L.R.* 2 April 1892.

41 *P.* 21 May 1892.

42 *L.C.* 4 June 1892.

43 *L.C.* 4, 5 July 1892.

44 *L.D.P.* 4 Feb. 1892; *L.R.* 25 June 1892; H. Miller, *Church Association: Scheme of Future Policy*, 1892; E. R. Norman, *op. cit.*, pp. 110–21, 223–5; Benson, *op. cit.*, ii, chap. vii.

45 *T.* 15 Sept. 1891.

46 W. J. Oldham, *The Ismay Line*, 1961, pp. 98–99.

47 *L.R.* 19 Sept., 14 Nov. 1891.

48 *L.R.* 2 Jan. 1892.

49 *P.D.*, 4th ser., vol. 153, cols. 1141–2; *T.* 15 April 1926.

50 R. Bean, 'Employers Associations in the Port of Liverpool, 1890–1914', *International Review of Social History*, xxi, 1976, pt. 3; *L.D.P.* 10 March 1892; Orchard, *op. cit.*, p. 405. Houston's liberality was not exceptional: the brewers, Cain and Walker, each gave £250.

51 *L.D.P.* 5 Nov. 1891.

52 S. Salvidge, *Salvidge of Liverpool*, 1934, p. 15.

53 *L.R.* 23 Feb. 1889.

54 *L.D.P.* 12 Feb. 1892.

55 *L.D.P.* 6 Feb., 1, 10 March 1892.

56 *L.D.P.* 17 March 1892; *L.R.* 19 March 1892.

57 *L.R.* 26 March 1892; *L.D.P.* 23 April 1892.

58 *P.S.* 4 June 1892.

59 *L.R.* 25 June 1892.

60 *T.* 24 June 1892.

61 *L.C.* 2 June 1892. Curtis, *op. cit.*, p. 133 n.32 wrongly dates this speech 1886.

62 See Sandys's speech in West Derby, *L.C.* 4 June 1892; *L.R.* 4 June 1892. The 14th Earl of Derby used a similar phrase about Catholics in the 1865 General Election—see R. Blake, *The Conservative Party from Peel to Churchill*, 1970, p. 87.

63 *L.R.* 6 Aug. 1892.

64 *P.S.* 16 Sept. 1892. The Home Secretary was Herbert Matthews.

65 *P.S.* 25 March 1893.

66 *L.C.* 22 Jan. 1892.

67 *L.C.* 6 July 1892. Cf. *P.S.* 23 July 1892; Lucas, *op. cit.*, p. 100; Dicey *op. cit.*, pp. 182–3; P. Buckland, *Ulster Unionism and the Origins of Northern Ireland 1886–1922*, Dublin and New York, 1973, p. 11.

68 Benson, *op. cit.*, ii, p. 348.

69 *L.D.P.* 4 Nov. 1891.

70 *L.C.* 30 April 1891; *The Radical Programme*, *op. cit.*, chap. vii.

71 *L.R.* 2 May 1891; *P.D.*, 3rd ser., cccliv, 1234–7, W. F. Lawrence, 1906–7, W. H. Cross.

72 *L.R.* 25 April 1891.

73 *L.C.* 30 April 1891. Cf. McDowell, *op. cit.*, p. 143.

74 Gardiner, *op. cit.* ii, p. 105. For the argument about the value of temperance workers in the Liberal ranks see Harcourt to W. S. Caine, 1 Aug. 1892; Caine to Harcourt, 2 Aug. 1892, Harcourt MSS. 220, fols. 121–6.

75 Open letter, A. B. Forwood to Revd. J. S. Drummond, 18 Nov. 1885. Cf. *P.P.* 1877, xi, Qs. 503–5, E. Lawrence.

76 *P.P.* 1897, xxxv, Qs. 11446, 12002–4, 12047–8, Miss H. M. Johnson.

77 Forwood writing to *L.C.*, 24 Aug. 1892; *L.C.* 21 April 1892.

78 *L.C.* 11 July 1892; *P.* 16 July 1892; correspondence of Revd. C. Aked and Sir William Harcourt, *L.D.P.* 12 April 1892.

79 A. B. Forwood to Lord Salisbury, 15 July 1892, Salisbury MSS.

80 Lord Wolmer to A. Akers-Douglas, 27 July 1888, quoted in Chilston, *Chief Whip*, pp. 141–2.

81 *L.C.* 28 Aug. 1891.

82 W. Oulton to Lord Derby, 23 June 1890, Derby MSS.

83 *T.* 17 Jan. 1890. Cf. Sanderson and Roscoe, *op. cit.* ii, p. 196; Cooke and Vincent, *op. cit.*, p. 439; Brodrick, *Literary Fragments*, pp. 536, 550–1, 557.

84 *L.C.* 20 Feb. 1890. The Committee was composed of equal numbers from both parties. The Conservatives included representatives of all sections—Forwood, Edward Lawrence, John Houlding, Charles Wycherley, Harry Thomas.

85 See speech to the Maghull Conservative Association, *L.C.* 29 Aug. 1890.

86 A. Bencke to Lord Derby, 14 April 1892, Derby MSS.

87 Idem, 31 March 1892.

88 Steel was Liverpool born of Scots parents; a former director of the Cotton Association; chairman of Wallasey Local Board in 1891.

89 Bencke to Derby, 31 March 1892, Derby MSS.

90 Lord Sefton to Lord Derby, 8 April 1892, Derby MSS.

91 *L.C.* 28 Aug. 1891; *T.* 5 April 1892; *L.D.P.* 5 April 1892.

92 A. B. Forwood to Schomberg McDonnell (Salisbury's political secretary), 24 July 1895. Forwood, however, recommended Ismay for a baronetcy in 1897—A. B. Forwood to Lord Salisbury, 20 March 1897, Salisbury MSS—an honour which Ismay refused. Sir William Forwood remembered Ismay more affectionately, see Forwood, *Reminiscences*, pp. 40–42.

93 Mersey, *op. cit.*, pp. 18, 89.

94 *T.* 23, 25 June 1892. On Jones see P. N. Davies, 'The African Steam Ship Company', in J. R. Harris, *op. cit.*, chap. viii. Among other claims to fame, Jones is remembered as one who did much to promote the banana in Britain.

95 *T.* 29 June 1892. Bigham's maiden parliamentary speech in 1897 was described by J. J. Clancy (Nationalist, Dublin Co. North) as 'the kind of speech that almost filled Irish members with despair . . . that the ABC of the Irish case still needed to be dinned into the skulls and intellects of hon. Members opposite'. *P.D..*, 4th ser., xlviii, 161–6.

96 *L.M.* 7 May 1889 et seqq.; Gardiner, *op. cit.* ii, p. 77.

97 *L.R.* 11 May 1889, 8 Feb. 1890.

98 *L.R.* 3 Jan. 1891.

99 *L.D.P.* 7, 13 July 1892; *L.C.* 8 July 1892; letters in *L.C.* 19 Feb., 7 July 1892, *L.D.P.* 18, 23 Feb. 1892.

100 *L.C.* 1 July 1892.

101 *P.* 18 June 1892; Robert Holt's diary, 5 July 1892.

102 Hamilton retired after a hunting accident in Scotland, *L.D.P.* 13 Oct. 1887; *L.C.* 6 Aug. 1888. On the Liberals' unpreparedness, Robert Holt, diary, 5 Aug. 1888.

103 *T.* 6 Aug. 1888; *L.R.* 15 Sept. 1888.

104 *L.R.* 18 May, 14 Dec. 1889, 21 June, 12, 26 July 1890.

105 *L.D.P.* 30 March 1892; *L.R.* 30 July 1892; Richard Rutherford to Lord Derby, 18 July 1929, Derby MSS., for Smith's share dealings. Rutherford described Smith as 'in every respect mercenary'.

106 *P.* 25 June 1892.

107 *T.* 14 Jan. 1888. Gibson had tried to advance George Wyndham, then Balfour's private secretary and without a seat in Parliament—see Wyndham's letter to his mother, 5 Feb. 1888, Mackail and Wyndham, *op. cit.*, i, p. 218, where Mattinson is misspelt. J. Biggs-Davison, *George Wyndham. A Study in Toryism*, 1951, p. 50 wrongly dates the by-election.

108 *T.* 16 Jan. 1888. Wilson was also a miner, and had been M.P. Houghton-le-Spring, 1885–6.

109 *T.* 21, 26 Jan. 1888.

110 *T.* 18 Jan., 4 Feb. 1888; *L.R.* 21 Aug. 1888. For Mattinson's species of Tory Democratic opinions see M. W. Mattinson to Lord R. Churchill, 30 Dec. 1886, Churchill, MSS. RCHL 1/18/2256.

111 *The Tory*, 25 June 1892; *L.D.P.* 17 June 1907; *P.D.*, 4th ser., cxviii, 965.

112 *L.R.* 31 Jan., 26 Sept. 1891.

113 *L.R.* 26 March 1892; *L.D.P.* 25 March 1892; Winskill and Thomas, *op. cit.*, pp. 82–83.

114 *L.R.* 2 April 1892.

115 D. Keir, *The Bowring Story*, 1962, p. 201.

116 *L.D.P.* 21 Jan. 1892; Robert Holt's diary, 5 July 1892.

117 Resolution of the Liverpool N.U.D.L. 15 April 1891, Picton Library, Liverpool 331 TRA/5/3/11.

118 *T.* 10 Aug. 1891. The L.T.C. had long considered West Derby. In 1885 the secretary, Alexander Clarke, believed that Labour's prospects were good because 'it was a thorough working-class constituency'. *Report, 18th Annual T.U.C. 1885*, p. 33. Strangely, however, though Matkin initiated Labour's municipal contests in West Derby ward in 1889, and Morrissey won Kensington ward in 1905 (part of West Derby parliamentary constituency), Labour did not fight West Derby in a General Election until after the First World War. It was in Edge Hill (part of the redistributed West Derby constituency) that Labour won its first parliamentary seat in Liverpool in 1923. See Chapter 16.

119 L.T.C. Minute Book IV, 4 Sept. 1891. Reeves repeated, and Threlfall denied, these allegations at meetings on 16 and 30 March 1892. Reeves had joined the L.E.A. in

1890, as the representative of a Bootle branch of the Knights of Labour, endeavouring to ginger the L.E.A. into a more radical position. In 1892 Reeves was president of Kirkdale L.E.A.—H. Pelling, 'The Knights of Labour in Britain, 1880–1901', *Ec.H.R..*, 2nd ser., vol. 9, 1956–7, p. 327; Bellamy and Saville, *Dictionary of Labour Biography*, i, p. 284.

120 *P.* 2 July 1892.

121 T. R. Threlfall, 'The Political Future of Labour', *Nineteenth Century,* xxxv, Feb. 1894, pp. 204–5; K. O. Morgan, *Keir Hardie*, 1975, chaps. i, ii.

122 T. R. Threlfall, 'The Trades Union Congress and the Rocks Ahead', *Nineteenth Century*, xxxii, Oct. 1892, p. 620.

123 *P.* 2 July 1892.

124 *L.D.P.* 2 April 1892.

125 *P.* 18 June 1892.

126 *P.* 2 July 1892.

127 L.T.C. Minute Book IV, 4 July 1892.

128 *L.D.P.* 6 April 1892.

129 There were seventeen questions on a variety of topics, including land reform, electoral reform, unemployment, and working conditions in public and private enterprise employment. The questionnaire was issued less than a week before polling day (5 July) and, of the eighteen candidates contesting Liverpool, only nine (four Liberals', four Unionists', and T. P. C'Connor's) replies are recorded in the L.T.C. Minutes. Later, in its *Annual Report 1892–3*, the L.T.C. announced that the replies 'were so very much alike in most points that the Council could not make any distinction between the various candidates, and decided to make no recommendations thereon'. This, as the actual replies show, was not true—the Liberals, with the exception of W. B. Bowring, were markedly more willing to detail their labour sympathies than were the Conservatives, with the exception of V. S. Fitzgerald. The questionnaire, then, while it was too incomplete and too late to have much impact on the course of the elections, is interesting for its reflection of two tendencies—that most Conservatives were sufficiently secure to ignore or oppose declared labour aspirations; and that the L.T.C. preferred not to make distinctions between the established parties.

130 *P.* 2 July 1892.

131 *L.D.P.* 28, 29 July 1892.

132 *L.C.* 11 Oct. 1887.

133 *L.R.* 4, 18 July 1891.

134 *L.D.P.* 18 May, 16 Oct. 1891.

135 *L.D.P.* 24 March 1892. On O'Connor's initial Radicalism, see Brady, *op. cit.*, pp. 70–82. H. W. Massingham and G. B. Shaw had been at odds with O'Connor during his editorship of *The Star* (1888–90) over what they considered his uncritical Liberalism and 'indifference on the social question'. See D. H. Laurence (ed.), *Bernard Shaw: Collected Letters 1874–1897*, 1965, pp. 183–6, 233, 245.

136 *The Tory*, 2 July 1892.

137 *L.C.* 29 April 1890.

138 Hamilton, *op. cit.*, pp. 35, 87–88. Cf. Forwood, *Recollections*, pp. 75–77.

139 A. J. Balfour to Lord Salisbury, Aug. 1891 quoted in J. P. Cornford, 'The Parliamentary Foundations of the Hotel Cecil', in R. Robson (ed.), *Ideas and Institutions of Victorian Britain*, 1967, p. 297. Curiously Salvidge, Forwood's successor as leader of Liverpool Conservatism, was as forgettable to Joseph Chamberlain as Forwood had been to Balfour—see Salvidge, *op. cit.*, p. 55; H. Jager, *Brief Life*, Liverpool, 1934, p. 120.

140 *P.D.*, 4th ser., ix, 16.

141 *L.D.P.* 13 July 1892.

142 *L.D.P.* 19, 26, 27, 28 July 1892.

143 *The Tory*, 16 July 1892.

144 *L.D.P.* 26 July 1892.
145 *L.D.P.* 22, 23, 25 July 1892; *L.R.* 30 July 1891.
146 *L.R.* 17 Sept. 1892.

CHAPTER 9

1 Quotations from *L.R.*, 8 Nov. 1890 and Annie Besant, 'Industry under Socialism', *Fabian Essays*, 1889, 6th edition, 1962, p. 189.

2 *The Tory*, 15 Oct. 1892.

3 *P.* 8 Oct. 1892; *The Tory*, 10 Sept. 1892.

4 *L.C.* 28 April 1892.

5 *L.C.* 12 May 1892.

6 *L.C.* 28 May 1892. Cf. Forwood's speech during an amendment to the Municipal Corporations Act (1882), *P.D.*, 4th ser., iv. 597–662.

7 E. R. Pease, *The History of the Fabian Society*, 1916, pp. 95–97, 102.

8 This was noteworthy (Sexton was I.L.P. member no. 92) since there were 1,000 registered members by the end of June 1892. See J. Burgess, 'The Independent Labour Party: Its Origin and Early History', articles in *The Clarion*, 3 Sept. 1909 to 28 Jan. 1910; Sexton, *op. cit.*, p. 150.

9 A. M. McBriar, *Fabian Socialism and English Politics 1884–1918*, Cambridge, 1966 edition, p. 167. He gives no source for the statement.

10 *Liverpool Fabian Society, Circular No. 6*, 1 May 1893, British Library.

11 McBriar, *op. cit.*, pp. 280–5, 303; *Liverpool Fabian Tracts, No. 2 Strike or Legislate? An Appeal to Trades Unionists*, 1894; and Sexton in *Manchester Empire News*, 17 Jan. 1926.

12 J. Keir Hardie, 'Mr Chamberlain's Programme', *Nineteenth Century*, xxxii, Dec. 1892, p. 890. Marx's *Capital*, 1867, became available in English translation in the 1880s, but Hardie claimed to owe more to Robert Burns—see W. Stewart, *J. Keir Hardie*, 1921, p. 19.

13 *L.D.P.* 29 Oct. 1892.

14 *P.* 8 Oct. 1892; L.T.C. Minute Book V, 28 Sept., 26 Oct. 1892.

15 *L.D.P.* 1 Nov. 1892. Chamberlain's manifesto, entitled 'The Labour Question', appeared in the November issue of *Nineteenth Century* but was widely discussed in the press in October. Chamberlain in fact gave less than ten lines, out of thirty-three pages, to a consideration of anti-alien legislation (p. 705). Neither Thomas Burt, H. H. Champion, Sam Woods, nor Keir Hardie, in their critical reviews of Chamberlain's article, *Nineteenth Century*, Dec. 1892, pp. 864–99, nor P. Fraser, *Joseph Chamberlain*, pp. 143–4, in his summary of the article, mention anti-alien legislation, although arguably it was among the most popular of Chamberlain's points.

16 L.T.C. Minute Book V, 28 Sept. 1892. Only three delegates—one was Councillor Taggart—opposed the resolution; and the L.T.C. pursued the point by organizing demonstrations and by getting the local Conservative M.P.s, Stock and Lawrence, to press the matter in Parliament, *L.T.C. Annual Report, 1892–3*, pp. 7–8.

17 *L.D.P.* 21 Oct. 1892.

18 *P.* 1 Oct. 1892.

19 *L.R.* 29 Oct. 1892; Maddock, *op. cit.*, p. 125. Denials from Conservatives in *P.* 8 Oct. 1892, and from Kaney in *L.D.P.* 27 Oct. 1892.

20 *L.D.P.* 27 Oct. 1892.

21 *L.D.P.* 29, 31 Oct. 1892.

22 *L.D.P.* 13 Oct. 1892.

23 *L.D.P.* 24 Oct. 1892. See Crane's address, *The Tory*, 29 Oct. 1892, and letter, *L.D.P.* 29 Oct. 1892.

24 Lynksey's speeches, *L.D.P.* 24, 28 Oct. 1892.

25 *The Tory*, 5 Nov. 1892.

26 *L.R.* 6 Feb. 1892; correspondence between the Conservative Councillor G. H. Ball, and Archibald Williamson, *L.D.P.* 20 Oct. 1892.

27 *L.D.P.* 2 Nov. 1892.

28 *P.* 19 Nov. 1892; R. D. Holt to J. Bryce, 21 Sept. 1892, E. Evans to J. Bryce, 19 Sept., 18, 30 Oct. 1892, 1 Jan. 1893, Bryce MSS. UB 34; E. Evans to J. Bryce, 10 Nov. 1892, ibid. UB 35.

29 *L.M.* 12 Nov. 1892; *L.D.P.* 15 Nov. 1892. James Picton, the chairman of the Library Committee from its inception in 1850 until his death in 1889, had established its tradition of non-party politics—see B. D. White, *op. cit.*, pp. 79–81.

30 *L.C.* 3 June 1890; *L.C.* 11 Nov. 1892. The Nationalists continued to criticize the Corporation's housing policy—see Councillor Kelly in *L.C.* 30 Jan. 1893.

31 *L.D.P.* 21 Jan. 1893.

32 *L.C.* 2 Feb. 1893.

33 *L.C.* 2 March 1893.

34 *L.C.* 18 April 1893.

35 *The Tory*, 8 Oct. 1892.

36 *L.R.* 30 Aug., 11 Oct. 1890. On earlier attempts to revise the ward distribution see *L.D.P.* 2 Oct. 1895, and Watkinson, *op. cit.*, pp. 430, 451.

37 *L.C.* 30 Jan. 1893.

38 *T.* 22 Feb. 1893; *P.D.*, 4th ser., ix, 19–21.

39 *L.D.P.* 13, 23 Dec. 1892; *T.* 19 Dec. 1892.

40 Sir G. Baden-Powell to A. J. Balfour, 26 June, 5 July, 17 Aug., 3 Sept. 1895; A. Akers-Douglas to J. S. Sandars, 27 Aug. 1895, Sandars MSS. c.726, fols. 118–19, 177–8; c. 727, fols. 9–19.

41 *L.D.P.* 26 Dec. 1892, cited in Sir Charles Petrie, *Walter Long and His Times*, 1936, p. 50.

42 Petrie, *op. cit.*

43 A. B. Forwood to Lord Salisbury, 5 Jan. 1893, Salisbury MSS.

44 Idem 7 Jan. 1893. In fact Forwood failed to move with the New Year and the letter is dated 1892.

45 Viscount Long, *Memories*, 1923, p. 105. Cf. Lowther's opinions about Long, from a letter to R. D. Blumenfeld, 7 Sept. 1909, quoted in K. D. Brown, 'The Anti-Socialist Union', in K. D. Brown (ed.), *Essays in Anti-Labour History*, 1974, p. 250.

46 *T.* 2 Jan. 1893.

47 *T.* 3, 4 Jan. 1893; *L.D.P.* 5 Jan. 1893.

48 *T.* 30 Dec. 1892, 2 Jan. 1893.

49 *L.D.P.* 5 Jan. 1893.

50 *L.D.P.* 6 Jan. 1893. Several prominent Liberals—and Nonconformists—were actively associated with the Liverpool diocesan branch of the Church of England Temperance Society. Samuel Smith and W. S. Caine had been; and Sir Edward Russell was a vice-president from 1894.

51 *L.D.P.* 4, 7, Jan. 1893. The chairman of West Derby Liberal Association, Robert Holt, would have preferred Frederick Smith, the candidate in 1892, to fight again. See Robert Holt to Richard Holt, 12 Jan. 1893, 14/1/150.

52 *L.D.P.* 11 Jan. 1893; *The Tory*, 14 Jan. 1893.

53 *L.D.P.* 10 Jan. 1893; *T.* 9 Jan. 1893.

54 *L.D.P.* 11 Jan. 1893; *L.R.* 21 Jan. 1893.

55 Quoted in Balfour, *op. cit.*, p. 195.

56 *P.D.*, 4th ser., xi, 516–22.

57 Ibid. 524–5.

58 *T.* 29 Oct. 1892. Liverpool Chamber of Commerce had been reconstituted in 1878 after accusations that it was too political—see Forwood, *Recollections*, p. 80.

59 Churchill had refused to appear in 1885—see above Chapter 4. Stanley Salvidge gives the impression that his father was the moving spirit behind Churchill's visit in 1893—see Salvidge, *op. cit.*, pp. 16–18, 271–3. Houston, Mattinson, and Forwood, however, were all involved—see A. Salvidge to Lord R. Churchill, 3 March 1893, Salvidge MSS; M. W. Mattinson to Lord R. Churchill, 19 Feb. 1893, and A. B. Forwood to Lord R. Churchill, 28 March 1893, Churchill MSS, RCHL 1/29/4094, 4158.

60 Long, *op. cit.*, p. 108. See also the Duke of Bedford to Viscount Wolmer, 22 Oct. 1893, 2nd Earl of Selbourne MSS., Box 13, fols. 136–7, for a description of Churchill at this time.

61 *L.D.P.* 7, 8 April 1893.

62 *P.S.* 18 Feb. 1893. Miss Cusack later wrote an autobiography, parts of which are recounted in W. Walsh, *The Secret History of the Oxford Movement*, 4th edition, 1898, pp. 186–7.

63 *P.S.* 29 June 1889; *L.C.H.* 1 May 1903; *P.S.* 17 April 1909; *Police (Liverpool Inquiry) Act 1909, Proceedings*, *op. cit.*, Q. 13970. For the vigilance of Colonel Sandys and Samuel Smith in these matters, see *P.D.*, 4th ser., x, 1503–4, xii, 1239–40, lxv, 256–7.

64 Walsh, *op. cit.*, pp. 167–70, 189. Cf. G. Best, 'Popular Protestantism in Victorian Britain' in Robson, *op. cit.*, pp. 115–42.

65 *P.S.* 8 April 1893.

66 *L.C.* 25 May 1893. The Junior Conservative Club in Liverpool was founded in 1883—see *T.* 27 June 1883.

67 *L.C.* 13 July 1893.

68 *L.C.* 20 Oct. 1893.

69 Ibid. and *L.C.* 9 Nov. 1893.

70 Robert Holt to Richard Holt, 2, 9 Feb., 30 Sept. 1893, Liverpool City Library references, 920 DUR 14/1/153, 154, 168; Robert Holt's diary, 5 April, 26 Sept., 19, 26 Oct. 1893, 17 Jan., 7 Feb. 1894, 1 Nov. 1895, 5, 6 Feb., 9 Nov. 1896, 6 Jan., 6 Oct. 1897, 4 May, 26 Oct. 1898. Interview with Salvidge, *L.R.* 3 Feb. 1894.

71 This was in 1894. At its foundation in 1868 the W.M.C.A. had 1,600 paying members; at its height in the early 1900s it had about 8,000 members—see *P.P.* 1868–9, viii, Q. 3379, A. B. Forwood; B. Whittingham Jones, *op. cit.*

72 Fried and Elman, *op. cit.*, p. 214.

73 *L.R.* 3 Feb. 1894; A. T. Salvidge to Lord Derby, 29 June 1914, Derby MSS.

74 *L.C.* 7 Dec. 1887.

75 *L.C.* 22 Dec. 1893. Cf. Forwood's address to the executive of the Constitutional Association, *L.C.* 25 Oct. 1889.

76 L.T.C. Minute Book V, 30 Nov. 1892.

77 William Chadwick, in ibid., 4 Dec. 1892.

78 Letter from 'Citizen', 13 Dec. 1892. Maddock, *op. cit.*, p. 127, assumes that the letter was written by Sam Reeves. Sexton, however, used this nom-de-plume as *The Clarion*'s Liverpool correspondent in the 1890s.

79 *P.D.*, 4th ser., ix, 1605; Sexton, *op. cit.*, p. 151. The President of the Board of Trade was A. J. Mundella. Cf. R. Davidson, 'Llewellyn Smith, the Labour Department and Government Growth 1886–1909', in G. Sutherland (ed.), *Studies in the Growth of Nineteenth-century Government*, 1972, pp. 227-62.

80 L.T.C. Minute Book V, 25 Jan. 1893. This was Sexton's first recorded appearance at the L.T.C.

81 Ibid., 3 March 1893.

82 Ibid., 27 Dec. 1893; Hamling, *op. cit.*, p. 28; *L.T.C. Annual Report 1893–4*, p. 6; Maddock, *op. cit.*, pp. 139–41.

83 *L.R.* 4 March 1893.

84 F. Brockway, *Socialism over Sixty Years*, 1946, p. 43.

85 Keir Hardie's estimate, cited in G. D. H. Cole and R. Postgate, *The Common People 1746–1946*, 1966 edition, p. 436.

86 J. Burns, 'The Unemployed', *Nineteenth Century*, Dec. 1892, pp. 852–4. The official figures, from trade unions which paid unemployment benefits, are 7·5 per cent unemployed—see Clegg, Fox, and Thompson, *op. cit.*, pp. 488–9.

87 *L.D.P.* 12 April 1893.

88 Simey, *op. cit.*, chaps. vi–vii; letters from W. Grisewood and W. Rathbone in *L.D.P.* 18 Sept. 1894; W. Rathbone, *Local Government and Taxation*, 1875, pp. 30–31; *P.D.*, 3rd ser., ccxxxviii, 608–9, ccxcix, 1424–7, W. Rathbone; P. d'A. Jones, *The Christian Socialist Revival, 1877–1914*, Princeton, 1968, pp. 397–8.

89 Quotations from T. S. Simey in Keeling, pp. 29, 38–39; and Eleanor Rathbone in M.D. Stocks, *Eleanor Rathbone*, 1949, pp. 45, 51.

90 Diary 22 April 1884, in Webb, *My Apprenticeship*, p. 129.

91 Article by 'Citizen' in *The Trade Unionist*, 9 Jan. 1892.

92 Sexton, *op. cit.*, p. 18; W. Poulson to J. Bryce, 12 Nov. 1892, Bryce MSS. UB 35.

93 *The Trade Unionist*, *op. cit.*; *P.D.*, 5th ser., vol. 217, 1082.

94 *L.D.P.* 14 April 1893.

95 Letter from Joe Hart, *L.D.P.* 13 April 1893.

96 *L.D.P.* 21 Aug. 1894.

97 Sidney Webb's figures, quoted *L.R.* 18 March 1893.

98 Birrell, *Things Past Redress*, p. 56; Picton, *Memorials*, ii, p. 225; *P.* 3 April 1886. Liverpool always had one of Britain's largest workhouses, with a capacity for 600 paupers in 1777, 1,750 by 1834. The Brownlow Hill workhouse was the second on that site. See Farrer and Brownbill, *op. cit.* iv, p. 34; Lewis, iii, p. 109; G. Chandler, *Liverpool*, 1957, pp. 391–6, 415; Clapham, *op. cit.* i, pp. 355–8; Midwinter, *Old Liverpool*, chap. 4.

99 *P.D.*, 5th ser., vol. 112, 1895–1901, vol. 131, 2688–91, vol. 134, 1036–43, vol. 135, 2347–8, N. Raw. For an experiment in the 1830s in Liverpool, to achieve a more dedicated class of nurses, see K. Curry (ed.), *New Letters of Robert Southey*, Cambridge, 1965, vol. ii, p. 350.

100 N. Hawthorne, *Our Old Home*, 1863, ii, pp. 211–34; Midwinter, *Social Administration*, p. 13 ff.; C. Dickens, *The Uncommercial Traveller and Reprinted Pieces Etc.*, Oxford, 1958 edition, chap. viii; Heasman, *op. cit.*, pp. 237–8; Eli Brooks in *L.D.P.* 13 Sept. 1894; *P.* 3 April 1886, 7 Jan. 1905; H. Peet, *Two Centuries' Records of Liverpool Parish: Our Poor-Law History*, Liverpool, 1898. The Bodleian Library copy of Peet's pamphlet includes an additional note by the author on conditions in the workhouse in 1899. On the confusion in Liverpool's Poor-Law administration, through the variety of boundaries and franchises, see H. Hagger's paper to the Poor Law conference of 1877, in W. Rathbone, A. Pell, and F. C. Montague, *Local Government And Taxation*, 1885, pp. 67–69. *T.* 11 March 1885; *P.* 18 Jan 1902.

101 *Liverpool Citizen*, 22 Jan. 1890.

102 O'Mara, *op. cit.*, p. 7.

103 *L.D.P.* 28 Aug. 1894. Note the Webbs's interview with Hagger, 1899, Webb Local Government Collection, vol. 148.

104 *L.D.P.* 14 April 1893.

105 *L.D.P.* 17, 21, 22 April 1893.

106 *L.D.P.* 2 April 1893.

107 L.T.C. Minutes, 26 May 1893.

108 *L.D.P.* 24 April 1893.

109 *L.D.P.* 25, 26, 27 April 1893. Havelock Wilson earlier claimed that 1,000 of the 2,000 blacklegs in Hull came from Liverpool, *L.D.P.* 17 April 1893.

110 *L.D.P.* 26 April 1893; *P.D.*, 4th ser., xi, 439–42, J. Havelock Wilson.

111 *L.C.* 6 May 1893; letter from Joe Hart, *L.M.* 13 May 1893.

112 *L.C.* 14 Oct. 1893.

113 L.T.C. Minutes, 24 May 1893.

114 *L.C.* 14 Oct. 1893.

115 *L.M.* 27 Nov. 1893.

116 *L.M.* 2 Dec. 1893; letter from 'Lex', *L.C.* 28 Dec. 1893. See also letter from the Lord Mayor to J. E. Atkinson (secretary of the Unemployed Association) describing the Council's limited powers, *L.D.P.* 9 March 1894.

117 *L.D.P.* 9 Dec. 1893.

118 *L.D.P.* 4 Jan. 1894; Hamling, *op. cit.*, p. 31; Sexton, *op. cit.*, p. 150; *Forward*, 25 May 1912.

119 *L.D.P.* 5, 6, 10, 13, 23, 27 Jan. 1894.

120 *L.D.P.* 26 Jan. 1894.

121 B. Disraeli, *Sybil: The Two Nations*, 1927 edition, p. 403. Cf. Palmerston's definition of 'deputation': 'a noun of multitude signifying many but not much'—quoted in J. Ridley, *Lord Palmerston*, 1970, Panther edition, 1972, p. 772.

122 *L.C.* 26 Jan., 1 Feb. 1894.

123 Letter in *L.M.* 27 Jan. 1894. Three radical clergymen, R. A. Armstrong (Unitarian), C. F. Aked (Baptist), and C. W. Stubbs (vicar of Wavertree, afterwards Bishop of Truro), made a similar suggestion in their journal, the *Liverpool Pulpit*—see I. Sellers, *Salute to Pembroke 1838–1931*, 1960, pp. 18–19.

124 *L.D.P.* 27 Oct. 1894.

125 *L.D.P.* 13 Sept. 1894. On Bain and the Town Mission see Sellers, 'Liverpool Nonconformity' pp. 31–32, 35–36.

126 *L.D.P.* 18 Sept. 1894.

127 *L.D.P.* 24 July 1894. 1,851 members were in Liverpool itself. Taggart suspected that unemployment in Liverpool, while severe, was less than in Birkenhead, where shipbuilding was practically halted.

128 *L.D.P.* 31 July 1894.

129 *L.D.P.* 28 Aug. 1894.

130 *L.D.P.* 31 July 1894.

131 *L.D.P.* 27 Oct. 1894.

132 *L.D.P.* 28 Aug. 1894.

133 *L.D.P.* 13 Sept. 1894.

134 *L.D.P.* 24 July 1894.

135 *L.D.P.* 13 Sept. 1894.

136 *L.D.P.* 27 Oct. 1894.

137 *L.D.P.* 13 Sept. 1894.

138 *L.D.P.* 31 July 1894.

139 *L.D.P.* 17, 31 July, 28 Aug., 13 Sept. 1894.

140 *L.D.P.* 27 Oct. 1894. Cf. *P.P.* 1892, xxxvi, Qs. 13579, 13606, Sexton; A. Harrison, *op. cit.*, pp. 33–45.

141 Sexton in *L.D.P.* 21 Aug. 1894. Report in *L.D.P.* 27 Oct. 1894.

142 Letter in *L.D.P.* 18 Sept. 1894.

143 *L.D.P.* 21, 28 Aug. 1894.

144 *L.D.P.* 17 July 1894; *L.M.* 18 Dec. 1895.

145 Robert Holt's diary, 18, 23 Feb., 19 March, 29 Sept. 1893; Wade's letter, *L.D.P.* 18 Sept. 1894.

146 *Clarion*, 15 Sept., 8 Dec. 1894; C. A. Collins, *op. cit.*, pp. 332–3. Eventually a relief fund was opened. £1,600 was collected by February 1895, *L.M.* 25 Feb. 1895.

147 E. Evans to J. Bryce 8 and 24 Nov. 1892; R. D. Holt to J. Bryce 2 Oct. 1892, Bryce MSS. UB 34, 35; *P.D.*, 4th ser., xi, 1128–30, A. B. Forwood and J. Bryce.

148 *L.C.* 22 Dec. 1893; *P.D.*, 4th ser., xxiv, 468–9, A. B. Forwood.

149 *L.C.* 5 April 1894.

150 *L.R.* 12 May 1894. Forwood also implicated the President of the Local Government Board, Shaw-Lefevre, *P.D.*, *op. cit.* 475, 1183, 1624–34.

151 *L.C.* 8 May 1894.

152 In 1865, in the visitors' book at Raby Castle—see R. R. James, *Rosebery*, 1963, p. 42.

153 *L.C.* 11 May 1894; Forwood in *L.C.* 10 May 1894.

154 *L.C.* 26 Oct. 1894.

155 *T.* 29 Sept. 1894.

156 L.T.C. Minutes, 26 Sept. 1894; Robert Holt's diary, 1 Nov. 1894.

157 L.T.C. Minutes, 25 July 1894. The reference, probably, was to Hardie's famous intervention in June 1894 when he opposed the vote of congratulations to the Queen upon the birth of a child (the future Edward VIII) to the Duchess of York, after Parliament had declined to take cognizance of the mining disaster at Cilfynydd—see Stewart, *op. cit.*, pp. 88–90; Cole and Postgate, *op. cit.*, p. 436.

158 *L.D.P.* 27 Sept. 1894.

159 *L.T.C. Annual Report 1894–5*, p. 10.

160 Manifesto in *L.D.P.* 17 Aug. 1894. These figures included Nationalist councillors, the vast majority of whom resembled their Liberal and Conservative counterparts in being middle-class (professional or business) and non-resident representatives. B. O'Connell, *op. cit.*, p. 131. The magnified Council, following the redistribution of wards in 1895, perpetuated these characteristics. It was stated in 1907 that of 137 Council members, only 25 lived in the wards they represented. Fifty lived outside the city, and 44 in the 6 richest residential wards. Of the 80 representatives of the 20 working-class wards, only 8 lived in those wards. See Lowell, *op. cit.*, ii, p. 156 n.3.

161 L.T.C. Minutes, 29 Aug. 1894.

162 *L.R.* 3 Nov. 1894.

163 *L.D.P.* 28 Nov. 1894.

164 *Labour Chronicle*, 1 Jan. 1895. Cf. H. Collins, 'The Marxism of the Social Democratic Federation', in A. Briggs and J. Saville (eds.), *Essays in Labour History 1886–1923*, 1971, pp. 47–69.

165 *L.T.C. Annual Report 1894–5*; J. E. Mortimer, *History of the Boilermakers' Society*, 1973, vol. i, on demarcation disputes in the shipyards.

CHAPTER 10

1 Opinions about Sir A. B. Forwood—*Lancashire Leaders Social and Political*, ii, p. 4; Robert Holt's diary, 6 Jan. 1897; Orchard, *Legion*, p. 307; *P.D.*, 4th ser., iv, 640–1, S. Smith.

2 *T.* 4 July 1895.

3 *T.* 10 July 1895; *L.D.P.* 13 July 1895.

4 *L.D.P.* 15 July 1895.

5 *L.C.* 12 July 1895. The illiterate voters of Liverpool are numbered in *P.P.* 1886, lii, pp. 609, 632; *P.P.* 1893–4, lxx, p. 710; *P.P.* 1896, lxvii, p. 312; *P.P.* 1906, xcvi, p. 7. Scotland Division had the highest proportion of illiterate voters in English urban seats.

6 *L.D.P.* 29 Oct., 2 Nov. 1892.

7 *T.* 29 June 1894.

8 Forwood to Salisbury, 3 July 1895, Salisbury MSS.; Salisbury to Forwood, 30 June 1895, Forwood MSS.; Forwood to Schomberg McDonnell, 4 July 1895, Salisbury MSS.

9 *Sun*, 31 July 1895, cutting in Forwood MSS.

10 J. Chamberlain, 'The Labour Question', *Nineteenth Century*, Nov. 1892, p. 695. The Employers' Liability Act (1880) had been Chamberlain's responsibility and he had then argued against the abolition of the doctrine of 'common employment'. His detractors now did not miss this point—see T. Burt, 'Mr Chamberlain's Programme', ibid., Dec. 1892, pp. 369–70. For a review of the Act see *T.* 14 Oct. 1884; *P.P.* 1892, xxxvi, pt. ii, Q. 13585, Sexton; W. C. Mallalieu, 'Joseph Chamberlain and Workmen's Compensation', *Journal of Economic History*, x, 1950, pp. 45–57.

11 Pamphlet, *Mr. A. B. Forwood on the 'Compensation to Workmen (Accidents) Bill'*, 1894.

12 Ibid.; *P.D.*, 4th ser., xi, 1182–90, xx, 59–61; *Ormskirk Advertiser*, 29 Oct. 1886; Forwood's letter, *T.* 25 July 1898. However, Forwood's maiden parliamentary speech in 1886 had opposed the inclusion of seamen in the existing (1880) legislation—*P.D.*, 3rd ser., cccii, 1104–8. For the provisions of the 1897 Act see Halévy, v, pp. 232–3.

13 J. Keir Hardie, 'Mr Chamberlain's Programme', *Nineteenth Century*, Dec. 1892, p. 886.

14 S. and B. Webb, *Industrial Democracy*, 1920 edition, p. 388. Cf. diary, 7 May 1897, in B. Webb, *Our Partnership*, 1948, pp. 138–9.

15 For the dockers' anger at exclusion, Sexton, *Agitator*, chap. xvii; J. Sexton, *A Criticism of the Workmen's Compensation Act*, Liverpool, 1900; Forwood's pamphlet, *op. cit.* Tom Austin was a cabinet-maker by trade. Forwood's Liverpool Conservative colleagues, representing various shipowners' associations, were decidedly hostile to the inclusion of seamen in Employers' Liability legislation—*P.D.*, 4th ser., xlviii, 1683–4, Lawrence, 1697–8, Warr, lxvii, 106–8, MacIver.

16 Cutting in Picton Library, Liverpool, initialled W.G., reference H.Q. 331 88 TRA. This may have been W. Gerrard, secretary of the L.L.R.C. The candidate referred to was Joseph Goodman, although in fact he was not the only Labour candidate in 1894. Sam Reeves, representing the L.T.C., polled 11,190 votes, the highest yet by any Labour candidate but still appreciably below election.

17 *L.D.P.* 19, 20, 21 Oct. 1892.

18 *L.D.P.* 22 Oct. 1892.

19 George Nelson in *L.T.C. Annual Report 1908–9*, p. 14; *P.D.*, 5th ser., lxii, 140–1, 1564–6, 1614–16, lxxi, 1830. The transference of supervision of voluntary schools to the City Council, and their support from the rates, had been attempted in the Elementary Education (Permissive Rates Aid) Bill, 1897, introduced by Liverpool M.P.s with an avowed distrust of the government Education Department—*P.D.*, 4th ser., xli, 1187–8, xlv, 300; B. D. White, *op. cit.*, pp. 147–8. Rate-aid was preferred to State-aid in Liverpool.

20 *L.C.* 11, 15 July 1895.

21 Forwood's speeches in *L.C.* 30 Oct. 1890, 20 Sept. 1894, *L.D.P.* 9 July 1895.

22 On the pressures placed upon Catholics to support Conservative candidates in 1895, see Halévy, *op. cit.*, p. 189 n.1; *P.D.*, 4th ser., xl, 1205–14, T. P. O'Connor.

23 L. OBroin, *The Chief Secretary*, 1969, p. 35; *L.D.P.* 10 May 1894. See J. Powell Williams to Viscount Wolmer, 4 March 1894, 2nd Earl of Selborne MSS, Box 13, fols.

140–2, for the fear that the 'G. O. Madman' (Gladstone) might successfully fight a Peers versus People campaign in the north on account of the Lords' rejection of Asquith's Bill. On Gladstone's and Rosebery's failure to rally the Liberal party against the House of Lords, see P. Stansky, *Ambitions and Strategies*, Oxford, 1964.

24 *L.C.* 5 Feb. 1894.

25 R. McKenzie and A. Silver, *Angels in Marble*, 1968, pp. 54–55. It should be observed, however, that the distribution on the whole favoured the Unionists because their advantages in small seats offset Ireland's over-representation—Blewett, *op. cit.*, pp. 367–8.

26 *L.C.* 10 May 1894. This was Smith's debut on a party platform. Part of the speech is quoted in Earl of Birkenhead, *Frederick Edwin, Earl of Birkenhead: The First Phase*, 1933, pp. 39–40.

27 *L.C.* 28 Jan. 1893.

28 Sandys to Salisbury, 16 July 1895, Salisbury MSS. What Sandys considered 'a healthy social reform' was a Bill to inflict corporal punishment on persons guilty of sexual offences—*P.D.*, 4th ser., lxxxi, 591–2.

29 Sandys to Salisbury, 16 July 1895, 7 Sept. 1897, Salisbury MSS. These letters can be recommended as classics to connoisseurs of nineteenth-century Conservative reaction and retired colonels.

30 John Houlding in *L.C.* 28 June 1895.

31 *L.C.* 6 July 1895. For the Nationalists' views, *P.D.*, 4th ser., xxxiv, 1183, W. Redmond, lxxix, 970–4, lxxxvii, 712–4, T. P. O'Connor. Interestingly Carson also opposed the Cromwell statue, calling him a 'murderer'. E. Majoribanks, *The Life of Edward Carson*, i, 1932, p. 278.

32 The I.N.L.'s manifesto, issued by T. P. O'Connor, recognized in Lord Salisbury's Irish policy 'the Cromwellian spirit of extermination, modified to suit the Victorian era . . .', *T.* 11 July 1895.

33 *L.C.* 8 July 1895.

34 *L.C.* 10, 12 July 1895.

35 *L.C.* 8 July 1895; Sir G. Baden-Powell to A. J. Balfour, 26 June, 5 July, 17 Aug., 3 Sept. 1895; A. Akers-Douglas to J. E. Sandars, 27 Aug. 1895, Sandars MSS. c. 726, fols. 118–19, 177–8, c. 727, fols. 9–19.

36 *L.C.* 16 July 1895.

37 Letter from the N.U.D.L. in *L.D.P.* 11 July 1895. Baden-Powell argued that dock work should be included in Merchant Shipping legislation, to avoid confusion in inspection—*P.D.*, 4th ser., xxv, 153–4.

38 Johnson's dye-works in Bootle and Kirkdale introduced one of the first industrial welfare departments—Willett, *op. cit.*, p. 101; W. Poulson to J. Bryce, 23 Dec. 1893, Bryce MSS. UB 35.

39 *L.D.P.* 10 July 1895.

40 *L.D.P.* 9 July 1895.

41 *L.C.* 12 July 1895.

42 *L.D.P.* 19 July 1895; W. H. Watts' letter, *L.C.* 20 July 1895.

43 *L.D.P.* 17 July 1895.

44 *L.C.* 10, 15 July 1895; *L.D.P.* 9, 10, 16 July 1895.

45 *L.D.P.* 17 July 1895.

46 *L.D.P* 16 Aug. 1894, 13 July 1895. Vaughan was in Liverpool to consecrate the new bishop, Dr. Whiteside.

47 Unionists also objected to the favour which successive Liberal Lord Mayors, R. D. Holt and W. B. Bowring, had accorded Unitarian ministers. They had displaced Anglican clergy at official occasions of the Corporation—see *L.C.* 12, 15, 18 Sept. 1894; L. P. Jacks, *The Confessions of an Octogenarian*, 1942, p. 144.

48 *L.C.* 11 July 1895.

49 *L.D.P.* 15 July 1895.

50 *L.D.P.* 20 July 1895.

51 Letter from E. Gearing, *L.D.P.* 25 July 1895.

52 Letter from Doughan, *L.D.P.* 22 July 1895.

53 *T.* 23 July 1895; P. Harnetty, 'The Indian Cotton Duties Controversy, 1894–1896', *E.H.R.* lxxvii, Oct. 1962, pp. 684–702.

54 *L.D.P.* 4 July 1895. For an example of Stock's incoherent rhetoric, see his speech in opposition to the disestablishment of the Church in Wales—*P.D.*, 4th ser. xxxii, 217–20.

55 *L.D.P.* 5, 10, 19 July 1895.

56 Webb, *My Apprenticeship*, p. 188 n.1; Lord Rosebery to R. D. Holt, 23 May 1895; Holt to Rosebery, 24 May 1895, Rosebery MSS. 10130, fol. 125, 10157, fols. 170–3; Robert Holt's diary, 24 May 1895.

57 Beatrice Webb's diary, vol. 20, October 10, 1899, Webb MSS.; Robert Holt's diary, 1 July 1895.

58 H. Dalton, *Call Back Yesterday*, 1953, p. 56.

59 *L.D.P.* 17, 19 July 1895.

60 T. P. O'Connor's phrase in *L.D.P.* 15 July 1895.

61 Gardiner, *op. cit.* ii, pp. 369–70; letter from A. W. in *L.C.* 15 July 1895. Cf. Rowntree and Sherwell, *op. cit.*, pp. 103–6, 502–9.

62 *L.C.* 5 July 1895; *L.D.P.* 8 July 1895; H. C. G. Matthew, *The Liberal Imperialists*, Oxford, 1973, pp. 238–9.

63 *L.D.P.* 18 July 1895; *T.* 27 June 1895.

64 *Clarion* 1, 8 Dec. 1894. Sexton was an amateur actor in his youth.

65 Sexton, *op. cit.*, chap. xx; Maddock, *op. cit.*, p. 82.

66 *L.D.P.* and *L.C.* 8 July 1895.

67 *L.R.* 4 Feb. 1893.

68 Forwood's letter, *T.* 30 July 1895.

69 *T.* 18 Oct. 1895.

70 *L.C.* 17 Oct. 1895; *L.M.* 31 Oct. 1895.

71 *L.D.P.* 17, 22, 28 Oct. 1895.

72 *L.C.* 29 Oct. 1895.

73 *L.D.P.* 22 Oct. 1895.

74 *L.M.* 28 Oct. 1895.

75 *L.M.* 31 Oct. 1895.

76 Forwood to Salisbury, 7 Dec. 1895, Salisbury MSS; Robert Holt's diary, 5, 6 Feb., 9 Nov. 1896.

77 *L.C.* 2 Nov. 1896.

78 *L.C.* 2, 9, Nov. 1895; Forwood to Salisbury, 2 Nov. 1895, Salisbury MSS.

79 *L.T.C. Annual Report 1895–6.* p. 5; Maddock, *op. cit.*, p. 136.

80 L.T.C. Minutes, 25 Sept. 1895. Reeves had ceased working as a coremaker and taken over a newsagent's and tobacconist's business in Scotland Road, to free himself for political work—see Bellamy and Saville, *op. cit.*, i, pp. 282–5; Maddock, *op. cit.*, pp. 249–50.

81 The charge of drunkenness was dropped but Matkin was convicted of technical assault and fined £1 with costs. Robert Gladstone, a J.P. of thirty-one years' experience, resigned when the Chancellor of the Duchy of Lancaster, Lord James of Hereford, decided to retain Matkin's name on the Commission. James's decision was reached after consulting Liberal leaders in Liverpool. See *T.* 30 Dec. 1895, 1 Feb. 1896; Gladstone's letter, *L.D.P.* 10 Jan. 1896; Lord Derby to R. D. Holt, 20 Jan. 1896, Holt MSS.

82 *L.M.* 20 Nov. 1895.

83 *L.M.* 11 Nov. 1895; Robert Holt's diary, 11 Nov. 1894, 25 Sept., 9, 10, 17 Nov. 1895, 23 Jan. 1896. Derby sought to placate the Irish by inviting Dr. Commins to be his deputy mayor. Commins had declined the Lord Mayoralty in 1894. See Watkinson, *op. cit.*

84 *L.C.* 30 Jan. 1896.

85 Salvidge was already a member of Hoylake and West Kirby Local Board (where he lived). This body met in the evenings, unlike Liverpool City Council, and Salvidge at this juncture was reluctant to sacrifice business time.

86 S. Salvidge, *op. cit.*, p. 28.

87 B. D. White, *op. cit.*, pp. 171–2; *L.D.P.* 22 Oct. 1895.

88 *P.P.* 1904, xxxii, Qs. 5723–7, Horsfall. Cf. Carter, *op. cit.*, p. 29.

89 Picton, *Memorials*, ii, p. 503.

90 J. R. Jones, *op. cit.*, pp. 168–9.

91 *Liverpool Town Planning and Housing Exhibition 1914*, p. 118.

92 Cf. *P.D.*, 4th ser., cxx, 944–5, J. Keir Hardie. Another consequence was that housing questions in Liverpool gradually became removed from party politics—B. O'Connell, *op. cit.*, pp. 85–86.

93 B. D. White, *op. cit.*, pp. 136–7.

94 *L.R.* 20 May 1899; J. Samuelson, *The Children of our Slums*, 1911, pp. 4–5.

95 Pumphrey, *op. cit.*, p. 150.

96 *Liverpool Town Planning and Housing Exhibition 1914*, p. 123. The deputy surveyor had previously observed that 'the adoption of this principle [restricting Council houses to the dispossessed] had in many cases necessitated dwellings being kept unoccupied for a considerable time, notwithstanding the fact that in every case the Corporation dwellings could readily have been let, but not to the right class of tenant'—see Hope, *City of Liverpool*, p. 168.

97 A. Sutcliffe (ed.),, *Multi-Storey Living*, 1974.

98 *Liverpool Town Planning and Housing Exhibition 1914*, p. 125.

99 *L.R.* 25 July 1893; *P.D.*, 4th ser., vol. 120, cols. 939–44. The Corporation had 66 one-room dwellings, 397 two-roomed, 143 three-roomed, and 16 four-roomed. The maximum rent was 5*s.* 6*d.* See J. F. J. Sykes, article on working-class housing, *J.S.S.*, vol. 64, June 1901, pp. 223, 242–3, 249.

100 B. D. White, *op. cit.*, p. 138.

101 Ibid., pp. 160–1; Hope, *op. cit.*, pp. 115–27; *P.D.*, 3rd ser., ccclii, 249–51, Forwood; S. A. Munro, 'Tramway Companies in Liverpool, 1859–1897', *T.H.S.L.C.*, vol 119, pp. 181–212.

102 *L.C.* 7 May 1897. The Town Clerk, Harcourt Clare, claimed the credit for this decision, after Forwood's death—see his interview with the Webbs, 1899, Webb Local Government Collection, vol. 148.

103 B. D. White, *op. cit.*, p. 162; *P.D.*, 4th ser., lix, 194–6, Forwood. By 1902 the trams were using two-thirds of all electrical units supplied in Liverpool—Hope, *op. cit.*, p. 113.

104 R. A. Hampson to A. B. Forwood, 10 May 1898, Forwood MSS.

105 *L.D.P.* 6 May 1898; Robert Holt's diary, 4 May 1898.

106 J. Thompson to A. B. Forwood, 14 May 1898, Forwood MSS.

107 A. T. Salvidge to A. B. Forwood, 11 May 1898, ibid.

108 *L.D.P.* 8 Oct. 1896, 4 Nov. 1897.

109 *L.R.* 5 Aug. 1899.

110 Most of the City Engineer's work after 1894 was done by men directly employed by the Corporation, after experience of shoddy and expensive work from contractors—see R. C. K. Ensor (ed.), *Modern Socialism*, 1910 edition, pp. 253–4.

111 *L.R.* 19 Aug. 1899.

112 *P.D.* 4th ser., cxxxii, 709; Dyos and Aldcroft, *op. cit.*, Map 16 on the tram flow in Liverpool.

113 The trams deprived the Overhead Railway—the 'Dockers' Umbrella'—of perhaps 1½ to 2 million passengers annually between 1900 and 1912. Sir William Forwood's criticisms also had a class bias: he complained that the suburbs lost their character as small property was built following the trams' intrusion. Large ratepayers reacted by moving to Cheshire. The Overhead Railway was closed in 1956 and afterwards demolished. See C. E. Box, *The Liverpool Overhead Railway 1893–1956*, 1962 edition; Forwood, *Recollections*; Robert Holt's diary, 25 Oct. 1897.

114 B. D. White, *op. cit.*, pp. 162–3.

115 The last horse-tram in Liverpool—as Manchester—ran in 1903. Liverpool's electric trams were phased out between 1948 and 1957. See R. E. Blackburn, *Liverpool Tramways 1943 to 1957*, 1968.

CHAPTER 11

1 Epigraphs: H. Walpole, *The Crystal Box*, privately printed, Glasgow, 1924, p. 63; *P.D.*, 4th ser., lxvi, 416, C. M'Arthur. Quotations in the introduction: Taylor in *The Guardian*, 19 Oct. 1898; Charles Booth in P. Keating, *Into Unknown England*, 1976, pp. 112–40.

2 P.P. 1898, xxxvi, Qs. 26262–815; Nott-Bower, *op. cit.*, p. 137.

3 D. J. Oddy, 'Working-Class Diets in Late Nineteenth Century Britain', *Ec.H.R.*, 2nd ser., xxiii, no. 2, 1970, pp. 314–23; A. E. Dingle, 'Drink and Working-Class Living Standards in Britain 1870–1914', ibid. xxv, no. 4, 1972, pp. 608–22.

4 *L.D.P.* 21 April 1896, 14 April 1897; *L.M.* 10, 27 April 1896; W. D. Morrison and G. B. Wilson, articles on the variations in criminal statistics, in *J.S.S.*, vol. 60, March 1897, pp. 1–32, vol. 75, Jan. 1912 pp. 183–247.

5 Letter from E. Jones, *T.* 24 Oct. 1894.

6 *P.P.* 1896, ix, Q. 544.

7 *L.M.* 29 Jan. 1896; J. M. Swift, *The Story of Garston and its Church*, Garston, 1937, pp. 202–3.

8 J. and B. Braddock, *The Braddocks*, 1963, p. 9.

9 On the founder and first chairman, T. F. A. Agnew (the Bank of England's agent in Liverpool) see Orchard, *Legion*, pp. 124–7. England's first Children's Hospital was opened in Liverpool in 1851, preceding the more famous (London) Great Ormond Street Hospital by a year; but it became so insanitary that it needed entirely rebuilding by 1896—B. D. White, *op. cit.*, p. 125; Abel-Smith, *op. cit.*, pp. 24–25. The N.S.P.C.C. was established in 1889. Legislation on child neglect, in 1889, 1894, and 1904, advanced the movement towards protection.

10 *Liverpool S.P.C.C., First Annual Report 31 March 1884*, p. 11.

11 Ibid. p. 12; Samuelson, *Children of our Slums*, p. 25. The Liverpool S.P.C.C. ministered to 297,857 children in its first fifty years' work, *T.* 19 April 1933.

12 *P.P.* 1896, xliii, Qs. 16207–375, S. Smith; S. Smith, 'Social Reform', *Nineteenth Century*, May 1883, p. 907; *P.D.*, 4th ser., lxxi, 597, lxxii, 235–9, S. Smith; *Liverpool School Board, Report for the Three Years ending 25 November 1900*, p. 31. Canadians, who received the bulk of these children, preferred the destitute child sent by philanthropic societies to the pauper child sent by work-houses. The latter, it was believed, were tainted, had 'bad blood', 'bad morals', and 'might corrupt that new country'. Only seventy-eight children were sent abroad in 1898 by thirty-one Boards of Guardians, through ten different

agencies. The Bondfield Report, 1924, virtually ended the assisted emigration of children under fourteen years old.

13 O'Mara, *op. cit.*, pp. 5–6.

14 Forwood, *Recollections*, pp. 211–12; Hope, *City of Liverpool*, pp. 80–81, 271–4; Heasman, *op. cit.*, p. 100.

15 On the *Clarence*, *P.P.* 1899, xliv, p. 154; *P.D.*, 4th ser., xxxi, 51, 1250, xxxii 470, 920, xcviii, 556–7; Hope, *op. cit.*, p. 271. On the *Akbar P.P.* 1911, lxxii, pp. 461–85; *P.D.*, 5th ser. xxi, 2076–9, 2159–202; R. S. Churchill, *Winston S. Churchill, II Companion Pt. 2, 1907–11*, 1969, p. 1051; J. Symons, *Horatio Bottomley*, 1955, pp. 105–7. At least one trainee remembered the *Akbar* fondly—see letter from Samuel Golightly, *Spectator*, 19 Dec. 1970—because the new premises at Heswall, where the school moved in 1909, were relatively lavish. *P.P.* 1910, lvii, p. 493.

16 See W. Parsons, 'The Story of the Fresh Air Fund', *The Poor in Great Cities*, 1896; Samuelson, *op. cit.*, p. 7; Barnett, *op. cit.*, chap. xv.

17 B. Simon, *Education and the Labour Movement*, 1965, p. 135.

18 Quoted in Samuelson, *op. cit.*, p. 31.

19 *L.R.* 7 Oct. 1899. On Lee Jones's work see Simey, *op. cit.*, pp. 119–22.

20 *P.* 15 Sept. 1900.

21 O'Mara, *op. cit.*, p. 82. F. Shaw, *My Liverpool*, 1971, p. 114, gives a different picture.

22 S. Hocking, *My Book of Memory*, pp. 78–79; *D.N.B. 1931–1940*, pp. 436–7; P. J. Keating, *The Working Classes in Victorian Fiction*, 1971, pp. 43–45. New editions of *Her Benny* have appeared in 1966 and 1868.

23 S. K. Hocking, *Her Benny*, 1879, p. 12. For Hocking's claims to realism see S. K. Hocking, *Dick's Fairy: A Tale of the Streets*, 1883, preface.

24 Hocking recognizes this in *Cricket: A Tale of Humble Life*, 1886, chap. iv. The novel in other respects repeats the formula of *Her Benny*. On the myth of upward social mobility see G. L. P. Anderson, 'A Study of Clerical Labour in Liverpool and Manchester 1850–1914', unpublished D. Phil. thesis, Lancaster, 1974, pp. 89–106.

25 Quoted in Samuelson, *op. cit.*, pp. 14. Cf. *An Illustrated and Descriptive History of the Liverpool and Bootle Police*, Liverpool, 1910, p. 15; J. B. Mays, *Growing Up in the City*, Liverpool, 1964 edition; Tobias, *op. cit.*, pp. 167–72.

26 *P.P.* 1904, xxxii, Qs. 2107–8, Dr. Young; R. M. Barrett, 'The Treatment of Juvenile Offenders', *J.S.S.*, June 1900, pp. 185, 192–3, 256–60.

27 Hope, *op. cit.*, pp. 97–98; *An Illustrated and Descriptive History of the Liverpool and Bootle Police*, *op. cit.*; Samuelson, *op. cit.*, pp. 59–66; S. Reynolds and B. T. Woolley, *Seems So! A Working-Class View of Politics*, 1911, chap. x. The first Police-Aided Clothing Association was in Edinburgh in 1892. As well as providing a much-needed charity, it partly checked the poor man's belief that the police were his enemy—*P.P.* 1920, xxii, Qs. 1983–6, Dunning. The Liverpool Association ceased in the early 1940s.

28 Samuelson, *op. cit.*, p. 1; C. Hassall, *Edward Marsh*, 1959, p. 223; Keeling, *op. cit.*, pp. 47–52.

29 Letter in *L.M.* 29 Jan. 1896.

30 *L.M.* 8, 25 Oct. 1897; *Church of England Purity Society, 4th Annual Report, April 1887*, p. 26.

31 H. M. Johnson, *Children and Public-Houses*, Nottingham, 1897 edition, pp. 9–10. By the Child Messengers' Act (1901) the age was raised to fourteen. This and other regulations were codified in the so-called Children's Charter (1908), although working men criticized it as 'the outcome of sentimentality and ignorance, engineered by well-meaning busybodies'—see Reynolds and Woolley, *op. cit.*, p. 39 and chap. iv.

32 The Chief Inspector of Reformatories, quoted in 'Memorandum on the

Regulation of Street Trading by Children at Liverpool and Elsewhere 1898–1905', Public Record Office HO45/10172/B27657. See also Nott-Bower, *op. cit.*, pp. 98–99.

33 *P.D.*, 5th ser., vol. 234, 1989–2001. The Liverpool Acts prefigured national legislation regulating the employment of children, in 1903 and 1933.

34 M. W. Flinn (ed.), *Report on the Sanitary Condition of the Labouring Population of Great Britain by Edwin Chadwick, 1842*, Edinburgh, 1965, pp. 251–2.

35 *P.P.* 1904, xxxii, Q. 2092, Dr. Young. On theories of urban degeneration see Stedman Jones, *op. cit.*, chaps. 6, 16, 18.

36 *P.P.* 1904, *op. cit.*, Qs. 8957 ff, Appendix xxvi, table iii, Dr. J. Wiglesworth, Appendix IX B, E. W. Hance, Q. 2120, Dr. Young. Cf. *P.P.* 1894, xxxv, p. 24; H. R. Jones, 'The Perils and Protection of Infant Life', *J.S.S.*, vol. 57, 1894, pp. 1–103.

37 T. McKeown and R. Record, 'Reasons for the Decline of Mortality in England and Wales during the Nineteenth Century', in Flinn and Smout, *op. cit.*, pp. 218–50.

38 Churchill quoted in Addison, *Road to 1945*, p. 228; *P.P.* 1904, *op. cit.*, Q. 2122, Dr. Young, 12143, Dr. Vincent; R. Boyce and C. S. Sherrington (eds), *The Thompson Yates Laboratories Report*, Liverpool, 1901, iv, pt. 1, p. 169.

39 F. W. Hirst, *Gladstone as Financier and Economist*, 1931, p. 90; D. W. Howell, 'The Impact of Railways on Agricultural Development in Nineteenth Century Wales', *The Welsh History Review*, vol. 7, June 1974; T. M. Shallcross, *op. cit.*, pp. 35–37. The Liverpool Health Department in 1903 consisted of 145 persons altogether, including permanent and temporary clerical staff—see Hope, *op. cit.*, p. 157.

40 Boyce and Sherrington, *op. cit.*, p. 171. Dairy companies only began to employ bacteriologists from the 1920s and, though Corporation improvements continuously bit into the cowkeepers' space, there were still 276 cowsheds in the city in 1929. See J. Hanson, *A Rolling Stone*, Liverpool, 1939, concerning the founder of Hanson's Model Dairy in Edge Lane; H. Forrester, *Twopence to Cross the Mersey*, 1974, p. 170; *P.D.*, 5th ser., vol. 241, 2163–6; McKeown and Record, *op. cit.*, p. 250, n.28.

41 *P.D.*, 5th ser., vol. 112, 1895–1901, vol. 116, 2274, vol. 117, 682–4, vol. 131, 2688–91, vol. 134, 1036–43; Brand, *op. cit.*, p. 69. The first Ministry of Health Order regarding the pasteurization of milk was issued in 1922.

42 *L.C.* 6 Sept. 1899; *L.M.* 5 Oct. 1899; letters and articles in all Liverpool dailies from 10 Oct. 1889; Carter, *op. cit.*, pp. 25–27. The Webb Local Government Collection, vol. 148, contains numerous complaints against butchers and slaughter-house men, 1817–35.

43 *L.C.* 15 Oct., 5 Nov. 1889.

44 *L.D.P.* 12 Feb., 30 April, 6 May 1890; *L.M.* 3, 12, April, 7 May 1890; Robert Holt, diary, 7 May 1890.

45 *T.* 21 April 1926. The new abattoir, opened in 1931 near the old Stanley Market, had a long and complicated background. Its accommodation was considered inadequate only four years after its opening—see *T.* 10 Jan. 1923, 13 Dec. 1927, 15 Sept. 1931, 19 Sept. 1935; B. D. White, *op. cit.*, pp. 59–60, 118–19; *P.D.*, 4th ser., xxx, 1554–6, xxxviii, 719–29, xl, 1088–9, lvi, 1179, 5th ser., vol. 167, 1468.

46 Both the Corporation and private companies employed full-time rat-catchers. Some figures indicate the scale of operations. Before 1914 the Bootle rat-catcher killed over 1,000 rats per month; and in the St. John's Market, which the Liverpool Corporation had built in the early 1820s, some 10,000 rats were killed each year. In 1927 rat-catchers killed 36,000 rats on ships and quays in Liverpool, and 7,100 rats were examined by the city bacteriologist for possible plague infection. See *L.C.* 29 May 1907; *L.D.P.* 3, 6 March 1911; *T.* 17 Oct. 1927; J. F. D. Shrewsbury, *A History of Bubonic Plague in the British Isles*, 1971, pp. 531–2.

47 Sir D. Gamble to Lord Derby, 12 Dec. 1890, Derby MSS.

48 See Diggle, *op. cit.*, pp. 30, 122–4, 135, 329.

49 Church Association, *The Ritualistic Clergy List*, 1902 edition.

50 Over twelve million copies were distributed in Ryle's lifetime—M. L. Loane, *John Charles Ryle 1816–1900*, 1953, p. 221; *L.R.* 21 Oct. 1899.

51 Loane, *op. cit.*, p. 49; *The Church Association Monthly Intelligencer*, Nov. 1881 pp. 307–8, 317–25. An autobiographical fragment, dictated by J. C. Ryle in 1873, largely composes chapter 1 of M. H. Fitzgerald, *A Memoir of Herbert Edward Ryle*, 1928.

52 J. C. Ryle, 'First Visitation Charge, 19 Oct. 1881' in *Visitation Charges, Diocesan Addresses and Special Sermons*, 1903, pp. 30–31; J. C. Ryle, *Can They Be Brought In?*, 1883, pp. 19, 44. Cf. G. Haw (ed.), *Christianity and the Working Classes*, 1906, chap. xi.

53 J. C. Ryle, *Brotherhoods*, 1890, pp. 3–4.

54 W. Walsh to Sir W. V. Harcourt, 6 March 1903, Harcourt MSS. dep. 244 f.13.

55 J. C. Ryle, *Third Visitation Charge, 27 Oct. 1887*; Ryle in *The Guardian*, 17 Aug., 16 Nov. 1898.

56 J. C. Ryle, *Fourth Visitation Charge, 4 Nov. 1890.*

57 R. W. Church, to Dr. Paget, 3 Feb. 1889, in M. C. Church (ed.), *The Life and Letters of Dean Church*, 1895, p. 336. Cf. Gladstone's opinion in *Hamilton's Diary*, i, p. 189. The Bishop of Lincoln was Edward King, who was prosecuted for Ritualist practices.

58 *P.S.* 25 May 1889, 31 March 1894; resolution of Liverpool branch of the Church Association in *The Church Association Monthly Intelligencer*, March 1881, pp. 82–83.

59 Sir A. B. Forwood to Lord Salisbury 11 Nov. 1897, Salisbury MSS.

60 *T.* 16 April 1880; *The Church Association Monthly Intelligencer*, Jan. 1880, pp. 14–25, May 1880, p. 135.

61 *L.M.* 19 July 1898; *L.C.* 7 May 1903. The living of St. Thomas's was once in the Gladstones' gift. For Wakeford's view that ritualism revived many dormant churches, see his letter to *The Guardian*, 10 Aug. 1898.

62 *Police (Liverpool Inquiry) Act 1909, Proceedings*, pp. 740–50.

63 See Public Record Office HO45 10160/B24058/7. More immediately the anti-ritualist movement grew in reaction to the efforts of Lord Halifax and others to establish a rapport between the Churches of England and Rome, 1894–6. See L. Creighton, *Life and Letters of Mandell Creighton*, 1904, ii, pp. 176–80.

64 On Archdeacon W. F. Taylor see *L.R.* 22 May 1886; C. H. Dant, *Distinguished Churchmen and Phases of Church Work*, 1902, p. 361; *The Church Association Monthly Intelligencer*, Nov. 1871, pp. 307–11, Feb. 1880, pp. 58–59, March 1881, p. 82, June 1881, pp. 180–92, April 1883, p. 94.

65 *P.D.*, 4th ser., cxxxiv, 964.

66 *L.R.* 13 May 1899; *P.* 1 Nov. 1902.

67 *T.* 20 Aug. 1898.

68 Sir E. Russell to H. Gladstone, 11 March 1888, Viscount Gladstone Papers B. L. Add. MSS. 46,053, fols. 21–23.

69 *T.* 13 Aug. 1898 ff.; letters in *T.* 26, 29 Aug. 1898.

70 *T.* 23 Aug. 1898; letters in *T.* 29 Aug. 1898; Robert Holt's diary, 24 Aug. 1898.

71 Walsh, *op. cit.*, pp. 273, 315, 358, 362–3. Harcourt's Protestant letters to *The Times* in 1898 boosted Walsh's sales—W. Walsh to Sir W. V. Harcourt, 14 Nov. 1898, Harcourt MSS. 238, fols. 35–38. Walsh's Liverpool lecture in *L.C.* 29 Oct. 1898. Evidently inspired by Walsh a series of articles, entitled 'Secret Societies in the Church of England', began in *L.C.* 5 Nov. 1898.

72 *L.C.* 13, 20, Oct. 1898. By contrast, in Oxford, there was a move to prevent the purchase of Walsh's book for the Union library—Brodrick *Memories*, p. 99.

73 *L.C.* 29 Oct. 1898.

74 Griffiths, *op. cit.*

75 *L.C.* 1, 3 Nov. 1898.

76 *L.C.* 4 Oct. 1898.

77 *L.C.* 12, 13, 14, 18 Oct. 1898.

78 See Salvidge's letter in *L.C.* 12 Oct. 1898, and his published correspondence with John Metcalfe, representing the Orangemen, in *L.C.* 31 Oct. 1898.

79 *L.C.* 2 Nov. 1898.

80 *L.D.P.* 2, 5 Nov. 1897; *L.C.* 29 Oct. 1898.

81 *T.* 12 Jan. 1899. Privately Salisbury considered the Protestant agitation 'very superficial', although he regretted 'the anarchy' which Ritualists had introduced into the Church. See his letters to Canon MacColl, of Ripon, 1 Aug. 1898 and 9 Feb. 1899, quoted in Russell, *MacColl*, p. 219.

82 Charles M'Arthur (Liberal Unionist) represented Exchange after Bigham was elevated to the judicial bench, 1897; David MacIver represented Kirkdale after Baden-Powell's death, 1898.

83 E. Ashby and M. Anderson, *Portrait of Haldane at Work on Education*, 1974, pp. 61–71; R. B. Haldane, *An Autobiography*, 1929, pp. 90, 140; Alsop, *op. cit.*, chap. iii, for the establishment of Liverpool University. For a disapproving view, see Robert Holt's diary, 27 Jan. 1902.

84 *L.R.* 4 Feb. 1899.

85 *T.* 12 Jan. 1899.

86 *L.R.* 4 March 1899.

87 *L.R.* 28 Jan. 1899.

88 *L.R.* 11 March 1899.

89 *T.* 27 March, 1 April 1899.

90 *T.* 11 May 1899; *P.D.*, 4th ser., lxxi, 231–43.

91 Lord F. Stanley to Sir W. V. Harcourt, 9 May 1899, Harcourt MSS. 241, fols. 26–30. Not all Evangelicals supported the Bill. Colonel Saunderson opposed it, believing that, being badly devised, it would destroy the Church—Lucas, *op. cit.*, p. 302. Cf. A. E. Gathorne-Hardy (ed.), *Gathorne Hardy First Earl of Cranbrook*, 1910, ii, p. 370.

92 *T.* 13, 16, 17, 18, 22 May 1899; Russell, *MacColl*, p. 223.

93 *T.* 19, 20 May 1899. This was a policy strongly pressed by Samuel Smith—see *P.D.*, 4th ser., xxxii, 658–63, xlvi, 27–38.

94 *T.* 25, 26 May 1899.

95 *T.* 27, 29 May 1899. There were an estimated 800 Catholic voters.

96 *T.* 27, 31 May 1899.

97 Quoted in S. Salvidge, *op. cit.*, p. 33.

98 *T.* 24 March, 4 May 1899.

99 *T.* 18 Aug., 8, 15 Sept. 1899.

100 *T.* 16 Sept. 1899.

101 *L.R.* 29 April 1899. Chesterton quoted in A. J. P. Taylor, *English History 1914–1945*, 1965, Pelican edition, 1970, p. 71 n.

102 *L.R.* 11 March, 29 April 1899.

103 *T.* 30, 31 May, 1 June 1899; *L.R.* 17 June 1899.

104 Quoted in Salvidge, *op. cit.*, p. 30.

105 *L.C.* 3 Nov. 1898, 14 Nov. 1899.

106 *L.C.* 13 Nov. 1899.

107 *L.C.* 14, 16 Nov. 1899.

108 *L.C.* 15 Nov. 1899.

109 *L.C.* 20, 22 Nov., 1 Dec. 1899.

110 Colonel Morrison in *L.C.* 27 April 1899.

111 Letter from Austin Taylor, *L.C.* 24 Nov. 1899.

112 *L.C.* 22 Nov. 1899.

113 On the Laurence family see *Pen and Ink Sketches of Liverpool Town Councillors*, 1866, pp. 117–23, 191.

114 *L.C.* 5 Dec. 1899.

115 *L.C.* 15 Dec. 1899.

116 *L.C.* 5 Dec. 1899.

117 *L.C.* 14 Dec. 1899. Thompson strongly favoured Stanley's leadership—see his letter in *L.C.* 30 Nov. 1899.

118 *L.C.* 6, 8, Dec. 1899; *L.R.* 16 Dec. 1899.

119 Robert Holt's diary, 6 Dec. 1899.

120 *L.C.* 12 Dec. 1899.

121 Letter from John Ashworth, *L.C.* 13 Dec. 1899; rejoinder in *L.C.* 14 Dec. 1899.

122 *L.C.* 15 Dec. 1899.

123 *T.* and *L.C.* 19 Dec. 1899.

124 *T.* 19 July 1900; Salvidge, *op. cit.*, pp. 34–35.

125 *L.C.* 16 Oct. 1899.

126 See Salvidge's praise of Higginbottom in *L.C.* 15 Dec. 1899.

127 *T.* 21 July 1900. In his autobiography Long omits to mention his forced retirement from West Derby; moreover, he describes the constituency organization as 'about as perfect as it could be', working harmoniously under the chairman, Alderman Cookson. In fact the crisis in 1899–1900 eliminated Cookson as completely as Long himself. See Long, *op. cit.*, pp. 103–4.

128 *P.* 26 July 1884; *T.* 22 Feb. 1894, 13 Sept. 1900. See also P. F. Clarke, *op. cit.*, pp. 232–3. Altogether some 20 per cent of seats in Britain, excluding Ireland, were uncontested by Liberals.

129 *T.* 11 Sept. 1899; Robert Holt's diary, 19 Sept. 1900.

130 *T.* 3, 12 Nov. 1897.

131 *L.C.H.* 3 Feb. 1899.

132 *L.C.H.* 10, 17 Feb. 1899; *L.R.* 20 May 1899.

133 *L.C.H.* 24 Feb., 24 March 1899.

134 *L.R.* 24 June 1899.

135 Sir E. Russell to Sir H. Campbell-Bannerman, 3 Nov. 1899, Campbell-Bannerman Papers, B.L. Add. MSS. 41235, fols. 95–99.

136 A. H. Bencke to Lord Rosebery, 18 Feb. 1900, Rosebery MSS. 10057, fol. 21; Matthew, *op. cit.*, p. 139.

137 *L.C.* 30, 31 Oct., 5, 7, Nov. 1899.

138 *L.C.* 6 Nov. 1899; *L.R.* 11 Nov. 1899.

139 *P.* 6 Jan. 1900.

140 *P.* 18 Jan. 1902. J. W. Auld, 'The Liberal Pro-Boers', *The Journal of British Studies*, xiv, no. 2, May 1975, pp. 78–101, enumerates 45 pro-Boer Liberal M.P.s. using three criteria in the definition: their view that the war was unjust as well as unnecessary or unwise; their activity in peace organizations; their parliamentary votes, especially against war supplies.

141 For Mrs. Mole's work, organizing women in trade unions, see Hamling, *op. cit.*, p. 24; Maddock, *op. cit.*, p. 249. She came to Liverpool in 1879, the wife of a wealthy fruit merchant and Socialist; fought the sweating system; died 1912.

142 Quoted in *L.R.* 21 July 1900. The *Labour Chronicle*, founded by the Liverpool Fabians and I.L.P. in 1899, was taken over by the L.T.C. and edited by Arthur Short—see L.T.C. Minutes, May, July 1899, October 1900; *L.T.C. Annual Report 1899–1900*.

143 *L.C.* 28 Oct., 4 Nov. 1899; J. Sexton, *A Criticism of the Workmen's Compensation Act*, Liverpool, 1900.

144 C. Ensor Walters (ed.), *The Social Mission of the Church*, 1906, pp. 167–8.

145 *L.R.* 31 Jan. 1900. Cf. Sellers, *op. cit.*, pp. 142–5, 263; I. Sellers 'Nonconformist Attitudes in Later Nineteenth-Century Liverpool', *T.H.S.L.C.*, vol. 114, 1962.

146 W. Robertson Nicoll, '*Ian MacLaren*': *Life of the Rev. John Watson*, 1908, pp. 263, 271–2. See also W. Robertson Nicoll, *Princes of the Church*, 1921, pp. 204–16; R. Hart-Davis, *Hugh Walpole*, 1952 edition, p. 43.

147 *L.R.* 21 July 1900; B. Gardiner, *Mafeking: A Victorian Legend*, 1966, p. 9; Robert Holt's diary, 1 March, 18, 19 May 1900; Richard Holt's diary, 1 March, 18, 19 May 1900.

148 Quoted in *L.R.* 16 June 1900. Morley's speech, separating imperialism from the politics of social reform, was interpreted as a bid for Labour support—see Hamer, *J. Morley*, pp. 315–16; Morgan, *Keir Hardie*, p. 107.

149 W. S. Blunt, *My Diaries*, New York, 1921, ii, p. 72.

150 Sir E. Russell to Sir H. Campbell-Bannermann, 4 Dec. 1899, Campbell-Bannerman Papers, B.L. Add. MSS. 41235, fol. 120. Russell had used a similar version of this phrase in a letter to Lord Rosebery, 1 Dec. 1899, Rosebery MSS. 10112, fols. 239–40.

151 *L.R.* 6 Oct. 1900.

152 Robert Holt's diary, 4 Oct. 1900; *L.R.* 15 Sept. 1900; S. Smith to Sir V. Harcourt, 8 Sept. 1898, Harcourt MSS. 237, fols. 32–37. Cf. Smith's prediction during the Benefices Bill debate in 1898—'We are nearing the time when a General Election will turn upon this question [Ritualism] more than any other.' *P.D.*, 4th ser., lix, 1036.

153 Sir E. R. Russell to Lord Rosebery, 13 July 1898, Rosebery MSS. 10111, fols. 72–75; Sir E. R. Russell to Sir W. V. Harcourt, 17, 24 Oct., 25 Nov. 1898; A. Taylor to Harcourt, 5 Dec. 1898, Harcourt MSS. 237, fols. 125–8, 147–8, 238, fols. 74–75, 239, fol. 33.

154 *L.C.* 30 Nov. 1899. Cf. D. W. R. Bahlman, 'The Queen, Mr. Gladstone, and Church Patronage', *Victorian Studies*, 1959–60, pp. 349–80.

155 Gardiner, *op. cit.* ii, pp. 521–2. Harcourt, however, supported the 1903 Church Discipline Bill, see *P.D.*, 4th ser., cxix, 776–86. On Harcourt's isolation, as an ultra-Protestant, among men of ministerial rank, see Russell, *MacColl*, chap. ix.

156 S. Smith to Harcourt, 31 Dec. 1898, 6 Jan. 1899, Harcourt MSS. 240, fols. 58–61.

157 *T.* 9 March 1900; W. Rathbone to A. Warr, 23 Oct. 1899, enclosed in W. Long to Lord Salisbury, 29 Oct. 1899, Salisbury MSS.

158 *L.C.* 27 Nov. 1899; *T.* 14 April 1900.

159 Quoted in J. B. Lancelot, *Francis James Chavasse, Bishop of Liverpool*, Oxford, 1929, p. 149.

160 *L.C.* 11 Oct., 15 Nov. 1899; *P.* 11 Aug. 1900.

161 *L.C.* 21 Oct. 1899.

162 *P.* 6 Oct. 1900. For a character sketch of the 6th Earl Portsmouth, formerly Viscount Lymington, M.P. Barnstaple (1880–5) and Devon North (1885–91), see Lord Newton, *Retrospection*, 1941, p. 5.

163 *L.R.* 22, 29 Sept. 1900.

164 See Houston's autobiographical admissions in *P.D.*, 4th ser., cliii, 1141–2; *L.C.* 25 Sept. 1900.

165 R. D. Holt to H. Gladstone, 27 Jan. 1903, Viscount Gladstone Papers, B.L. Add. MSS. 46060, fol. 109. See also L.T.C. Minutes, 29 Aug. 1900; and Higginbottom's maiden parliamentary speech, against the Miners (Eight Hours) Bill, in *P.D.*, 4th ser., lxxxix, 1383–4.

166 *L.R.* 29 Sept. 1900.

167 See *L.C.* 4 to 11 Nov. 1897; *T.* 20 Oct. 1897. M'Arthur defeated the shipowner, Russell Rea. The Liverpool Liberals wanted Rea to fight another local seat, probably Kirkdale, in 1900, but he was pledged to Gloucester. Robert Holt's diary, 2 Dec. 1898.

168 *T.* 28 Oct. 1897; *Liverpool Steam Ship Owners' Association, Annual Report 1910*, p. 14; *Dod's Parliamentary Companion.*

169 B. O'Connell, *op. cit.*, pp. 123–4.

170 *L.C.H.* 14 April 1899.

171 *L.R.* 24 June 1899; *P.* 1, 22, 29 Sept., 6 Oct. 1900; Viscount Gladstone, *op. cit.*, p. 186; W. B. Gwynn, *Democracy and the Cost of Politics in Britain*, 1962, p. 141; Lord Birkenhead, *Contemporary Personalities*, 1924, pp. 259–66.

172 L.T.C. Minutes, 2 Oct. 1900.

173 *L.R.* 29 Sept. 1900.

174 *L.R.* 6 Oct. 1900.

175 *P.* 10, 17 Nov. 1900.

CHAPTER 12

1 Dicey, *op. cit.*, p. 187; Smith, *Life Work*, p. 43; A. Dru (ed.), *The Journals of Kierkegaard 1834–1854*, Fontana edition, 1965, p. 233.

2 Richard Holt's diary, 15 Nov. 1900; *P.* 15, 22 Dec. 1900.

3 Sir E. R. Russell to Lord Rosebery, 22 Jan. 1901, Rosebery MSS. 10114, fols. 24–25; *P.S.* 2 Feb. 1901; Sellers, *Salute to Pembroke*, p. 19.

4 *T.* 25 April 1901; S. Smith to H. Gladstone, 29 March 1901, Viscount Gladstone Papers, B.L. Add. MSS. 46058, fol. 234.

5 *T.* 14 Feb. 1901; *P.S.* 6 April 1901.

6 Chavasse in *Church and Reform*, 1902, pp. ix-xiii; *L.C.* 8 April 1901. Chavasse, however, continued to be one of the few bishops in the Church Association's good books—*Church Association Annual Report, 1912–13*, p. 11.

7 Chadwick, *op. cit.* ii, pp. 390–1. By 1901 the cathedral fund amounted to £143,000, but the Diocesan Committee was divided over the question of a site. Kensington fields, Monument Place, and St. John's churchyard, were each canvassed before St. James's Mount was fixed. St. Peter's, in Church Street, was used as the pro-cathedral: this was demolished in 1923 to make way for Woolworth's. See Sir W. B. Forwood, *The Liverpool Cathedral: The Story of its Foundation 1895–1914*, Liverpool, 1925; *Liverpool Cathedral: The Protest by the Liverpool Cathedral Petition Committee,* Liverpool, 1901; Sir F. Radcliffe, 'Some Notes on the First Scheme for a Liverpool Cathedral', *The Liverpool Review*, vol. v, no. 7, July 1930, pp. 291–7.

8 Revd. J. McKinney in *L.C.* 15 July 1901. Cf. J. Bateman, *The Church Association*, 1880, pp. 44–53. However, C. W. Stubbs, then vicar of Wavertree, argued powerfully for cathedrals as centres of social work as well as of religion—see C. W. Stubbs, *Saint Nicholas at the Port*, Liverpool, 1893; *The Cathedral Chapter of Liverpool*, 1904, and *Christ and Economics*, 1893, pp. 45, 88–89; E. H. Sedding *Charles William Stubbs D.D., Fourth Bishop of Truro*, Plymouth, 1914, pp. 23–60.

9 *Police (Liverpool Inquiry) Act 1909, Proceedings*, pp. 665, 684–5.

10 Ibid., pp. 674–6, 759, 761; *L.C.* 17, 27, 28 May, 1 June 1901; *T.* 3 June 1901.

11 *P.* 11 Oct. 1902.

12 *L.C.* 15, 16, 17 July 1901.

13 *L.C.* 29 July 1901.

14 *P.S.* 3, 17 Aug. 1901.

15 *T.* 31 Aug. 1901; *L.D.P.* 25, 29, Oct., 1 Nov. 1901.

16 *L.D.P.* 2 Nov. 1901.

17 *L.D.P.* 31 Oct. 1901; Shrewsbury, *op. cit.*, pp. 531–2.

18 *L.D.P.* 7 Nov. 1901.

19 *P.* 12 April 1902.

20 Quoted in J. Wentworth Day, *Lady Houston D.B.E.*, 1958, p. 40. Poppy was progressively 'Mrs.' Gretton, Lady Brinckman, and Lady Byron, before she married Houston in 1924.

21 *P.D.*, 4th ser., lxxxii, 1068–87; W. Camp, *The Glittering Prizes*, 1960, p. 34 ff.; Lord Birkenhead, *The Life of F. E. Smith*, 1959, pp. 71–72. In Houston's favour it might be noted that some of his ships transported troops to South Africa free of charge—see *L.D.P.* 17 Oct. 1899.

22 A. T. Salvidge to Lord Derby, 14 Dec. 1921. Houston's and Derby's mutual hatred was even more extreme—Derby to Salvidge, 21 June 1917, 9 Dec. 1921, Derby MSS.

23 *P.* 18 Jan. 1902.

24 Letter signed C.A.T. in *L.D.P.* 6 Nov. 1902.

25 *L.C.* 15 April 1901.

26 *L.C.* 15 May 1902. For the disputed effects of the corn duties on food prices see *P.D.*, 4th ser., cxxiii, 344, cxxiv, 131–5, M'Arthur and MacIver.

27 *P.S.* 24 May 1902.

28 *P.S.* 12 July 1902.

29 *L.C.* 29 May 1901; *P.* 19 July 1902.

30 Walsh, *op. cit.*, pp. 38–39.

31 *The Church Association Monthly Intelligencer*, Jan. 1882, pp. 23–24, June 1883, p. 168, July 1883, pp. 180–2, Aug. 1883, p. 212; *Truth*, 29 Aug., 19 Sept. 1889, 11 Jan. 1894; J. Britten, *A Prominent Protestant*, 1898, pp. 3–4, 7–9; Thorold, *op. cit.*, p. 452; R. D. Blumenfeld, *R.D.B.'s Diary 1887–1914*, 1930, p. 176. On the Catholic Truth Society, founded by James Britten in 1884, see Inglis, *op. cit.*, pp. 137–40.

32 Creighton, *op. cit.*, ii, p. 215.

33 Ibid., pp. 287–94, 313–14, 424; J. G. Lockhart, *Charles Lindley, Viscount Halifax*, 1936, vol. ii, pp. 133–7; Lord Birkenhead, *Halifax*, 1965, p. 61; Prestige, *op. cit.*, pp. 227–36; Smith, *Life Work*, p. 394; *P.D.*, 4th ser., lix, 469–80, Smith; *P.S.* 27 April 1901; *The Church Annual Log-Book*, 1902, pp. 360, 397; *T.* and *L.D.P.* 9 Oct. 1902; *P.* 11 Oct. 1902; *The Guardian*, 5 Jan. 1898 *et. seqq.*

34 *P.S.* 6, 13, 20 April 1901.

35 *P.S.* 23 Aug. 1902.

36 *P.S.* 13 Sept. 1902.

37 *P.S.* 11 Oct. 1902.

38 *P.* 13 Sept. 1902; *T.* 9 Sept. 1902.

39 *P.* and *P.S.* 20 Sept. 1902.

40 *T.* 11 Sept. 1902.

41 *T.* 22, 23 Sept, 1902.

42 *P.* 13 Sept. 1902.

43 *P.* 4 Oct. 1902; *T.* 26 Sept. 1902. Birkenhead, *Halifax*, p. 61 wrongly describes the weapon as 'a well-aimed brick'.

44 His death was unexpected. The wound over his eye was healing and on 5 October Kensit even conducted a service in the hospital—*L.D.P.* 6 Oct. 1902; *The Guardian*, 5, 26 Nov. 1902.

45 J. C. Wilcox and J. A. Kensit, *Contending for the Faith*, 1939, pp. 60–61; *T.* 10 Oct. 1902.

46 *The Guardian*, 1, 15 Oct. 1902.

47 He is wrongly named 'McKeevan' in Birkenhead, *Birkenhead*, p. 107.

48 Robert Holt's diary, 15 Dec. 1902; *The Guardian*, 17 Dec. 1902; *L.C.* 22 June, 22 July 1903.

49 *T.* 3 Dec. 1902. The Church Association made the same point—*Church Association, Annual Report 1902*, pp. 16–17.

50 *L.C.* 9 Jan. 1903.

51 J. A. Kensit, *What I Saw in Rome*, 1924, p. 59. Cf. *P.S.* 11 Oct. 1902.

52 *T.* 13 Oct. 1902.

53 *P.S.* 20 Dec. 1902.

54 Sir C. Petrie, *The Life and Letters of the Right Hon. Sir Austin Chamberlain*, 1939, vol. i, pp. 97–98.

55 *T.* 23, 31 Aug. 1901; E. Evans to H. Gladstone, 15 Aug. 1901, Viscount Gladstone Papers, B.L. Add. MSS 46059, fol. 27.

56 *T.* 17, 31 Dec. 1901; Matthew, *op. cit.*, chaps. iii, viii.

57 Lord Rosebery to Lord Sefton, 11 Aug. 1902, copy, Rosebery MSS. 10131 p. 311.

58 *P.* 1 Feb. 1902.

59 *T.* 24 Jan. 1902, 25 Feb. 1902. See also E. Evans to Sir H. Campbell-Bannerman, 20 Feb. 1902, and Sir E. Russell to the same, 21 Dec. 1901, B.L. Add. MSS. 41237, fol. 5., 41241, fols. 236–9, 240b; J. Wilson, *C. B.; A Life of Sir Henry Campbell-Bannerman*, 1973, chaps. 23–25; Blumenfeld, *op. cit.*, pp. 171–2; J. L. Hammond, *C. P. Scott*, 1934, pp. 77–78.

60 *T.* 8 May 1902; Sellers, 'Liverpool Nonconformity', pp. 349–50; *Daily News*, 20 Feb. 1903; Robert Holt's diary, 21 July, 13 Nov., 20 Dec. 1901, 10 Jan., 14, 15, 23 Feb. 1902; Richard Holt's diary, 19 Dec. 1901, 14, 15, 21, 25 Feb., 24 March, 14 May 1902.

61 Bryce quoted in H. A. L. Fisher, *James Bryce*, 1927, vol. i, p. 325; Matthew pp. 94–97, 231–5; E. G. Sandford (ed.), *Memoirs of Archbishop Temple*, 1906, vol. ii, pp. 377–82; G. K. A. Bell, *Randall Davidson*, Oxford, 1935, vol. i, pp. 372–80; Halévy, *op. cit.*, v, pp. 202–4.

62 B. D. White, *op. cit.*, pp. 147–8; *P.D.*, 4th ser., cv, 950–3, T. P. O'Connor, cxii, 225–7, C. M'Arthur; Smith, *Life Work*, pp. 463–4; Sellers, 'Liverpool Nonconformity' pp. 352–4; Sellers, *Salute to Pembroke*, p. 23.

63 *L.C.* 5, 6, 10, 11 Feb. 1902.

64 K. Martin, *Father Figures*, Penguin, 1969, p. 43.

65 *P.* 1 Nov. 1902. Taylor soon gave clear warning that he opposed any interference with the free movement of foods and raw materials—'I am not "a free trader": I am "a convinced free trader".' *P.D.*, 4th ser., cxxiii, 398–404.

66 *P.* 1 Nov. 1902; *P.D.*, 4th ser., cxiv, 1415–20, cxv, 553–4.

67 *L.D.P.* 29 Oct. 1902.

68 *T.* and *L.D.P.* 30 Oct. 1902. Williams was vice-chairman of Granby ward Conservative Association and a member of the East Toxteth divisional council; Lloyd was chairman of the High Park Street Conservative club.

69 *T.* and *L.D.P.* 1 Nov. 1902 differ slightly in their enumerations.

70 O. C. Williams in *P.* 15 Nov. 1902.

71 *L.D.P.* 1 Nov. 1902.

72 See McGuffie's letters in *L.C.* 8 Feb. 1902; *L.M.* 10, 24 May, 19 Sept. 1902; *L.D.P.* 23 July 1902; Swift, *op. cit.*, chaps. viii, x.

73 *L.D.P.* 1 Nov. 1902.

74 *L.D.P.* 29 Oct. 1902.

75 *L.D.P.* 30, 31 Oct. 1902. See also letters from P. Lloyd and H. Burley in *L.D.P.* 1, 3 Nov. 1902.

76 *L.D.P.* 28 Oct. 1902.

77 *P.S.* 1 Nov. 1902.

78 *P.* 8 Nov. 1902.

79 *T.* 6 Nov. 1902.

80 *L.D.P.* 3 Nov. 1902.
81 *L.D.P.* 5, 6 Nov. 1902.
82 *T.* 6 Nov. 1902; *The Guardian*, 12 Nov. 1902; *P.* 6 Dec. 1902.
83 *P.* 15 Nov. 1902.
84 Letter from 'Unionist' in *L.D.P.* 6 Nov. 1902.
85 *L.D.P.* 6 Jan. 1903.
86 *P.* 22, 29 Nov. 1902.
87 H. R. Rathbone in *T.* and *L.D.P.* 12 Jan. 1903.
88 *L.D.P.* 24 Jan. 1903; Robert Holt's diary, 20 Jan. 1903.
89 *T.* 12 Jan. 1903; *L.D.P.* 13 Jan. 1903. A small majority of the Finance Committee of Liverpool City Council called for the taxation of unoccupied land and houses, as did many large municipalities and most Liberals. Rutherford promoted the Land Values Bill 1904; and Austin Taylor and J. S. Harmood-Banner were other Liverpool Conservatives supporting such legislation. J. H. Stock voiced the opposition of the Mersey Docks and Harbour Board. See *P.D.*, 4th ser., cxxxi, 866–71, 910–11; cxlv, 216–19, 240–4.
90 *T.* 16, 19, 20 Jan. 1903; *Daily News*, 19 Jan. 1903; and report of 15th Conference of Lancashire and Cheshire Working Men's Federation, in *L.D.P.* 25 May 1903.
91 Robert Holt's diary, 7, 8 Jan. 1903; Richard Holt's diary, 7, 8 Jan. 1903.
92 Beatrice Webb's diary, vol. 20, 10 Oct. 1899, Webb MSS.
93 Robert Holt's diary, 23 July 1892, 1 Oct. 1899; Richard Holt's diary, 15 April 1900, 12 March 1903.
94 *T.* 9, 12 Jan. 1903; *L.C.H.* 16, 23, 30 Jan 1903.
95 *L.C.* 15 Jan. 1903; Richard Holt's diary, 31 Dec. 1901.
96 *L.C.* 10 Jan. 1903.
97 *L.D.P.* 8 Jan. 1903; *L.C.H.* 9 Jan. 1903; *P.S.* 17 Jan. 1903.
98 *L.C.* 15 Jan. 1903.
99 *Daily News*, 19 Jan. 1903.
100 The contests, in Edge Hill, Low Hill, and Kensington, in 1902 were straight fights against Conservatives. Some of the anti-Conservative vote was, therefore, Liberal; moreover, personal influences were unquantifiable—for example R. C. Faulkner, bearing Labour's standard in Edge Hill, was formerly active in the W.M.C.A.
101 *L.D.P.* and *L.C.* 3 Jan. 1903.
102 *T.* 7 Jan. 1903.
103 *L.D.P.* 13 Jan. 1903.
104 Sellers, *Salute to Pembroke*, p. 14; *L.R.* 16 April 1892.
105 Aked, *op. cit.*, pp. 185, 192–5; Revd. J. Watson to Revd. C. Aked, 8 May 1893, in Nicoll, *op. cit.*, pp. 161–3.
106 C. Cross, *Philip Snowden*, 1966, p. 61; M. A. Hamilton, *Remembering My Good Friends*, 1944, p. 114; M. I. Cole (ed.), *Beatrice Webb's Diaries 1924–1932*, 1956, p. 3 et seqq. Mrs Snowden later told C. P. Scott, 'The *Manchester Guardian* represents my views'—T. Wilson (ed.), *The Political Diaries of C. P. Scott 1911–28* diary, 27–30 Nov. 1924, p. 472.
107 *T.* 9 Jan. 1903.
108 Glasier's letter in *L.D.P.* 24 Jan. 1903; J. Keir Hardie in *Labour Leader*, 17 Jan. 1903.
109 *L.D.P.* 8 Jan. 1903. Cf. F. Bealey and H. Pelling, *Labour and Politics 1900–1906*, 1958, p. 138; McBriar, *op. cit.*, pp. 315–16; R. McKibbin, *The Evolution of the Labour Party 1910–1924*, Oxford, 1974, pp. 100–3.
110 *L.D.P.* 9 Jan. 1903.
111 *T.* 10, 17 Jan. 1903.
112 *T.* 20 Jan. 1903.
113 Bealey and Pelling, *op. cit.*, p. 139; W. B. Gwynn, *op. cit.*, pp. 174–5.

114 *L.D.P.* 21 Jan. 1903.

115 *L.D.P.* 17 Jan. 1903; *L.R.* 24 Jan. 1903; R. D. Holt to H. Gladstone, 27 Jan. 1903, Viscount Gladstone Papers, B.L. Add. MSS. 46060, fol. 109; Robert Holt's diary, 7, 8, 20 Jan. 1903; Richard Holt's diary, 7, 8 Jan. 1903.

116 This is the second verse. In full in *L.D.P.* 22 Jan. 1903.

117 *L.D.P.* 24 Jan. 1903.

118 *L.D.P.* 19 Jan. 1903; McGuffie's letter to Austin Harford in *L.C.* 31 Jan. 1903.

119 *L.C.* 4 Feb. 1903.

120 See McGuffie's letter to his constituents in *L.D.P.* 30 Oct. 1905. On Bell see Orchard, *Legion*, p. 161.

121 *L.R.* 24 Feb. 1903.

122 *T.* 11 Nov. 1902.

123 *L.C.* 5 March 1903.

124 Wise's letter in *L.C.* 26 March 1903; *L.D.P.* 7 March 1903.

125 *L.D.P.* 6 March 1903; *L.C.H.* 13 March 1903.

126 *P.S.* 4 April 1903, 9 May 1903; *L.C.* 28 April 1903.

127 *L.R.* 4 April 1903.

128 *P.S.* 11 April 1903.

129 R. Griffiths, *op. cit.*, p. 11; R. F. Henderson, *George Wise of Liverpool*, privately printed, Liverpool Protestant Party, *c.* 1967, pp. 8–11.

130 *L.C.* 20 April 1903. See also interview with Wise in *L.C.* 8 June 1903.

131 *P.S.* 2 May 1903; *L.R.* 9 May 1903; *L.C.* 15 May 1903; Griffiths, *op. cit.*, p. 12.

132 Interview with Wise in *L.C.* 23 April 1904.

133 *L.C.* 21, 23 April 1903; *P.D.*, 4th ser., cxxii, 199–200, J. Cullinan and A. Akers-Douglas.

134 *L.C.* 28 April 1903.

135 When 'Red Indian' acts became popular in circuses in the 1850s, George Sanger recruited his first ten 'savages' (two were women) from Liverpool slums—see G. Sanger, *Seventy Years a Showman*, 1926 edition, chap. xxxiv.

136 The Revd. Weir Miskimmin in *L.C.* 2 May 1903. See also *The Church Association Annual Report 1902*, p. 5.

137 J. Brent in *L.C.* 6 May 1903.

138 *L.C.* 23 April, 2 May 1903; *P.S.* 25 April 1903.

139 *L.R.* 16 May 1903.

140 *L.D.P.* 14 May 1903.

141 *P.S.* 4 April 1903.

142 *L.D.P.* 14 May 1903.

143 *L.C.* 23, 28 May 1903; *L.D.P.* 20, 27 May 1903.

144 *P.S.* 13 June 1903.

145 *L.C.* 11, 14 July 1903; *L.R.* and *P.S.* 18 July 1903. An Independent Orange Institution had been established in June 1903, angry at the betrayal of the Protestant democracy by 'Orange leaders whose address is Carlton Club'—see *Orangeism: Its History and Progress: A Plea for First Principles*, Dublin, 1904.

146 *P.S.* 5 Sept. 1903.

147 H. Johnson, *Stories of Great Revivals*, 1906, p. 380. Torrey and Alexander returned to Liverpool between November 1904 and January 1905—see W. T. Stead, *The Revival of 1905*, 1905, pp. 79–99.

148 *L.C.* 15, 17, 19 Sept. 1903.

149 *L.D.P.* 3 Nov. 1903.

150 *L.C.* 22 June 1903. For the controversy over the respective pastoral diligence of Wise, Catholic priests, and Anglican clergy, see *L.C.* 25, 26, 30 June, 3, 8, 9 July 1903.

151 *L.R.* 24 Oct. 1903.

152 *L.C.H.* 30 Jan., 20 Feb. 1903; *L.C.* 14 Feb. 1903.

153 *L.D.P.* 9 March 1903. For an earlier version, see Wakeford's letter to *The Guardian*, 3 Aug. 1898. The Bishop of Liverpool had the measure of Wakeford's impulsive character in a letter of 15 Dec. 1910, when Wakeford was among the candidates to succeed Scott Holland as a Canon of St. Paul's, Asquith MSS. 22, fol. 51.

154 *P.S.* 21 March 1903; *P.D.*, 4th ser., cxix, 772–6, W. W. Rutherford.

155 Wakeford in *L.R.* 22 April 1899.

156 *L.R.* 8 Sept. 1900.

157 *L.R.* 29 April 1899.

158 *L.R.* 22 Sept. 1900. Cf. Bateman, *op. cit.*, p. 70.

159 *L.D.P.* 15 Oct. 1903; *L.C.* 26 Sept. 1903.

160 Wise in *L.D.P.* 21 Dec. 1903.

161 *L.R.* 31 Oct. 1903.

162 *L.D.P.* 5 Oct. 1903.

163 B. D. White, *op. cit.*, pp. 173–6.

164 *L.D.P.* 1 Dec. 1903.

165 *L.C.* 3 Aug. 1903.

166 *L.D.P.* 12 Nov. 1903; *L.C.H.* 6 Nov. 1903.

167 J. Amery, *The Life of Joseph Chamberlain*, vol. 6, 1969, pp. 488–93; Robert Holt's diary, 28 June, 25, 30 Oct., 6, 18 Nov. 1903.

168 *L.D.P.* 31 Oct. 1903.

169 *L.C.* 12 Sept. 1903; *L.D.P.* 20 Oct. 1903; *L.R.* 31 Oct. 1903.

170 Joseph's estimate in *L.R.* 31 Oct. 1903.

171 *L.R.* 14 Nov. 1903; Robert Holt's diary, 6, 9 Nov. 1903. In Hampson's case the Mayoralty paid handsomely for he received a baronetcy (despite the Prime Minister's belief that a knighthood was adequate) in 1904 when the King visited Liverpool to lay the foundation stone of the Anglican Cathedral. See J. S. Sandars to Lord Knollys, 7 July 1904, Sandars MSS. c. 720, fols. 73–75, copy.

172 Williams belonged to the Scotland constituency branch of the W.M.C.A.; Griffiths wrote a pamphlet biography of Wise in 1909.

173 *P.S.* 14 Nov. 1903.

174 *L.C.* 12 Nov. 1903; *L.R.* 21 Nov., 12 Dec. 1903.

175 *L.D.P.* 5 Oct. 1903; *P.S.* 28 March, 29 Aug., 14 Nov. 1903.

176 *L.D.P.* 24 Nov. 1903; *T.* 30 Nov. 1903. The Bishop of Chester was Dr. Jayes.

177 *P.S.* 5 Dec. 1903.

178 Ibid.

179 J. Morris to Lord Derby, 17 May 1903, quoted in R. S. Churchill, *Lord Derby*, 1959, p. 82.

180 *L.D.P.* 20 Nov., 4 Dec. 1903; Salvidge, *op. cit.*, pp. 60–61.

181 *L.D.P.* 8 Dec. 1903.

182 *L.D.P.* 19 Nov. 1903.

183 *P.S.* 21 Nov. 1903.

184 *L.D.P.* 18, 20, 23 Nov. 1903.

185 *L.D.P.* 15, 27, 28 Nov., 30 Dec. 1903.

186 *L.D.P.* 28 Nov. 1903.

187 Letter from T. Watkinson (vice-chairman of Edge Hill W.M.C.A.) in *L.D.P.* 1 Dec. 1903.

188 *L.D.P.* 8 Dec. 1903, 23 April 1904.

189 *L.D.P.* 28 Nov., 8 Dec. 1903.

190 Letter from J. Glynn in *L.D.P.* 11 Dec. 1903.

191 *L.D.P.* 15 Dec. 1903.
192 *L.D.P.* 18 Dec. 1903.

CHAPTER 13

1 W. Jeans, *Parliamentary Reminiscences*, 1912, p. 8; Connolly quoted in Greaves, *op. cit.*, p. 63.

2 Henderson, *op. cit.*, p. 13. Lord Derby was the reversioner of the property. The Church appealed to him in 1921 for a reduction in the renewal fine—R. Briggs to Derby, 27 July 1921; Derby to Salvidge, 23 Aug. 1921, Derby MSS.

3 Griffiths, *op. cit.*, p. 15 estimated 1,300 Bible Class members in 1909; the Judicial Inquiry in 1910 reckoned 'over 1,600'—*Police (Liverpool Inquiry) Act 1909, Proceedings*, p. 43.

4 *Inquiry*, *op. cit.*, pp. 43, 721.

5 Whittingham-Jones, *op. cit.*, pp. 49–51.

6 Sir E. R. Russell to R. B. Haldane, 23 July 1913, Haldane MSS. 5910, fols. 78–79; Sir E. R. Russell, *Arrested Fugitives*, 1912, chap. xi; *P.S.* 28 March 1908. Likewise, the Free Church Council had been tempted to join Kensit's anti-Ritualist movement. See A. G. Gardiner, *Life of George Cadbury*, 1923, pp. 184–5.

7 *P.S.* 3 Aug. 1907.

8 *Inquiry*, *op. cit.*, pp. 114, 116, 1408–9, 1436 and Qs. 14843–6, 19787.

9 *L.C.* 23, 27, 29 April, 2 May 1904.

10 *L.D.P.* 30 April, 3 May 1904.

11 *L.C.* 3 May 1904.

12 *T.* 28 March, 18 April, 23 May 1904; *L.C.* 1, 19 April 1904.

13 *L.C.* 4 May 1904.

14 *L.D.P.* 4 May 1904.

15 *L.D.P.* 25 April 1904.

16 Wise reportedly considered Roberts 'a most fascinating psychological study', quoted in G. Hughes, *Evan Roberts, Revivalist: Story of the Liverpool Mission*, Dolgelly, 1905, p. 66.

17 Author's conversation with Ralph Rattray (b. 1884). Rattray gave evidence to the Liverpool Inquiry in 1910 (p. 449 ff.). He was then a chain-worker and Wiseite; later he became a Conservative councillor and alderman.

18 *L.D.P.* 8 Sept. 1904.

19 *P.S.* 28 Nov. 1903.

20 *L.R.* 7 Nov. 1903.

21 *L.D.P.* 3 Dec. 1903, 21 June, 8 Aug. 1904.

22 *L.D.P.* 10 June 1904; *L.M.* 18 June 1904.

23 Sectarian riots brought benefit to ordinary constables in that the prolonged periods of extra duty led to the first definite recognition of overtime payment—*P.P.* 1920, xxii, Qs. 1495, 1499, Dunning.

24 *Liverpool Police, Annual Report*, 1903, p. 27; ibid., 1904, pp. 19–20.

25 *L.D.P.* 25 April 1904.

26 *L.D.P.* 4 May 1904; *T.* 6 Sept. 1904.

27 *T.* 8 Sept. 1904.

28 *Municipal Journal*, 16 Sept. 1904; H045 10094 B9051/29, Public Record Office. On the limitations of bye-laws see W. O. Hart, *Hart's Introduction to the Law of Local Government and Administration*, 6th edition, 1957, chap. viii.

29 *T.* 11 Oct. 1904.

30 *L.D.P.* 14 Oct. 1904.

31 *T.* 2 Feb. 1905; *L.C.* 27 March 1905; *P.S.* 5, 19 Aug. 1905; *L.D.P.* 5 Sept. 1905; *P.S.* 30 Sept. 1905.

32 Quoted in Salvidge, *op. cit.*, p. 47.

33 *L.R.* 7 March 1903; *L.D.P.* 24 Dec. 1903.

34 F. E. Smith, *Speeches 1906–1909*, Liverpool, 1910, p. 5.

35 *P.D.*, 4th ser., cxxxiii, 691–2. That a Royal Commission rather than a Select Committee of the Commons was set up was due to the Archbishop of Canterbury's influence. Ritualists would not have relished appearing before a Select Committee 'made up of such rascals as Austen (*sic*) Taylor'—H. W. Hill, secretary of the English Church Union, quoted in R. Lloyd, *The Church of England 1900–1965*, 1966, p. 138. As it was Ritualists considered the Royal Commission unsympathetic, with only three moderately High Church members. Not that this pleased Liverpool's Evangelicals—the prevailing influence was Broad Church. In party terms the members were twelve Conservatives and two Liberals. See G. W. E. Russell, *A Pocketful of Sixpences*, 1907, chap. 38.

36 *P.D.*, 4th ser., lix, 474, S. Smith, lxxi, 285–96, A. J. Balfour.

37 *P.D.*, 4th ser., cxxxiii, 760–71.

38 *L.C.* 23, 28 April 1904.

39 *L.M.* 23 April 1904; *L.D.P.* 20 Oct. 1904.

40 Herbert Gladstone quoted in H. W. McCready, 'Home Rule and the Liberal Party, 1899–1906', *Irish Historical Studies*, xiii, no. 2, Sept. 1963, p. 323. See also Matthew, *op. cit.*, chap. viii.

41 *L.C.* 7 May 1904.

42 *L.D.P.* 6 Sept. 1904.

43 George Wyndham to his mother, 24 Jan. 1906, in Mackail and Wyndham, *op. cit.*, ii, pp. 537–9.

44 *P.* 18 Feb. 1905; J. Chamberlain to A. T. Salvidge, 9 March 1905, quoted in Salvidge, *op. cit.*, p. 67. Amery, *op. cit.*, vol. 6, p. 668, also cites this letter, but incorrectly writes of 'the Eastern division of Liverpool' instead of Everton.

45 *L.M.* 31 Oct. 1895.

46 *P.* 25 Feb. 1905.

47 *T.* 20 Feb. 1905.

48 *L.D.P.* 18 Jan. 1906.

49 *P.S.* 10 June 1905.

50 *P.* 8 April 1905; *L.D.P.* 21 Nov. 1905.

51 *P.* and *P.S.* 20 May 1905.

52 *P.S.* 15 July 1905.

53 *L.D.P.* 10 Oct. 1905; *P.S.* 14 Oct. 1905.

54 *P.S.* 18 March 1905.

55 *P.S.* 21 Oct. 1905.

56 *P.S* 14 Oct. 1905.

57 *P.S.* 23 Dec. 1905.

58 *L.D.P.* 24 Oct. 1905.

59 *L.D.P.* 28 Oct. 1905. The authorities denied that any bitter anti-semitic feeling existed in Liverpool—see *P.P.* 1903, ix, Q. 21450, Dr. Hope.

60 On Cohen, see A. Briggs, *Friends of the People: The Centenary History of Lewis's*, 1956, pp. 8–9 and chap. v.

61 *L.D.P.* 25 Oct. 1905.

62 *P.* 28 Oct. 1905.

63 *L.D.P.* 26 Oct. 1905.

64 *L.D.P.* 24 Oct. 1905. The Corporation's interest in Rivington went back to the 1840s. There were real fears of pollution—see Hope, *City of Liverpool,* pp. 226–31.

65 *L.D.P.* 17 Oct. 1905.

66 The general rate in the pound was as follows, in shillings and pence:

	1893	*1895*	*1905*
Liverpool	4–0¾	3–11½	6–3¾
Kirkdale	5–0½	4–7¾	6–7¾
Everton	4–11	4–9¼	7–0¾
West Derby	5–1½	4–9¼	7–3½
Toxteth Park	4–9½	4–6½	6–10

(*L.D.P.* 24 Oct. 1905).

67 B. D. White, *op. cit.*, p. 191; *L.D.P.* 31 Oct., 8 Nov. 1905; *Liverpool Citizen*, 7 July 1906. It is of course true, considering the magnitude of Liverpool's problems, that its record was deserving of some credit; nevertheless, it invariably remained behind the national average—see Clapham, *op. cit.*, iii, p. 493, iv, pp. 438, 461.

68 *P.S.* 11 Nov. 1905.

69 Sexton, *Agitator*, p. 109.

70 *P.* 26 Aug. 1905.

71 L. H. Powell, *The Shipping Federation 1890–1950*, 1950.

72 *P.* 15 July 1905. Larkin, *op. cit.*, p. 10 wrongly nominates the mayor, 'Sir Edward Lee'.

73 Quoted in Larkin, *op. cit.*, p. 11.

74 *L.C.* 16 Aug. 1905.

75 *P.* 26 Aug. 1905; *L.D.P.* 22 Aug. 1905.

76 *L.D.P.* 7 July 1905; *P.D.*, 4th ser., cxlviii, 1117, cxlix, 380–1, 852, cl. 1149, 1379; *P.* 29 July 1905; L.L.R.C. Minutes, 5 July 1905. Probably half of Harrison's blacklegs were in lodging-houses where conditions, according to the Health Committee, were verminous—see *P.D.*, 4th ser., cli, 59–60; *Liverpool Opinion*, 7 July 1906. The strike is not mentioned in F. E. Hyde, *Shipping Enterprise and Management, 1830–1939: Harrison's of Liverpool*, Liverpool, 1967.

77 *P.* 5, 12 Aug. 1905; letter from Sexton, *L.C.* 4 May 1905.

78 *L.D.P.* 11 Aug. 1905 mentioned Councillor E. J. Chevalier, Salvidge's co-director of Bent's Brewery.

79 *P.* 26 Aug., 2 Sept. 1905.

80 Who persuaded the dockers to return is a mystery—see Larkin, *op. cit.*, p. 10.

81 Ibid., pp. 11–12. Larkin was to leave the N.U.D.L. in 1908 and establish the Irish Transport and General Workers' Union.

82 *L.D.P.* 28 Oct. 1905.

83 *P.P.* 1894, xxxv, Q. 3577. Cf. *P.P.* 1892, xxxvi, Q. 13605, Sexton.

84 B. D. White, *op. cit.*, chap. vi; Pumphrey, *op. cit.*, pp. 88–89; L. Lacey (ed.), *The History of Liverpool from 1207 to 1907: Some Notes*, Liverpool, 1908; Dyos and Aldcroft, *op. cit.*, pp. 269–73; *P.D.*, 5th ser., vol. 213, 1958–9, vol. 245, 1673; R. Ornsby, *Memoirs of James Robert Hope-Scott*, 1884, vol. ii, pp. 121–7.

85 Interview with M. H. Burton, Webb Local Government Collection, vol. 148; Forwood, *Recollections*, pp. 37–38; *P.D.*, 5th ser., vol. 113, 1788.

86 *P.D.*, 4th ser., lxxxiii, 214, W. F. Lawrence.

87 Ibid. xxxviii, 723–4, T. P. O'Connor, lxxxiii, 207–12, W. Field and W. Moore, lxxxiv, 886–8, P. O'Brien. The volume of Liverpool trade continued to increase after the completion of the Manchester Ship Canal.

88 *P.* 10 March 1906; Hyde, *Liverpool and the Mersey*, pp. 126–8; *P.D.*, 4th ser., cxxxviii, 117–36; A. Temple Patterson, *A History of Southampton 1700–1914*, vol. iii, Southampton, 1975, chaps. ix, xi.

89 *P.* 22 April 1905. The Corporation and Docks Board clashed in 1904 over the Land Values Bill, and in 1906–7 the Council sought official representation on the Board—*P.D.*, 4th ser., cxxxi, 910–1; S. Mountfield, *Western Gateway: A History of the Mersey Docks and Harbour Board*, Liverpool, 1965, pp. 103–4; Lacey, *op. cit.*, p. 60.

90 Richard Holt's diary, 18 March 1901.

91 Salvidge, *op. cit.*, pp. 18, 43. T. P. O'Connor, with his argument furnished by Sexton, provided a parliamentary voice in this question—*P.D.*, 4th ser., xcv, 142, cxxiv, 594–5.

92 *L.C.* 31 Jan., 2 Feb. 1905; *L.D.P.* 25 Oct 1905; *P.D.*, 5th ser., xcv, 1182–3.

93 *P.* 18 Nov. 1905.

94 J. W. Boyce, 'The Belfast Protestant Association and the Independent Orange Order, 1901–10', *Irish Historical Studies*, xiii, Sept. 1962, pp. 117–52; Larkin, *op. cit.*, Appendix D; Buckland, *op. cit.*, pp. 28–31.

95 *L.D.P.* 24 Nov. 1905.

96 *P.* 14 Nov. 1905.

97 *L.D.P.* 10, 12 Oct. 1905.

98 *P.* 9 Dec. 1905.

99 *P.* 2 Sept. 1905.

100 *L.D.P.* 27 Oct. 1905.

101 *P.P.* 1868–9, viii, Qs. 1600–1930, T. Trippier.

102 Sexton's first municipal contest, a by-election in Brunswick Ward in 1902, had involved his fighting not only a Liberal, E. Beloe, but also one of the more progressive Nationalists, a master-porter and stevedore, Tom Byrne, at a time when Byrne was out of favour with the parish priest—see *P.* 12, 26 July 1902.

103 *L.D.P.* 1 Nov. 1905; *Sunday Chronicle* 9 Dec. 1906; P. J. Waller, 'Racial Phobia: The Chinese Scare 1906–14', in *Essays presented to C. M. Bowra*, Oxford, 1970, pp. 95–96.

104 *L.D.P.* 10 Oct. 1905.

105 *L.D.P.* 3, 4 Oct. 1905. The election of a city auditor was usually thought a 'disgraceful farce', with few electors voting. See Richard Holt's diary, 1 March 1900.

106 *L.D.P.* 4 Oct. 1905; *P.* 28 Oct. 1905. John Stewart Ratcliffe was a musician, and represented the Musicians Union on the L.T.C.

107 *L.D.P.* 24 Nov. 1905.

108 *L.D.P.* 26, 31 Oct. 1905.

109 *Clarion*, 8, 15 Dec. 1905. Cf. G. D. H. Cole, *A History of the Labour Party from 1914*, 1951 edition, p. 453.

110 *L.D.P.* 23 Dec. 1905; *P.* 16 Dec. 1905.

111 *P.* 18 Nov., 9 Dec. 1905; *L.D.P.* 10 Nov. 1905; *L.C.* 11 Nov. 1905.

112 *L.D.P.* 11 Oct. 1905.

113 *L.D.P.* 14, 27 Oct. 1905.

114 Quoted in S. J. Chapman and H. M. Hallsworth, *Unemployment*, Manchester, 1909, p. 9. See also K. D. Brown, *Labour and Unemployment 1900–1914*, Newton Abbot, 1971, chaps. 2 and 3.

115 *P.D.*, 4th ser., vol. 176, cols. 615–16, vol. 197, col. 1088. On labour colonies see R. Postgate, *The Life of George Lansbury*, 1951, pp. 68–71, 77–87; K. D. Brown, *op. cit.*, p. 81.

116 D. I. Mackay, D. J. C. Forsyth, and D. M. Kelly, 'The Discussion of Public Works Programmes, 1917–1935: Some Remarks on the Labour Movement's Contribution',

International Review of Social History, ix, 1966 pp. 8–17; E. Phelps Brown's review of K. D. Brown, *op. cit.* in *Ec.H.R.*, 2nd ser., xxv, no. 1., 1972, pp. 174–5.

117 *L.D.P.* 16, 23 Dec. 1905.

118 See Inglis, *op. cit.*, pp. 206–7 for Hyndman's past controversy with Booth; K. D. Brown, *op. cit.*, chap. 1 on the S.D.F.'s agency in bringing unemployment to national attention.

119 *P.* 24 Feb., 5 June 1906.

120 *Liverpool Weekly Post*, 20 Jan., 10, 17 Feb. 1906.

121 *L.L.R.C. Annual Report, 1906*; L.L.R.C. Minutes, 2 and 9 May 1906, and enclosed letter from E. Pickmere, the Town Clerk and secretary of the Unemployed Committee, to W. Gerrard, secretary of the L.L.R.C., 16 June 1906. See also Halévy, *op. cit.*, v, pp. 370–1; K. D. Brown, 'Conflict in Early British Welfare Policy', *J.M.H.*, vol. 43, no. 4, Dec. 1971, pp. 615–29.

122 *Liverpool Opinion*, 2 June 1906. On the symbolic importance of Will Crooks see C. F. G. Masterman, *The Condition of England, 1909*, 1960 edition, pp. 113–16.

123 *Liverpool Weekly Post*, 6 Jan. 1906.

124 As the first Labour candidate the Boilermakers' ever ran, Conley was compelled to mute his past Liberal faith. The Union, with 50,000 members in 1905, was £415,000 in credit—see H. Pelling, *Popular Politics and Society in Late Victorian Britain*, 1968, p. 61; J. E. Mortimer, *op. cit.*, pp. 146–9.

125 L.L.R.C. Minutes, 3 Nov. 1903.

126 *L.R.* 12 Dec. 1903.

127 L.L.R.C. Minutes, 1 Feb., 7 March 1905.

128 *L.D.P.* 12 Oct. 1905; *Liverpool Weekly Post*, 6 Jan. 1906.

129 *L.D.P.* 15 Jan. 1906.

130 L.L.R.C. Minutes, 4 July 1906.

131 Ibid., 1 Feb. 1905.

132 *L.D.P.* 30 Dec. 1905. Cf. Simon, *op. cit.*, pp. 255–6.

133 *Liverpool Weekly Post*, 6 Jan. 1906.

134 *L.D.P.* 23 Dec. 1905. Cf. Houston's own account, *P.D.*, 4th ser., cliii, 1141–2.

135 J. Saville, 'Trade Unions and Free Labour: The Background to the Taff Vale Decision', in Flinn and Smout *op. cit.*, p. 266; Sexton, *Agitator*, pp. 203–4; F. Bower, *Rolling Stonemason*, 1936, p. 169; Larkin, *op. cit.*, pp. 12–13; *P.D.*, 4th ser., clii, 600, R. Houston.

136 See for example the speech reported in *L.D.P.* 16 Jan. 1906, parts of which can be read in Larkin, *op. cit.*, pp. 13–14.

137 *P.* 13 Jan. 1906. Under 2 per cent of Houston's crews were foreigners, recruited abroad to replace deserting British seamen. Houston demanded legislation to compel British vessels sailing from British ports to engage at least 75 per cent British subjects. One of the special targets was Alfred Holt & Co., working the Liverpool–China trade with, according to David MacIver, 2,000 Chinese among the crews. However, Houston and MacIver distorted the general picture by particular examples because employment in British vessels was annually moving towards their goal. Between 1901 and 1910 the proportion of British seamen increased from 69·7 to 73·2 per cent, see *P.D.*, 4th ser., cliv, 603–4, clxiii, 79, clxv, 1039, clxxxv, 618–55; *Liverpool Steam Ship Owners' Association, Annual Report, 1911*, Table VI.

138 *L.D.P.* 16 Jan. 1906; *P.* 27 Jan. 1906, 11 Feb. 1911.

139 *P.* 3 Feb. 1906.

140 Robert Holt's diary, 16 March, 1 Nov. 1897, 1 Nov. 1898, 6 Feb. 1901, 18 May 1904, 21 Jan. 1906.

141 *L.D.P.* 9 Dec. 1905; Lord Reading, *Rufus Isaacs, First Marquess of Reading 1860–1914*, 1942, p. 147.

142 *L.D.P.* 8 Dec. 1905. Brewers might also manipulate the Licensing Act by securing compensation for an unprofitable pub which they wished to close anyway—see C. Fenby, *The Other Oxford*, 1970, pp. 91–92.

143 *L.D.P.* 9 Dec. 1905.

144 *L.D.P.* 11 Dec. 1905. For Forwood's views on licensing reform see Samuelson, *Drink and Compensation*, pp. 31–33.

145 *P.* 4 Nov. 1905.

146 Chamberlainite shipowners MacIver defined as those engaged in the general cargo trade, carrying especially British manufactured goods. Free traders he defined as those in minor traffic, such as the coal trade, or those with vested interests in cosmopolitan capital, like bankers, brokers, and middlemen. The Liverpool Tariff Reform League included many prominent shipowners—Sir Alfred Jones, Aubrey Brocklebank, R. W. Leyland, and two chairmen of the Steam Ship Owners' Association, A. S. Collard and Beckett Hill. See *P.D.*, 4th. ser., cxli, 208–16, cxliii, 1619–25.

147 *L.D.P.* 16 Jan. 1906. The cotton seasons from 1904 to 1907 brought 'unexampled prosperity', with plentiful raw materials, high production and consumption, increased profits and wages; and in December 1906 the Prince of Wales opened a new Liverpool Cotton Exchange—see *Ellison's Annual Review of the Cotton Trade*, 1904–5, 1905–6, 1906–7.

148 Forwood, *Recollections*, pp. 152–3; *P.* 3 June 1905. MacIver claimed that since the family firm, Leach, Harrison, and Forwood, was no longer independent but simply agent to the Hamburg-American Company, Forwood had ceased to have title as a Liverpool shipowner—*P.D.*, 4th. ser., cxli, 210–11. On the weaknesses of the Free Food League, see R. A. Rempel, *Unionists Divided*, Newton Abbot, 1972, p. 46 ff.

149 Mackail and Wyndham, *op. cit.* ii, pp. 534–5, 594–6.

150 Tressell, *op. cit.*, p. 23.

151 *Liverpool Steam Ship Owners Association, Annual Report 1903*, pp. 4–8. Some protection had already been achieved since 1850 through conference rings and passenger pools; but marine insurance, 'light' dues and liability legislation were impositions which many British shipowners complained of, and by 1900 several large Liverpool companies owned vessels which traded under Belgian and Dutch flags 'because there are certain privileges obtainable thereby as well as exemptions from conditions of unreasonable Board of Trade interference with shipping which they do not find under the British flag'. See *P.D.*, 4th. ser., lv, 157–61, lxiii, 26–28, lxvii, 106–8, lxxx, 1366–72, D. MacIver and C. M'Arthur; A. H. John, *A. Liverpool Merchant House*, 1959, p. 60; Dyos and Aldcroft, *op. cit.*, chap. 9.

152 *L.D.P.* 16 Jan. 1906.

153 *L.C.* and *L.D.P.* 17 Jan. 1906.

154 Quoted in *L.D.P.* 30 Dec. 1905.

155 Richard Holt's diary, 19 Jan. 1904; letter from A. Haywood in *L.D.P.* 16 Jan. 1906. See *P.D.*, 4th ser., cxliii, 1629–32 for M'Arthur's confusion. M'Arthur became progressively more Balfourian as it became clear that he would face Liberal opposition—Rempel, *op. cit.*, pp. 144, 160–1.

156 The polling day, Tuesday, 16 January 1906, chosen by the Conservative agent, was most objectionable to the Nationalist organizers because of the particular conditions of port work—see F. L. Crilly in *L.D.P.* 9 Jan. 1906.

157 *T.* 27 Jan. 1905.

158 *L.D.P.* 20 Nov. 1905.

159 T. P. O'Connor to J. Redmond, 30 Oct. 1905, quoted in D. Gwynn, *The Life of John Redmond*, 1932, p. 115. See also B. O'Connell, *op. cit.*, p. 166.

160 Speech at Sunderland, *L.D.P.* 9 Nov. 1905.

161 Petrie, *Chamberlain*, ii, p. 174; Sir A. Chamberlain, *Politics from Inside*, 1936, p. 39; Rempel, *op. cit.*, pp. 144–5. Carson, however, spoke at a Liverpool rally organized by Salvidge—see *L.D.P.* and *L.C.* 12 Jan. 1906.

162 *P.* 17, 24 June 1905.

163 *L.D.P.* 25 Nov. 1905. On the eve of polling Lawrence finally threw over Chamberlain's fiscal policy—*L.D.P.* 16 Jan. 1906.

164 J. E. B. Seely, *Adventure*, 1930, pp. 105–6; Rempel, *op. cit.*, *passim* on the Hughligans. Seely had undertaken to fight Abercromby, paying his own expenses, early in 1905, though Richard Holt had been approached before him. See Richard Holt's diary, Dec. 1904; and Seely to H. Gladstone, 10 Jan. 1905, Viscount Gladstone Papers. B.L. Add. MSS. 46061, fol. 109. On the relative importance of free trade and Chinese labour as issues in Abercromby, see *P.D.*, 4th. ser., cliii, 1143. Education was also important see *L.D.P.* 27 Nov. 1905.

165 *L.D.P.* 16 Jan. 1906; *L.C.* 20 Dec. 1899.

166 *L.D.P.* 30 Nov. 1905; Seely, *op. cit.*, p. 110.

167 Some Liverpool Unionists—Salvidge and M'Arthur, for instance—who demanded an Aliens Bill, nevertheless joined in the protests of the Jewish community against the Russian pogroms—see *L.D.P.* 21 Nov. 1905; P. Ettinger, *'Hope Place' in Liverpool Jewry*, Liverpool, 1930, pp. 88–89.

168 *P.* 13 Jan. 1906. Also quoted in Birkenhead, *F.E.*, 1933 and 1959, *op. cit.*, whose descriptions of the election contain several minor inaccuracies.

169 *P.S.* 3 March 1906; Lady Cynthia Asquith, *Diaries 1915–1918*, 1968, entry, 10 May 1917. These suspicions were endorsed on 26 June 1906, during the Education Bill debate, when Smith 'expressed no opinion on any side of the religious question which had convulsed Liverpool opinion so long and bitterly, but he would say that any proposal which would make it necessary for candidates to state at municipal elections whether they would vote for special facilities to Roman Catholics or Protestants was calamitous and reactionary'. None the less, that same day, Smith voted for the Monastic and Conventual Institutions Bill, 'this ignoble attempt to revive the embers of dying bigotry', T. P. O'Connor dubbed it. *P.D.*, 4th ser., clix, 802, 826. See also H. A. Taylor, *Jix, Viscount Brentford*, 1933, pp. 67–69.

170 Aspinall, *op. cit.*, p. 132. Cf. H. Jager, *op. cit.*, p. 110.

171 J. S. Sandars's biographical notes on Smith, written *c.* 1918–19, Sandars MSS. c. 771, fol. 3.

172 *P.* 10 June, 8 July 1905, 20 Jan. 1906.

173 *L.D.P.* 16 Jan. 1906; *P.* 6 May 1905, 20 Jan. 1906.

174 *L.R.* 3 March 1888.

175 *L.D.P.* 25 Oct. 1905.

176 *P.* 9 Dec. 1905.

177 *L.D.P.* 1 Dec. 1905.

178 *L.D.P.* 15 Jan. 1906.

179 *P.* 13 Jan. 1906.

180 *P.* 6 Jan. 1906.

181 *L.D.P.* 25 Dec. 1905; Robert Holt's diary, 17 April 1905; Richard Holt's diary, 6 March 1905.

182 *L.T.C. Annual Report, 1902–3*, pp. 10–12.

183 Not the 'slavery' aspect, but that foreign labour was used in preference to British labour, most excited Rutherford—see *L.C.* 8 Jan., 25 April 1904; *L.D.P.* 28 Dec. 1905; *P.D.*, 4th. ser., cxxx, 76–78.

184 *The Liberal Outlook*, Oct. 1904.

185 *L.D.P.* 28 Dec. 1905.

186 *L.C.* 25 April 1904; *L.D.P.* 1 Dec. 1905; *P.D.*, 4th. ser., cliii, 295–6, clv, 330, clxvii, 132.

187 *L.D.P.* 18, 19 Oct. 1905. There was uncertainty about Rutherford's actual words. The report in *P.S.* 21 Oct. 1905 construes the speech as a model of toleration.

188 *P.* 1 July 1905.

189 *L.D.P.* 25 Nov. 1905.

190 *L.D.P.* 19 Oct. 1905.

191 *L.D.P.* 16 April 1904; Lord E. Stanley to J. S. Sandars, 13 Oct. 1903, Sandars MSS. c. 745, fols. 115–16.

192 *P.* 25 March 1905.

193 Quoted in Salvidge, *op. cit.*, pp. 63–64.

194 *L.D.P.* 23 Jan. 1906.

195 *P.S.* 10, 17 March 1906.

196 Quoted in Salvidge, *op. cit.*, pp. 70–71.

197 *P.* 10 Feb. 1906.

198 Lord E. Stanley to J. S. Sandars, 13 Oct. 1903, Sandars MSS. c. 745, fols. 115–16; A. Chamberlain to J. Chamberlain, 12 March 1908, in Chamberlain, *op. cit.*, p. 97.

199 *L.D.P.* 18 Jan. 1906.

200 *L.D.P.* 8 Jan. 1906.

201 *L.D.P.* 16 Jan. 1906.

202 *Church Association Annual Report, 1904*, pp. 19–23; ibid. 1905, pp. 24–27; *T.* 6 April 1905; Church Association, *Protestantism before Party Politics*, 1906, p. 6. Kensit won 4,963 votes as a Protestant in Brighton in 1900.

203 *P.S.* 8, 22 July 1905. The Church Association was £800 in debt at the end of 1904. It launched another appeal for £20,000 early in 1906—*P.S.* 7 Jan. 1905, 6 Jan. 1906.

204 The N.P.L. had only a handful of members in Liverpool by 1905–6. Nationally its paper membership was 8,119, and it ran down rapidly thereafter.

205 *Protestantism before Party Politics*, pp. 15, 38–40.

206 *L.D.P.* 31 Oct. 1905, 15 Jan. 1906; *P.S.* 3 March, 14 July 1906.

207 *Church Association Annual Report, 1906*, pp. 6–8; *P.S.* 14, 28 July 1906; Prestige, *op. cit.*, pp. 293–7.

208 *P.S.* 14 July 1906. Cf. *P.P.* 1906, xxxiv, Qs. 22024, 22063, 22116–21, F. J. Chavasse. The Diocesan Board of Education had refused a grant to St. Thomas's in 1902, after the vicar, E. Underhill, persisted in disobeying archepiscopal injunctions with regard to the use of incense—*The Church Annual Log-Book, 1902*, pp. 220, 474.

209 Lloyd, *op. cit.*, pp. 137–41.

210 *P.* 18 Feb. 1905.

211 *L.D.P.* 17 Nov. 1905, 18 Jan. 1906.

212 *Clarion*, 2 Feb. 1906.

213 Viscount Morpeth in Lord Malmesbury (ed.), *The New Order: Studies in Unionist Policy*, pp. 28–30; McKibbin, *op. cit.*, pp. 84–85.

214 Malmesbury in Malmesbury, *op. cit.*, p. 13.

215 R. McNeill in ibid., p. 321.

216 Masterman, *op. cit.*, p. 53.

217 *L.D.P.* 7 Nov. 1905. Cf. John Edwards in *L.D.P.* 10 Nov. 1905; Lord Newton, *op. cit.*, p. 149.

218 *P.* 17 March 1906.

219 B. D. White, *op. cit.*, pp. 188–9.

220 *L.D.P.* 29 Dec. 1905.

CHAPTER 14

1 Lord Hugh Cecil to Lord Rosebery, 7 Feb. 1910, Rosebery MSS. 10122, fols. 48–49.

2 Two reactions to the 1907 Kirkdale by-election—the Duke of Rutland, quoted in E. Pomeroy, *Salvation by Legislation or Are We All Socialists?*, 1909; Frank Rose, in *Clarion*, 4 Oct. 1907.

3 *P.S.* 14 April 1906.

4 *Liverpool Inquiry*, *op. cit.*, pp. 764–5.

5 *P.S.* 26 Feb. 1907 et seqq.

6 *P.* 19 May, 16 June 1906.

7 *P.S.* 15 Sept. 1906.

8 Significantly Labourites designated Conservatives 'the Protestant' party, as distinct from the Wiseites, the 'Ultra-Protestant' party, *L.T.C. Annual Report, 1906–7*, p. 6.

9 Mary Bamber, Bessie Braddock's mother, was one who made up the broth—see J. and B. Braddock, *op. cit.*, chap. 1; *P.D.*, 5th ser., vol. 444, cols. 1635–6, Mrs Braddock.

10 Halévy, *op. cit.*, vi, pp. 65–69; *L.C.* 2 Nov. 1906; Robert Holt's diary, 1 Nov. 1906; Richard Holt's diary, 1 Nov. 1906; G. K. A. Bell, *op. cit.*, i, chap. xxix; Prestige, *op. cit.*, pp. 287–9; OBroin, *op. cit.*, pp. 5–6.

11 *L.C.* 13 April 1905, 20 July 1906.

12 *L.D.P.* 14 Sept. 1906.

13 *L.D.P.* 18 Sept. 1906 ff.; *L.C.* 26 Sept. 1906 ff.

14 *L.D.P.* ibid. Four years earlier Lee Jones recorded his own estimate of the causes of poverty in Liverpool: 45 per cent from unemployment or irregular employment; 15 per cent from drink; 10 per cent from sickness striking the breadwinner; 10 per cent from the death of the breadwinner; 10 per cent from improvidence (i.e. early marriages, bad household management); 5 per cent from indolence; 5 per cent from vice. *P.* 18 Jan. 1902.

15 *L.D.P.* 25 Sept. 1906.

16 *L.C.* 2 Oct. 1906.

17 *L.D.P.* 19 Sept. 1906.

18 *L.C.* 2 Oct. 1906.

19 *L.D.P.* 26 Sept. 1906. The Housing Association reckoned that 9,000 court-houses and 3,000 cellar dwellings awaited removal. To some extent, however, the Corporation's satisfaction was justified: Liverpool had provided more municipal housing than any authority except the L.C.C. In 1895 373 Corporation tenements housed 1,164 persons who paid £3,843 in rent; by 1907 2,046 tenements housed 7,566 persons who paid £17,218 in rent. See *L.D.P.* 18 Oct. 1906; letter from one council tenant critical of conditions in council houses, *L.D.P.* 30 Nov. 1903; and F. W. Hirst's edition of G. R. Porter, *The Progress of the Nation*, 1912, p. 101.

20 *L.C.* 13 Oct. 1906. Petrie had succeeded Royden as president of the Constitutional in 1906, on the ground that he was 'the least objectionable selection'—F. E. Smith to A. T. Salvidge, 20 May 1906, Salvidge MSS. The version quoted in Salvidge, *op. cit.*, p. 72 differs in one respect from the original: for 'MacIver who is moreover though charming, not taken seriously enough', read 'MacIver who is moreover though charming rather a laughing stock'.

21 *L.C.* 31 Oct. 1906. The Conservatives' attitude to Dr. Hope changed in time. In 1911 Dr. Hope strongly criticized general strikes (see Chapter 15); and in 1922 Salvidge recommended Hope for a knighthood, writing that he had been 'a very good man for Liverpool and, in his profession, first-rate'. Sir A. T. Salvidge to Lord Derby, 21 Sept. 1922, Derby MSS.

22 *L.C.* 2 Nov. 1906.

23 *L.C.* 28 Oct. 1899; *L.D.P.* 23 July, 25 Sept. 1906.

24 Asquith in 1907, quoted in B. E. V. Sabine, *A History of Income Tax*, 1966, p. 146.

25 The articles begin in *L.D.P.* 20 April 1907. The quotation is from the summarizing editorial, *L.D.P.* 4 May 1907.

26 Waller in *Essays to C. M. Bowra*, pp. 88–100; L.T.C. Minutes, 9 and 27 Jan. 1907. Cf. B. Gainer, *The Alien Invasion*, 1972; Priestley, *op. cit.*, pp. 240–4.

27 L.L.R.C. Minutes, 28 Sept., 3 Oct. 1906.

28 Short was eventually made a freeman of the L.L.R.C. in recognition of his work—see L.L.R.C. Minutes, 5 March 1913; *The Transport Worker*, Nov. 1911.

29 See Pelling, *Popular Politics*, chap. 8. Both victors, P. Curran and V. Grayson, were soon ruined by drink.

30 *Clarion* 27 Sept. 1907.

31 *T.* 27 Sept. 1907.

32 Quoted in Salvidge, *op. cit.*, p. 76.

33 *L.L.R.C. Annual Report 1907*, p. 5.

34 *T.* 2 Sept. 1907.

35 *T.* 28 Sept. 1907.

36 *Clarion*, 20, 27 Sept. 1907; L. Thompson, *Robert Blatchford*, 1951, p. 188. Cf. 'Truth Stands', *The Socialist Fraud*, 1907; F. Bibby, *Trade Unionists and Socialism*, Manchester, 1907.

37 *P.S.* 12 Dec. 1903.

38 *P.S.* 28 Sept. 1907. Cf. *P.D.*, 4th ser., clxxxiv, 1466, F. E. Smith.

39 *Clarion*, 11 Oct. 1907.

40 See Rosebery's letter in *T.* 15 Oct. 1907. Govan went Unionist in 1906, one of only five seats to do so which had not been Unionist in 1900. See Kinnear,*op. cit.*, p. 30.

41 *T.* 11 Sept. 1907; A. P. Mooney, *Some Economic Criticisms of Socialism*, and *Some Ethical Criticisms of Socialism*, Catholic Truth Society, 1908.

42 *T.* 11, 12 Sept. 1907. Cf. *P.D.*, 4th. ser., clvi, 1041–9, T. P. O'Connor; and O'Connor quoted in Blewett, *op. cit.*, p. 59.

43 *T.* 30 Sept. 1907.

44 *T.* 10 Oct. 1907.

45 Salvidge, *op. cit.*, p. 80.

46 Quoted in *P.S.* 19 Oct. 1907.

47 *Clarion*, 4 Oct. 1907. Cf. Arthur Henderson in G. Haw (ed.), *Christianity and the Working Classes*, 1906, chap. v.

48 *Clarion*, 11 Oct. 1907.

49 *L.D.P.* 2 Nov. 1907; Robert Holt's diary, 27 Oct. 1907.

50 L.L.R.C. Minutes, 5 Feb. 1908.

51 Ibid. 7 Oct. 1908. Walker described his Protestant Labour Club thus: 'It labours by day and discusses Protestantism in the evening.' *Liverpool Inquiry*, *op. cit.*, p. 314.

52 *L.D.P.* 27 Oct. 1908.

53 L.L.R.C. Minutes, 4 Nov. 1908.

54 Quoted in T. L. Drinkwater, 'A History of the Trade Unions and Labour Party in Liverpool, 1911 to the Great Strike', B.A. thesis, Liverpool University, 1940, p. 7. See also *L.D.P.* 30 Oct. 1908.

55 *L.D.P.* 2, 3, Nov. 1908; L.L.R.C. Minutes, 4 Nov. 1908. Grayson was born in Liverpool on 5 September 1881. His parliamentary antics on behalf of the unemployed brought his expulsion from the House in October 1908, see R. Groves, *The Strange Case of Victor Grayson*, 1975; McKibbin, *op. cit.*, pp. 50–51.

56 Salvidge in *L.D.P.* 27 Oct. 1908. Cf. *Annual Register 1907*, p. 236.

57 *L.D.P.* 31 Oct. 1908; G. K. A. Bell, *op. cit.* i, chap. xxix; Halévy, *op. cit.* vi, pp. 70–73.

58 *L.D.P.* 3 Nov. 1908; Robert Holt's diary, 1 Nov. 1907.

59 *P.S.* 18 April 1908; Blewett, *op. cit.*, p. 50. Chavasse, a total abstainer from 1871, had made a spectacle of himself in 1904 when he declared that he would not accept a farthing from men whose fortune was made from degrading their fellows, only to learn that the cathedral fund had received donations from breweries as well as from property owners with drink interests—see 'Veritas', *The Attitude of the Anglican Church on the Question of Alcoholic Drinks*, 1908, pp. 36–38.

60 *P.D.*, 4th ser., clxxxviii, 522, cxci, 854. See also the letter from a Liverpool Conservative businessman, A. Bevan to Lord Derby, 12 Nov. 1910, advocating a programme which included larger old age pensions as 'an attractive counterblast to the present Socialistic offers of the Radical party'. Letter now in Sandars MSS. c. 762, fols. 36–39.

61 The Sun Hall was built for £30,000 in 1905 by Heber Radcliffe to bring religion to poor people outside the churches. Woolworth's now occupies the site. See E. Green, *My Father's Faith: The Story of Heber Radcliffe*, Guildford, 1969. I owe this source to Richard Shackleton.

62 *P.S.* 16 Nov. 1907, 15, 22, 29 Feb. 1908; Wise's letter in *L.D.P.* 1 Nov. 1907, cited in Maddock, *op. cit.*, p. 199.

63 This was essentially the Church Discipline Bill retraced, after Austin Taylor had failed with the original bill in February 1907—see Church Association pamphlet no. 390, *Obstructing the Bill*, 1908; *P.D.*, 4th. ser., vol. 169, cols. 856–8, vol. 184, cols. 303–80; L. Masterman, *C. F. G. Masterman*, 1939, pp. 97–99.

64 *Liverpool Inquiry*, *op. cit.*, p. 63. From their protests Protestants discovered that certain penal sections of the Catholic Emancipation Act (1829) were still enforceable, regarding public processions of Catholic images and vestments—ibid., pp. 50, 57; Asquith MSS., fols. 91–195; *Church Association Annual Report, 1908* pp. 13–17.

65 William Redmond won leave to introduce a Roman Catholic Disabilities Bill in November 1908—*P.D.*, 4th. ser., cxcvii, 134–40. See also Church Association pamphlets, no. 404, *The King's Protestant Declaration: Why it must not be altered*, 1910; no. 405, *Alter the King's Declaration? No.*

66 *P.S.* 23 Jan. 1909.

67 *P.S.* 5 June 1909.

68 *Liverpool Inquiry*, *op. cit.*, p. 12.

69 Liverpool's tiny Italian colony was located around Gerard Street, one of the city's worst districts which ran between Byrom Street and Christian Street and is now demolished. The Italians mostly engaged in ice cream manufacture, organ-grinding, and moulding in plaster of Paris. See *P.P.* 1903, ix, Q. 21462, Dr. Hope; C.C. Abbott (ed.), *Further Letters of Gerard Manley Hopkins*, Oxford, 1956 edition, p. 157.

70 *Liverpool Inquiry*, *op. cit.*, pp. 69, 92, 353, 696, 722–3.

71 Ibid., p. 158, S. G. Thomas.

72 Ibid., p. 94. Thomas later withdrew an allegation of brutality against Smith, owing to the uncertainty of recognition in the fighting, p. 297. Smith had used rough tactics in a sectarian disturbance before—*P.D.*, 4th. ser., cxxii, 199–200.

73 *Liverpool Inquiry*, *op. cit.*, Qs. 20271–2. Fitzgerald ran a mission on St. Domingo Road.

74 Ibid., Qs. 20865–7, Father Keohan.

75 Ibid., pp. 608, 614, Revd. Sherwood Jones.

76 Ibid., p. 77 ff.

77 Ibid., pp. 636–8.

78 Ibid., p. 474.

79 Ibid., p. 1117.

80 Ibid., p. 77. The councillors were Lloyd and Utting.
81 Ibid., Q. 16686. Cf. the Garston riot, in *L.D.P.* 2 April 1907.
82 Ibid., p. 594.
83 Ibid., pp. 449–50.
84 Ibid., p. 69.
85 Ibid., p. 1050.
86 Ibid., Qs. 20211, 20060. Fitzgerald was quite capable of defending himself in a fight—see *L.D.P.* 11 Jan. 1910.
87 Ibid., Qs. 20229–40.
88 Ibid., Qs. 20713–32. Note evidence of Father Penswick and Dr. O'Sullivan.
89 *P.S.* 26 June 1909.
90 *Liverpool Inquiry*, *op. cit.*, pp. 35, 863, 1325.
91 Ibid., pp. 167, 768.
92 *T.* 16 Aug. 1909. *P.S.* 21 Aug. 1909 estimated 150,000 people.
93 *P.S.* 14 Aug. 1909.
94 *P.S.* 21 Aug. 1909.
95 *T.* 19 Aug. 1909; *P.S.* 28 Aug. 1909.
96 *Liverpool Inquiry*, *op. cit.*, p. 67.
97 Ibid., pp. 42, 211–12, 220–4, 238, 303. Thomas afterwards apologized.
98 *T.* 30 Aug. 1909. The chairman was J. P. Reynolds, M.P. Liverpool Exchange 1929–33.
99 *P.S.* 18 Sept. 1909.
100 *P.S.* 25 Sept. 1909.
101 *Liverpool Inquiry*, *op. cit.*, p. 729.
102 Ibid., evidence of Constables Cummins and Orrell. Pollock was president of the Imperial Protestant Defence League.
103 Ibid., pp. 928–9.
104 *P.S.* 11 Dec. 1909.
105 *P.S.* 4 April 1908, 15, 22, 29 Jan. 1910. The classic Unionist case is A. V. Dicey, *England's Case against Home Rule*, 1886.
106 *P.S.* 18 Dec. 1909, 15 Jan., 7 May 1910.
107 *L.D.P.* 13 Jan. 1910.
108 *L.D.P.* 12 Jan. 1910.
109 *P.S.* 1 Jan. 1910. Nationally the Church Association's activities in the 1910 Elections were inconsiderable compared with 1906. It still extracted pledges from several hundred M.P.s; but the repeated failure to secure legislation was depressing, and the death of Henry Miller, the secretary, removed the organization's linchpin.
110 *T.* 1 Jan. 1910; Blewett, *op. cit.*, pp. 340–3.
111 *L.D.P.* 14 Jan. 1910; *T.* 18 Jan. 1910.
112 *L.D.P.* 15, 17 Jan. 1910.
113 *T.* and *M.G.* 18 Jan. 1910; Blewett, *op. cit.*, pp. 342, 350.
114 *L.D.P.* and *M.G.* 18 Jan. 1910.
115 *L.D.P.* 19 Jan. 1910.
116 Quoted in Salvidge, *op. cit.*, pp. 123–6.
117 Churchill, *Winston S. Churchill*, ii, 1967, pp. 280–1; Halévy, *op. cit*, vi, pp. 286, 292; Mackail and Wyndham, *op. cit.* ii, pp. 627–8; W. N. Calkins, 'A Victorian Free Trade Lobby', *Ec.H.R.*, 2nd ser., xiii, 1960–1, p. 104; B. K. Murray, 'The Politics of the "People's" Budget', *The Historical Journal*, xvi, no. 3, 1973, pp. 559–60.
118 Salvidge, *op. cit.*, pp. 84–85.
119 Booth, Beazley, and Norman Hill, in *M.G.* 18 Jan. 1910.
120 *L.D.P.* 18 Jan. 1910.

121 Chamberlain, *op. cit.*, pp. 228–9.
122 *L.D.P.* 1 Jan. 1910; L.T.C. Minutes, 12 Jan. 1910.
123 *L.D.P.* 19 Jan. 1910.
124 L.L.R.C. Minutes, 2 Sept. 1908.
125 *L.C.* 12 July 1910.
126 *L.D.P.* 3 Jan. 1910; *Manchester Empire News*, 31 Jan. 1926. Sexton's candidature was endorsed by the Liberals—Maddock, *op. cit.*, p. 202. Allegedly the Unionists profited from personations—Blewett, *op. cit.*, p. 372.
127 *L.D.P.* 7 Jan. 1910.
128 Salvidge, *op. cit.*, pp. 88–90.
129 Birkenhead, *F.E.*, 1959, p. 151.
130 *T.* 17 Jan. 1910; Blewett, *op. cit.*, p. 221.
131 See the episode of the draft Licensing Bill (1908), which was mislaid by Herbert Gladstone and which Rutherford returned to him after some delay, Viscount Gladstone Papers, B.M. Add. MSS. 46065, fols. 113–8.
132 *L.D.P.* 15 Jan. 1910; *T.* 19 Jan. 1910.
133 *P.S.* 7 March 1908.
134 *L.D.P.* 6, 11, 14, 15 Jan. 1910.
135 F. Elias, *John Lea, Citizen and Art Lover*, Liverpool, 1927, pp. 60, 63. Elias was Lea's nephew.
136 *L.D.P.* 4, 13 Jan. 1910; Lord Birkenhead, *Law, Life, and Letters*, 1927, vol. i, chap. ix.
137 Chaloner's wife was a lineal descendent of the engineer of Liverpool's first enclosed dock—see H. Peet, *Thomas Steers*, pp. 41–42.
138 Quoted in Petrie, *Long*, pp. 122–8.
139 Chaloner (as Lord Gisborough) was president of the Church Association, 1919–24.
140 J. E. B. Seely to H. Gladstone 24 Jan. 1910, Viscount Gladstone Papers, B.L. Add. MSS. 46068, fol. 231. T. P. O'Connor would not accept that it was the Irish who failed Seely—T. P. O'Connor to J. E. B. Seely, 18 Jan. 1910, Mottistone MSS. 1, fol. 246.
141 *L.D.P.* 14 Jan. 1910.
142 *T.* 18 Jan. 1910. Scott had practised law in Liverpool before 1906. F. E. Smith was among his pupils: the hen, Scott observed, had hatched out a very large duck. *D.N.B.* 1941–50, p. 763.
143 *Liverpool Inquiry*, *op. cit.*, Qs. 16571–80.
144 Ibid., Qs. 16498–505; *T.* 13 Sept. 1910.
145 *Liverpool Inquiry*, *op. cit.*, Report, pp. 65, 70, Proceedings, Qs. 22394–6.
146 *T.* 27 June 1910.
147 *L.C.* 14 July 1910.
148 *P.* 7 Oct. 1911.
149 *L.C.* 12 July 1910; *T.* 15 July 1910.
150 *L.C.* 11, 14 July 1910.
151 *T.* 13 July 1910.
152 *L.C.* 13 July 1910.
153 *L.C.* 14 July 1910.
154 *T.* 20 July 1910.
155 *L.C.* 11 July 1910.
156 *T.* 15 July 1910.
157 *L.C.* 19, 20 July 1910.
158 *L.C.* 15, 16, 18 July 1910. On the Anti-Socialist Union, founded in 1908, see Blumenfeld, *op. cit.*, pp. 224–5.

159 *L.C.* 12, 20 July 1910.

160 *L.C.* 12, 15 July 1910. It was also an illegal formulation, according to the ruling of Labour's N.E.C. Information from Dr. R. McKibbin.

161 *T.* 19 July 1910; *L.C.* 16 July 1910.

162 *L.C.* 19 July 1910.

163 *L.C.* 20 July 1910.

164 *T.* 20 July 1910. Eleven per cent of the electorate had moved since the last register.

165 *L.C.* 15 July 1910.

166 *T.* 21 July 1910.

167 *L.C.* 21 July 1910.

168 *T.* 21 July 1910.

169 *P.D.*, 5th. ser., xviii, 489, 850, xix, 2547; H. Nicolson, *King George the Fifth*, 1952, pp. 162–3.

170 *Church Association Annual Report, 1910–11*, p. 8; *P.S.* 9 July 1910.

171 *T.* 26 Sept. 1910.

172 *T.* 3 Oct. 1910; *P.S.* 13 Aug., 2 Sept., 8 Oct. 1910.

173 *T.* 21 Oct. 1910.

174 Quoted in F. Shaw, *You Know Me Anty Nelly?: Liverpool Children's Rhymes*, 1970 edition, p. 55. 'Scotty Road' is Scotland Road.

175 *Liverpool Inquiry*, *op. cit.*, p. 163.

176 McKibbin, *op. cit.*, pp. 20–21.

177 His conversion to Labour Whitley attributed to the influence of Oxford, Sidney Webb, and H. G. Wells. The Bulley family was active in Labour politics in Cheshire—J. M. Lee, *op. cit.*, pp. 170–1; Cole, *Beatrice Webb's Diaries 1912–1924*, p. 70.

178 Instead of Salvidge—see Salvidge, *op. cit.*, pp. 96–97.

179 Sexton, *Agitator*, p. 169.

180 *L.C.* 26 April 1911.

181 *T.* 14 Nov. 1910. There was no more testing register than that of December 1910 in any general election between 1885 and 1918. There were 25,000 removals in Liverpool between August 1909 and December 1910, over 30 per cent of the electorate. About 21,000 were successfully traced. See N. Blewett, 'The Franchise in the United Kingdom, 1885–1914', *Past and Present*, no. 32, 1965, p. 37; and Blewett, *The Peers, the Parties and the People*, p. 282.

182 *L.D.P.* 19 Nov. 1910.

183 *M.G.* 6 Dec. 1910; Lord Derby to J. S. Sandars, 13 Nov. 1910, with enclosure, A. Bevan to Derby, 12 Nov. 1910, Sandars MSS. c. 762, fols. 34–39.

184 *M.G.* 9 Dec. 1910. Cf. Earl Winterton, *Orders of the Day*, 1953, p. 50; Brady, *op. cit.*, pp. 415–16.

185 Salvidge to Derby, 6 Jan. 1911, Derby MSS.; Alsop, op. cit., p. 144; Salvidge, *op. cit.*, p. 100; *P.* 14 Jan. 1911 on Robertson Dunn, the reorganizer of Exchange Unionism.

186 L.L.R.C. Minutes, 25 Nov. 1910. A small grant was made from central funds towards this contest—W. B. Gwynn, *op. cit.*, p. 196.

187 L.L.R.C. Minutes, 2 Feb., 4 May, 1 June 1910; McKibbin, *op. cit.*, pp. 5, 15.

188 Petrie, *Chamberlain*, ii, pp. 266–73.

189 Salvidge, *op. cit.*, pp. 102–44. However, see Buckland, *op. cit.*, chap. iv.

190 Salvidge, *op. cit.*, p. 105.

191 *T.* 16 Jan. 1911.

192 Quoted in Salvidge, *op. cit.*, pp. 106–7.

193 R. B. Jones, 'Balfour's Reform of Party Organization', *Bulletin of the Institute of Historical Research*, May 1965, pp. 94–101; Blewett, *op. cit.*, pp. 266–82; Salvidge to Derby, 24 Jan., 8 Feb., 25 May 1911; Derby to Salvidge, 13 Jan. 1911, Derby MSS.

CHAPTER 15

1 Gosling, *op. cit.*, p. 153; James Connolly quoted in Greaves, *op. cit.*, p. 398; Richard Holt's diary, 22 Aug. 1911; F. E. Smith writing to Austen Chamberlain, 20 Oct. 1910, about Home Rule, quoted in Birkenhead (1959), p. 156.

2 Lord Derby to Colonel T. M. Sandys, 27 Feb. 1911, Bonar Law MSS. 21/4/21; Churchill, *Derby*, pp. 120–3; R. Blake, *The Unknown Prime Minister*, 1955, pp. 66–68.

3 Sir A. Salvidge to Lord Derby, 25 Oct. 1918, Derby MSS.; Jager, *op. cit.*, p. 211.

4 C. F. Bell to T. W. A. Bagley, Bonar Law MSS. 18/7/165.

5 *T.* 17 March 1911.

6 *T.* 18, 20 March 1911; *Church Association Annual Report, 1910–11*, p. 21. Max Muspratt's evident Irish support earned him the nickname 'Mick Mucksprattt' from R. P. Houston. Author's conversation with Sir Charles Petrie.

7 *L.D.P.* 28 March 1911.

8 *L.D.P.* 18 March, 26 April 1911.

9 *L.D.P.* 27 April 1911. On Rogers see Sellers, *op. cit.*, *T.H.S.L.C.* 1962, pp. 227–8.

10 *L.D.P.* 28 March 1911.

11 *P.S.* 18 Feb. 1911.

12 *L.C.* 1 May 1911; *L.D.P.* 2 May 1911.

13 *L.D.P.* 19, 30 June 1911; *L.D.P.* 7 July 1911.

14 *L.D.P.* 24 July 1911. Of eight M.P.s known to be sympathetic to an anti-Mormon crusade six were from Liverpool—F. E. Smith, Harmood-Banner, Houston, Chaloner, Scott, and Marshall Hall, *M.A.P.* 1 July 1911.

15 *L.D.P.* 20 June, 8 July 1911.

16 *L.D.P.* 8, 11 July 1911.

17 *P.S.* 4 June 1910; D. A. Roberts, 'Religion and Politics in Liverpool since 1900', M.Sc. Econ. thesis, London University, 1965, p. 61.

18 Letter from Wise, *L.C.* 31 July 1911. Cf. Wise in *P.S.* 9 April 1910.

19 *L.D.P.* 2, 10 Aug. 1911.

20 Bower, *op. cit.*, p. 195; T. Mann, *Memoirs*, 1923, p. 263.

21 Quoted in G. D. H. Cole, *The World of Labour*, 1915 edition, p. 3.

22 J. R. MacDonald, *Syndicalism*, 1912, p. 45. Cf. H. M. Hyndman, *Further Reminiscences*, 1912, chap. xix.

23 Chamberlain, *op. cit.*, pp. 404–5; M. Cole in Briggs and Saville, *op. cit.*, p. 266.

24 *T.* 7 Sept. 1912. Cf. Morgan, *Wales in British Politics*, pp. 253–5; and Fred Bower in *Forward*, 27 Dec. 1912. By contrast R. Holton, 'Syndicalism and Labour on Merseyside 1906–14', in Hikins *op. cit.*, pp. 121–50, emphasizes the importance of ideologically committed 'Syndicalists' or 'revolutionaries'.

25 *T.* 16 Jan. 1911; Morgan, *Keir Hardie*, pp. 89–90; B. Mogridge, 'Militancy and Inter-Union Rivalries in British Shipping, 1911–1929', *International Review of Social History*, vi, 1961, pp. 380–1. Description of Mann by R. B. Cunninghame Graham, 'With the North-East Wind', in H. S. Milford (ed.), *Selected Modern English Essays*, Oxford, 1925, p. 126.

26 R. Bean, 'Employers Association in the Port of Liverpool, 1890–1914', *op. cit.*

27 Clegg, Fox, and Thompson, *op. cit.*, p. 451; *The Transport Worker* Nov. 1911.

28 On Cotter, *The Transport Worker*, Oct. 1911; Mogridge, *op. cit.*, pp. 391–2.

29 Mann, *op. cit.*, p. 259.

30 *P.* 24 June 1911.

31 *L.D.P.* 26 June 1911.

32 *Labour Leader*, 16, 23 June 1911. The Shipping Federation in July 1910 had refused the N.S.F.U.'s request for a National Conciliation Board, composed of masters and men, to consider wages and conditions.

33 Ibid. 7, 14 July 1911. *P.P.* 1912–13, xlvii (cd.6472), pp. 144–50 gives the details of the shipowners' and dockers' leaders' agreement.

34 *P.* 8 July 1911.

35 *Labour Leader*, 7 July 1911.

36 *The Transport Worker*, Aug. 1911.

37 H. V. Marrot, *The Life and Letters of John Galsworthy*, 1935, pp. 309–10, 637–8; L.L.R.C. Minutes, 1 April 1914. The censure was not carried, by sixteen votes to fifteen. Suffragettes were also offended by Sexton's play—see G. W. Goldie, *The Liverpool Repertory Theatre, 1911–1934*, Liverpool, 1935, pp. 92–93.

38 J. Sexton, *The Riot Act*, 1914, p. 33; review in *T.* 4 Feb. 1914.

39 Ibid., p. 73.

40 Ibid., p. 15.

41 Sexton, *Agitator*, p. 152.

42 Sexton, *Riot Act*, pp. 26–27.

43 Ibid., pp. 24–25. See also Cunliffe's soliloquy about the working man who 'rises', ibid., p. 75.

44 *The Transport Worker*, Aug. 1911; report from the Head Constable of Liverpool, 21 Aug. 1911, Public Record Office HO 45/10655/212470/238. The Mersey Carters' were not affiliated to the L.T.C.

45 W. H. Billal Quilliam, vice-president of the Carters', in *The Transport Worker*, Aug. 1911. The Mersey Quay and Railway Carters' Union grew in members from 3,362 in December 1905, to 5,083 in December 1910, to 7,301 in December 1911—*P.P.* 1906, cxii, p. 585; *P.P.* 1911, lxxvi, p. 736; *P.P.* 1912–13, lxxxii, p. 1000. Carters and motor-drivers later organized a single union, the Liverpool and District Carters' and Motor-men's Union. Four or five thousand horse carters still operated in Liverpool in 1935, when their fear of being replaced by motor lorries was accentuated by new traffic regulations. Before then horse traffic remained viable because of the taxation of heavy motor vehicles—D. C. Jones, *op. cit.*, ii, pp. 177–89; *P.D.*, 5th. ser., vol. 278, 1425–6, vol. 304, 1827, 2829–30.

46 Sexton, *Agitator*, chaps. xxxi, xxxiii; Rathbone (1903–4), *op. cit.*, pp. 54–56; *P.P.* 1892, xxxv, Qs. 261–70, F. Brien; R. Williams, *The First Year's Working of the Liverpool Docks Scheme*, 1914, p. 130.

47 Phelps Brown, *op. cit.*, pp. 298–302, 321–4.

48 *P.D.*, 5th. ser., xxix, 2305–6, C. Money.

49 *T.* 7, 8 Aug. 1911; L.T.C. Minutes, 9 Aug. 1911. 349 porters remained 'loyal' throughout the strike—HO45/10655/212470/167.

50 G. Blaxland, *J. H. Thomas*, 1964, p. 68. Many perhaps shared the attitude of Harry Pollitt's father that union leaders, 'getting their feet under the table', were interested in a soft job and money for themselves—see H. Pollitt, *Serving my Time*, 1940, p. 30.

51 HO45/10654/212470/1a.

52 Ibid. for the original; HO45/10657/212470/427a for the proof correction. The correspondence was published in November 1911, following a question in the Commons from Keir Hardie.

53 *P.D.*, *op. cit.* 2328, W. S. Churchill.

54 Ibid. 2335–6, J. Keir Hardie. However, Tillett, *Memories*, p. 244 eulogized Churchill. See also Phelps Brown, *op. cit.*, p. 303.

55 *T.* 11, 12 Aug. 1911. Cf. Sexton, *Riot Act*, Act I, scene 3, for the meeting of the magistrates. Sexton opposed the military intervention and refused to perform any magisterial duties while troops remained in Liverpool.

56 *T.* 12 Aug. 1911; HO45/10654/212470/7a; *P.P.* 1912–13, xlvii, p. 28.

57 Sexton, *Agitator*, p. 224.

58 Mann, *op. cit.*, p. 266; *P.D.*, *op. cit.*, 1989. W. S. Churchill. J. H. Thomas on 22 August dissociated himself and his union from the demonstration, asserting that it was arranged 'not in connection with the strike, not in the least in connection with the railway dispute, but for the purpose of celebrating the victory of the dockers'. *P.D.*, *op. cit.* 2303.

59 The first story is recounted, with different embellishments, by Bower, *op. cit.*, pp. 195–6, Mann, *op. cit.*, p. 273, Thomas (*P.D.*, *op. cit.*), and E. Tupper, *Seamen's Torch*, 1938, chap. v. The second is the official view, of the police and Home Office—*P.D.*, *op. cit.* 1989, W. S. Churchill.

60 Mann, *op. cit.*, p. 274.

61 *T.* 15 Aug. 1911.

62 *P.D.*, *op. cit.* 2298, J. R. MacDonald.

63 *L.C.* 14, 15 Aug. 1911.

64 *L.C.* 5 Sept. 1911.

65 *P.* 19 Aug. 1911.

66 HO45/10654/212470/27.

67 Churchill read the Head Constable's report to the House of Commons—*P.D.*, *op. cit.* 1756. A truncated version is quoted in Churchill, *Winston S. Churchill*, ii, 1967, pp. 381–2. The significant first sentence is omitted: 'You need not attach any very great importance to the rioting last night.' This spoils the story of the young Home Secretary resolute in the face of revolution.

68 *P.D.,op. cit.* 1757.

69 Ibid. 2315–16.

70 Ibid. 1990; HO 45/10655/212470/185. The dead, symbolically, were a docker and carter, respectively Michael Prendergast, aged twenty-nine, and John Sutcliffe, aged twenty.

71 *L.D.P.* 1 Sept. 1911.

72 *T.* 16 Aug. 1911; Churchill, *op. cit.*, p. 382.

73 HO 45/10657/212470/390–1.

74 H. R. Hikins, 'The Liverpool General Transport Strike, 1911', *T.H.S.L.C.*, vol. 113, 1962, p. 194 states that the Strike Committee's permits 'meant nothing less than working-class control of the means of distribution'. Their control, however, was for limitation more than operation.

75 HO 45/10654/212470/25; HO 45/10655/212470/179.

76 *T.* 16 Aug. 1911.

77 *T.* 17 Aug. 1911.

78 *P.* 19 Aug. 1911.

79 *Daily Mail*, 28 Aug. 1911.

80 *L.D.P.* 12 Sept. 1911.

81 *P.* 2 Sept. 1911. The official statistics are 340 crimes of riot and riotous damage to property in 1911—*Liverpool Police, Annual Report 1911*, p. 12.

82 *T.* 17 Aug. 1911.

83 HO 45/10654/212470/120; Sir C. Petrie to Lord Derby, 30 Aug. 1911, Derby MSS. The account of one hearty, public-school, Oxonian stoker was printed in *L.D.P.* 28 Aug. 1911. Richard Holt's younger brother, Ted, was another volunteer—see Richard Holt's diary, 23 Aug. 1911.

84 Out of 7,991 consumers of electricity in Liverpool by 1910, 1,933 were domestic—

see H. C. Morton, 'A Technical Study of Housing in Liverpool 1760–1938', M.Arch. thesis, Liverpool University, 1967, vol. B, 1203. Branches of the E.T.U. were in their infancy on Merseyside in 1911—see Lord Citrine, *Men and Work*, 1964, pp. 38–40. On the Liverpool United Gaslight Company—which had not been municipalized—see B. D. White, *op. cit.*, pp. 163–5; *P.D.*, 5th. ser. lxiv, 1330–74.

85 *L.C.* 31 Aug. 1911.

86 HO 45/10654/212470/31.

87 *T.* 19 Aug. 1911; Hyndman, *op. cit.*, p. 464; *P.* 1 July, 19 Aug. 1911.

88 HO 45/10655/212470/141; O'Connor in *T.* 21 Aug. 1911. On the settlement and its effects, Alderman, *op. cit.*, p. 209 ff. O'Connor had been considered for the position of industrial arbitrator, once before, by Lloyd George during the music-hall employees' strike of 1907; but he had then refused. See Halévy *op. cit.*, vi, p. 107.

89 HO 45/10655/212470/238; *T.* 22 Aug. 1911.

90 HO 45/10657/212470/390.

91 *L.D.P.* 21, 24 Aug. 1911; *T.* 23 Aug. 1911; HO 45/10655/212470/204. The official estimate of the number of tramwaymen who struck was 250 or 300; but the strikers themselves claimed 967, about one-third of the total employed in the tramway service—see HO 45/10655/212470/238; A. T. Salvidge to Lord Derby, 4 Sept. 1911, Derby MSS.; *L.D.P.* 24 Aug. 1911. Councillor John Gordon (Conservative) reckoned 450, *L.D.P.* 28 Oct. 1911.

92 See L.T.C. Minutes, 31 March, 28 April 1897. Those tramwaymen who had affiliated to the L.T.C. in 1900 proved to be militant Socialists for most of the two years they remained.

93 *T.* 24 Aug. 1911. This was a bluff for, Sam Reeves told J. Bruce Glasier, the dockers were unwilling to support the tramwaymen—see L. Thompson, *The Enthusiasts*, 1971, p. 171.

94 Askwith was Chief Industrial Commissioner, 1911–19.

95 Salvidge, *op. cit.*, pp. 115–16.

96 The resolution was actually framed by Sir Charles Petrie (who was abroad during the worst of the strike) and this was probably decisive in winning the Committee's approval. However, the press (and, afterwards, Salvidge's son and biographer) gave all the credit to Salvidge for ending the deadlock. This exacerbated the tensions in Petrie's and Salvidge's dual leadership. Both men gave versions of their roles in letters to Lord Derby—Petrie, 30 Aug. 1911; Salvidge 4, 12, 14 Sept. 1911, Derby MSS.

97 *T.* 25 Aug. 1911.

98 *L.D.P.* 25 Aug. 1911.

99 *T.* 25 Aug. 1911; Richard Holt's diary, 22 Aug. 1911.

100 *L.D.P.* 12 Oct. 1911; HO45/10657/212470/391; *P.P.* 1912–13, xlvii, pp. 176–7.

101 So too did Sandhills Ward Liberal Association—HO 45/10657/212470/394.

102 *L.D.P.* 5 Oct. 1911. This was a common practice. The *Daily Post* established a fund to reward 'loyal' railwaymen, to which Lord Derby subscribed £100; and directors of the Lancashire and Yorkshire Railway granted double pay to those who had worked through the strike—*L.D.P.* 3 Oct. 1911; R. Roberts, *The Classic Slum*, Manchester, 1971, p. 75. The Watch Committee was entitled to award gratuities to constables under the 1859 County and Borough Police Act.

103 *L.D.P.* 18 Oct. 1911; letter from Dr. W. A. Aikin, *T.* 27 Oct. 1911.

104 *L.D.P.* 23, 30, 31 Oct. 1911.

105 Prof. Moore in *L.D.P.* 11, 13, 18 Nov. 1911.

106 *Liverpool Steam Ship Owners Association, Annual Report 1911*, p. 22; *L.D.P.* 4 Oct. 1911; *Liverpool Express*, 20, 23 Oct. 1911; Gwynn, *op. cit.*, pp. 200–2.

107 F. E. Smith to A. J. Balfour, 30 Oct. 1910, Sandars MSS, c. 761, fols. 291–6. Smith

in common with many Conservatives preferred to pay M.P.s rather than reverse Osborne—Blewett, *op. cit.*, p. 163.

108 Webbs quoted in J. Saville, 'Trade Unions and Free Labour: The Background to the Taff Vale Decision', reprinted in Flinn and Smout, *op. cit.*, p. 252.

109 *The Transport Worker*, Nov. 1911. Altogether union membership increased by about half a million in 1911, over a quarter of a million being concentrated in twelve unions, mostly of transport workers. *P.P.* 1912–13, lxxxii, pp. 984–5.

110 Sexton, *Agitator*, pp. 267–8; D. F. Wilson, *Dockers*, 1972, *passim*; G. A. Phillips, 'The Triple Industrial Alliance in 1914', *Ec.H.R.*, 2nd ser. xxiv, Feb. 1971.

111 *L.C.* 13 Sept. 1911; *Labour Leader*, 14 July 1911. The N.U.D.L.'s funds at the beginning of 1911 stood at £11,795, at the end of 1911 at £8,689. The union had paid out £10,978 in strike benefits; but the membership nationally increased from 14,253 to 45,460. *P.P.* 1912–13, lxxxii, pp. 1000–1.

112 *L.C.* 13 Sept. 1911. Cf. Kyffin-Taylor's essay on the housing problem in *Town Planning Review*, viii, April 1920, pp. 105–16.

113 *L.D.P.* 3 Oct. 1911.

114 A. T. Salvidge to Lord Derby, 12 and 14 Sept. 1911, Derby MSS.

115 *L.D.P.* 13 Sept. 1911.

116 Cf. Wise's preferred list of members in *L.D.P.* 13 Sept. 1911. Churchill, *Derby*, *op. cit.*, p. 137 describes the conference as 'one of Derby's first acts as Lord Mayor'. The authorship was not his; moreover, Derby did not become Lord Mayor of Liverpool until 10 November 1911, and the conference first met on 9 October.

117 A. Harford in *L.C.* 19 Oct. 1911.

118 *L.D.P.* 13, 17 Oct. 1911.

119 *L.C.* 15, 20 Oct. 1911; *L.D.P.* 12 Jan. 1912.

120 Francis Caldwell, the former Assistant Head Constable, succeeded Dunning—*L.D.P.* 1, 19 Dec. 1911, 10 Jan. 1912.

121 *L.D.P.* 10 Oct. 1911.

122 *L.D.P.* 3 Oct. 1911.

123 See letter from T. Peters, *L.C.* 14 Sept. 1906; and discussions about policemen's wages and conditions, *L.C.* 11 Sept. 1890, 29 Jan. 1912; *L.M.* 2, 9 June 1896. The conditions of police service in Liverpool, introduced in 1902 and framed from Dunning's experience of the R.I.C., included a declaration that 'I do not and will not belong to or subscribe money to the funds of any political or Party Society'. *P.P.* 1920, xxii, Report, pp. 26–27, Minutes, Qs. 1511, 10305–409, Dunning, 3786, Smithwick, 3882, Addis. The National Union of Police and Prison Officers was founded in 1913.

124 *P.* 28 Oct. 1911.

125 *L.D.P.* 25 Oct. 1911.

126 *L.D.P.* 28 Oct. 1911.

127 *P.S.* 26 Aug. 1911. Cf. the reflections on the London Dock Strike, 1889, and on the strike at Manningham Mills, Bradford, 1891, in *P.S.* 14, 21 Sept. 1889, 18 April, 9 May 1891.

128 *P.S.* 19 Aug. 1911; *P.* 2 Sept. 1911.

129 *L.D.P.* 9 Nov. 1911, quoted in D. A. Roberts, *op. cit.*, p. 63.

130 *L.C.* 25 Oct. 1911.

131 Quoted in E. Longford, *Wellington: Pillar of State*, Panther edition, 1975, p. 68.

132 *L.D.P.* 14 Oct. 1911.

133 *P.* 18 Nov. 1911; *The Transport Worker*, Dec. 1911.

134 *T.* 5 Dec. 1911; Winterton, *op. cit.*, p. 73. Privately one of the apostles of the planned revival, Seely, despaired of Liberalism in Liverpool—see letter to H. Gladstone, 24 Jan. 1910, Viscount Gladstone Papers, B.L. Add. MSS. 46068, fol. 231.

135 C. P. Scott to L. T. Hobhouse, 19 June 1914, quoted in Wilson, *C. P. Scott*, p. 88.

136 Chamberlain, *op. cit.*, p. 430.

137 *Forward*, 22 June 1912; Swift, *op. cit.*, pp. 190–1.

138 See Bower, *op. cit.*, pp. 180–2; Mann, *op. cit.*, pp. 289–90; Thompson, *The Enthusiasts*, pp. 174–5.

139 *Forward*, 13 July 1912; Bower, *op. cit.*, p. 121; Swift, *op. cit.*, p. 202.

140 Inglis, *op. cit.*, p. 219.

141 *L.C.* 15, 16 Aug., 12 Sept. 1912; *L.D.P.* 16 Aug. 1912; and petition to the Lord Mayor, with depositions of twenty-six witnesses or victims, in Picton Library, Liverpool 331/TRA 5/8/3.

142 *Forward*, 4 May, 1 June 1912; Sexton *Agitator*, p. 226. Six clearing-houses replaced about sixty stands.

143 *P.D.*, 5th. ser., vol. 118, 323–4; *Forward* 29 June, 6, 13 July 1912.

144 *Forward*, 20 July 1912.

145 Ibid. 27 July 1912; *Liverpool Steam Ship Owners Association, Annual Report, 1912*, pp. 11–12.

146 *Forward*, 2 Aug. 1912.

147 The libel is in full in *Forward*, 20 July 1912, in part in *T.* 18 July 1912.

148 Sexton, *Agitator*, chap. xxix; *Manchester Empire News*, 24 Jan. 1926; L.T.C. Minutes, 10 Nov. 1909.

149 Sexton, *Agitator*, chap. xlii; L.L.R.C. Minutes, 10 July 1912; L.T.C. Minutes, 9 Oct 1912.

150 *Forward*, 25 Oct. 1912; apology, ibid. 8 Nov. 1912.

151 Ibid. 1 Nov. 1912.

152 R. Williams, *The Liverpool Docks Problems*, Liverpool, 1912, pp. 6–9, 15; *P.D.*, 5th. ser., vol. 132, col. 99.

153 R. Williams, *The First Year's Working of the Liverpool Docks Scheme*, 1914, p. 83; K. D. Brown, *op. cit.*, p. 126; Wilson, *Dockers*, chap 3. Goole and Grimsby later imitated the Liverpool clearing-house system, see A. G. Gardiner's article, 'Morning at the Docks: A London Scandal and a Liverpool Example', *Daily News*, 23 May 1914.

154 Williams (1912), p. 18, (1914), pp. 13, 98 and Tables 6–6a.

155 Ibid. (1914), p. 11.

156 Ibid., pp. 18–19, 85–95.

157 *T.* 9 Jan., 21, 28 April 1913; Williams (1914), pp. 14–15. The strikers wanted more pay for Saturday work, rather than a half-day holiday.

158 *T.* 8 May 1913.

159 *T.* 20 May 1913.

160 *T.* 26 Nov. 1913.

161 *T.* 17, 18 Nov. 1913.

162 See S. O'Casey, *Drums under the Windows*, 1945, chapter entitled 'Prometheus Hibernica'; and A. G. Gardiner in *Daily News*, 22 Nov. 1913.

163 See Larkin's speeches in *T.* 11 Oct., 17, 22, 26, 27 Nov., 1 Dec. 1913.

164 *T.* 2 Sept. 1913; *46th Annual T.U.C. Report, 1913*, pp. 67–68.

165 L.T.C. Minutes, 8 Oct. 1913.

166 *T.* 17 Nov. 1913.

167 *T.* 2 Dec. 1913. The meeting which Larkin addressed was held under the auspices of the B.S.P. and Clarion Club, although the L.L.R.C., by thirteen votes to nine, agreed to be represented (L.L.R.C. Minutes, 19 Nov. 1913). On Havelock Wilson and the Shipping Federation, B. Mogridge, 'Militancy and Inter-Union Rivalries in British Shipping, 1911–1929', *International Review of Social History*, vi, 1961, pp. 375–412.

168 L.T.C. Minutes, 12 Nov. 1913.

169 Report of Sexton's clash with Larkin, *T.* 10 Dec. 1913.

170 Seven municipal contests involved Labour candidates in 1910, eleven in 1911, twelve in 1912, (including one by-election in each year), and ten in 1913 (including three by-elections). Only five wards were fought on every occasion—Edge Hill, Low Hill, Kensington, Kirkdale, and Wavertree West.

171 *L.C.* 1 Nov. 1912.

172 *L.C.* 31 Oct. 1912.

173 *L.C.* 1 Nov. 1912.

174 L.L.R.C. Minutes, Nov. 1912.

175 A. T. Salvidge to Lord Derby, 19 April 1913, Derby MSS.

176 L.L.R.C. Minutes, 25 Oct. 1913, 2, 7, 24 Feb., 7, 14 April, 9, 13, 27 May, 3, 11 June 1914. Left-wing fringe groups in Liverpool can be fleetingly glimpsed in *The Anarchist*, 10 Nov. 1894, 24 May, 14 June, 12 July, 9 Aug., 29 Nov. 1912.

177 *L.C.* 1 Nov. 1912.

178 *P.D.*, 5th. ser., lxii, 1892–1903; Salvidge, *op. cit.*, p. 122.

179 L.L.R.C. Minutes, 21 May 1913.

180 L.L.R.C. Minutes, 6 Aug., 3, 24 Sept., 1, 25 Oct., 5 Nov. 1913. During the war Murphy took a somersault: he joined the W.M.C.A., rising to become a member of its Central Committee, and in the 1920s he was a co-founder of the Constitutional Labour League, which was fascist in character—see J. Murphy to Lord Derby, 14 Oct. 1926; Salvidge to Derby, 18 Oct. 1926, Derby MSS.

181 ÓBroin, *op. cit.*, p. 75; *Forward*, 18 May 1912. This was somewhat unfair to the pro-Labour section of the Nationalists who, led by Harford and J. O'Shea, had been the engine of the Housing Committee for the past four years—see B. O'Connell, *op. cit.*, pp. 85–86.

182 L.L.R.C. Minutes, 15 Nov., 3 Dec. 1913.

183 Ibid. 19 Nov. 1913 for reprimands to Councillors for their slackness.

184 *P.D.*, 5th. ser., lxiv, 1330–74, lxv, 782–98. Profit-sharing schemes were widespread in the gas industry—see E. Bristow, 'Profit-Sharing, Socialism, and Labour Unrest', in K. D. Brown (ed.), *Essays in Anti-Labour History*, chap. 11.

185 L.L.R.C. Minutes, 19 May, 26 June 1914.

186 Ibid. 18 Sept. 1914. The L.L.R.C.'s executive on 30 August 1912 had recommended that, in the event of international war, a strike be supported.

187 Quoted in M. Ostrogorski, *Democracy and the Organization of Political Parties*, 1902, vol. ii, p. 428.

188 A Bishoprics Bill, creating three new dioceses—Sheffield, Chelmsford, and St. Edmundsbury and Ipswich—passed in mid-1913. See R. Lloyd, *op. cit.*, pp. 232–3; *Church Association Annual Report*, 1912–13, p. 21.

189 F. E. Smith to A. J. Balfour, 30 Oct. 1910, Sandars MSS. c. 761, fols. 291–6; *L.D.P.* 4 Oct. 1911.

190 *L.D.P.* 9 Oct. 1911.

191 A. T. Salvidge to Lord Derby, 28 July 1911, Derby MSS.

192 Idem 24 Aug. 1912.

193 Idem 6 Dec. 1913.

194 D. A. Roberts, *op. cit.*, p. 70; Montgomery Hyde, *Carson*, 1953, p. 323; ÓBroin, *op. cit.*, pp. 65–66.

195 Quoted in I. Colvin, *Life of Lord Carson*, vol. 2, 1934, p. 225.

196 Quotations from Salvidge's speeches from newspaper cuttings which Salvidge enclosed in a letter to Lord Derby, 29 June 1914, Derby MSS. For Conservative allegations that the Liberal Government had created a spoils system in public offices for

members of the Labour movement, see Halévy, *op. cit.*, vi, pp. 446–8; on Irish jobbery, see Ó Broin, *op. cit.*, pp. 83, 155.

197 T. W. A. Bagley to A. Bonar Law, 3 Jan. 1912, Bonar Law MSS. 25/1/7.

198 See Salvidge's correspondence with F. E. Smith, Dec. 1912, quoted in Salvidge, *op. cit.*, 125–30.

199 Quoted in Petrie, *Chamberlain*, i, p. 329.

200 J. W. Hills, W. J. Ashley, and M. Woods, *Industrial Unrest: A Practical Solution*, 1914.

CHAPTER 16

1 Chapter title is from R. B. Haldane to J. R. MacDonald, 24 Dec. 1923, quoted in Haldane, *op. cit.*, p. 321. The epigraphs are as follows: Beatrice Webb to Tom Jones, 16 March 1920, and Stanley Baldwin, 26 April 1926, both concerning the Lloyd George Coalition, quoted in T. Jones (K. Middlemas, ed.), *Whitehall Diary*, 1969, vol. i, p. 106, and vol. ii, p. 23; R. Strausz-Hupé, 'Maxims', *Encounter*, xlvi, March 1976, p. 38.

2 *T.* 11 Nov. 1922. Cf. F. C. Stanley, *The History of the 89th Brigade 1914–1918*, Liverpool, 1919.

3 R. Roberts, *op. cit.*, p. 3.

4 *T.* 20 Sept. 1915.

5 A. T. Salvidge to Lord Derby, 23 March 1915, 24 Aug. 1916, Derby MSS.; *T.* 7 Feb. 1916; Salvidge, *op. cit.*, chap. x; A. Marwick, *The Deluge*, Penguin, 1967, pp. 65–71; J. B. Priestley, *op. cit.*, p. 20; J. Samuelson, *Drink and the War*, Liverpool, 1917; O'Mara, *op. cit.*, p. 192; Jones, *Whitehall Diary*, ii, pp. 88, 205; Dalton, *op. cit.*, p. 172.

6 *T.* 6, 15, 23 Jan., 20 Feb., 17 Dec. 1915; Mountfield, *op. cit.*, chap. 14; Forwood, *Reminiscences*, pp. 55–86; *P.D.*, 5th. ser., lxix, 1208–21, lxx, 1123–4, lxxi, 272–3, 1239–41, lxxii, 174–5, 658–9, lxxvii, 631–2, 1504–6, lxxxvii, 891, 1250, xc, 891–2, 1654–5, vol. 117, 823–7, 1612, vol. 119, 1102, vol. 121, 353–5, vol. 123, 9–10, vol. 126, 1105.

7 *T.* 9 Sept. 1915; Sexton, *Agitator*, chap. xxxv.

8 L.L.R.C. Minutes, 18 Sept., 7 Oct. 1914; *T.* 1, 2, 14 April 1915, 27 Jan., 10 June 1916; Lloyd George's foreword in Sexton, *Agitator*, p. 9.

9 *T.* 5 June 1915; Lord Beveridge, *Power and Influence*, 1953, pp. 134–5.

10 *T.* 22 April 1915, 14 March 1916, 1 Jan., 19 March 1917, 15 Feb., 27 March, 20 July 1918; *P.P.* 1917–18, xv, pp. 13–28; *P.D.*, 5th. ser., lxxxvi, 1572–4, vol. 110, 338.

11 *T.* 9, 20 Oct. 1916, 25 May 1917.

12 Mogridge, *International Review of Social History*, 1961, pp. 389–90; *T.* 29, 30 Nov. 1917.

13 *T.* 10 May 1915.

14 *T.* 4 Jan., 19 Feb. 1915.

15 *P.D.*, 5th ser., lxxxvii, 892–3, xciii, 119–26, xcviii, 1708–21, vol. 120, 229; *T.* 21 Nov., 2 Dec. 1916. For a time the crews of captured submarines were treated differently from other P.O.W.s—Nicolson, *op. cit.*, pp. 272–3.

16 *T.* 10 May 1915.

17 *T.* 10, 11, 12, 13 May, 2 Dec. 1915, 30 March 1916, 2 July, 1, 27 Aug. 1918. An Aliens Restriction Bill, although welcomed by such as Lord Birkenhead, was defeated in the House of Lords in 1919—Lord Newton, *op. cit.*, pp. 277–9.

18 *P.D.*, 5th. ser., lxviii, 707–15, lxxvii, 1348–52, lxxviii, 400–1, 803–6, 1092–3, 1172–3, 1189–90, lxxxii, 65–67, 143–54, 1155–8, lxxxiii, 1118–20, xcii, 2533, vol. 108, 1117–18, 1142–7. See also Richard Holt's diary, 19 July 1914, 6, 20 June, 19 Sept., 24 Oct. 1915, 9 Jan., 4 Feb., 6 Aug. 1916, 22 Nov. 1917.

19 *T.* 2 Aug. 1918; R. F. Henderson, *op. cit.*, pp. 23–24. A. J. Ashton, K.C., the Commissioner who investigated Wise's part in the sectarian riots in 1909–10, accepted the rumours about Wise's origins, stating that he was a German Jew, once Weiss; and this encouraged Ashton to make anti-semitic remarks—see A. J. Ashton, *As I Went on my Way*, 1924, pp. 238–41.

20 *P.D.*, 5th ser., lxix, 85–86; *Church Association Annual Report*, 1914–15, p. 14, 1915–16, pp. 7–8; Henderson, *op. cit.*, pp. 22–26. Liverpool Irishmen in fact had a remarkable record of patriotism, the Liverpool U.I.L. boasting that 25,000 had joined the forces by November 1915—B. O'Connell, *op. cit.*, p. 93.

21 Quoted in Henderson, *op. cit.*, p. 30.

22 Kyffin-Taylor, disliking Westminster and being a lax M.P., had long wanted release. The Unionist party, however, had not wanted another by-election in Kirkdale, and Kyffin-Taylor was held there with some financial inducement. Unbeknown to the Conservatives, the L.L.R.C. was also reluctant to fight Kirkdale again, until the Home Rule question was resolved. See A. T. Salvidge to Lord Derby, 17 June 1912, 15, 17 Nov., 8 Dec. 1914, Sir C. Petrie to Derby, 19 April, 21 June 1912, 6 Nov. 1913, Derby MSS.; L.L.R.C. Minutes, 28 Nov., 3, 19 Dec. 1913, 7 Jan., 4, 18 Feb., 27 March, 16 April, 1 May, 26 June 1914.

23 Marshall Hall had decided to retire in 1913, from personal and professional reasons. Rankin was absent on active service both at his first election in 1916 and at his re-election in 1918. Salvidge to Derby, 7 Feb. 1916, Derby MSS., notes the aborted opposition to Rankin from the Orange clergyman, Theodore Howard.

24 Salvidge, *op. cit.*, p. 257.

25 For O'Connor's views on moral standards in films, *P.D.*, 5th. ser., vol. 138, 256–8; Marwick, *op. cit.*, p. 151.

26 *P.D.*, 5th ser., lxxv, 1571–8, lxxxv, 2558–69, lxxxvi, 609–20, xci, 425–42, vol. 110, 1962–76, vol. 114, 1438–55, vol. 119, 2065–74, vol. 125, 576–83, 1148–51, 1171–8, vol. 126, 741–7, vol. 127, 966–76, vol. 139, 2681–90; T. P. O'Connor to Viscount Gladstone, 6 Nov. 1923, B.L. Add. MSS. 46085, f. 128.

27 *T.* 27 Oct. 1920; R. Roberts, *op. cit.*, p. 167; J. Whittaker, *I, James Whittaker*, 1934, pp. 121–5; O'Mara, *op. cit.*, p. 190 ff.

28 *T.* 18, 19 Oct. 1916; Whittaker *op. cit.*, p. 168; H. R. Poole, *The Liverpool Council of Social Service 1909–1959*, Liverpool, 1960, pp. 23–24, 37–38, 41; M. H. Lloyd Davies, 'Juvenile Delinquency and its Prevention', *The Liverpool Review*, June 1930, pp. 211–14. The last Head Constable, Dunning, had written, 'Personally I am glad to see the increased use of the birch, as there are many boys for whom it is the best treatment, and some offences to which it is peculiarly suitable, indecency for instance'. *An Illustrated and Descriptive History of the Liverpool and Bootle Police*, Liverpool, 1910.

29 The Central Control Board's liquor traffic restrictions operated in Liverpool from 16 August 1915, and an effect upon the annual number of convictions for drunkenness was registered immediately, with 9,155 convictions in 1915, 6,138 in 1916, 3,769 in 1917, and 2,589 in 1918. A rise ensued in the 1920s, only to fall again in the 1930s. See *P.P.* 1919, xlii, p. 352; *T.* 15 Jan. 1919, 6 April 1926, 10 April 1930; *P.D.*, 5th ser., vol. 321, 3054–5, vol. 326, 2446.

30 Quotations in the previous dozen paragraphs are from the diaries of Robert and Richard Holt, vols. 6–11 *passim*; additional quotations from Robert to Richard Holt, 11 June 1893; Beatrice Webb's diary, vol. 20, 10 Oct. 1899; and Forwood, *Recollections*, pp. 20, 60–62. See also G. Findlay Shirras and L. Rostas, *The Burden of British Taxation*, Cambridge, 1942.

31 *T.* 16 June 1917; Salvidge to Derby, 12, 18 June 1917; Derby to Salvidge, 21 June 1917, Derby MSS.

32 *T.* 15, 21 June 1917; Salvidge to Derby, 19 June 1917, Derby MSS. Hughes's contest was the first advanced by the N.F.D.S.S., which went on to sponsor or approve some thirty-two candidates altogether (mostly in the 1918 General Election) before merging into the British Legion at its foundation in 1921.

33 *T.* 25, 26, 27, 28 June 1917; Derby to Salvidge, 25 June 1917, Derby MSS.

34 Salvidge to Derby 20, 30 June, 14 July 1917, Derby MSS; Salvidge, *op. cit.*, pp. 277–8; *T.* 25 June 1917.

35 *P.D.*, 5th ser., xciii, 2359–64, xciv, 810–17, 822, xcv, 1144–55; *T.* 12, 13 June, 5 July 1917. F. E. Smith's pronouncements were similar to Scott's—*P.D.*, 5th ser., xciv, 794–8, xcv, 1245–50, xcix, 1422–7; Birkenhead (1959), pp. 322–3.

36 Salvidge to Derby, 2 June 1917, Derby MSS.

37 Idem 23, 31 Aug. 1917.

38 *T.* 5 April 1918.

39 Salvidge to Derby, 9 April 1918; Derby to Salvidge, 20 April 1918, Derby MSS.; *P.D.*, 5th ser., vol. 106, 81–87. T. P. O'Connor's opinions changed altogether by 1920, owing to the continuing problems of sectarian minorities in Ireland; and henceforward he favoured proportional representation generally. *P.D.*, 5th ser., vol. 110, 2443–5, vol. 136, 814–19, 883–8, vol. 172, 2033–8.

40 *P.P.* 1917–18, xiii, pp. 400–1. The municipal electorate, 1911–21, more than doubled in Liverpool, from 26 per cent to 61 per cent of the population over twenty years of age. See table in Budge and O'Leary, *op. cit.*, p. 175.

41 Salvidge to Derby, 19 Nov. 1918, 11 July 1919, Derby MSS.

42 F. E. Smith to D. Lloyd George, 19 Dec. 1918. Lloyd George MSS. F/4/7/6/.

43 Salvidge, *op. cit.*, p. 143.

44 Salvidge to Derby, 23 Nov., 3 Dec. 1918, Derby MSS.

45 On Raw's adoption by Salvidge see *T.* 2, 5 Feb. 1935; Salvidge to Derby, 31 Dec. 1918, Derby MSS.

46 Salvidge, *op. cit.*, p. 163.

47 Quoted in Maddock, *op. cit.*, p. 213; D. A. Roberts, *op. cit.*, p. 76; Drinkwater, *op. cit.*, p. 39; *Church Association Annual Report, 1918–9*, p. 10.

48 *Daily News*, 7 Dec. 1918 (cutting in A. G. Gardiner papers); Lord Newton, *Retrospection*, 1941, pp. 277–9; T. W. E. Roche, *The Key in the Lock*, 1969, pp. 79–99.

49 *P.D.*, 5th ser., lxviii, 855–7, lxxiv, 1112–30, vol. 110, 3290–2, vol. 112, 1510–5, vol. 121, 2034–42, vol. 129, 630, vol. 131, 2300–1, 2546–7, vol. 142, 214–18, vol. 153, 1927–9, vol. 194, 1661–3, vol. 197, 1326, vol. 200, 2285; B. E. V. Sabine, *A History of Income Tax*, 1966, p. 152.

50 Jones, *Whitehall Diary*, i, pp. 114–15; Dalton, *op. cit.*, chap. vii; McKibbin, *op. cit.*, *passim*; Richard Holt's diary, 2 Jan. 1918.

51 The L.L.R.C. formally adopted the title in 1917.

52 R. Baxter, 'The Liverpool Labour Party, 1918–1963', D.Phil. thesis, Oxford, 1969, p. 38.

53 *L.L.R.C. Annual Report, 1916*, p. 6. Illness eventually removed Hoey, the Plumbers' delegate, in 1921.

54 Maddock, *op. cit.*, pp. 216–26. Sexton defeated Rigby Swift, himself a Liverpudlian—see E. S. Fay, *The Life of Mr. Justice Swift*, 1939, pp. 9–12.

55 Drinkwater, *op. cit.*, p. 33; A. Clinton, 'Trade Councils during the First World War', *International Review of Social History*, xv, 1970, pp. 202–34.

56 Drinkwater, *op. cit.*, pp. 57–58; Maddock, *op. cit.*, pp. 227–39.

57 Quoted in Salvidge, *op. cit.*, p. 173. Hall's biographer writes, improbably, 'By the end of the war his reputation stood so high that he was spoken of as a future Foreign Secretary'—Sir W. James, *The Eyes of the Navy*, 1955, p. 175.

58 *T.* 24 Jan., 24, 26 Feb. 1919; T. Carlyle, 'Chartism' (1839), in *Critical and Miscellaneous Essays*, 1869, v, p. 407.

59 Pollitt, *op. cit.*, p. 96; Martin, *op. cit.*, p. 87; Jones, *Whitehall Diary*, i, pp. 99–103; B. Thomson, *Queer People*, 1922, p. 276.

60 *P.D.*, 5th ser., vol. 112, 361–7, vol. 119, 1235–40; *T.* 14 Feb. 1919. Cf. Lord Derby's observation that Sexton was 'a very straight little man and not at all the sort to countenance Bolshevism', quoted in Salvidge, *op. cit.*, p. 169.

61 Ordinary constables after the war earned less than the lowest class of dock labour; and 'engineers, draughtsmen, and others of equal social status to ourselves' received at least twice as much. *P.P.* 1920, xxii, Qs. 3563–5, 3615, Sgt. Miles, 3682, P. C. Smithwick, 3922, Chief Inspector Duckworth.

62 *T.* 2 Aug. 1919; Maddock, *op. cit.*, p. 170.

63 R. Graves and A. Hodge, *The Long Weekend*, 1940; Four Square edition, 1965, p. 31.

64 M. Toole, *Mrs. Bessie Braddock M.P.*, 1957, p. 58; G. W. Reynolds and A. Judge, *The Night the Police went on Strike*, 1968, *passim*; *P.D.*, 5th ser., vol. 166, 1692–716, vol. 173, 1661–2.

65 *T.* 4 Aug., 21 Oct. 1919; O'Mara, *op. cit.*, p. 233; diary, 31 Aug. 1918, in Lady Cynthia Asquith, *Diaries 1915–1918*, 1968; *P.D.*, 5th ser., vol. 119, 369–70.

66 *T.* 5 Aug. 1919. One of the Birmingham strikers who subsequently lost his pension rights after twenty-four years service, was Sergeant Taylor. Taylor had escorted Lloyd George from Birmingham Town Hall during the Boer War.

67 Sir N. Macready, *Annals of an Active Life*, 1924, ii, p. 411.

68 Tramwaymen in the Municipal Employees Association opposed the company union, the Transport and Vehicle Workers' Union, *T.* 10 July 1918, 9 Aug. 1919. There was a suspicion of Tory jobbery through the W.M.C.A.'s links with the T.V.W.U.—see D. E. Baines and R. Bean, 'The General Strike on Merseyside, 1926', in J. R. Harris (ed.), *op. cit.*, p. 249.

69 *T.* 5, 11, 15, 16, 19 Aug. 1919. Both Sexton and James O'Grady, the two Labour M.P.s on the Desborough Commission, criticized the 1919 Police Act, which differed from their recommendations regarding the standing of the Police Federation—*P.D.*, 5th ser., vol. 118, 813–17, 2446–7.

70 Quoted in Salvidge, *op. cit.*, p. 177. Cf. Jones, *Whitehall Diary*, i, p. 103.

71 Reynolds and Judge, *op. cit.*, p. 194; V. L. Allen, 'The National Union of Police and Prison Officers', *Ec.H.R.*, 2nd ser., xi, no. 1, 1958, pp. 133–43; Drinkwater, *op. cit.*, pp. 73–74; M. Cowling, *The Impact of Labour 1920–1924*, Cambridge, 1971, p. 373; H. Hessell Tiltman, *James Ramsay MacDonald*, 1929, p. 195. Salvidge endeavoured to secure back-pay and pensions for strikers—see J. H. Hayes to Sir A. T. Salvidge, 21 Oct. 1925, Salvidge MSS., which differs in minor particulars from the version quoted in Salvidge, *op. cit.*, pp. 285–6. Salvidge's sympathy was real as much as politic, believing that the strikers were, 'in the main, badly advised and shockingly led'. Salvidge to Derby, 2 Feb. 1921, Derby MSS. For Hayes's continuing efforts to wring concessions from the Home Office, *P.D.*, 5th ser., vol. 119, 2051–3, vol. 125, 706–7, vol. 166, 1692–716, vol. 173, 1635–47, vol. 196, 1023–51.

72 Salvidge to Derby, 7 Feb., 12 Aug. 1919, Derby MSS.; Baxter, *op. cit.*, p. 254; Toole, *op. cit.*, p. 67.

73 Salvidge to Derby, 3 Nov. 1920, Derby MSS.

74 R. Briggs to Salvidge, 17 July 1921, copy Derby MSS.

75 A. T. Salvidge to Lord Derby, 24 Jan. 1917, Derby MSS.; *L.D.P.* quoted in D. A. Roberts, *op. cit.*, pp. 79–80; D. C. Jones, *op. cit.*, iii, chap. 11.

76 *T.* 18, 29 Jan. 1917, 25 July 1918, 31 Dec. 1919, 1 Jan. 1920, 4 Jan., 4, 7 Feb., 11,

12 March, 16 May, 1921; C. L. Mowat, *Britain between the Wars 1918–1940*, 1955, Methuen paperback, 1968, pp. 77, 80; Salvidge to Derby, 14 Jan. 1915, 13, 19, 23, 24 Jan. 1917; Derby to Salvidge, 19 Jan. 1917, Derby MSS.; *P.D.*, 5th ser., vol. 127, 21–22, vol. 135, 654–5, vol. 139, 1225–6.

77 Churchill, *Derby*, pp. 405–21; Salvidge, *op. cit.*, pp. 199–200, 212; Salvidge to Derby, 28 June 1916, Derby MSS. See also Waldorf Astor to J. L. Garvin, two letters, undated [Nov. 1921]; and Lord Derby to Austen Chamberlain, 14 Nov. 1921. Dr. K. O. Morgan kindly supplied me with these references.

78 *T.* 26 May 1922. Wilson was M.P. for North Down.

79 *P.D.*, 5th ser., vol. 150, 1335–9.

80 Quoted in Baxter, *op. cit.*, p. 16.

81 *T.* 19 Oct. 1915; D. C. Jones, *op. cit.* i, p. 260. The provision of school meals was also curtailed—Marwick, *op. cit.*, p. 214.

82 T. Jones to Sir M. Hankey, 27 Feb. 1919, in Jones, *Whitehall Diary*, i, pp. 79–80.

83 *T.* 22 Aug., 20 Sept. 1919, 3 March 1920; *P.D.*, 5th ser., vol. 133, 1571–2, vol. 189, 1846–55.

84 D. C. Jones, *op. cit.* i, pp. 261–2; Pumphrey, *op. cit.*, p. 152; *P.D.*, 5th ser., vol. 345, 49, 594, vol. 346, 480–1. For comparative purposes it might be noted that in 1974 when the Merseyside Metropolitan County Council was created the Liverpool Corporation owned about 99,000 houses and flats.

85 *T.* 9 Oct. 1920, 25 Nov. 1926, 23 March 1929, 5 Jan. 1932.

86 *T.* 28 Jan. 1927, 3 Jan. 1929.

87 D. C. Jones, *op. cit.* i, chap. 14; *P.D.*, 5th ser., vol. 331, 2154–7.

88 *T.* 8 Nov. 1927, 18 Feb. 1928, 1 Feb. 1933. By mid-1937 over 20 per cent of the Corporation's housing stock was in flats—Pumphrey, *op. cit.*, p. 150.

89 *T.* 30 July 1928, 1, 7 Jan. 1932, 7 July 1933, 2, 22 Oct. 1936, 17 Sept. 1937; W. G. Holford and W. A. Eden, *The Future of Merseyside*, Liverpool, 1937, pp. 19–32; *P.D.*, vol. 345, *op. cit.*

90 G. D. H. Cole, *Local and Regional Government*, 1947, p. 47; *P.D.*, 5th ser., vol. 274, 56–57, 74–78, vol. 275, 238–40, 276–8, vol. 280, 2413–14, vol. 285, 2088, vol. 297, 2115–20, vol. 307, 490–7.

91 D. C. Jones, *op. cit.* i, chaps. 13, 14. A survey of working-class houses in Liverpool in 1935–6 revealed that 11,554 families were living in overcrowded conditions—see L. H. Keay, 'Housing', in *The Liverpool Quarterly*, April 1937, pp. 79–83.

92 *P.D.*, 5th ser., vol. 414, cols. 1256–60, Mrs. Braddock.

93 E. S. Griffith, *The Modern Development of City Government in the United Kingdom and the United States*, Oxford, 1927, i, p. 381; Salvidge to Derby, 12 Aug. 1921, Derby MSS; *P.D.*, 5th ser., vol. 155, 373–4.

94 D. C. Jones, *op. cit.* ii, p. 234; *P.D.*, 5th ser., vol. 133, 1108, vol. 138, 383; J. J. Astor *et al.*, *The Third Winter of Unemployment*, 1922, pp. 330–2. One reflection of the slump in Liverpool was the fall in the number of passengers on the Overhead Railway from over 16 million in 1920 to under 10 million in 1921—see Box, *op. cit.*, pp. 137–8.

95 Salvidge to Derby, 11 Sept., 13 Dec. 1922, 16 April 1923; Derby to Salvidge, 16, 17 April 1923, Derby MSS.; *L.D.P.* 12, 20 Jan. 1923. The East Lancashire Road opened in 1933. It cost £2¾ million of which the Ministry of Transport paid over £2 million; but Liverpool Corporation contributed £275,000, Bootle £27,000, and the Docks Board £76,000. No more than 1,300 men were employed on the road at any time, and only a proportion of these were Liverpudlians—*P.D.*, 5th ser., vol. 211, 2317–18, vol. 252, 384, vol. 304, 2644.

96 *T.* 8, 10, 14 Sept. 1921; Toole, *op. cit.*, p. 68 ff.

97 *T.* 1 Oct. 1921; J. and B. Braddock, *op. cit.*, chap. 3. Earlier in 1921 Hemmerde

had discredited evidence which the police brought against some Sinn Feiners; and he alleged that from 1921 the Liverpool Corporation, guided by Salvidge, ostracized him professionally and socially. The Labour party demanded an inquiry, but Hemmerde had personal enemies in all parties, and the matter was officially closed in 1936—see *T.* 3 Aug., 29 Sept., 4 Dec. 1934, 18 May 1935, 4 May 1936; Baines and Bean, in J. R. Harris, *op. cit.*, pp. 245, 269; Sir Thomas White to Derby, 23 Oct. 1934; Derby to L. Holt, 1, 3, 9 Nov. 1934; Holt to Derby, 9 Nov. 1934, Derby MSS.

98 Jones, *Whitehall Diary*, i, p. 73; J. and B. Braddock, *op. cit.*, chap. 4; Gallacher, *op. cit.*, pp. 167, 205–6; R. Bean, 'Liverpool Shipping Employers and the Anti-Communist Activities of J. M. Hughes 1920–25', *Bulletin of the Society for the Study of Labour History*, 1977.

99 A. J. P. Taylor, *op. cit.*, p. 254.

100 *T.* 26 Feb. 1921, 7 Jan. 1922; Salvidge to Derby, 13 Jan. 1922, Derby MSS.

101 According to J. C. C. Davidson's record of the Carlton Club meeting, Hall, Pennefather, Raw, and Rutherford, voted to fight the next election independently—R. R. James, *Memoirs of a Conservative*, 1969, pp. 129–33. According to Austen Chamberlain's list, Raw was not present to vote. However, this list, as reprinted by Kinnear, records as M.P. Liverpool Exchange, E. Pollock. In fact Leslie Scott represented Liverpool Exchange and Ernest Pollock represented Warwick and Leamington—M. Kinnear, *The Fall of Lloyd George*, 1973, Appendix 1.

102 *Liverpool Echo*, 2 Nov. 1922, quoted in D. A. Roberts, p. 91.

103 Salvidge to Derby, 16 Oct. 1922, Derby MSS.; Churchill, *Derby*, pp. 440–6. There was no Lloyd George Liberal constituency organization in Liverpool, 1920–2. The Junior Reform Club declared its preference for 'reunion' candidates who would defend Liberal principles and not prejudge the leadership question; but Lloyd George Liberals apparently backed the Conservatives in Liverpool Wavertree, East Toxteth, Exchange, and Edge Hill in 1922. See Kinnear, *British Voter*, pp. 89, 94, 97.

104 Churchill, *Derby*, pp. 465–82; James, *Memoirs of a Conservative*, pp. 185–90. Lloyd George and Tom Jones assumed that Derby wanted to become Foreign Secretary on the collapse of the Coalition. Jones, *Whitehall Diary*, i, pp. 212–13.

105 Derby's youngest son, Oliver Stanley, had declined nomination in Wavertree in March, having ambitions at the bar still, though Derby wishfully considered his chances of displacing Smith even in October—Salvidge to Derby, 28 March, 2 Nov. 1922; Derby to Salvidge, 25 Oct. 1922, Derby MSS.

106 Stocks, *op. cit.*, pp. 91–92. Miss Rathbone would have preferred to have contested Wavertree but Richard Holt, the local Liberal leader, would not make electoral compacts either with the Women's Citizen's Association or with Labour. E. F. Rathbone to R. D. Holt, 17, 24 Aug. 1921 (14/27/306–7); Holt's diary, 24 July 1921.

107 *T.* 7, 8 Nov. 1922; *D.N.B. 1931–40*, pp. 222–3; Salvidge to Derby, 13, 18, 29 Nov., 6 Dec. 1922; Derby to Salvidge, 19 Nov. 1922, Derby MSS. Draft of letter to Bonar Law from the Law Officers of the Coalition Government, 23 Oct., 1922; notes of interview with S. Baldwin, 12 Nov. 1924 (Scott MSS.). The papers of Sir Leslie Scott are deposited by courtesy of Lady Pim at the Modern Records Centre, University of Warwick.

108 Drinkwater, *op. cit.*, p. 59.

109 M. Toole, *Our Old Man*, 1948, pp. 50–52.

110 *T.* 10 Jan. 1923; Salvidge to Derby, 10, 13, 14, 15, 17, 20, 23, 26, 28 Feb. 1923; Derby to Salvidge, 12, 13, 14, 16, 21 Feb., 1, 16 March 1923, Derby MSS.; *P.D.*, 5th ser., vol. 160, 1238, vol. 162, 2318–19.

111 Salvidge's speech to Edge Hill Unionist Divisional Council, 19 Feb. 1923, Derby MSS.; W. J. Brown, *So Far . . .*, 1943, chap. xiii; McKibbin, *op. cit.*, p. 146.

112 *T.* 7 March 1923. Colonel Stanley and Sir Arthur Griffith-Boscawen failed in East Willesden and Mitcham.

113 Drinkwater, *op. cit.*, p. 67; Bellamy and Saville, *op. cit.* i, p. 284.

114 B. Donoughue and G. W. Jones, *Herbert Morrison*, 1973, pp. 98–103.

115 Pollitt, *op. cit.*, pp. 200–2; Drinkwater, *op. cit.*, p. 72.

116 Baxter, *op. cit.*, p. 20; B. O'Connell, *op. cit.*, p. 153; *P.D.*, 5th ser., vol. 136, 814–19, 883–8, vol. 162, 2200, vol. 163, 1552, vol. 172, 2033–8, vol. 176, 2603–9, vol. 177, 94–108, 409–17, vol. 185, 1776–81, vol. 186, 2486–91, vol. 195, 328–31, vol. 198, 2751–6.

117 Derby's memorandum to the King, 18 Nov. 1922, quoted in Churchill, *Derby*, p. 480.

118 Kinnear, *Fall of Lloyd George*, pp. 30, 200; Kinnear, *British Voter*, pp. 42, 110. Salvidge was not surprised by the Bootle result: the Conservative candidate was badly chosen, unpopular as an ex-Liberal. Salvidge to Derby, 18 Nov. 1922, Derby MSS.

119 Salvidge, *op. cit.*, p. 253; Churchill, *Derby*, p. 533. Baldwin spoke in Liverpool on 3 December 1923.

120 *T.* 21 Nov. 1923.

121 Quoted in Salvidge, *op. cit.*, p. 255.

122 Jones, *Whitehall Diary*, i, p. 259. However, in common with the majority of Baldwin's senior colleagues, Hall had advised against an election in 1923. His acceptance of Bonar Law's invitation to be Principal Agent his biographer describes as 'one of the few big mistakes he made in his life'. Salvidge was surprised by his appointment. Hall left the job within the year. Sir W. James, *op. cit.*, p. 183; Salvidge to Derby, 15 March 1923, Derby MSS.; C. Cook, *The Age of Alignment*, 1975, chap. 7; James, *Memoirs of a Conservative*, p. 183 n.l.

123 *T.* 5 Dec. 1923. Jones's ambitions for a united, God-fearing, and civilized city can be read in *The Liverpool Review*, vol. i, no. 8, Aug. 1930, pp. 342–4.

124 Salvidge, *op. cit.*, p. 254.

125 *T.* 29 Nov. 1923; Churchill, *Derby*, pp. 538–9. On the capital levy, Kinnear, *Fall of Lloyd George*, pp. 169–72; Tiltman, *op. cit.*, pp. 140, 158–60.

126 O'Connor regarded Mosley as 'the man who really began the breakup of the Black and Tan savagery'—quoted in Sir O. Mosley, *My Life*, 1968, p. 157.

127 *T.* 5 Dec. 1923.

128 Churchill, *Derby*, pp. 541, 547.

129 *T.* 18 Jan. 1924.

130 *T.* 24 Jan. 1924.

131 Salvidge, *op. cit.*, chaps. xviii, xix; Churchill, *Derby*, pp. 560–6.

132 *T.* 13 Feb. 1924; R. T. McKenzie, *British Political Parties*, 1955, pp. 114–21, 238–40.

133 D. A. Roberts, *op. cit.*

134 Salvidge to Derby, 9 May 1924, Derby MSS.

135 *T.* 7 May 1924.

136 Salvidge, *op. cit.*, pp. 269–79; *T.* 8, 9, 14 May 1924.

137 *T.* 21 May 1924.

138 *T.* 22 May 1924.

139 *P.D.*, 5th ser., vol. 200, 1466–7; *T.* 12 May 1924; Salvidge to Derby, 19, 23 May 1924, Derby MSS. The budget reduced duties on sugar, tea, coffee, and cocoa, and reduced the entertainment tax.

140 Drinkwater, *op. cit.*, pp. 61–62; Baxter, *op. cit.*, pp. 22–23.

141 In Barton's view only six of the thirty-seven wards had functioning Labour parties. He remained secretary until 1948. Nationally the picture reveals a similar intensive revitalization of existing resources—the number of branches rose from 637 in 1923 to 1,028 in 1925, although party membership remained between 26,000 and 30,000. The crucial factor was the enthusiasm of trade unionists, whose extemporized activities in

elections did much to offset Labour's want of regular constituency and ward organization. See Baxter, *op. cit.*, pp. 33–34; Cole, *Labour Party from 1914*, p. 142; McKibbin, *op. cit.*, chap. vii.

142 *P.D.*, 5th ser., vol. 177, 672–8; Jones, *Whitehall Diary*, i, pp. 290–8.

143 Salvidge to Derby, 8, 10, 16 July 1924; Derby to Salvidge, 5 Aug. 1925, Derby MSS.

144 *T.* 17 Oct. 1924, 31 Aug. 1927, 30 March 1931; Salvidge to Derby, 20 Aug. 1924, Derby MSS.; Cook, *op. cit.*, chap. 3.

145 A. Bevan, *In Place of Fear*, 1952, p. 26; *T.* 8 Dec. 1924. Churchill's 1925 budget in fact did both—cutting income tax and super-tax, and extending the network of pensions and insurance.

146 M. Gilbert, *Winston S. Churchill*, vol. v, *1922–1939*, 1976, chaps 13–14; H. Finer, *English Local Government*, pp. 409–17; K. J. Hancock, 'The Reduction of Unemployment as a Problem of Public Policy, 1920–29', *Ec.H.R.*, 2nd ser., xv, 2, 1962, pp. 328–43; W. O. Hart, *Hart's Introduction to the Law of Local Government and Administration*, 6th edition, 1957, chap. vi; Cole, *Local and Regional Government*, pp. 223–4.

147 Salvidge to Derby, 8, 26 May, 6 Aug., 9 Oct. 1925, Derby MSS.; *T.* 31 Jan. 1925, 14 March 1925; Salvidge, *op. cit.*, chap. xx; Pumphrey, *op. cit.*, pp. 32–36.

148 *T.* 13 Oct., 17 Dec. 1925; Richard Holt's diary, 15 Feb. 1925.

149 Sir Thomas White to Derby, 5 May 1924, enclosing letter from Arthur Collins, Derby MSS; *T.* 27 Feb., 4, 22 March 1932, 24 March, 28 April, 13, 26 June 1934, 9 Jan., 13 Feb. 1936; G. L. Reakes, *Man of the Mersey*, 1956, pp. 48–49. The maintenance of the tunnel was equal to a 6*s*. 4*d*. rate in Liverpool and a 3*s*. 9*d*. rate in Birkenhead by 1937. The local authorities tried to get the government to take responsibility, arguing that the tunnel constituted a trunk road, not merely a local amenity.

150 G. Thayer, *The British Political Fringe*, 1965, p. 227; *P.D.*, 5th ser., vol. 189, 1192.

151 *P.D.*, 5th ser., vol. 136, cols. 814–19; D. C. Jones, *op. cit.* iii, pp. 81–84. By 1932 Liverpool had seven schools in the first category, and twenty-eight in the second—Pumphrey, *op. cit.*, p. 164.

152 *P.D.*, 5th ser., vol. 296, 550–1; A. Zimmern to Tom Jones, 7 Jan. 1917, in Jones, *Whitehall Diary*, i, p. 20; G. K. A. Bell, *op. cit.* ii, chap. lxxi; Mowat, *op. cit.*, pp. 206–8.

153 D. A. Roberts, *op. cit.*, p. 104; *T.* 10 Aug. 1925.

154 Bell, *op. cit.*, pp. 1325–60; F. A. Iremonger, *William Temple*, 1948, pp. 247–59; E. A. Knox, *Reminiscences of an Octogenarian 1847–1934*, 1935, chap. xvi.

155 *T.* 13 Aug. 1925.

156 *T.* 6 Oct. 1925; H. A. Taylor, *op. cit.*, pp. 181–2; Derby to Salvidge, 6 Oct. 1925, Derby MSS.

157 D. A. Roberts, *op. cit.*, p. 103.

158 Baines & Bean in J. R. Harris, *op. cit.*, pp. 239–75.

159 Tramwaymen and power workers were rewarded with about £10,000 in gratuities—about a week's extra pay—for remaining at work, although Salvidge was not anxious to single out groups or individuals in this way—Salvidge to Derby, 16, 17, 20, 21 May 1926, Derby MSS.

160 Quoted in J. Symons, *The General Strike*, 1957, pp. 103, 141.

161 *P.D.*, 5th ser., vol. 200, 391; Drinkwater, *op. cit.*, p. 88.

162 Martin, *op. cit.*, pp. 160–1. Cf. Cole (ed.), *Beatrice Webb's Diaries 1924–1932*, pp. 145–6; Jones, *Whitehall Diary*, ii, *passim*; Richard Holt's diary, 8, 16 May 1926.

163 Baxter, *op. cit.*, pp. 41–42; *T.* 15 June 1926; Richard Holt's diary, 9 May 1927.

164 Salvidge to Derby, 24 Sept. 1926, Derby MSS.; *T.* 6 Jan., 8 July 1926, 8 Sept. 1927.

165 Salvidge to Derby, 7 Dec. 1922, enclosing letter from J. W. Laird, Derby MSS.;

Richard Holt's diary, 1 Feb. 1927; *T.* 31 Jan. 1927. The Gladstone Docks commemorated Robert Gladstone, the Docks Board's chairman, rather than W. E. Gladstone, the Prime Minister.

166 *T.* 14 Oct. 1925, 25 Jan. 1926; *P.D.*, 5th ser., vol. 210, 1038, vol. 217, 1050.

167 *P.D.*, 5th ser., vol. 125, 1798–9, vol. 131, 909–11, vol. 143, 470–3, 1932–8, vol. 145, 1766–9, vol. 170, 2042–6, vol. 172, 1406–7, vol. 192, 1942–3, vol. 204, 2059, vol. 205, 1922–7, vol. 259, 357–9, vol. 260, 398–9, 1956–62, vol. 269, 281–2, vol. 270, 242–3, vol. 272, 1430–1, vol. 277, 221, vol. 287, 553–4, vol. 299, 1796, vol. 319, 1901–4, vol. 325, 1350, vol. 326, 2232.

168 Ibid., vol. 150, 859, vol. 161, 137–42, vol. 245, 588–9, vol. 304, 1985, vol. 314, 582, vol. 342, 176–9, vol. 343, 1092–3; *P.P.* 1937–8, xiii, p. 224; Keeling, *op. cit.*, p. 15.

169 *P.D.*, 5th ser., vol. 180, 1606, vol. 211, 71–75, vol. 283, 1043–4, vol. 284, 877–80, vol. 297, 82–84, vol. 315, 599–698, vol. 317, 180–7; Keeling, *op. cit.*, pp. 42–43, 46.

170 *P.D.*, 5th ser., vol. 180, 1587–8, vol. 193, 710–12, vol. 194, 1926–7, vol. 226, 574–5, vol. 237, 576–7, vol. 244, 1018–19, vol. 247, 1123–4, vol. 252, 534, 2214–15.

171 *T.* 29 Sept. 1927. For Salvidge's view that the Guardians' action might do 'incalculable harm' to the Conservatives' municipal prospects, see Salvidge to Derby, 27 Oct. 1927, Derby MSS.

172 *T.* 27 Oct., 29 Dec. 1927.

173 D. A. Roberts, *op. cit.*, p. 106; *T.* 24 Nov. 1927.

174 *T.* 28 Jan. 1928; *P.D.*, 5th ser., vol. 218, 1047–53. On the Malines conversations, between Lord Halifax and Cardinal Mercier, see Bell, *op. cit.*, p. 1300; Lockhart, *op. cit.* ii, chaps. xviii–xxii; Lloyd, *op. cit.*, pp. 414–24. On the Prayer Book debates, see H. A. Taylor, *op. cit.*, chap. xxvii.

175 D. A. Roberts, *op. cit.*, p. 107. Downey was the second Irish-born bishop (the first Irish-born archbishop) of Liverpool. Bernard O'Reilly, bishop from 1873 to 1894, was the other.

176 Chilcott admired Salvidge as 'the King of Liverpool'—quoted in Salvidge, *op. cit.*, p. 293.

177 *T.* 8, 22, 23, 25, 28 April 1927; Salvidge to Derby, 23 March 1927, Derby MSS. Winston Churchill's letter to Salvidge, reporting Baldwin's opinion, is partly quoted in Salvidge, *op. cit.*, pp. 301–2, and dated 10 April 1927. The original survives in the Salvidge Papers, dated 31 March 1927; moreover, it includes criticisms of Scott, especially that he 'had used his [Baldwin's] name, and conveyed an impression that the Central Office was also favourable to the Scott movement . . . ' . The full text is published in M. Gilbert, *Winston S. Churchill, Companion Volume V: Part I 1922–1929*, 1979, pp. 973–4.

178 Memorandum by Liverpool M.P.s, 24 March 1927, Copy, Derby MSS.; Earl of Kilmuir, *Political Adventure*, 1964, p. 42.

179 Quoted in Salvidge, *op. cit.*, pp. 293, 300–1.

180 *P.D.*, 5th ser., xciii, 2359–64, xciv, 810–17, 822, xcv, 1144–55, vol. 113, 1995–2002, vol. 114, 1813–19, 2281–97, vol. 117, 1033–6, 1062, 1481–3, 1561–3, vol. 179, 217–28, vol. 189, 1846–55, vol. 193, 1559–60, vol. 194, 1605–13, vol. 205, 1521–7, vol. 207, 839–47; Scott to Sankey, 11 June 1929, Sankey MSS. c. 536, fol. 108. For Scott's thoughts on Land Transfer see Public Record Office, L.C.O.2/509 X/J.69.52; L.C.O.2/449 X/J. 6631. I owe this reference to Dr. A. Offer. See also Scott MSS. 119/3/P/BA, CH, GEN, LI, RE, TP; and P. B. Johnson, *Land fit for Heroes*, Chicago, 1968, pp. 65, 189, 413–16.

181 *P.D.* 5th ser., vol. 188, 1433–7, vol. 189, 567–8, vol. 222, 988–90, vol. 236, 303–10, vol. 238, 1977–82, vol. 241, 2163–6, vol. 268, 1355–6, vol. 272, 1709–12, vol. 275, 1044–5, vol. 278, 437–43, vol. 280, 604–6; and G. C. Abbott, 'A Re-examination of the 1929 Colonial Development Act', *Ec.H.R.*, 2nd ser., xxiv, 1971, pp. 68–81.

182 *P.D.*, 5th ser., vol. 160, 918–24, vol. 192, 433–7. On the other hand Cohen threatened to vote with Labour against the Conservative government on pensions questions in June 1923, and did so in May 1925. See G. Wootton, *The Official History of the British Legion*, 1956.

183 Jones, *Whitehall Diary*, ii, pp. 155, 192. Sir Robert Horne had been Minister of Labour, President of the Board of Trade, and Chancellor of the Exchequer in the Lloyd George Coalition Government. On the disreputable side of Chilcott, see S. Roskill, *Hankey, Man of Secrets, II, 1919–1931*, 1972, pp. 420–3, and T. Cullen, *Maundy Gregory, Purveyor of Honours*, 1974, chap. ix.

184 *P.D.*, 5th ser., vol. 189, 572–5, vol. 191, 553–9, vol. 192, 1649, vol. 198, 2801, vol. 200, 2100, vol. 214, 1007–18, vol. 215, 1777. Tawney, the historian, was a pioneer of the W.E.A. He had been a member of the Sankey inquiry into the coal industry in 1919; and the Labour party's electoral manifesto, *Labour and the Nation*, 1929, reflected much of his political thought.

185 Ibid., vol. 171, 2291–7, vol. 193, 1510–11, vol. 195, 1023–6, vol. 202, 2129–34, vol. 249, 691–2.

186 Sir J. Sandeman Allen to Dr. R. I. Richardson, 19 Dec. 1928, copy, Derby MSS.

187 Sir J. Reynolds quoted in Salvidge to Derby, 16 June 1928; Allen's memorandum for Lord Stonehaven, copy enclosed in Allen to Derby, 27 Aug. 1931, ibid.

188 Salvidge to Derby, *op. cit.*

189 Salvidge to Derby, 13 May 1924, 24 Sept. 1926, ibid.

190 Memoranda, by Salvidge 14 March 1927, and by the Liverpool M.P.s, 24 March 1927, copies, Derby MSS.

191 R. Rutherford to Derby, 19 Jan., 21 Dec. 1929, ibid.

192 Allen to Derby, 5 April 1927; Cf. J. A. Tinne to Derby, 5 Jan. 1929, ibid.

193 Salvidge to Derby, 17, 23, 29 March, 5 April 1927, 28 July, 4 Aug. 1928; Derby's notes of a conversation with Salvidge, 23 March 1927, ibid.

194 Derby to Lord Birkenhead, 8 April 1927; Derby to H. R. Topping, 20 June 1928; Derby to Tinne, 4 Jan., 14 March 1929; Derby to Lord Stanley, 12 March 1929, copies, ibid.

195 *L.D.P.* 22 April 1927; Salvidge to Derby, 19 May 1927, Derby MSS.

196 Memoranda, by Derby and Allen, regarding the conference at the Conservative Club, 28 May 1927; Derby to Salvidge, 20 July, 2 Sept. 1927, copies, Derby MSS.

197 Sir L. Scott to Derby 1 April 1927, ibid.

198 Derby's and Allen's memoranda, 28 May 1927; Allen to Derby, 2, 5 June 1927; Derby to J. C. C. Davidson, 2 April, 31 May 1927, copies, ibid.

199 Derby to Allen, 3 June 1927; Davidson to Derby, 2 Sept. 1927; Salvidge to Derby, 15, 16 Nov. 1927; Derby's memorandum regarding the conference at the Conservative Club, 19 Nov. 1927, copies, ibid.

200 Derby to Salvidge, 30 May 1927, copy, ibid.

201 James, *Memoirs of a Conservative*, p. 73; Derby to Salvidge, 9 Dec. 1921, copy, Derby MSS. The Prime Minister in question was Lloyd George. An important conference on Anglo-Irish relations was held at Gairloch in September 1921.

202 Salvidge to Scott, 25 March 1927, enclosed in Scott to Derby, 27 March 1927; W. Russell to Derby, 6 April 1927, Derby to Russell, 7 April 1927; *L.D.P.* 14, 22 April 1927, copies, Derby MSS.

203 Derby to Allen 20, 31 May 1927; Allen to Derby, 2 June 1927; Derby to Davidson, 10 Sept, 31 Oct. 1927, copies, ibid.

204 Derby to Allen, 24 Oct. 1927; Derby's memorandum, 19 Nov. 1927, ibid.

205 Churchill, *Derby*, pp. 578–9; Derby to Reynolds, 23 Nov. 1927; Reynolds to Derby, 24 Nov. 1927; Derby to Salvidge, 15 May 1928; Derby to H. R. Topping, 20 June 1928; Allen to Derby, 7 Sept. 1928; Derby to Allen, 25 Oct. 1928, Derby MSS.

206 Salvidge to Derby, 12 March, 5 April 1928; Derby to Topping, *op. cit.*; E. Stacey to Derby, 16 Dec. 1929, ibid.

207 Salvidge to Derby, 12 Sept., 2, 5, 20 Oct. 1928; Derby to Salvidge, 15, 27 Sept., 4, 6, 13, 23 Oct. 1928; Derby to Reynolds, 15 Sept. 1928; Reynolds to Derby, 18 Sept. 1928; Derby to Allen, 12, 21 Sept., 4 Oct. 1928; Allen to Derby, 26, 29 Sept. 1928, ibid.

208 Quoted in Salvidge, *op. cit.*, p. 9. The original survives in the Salvidge Papers, dated 6 Dec. 1928—i.e. Salvidge was not dead when Garvin made his appreciation as the biography implies.

209 Derby to Sir Warden Chilcott, 25, 26 Feb. 1929, copies, Derby MSS.

210 Derby to Birkenhead, 22 Dec. 1928, copy, ibid.

211 Sir C. Petrie, *Scenes of Edwardian Life*, 1965, p. 66; Sir C. Petrie, *The Victorians*, 1960, p. 94. J. C. C. Davidson claimed that Salvidge actually confessed to having taken party funds—James, *Memoirs of a Conservative*, p. 117.

212 Author's conversation with Sir Charles Petrie.

213 Lloyd George, quoted in Jones, *Whitehall Diary*, iii, p. 168.

214 Derby to Allen, 2 Jan. 1929, copy, Derby MSS.

CHAPTER 17

1 The phrase 'sectarian cobwebs' is from Campbell-Bannerman's election address of 1900, quoted in Wilson, *C–B*, p. 334. The epigraph is compiled from MacDonald's speech at Sunderland, November 1921, quoted in Tiltman, *op. cit.* p. 138; and from Beatrice Webb's diary, April 1927, in M. I. Cole (ed.), *Beatrice Webb's Diary 1924–1932*, 1956, p. 138.

2 E. S. Murch to Derby, 12 Feb. 1923, Derby MSS.

3 Allen to Derby, 17 Dec. 1928, ibid.

4 Derby to Birkenhead, 8 April 1927, ibid.

5 Derby to Allen, 2 Jan. 1929, ibid.

6 Allen to Derby, 13, 17 Dec. 1928, ibid.

7 Reynolds to Derby, 22 April, 20 Sept. 1929, ibid.

8 Derby to Sir M. Muspratt, 21 Jan. 1929, ibid.

9 Derby to M. H. Maxwell, 1 Jan. 1929; Derby to Scott, 3 Jan. 1929; Allen to Derby, 14 Jan. 1929; Derby to Allen, 22 Jan. 1929; Derby to R. Rutherford, undated memorandum (Jan. 1929); Rutherford to Derby, 31 Jan. 1929; Murch to Derby, 29 Jan., 1 Feb. 1929, ibid.

10 Derby to Maxwell, 2 Jan. 1929, ibid.

11 White to Derby, 8 Feb. 1929, ibid.

12 Derby to Salvidge, 14 March 1928; Derby to Sir P. Bates, 20 Dec. 1929; Bates to Derby, 29 Dec. 1928; Sir Thomas Royden to Derby, 14 Jan. 1929, ibid.

13 Allen to Derby, 15 Jan. 1929, ibid.

14 Derby to Allen 17, 22 Jan. 1929; Derby to White, 13 Jan. 1929, ibid.

15 Derby's and Allen's memoranda of the conference at the Conservative Club, 28 May 1927; R. Rutherford to Derby, 27 Jan. 1929, ibid.

16 Derby to Murch, 26 Feb. 1929, ibid.

17 Allen to Derby, 26 March, 1929, ibid.

18 Murch to Derby, 4, 13 Feb. 1929, ibid.

19 Jones, *Whitehall Diary*, ii, pp. 14–18, 101–2; Brown (ed.), *Essays in Anti-Labour History*, pp. 61–64, 286–8; *P.D.*, 5th. ser., vol. 272, 627, Sir R. Rankin, vol. 330, 1420–4, B. V. Kirby; *T.* 12, 15 March 1929. Lloyd George spoke of Melchett as Judas after 1926—Winterton, *op. cit.*, p. 132.

20 Mond's views are mostly taken from his attack on the 1930 budget—*P.D.*, 5th ser., vol. 235, 1446–57, vol. 237, 2817–23, vol. 240, 471–7, vol. 244, 1751–61.

21 *T.* 16 March 1929.

22 H. Mond to Derby, 8 March 1929, Derby MSS.

23 *P.D.*, 5th ser., vol. 125, 2113–14, J. B. Cohen. See also Jones, *Whitehall Diary*, ii, p. 98.

24 Allen to Derby, 3 Jan. 1929; G. Watson to Derby, 4 June 1929, 10 Feb. 1930; Derby to Watson, 12 Feb. 1930; Murch to Derby, 5, 9, 19, 23, 27 March, 2 April, 1929, Derby to Murch 6, 9, 14 March, 4 April 1929, Derby MSS.; *P.D.*, 5th. ser., vol. 247, 882–7.

25 *T.* 8 March 1928, 28 May 1929; *P.D.*, 5th. ser., vol. 244, 1146–9.

26 Scott to Derby, 11 April 1929, Derby MSS.

27 Reynolds to Derby 7, 20 Sept., 8 Oct. 1929, ibid. See also Murch to Scott, 12 April 1929; Reynolds to Scott, 11 April, 31 May, 5 June 1929 (Scott MSS. 119/3/S/LI).

28 *T.* 30 May, 13 June 1929.

29 Allen to Derby, 6 June 1929; White to Derby, 29 April 1933, Derby MSS.

30 Derby to White, 31 Jan., 12 Feb. 1929; White to Derby, 2 Feb. 1929, ibid.

31 *T.* 1, 7 June 1928. On Margaret Beavan's work, see *Living Hands: Fifty Years of Child Welfare Service in Liverpool 1907–1957*; and I. Ireland, *Margaret Beavan of Liverpool*, Liverpool, 1938.

32 M. Beavan to Derby, 2 Dec. 1928, 12 Jan., 25, 27 March, 5, 29 April, 1, 6, 11 June, 10 Dec. 1929; Derby to Beavan, 4 Dec. 1928, 17, 29 Jan., 12 June 1929; Derby to Allen, 3 June 1929, Derby MSS.

33 Ireland, *op. cit.*, chap. xxi. Derwent Hall Caine's elder brother was Conservative M.P. for East Dorset, 1922–31.

34 Sandham was thought 'one of the best speakers in the Labour party'—*Times Election Supplement*, 1 June 1929.

35 Beavan to Derby, 18 June 1929, Derby MSS. Arthur Greenwood, the new Minister of Health, gave a similar explanation of Labour's victory—'. . . their persistent weekly propaganda, the speeches being discussed the following day in workshop and factory, the machinery of trade union organization helping the agents to trace removals of voters, the growth of the feeling among working men that "Labour" is naturally their Party, the idealism which has not been chilled by office and trial and disappointment'. Jones, *Whitehall Diary*, ii, p. 188.

36 Derby's notes on the seven M.P.s' crisis, undated (May 1927); Derby to Davidson, 31 May 1927; Rutherford to Derby, 26 May 1929; Allen to Derby, 26 March 1929; Derby to Allen, 30 March 1929; Derby to J. A. Tinne, 15 April 1929; Derby to E. Stacey, 28 April 1929, Derby MSS.

37 Derby to Allen, 17, 19 Dec. 1929; Derby to White, 2 Jan. 1930, ibid.

38 Allen to Derby, 2 June 1927, ibid.

39 Tinne to Derby, 11 March 1929; Derby to Stacey, 28 April 1929; E. Haigh to Derby, 29 April 1929, ibid.

40 J. F. Brakell to Derby, 26 April 1929; Derby to Sir M. Muspratt, 22 May 1929, ibid.

41 Davidson to Derby, 30 June, 11, 15 July 1927; Derby to Davidson 1 July 1927, ibid.

42 Derby to Scott, 3 Jan. 1929, ibid.

43 Derby to White, 13 Jan. 1929, ibid.

44 Derby to Scott, 3 Jan. 1929; Derby to Stacey, 22 26 April 1929; Derby to Tinne, 13 June 1929, ibid.

45 Muspratt to Derby, 10 Jan. 1930; Derby to White, 23 Jan. 1930, ibid.

46 J. Pearson and others to Derby, 31 Jan., 7, 19 Feb. 1930; Derby to Pearson, 15, 18 Feb. 1930; White to Derby, 12 Feb., 14 April 1930, ibid. Rushton had been Lord Mayor of Liverpool, 1923–4.

47 Derby to White, 3 June 1929, ibid.

48 White to Derby, 14 June 1929; Allen to Derby 6, 17 June 1929, ibid.

49 Derby's notes for a speech to the Constitutional, 3 Oct. 1929, ibid.

50 Derby to Topping, 28 Nov. 1929; Derby to Tinne, 19 Dec. 1929, ibid.

51 Allen to Derby, 21 Dec. 1929; Derby to all constituency chairman, 31 Dec. 1929; White to Derby, 6 Jan. 1930, ibid.

52 White to Derby, 30 Jan., 7 Feb. 1930; Derby to White, 3, 12 Feb. 1930; Derby to Stacey, 3 Feb. 1930, ibid.

53 Derby to White, 13, 31 March, 9 April 1930; White to Derby, 6, 27 March, 14 April 1930; Derby to Allen, 31 March 1930, ibid.

54 Derby to Stacey, 8 April 1930; Derby to White, 9 April 1930, ibid.

55 Stacey to Derby, 28 Oct., 17 Dec. 1930; White to Derby, 15 Jan. 1934, ibid.

56 The joke was made by T. J. Condon, M.P. Tipperary E., in 1893—*P.D.*, 4th ser., xv, 732.

57 *P.D.*, 5th ser., vol 234, 538–42, vol. 257, 891–956, vol. 272, 826–7, vol. 276, 595, 600–2, vol. 278, 2173–5, vol. 304, 1138–40, vol. 317, 1048, vol. 318, 652–4.

58 Baxter, *op. cit.*, pp. 203, 214–15.

59 Ibid., p. 246.

60 £122,000 had been subscribed to the Cathedral fund during Keating's archepiscopate—F. Gibberd, *Metropolitan Cathedral of Christ the King Liverpool*, 1968, pp. 152–3.

61 *T.* 1, 28 March 1930.

62 R. F. Henderson, *The Startling History of the New Liverpool Roman Catholic Cathedral*, 1967, p. 4; *T.* 2 June 1930. By contrast the Anglican Cathedral Committee bought the fourteen-acre site, St. James's Mount, from the Corporation for £20,000 under thirty years before—Forwood, *Recollections*, p. 197.

63 *T.* 6, 12 June 1930.

64 Baxter, *op. cit.*, pp. 49–58.

65 D. A. Roberts, *op. cit.*, pp. 114–15.

66 *T.* 3 May 1930. Disputes between local Labour parties and Labour councillors concerning the party line were quite common in the 1920s. The Liverpool dispute was the last straw, which induced the N.E.C., under Herbert Morrison's influence, to authorize model standing orders to guide local parties. See Donoughue and Jones, *op. cit.*, p. 136.

67 J. and B. Braddock, *op. cit.*, pp. 69–72; Toole, *Mrs. Braddock*, pp. 97–98.

68 R. Bevins, *The Greasy Pole*, 1965, p. 13; Shaw, *My Liverpool*, pp. 143–51.

69 Baxter, *op. cit.*, pp. 230–1.

70 Bevins, *op. cit.*, p. 11.

71 Baxter, *op. cit.*, pp. 64–67.

72 Bevins, *op. cit.*, pp. 12–14.

73 J. H. Whyte, 'The Influence of the Catholic Clergy on Elections in Nineteenth-Century Ireland', *E.H.R.*, ccxcv, April 1960, pp. 239–59.

74 White to Derby, 13 Oct. 1930, Derby MSS.

75 The Cenotaph was unveiled in front of St. George's Hall on Armistice Day, 1930. No Catholic dignitaries were present.

76 *T.* 13 Nov., 3 Dec. 1930; *The Liverpool Review*, 1930, pp. 234, 438, 459–64, 507–8. A dispensation for a Catholic to marry a non-Catholic was virtually impossible in Liverpool before Whiteside's death in 1921—J. C. Heenan, *A Crown of Thorns*, 1974, chap. 16.

77 *T*. 15 Nov. 1930.

78 *T*. 3, 4 Dec. 1930.

79 *T*. 2 March 1931.

80 *T*. 14, 15, 16, 22 Jan., 4 March 1931.

81 *T*. 23 June 1930.

82 *P.D.*, 5th ser., vol. 247, 193–260, vol. 308, 1246–50; Snell, *op. cit.*, pp. 243–4. The Bill was finally rejected by the House of Lords in March 1931, and the President of the Board of Education, C. P. Trevelyan, resigned.

83 *T*. 24, 26 Jan. 1931.

84 *T*. 22, 30 Jan., 5 Feb. 1931.

85 On the in-fighting behind the candidature, White to Derby, 15 Jan. 1931, Derby to White, 31 Dec. 1930, 19 Jan. 1931, Derby MSS.; *T*. 14 Jan. 1931; Gilbert, *Churchill*, v, p. 391, n.l.

86 *T*. 22, 29 Jan., 3, 4 Feb. 1931.

87 *T*. 2 March 1931; Jones, *Whitehall Diary*, i, pp. 311–12, ii, pp. 96, 99, 265.

88 On Treleavan, see Bevins, *op. cit.*, p. 12.

89 *T*. 6, 8, 11, 23 June 1931; J. A. Tinne to Derby, 11 March 1929, Derby MSS.

90 *T*. 13, 18, 23 June 1931.

91 *P.D.*, 5th ser., vol. 259, 367–72, vol. 275, 426–8, vol. 283, 937–8, vol. 286, 969, vol. 288, 1222–5; M. Cowling, *Impact of Hitler*, Cambridge, 1975, p. 358.

92 White to Derby, 25 June 1931, Derby MSS.

93 *T*. 19 Oct. 1931.

94 J. H. Thomas to Derby, 9 Oct. 1931; Derby to Thomas, 12 Oct. 1931, Derby MSS. Everton and South-East Essex were the only constituencies where a National Labour candidate fought both Labour and Conservative opponents. In Everton the Conservative poll fell from 12,667 in 1929 to 12,186 in 1931. Hall Caine's poll of 14,234 in 1929 both dwindled and divided in 1931, into 4,950 National Labour and 7,786 Labour votes. See R. Bassett, *Nineteen Thirty-One*, 1958, p. 332.

95 *T*. 22 Oct. 1931; Derby to White, 12 Oct., 4 Nov. 1931; White to Derby, 3 Nov. 1931, Derby MSS.

96 *T*. 21, 29 Aug., 25 Sept. 1931. Liverpool Corporation appointed an Economy Committee in the depression years to scrutinize all expenditure over £1,000. Pumphrey, *op. cit.*, p. 204.

97 *T*. 24 Sept., 10 Nov. 1931.

98 *P.D.*, 5th ser., vol. 256, cols. 878–80.

99 *T*. 10 Nov. 1930, 14 Sept., 13 Oct. 1931; Derby to W. Russell, 3 June 1929; White to Derby, 29 April 1933, Derby MSS.

100 *T*. 7 Sept. 1933. Others, without Longbottom's sectarian animus, like Sir John Sandeman Allen and Eleanor Rathbone, also made a connection between Irish immigration and Liverpool's slum and unemployment problems. Moreover, the Society of St. Vincent de Paul urged its Irish branches not to send seekers for work to Liverpool. In 1921 there were 28,700 Merseyside residents who were born in the Irish Free State, in 1931 30,500. 56·8 per cent of Irish immigrants were unskilled and it was found from a study of three depression years in Liverpool that 87 per cent of the public assistance was expended on people of Irish extraction. This included persons born in the city of Irish parents as well as recent arrivals from Ireland—D. C. Jones, *op. cit.* i, chap. 11; *T*. 5 Aug. 1936. See also *P.D.*, 5th ser., vol. 280, 604–6.

101 *P.D.*, 5th ser., vol. 229. 1203–6, vol. 236, 1613–15, vol. 237, 1703–6, vol. 242, 42–44, 309–30, 741–69; Winterton, *op. cit.*, pp. 162–3.

102 White to Derby, 3 Nov. 1931, Derby MSS.

103 D. C. Jones, *op. cit.* ii, pp. 7, 366–9.

104 Ibid., pp. 63, 67; Hyde, *Shipping Enterprise and Management*, pp. 166–7; *T*. 4 Dec. 1931.

105 D. C. Jones, *op. cit.* ii, p. 82; R. Lawton and C. M. Cunningham (eds.), *Merseyside: Social and Economic Studies*, 1970, pp. 60–61.

106 D. C. Jones, *op. cit.* ii, pp. 10–11.

107 *T*. 20 May 1927.

108 D. C. Jones, *op. cit.* ii, p. 359.

109 *P.D.*, 5th ser., vol. 323, 1249, vol. 331, 1300–1, 1416, vol. 345, 2728–32, vol. 348, 1296–7.

110 D. C. Jones, *op. cit.* ii, p. 403; D. C. Jones, *Trade Revival in a Depressed Area*, Liverpool, 1937, chap. ix: *T*. 3 March, 5 Aug. 1936, 25 Jun. 1939. On shipbuilding see *Britain in Recovery*, British Association, 1938, p. 345.

111 Hyde, *Liverpool and the Mersey*, p. 170.

112 *T*. 26 Feb. 1935; Poole. *op. cit.*, chap. v.

113 *P.D.*, 5th ser., vol. 265, 1964–5, 2197–9, vol. 302, 2128; Pilgrim Trust, *Men without Work*, Cambridge, 1938, pp. 29, 90–91, 97; *The Liverpool Quarterly*, Oct. 1937, pp. 171–4, Jan. 1938, pp. 3–5.

114 *T*. 28 Nov. 1936, 9 March 1939; *P.D.*, 5th ser., vol. 307, 2164, vol. 342, 1193–5.

115 *T*. 3 Dec. 1932, 8 March 1933; White to Derby, 16 Dec. 1931, Derby MSS.

116 W. Hannington, *Unemployed Struggles 1919–1936*, 1936, pp. 233–7; W. Hannington, *Never On Our Knees*, 1967, pp. 252–4; T. Lane, 'Some Merseyside Militants of the 1930s' in Hikins, *op. cit.*, pp. 153–77; *T*. 20 Sept. 1932.

117 *P.D.*, 5th ser., vol. 256, 1947–62.

118 *T*. 22, 23, 26, 27 Sept., 28, 29 Oct., 11 Nov., 6, 7 Dec. 1932.

119 J. and B. Braddock, *op. cit.*, p. 11.

120 *T*. 28 Oct., 23 Nov. 1933.

121 See table of councillors' occupations in D. C. Jones, *op. cit.* ii, p. 5. This can be compared with the table of occupations of Liverpool Councillors in 1870, 1880, 1890, 1900, 1910, and 1922 in Griffith, *op. cit.* ii, p. 675. For the composition of the early Victorian Council see *L.M.* 16 Nov. 1849, in Webb Local Government Collection, vol. 148.

122 *T*. 9, 11 Jan. 1933.

123 *T*. 17, 21, 23, 29 Dec. 1932, 6, 11, 13 Jan. 1933; Goldie, *op. cit.*, pp. 209–10.

124 White to Derby, 13 Dec. 1932, 4, 25 Jan. 1933, 15 Jan. 1934, Derby MSS.

125 D. A. Roberts, *op. cit.*, p. 122.

126 *T*. 2, 22 June, 3 Aug., 29 Sept., 11 Oct. 1932.

127 *T*. 22, 23 Feb., 10 March 1933; *P.D.*, 5th ser., vol. 275, 1175.

128 *T*. 13, 22 April, 5 May, 23 June 1933.

129 For example, only £60,000 went towards the relief of Scotland. *T*. 14, 21 July 1933; *P.D.*, 5th ser., vol. 280, 545–8.

130 *T*. 7 July 1933.

131 *T*. 11 Dec. 1933; White to Derby, 9 May 1932, 29 Dec. 1933, 10, 12 Dec. 1934, Derby MSS.; letter from W. Walker in *T*. 11 Dec. 1933. The housing subsidy did not distinguish between rich and poor areas or between local authorities with large and small housing programmes; and the lowering of the subsidy in 1930 meant higher rents and less local authority activity. See H. W. Richardson and D. H. Aldcroft, *Building in the British Economy between the Wars*, 1968, pp. 182–3, on Liverpool's record; and *P.D.*, 5th ser., vol. 264, 773–4, vol. 273, 624–31, vol. 274, 56–57, 74–78, vol. 275, 238–40, 276–80.

132 *T*. 4 Sept. 1934, 3 March 1936; *P.D.*, 5th ser., vol. 274, 1171, vol. 275, 1019–22, vol. 286, 969, vol. 307, 1210–13.

133 *P.D.*, 5th ser., vol. 298, 1611–14, 2102–3, vol. 299, 581, vol. 301, 1206–8, 1237–43, vol. 303, 15–16, vol. 307, 1245–9, vol. 326, 293–5; *P.P.* 1937–8, xiii, pp. 223–8.

134 *T.* 14 March 1936.

135 Lane in Hikins, *op. cit.*, pp. 160, 170–1, notes that Orangemen co-operated in the unemployed demonstrations in Birkenhead in 1932.

136 *T.* 16 July 1932.

137 *T.* 17 Oct. 1932.

138 *T.* 8 Oct. 1932. The file was presented to the Protestant Truth Society by Lady Birkenhead after her husband's death. F. E. Smith had been prosecuting counsel at McKeever's trial—see p. 192.

139 *T.* 13, 14 Sept., 28 Nov. 1932, 27 Feb., 5 May 1933.

140 *T.* 15, 25, 29 Sept. 1933.

141 *Church Association Annual Report, 1924–5*, p. 10.; C. E. Raven, *Liverpool Cathedral*, Oxford, 1933; Redfern MSS. 24174 (22). Various non-Anglicans had contributed to the Cathedral fund—G. S. Spinks, E. L. Allen, and J. Parkes, *Religion in Britain since 1900*, 1952, p. 88.

142 *T.* 25 Sept. 1923.

143 *T.* 23 Sept. 1933.

144 *T.* 9 Jan. 1934; Iremonger, *op. cit.*, pp. 467–73. See also Lord Hugh Cecil's letter in *M.G.* 17 Nov. 1933; Lord Halifax and the Bishop of Liverpool in *T.* 2, 6, 9, 12 Jan. 1934.

145 *T.* 9 June 1934. Reactions of the Bishop, Dr. Dwelly, Prof. Raven, Dr. Jacks, and Canon Bezzant in *T.* 18, 25, 26 June, 3 July 1934. See also Jacks, *op. cit.*, chap. 26; H. H. Henson, *Retrospect of an Unimportant Life*, Oxford, 1943, vol. ii, chap. xxv; A. R. Ellis (ed.), *Lawrence Redfern*, Bournemouth, 1968, pp. 36–52; L. P. Jacks, C. E. Raven, and F. W. Dwelly, *Two Letters*, Oxford, 1934.

146 W. R. Inge to L. Redfern, 15 Aug. 1934, Redfern MSS. 24174 (20).

147 Quoted in D. A. Roberts, *op. cit.*, p. 123.

148 See Richardson's, 'Ambitions for Liverpool', *The Liverpool Review*, May 1930, pp. 174–6. Richardson's political activities had several times cost him promotion in the Post Office—*P.D.*, 5th ser., xciv, 78–81.

149 Sir Frederick Bowring had two terms as Lord Mayor, 1925–7. His donations led the movement to extend the Walker Art Gallery—*T.* 30 Nov. 1925.

150 J. and B. Braddock, *op. cit.*, p. 137; Toole, *Mrs. Braddock*, p. 109; Baxter, *op. cit.*, pp. 354–5.

151 Allen to Derby, 4, 13 April, 27 Aug. 1931 (all with enclosures); White to Derby, 4, 12 April 1933, 30 March 1935; Derby to White, 28 March 1935, Derby MSS.

152 *T.* 6 Dec. 1934.

153 *T.* 30 Jan. 1935.

154 In 1935 India was granted a limited degree of Dominion status. Winston Churchill not only regretted that Randolph stood in Wavertree without consulting him, he also disapproved of Randolph widening the issue from the India Bill to that of Conservatism versus the National Government—Gilbert, *Churchill*, v, chap. 30, Randolph's contest greatly offended Conservative society—see R. R. James (ed.), *Chips: The Diaries of Sir Henry Channon*, 1967, pp. 23–26.

155 *T.* 30 Jan. 1935; Jones, *Whitehall Diary*, ii, pp. 67–68, 176.

156 White to Derby, 10, 12, 21 Dec. 1934, 6 Feb., 28 Aug. 1935, Derby MSS.

157 White won £1,000 damages and costs—*T.* 16 July 1935.

158 *T.* 26 Jan., 2, 6 Feb. 1935; John Reynolds to Derby, 28 Dec. 1932, Derby MSS.

159 *T.* 26, 28 Jan., 5 Feb. 1935.

160 *T.* 29 Jan., 4 Feb. 1935; White to Derby, 6 Feb. 1935, Derby MSS.

161 *P.D.*, 5th ser., vol. 297, 2115–20.

162 *T.* 5 Feb. 1935.

163 White to Derby, 22 April, 16, 26 June 1933, 1 Dec. 1934, Derby MSS.; *T.* 8 Feb. 1935; Randolph Churchill in *T.* 27 Feb. 1935.

164 *T.* 23 Feb., 12 March 1935.

165 *T.* 18, 19 March, 3 April, 1 May 1935.

166 Although considered Salvidge's protégé politically, Maxwell Fyfe made no mention of him and little of Liverpool politics in his autobiography, see Kilmuir, *op. cit.* 1964.

167 *T.* 10 July 1935; White to Derby, 20 July 1935, Derby MSS.

168 White to S. Baldwin, 17 May 1935, copy; White to Derby, 7 Nov. 1935, Derby MSS.

169 *T.* 16, 30 Oct. 1935; White to Derby, 28 Aug., 25, 30 Sept. 1935; Derby to White, 26, 29 Aug., 22 Sept., 1, 10, 23 Oct., 8 Nov. 1935, Derby MSS.; Gilbert, *Churchill*, v, chap. 28.

170 *T.* 4, 6 Nov. 1935.

171 On MacDonald see H. G. Wells quoted in Dalton, *op. cit.*, p. 187; on Baldwin see Martin, *op. cit.*, p. 203; Cowling, *Impact of Hitler*, p. 52.

172 Letter from John Beattie, *The Listener*, 19 March 1970.

173 Toole, *Mrs. Braddock*, pp. 116–17; *P.D.*, 5th. ser., vol. 307, 490–7, 1217–19.

174 *T.* 14 Nov. 1935.

175 White to Derby, 28 Aug., 7 Nov. 1935, Derby MSS.

176 Toole, *op. cit.*, p. 109; *T.* 30 July 1936.

177 White to J. J. Shute, 8 Nov. 1935, copy; White to Derby, 7, 9 Nov. 1935, Derby MSS.

178 White to Derby, 29 April 1933, ibid.

179 T. 3 Jan. 1936; *P.D.*, 5th ser., vol. 308, 1222–5, 1246–50, vol. 312, 2067–71.

180 *T.* 12, 27; 30 March 1936.

181 *T.* 7 March 1936; Keeling, *op. cit.*, pp. 64–67.

182 Baxter, *op. cit.*, p. 77.

183 *T.* 17 Dec. 1936.

184 *T.* 12 Oct. 1936; *P.D.*, 5th ser., vol. 303, cols. 809–10.

185 *T.* 11, 19 Oct., 8 Dec. 1937, 8 Feb. 1938; Mosley, *op. cit.*, pp. 312–13; C. Cross, *The Fascists in Britain*, 1961, p. 185.

186 Whittingham-Jones, *op. cit.*, p. 2, 15.

187 White to Derby, 11, 25 June, 30 Sept. 1936; Derby to White, 12, 29 June 1936, Derby MSS.

188 *T.* 21, 24 Dec. 1937; *P.D.*, 5th. ser., vol. 307, 1941–2.

189 Sir J. Sandeman Allen to Derby, 17 Dec. 1928; D. Maxwell Fyfe to Derby, 31 Jan. 1938; Derby to Maxwell Fyfe, 25 Feb. 1938; Derby to Winterton, 20 June 1938, Derby MSS.

190 Baxter, *op. cit.*, pp. 83–84.

191 *T.* 9 July 1938; *P.D.*, 5th ser., vol. 328, 686–90, vol. 330, 1326, vol. 334, 1299, vol. 338, 1510–15, vol. 341, 1944–5, vol. 342, 1362–3, vol. 343, 399–400, 1384. A precedent existed for the Board's action, in Merionethshire in 1908—see A. C. F. Beales, 'The Struggle for the Schools', in G. A. Beck (ed.), *The English Catholics 1850–1950*, 1950, p. 393.

192 *T.* 29 Oct. 1938.

193 Baxter, *op. cit.*, p. 221; Stafford Cripps Papers—letters from J. T. Battle, 30 Jan. 1937; Herbert Jones and A. Jones, 30 Sept. 1937; G. Shepherd, 8 and 24 Feb. 1938; Herbert Morrison, 28 Nov. 1938; and Cripps to Shepherd 18 and 21 Feb. 1938. Files 763/514 and 779/502. Dr. J. S. Rowett kindly referred me to these letters.

194 *T.* 11 Feb. 1939.

195 *P.D.*, 5th ser., vol. 350, cols. 354–8, 1497–1502; *T.* 23 July 1938; letter from A. C. Wardle, *T.* 2 Sept. 1938. By 1939–40 Liverpool had 200 elementary schools, accommodating 162,000 pupils. 101 were absolutely controlled by the L.E.C.; 99 (45 Anglican, 52 Catholic, 1 Methodist, 1 Hebrew) were managed by denominationalists but maintained by the L.E.C. Of 22 secondary schools, 12 were directly run, and 10 aided, by the L.E.C. Pumphrey, *op. cit.*, pp. 160–1.

196 *T.* 2 Jan. 1939.

197 *T.* 25 Jan. 1939.

198 *T.* 15 Aug. 1939.

199 *T.* 4 Aug. 1939.

200 *P.D.*, 5th ser., vol. 350, cols. 1654–6; *T.* 31 July, 26, 28, 30 Aug. 1939. By contrast Welsh Nationalists claimed the support of 5,000 Liverpool Welsh for their arson attacks—see Saunders Lewis, 'Why We Burnt the Bombing School', in R. Reynolds (ed.), *British Pamphleteers*, 1951, p. 294.

201 *T.* 29 July 1939.

CHAPTER 18

1 C. B. A. Behrens, *Merchant Shipping and the Demands of War*, 1955, pp. 139–42 emphasizes that the air attacks hardly upset Liverpool's war effort. See also J. and B. Braddock, *op. cit.*, p. 88; R. Whittington-Egan, *Liverpool Roundabout*, Liverpool, 1957, pp. 329–94; Mountfield, *op. cit.*, chap. 18; Woods and Brown, *op. cit.*, pp. 224–6; H. Jager, *The Rise and Ascent of Number Two Platoon (Home Guard)*, 1945.

2 Derby to A. E. Shennan, 10 Sept. 1943; Sir J. Reynolds to Derby, 7, 20 Sept., 8 Oct. 1929; Derby to Reynolds, 25 Sept. 1929; Derby to White, 18 Oct. 1929, Derby MSS. One of the leaders of the Home Rule Council faction, Dr. Commins, had been offered the Lord Mayoralty in 1894, during the Liberals' period of Council rule, but he had refused.

3 Baxter, *op. cit.*, pp. 94–96.

4 Ibid., pp. 88–89, 104; *P.D.*, 5th ser., vol. 353, 1049.

5 J. Brothers, *Church and School*, Liverpool, 1964, p. 158; D. Nicholls, *Church and State in Britain since 1820*, 1967, pp. 211–14; J. G. Lockhart, *Cosmo Gordon Lang*, 1949, pp. 367–9; Iremonger, *op. cit.*, pp. 569–76.

6 The average turn-out in England was 73 per cent, the average swing to Labour in Britain 12 per cent. R. B. McCallum and A. Readman, *The British General Election of 1945*, Oxford, 1947, pp. 293–5. The relatively low swing to Labour in Liverpool in 1945 is explained by the relatively high Labour poll there in 1935.

7 West Rhondda (Labour) and Armagh (Unionist) were the other two.

8 McCallum and Readman, *op. cit.*, p. 151. Cf. Kilmuir, *op. cit.*, p. 84.

9 Toole, *Mrs Braddock*, p. 126. In her maiden speech at Westminster Mrs. Braddock attributed her success to concern for housing—*P.D.*, 5th ser., vol. 414, cols. 1256–60.

10 D. E. Butler, *The Electoral System in Britain since 1918*, Oxford, 1963 edition, p. 147. For Mrs. Braddock's view, *P.D.*, 5th ser., vol. 449, cols. 1682–3.

11 Circumstances were not unchanging. By the boundary revision in 1950 the electorate of Exchange was practically doubled. On Mrs. Braddock's feuds see Toole, *op. cit.*, p. 193 ff.; J. and B. Braddock, *op. cit.*, p. 90 ff.; Baxter, *op. cit.*, pp. 120–4; A. Ranney, *Pathways to Parliament*, 1965, pp. 188–90; obituary in *T.* 14 Nov. 1970.

12 Baxter, *op. cit.*, *passim*; R. Hattersley in *Guardian*, 15 Dec. 1970; *The Economist*, 3 Jan. 1970.

13 H. G. Nicholas, *The British General Election of 1950*, 1951, p. 41.

14 Except West Derby.

15 On the problems of defining marginal seats, see J. Rasmussen, 'The Implications of Safe Seats for British Democracy', in R. Rose (ed.), *Policy-Making in Britain*, 1969, pp. 30–47; Kinnear, *British Voter*, p. 114.

16 Maxwell Fyfe, as the Lord Chancellor, had become Lord Kilmuir.

17 Raikes resigned the Conservative whip over Suez. Like other right-wingers, he wanted the Government to dispute Nasser's control of the Canal—Ranney, *op. cit.*, p. 85.

18 See, however, the pro-Conservative article by Michael Canning in *The Irish Post*, 6 June 1970.

19 *T.* 1 April 1971.

20 See *T.* 2 April 1971. The by-election recorded 1·7 per cent swing to Labour. Result: Marsden, 6,795; Porter, 1,751; Mahon, 981.

21 *Guardian*, 15 Oct. 1971.

22 Heenan, *op. cit.*, chap. 16; K. Sim in *New Statesman*, 21 July 1972 on the surviving outward symbols of sectarianism in Liverpool.

23 Militant Protestantism was also stirred by Pope John XXIII's inclination towards ecumenicalism. The Revd. Ian Paisley sprang to prominence in the so-called 'tricolour riots' in Belfast, in October 1964—Liam de Paor, *Divided Ulster*, Penguin, 1970, p. 160 ff.; A. Boyd, *Holy War in Belfast*, 1969, chap. 11.

24 D. A. Roberts, *op. cit.*, pp. 146–7.

25 Letter to the author, 22 Nov. 1971.

26 T. McWilliam to the author, 9 July 1969.

27 Liverpool's wards were redistributed in 1953, the first time since 1894–5. Everton, Abercromby, and Vauxhall had lost half their populations between 1931 and 1951, and another 20 per cent between 1951 and 1961. Orangemen were among the few to oppose the slum clearance programme initiated in 1955, seeing in the scattering of Netherfield and St. Domingo Protestants a Catholic plot. However, although some 20 to 30 per cent of Merseyside was Catholic, compared with a national average of 8 per cent, in no Liverpool constituency in 1970 did Irish-born electors constitute above 5 per cent. See T. W. Freeman, *The Conurbations of Great Britain*, Manchester, 1966 edition, p. 113; D. M. Muchnick, *Urban Renewal in Liverpool*, 1970, pp. 87–88, 100–5; D. Butler and M. Pinto-Duschinsky, *The British General Election of 1970*, 1971, p. 417.

28 E. Heffer's article in *New Statesman* 4 May 1973. Replies from H. Davies and G. Tope, ibid. 11, 25 May 1973. For the controversy concerning the Labour party, ward organization, and social class, see B. Hindess, *The Decline of Working Class Politics*, 1971, and R. Baxter's refutation in *Political Studies*, xx, March 1972, pp. 97–107.

29 Some of McKinsey and Company's recommendations to Liverpool Corporation are given in R. Greenwood and J. D. Stewart, *Corporate Planning in English Local Government*, 1974, pp. 115–25, 225–33, 515–25. The Liverpool Planning Department (established 1962), in conjunction with the National Building Agency, produced a programme of three stages in which all slums and short-life areas would be progressively eliminated between 1966 and 1991. For a critique see Muchnick, *op. cit.*; for earlier initiatives see R. Bradbury's articles in *Town Planning Review*, xxii, April 1951, pp. 45–71, xxvii, Oct. 1956, pp. 145–63, and G. Shankland, 'The Central Area of Liverpool', ibid. xxxv, July 1964, pp. 105–32; J. F. Smith, G. Hemm, and A. E. Shennan, *Liverpool, Past, Present, Future*, Liverpool, 1948, pp. 65–81. In January 1981 the Housing committee proposed to invest £9m. in reconditioning 7,000 derelict properties, thus virtually halting its building of new houses in 1981–2.

30 *Sunday Times*, 5 Nov. 1972.

31 *Liverpool Constitutional Association Centenary Souvenir*, Liverpool, 1948, p. 77; note in author's possession, Nov. 1971.

32 See various essays from *Proper Studies*, 1927, *Music at Night*, 1931, and *The Olive Tree*, 1936, reprinted in A. Huxley, *Stories, Essays and Poems*, 1937.

33 *T.* 22 April 1972; *Guardian*, 15 May 1972, 4 June 1973, 24 June 1974; H. Channon, *Portrait of Liverpool*, 1972 edition, preface and pp. 134–8; *P.D.*, 5th ser., vol. 307, col. 1,921; *Sunday Times*, 16, 30 May 1976; *Guardian*, 3 March 1977, 17 March 1978, 24 Jan. 1981.

34 *Guardian*, 30 Nov. 1970, 21 March, 4 June 1973; *Sunday Times*, 5 Nov. 1972, 18 Jan. 1976; Lawton and Cunningham *op. cit.*, p. 53; Cole, *Local and Regional Government*, p. 159.

35 W. Plomer (ed.), *The Diary of the Rev. Francis Kilvert*, 1939, vol. ii; *Guardian*, 27 March 1976.

36 B.B.C. television programme, 'Anno Domini', 1975; reporter Peter France.

37 A. H. Richmond, *Colour Prejudice in Britain*, 1954; R. May and R. Cohen, 'The Interaction between Race and Colonialism: A Case Study of the Liverpool Race Riots of 1919', *Race and Class*, xvi, 2 (1974), pp. 111–26; *Observer*, 13 Aug. 1972; 'Linacre Lane', *The ABZ of Scouse*, Liverpool, 1966, reprinted 1970.

38 *Guardian*, 13 Jan. 1977; *Sunday Times*, 16 Jan. 1977; *Observer*, 30 Jan. 1977.

39 *Sunday Times*, 30 Jan. 1977.

APPENDIX 1

Boundaries of Liverpool Parliamentary Constituencies from 1885

1 1885–1918

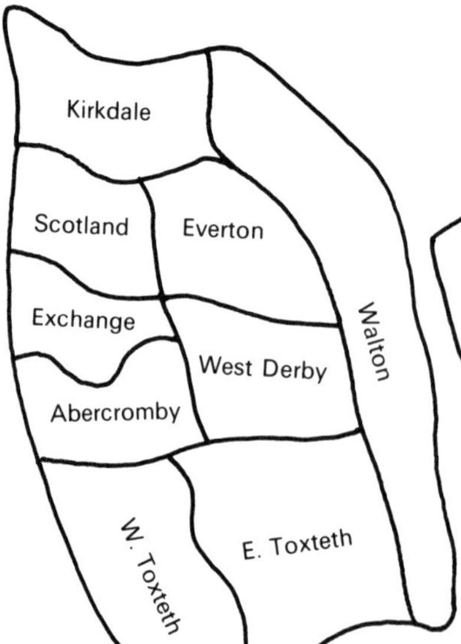

2 1918–49

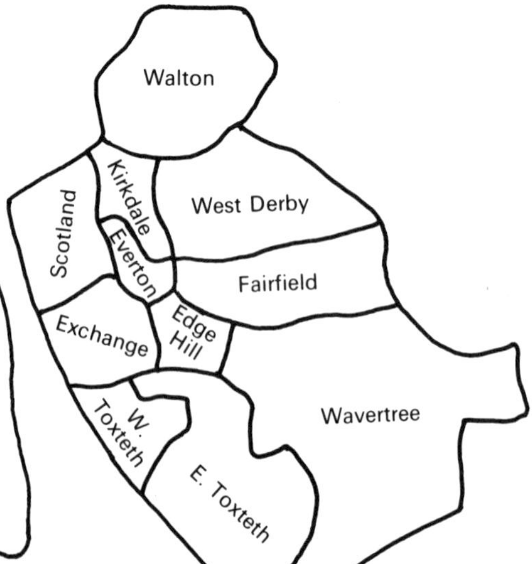

Source: F. W. S. Craig (ed.), *Boundaries of Parliamentary Constituenceies, 1885–1972,* Chichester, 1972, pp. 189, 191, 193, 195, 197

3 1950–5

4 1955–70

5 1971–

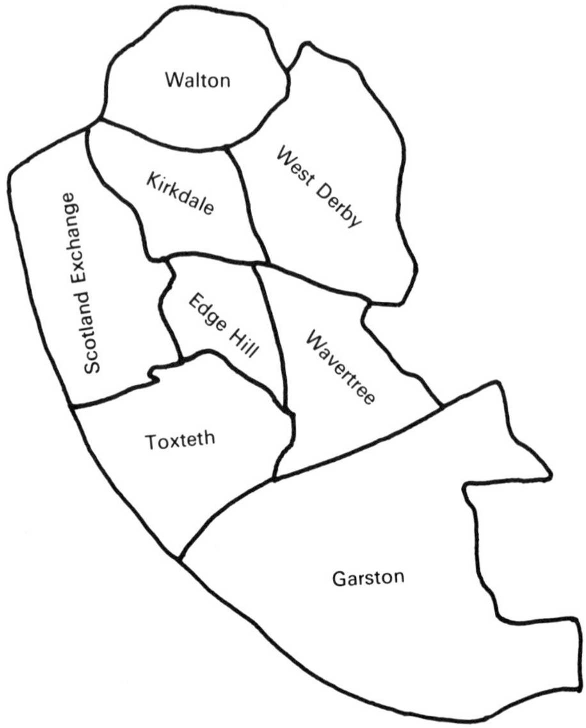
Walton
West Derby
Kirkdale
Scotland Exchange
Edge Hill
Wavertree
Toxteth
Garston

APPENDIX 2

Parliamentary Constituencies and Municipal Wards in Liverpool from 1885[1]

A. 1885–95

Parliamentary Constituency	*Wards*
Abercromby	Abercromby, Rodney Street, Great George's, Pitt Street, St. Peter's, Castle Street
East Toxteth	North Toxteth (part)
Everton	Everton (part)
Exchange	Lime Street, St. Anne's, Exchange, St. Paul's, Vauxhall
Kirkdale	Everton (part)
Scotland	Scotland
Walton	Everton (part); parts of Walton and Wavertree parishes
West Derby	West Derby
West Toxteth	South Toxteth, North Toxteth (part)

B. 1895–1918

Parliamentary Constituency	*Wards*
Abercromby	Abercromby, Great George, St. Peter's, Castle Street
East Toxteth	Granby, Princes Park, Sefton Park East, Sefton Park West (part)
Everton	Everton, Netherfield, St. Domingo (part)
Exchange	Exchange, Vauxhall, St. Anne's
Kirkdale	Kirkdale, Sandhills, St. Domingo (part)
Scotland	North Scotland, South Scotland
Walton	Anfield, Breckfield, Fairfield, Wavertree West, West Derby (part)
West Derby	Edge Hill, Low Hill, Kensington
West Toxteth	Brunswick, Dingle, Sefton Park West (part)

1 Two comprehensive ward redistributions have taken place in Liverpool in the last hundred years, in 1895 and 1955. In addition the boundaries of the city have been extended from time to time. In 1895 Greater Liverpool was formed by the inclusion of Walton, Wavertree, and further parts of West Derby and Toxteth Park; in 1902 Garston was included, in 1905 Fazakerley, and in 1913 Allerton, Childwall, Little Woolton, and Much Woolton.

C. 1918–49

Parliamentary Constituency	*Wards*
East Toxteth	Aigburth, Granby, Sefton Park East, Sefton Park West
Edge Hill	Edge Hill, Low Hill, Kensington (part)
Everton	Everton, Netherfield
Exchange	Abercromby, Castle Street, Exchange, Great George, St. Anne's, St. Peter's, Vauxhall (part)
Fairfield	Fairfield, Old Swan, Kensington (part)
Kirkdale	Kirkdale, St. Domingo
Scotland	North Scotland, South Scotland, Sandhills, Vauxhall (part)
Walton	Fazakerley, Walton, Warbreck
Wavertree	Allerton, Childwall, Little Woolton, Garston, Much Woolton, Wavertree, Wavertree West
West Derby	Anfield, Breckfield, West Derby
West Toxteth	Brunswick, Dingle, Princes Park

D. 1950–70

Parliamentary Constituency	*Wards*
Edge Hill	1950–5 Edge Hill, Fairfield, Kensington, Low Hill
	1955– Picton, Fairfield, Kensington, Smithdown
Exchange	1950–5 Abercromby, Brunswick, Castle Street, Exchange, Granby, Great George, St. Anne's, St. Peter's, Vauxhall
	1955– Abercromby, Central, Granby, Low Hill, St. James
Garston	1950–5 Aigburth, Allerton, Childwall, Garston, Little Woolton, Much Woolton
	1955– Aigburth, Allerton, St. Mary's, Speke, Woolton
Kirkdale	1950–5 Anfield, Breckfield, Kirkdale
	1955– Anfield, Breckfield, Melrose, Tuebrook, Westminister
Scotland	1950–5 Everton, Netherfield, North Scotland, South Scotland, St. Domingo, Sandhills
	1955– Everton, Netherfield, Vauxhall, St. Domingo, Sandhills
Toxteth	1950–5 Dingle, Princes Park, Sefton Park East, Sefton Park West
	1955– Dingle, Princes Park, Arundel, St. Michael's
Walton	1950–1 Fazakerley, Walton, Warbreck, and part of West Lancashire
	1951–5 As above but alteration to the West Lancashire part
	1955– County, Fazakerley, Pirrie, Warbreck
Wavertree	1950–5 Old Swan, Wavertree, Wavertree West
	1955– Broadgreen, Childwall, Church, Old Swan
West Derby	1950–5 Croxteth, West Derby
	1955–64 Croxteth, Clubmoor, Dovecot, Gillmoss
	1964– As above but Liverpool County Borough altered

E. 1971–

Parliamentary Constituency	*Wards*
Edge Hill	As 1955—plus Low Hill
Kirkdale	As 1955—plus St. Domingo
Scotland-Exchange	Abercromby, Central, Everton, Netherfield, St. James, Sandhills, Vauxhall
Toxteth	As 1955—plus Granby

Garston, Walton, Wavertree, and West Derby, parliamentary constituencies, no change.

Source: F. W. S. Craig (ed.), *Boundaries of Parliamentary Constituencies, 1885–1972*, 1972.

APPENDIX 3

Biographical Notes

ADAM, James de Bels (1849–97), born Liverpool; mother of Belgian ancestry; Scots father, who established prosperous firm of fruit brokers which James took over in 1887, having previously worked with Lamport and Holt, shipowners; director of two insurance companies; assisted formation of Liverpool Fruit Porters' Union; Presbyterian; leading Freemason; Conservative councillor 1889; mayor 1891–2.

AGGS, William Hanbury (1870—), born London; educated Uppingham and Cambridge; northern circuit barrister; resigned from Conservative party as free trader 1904; advocate of Church Discipline Bill; Liberal candidate Liverpool Everton 1905, 1906, and January 1910.

AKED, Charles Frederick (1864–1941), born Nottingham; junior clerk, auctioneer's assistant; became Baptist minister in 1886 preaching a Social Gospel; ministries in Derbyshire, Leicestershire, and St. Helens; pastor of Pembroke Street Baptists, Liverpool 1890–1906; made lecture tours of America from 1895 and received D.D.; professed Fabian; emigrated to take over Baptist Chapel on New York's Fifth Avenue at (reputed) stipend of £5,000; afterwards renewed his old radicalism during ministries in San Francisco, Kansas City, and Los Angeles.

ALLDRITT, Walter (b. 1918), educated Liverpool University (W.E.A.); Labour councillor from 1955; J.P. 1958; M.P. Liverpool Scotland 1964–71; regional secretary National Union of General and Municipal Workers from 1970.

ALLEN, John Sandeman (1865–1935), born Croydon; educated Brighton, Edinburgh, Germany; underwriter; manager, Union Marine Insurance Company; Liverpool representative on War Committee of Chamber of Shipping; committee member of Lloyds Register; chairman Liverpool Chamber of Commerce 1923–6; vice-president Royal Empire Society; chairman Joint East Africa (Advisory) Board; Conservative councillor from 1921; M.P. Liverpool West Derby 1924–35; knighted 1928; one of his sons was Conservative M.P. Birkenhead West.

ARMSTRONG, Richard Acland (1843–1905), born Clifton, son of Unitarian minister (a convert from the Church of Ireland); entered ministry, serving first at Banbridge in Ireland 1866–9; Nottingham 1870–83; Hope Street, Liverpool, from 1883; made Lord Mayor's private chaplain by W. B. Bowring (q.v.) 1893–4; decided Liberal; temperance activist; instigator of Purity Crusade 1891; member of Corporation commission into unemployment in Liverpool; advocated municipal farm colonies. His son, Francis Edwin Armstrong (1879–1921), was an expert on coal industry and Professor of Mining at Sheffield.

ATKIN, Peter Wilson (1859–1931), born Birkenhead, son of leading local Liberal and building merchant; educated Mill Hill and Cambridge; rowing blue; barrister; member of committee, Birkenhead Charity Organization Society; active in child charities; Liberal candidate Liverpool Everton 1892; Congregationalist.

ATKINSON, Thomas (d. 1922), dock foreman shipwright; one of Salvidge's (q.v.) lieutenants in the W.M.C.A.; Birkenhead town councillor; Deputy-Recorder of Liverpool; Stipendiary Magistrate of Salford 1913–31; arbitrator Manchester Ship Canal strike 1916; left £1,137.

BADEN-POWELL, Sir George Smyth (1848–98), son of Professor of Geometry at Oxford; mother an admiral's daughter; educated St. Paul's, Marlborough, Balliol College, Oxford; home, Hyde Park; diplomat and colonial administrator; author of works on empire and trade; Conservative M.P. Liverpool Kirkdale 1855–98; recreations: yachting, shooting, big-game hunting, golf, cricket.

BAILY, Laurence Richardson (c. 1815–87), born London, married Liverpool woman; lived Allerton Hall; Board of Trade nominee on Docks Board; director, Great Northern Railway, Buffalo and Lake Huron Railway, Pacific Steam Navigation Co., British and Continental African Co.; chairman, Reliance Marine Insurance Co.; Conservative candidate Sunderland 1874; M.P. Liverpool Exchange 1885–6; supporter of Additional Curates Society.

BALDWIN, Stanley (1887–1947), cr. Earl 1937; ironfounder, succeeded father as Conservative M.P. Worcestershire (West or Bewdley) 1908–18, Bewdley 1918–37; Joint Financial Secretary to Treasury 1917–21, President of Board of Trade 1921–2, Chancellor of Exchequer 1922–3, Prime Minister 1923–4, 1924–9, 1935–7; Lord President of Council 1931–5.

BALFOUR, Alexander (1824–86) born Fifeshire; settled in Liverpool 1844; business partnership with Stephen Williamson (q.v.); pillar of Canning Street Presbyterian Church; friend and associate of Samuel Smith (q.v.) in charitable works; president, Liverpool Y.M.C.A. for fifteen years; secretary, Mersey Mission to Seamen; member, Liverpool Council of Education; president, Popular Control and Sunday-Closing Association (but no teetotaller).

BALFOUR, Arthur James (1848–1930), cr. Earl 1922; nephew of Lord Salisbury (q.v.); Conservative M.P. Hertford 1874–85, Manchester East 1885–1906, City of London 1906–22; President of Local Government Board 1885–6; Secretary for Scotland 1886–7; Chief Secretary for Ireland 1887–91; First Lord of Treasury 1891–2, 1895–1905; Prime Minister 1902–5; First Lord of Admiralty 1915–16; Foreign Secretary 1916–19; Lord President of Council 1919–22, 1925–9.

BALFOUR, Charles B. (1862–1921), cousin of A. J. Balfour (q.v.); officer in Scots Guards during Egyptian campaign 1882; Conservative candidate Roxburghshire 1885, Berwickshire 1892, Lancashire South-West (Southport) 1899; M.P. Middlesex (Hornsey) 1900–10; director, Barclays' Bank and Scottish Widows' Fund Life Assurance Society; Lord-Lieutenant, Berwickshire 1917.

BALL, Joseph (1831–1907), jeweller and watchmaker with shop in London Road; leading Orangeman in 1870s and advocate of retrenchment in municipal government; councillor 1878; Lord Mayor 1905–6, but thought by R. D. Holt (q.v.) 'hardly the type of man for the first position in a great commercial centre like Liverpool'; founder of Protestant Burial Society.

BARTLETT, Ellis Ashmead (1849–1902), knighted 1892; American parents; educated Oxford; Conservative M.P. Eye 1880–5, Sheffield Ecclesall 1885–1902; civil servant in Education Department 1877–80; supported Gladstone on Bulgarian atrocities, Northcote on N.U.C.C.A.; Civil Lord of Admiralty 1885–6, 1886–92; chairman, N.U.C.C.A. 1886–8. Worked hard for the party in the provinces but considered by Lord Salisbury (q.v.) to have no weight in Parliament and by A. J. Balfour (q.v.) to have no administrative sense.

BARTLETT, William (1837–1917), Conservative councillor, active regarding insanitary property; out of sympathy with Protestant agitation; solicitor, in partnership with Edwin Berry, who acted for several brewers, and was a power in the Walton Conservative Association; left £72,553.

BARTON, Sam ('Sandy') (1860–1921), born Dumfriesshire; married at eighteen; railway clerk in Liverpool; joined W.M.C.A., Dingle branch 1886; secretary W.M.C.A. 1900–; vigorous organizer of whom Salvidge (q.v.) wrote to Lord Derby (q.v.) in 1917: 'He is a good man in many ways but has absolutely no sense of proportion and is given at times to writing letters which are nothing less than impudent. I have had several of these epistles and on one occasion brought his conduct before the executive officers of the association. The only way to keep him in hand is to have no nonsense and speak to him straight.' J.P.; left £374.

BEACH, Sir Michael Edward Hicks (1837–1916), 9th Bart., cr. Viscount St. Aldwyn 1906, Earl 1915; Conservative M.P. Gloucestershire East 1864–85, Bristol West 1885–1906; junior minister, Poor Law Board and Home Office 1868; Chief Secretary for Ireland 1874–8, 1886–7; Colonial Secretary 1878–80; Chancellor of Exchequer 1885–6, 1895–1902; President of Board of Trade 1888–92.

BEARD, Charles (1827–88), born Manchester; Unitarian minister at Renshaw Street, Liverpool; special correspondent, *Daily News*, during Lancashire Cotton Famine; leader-writer, *Liverpool Daily Post* until 1886; influential in Liverpool Liberal party until opposed Irish Home Rule; promoter of Victoria University; theological historian; opposed disestablishment of Church of England; affected to tears by own sermons and speeches; advocate of extended franchise; gave popular lectures in Rotunda Theatre to working-class audiences.

BEAVAN, Margaret (*c.* 1876–1931), born Liverpool; educated Royal Holloway College; founded Liverpool Open-Air Hospital for Children, Leasowe, 1914; pioneer of Child Welfare Association which co-ordinated several voluntary bodies in Liverpool and established its own maternity home and welfare clinics; J.P. 1920; Coalition Liberal councillor 1920; joined Conservatives 1924; Liverpool's first female Lord Mayor 1927–8; candidate Liverpool Everton 1929; nicknamed 'the Mighty Atom' by Salvidge (q.v.).

BENCKE, Albert H. (1847–), born Liverpool; father flax and hemp broker and former Wurtemburg Consul; educated Brasenose College, Oxford; lawyer; treasurer,

West Derby Liberal Association 1878, South-West Lancashire Liberal Registration Society 1879–85; Whig; promoted Liverpool Liberal Unionist Association 1886 but early shunted aside; retained membership of Liverpool Reform Club; admirer of Lord Rosebery (q.v.) after his retirement as Liberal leader.

BEVINS, John Reginald (b. 1908), born Liverpool; in insurance business; served in Second World War, ending with rank of major; election agent to Treleavan (q.v.) in Wavertree 1929; Labour councillor 1935–8; Conservative councillor 1938–50; contested Liverpool West Toxteth 1945, Edge Hill 1947; M.P. Liverpool Toxteth 1950–64; Postmaster-General 1959–64.

BIGHAM, John Charles (1840–1929), born Liverpool; father oil importer, member of Dock Board and Liberal councillor Scotland Ward 1849–52; educated abroad; Catholic convert 1857; barrister on northern circuit specializing in commercial law; Liberal candidate Liverpool East Toxteth 1885, Liberal Unionist candidate Liverpool Exchange 1892; M.P. Liverpool Exchange 1895–7, retiring on appointment as judge; knighted; when created Viscount Mersey joked that he was leaving the style of Lord Atlantic for F. E. Smith (q.v.).

BINGHAM, Richard Martin (b. 1915), educated Harrow and Cambridge; lawyer on northern circuit; served in war, ending with rank of major; Conservative councillor 1946–9; M.P. Liverpool Garston 1957–66; Recorder of Oldham 1960–71; circuit judge 1972.

BIRRELL, Augustine (1850–1933), son of minister of Pembroke Place Baptists, Liverpool; Fellow of Trinity Hall, Cambridge; barrister and literary essayist; Liberal candidate Liverpool Walton 1885; M.P. Fifeshire West 1889–1900, Bristol North 1906–18; President of Board of Education 1905–7; Chief Secretary for Ireland 1907–16; President, National Liberal Federation 1902–5; recreation: book-hunting.

BLAIR, William Richard (1874–1932), born Liverpool, son of book-keeper; began work in shipping firm but joined Liverpool Co-operative Society 1902; secretary 1905–19, seeing its membership grow from 3,000 to 50,000, and sales from £55,000 to £1½ million; member of Co-operative Wholesale Society's Board 1919–32; co-opted member Liverpool Education Committee; Labour councillor from 1911; favourably impressed Beatrice Webb (q.v.) when they met in 1921.

BLATCHFORD, Robert Peel Glanville (1851–1943), born Maidstone; parents, actors; apprentice brushmaker; joined army and left as sergeant 1878; clerk; journalist, *Sunday Chronicle* 1885–91; founder and editor *Clarion*; individualist Socialist.

BLIGH, Alexander M. (1834–1922), born Co. Galway of farming stock; educated Queen's College, Galway, Dublin, and London where he qualified as a doctor; a founder of Irish Home Rule movement in Liverpool; councillor 1876–92, 1898–1902, alderman 1892–8, 1902–3; member of Corporation Health Committee; anti-Parnellite.

BLUNT, Wilfrid Scawen (1840–1922), born Petworth House; married daughter 1st Earl of Lovelace; Catholic; diplomat; Home Ruler, twice tried to enter Parliament, as Conservative 1885, as Liberal 1886; imprisoned in Ireland for two months 1888; writer, roué, breeder of Arab horses; owner of 2,000 acres.

BOLD, Thomas (1805–83), son of minister of St. Catherine's, Liverpool; shipbroker; related to Ewart family; Tory Alderman, 1852–68.

BOND, John (1826–99), born London; Chartist; moved to Liverpool 1859; piano manufacturer; Anglican; secretary, Liverpool branch Reform League 1866–7; active Lime Street ward, which he contested for L.E.A. 1889; sought magistracy from Liberal Government as reward for party service 1893–4.

BOWRING, William Benjamin (1837–1916), born Newfoundland; Unitarian; head of well-established Liverpool shipowners in American and Canadian trades; director, Alliance Marine Assurance Co., and North-Western Bank; deputy-chairman Parnell Expenses Fund 1888; president, Liverpool Domestic Mission, and United Kingdom Temperance Society; chairman Liverpool Peace Society; member Mersey Docks and Harbour Board 1884–92; Liberal councillor St. Peter's ward (once represented by his father); Lord Mayor 1893–4; Liberal candidate Liverpool Abercromby 1892, Liverpool Exchange 1895; knighted 1907; burly figure, punctual habits, austere manner; presented Roby Hall Estate to City of Liverpool, 1906.

BRADDOCK, Elizabeth ('Bessie') Margaret (1899–1970), *née* Bamber; born Liverpool; mother, active Socialist (later Communist) worker, national organizer of N.U.D.A.W.; clerk in Warehouse Workers Union; foundation member Communist party and treasurer Liverpool branch 1919; left C.P. 1924; married Jack Braddock (q.v.) 1922; Labour councillor 1930–55, alderman 1955–61; president L.T.C. and L.P. 1944; M.P. Liverpool Exchange 1945–70; recreations: reading, house-keeping.

BRADDOCK, John ('Jack') (1893–1963), born Hanley; father, Socialist and maker of baths and wash-basins; moved to Liverpool 1915; wagon-repairer, unemployed for six years after war; agent Co-operative Insurance Society; married 1922; foundation member Communist Party and leader Liverpool branch 1919–21; left C.P. 1924; Labour Councillor for Everton from 1929; declined Labour nomination to contest Everton parliamentary seat 1935; deputy leader Liverpool Labour party 1943; leader from 1948.

BRAMLEY-MOORE, John (1800–86), born Pontefract; moved to Liverpool 1835; established firm of Brazilian merchants; chairman Docks Committee 1843–8; mayor 1848; director, London & North-Western Railway; financial interests in other railways and banks; Conservative; two sons—one, a clergyman; the other, **John Arthur** (1840–99), carried on family business and made occasional platform appearances as Evangelical churchman who initially patronized George Wise (q.v.) in Liverpool.

BRASSEY, Sir Thomas (1836–1918), son of railway contractor; educated Rugby and Oxford; qualified barrister; J.P. and deputy-lieutenant of Sussex (where he lived); Liberal candidate Birkenhead 1861, Devonport 1865 (which he had formally represented for three weeks); M.P. Hastings 1868–86; Civil Lord of Admiralty 1880–4; candidate Liverpool Abercromby and St. Andrew's District 1886; one of few leading Liberal members of Imperial Federation League; cr. Lord Brassey 1886, 1st Earl 1911; Governor of Victoria 1895–1900; yachtsman.

BRIGHT, Allan Heywood (1862–1941), born Liverpool; educated Harrow; father in great firm of general merchants, Gibbs, Bright & Co. who owned the *Great Britain* when it was the largest ship afloat; partner in firm of iron and tinplate merchants and colliery agents; Liberal candidate Exeter 1899, Shropshire West (Oswestry) 1901, Stalybridge

1910; Liberal M.P. Oswestry 1904–6; author of *New Light on Piers Plowman*; lived Herefordshire.

BROCKLEBANK, Clement Edmund Royds (1882–1949), born Kent; educated Eton and Oxford; Conservative candidate Smethwick 1923, Birkenhead East 1929; M.P. Nottingham East 1924–9, Liverpool Fairfield 1931–45; Parliamentary Private Secretary to Under-Secretary Home Office 1927–9, to Minister of Health 1934–5, to Malcolm MacDonald 1935–41, to Sir John Anderson 1941–5; lived Bradford-on-Avon; knighted 1937.

BROCKLEBANK, Thomas (1814–1906), born Cumberland; family business of merchants and shipowners established from the Whitehaven Brocklebanks; churchman—gave £10,000 to Liverpool Cathedral fund; director Liverpool and London Globe Insurance Co.; two country seats, at Allerton and Irton; chairman, South-West Lancashire Liberal Association before 1885; Liberal Unionist 1886; cr. baronet 1885, apparently through the influence of the former Lord Ramsay (q.v.), whose election campaign in 1880 Brocklebank materially assisted. His son, also **Thomas** (1885–1911), continued the family business; director North and South Wales Bank; treasurer Liverpool Liberal Unionist Association.

BROWN, Alexander Hargreaves (1844–1922), grandson of Sir William Brown (donor of Liverpool City Library); born Yorkshire; houses in Liverpool and Grosvenor Gardens, London; partner Brown, Shipley & Co. Bank, of Liverpool and London, before its Liverpool business taken over by Bank of Liverpool; philanthropist—gave £10,000 to University College, Liverpool; built St. Benedict's Church, Everton; president Liverpool Royal Infirmary 1884–90 and took lead in finding it new buildings; Liberal M.P. Wenlock 1868–85, Shropshire (Wellington) 1885–1906 (from 1886 Liberal Unionist); cr. baronet 1902.

BROWNE, Edward (1825–98), born Co. Meath; corn merchant; Catholic member Liverpool School Board 1870–9; Liberal Unionist; left £20,290.

BROWNING, Oscar (1837–1923), historian; Fellow of King's, Cambridge; briefly taught at Liverpool College; Liberal candidate Lambeth Norwood 1886, Eastern Worcestershire 1892, Liverpool West Derby 1895, with 'penchant for four-figure defeats'.

BRUNNER, (Sir) John T. (1842–1919), born Everton, son of Revd. John Brunner (of Swiss extraction); Manx mother; built great chemical firm in partnership with Ludwig Mond, at Winnington, the forerunner of I.C.I.; radical Liberal and subscriber to Irish Land League; M.P. Northwich 1885–6, 1887–1910; benefactor University College, Liverpool; shareholder in several Liberal newspapers. His brother, **Joseph** (d. 1892) was an agent of Brunner, Mond; Liverpool J.P.; Liberal candidate West Toxteth ward 1891.

BUCHAN-HEPBURN, Patrick George Thomas (1901–74), youngest son of 4th baronet; educated Harrow and Cambridge; attaché British Embassy, Istanbul 1925–7; member London County Council 1930–1; one-time private secretary of Winston Churchill (q.v.); Conservative candidate Wolverhampton East 1929; M.P. Liverpool East Toxteth 1931–50; Parliamentary Private Secretary to Oliver Stanley (q.v.) in his various ministries in National Government; Whip 1945–55; M.P. Beckenham 1950–7; Minister of Works 1955–7; cr. Baron Hailes; Governor-General West Indies 1958–62;

alone among the fifteen in Eden's cabinet to be interviewed by Lord Salisbury, who favoured Butler's, not MacMillan's, succession.

BURDEN, Charles, Liverpool policeman who lost job after 1919 strike; Labour councillor first in Liverpool then in Wallasey; lived Moreton, Cheshire; Labour candidate Liverpool East Toxteth 1924, 1931.

BURGESS, William James (1854–), born Frodsham; senior partner general produce merchants, Liverpool; Conservative councillor 1891; member executive Liverpool Constitutional Association; chairman of its political committee 1899; strong supporter of Church of England schools and Church of England Temperance Society; president Liverpool Divisional Council Primrose League.

BURKE, Thomas, born Connemara; metals and furs business Liverpool; Nationalist Councillor Vauxhall ward; chairman Liverpool Central branch I.N.L.; organizer Irish language and Hibernian societies; author of *Catholic History of Liverpool.*

BUTT, Isaac (1813–79), born Co. Donegal; educated Trinity College, Dublin; Whately Professor Political Economy there 1836–41; barrister; M.P. Harwich 1852, Youghal 1852–65, Limerick 1871-death; ran counter agitation to Repeal Association 1843; defended Fenian prisoners 1863–9; leader of Home Rule party 1871–9; Protestant.

BYRNE, Pat (1850–90), Irish-born; wealthy Liverpool publican; bachelor, known as 'Dandy Pat'; Irish Nationalist councillor from 1883, who took up question of scavengers' wages; benefactor Catholic churches, schools, charities; bequeathed employees £5 for every year in his service.

CAIN, Robert, wealthy brewer with premises in Stanhope Street; self-made; strong Conservative, styled 'King of the Toxteths'; employed about 300 people in 1890s.

CAINE, Derwent Hall (1891–1971), son of novelist; managing director of 'The Readers Library'; Labour candidate Reading 1922, Clitheroe 1924; M.P. Liverpool Everton 1929–31; joined National Labour party 1931; knighted 1933; cr. baronet 1937.

CAINE, William Sprotson (1842–1903), iron-master; Baptist, brother-in-law of Liverpool minister, Revd. Hugh Stowell Brown; teetotaller, prominent in United Kingdom Alliance, British Temperance League, Band of Hope; Liberal candidate Liverpool 1873, 1874; M.P. Scarborough 1880–85; Civil Lord of Admiralty 1884–5; Liberal candidate Middlesex (Tottenham) 1885; Liberal M.P. Barrow 1886, Liberal Unionist M.P. Barrow 1886–90; rejoined Gladstonian Liberals; Liberal M.P. Bradford East 1892–5, Cornwall North-West (Camborne) 1900–3.

CAMERON, Alexander Gordon (1876–1944), born Oban; member Amalgamated Society of Carpenters and Joiners; Labour candidate Liverpool Kirkdale, January and July 1910, Durham Jarrow December 1910; M.P. Widnes 1929–31; became building contractor; lived Brixton, London.

CAMPBELL, Herbert (1830–1903), senior partner cotton brokers, established by grandfather; Conservative councillor 1886–98; chairman West Toxteth Divisional Association; active in Scripture Readers' Society and Liverpool Royal Southern Hospital; left £46,000.

CAMPBELL-BANNERMAN, Henry (1836–1908), son of a Lord Provost of Glasgow; educated Glasgow and Cambridge; Liberal M.P. Stirling Burghs 1868–1908; Financial Secretary to War Office 1871–4, 1880–2; Parliamentary Secretary to Admiralty 1882–4; Chief Secretary for Ireland 1884–5; Secretary of State for War, 1886, 1892–5; knighted 1895; leader of Conservative party in House of Commons 1899–1908; Prime Minister 1905–8.

CANNING, George (1770–1827), born London; educated Eton and Oxford; originally a Whig; Pittite supporter and junior minister during French Revolution; entered Parliament 1794; Tory M.P. Liverpool 1812–23; Foreign Secretary 1807–9, 1822–7; Prime Minister 1827.

CARSON, Edward Henry (1854–1935), born Dublin; Presbyterian; Orangeman from age nineteen; lawyer; Crown prosecutor in Ireland; retained against Oscar Wilde 1895; Conservative M.P. Dublin University 1892–1918, Belfast 1918–21; Solicitor-General for Ireland 1892; Solicitor-General for England 1900–5; leader Ulster Unionists 1910; Attorney-General 1915; First Lord of Admiralty 1916–17; member War Cabinet 1917–18; made life peer and Lord of Appeal 1921.

CHADWICK, Edwin (1800–90), qualified lawyer; friend and disciple of Bentham; social reformer; chief commissioner for poor law 1833, secretary poor law commissioners 1834–46; member, sanitary commission 1839, 1844, and board of health 1848–54; knighted 1889.

CHALONER, Richard Godolphin Walmesley (1856–1938), brother Walter Long (q.v.); educated Winchester; entered army 1878, serving in India and Afghanistan; by royal licence took name Chaloner under will of Admiral Chaloner 1888; adjutant North Somerset Yeomanry Cavalry; commander 1st Battalion Imperial Yeomanry in Boer War; Conservative M.P. Wiltshire Westbury 1895–1900, Liverpool Abercromby January 1910–17; cr. Baron Gisborough 1917; president Church Association 1919–24.

CHAMBERLAIN, Joseph (1836–1914), screw manufacturer; mayor Birmingham 1873–6; Liberal M.P. Birmingham 1876–85, Birmingham West 1855–1914 (Liberal Unionist from 1886); President of Board of Trade 1880–5; President of Local Government Board 1886); Colonial Secretary 1895–1903. One son **(Arthur) Neville** (1869–1940), was Postmaster-General 1922–3; Paymaster-General 1923, Minister of Health 1923, 1924–9, 1931, Chancellor of Exchequer 1923–4, 1931–7, Prime Minister 1937–40. Another son, **(Joseph) Austen** (1863–1937), was Postmaster-General 1902–3, Chancellor of Exchequer 1903–5, 1919–21, Secretary for India 1915–17, was in cabinet 1918–19, leader of Conservative party in Commons 1921–2, Foreign Secretary 1924–9, 1st Lord of Admiralty 1931.

CHAVASSE, Francis James (1846–1928), born Sutton Coldfield; father doctor; educated Oxford; ministered in Holloway and Oxford; Principal Wycliffe Hall, Oxford 1889–1900; second Anglican Bishop of Liverpool 1900–23; consecrated twenty-four new churches in diocese (including Lady Chapel of Cathedral); diminutive 5 feet 3 inches, often in poor health; strong dislike of smoking; teetotaller from 1871; evangelical—as bishop never adopted the Eastward position though it was legal to do so, following the Lincoln Judgement 1890; together with the Bishop of Manchester, the only bishop to protest against the inclusion of Prayers for the Departed in the official Forms of Prayer, 1917; one of his twin sons awarded a Bar to the V.C., posthumously 1917; the other became Bishop of Rochester.

CHERRY, Richard Robert (1859–1923), born Waterford; father solicitor; educated Trinity College, Dublin; lawyer; Liberal candidate Liverpool Kirkdale 1900; M.P. Liverpool Exchange 1906–9; Protestant, Home Ruler; Attorney-General for Ireland 1905–9; Lord Justice of Appeal for Ireland 1909–14; Lord Chief Justice of Ireland 1914–16.

CHILCOTT, Warden Stanley (1871–1942), director several city companies; yachting friend F. E. Smith (q.v.); served with Royal Naval Air Service and Ministry of Munitions during war; lieutenant-commander; knighted 1922; Conservative M.P. Liverpool Walton 1918–29; disliked by J. C. C. Davidson, Lord Derby, Leslie Scott, and Sandeman Allen (q.v.).

CHILDERS, Hugh Culling Eardley (1827–96), educated Cambridge; government agent Australia 1850s; Liberal M.P. Pontefract 1860–85, South Edinburgh 1886; First Lord of Admiralty 1868–71; Chancellor of Duchy of Lancaster 1872–3; Secretary of State for War 1880–2; Chancellor of Exchequer 1882–5; Home Secretary 1886.

CHURCHILL, Lord Randolph (1849–95), third son of 7th Duke of Marlborough; Conservative M.P. Woodstock 1874–85, Paddington South 1885–94; Secretary for India 1885–6; Chancellor of Exchequer 1886; exponent of 'Tory Democracy'.

CHURCHILL, Randolph Frederick Edward Spencer (1911–68), son of Winston Churchill (q.v.); educated Eton and Oxford; journalist, author, lecturer; Independent Conservative candidate Liverpool Wavertree February 1935; Conservative candidate Liverpool West Toxteth November 1935, Ross and Cromarty 1936; M.P. Preston 1940–5; served in war, rank of captain; twice married.

CHURCHILL, Winston Leonard Spencer (1874–1965), knighted 1953; son of Lord Randolph Churchill (q.v.); Conservative M.P. Oldham 1900–4; Liberal M.P. Oldham 1904–6, Manchester North-West 1906–8, Dundee 1908–22; Conservative M.P. Essex (Epping) 1924–45, Woodford 1945–64; Under-Secretary of State for Colonies 1905–8; President of Board of Trade 1908–10; Home Secretary 1910–11; First Lord of Admiralty 1911–15, 1939–40; Chancellor of Duchy of Lancaster 1915; Minister of Munitions 1917–19; Secretary of State for War and Air 1919–21; Colonial Secretary 1921–2; Chancellor of Exchequer 1924–9; Prime Minister 1940–5, 1951–5.

CLANCY, Joseph, hotel proprietor; chairman Michael Davitt branch I.N.L., St. Anne's ward; anti-semitic; criticized 'Socialist-Atheist' element of Labour party; leader Liberal-Catholic Nationalist rump (the Catholic Representation Association) after P. J. Kelly (q.v.) made pact with Labour 1924–5.

CLARE, Harcourt E. (1854–1922), born Leicestershire; educated Repton; entered Liverpool Corporation 1880; Deputy Town Clerk 1883, Town Clerk of Liverpool June 1895; Clerk of Lancashire County Council 1899; knighted 1916.

CLEARY, Joseph Jackson (b. 1902) born Liverpool; social worker; Labour councillor; candidate East Toxteth 1929, West Derby 1931; M.P. Wavertree 1935; Methodist lay preacher; deputy leader Labour Council group 1935–43; alderman 1941; Lord Mayor 1949–50; soccer and tennis enthusiast; knighted 1965; Freeman of Liverpool 1970.

CLITHEROW, Richard (1902–47), born Liverpool; educated Liverpool schools and university; pharmacist and dentist; Conservative councillor Fairfield ward 1937–45 (switching to Labour during war); Labour M.P. Liverpool Edge Hill 1945–7; served with Royal North-West Mounted Police 1919–22.

COHEN, Jack Benn Brunel (1886–1965), son of Louis Cohen (q.v.); educated Cheltenham; married daughter Sir Stuart Samuel; lost both legs Ypres 1917; hon. treasurer British Legion 1921–30, 1932–46; vice-chairman 1930–2; Conservative M.P. Liverpool Fairfield 1918–31; chairman Remploy Ltd. 1955; knighted 1943.

COHEN, Louis (1846–1922), father New South Wales M.P.; Jew; partner David Lewis (1823–85), founder Lewis department stores; Conservative councillor 1895; Lord Mayor 1899–1900; charitable—subscribed £1,000 to Liverpool University, Liverpool Anglican Cathedral, Queen's Memorial, and £50 per week unemployed relief fund 1904–5; chairman Hospital Saturday Fund, president Dental Hospital; keen supporter Volunteer Corps; cast controversial vote Council debate dock strike 1905.

COLLIN, Daniel Shilton (1851–97), born Maryport; father and wife temperance workers; secretary (Liverpool) Popular Control Association; president Liverpool Direct Veto League; member council United Kingdom Alliance; drew Drink Map of Liverpool; co-founder Liverpool Vigilance Committee; church-worker with Revd. Richard Hobson at St. Nathaniel's; tea dealer; Independent Liberal candidate Birmingham East 1892, Liberal candidate Liverpool West Derby 1893; moved to London 1895.

COMMINS, Andrew (1832–1916), born Co. Carlow; father farmer; educated Queen's College, Cork, and London University; barrister Northern Circuit; one-time Professor of Political Economy; keen student chemistry; Denvir (q.v.) wrote that he 'was a man of such wide attainments that I think there was a general belief amongst Liverpool Irishmen that he knew EVERYTHING'; co-founder Home Rule Confederation 1870, *United Irishman* 1874; president H.R.C. 1875–6; withdrew as Home Rule candidate Liverpool by-election 1873; councillor 1876–92, alderman 1892–1913; M.P. Roscommon 1880–5, Roscommon South 1885–92, Cork County South-East 1893–1900; member Financial Reform Association 1871–1913.

CONLEY, James (1859–), born South Shields; boilermaker; moved to Partick, Scotland; trade union official and J.P.; Labour candidate Liverpool Kirkdale 1906.

CONNOLLY, Lawrence (1828–1903), born Co. Dublin; father farmer; settled Liverpool 1857; fruit broker and commission merchant; Liverpool's first Home Rule councillor, 1875–86; M.P. Longford County South 1885–8, retiring because of health; property speculator and developer New Brighton, where lived; left £78,000 personalty.

COOKSON, Edward H. (1837–1922), merchant shipowner African trade—said by one Labour critic to have 'made his money out of the blacks . . . [and] sold to them bad rum in return for palm oil'; prominent Freemason; Conservative councillor; chairman West Derby Divisional Association; mayor 1888–9; Orangeman but tied too closely to Walter Long (q.v.) in Church Discipline Bill crisis 1899–1900; left £244,438.

COTTER, Joe (1877–), born Liverpool; Irish father, English mother; orphaned at age two and a half; worked coal-mine and advertising firm in teens; married at twenty-one; went to sea as cook; steward on Cunard's *Mauretania*; lost job to foreign labour 1909;

founded Ships' Cooks and Stewards Union; studied economics; member Liverpool Strike Committee 1911; vice-president L.T.C. 1913; made C.B.E. 1920.

COX, James Bell (1837–1923), born Norfolk; educated Merchant Taylor's and Cambridge; curate/vicar St. Margaret's, Liverpool 1869–1921—church without parish endowments, drawing congregation from many areas and relying on contributions like dissenting community; prosecuted by Dr. Hakes (q.v.) for Ritualist practices; imprisoned for contempt of court 1887; member Liverpool School Board 1888–91.

CRANBORNE, Viscount (1861–1947), succeeded as 4th Marquess of Salisbury in 1903; Conservative M.P. Lancashire North-East (Darwen) 1885–92, Rochester 1893–1903; Under-Secretary Foreign Affairs 1900–3, Lord Privy Seal 1903–5, 1924–9, President of Board of Trade 1905, Chancellor of Duchy of Lancaster 1922–3.

CRAWSHAW, Richard (b. 1917), educated Pendleton Grammar School and Cambridge; clerk 1931–3; engineer 1933–6; theological student 1936–9; army 1939–45, lieutenant-colonel Parachute Regiment, T.A.; lawyer, northern circuit; Labour councillor Liverpool 1948–65; M.P. Toxteth 1964; one-time holder non-stop walking record; among sixty-nine Labour M.P.s to vote for entry into E.E.C. October 1971.

CREMLYN, John William Jones (1875–), born Bootle; lawyer, northern circuit; changed name from Jones to Cremlyn, the name of his father's house and estate (father Anglesey man) 1897; Conservative candidate Liverpool West Toxteth 1935.

CRITCHLEY, Alexander (1893–1974), Liverpool accountant, related to Holts (q.v.); councillor from 1925; Conservative M.P. Liverpool Edge Hill 1935–45.

CROSFIELD, William (1838–1909), family firm Stanley Street, Liverpool; prominent Congregationalist, locally and nationally; promoter Ragged Schools, Mersey training ships, University College, Liverpool and Mansfield College, Oxford; member executive Liberation Society; Whiggish—'Mr. Crosfield, though not averse to serving on public bodies, shrinks apparently from the peculiar toil of soliciting votes'; Liberal candidate Warrington 1885, Lincoln 1886; M.P. Lincoln 1892–5.

CROSS, William (1830–1908), doctor, qualified from St. Andrews, 1862; practice at 29, Islington, Liverpool; Conservative councillor; advocated municipalized gas.

CROSS, William H. (1856–92), father R. A. Cross (Viscount Cross: Home Secretary; Secretary of State for India); educated Rugby and Oxford; barrister; Conservative M.P. Liverpool West Derby 1888–92; took up postal workers' cause; died typhoid.

CURZON, George Nathaniel (1859–1925), 5th Baron Scarsdale, Marquess Curzon of Kedleston; Conservative M.P. Lancashire South-West (Southport) 1886–98; among few Tories to demand local option and Sunday closing 1892 General Election; Under-Secretary of State India 1891–2; Under-Secretary Foreign Affairs 1895–8; Viceroy and Governor-General of India 1898–1905; Lord Privy Seal 1915–16; Lord President of Council 1916–19; Foreign Secretary 1919–24.

DAVID, Albert Augustus (1867–1950), born Exeter, father clergyman; Fellow of Queen's College, Oxford; master Bradfield College and Rugby School; Examining Chaplain to Bishop of Liverpool 1901; Headmaster Clifton College 1905–9, and Rugby 1909–21; co-founder of Life and Liberty Movement 1917 (seeking greater self-government for the Church); recommended by Archbishop of Canterbury, Randall Davidson, to the see of Hereford, but the Prime Minister, Lloyd George (q.v.) elevated H. H. Henson, 1917; Bishop of St. Edmundsbury and Ipswich 1921–3; third Bishop of Liverpool 1923–44; keen angler and gardener; retired to Cornwall.

DAVIDSON, John Colin Campbell (1889–1970), born Aberdeen; educated Westminster and Cambridge; lawyer, private secretary various ministers 1910–27; Conservative M.P. Herts. (Hemel Hempstead) 1920–3, 1924–7; chairman Conservative party 1927–30; Chancellor of Duchy of Lancaster 1931–7; Viscount 1937.

DAVITT, Michael (1846–1906), born Ireland; family evicted 1852; began work Lancashire cotton factory 1856; lost right arm by machinery 1857; entered printing trade; Fenian 1865; imprisoned 1870–7; founded Irish Land League 1879; re-imprisoned 1881–3; election as M.P. (Co. Meath) quashed 1882 by special vote of Parliament; arbitrator Liverpool dock strike 1890; Nationalist M.P. North Meath 1892, unseated on petition; M.P. North-East Cork 1892–3, resigned owing to bankruptcy proceedings; M.P. East Kerry and South Mayo 1895; 1899 resigned; journalist and publicist.

DENVIR, John (1834–1916), born Co. Antrim; second cousin Bishop of Down and Connor; moved to Liverpool as child; intended priesthood; became joiner and builder; teetotaller, working with Father Nugent (q.v.); journalist and publisher—at different times manager *Northern Press*, *Catholic Times*, *United Irishman*, and *Irish Programme*; joined Fenians 1866, taking part in raid on Chester Castle; founder Home Rule movement Liverpool; secretary Catholic Club 1873; general secretary Home Rule Confederation 1875–6; secretary Liverpool Land League; left Liverpool 1885 as general organizer I.N.L.

DERBY, 15th Earl (1826–93), son of 14th Earl; as Edward Henry (Lord) Stanley Conservative M.P. King's Lynn 1848–69; Under-Secretary Foreign Affairs 1852; Secretary for Colonies 1858, 1882–5; President of Board of Control 1858; Secretary of State for India 1858–9; Foreign Secretary 1866–8, 1874–8; joined Liberals 1880; Liberal Unionist 1886; largest private landowner in Liverpool (principally Kirkdale-Bootle).

DERBY, 16th Earl (1841–1908), brother 15th Earl; as Frederick Arthur Stanley Conservative M.P. Preston 1865–8, North Lancashire 1868–85, Blackpool 1885–6; Civil Lord of Admiralty 1868; Financial Secretary War Office 1874–7, Treasury 1877–8; Secretary of State for War 1878–80, Colonies 1885–6; President of Board of Trade 1886–8; Governor-General of Canada 1888–93; Freedom of Liverpool 1904.

DERBY, 17th Earl (1865–1948), eldest son of 16th Earl; as Edward (Lord) Stanley Conservative M.P. Lancashire South-East (Westhoughton) 1892–1906; Junior Lord of Treasury (Whip) 1895–1900; Financial Secretary War Office 1900–3; Postmaster-General (in Cabinet) 1903–5; Director of Recruiting 1915; Secretary of State for War 1916–18, 1922–4; Ambassador to France 1918–20; Lord Mayor of Liverpool 1911–12, Freeman 1912; Lord Lieutenant of Lancashire; chairman Liverpool Chamber of Commerce for thirty-two years; president Merseyside Hospitals Council.

DEVLIN, Joseph (1871–1934), Belfast Catholic; journalist *Irish News* and *Freeman's*

Journal; secretary Belfast branch Young Ireland Society and U.I.L.; founding president Ancient Order of Hibernians 1905; organizer National Volunteers 1913; unmarried; celebrated, though nervous, orator; Nationalist M.P. West Belfast 1906–18; declined leadership Nationalist party 1918; M.P. Belfast Falls 1918–22; Independent candidate Liverpool Exchange 1922; elected to Northern Ireland parliament 1921 but did not take seat until 1925; withdrew with other Catholic M.P.s 1932.

DOEG, Charles (1847–1895), born Devon; newspaper compositor; moved to Liverpool 1882, working on *Liverpool Daily Post*; president L.T.C. 1890–1; advocated anti-alien legislation.

DOUGHAN, James A. (1841–1891), born Liverpool; Catholic; merchant North African trade; member Liverpool School Board 1885–92; chairman of its Finance Committee; Home Rule councillor 1891; active Catholic child charities.

DOWDALL, Harold Chaloner (1868–1955), born Liverpool; educated Rugby and Oxford; chairman East Toxteth Divisional Conservative Association; Lord Mayor 1908–9; subject of a controversial picture by Augustus John; lawyer, eventually Lancashire County Court Judge 1921–40; first chairman Liverpool Council of Social Service 1909–17; Chancellor Diocese of Liverpool 1913–48, Bristol 1919–48; first chairman Legal Board of National Assembly of Church of England 1923–8.

DOWNEY, Richard (1881–1953), born Kilkenny; educated St. Edward's, Liverpool; Professor Catholic colleges, including Upholland; Catholic Archbishop of Liverpool 1928–53.

DUNCAN, David (1831–86), born Perthshire; moved Liverpool 1849; shipowner, associated with Stephen Williamson (q.v.) and Alexander Balfour (q.v.), leaving them 1862; director several South American companies, Royal Insurance Co., British & Foreign Marine Insurance Co.; lived Gayton Hill, Eston, and James Street, Liverpool; J.P. Cheshire; Liberal M.P. Barrow 1885, unseated after petition proving illegal employment of voters; M.P. Liverpool Exchange 1886; Nonconformist; left £180,000.

DUNN, James Anthony (b. 1926), born Liverpool; educated L.S.E.; youth club worker; Catholic; member T.G.W.U.; Labour councillor 1958–66; M.P. Liverpool Kirkdale 1964–; Labour Whip 1971.

DUNNICO, Herbert (1876–1953), born in poverty North Wales; worked in factory and coal-mine as boy; Baptist minister; at Kensington Chapel, Liverpool where his Fabianism upset congregation 1906–14; potential I.L.P. candidate Liverpool West Derby 1917; Labour M.P. Consett 1922–31; Deputy Chairman Ways and Means Committee 1929–31; Deputy-Speaker 1929–31; belated convert National Labour party 1935; knighted; liked bowling and soccer.

DUNNING, Leonard (1860–1941), father London solicitor, with Liverpool connections; educated Eton and Oxford; studied for the bar but joined police; District Inspector R.I.C. 1882–95; Assistant Head Constable Liverpool 1895–1902; Head Constable 1902–11; H.M. Inspector of Constabulary, Home Office, 1912–30; knighted 1917, cr. baronet 1930.

DYKE, Sir William Hart (1837–1931), 7th bart.; M.P. West Kent 1865–8, Mid Kent

1868–85, Dartford 1885–1906; Whip 1868; Patronage Secretary to Treasury (Chief Whip) 1874–80; Chief Secretary for Ireland 1885–6; Vice-President Committee of Council (Education) 1887–92; large landowner Kent; tennis and racquets player.

EARLE, Arthur (1838–1919), son of Sir Hardman Earle (1791–1877); family prominent in Liverpool for two centuries; educated Harrow; oil merchant; director Bank of Liverpool and two big insurance companies; lived Childwall Lodge; secretary General Committee Liverpool Diocese; prominent contributor Liberal party; chairman Liverpool Reform Club 1882; Liberal Unionist candidate Liverpool Scotland 1886; brother of Sir Thomas Earle and Major-General William Earle (killed on the march to Khartoum); recreations, hunting, motoring, and travelling the world; liked by Richard Holt (q.v.) despite some 'curious failings—inquisitive to impertinence and mean to comicality about small things'.

EDWARDS, John (d. 1922), iron-founder; chairman Liverpool Fabian Society; sometime editor *Labour Chronicle*; left £6,511.

ELIAS, Owen (1806–80), Welsh builder, self-made, whose model cottages appeared throughout Kirkdale, Everton, and Walton; known as 'King of Everton'; deacon Calvinistic Methodist Connection; claimed to have 'no public gifts' but prominent in Welsh religious life Liverpool; inclined to prohibit public houses on his estates.

EVANS, Edward (1846–1917), knighted 1906; director great firm of wholesale druggists; lived Spital Old Hall, Bromborough; secretary West Cheshire Liberal Association; secretary Parnell Expenses Fund (to fight *The Times*–Pigott forgeries); chairman Liverpool Reform Club; president Liverpool Liberal Federal Council from 1889; chairman National Liberal Federation from 1894; golfer; refused to stand for Parliament.

FARRIE, Hugh (1857–1918), father senior employee of T. H. Ismay (q.v.); chief leader-writer *Liverpool Daily Post*; inaugurated famous inquiry into slums 1882–3; novelist; Baptist; left *Daily Post* 1891; took over *Porcupine* and *Liverpool Citizen*.

FITZGERALD, J. V. Vesey (1848–   ), Anglo-Irish landed family; educated Rugby and Oxford; Conservative candidate Liverpool Scotland 1892.

FITZROY, Ernest J. A. (1834–1916), vicar St. Jude's Liverpool, whose ritualism excited riots 1882; charged before Lord Penzance's court with drunkenness and immorality 1884; suspended from ministry for three years; later held in restraint in asylum; released into poverty; convicted of theft of baggage Euston Station 1894.

FORWOOD, Arthur Bower (1836–98), cr. bart. 1895; merchant shipowner; councillor 1871, mayor 1878–9; chairman Liverpool Constitutional Association from 1880; Conservative candidate Liverpool 1882; M.P. Lancashire South-West (Ormskirk) 1885–98; Parliamentary and Financial Secretary to Admiralty 1886–92; Privy Councillor 1892. Twice married into Liberal families—first to a Liverpool Crosfield; second to niece of Sir Edward Baines (of the *Leeds Mercury*).

FORWOOD, William Bower (1840–1928), brother of Arthur Forwood (q.v.); knighted 1883; shipowner; director Cunard's and Bank of Liverpool; co-founder and first chairman Liverpool Overhead Railway; president Joint Committee on Railway Rates; Conservative member of City Council for fifty-eight years (the vast majority of these years as a pitchforked alderman); chairman Southport Conservative Association; founder and president Unionist Free Food League in Liverpool 1903; chairman Lancashire Quarter Sessions 1890–1910; chairman Liverpool Cathedral Fund 1900–13; mayor 1880–1; Freedom of the city, 1902; Lord Mayor 1903; yachtsman.

FYFE, David Maxwell (1900–67), Scots-born lawyer; educated Edinburgh and Oxford; married Liverpudlian; founder and editor *Oxford Review*; Conservative candidate Wigan 1924; lawyer northern circuit 1922–34; Q.C. 1934; M.P. Liverpool West Derby 1935–54; Recorder of Oldham 1936–42; Solicitor-General 1942–5; Attorney-General 1945; Deputy Chief Prosecutor Nuremberg War Trials 1945–6; deputy-chairman Liverpool Constitutional Association from 1934, president from 1952; Home Secretary 1951–4; knighted 1942; Lord Chancellor 1954–62; cr. Earl (Kilmuir) 1962.

GAMBLE, Sir David (1823–1907), son of Irish Presbyterian who quit ministry for manufacture, setting up chemical business with E. K. Muspratt; churchman; subscriber to Anti-Corn Law League, and Irish famine relief fund; benefactor numerous hospitals, churches, schools; mayor St. Helens seven times; Liberal candidate St. Helens 1885; Liberal Unionist 1886; member founding committee Liverpool Unionist Free Food League 1903; cr. baronet 1897.

GEORGE, David Lloyd (1863–1945), cr. Earl 1945; born Manchester, raised in North Wales; solicitor; Liberal M.P. Caernarvon Boroughs 1890–1945 (Independent Liberal from 1931); President of Board of Trade 1905–8; Chancellor of Exchequer 1908–15; Minister of Munitions 1915–16; Secretary of State for War 1916; Prime Minister Coalition Government 1916–22.

GIBBINS, Joe (1888–1965), born Toxteth; educated St. Thomas Church of England School and Liverpool University Evening Classes; secretary Liverpool Boilermakers' Union; Labour M.P. Liverpool West Toxteth 1924–31, 1935–50.

GIBSON, John George (1846–1923), born and educated Dublin; lawyer Leinster circuit; Q.C. 1880; Conservative M.P. Liverpool Walton 1885–8; Solicitor-General and Attorney-General for Ireland 1885–9; Irish Judge 1888–1921; brother of Rt. Hon. E. Gibson (Attorney-General for Ireland 1875–80; cr. Lord Ashbourne 1885).

GLADSTONE, Robert (1833–1919), eldest son of a Dumfriesshire Gladstone; married daughter of Robertson Gladstone of Liverpool (one of the Liberal Prime Minister's brothers, and founding president Financial Reform Association; died 1875); educated Eton and Edinburgh University; chairman Mersey Docks and Harbour Board 1899–1911; in India and China trade; treasurer Liverpool University College; Freeman of Liverpool; Liberal who voted Conservative for first time in January 1910, although instrumental in securing unopposed return of W. F. Lawrence (q.v.) 1895; 'one of the old school—a classical scholar to the last who kept up his regular reading of Greek and Latin' (Richard Holt, diary 16 July, 1919).

GORST, John Eldon (1835–1916), barrister; Conservative M.P. Cambridge, 1866–8, Chatham 1875–92, Cambridge University 1892–1906; Liberal candidate Preston (his birthplace) January 1910; Conservative agent 1870–4, 1880–2; secretary N.U.C.C.A. 1871–7; Solicitor-General 1885–6; Under-Secretary for India 1886–91; Financial Secretary to Treasury 1891–2; Vice-President Committee of Council (Education) 1895–1902.

GOSCHEN, George Joachim (1831–1907), cr. Viscount 1900; father banker; Liberal M.P. City of London 1863–80, Ripon 1880–5, Edinburgh East 1885–6; Liberal Unionist candidate Liverpool Exchange 1887; Liberal Unionist M.P. St. George's, Hanover Square 1887–1900; Paymaster-General 1865–6; Chancellor of Duchy of Lancaster 1866; President Poor Law Board (in Cabinet) 1868–71; First Lord of Admiralty 1871–4, 1895–1900; Chancellor of Exchequer 1887–92.

GOSS, Alexander (1814–72), second Catholic Bishop of Liverpool 1856–72; born Ormskirk; Protestant father; educated Ushaw and Rome; professor and vice-president St. Edward's College, Liverpool 1843–53; as bishop put great effort into provision of Catholic schools; Conservative; ecclesiastical historian; 6 feet 3 inches tall.

GRANT, Jacob R. (b. 1847), house furnisher; hire-purchase and money-lending business; Jew; Liberal councillor St. Anne's ward 1890–9, resigning that and vice-presidency Exchange Divisional Liberal Association, in protest against Irish pro-Boers; active on behalf of distressed dockers and Corporation scavengers; promoted Fair-Wages clause in Corporation contracts.

GRAVES, Samuel Robert (1818–73), father Irish magistrate; mayor Liverpool 1860–1; councillor Pitt Street ward; shipowner; uncompromising churchman; Conservative M.P. Liverpool, 1865–73; potential minister at Admiralty 1868; one of daughters married son of Sir Edward Bates, the Liverpool shipping magnate and M.P. Plymouth singled out for attack by Samuel Plimsoll (q.v.) 1875.

GRIFFITH, Ellis Jones (1860–1926), born Anglesey; educated University College, Aberystwyth, and Cambridge; Fellow of Downing College, Cambridge; barrister; Liberal candidate Liverpool West Toxteth 1892; M.P. Anglesey 1895–1918, Carmarthen 1923–4; Recorder of Birkenhead 1907–12; under-secretary Home Office 1912–15; cr. baronet 1918.

GROGAN, William (1871–1928), born Liverpool; Irish Nationalist of independent nature, pressing working-class causes; councillor from 1920, first as Nationalist, then Labour; Independent Nationalist candidate Liverpool Exchange 1923.

GUION, Stephen Barker (1820–85), American-born, naturalized Briton; steamship owner (founded Guion Line 1866); ruined by competition of Cunard's; Liberal councillor Exchange ward 1869–85; declined Liberal candidature Liverpool by-election 1882; president Liverpool Liberal Nine Hundred; member Docks Board.

GUTHRIE, Alexander (1845–), son of Scottish divine, Thomas Guthrie; business partner with Alexander Balfour (q.v.); chairman Liverpool branch United Kingdom Alliance; prominent in Purity Crusade; brother-in-law of Stephen Williamson (q.v.).

HAKES, James (1822–1902), doctor, practising in Hope Street, Liverpool; member Liverpool School Board 1873–91, vice-chairman 1888–91; stalwart Church Association, Protestant Alliance, and Church Missionary Society; spent £3,000 in prosecution of Revd. Bell Cox (q.v.) for Ritualist practices; Bell Cox called him a fine foe and true friend; *Liverpool Review* called him a 'bigoted busybody'.

HALL, Edward Marshall (1859–1927), born Brighton, son of doctor; educated Rugby and Cambridge; barrister, mainly in London and south-east circuit; friend of Horatio

Bottomley; Conservative M.P. Lancashire South-West (Southport) 1900–6; Liverpool East Toxteth January 1910–16, resigned on appointment as Recorder of Guildford; keen shot and golfer.

HALL, Sir William Reginald (1870–1943), career in Navy, rising to Admiral; war-time Director of Naval Intelligence; Conservative M.P. Liverpool West Derby 1919–23; principal agent Conservative party March–December 1923; M.P. Eastbourne 1925–9.

HAMILTON, Lord Claud (1843–1925), second son of 1st Duke of Abercorn; Orangeman; Conservative M.P. Londonderry 1865–8, King's Lynn 1869–80, Liverpool 1880–5, Liverpool West Derby 1885–8 retiring after hunting accident; M.P. Kensington South 1910–18; Lord of Treasury 1868; chairman N.U.C.C.A. 1876–9; chairman Great Eastern Railway; member Council Anti-Socialist Union 1909–11. Younger brother, Lord George Hamilton: junior minister in Disraeli's 1874–80 Government, First Lord of Admiralty 1885–6, 1886–92, Secretary of State for India, 1895–1902. Family connections throughout peerage—his mother, daughter of Duke of Bedford; his step-grandfather, the Prime Minister, Lord Aberdeen; his sisters Countess of Lichfield, Countess of Durham, Countess of Mount Edgecombe, Duchess of Buccleuch, Marchioness of Winterton, Marchioness of Blandford, and Marchioness of Lansdowne.

HAMPSON, Robert Alfred (1852–1919), solicitor; Conservative party Whip Liverpool Council; leader of Council 1901–2; secretary Liverpool Cathedral Committee; chairman Everton Divisional Conservative Association from 1902; Lord Mayor 1903–4; knighted 1904; chairman C. Tinling & Co., proprietors *Liverpool Courier* and *Liverpool Evening Express*; lived Ulverston.

HARCOURT, Sir William George Granville Venables Vernon (1827–1904), grandson of Archbishop of York; barrister; Whewell Progessor of International Law Cambridge 1867–77; Liberal M.P. Oxford 1868–80, Derby 1880–95, Western Monmouthshire 1895–1904; Solicitor-General 1873–4; Home Secretary 1880–5; Chancellor of Exchequer 1886, 1892–5; leader of Liberal party in House of Commons 1894–8.

HARDIE, James Keir (1856–1915), born Lanarkshire, son of ship's carpenter; miner; educated at night school; moved from temperance work to trade unionism; founded Scottish Labour Party 1888, I.L.P. 1893; Labour candidate Mid Lanark 1888, Bradford East 1896, Preston 1900; M.P. West Ham South 1892–5, Merthyr Tydfil 1900–15.

HARFORD Austin (1863–1944), cloth and woollen merchants' business in Richmond Street; Nationalist councillor from 1899; with brother, Frank, broke the control which Lynskey (q.v.) exercised over Liverpool Nationalist party; withdrew candidature Liverpool Scotland 1900; deputy-chairman Housing Committee 1907–24 (acting chairman during war); first Catholic Lord Mayor of Liverpool 1943–4.

HARGROVE, Jonathan (1850–1905), born Whitehaven; Wesleyan; Liverpool firm of loading brokers; Liberal; subscribed towards expenses of labour candidates; inaugurated fund to relieve strikers' families during dockers' strike 1890; teetotaller; treasurer Liverpool and District Veto League; fought Durham (Houghton-le-Spring) as Independent Liberal 1892 when local Liberal association selected H. T. Fenwick, a brewer and critic of Newcastle Programme; 1897–8 fought two Council seats in Liverpool against Conservative candidates with brewing connections—Colonel W. Hall Walker and Edwin Berry.

HARMOOD-BANNER, John Sutherland (1847–1927), born Liverpool; educated Radley; family business of accountants; grandfather founder of Liverpool Exchange; father onetime chairman Liverpool & Harrington Water Co., and Gas and Coke Co., and town councillor; two brothers Anglican clergymen; married daughter Thomas Knowles, Conservative M.P. Wigan 1874–82; director Pearson, Knowles Coal & Iron Co., chairman 1895; director of five other companies; auditor Lancs. & Yorks. Railway Co., and Bank of Liverpool; Conservative councillor Exchange ward from 1895; chairman Corporation Finance Committee; M.P. Liverpool Everton 1905–24; Lord Mayor Liverpool 1913; knighted 1924.

HAYES, John ('Jack') Henry (1889–1941), father Wolverhampton Police Inspector; sergeant Metropolitan Police 1909–19; general secretary N.U.P.P.O.; member I.L.P.; Liverpool councillor 1919; first Labour M.P. in Liverpool (Edge Hill) 1923–31; parliamentary secretary Minister of Pensions 1924; junior Whip 1925–31; vice-chamberlain H.M. Household 1929–31; secretary British Optical Society and Registrar Joint Council of Qualified Opticians.

HEENAN, John Carmel (1905–76), born Ilford; parish priest, Barking and London's East End; Bishop of Leeds 1951; Archbishop Liverpool 1957; Archbishop Westminster 1963; Cardinal 1965.

HEFFER, Eric Samuel (b. 1922), born Hertford; carpenter and joiner; president L.T.C. & L.P. 1959–60, 1964–5; Labour councillor 1960–6; M.P. Liverpool Walton 1964–.

HEMELRYK, Paul Edward Joseph (1840–1919), born Leyden, Holland; Catholic merchant family; settled in Liverpool 1862; married 1874 and fathered nine children; partner with Hornby family (q.v.) in cotton merchant firm; introduced polo locally; active in establishing direct telegraphic links with continent; Dutch Vice-Consul Liverpool 1885–9; Liberal before 1886; president Wavertree branch W.M.C.A. 1886–90; resigned in protest at anti-Catholic tone; president Liverpool Council of St. Vincent de Paul's Society; left £141,288.

HEMMERDE, Edward George (1871–1948), born Peckham, father merchant banker; educated Winchester and Oxford; Recorder of Liverpool from 1909; Liberal candidate Winchester 1900, Shrewsbury 1906, Portsmouth December 1910, Liberal M.P. Denbighshire East 1906–10, Norfolk North-Western 1912–18; chambers at Inner Temple bombed in December 1917 while in Parliament pleading for fair treatment for Germany; Labour M.P. Crewe 1922–4; at odds with Liverpool Corporation from 1921; playwright under pseudonym Edward Denby.

HERRING, Richard Francis (1858–1916), born London, son of vicar; educated St. Paul's, London and Durham Universities; Greek scholar; copious contributor to ecclesiastical journals; curacy Morpeth; vicar St. John the Baptist, Toxteth, from 1886, a church whose congregation had declined under Revd. James Hassall, a man of private means (he left £49,000 but spent nothing on the church); Herring made St. John's a thriving place of worship; stoned and mobbed by anti-Ritualists; services held under police protection 1886–7; active in Early Closing and Co-operative movements; outspoken critic of Unitarianism.

HIGGINBOTTOM, Samuel Wasse (1853–1902), born Dukinfield, Cheshire; worked on railways, in mines; began commercial career Liverpool 1874; made fortune as mine owner and steamship owner (in Isle of Man traffic); Conservative councillor Edge Hill 1895; M.P. Liverpool West Derby 1900–2; Wesleyan Methodist, supporter of several chapels, churches, and charities in West Derby; 'a man of affairs rather than of words'; key figure in Protestants' expulsion of Walter Long (q.v.); described his recreations thus: 'fond of horses and driving, but practically never took any physical exercise, his principal hobby being local municipal government and politics'.

Hill, Charles Alexander (1867–), born Liverpool, son of merchant in Brazilian trade; educated Rugby and Cambridge; surgeon Consumption Hospital, Mount Pleasant; consulting physician to several life insurance companies; concerned with housing question as key to consumption; mountaineer and cyclist; Conservative councillor; straightforward Protestant—'Ritualism he could not understand. If a person was Protestant let him stick to the Protestant religion and not ape something else'—but defeated by Protestant candidate St. Domingo 1905.

HILLS, John Waller (1867–1938), born Highmead Castle, Cumberland; educated Eton and Oxford; family friend of novelist, John Galsworthy; served in army, wounded; lieutenant-colonel; Unionist M.P. Durham 1906–22; Financial Secretary to Treasury 1922–3; Conservative candidate Liverpool Edge Hill March 1923; M.P. Ripon 1925–38; died before his intended nomination to baronetcy.

HOCKING, Silas Kitto (1850–1935), born Cornwall; married Liverpool woman; minister United Methodist Free Church 1870–96, spending some years in Toxteth; novelist; Liberal candidate Mid Bucks 1906, Coventry 1910; enthusiast of golf, bowls, and travelling.

HOGAN, Luke, chairman of Liverpool Council of Action during General Strike; trade union official (N.U.D.A.W.); leader Liverpool Labour party from 1930; Lord Mayor 1945–6; defence of Liverpool Cotton Exchange from closure by Labour Government brought his downfall from leadership 1948; resigned Labour party 1950; sat as Independent Catholic councillor.

HOLT, Alfred (1829–1911), brother of Robert Holt (q.v.); civil engineer, equipped ship with compound engines to carry 3,000 tons cargo non-stop Liverpool to Mauritius 1865; founder Ocean Steamship Co (trading to the Orient); chairman Liverpool Steam Ship Owners Association 1876; member and chairman Mersey Docks & Harbour Board, resigned 1890 disputing policy.

HOLT, Richard Durning (1868–1941), son of Robert Holt (q.v.); educated Winchester and Oxford; partner, Alfred Holt & Co., bringing enterprise to a then flagging concern; member 1896, chairman Mersey Docks and Harbour Board 1927–9, 1930–41; chairman Elder Dempster Lines from 1932; deputy chairman Martins Bank Ltd. 1934; Liberal candidate Liverpool West Derby 1903, 1906; M.P. Hexham 1907–18; treasurer and president Free Trace Union; baronet 1935.

HOLT, Robert Durning (1832–1908), leader Liverpool Liberal party 1879–89; one of five brothers, including George (died 1874; partner in Lamport & Holt, shipowners and merchants chiefly in South American trade) and Alfred (q.v.); senior in George Holt & Co., cotton brokers established by his father (1790–1861) in 1821; director Bank of Liverpool; Unitarian; brother-in-law of Beatrice Webb (q.v.); first Lord Mayor of

Liverpool 1892–3; refused baronetcy from Rosebery's government; member Royal Commission on Government of London 1893–4; Freedom of Liverpool 1904'

HORNBY, Frank (1863–1936), self-made businessman, founder of Meccano; Conservative councillor; M.P. Liverpool Everton 1931–5.

HORNBY, Henry Hugh (1832–1913), old Liverpool family; brother of T. D. Hornby (q.v.); partner with brother and P. E. J. Hemelryk (q.v.), cotton brokers'; director Bank of Liverpool, and Royal Insurance Co.; treasurer Liverpool Central Relief and Charity Organization Society; Liberal Unionist Councillor, resigned in protest at Liberal ward redistribution 1894; returned to Council 1895; alderman 1896; chairman Watch Committee 1890–4, 1895–9; left £71,121.

HORNBY, Thomas Dyson (1822–89), chairman Docks Board 1876–89; Hornby Dock bore his name; leading part in Liberal Unionist Association; left £159,533.

HOULDING, John (1833–1902), hotel proprietor and brewer, prominent in Everton public life; Guardian 1872; councillor 1884; member Everton Burial Board; on management committee Stanley Hospital; chairman Everton Conservative Association 1885–1902; potential parliamentary candidate; president Liverpool Carters Union; member Liverpool Land and House Owners Association; Lord Mayor 1897–8; Orangeman; Freemason; football enthusiast, playing key role in foundation of both Liverpool F.C. and Everton F.C.; left £45,000.

HOULDSWORTH, William Henry (1834–1917), cr. bart. 1887; mill-owner and landowner; born Manchester; Scots parents; Conservative M.P. Manchester 1883–5, Manchester North-West 1885–1906; opponent of Churchill (q.v.) in N.U.C.C.A. controversy; member Royal Commissions on Depression of Trade, and Liquor Licensing Laws.

HOUSTON, Robert Paterson (1853–1926), born Bootle of Renfrewshire family; educated Liverpool College; apprenticed as engineer and shipbuilder; began as ship owner (with one ship) 1881; established Houston Line trading principally to River Plate; breaker of conference rings; Dewar, the whisky millionaire, called him the 'Robber Baron'; *The Times* described business career as 'one of the most striking individual achievements in the modern history of shipping'; Conservative M.P. Liverpool West Toxteth 1892–1924, known for treating of constituents; retired to Jersey to escape death duties; wife financed the Spitfire prototype.

HOWARD, Theodore A. (1852–1922), vicar St. Matthew's, Toxteth; chaplain Liverpool Orange Lodge; quarrelled with George Wise (q.v.) 1903.

HUGHES, John (1830–95), son of Welsh labourer; born Liverpool; began as office boy; solicitor, tied closely with drink interests; Conservative councillor 1871; mayor 1881–2; chairman Watch Committee 1883–90, Water Committee 1891–2.

HUGHES, Thomas (1838–1923), knighted 1898; born Liverpool; large firm timber merchants Warwick St., Brunswick Dock; Conservative councillor North Toxteth 1878; mayor 1889; alderman 1891; Lord Mayor 1896–7; independent, and brusque manner; leader City Council 1898–9; resigned from Council, an anti-Salvidge Conservative 1900;

long-serving chairman Watch Committee and Licensing Committee, acknowledged by Samuel Smith (q.v.) as 'one of the greatest of Liverpool's social reformers'.

HUME, Abraham (1814–84), born Co. Down; educated Belfast, Glasgow University and Trinity College, Dublin; curate Liverpool 1843–7; first vicar Vauxhall, Liverpool 1847; antiquarian; made statistical inquiries into physical and spiritual condition of Liverpool; explored Chile and Peru for South American Missionary Society 1867; vice-chairman Liverpool School Board 1870–6; secretary bishopric committee 1873–80; co-founder Historic Society of Lancashire and Cheshire 1848.

ISMAY, Thomas Henry (1837–99), born Cumberland; father shipowner and shipbuilder; Broad Churchman; senior in Ismay, Imrie & Co.; founder White Star Line, giving Cunard and Inman Lines their first real competition in Atlantic traffic; director London and North Western Railway and several insurance companies; member several Royal Commissions; Liberal Unionist; declined candidature Liverpool Exchange 1892; Deputy Lord Lieutenant and High Sheriff of Cheshire; keen traveller and yachtsman.

JACOB, Albert Edward (1858–1929), Dublin-born, biscuit manufacturer; first Liberal councillor Aigburth ward 1901–12; Conservative councillor from 1918; alderman 1925; Conservative M.P. Liverpool East Toxteth 1924–9; advocate of empire trade; vice-president Federation of British Industries.

JELLICOE, E. G., Welsh-born barrister; practised in New Zealand for twenty-five years; aggressive critic of Boer War; Liberal candidate Liverpool Walton 1906; Independent Liberal January 1910.

JOHNSON, Benjamin Sands (1865–1937), owned large dyeworks in Kirkdale-Bootle; mayor Bootle 1893–5; in Band of Hope, Men's Bible Class work; campaign chairman for T. R. Threlfall (q.v.) 1892; Liberal candidate Liverpool Kirkdale 1895; art collector; paternalistic employer with one of country's first industrial welfare departments; pronounced 'all right' by Jack Braddock (q.v.); lent Braddock £150 to set up as agent Co-operative Insurance Society; leader Liverpool Liberal party 1910; knighted 1910; voted Conservative by 1929.

JONES, Alfred Lewis (1846–1919), born Carmarthen of middle-class family; clerk with Laird's 1859; shipping insurance broker 1878; senior partner Elder Dempster Lines; president Liverpool Chamber of Commerce; chairman Bank of West Africa; founder Liverpool School of Tropical Medicine; member Tariff Commission 1904; knighted 1901; potential Conservative candidate for several Liverpool seats.

JONES, Charles William (1840–1908), shipowner in Lamport and Holt's; Liberal councillor; member Licensing Committee; Unitarian; donated recreation ground to University College.

JONES, Charles Sydney (1872–1947), born Liverpool, son of Charles William Jones (q.v.); educated Charterhouse and Oxford; director Ocean Steam Ship Co. (Blue Funnel Line); treasurer Liverpool University; High Sheriff Lancashire; president British and Foreign Unitarian Association 1921; Liberal councillor; Liberal M.P. Liverpool West Derby 1923–4; Lord Mayor 1938–42; knighted 1937; unmarried.

JOSEPH, Francis ('Frank') L'Estrange (1870–1951), born Liverpool; left school at twelve; became head of great coal, iron, and timber combine; active in Liverpool Food and Betterment Association; temperance advocate; Liberal Councillor 1903–13; Liberal candidate Liverpool Walton January 1910, Coalition Liberal candidate Liverpool Fairfield, 1918; acting secretary to Auckland Geddes 1917–18; High Sheriff Staffordshire 1932–3; President North Staffordshire Chamber of Commerce 1922–32, Federation of British Industries 1935, Society of British Gas Industries 1939–46; director Imperial Airways Ltd.; director Midland Bank; member various trade missions; knighted 1922; cr. baronet 1942.

KANEY, Edward, pattern-maker; delegate Liverpool branch A. S. E. from 1876; Fabian and I.L.P. member; Trades Council candidate South Toxteth 1892.

KEARNEY, Patrick (1850–1902), president Joseph Biggar Branch I.N.L.; brother-in-law of Lynskey (q.v.); Councillor S. Scotland ward.

KEATING, Frederick William (1859–1928), born Birmingham; ordained 1882; Catholic Bishop of Northampton 1907–21; Archbishop Liverpool 1921–8; raised £122,000 towards cathedral.

KELLY, Patrick J. (1869–1936), Irish born; settled Liverpool about 1885; insurance agent and trade union organizer; Independent Nationalist candidate Everton ward by-election 1892; Nationalist councillor 1914–24; imprisoned 1921 as Sinn Feiner; pro-Labour.

KELLY, Thomas (1858–95), onetime labourer; commission agent Royal Liver Insurance Co.; Nationalist councillor 1890; temperance champion; pronounced Catholic; *Porcupine* called him 'the Tim Healy of the Council'; pestered Liberal party for magistracy 1894; brother of P. J. Kelly (q.v.).

KENSIT, John (1853–1902), born Bishopsgate, London; renowned anti-Ritualist; founder Wycliffe Preachers and Protestant Truth Society; Independent (Protestant) candidate Brighton 1900; died of double pneumonia, accelerated by shock after injury received at Mersey ferry. His son, **John A.**, continued his work, for example his nostrum to maintain English family life: 'keep the priest on the street side of the threshold'.

KIRBY, Bertie Victor (1887–1953), born Cheltenham; elementary education; served in both wars in all ranks to captain; Liverpool district secretary National Union of Clerks; president L.T.C. & L.P.; wanted for the L.T.C. greater power to control councillors' votes; councillor from 1924; alderman 1939; deputy leader Labour Council group early 1930s; Labour M.P. Liverpool Everton 1935–50.

KYFFIN-TAYLOR, George (1863–1949), third son of Revd. W. F. Taylor (q.v.); educated Liverpool College; solicitor; chairman northern council Church Association 1905; committee member Protestant Reformation Society; joined Volunteers as private 1885; later colonel 1st West Lancashire Brigade Royal Field Artillery (Volunteers); Director National Service, North-West Region 1918; councillor Everton 1904–19; chairman Housing Committee 1907–19; Conservative M.P. Liverpool Kirkdale 1910–15; received financial support from Lord Derby (q.v.) as M.P.; Housing Commissioner for Lancashire and Cheshire 1919–22.

LAIRD, John (1805–74), born Greenock; established shipbuilders Birkenhead;

Birkenhead's first M.P. (Conservative) 1861–74; brother of African explorer, MacGregor Laird (1808–61).

LARKIN, James ('Jim') (1876–1947), born Liverpool; father died of consumption 1883; began work at eleven; ran away to sea 1893; casual docker; joined Liverpool I.L.P.; foreman docker with T. & J. Harrison 1903–5; branch leader N.U.D.L.; election agent for Sexton (q.v.) 1906; founded Irish Transport and General Workers Union; linchpin Dublin workers' epic strike 1913; in America 1914–23 (imprisoned two years alleged treason); deported; Catholic; teetotaller; non-smoker.

LAUGHLAND, Vint, born Southampton; at college in America; pastor of Pembroke St. Baptist Chapel, 1920; Socialist; active Liverpool Unemployed Workers Movement; Labour candidate Liverpool Wavertree 1922, 1923; left Liverpool for America 1924.

LAW, Andrew Bonar (1858–1923), born New Brunswick; father Presbyterian minister; in iron trade; Conservative M.P. Glasgow Blackfriars 1900–6; Camberwell (Dulwich) 1906–10, Lancashire South-West (Bootle) 1911–18, Glasgow Central 1918–23; Parliamentary Secretary Board of Trade 1902–5; leader Conservative party 1911–21, 1922–3; Colonial Secretary 1915–16; Chancellor of Exchequer 1916–19; Lord Privy Seal 1919–21; Prime Minister 1922–3.

LAURENCE, Edward (1825–1909), family wealthy brewers; father mayor Liverpool 1844; general merchant, trading to India; Conservative councillor 1861–7, mayor 1864–5; Conservative candidate Lancaster 1865; retired from conspicuous political activity; vice-president Liverpool College; chairman council University College; active in hospital, blind, and orphan asylum work; treasurer Church of England Temperance Society; chairman Liverpool Gas Co.; director Overhead Railway; returned to City Council 1892; stop-gap president Liverpool Constitutional Association 1898–9.

LAWRENCE, T. D. (1846–), born Sheffield; Quaker; owner temperance hotel Lime Street ward; Liberal councillor 1890; member Licensing Committee established to administer 1904 Act; Poor Law Guardian.

LAWRENCE, William Frederick (1844–1935), born Liverpool; Jamaican interests; educated Eton and Oxford; barrister, mostly non-practising; lived Wiltshire 1880–; J. P. Wiltshire; Conservative M.P. Liverpool Abercromby 1885–1906.

LEA, John (b. 1850), colliery owner and coal merchant; Liberal councillor 1890; Lord Mayor Liverpool 1904–5; active in temperance and purity campaigns; Scots Presbyterian; Liberal candidate Liverpool East Toxteth Jan. 1910; member Council Liverpool University; succeeded Philip Rathbone (q.v.) chairman Walker Art Gallery; lampooned by Sandon Group (which included Augustus John) for philistinism.

LESTER, T. Major (1829–1903), born London; educated Christ's College, Cambridge; vicar St. Lawrence, Kirkdale, from 1855; founder, Superintendent, and Treasurer Kirkdale Industrial Ragged Schools and Homes from 1856; chairman Liverpool Self-Help Emigration Society from 1880; member (from 1885) and chairman (from 1891) Liverpool School Board; active on Stanley Hospital and Kirkdale Burial Board; died poor man but raised £1 million for charity.

LEVER, William Hesketh (1851–1925), born Bolton; son of wholesale grocer; became world's biggest soap producer after building Port Sunlight Works, Bebington, 1888–9; Liberal candidate Birkenhead 1892, 1894, 1895, Cheshire (Wirral) 1900, Lancashire South-West (Ormskirk) January 1910; M.P. Cheshire (Wirral) 1906–10. Lloyd George (q.v.) ranked him and nearly all big businessmen as political 'bletherers'; Nonconformist; introduced profit-sharing in his business; theatre patron; bought island of Lewis 1918; baronet 1911, baron 1917, viscount 1922.

LEYLAND, Ralph Watts (1842–1921), father Liverpool builder; underwriter, established firm of shipowners and marine insurance brokers; lived Upton Major, Cheshire; horseman; moved from Liberal to Conservative via Liberal Unionists within three years; councillor Exchange ward.

LOCKHART, William P. (1837–93), born Liverpool; father merchant in Spanish trade; Baptist; president Liverpool branch Band of Hope; lay minister Toxteth Tabernacle (erected by Lockhart's Nonconformist friends) from 1871; manager Liverpool Investment Building Society; Liberal Unionist.

LOGAN, David Gilbert (1871–1964), born Liverpool; Scots father, Irish mother; married Irish school-teacher; Nationalist Councillor; joined Labour 1923; pawnbroker; general secretary trade union pawnbrokers' assistants (his foundation); alderman 1929–35; Labour M.P. Liverpool Scotland 1929–64; founder member Knights of St. Columba in England.

LONG, Walter Hume (1854–1924), cr. viscount 1921; squire; Conservative M.P. Wiltshire (North) 1880–5, Wiltshire (East or Devizes) 1885–92, Liverpool West Derby 1893–1900, Bristol South 1900–6, County Dublin South 1906–10, Strand 1910–18, Westminister (St. George's) 1918–21; Parliamentary Secretary Local Government Board 1886–92; President Board of Agriculture 1895–1900; President Local Government Board 1900–5, 1915–16; Chief Secretary for Ireland 1905; contestant Conservative leadership 1911; Colonial Secretary 1916–19; First Lord of Admiralty 1919–21.

LONGBOTTOM, H. D. (1886–1962), assistant to George Wise (q.v.) 1913–16; pastor Queen's Walk Congregational Church, Nottingham 1916, then Leytonstone Baptists; pastor Protestant Reformers' Memorial Church 1919-death; Protestant candidate Liverpool Kirkdale 1931, 1935, 1945; Lord Mayor 1950–1; long-serving chaplain Orange Order; Grand Master 1946–56; Imperial Vice-President 1956–61, expelled.

LOVELL, John (1835–90), born Farnham, Surrey; father small tradesman; reporter Surrey, Sheffield, and Birmingham newspapers; editor *Cassell's Magazine* 1868; managed Press Association (virtually his creation) eleven years; editor and business manager *Liverpool Mercury* 1879–90; Radical Liberal; bibliomaniac; weighed 20 stones.

LOWNDES, Frederick W. (1838–1919), doctor Lock Hospital from 1875; chief surgeon Liverpool police, 1877–1911; nephew of Tory alderman, J. G. Livingston; friend of J. A. Willox (q.v.).

LOWRY, James, born Belfast; retail and wholesale grocer; agent and manager Pioneer Life Assurance Co.; temperance worker; president L.T.C.; Conservative candidate Great George ward 1892; W.M.C.A. prospective candidate, 1874, 1885; chairman Liverpool Select Vestry; appointed Government Inspector of Poor Law, 1901; Methodist.

LUNDIE, Robert Henry (1823–95), Presbyterian minister, Fairfield, Liverpool from 1866; descended from line of Scots ministers; graduated Edinburgh University 1848; minister Birkenhead 1850–66; twice Moderator English Presbyterian Church; president Liverpool Vigilance Committee; biographer of Alexander Balfour (q.v.).

LYNCH, James, Secretary Liverpool Province of Orangemen 1880s and 1890s; printer and publisher with offices at Low Hill; editor *Loyal Orangeman* and *Protestant Standard.*

LYNSKEY, George Jeremy (1861–1921), born Co. Galway; father large farmer; brother priest, two sisters nuns; educated Tuam, Limerick, London University; solicitor Liverpool; secretary Young Ireland Society branch; I.N.L. organizer and registration agent Merseyside 1887; married sister of Patrick Kearney (q.v.); councillor 1889; alderman 1913; noted but infrequent debater; on Finance and Water Committees; hounded during Irish faction-fighting 1890s; returned to favour as Catholics' counsel during Wiseite disturbances; left £19,000.

M'ARTHUR, Charles (1843–1910), average adjuster; Bristol born, married daughter of Liverpool man; president Liverpool Chamber of Commerce; anti-Ritualist; Liberal Unionist M.P. Liverpool Exchange 1897–1906, Unionist M.P. Liverpool Kirkdale 1907–10; believed that 'a true Liberalism, in the time-honoured sense of the words, was consistent with a true Conservatism'.

MACARTNEY, William Grey Ellison (1852–1924), Ulster landowner; Conservative M.P. Antrim South 1885–1903; candidate Liverpool Scotland 1895; Financial Secretary to Admiralty from 1895; Deputy Master of the Mint 1903.

MACDONALD, James Ramsay (1866–1937), journalist; joined I.L.P. 1894; Labour M.P. Leicester 1906–18, Glamorganshire (Aberavon) 1922–9, Durham (Seaham) 1929–31; National Labour M.P. Durham (Seaham) 1931–5, Scottish Universities 1936–7; chairman I.L.P. 1906–9; leader P.L.P. 1911–14; Foreign Secretary 1924; Labour Prime Minister 1924, 1929–31; Prime Minister National Government 1931–5; Lord President of Council 1935–7.

MACIVER, David (1840–1907), father co-founder Cunard; senior partner shipowning business trading to Argentine; director G. W. R. and other railway companies; tariff reformer from 1870s; Conservative M.P. Birkenhead 1874–85, Liverpool Kirkdale 1898–1907; Liverpool councillor 1873–9, defeated by Samuel Smith (q.v.); pitchforked alderman 1880–92, retiring to fight (and lose to) R. D. Holt (q.v.) Exchange ward; Presbyterian; first wife (died 1869) daughter Robert Rankin, shipowner and chairman Mersey Docks and Harbour Board; brother-in-law (Sir) James Rankin, Conservative M.P. Leominster 1880–5, 1886–1906.

MACLEAN, James Mackenzie (1835–1906), journalist; one-time editor *Newcastle Chronicle*, part owner *Western Mail*; Conservative M.P. Oldham 1885–92, Cardiff District 1895–1900; supporter of Lord Randolph Churchill (q.v.) in N.U.C.C.A., but rallied to Lord Salisbury (q.v.).

MADDEN, Thomas John (1853–1915), born Belfast; curate Christ Church, Everton 1879–83; vicar Barrow 1885–8, St. Luke's, Liverpool 1889; hon. chaplain to Bishop of Liverpool 1891; Archdeacon Warrington 1895–1906; Archdeacon Liverpool from 1906; vicar Christ Church, Southport from 1913; various publications, including *Follies and Fallacies of Betting and Gambling*; recreations: fishing, yachting, rowing, astronomy.

MADDOCKS, Fred, speaker St. Domingo Pit, specializing in anti-Catholic insinuation, for example, 'where there is a nunnery you find a monastery, and where you find both you find a Catholic orphanage'; Protestant councillor 1903; announced intention to join Labour November 1905.

MAHON, Peter (b. 1909), son of Alderman Simon Mahon of Bootle; Labour councillor Bootle 1933; mayor 1954–5; chairman or deputy chairman various Corporation committees; member national committee T.G.W.U.; Labour M.P. Preston South 1964–70; talked out first Abortion Bill 1966; Against Abortion candidate Liverpool Scotland, April 1971; expelled from Labour party; joined Liberal party January 1973.

MAHON, Simon (b. 1914), brother of Peter Mahon (q.v.); general contractor; Labour alderman Bootle; chairman Housing Committee; M.P. Bootle 1955–; mayor 1962; opposition Whip 1959–61.

MANN, Tom (1856–1941), born Warwickshire mining district; farm and pit worker as boy; apprenticed engineer Birmingham; moved to London 1877; joined A.S.E. 1881 (General Secretary 1918–21), S.D.F. 1885; four times parliamentary candidate; travelled world Socialist propagandist 1897–1910; syndicalist; active Liverpool strikes 1911–12.

MARSH, Nicholas Kenrick (1824–93), doctor with large practice at 44, Bedford St. (Abercromby Square); churchman—pillar of St. Saviour's for thirty years; Conservative councillor Abercromby.

MATHESON, Thomas (1823–), born Edinburgh; lawyer's son; in India and China trade; prominent evangelical Liverpool; chairman committee organized Moody's and Sankey's visit 1875; director British Workman Public House Co.; teetotal from 1864; three times married; Liberal Unionist.

MATKIN, William (1845–1920), born Lincolnshire, son of builder; moved London; foreman joiner; member A.S.C. & J. early 1870s, General Secretary from 1884; secretary Liverpool branch Labour Electoral Association 1887; retired from Liverpool Trades Council 1897 on becoming Liberal agent; member T.U.C. Parliamentary Committee 1871, 1890–1, 1911–15; President T.U.C. (held in Liverpool) 1890; Liverpool's first working-class J.P. 1892; convicted of technical assault on police constable 1896.

MATTINSON, Miles Walker (1854–1944), born Newcastle; barrister Northern Circuit; Conservative candidate Carlisle 1880, Dumfries Burghs 1885, 1886, Bolton 1910; M.P. Liverpool Walton 1888–92; Recorder of Blackburn 1886–1922; member council N.U.C.C.A. and Churchillite Tory Democrat; Q.C. 1897; knighted 1922.

MAXWELL, Maxwell Hyslop (–1937), born Liverpool; family business North American merchants; educated Uppingham; director Cunard Steamship Co.; Royal Insurance Co., Liverpool, London and Globe Insurance Co., Buffalo and Lake Huron Railway, Liverpool Overhead Railway; Conservative councillor; long-serving chairman Watch Committee from 1900.

McARDLE, Charles (1833–1906), cotton merchant; Nationalist Councillor 1876–84; left £10,000 personalty.

McCARTHY, Justin (1830–1912), born Cork; journalist *Liverpool Daily Post* 1852–60;

editor *Morning Star* 1864–8; leader-writer *Daily News* from 1870; novelist and historian; Nationalist M.P. Longford County 1879–86, Derry City 1886–92, Anti-Parnellite North Longford 1892–1900; chairman Irish Parliamentary party 1890–6.

McCOMB, James (1852–1908), born Liverpool; Baptist; secretary Liverpool Liberal Association 1876–85 and South-West Lancashire Liberal Association to 1881; agent Liverpool Liberal Unionist Association 1886–1907.

McCRACKEN, Thomas (1850–1917), born Belfast, son of builder; wine and spirit merchant West Derby Road and Myrtle Street, Liverpool; Freemason; Orangeman, although known contributor Catholic charities; chairman Low Hill branch W.M.C.A. 1880; co-founder Junior Conservative Club 1880; co-secretary Hot-Pot fund; quarrelled with Arthur Forwood (q.v.) and Liverpool Tory party, and with Harry Thomas (q.v.) and Orange Order, 1889–1892; kept unusual pets, donkey and St. Bernard dog.

McGUFFIE, Peter (1850–1911), shipowner; anti-Salvidge Conservative councillor 1896–1905; temperance advocate; promoted industrial development of Garston; sympathized with Irish Home Rule; expelled Liverpool Conservative party 1903.

McKINNEY, James (1848–1918), born co. Tyrone; curate and vicar of parishes in co. Donegal, 1871–6; vicar St. Silas, Liverpool, from 1893, increasing congregation from average fifty to near 2,000; Orangeman; proclaimed rightness of Boer War and 'its ultimate benefit to England, Africa, and Mankind'; broke with Wise (q.v.) and National Protestant Electoral Federation 1903.

McMILLIN, Samuel (1840–1919), Ulster Presbyterian; Liberal Home Ruler; joiner, builder, cabinet-maker and second-hand furniture dealer Liverpool's Cheapside; chairman Rodney Street Liberal committee; councillor St. Anne's 1888; attacked municipal extravagance.

M'NEILE, Hugh (1795–1879), father Sheriff Antrim; married a daughter of Archbishop of Dublin, Magee, 1822; vicar St. Jude's, Liverpool 1834, St. Paul's 1848; canon Chester Cathedral 1845, canon residentiary 1860; Dean of Ripon 1868–75; retired to Bournemouth; great orator and political Protestant; co-founder Liverpool College, Shaw Street, 1840; niece married Hugh Cairns (later Lord Chancellor) 1856.

MEADE-KING, Richard R. (1850–1906), general broker, importing petroleum; prominent Liverpool Kyrle Society, seeking to extend popular recreational facilities; extensively read and travelled; Liberal councillor 1891; on Health Committee, Parks, Garden and Improvement Committee, Library, Museum, and Arts Committee.

MELLY, George (1830–94), educated Rugby; connected through mother with Liverpool Brights and Manchester Gregs; senior partner general merchants, Liverpool and London; chairman Globe Insurance Co.; director Bank of Liverpool and Union Marine Insurance Co., member Docks Board; Liberal candidate Preston 1862, Stoke 1865; M.P. Stoke 1868–75; deputy-lieutenant Lancashire.

MILLIGAN, George Jardine (1868–1925), born Liverpool, son of compositor; barman, then casual docker afterwards White Star regular; leader North-end dockers and Sexton's deputy, N.U.D.L.; Catholic; anti-Socialist; joined British Empire Union; O.B.E. 1917, J.P. 1924; author of *Life Through Labour's Eyes*, 1911.

MOND, Alfred (1868–1930), cr. bart. 1910; Baron Melchett 1928; creator and head I.C.I.; advocated industrial rationalization and profit-sharing; Liberal M.P. Chester

1906–10, Swansea 1910–18, Swansea West 1918–23, Carmarthen 1924–8; First Commissioner of Works 1916–21; Minister of Health 1921–2; joined Conservative party 1926 from hostility to Lloyd George's Land Campaign and Socialism; Zionist.

MOND, Henry (1898–1949), son of Alfred (q.v.); educated Winchester; director I.C.I. and International Nickel Company of Canada, etc.; Liberal M.P. Isle of Ely 1923–4; Conservative M.P. Liverpool East Toxteth 1929–30; 2nd Baron Melchett.

MORLEY, John (1838–1923), cr. viscount 1908; born Blackburn; journalist, man-of-letters, Gladstone's official biographer; Liberal M.P. Newcastle 1883–95, Montrose Burghs 1896–1908; Chief Secretary for Ireland 1886, 1892–5; Secretary of State for India 1905–10, 1911; Lord President of Council 1910–14; resigned on outbreak of war.

MORRIS, Artro, Liverpool solicitor; father High Sheriff Merionethshire; Liberal candidate Wallasey 1922, 1923, Liverpool Wavertree 1935.

MORRIS, Isaac (1845–1917), born Shropshire; partner Liverpool paint manufacturing business; onetime Birkenhead councillor; chairman Abercromby Conservative Divisional Council; Liverpool councillor 1886–9.

MORRISSEY, John Wolfe Tone, insurance agent; elective city auditor 1901; Labour councillor 1905–8; teetotaller; pacifist; devout Catholic. His wife (d. 1912), prominent in I.L.P. and Co-operative movement; co-founder W.S.P.U. in Liverpool; twice imprisoned suffragette activities.

MURPHY, James, delegate Lithographic Society on L.T.C.; attached to No. 12 branch N.U.D.L. during 1911 strike—member Strike Committee.

MUSPRATT, Max (1872–1934), knighted 1922; director I.C.I. after family chemical business merged with Brunner, Mond; parliamentary candidate Widnes 1885; Liverpool City councillor from 1903; Liberal M.P. Liverpool Exchange January–December 1910; candidate Bootle 1911; Lord Mayor Liverpool 1917; leader Coalition Liberals in City Council from 1918; chairman Merseyside Council of Centre Liberals; President Federation of British Industries 1926; joined Conservatives 1926.

NALL-CAIN, Arthur Ronald (1904–67), born Liverpool; father Sir Charles Nall-Cain, chairman Walker-Cain, brewers; educated Eton and Oxford; golf blue; barrister; lived Hertfordshire; Conservative M.P. Liverpool Wavertree 1931–4; succeeded father Lord Brocket 1934.

NAYLOR-LEYLAND, Herbert Scarisbrick (1864–99), nephew of Lord Scarisbrick; landowner Southport district; captain 2nd Life Guards 1882–95; Conservative M.P. Colchester 1892–5; joined Liberal party and received baronetcy 1895; Liberal candidate Southport 1895; M.P. Southport 1898–9.

NELSON, George, delegate Typographical Society on L.T.C.; secretary Liverpool Fabian Society 1892; co-opted member Liverpool Education Committee; Labour candidate Liverpool West Derby 1918, 1919.

NEVILLE, Ralph (1848–1918), doctor's son, born Esher; educated Tonbridge and Cambridge; commercial lawyer; Q.C. 1888; Liberal candidate Liverpool Kirkdale 1885, Liberal M.P. Liverpool Exchange 1887–95; president Garden City Association; High Court Judge from 1906; knighted 1906.

NICHOLSON, William, district secretary National Seaman's and Firemen's Union; L.T.C. candidate Everton ward 1890.

NORTHCOTE, Sir Stafford Henry (1818–87), son of 7th baronet; educated Eton and Oxford; barrister; Gladstone's private secretary 1840s; Conservative M.P. from 1855; President Board of Trade 1866; secretary for India 1867; governor Hudson's Bay Company 1869–74; Chancellor of Exchequer 1874–80; leader Conservative party House of Commons 1880–5; cr. Earl of Iddesleigh 1885; Foreign Secretary 1886.

NUGENT, James (1822–1905), born Liverpool; educated Durham and Rome; priest in Liverpool 1848; Father Mathew's successor as leading Catholic temperance champion; first Catholic chaplain Walton Gaol (appointed under Act of 1863)—'twenty years penal servitude' he called it 1886; founded Catholic Institute, Hope Street, Boys' Refuge, St. Anne Street; popularized Penny Savings Banks among Liverpool Irish poor; active in assisted emigration societies; Monsignor 1892.

O'BRIEN, John T. (1848–), Irish-born; moved Liverpool c. 1860; coach-builder; in S.D.F. and Unemployed movements; contested five wards simultaneously 1893 but sentenced to six months' hard labour because forged nomination papers; attempted to contest Exchange parliamentary constituency 1895; candidate Abercromby ward 1898, 1899.

O'CONNOR, Thomas Power ('Tay Pay') (1848–1929), born Athlone; father former army officer and billiards saloon keeper; mother a Galway Power, her father captain in Wellington's Peninsula army; educated Queen's college, Galway; journalist, *Daily Telegraph, New York Herald, Pall Mall Gazette, Freeman's Journal*; editor London *Star* 1888, *M.A.P.* 1898, and *T.P.s Weekly* 1902; popular biographer; member Lambeth Radical Association; Home Rule M.P. Galway 1880–5, Liverpool Scotland 1885–1929; president Irish National League of Great Britain 1883; president Trade Board of Film Censors 1916; Privy Councillor 1924.

OGDEN, Eric (b. 1923), educated Middleton Grammar School; merchant seaman 1942–6; in textile industry 1946–52; National Coal Board 1952–64; Labour councillor Middleton 1958–65; first N.U.M. sponsored candidate outside mining area; Labour M.P. Liverpool West Derby 1964–.

O'MARA, Pat (1900–), born Liverpool slums; Irish stock; brutal, broken, home life described in *Autobiography of a Liverpool Irish Slummy* (1934); went to sea 1914; became taxi-driver in Baltimore.

O'REILLY, Bernard (1824–93), born Co. Meath; worked among Liverpool Irish poor from ordination 1847, initially St. Patrick's Mission, then St. Vincent de Paul; third Catholic Bishop of Liverpool 1873; solid, rather retiring figure but Tory inclined; founded diocesan seminary Upholland 1883.

O'SHEA, William Henry (1840–1905), Home Rule M.P. County Clare 1880–5, Galway 1886; intermediary between Parnell (q.v.) and Liberal leaders 1882–4; obtained divorce (November 1890) from wife, who married Parnell, the co-respondent, June 1891.

OULTON, William (*c.* 1840–1913), shipowner, and contractor to railway companies; chairman Adelphi Bank Ltd.; chairman Liverpool Reform Club, turned Liberal Unionist 1886; three times failed to gain election to City Council as Liberal but made it as Liberal

Unionist 1895; Lord Mayor 1898–9; sat for two decades on Liverpool School Board; afterwards pillar of Liverpool Education Committee; one of Unionist licensing magistrates whose libel action against Sir Edward Russell (q.v.) failed 1905; alderman 1904; left £85,924.

PANNELL, Norman Alfred (1901–76), merchant, with John Holt & Co. (Liverpool) Ltd., West Africa 1930–45; member Nigerian Legislative Council 1944–5; Finance Manager, Liverpool, 1945–50; Conservative councillor, Liverpool 1952–7, 1967–70, Cheshire 1970–, Merseyside Metropolitan County, 1973–; governor, Liverpool Bluecoat School 1953–; M.P. Liverpool Kirkdale 1955–64.

PARKIN, George (1844–1909), born Bristol; engine-fitter; delegate A.S.E. on Liverpool Trades Council; twice president L.T.C.

PARNELL, Charles Stewart (1846–91), born Co. Wicklow; Anglo-Irish Protestant father, American mother; educated Cambridge; Home Rule M.P. Meath 1875–80, Cork 1880–91; leader Irish Home Rule party 1877; imprisoned 1881; libelled by *The Times* 1889; politically ruined as co-respondent in divorce suit filed by O'Shea (q.v.).

PATTERSON, John (1822–90), Liberal, from 1886 Liberal Unionist; leader Ulster Presbyterians Liverpool; temperance activist; corn merchant, philanthropist and evangelist—often leading merchants' noon-day prayer meetings in Common Hall, Hackins Hay.

PAULL, Edward (d. 1908), grocery and bakery business; Liberal councillor; advocated leasehold enfranchisement and taxation of ground rents; Liberal candidate Liverpool East Toxteth 1892; left £13,076.

PENNEFATHER, John de Fonblanque (1856–1933), knighted 1924; born Co. Tipperary, father army major; senior partner large Anglo-American firm cotton brokers Liverpool; ex-M.F.H., landowner and farmer; Conservative candidate Monmouthshire North 1900; M.P. Liverpool Kirkdale 1915–29; various publications, including 'The Capital Levy Exposed' and 'Safeguarding Employment'.

PERCY, Earl (1846–1918), Conservative M.P. Northumberland (North) 1868–85; Treasurer of Household 1874–5; Lord Lovaine of Alnwick 1887, 7th Duke of Northumberland 1899; opponent of Lord Randolph Churchill (q.v.) in N.U.C.C.A.

PETRIE, Charles (1853–1920), Scots-Irish parentage, born Co. Mayo; educated Wesley College, Dublin; attended Presbyterian services Liverpool; wholesale fish and game merchant; director Cold Storage and Ice Co.; councillor 1890; leader Conservative party in City Council 1899; chairman Liverpool Constitutional Association 1906–19; Lord Mayor 1901–2; knighted; keen on golf and shooting. His son, the historian, described his politics as 'a little bit and not too far'.

PICTON, James Allanson (1805–89), born Liverpool; father joiner and timber merchant, bankrupt; architect; authority on land arbitration; Whig councillor from 1849; Congregationalist but undenominational in temper; originated Liverpool public library and museum 1852; member Liverpool Vigilance Committee; knighted 1881; eldest son Liberal M.P. Leicester 1884–94; antiquarian, author of *Memorials of Liverpool* (1873).

PLATT, James, Liverpool cotton merchant; director several companies; resident Flintshire; Conservative candidate Liverpool Wavertree 1935.

PLIMSOLL, Samuel (1824–98), born Bristol; clerk; hon. sec. Great Exhibition 1851; coal merchant London from 1852; Liberal M.P. Derby 1868–80; 'the Sailor's Friend', promoting legislation against unseaworthy ships; Liberal candidate Liverpool 1880; president Sailors' and Firemens' Union 1890; evangelical Protestant; Congregationalist.

PURBRICK, Reginald (1877–1950), born Melbourne of Midlands stock; in business Australia thirty years, controlling condensed milk and diary products; three times amateur walking champion Victoria; retired from business 1921; Conservative M.P. Liverpool Walton 1929–45.

RADCLIFFE, David (1834–1907), born Netherton, Yorkshire; engineering and brass foundry business Liverpool; director North Western Bank, Liverpool Electric Supply Co., Lancashire & Yorkshire Railway; chairman Liverpool United Tramways & Omnibus Co.; Conservative councillor and Alderman; mayor 1884–6; conspicuous entertainment and treating of working people; knighted 1886.

RAIKES, Henry Cecil (1838–91), grandson of chancellor Chester Diocese; barrister; Conservative M.P. Chester 1868–70, Preston 1882, Cambridge University 1882; Postmaster-General 1886–91.

RAMSAY, Lord John William (1847–87), served Navy 1861–79; Liberal candidate Liverpool February 1880; M.P. Liverpool April–August 1880; succeeded father (staunch Tory) as 13th Earl of Dalhousie; Secretary for Scotland 1886.

RANKIN, James Stuart (1880–1960), son of John Rankin (1845–1928), chairman Rankin, Gilmour & Co., shipowners, and Bank of Liverpool; educated Sedbergh (of which father was a governor) and Oxford; Conservative Councillor; candidate Stockport January 1910; M.P. Liverpool East Toxteth 1916–24.

RANKIN, Robert (1877–1960), elder brother of James Rankin (q.v.); educated Sedbergh and Cambridge; Conservative candidate Liverpool Kirkdale 1929; M.P. Liverpool Kirkdale 1931–45; member Royal Empire Society; vice-president Liverpool School of Tropical Medicine; cr. baronet 1937; High Sheriff of Lancashire 1948–9.

RATHBONE, Eleanor Florence (1872–1946), daughter of William Rathbone (q.v.); educated Kensington High School, Liverpool and Oxford Universities; Liverpool's first female councillor 1909–34; statistical inquiry into dock labour Liverpool 1903; succeeded Mrs. Fawcett president National Union for Equal Citizenship 1919–29; advocated child allowances; Independent candidate Liverpool East Toxteth 1922; M.P. Combined English Universities 1929–46.

RATHBONE, Herbert Reynolds (1862–1930), fifth son of P. H. Rathbone (q.v.); educated Clifton and Oxford; lawyer; active in education and nursing; Liberal councillor Sefton Park West from 1900; candidate Liverpool East Toxteth 1902; Lord Mayor 1913–14.

RATHBONE, Hugh Reynolds (1862–1940), son of Richard Rathbone; married his cousin, a daughter of William Rathbone (q.v.); educated Eton and Cambridge; member

Docks Board 1905–33; one of Liverpool's largest grain merchants; Liberal M.P. Liverpool Wavertree 1923–4.

RATHBONE, Philip Henry (1828–95), youngest brother of William Rathbone (q.v.); underwriter; president Liverpool Chamber of Commerce 1865, and for next twenty years chairman Commercial Law Committee which examined all legislation affecting Liverpool trade; 1857–9 organized committee of inquiry into trade unions, serving with Thomas Hughes, Sir James Kay-Shuttleworth, W. E. Forster, and F. D. Maurice; Liberal councillor 1867; Alderman 1892; chairman Library, Museum and Arts Committee from 1871; chairman Walker Art Gallery 1886-death; poetaster.

RATHBONE, Samuel Greg (1823–1903), brother of William Rathbone (q.v.); established China connections for family merchant business; Liberal councillor 1862–77; chairman Liverpool School Board 1870–91.

RATHBONE, William (1819–1902), educated by father of John Brunner (q.v.); long-serving member Select Vestry; retired family shipowning and merchant business 1868; keen interest local government reform; promoted Liverpool Central Relief and Charity Organization Society; benefactor on broad scale—founder District Nursing, champion episcopal see and university for Liverpool, etc.; Unitarian; out of sympathy with extreme temperance and Home Rule factions; Liberal M.P. Liverpool 1868–80; defeated Lancashire South-West 1880; M.P. Caernarvonshire 1880–95; Freeman of Liverpool 1891.

RAW, Nathan (1866–1940), specialist in tuberculosis and insanity; head of Liverpool's Poor Law Infirmary 1897; lieutenant-colonel in First World War; supported evangelical work at Sun Halls, Kensington, and Bootle; Conservative M.P. Liverpool Wavertree, 1918–22.

REDFERN, Lawrence (1888–1967), Unitarian minister, Norwich 1914–18; Ullet Road, Liverpool 1918–50; Bournemouth 1950–60; at centre of Liverpool Cathedral controversy 1933.

REDMOND, John Edward (1856–1918), born Co. Wexford; lawyer; Home Rule M.P. New Ross 1881–5, Wexford North 1885–91, Waterford 1891–1918 (as Parnellite Nationalist 1891–1900); leader Irish National party 1900; condemned Easter Rising 1916.

REEVES, Sam (1862–1930), born, probably Glasgow; educated church schools Liverpool; worked on building north-end docks; coremaker (ironmoulder); newsagent and tobacconist Scotland Road from 1895; S.D.F., Fabian, I.L.P., member; widely read; president L.T.C. 1894; elective auditor 1906; forty-one times defeated candidate for Council, School Board, and Parliament (Lancashire Waterloo 1918); councillor Bootle from 1928; anti-Communist.

REYNOLDS, James Philip (1865–1932), English Catholic; cotton broker; director several insurance and banking companies; chairman David Lewis Social Club and outer Liverpool branch N.S.P.C.C.; Conservative councillor, Castle Street; chairman Catholic Emergency Association 1909; High Sheriff Lancashire 1927–8; Privy Chamberlain to Pope 1929; Conservative M.P. Liverpool Exchange 1929–32; knighted 1920.

RICHARDSON, Benjamin Ward (1828–96), London surgeon; author of various works, including urban utopian model, *Hygeia* (1875); research in anaesthetics, heart diseases, cholera, consumption, and public health; temperance advocate; Liberal candidate Liverpool Walton 1892; favoured tobacco as 'the least injurious' vice; knighted.

RICHARDSON, F. T., Liverpool's first Labour mayor 1934–5; post-office worker; councillor from 1911; member Watch, Education, and Co-ordination Committees; represented Duchy of Lancaster on Court of Governors Liverpool University; People's Warden St. Mark's, Edge Lane.

ROBERTS, Aled Owen (1889–1949), born Liverpool; insurance broker and underwriter; acted in insurance matters for Presbyterian Church of Wales; member Merseyside & N. Wales Electricity Board; Liberal candidate Liverpool East Toxteth (twice) 1929, Kirkdale 1945; councillor from 1936; M.P. Denbighshire, Wrexham 1931–5.

ROBERTS, William (1851–1921), large employer of carters; Orangeman; churchwarden St. Andrew's, Liverpool; member Liverpool School Board 1891; Tory councillor and alderman.

ROBINSON, William Albert (1877–1949), leader Liverpool Labour party 1917–30; delegate National Heating Engineers and Whitesmiths Union; later political secretary N.U.D.A.W.; city councillor (later alderman) from 1911; Labour candidate Liverpool West Toxteth 1918, Wavertree 1924, Exchange 1929, Shipley 1930, 1931; joined National Labour party 1931, chairman 1935; National Labour M.P. St. Helens 1935–45; Catholic convert.

ROSCOE, William (1753–1831), lawyer, banker, botanist, and biographer (*Lorenzo de Medici*, 1795; *Leo the Tenth*, 1805); an editor of Pope; Whig M.P. Liverpool 1806–7; anti-slavery; first president Liverpool Royal Institution 1817; bankrupt 1820; collector of books and prints, part of which went to Liverpool Athenaeum.

ROSEBERY, Earl of (1847–1920), born Archibald Philip Primrose; son of Lord Dalmeny; succeeded grandfather as 5th Earl of Rosebery 1868; married Hannah Rothschild 1878; Under-Secretary to Home Office 1881–3; First Commissioner of Works 1883–5; Lord Privy Seal 1885; Foreign Secretary 1886, 1892–4; first chairman L.C.C. 1889; Prime Minister 1894–5; resigned Liberal leadership 6 October 1896; president Liberal League 1902; opposed Lloyd George's 'People's Budget' and Parliament Act; cr. Earl of Midlothian 1911; three times his horses won Derby.

ROUSE, Charles, delegate Amalgamated Society of Carpenters and Joiners on the L.T.C.; Labour candidate Great George ward 1892; secretary L.T.C. 1892–94.

ROYDEN, Thomas Bland (1832–1917), born Liverpool; both parents members of shipbuilding families, though father self-made; served apprenticeship as shipwright; took over 1860 when father unwilling to change from wood to iron; Conservative councillor 1873; mayor 1878–9; member Royal Commissions on shipping; founder Indra steamship line; deputy-chairman Cunard; director Lancashire and Yorkshire Railway, and Midland Bank; Conservative M.P. West Toxteth 1885–92; re-entered Council 1903 during Protestant crisis; Alderman 1904; cr. baronet 1905; president Liverpool Constitutional Association 1904–6; father of **Maude** (1876–1956), the preacher, and of **Sir Thomas** (1871–1950), Conservative M.P. Bootle 1918–22, chairman Cunard 1922–30 and London, Midland and Scottish Railway from 1941.

RUSSELL, Edward Richard (1834–1920), Cockney born, son of bookbinder and governess; grandfather minor composer church music; assistant librarian, school usher, clerk; assistant-editor *Liverpool Daily Post* 1860–5; freelance reporter London and leader-writer for several provincial papers 1865–9; editor *Liverpool Daily Post* from 1869; cultivated friendship with various leaders of Liberal party, at some cost of personal consistency; anti-Ritualist; attended Presbyterian church Sefton Park; described himself to Joseph Chamberlain (q.v.) 1881 as 'the broadest of Broad Churchmen'; influential figure Liverpool literary and philomathic circles; Liberal M.P. Glasgow Bridgeton 1885–7; life member Court of Liverpool University and life Governor University College, Aberystwyth; first chairman Liverpool Reform Club; author of literary and philosophical essays; knighted 1893; cr. Baron Russell 1919.

RUTHERFORD, Sir John Hugo (1887–1942), son of W. W. Rutherford (q.v.); solicitor; councillor from 1922; Conservative candidate Liverpool Edge Hill 1929; M.P. Liverpool Edge Hill 1931–5.

RUTHERFORD, William Watson (1853–1927), born Liverpool; educated Merchant Taylors', Great Crosby, and London University; solicitor; Freemason; Orangeman; Presbyterian; Conservative councillor 1895–1909; candidate Liverpool Scotland 1900; Lord Mayor 1902–3; chess-player; reputedly *The Times*'s Liverpool correspondent; Conservative M.P. Liverpool West Derby 1903–18, Edge Hill 1918–23; honorary member A.S.R.S.; Orange Grand Master of England 1912; knighted 1918; cr. baronet 1923.

RYLE, John Charles (1816–1900), born Macclesfield; son of M.P. Macclesfield; at Eton with Viscount Sandon (q.v.); keen cricketer at Oxford; claimed never to have said prayers or read Bible from age seven to twenty-one; commission Cheshire yeomanry; studied law; ambition of Tory M.P.; 1841 father—a banker—bankrupt; December 1841 Ryle ordained; wrote evangelical tracts; country parson in East Anglia; first Bishop of Liverpool 1880; consecrated forty-four churches, opened fifty-nine mission rooms, and doubled number of curates and confirmations; towering figure, 6 feet 3½ inches; married three times; slight stroke 1891; a son successively Bishop of Exeter, Bishop of Winchester, and Dean of Westminster; a grandson Gilbert Ryle, philosopher.

SALISBURY, 3rd Marquess of (1830–1903), born Lord Robert Arthur Talbot Gascoyne-Cecil; Viscount Cranborne 1865–8; Conservative M.P. Stamford 1853–68; Secretary of State for India 1866–7 (resigning in disapproval of Reform Act), and 1874–8; Foreign Secretary 1878–80, 1885–6, 1887–92, 1895–1900; Prime Minister 1885–6, 1886–92, 1895–1902.

SALVIDGE, Archibald Tutton (1863–1928), second son of Liverpool brewer; educated Wesleyan primary school and Liverpool Institute; Managing Director Bent's Brewery; vice-chairman W.M.C.A. 1888–92, chairman 1892–1928; councillor 1896, alderman 1898; chairman N.U.C.C.A. Norwich conference 1913; declined Lord Mayoralty 1910; president Liverpool Constitutional Association 1919-death; knighted 1916; Privy Councillor 1922; Freeman of Liverpool 1925.

SAMUELSON, James (1829–1918), born Hull, son of forwarding agent; moved to Liverpool as child; Unitarian; non-practising barrister; in business as seed-crusher and oil cake manufacturer, involving workers in co-operative scheme; student of labour problems, trade union organization, arbitration schemes, temperance, and technical education; Liberal candidate Birkenhead 1874, Liverpool Kirkdale 1885, Renfrewshire

East 1886. One brother, **Edward**, tobacco broker, Tory councillor from 1864, Mayor 1872, and 'Father' of Council when retired 1895; another brother, **Sir Bernard**, Liberal M.P. Banbury 1865–95.

SANDHAM, Elijah (1875–1944), born Chorley where organized Care Committee for Consumptives; stump orator; I.L.P.-er; Labour M.P. Liverpool Kirkdale 1929–31.

SANDON, Viscount (1831–1900), 3rd Earl of Harrowby 1882; Liberal–Conservative (Palmerstonian) M.P. Lichfield 1856–9; Conservative M.P. Liverpool 1868–82 (which his father represented, 1831–47); member London School Board; Vice-president Committee of Council (Education) 1874–8; President Board of Trade 1878–80; Lord Privy Seal 1885–6; evangelical Protestant.

SANDYS, Thomas Myles (1837–1911), father naval captain East India Co.; educated Shrewsbury; lived Graithwaite Hall, Ulverston, and Jermyn Street, London; soldier, serving during Indian mutiny; colonel 3rd Battalion Royal North Lancashire Regiment, retiring 1897; Orangeman; Conservative M.P. Lancashire South-West (Bootle) 1885–1911.

SCOTT, Leslie Frederick (1869–1950), son of Sir John Scott, K.C.M.G.; educated Rugby and Oxford; lawyer northern circuit (it was in his Liverpool chambers that F. E. Smith (q.v.) began); moved London 1906; K.C. 1909; promoted international unification of maritime law; Conservative candidate Liverpool Exchange January 1910; M.P. Liverpool Exchange December 1910–29; Solicitor-General 1922; founder 1924 Club; led M.P.s' revolt against Salvidge (q.v.) 1927; widely interested in social and industrial reform; chairman Agricultural Organization Society 1917–22; member Lloyd George's Reconstruction Committee; chairman Land Acquisition Committee.

SEELY, John ('Jack') Edward Bernard (1868–1947), cr. Baron Mottistone 1933; lawyer; served in Boer War; Conservative M.P. Isle of Wight 1900–4; Liberal M.P. Isle of Wight 1904–6, 1923–4, Liverpool Abercromby 1906–10, Derbyshire (Ilkeston) 1910–22; Under-Secretary of State for Colonies 1908–11; Under-Secretary of State for War 1911–12; Secretary of State for War 1912–14; Parliamentary Under-Secretary of State Ministry of Munitions 1918–19; Under-Secretary of State for Air 1919.

SEFTON, 4th Earl (1835–97), born Croxteth Hall, styled Viscount Molyneux 1838–55; educated Eton; joined Grenadier Guards, serving in Crimea; retired 1858; Lord-Lieutenant of Lancashire 1858–95; deprived of power of recommending magistrates, because pro-Unionist bias 1893–5; Whig, from 1886 Liberal Unionist.

SEFTON, William H. (b. 1915), born and educated Liverpool; docker's son; onetime plumber and insurance agent; became partner in garage; councillor from 1953; Bevanite; leader Liverpool Labour party from 1963; chairman, Merseyside County Council 1974–7; chairman, North West Economic Council, from 1975; chairman, Runcorn Development Corporation, from 1974; cr. life peer, 1978.

SEXTON, James (1856–1938), born Newcastle of Irish stock; elementary education St. Helens; started work Pilkington's glass works; went to sea aged thirteen; docker, incapacitated by accident; coal dealer; general secretary National Union of Dock Labourers from 1893; author and journalist; T.U.C. representative Consumers' Council at Ministry of Food 1918; national supervisor docks section T.G.W.U. after merger with

N.U.D.L.; Labour M.P. St. Helens 1918–31; supported proportional representation 1918; described by 17th Earl of Derby (q.v.) as 'a very straight little man and not at all the sort to countenance Bolshevism'; knighted 1931; member T.U.C. parliamentary committee 1900–23, General Council 1923–.

SHAW, Peter Stapleton (1888–1953), cousin of Ronald Nall-Cain (q.v.); director Walker Cain, brewers, and other companies; served in Tank Corps and War Office during First World War; rank of major; Conservative M.P. Liverpool Wavertree 1935–45.

SHENNAN, Alfred Ernest (1887–1959), educated Birkenhead; chartered architect; Conservative councillor from 1920, Alderman 1934; leader Liverpool Conservative party from 1938; Freedom of Liverpool 1946; member commission to examine working of Ecclesiastical Dilapidations Measures 1923–9, 1958–9; knighted 1952.

SHORT, Arthur W., joiner; worked in Canada and America ten years; active in Knights of Labour; returning to Liverpool joined A.S.C.J. and Bootle I.L.P.; editor *Labour Chronicle* until collapse under libel suits; organizer Warehouse Workers Union; President and Secretary Bootle L.R.C.; Labour councillor Linacre ward, Bootle, from 1902; secretary L.L.R.C. 1907–12; Freeman of L.L.R.C. 1913.

SHUTE, John Joseph (1873–1948), knighted 1935; born Liverpool; unmarried; Catholic; colonel in Territorials in France during First World War; partner Sir James Reynolds (q.v.); Conservative M.P. Liverpool Exchange 1933–45; chairman, Combined Egyptian Mills Ltd., United Trades Association (Liverpool), and Liverpool Repertory Theatre.

SILVERMAN, Samuel Sydney (1895–1968), born Liverpool; imprisoned for pacifist activities; educated Liverpool University; University lecturer in Finland; admitted as solicitor 1927; friend and ally of Braddocks (q.v.); candidate Liverpool Exchange 1933; M.P. Nelson and Colne 1935–; member Labour party N.E.C. from 1956; fought against capital punishment for thirty years, succeeded with 1964 Bill.

SIMPSON, William (1829–83), born Lancaster; father carpenter; moved to Liverpool; emigrated to America; spoke thereafter with American accent; up and down business career, in shipping, catering, and zoo management; teetotaller; Anglican; active in W.M.C.A. from foundation; quarrelled with Tory leaders concerning denominational education 1869–70; Independent candidate, with Orange and Trades Council support, Liverpool 1874; joined Liberal party 1878–9; purity crusader; conciliator 1879 dockers strike; originator Christmas Hot-Pot Fund; Liberal councillor West Derby ward 1879–80, unseated after judged ineligible on register; Liberal candidate Preston 1882.

SMITH, Frederick Edwin (1872–1930), born Birkenhead; educated locally and Wadham College, Oxford; lawyer; Fellow Merton College, Oxford; K.C. 1908; Conservative M.P. Liverpool Walton 1906–18, Liverpool West Derby 1918–19; Solicitor-General 1915; Attorney-General 1915–19; Lord Chancellor 1919–22; Secretary of State for India 1924–8; left Government for City directorships; knighted 1915; Lord Birkenhead 1919, Viscount 1921, Earl 1922.

SMITH, Frederick R. (1850–   ), born Ashby-de-la-Zouch; moved Liverpool 1872; Anglican; solicitor; shrewd speculator in stock market; potential local Liberal leader but insufficient self-control; councillor 1884; alderman 1892; candidate Liverpool West Derby 1892; declined Lord Mayoralty 1904.

SMITH, Harold (1876–1924), brother of F. E. Smith (q.v.); partner Liverpool and Birkenhead firm of auctioneers and valuers until 1908; lawyer; moving spirit Birkenhead W.M.C.A.; Conservative candidate Huddersfield January 1910; M.P. Warrington December 1910–18, Liverpool Wavertree 1922–3; Recorder of Blackburn from 1922.

SMITH, James Barkeley (1829–98), timber merchant; family firm libelled by Samuel Plimsoll (q.v.) concerning wooden ships; director Liverpool United Gas Co.; deputy chairman Maritime Assurance Co.; Conservative councillor 1878; long-serving chairman Health Committee; leader Conservative party in City Council 1886; cultivated man, but high and dry politically; left £98,000.

SMITH, Samuel (1836–1906), born Kirkcudbright; cotton merchant; president Liverpool Chamber of Commerce 1876; Liberal councillor 1879–83; M.P. Liverpool 1882–5, Flintshire 1886–1906; attended Presbyterian church, Canning Street, Liverpool; active in philanthropic, purity, anti-Ritualist, and emigration societies; erected Liverpool Gordon Institute for seamen to commemorate his only son, Gordon, who died of typhoid 1898.

STACEY, Ernest (1896–1973), born Blundellsands; educated Oundle and Liverpool University; served army 1914–17; mentioned in dispatches 1916; invalided as result of wounds; engineering training; stockbroker from 1919; founder and leader 1924 Club; director various companies 1930–44; breeder of shorthorns 1941–53; chairman Liverpool Conservative Association, 1956–66; knighted 1958.

STANLEY, Lord Edward Montagu Cavendish (1894–1938), eldest son of 17th Earl of Derby (q.v.); educated Eton and Oxford; captain Grenadier Guards; Conservative M.P. Liverpool Abercromby 1917–18, Fylde 1922–38; deputy-chairman Conservative party 1927–9; Junior Lord of Treasury, 1924–7; Parliamentary and Financial Secretary, Admiralty, 1931–5, 1935–7; Parliamentary Under-Secretary, India Office 1937–8; Dominions Secretary 1938; chairman and president, Junior Imperial League, 1927–33.

STANLEY, Oliver Frederick George (1896–1950), son of 17th Earl of Derby (q.v.); educated Eton; lawyer; Conservative candidate Liverpool Edge Hill 1923; M.P. Westmorland 1924–45, Bristol West 1945–50; Parliamentary Under-Secretary Home Office 1931–3; Minister of Transport 1933–4; Minister of Labour 1934–5; President Board of Education 1935–7; President Board of Trade 1937–40; Secretary for War 1940; Colonial Minister 1942–5.

STEPHENS, Thomas English (1838–1912), born Worcester; educated Liverpool College and London University; qualified lawyer; partner in drapery and silk mercery; Liverpool councillor 1879; chairman Wallasey Local Board 1881–6; secretary Liverpool Liberal Association 1881–5; companion investigator with Hugh Farrie (q.v.) of 'Squalid Liverpool' articles 1882–3; withdrew candidature Liverpool Exchange 1885 amid Liberal-Irish machinations; Liberal candidate Plymouth 1886, Mid Worcestershire 1892; left Liverpool for London *c.* 1887; committed suicide in National Liberal Club.

STEWARD, Harold MacDonald (1904–77), born Rainhill; educated Technical College, St. Helen's; consulting engineer; radar research during war; Conservative councillor Liverpool from 1953, alderman 1961–; leader Liverpool Conservative party 1964; chairman Merseyside Passenger Transport Authority 1969; candidate Liverpool Edge Hill 1951; M.P. Stockport South 1955–64; knighted 1972.

STITT, Samuel (1816–98), born Whitehaven, of Scots stock; father iron merchant, shipowner and member first reformed Town Council Liverpool 1835; vice-president Docks Board; chairman British & Foreign Marine Insurance Co.; leading Presbyterian layman Liverpool; Liberal candidate Birkenhead 1874; Liberal Unionist 1886. Brother, **John Johnson** (1826–89), business partner; Congregationalist; City councillor.

STOCK, James Henry (1855–1907), father accumulated fortune Liverpool cotton market; educated privately and Oxford; lawyer; keen rider, hunter, angler, polo player; four residences—London, Lancashire, Cheshire, and Scotland; Conservative M.P. Liverpool Walton 1892–1906; hon. lieutenant-colonel Lancashire Hussars Imperial Yeomanry.

STONES, Albert, Protestant lecturer from London hired by George Wise Crusade 1903; paid £2.10*s*., plus 15*s*. for lodgings, per week; broke with Crusade April 1904.

TAGGART, John Gregory (1861–1925), born Co. Tyrone; moved Liverpool 1866; as boy worked in mines in north-east; returned Liverpool 1879; labourer Tate's refinery; estate agent's collector; district secretary Gasworkers' and General Labourers' Union 1889; attended evening classes, winning Queen's prizes in chemistry, mathematics, acoustics, electricity, applied mechanics, physiology; accomplished musician; Home Ruler from 1878; anti-Parnellite; Liverpool's first working-class councillor 1888; member Housing and Baths Committees; described by *Porcupine* (no friend) 1906 as 'the ablest of the Irish Nationalists [who] knows more about municipal administration, perhaps, than even the Town Clerk'; teetotaller; pro-Boer; alderman 1906; established estate agent's business; promoter Catholic schooling; denounced pact with Labour 1919 and supported Liberals.

TATE, Henry (1819–99), cr. bart. 1898; born Chorley; made fortune in sugar trade Liverpool and London; art collection left to nation, together with £80,000 towards a building (Tate Gallery); benefactor Liverpool University College; Freedom of Liverpool 1891.

TAYLOR, Austin (1858–1955), second son of Revd. W. F. Taylor (q.v.) and brother of G. Kyffin-Taylor (q.v.); educated Liverpool College and Cambridge; shipowner (retired 1912); member Liverpool Philomathic Society; Conservative councillor 1892–5, 1900–3; founder Laymen's League; Conservative M.P. East Toxteth 1902–6; Free Trader, turned Liberal M.P. East Toxteth 1906–10; published addresses on Burke, Ibsen, and French Revolution; chairman Westminster Hospital 1925–8.

TAYLOR, William Francis (1821–1906), Irish-born; educated Trinity College, Dublin; tutor in family of Lord Anally; ordained 1848; preaching impressed M'Neile (q.v.); through his influence vicar St. John's, Liverpool 1851, St. Silas 1861–70, St. Chrysostom's 1870–90, St. Andrew's 1890–1906; canon Chester; Rural Dean Walton 1886–95; Archdeacon Warrington 1889–95; Archdeacon Liverpool 1895–1906; controversialist—against Bradlaugh and Ritualism; stalwart Church Association; cut out for bishopric until evangelicalism unfashionable; Canon Woodward described him as another Luther.

THOMAS, Harry (1858–), born Liverpool; father in provision trade, opened Thomas's Restaurant, Dale Street; educated Halton Grammar School, Cheshire; left clerical job preferring to work with hands; apprentice plumber; began business Cheapside 1883; Orangeman (like father) 1875; Provincial Grand Secretary Liverpool Province 1882, Provincial Grand Master 1886; Deputy Grand Master of England 1885–9; Grand Treasurer of England from 1889; Conservative party polling district secretary; member Liverpool School Board 1888–91.

THOMAS, James Henry (1874–1949), born Newport; railwayman; president A.S.R.S. 1910, general secretary N.U.R. 1911–31; Labour M.P. Derby 1910–36 (National Labour from 1931); Colonial Secretary 1924, 1935–6; Lord Privy Seal 1929–30; Dominions Secretary 1930–5; left public life after revealing budget secrets.

THOMAS, John (1853–1913), born Liverpool; self-made man, joiner and builder; Guardian; Liberal; temperance advocate; founder Toxteth Relief Society 1886; candidate South Toxteth ward 1888, 1889; hon. pastor Garston Baptist Tabernacle.

THOMAS, John (1859–), born Glamorganshire; physically tiny; in poor health having worked in mine to support widowed mother; Baptist minister 1887; graduate London University; from 1892 minister Myrtle Street, Liverpool; Kensit supporter and Wiseite; uncompromising patriot during Boer War; refused to pay rates in protest against Education Act 1902.

THOMPSON, James (1848–), Derbyshire born; Conservative agent Wolverhampton 1879–86, Liverpool 1886–1913; influential in reconciling Protestant and Conservative quarrels after Forwood's death; reputedly diabetic.

THRELFALL, T. R. (1852–), born Liverpool; compositor; settled in Southport; councillor there; president T.U.C. 1885; secretary L.E.A.; Lib-Lab candidate Sheffield (Hallam) 1886, Liverpool Kirkdale 1892.

TILLETT, Ben (1860–1943), born Bristol; served Royal and Merchant Navies; settled in London; organized Dock, Wharf Riverside, and General Labourers' Union; general secretary 1887–1921; Labour M.P. Salford North 1917–24, 1929–31; member T.U.C. General Council 1921–31 (chairman 1928–9); I.L.P. candidate Bradford West 1892, Lancashire South-East (Eccles) 1906; Socialist candidate Swansea January 1910.

TINNE, John Abraham (1877–1933), born British Guiana; family planters for five generations; educated Eton and Oxford; partner in Sandbach, Tinne & Co., traders to Canada and West Indies; director Liverpool Gas Co.; chairman Liverpool West Indian Association; chairman Liverpool Citizen's Institute; treasurer Liverpool School of Tropical Medicine; lived Daresbury Hall, near Warrington; Conservative M.P. Liverpool Wavertree 1924–31; Parliamentary Private Secretary to President of Board of Trade 1927–8.

TISSYMAN, Robert, Liverpool policeman; lost job (and pension) by striking 1919; member Unemployed Workers Movement, expelled from L.T.C. & L.P. in 1923 when an Unemployed candidate in municipal elections; soon Labour councillor, suspended from Council chamber twice, 1926 and 1927; at centre of internecine party disputes Edge Hill 1930.

TOBIN, Alfred Aspinall (1855–1939), born of well-established Liverpool merchant family (onetime slavers); educated Rugby and Oxford; barrister; Recorder of Salford 1904–15; Conservative candidate Liverpool Scotland 1906, tariff reformer; M.P. Preston January 1910–15; County Court Judge 1915–35.

TOOLE, Joseph (1887–1945), born Salford; Catholic; newsboy, then labourer; Labour councillor; Lord Mayor of Manchester 1936–7; candidate Liverpool Everton 1923; M.P. Salford South 1923–4, 1929–31.

TOPPING, Hugh Robert (1877–1952), born Dublin; secretary and agent various Conservative Associations 1904–27; principal national agent 1927–45; knighted 1934.

TORR, John (1813–80), Liverpool merchant, partner T. & H Littledale & Co.; member Docks Board, Council of Royal Agricultural Society; chairman Liverpool College; leader in Liverpool Cathedral Fund (to which he promised £10,000); with William Rathbone (q.v.) promoted amalgamation of local charities in Liverpool Central Relief and Charity Organization Society; Conservative M.P. Liverpool 1873–80; left £1¼ million.

TRELEAVAN, Samuel Lewis, born Torquay; insurance agent in Midlands; Nonconformist; fond of Samuel Smiles's precepts; Labour candidate Liverpool Wavertree 1929, 1931.

UTTING, John (b. 1852), doctor; councillor from 1899; chairman Port Sanitary and Hospitals Committee; promoted Fazakerley Hospital; instrumental in providing Kirkdale with Free Library and recreation grounds; Wiseite sympathizer; Freemason; Lord Mayor 1918.

WAKEFORD, John, perpetual curate St. Margaret's, Anfield, from 1893; member English Church Union; debater with Wise (q.v.); preached admissibility of confessional practices but, despite the Wiseites' allegations, unsympathetic to Rome; wrote in parish magazine 1908 about the 'terrible blasphemies and profanities' of Catholic services and the illiberal nature of Catholic régimes in Europe; critic of social snobbery and privileges of Anglican episcopal bench; urged Church to stand out for social justice by supporting such as the early closing of shops movement; candidate to succeed Scott Holland as canon of St. Paul's 1910; afterwards Archdeacon of Stow and Precentor at Lincoln Cathedral; ruined 1921 when found guilty of having committed adultery and passed worthless cheques in Bull Hotel, Peterborough.

WALKER, Andrew Barclay (1824–93), knighted 1877, cr. bart. 1886; councillor 1867, alderman 1872, mayor 1873–4, 1876–7; brewing magnate, described by Viscount Sandon as 'a very wealthy respectable and unpretending man, and a staunch Conservative'; donated to Liverpool Corporation the Art Gallery which bears his name; Freeman of Liverpool 1889; left about £3 million personalty.

WALKER, John, contractor; Orangeman; founder and president Protestant Labour Club ('It labours by day, and discusses Protestantism in the evening'); Protestant councillor Netherfield ward 1909 at seventh attempt; knocked unconscious during 1909 riot, probably by Catholics, though Walker accused the police; bound over to keep peace for six months.

WARR, Augustus Frederick (1847–1908), born Liverpool; father rector of Childwall and honorary canon of Liverpool; commercial lawyer with shipping interests; Conservative councillor from 1894; M.P. Liverpool East Toxteth 1895–1902; advised closest friend, 'whenever they met, not to enter on a political career as it was unsatisfactory'; leader of movement to found Liverpool University; dissented from W.M.C.A.'s and Laymen's League's initiative regarding Church Discipline.

WATSON, John (1850–1907), born Manningtree; educated Edinburgh University and Germany; clergyman Free Church of Scotland; minister Sefton Park Presbyterian Church, Liverpool 1880–1905; Conservative; Moderator of Synod, Presbyterian Church of England, 1900; compulsive organizer—of Sunday Schools, country holiday funds, Bible Guilds; secretary Liverpool Evangelical Alliance; writer of popular tales under pseudonym, Ian MacLaren.

WATTS, William Herbert (1825–1922), father Baptist preacher; born Warminster; moved Liverpool about 1854; senior partner drapery and house furnishing business; Liberal councillor 1889; advocated retrenchment; lost libel suit against A. B. Forwood (q.v.) 1893; Lord Mayor 1894–5; lived Elm Hall, Wavertree; keen angler; member Liverpool Land and House Owners Association; successfully sued *Liverpool Courier* for libel after 1895 municipal elections.

WEBB, Beatrice (1858–1943), *née* Potter; daughter chairman Great Western Railway; contributor to Charles Booth's social and industrial survey of London poor; member Government commissions, including Poor Law (1905–9) and Reconstruction (1917–8); Fabian Socialist; author (with husband Sidney) of monumental works on trade union history, local government, poor law, etc.

WHITE, Thomas (1877–1938), born Liverpool; cabin boy; later ship's steward, licensed victualler and paper merchant; teetotaller and non-smoker; Poor Law Guardian and rating expert; chairman National Union of Assessment Committees and other valuation bodies; noticed by Salvidge (q.v.) 1917 as 'a born electioneer, who is making himself very useful to me and I shall do all I can for him'; Conservative councillor from 1919; Orangeman; twice defeated candidate Liverpool West Toxteth 1924; knighted 1928; leader Liverpool Conservative party 1928–38; chairman and managing director Bent's Brewery Co. from 1929; chairman local board Eagle, Star, and British Dominions Insurance Co.; buried at sea by Pastor Longbottom (q.v.).

WHITESIDE, Thomas (1857–1921), fourth Catholic Bishop of Liverpool 1894, first Archbishop 1911–21; old Lancashire family; educated Ushaw, Liverpool, and Rome; Unionist in politics; rarely intervened in municipal affairs; Nationalists checked his attempt to control list of Catholic members for School Board 1897.

WHITLEY, Edward (1825–92), solicitor, like father; educated Rugby; Liverpool councillor and alderman 1865–death; mayor 1868–9; Conservative M.P. Liverpool 1880–5, Liverpool Everton 1885–92; member Central Committee and opponent of Lord Randolph Churchill (q.v.) in National Union controversy; family ties with brewers, Greenall, Whitley & Co.; lived Rhyl from April 1890; Sunday School teacher forty years; tea-party politician.

WILLIAMS, William (1813–86), born Anglesey; apprenticed millwright; moved Liverpool as joiner; set up building business, building several warehouses north Liverpool; active Welsh Calvinistic Methodist Connection, Fitzclarence Street; Whig councillor Scotland ward 1863–75, St. Paul's ward 1877–80; member Health and Watch Committees.

WILLIAMSON, Archibald (1860–1931), son of Stephen Williamson (q.v.); educated Edinburgh University; partner in Balfour, Williamson & Co., merchants and shipowners; patron of temperance and nursing associations; director marine insurance and various Latin American railway, mining, and oil companies; City councillor; declined Liberal candidature Liverpool Exchange 1895; candidate Elgin and Nairn 1900; Liberal then Coalition Liberal M.P. Elgin and Nairn 1906–22; refused chairmanship Port of London Authority, with peerage 1909; Privy Councillor 1918; Financial and Parliamentary Secretary to War Office 1919–22; created Lord Forres 1922; very wealthy, owning what Richard Holt (q.v.) called a 'palace', Belgrave Square, London.

WILLIAMSON, Stephen (1827–1903), born Fifeshire; partner Balfour, Williamson & Co., Liverpool; benefactor various charities; Liberal M.P. St. Andrew's District 1880–5, Kilmarnock District 1886–95.

WILLINK, William Edward (1856–1924), son of vicar of St. Paul's, Tranmere; educated Liverpool College and Cambridge; architect; Conservative; elected to Council for North Toxteth 1890 as Temperance candidate, returned to Conservative fold; promoted technical education.

WILLMER, Charles (1819–97), newspaper proprietor; active Liberal, first in Liverpool (Abercromby and St. Peter's wards) then Birkenhead, being a councillor there 1878 and mayor 1891–2; owned *Birkenhead News* (1877), *Cheshire Observer*, and *Liberal* (later *Liverpool*) *Review* (1870); turned Liberal Unionist 1886 but newspapers remained Gladstonian, edited by sons, Frederick (1851–91) and Charles (1848–1903).

WILLOX, John Archibald (1842–1905), born Edinburgh, son of journalist; educated Liverpool College; worked way up on *Liverpool Courier* from 1865 and presided over its transformation to daily paper; Conservative M.P. Liverpool Everton 1892–1905; married widow of Thomas Cope, tobacco manufacturer; president National Protestant Union 1904; knighted.

WILSON, Clyde Tabor (1889–1971), born Birkenhead; father doctor; educated Rugby and Cambridge; barrister; member London County Council 1925–35; Conservative M.P. Liverpool West Toxteth 1931–5; Metropolitan Police magistrate 1935–62.

WILSON, Joseph Havelock (1859–1929), born Sunderland; founder Seamen's and Fireman's Union 1887; general secretary or president until death (union becoming National Union of Seamen); member T.U.C. Parliamentary Committee 1889–98, 1918–19; (Lib-)Labour candidate Bristol East 1890; M.P. Middlesborough 1892–1900, 1906–10, South Shields 1918–22.

WISE, George (1856–1917), born Bermondsey; collateral descendent on mother's side of John Pounds, cobbler and accredited originator of Ragged Schools; baptized 1873; worker in Metropolitan Tabernacle and Dockhead Mission Hall; confirmed into Church of England 1878 after reading Ryle's tract, *What Do We Owe to the Reformation?*; brief period of scepticism; lecturer Christian Evidence Society 1882; attended University Extension classes; Queen's prizeman in physiology; moved to Liverpool 1888; worked for Christian Evidence and Y.M.C.A.; Protestant crusader and menace to authorities; Protestant councillor Kirkdale ward 1903–6; pastor Protestant Reformers' Memorial Church 1903–17.

WOODCOCK, Herbert Charles (1871–1950), Bristol merchant and alderman;

commanded 6th Battalion Gloucester Regiment from 1911; Conservative M.P. Gloucestershire (Thornbury) 1922–3, Liverpool Everton 1924–9; keen soccer player and swimmer.

WOOLLAM, John Victor (b. 1927), educated Liverpool University; barrister; Conservative candidate Liverpool Scotland 1950; M.P. Liverpool West Derby 1954–64; Personal Private Secretary to Minister of Labour 1960–2; stamp collector.

WORMS, Baron Henry de (1840–1903), Baron of Austrian Empire; born London of Jewish extraction, related to Rothschilds; educated London University; lawyer; Conservative M.P. Greenwich 1880–5, Liverpool East Toxteth 1885–95; parliamentary secretary Board of Trade 1885, 1886–8; under-secretary for Colonies 1888–92; opponent of Lord Randolph Churchill (q.v.) in National Union controversy; created Lord Pirbright 1895; opponent of sugar bounties; president Anglo-Jewish Association 1872–86; gourmet; twice married (divorcing first wife, eldest daughter of Baron von Todesco, 1886); left Jewish community 1886 when daughter married contrary to Jewish observance; buried in Anglican churchyard near Guildford.

WORTLEY, Charles Stuart (1851–1926), barrister; Conservative M.P. Sheffield 1880–5, Sheffield (Hallam) 1885–1916; Under Secretary Home Office 1885–6, 1886–92; peer 1917.

WYCHERLEY, Charles (–1893), butcher's agent and owner of carting business; prominent St. Silas's church; Freemason; Orangeman; chairman W.M.C.A.

YATES, John (1807–87), born Haslingden; solicitor, like father; converted to Catholicism while at school; served on Liverpool Town Council, Select Vestry, School Board and bench of magistrates; Tom Burke (q.v.) wrote of him, 'No church or school was created, no charitable movement founded, no social reform inaugurated, during his long life in Liverpool, without his name being prominently associated with it, either in the shape of money, work or advice'; Whig Home Ruler, critical of Parnell (q.v.).

YOUNG, Sir Edward Hilton (1879–1960), cr. Baron Kennet 1935; younger son of 3rd baronet; barrister; Liberal M.P. Norwich 1915–23, 1924–9; Conservative M.P. Kent (Sevenoaks) 1929–35; Financial Secretary to Treasury 1921–2; Parliamentary Secretary to Department Overseas Trade 1931; Minister of Health 1931–5. Lloyd George's land proposals propelled Young's movement from Liberalism to Conservatism.

Bibliography

Unless otherwise stated the place of publication in each case is London.

Works of reference and official publications

Bellamy, J. M., and Saville, J., *Dictionary of Labour Biography*, vol. 1, 1972, vol. 2, 1974.
Craig, F. W. S. (ed), *British Parliamentary Election Results, 1885–1918*, 1974.
——*British Parliamentary Election Results, 1918–1949*, Glasgow, 1969.
——*British Parliamentary Election Results, 1950–1970*, Chichester, 1971.
——*Boundaries of Parliamentary Constituencies, 1885–1972*, Chichester, 1972.
Cross, F. L., and Livingstone E. A. (ed.), *The Oxford Dictionary of the Christian Church*, Oxford, 1974.
Dictionary of National Biography.
Dod's Parliamentary Companion.
Lancashire Leaders Social and Political, 2 vols., Exeter, 1897.
Orchard, B. G., *Liverpool's Legion of Honour*, Birkenhead, 1893.
Parliamentary Debates (Hansard).
Parliamentary Papers.
Vincent, J., and Stenton, M. (eds.), *McCalmont's Parliamentary Poll Book 1832–1918*, Brighton, 1971.
Who Was Who.
Who's Who.

Newspapers and periodicals

Contemporary Review
Fortnightly Review
The Anarchist
The Church Association Monthly Intelligencer
The Clarion
The Guardian
The Irish Programme
The Labour Leader
The Nationalist
The Nineteenth Century
The Quarterly Review
The Times
The Transport Worker
Liverpool Courier
Liverpool Catholic Herald
Liverpool Citizen
Liverpool Daily Post
Liverpool Mercury
Liverpool Opinion
Liverpool Review
Manchester Guardian
North Liverpool Times
Porcupine
Protestant Standard

Manuscript and original sources

Particular papers in the following collections have been consulted with reference to Liverpool men or Liverpool affairs:

H. H. Asquith
James Bryce
Sir Henry Campbell-Bannerman
Joseph Chamberlain
Lord Randolph Churchill
15th, 16th, and 17th Earls of Derby
T. E. Ellis
Sir A. B. Forwood
A. G. Gardiner
D. Lloyd George
Robertson Gladstone
W. E. Gladstone
Viscount Gladstone
Ellis Griffith
R. B. Haldane
Sir W. V. Harcourt
2nd Earl of Harrowby
Robert and Richard Holt
Andrew Bonar Law
George Melly
Lawrence Redfern
5th Earl of Rosebery
3rd Marquis of Salisbury
Sir Archibald Salvidge
J. S. Sandars
Lord Sankey
Sir Leslie Scott
J. E. B. Seely
2nd Earl of Selborne
Samuel Smith
Beatrice Webb
Roman Catholic Archdiocese of Liverpool
Liverpool Steam Ship Owners Association

Books and articles

General background

Acton, W., *Prostitution*, 2nd edition, 1870.
Addison, P., *The Road to 1945*, 1975.
Amery, J., *The Life of Joseph Chamberlain*, vols. 5–6, 1969.
Amery, L. S., *My Political Life*, 1953.
Anderson, M., *Family Structure in Nineteenth Century Lancashire*, Cambridge, 1971.
Austin, A., *The Autobiography of Alfred Austin 1835–1910*, 1911, 2 vols.
Bahlman, D. W. R., *The Diary of Sir Edward Hamilton*, Oxford, 1972, 2 vols.
Baker, J. J., *The Economy of Temperance*, 1909.
Balfour, A. J., *Chapters of Autobiography*, 1930.
Bassett, R., *Nineteen Thirty-One*, 1958.
Bealey, F., and Pelling, H., *Labour and Politics 1900–1906*, 1958.
Bell, E. Moberly, *Octavia Hill*, 1942.
Bell, G. K. A., *Randall Davidson*, 1938.
Benson, A. C., *The Life of Edward White Benson, Archbishop of Canterbury*, 1900, 2 vols.
Birkenhead, Lord, *Halifax*, 1965.
Blake, R., *The Unknown Prime Minister*, 1955.
Blatchford, R., *Merrie England*, 1894.
Blewett, N., *The Peers, the Parties, and the People: The General Election of 1910*, 1972.
Blumenfeld, R. D., *R. D. B.'s Diary, 1887–1914*, 1930.
Blunt, W. S., *My Diaries*, 2 vols., New York edition, 1921.
Bowen, D., *The Idea of the Victorian Church*, Montreal, 1968.
Brand, J. L., *Doctors and the State*, Baltimore, 1965.
Briggs, A., *Victorian Cities*, 1963.
——and Saville, J., *Essays in Labour History 1886–1923*, 1971.

Brodrick, G. C., *Political Studies*, 1879.
——*Literary Fragments*, 1891.
——*Memories and Impressions 1831–1900*, 1900.
Brown, B. H., *The Tariff Movement in Great Britain 1881–1895*, 1943; new edition 1966.
Brown, K. D., *Labour and Unemployment 1900–1914*, Newton Abbot, 1971.
——(ed.), *Essays in Anti-Labour History*, 1974.
Brown, E. H. Phelps, *The Growth of British Industrial Relations*, paper edition, 1965.
Buckland, P., *Irish Unionism: Two, Ulster Unionism and the Origins of Northern Ireland 1886–1922*, Dublin and New York, 1973.
Buckle, G. E., *The Life of Benjamin Disraeli, Earl of Beaconsfield*, vols. v, vi, 1920.
Budge, I., and O'Leary, C., *Belfast: Approach to Crisis*, 1973.
Bullock, S. F., *Robert Thorne: The Story of a London Clerk*, 1907.
Burnett, J., *Plenty and Want*, 1966.
Cecil, G., *Life of Robert, Marquis of Salisbury*, vol. iii, 1931, vol. iv, 1932.
Chadwick, O., *The Victorian Church*, part ii, 1970.
Chilston, Viscount, *W. H. Smith*, 1965.
Church, M. C., *The Life and Letters of Dean Church*, 1895.
Clapham, J. H., *An Economic History of Modern Britain*, vols. i–iii, Cambridge, 1926, 1932.
Clegg, H. A., Fox, A., and Thompson, A. F., *A History of British Trade Unions since 1889*, vol. i, Oxford, 1964.
Cole, G. D. H., *Local and Regional Government*, 1947.
Colson, P. (ed.), *Lord Goschen and His Friends*, 1946.
Cook, C., *The Age of Alignment*, 1975.
Cooke, A. B., and Vincent, J., *The Governing Passion*, Brighton, 1974.
Cooper, C. A., *An Editor's Retrospect*, 1896.
Cornford, J. P., 'The Transformation of Conservatism in the late Nineteenth Century', *Victorian Studies*, 1963–4.
Cowling, M., *The Impact of Hitler*, Cambridge, 1975.
Creighton, L., *Life and Letters of Mandell Creighton*, 2 vols., 1904.
Critchley, T. A., *A History of the Police in England and Wales 900–1966*, 1967.
Crossick, G. (ed.), *The Lower Middle Class in Britain*, 1977.
Cruickshank, M., *Church and State in English Education*, 1963.
Curtis, L. P., *Anglo-Saxons and Celts*, New York, 1968.
Dalton, H., *Call Back Yesterday*, 1953.
Dewar, M. W., *Why Orangeism?*, 1958.
——Brown, J., and Long, S. E., *Orangeism? A New Historical Appreciation*, 1967.
Dicey, A. V., *England's Case against Home Rule*, 1886; new edition, Brighton, 1973.
Diggle, J. W., *The Lancashire Life of Bishop Fraser*, People's edition, 1891.
Donoughue, B., and Jones, G. W., *Herbert Morrison*, 1973.
Dugdale, B. E. C., *Arthur James Balfour, 1st Earl of Balfour*, vol. i, 1936.
Dyos, H. J., and Aldcroft, D. H., *British Transport*, Leicester, 1969.
——and Wolff, M. (ed.), *The Victorian City*, 2 vols., 1973.
Elliott, A. D., *The Life of George Joachim Goschen, First Viscount Goschen, 1831–1907*, 2 vols., 1911.
Ellis, H., *Impressions and Comments*, 1914.
Escott, T. H. S., *England: its People, Polity, and Pursuits*, 1885.
——*Randolph Spencer-Churchill*, 1895.
Feuchtwanger, E. J., *Disraeli, Democracy, and the Tory Party*, Oxford, 1968.
Finer, H., *Municipal Trading*, 1941.
——*English Local Government*, 3rd edition, 1946.

Flinn, M. W., and Smout, T. C. (eds.), *Essays in Social History*, Oxford, 1974.

Fisher, H. A. L., *James Bryce*, 2 vols., 1927.

Fried, A., and Elman, R. M. (eds.), *Charles Booth's London*, 1969.

Garvin, J. L., *The Life of Joseph Chamberlain*, vols. 1–2, 1932–3.

Gathorne-Hardy, A. E. (ed.), *Gathorne Hardy First Earl of Cranbrook, A Memoir*, 2 vols, 1910.

Gilbert, B. B., *British Social Policy, 1914–1939*, 1970.

Gilbert, M., *Winston S. Churchill*, vol. v, 1976.

Gladstone, Viscount, *After Thirty Years*, 1928.

Gooch, G. P., *Life of Lord Courtney*, 1920.

Gorst, H. E., *The Fourth Party*, 1906.

Gosling, H., *Up and Down Stream*, 1927.

Greaves, C. D., *The Life and Times of James Connolly*, 1961, paperback, 1972.

Greenwood, W., *How the Other Man Lives*, 1939.

Griffith, E. S., *The Modern Development of City Government in the United Kingdom and the United States*, 2 vols., Oxford, 1927.

Gwynn, D., *The Life of John Redmond*, 1932.

Gwynn, W. B., *Democracy and the Cost of Politics in Britain*, 1962.

Haldane, R. B., *An Autobiography*, 1929.

Halévy, E., *A History of the English People in the Nineteenth Century*, vols. v–vi, paperback edition, 1961.

Hamer, D. A., *John Morley*, Oxford, 1968.

—— *Liberal Politics in the Age of Gladstone and Rosebery*, Oxford, 1972.

Hamilton, M. A., *Remembering My Good Friends*, 1944.

Hammond, J. L., and B., *James Stansfeld*, 1932.

——, —— *The Bleak Age*, 1947.

Handley, J. E., *The Irish in Scotland 1798–1845*, Cork, 2nd edition, 1945.

—— *The Irish in Modern Scotland*, Cork, 1947.

Hanham, H. J., *Elections and Party Management*, 1959.

Harrison, B., *Drink and the Victorians*, 1971.

Harrison, R., *Before the Socialists*, 1965.

Hasluck, E. L., *Local Government in England*, Cambridge, 2nd edition, 1948.

Haw, G. (ed.), *Christianity and the Working Classes*, 1906.

Heasman, K., *Evangelicals in Action*, 1962.

Hennock, E. P., *Fit and Proper Persons*, 1973.

Henson, H. H., *Retrospect of an Unimportant Life*, vol. ii, Oxford, 1943.

Hill, R. L., *Toryism and the People 1832–1846*, 1929.

Hirst, F. W., *Early Life and Letters of John Morley*, 2 vols., 1927.

—— *Gladstone as Financier and Economist*, 1931.

Hobson, J. A., *Problems of Poverty*, 1895.

Howard, C. H. D., 'The Parnell Manifesto of 21st November, 1885, and the Schools Question', *E.H.R.*, January 1947.

Hyndman, H. M., *Further Reminiscences*, 1912.

Inglis, K. S., *Churches and the Working Classes in Victorian England*, 1963.

Iremonger, F. A., *William Temple, Archbishop of Canterbury*, Oxford, 1948.

Jackson, J. A., *The Irish in Britain*, 1963.

James, R. R., *Lord Randolph Churchill*, 1959.

—— *Memoirs of a Conservative*, 1969.

Jeans, W., *Parliamentary Reminiscences*, 1912.

Jones, G. S., *Outcast London*, Oxford, 1971.

Jones, T. (Middlemas, K., ed.), *Whitehall Diary*, vols. 1–2, Oxford, 1969, vol. 3, 1971.

Jowett, F. W., *The Socialist and the City*, 1907.

Kebbel, T. E., *A History of Toryism*, 1886; Brighton, 1972.
Kinnear, M., *The British Voter*, 1968.
—— *The Fall of Lloyd George*, 1973.
Knox, E. A., *Reminiscences of an Octogenarian 1847–1934*, 1935.
Koss, S., *Fleet Street Radical*, 1973.
Lambert, R., *Sir John Simon, 1816–1904 and English Social Administration*, 1963.
Lloyd, R., *The Church of England, 1900–1945*, 1966.
Lockhart, J. G., *Viscount Halifax*, 2 vols., 1936.
Lowther, J. W., *A Speaker's Commentaries*, 2 vols., 1925.
Lucas, R., *Colonel Saunderson M.P.*, 1908.
Lucy, H. W., *A Diary of the Salisbury Parliament 1886–1892*, 1892.
Lyons, F. S. L., *The Fall of Parnell 1890–91*, 1960.
McBriar, A. M., *Fabian Socialism and English Politics 1884–1918*, Cambridge, paperback edition, 1966.
McCallum, R. B., and Readman, A., *The British General Election of 1945*, Oxford, 1947.
McDowell, R. B., *British Conservatism 1832–1914*, 1959.
McKibbin, R. I., *The Evolution of the Labour Party 1910–1924*, Oxford, 1975.
Malmesbury, Lord (ed.), *The New Order*, 1908.
Marsh, P. T., *The Victorian Church in Decline*, 1969.
Martin, K., *Father Figures*, 1966; Penguin edition, 1969.
Marwick, A., *The Deluge*, 1967.
Masterman, C. F. G., *The Condition of England*, 1909, new edition, 1960.
Masterman, L., *C. F. G. Masterman*, 1939.
Mather, F. C., *Public Order in the Age of the Chartists*, Manchester, 1959.
Matthew, H. C. G., *The Liberal Imperialists*, Oxford, 1973.
Morgan, K. O., *Wales in British Politics, 1868–1922*, 2nd edition, 1970.
—— *Keir Hardie*, 1975.
Mortimer, J. E., *History of the Boilermakers' Society*, vol. 1, 1973.
Mosley, Sir O., *My Life*, 1968.
Mowat, C. L., *Britain between the Wars 1918–1940*, 1955, paperback, 1968.
—— *The Charity Organization Society, 1869–1913*, 1961.
Mumford, L., *The City in History*, 1961; Pelican edition, 1966.
Murray, A. C., *Master and Brother*, 1945.
Namier, L., and Brooke, J., *The History of Parliament: The House of Commons 1754–1790*, vol. 1, 1964.
Newton, Lord, *Retrospection*, 1941.
Nicolson, H., *King George the Fifth*, 1952.
Norman, E. R., *Anti-Catholicism in Victorian England*, 1968.
Ó Broin, L., *The Chief Secretary*, 1969.
Pease, E. R. *The History of the Fabian Society*, 1916.
Pelling, H., *America and the British Left*, 1956.
—— *Social Geography of British Elections 1885–1910*, 1967.
—— *Popular Politics and Society in Late Victorian Britain*, 1968.
Pollitt, H., *Serving My Time*, 1940.
Ponsonby, A., *Henry Ponsonby*, 1942.
Prestige, G. L., *The Life of Charles Gore*, 1935.
Raikes, H. S. J., *The Life and Letters of Henry Cecil Raikes*, 1898.
Ranney, A., *Pathways to Parliament*, 1965.
Redford, A., *Labour Migration in England, 1800–50*, Manchester, 1926.
Rempel, R. A., *Unionists Divided*, Newton Abbot, 1972.
Reynolds, S. and Woolley, B. and T., *Seems So!*, 1911

Reynolds, S., *A Poor Man's House*, 1909.
Roberts, R., *The Classic Slum*, Manchester, 1971.
Robson, R. (ed.), *Ideas and Institutions of Victorian Britain*, 1967.
Rowntree, J., and Sherwell, A., *The Temperance Problem and Social Reform*, 1899.
Russell, G. W. E., *A Pocketful of Sixpences*, 1907.
—— *Malcom MacColl*, 1914.
Sanger, G., *Seventy Years a Showman*, 1910; 1926 edition.
Sedgwick, R., *The History of Parliament: The House of Commons 1715–1754*, vol. 1, 1970.
Selborne, Lord, *Memorials Part II Personal and Political 1865–1895*, 2 vols., 1896.
Shrewsbury, J. F. D., *A History of Bubonic Plague in the British Isles*, 1971.
Simon, B., *Education and the Labour Movement*, 1965.
Sims, G. R., *How the Poor Live and Horrible London*, 1889.
Smith, H. Llewellyn, and Nash, V., *The Story of the Dockers' Strike*, 1890.
Smith, P., *Disraelian Conservatism and Social Reform*, 1967.
—— (ed.), *Lord Salisbury on Politics*, Cambridge, 1972.
Snell, Lord, *Men, Movements, and Myself*, 1936.
Spinks, G. S., Allen, E. L., and Parkes, J., *Religion in Britain since 1900*, 1952.
Spinner, T. J., *George Joachim Goschen*, Cambridge, 1973.
Stewart, W., *J. Keir Hardie*, 1921.
Tarn, J. N., *Five Per Cent Philanthropy*, Cambridge, 1973.
Taylor, H. A., *Jix, Viscount Brentford*, 1933.
Taylor, A. J. P., *English History 1914–1945*, 1965, paperback, 1970.
Thompson, L. *Robert Blatchford*, 1951.
Thompson, P. *Socialists, Liberals, and Labour*, 1967.
Thorold, A. L. *The Life of Henry Labouchere*, 1913.
Tiltman, H. H., *James Ramsay MacDonald*, 1929.
Tobias, J. J., *Crime and Industrial Society in the Nineteenth Century*, paperback, 1972.
Tressell, R., *The Ragged Trousered Philanthropist*, 1914; Panther edition, 1967.
Vincent, J., *The Formation of the British Liberal Party 1857–68*, 1966, paperback, 1972.
Webb, B., *My Apprenticeship*, 1926.
Weber, A. F., *The Growth of Cities in the Nineteenth Century*, New York, 1899, paperback, 1967.
White, A., *The Problems of a Great City*, 1886.
Wilson, J., *C. B.: A Life of Sir Henry Campbell-Bannerman*, 1973.
Wilson, J. Havelock, *My Stormy Voyage Through Life*, 1925.
Wilson, T. *The Downfall of the Liberal Party 1914–1935*, 1966, paperback, 1968.
—— (ed.), *The Political Diaries of C. P. Scott 1911–1928*, 1970.
Winterton, Earl, *Orders of the Day*, 1953.

Aspects of Liverpool

Abbott, C. C. (ed.), *The Correspondence of Gerard Manley Hopkins and Richard Watson Dixon*, Oxford, 1935.
—— *Further Letters of Gerard Manley Hopkins*, Oxford, 1956 edition.
Aked, C. F., *Changing Creeds and Social Struggles*, 1893.
Alsop, Mrs. J. W., *The Life of James W. Alsop*, Liverpool, 1926.
Anderson, G. L. P., 'A Study of Clerical Labour in Liverpool and Manchester 1850–1914' (unpublished D.Phil. thesis, Lancaster, 1974).
Armstrong, G. G., *Richard Acland Armstrong: A Memoir*, 1906.
Armstrong, R. A., *Our Duty in the Matter of Social Purity*, 1885.
—— *The Deadly Shame of Liverpool*, Liverpool, 1890.

Ashton, A. J., *As I Went on My Way*, 1924.
(Aspinall, J.), 'An Old Stager' *Liverpool a Few Years Since*, 1852.
Baines, T., *Liverpool in 1859*, 1859.
Balfour, A., *Licence Reform*, 1876.
Balleine, G. R., *A History of the Evangelical Party in the Church of England*, 1908, new edition, 1933.
Bateman, J., *The Church Association*, 1880.
Baxter, R., 'The Liverpool Labour Party, 1918–1963' (unpublished D.Phil. thesis, Oxford, 1969).
—— 'The Working Class and Labour Politics', *Political Studies*, xx, March 1972.
Bean, R., 'The Liverpool Dock Strike of 1890', *International Review of Social History*, xviii, 1973, pt. 1.
—— 'Employers Associations in the Port of Liverpool, 1890–1914', ibid. xxi, 1976, pt. 3.
Bean, W., *The Parliamentary Representation of the Six Northern Counties of England*, Hull, 1890.
Beck, G. A. (ed.), *The English Catholics 1850–1950*, 1950.
Behrend, A., *Portrait of a Family Firm: Bahr, Behrend & Co. 1793–1945*, Liverpool, 1970.
Behrens, C. B. A., *Merchant Shipping and the Demands of War*, 1955.
Bell, S. P. (ed.), *Victorian Lancashire*, Newton Abbot, 1974.
Bevins, R., *The Greasy Pole*, 1965.
Birkenhead, 1st Earl, *Contemporary Personalities*, 1924.
Birkenhead, 2nd Earl, *Frederick Edwin, Earl of Birkenhead*, 1933.
—— *The Life of F. E. Smith*, 1959.
Birrell, A. *Some Recollections of Early Liverpool*, Liverpool, 1924.
—— *Things Past Redress*, 1937.
Black, R. D. C., and Konekamp, R. (eds.), *Papers and Correspondence of William Stanley Jevons*, 2 vols., 1972–3.
Blackburn, R. E., *Liverpool Tramways*, 1968.
Bower, F., *Rolling Stonemason*, 1936.
Box, C. E., *The Liverpool Overhead Railway 1893–1956*, revised edition, 1962.
Boyce, R., and Sherrington, C. S., *The Thompson Yates Laboratories Report*, vol. iv, Liverpool, 1901
Braddock, E., and Braddock, J., *The Braddocks*, 1963.
Brady, L. W., 'T. P. O'Connor and Liverpool Politics 1880–1929', (unpublished D.Phil. thesis, Liverpool, 1968).
Briggs, A., *Friends of the People: The Centenary History of Lewis's*, 1956.
Bright, J., *Selected Speeches*, Everyman edition, 1907.
Britten, J., *A Prominent Protestant*, 1898.
Brothers, J., *Church and School*, Liverpool, 1964.
Brown, H. S., *Twelve Lectures to the Men of Liverpool*, Liverpool, 1859.
—— *Lectures to Working Men*, 1870.
Brown, W. H., *A Century of Liverpool Co-operation*, Liverpool, 1929.
Buer, M. C., *Health, Wealth, and Population in the Early Days of the Industrial Revolution*, 1926.
Bullock, C., *Hugh M'Neile and Reformation Truth*, 1882.
Burke, T., *Catholic History of Liverpool*, Liverpool, 1910.
Caine, W. S. (ed.), *Hugh Stowell Brown: His Autobiography*, 1887.
Camp, W., *The Glittering Prizes*, 1960.
Carlson, R. E., *The Liverpool and Manchester Railway Project 1821–1831*, 1969.
Carter, W., *Some Results of Recent Sanitary Legislation*, Liverpool, 1886.
Chalkin, C. W., *The Provincial Towns of Georgian England*, 1974.
Chamberlain, A., *Politics from Inside*, 1936.
Chandler, G., *Liverpool*, 1957.

Chapman, S. D. (ed.), *The History of Working-Class Housing*, Newton Abbot, 1971.
Checkland, S. G., *The Gladstones*, Cambridge, 1971.
Chilston, 3rd Viscount, *Chief Whip*, 1961.
Churchill, R. S., *Lord Derby*, 1959.
—— *Winston S. Churchill*, vol. ii, 1967, Companion parts 2 and 3, 1969.
Churchill, W. S., *Lord Randolph Churchill*, 2nd edition, 1907.
Citrine, Lord, *Men and Work*, 1964.
Clarke, P. F., *Lancashire and the New Liberalism*, Cambridge, 1971.
Clemens, P. G. E., 'The Rise of Liverpool 1665–1750', *Ec.H.R.*, 2nd ser., xxix, May 1976.
Collins, C. A., 'Politics and Electors in Nineteenth Century Liverpool' (unpublished M.A. thesis, Liverpool, 1974).
Cole, G. D. H., *The World of Labour*, 2nd edition, 1915.
—— *A History of the Labour Party from 1914*, 2nd edition, 1951.
Cole, M., *Growing Up into Revolution*, 1949.
—— (ed.), *Beatrice Webb's Diaries 1912–1924*, 1952.
—— *Beatrice Webb's Diaries 1924–1932*, 1956.
Conor, J. R., *The Struggles of an Infant Parish*, 1854.
Cowell, P., *Liverpool Public Libraries*, 1903.
Cullen, L. M., *Anglo-Irish Trade 1660–1800*, Manchester, 1968.
Currie, W. W. (ed.), *Memoir of the Life, Writings, and Correspondence of James Currie M.D., F.R.S., of Liverpool*, 2 vols., 1831.
Dart, C. H., *Distinguished Churchmen and Phases of Church Work*, 1902.
Davies, A. T., *A Survey of Liverpool's 144 Lapsed Licenses and What It Teaches*, 1897.
—— *The Relation of Municipal Action to Morals*, 1899.
Day, J. Wentworth, *Lady Houston D.B.E.*, 1958.
Department of Economic Affairs, *The Problems of Merseyside*, 1965.
Denvir, J., *The Irish in Britain*, 1892.
—— *The Life Story of an Old Rebel*, Dublin, 1910.
Devlin, C. (ed.), *The Sermons and Devotional Writings of Gerard Manley Hopkins*, Oxford, 1959.
Drinkwater, T. L., 'A History of the Trade Unions and Labour Party in Liverpool 1911 to the Great Strike' (unpublished B.A. thesis, Liverpool, 1940).
Elias, F., *John Lea, Citizen and Art Lover*, Liverpool, 1927.
Ellis, A. R. (ed.), *Lawrence Redfern*, Bournemouth, 1968.
Ellison, T., *Gleamings and Reminiscences*, Liverpool, 1905.
Emerson, R. W., *Journals and Miscellaneous Notebooks*, vol. x, Harvard, 1973.
Ettinger, P., *'Hope Place' in Liverpool Jewry*, Liverpool, 1930.
Evans, J., *The Conways*, 1966.
—— *Lancashire Authors and Orators*, 1850.
Farrer, W., and Brownbill, J. (eds.), *The Victoria History of the County of Lancaster*, vol. ii, 1908, vol. iii, 1907, vol. iv, 1911.
Fay, C. R., *Life and Labour in the Nineteenth Century*, 1920; Cambridge, 1947.
—— *Huskisson and his Age*, 1951.
—— *Round About Industrial Britain 1830–1860*, Toronto, 1952.
Fay, E. S., *The Life of Mr. Justice Swift*, 1939.
Fitzgerald, M. H., *A Memoir of Herbert Edward Ryle*, 1928.
Forrester, H., *Twopence to Cross the Mersey*, 1974.
Forwood, A. B., 'Democratic Toryism', *Contemporary Review*, Febuary 1883.
—— 'Redistribution: Electoral Districts', ibid., Oct. 1884.
—— *The Dwellings of the Industrial Classes in the Diocese of Liverpool and How to Improve Them*, Liverpool, 1883.

Forwood, W. B., *Recollections of a Busy Life*, Liverpool, 1910.
——*Reminiscences of a Liverpool Shipowner 1850–1920*, Liverpool, 1920.
—— *The Liverpool Cathedral: The Story of its Foundation 1885–1914*, Liverpool, 1925.
Francis, G. H., *Orators of the Age*, 1847.
Fraser, D., *Urban Politics in Victorian England*, Leicester, 1976.
Freeman, T. W., *The Conurbations of Great Britain*, Manchester, revised edition, 1966.
Fry, M., *Autobiographical Sketches*, 1975.
Fyfe, H., *T. P. O'Connor*, 1934.
Gardiner, A. G., *The Life of Sir William Harcourt*, 2 vols., 1923.
Gibberd, F., *Metropolitan Cathedral of Christ the King Liverpool*, 1968.
Gladstone, W. E., *Address Delivered at Liverpool College Dec. 21st 1872*, 1873.
Goldie, G. W., *The Liverpool Repertory Theatre, 1911–1934*, Liverpool, 1935.
Green, E., *My Father's Faith*, Guildford, 1969.
Gregory, B., *Autobiographical Recollections*, 1903.
Grey-Edwards, A. H., *A Great Heart or the Life of Canon Major Lester*, 1906.
Griffiths, R., *Life Story of Pastor George Wise*, Toxteth, 1909.
Gummer, S., *The Chavasse Twins*, 1963.
Halle, K. (ed.), *Randolph Churchill, The Young Pretender*, 1971.
Hamilton, Lord G., *Parliamentary Reminiscences and Reflections 1886–1906*, 1922.
Hamling, W., *A Short History of the Liverpool Trades Council 1848–1948*, Liverpool, 1948.
Hannington, W., *Unemployed Struggles 1919–1936*, 1936.
——*Never on our Knees*, 1967.
Hanson, J., *A Rolling Stone*, Liverpool, 1939.
Harries, W. T., *Landmarks in Liverpool History*, 1946.
Harris, C. M., *Problems of Local Government*, 1911.
Harris, J. R. (ed.), *Liverpool and Merseyside*, 1969.
Harrison, A., *Women's Industries in Liverpool*, 1904.
Hart-Davies, R., *Hugh Walpole*, 1952.
Hawthorne, N., *Our Old Home*, 2 vols, 1863.
——*Passages from the English Notebooks of Nathaniel Hawthorne*, 2 vols., 1870.
Heenan, J. C., *Not the Whole Truth*, 1971.
——*A Crown of Thorns*, 1974.
Henderson, R. F., *George Wise of Liverpool*, Liverpool, 1967.
Henderson, W. O., *The Lancashire Cotton Famine 1861–65*, Manchester, 2nd edition, 1969.
Herdman, W. G., *Pictorial Relics of Ancient Liverpool*, 2 vols., Liverpool, 1878.
Hikins, H. R., 'The Liverpool General Transport Strike, 1911', *T.H.S.L.C.*, vol. 113, 1962.
——(ed.), *Building the Union*, Liverpool, 1973.
Hindess, B., *The Decline of Working Class Politics*, 1971.
Hobson, R., *What Hath God Wrought*, 1903.
Hocking, S. K., *Her Benny*, 1879.
——*Cricket: A Tale of Humble Life*, 1886.
——*My Book of Memory*, 1923.
Holford, W. G., and Eden, W. A., *The Future of Merseyside*, Liverpool, 1937.
Holt, A. (ed.), *Merseyside*, Liverpool, 1923.
——*A Ministry to the Poor*, Liverpool, 1936.
——*Walking Together*, 1938.
Holt, R. V., *The Unitarian Contribution to Social Progress in England*, revised edition, 1952.
Hope, E. W. (ed.), *City of Liverpool*, Liverpool, 1903.
——*Health at the Gateway*, Cambridge, 1931.
Hughes, G., *Evan Roberts, Revivalist: Story of the Liverpool Mission*, Dolgelly, 1905.

Hughes, J., *Liverpool Banks and Bankers 1760–1837*, Liverpool, 1906.
Hughes, J. Q., *Seaport*, 1964.
—— *Liverpool*, 1969.
Hume, A., *Suggestions for the Advancement of Literature and Learning in Liverpool*, Liverpool, 1851.
—— *The Church of England: The Home Missionary to the Poor*, 1862.
—— *Ecclesiastical History of Liverpool*, Liverpool, 1881.
Hyde, F. E., and Harris, J. R., *Blue Funnel*, Liverpool, 1956.
—— —— *Shipping Enterprise and Management, 1830–1939: Harrison's of Liverpool*, Liverpool, 1967.
—— —— *Liverpool and the Mersey*, Newton Abbot, 1971.
Ireland, I. A., *Margaret Beavan of Liverpool*, Liverpool, 1938.
Jacks, L. P., *The Confessions of an Octogenarian*, 1942.
Jager, H., *Brief Life*, Liverpool, 1934.
Jaggard, W., *Liverpool Literature*, Liverpool, 1905.
James, W., *The Eyes of the Navy*, 1955.
Jevons, W. S., *The State in Relation to Labour*, 1882.
Johnson, G. W., and L. A. (eds.), *Josephine Butler: An Autobiographical Memoir*, 1911.
Johnson, H., *Stories of Great Revivals*, 1906.
Johnson, H. M., *Children and Public-Houses*, Nottingham, 3rd edition, 1897.
Jones, D. Caradog (ed.), *The Social Survey of Merseyside*, 3 vols., 1934.
Jones, J. R., *The Welsh Builder on Merseyside*, Liverpool, 1946.
Jones, T., *Henry Tate 1819–1899*, revised edition, 1960.
Keeling, D. C., *The Crowded Stairs*, 1961.
Keir, D., *The Bowring Story*, 1962.
Kellett, J. R., *The Impact of Railways on Victorian Cities*, 1969.
Kilmuir, Earl of, *Political Adventure*, 1964.
Koss, S., *Sir John Brunner, Radical Plutocrat 1842–1919*, Cambridge, 1970.
Lacey, L. (ed.), *The History of Liverpool from 1207 to 1907: Some Notes*, Liverpool, 1908.
Lancaster, H. B., *Liverpool and Her Potters*, Liverpool, 1936.
Lancelot, J. B., *Francis James Chavasse, Bishop of Liverpool*, Oxford, 1929.
Larkin, E., *James Larkin*, 1965.
Latham, F. A., *Timber Town*, Liverpool, 1967.
Lawton, R., 'The Population of Liverpool in the Mid-Nineteenth Century', *T.H.S.L.C.*, vol. 107, 1956.
—— and Cunningham, C. M. (eds.), *Merseyside Social and Economic Studies*, 1970.
—— and Pooley, C. G., 'David Brindley's Liverpool', *T.H.S.L.C.*, vol. 125, 1974.
Lee, J. M., *Social Leaders and Public Persons*, Oxford, 1963.
Leverhulme, 2nd Viscount, *Viscount Leverhulme*, 1927.
Lewis, W., *Clarke Aspinall*, 1893.
Lewis, S., *A Topographical Dictionary of England*, vol. iii, 1831.
Liverpool and Slavery by a Genuine 'Dicky Sam', 1884, reprinted Newcastle, 1969.
Liverpool Cathedral: The Protest by the Liverpool Cathedral Petition Committee, Liverpool, 1901.
Liverpool Constitutional Association Centenary Souvenir, Liverpool, 1948.
The Liverpool Irishman: or Annals of the Irish Colony in Liverpool, Liverpool, 1906
Liverpool Town Planning and Housing Exhibition 1914, Liverpool, 1914.
Loane, M. L., *John Charles Ryle 1816–1900*, 1953.
Long, Viscount, *Memories*, 1923.
Lowell, A. L., *The Government of England*, 2 vols., new edition, 1920.
Lowndes, F. W., *Prostitution and Venereal Diseases in Liverpool*, 1886.
Lundie, R. H., *Alexander Balfour*, 2nd edition, 1889.

McCarthy, J., *The Story of an Irishman*, 1904.
—— and Praed, Mrs. Campbell, *Our Book of Memories*, 1912.
MacDonagh, O., *A Pattern of Government Growth 1800–60*, 1961.
MacDonald, J. R., *Syndicalism*, 1912.
Mackail, J. W., and Wyndham, G., *Life and Letters of George Wyndham*, 2 vols., 1924.
McLachlan, H., *Records of a Family 1800–1933*, Manchester, 1935.
MacRitchie, W., *Diary of a Tour through Great Britain in 1795*, 1897.
Maddock, S., 'The Liverpool Trades Council and Politics 1878–1918' (unpublished M.A. thesis, Liverpool, 1959).
Mann, T., *Memoirs*, 1923.
Masefield, J., *The Wanderer of Liverpool*, 1930.
Masterman, L. (ed.), *Mary Gladstone (Mrs. Drew) Her Diaries and Letters*, 1930.
Mayer, J. P. (ed.), *Alexis de Tocqueville, Journeys to England and Ireland*, 1958.
Mays, J. B., *Growing up in the City*, Liverpool, revised edition 1964.
Melly, G., *The Children of Liverpool and the Rival Schemes of National Education*, Liverpool, 1869.
—— *Recollections of Sixty Years 1833–1893*, Coventry, 1893.
Melville, H., *Redburn: His First Voyage*, 2 vols., 1849.
Mersey, Viscount, *A Picture of Life 1872–1940*, 1941.
Midwinter, E. C., *Law and Order in Early Victorian Lancashire*, Borthwick Papers no. 34, York, 1968.
—— *Social Administration in Lancashire 1830–1860*, Manchester, 1969.
—— *Old Liverpool*, Newton Abbot, 1971.
Mogridge, B., 'Militancy and Inter-Union Rivalries in British Shipping, 1911–1929', *International Review of Social History*, vi, 1961.
Moody, T. W., 'Michael Davitt and the British Labour Movement, 1882–1906', *T.H.S.L.C.*, vol. 3, .1953.
Morgan, E., *Memoir of the Reverend John Elias*, Liverpool, 1844.
Morley, J., *The Life of William Ewart Gladstone*, 2 vols., 1911 edition.
Morton, H. C., 'A Technical Study of Housing in Liverpool 1760–1938' (unpublished M.Arch. thesis, Liverpool, 1967).
Moser, C. A., and Scott, W., *British Towns*, 1961.
Mountfield, S., *Western Gateway*, Liverpool, 1965.
Muchnick, D. M., *Urban Renewal in Liverpool*, 1970.
Muir, D. E., *Lift the Curtain*, 1955.
Muir, R., *A History of Liverpool*, Liverpool, 1907.
Munford, W. A., *William Ewart M.P. 1798–1869*, 1960.
Murphy, J., *The Religious Problem in English Education*, Liverpool, 1959.
Muspratt, E. K., *My Life and Work*, 1917.
Newton, J., *W. S. Caine, M.P.*, 1907.
Nicholl, W. R., '*Ian MacLaren*': *Life of the Rev. John Watson*, 1908.
Nott-Bower, J. W., *Fifty-Two Years a Policeman*, 1926.
O'Brien, R. B., *The Life of Charles Stewart Parnell 1846–1891*, 2 vols., 1898.
—— *The Life of Lord Russell of Killowen*, 1901, Nelson's Shilling edition, 1909.
O'Connell, B., 'The Irish Nationalist Party in Liverpool, 1873–1922' (unpublished M.A. thesis, Liverpool, 1971).
O'Connor, T. P., *Memoirs of an Old Parliamentarian*, 2 vols., 1929.
Oldham, W. J., *The Ismay Line*, 1961.
O'Malley, W., *Glancing Back*, 1933.
O'Mara, P., *The Autobiography of a Liverpool Irish Slummy*, 1934.
The Orange Institution, 1813.

——*Orangeism: Its History and Progress: A Plea for First Principles*, Dublin, 1904.
Orchard, B. G., *The Clerks of Liverpool*, Liverpool, 1871.
Orr, J. E., *The Second Evangelical Awakening in Britain*, 1949.
Ostrogorski, M., *Democracy and the Organization of Political Parties*, 2 vols., 1902.
Parkinson, C. N., *The Rise of the Port of Liverpool*, Liverpool, 1952.
Pearson, S., *Service in Three Cities*, 1891.
Peet, H., *Two Centuries' Records of Liverpool Parish: Our Poor-Law History*, Liverpool, 1898.
—— *Thomas Steers*, 1932.
Petrie, Sir C., *Walter Long and his Times*, 1936.
—— *The Life and Letters of the Right Hon. Sir Austen Chamberlain*, 2 vols., 1939.
——*Chapters of Life*, 1950.
—— *The Victorians*, 1960.
——*Scenes of Edwardian Life*, 1965.
Picton, J. A., *Memorials of Liverpool*, 2 vols., Liverpool, 1903 edition.
——*Sir James A. Picton*, 1891.
Pilgrim Trust, *Men Without Work*, Cambridge, 1938.
Poole, H. R., *The Liverpool Council of Social Service 1909–1959*, Liverpool, 1960.
Powell, L. H., *The Shipping Federation 1890–1950*, 1950.
——*History of the Liverpool Steam Ship Owners' Association, 1858–1958*, 1958.
Priestley, J. B., *English Journey*, 1934.
Pumphrey, G. H., *The Story of Liverpool's Public Services*, Liverpool, 1940.
Raffles, T. S., *Memoirs of the Life and Ministry of the Rev. Thomas Raffles*, 1864.
Rathbone, E. F., *William Rathbone*, 1905.
Rathbone, W., *Local Government and Taxation*, 1875.
——*Speeches Delivered by Mr. William Rathbone, M.P.*, Carnarvon, 1882.
——, Pell, A., and Montague, F. C., *Local Government and Taxation*, 1885.
Reading, 2nd Marquis of, *Rufus Isaacs, First Marquis of Reading 1860–1914*, 1942.
Reakes, G. L., *Man of the Mersey*, 1956.
Reilly, C. H., *Scaffolding in the Sky*, 1938.
Reynolds, G. W., and Judge, A., *The Night the Police went on Strike*, 1968.
Richardson, H. W., and Aldcroft, D. H., *Building in the British Economy Between the Wars*, 1968.
Roberts, D. A., 'Religion and Politics in Liverpool since 1900' (unpublished M.Sc. Econ. thesis, London, 1965).
Roderick, G. W., and Stephens, M. D., *Scientific and Technical Education in Nineteenth-Century England*, Newton Abbot, 1972.
Rogers, S., *Through Fifty Years*, Liverpool, 1927.
Rolo, P. J. V., *George Canning*, 1965.
Russell, Sir E. R., *That Reminds Me*, 1899.
——*Arrested Fugitives*, 1912.
Ryle, J. C., *Can They Be Brought In?*, 1883.
—— *Visitation Charges, Diocesan Addresses, and Special Sermons*, 1903.
Sadler, M. E., *Report on Secondary Education in Liverpool*, 1904.
Salvidge, S., *Salvidge of Liverpool*, 1934.
Samuelson, J., *Boards of Conciliation in Labour Disputes*, 1891.
—— *The Civilization of our Day*, 1896.
——*Drink and Compensation*, 1903.
——*James Samuelson's Recollections*, 1907.
—— *The Children of our Slums*, 1911.
——*Drink and the War*, Liverpool, 1917.
Sanderson, F. E., 'Liverpool and the Slave Trade: A Guide to Sources', *T.H.S.L.C.*, vol. 124, 1972.

Sanderson, T. H., and Roscoe, E. S., *Speeches and Addresses of Edward Henry, XVth Earl of Derby*, 2 vols., 1894.
Sayers, R., *The History of Everton*, Liverpool, 1830.
Scott, D., *Liverpool*, 1907.
Sedding, E. H., *Charles William Stubbs, D.D., Fourth Bishop of Truro*, Plymouth, 1914.
Seely, J. E. B., *Adventure*, 1930.
Sellers, I., 'William Roscoe, The Roscoe Circle, and Radical Politics in Liverpool, 1787–1807,' *T.H.S.L.C.*, vol. 120, 1968.
——*Salute to Pembroke 1838–1931*, 1960.
——'Liverpool Nonconformity 1786–1914' (unpublished D.Phil. thesis, Keele, 1969).
Sexton, J., *A Criticism of the Workmen's Compensation Act*, Liverpool, 1900.
——*The Riot Act*, 1914.
——*Sir James Sexton, Agitator*, 1936.
Shallcross, T. M., *Municipal Shortcomings: the Example of Liverpool*, 1904.
Shaw, F., '*You Know Me Anty Nelly?: Liverpool Children's Rhymes*, 1970.
——*My Liverpool*, 1971.
Shimmin, H., *Liverpool Sketches*, 1863.
——*The Sanitary Aspect of Philanthropy*, Liverpool, 1866.
Simey, M. B., *Charitable Effort in Liverpool in the Nineteenth Century*, Liverpool, 1951.
——, and Simey, T. S., *Charles Booth*, Oxford, 1960.
Smith, F. E., *Speeches Delivered in the House of Commons and Elsewhere 1906–1909*, Liverpool, 1910.
Smith, G. A., *The Life of Henry Drummond*, 1902 edition.
Smith, S., *My Life-Work*, 1902.
Smith, W. (ed.), *A Scientific Survey of Merseyside*, Liverpool, 1953.
Southey, R., *Letters from England*, 1951 edition.
Stanley, F. C., *The History of the 89th Brigade 1914–1918*, Liverpool, 1919.
Stead, W. T., *The Revival of 1905*, 1905.
Stocks, M. D., *Eleanor Rathbone*, 1949.
Stonor, R. J., *Liverpool's Hidden Story*, Birchley Hall, 1957.
Stubbs, C. W., *The Church and Democracy*, Cambridge, 1881.
——*'For Christ and City!': Liverpool Sermons and Addresses*, 1890.
——*Christ and Economics*, 1893.
——*Saint Nicholas at the Port*, Liverpool, 1893.
——*The Cathedral Chapter of Liverpool*, 1904.
——(Freeman, H., ed.), *Some Sermons, Speeches, and Pastoral Letters*, 1915.
Sutcliffe, A. (ed.), *Multi-Storey Living*, 1974.
Swift, J. M., *The Story of Garston and its Church*, Garston, 1937.
Taplin, E. L., *Liverpool Dockers and Seamen, 1870–1890*, Hull, 1974.
Taylor, W. Cooke, *Notes of a Tour in the Manufacturing Districts of Lancashire*, 1841–2, 1968 edition.
Thayer, G., *The British Political Fringe*, 1965.
Thom, D., *Why is Popery Progressing?*, 1835.
Thompson, L., *The Enthusiasts*, 1971.
Thornton, R. D., *James Currie, the Entire Stranger and Robert Burns*, 1963.
Thwaite, B. H. (ed.), *Guide to Liverpool and its International Exhibition*, Liverpool, 1886.
Tiffen, H. J., *A History of the Liverpool Institute Schools 1825–1935*, Liverpool, 1935.
Tillett, B., *The Dock Labourers' Bitter Cry*, 1889.
——*Memories and Reflections*, 1931.
Tirebuck, W., *Dorrie*, 1891.
Toole, M., *Our Old Man*, 1948.

——*Mrs. Bessie Braddock, M.P.*, 1957.
Tupper, E., *Seamen's Torch*, 1938.
Vigier, F., *Change and Apathy: Liverpool and Manchester during the Industrial Revolution*, Massachusetts, 1970.
Walker, R. B., 'Religious Changes in Liverpool in the Nineteenth Century', *The Journal of Ecclesiastical History*, xix, October 1968.
Walmsley, H. M., *The Life of Sir Joshua Walmsley*, 1879.
Walpole, H., *The Crystal Box*, Glasgow, 1924.
Walsh, W., *The Secret History of the Oxford Movement*, 4th edition, 1898.
Ward, C. K., *Priests and People*, Liverpool, revised edition 1965.
Watkinson, C. D., 'The Liberal Party on Merseyside in the Nineteenth Century' (unpublished D.Phil. thesis, Liverpool, 1967).
Miss Weeton's Journal of a Governess, 2 vols., Newton Abbot, 1969.
Whibley, C., *Lord John Manners and his Friends*, 2 vols., 1925.
White, B. D., *A History of the Corporation of Liverpool 1835–1914*, Liverpool, 1951.
Whittaker, J., *I, James Whittaker*, 1934.
Whittingham-Jones, B., *The Pedigree of Liverpool Politics: White, Orange, and Green*, Liverpool, 1936.
Whittington-Egan, R., *Liverpool Roundabout*, Liverpool, 1957.
——*Liverpool Soundings*, Liverpool, 1969.
Wilcox, J. C., and Kensit, J. A., *Contending for the Faith*, 1939.
Willett, J., *Art in a City*, 1967.
Williams, G., *History of the Liverpool Privateers with an Account of the Liverpool Slave Trade*, 1897.
Williams, R., *The Liverpool Docks Problem*, Liverpool, 1912.
——*The First Year's Working of the Liverpool Docks Scheme*, 1914.
Willmer, W., *Family Business*, Birkenhead, 1961.
Winskill, P. T., *Temperance Standard Bearers of the Nineteenth Century*, 2 vols., 1897.
——and Thomas, J., *History of the Temperance Movement in Liverpool and District*, Liverpool, 1887.
Woods, E. C., and Brown, P. C., *The Rise and Progress of Wallasey*, 1960 edition.
Woolton, Earl of, *Memoirs*, 1959.

Index

The index is divided into two parts, an Index of Persons and a General Index. Page numbers in bold type refer to entries in Appendix 3, Biographical Notes.

A. INDEX OF PERSONS

B. GENERAL INDEX